Encyclopedia of
American Opera

Encyclopedia of American Opera

Ken Wlaschin

McFarland & Company, Inc., Publishers
Jefferson, North Carolina, and London

ALSO BY KEN WLASCHIN

Encyclopedia of Opera on Screen:
A Guide to More Than 100 Years of Opera
Films, Videos, and DVDs (Yale, 2004)

Gian Carlo Menotti on Screen:
Opera, Dance and Choral Works on Film,
Television and Video (McFarland, 1999)

LIBRARY OF CONGRESS CATALOGUING-IN-PUBLICATION DATA

Wlaschin, Ken.
Encyclopedia of American opera / Ken Wlaschin.
p. cm.
Includes bibliographical references and index.

ISBN 0-7864-2109-6 (illustrated case binding : 50# alkaline paper) ∞

1. Opera — United States — Encyclopedias. I. Title.
ML102.O6W53 2006 782.10973'03 — dc22 2005027667

British Library cataloguing data are available

Cover photograph ©2006 Pictures Now

Manufactured in the United States of America

McFarland & Company, Inc., Publishers
Box 611, Jefferson, North Carolina 28640
www.mcfarlandpub.com

Contents

Introduction

This is a reference book on American operas and operettas and their composers, librettists, singers, arias and source authors with information on the recordings and videos made of them. Entries range from ballad operas and composers of the eighteenth century to modern minimalists and video opera artists. Recordings are listed since 1893. Each opera entry provides information on plot, history, premiere and cast, and is followed by a chronological listing of recordings and videos. There are entries on approximately 750 operas and 1000 people. Cross-references are indicated by SMALL CAPITALS.

American opera is in a period of rapid growth and is currently the most important opera in the world. Never has there been a larger or more receptive audience for opera, and never have so many new operas been composed. American operas are televised and broadcast on a regular basis, and CDs of American operas are issued in increasing numbers. There is an American opera on stage somewhere in the United States every day. The main supporters of American opera are not the traditional older audiences interested mostly in nineteenth century European opera but younger audiences fascinated by new ideas, sounds and structures.

American opera goes back a long way. Operas were being composed by Americans as early as 1730, and there is a modern recording of one dating from 1767, but they did not come into prominence until the beginning of the twentieth century. Dozens were composed and staged between 1900 and 1930 as composers tried to create an American identity for opera. The Metropolitan Opera alone produced seventeen new American operas during that period. None of them caught fire, but many were well received and some of the music was excellent, as we can hear in recordings. However, the model was still the European opera, which was not the right model.

The "American opera," when it finally emerged, did not come out of the opera house but out of Broadway and other nontraditional venues. The first two great American operas were staged in the mid–1930s with all-black casts and were not at all like European grand opera. Indeed they were so different — and so *American* — that many contemporary critics refused to accept them as "real" operas. Yet they were the pioneers that blazed the trail for the American operas that followed.

The first of these pioneering works was Virgil Thomson's avant-garde *Four Saints in Three Acts* with an original libretto by Gertrude Stein. Staged in 1934 at the Wadsworth Atheneum in Hartford, Connecticut, by the Friends and Enemies of American Opera, it did not seem very American at first sight. Although it had an all-black cast, they did not portray African Americans but white Spanish saints in sixteenth-century Spain. It was totally unrealistic, with a set design based on cellophane, and had no discernable plot. The libretto was criticized as pure nonsense, and the entire work seemed playful in tone. The music, however, was clearly American, a potpourri of nineteenth-century church and popular music synthesized out of the composer's Kansas City youth. *Four Saints* expanded the notion of what American opera could be and showed that opera could be serious without being heavy. It proved that American opera could be nontraditional, and it influenced avant-garde composers from John Cage to Philip Glass.

Next was George Gershwin's Broadway folk opera *Porgy and Bess*. It was staged in 1935 at the Alvin Theater in New York with a libretto by DuBose Heyward and Ira Gershwin based on a book by Heyward. *Porgy and Bess* was realistically American in setting, subject and ambience, with its all-black cast portraying poor African Americans in Charleston, South Carolina, in the 1920s. The music showed strong influence from blues and jazz, was memorably melodic and did not sound difficult to the nonoperatic public. Its tragic love story was told in a simple, emotional style. *Porgy and Bess* was so popular that many critics felt it could not possibly be an opera. It set new standards.

Thanks to these works, folk opera became an accepted genre with such notable descendants as Kurt Weill's *Down in the Valley*, Douglas Moore's *The Ballad of Baby Doe* and Carlisle Floyd's *Susannah*. It was also a model for operas based on gritty American novels and plays, like Floyd's *Of Mice and*

Men from the John Steinbeck novel and André Previn's *A Streetcar Named Desire* from the Tennessee Williams play.

After the Thomson and Gershwin operas showed how it could be done, American opera began to blossom. In 1937 Marc Blitzstein created a political scandal with *The Cradle Will Rock* and Gian Carlo Menotti attracted attention with *Amelia Goes to the Ball*. In 1939 African American composer William Grant Still completed his *Troubled Island* and Douglas Moore composed the popular *The Devil and Daniel Webster*. After a lull caused by World War II, American opera took off again with Menotti's *The Medium*, Thomson's *The Mother of Us All* and the first operas of Lukas Foss and Carlisle Floyd. By 1948 the New York City Opera was presenting new American operas and by 1951 NBC was commissioning American operas for television, starting with Menotti's *Amahl and the Night Visitors*.

What makes an opera American? For purposes of this book, an American opera is written in English by an American-born composer or by a foreign-born composer living and working in the United States. Gershwin and Thomson were born in the U.S. and wrote American operas. Gian Carlo Menotti was born in Italy but lived for 30 years in the U.S., where he wrote American operas. Kurt Weill was born in Germany but moved to the U.S., where he wrote American operas.

What makes an opera an opera? The traditional definition is that it is staged sung drama, a form of music theater in which music is the dominant element. However, defining opera has become difficult in recent years as composers and librettists have stretched the form into new shapes. At one end, opera has encroached on the Broadway musical with operas like Gershwin's *Porgy and Bess*. At the other end, composers have created experimental operas that defy traditional categorization. American operas tend to be chamber works rather than grand opera, so most are not staged in large opera houses, even though New York City Opera and Houston Grand Opera have encouraged them.

Broadway producers used to label operas like Marc Blitzstein's *Regina* as "musicals" because that made them easier to sell. However, an opera is recognizably different from a musical or an operetta even when presented on Broadway. Weill's *Street Scene*, for example, is an opera, and modern recordings of the work are by opera singers. Leonard Bernstein's *West Side Story*, on the other hand, is not an opera, even though it was written by an opera composer and has been recorded by opera singers. Bernstein's *Candide* is a borderline case, a combination of opera and operetta with arias modeled on Gounod and Puccini.

American avant-garde operas come in a variety of styles, from Robert Ashley's videos to Meredith Monk's happenings and Todd Machover's high tech experiments, but they are quite different from their European counterparts. The most popular have been the minimalist operas of Philip Glass, which have attracted an international audience and exerted a powerful influence. Glass has even written operas based on films by Jean Cocteau. Is it an opera if the libretto is a film? Glass's admirers think so. Sometimes it is best to consider a musical work an opera if it calls itself an opera.

Entries in this encyclopedia cover the following topics:

Operas

This encyclopedia includes entries on operas written and composed by Americans (including naturalized Americans like Menotti and Weill) and operas created by non–Americans for American opera houses (Prokofiev's *The Love for Three Oranges* is not usually thought of as an American opera, but it was written by a composer living in the United States and was commissioned and premiered by an American opera company). There are also entries on avant-garde and multi-media operas, video operas, "movie operas" (operas created for films) and "Americanized operas" (English-language operas with American plots using music from European operas*)*. The earliest opera with an entry is American-born James Ralph's *The Fashionable Lady* staged in London in 1730.

Audio and Video Recordings

Information on recordings is an essential part of this encyclopedia. American opera must be seen and heard to be appreciated, and often the only way to do this is through recordings. Every known audio and video recording made of music from an American opera created for 78, 45, LP, tape, CD, VHS, DVD or RV is listed, though heavily recorded popular operettas have selective listings. Most libraries have audio-video collections, the Museum of Television and Radio (MTR) in New York and Los Angeles has viewable copies of telecasts, and the New York Public Library for the Performing Arts at Lincoln Center (NYPL) has recordings and videos. Many specialized companies make available off-air and live concert recordings and videos. The earliest American opera that has been recorded is Thomas Barton's satirical *The Disappointment,* published in Philadelphia in 1767 and recorded in Washington, D.C., in 1976. The first recording of an aria from an American comic opera was made in 1893: George J. Gaskin singing "O, Promise Me," from Reginald De Koven's *Robin Hood*. The first recording of an aria from an American opera was made in 1911: Alice Nielsen singing "Chonita's Prayer" from Frederick S. Converse's *The Sacrifice*.

Comic Operas

American comic operas, operettas and other music theater works sung on stage or recorded by opera singers have entries. The first notable American comic opera was Reginald De Koven's *Robin Hood* (1890), set in England. Operetta settings quickly became Americanized, reflecting United States locations and events: Victor Herbert's *Naughty Marietta* (1910) is set in New Orleans, John Philip Sousa's *The Glass Blowers* (1913) in the Spanish-American War, Sigmund Romberg's *My Maryland* (1926) during the American Civil War, and Rudolf Friml's *White Eagle* (1927) in the American West. Librettist Oscar Hammerstein II helped create a new kind of American operetta working with composers Jerome Kern on *Show Boat* (1927*)* and Richard Rodgers on *Oklahoma* (1943). Leonard Bernstein mixed opera with operetta in *Candide* (1956) and Frank Loesser created an opera disguised as a Broadway musical in *The Most Happy Fella* (1956). Many American operettas have moved from Broadway into the opera house repertory, especially in the regional theaters.

Arias

The book includes entries for the most popular American opera arias. They are not rare, but the best known are not usually thought of as arias because they are sung in English; "Summertime," for example, is the most famous aria from an American opera but is rarely referred to as such. The current *New Grove Dictionary of Opera* includes arias and ensembles from only two American operas (*Porgy and Bess* and *The Rake's Progress*) in its aria listings, but that will change. American opera arias have provided the basis of several record albums in recent years, including historical anthologies of older arias that provide an overview of the development of American opera, and recital albums by major singers like Renée Fleming and Dawn Upshaw. There are now several books devoted to American arias, including the Schirmer series *American Aria Anthology* and the Robert Larsen series of arias for bass, baritone, tenor. mezzo-soprano, soprano and coloratura soprano. Martial Singher analyzes arias from *Susannah, The Consul, The Medium* and *The Old Maid and the Thief* in classic *An Interpretive Guide to Operatic Arias*, and Richard Walters gives words and music for eleven in *Opera American Style*.

American States

There is a tendency to think of opera as an art form located primarily in New York City because it has the largest and most publicized opera companies, but this is far from true. Opera is genuinely national, and there are dozens of excellent opera companies in other states. Most American operas have premiered outside New York, including *Four Saints in Three Acts* in Connecticut, *Porgy and Bess* in Massachusetts, *The Ballad of Baby Doe* in Colorado, *Susannah* in Florida, *Nixon in China* in Texas and *A Streetcar Named Desire* in California. To avoid New York centrism and emphasize the regional strength of American opera, each of the fifty U.S. states and the District of Columbia has its own entry with information about its opera companies, premieres, composers and singers.

Companies

The first major company to present an American opera was Boston Opera, which premiered Walter Damrosch's *The Scarlet Letter* in 1896. The Metropolitan Opera began in 1910 when it staged Frederick Converse's *The Pipe of Desire*, and Chicago Opera premiered four American operas in the 1920s. San Francisco Opera did not premiere one until 1961. Most American opera companies today present American operas on a regular basis and often commission them. The most active in recent years are Houston Grand Opera, New York City Opera, Chicago Lyric Opera, Lyric Opera of Kansas City, Minnesota Opera, San Francisco Opera, Santa Fe Opera and the Metropolitan Opera.

Singers

Opera singers have entries only if they sang or recorded music from American operas, and their careers are described only in relation to American opera. Many well-known singers have created roles in American operas. In early years, they included Mary Garden, John McCormack, Frances Alda, Maggie Teyte, Ernest Schumann-Heink, Lawrence Tibbett and Helen Traubel. In recent times, they have included Leontyne Price, Marilyn Horne, Teresa Stratas, Renée Fleming, Frederica Von Stade, Thomas Hampson, Jerry Hadley, Dawn Upshaw and Susan Graham. Many others have made recordings of American opera arias, including legends like Amelita Galli-Curci and Rosa Ponselle. The singers who created the most roles in American operas are Elaine Bonazzi (15 premieres from 1958 to 1993) and John Reardon (15 premieres from 1954 to 1985).

Authors

American authors whose works have been the basis for an opera have entries. The most popular are Edgar Allan Poe, Nathaniel Hawthorne, Herman Melville, O. Henry and Gertrude Stein. The first American opera based on a story by an American writer was C. E. Horn's *Ahmed al Kamel; or, The Pilgrim of Love,* libretto by Henry J. Finn from Washington Irving's *Tales of the Alhambra,* which premiered at the New National Opera House in New York on October 12, 1840. The first American grand opera to be based on an American work was George Frederick Bristow's *Rip Van Winkle* (1855), also from a Washington Irving story. Modern American writers have become quite popular with composers of major operas in recent years, including Tennessee Williams (André Previn's *A Streetcar Named Desire*), F. Scott Fitzgerald (John Harbison's *The Great Gatsby)* and Arthur Miller (William Bolcom's *A View from the Bridge).*

Special Subjects

The following subjects concerning aspects of American opera have entries: African American Opera, Americanized Operas, Arias, Duets and Ensembles, Asian American Opera, Bispham Memorial Medal, Colleges and Universities, Film and American Opera, First American Operas, First U.S. Opera Recordings, First U.S. Operas on Radio, First U.S. Operas on TV, First U.S. Operetta Recordings, Jazz Operas, Latin American Opera, Librettists, Longest American Opera, Movie Operas, Native American Opera, Operas Based on Movies, Pulitzer Prizes for Operas, Radio and American Opera, Singers, Science Fiction Operas, Shakespeare Operas, Television and American Opera, Television Opera Directors, Women Composers, Women Librettists.

Following the main text is a selective bibliography listing books devoted to various aspects of American opera and operetta. It includes works on operas, composers, librettists, singers, and opera companies. It does not list scores and librettos.

I would to thank all those many people who have helped me in the creation of this encyclopedia and have provided information and photographs. They are too many to list individually, but they include American opera company officials, composers, librettists, directors, singers and writers whose work I have drawn upon. They include as well my understanding wife, Maureen Kennedy Martin, to whom I dedicate this book.

Ken Wlaschin
Palm Springs, California

A

A'AGITA *1983 opera by Giteck*

Janice Giteck's 60-minute "ceremonial opera" *A'Agita*, libretto by R. Gitech based on Pima and Papago Native American mythologies, premiered at the Cornish Institute in Seattle, Washington, in May 1983. It was performed by three singer-actors, a dancer and eight musician-actors of the Port Costa Players who toured it around the West in Europe.

ABBOTT, EMMA *American soprano (1850–1891)*

Emma Abbott, one of the most famous sopranos in America in the late 19th century, made an important contribution to American opera by popularizing opera sung in English. She toured to places where opera had never been heard, inaugurated operas houses in small Western towns from Iowa to Utah and helped opera shed its reputation as an esoteric art form that could only be appreciated by an Eastern elite. While she did not sing American operas (there weren't many around at the time), she opened the door for their eventual acceptance.

THE ABDUCTION OF FIGARO *1984 opera by Schickele*

Foolish Figaro appears to be dying, worried wife Susanna Susannadonna can't cope and desperate Donna Donna is on the prowl for Donald Giovanni. It sounds like Gianni Schicchi mixed with Mozart in Cloud Cuckoo Land, and it is. Peter Schickele's bizarre but very funny opera *The Abduction of Figaro,* credited to the imaginary P. D. Q. Bach, is a fantastic and very effective send-up of mostly Mozart operas with parodies of its more famous numbers, like the trio from *Così fan tutte* that ends Act I. *The Abduction of Figaro* was premiered by Minnesota Opera at the Orpheum Theater, Minneapolis, on April 24, 1984. Arthur Kraemmer was Figaro, Dana Krueger was Susanna Susannadonna, Marilyn Brustadt was Donna Donna, Bruce Ford was Peccadillo, Lisbeth Lloyd was Blondie, Michael Burt was Donald Giovanni, Jack Walsh was Schlepporello, LeRoy Lehr was Al Donfonso, Pasha Shaboom and Papa Geno, Will Roy was Captain Kadd, and John Ferrante was Opec. Larry Hayden arranged the choreography, John Lee Beaty designed the sets, Gail Bakko coordinated the costumes, Michael Montel was stage director and Schickele conducted the Minnesota Opera Orchestra, Chorus and Ballet. The work is scored for a normal orchestra with the addition of ukulele and electric and steel guitars.

1984 Minnesota Opera. The Minnesota Opera premiere performance at the Orpheum Theater in Minneapolis was videotaped live with the cast as above including Arthur Kraemmer as Figaro, Dana Krueger as Susanna Susannadonna, Marilyn Brustadt as Donna Donna and Bruce Ford as Peccadillo. The composer conducts the Minnesota Opera Orchestra. Kaye S. Lavine directed the 144-minute video. VAI VHS/DVD. (The DVD version includes a 1972 interview with Schickele).

ABELARD AND HELOISE *1982 opera by Ward*

At the funeral of free-thinking French scholar-monk Peter Abelard in 1142, his former pupil Heloise and his friend Peter the Venerable remember his life. Heloise had a love affair with Abelard and secretly married him but when she became pregnant, their affair became a public scandal. Heloise's uncle, the Canon of Notre Dame, had Abelard castrated and Heloise incarcerated in a nunnery. Abelard's conservative rival Bernard, the Abbot of Clairvaux, succeeded in getting Abelard condemned for heresy but Abelard's ideas triumph in the end. Robert Ward's lyrical three-act opera *Abelard and Heloise,* libretto by Jan Hartman based on the lovers' letters, was commissioned by Charlotte Opera which premiered it in Charlotte, North Carolina, on February 19, 1982. Jerold Norman was Abelard, Nancy Shade was Heloise, Malcolm Smith was Bernard, Vern Sutton was Heloise's uncle Fulbert, Timothy Braden was Peter, Chester Ludgin was Denys, William Beck was Thibault and Phyllis Tektonidis was the Prioress/Berthe. Rhoda Levine staged the opera and Richard Marshall conducted the orchestra. Ward's neo-romantic score is melodious and includes Gregorian chants to enhance the period setting. Charlotte Opera videotaped the premiere.

1991 William Stone. William Stone sings the baritone aria "Condemn Not, Oh Woeful Man," a defense of Peter Abelard sung by his friend Peter the Venerable, who refuses to condemn him. Thomas Warburton accompanies on piano on the album *Robert Ward: Arias and Songs.* Bay Cities CD.

ABIGAIL ADAMS *1987 opera by Owen*

Abigail Smith Adams, wife of President John Adams and mother of President John Quincy Adams, experiences historic events during and after the American Revolution. Her reactions and those of her husband and son are experienced through the letters they exchange. Richard Owen's two-act opera *Abigail Adams,* libretto by the composer based on those letters, was premiered by New York Lyric Opera on March 18, 1987, as part of the Bicentennial celebrations. Abigail's letters, which date from 1762 to 1845, were published in 1876 by her grandson and paint a vivid picture of her life and times.

ABORN, LORA *American composer (1907–)*

New York native Lora Aborn based her two one-act operas on popular works of literature. THE GIFT OF THE MAGI, libretto by the composer based on the O. Henry story, premiered in Oak Park, Illinois, in 1975. *The Secret Life of Walter Mitty,* libretto by the composer based on the James Thurber tale, was premiered In Oak Park in October 1976. Aborn, who studied at Oberlin and in Chicago, also created a number of full-length ballets presented in operas houses. Three of her songs are on mezzo-soprano Jennifer Larmore's 1997 album *My Native Land: A Collection of American Songs.*

ABOVE THE CLOUDS *1922 musical by Johnstone*

A Hollywood star goes East to straighten out problems at a school which is misusing her name. The role was played on Broadway by opera soprano Grace Moore before she became a Metropolitan Opera diva and a genuine Hollywood star. Tom Johnstone's musical *Above the Clouds,* libretto by Will B. Johnstone premiered at the Lyric Theater on Broadway on January 9, 1922. Moore played movie star Jean Jones, J. Herbert Blake played the crook running the school and Hal Van Rensallear played a patriotic war hero screenwriter.

ABRAVANEL, MAURICE *American conductor (1903–1993)*

Maurice Abravanel became a friend of Kurt Weill in Berlin in the 1920s and was closely associated with his American career, conducting the Broadway premieres of five of his music theater works. He led the orchestra for KNICKERBOCKER HOLIDAY in 1938, LADY IN THE DARK in 1941, ONE TOUCH OF VENUS in 1943, THE FIRE-

BRAND OF FLORENCE in 1945 and STREET SCENE in 1947 and made the recording of the radio version of DOWN IN THE VALLEY in 1945. In 1949 he conducted the premiere of Marc Blitzstein's opera REGINA. Abravanel, born in Greece in a Jewish family, made his conducting debut in Berlin in 1924 after studying with Weill. After Hitler came to power, he moved to America and conducted at the Metropolitan Opera from 1936 to 1938. He was awarded the Kurt Weill Foundation's distinguished achievement award in 1990.

ACADEMY OF MUSIC   *American opera houses*

There are several American theaters called the Academy of Music that have staged premieres of American operas and they are sometimes confused. The oldest opera house still in regular use in the United State is Philadelphia's Academy of Music, opened in 1851, which hosted premieres of William Henry Fry's *Notre Dame de Paris* in 1864, Johann H. Bonawitz's *The Bride of Messina* in 1874, Wassili Leps' *Andron* in 1905 and Gian Carlo Menotti's THE OLD MAID AND THE THIEF in 1941. The New York Academy of Music, which opened in 1854, was New York City's leading opera house before the Met and the site of premieres of Charles Hopkins' operatic oratorio *Samuel* in 1877, and Max Maretzek's *Sleepy Hollow: or, The Headless Horseman* in 1879. The Baltimore Academy of Music presented Dudley Buck's controversial DESERET in 1880, Victor Herbert's *The Tattooed Man* in 1907 and Herbert's SWEETHEARTS in 1913. The Brooklyn Academy of Music is on the cutting edge of American opera. John Adams' THE DEATH OF KLINGHOFFER had its U.S. premiere there in 1991 and his NIXON IN CHINA was staged there in 1999. Philip Glass's EINSTEIN ON THE BEACH was presented in 1984, HYDROGEN JUKEBOX in 1991, MONSTERS OF GRACE in 1998 and DRACULA in 1999. Meredith Monk's ATLAS was staged in 1993. Tom Wait's THE BLACK RIDER in 1994. Robert Ashley's NOW ELEANOR'S IDEA in 1995 and Steve Reich's HINDENBURG in 1998. The Boston Academy of Music, based at the Emerson Majestic Theater, has staged Samuel Barber's VANESSA, Richard Rodgers' SOUTH PACIFIC and Kurt Weill's LADY IN THE DARK.

THE ACCUSED   *1961 opera by Strauss*

John Strauss's 30-minute one-character opera *The Accused*, libretto by Sheppard Kerman, premiered on CBS television on May 7, 1961. Soprano Patricia Neway played a woman accused of being a witch in Puritan Salem. During her trial she attacks the closed minds of her accusers and reveals she is pregnant. John McGiffert produced the opera for the *Camera Three* series. Neil De Luca designed the set, Julius Rudel conducted the orchestra, and John Desmond directed the telecast. This was the only opera composed by Strauss who wrote songs for the off-Broadway show *The Littlest Revue* and worked as a TV pianist and conductor.

THE ACHILLES HEEL   *1993 youth opera by Bohmler*

A group of teenagers learn lessons about the meaning of tolerance. Craig Bohmler's short youth opera *The Achilles Heel,* libretto by Mary Carol Warwick, was premiered by Houston Grand Opera on February 22, 1993, at the Houston Community College. Clifton Hazel Wood was Achilles, Elizabeth Jones was Mother, Jon Kolbet was Harry, Nancy Bruffett was Miffie and Teri Hansen was Cassie. Craig Sapin designed the set and costumes, Eileen Morris directed and Ward Holmquist conducted.

ADAMO, MARK   *American composer (1968–)*

Mark Adamo's first opera LITTLE WOMEN, based on the novel by Louisa May Alcott and composed to his own libretto, has become one of the most popular recent American operas. After its premiere at Houston Grand Opera's Opera Studio in March 1998, it was revived, broadcast, telecast, staged by other companies, and issued on CD. Adamo also created an orchestral version of the opera titled *Alcott Portraits.* His second opera, LYSISTRATA or *The Nude Goddess,* libretto by the composer based on the ancient Greek comedy by Aristophanes, was commissioned by Houston Grand Opera and given a workshop production in Houston in 2003 but not scheduled for production. A graduate of New York University and the Catholic University of America, Adamo is composer in residence at New York City Opera.

ADAMS, JOHN   *American composer (1947–)*

John Adams, one of the most popular modern American composers, writes operas about contemporary events, usually in collaboration with stage director Peter Sellars. Together they originated what has became known as the "CNN opera." Their first was NIXON IN CHINA (1987) one of the most publicized modern operas and the first to feature contemporary politicians like President Nixon and Chairman Mao in an operatic context. Its revival by the English National Opera confirmed its status as a modern classic. The controversial THE DEATH OF KLINGHOFFER (1991), based on the hi-jacking of the cruise ship Achille Lauro by Arab terrorists, attempts to show the reasons for the hijacking and presents the arguments on both sides. It was attacked by those who object to sympathetic portrayals of this kind. I WAS LOOKING AT THE CEILING AND THEN I SAW THE SKY (1995) is an operatic reaction to a Los Angeles earthquake. EL NIÑO (2000), a Nativity opera/oratorio featuring dance and film as well as singing, premiered at the Theatre de Châtelet in Paris and has been widely staged. *Doctor Atomic,* libretto by Alice Goodman about Manhattan Project director J. Robert Oppenheimer, was commissioned by San Francisco Opera and Lyric Opera of Chicago for presentation in September 2005 in a Sellars production. Adams, who was born in Worcester, Massachusetts, and began his music studies at Dartmouth and Harvard, made his reputation on the West Coast as a teacher at the San Francisco Conservatory of Music. After he founded the New Music Ensemble, he created much-played chamber works like the string septet *Shaker Loops* and *The Chairman Dances.* Adams' popularity in the opera world has continued to grow as his operas are listener-friendly in a melodic minimalist style and highly singable with real arias.

1999 The John Adams Earbox. This is a large (ten CDs) anthology of works by Adams includes excerpts from *Nixon in China, The Death of Klinghoffer* and *I Was Looking at the Ceiling and Then I Saw the Sky.* Nonesuch CD box. **2003 John Adams: A Portrait.** The first part of this DVD is a 50-minute documentary with comments from Adams, Peter Sellars and Alice Goodman, sequences of the making of the Channel 4 film *The Death of Klinghoffer,* and scenes from *Nixon in China* and *El Niño.* The second part is a concert of American music at the Théâtre du Châtelet in Paris in 2000. 134 minutes. Arthaus DVD.

ADAMS, JOHN LUTHER   *American composer (1953–)*

John Luther Adams, the leading Alaskan classical composer, has created many of his musical works around Native American and Alaskan legends. His opera trilogy *Giving Birth to Thunder, Sleeping with His Daughter* and *Coyote Builds North America,* composed to Indian stories dramatized by Barry Lopez, was premiered in Juneau, Alaska, in 1987. He has worked as resident composer with Anchorage Opera and his EARTH AND THE GREAT WEATHER was staged by Anchorage Opera on May 12, 1995. Adams was born in

Meridian, Mississippi, but has spent much of his professional life in Alaska.

ADAMS, LESLIE   *American composer (1932–)*

Leslie Adams found an innovative manner of getting attention for his opera BLAKE, the story of an African American slave on a southern plantation at the time of the Civil War. He arranged with friends to present arias from it in recitals in concert halls in 1983, long before it was finished. The opera became known around the country through the arias sung in these concerts and was eventually given a full performance in Baltimore in 1997. Adams, a native of Cleveland, Ohio, is best known for his instrumental and choral work.

ADDISON, ADELE   *American soprano (1924–)*

Adele Addison created the role of Pertolete in Seymour Barab's opera CHANTICLEER in 1956 and sings the role of Bess in the 1959 film of George Gershwin's PORGY AND BESS, dubbing for Dorothy Dandridge. Addison, a native New Yorker, has made several recordings of works by Handel and was the first singer to perform Lukas Foss's *Time Cycle*. She sang the role of Deborah in the New York production of Richard Owen's church opera A FISHERMAN CALLED PETER.

ADLER, PETER HERMAN   *American conductor (1899–1990)*

Peter Herman Adler, one of the founders of NBC Opera Theatre, was born in Czechoslovakia and completed his music studies in Prague. He was made music director of Bremen State Opera and the Ukrainian State Philharmonic but emigrated to America in 1939 after the German invasion. He began conducting with the New York Philharmonic in 1940 and became music and artistic director of NBC Opera Theater in 1949 where he worked with producer SAMUEL CHOTZINOFF and director KIRK BROWNING. He conducted the world premieres of Gian Carlo Menotti's AMAHL AND THE NIGHT VISITORS and MARIA GOLOVIN, Norman Dello Joia's THE TRIAL AT ROUEN and Leonard Kastle's DESERET, and the TV premieres of Kurt Weill's DOWN IN THE VALLEY, Leonard Bernstein's TROUBLE IN TAHITI, Menotti's THE SAINT OF BLEECKER STREET and Lukas Foss's GRIFFELKIN. He was music director of the Baltimore Symphony Orchestra from 1959 to 1968 and then music director of National Educational Television. With Browning, he created the NET OPERA Company which commissioned and premiered Thomas Pasatieri's THE TRIAL OF MARY LINCOLN and Jack Beeson's MY HEART'S IN THE HIGHLANDS. Original NET Opera production ended in 1973 when Hans Warner Henze's RACHEL THE CUBANA busted its budget. Adler began to conducted at the Metropolitan Opera in 1972 and headed the American Opera Center at the Juilliard School from 1973 to 1981.

ADLER, RICHARD   *American composer (1921–)*

New Yorker Richard Adler created two popular Broadway musicals with fellow New Yorker Jerry Ross (1926–1955). *The Pajama Game* (1954), libretto by George Abbott and Richard Bissell, revolves around a pajama factory manager's love affair with a union official; it was filmed with John Raitt and Doris Day. *Damn Yankees* (1955), libretto by Abbott and George Wallop, is a baseball-oriented version of the Faust legend centering around a Washington Senators fan who will do anything to help his team beat the Yankees; it was filmed with star Gwen Verdon. There are cast albums of both. For television, Adler composed two operetta-like musicals in 1958. LITTLE WOMEN, based on Louisa May Alcott's novel,

was telecast with Met soprano Risë Stevens as the mother of the March girls. THE GIFT OF THE MAGI, based on the story by O. Henry, was televised with Gordon MacRae and Sally Ann Howes as the young lovers.

ADLER, SAMUEL   *American composer (1928–)*

Samuel Adler composed three operas and helped reconstruct the first American opera, Andrew Barton's 1767 THE DISAPPOINTMENT. Adler's best-known opera is THE OUTCASTS OF POKER FLAT, libretto by Judah Stampfer based on the Bret Harte story, which premiered at North Texas State University in Denton on June 8, 1962. *The Wrestler*, libretto by Stampfer based on the Biblical story of Jacob, premiered at Southern Methodist University in Dallas in 1972. *The Lodge of Shadows*, libretto by Jerrold Ramsey telling a Native American version of the Orpheus legend, premiered in Fort Worth in 1988. Adler, a prolific composer of all types of music, was born in Mannheim but his family moved to America when he was a child. He was a professor at North Texas State University from 1957 to 1966 and associated with the Eastman School of Music from 1966 until his retirement.

ADOLPHE, BRUCE   *American composer (1955–)*

Bruce Adolphe, a Juilliard-trained New Yorker, began his operatic career with an opera based on a story by Edgar Allan Poe but afterward turned to Jewish history for inspiration. THE TELL-TALE HEART (1982) is a one-act work based on Poe's tale about a young man who kills his landlord but becomes convinced the man's heart is beating beneath the floor. *Mikhoels the Wise* (1982), libretto by Mel Gordon, is the story of a Russian Jewish actor who became famous in the Soviet Union but was murdered by Stalin when he interceded for Russian Jews. It was premiered by Jewish Opera at the 92nd Street YMCA in New York in 1982 with Erie Mills as Sincha. *The False Messiah*, libretto by Mel Gordon about the rise and fall of a false Jewish messiah in 17th century Turkey, premiered at the 92nd Street YMCA in 1983. Adolphe's musical style varies according to the opera but is generally accessible in the manner of Kurt Weill.

THE ADVENTURES OF MARCO POLO   *1958 TV operetta by Warnick/Pahl/Rimsky-Korsakov*

The success of Alfred Drake in the Broadway operetta KISMET, based on themes by Russian composer Alexander Borodin, inspired TV producer Max Liebman to create a similar operetta for Drake based on themes by Russian composer Nikolai Rimsky-Korsakov. Many of the tunes were borrowed from Rimsky-Korsakov operas, like "The Garden of Imagining" taken from *Le Coq d'Or*. Clay Warnick and Mel Pahl adapted the music, Edward Eager wrote the lyrics and Neil Simon and William Friedberg wrote the book. The story is basic: Venetian traveler Marco Polo goes East to China and has romantic adventures meeting Kubla Khan and experiencing the glory of Xanadu. The operetta was televised on NBC on April 14, 1956. Drake sang the role of Marco Polo opposite his *Kismet* co-star Doretta Morrow and supporting players Paul Ukena and Ray Drakely. Frederick Fox designed the sets, Paul Dupont created the costumes, James Starbuck arranged the choreography, Irwin Kostal arranged the orchestrations, Charles Sanford conducted the orchestra and Max Liebman directed.

1956 Original cast album. The original cast recorded 13 numbers from the operetta under the supervision of Goddard Lieberson for an LP which is now a CD. Most of the songs are performed by Drake and Morrow. Columbia LP/DRG CD.

AFRICAN AMERICAN OPERA

The first African American opera composer was probably JOHN THOMAS DOUGLASS, whose *Virginia's Ball* was staged in New York in 1868. More successful was his contemporary EDMOND DÉDÉ, a New Orleans-born Creole composer who moved to France and composed light operas staged in the 1870s. HARRY LAWRENCE FREEMAN was the first African American to compose a substantial number of dramatic operas beginning with THE MARTYR staged in Denver in 1893. SCOTT JOPLIN toured his lost opera A GUEST OF HONOR in 1903 but his splendid TREEMONISHA, written in 1911, was not produced until 1975. LOUISA MELVIN DELOS MARS was the first African American woman composer to write an operetta and have it staged and published; she premiered *Leoni, The Gypsy Queen* in Providence, Rhode Island on December 4, 1889. SHIRLEY DUBOIS GRAHAM was the first African American woman opera composer and her grandiose TOM-TOM was premiered in Cleveland in 1932. WILLIAM GRANT STILL was the first African American composer to have an opera staged by a major opera company; his TROUBLED ISLAND was premiered at New York City Opera in 1949. ULYSSES KAY was highly praised for his historic opera FREDERICK DOUGLASS, staged in 1989. The best-known living African American composer is ANTHONY DAVIS, who has written four operas, including AMISTAD and X, THE STORY OF MALCOLM X. Other African American composers with entries in this encyclopedia include LESLIE ADAMS, NOA AIN, ANTHONY BRAXTON, LESLIE SAVOY BURRS, HALL JOHNSON, JAMES P. JOHNSON, JULIA PERRY and CLARENCE CAMERON WHITE. The opera company OPERA EBONY was founded in 1873 to help produce operas by African Americans. All-black opera companies producing classic European operas were formed in the 19th century because black singers were not allowed to sing with white companies. Many notable singers began their careers in these companies including TODD DUNCAN, the creator of Porgy. Julius Eichberg's comic opera *The Doctor of Alcantara*, the first American opera staged by an African American opera company, was presented by the Original Colored American Opera Troupe of Washington, D.C., in Washington and Philadelphia in 1873. Jan Schmidt-Garre and Marieke Schroeder's 2000 documentary *Aida's Brothers and Sisters: Black Voices in Opera* describes the history of black opera singers in America with commentary from Rosalyn Story. Singers discussed include KATHLEEN BATTLE, GRACE BUMBRY, SIMON ESTES, BARBARA HENDRICKS, ROBERT MCFERRIN, JESSYE NORMAN, LEONTYNE PRICE, PAUL ROBESON and SHIRLEY VERRETT.

AGEE, JAMES   *American writer (1909–1955)*

James Agee, one of America's most perceptive film critics and a fine screenwriter (*The African Queen, The Night of the Hunter*), received a posthumous Pulitzer Prize for his semi-autobiographical 1957 novel *A Death in the Family*. It tells the story of a young boy and his dysfunctional family in Knoxville, Tennessee, in 1915. William Mayer based his 1983 opera A DEATH IN THE FAMILY on a stage version of the novel. Samuel Barber's composition for soprano, *Knoxville: Summer of 1915,* is based on a poem in the novel.

AHLSTROM, DAVID   *American composer (1927–)*

David Ahlstrom composed two playful and tonal chamber operas to texts by Gertrude Stein. THREE SISTERS WHO ARE NOT SISTERS premiered in Cincinnati in 1953 and DR. FAUSTUS LIGHTS THE LIGHTS premiered in San Francisco in 1982. Ahlstrom, a New Yorker who moved to San Francisco and founded VOICES/SF Bay Area Youth Opera in 1982, has also composed operas to texts by e. e. cummings, William Saroyan and Boccaccio. The cummings opera *america i love you*, which gets its title us from the poem "next to of course god america i love you land of the pilgrims and so forth," was premiered in New Orleans in 1981. The Saroyan opera *My Heart's in the Highlands* was composed in 1990 but is less well known than the 1970 version by Jack Beeson. The Boccaccio opera, *Wicked Was He That Took Away the Flower,* is based on a tale in the *Decameron* about a brother who kills his sister's lover.

AHMED AL KAMEL   *1840 ballad opera by Horn*

Moslem Prince Ahmed al Kamel learns about love from the birds, a dove, an owl and a parrot. He uses a magic carpet to rescue and win a Christian princess. C. E. Horn's *Ahmed al Kamel; or, The Pilgrim of Love*, libretto by Henry J. Finn based on one of the tales in Washington Irving's *The Legends of the Alhambra* (1832), premiered at the New National Opera House in New York City on October 12, 1840. It is believed to be the first American ballad opera based on an American literary work.

AIKEN, DAVID   *American baritone (1917–)*

David Aiken created major roles in two operas by Gian Carlo Menotti. He was King Melchior in AMAHL AND THE NIGHT VISITORS when it premiered on television in 1951 and he created the role of Carmela's bridegroom Salvatore in THE SAINT OF BLEECKER STREET on Broadway in 1954. He is featured on the cast recordings of both. He played Mr. Kofner in a 1951 BBC TV production of Menotti's THE CONSUL and sang the role on stage at New York City Opera in 1953. He has also produced *Amahl and the Night Visitors* on stage. Aiken, a native of Benton, Illinois, sang the St. Louis Municipal Opera before World War II and later with New York City Opera.

AILEY, ALVIN   *American dancer/choreographer (1931–1989)*

Dancer Alvin Ailey formed his own company in 1958 and quickly won world recognition, especially dancing to music by Samuel Barber. He choreographed two American operas at the Met, Barber's ANTONY AND CLEOPATRA for the 1966 world premiere opening the new opera house and Virgil Thomson's FOUR SAINTS IN THREE ACTS for a Mini-Met production in 1973. He was also the choreographer for Leonard Bernstein's MASS at the Kennedy Center in 1971. Ailey, born in Rogers, Texas, began his company with black dancers only but decided to integrate it in 1962.

AIN, NOA   *American composer (1941–)*

Noa Ain had notable success with her opera THE OUTCAST, a retelling of the Biblical story of Ruth, premiered by Opera Ebony in 1990 and produced by Houston Grand Opera in 1994. *Trio*, a one-act gospel-style work about a woman expecting a baby and its effect on her relations with mother and grandmother, was presented at the American Music Theater Festival in Philadelphia in 1984. *Bring on the Bears* was staged at the Lenox Arts Center in Stockbridge, Massachusetts. in 1982. Ain's other operas, all composed to her own librettos, are *Angels' Voices, Possessed* and *George and Her Friends*.

AINADAMAR   *2003 opera by Golijov*

At the end of her life Catalan actress Margarita Xirgu remembers working with Spanish poet-playwright Federico Garcia Lorca. She starred in the 1927 production of his play *Mariana Pineda* and it made them both famous. Lorca was captured and executed by Fascist soldiers at Ainadamar in August 1936 during the Spanish

Civil War. Ainadamar is a Moorish word meaning Fountain of Tears. Osvaldo Golijov's chamber opera *Ainadamar*, libretto by David Henry Hwang, premiered at the Tanglewood Festival in August 2003. Soprano Dawn Upshaw played the aging Margarita Xirgu, mezzo-soprano Kelly O'Connor played Lorca and soprano Amanda Forsythe played Margarita as a young woman. Robert Spano conducted the orchestra. The opera was reprised at the Walt Disney Concert Hall in Los Angeles on February 29, 2004. Golijov creates melodic music partially derived from his Argentine-Jewish background and the opera was warmly received.

"AIN'T IT A PRETTY NIGHT!" *Soprano aria: Susannah (1955). Words and music: Carlisle Floyd*

Eighteen-year-old Susannah observes the sky from her Appalachian home and sings about the stars looking down and the places she's never been. "Ain't it a pretty night!" she says "The sky's so dark and velvet-like." She dreams of leaving the valley to see what's beyond the mountains and wonders if she would be lonesome if she did. Carlisle Floyd's touching aria from his opera SUSANNAH has become a favorite of American sopranos. It was introduced by Phyllis Curtin in the premiere production at Florida State University and then reprised at New York City Opera; her version is on record. The aria is sung by Cheryl Studer in a Lyons Opera production of the complete opera, which is on CD, and by Dawn Upshaw, Renée Fleming and Helen-Kay Eberley on albums devoted to American opera music. "Ain't It a Pretty Night" is one of the American opera arias analyzed in Martial Singher's book *An Interpretive Guide to Operatic Arias* and is featured in Richard Walters' collection *Opera American Style*.

AITKEN, HUGH *American composer (1924–)*

Hugh Aitken has composed a large amount of orchestral and choral music and two operas. FABLES (1975), libretto by the composer, is based on La Fontaine's version of Aesop's *Fables* and features ten of the moral fables presented by four singers. *Felipe* (1980), libretto by L. Tapia based on Cervantes' Spanish tale *El viejo celoso*, deals with an attempt at seduction in 16th century Seville. New York native Aitken studied at Juilliard with opera composer Robert Ward and headed the music department of William Paterson College in Wayne, NJ.

AKHNATEN *1984 opera by Glass*

Akhnaten was voted the third most popular opera of the 20th century by readers of BBC Music Magazine in a poll published in December 1999. Its protagonist is the Egyptian Pharaoh Akhnaten who created a monotheist religion in 1875 BC and ignored the traditional gods of the land. His subjects eventually rebel and restore polytheism. Philip Glass's three-act opera *Akhnaten,* libretto by Shalom Goldman, Robert Israel, Richard Riddell, Jerome Robbins and the composer, was premiered by Stuttgart State Opera on March 24, 1984, at the Wurttemberg Theater. Paul Esswood sang the role of Akhnaten, Milagro Vargas was Nefertiti and Melina Liebermann was Queen Tye. Achim Freyer staged the opera and Dennis Russell Davies conducted the Stuttgart State Opera Orchestra and Chorus. *Akhnaten,* which includes sections written in Akkadian, Egyptian and Biblical Hebrew, has a countertenor protagonist and is composed for twelve soloists, chorus, narrator and orchestra. It was staged by Houston Grand Opera and New York City Opera in 1984, by English National Opera in 1985 and 1987 and by Boston Lyric Opera and Chicago Opera Theater in 2000. It is the third of Glass's trilogy of historical "portrait" operas following *Einstein on the Beach* and *Satyagraha*.

1984 A Composer's Notes. *A Composer's Notes: Philip Glass The Making of an Opera* is a film about productions of *Akhnaten* in Germany and America in 1984. The Stuttgart State Opera production is directed by Achim Freyer with Paul Esswood as Akhnaten, Milagro Vargas as Nefertiti and Dennis Russell Davies as conductor. The Houston Grand Opera production is directed by David Freeman with Christopher Robson as Akhnaten, Marta Senn as Nefertiti and John DeMain as conductor. Michael Blackwood directed the 87-minute film with Mead Hunt as his cinematographer. VAI VHS. **1987 Stuttgart State Opera.** Paul Esswood sings the role of Akhnaten in this complete recording of the Stuttgart State Opera production. Milagro Vargas is Nefertiti, Melina Liebermann is Queen Tye, Tero Hannula is Horemhab, Helmut Holzapfel is the High Priest of Amon, Cornelius Hauptmann is Aye and the Daughters of Akhnaten are Victoria Schneider, Lynn Wilhelm-Königer, Maria Koupilová-Ticha, Christina Wahtler, Geraldine Rose and Angelika Schwarz. Davis Warrilow is the narrator Scribe. Dennis Russell Davies conducts the Stuttgart State Opera Orchestra and Chorus. Sony Classical CD box.

ALABAMA *American state (1819–)*

Opera in Alabama dates back to the early 1800s when touring companies from New Orleans presented operas in French. It is the setting for Kurt Weill's folk opera DOWN IN THE VALLEY, in which the hero escapes from Birmingham Jail, and for Robert Greenleaf's UNDER THE ARBOR, which takes place by the Chattahoochee river. Alabama-born opera singers include James Atherton.

Birmingham: Birmingham Opera Theatre staged Scott Joplin's TREEMONISHA in 1996 at the Alabama Theater. P. Wishart's *Two in the Bush* was presented by the University of Alabama in 1959 and Wishart's *The Captain* in 1960. Robert Greenleaf's UNDER THE ARBOR was premiered in 1992. Alabama Operaworks and Opera Birmingham are based in Birmingham.

Florence: Opera South is based in Florence.

Huntsville: Huntsville Opera Theater presents its opera productions at the Von Braun Civic Center Playhouse.

Mobile: The major opera company in Alabama is Mobile Opera, founded in 1947. It concentrates on European opera but it produced Douglas Moore's THE DEVIL AND DANIEL WEBSTER in 1948, Moore's THE BALLAD OF BABY DOE in 1990 and Aaron Copland's THE TENDER LAND in 2000. Baritone Julian Patrick made his debut with Mobile Opera in 1950.

Montgomery: Huntington College. located in Montgomery, presents operas through its Department of Music, Dance and Fine Art.

Tuscaloosa: Bruce Neely's *Pyramus and Thisbee* was premiered at Alabama University in Tuscaloosa in 1965.

ALASKA *American state (1959–)*

American operas were not staged in Alaska until very recently. The first seems to have been Willard Straight's three-act *Toyon of Alaska,* libretto by Frank Brink, premiered in Anchorage on July 7, 1967.

Anchorage: Anchorage Opera, which presents operas in the Discovery Theater, was founded in 1975. Its second production was Douglas Moore's THE BALLAD OF BABY DOE, staged in 1976, and it has since presented Leonard Bernstein's CANDIDE and Stephen Sondheim's SWEENEY TODD. Resident composer JOHN LUTHER ADAMS has created several works around Alaska legends including EARTH AND THE GREAT WEATHER premiered in 1995.

Douglas: Alan Chapman's *The Lady That's Known as Lou,* libretto by Gordon Duffey, centers around the heroine of Robert

Service's poem *The Shooting of Dan McGrew* and was premiered in Douglas in 1985.

Juneau: Juneau Lyric Opera, founded in 1975, includes American operas and operettas in its repertory. Past programs have included Leonard Bernstein's CANDIDE, Meredith Willson's THE MUSIC MAN and Stephen Sondheim's A LITTLE NIGHT MUSIC.

ALBANESE, LICIA   *American soprano (1913–)*

Licia Albanese, who appeared in a stage production of Deems Taylor's opera PETER IBBETSON at the Empire State Festival in 1960, performs an aria from it on a radio broadcast, available on CD. Albanese, who was born in Italy, came to the U.S. in 1940 and participated in the first U. S. opera telecast. She can be seen on screen as herself in the 1956 Mario Lanza film *Serenade*.

ALBEE, EDWARD   *American playwright/librettist (1930–)*

Edward Albee is best known for plays like *Who's Afraid of Virginia Woolf?* but he also wrote opera librettos. They were created for William Flanagan who composed incidental music for Albee's plays *The Sandbox* and *The Ballad of the Sad Café*. BARTLEBY, based on the Herman Melville novella, was written by Albee in collaboration with I. J. Hinton and premiered at York Playhouse in New York January 24, 1961. *The Ice Age* was commissioned by New York City Opera in 1967 but never completed. Albee, born in Virginia but brought up in Larchmont, NY, found success with his first play, the 1958 *The Zoo Story*.

ALBERGHETTI, ANNA MARIA   *American soprano (1936–)*

Anna Maria Alberghetti began her public career by portraying Monica in Gian Carlo Menotti's 1951 film THE MEDIUM with memorable performances of the arias "THE BLACK SWAN" and "MONICA'S WALTZ." She also starred in a 1967 TV production of the operetta KISMET with José Ferrer. Paramount Pictures thought she might be another Deanna Durbin and had her perform opera arias in the Bing Crosby musical *Here Comes the Groom* and the Lauritz Melchior musical *The Stars Are Singing*. It didn't happen. The high point of her later career was a Tony for the Broadway music *Carnival*. Alberghetti, who was born in Italy, moved to America after her success in *The Medium*, which was shot in Rome.

ALBERT, DONNIE RAY   *American bass-baritone (1950–)*

Donnie Ray Albert sings the role of Porgy in Houston Grand Opera's 1976 Grammy-winning recording of George Gershwin's PORGY AND BESS. After studies in Louisiana, he made his first professional singing appearance as Parson Alltalk in Houston Grand Opera's production of Scott Joplin's TREEMONISHA in 1975. He also sang Father Lestant in William Grant Still's A BAYOU LEGEND, though he did not create the role. Albert, born in Baton Rouge, Louisiana, studied at Louisiana State and Southern Methodist universities.

ALBERTS, EUNICE   *American contralto (1927–)*

Eunice Alberts created roles in two American operas. She was the Elderly Woman in David Tamkin's THE DYBBUK at the New York City Opera in 1951 and Rebecca Nurse in Robert Ward's THE CRUCIBLE at the NYCO in 1961. She sang the role of Sally in the first recording of Samuel Barber's A HAND OF BRIDGE in 1960. On stage she portrayed Lulu in Lukas Foss's THE JUMPING FROG OF CALAVERAS COUNTY, Miss Todd in Gian Carlo Menotti's THE OLD MAID AND THE THIEF, Augusta Tabor in Douglas Moore's THE BALLAD OF BABY DOE and Baba the Turk in Igor Stravinsky's THE RAKE'S PROGRESS. Alberts, who was born in Boston, made her debut with NYCO in 1951.

ALBRIGHT, WILLIAM   *American composer/pianist (1944–1998)*

William Albright is best known for his work in reviving interest in ragtime and the music of Scott Joplin but he also composed two operas. *Cross of Gold,* libretto by the composer, was presented in Chicago in 1975. *The Magic City*, libretto by G. Garrett, was commissioned by the University of Michigan in 1978 and gained him a Guggenheim Fellowship. He has written other vocal music but his best-known compositions are for organ and piano. Albright, born in Gary, Indiana, studied at Juilliard, Michigan University and the Paris Conservatory and began teaching music at Michigan in 1982.

ALCOTT, LOUISA MAY   *American novelist (1832–1888)*

Louisa May Alcott wrote many novels and stories, including potboiler thrillers under a pseudonym, but she is best known for her semi-autobiographical 1868 classic LITTLE WOMEN. There are four musical versions of it. Eleanor Everest Freer's *Scenes from Little Women* premiered at the Musicians' Club of Women in Chicago April 2, 1934. Risë Stevens sang the role of the mother in Richard Adler's *Little Women* on CBS television in 1958. William Dyer's musical *Jo* opened at the Orpheum Theatre in New York in 1964. Mark Adamo's opera *Little Women,* which premiered at the Houston Opera Studio in 1998, was revived in Houston in March 2000 and staged in Central City in 2001.

ALDA, FRANCES   *American soprano (1883–1952)*

Soprano Frances Alda, who married Metropolitan Opera general manager Giulio Gatti-Casazza in 1910, starred in three American operas that premiered at the Met. In 1913 she created the role of Roxane in Walter Damrosch's CYRANO. In 1914 she starred as Madeleine in Victor Herbert's MADELEINE and recorded her aria

Soprano Frances Alda

"A Perfect Day." In 1920 she created the role of Cleopatra in Henry Hadley's CLEOPATRA'S NIGHT. Chicago newspaper magnate Harold McCormick hired Alda to train Ganna Walska, the opera singer who was the prototype for the opera singer in *Citizen Kane*; it didn't help much as Walska was pelted with vegetables at the performance. Alda was born in Christchurch, New Zealand, and became an American citizen in 1939 Her entertaining autobiography is titled *Men, Women and Tenors.*

ALDEN, CHRISTOPHER *American director (1949–)*

Christopher Alden, twin brother of David, directed the premiere of Anthony Davis's TANIA in Philadelphia in 1992, Stewart Wallace's HARVEY MILK in Houston in 1995 and Wallace's HOPPER'S WIFE in Long Beach in 1997. His Glimmerglass Opera production of Virgil Thomson's THE MOTHER OF US ALL was hailed by critics as a theatrical masterpiece when it was reprised by New York City Opera in 2000. He has been director of production at Long Beach Opera and associate director at opera at the Academy in New York City.

ALDEN, DAVID *American director (1949–)*

David Alden, twin brother of Christopher, directed the premiere of Conrad Susa's THE LOVE OF DON PERLIMPLIN in Purchase, NY, in 1984 and William Bolcom's CASINO PARADISE in Philadelphia in 1990. He created a punk version of Igor Stravinsky's THE RAKE'S PROGRESS in Amsterdam in 1982 and staged the innovative revival of John Philip Sousa's THE GLASS BLOWERS at Glimmerglass in 2000. He was assistant director on Carlisle Floyd's BILBY'S DOLL at Houston Grand Opera in 1976.

ALEXANDER, ROBERTA *American soprano (1949–)*

Roberta Alexander won acclaim singing the role of Bess in the Metropolitan Opera's 1986 production of George Gershwin's PORGY AND BESS after taking over the role from Grace Bumbry. She is featured as Bess on two recordings, one with Simon Estes as Porgy and Leonard Slatkin conducting the Berlin Radio Symphony Orchestra, the other with Gregg Baker as Porgy with Zubin Mehta conducting the New York Philharmonic Orchestra. She performs arias from Leonard Bernstein's CANDIDE and MASS on her 1991 album *Bernstein: Songs* and from Samuel Barber's ANTONY AND CLEOPATRA and VANESSA on her 1992 album *Barber: Songs and Arias.* She has also recorded an album of songs by Aaron Copland. Alexander, who was born in Lynchburg, Virginia, studied in Michigan and Europe and made her debut in the Netherlands.

ALFRED *1757 masque by Smith*

William Smith's masque *Alfred,* subtitled *An Oratorial Exercise,* is the first opera-like music drama by an American presented in America. Smith, Provost of the College of Philadelphia, adapted Thomas Arne's *The Masque of Alfred* about 9th century English King Alfred the Great for presentation at his college in during the Christmas holidays in 1756 and in January 1757. It was in three acts with prologue and epilogue, the actor/singers wore costumes and some of the music was original. Jacob Duché played King Alfred, his wife Elizabeth (sister of composer Francis Hopkinson), Miss Lawrence sang the female parts and college students took the other roles. John Palmer conducted the chamber orchestra which included harpsichord, violins, cello and flute. Composer Francis Hopkinson is said to have played the harpsichord. The libretto was published in the *Pennsylvania Gazette* in January and February 1757.

ALGLALA *1923 opera by DeLeone*

Chippewa maiden Alglala is wooed by young brave Ozawa-animiki but falls in love with white fugitive Ralph. When jealous Ozawa-animiki threatens to harm the couple, Alglala hits him with an axe. They flee the village but her father Namegos sends warriors in pursuit. Francesco DeLeone's one-act opera *Alglala: A Romance of the Mesa,* libretto by Cecil Fanning, was premiered by Cleveland Grand Opera at the Akron Armory in Akron, Ohio, on May 24, 1923. Mabel Garrison was Alglala, Edward Johnson was Ralph, Francis Sadler was Namegos and librettist/baritone Cecil Fanning was Ozawa-animiki. Carl Grossman conducted the Cleveland Symphony Orchestra. Composer and librettist are both Ohio natives. The opera was reprised in Cleveland in 1924, won the Bispham Medal that year and was reprised again in Chicago in 1936. *Alglala* was one of the first American operas presented on radio. It was broadcast by NBC's National Grand Opera Company on February 4, 1929, with Cesare Sudaro conducting the Grand Opera Orchestra.

ALICE IN WONDERLAND *Music theater based on Carroll fantasies*

Alice falls down a rabbit hole and is involved in a series of surrealistic adventures with the White Rabbit, The Queen of Hearts, the Mad Hatter, the Cheshire Cat and other strange creatures. Lewis Carroll's novels *Alice in Wonderland* (1865) and *Through the Looking Glass* (1872) have been popular with American composers but have not inspired a full-scale opera.

1966 Moose Charlap. Moose Charlap's musical *Through the Looking Glass,* libretto by Albert Simmons based on the Lewis Carroll novel, premiered on NBC Television on November 6, 1966. The starry cast included Judi Rolin as Alice, Nanette Fabray, Jack Palance, Jimmy Durante, Robert Coote and Agnes Moorehead. Alan Handley directed and Harper MacKay was music director. RCA LP/Sultan VHS. **1976 Robert Chauls.** Robert Chauls' 90-minute comic opera *Alice in Wonderland,* libretto by the composer based on the Lewis Carroll novel, was premiered by Valley Opera in Van Nuys, California, on January 16, 1976, and reprised at Lake George in 1980. **1978 Micki Grant.** Micki Grant's *Alice,* libretto by Vinnette Carroll based on *Alice in Wonderland,* opened at the Forrest Theater in Philadelphia on May 31, 1978. The large cast was headed by Debbie Allen as Alice, Alice Ghostley as the White Queen and Paula Kelly as the Black Queen. Joyce Brown was conductor and Vinnette Carroll directed. **1985 Steve Allen.** Steve Allen's four-hour *Alice in Wonderland,* libretto by Pulitzer Prize-winning playwright Paul Zindel based on *Alice in Wonderland* and *Through the Looking Glass,* premiered on CBS Television December 9 and 10, 1985. It was a lavish spectacle produced by Irwin Allen with an all-star cast headed by Natalie Gregor as Alice, Jayne Meadows as the Queen of Hearts, Sammy Davis Jr. as the Caterpillar and Pat Morita as the Cheshire Cat. Harry Harris directed and Morton Stevens conducted the orchestra. Warner VHS/Columbia LP.

ALLAN, LEWIS *American songwriter/librettist (1903–1986)*

"Lewis Allan," the penname of Abel Meeropol, wrote librettos for operas by ELIE SIEGMEISTER, LEHMAN ENGEL, ROBERT KURKA, and MARTIN KALMANOFF, but is best remembered for writing two famous songs: "Strange Fruit," made popular by Billie Holiday, and "The House I Live In," made popular by Frank Sinatra. For Siegmeister he wrote the one-act folk opera *Darling Corie,* based on the tragic ballad, and it premiered at Hofstra University in 1954. For Engel he wrote *Golden Ladder,* a musical presented in Cleveland in 1953; MALADY OF LOVE, an opera about a psycho-analyst seduced by a patient which premiered in New York in 1954; and THE SOLDIER, an opera based on Roald Dahl's story about a crazed ex-soldier that was presented in New York in 1956. For Kurka he wrote the very successful three-act THE GOOD SOLDIER SCHWEIK, based on the novel by Jaroslav Hašek, which premiered at New York City Opera in 1957. For Kalmanoff he wrote THE INSECT COMEDY, an opera based on the play by Karel and Josef Capek; it was completed in 1977 but did not premiere at Hunter College in New York until 1997. Allan, who was born and brought up in the Bronx and taught for more than 25 years at DeWitt Clinton School, was a stout defender of Julius and Ethel Rosenberg and adopted their children when the couple were executed as Soviet spies in 1953.

ALLEN, BETTY   *American mezzo-soprano (1930–)*

Bette Allen created the role of Monisha in Scott Joplin's TREEMONISHA in Houston and sings the role on the cast recording. She is Commère in the 1982 recording of Virgil Thomson's FOUR SAINTS IN THREE ACTS, the opera in which she had made her debut in 1952, and she sings excerpts from it in documentary films about Thomson and Gertrude Stein. She sang Queenie in Jerome Kern's SHOW BOAT at New York City Opera in 1954. In 1979 she became executive director of the Harlem School of the Arts. Allen, born in Campbell, Ohio, has also sung with San Francisco Opera and Canadian Opera.

ALLEN, CHET   *American boy soprano (1940–1984)*

Chet Allen created the role of Amahl in the first TV opera, Gian Carlo Menotti's 1951 AMAHL AND THE NIGHT VISITORS, and is on the original cast recording. His success led to a Hollywood film, Douglas Sirk's *1952 Meet Me at the Fair*, in which he played an orphan befriended by Dan Dailey. He was also featured in Enzo Pinza's operatic 1953 TV series *Bonino*. Allen, a treble discovered by Menotti in the Columbus Boys Choir, continued to sing with that group until 1956. He was unable to cope with the loss of fame and committed suicide in 1984.

ALLEN, PAUL HASTINGS   *American composer (1883–1952)*

Boston-born composer Paul Hastings Allen composed twelve operas, most of them with Italian librettos and premiered in Italy. After graduating from Harvard in 1903, he moved to Florence where his opera *O munasterio* was performed in 1911. *Il filtro* was staged in Genoa on October 26, 1913. His major opera, the three-act *L'Ultimo del Moicano*, libretto by Zangarini based on James Fenimore Coopers novel THE LAST OF THE MOHICANS, was premiered in Florence in 1916 and published by Ricordi. The one-act *Milda* was premiered in Venice on June 14, 1913. He served with the U. S. diplomatic service during World War I and returned to Boston in 1920. Allen's other operas include *Cleopatra* (1921), based on the play by Sardou, and *La piccola Figaro* (1931) which was retitled *Mamzelle Figaro* and performed in Lindenhurst, NY, on March 20, 1948.

ALTHOUSE, PAUL   *American tenor (1889–1954)*

Paul Althouse, the first American tenor to sing at the Metropolitan Opera without first gaining a reputation in Europe, created roles in four American operas at the Met. He was François in Victor Herbert's MADELEINE in 1914, the Squire in Reginald De Koven's THE CANTERBURY PILGRIMS in 1917, Lionel Rhodes in Charles Cadman's SHANEWIS in 1918 and Stephen Pauloff in Joseph

Tenor Paul Althouse, ca. 1936

Breil's THE LEGEND in 1919. Althouse, born in Reading, Pennsylvania, made his Met debut in 1913 and continued to sing there until 1940. Afterwards he was a voice teacher and his pupils included Richard Tucker and Eleanor Steber.

ALTMAN, ROBERT   *American film/opera director (1925–)*

Hollywood filmmaker Robert Altman has been involved with three American operas. The first was *The Rake's Progress,* which he directed for Lyons Opera in France and then for the University of Michigan in Ann Arbor. William Bolcom saw it and invited Alt-

Director Robert Altman

Des Moines Metro Opera staged Gian Carlo Menotti's popular Christmas opera Amahl and the Night Visitors in 2003. Photograph courtesy of Des Moines Metro Opera.

man to collaborate on his opera MᴄTᴇᴀɢᴜᴇ; Altman co-wrote the libretto and staged it for Lyric Opera of Chicago in October 1992. The collaboration was so well received that Lyric Opera of Chicago commissioned Bolcom and Altman to turn Altman's 1978 film A Wᴇᴅᴅɪɴɢ into an opera and it was premiered in 2004. Altman's other films include *M.A.S.H.*, *Nashville*, *Gosford Park*, *Short Cuts*, and *The Player*.

AMAHL AND THE NIGHT VISITORS   *1951 TV opera by Menotti*

Amahl, a crippled boy with a crutch, and his loving mother are visited on Christmas Eve by the Three Kings, Melchior, Balthazar and Kaspar, on their way to Bethlehem with valuable gifts. The family is desperately poor but offers hospitality with the help of neighbors. When the Kings are asleep, the mother is tempted by the treasure and is caught taking a piece of gold by the Page. When Amahl learns why the Kings are taking their treasures as gifts, he offers his crutch as a present for the Holy Child. He is miraculously healed and joins the Kings on their visit. *Amahl and the Night Visitors*, the first opera created for television, was written, composed and staged by Gian Carlo Menotti for NBC Opera Theatre as a hour-long Christmas Eve special and premiered December 24, 1951. Rosemary Kuhlmann created the role of Mother, Chet Allen was Amahl, David Aiken was Melchior, Leon Lishner was Balthazar, Andrew McKinley was Kaspar and Francis Mona-

chino was the Page. Samuel Chotzinoff produced, Thomas Schippers conducted the NBC Orchestra, Eugene Berman designed the costumes and sets, John Butler created the choreography and Kirk Browning directed the live telecast. Chotzinoff, who had commissioned the opera, had also commissioned Menotti's radio opera *The Old Maid and the Thief* in 1939. Menotti has said he was inspired to create the opera by Bosch's painting *Adoration of the Magi*. *Amahl* proved so popular it was repeated annually for years in the Hallmark Hall of Fame series. It was quickly adapted for the stage and received its theatrical premiere at Indiana University School of Music in Bloomington on February 21, 1952. Marilyn Rights sang the Mother, Ronald Jennings was Amahl, Jack DeLon was Kaspar, James Serviss was Melchior, Don Vogel was Balthazar and Don Slagel was the Page. Hans Busch staged the opera and Ernst Hoffman conducted. The first professional stage production was at New York City Opera on April 9, 1952, with Kuhlmann and Allen reprising the roles they created on TV and Lawrence Winters, Michael Pollock and Richard Wentworth as the three kings while Thomas Schippers conducted. *Amahl* became very popular with church, school and community groups and has been staged more often than any other American opera. It has also been popular with television companies around the world.

1951 NBC Opera Theatre. The NBC Opera Theatre premiere was telecast live on December 24, 1951. Rosemary Kuhlmann is Mother, Chet Allen is Amahl, David Aiken is Melchior, Leon

Lishner is Balthazar, Andrew McKinley is Kaspar and Francis Monachino is the Page. Thomas Schippers conducts the NBC Orchestra and Chorus and Kirk Browning directed for television. Videos at UCLA and Museum of Television and Radio. **1952 NBC Opera Theatre.** The NBC Opera Theatre premiere cast recorded the opera in a studio on January 4 and 10, 1952. Rosemary Kuhlmann is Mother, Chet Allen is Amahl, David Aiken is Melchior, Leon Lishner is Balthazar Andrew McKinley is Kaspar and Francis Monachino is the Page. Thomas Schippers conducts the NBC Orchestra and Chorus. RCA Victor/HMV LP and RCA CD. **1952–1954 NBC Opera Theatre.** *Amahl and the Night Visitors* was presented eight times in the Hallmark Hall of Fame series. The premiere cast sang in an Easter telecast on April 13, 1952, then Bill McIver replaced Chet Allen as Amahl. Videos at UCLA. **1953 Italian radio.** Giulietta Simionato sings the role of Mother in this recording of an Italian RAI radio broadcast of the opera on May 9, 1953. Leopold Stokowski conducts the RAI Orchestra. Omega Opera Archives CD. **1954 BBC Television.** Gladys Whitred is Mother with Charles Vignoles as Amahl in this production telecast by BBC December 20, 1954. John Lewis is Kaspar, John Cameron is Melchior, Scott Joyn is Balthazar and Edric Connor is the Page. Christian Simpson directed and Stanford Robinson conducted the Wigmore Ensemble. 50 minutes. Video in BBC archive. **1963 NBC Opera Theater.** Martha King is Mother in this 1963 NBC Opera Theater TV production. Kurt Yaghjian is Amahl, John McCollum is Kaspar, Richard Cross is Melchior, Willis Patterson is Balthazar, and Julian Patrick is the Page. Herbert Grossman conducts the NBC Orchestra. Kirk Browning directed the telecast. Video at MTR/Soundtrack RCA LP. **1963 Teatro Comunale, Florence.** Giulietta Simionato sings the role of the Mother in this live recording of a stage production of the opera at the Teatro Comunale in Florence, Italy. Leopold Stokowski conducts the Teatro Comunale Orchestra. Live Opera audiocassette. **1978 Brown film.** Teresa Stratas sings Mother in this film shot in Israel with Arvin Brown directing. Robert Sapolsky is Amahl, Giorgio Tozzi is Melchior, Willard White is Balthazar and Nico Castel is Kaspar. Ivy Baker Jones designed the costumes and Jesus Lopez-Cobos conducts the Ambrosian Opera Chorus and Philharmonia Orchestra. 52 minutes. VAI VHS and CD. **1986 Royal Opera House.** Menotti recorded his Royal Opera House production at the Sadler Wells Theatre in London on December 21, 1986. Lorna Haywood is Mother, James Rainbird is Amahl, John Dobson is Kaspar, Donald Maxwell is Melchior, Curtis Watson is Balthazar and Christopher Painter is the Page. David Syrus conducts the Royal Opera House Orchestra and Chorus. MCA and Jay CD.

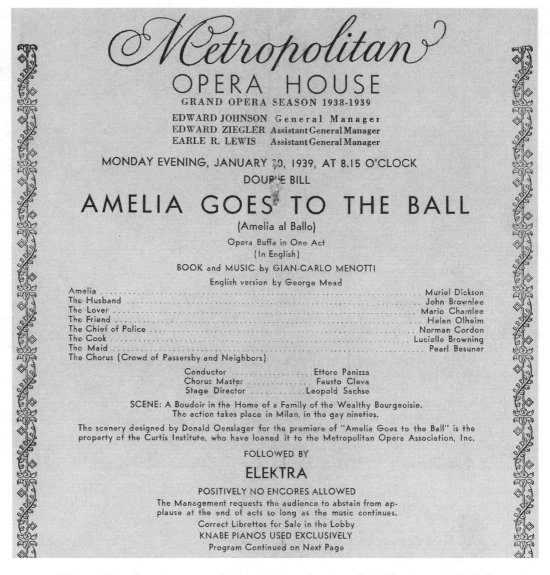

Metropolitan Opera program for its 1938 production of *Amelia Goes to the Ball.*

AMATO, PASQUALE   *American baritone (1878–1942)*

Pasquale Amato created the role of Cyrano in Walter Damrosch's opera CYRANO DE BERGERAC at the Metropolitan Opera in 1913 though he is more remembered for creating the role of Jack Rance in the world premiere of Puccini's *La Fanciulla del West* at the Met in 1910. Amato made his debut in his native Naples in 1900, first sang at the Met in 1908, and stayed with the company until 1921. He left many recordings but none of arias from American operas.

AMELIA GOES TO THE BALL (AMELIA AL BALLO)
1937 opera by Menotti

Amelia is looking forward to going to a fancy ball. It seems it may not be possible when her husband finds out about her lover upstairs and he ends up in hospital while the lover goes to prison. However, Amelia persuades the investigating police inspector to take her. Gian Carlo Menotti's comic opera *Amelia Goes to the Ball* (*Amelia al Ballo*), his first stage success, has an Italian libretto by the composer but the opera was premiered in English in a translation by George Mead at the Philadelphia Academy of Music on April 1, 1937. Margaret Daum sang the title role, William Martin was her lover, Conrad Mayo played her husband, Edwina Eustis was Amelia's Friend, Leonard Treash was the Police Chief, Wilburta Horn was the Cook and Charlotte Daniels was the Maid. Fritz Reiner conducted the Curtis Institute Orchestra. The Metropolitan Opera staged the opera the following year, on March 3, 1938, with Muriel Dickson as Amelia, Mario Chamlee as the Lover, John Brownlee as the Husband, Helen Olheim as the Friend, Norman Cordon as the Police Chief, Lucille Browning as the Cook and Charlotte Symons as the Maid. Donald Oenslager designed the set, Leopold Sachse directed the production and Ettore Panizza conducted the Metropolitan Opera Orchestra. The opera continues to be staged and seems to have entered the repertory.

1937 Curtis Institute of Music. Most of the original cast sang in a CBS broadcast of the opera from the Curtis Institute of Music in Philadelphia on May 2, 1937. Margaret Daum is Amelia, Conrad Mayo is the Husband, William Martin is the lover, Elsie MacFarlane is the Friend, Charlotte Daniels is the Maid and Wilburta Horn is the Cook. Edward Krug is the Announcer and Sylvan Levin conducts the Curtis Institute Symphony Orchestra and Chorus. Pearl 2-CD (with *The Medium* and *The Telephone*). **1939 Philadelphia Orchestra.** Eugene Ormandy leads the Philadelphia Orchestra in a recording of the Overture to the opera made on January 8, 1939. It was reissued in 1995 on the Smithsonian CD *Great American Orchestras* and in 2000 on the Pearl CD *Gian Carlo Menotti.* **1954 Teatro alla Scala.** Margherita Carosio sings Amelia in this recording sung in Italian based on a 1954 La Scala production. Giacinto Prandelli is the Lover, Rolando Panerai is the Husband, Maria Amandini is the Friend, Enrico Campi is the Chief of Police and Silvana Zanolli and Elena Mazzoni are the two maids. Nino Sanzogno conducts the Teatro alla Scala Orchestra and Chorus. Columbia and Angel LP/Odeon and Testament CD. **1961 Columbia Symphony Orchestra.** Thomas Schippers leads the Columbia Symphony Orchestra in a recording of the Overture made at the Manhattan Center in 1961. It's on the album *Opera Overtures.* Columbia LP/Sony Classics CD. 1978 Leontyne Price. Leontyne Price sings the aria "While I waste these precious hours" accompanied by the New Philharmonia Orchestra conducted by Nello Santi. It's on the albums *Prima Donna/ Volume 4* (RCA Victor LP) and *The Prima Donna Collection* (RCA CD). **1991 Metropolitan Opera Orchestra.** James Conlon leads members of the Metropolitan Opera Orchestra in the Overture at a gala concert at Avery Fisher Hall November 10, 1991. The concert, titled *A Salute to American Music,* is on a RCA Victor CD.

AMERICAN INDEPENDENT *1781 opera/oratorio by Hopkinson*

Francis Hopkinson's patriotic *America Independent,* later renamed *The Temple of Minerva,* was one of the first American oratorios staged in America. A through sung "oratorial entertainment," it was created to celebrate the American victory over the British. It was premiered in Philadelphia on March 21, 1781, at the home of the French ambassador to the Continental Congress. Hopkinson wrote the words and arranged the music pasticcio style, meaning he borrowed it from Handel, Arne and Thomas. It consists of thirteen musical numbers in four scenes sung by four

characters. It was published in two versions in Philadelphia in 1781 and reconstructed by Gillian Anderson in 1979. Hopkinson, one of the signers of the Declaration of Independence, claimed to be America's first native composer.

1982 Isaiah Thomas Singers. The Isaiah Thomas Singers sing "Great Minerva" from *American Independent* aka *The Temple of Minerva.* The music is based on Handel's "See the Conquering Hero Comes" from *Judas Maccabaeus.* David P. McKay directs the singers and Stephen Long accompanies on organ. It's on the album *The Cantata in Early American Music.* Folkways Records LP.

AMERICANIZED OPERAS *American operas based on European operas*

Some European operas have been "Americanized," that is turned into American operas with new English-language librettos featuring American characters in American stories singing new words to old music. The most successful is Oscar Hammerstein's CARMEN JONES (1943) in which Bizet's tale of Spanish gypsies is transmuted into a story about African Americans during World War II. Charles Friedman used Verdi's *Aida* as the basis for MY DARLIN' AIDA (1952) with the story re-set in the American South during the Civil War. Victor Herbert's THE MAGIC KNIGHT, a spoof based on *Lohengrin* with the knight arriving in a cab pulled by a swan, was popular with the critics when it opened on Broadway in 1906 but went over the heads of the audiences. The earliest work of this kind is William Mitchell's *The Roof Scrambler,* a parody of *La Sonnambula* presented in New York in 1839. (Peter Sellars has staged several operas in updated American settings, including *The Marriage of Figaro* in Trump Tower, but they cannot be considered "Americanized operas" as they were still sung in Italian and the librettos were not changed.)

AN AMERICAN TRAGEDY *2005 opera by Picker*

Theodore Dreiser's 1925 novel *An American Tragedy,* about a tragic love triangle which leads to an ambitious young man drowning a poor pregnant girlfriend so he can marry a wealthy girlfriend, was the basis of this opera by composer Tobias Picker using a libretto by Gene Scheer. It premiered at the Metropolitan Opera on December 2, 2005, with Nathan Gunn as the murderous Clyde, Patricia Racette as the victim Roberta and Susan Graham as the wealthy Sondra. Francesco Zambello directed and James Conlan conducted. The opera, which had mixed reviews, was broadcast by the Met. The novel was also the basis of Hollywood films made in 1931 and 1951.

AMES, ROGER *American composer (1944–)*

Roger Ames collaborated with librettist Laura Harrington on three operas. HEARTS ON FIRE, about a young girl's coming of age, was premiered by the New Music Ensemble in Minneapolis in 1995 and warmly received. Earlier they had collaborated on *Angel Face,* performed in St. Paul and Omaha in 1988, and *Martin Guerre,* staged in New York in 1989. Ames, a native of Cooperstown, New York, began his operatic career in 1980 with *Amarantha* based on the Wilbur Steele story "How Beautiful with Shoes" and performed in Connecticut, New York and Maryland. He received an NEA grant in 1976 for the opera *Amistad* based on the same historical events as Anthony Davis's 1997 opera of the same title.

AMISTAD *1997 opera by Davis*

African prisoners on the slave ship Amistad rebel while being transported to America in the early 19th century and end up being tried in an American court. Anthony Davis's opera *Amistad,* libretto by his poet cousin Thulani Davis, was premiered by Lyric Theater of Chicago on November 29, 1997. Mark S. Doss was slave leader Cinque, Thomas Young was Trickster God, Florence Quivar was Goddess of the Waters, John Daniecki was abolitionist Tappan, Stephen West was John Quincy Adams, William Watson was President Martin Van Buren, Kimberly Jones was Margru, Eugene Perry was Antonio, Mark Baker was Navigator, Wilbur Pauley was Don Pedro, Anisha M. McFarland was Bahia, David Lee Brewer was Kinna, E Mani Cadet was Kaleh, Patrick Blackwell was Burnah, Timothy Robert Blevins was Grabeau and Kevin Maynor was Cook. George C. Wolfe directed, Riccardo Hernandez designed the set and Dennis Russell Davies conducted. Steven Spielberg's film about the same revolt also premiered in 1997.

1997 Lyric Opera of Chicago Commentary. Critical analysis by Alfred Glasser of *Amistad* on audiotape in the Women's Board of Lyric Opera Commentaries series. It is basically an interview with composer Davis including historical background to the opera and information about the composer. Lyric Opera Commentaries audiocassette.

L'AMORE DI FATIMA   *1949 "movie opera" by Castelnuovo-Tedesco*

Italian American composer Mario Castelnuovo-Tedesco created the opera *L'Amore di Fatima* (Fatima's Love) for the 1949 film *Everybody Does It*. It tells the story of an Aida-like love affair between Solomon and Fatima. Paul Douglas sings the baritone role of Salimano (Solomon) with Linda Darnell as the sexy Fatima when the opera is premiered by the American Scala Opera Company. The premiere turns into a comic disaster. Douglas, wearing ridiculous horned helmet and beard, takes so many pills and potions to quell his nerves that he collapses. He pulls down the set, falls into the orchestra pit and the audience roars with laughter. Douglas's opera career is over but he doesn't mind. He had been persuaded to sing by Darnell because of his fine voice but it is Douglas's wife (Celeste Holm) who wanted to be an opera singer. Douglas's voice is dubbed by New York City Opera baritone Stephen Kemalyan and Darnell is dubbed by San Francisco Opera soprano Helen Spann. The Italian opera singers are Trina Varela, Baldo Minuti, Antonio Filauri, Mario Siletti and Alfonso Pedroza. The film was based on James Cain's story *Career in C Major*. Edmund Goulding directed for Twentieth Century Fox. Fox VHS.

AMOUR ET GLOIRE   *1943 "movie opera" by Ward*

A count woos a princess on a grandiose double-stairway and then goes off to war in this opera about love and glory. Composer Edward Ward and librettist George Waggner created the "French" opera *Amour et Gloire* (aka *Ghislaine D'Armanae*) for the 1943 MGM movie *The Phantom of the Opera*. About eight minutes of the opera are seen on stage at the Paris Opera House, including opening chorus, soprano and baritone arias and duet. The music sounds familiar because it's based on themes by Chopin. In the film the soprano role is sung in the first act by Paris Opera diva Biancarolli (Jane Farrar) partnered by house baritone Anatole Garon (Nelson Eddy). After the Phantom slips a knockout drug in her drink, she is replaced by understudy Christine DuBois (Susanna Foster) who hits sizzling high notes and wows the audience and conductor. The other opera created for the movie is called LE PRINCE MASQUE DE LA CAUCASIE. The opera sequences were staged by Wilhelm Von Wymetal Jr. of the Metropolitan Opera and Lester Horton while Arthur Lubin directed the 93-minute color movie for Universal. MCA Universal VHS.

Linda Darnell in the movie opera *L'Amore di Fatima* created for the 1949 film *Everybody Does It.*

AMRAM, DAVID   *American composer (1930–)*

David Amram's opera THE FINAL INGREDIENT, about a Passover meal in a concentration camp, was telecast in 1965 and has remained so popular its soundtrack has been released on CD. His second opera, TWELFTH NIGHT, based on the Shakespeare play as revised by Joseph Papp, was staged at the Lake George Opera Festival. The Philadelphia-born composer has created music for theater and cinema as well as the opera house. He began composing for Ford's Theater in Washington and then became music director of Joseph Papp's Shakespeare Festival in New York. His film scores include *Splendor in the Grass* and *The Arrangement* for Elia Kazan and *The Manchurian Candidate* for John Frankenheimer. He has become a cult figure for Beat Generation admirers because of his collaboration with Jack Kerouac on the 1959 avant-garde film *Pull My Daisy.*

AND DAVID WEPT   *1971 opera by Laderman*

King David, now old, weeps over a great evil he committed as a young man. A married woman called Bathsheba had bathed nude on the roof of her house in order to seduce him. She succeeded but then became pregnant and was afraid she would be condemned as an adulteress as she was no longer with her husband, Uriah the Hittite. Uriah refuses to cooperate in a cover-up so David sends him off to war to be killed. The Prophet Nathan denounced David. The love triangle protagonists tell their story in flashback as dancers re-enact it. Ezra Laderman's 50-minute Biblical opera *And David Wept*, libretto by Joseph Darion loosely based on the book of Samuel in the Bible, premiered on CBS Television on April 8, 1971, on a commission from CBS News. Rosalind Elias sang the role of Bathsheba, Ara Berberian was Uriah and Alfredo Antonini conducted the CBS Orchestra. The opera was given its stage premiere at the 92nd Street YMHA in New York City on May 31, 1980.

AND GOD CREATED WHALES   *2000 semi-opera by Eckert.*

A composer (Rinde Eckert), is alone in a room trying to write an opera based on *Moby Dick* and is helped by a Muse (Nora Cole). As he is losing his memory, he carries a tape recorder which gives instructions on how to finish the opera. The Muse also plays an opera singer and the Pequod sailors, including harpooner Queequeg. She ends the piece singing Ishmael's final words. Rinde Eckert's 75-minute experimental semi-opera *And God Created Whales*, libretto by the composer, was premiered by Foundry Theater at Culture Project Theater in New York on September 15, 2000. The production was staged by David Schweizer with lighting by Kevin Adams. See also MOBY DICK.

AND THE WALLS CAME TUMBLING DOWN   *1976 opera by Roosevelt*

Joseph is the leader of a community of freed slaves in 1664 New Amsterdam but the Dutch colony is being bombarded by the British. Joshua supports the Dutch, who lose and is hanged as a traitor by the victors. Joseph Willard Roosevelt's 55-minute opera *And the Walls Came Tumbling Down*, libretto by Lofton Mitchell, was premiered at the Harlem School of Arts in New York City on March 16, 1976. It is an unusual opera both because of its subject, the little-known black community in early Manhattan, and its creators, a noted African American playwright (Mitchell wrote the hit musical *Bubbling Black Sugar*) and a direct descendent of a New Amsterdam colonist (Roosevelt's grandfather was President Theodore Roosevelt).

ANDERSON, BETH   *American composer (1950–)*

Beth Anderson studied with John Cage and Robert Ashley and her operas reflect their unconventional ideas about music theater. Her chamber opera *Queen Christina*, which mixes singers, pop music and tape collage in a portrait of the Swedish monarch, premiered at Mills College in Oakland, CA, on December 1, 1973.

Zen Piece, presented at the New York avant-garde center The Kitchen in 1976, poses gnomic questions. *Soap Tuning* (1976), based on TV soap operas, uses quotes from these shows as its non-narrative libretto. *Riot Rot* (1984) mixes one singer, two narrators, tape, film, electronic music and traditional instruments into a portrait of New York street riots. Anderson, born in Lexington, Kentucky, has also composed an oratorio (*Joan*, premiered in 1974) and other vocal and instrumental music.

ANDERSON, JUNE   *American soprano (1952–)*

June Anderson has won many admirers for her portrayal of Cunegonde in the 1989 operatic recording of CANDIDE, especially on the coloratura aria GLITTER AND BE GAY. She sings the role of the First Lady in the 2000 recording of Bernstein's *A White House Cantata*, the concert version of his musical *1600 Pennsylvania Avenue*. The Boston-born singer made her debut at the New York City Opera in 1978 and has been heard around the world, especially in *bel canto* roles.

ANDERSON, LAURIE   *American composer (1947–)*

Laurie Anderson composes multi-media musical stage works with affinities to experimental opera which can be described as solo operas. Her music has similarities to that of Glass and Reich and she is featured on the recording of Glass/Wilson opera THE CIVIL WARS. Her first notable production was the l2-hour epic *The Life and Times of Josef Stalin* presented at BAM in 1973. Her minimalist aria "O Superman (for Massenet)," a pop hit in England in 1981 and early evidence of her interest in opera, comes from her 1981 debut album *Big Science* and is part of her 1982 epic UNITED STATES, recorded live in performance at BAM. Her opera *Empty Places* premiered at the Spoleto Festival USA in 1989 and her opera about MOBY DICK was first performed there in 1999. Anderson, born in Chicago, Illinois, trained as a violinist and features her electronic violin in her shows but she is also a poet and writes her own librettos. Like poet e. e. cummings, she is a romantic in avant-garde disguise.

ANDERSON, MAXWELL   *American playwright (1888–1959)*

Maxwell Anderson, whose plays range from the rough-spoken 1924 *What Price Glory* to verse dramas like the 1935 *Winterset*, also wrote librettos for Kurt Weill. The 1938 KNICKERBOCKER HOLIDAY was based on the writings of Washington Irving while the 1949 LOST IN THE STARS was based on Alan Paton's novel about South Africa, *Cry, the Beloved Country.*

ANDERSON, T. J.   *American composer (1928–)*

Thomas Jefferson Anderson created three musical theater works and orchestrated the score for Scott Joplin's TREEMONISHA when it was belatedly premiered in concert form in 1972. *The Shell Fairy*, an operetta with libretto by S. Beattie after a play by C. M. Pierce, was composed in 1967 while *Re-creation*, libretto by Leon Forrest for three speakers and dancer, was composed in 1978. The opera *Soldier Boy, Soldier*, libretto by Forrest, premiered at Indiana University in 1982. *Thomas Jefferson's Minstrels* was performed in Medford, MA, in 1983 and its variant *Thomas Jefferson's Orbiting Minstrels and Contraband* was staged at Northern Illinois University on February 12, 1986. Anderson, the first black composer in residence at Atlanta Symphony Orchestra, was born in Coatesville, PA, and studied at West Virginia State, Pennsylvania State and Iowa University. His use of jazz in music theater reflects his years in a jazz orchestra.

Soprano Julie Andrews

ANDREWS, JULIE   *British-born American soprano* (1935–)

Julie Andrews created the roles of Eliza Doolittle in Frederick Loewe's American operettas MY FAIR LADY (1956) and Guenevere in CAMELOT (1960) and played Maria in Robert Wise's superb 1965 film of Richard Rodger's operetta THE SOUND OF MUSIC. She recorded Rudolf Friml's operetta ROSE-MARIE with opera singer Giorgio Tozzi and sang an aria from Reginald De Koven's comic opera ROBIN HOOD in her film *S.O.B.* She won an Academy Award for her performance in *Mary Poppins* in 1964. Andrews, born in Walton-on-Thames, began her stage career as a child. She is married to director Blake Edwards.

ANGEL FACE   *1919 operetta by Herbert*

A vial of a miraculous rejuvenating medicine containing monkey gland juice has amazing effects on those who try it. Victor Herbert's operetta *Angel Face*, libretto by Harry B. Smith, premiered at the Colonial Theater in Chicago on June 8, 1919, and opened in New York at the Knickerbocker Theater on December 29, 1919. Jack Donahue, Marguerite Zender, Tyler Brooke, Minerva Grey and John E. Young starred. The operetta is forgotten today except for its one hit song which has became a Herbert standard. Robert B. Smith's lyrics to "I Might Be Your Once-in-a-While" still evoke the period and the tune is a delight. All the recordings from this show are of this song.

1920 Olive Kline. Soprano Olive Kline of the Victor Light Opera Company recorded the show's hit song "I Might Be Your Once-in-a-While" for a Victor 78 record in 1920. **1993 Jerry Hadley.** Metropolitan Opera tenor Jerry Hadley sings "I Might Be Your Once-in-a-While" with the American Theater Orchestra led by Paul Gemignani. It's on his 1993 album *Golden Days.* BMG RCA Victor CD. **1999 Joan Morris.** Joan Morris sings "I Might Be Your Once-in-a-While" accompanied on piano by William Bolcom on their album *Moonlight Bay: Songs Is as Songs Was.* Albany CD.

ANGEL LEVINE   *1985 opera by Siegmeister*

An African American angel comes to the aid of a poor but skeptical Jewish tailor in 1940s New York City. Elie Siegmeister's one-act opera *Angel Levine*, libretto by Edward Mabley based on a story by Bernard Malamud, was premiered at the 92nd Street YMCA in New York on October 5, 1985. Baritone Richard Frisch starred as the tailor Nathan Manischevitz. The opera was revived in a more lavish production at the Center for Contemporary Opera in New York in 1999 with Frisch again taking the role of the tailor opposite Sam McKelton as the Angel.

THE ANGEL OF SHILOH   *1906 fictional American opera by Muhlheim*

Eric Muhlheim's *The Angel of Shiloh*, libretto by the composer, is an imaginary American opera that would have been "the great American opera" if it had actually opened Oscar Hammerstein's Manhattan Opera House in New York on December 3, 1906. The opera, set in the American Civil War, centers around the love of a disfigured hero for a beautiful woman. French diva Christine de Chagny sings the role of the heroine Eugenie, composer Muhlheim sings the role of her suitor Miles and Alessandro Gonci is his rival Joshua. Cleofonte Campanini conducts. The opera was reviewed (fictionally) in *The New York Times* by Gaylord Spriggs who calls it "the great American opera." *The Angel of Shiloh* is the creation of Frederick Forsythe who describes it in detail in his 1999 novel *The Phantom of Manhattan.* The mysterious composer/singer is none other than the Phantom of the Paris Opera who escaped to America to continue his operatic saga. In the real world the opera that opened the Manhattan Opera House in 1903 was Bellini's *I Puritani,* but Campanini was the conductor and Gonci did sing opposite a French soprano named Regina Pinkert.

ANGLE OF REPOSE   *1976 opera by Imbrie*

A divorced and much troubled historian looks at the hardships endured by his pioneering grandparents as he writes the story of what happened to them in California in the 1870s. Their experiences help him understand and cope with his own problems. Andrew Imbrie's three-act opera *Angle of Repose,* libretto by Oakley Hall based on a Pulitzer Prize-winning novel by Wallace Stegner, premiered at San Francisco Opera on November 6, 1976. Chester Ludgin sang the role of the historian Lyman Ward, Nancy Shade was Susan, Susanne Marsee was Shelly and Dale Duesing was Oliver. John Mauceri conducted. The score incorporates banjo tunes and other popular songs of the era.

ANNIE GET YOUR GUN   *1946 musical by Berlin*

Irving Berlin's tune-filled Broadway musical *Annie Get Your Gun* has entered the opera repertory and seems likely to become a standard work. Herbert and Dorothy Fields's libretto with the lyrics by Berlin is the highly romanticized story of sharpshooting star Annie Oakley and her competitive love affair with fellow sharpshooter Frank Butler in Buffalo Bill's touring Wild West Show. It premiered at the Shubert Theater in New Haven, CT, on March 28, 1946, and opened in New York at the Imperial Theater on May 16, 1946. Ethel Merman was Annie, Ray Middleton was Frank, Marty May was Charlie Davenport, Lea Penman was Dolly and William O'Neal was Buffalo Bill Cody. Jo Mielziner designed the sets, Joshua Logan directed and Jay S. Blackton conducted. The show was a huge hit with 1,147 performances on Broadway and

1,304 more in London. Houston Grand Opera presented it in 1992 with Cathy Rigby as Annie and Michael DeVries as Frank.

1946 Original Broadway cast. Ethel Merman is Annie opposite Ray Middleton as Frank in this original Broadway cast album with support from Robert Lenn and Kathleen Carnes. Jay Blackton conducts. Decca LP/MCA CD. **1947 Original London cast.** Dolores Gray sings Annie opposite Bill Johnson as Frank in this original London cast recording. Lew Stone conducts the orchestra. It on the album *Americans in London 1947–1951.* Encore CD. **1950 MGM film.** Betty Hutton stars as Annie with Howard Keel as Frank in this MGM film. Louis Calhern is Buffalo Bill, Keenan Wynn is Charlie Davenport and Benay Venuta is Dolly Tate, Charles Rosher photographed it, Sidney Sheldon wrote the screenplay, Adolphe Deutsch conducts the orchestra, and George Sidney directed the film. WB VHS/DVD and Soundtrack on Warner LP/CD. **1957 NBC Television.** Mary Martin sings Annie opposite John Raitt as Frank in this soundtrack recording of a 1957 NBC Television production. Louis Adrian conducts the orchestra and chorus. Capitol LP/Angel CD. **1963 Doris Day/Robert Goulet.** Doris Day sings Annie opposite Robert Goulet as Frank in this highlights recording with Franz Allers conducting orchestra and chorus. Renée Winters is Renée, Kelly Brown is Tommy, Leonard Stokes is Charlie, and the Jack and Jill Little People are Annie's brothers and sisters. Columbia LP. **1966 Lincoln Center.** Ethel Merman is Annie opposite Bruce Yarnell in this recording of a 1966 Lincoln Center revival with Franz Allers conducting the Lincoln Center Orchestra. Jerry Orbach sings the role of Charlie and Benay Venuta is Dolly. RCA Victor LP/CD. **1990 Kim Criswell/Thomas Hampson.** Kim Criswell, who sang the role on stage in England, sings Annie with Thomas Hampson as Frank in this highlights recording. John McGlinn conducts the London Sinfonietta. On CD. **1995 Judy Kaye/Barry Bostick.** Judy Kaye is Annie opposite Barry Bostick as Frank in this London studio highlights recording. John Owen Edwards conducts. Jay Records CD. **1998 Kiri Te Kanawa.** Kiri Te Kanawa performs songs from *Annie Get Your Gun* with the Abbey Road Ensemble led by Jonathan Tunick on her album *Songs of Irving Berlin.* Angel CD. **1999 Broadway revival.** Bernadette Peters sings Annie opposite Tom Wopat as Frank in this recording by the 1999 Broadway revival cast. Some of the lyrics are altered to make them more politically correct. EMI Angel CD.

ANTHEIL, GEORGE *American composer (1900–1959)*

George Antheil used to be known as the "bad boy of American music" because of the experimental nature of his early work. *Ballet mécanique* was considered the ultimate in avant-garde music in 1926 because it featured airplane propellers and electric bells. Antheil built his reputation in Europe in the 1920s and his most famous opera TRANSATLANTIC, a satire on American politics, was premiered in Frankfurt, Germany, in 1930. Minnesota Opera successfully revived it in 1998. Antheil's second opera HELEN RETIRES was considered unsuccessful when it premiered at the Juilliard School in 1934 and Antheil gave up writing for the operatic stage until the 1950s. He moved to Hollywood in 1936 and became a successful movie composer with scores for many notable films including Cecil B. DeMille's *The Plainsman* and Nicholas Ray's *In a Lonely Place.* He even partnered with actress Hedy Lamarr on the invention of a radio torpedo patented in 1941. He returned to opera in 1949 with VOLPONE, based on the play by Ben Jonson, which premiered at USC in Los Angeles in 1953. THE BROTHERS was staged at the University of Denver in Colorado in 1954. THE WISH, commissioned by Louisville Orchestra, was premiered by Kentucky Opera in 1955. VENUS IN AFRICA, written in 1954, was staged at the University of Denver in 1957. Antheil, who was born in Trenton, NJ, began his music studies at the age of 16 and headed for Europe and notoriety at the age of 22.

ANTHOLOGIES   See *ARIAS, DUETS AND ENSEMBLES*

ANTOINE, JOSEPHINE   *American soprano (1907–1971)*

Metropolitan Opera soprano Josephine Antoine created the role of Malibran in Richard Russell Bennett's opera MARIA MALIBRAN in 1935 and recorded "One Kiss" from Rudolf Friml's NEW MOON in 1940. Antoine, who was quite popular in the 1930s and 1940s, often sang arias from classic American operettas on the radio.

ANTONY AND CLEOPATRA   *1966 opera by Barber*

The greatest lovers of ancient history end up dead when Roman leaders object to their romance. Samuel Barber's opera based on Shakespeare's play opened the new Lincoln Center Metropolitan Opera House on September 16, 1966. The libretto consists of Shakespeare's words rearranged by Franco Zeffirelli and condensed into seventeen scenes. Leontyne Price created the role of Cleopatra, Justin Diaz was Antony, Rosalind Elias was Charmian, Belén Amparian was Iras, Jess Thomas was Octavius, Mary Ellen Pracht was Octavia, Ezio Flagello was Enobarbus, John Macurdy was Agrippa and Ron Bottcher was Scarus. Thomas Schippers conducted the Metropolitan Opera and Chorus. The premiere was dominated by director/designer Zeffirelli's staging and was disliked by most critics. Barber was devastated and never wrote another opera but he later revised *Antony and Cleopatra* with the help of Gian Carlo Menotti who created a simplified libretto. The new version was successfully staged at the Juilliard American Opera Center in February 1975 with Esther Hinds as Cleopatra and then presented at the Spoleto Festivals. Lyric Opera of Chicago mounted a production of the new version in 1991 with Catherine Malfitano as Cleopatra.

1966 Metropolitan Opera. The Metropolitan Opera premiere with Leontyne Price was broadcast by Texaco on September 16, 1966, and taped by the Met for its archive. It was re-recorded in May 1987 by the New York Public Library for the Performing Arts using the Met tapes. It is not available commercially but can be listened to at the Library. **1966 The New Met: Countdown to Curtain.** *The New Met: Countdown to Curtain* is a TV documentary about preparations for the premiere at the Met. Leontyne Price rehearses the role of Cleopatra with Franco Zeffirelli and Thomas Schippers and gets trapped inside a giant pyramid during the dress rehearsal. Zeffirelli experiences problems because of his ambitious design, Barber changes parts of the score at the last moment, Schippers makes the orchestra sight-read the changes and Rudolf Bing remains unflappable. Price is seen performing several arias on opening night, including "Give me my robe." Robert Drew directed this 60-minute NBC Bell Telephone Hour film. Kultur VHS. **1968 Leontyne Price.** Leontyne Price recorded two arias from the opera in 1968 with Thomas Schippers conducting the New Philharmonia Orchestra: "Give me some music" from Act I and "Give me my robe" from Act III. They're on several albums, including *Barber: Two Scenes from Antony and Cleopatra* (RCA LP), *Prima Donna* (RCA Decca CD), and *The Essential Leontyne Price: Her Greatest Roles* (BMG/Decca CD). **1977 Esther Hinds.** Esther Hinds, who sang Cleopatra in the Juilliard revival in February 1975, performs "Give Me My Robe" on *Happy Birthday, Samuel Barber,* a CBS Camera Three TV program. Roger England directed the March 6, 1977, telecast. Video at MTR. **1983 Spoleto**

Festival Italy. Esther Hinds sings Cleopatra opposite Jeffrey Wells as Antony in a complete recording of the opera based on performances staged by Menotti at the Festival of Two Worlds in Spoleto, Italy, in June 1983. Eric Halfvarson is Enobarbus, Jane Bunnell is Iras, Kathryn Cowdrick is Charmian and Robert Grayson is Caesar. Christian Badea conducts the Spoleto Festival Orchestra and Westminster Choir. The recording was distributed with the revised Menotti libretto. New World Records 3-LP box/ 2-CD box. **1983 Spoleto Festival USA.** Esther Hinds is Cleopatra in Menotti's revised version of *Antony and Cleopatra* presented at the Spoleto Festival USA in Charleston in 1983. Scenes from the opera are shown on the TV program *Festival! Spoleto USA.* Kirk Browning directed the telecast shown June 27, 1983. Video at New York Public Library. **1991 Lyric Opera of Chicago.** Catherine Malfitano is Cleopatra opposite Richard Cowan as Antony in this recording of a Lyric Opera of Chicago production by Elijah Mojinsky. Jacques Trussel is Octavius, Erick Halfvarson is Enobarbus, Wendy White is Charmian, Nancy Maultsby is Iras, Michael Wadsworth is Agrippa, Paul Kreider is Dolabella, Philip Zawisza is Eros and William Walker is Alexas. Richard Buckley conducts the Lyric Opera of Chicago Orchestra and Chorus. Custom Opera CD. **1991 Carol Vaness.** Carol Vaness sings the aria "Give Me My Robe" at a gala at Lincoln Center on November 10, 1991, with James Conlon conducting members of the Metropolitan Opera Orchestra. The concert, titled *A Salute to American Music,* is on a RCA Victor CD. **1992 Roberta Alexander.** Roberta Alexander sings the arias "Give Me Some

The revised version of Samuel Barber's *Antony and Cleopatra* was staged and recorded at the 1983 Spoleto Festival.

Music" and "She Looks Like Sleep" on her album *Barber: Scenes and Arias.* Edo de Waart conducts the Netherlands Radio Philharmonic Orchestra. Etcetera CD. **1992 Cambridge University Chamber Choir.** The Cambridge University Chamber Choir performs "My Lord, My Lord" (death of Anthony) and "She Looks

like Sleep" (death of Cleopatra) on the album *Barber: Choral Music.* Timothy Brown conducts. Gamut Classics CD. **1995 Dawn Upshaw.** Dawn Upshaw sings "Give Me Some Music" on her album *The World So Wide* accompanied by pianist David Zinman. Nonesuch CD. **1997 Jacque Trussel.** Jacque Trussel, who was

Octavius in the 1991 Lyric Opera of Chicago production of the opera, sings the aria "The breaking of so great a thing" on his album *Sounds and Sweet Airs.* It was recorded in 1997 at the Janáček Cultural Center in Haviov, Czech Republic, with Dennis Burkh conducting the Janáček Philharmonic Orchestra. Purchase Records CD. **2000 Alessandra Marc.** Alessandra Marc sings "Give me my robe" accompanied by the Dallas Symphony led by Andrew Litton on the album *Opera Gala.* Delos CD.

APOCALYPSE   *1990 opera by Shields*

The Woman journeys from conception to birth and is initiated by the goddess Seaweed who teaches her reverence for life. She meets and mates with the erotic god Shiva who teaches her sexuality. Alice Shields' experimental *Apocalypse, An Electronic Opera,* libretto by the composer in English, Greek, Gaelic and Sanskrit, is a multilingual opera for live and recorded singers. It was composed and premiered in 1990 at the Columbia University Electronic Music Centre using MIDI instruments and analog electronic music technology and was one of the first electronic operas composed in America. The composer, who has sung mezzo-soprano roles with professional opera companies sings many of the roles and plays the keyboards and synthesizers when *Apocalypse* is performed.

1993 Alice Shields. Composer Alice Shields sings the roles of Woman, Seaweed and Chorus and plays keyboards and synthesizers on a recording made at the Quality and PASS studios in New York. Baritone Michael Willson sings the role of Shiva while Jim Matus plays electric guitar. The recording, which consists of 67 scenes, is comprised primarily of the tape component that accompanies the opera when it is performed live. 68 minutes. CRI CD.

APOLLONIA   *1970 opera by Starer*

Apollonia has the gift of helping others realize their dreams. She concentrates her attention on mentally troubled opera singer Marius and becomes his lover but when he become a success, he leaves her. Robert Starer's opera *Apollonia,* libretto by Gail Godwin, was premiered by Minnesota Opera in St. Paul on May 22, 1979.

THE ARCHERS   *1796 opera by Carr*

Benjamin Carr's three-act *The Archers, or The Mountaineers of Switzerland,* is the first American ballad opera of which both libretto and music survive (two songs, a march and a rondo). William Dunlop based his libretto on the William Tell legend and wrote it eight years before the Schiller play that inspired Rossini's William Tell opera. *The Archers* premiered at the John Street Theater in New York City on April 18, 1896. Carr's other operas are lost but his appealing style can be experienced in a recording of his song cycle *The Lady of the Lake.*

ARGENTO, DOMINICK   *American composer (1927–)*

Dominick Argento has created a large number of popular American operas, many premiered by Minnesota Opera and seven with librettos written by John Olon-Scrymgeour. *Sicilian Limes,* libretto by Olon-Scrymgeour based on a Pirandello story, was first performed at the Peabody Conservatory in Baltimore and the New School for Social Research in New York in 1954. THE BOOR, libretto by Olon-Scrymgeour based on the Chekhov story about a woman falling in love with her boorish neighbor, premiered at the Eastman School of Music in Rochester May 6, 1957. COLONEL JONATHAN THE SAINT, libretto by Olon-Scrymgeour about a woman in love with a dead soldier, was composed in 1961 but not premiered until December 31, 1971, when it was staged by Lyric

Opera at Loretta Heights College in Denver, Colorado. CHRISTOPHER SLY, libretto by John Manlove based on an incident in Shakespeare's *The Taming of the Shrew,* premiered at the University of Minnesota in Minneapolis on May 31, 1963. THE MASQUE OF ANGELS, libretto by Olon-Scrymgeour about a group of angels involved in a romance, was premiered by Center Opera in Minneapolis on January 9, 1964. THE SHOEMAKER'S HOLIDAY, libretto by Olon-Scrymgeour based on the Thomas Dekker play about love and a shoemaker, was premiered by Minnesota Opera June 1, 1967. POSTCARD FROM MOROCCO, libretto by John Donahue, is a surrealistic tale about people waiting at a strange train station which was premiered by Minnesota Opera on October 14, 1971. JONAH AND THE WHALE, a dramatic oratorio with libretto by the composer based on a 14th century poem about the Bible character, was premiered in Minneapolis March 9, 1974. A WATER BIRD TALK, a monodrama for baritone with a libretto by the composer based on Chekhov and Audubon, is the story of a henpecked lecturer who mixes up birds and his life; it was premiered by New Opera Theatre at the Brooklyn Academy of Music on May 19, 1977. THE VOYAGE OF EDGAR ALLAN POE, libretto by Charles Nolte about an imaginary trip Poe might have taken on the day of his death, was premiered by Minnesota Opera Studio on April 24, 1976. The monodrama MISS HAVISHAM'S WEDDING NIGHT, libretto by Olon-Scrymgeour based on scenes in Charles Dickens' *Great Expectations,* was premiered by Minnesota Opera on May 1, 1981. MISS HAVISHAM'S FIRE (1979), libretto by Olon-Scrymgeour, featured the same character in a full-length opera and was premiered at New York City Opera March 22, 1979. It was not well received at its first performance but was acclaimed in a shorter revised version presented by Opera Theatre of St. Louis in June 2001. CASANOVA'S HOMECOMING, libretto by the composer based on the memoirs of the 17th century rake, was premiered by Minnesota Opera on April 12, 1985. THE ASPERN PAPERS. libretto by the composer based on the Henry James novella, was premiered by Dallas Opera on November 19, 1988. THE DREAM OF VALENTINO, libretto by Charles Nolte about the movie star Rudolph Valentino, was premiered by Washington Opera on January 15, 1994. Argento, who was born in York, Pennsylvania, was professor of music at the University of Minnesota for many years and helped create Minnesota Opera in 1964. He won the Pulitzer Prize for Music in 1975 for his song cycle *From the Diary of Virginia Woolf.*

ARIA DA CAPO   *American operas based on Millay play*

Intellectual Pierrot and flapper Columbine, two light-hearted characters out of commedia dell'arte, talk trivialities and enjoy themselves at a fancy meal. Cothurnus, the Masque of Tragedy, comes on and encourages rustic shepherds Corydon and Thyris to become rivals, build a wall, begin a war and eventually kill each other. Pierrot and Columbine come back and repeat their opening lines while ignoring the carnage. Edna St. Vincent Millay's one-act anti-war play *Aria da Capo* was premiered by the Provincetown Players in New York on December 5, 1919, and was widely acclaimed. Its pacifist message has helped make to be popular with modern American composers.

1951 Burdette Fore. Burdette Fore's *Aria da Capo,* libretto by the composer based on the Millay play, was premiered at the College of the Pacific in Stockton, California, on May 19, 1951. **1955 Cardon Burnham.** Cardon Burnam's *Aria da Capo,* libretto by the composer based on the Millay play, was premiered in New Orleans on April 17, 1955. **1960 Alan Blank.** Alan Blank's 50-minute opera *Aria da Capo* is an exact setting of the Millay play composed for five soloists and a 10-piece chamber orchestra. **1967 John Bilota.** John Bilota's 60-minute opera *Aria da Capo*, libretto by the composer based on the Millay play, was a finalist at the New York City Opera competition. It is composed for five singers and a 19-piece chamber orchestra. **1969 Robert Baksa.** Robert Baksa's 80-minute opera *Aria da Capo*, libretto by the composer based on the Millay play, was premiered at the Lake George Opera Festival in New York in August 1969 and reprised at the Academy of Vocal Arts in Philadelphia in 1881. Baksa's version, creaed for a 17-piece chamber orchestra, includes a Prologue with Stage Manager. **1976 Bern Herbolsheimer.** Bern Herbolsheimer's opera *Aria da Capo*, libretto by William Lewis based on the Millay play, won first prize in the National Opera Association's New Opera Competition and was premiered in Seattle, Washington on November 5, 1976. **1980 Larry A. Smith.** Larry A Smith's one-act opera *Aria da Capo*, a setting of the play by Millay, was commissioned by Chamber Opera Theatre of Chicago and premiered by that company on June 11, 1980. **1981 José-Luis Greco.** José-Luis Greco's 45-minute opera *Aria da Capo*, libretto by the composer based on the Millay play, was premiered by Encompass Music Theatre at the Good Shepherd Faith Church in New York on May 13, 1981, with Buck Ross directing and Greco conducting the chamber orchestra. **1990 Brent Weaver.** Brent Weaver's 40-minute opera *Aria da Capo*, libretto by the composer based on the play by Millay, was premiered at Clayton State College in October 1990. **1995 Joel E. Naumann.** Joel E. Naumann's 39-minute opera *Aria da Capo*, libretto by the composer based on the Millay Play, was composed for five singers and a seven-piece chamber orchestra. **1997 Lawrence Axelrod.** Lawrence Axelrod's 61-minute opera *Aria da Capo*, libretto by the composer based on the Millay play, was premiered on March 25 1997.

ARIA DATABASE   *Internet opera website*

The web-based Aria Database (www.aria-database. com) features lyrics of a large number of opera arias, mostly European. Twelve American operas are featured with their lyrics: Leslie Adam's BLAKE, Samuel Barber's VANESSA, Leonard Bernstein's CANDIDE and TROUBLE IN TAHITI, Aaron Copland's THE TENDER LAND, Carlisle Floyd's SUSANNAH, George Gershwin's PORGY AND BESS, Gian Carlo Menotti's THE CONSUL, THE OLD MAID AND THE THIEF and THE SAINT OF BLEECKER STREET, Douglas Moore's THE BALLAD OF BABY DOE and Kurt Weill's LOST IN THE STARS.

ARIAS, DUETS AND ENSEMBLES

The most popular American opera arias, duets and ensembles have their own entries in this encyclopedia. While American opera arias are not rare, the best known, like "Summertime," are not usually thought of as arias because they are sung in English. They have been the basis of several record albums in recent years, including historical anthologies of older arias that provide an overview of American opera of the early 20th century. There are now several books for singers featuring their words and music including the four-volume *G. Schirmer America Aria Anthology, American Arias for Sopranos, Opera American Style* and the Robert Larsen series devoted to arias for bass, baritone, tenor. mezzo-soprano, soprano and coloratura soprano. Record albums, LPs and CDs featuring arias from more than one opera are listed below; albums with arias by one composer are listed under that composer's name.

1978 Towards an American Opera 1911–1954. Pioneering anthology of arias from American operas from the 78 era performed by notable opera singers. There are two are from Victor Herbert's NATOMA: Alma Gluck sings "I list the trill" and John

McCormack "No country can my own outvie." Lawrence Tibbett sings four arias from three operas: "Oh, Caesar, great wert thou" and "Nay, Maccus, lay him down" from Deems Taylor's THE KING'S HENCHMAN, "Standin' in the need of prayer" from Louis Gruenberg's THE EMPEROR JONES and "Oh, 'tis an Earth defiled" from Howard Hanson's MERRY MOUNT. Patricia Neway sings "To this we've come" from Gian Carlo Menotti's THE CONSUL. Finally here are numbers from two operas by Aaron Copland: "Two Willow Hill," "Sextet," "Jeff's Song" and "Queenie's Song" from THE SECOND HURRICANE are performed by high school students led by Leonard Bernstein; and "It promises to be a fine night" and "The promise of living" from THE TENDER LAND sung by Joy Clements, Claramae Turner, Richard Cassilly, Richard Fredericks and Norman Treigle. With notes by Patrick J. Smith. New World LP.

1983 Helen-Kay Eberley: American Girl. American soprano Helen-Kay Eberley sings arias from seven American operas with piano accompaniment by Donald Isaak: "Do not utter a word" from Samuel Barber's VANESSA; "Thank you, thank you all" from Aaron Copland's THE TENDER LAND; "Ain't it a pretty night" and "Come back, oh summer" from Carlisle Floyd's SUSANNAH; "No, I haven't been well" from Lee Hoiby's SUMMER AND SMOKE; "Bravo! And after the theatre, supper and dance" from Gian Carlo Menotti's THE MEDIUM; "Steal me, oh sweet thief" from Menotti's THE OLD MAID AND THE THIEF; "Willow, where we met together" and "Gold is a fine thing" from Douglas Moore's THE BALLAD OF BABY DOE. Eb-Sko LP.

1989 Dawn Upshaw: Knoxville: Summer of 1915. Dawn Upshaw sings arias from two American operas accompanied by the Orchestra of St. Luke's led by David Zinman: "What a curse for a woman is a timid man" from Gian Carlo Menotti's THE OLD MAID AND THE THIEF and "No word from Tom" from Igor Stravinsky's THE RAKE'S PROGRESS. The album also features Samuel Barber's tone poem "Knoxville: Summer of 1915" based on a poem by James Agee. Elektra/Nonesuch CD.

1991 A Salute to American Music. Arias, ensembles and instrumental numbers from American operas and music theater are performed in a televised Richard Tucker Foundation concert in Lincoln Center on November 10, 1991: "Give me my robe" from Samuel Barber's ANTONY AND CLEOPATRA; "Must the winter come so soon?" from Barber's VANESSA; "Make our garden grow" from Leonard Bernstein's CANDIDE; "Maria" from Bernstein's WEST SIDE STORY; "Rain Quartet" from Marc Blitzstein's REGINA; ""Ice Cream Sextet" from Blitzstein's STREET SCENE, "Hear me, O Lord" from Carlisle Floyd's SUSANNAH; "Leavin' for the promised land" from George Gershwin's PORGY AND BESS; "Too weak to kill the man I hate" from Marvin Davy Levy's MOURNING BECOMES ELECTRA; "Overture" from Gian Carlo Menotti's AMELIA GOES TO THE BALL; "I've got a ram, Goliath" from Douglas Moore's THE DEVIL AND DANIEL WEBSTER; "If I loved you" from Richard Rodger's CAROUSEL; "Fanfare" from Igor Stravinsky's THE RAKE'S PROGRESS; and "September Song" from Kurt Weill's KNICKERBOCKER HOLIDAY. The singers are Renée Fleming, Paul Groves, Jerry Hadley, Karen Holvik, Marilyn Horne, Jeff Mattsey, Robert Merrill, Sherrill Milnes, Maureen O'Flynn, Phyllis Pancella, Leontyne Price, Samuel Ramey, Daniel Smith, Carol Vaness, Frederica von Stade, Denise Woods. James Conlon conducts and Price introduces each number. RCA CD.

1991 Lawrence Tibbett: Broadway to Hollywood. Lawrence Tibbett sings arias from three American operas and two movie operettas. Included are eight numbers from George Gershwin's PORGY AND BESS (recorded in 1935 with Helen Jepson featured on four numbers), "Oh Lord! standin' in the need of prayer" from

Louis Gruenberg's EMPEROR JONES (recorded 1934) and "Oh, 'tis an earth defiled" from Howard Hanson's MERRY MOUNT (recorded 1934). The movie operettas are *The Rogue Song* (1930) and *The Prodigal* (1931). Nimbus Records CD.

1993 Souvenirs from American Operas. An anthology of rarely-heard arias and ensembles from eleven classic American operas taken from 78 records and radio broadcasts going back to 1911. Charles Wakefield Cadman's SHANEWIS: "Spring Song of the Robin Woman" and "Ojibway Canoe Song" sung by Elsie Baker (1925); Frederick Converse's THE SACRIFICE: "Chonita's Prayer" sung by Alice Nielsen (1911); Walter Damrosch's CYRANO DE BERGERAC: "Balcony Scene" sung by Agnes Davies, Earl Wrightson and Felix Knight (1942); Louis Gruenberg's THE EMPEROR JONES: "Oh, Lawd, Lawd" sung by Lawrence Tibbett (1934); Richard Hageman's CAPONSACCHI: "I know you better" and "Who are you?" sung by Helen Jepson (1937); Howard Hanson's MERRY MOUNT: "Oh, 'tis an earth defiled" sung by Lawrence Tibbett (1934); Victor Herbert's MADELEINE: "A perfect day" sung by France Alda (1914); Victor Herbert's NATOMA: "No country can my own outvie" sung by John McCormack (1912), "When the sunlight dies" sung by Reinald Werrenrath (1912), "I list the trill in golden throat" sung by Alma Gluck (1912); "Vaquero's Song" sung by Earl Cartwright (1912) and "Gentle maiden" sung by Jan Peerce (1935); Horatio Parker's MONA: "Thy golden heart wide open" sung by Arlene Saunders and Enrico Di Giuseppe (1961); Deems Taylor's THE KING'S HENCHMAN: "O Caesar, great wert thou" sung by Lawrence Tibbett (1928), "Eadgar! Eadgar!" sung by Tibbett (1934) and "God willing we leave this house tonight" sung by Vivian Della Chiesa and Jan Peerce (1942); Deems Taylor's PETER IBBETSON: "I could never dedicate my days" sung by Licia Albanese (1960). IRRC CD.

1993 Lesley Garrett: Prima Donna. Lesley Garrett sings three arias from American operas in this collection with Ivor Bolton conducting: "Summertime" from George Gershwin's PORGY AND BESS; "I want to be a prima donna (Art is calling me)" from Victor Herbert's THE ENCHANTRESS; and "What good would the moon be?" from Kurt Weill's STREET SCENE. Silva America CD.

1994 Dawn Upshaw: I Wish It So. Dawn Upshaw sings arias and songs from Broadway operas and American music theater works with an orchestra conducted by Eric Stern: "Glitter and be gay" from Leonard Bernstein's CANDIDE; "My new friends" from Bernstein's *The Madwoman of Central Park West*"; I feel pretty" from Bernstein's WEST SIDE STORY; "I wish it so" from Marc Blitzstein's JUNO; "Never get lost" from Blitzstein's REUBEN, REUBEN; "In the clear" from Blitzstein's NO FOR AN ANSWER; "There won't be trumpets" from Stephen Sondheim's *Anyone Can Whistle*; "Take me to the world" from Sondheim's *Evening Primrose*; "The girls of summer" from Sondheim's *The Girls of Summer;* "Like it was" from Sondheim's *Merrily We Roll Along*; "What more do I need?" from Sondheim's *Saturday Night*; "My ship" and "The Saga of Jenny" from Kurt Weill's LADY IN THE DARK; "Stay well" from Weill's LOST IN THE STARS; and "That's him" from Weill's ONE TOUCH OF VENUS. Elektra Nonesuch CD.

1994 Jerry Hadley: Golden Days. Tenor Jerry Hadley sings eighteen arias from American comic operas and operettas with backing from the Harvard Glee Club and Paul Gemignani, who conducts the American Theatre Orchestra. The numbers are from Victor Herbert's ANGEL FACE, NAUGHTY MARIETTA, THE ONLY GIRL, PRINCESS PAT and THE RED MILL; Sigmund Romberg's THE DESERT SONG, THE NEW MOON and THE STUDENT PRINCE and Rudolf Friml's THE FIREFLY and THE VAGABOND KING. RCA Victor CD.

1994 David Zinman: Dance Mix. Instrumental pieces from American operas by modern American composers performed by the Baltimore Symphony Orchestra led by David Zinman. Included are pieces from John Adams' NIXON IN CHINA, Dominick Argento's THE DREAM OF VALENTINO, Leonard Bernstein's WEST SIDE STORY and John Harbison's THE GREAT GATSBY. Argo CD.

1995 Dawn Upshaw: The World So Wide. Dawn Upshaw sings arias from eight American operas accompanied by pianist David Zinman: "This is prophetic" from John Adams' NIXON IN CHINA; "Give me some music" from Samuel Barber's ANTHONY AND CLEOPATRA; "What a movie" from Leonard Bernstein's TROUBLE IN TAHITI; "Laurie's Song" from Aaron Copland's THE TENDER LAND; "Ain't it a pretty sight" from Carlisle Floyd's SUSANNAH; "Oh Yemanja" (Mother's Prayer) from Tania León's SCOURGE OF HYACINTHS; "Willow Song" from Douglas Moore's THE BALLAD OF BABY DOE; and "Lonely House" from Kurt Weill's STREET SCENE. Nonesuch CD.

1999 Renée Fleming: I Want Magic. Renée Fleming sings arias from nine American operas with James Levine conducting the Metropolitan Opera Orchestra: "Do not utter a word" from Samuel Barber's VANESSA; "Glitter and be gay" from Leonard Bernstein's CANDIDE; "Ain't it a pretty night" and "The trees on the mountains" from Carlisle Floyd's SUSANNAH; "I have dreamt" from Bernard Herrmann's WUTHERING HEIGHTS; "The Letter Song" from Douglas Moore's THE BALLAD OF BABY DOE; "Monica's Waltz" from Gian Carlo Menotti's THE MEDIUM; "My man's gone now" and "Summertime" from George Gershwin's PORGY AND BESS; and "No word from Tom" from Igor Stravinsky's THE RAKE'S PROGRESS. Fleming has starred in stage productions of the American operas *Susannah* and A STREETCAR NAMED DESIRE. London CD.

ARIZONA *American state (1912–)*

Opera has become popular in Arizona in recent years and several American operas have premiered there. Arizona Opera, founded in 1971 and based in Phoenix, is the major opera company of the state presenting operas in Phoenix, Tucson, and Flagstaff. Arizona opera people include composer Ulysses Kay, born and brought up in Tucson, and baritones Herbert and Eugene Perry, who made their debuts at Arizona Opera in Phoenix.

Flagstaff: Arizona Opera presents its productions in Flagstaff at the Ardrey Auditorium

Phoenix: Grant Fletcher's opera The *Sack of Calabasas,* based on a story by J. M. Myers and set in Calabasas, was premiered in Phoenix in 1964. It's set in 1882 and tells the story of a preacher who swindles people expecting to get rich when the railroad arrives. Arizona Opera presents four operas a year in Phoenix, most from the standard repertory, though Sergey Prokofiev's THE LOVE FOR THREE ORANGES was staged in 1981, Douglas Moore's THE BALLAD OF BABY DOE in 1982 and Gian Carlo Menotti's THE CONSUL in 2004. Arizona State University's Lyric Opera company presents operas in Phoenix and Tempe.

Scottsdale: Joseph Esile premiered two of his operas at Scottsdale Opera, *Still Dark Clouds* in 1960 and *Sara* in 1963. Both have librettos by Frank Langer.

Tempe: Arizona State University's Lyric Opera company presents operas in Tempe and Phoenix. Seymour Barab's one-act *Who Am I?* premiered in 1971 and Kirke Mechem's three-act TARTUFFE was staged in 1981.

Tucson: University of Arizona Opera has premiered several operas in Tucson: John Davis's *The Pardoner's Tale*, libretto by the composer based on Chaucer, and Henry Johnson's *The Mountain,* libretto by David Grozier, were both staged in 1967. Dee Strickland Johnson's *MacLeod O'Dunatore*, libretto by the composer, premiered in 1968. W. Garza's *The Blue Angel*, libretto by the composer, was staged in 1973. Thomas Pasatieri's *Maria Elena,* based on a Mexican story, was premiered on April 6, 1983. Arizona Opera presents its productions in Tucson as well as Flagstaff and Phoenix.

ARKANSAS   *American state (1836–)*

Arkansas is the location of SCOTT JOPLIN's opera TREEMONISHA which is set on a plantation near Texarkana; Joplin was born just across the river in Texas. Seven American operas have been premiered at the summer arts festival in Eureka Springs. Arkansas-born opera people include composer James Sellars (Fort Smith), baritone Robert McFerrin (Marianna), bass William Warfield and soprano Barbara Hendricks (Stephens). Contralto Lili Chookasian made her debut at Arkansas Opera and conductor/director Sarah Caldwell was educated at the University of Arkansas.

Bentonville: Isaac Van Grove created a number of religious operas for Arkansas summer festivals including *The Other Wise Man* premiered in Bentonville in 1959.

Conway: Howard Groth's *Petruchio*, an operatic version of Shakespeare's *The Taming of the Shrew*, was premiered in Conway in 1954.

Eureka Springs: Opera in the Ozarks, the summer festival at Inspiration Point Fine Arts Colony in Eureka Springs, is known for staging American operas, many of great rarity. Its premieres include N. Solomon Burnand's *Pickwick* (1956), Anne Reiners' *Cindy* (1964), Isaac Van Grove's religious operas *The Shining Chalice* (1964), *Ruth* (1966) and *The Prodigal* (1976), Eusebia Hunkins' choral dance opera *Child of Promise* (1965) and William J. McDaniel's *The Green Tint* (1975). The festival has also presented Samuel Barber's A HAND OF BRIDGE, Charles Wakefield Cadman's SHANEWIS, THE WILLOW TREE and *The Prodigal Son*, John Duke's *Captain Lovelock,* Carlisle Floyd's SUSANNAH, Charles Haubiel's *Sunday Costs Five Pesos,* Gerald Humel's *The Proposal,* Eusebia Hunkins' *Smoky Mountain,* Meyer Kupferman's *Draagenfoot Girl,* Bohuslav Martinů's WHAT MEN LIVE BY, Gian Carlo Menotti's AMAHL AND THE NIGHT VISITORS, THE MEDIUM, THE OLD MAID AND THE THIEF and THE TELEPHONE, Henry Mollicone's THE FACE ON THE BARROOM FLOOR, Thomas Pasatieri's SIGNORE DELUSO, Stephen Paulus's THE VILLAGE SINGER, Julia Smith's *The Gooseherd and the Goblin,* Stephen Sondheim's A LITTLE NIGHT MUSIC, Randall Thompson's SOLOMON AND BALKIS, Isaac Van Grove's *Miracles of Our Lady, Noe's Fludde* and *The Other Wise Men,* Robert Ward's THE CRUCIBLE, Kurt Weill's DOWN IN THE VALLEY and STREET SCENE and Alex Wilder's SUNDAY EXCURSION.

Fayetteville: Two operas were premiered at the Fine Arts Center at University of Arkansas in Fayetteville, Arthur Kreutz's *Acres of Sky* on November 16, 1950, and J. P. Rameau's mythological *Io* in 1981.

Hot Springs: The Hot Springs Musical Festival is noted for the adventurous programming of conductor Richard Rosenberg. His pioneering album of music by Edmond Dédé was recorded at the festival in 1999, his "saynéte comique" FRANÇOISE ET TORTILLARD. Jerome Moross's opera-ballets *Willie the Weeper* (from BALLET BALLADS) and *Frankie and Johnnie* were recorded in 2001.

Little Rock: Arkansas Opera Theater, founded in 1973 by Anne Chotard to present operas in English, has commissioned three operas. William Underwood's one-act children's opera *Jorinda and Joringle,* libretto by the composer, premiered in 1977. LIBBY LARSEN's *Clair de Lune,* libretto by Patricia Hampl about a woman aviator, premiered on February 22, 1985. Raymond Pannell's *As Long as a Child Remembers*, libretto by the composer, was premiered on April 10, 1986. Arkansas Opera was reorganized as Opera Theatre at Wildwood in 1989 and is now park of Wildwood Park for the Performing Arts. Voice and Opera at the University of Arkansas stages operas as part of its program

Henderson: William Underwood's one-act opera *A Medicine for Melancholy*, libretto by the composer based on a story by Ray Bradbury, was premiered at Henderson State College on April 20, 1974. Soprano Irene Calloway Harrower, who made her debut at the Rome Opera, graduated from Henderson College in 1949.

Fayetteville: The University of Arkansas in Fayetteville has organized a number of opera workshops and productions. Arthur Kreutz's ballad opera *Acres of Sky* was premiered in Fayetteville in 1951 and Robert Boury's *Bowl, Cat and Broomstick* in 1989.

Siloam Springs: John Brown University Opera Workshop presented Leonard Bernstein's TROUBLE IN TAHITI on January 27, 2000, in the Jones Recital Hall.

ARLEN, HAROLD   *American composer (1905–1986)*

Harold Arlen is best known for the movie *The Wizard of Oz* and its song "Over the Rainbow" but he also wrote for the stage, including a little-known opera called *Free and Easy.* Composed in 1954 and based on his 1946 stage musical *St. Louis Woman*, it was premiered in Amsterdam on December 22, 1959, and staged in Paris in February 1960 but was not brought to America. St. Louis Opera used Arlen's film score when it presented *The Wizard of Oz* as a stage musical in 1942. Arlen's partnership with lyricist E. Y. Harburg on *Wizard* continued in the stage musicals *Bloomer Girl* (1944) and *Jamaica (1957).* His other stage musicals include *Saratoga* (1959) with Johnny Mercer and *House of Flowers* (1954) with Truman Capote. Arlen, who was born in Buffalo, New York, began his composing career working in nightclubs like Harlem's Cotton Club and writing songs for revues.

ARLESIANA   *1939 "movie opera" by Pokrass*

Arlesiana was composed by Sam Pokrass to a libretto by Armando Hauser for the 1939 Twentieth Century-Fox film *Wife, Husband and Friend.* *Arlesiana* is seen on stage twice, first with opera diva Binnie Barnes in her glory singing her big aria, the second time with would-be opera baritone Warner Baxter drunkenly disgracing her in his big scene. Opera soprano Nina Koshetz provides the singing voice for Barnes while Emery Darcy sings for Baxter. He's actually a building contractor and it's his wife Loretta Young who wants to be an opera singer (her singing is by Tatiana Chavrova). Unfortunately he has a better voice. The 75-minute black-and-white film is based on James Cain's story *Career in C. Major* and was filmed again in 1949 as *Everybody Does It* with another movie opera.

"ART IS CALLING FOR ME"   *Soprano aria: The Enchantress (1911). Words by Harry B. Smith. Music by Victor Herbert.*

THE ENCHANTRESS, an almost forgotten comic opera by Victor Herbert, has a wonderfully funny and effective parody of an operatic aria that has become a favorite of modern female opera singers. "Art is Calling for Me" ("I Want to be A Prima Donna") was introduced by Louise Bliss portraying a would-be coloratura opera singer who tells us she wants to be a "peachy, screechy cantatrice" like Luisa Tetrazzini. The memorable words are by Harry B. Smith. Beverly Sills sings the aria on a 1975 recording, Lesley Garrett features it on 1992 album *Prima Donna*, Kiri Te Kanawa performs it on 1989 and 1994 concert videos and albums and Virginia Croskery sings it on a 1999 album.

ARVEY, VERNA   *American librettist (1910–1987)*

White Jewish concert pianist/journalist Verna Arvey was hired by African American composer William Grant Still as his press secretary in 1934. She premiered his piano tone poem *Kaintuck'* in 1935 and performed others in concert, wrote articles about him for newspapers, helped him get a job conducting at the Hollywood Bowl and married him in 1939. She began writing his librettos in 1937, the first being TROUBLED ISLAND on which she collaborated with Langston Hughes. She is sole librettist of A BAYOU LEGEND, HIGHWAY 1 USA, *Costaso, Mota, The Pillar* and MINETTE FONTAINE.

ASCHAFFENBURG, WALTER   *American composer (1922–)*

Walter Aschaffenburg's opera BARTLEBY, composed to a libretto by film scholar Jay Leyda based on Herman Melville's novella, was premiered in Oberlin in 1964. Aschaffenburg, who was born in Essen, Germany, emigrated to the U.S. in 1938 and became an American citizen. This was his only opera.

ASHLEY, ROBERT   *American composer (1930–)*

Robert Ashley's video operas have helped change the concept of "opera" for admirers in the avant-garde world but he has also created non-traditional stage operas like BALSEROS (1997), about the Cuban raft people. He is considered by some to be the first opera composer of the post-stage world and he has promoted the idea that video artists should create re-viewable works of art which can be experienced over and over. Ashley, who is a native of Ann Arbor, has been composing video operas since 1964, mixing music with spoken and written texts and experimental imagery. THAT MORNING THING was premiered at Ann Arbor in 1968 and *In Memoriam Kit Carson* at Mills College in Oakland in 1971. MUSIC WITH ROOTS IN THE AETHER (1976) involves the music of six other composers. PERFECT LIVES (1980) has been telecast in England and America. IMPROVEMENT (1992) is on CD. EL/AFICIONADO (1995) and YOUR MONEY MY LIFE GOODBYE (1998) have been recorded.

Composer Robert Ashley

DUST (1999) features homeless street people. Ashley's operas mostly belong to three groups: ATALANTA (ACTS OF GOD), *Perfect Lives* and NOW ELEANOR'S IDEA.

ASHOKA'S DREAM   *1997 opera by Lieberson*

Incidents in the life of the enlightened Third Century BC Indian Emperor Ashoka. He begins as a cruel ruler but after a devastating battle becomes a Buddhist and attempts to bring peace to his empire. Peter Lieberson opera *Ashoka's Dream*, libretto by Douglas Penick, premiered at Santa Fe Opera on July 26, 1997. Kurt Ollmann was Ashoka, Clare Gormley was Ashoka's first wife Laksmi, Lorraine Hunt-Lieberson was his second wife Triraksha, Paul Kreider was the Sage who teaches Ashoka enlightened leadership and Mark Thomsen was Girika. The Four Ministers were sung by Greer Grimsley, Beau Palmer, John Atkins and Bruce Baumer and the Four Elements were played by Patricia Johnson, Sara Seglem, Christine Abraham and Beth Clayton. Stephen Wadsworth directed and Richard Bradshaw conducted. The opera was very favorably received.

2000 Lorraine Hunt-Lieberson. Lorraine Hunt-Lieberson performs Triraksha's aria from *Ashoka's Dream* on stage in London. It's on the album *Lorraine Hunt-Lieberson: Live from Wigmore Hall.* BBC Legends CD.

ASIAN AMERICAN OPERAS

Asian American composers, librettists and conductors have grown in prominence and prestige in recent years and are making important contribution to American opera. Chinese-born American composer Tan Dun had great success with MARCO POLO in 1996, PEONY PAVILION in 1998, and TEA in 2003. Chinese-born American composer Bright Sheng has won admiration for THE SONG OF MAJNUN, staged by Lyric Opera of Chicago in 1992, and THE SILVER RIVER, presented in Santa Fe in 1997. Los Angeles-born Chinese American writer David Henry Hwang, who wrote the libretto for *The Silver River,* has also written librettos for Philip Glass, including THE VOYAGE (1992), 1000 AIRPLANES ON THE ROOF (1988) and *The Sound of Voice* (2003) and for Osvaldo Golijov's AINADAMAR (2003). Chinese American Michael Ching, popular as conductor as well as composer, has created a number of successful operas, including BUOSO'S GHOST and CUE 67. Chinese American Evan Chen's *Bok Choy Variations,* libretto by Chinese American Fifi Servoss, premiered in St. Paul in 1995. Chinese American Nathan Wang's one-act opera ON GOLD MOUNTAIN, libretto by Lisa See based on her book about her grandfather, was premiered by Los Angeles Opera in 2000. Chinese American composer Jason Kao Hwang's *The Floating Box* premiered in New York in 2001. Chinese-born American conductor Seiji Ozawa has recorded two American operas and Japanese American conductor Kent Nagano has recorded three American operas, premiering John Adams' THE DEATH OF KLINGHOFFER in 1991 and EL NIÑO in 2000 and conducting the first complete recording of Carlisle Floyd's SUSANNAH in 1994.

THE ASPERN PAPERS   *1988 opera by Argento*

1895 near Lake Como. An aging opera singer, who had been the mistress of a famous opera composer in the 1830s, lives in a lakeside villa and takes in lodgers to pay expenses. A new lodger makes a play for her unmarried niece but it looks like he is really trying to find a lost opera composed for the singer back- in 1835. The narrative shifts between past and present as the story unfolds. Dominick Argento's *The Aspern Papers,* libretto by the composer based on a novella by Henry James, shifts the location of the story from Venice to Lake Como and makes Aspern an opera composer instead of a poet. *The Aspern Papers* was premiered by Dallas Opera on November 19, 1988, with Elisabeth Söderstrom as the former diva Juliana, Frederica von Stade as her niece Tina, Richard Stilwell as the Lodger, Neil Rosenshein as Aspern, Katherine Ciesinski as Sonia, Eric Halfvarson as Barelli, Erick Johnson as the Gardener, Joan Gibbons as Olimpia and John Calvin West as the Painter. Mark Lamos staged the opera, John Conklin designed the sets and costumes Nicola Rescigno conducted the Dallas Symphony Orchestra. Minnesota Opera revived the opera in January 1991 and its production was broadcast on BBC Radio in England on June 3, 1991.

1988 Dallas Opera. Elisabeth Söderstrom plays diva Juliana in this videotape of the Dallas Opera premiere The cast is as listed above with Frederica von Stade as Tina, Richard Stilwell as the Lodger, Neil Rosenshein as Aspern and Katherine Ciesinski as Sonia. Nicola Rescigno conducts the Dallas Symphony Orchestra. The two-hour opera, directed by Kirk Browning using cinematic superimpositions, was taped in November 1988 and telecast on June 9, 1989. Premiere Opera VHS/video at MTR.

ATALANTA (ACTS OF GOD)   *1982 opera by Ashley*

In Greek mythology, Atalanta was a swift-running virgin huntress who avoided marriage by winning races against her suitors. She is finally defeated by a suitor who is given golden apples by Aphrodite to drop along the way. Robert Ashley's video opera *Atalanta (Acts of God),* libretto by the composer, is only loosely connected to the myth. It was premiered in 1985 at the Museum of Contemporary Art in Chicago in three 90-minute episodes, each about a different person.

1984 Atalanta Strategy. Seven scenes from the second episode titled *Willard*: "The Immigration Office" with Ronald Vance, Willem Dafoe, Norman Frisch, Jim Johnson, Anna Kohler, Payton, Annie Roth, and Kate Valk; "The Interview" with Ashley talking to Jeffrey M. Jones; "The Flying Saucer" with Kate Valk and Ron Vawter as aliens in a space ship discussing humans; "Willard Anecdote and Chorales" with voice-over narration by Ashley and chorus by Rebecca Armstrong and David Van Tiegham; "Character Reference"(with Ashley; "The Mule in the Tree" with Jacqueline Humbert; and "The Mystery of the River" with Margaret Ahrens and Marjorie Merrick. Lawrence Brickman designed and directed the 28-minute video. Lovely Music VHS. **1985 Teatro Olimpico, Rome.** This recording of a live performance of the opera with the Chicago cast was made at the Teatro Olimpico in Rome, Italy, in 1985. The performers are Ashley, Thomas Buckner, Jacqueline Humbert, Paul Shorr, Carla Tatò and "Blue" Gene Tyranny. Lovely Music LP/CD box.

ATHALIAH   *1964 opera by Weisgall*

Usurper Queen Athaliah is overthrown by soldiers loyal to her grandson, seven-year-old boy king Joas (Johoash), and the house of David. The uprising is organized by his aunt Yehosheba and high priest Yehoyada. Hugo Weisgall's two-act opera *Athaliah*, libretto by R. F. Goldman based on Racine's 1691 play *Athalie* derived from a story in the Bible, was premiered by the Concert Opera Association at the Philharmonic Hall in New York City on February 17, 1964. Shirley Verrett was Athaliah, Irene Jordan was Yehosheba, John Reardon was Yehoyada, Raymond Michalski was Abner and William Lewis was Mattan. Thomas Sherman conducted.

ATHERTON, JAMES   *American tenor (1943–1987)*

James Atherton created the role of Pacheco in Thomas Pasatieri's

INES DE CASTRO in Baltimore in 1976 and sang the role of Jo the Loiterer in the Santa Fe Opera recording and telecast of Virgil Thomson's THE MOTHER OF US ALL in 1977. Born in Montgomery, Alabama, he made his debut with San Francisco Opera in 1971 and has sung with several American companies, including the Met. He has also worked as an opera director.

ATKINSON, DAVID   *American baritone (1921–)*

David Atkinson created and performed roles in a number of American operas and operettas. He created playwright Clyde Hallam in the premiere of Sigmund Romberg's THE GIRL IN PINK TIGHTS on Broadway on March 5, 1954, Dr. Gregg in the premiere of Douglas Moore's GALLANTRY at Columbia University on March 19, 1958, and Lt. Henry Lukash in the premiere of Robert Kurka's THE GOOD SOLDIER SCHWEIK at New York City Opera on April 23, 1958. He helped popularize Leonard Bernstein's TROUBLE IN TAHITI singing the role of Sam on NBC Television in 1962, recording the opera in 1953 and reprising the role at New York City Opera in 1958. He played Pantaloon at NYCO in the first professional production of Robert Ward's HE WHO GETS SLAPPED in 1959 and Larry Foreman in the NYCO production of Marc Blitzstein's THE CRADLE WILL ROCK in 1960. On Broadway he created the role of Oliver J. Oxheart opposite Carol Channing in James Mundy's *The Vamp* in 1955, took over the lead role of Don Quixote in Mitch Leigh's MAN OF LA MANCHA in 1965 and sang Tommy in the 1957 revival of Frederick Loewe's BRIGADOON in 1957. He sang in the Paper Mill Playhouse productions of Sigmund Romberg's THE DESERT SONG and the Wright/Forrest *Song of Norway* in 1951. He can be heard on several recordings: in addition to *Trouble in Tahiti,* there are cast albums of *The Cradle Will Rock* (1960) and *The Girl in Pink Tights* (1954) and 1952 studio highlight albums of Richard Rodger's OKLAHOMA and Romberg's THE DESERT SONG.

ATLAS   *1991 opera by Monk*

Atlas tells the story of a woman explorer (Alexandra David-Neel was the inspiration) and her journeys. She struggles with demons while she searches for spiritual values in a world that has lost it sense of wonder. The characters do not sing comprehensible words but textless vocalese. Avant-garde composer Meredith Monk achieved respectability in the traditional opera world when the three-act *Atlas*, libretto by the composer, premiered at Houston Grand Opera February 22, 1991. It featured nineteen singers/actors in multiple roles with Alexandra portrayed by different women in each act. In Part I: *Personal Climate*, Dina Emerson played her at age 13 and Meredith Monk played her from age 25 to 40. In Part II: *Night Travel* she is portrayed by Monk as a mature woman. In Part III: *Invisible Night,* she is played by Sally Gross as the age of 60. The other performers in multiple roles from explorers to demons included Wendy Hill, Thomas Bogdan, Dina Emerson, Ching Gonzalez, Allison Easter, Chen Shizheng, Stephanie Kalm, Robert Een, Katie Geissinger, Victoria Boomsma, Wilbur Pauley, Janis Brenner, Randall Wong, Carlos Arévalo, Emily Eyre, Dana Hanchard. Yoshio Yabara designed the sets and costumes, Beverly Emmons designed the lighting, Monk directed with Pablo Velo and Wayne Hankin conducted the Houston Grand Opera Orchestra. *Atlas* was commissioned by Houston in collaboration with Walker Arts Center, Wexner Arts Center and American Music Theater Festival.

1992 Meredith Monk Ensemble. Meredith Monk directed a recording of the opera in a New York studio in June 1992 with a cast that included most of the Houston Opera performers, all taking multiple roles Dina Emerson is Alexandra at 13, Meredith Monk is mature Alexandra, Wendy Hill is Mother, Thomas Bogdan is Father and the other singers are Victoria Boomsma, Janis Brenner, Shi-Zheng Chen, Carlos Arávalo, Kathleen Carroll, John Cipolla, Allison Easter, Robert Een, Emily Eyre, Arthur Fiacco, Katie Geissinger, Ching Gonzalez, Dana Hanchard, Wayne Hankin. Bill Hayes, Susan Iadone, Stephen Kalm, Darryl Thomas Kubian, Steve Lockwood, Robert Osborne, Wilbur Pauley, Thad Wheeler, James F. Wilson and Randall K. Wong. Wayne Hankin conducts the chorus and instrumental ensemble. ECM 2-CD set.

ATWATER KENT PROGRAM   *American radio series (1925–1931)*

The Atwater Kent Program was an early radio series devoted to classical music and opera. Its performers included several singers associated with contemporary American operas, like Lawrence Tibbett and George Cehanovsky (THE KING'S HENCHMAN), Mabel Garrison (ALGLALA), and Frances Alda (MADELEINE) and arias from their operas were occasionally featured.

AUDEN, W. H.   *Anglo-American librettist (1907–1973)*

W. H. Auden, America's finest opera librettist, has seen his poetic reputation rise enormously in recent years with his poems quoted in movies and on the internet. Auden left England for America in 1940, became an American citizen not long after and wrote all his librettos in the U.S.A. He began by collaborating with Benjamin Britten on the neglected opera/operetta PAUL BUNYAN in 1941 but had his greatest success with Igor Stravinsky's 1948 THE RAKE'S PROGRESS. It was written in collaboration with his lifetime companion Chester Kallman whom Auden said had made him into an "opera addict." Their other opera librettos include LOVE'S LABOUR'S LOST, an adaptation of a Shakespeare play for Nicolas Nabokov which premiered in America, and Hans Werner Henze's *Elegy for Young Lovers* and *The Bassarids*, both of which were premiered in Germany. Auden and Kallman also wrote English-language versions of operas by Weill and Mozart.

THE AUDIENCE   *1982 opera by Dembo*

A woman gets up from the audience, goes onto the stage and begins to sing. Her husband enters and complains. Her voice teacher arrives and joins him in a duet. Finally the husband gives in and all three perform a trio for the audience. Royce Dembo's post-modern one-act opera *The Audience*, libretto by Glen Miller, was premiered by Soho Repertory in New York on May 7, 1982.

AUSTIN, LARRY   *American composer (1930–)*

Larry Austin, a leader in the computer and electronic music field, has composed a number of experimental operas/musical theater pieces. *Roma: A Theater Piece in Open Style for Improvisation Ensemble and Tape* was performed at the University of California, Davis, January 9, 1966. *The Maze: A Theater Piece in Open Style for Three Percussionists, Dancers, Tapes, Machines and Projections,* was presented at UC Davis, March 3, 1966. *Agape*, libretto by the composer based on the Bible and described as a celebration for priests, musicians, dancers, rock band, actors and poets, was presented at SUNY, Buffalo, on February 25, 1970. *Catalogo Voce*, a mini-opera for bass-baritone, tape and slides, was premiered in New York on June 13, 1979. *Euphonia: A Tale of the Future*, two-act opera with libretto by T. Holliday after Berlioz composed for soloists, chorus, chamber orchestra, tape and digital synthesizer, was premiered at Potsdam, New York, April 1, 1982. Austin, born in Duncan, Oklahoma, has founded several institutions to promote experimental music and taught at the University of South Florida in Tampa, and the University of North Texas in Denton.

AZARA   *1898 opera by Paine*

In medieval Provence Gontran asks for the hand of the captive Saracen woman Azara who has been converted to Christianity. When he is refused, he frees the Saracen chief Malek who takes Azara prisoner because he knows she is the daughter of the Caliph. Azara escapes and returns in disguise but is pursued by Malek. John Knowles Paine's three-act grand opera *Azara*, libretto by the composer based on the 13th century French troubadour tale *Aucassin et Nicolette,* was written for American soprano Emma Eames with the hope of having it staged at the Metropolitan Opera. Paine was one of the most respected composers in America at the end of the 19th century and Eames one of the most important singers but that was not enough to convince the Met to stage an American opera. *Azara* was given a concert performances at Chickering Hall in Boston in 1903 and was favorably reviewed but it was never staged.

AZORA   *1917 opera by Hadley*

An Aztec princess is ready to die for her love but is saved by the power of her Christian faith. Henry Hadley's "legendary" opera *Azora, Daughter of Montezuma*, libretto by David Stevens, is a kind of Christian version of *Aida* and ends with a solemn *Gloria in Excelsis Deo*. It was premiered by the Chicago Opera Company at the 4000-seat Auditorium on December 26, 1917, with Anna Fitziu as Azora, Forrest Lamont as Prince Xalea, Arthur Middleton as Ramatzin, Frank Preisch as Canek and James Goddard as Montezuma. It was reprised in New York at the Lexington Theater in 1918 with the same cast.

B

BABBITT, MILTON   *American composer (1916–)*

Milton Babbitt, the leading proponent of 12-tone compositional theory and practice in the U. S. and one of the most influential figures in modern American music, composed one early music theater work. *Fabulous Voyage*, libretto by the composer with R. S. Childs and R. H. Kock based on Homer's *The Odyssey*, was completed in 1946 but not premiered until January 27, 1989, when it was presented at the Juilliard School of Music in New York. *Three Theatrical Songs* from *Fabulous Voyage* for voice and piano were also prepared in 1946: "Penelope's Night Song," "Now You See It" and "As Long as It Isn't Love." Babbitt, who was born in Philadelphia and headed the Columbia-Princeton Electronic Music Center for many years, was awarded a special Pulitzer Prize in 1982 for his life's work.

BABES IN TOYLAND   *1903 operetta by Herbert*

Victor Herbert's delightful operetta *Babes in Toyland* has memorable music, a clever libretto by Glen MacDonough and a charming fairy tale setting. Two children, Alan and Jane, the "babes" of the title, escape from a wicked uncle to Toyland and are helped by nursery rhyme characters. The best-known numbers are the oft-recorded "Toyland," introduced by Bessie Wynn, and the "March of the Toys." *Babes in Toyland* premiered at the Grand Opera House in Chicago on September 17, 1903, and opened in New York at the Majestic Theater on October 13, 1903. William Norris played Alan, Mabel Barrison was Jane, George W. Denham was evil Uncle Barnaby, Amy Ricard was Contrary Mary, Bessie Wynn was Tom Tom, Nella Webb was Bo-Peep, Nellie Daly was Jill, Susie Kelleher was Red Riding Hood and Dore Davidson was the Toymaker. Max Hirschfeld conducted. The quality of the music is amply demonstrated in a 1996 Razumovsky Symphony recording featuring the nearly forgotten fifteen-minute prelude. There are many, many recordings and six screen versions and the operetta continues to be revived on stage, including a Houston Grand Opera production in 1991.

1904 Corrine Morgan. Contralto Corrine Morgan teams with the Haydn Quartet in this recording of "Toyland" made for a Victor 78 in 1904. **1911 Victor Light Opera.** Victor Light Opera Company vocalists sing a medley of songs for the Victor 78 record *Gems from Babes in Toyland.* It on the AEI CD album *Babes in Toyland.* **1911 and 1913 Victor Herbert.** Victor Herbert conducts his orchestra in Victor and Edison recordings in 1911 and 1913 of "March of the Toys," "The Toymaker's Shop," "The Military Ball" and "Selections from Babes in Toyland." They're on the AEI CD *Babes in Toyland* album. **1934 MGM film.** Stan Laurel is Stannie Dum, Oliver Hardy is Ollie Dee and tenor Felix Knight is

The 1934 film version of Victor Herbert's operetta *Babes in Toyland* was a visually effective production, retaining most of the stage score.

Tom Tom in this classic MGM film which retains most of the Herbert score. Charlotte Henry is Little Bo Peep, Johnny Downs is Little Boy Blue, Jean Darling is Curly Locks, Marie Wilson is Mary Quite Contrary, William Burress is the Toy Maker, Ferdinand Munier is Santa Claus and Virginia Karns is Mother Goose. The film was produced by Hal Roach, written by Nick Grinde and Frank Butler, photographed by Art Lloyd and Francis Corby and directed by Charles Rogers and Gus Meins. Harry Jackson was music director. Mark 56 soundtrack LP/Goodtimes VHS. **1935 Bessie Wynn.** Bessie Wynn, who created the role of Tom Tom, sings "Toyland" and "Go to Sleep, Slumber Deep" in a 1935 recording. It's on the AEI CD album *Babes in Toyland.* **1938 Nathaniel Shilkret.** Nathaniel Shilkret conducts the RCA Victor Chorus and Orchestra in a medley of songs from the operetta with Anne Jamison and Gladys Rice as soloists. It's on the RCA Victor LP *Victor Herbert Melodies.* **1944 Kenny Baker/Karen Kemple.** Kenny Baker and Karen Kemple as the principal singers in this recording of ten numbers from the musical with Alexander Smallens conducting the chorus and orchestra. Decca LP/CD. **1949 David**

Poleri/Marie Haddon. Robert Trendler leads the orchestra in this radio version of the operetta broadcast on October 24, 1949. David Poleri sings Alan's songs (speaking voice by Jonathan Hall), Marie Hadden sings Jane's songs (speaking voice by Mary Frances Desmond), Lois Faire is Contrary Mary, and Marion Claire narrates. AEI CD/Live Opera audiocassette. **1961 Disney film.** Ray Bolger is villain Barnaby, Annette Funicello is Mary Contrary and Ed Wynn is the Toymaker in this Disney film directed by Jack Donahue. Tommy Sands is Tom Piper, Tommy Kirk is Grumio, Kevin Corcoran is Boy Blue, Mary McCarty is Mother Goose, Ann Jillian is Bo Peep, Henry Calvin is Gonzorgo and Gene Sheldon is Roderigo. Ward Kimball, Joe Rinaldi and Lowell S. Hawley did the adaptation. Disney VHS/Disneyland LP. **1962 Lehman Engel.** Lehman Engel conducts orchestra and chorus in this highlights recording made for *The Reader's Digest* box set *Treasury of Great Operettas.* Mary Ellen Pracht is Jane, Jeanette Scovotti is BoPeep, Peter Palmer is Alan, Sara Endich is Mary, Patricia Kelly is the Fairy, and Mallory Walker is Tom Tom. Henri Rene created the arrangements. RCA LP box set. **1965 and 1975 André Koste-**

lanetz. André Kostelanetz conducts "Toyland" and "March of the Toys" with his own orchestra on the 1965 album *Music of Victor Herbert* (Columbia LP) and with the London Symphony Orchestra on the 1975 album *Music of Victor Herbert* (EMI LP). **1978 Kim Criswell.** Kim Criswell sings "I Can't Do the Sum" with the Cincinnati's University Singers and Theater Orchestra led by Earl Rivers. It's on the album *I Wants to Be an Actor Lady*. New World LP/CD. **1979 Bob Christianson.** Bob Christianson leads orchestra and singers in this cast album based on a 1979 stage production of the operetta as rewritten and revised by Shelly Markham and Annette Leisten. Babes in Toyland LP. **1980 Carolyn Mignini.** "Toyland" is sung by Carolyn Mignini and ensemble in the finale of the 1980 stage revue *Tintypes*. Pianist Mel Marvin plays piano. DRG CD. **1986 Clive Donner film.** Clive Donner's TV film stars Drew Barrymore, Richard Mulligan, Eileen Brennan, Keanu Reeves, Jill Schoelen and Pat Morita but very little of Herbert's score is used. "Toyland" and "March of the Wooden Soldiers" are heard but take second place to music by Leslie Bricusse. Paul Zindel wrote the adaptation. On VHS. **1986 Donald Hunsberger.** Donald Hunsberger leads the Eastman-Dryden Orchestra in numbers from the operetta on the album. *Victor Herbert: L'Encore*. Arabesque CD. **1989 Leonard Slatkin.** Leonard Slatkin leads the St. Louis Symphony Orchestra in "March of the Toys" on the album *Classic Marches*. RCA Victor CD. **1991 Lorin Maazel.** Lorin Maazel leads the Pittsburgh Symphony Orchestra in "March of the Toys" and "I Can't Do the Sum" on the album *Popular American Music*. Sony CD. **1996 Keith Brion.** Victor Herbert specialist Keith Brion leads the Razumovsky Symphony Orchestra in nine numbers from the operetta, including the little-heard 15-minute "Prelude." They're on the album *Victor Herbert: Babes in Toyland*. American Classics Naxos CD. **1997 Babes in Toyland anthology.** This fascinating anthology album features historic recordings of *Babes in Toyland*, including the Victor Herbert and Victor Light Opera Company selections from 1911, the "Toyland" recorded by Bessie Wynn in 1935 and the 1949 radio version. AEI CD. **1997 MGM film.** Colorful and enjoyable animated feature film version featuring the voices of James Belushi, Christopher Plummer, Catherine Cavadini, Lacey Chabert, Bronson Pincot, Charles Nelson Reilly, and Raphael Sbarge. It was designed by Toby Bluth, written by John Loy, and directed by Charles Grosvenor, Toby Bluth, and Paul Sabella with some new songs by Mark Waters. MGM-UA VHS. **1999 Virginia Croskery.** Virginia Croskery sings "Toyland" accompanied by the Slovak Radio Symphony Orchestra led by Keith Brion on the album *Victor Herbert: Beloved Songs and Classic Miniatures*. American Classics Naxos CD.

BABETTE   *1903 operetta by Herbert*

Babette is a Belgian woman who writes letters for a living. With the help of an adventurous soldier of fortune, she persuades the King of France to end Spanish control of the country. Victor Herbert's operetta *Babette*, libretto by Harry B. Smith, premiered at the National Theater in Washington, D.C., on November 9, 1903, and opened at the Broadway Theater in New York on November 16, 1903. Met soprano Fritzi Scheff, making her first appearance in light opera, starred as Babette with Eugene Cowles as her soldier friend Mondragon, Richie Ling as the painter Marcel and Errol Dunbar as the King of France. Scheff's singing was highly praised as was Herbert's music but the libretto was weak and the operetta has a short run. The operetta's "Butterfly Waltz Song" is modeled on an aria from Gounod's opera *Roméo et Juliette* called "Je Veux Vivre." Scheff had made her debut in this opera in 1897.

1911 Victor Herbert. Victor Herbert leads his orchestra in a performance of the number "There Once Was an Owl" from *Babette* for a Victor 78 record. **2000 Sweethearts.** Elizabeth Futral sings the "Butterfly Waltz Song" from *Babette* accompanied by the Rudolph Palmer Singers and Robert Tweten on piano. It's on the album *Sweethearts*. Newport Classics CD.

BACH, JAN   *American composer (1937–)*

Jan Bach, born in Forrest, Illinois, is best known for three one-act operas based on literary works. THE SYSTEM is a black comedy based on a story by Edgar Allan Poe that premiered in New York in 1974. *The Happy Prince* is fairy tale based on the story by Oscar Wilde; it premiered in Omaha, Nebraska, in 1980. THE STUDENT FROM SALAMANCA, a comic romp about a wife setting out to cuckold her husband based on a Cervantes story, was premiered by New York City Opera in 1980.

BACH, P.D.Q.   *Mythical German composer (1807–1742)*

Peter Schickele created this imaginary member of the Bach family and wrote parodistic pieces of baroque and classical music in his name. P.D.Q. Bach is said to have composed eight operas, starting with THE STONED GUEST in 1967. For details, see PETER SCHICKELE.

BACON, ERNST   *American composer (1898–1990)*

Ernest Bacon composed four music theater pieces in what he described as folk opera style. The best-known are the folk opera A TREE ON THE PRAIRIE, premiered at Converse College in Spartanburg, SC, where he was teaching, on May 2, 1942; and the 1949 folk opera A DRUMLIN LEGEND, libretto by Helene Carus, premiered in New York on May 4, 1949. Bacon is also known for his songs composed to poems by Emily Dickinson and Walt Whitman. The Chicago-born composer has won a number of musical awards, including two Guggenheim fellowships.

BACQUIER, GABRIEL   *French baritone (1924–)*

Gabriel Bacquier is best known for his impressive performances in classic roles in 19th century European operas but he also created a major character in an American opera. He portrayed Abdul, the presumed savage, in Gian Carlo Menotti's THE LAST SAVAGE when it premiered at the Paris Opera in 1963 as *Le dernier Sauvage*. Bacquier, who was born in Béziers, began his career in 1950 and has sung at most of the great opera houses.

BADEA, CHRISTIAN   *Romanian-born American conductor (1947–)*

Christian Badea has conducted and recorded a number of operas by Samuel Barber and Gian Carlo Menotti. He recorded Barber's ANTONY AND CLEOPATRA in Spoleto in 1983, conducted the Spoleto Festival telecast of Menotti's MARIA GOLOVIN in 1977, conducted the European premiere of Menotti's THE HERO in 1980 and conducted the Spoleto Festival telecast of THE MEDIUM in 1981. He was music director of the Spoleto Festival from 1978 to 1986 and became music director of the Savannah and Columbus Symphony Orchestras in 1983.

BAKER, ALAN   *American baritone (1936–)*

Lyric baritone Alan Baker, a native of Kansas City, Missouri, created roles in three American operas, including two that premiered on television. He was the Angel in the Ezra Laderman's SARAH on CBC TV in 1958, the Clown in Laderman's *Goodbye to the Clown* when it was premiered by Turnau Opera in 1960 and

Max in Amram's THE FINAL INGREDIENT on ABC TV in 1965. On stage he has played the Husband in Gian Carlo Menotti's *Amelia Goes to the Ball*. Baker, who studied at Juilliard and in Germany, made his debut with the Turnau Opera Company in 1959.

BAKER, GREGG   *American baritone (1955–)*

Gregg Baker made his debut at the Met in 1985 singing Crown in the first Metropolitan Opera production of Gershwin's PORGY AND BESS and then repeated the role at the Glyndebourne Festival the following year. He is featured on the Glyndebourne recording and video and a highlights recording with Roberta Alexander. In 1991 he was featured in a recording of CARMEN JONES and in 1996 in a recording of Gershwin's BLUE MONDAY. Baker, born in Memphis, Tennessee, began his career singing in *The Wiz* on Broadway, and went on to sing at the Met as Escamillo in *Carmen* and the High Priest in *Samson and Dalila*.

BAKER, MARK   *American tenor (1950–)*

Mark Baker created the role of Tom Buchanan in John Harbison's THE GREAT GATSBY at the Metropolitan Opera in 1999 and the Navigator in Anthony Davis's opera AMISTAD in Chicago in 1997. He sings the title role in a 1974 Chelsea Theater recording of Leonard Bernstein's CANDIDE.

BAL MASQUE   *1936 "movie opera" by Carbonara*

Metropolitan Opera soprano Mary Ellis sings the principal role in *Bal Masque*, an imaginary opera featured in the 1936 Paramount opera movie *Fatal Lady*. Gerard Carbonara and Victor Young composed the music to a libretto by Sam Coslow, Leo Robin and Max Terr while Boris Petroff staged it. The arias include "Je Vous Adore," and "The Death Song." *The New York Times* called the film "a prima donna's vehicle, duly affording Miss Ellis opportunities of singing choice bravura passages." Ellis plays an opera diva who runs away after accusations of murder and begins to sing under a false name. Back-stage intrigue and murder follow her to an opera house in South America but Walter Pidgeon finally solves the mystery. The film includes a second imaginary opera by Carbonara called ISABELLE. Edward Ludwig directed the movie for Paramount.

BALADA, LEONARDO   *American composer (1933–)*

Leonardo Balada's first opera, the satirical HANGMAN, HANGMAN! (1982), features a horse thief as hero and was based on an American cowboy ballad. *Zapata* (1984), about the life of the Mexican revolutionary, was commissioned by San Diego Opera. CRISTÓBAL COLÓN (*Christopher Columbus*/1986), a grand opera about Columbus's voyage, premiered in Balada's native Barcelona with José Carreras and Montserrat Caballé in the leading roles. *Death of Columbus* (1996) is a sequel to *Christopher Columbus* starting with his return from his voyage of discovery and ending with his death. THE TOWN OF GREED (1997), a sequel to *Hangman, Hangman!*, has been staged in both America and Spain. Balada, who came to America in 1956 as a student, remained to become a composer linking the music of Spain with that of the U.S.

BALALAIKA   *1939 "movie opera" by Stothart*

Balalaika is an imaginary opera based on music from Rimsky-Korsakov's *Scheherezade* that is staged at the Imperial Opera House in Moscow in the 1939 MGM operetta film *Balalaika*. It was devised by Herbert Stothart with help from musical pastiche masters Bob Wright and Chet Forest, the team that later transmuted Borodin's music into the operetta *Kismet*. Nelson Eddy and Ilona Massey are the singing stars of the movie set in Moscow and Paris at the time of the Russian revolution and based on a British stage operetta by Eric Maschwitz. William Axt conducts the music and Reinhold Schunzel directed the film. MGM-UA VHS/DVD.

BALK, HOWARD   *American director/librettist (1932–)*

Howard Balk, a native of St. Paul, was resident stage director for Minnesota Opera many years and mounted the premieres of seven American operas including three for which he wrote the libretto. They were Eric Stokes' HORSPFAL in 1968, Yale Marshall's *Oedipus and the Sphinx* in 1969 (libretto), Marshall's *The Business of Good Government* in 1970, John Gessner's *Faust Counter Faust* in 1971 (libretto), Philip Brunelle and William Huckaby's *The Newest Opera in the World* in 1974 (libretto), Conrad Susa's TRANSFORMATIONS in 1973 and Elliot Kaplan, Frank Lewin, Robert Karmon and Louis Phillips' multi-media work *Gulliver: A Spatialoperadramafilmevent* in 1975.

THE BALLAD OF BABY DOE   *1956 opera by Moore*

Colorado mining magnate Horace Tabor falls in love with Baby Doe McCourt in 1880 Leadville and leaves his domineering wife Augusta. He marries her in Washington while serving a term as Senator and President Chester Arthur attends the wedding reception. Tabor's fortune is tied to silver, however, and when pro-silver presidential candidate William Jennings Bryan loses the 1896 election, Tabor is ruined. Baby Doe remains faithful to him even after his death. Douglas Moore's opera *The Ballad of Baby Doe*, superb libretto by John Latouche, is based around real people and events. It premiered at the Central City Opera House in Colorado on July 7, 1956. Dolores Wilson was Baby Doe, Walter Cassel was Horace, Martha Lipton was Augusta, Beatrice Krebs was Mama McCourt and Lawrence Davidson was William Jennings Bryan. It was staged by Hanya Holm and Edward Levey with costumes, sets and lighting by Donald Oenslaveger and Emerson Buckley conducting.

The opera attracted major attention when it opened at New York City Opera April 3, 1958, with Beverly Sills as Baby Doe, a role that helped make her an operatic celebrity. Walter Cassel was Horace, Martha Lipton was Augusta, Beatrice Krebs was Mama McCourt and Joshua Hecht was William Jennings Bryan. Vladimir Rosing was the stage director and Emerson Buckley conducted. For a time *Ballad of Baby Doe* was considered the Great American Opera; during the 1976 Bicentenary celebrations there were five professional productions. It was revived in 2001 by New York City Opera with Elizabeth Futral as Baby Doe, Mark Delavan as Tabor and Joyce Castle as Augusta. Two of Baby Doe's arias have become popular as soprano recital pieces, the LETTER SONG and WILLOW SONG, and Augusta's aria AUGUSTA! AUGUSTA! HOW CAN YOU TURN AWAY? is also popular.

1958 New York City Opera. Beverly Sills sings Baby Doe in this classic recording by the New York City Opera cast. Walter Cassel is Horace, Frances Bible is Augusta, Joshua Hecht is William Jennings Bryan, Beatrice Krebs is Mama McCourt and Chester Ludgin is a bartender and a Denver politician. Emerson Buckley leads the New York City Orchestra and Chorus. MGM/Heliodor/ DGG 3-LP set and DG 2-CD set. **1958 Beverly Sills.** Beverly Sills sings the aria "Gold is a fine thing" with Emerson Buckley conducting the New York City Opera Orchestra on the 2000 album *The Art of Beverly Sills*. It's taken from the NYCO cast album. Universal CD. **1962 American Music Theater.** Beverly Sills re-creates her New York City Opera triumph as Baby Doe in this American Music Theater television program of highlights from the opera. Appearing on the show with Sills is composer Douglas Moore Alfredo Antonini conducted the CBS orchestra and Martin O'Carr directed. The 30-minute program was telecast on WCBS-TV on March 4, 1962. Video at MTR. **1969 New York City Opera.** Beverly Sills sings Baby Doe in this live recording of the opera as performed and broadcast by New York City Opera November 13, 1969. Muriel Greenspon is Augusta and Walter Cassel is Horace. Gustav Meier conducts the NYCO Orchestra and Chorus. Live Opera audiocassette. **1969 NYCO in Los Angeles.** Beverly Sills sings the role of Baby Doe in this live recording of the opera as performed by the New York City Opera in Los Angeles on December 1, 1969. Frances Bible is Augusta and Walter Cassel is Horace Tabor. Gustav Meier conducts the NYCO Orchestra and Chorus. Live Opera audiocassette. **1976 New York City Opera.** Ruth

Evelyn del la Rosa starred as Baby Doe in Des Moines Metro Opera's superb 1995 production of Douglas Moore's opera *The Ballad of Baby Doe.* Photograph courtesy of Des Moines Metro Opera.

Welting sings the role of Baby Doll in a recording of a New York City Opera production telecast on April 21, 1976. Francis Bible is Augusta, Richard Fredricks is Horace and Judith Somogi conducts the NYCO Orchestra and Chorus. On CD. **1983 Helen-Kay Eberley.** Helen-Kay Eberley sings the "Silver Aria" and the "Willow Song" accompanied by pianist Donald Isaak on her recital album *American Girl.* Eb-Sko LP. **1992 Cleveland Opera.** Sheryl Woods stars as Baby Doe in this recording of the opera as performed by Cleveland Opera on April 10, 1993. Joyce Castle is Augusta and Richard Stilwell is Walter. Anton Coppola conducts the Cleveland Opera Orchestra. Live Opera audiocassette. **1992 Lancaster Opera.** New York City Opera baritone John Darrenkamp stars as Horace Tabor opposite Andrea Rose Folan as Baby Doe in this production by the Lancaster Opera Company at the Fulton Theater in Lancaster, PA. This is a poor quality nonprofessional video shot from a balcony. Opera Dubs VHS. **1995 Dawn Upshaw.** Dawn Upshaw sings the "Willow Song" accompanied by pianist David Zinman on her album *The World So Wide.* Nonesuch CD. **1995 Eileen di Tullio.** Eileen di Tullio sings the Letter Song "Dearest Mama, I am writing" from *The Ballad of Baby Doe* on her album *The Art of Eileen di Tullio.* Legato CD. **1995 Des Moines Opera.** Evelyn del la Rosa sings Baby Doe in this highly enjoyable Des Moines Metro Opera production staged and conducted by Robert Larsen. Gwendolyn Jones is Augusta, Richard L. Richards is Horace Tabor, Anne Larson is Mama McCourt and Paul Geiger is William Jennings Bryan. The opera was telecast by Iowa Public Television. Opera Dubs/Premiere Opera VHS. **1996 Central City Opera.** Jan Grissom is Baby Doe in this recording made at the Central City Opera House where the opera premiered. Brian Steele is Horace, Dana Krueger is Augusta, Myrna Paris is Mama McCourt, Torrance Blaisdell is Chester A. Arthur and Mark Freiman is William Jennings Bryan. John Moriarty conducts the Orchestra and Chorus of the Central City Opera. Newport Classic 2-CD set. **1998 B. J. Ward.** B. J. Ward sings

"The Willow Song" with The New Synthony Orchestra on her album *Stand-Up Opera.* It was recorded at The Bakery in Los Angeles. BOS CD. **1998 Renée Fleming.** Renée Fleming sings "The Letter Song" on her recital album *I Want Magic.* James Levine conducts the Metropolitan Opera Orchestra. London Classics CD. **2000 Taking a Chance on Love.** The off-Broadway revue *Taking a Chance on Love.* based on the lyrics of John Latouche, closes with "Always Through the Closing" from *The Ballad of Baby Doe.* The singers are Eddie Korbich, Terry Burrell, Jerry Dixon and Donna English. Original Cast Records CD. **2002 B. J. Ward.** B. J. Ward sings "The Willow Song" with Sydney Waterman conducting on her album *Queen of the Night.* Summit CD.

BALLET BALLADS *1948 ballet-operas by Moross*

Composer Jerome Moross and librettist John Latouche cross genre boundaries with *Ballet Ballads,* three ballet-operas that premiered together on May 9, 1948, at the Experimental Theater in New York. *Susanna and the Elders,* like the more famous Carlisle Floyd opera, transposes the Biblical story into the American South. *Willie the Weeper* features a 12-tone saxophonist riding high on marijuana dreams. *The Eccentricities of Davy Crockett* tells the story of the frontier folk hero who said he caught a mermaid and certainly died at the Battle of the Alamo. A fourth ballet-opera, *Riding Hood Revisited,* was not included in this program. An earlier ballet-opera *Frankie and Johnny* was premiered in Chicago in 1938.

2000 Taking a Chance on Love. The off-Broadway revue *Taking a Chance on Love,* based around the lyrics and life of John Latouche, features *The Eccentricities of Davy Crockett* from *Ballet Ballads* plus the numbers "Mr. Nobody" and "Oh, Baby." The singers are Eddie Korbich, Terry Burrell, Jerry Dixon and Donna English. Original Cast Records CD. **2002 Hot Springs Music Festival.** The opera-ballet *Willie the Weeper* is performed by tenor John DeHaan at the Hot Springs Music Festival in Arkansas with orchestration created by Moross in 2000. The opera- ballet *Frankie* *and Johnny*, premiered in Chicago in 1938, is sung by Melisa Barrick, Denis Eddy and Diane Kesling. Richard Rosenberg conducts the Hot Springs Music Festival Chamber Chorus and Symphony Orchestra. Naxos CD.

BALLYMORE *1999 opera by Wargo*

Richard Wargo's two-part opera *Ballymore*, libretto by the composer, is based on Irish playwright Brian Friel's two-part play *Lovers* consisting of *Winners* and *Losers*. Ballymore is the name of the fictional town in northern Ireland where the stories are set. In the tragic *Winners* young lovers Mag and Joe enjoy a day together but balladeers tell us it will be their last before they die in an accident. In the comic *Losers* middle-aged couple Hanna and Andy have problems with her overly-religious mother following news from the Vatican that favorite saint Philomena has been decanonized. The opera, commissioned by Skylight Opera Theatre of Milwaukee and Opera Company of Philadelphia, was premiered by Skylight in Milwaukee on January 29, 1999. In *Winners* Alice Berneche was Mag, Jeffrey Picon was Joe and Neil Michael and Hillary Nicolson were the Ballad Singers. In *Losers* Leslie Fitzwater was Hanna, David Barron was Andy, Jennifer Clark was Kate Cassidy and Alicia Berneche was Cissie Cassidy. Carol Bailey designed the sets, Dorothy Danner directed and Richard Carsey conducted.

BALSEROS *1997 opera by Ashley*

Cuban raft people (the balseros of the title) tell the story of their dangerous flight from Cuba to Florida. Robert Ashley's opera *Balseros* includes 36 stories in Spanish and English in the long journey with a Cuban American couple as narrators. Maria Irene Fornes wrote the libretto based on interviews with rafters who made the journey. The opera was premiered by Florida Grand Opera in Miami Beach on May 16, 1997. The cast included Joan La Barbara, Thomas Buckner, Sam Ashley, Jacqueline Humbert, Demetra Adams, Mani Cadet, Christine Clark, David Dillar and Amy Van Roekel.

BALTHROP, CARMEN *American soprano (1948–)*

Carmen Balthrop plays Treemonisha in the 1975 video and 1982 recording of the Houston Grand Opera productions of Scott Joplin's opera TREEMONISHA; she also performed the role on Broadway and at Michigan Opera Theater. She created the role of Vanqui in Leslie Savoy Burrs VANQUI in Columbus in 1999 and Annie in Robert Greenleaf's UNDER THE ARBOR in Birmingham in 1992. She played Aurore in William Grant Still's A BAYOU STORY when it was filmed by Opera/South in 1981. Balthrop, who was born in Washington, D. C., made her opera debut in 1973 in Washington and first sang at the Metropolitan Opera in 1977.

BANDANNA *1999 opera by Hagen*

Latino police chief Miguel Morales has problems. He suspects his wife Mona of being unfaithful, his deputy Jake Lopez is allowing illegal immigrants to cross the border and labor organizer James Kane is out to get him. Daron Hagen's opera *Bandanna*, libretto by Paul Muldoon, is a version of the Otello story set in small town on the U.S./Mexico border. It was premiered by the University of Texas-Austin Opera Theater on February 25, 1999.

1999 North Texas Wind Symphony. The "Wedding Dances" from *Bandanna* are performed by the North Texas Wind Symphony conducted by Eugene Migliaro Corporon on the album *Sojourns*. Klavier CD. **2000 University of Nevada Opera.** Mark Thomsen is Police Chief Morales in this recording of a concert production by the University of Nevada Opera Theatre in Las Vegas

March 3, 2000. James Demler is Lopez, Paul Kreider is Kane, and Darynn Zimmer is Mona with support from Lesley DeGroot and Travis Lewis. Hagen conducts the Opera Theatre orchestra, chorus and mariachi ensemble. ARSIS CD.

BARAB, SEYMOUR *American composer (1921–)*

Chicago-born Seymour Barab is a prolific composer of one-act operas that have become popular with universities and semi-professional groups. CHANTICLEER, based on Chaucer's *The Nun's Priest's Story*, premiered in Aspen in 1956. The comic A GAME OF CHANCE was first presented at Augustana College in Illinois in 1957. *The Maladroit Door* was premiered at Manhattan School in 1950 with Johanna Meier starring as Blanche. *The Ransom of Red Chief*, based on an O. Henry story, was premiered in Newark, NJ, in 1964. PHILIP MARSHALL, based on Dostoevsky's *The Idiot*, was first performed in Chautauqua in New York in 1974. The teasing NOT A SPANISH KISS was premiered by the New York Singing Teachers Association in 1977. The quirky FORTUNE'S FAVORITES, based on an H. H. Munro story, was first staged at the Singer's Theater in 1981. The satiric *I Can't Stand Wagner*, based on a story by Evelyn Smith, was first presented at the Singer's Forum in New York in 1986. After Dinner Opera staged *At Last I've Found You* in 1983, *Fair Means or Foul* in 1983, *Out the Window* in 1985, *Predators* in 1985, *Passion in the Principal's Office* in 1987 and *Pizza with Mushrooms* in 1989. Barab also writes children's operas. *Little Red Riding Hood* (1958), libretto by the composer based on the Grimm fairy tale, was staged by L'Ensemble in 1980 and Louisiana Tech Opera Workshop in 1984. *The Toy Shop* (1978), libretto by the composer, was staged by Mobile Opera in 1979 and Chattanooga Opera in 1986. Eleven of Barab's operas have been videotaped though none have been released commercially.

DAS BARBECÜ *1993 Ring satire by Warrender*

Richard Wagner's *Der Ring des Nibelungen* transposed to the mythical land of East Texas and told with country-style music. Wotan is transformed into an oil tycoon and Siegfried into a cowboy while Erda runs a whore house and the Rhinemaidens have become tent show attractions. They battle for "A Ring of Gold in Texas" until Brünnhilde destroys the world by pitching the Ring back into the river. Scott Warrender's *Das Barbecü*, libretto by Jim Luigs, was commissioned by Seattle Opera which premiered it in 1993 in connection with its production of Wagner's Ring cycle. *Das Barbecü* has toured the country from New York to Dallas.

1994 Original cast album. The forty roles in the musical, from Wotan, Fricka and Siegfried to Valkyries and Rivermaidens, are played and sung by five people: Julie Johnson, J. K. Simmons, Jerry McGarity, Carolee Carmello and Sally Mayes. Bruce Kimmel produced this album version recorded in a New York studio with a mini-orchestra. Varese Sarabande CD.

BARBER, SAMUEL *American composer (1910–1981)*

Samuel Barber only composed two full-length operas but both were premiered at the Metropolitan Opera House. The Pulitzer Prize-winning VANESSA is considered by some to be one of the great American operas while ANTONY AND CLEOPATRA has found new life after its initial failure. Barber's other opera is the enjoyable trifle A HAND OF BRIDGE. All three operas are on CD. Barber was never a favorite of modernist critics and his consciously romantic style was deemed aggressively reactionary during his lifetime. However, his reputation has grown since his death and his operas continued to be revived. His "Adagio for Strings" is said to be the most popular American classical composition of the 20th century. Barber, the nephew of Met soprano Louise Homer was a child prodigy. He was born in West Chester, Pennsylvania, and studied at the Curtis Institute of Music where he formed a life-long attachment to Gian Carlo Menotti who wrote librettos for his operas.

BARLOW, HOWARD   *American conductor (1892–1972)*

Howard Barlow was known as a staunch advocate of American music and opera. He created an orchestra in 1923 consisting entirely of musicians born in the U.S.A. and was conductor/music director at CBS from 1927 to 1943. He conducted the stage premiere of Charles Cadman's THE GARDEN OF MYSTERY in 1925. He conducted the first American opera to be broadcast on radio, Deems Taylor's THE KING'S HENCHMAN, transmitted coast to coast by CBS September 18, 1927. He was music director/conductor of NBC's THE VOICE OF FIRESTONE radio and television series from 1943 to 1961 and he usually included arias from American operas and operettas. He can be seen on many of the videos of the Firestone telecasts.

Conductor Howard Barlow

BARLOW, SAMUEL   *American composer (1892–1982)*

Samuel Barlow was the first American to have an opera presented at the Opéra-Comique in Paris though he was greatly assisted in this achievement by having as librettist Paris theatrical favorite Sacha Guitry. Their one-act *Mon Ami Pierrot,* which premiered on January 11, 1935, revolves around the life of French opera composer Lully and the origin of the popular tune "Au clair de la lune." Barlow, a New Yorker who studied under Respighi in Rome, wrote two other operas, *Amanda* and *Eugenie,* but neither has been staged.

BARNES, EDWARD   *American composer (1960–)*

Edward Barnes' best-known opera, A PLACE TO CALL HOME dealing with the struggles of new immigrants in America, was premiered by L. A. Opera in 1992. His other opera written for L.A. Opera was *A Muskrat Lullaby* (1990). Barnes' first opera was *Feathertop,* libretto by Maurice Valency based on the story by Nathaniel Hawthorne, which premiered at the Juilliard School in 1980 and was reprised by Minnesota Opera, *The Frog Who Became a Prince* (1980) was staged by Virginia Opera with Pamela Coburn and

Michael Dash in the leading roles. *Zetabet* (1982), was commissioned by Sarah Caldwell and premiered by the Opera Company of Boston. The monodrama *The Vagabond Queen* was produced at McPherson College in McPherson, Kansas, in 1989 with Katherine Peters in the title role. *Papagayo* (1995) was premiered by San Diego Opera and *Mystery on the Docks* (1995) was first staged by Lyric Opera of Kansas City.

BARON, MAURICE   *American composer/conductor (1889–1964)*

Maurice Baron's only opera was the three-act *François Villon,* libretto by the composer based on the life of the French poet, which premiered on NBC Radio on April 14, 1940. Baron began his music studies in Lille, France, where he was born, and continued them in Boston where he was made assistant conductor if the Boston Opera. After a period working as a violinist and composing scores for silent movies like *Ben Hur* and *The Big Parade,* he went to Radio City Music Hall where he was staff composer and conductor from 1932 to 1949. Baron also composed an operetta (*The Enchanted Forest*), a ballet (*Susan at the Zoo*) and orchestral works.

THE BARRIER   *1950 opera by Meyerowitz*

Colonel Thomas Norwood lives with his African American housekeeper/mistress Cora Lewis and their three children on a Georgia plantation. Son William is well-behaved, daughter Sally is confused and son Robert is a rebel. Robert kills his father during a quarrel and flees. When a posse goes after him, he kills himself. Jan Meyerowitz's opera *The Barrier,* libretto by Langston Hughes, paints a harsh portrait of racial and family problems in the American South. The opera premiered at Columbia University in New York January 18, 1950, and moved to Broadway on February 11. Lawrence Tibbett headed the cast as Colonel Norwood with Muriel Rahn as Cora, Rawn Spearman as Bert, Marc Breuax, Wilton Clary, Reri Grist and Charlotte Holloman. Doris Humphrey directed, H. A. Condell designed the sets and Herbert Zipper conducted. The opera was revived in New York in 1953 and 1961. It was broadcast on Italian radio in 1959 (retitled *The Mulatto*) with the principal roles sung by Italo Tajo, Magda Laszlo, Giulio Fioravanti, Ornella Rovero and Mario Carlin. It was staged by Teatro San Carlo in Naples in 1971 and Darmstadt Staatsoper in 1996.

BARTHELME, DONALD   *American writer (1931–1989)*

Donald Barthelme, a leading light of the meta-fiction movement after the success of his 1964 collection *Come Back Dr. Caligari,* wrote the libretto for Stephen Dembski's 1986 mini-opera *The Show* based on his story. It was premiered on February 22, 1986, at the Hirschhorn Museum in Washington, D.C.

BARTHELSON, JOYCE   *American composer (1910–1986)*

Joyce Barthelson based her mostly comic operas on works by Chaucer, Shaw, Hawthorne. O. Henry and Aristophanes. She began to write opera in 1967 and was encouraged when her CHANTICLEER, based on Chaucer's "The Nun's Priest's Tale," won a major prize and was staged. She followed it with *Feathertop* (1965, based on the Hawthorne story) and *Greenwich Village, 1910* (1969, based on O. Henry's THE GIFT OF THE MAGI). Her other operas include THE KING'S BREAKFAST (1973, based on Maurice Baring's "Catherine Parr"), *The Devils's Disciple* (1977, based on the play by George Bernard Shaw), and LYISTRATATA (1981, based on the play by Aristophanes). Barthelson, who was born in Yakima, Washington, was also a music teacher and conductor.

BARTLEBY   *American operas based on Herman Melville story*

Bartleby the scrivener is hired by a lawyer in New York in the 1840s and works with two other clerks. Gradually he "prefers not to" do anything, not even leave the office, and is arrested and taken to prison. He prefers not to eat and dies. His story is narrated by a lawyer but no reasons are given his behavior. Herman Melville's memorable 1953 novella *Bartleby the Scrivener* has inspired several films and two American operas.

1961 William Flanagan. William Flanagan's *Bartleby,* his only completed opera, was composed to a libretto by playwright Edward Albee in collaboration with I. J. Hinton and premiered at the York Playhouse in New York City on January 24, 1961. The music is as dark as the subject matter but still melodious. **1964 Walter Aschaffenburg.** Walter Aschaffenburg's impressive opera *Bartleby* was composed to a libretto by film scholar Jay Leyda. It was premiered at Oberlin College Conservatory in Ohio on November 12, 1964.

BARTLETT, JOSEPHINE   *American mezzo soprano (1862–)*

Mezzo soprano Josephine Bartlett created roles in seven classic American operettas composed at the turn of the century She was Dame Durden in Reginald DeKoven's ROBIN HOOD in 1890 and premiered six Victor Herbert operettas. She was Felicie in *Prince Ananias* in 1894, The Mother Superior in THE SERENADE in 1897, Ortensia in *The Viceroy* in 1900, Eva in *Babette* in 1903, Mme. Cecile in MLLE. MODISTE in 1905 and Mother Justine in *The Prima Donna* in 1908.

BARTLETT, MICHAEL   *American tenor (1901–1978)*

Tenor Michael Bartlett starred in the premiere of CLARENCE LOOMIS's folk opera *Susanna, Don't You Cry* in 1939. After joining San Francisco Opera, he sang opposite Jarmila Novotná and played Romeo to Jeanette MacDonald's Juliette in a Chicago Opera production. The Massachusetts-born tenor had become widely known acting singing in movies beginning with *Love Me Forever* in 1935.

BARTON, ANDREW   *American librettist (?–?)*

Andrew Barton's THE DISAPPOINTMENT, OR THE FORCE OF CREDULITY is the first American opera or, to be more exact, the first American ballad opera written by an American for Americans. "Andrew Barton" is a rather mysterious figure and the name is probably a pseudonym as his opera was considered so dangerous it was banned. It was to premiere in Philadelphia in 1767 but authorities cancelled the performance saying its satirical elements and "personal elements" made it "unfit for the stage." Barton was able to publish his libretto before the ban, however, and it survived though the music for its eighteen songs was lost. The opera was never publicly performed in its era but in 1976 Samuel Adler reconstructed the music for a version presented at the Library of Congress.

BASKERVILLE, PRISCILLA   *American soprano (1962–)*

Brooklyn-born Priscilla Baskerville created the roles of Louise and Betty in Anthony Davis's X, THE LIFE AND TIMES OF MALCOLM X when it premiered at New York City Opera in 1986 and she sings the parts on the recording. The Brooklyn singer made her debut at the Metropolitan Opera singing Lily in PORGY AND BESS in 1985 and later returned to star as Bess. She has sung the role of Mary in Robert Ward's THE CRUCIBLE and many of the soprano roles in Puccini, Verdi and Mozart operas.

BATTLE, KATHLEEN   *American soprano (1948–)*

Kathleen Battle seems to have a fondness for the aria "Summertime" from George Gershwin's PORGY AND BESS. She sings it on her 1990 video *Kathleen Battle at the Metropolitan Museum,* her 1991 album *Kathleen Battle at Carnegie Hall* and her 1995 album *Honey and Rue* (which also features "I Loves You, Porgy"). She does not appear to have sung the Gershwin opera nor any other American opera on stage. Battle, born in Portsmouth, Ohio, made her debut with New York City Opera in 1976. She says she learned about opera through television.

A BAYOU LEGEND   *1941 opera by Still*

A Mississippi bayou community. Clothilde turns down suitor Leonce because she wants to marry Bazile. He agrees after she tells him he is the father of her unborn child. Bazile's true love, the spirit maiden Aurore, lets him know this is not true, so Bazile rejects Clothilde. She gets her revenge by accusing him of witchcraft. When the villagers hang him for the crime, his spirit rises up to join Aurore. William Grant Still's *A Bayou Legend,* libretto by his wife Verna Arvey based on a Biloxi, Mississippi, legend, was composed in 1941. It was not staged until November 15, 1974, when Opera/South premiered it at the Municipal Auditorium in Jackson, Mississippi. Juanita Waller sang Aurore, Barbara Conrad was Clothilde, Robert Mosely was Leonce, John Miles was Bazile, Naymond Thomas was Father Lestant. Donald Dorr designed the sets and directed the stage production while Leonard de Paur conducted the Opera/South Orchestra and Chorus.

1974 Opera/South. The Opera/South premiere of the opera was recorded with the cast as described above including Juanita Waller as Aurore, Barbara Conrad as Clothilde and Robert Mosely as Leonce. Leonard de Paur conducts the Opera/South Orchestra and Chorus. Audiocassettes from William Grant Still Music, 4 South San Francisco Street, Suite 422, Flagstaff, Arizona. **1979 Opera/South.** Still's opera was videotaped on location on a Mississippi bayou in 1979 with an Opera/South cast performing their roles in the natural setting of the opera. Carmen Balthrop is Aurore, Raeschelle Potter is Clothilde, Gary Burgess is Bazile and Peter Lightfoot is Leonce. Leonard de Paur conducts the Opera/South Orchestra and Chorus. John Thompson directed the video produced by Curtis W. Davis. Telecast on PBS June 15, 1981. Video at MTR.

BE GLAD THEN AMERICA   *1976 choral opera/oratorio by La Montaine*

The Town Crier introduces scenes showing the birth of the United States from the Boston Tea Party and the Battle of Lexington to the signing of the Constitution. Among those appearing on stage are Samuel Adams, Thomas Paine and Patrick Henry. John La Montaine's patriotic choral opera/oratorio *Be Glad Then America: A Decent Entertainment from the Thirteen Colonies,* libretto by the composer based on American Revolution documents, premiered at the Institute for the Arts and Humanistic Studies at Pennsylvania State University on February 6, 1976. Created for the American Bicentennial, it featured the 200-voice Penn State Chorus and was directed by Sarah Caldwell. Like the composer's church operas, it is a grand pageant quoting music from the period, especially that by William Billings.

BE NOT AFEARED   *Tenor aria: The Tempest (1986). Words: Mark Shulgasser. Music: Lee Hoiby*

Caliban's haunting aria "Be not afeared" was praised by critic John Briggs in *Opera News* as "the most beautiful aria written into an American opera for nearly fifty years." It was created by composer Lee Hoiby and librettist Mark Shulgasser for the 1986 opera THE TEMPEST, based on the play by Shakespeare. It was introduced on stage in Indianola, Iowa, by Jacque Trussel portraying Caliban and he sang it in revivals of the opera in Kansas City in 1988 and Dallas in 1993. In the aria the misshapen monster Caliban tells the butler Stephano and the jester Trinculo about the magic island on which they have landed. He says the isle is "full of noises, sounds and sweet airs that give delight and hurt not." Trussel used words from the aria as the title of his recital album *Sounds and Sweet Airs* on which he sings it with the Janáček Philharmonic Orchestra led by Dennis Burkh.

BEACH, AMY MARCY *American composer/pianist (1867–1944)*

Amy (Mrs. H. H.) Marcy Beach wrote only one opera, CABILDO, but she composed more than 300 works in other genres. She was the first American women to achieve success as a composer of large-scale classical music, including symphonies, concertos and choral works. Born in Henniker, NH, she was a child prodigy and a noted concert pianist. After her husband's death in 1911, she toured Europe playing her own compositions and was sometimes praised for being America's leading composer. Her opera *Cabildo*, set in New Orleans in 1812, features pirate Pierre Lafitte involved in a love story. It was completed in 1932 but not staged until 1945 and not recorded until 1995 when it was presented at Lincoln Center.

BEAGLE, PETER S. *American librettist/fantasy writer (1939–)*

Peter S. Beagle wrote the libretto for David Carlson's THE MIDNIGHT ANGEL based on his story "Come, Lady Death" in which Death is invited to a party. It was premiered by Opera Theatre of Saint Louis in 1993 with Elaine Bonazzi in the leading role. Beagle became popular with his first novel, *A Fine and Private Place* (1960), and there are many admirers of his fine fantasy novel *The Last Unicorn* (1982).

BEAST AND SUPERBEAST *1996 chamber operas by Martin*

Jorge Martin's *Beast and Superbeast*, libretto by Andrew Joffe, consists of four one-act chamber operas based on stories by Saki. In *The Interlopers* two enemies are trapped by a fallen tree and make peace before the wolves arrive. In *Sredni Vashtar* a sick boy makes a pet of a ferret which kills his beastly guardian. In *The Mappined Life* a young woman and her aunt compare their lives to that of animals in a zoo. In *Tobermary* a cat tells house party guests all the dirty secrets it has overheard. The opera quartet was premiered by the American Chamber Opera Company on June 21, 1996, with a cast headed by Bethany Reeves, Jessica Marsten, Lynn Norris, Lisa Pierce, Daniel Rawe, Pamela Phillips, Thomas L. Honnick, Keith J. Richards, Gustavo Camps, David Stoneman and Leslie Churchill Ward.

"BEAT OUT DAT RHYTHM ON A DRUM"

Mezzo-soprano aria: Carmen Jones (1943). Words: Oscar Hammerstein II. Music: Georges Bizet.

"Beat out dat rhythm on a drum" is the most memorable of the arias in Oscar Hammerstein's *Carmen Jones*, partially because "Chanson Bohemienne" in the original *Carmen* is less famous than other number but primarily because Hammerstein's words and arrangement are so effective. The aria is sung by Carmen's friend Frankie in Billy Pastor's café as she urges the band's drummer (jazz

great Cozy Cole in the original stage production) to beat out a dance rhythm for her. "I don't need no tune at all," she proudly proclaims. Hammerstein's adaptation is wondrous, respecting the original version and Bizet's music and yet refashioning it into something genuinely American. The aria is sung on the original Broadway cast album by Muriel Smith. who played Carmen on stage, but the most famous version is from the 1954 film where Pearl Bailey as Frankie sings it with incredible verve. English mezzo Elizabeth Welch performs it on a fine 1962 British recording of *Carmen Jones*.

BEATON, MORAG *Australian soprano (1942?–)*

Composer Bernard Herrmann selected the little known Australian soprano Morag Beaton to create the role of Cathy (Catherine Earnshaw) in the 1966 London recording of his opera WUTHERING HEIGHTS. Herrmann rehearsed the opera with her at the home of his friend Ursula Vaughan Williams, with whom he was staying, and recorded her singing it at Barking Town Hall. Beaton's only other recording is collaborating with Joan Sutherland on an album of Noël Coward songs.

BEATRICE *1959 opera by Hoiby*

Beatrice, a deeply religious novice in a 13th century Belgian convent, falls in love with a prince and leaves the convent to be with him. The Virgin Mary takes her place while the convent's statue of Mary disappears. The new Beatrice is proclaimed a saint when she performs a miracle. The real Beatrice returns many years later to die at the foot of the statue of Mary which reappears. Lee Hoiby's three-act opera *Beatrice,* libretto by Marcia Nardi based on Maurice Maeterlinck's *Soeur Béatrice*, was commissioned by WAVE in Louisville, Kentucky, to celebrate the opening of the WAVE Radio and Television Center. It premiered on WAVE-TV on October 23, 1959, under the direction of Burt Blackwell. It was staged a week later, October 30, at the Columbia Auditorium in Louisville by Kentucky Opera under the direction of Moritz Bomhard. Audrey Nossaman sang the role of Beatrice, Elizabeth Johnson was the Abbess, Richard Lohr was Bellidor, Robert Fischer was Father Justinian, David Clenny was Timothy, Bonnie Bounnell was Sister Eglantine and Mary Treitz was Sister Anna. Moritz Bomhard conducted the Louisville Orchestra and Chorus.

1959 Kentucky Opera. Audrey Nossaman stars as Beatrice in this recording of the Kentucky Opera production of *Beatrice* made at the time of the premiere with the premiere cast. Elizabeth Johnson is the Abbess, Richard Lohr is Bellidor, Robert Fischer is Father Justinian, David Clenny is Timothy, Bonnie Bounnell is Sister Eglantine and Mary Treitz is Sister Anna. Moritz Bomhard conducts the Louisville Orchestra and Chorus. Louisville Orchestra First Edition 2-LP set.

BEATRIX CENCI *1971 opera by Ginastera*

Roman Count Francesco Cenci, who inspires terror in his daughter Beatrix and second wife Lucrecia, organizes a masked ball in 1598 at which he rapes Beatrix. She avenges herself with the help of her stepmother and brother and has him killed. When this is discovered, all three are executed even though the Roman people consider their actions justified. Alberto Ginastera's violent two-act opera *Beatrix Cenci*, libretto by William Shand and Alberto Girri based on historical events, was commissioned by Washington Opera which premiered it September 10, 1971, at the Kennedy Center in Washington, D.C. Justino Diaz played Count Francesco Cenci, Arlene Saunders was Beatrix Cenci, Carol Smith was her stepmother Lucrecia and Grayson Hirst was the deceitful priest

Orsino. John Conklin designed the sets, Gerald Freedman directed and Julius Rudel conducted the Chorus and Orchestra of the Washington Opera Society. The opera was reprised with essentially the same cast and production crew at New York City Opera in March 1973. Gwendolyn Killebrew took over the role of Lucrecia and Gary Glaze was Orsino. It was not staged in Europe until 2000 when it was presented in Geneva where Ginastera had died in 1983. The Beatrix Cenci story was also told by Shelley in his verse play *The Cenci* which inspired a British opera by Berthold Goldschmidt.

BEAUTY AND THE BEAST   *American operas based on classic fairytale*

Beauty asks her father for a rose which he takes from the Beast's garden. The Beast threatens to kill him unless he sends Beauty to be his bride so Beauty agrees to live with the Beast. When she goes home for a visit and returns late, she find the Beast dying. She begs him to live and kisses him and he turns into a prince. Four American operas have been based on this popular fairytale. In addition to the two listed below titled *Beauty and the Beast,* there are also Robert Moran DESERT OF ROSES (1992) and Philip Glass's LA BELLE ET LA BÊTE (1994).

1938 Vittorio Giannini. Vittorio Giannini's one-act opera *Beauty and the Beast,* libretto by Robert A Simon, premiered on CBS radio on November 24, 1938, with Agnes Moorehead as narrator. Met tenor Charles Kullman sang the role of Beast, Genevieve Rowe was Beauty, Richard Hale was Father, Helen Van Loon and Lillian Knowles were Beauty's Sisters and Winston Bowe was Gatchkayon. The opera was staged at the Hartford School of Music in Hartford, Connecticut, on February 14, 1946. The 1938 broadcast was recorded off-air. Omega Opera Archives CD. **1974 Frank DiGiacomo.** Frank DiGiacomo's *Beauty and the Beast,* libretto by Emul P. Edmon and the composer, was premiered by Opera Theater of Syracuse in 1974. Christine Klemperer sang Beauty, William Black was Beast, Gayle Ross was First Sister, Donna Miller was Second Sister and Richard McCullough was Father. Terry Glaser directed the production, Anthony Salatino choreographed the Syracuse Ballet Theater dancers and Gary Sheldon conducted the Syracuse Symphony Orchestra. The opera was reprised by Opera Theatre of Syracuse in 1976 with its original cast and recorded with Gary Sheldon conducting. 20th Century LP box.

BED   *Soprano aria: Einstein on the Beach (1976). Word and Music: Philip Glass*

"Bed" is an aria for soprano with a single word or sound as lyric, she simply sings variations of "ah" as her voice floats above an organ accompaniment. It seems simple but it really isn't and it has even been compared to the opening of *Das Rheingold.* The opera EINSTEIN ON THE BEACH is scored simply for one soprano, small ensemble and small chorus. While no aria from a Philip Glass opera has become popular outside its theatrical context, his vocal music is always recognizable and "Bed" has been recorded by three different singers and a saxophone player. AKHNATEN and SATYAGRAHA may have more traditional arias but it was *Einstein on the Beach* that made Glass famous. It has a dream-like narrative revolving around the life of Albert Einstein but there is no real plot. Fol-

Christine Klemperer and William Black in the 1974 Syracuse premiere of Frank DiGiacomo's *Beauty and the Beast.*

lowing its premiere in Avignon in 1976, the opera was staged at the Met. "Bed" is on the recording of the complete opera made in a New York studio in 1978, sung by Iris Hiskey accompanied on organ by George Andoniadis. Her version is also on the CBS CD *Philip Glass: Songs from the Trilogy.* Patricia Schuman is the singer of the aria on the second complete recording of the opera made in 1993 while Janice Pendarvis sings it on the 1994 album *The Essential Philip Glass.* Jon Gibson performs it as a saxophone solo on his 1992 album *Jon Gibson — In Good Company.*

BED AND SOFA   *1996 "silent movie opera" by Pen*

A trio of working folk live in a one-room apartment in 1920s Moscow. The married couple sleep on the bed and their friend sleeps on the sofa. When the husband goes away for a time, the friend moves into the bed. When the husband returns, problems arise and the wife eventually decides to leave. Polly Pen's *Bed and Sofa,* described as a "silent movie opera," is based on a 1926 silent Soviet film directed by Abram Room and written by Victor Schlovsky. The 90-minute chamber opera with a libretto by Laurence Klavan premiered at the off-Broadway Vineyard Theater on February 1, 1996, in a production by André Ernotte. Terri Klausner played the wife Ludmilla, Michael X Martin was the husband Nikolai (Kolya) and Jason Workman was the friend Volodya. The taped narrator was Elizabeth Ogun and the taped vocals were by Polly Pen and Martin Moran. G. W. Mercier designed the sets and costumes, Phil Monat created the lighting and Alan Johnson played piano and led the four-piece orchestra.

1996 Vineyard Theater. The Vineyard Theater cast recorded the opera at the Smash Studios in New York. Terri Klausner sings the part of Ludmilla, Michael X Martin is Nikolai, Jason Workman is Volodya and the radio singers are Polly Pen and Martin Moran. Alan Johnson plays piano and directs the viola, cello and violin chamber orchestra. Varèse Sarabande CD.

BEESON, JACK   *American composer (1921–)*

Jack Beeson has become one of the most popular modern American opera composers because of his tuneful melodic style and interesting choice of American subjects. Like Carlisle Floyd, George Gershwin and Douglas Moore, he has helped define the modern American opera by the creation audience-friendly operas with memorable melodies. HELLO OUT THERE (1954), based on a story by William Saroyan, is a touching dialogue between a prisoner in a Texas jail and a young girl. THE SWEET BYE AND BYE (1956) revolves around an evangelical gospel sect similar to that led by Aimee Semple McPherson. LIZZIE BORDEN (1965), Beeson's most popular opera, tells the story of the legendary Massachusetts woman accused of axe murdering her parents. It has become one of the repertory classics of modern American opera MY HEART'S IN THE HIGHLANDS (1970), based on a play by William Saroyan, describes the adventures of a delightfully eccentric family in Fresco. CAPTAIN JINKS OF THE HORSE MARINES (1975) is based on a 1916 play by Clyde Fitch about a man who bets he can seduce a visiting opera singer. DR. HEIDEGGER'S FOUNTAIN OF YOUTH (1978) is a retelling of a Nathaniel Hawthorne story about a elixir that restores youth. SORRY WRONG NUMBER (1999) is an operatic version of a famous radio play by Lucille Fletcher. Most of Beeson's operas, which mix folk idioms with operatic lyricism, have been recorded and published. His early operas have librettos by Kenward Elmslie, the later ones by Sheldon Harnick. Beeson, who was born in Indiana, began composing for the stage in 1950 starting with *Jonah* based on the Biblical story. After that all his themes were American.

BEFORE BREAKFAST   *1980 opera by Pasatieri*

A woman in an apartment is unable to wake her husband Alfred. She puts on a record and recalls how they met, married and grew apart. She begin to scream until a policeman enters and finds there is nobody in the bedroom. Thomas Pasatieri's 40-minute one-act dramatic monologue *Before Breakfast*, libretto by Frank Corsaro based on the play by Eugene O'Neill, was premiered by New York City Opera on October 9, 1980, in the program *An American Trilogy*. Marilyn Zschau played the part of the Woman. Lloyd Evans designed the set, Frank Corsaro directed and Imre Pallo conducted the NYCO orchestra.

BEGGAR'S HOLIDAY   *1946 ballad opera by Ellington*

Duke Ellington's ballad opera *Beggar's Holiday* is an updating of John Gay's *The Beggar's Opera* with Macheath transformed into an American gangster. Librettist John Latouche, who later wrote the libretto for the opera *The Ballad of Baby Doe*, retained the cynical tone of the original and Ellington composed a notable score. It premiered at the Broadway Theater on December 26, 1946, with Alfred Drake starring as Macheath supported by Zero Mostel, Bernice Parks, Avon Long, Marie Bryant, Jet MacDonald, Herbert Ross and Mildred Smith. Oliver Smith designed the sets, Nicholas Ray directed and Max Meth was conductor. The opera's songs include "Brown Penny" (lyric based on a poem by W. B. Yeats), "When You Go Down by Miss Jenny" and "Take Love Easy."

1946 Original cast album. The original cast of the opera made a demonstration record in 1946, later released on an LP. The singers are Alfred Drake, Bernice Parks, Avon Long, Marie Bryan, Mil-

dred Smith, Jet MacDonald and Dorothy Johnson. Blue Pear LP. **1984 Richard Rodney Bennett.** Richard Rodney Bennett sings and plays "I've Got Me" from *Beggar's Holiday* on the recital album *Take Love Easy: The Lyrics of John Latouche.* Audiophile LP/CD. **2000 Terry Burrell/Jerry Dixon.** Terry Burrell and Jerry Dixon perform "Maybe I Should Change My Ways/Take Life Easy" from *Beggar's Holiday*" in the off-Broadway revue *Taking a Chance on Love.* The show was based around the lyrics of John Latouche. Original Cast Records CD.

BELL, DONALD   *Canadian bass-baritone (1934–)*

Donald Bell created the role of Heathcliff in Bernard Herrmann's undervalued opera WUTHERING HEIGHTS when it received its world premiere in the form of a 1966 London recording. Bell, born in British Columbia, studied in London and made his debut as a recitalist at Wigmore Hall in 1958. In 1990 he sang at Portland Opera in Christopher Drobyn's opera LUCY'S LAPSES.

BELL, MARION   *American soprano (1919–1997)*

Marion Bell created the role of Jennie Parsons in Kurt Weill's folk opera DOWN IN THE VALLEY when it premiered on July 15, 1948, at Indiana University in Bloomington, Illinois. She then starred in the 1950 NBC television production of the opera and recorded it under Weill's supervision. She is best known for creating the role of Fiona in the classic Frederick Loewe/Alan Jay Lerner musical BRIGADOON on Broadway in 1947 and she was married to Lerner for a time. She recorded a highlights version of Rudolf Friml's operetta ROSE MARIE in 1948 and has sung in many operettas on stage. Bell, who was born in St. Louis, made her operatic debut with San Francisco Opera in 1941 and sang with several opera companies. She was under contract to MGM for many years and can be seen in the Marx Brothers film *A Night at the Opera*, as the girl who pushes her way into the packed stateroom to phone her Aunt Minnie, and in *Ziegfeld Follies*, singing a duet from *La Traviata*.

BELL TELEPHONE HOUR   *American radio and TV series (1959–1968)*

The *Bell Telephone Hour*, which premiered on radio in 1940 and television in 1959, helped bring opera to the wider American public. It was rarely devoted to American opera but the 1966 TV program *The New Met: Countdown to Curtain* revolved around Samuel Barber's ANTONY AND CLEOPATRA. It would also occasionally feature singers performing American opera arias. Risë Stevens, for example, sang an aria from Victor Herbert's NATOMA on a 1952 radio program.

THE BELL TOWER   *1957 opera by Krenek*

Evil sorcerer Bannadonna is creating a great bell for a city's tower but is hated by his enslaved workers. When Giovanni tries to escape his workshop, Bannadonna kills him and uses his blood to complete the casting. Giovanni's daughter Una witnesses the murder but does nothing until the bell is put in the tower. When she tries to push Bannadonna off the tower, he turns her to stone but her statue strikes him dead and the bell cracks open. Ernst Krenek's grim one-act opera *The Bell Tower*, libretto by the composer based on a story by Herman Melville, premiered at the University of Illinois in Urbana on March 17, 1957. Manfred Capell was Bannadonna, Donna Sue Barton was Una, William Olson was Giovanni, Dan Macdonald and Donald Peascher were the Senators, Edward Levy and Bruce Govich were the Workmen and John Wilson was the Statue. John Garvey conducted.

BELLADONNA   *1997 opera by Rands*

Five women in a university town take part in a dinner party and talk of love, echoing Plato's *Symposium*. One is a professor in love with a student, one is a Chinese dissident, one is a divinity school graduate and two are transvestite opera singers. Bernard Rands' chamber opera *Belladonna*, libretto by Leslie Dunton-Downer, was premiered by Aspen Opera Theater in the Wheeler Opera House on July 29, 1999. The opera, which is scored for five soloists and two choruses, was commissioned by the Aspen Music Festival to celebrate the festival's 50th anniversary. The premiere cast of music students included Jennifer Aylmer as the infatuated professor, Makio Narumi as the Chinese dissident and Michael Maniaci as a diva in drag. Anne C. Patterson designed the sets, Edward Berkeley staged the opera and David Zinman conducted the 17-piece orchestra. Rands won the Pulitzer Prize for Music in 1984 for his song cycle *Canti del Sole*.

LA BELLE ET LA BÊTE   *1994 opera by Glass*

The 1946 French film *La Belle et la Bête* retells the fairy tale of Beauty and the Beast in a poetic manner with Josette Day as Beauty and Jean Marais as the Beast. Jean Cocteau wrote and directed it, cinematographer Henri Alekan created its stunning images and Georges Auric composed its superb score. Philip Glass's 1994 *La Belle et la Bête* is an attempt to make this movie into an opera. His 1993 stage opera *Orphée* had used the script of Cocteau's film *Orphée* as libretto. This time the opera was created to be presented with the actual film, live performers singing the words the actors recite on screen while the film is projected without sound. Whether the Glass music improves the words or the images dominate his atmospheric score is debatable, but it is certainly unusual. After premiering in Sicily on June 21, 1994, the opera was presented at the Brooklyn Academy of Music on December 8, 1994, with Glass leading the Philip Glass Ensemble. Alexandra Montano sang the role of La Belle, Gregory Purnhagen was La Bête, John Kuether was the Father, Ana Maria Martinez was Félicie, Hallie Neill was Adélaïde and Zheng Zhou was Ludovic.

1994 Philip Glass Ensemble. Mezzo-soprano Janice Felty sings Belle opposite baritone Gregory Purnhagen as the Beast in this recording of the opera made at the Looking Glass Studios in New York. John Kuether is the Father, Ana Maria Martinez is Félicie, Hallie Neill is Adélaïde and Zheng Zhou is Ludovic. Michael Riesman conducts the Philip Glass Ensemble with Philip Glass, Martin Goldray, Eleanor Sandresky and Riesman on keyboards, Jon Gibson on soprano saxophone/flute, Richard Peck on alto/soprano saxophone and Andrew Sterman on flute/piccolo/soprano sax/bass clarinet. There are also musicians playing violin, viola, cello, French horn, tenor trombone, bass trombone, tuba and bassoon. Electra Nonesuch CD box.

BELLOW, SAUL   *American novelist (1915–2005)*

Leon Kirchner's opera LILY is based on Saul Bellow's novel *Henderson the Rain King*. It premiered at New York City Opera on April 14, 1977, with Ara Berberian in the role of Henderson. Bellow won the Pulitzer Prize for *Humboldt's Gift* in 1975 and the Nobel Prize for Literature the following year. His central theme is seen as the search for identity in the modern world.

BENÉT, STEPHEN VINCENT   *American poet, writer, librettist (1898–1943)*

Stephen Vincent Benét, who explored American history and its legends through novels, stories and poems, wrote two librettos for composer Douglas Moore. The first was the 1935 "school operetta"
THE HEADLESS HORSEMAN, based on Washington Irving's *The Legend of Sleepy Hollow*, which premiered in Bronxville, New York, on March 4, 1937. The second was the 1939 opera THE DEVIL AND DANIEL WEBSTER based on his own 1937 story which also provided the basis for a 1941 movie. His story *Jacob and the Indians* was adapted by librettist E. Kinoy for an opera by Ezra Laderman that premiered at Woodstock in 1957. Benét won the Pulitzer Prize for his extraordinary verse novel JOHN BROWN'S BODY which was turned into an opera by Walter Schumann; it premiered in Los Angeles on September 21, 1953. Benét is also known for his much-quoted poem "American Names" (the names that never grow flat) and the story "Sobbin' Women," the basis of the MGM musical *Seven Brides for Seven Brothers*.

BENNETT, ROBERT RUSSELL   *American composer (1894–1981)*

Robert Russell Bennett, best known as the orchestrator of more than 300 Broadway musicals and films, also wrote operas, three with librettos by his music critic friend Robert A. Simon. MARIA MALIBRAN, which revolves around the famous diva's love life in New York in the 1820s, was produced on stage in New York in 1935. THE ENCHANTED KISS, a radio opera based on an O. Henry story, was broadcast on the Mutual Broadcasting System through WNYC in 1945 and produced on stage the same year. *Endymion*, a ballet-opera composed in 1927, was produced by fellow composer Howard Hanson at the Eastman School in 1935. *An Hour of Delusion*, a one-act opera composed to a libretto by Arthur Train Jr. in 1928, has not been performed. The "Music Box Operas" were created for the 1941/1942 radio program *Russell Bennett's Notebook* and based around familiar melodies including *Clementine, My Old Kentucky Home* and *The Man on the Flying Trapeze*. Bennett's last opera was *Crystal*, a story about modern cave-dwellers, was written in the early 1970s but has not been staged. Bennett's Broadway orchestrations include the first production of SHOW BOAT (used on a 1988 recording), OKLAHOMA!, SOUTH PACIFIC, MY FAIR LADY, KISS ME KATE and THE SOUND OF MUSIC.

BENTLEY, ERIC   *American writer/critic (1916–)*

Eric Bentley, one of America's leading theater critics and editors, also dabbled in opera. In 1979 he wrote the libretto for Martin Kalmanoff's opera ON THE HARMFULNESS OF TOBACCO, based on a Chekhov story, which was performed by the Manhattan Opera Singers in Tully Hall. Bentley, a notable translator of the plays of Brecht and Pirandello, also edited many important play collections.

BERBERIAN, ARA   *American bass (1935–)*

Ara Berberian created roles in six American operas, including three composed by Ezra Laderman for television. In 1958 he was Abraham in Laderman's TV opera SARAH. In 1962 he was a Citizen in Abraham Ellstein's GOLEM at the New York City Opera. In 1967 he was Galileo in Laderman's GALILEO GALILEI on television. In 1971 he was Uriah in Laderman's TV opera AND DAVID WEPT. In 1974 he was Creon on the CBS Television production of Benjamin Lee's MEDEA IN CORINTH. In 1977 he portrayed Henderson in the New York City Opera premiere of Leon Kirchner's opera LILY based on Saul Bellow's novel *Henderson the Rain King*. In 1991 he played Suleyman Pasha in John Corigliano's THE GHOST OF VERSAILLES AT THE MET. He also played the priest Don Marco in a reprise production of Gian Carlo Menotti's opera THE SAINT OF BLEECKER STREET. Berberian, who was born in Detroit, made his opera debut in 1958.

BERGSMA, WILLIAM *American composer (1921–)*

William Bergsma, a Californian who studied under Howard Hanson, composed two notable operas. THE WIFE OF MARTIN GUERRE (1956), libretto by Janet Lewis, is a somber but lyrical operatic version of the famous story of the 16th century French peasant who returned to his wife after eight years but was later denounced by her as an imposter. *The Murder of Comrade Sharik* (1973) is an 85-minute comic opera based on Mikhail Bulgakov's satirical Russian novel *Heart of a Dog,* in which a dog becomes an offensive Soviet citizen.

BERLIN, IRVING *American composer (1888–1989)*

Irving Berlin was primarily a great songwriter, words as well as music, but he also composed for musical theater and his great musical ANNIE GET YOUR GUN has entered the opera repertory in both America and Europe. Berlin, who was born in Russia as Israel Berlin, came to America aged five and learned his trade as a singing waiter and song plugger. He taught himself how to play piano and write songs and had his first hit in 1911 with "Alexander's Ragtime Band." He began to write for the stage in 1914, mostly for revues, and composed songs for twenty Broadway shows and several films. His first book musical was the moderately successful 1940 show *Louisiana Purchase.* Next was his biggest stage success. *Annie Get Your Gun*, libretto by Herbert and Dorothy Fields about Wild West Show sharpshooter Annie Oakley, opened in 1946 with Ethel Merman as Annie. It remains popular and has been recorded multiple times. *Miss Liberty* was less successful in 1949 but *Call Me Madam,* again starring Merman, was a big hit in 1950. The libretto by Howard Lindsay and Russell Crouse tells the story of a hostess with the mostes' who becomes the ambassador to a small European country. Berlin's final stage musical was the modestly successful political comedy *Mr. President*, composed to another libretto by Lindsay and Crouse.

BERMAN, EUGENE *Russian-born American designer (1899–1972)*

Russian-born American designer Eugene Berman created the costumes and sets for Gian Carlo Menotti's AMAHL AND THE NIGHT VISITORS for its NBC TV world premiere on December 24, 1951, Although he was already well known, these designs made him truly famous and he began to work at the Met and La Scala. He had earlier designed sets for Menotti's 1942 opera THE ISLAND GOD when it was to be produced at the Met but they were rejected. After *Amahl* Berman worked as stage designer at the Met from 1951 to 1963 and at La Scala in the 1950s.

BERNSTEIN, LEONARD *American composer/conductor (1918–1990)*

Leonard Bernstein created music theater works that occupy an ambiguous area between opera and Broadway. The "musicals" CANDIDE, WEST SIDE STORY, ON THE TOWN, WONDERFUL TOWN and MASS have been staged by opera companies while the "operas" TROUBLE IN TAHITI and A QUITE PLACE have been staged rather like musicals. Bernstein filmed his musicals with opera singers and he recorded many of his theatre pieces in an operatic manner. He was, of course, a notable conductor but he did not normally conduct his own Broadway productions. He did conduct the first performance of *Candide* in 1956 and the premiere of his friend Lukas

Composer Irving Berlin

Foss's INTRODUCTIONS AND GOODBYES in 1960. He often worked on television, especially *Omnibus*, and there are over 300 Bernstein TV programs at the Museum of Television and Radio.

1963 Popular Music of Leonard Bernstein. The album *Alfred Drake and Roberta Peters Sing the Popular Music of Leonard Bernstein* includes "Best of All Possible Worlds" and "Glitter and Be Gay" from *Candide* and songs from *West Side Story, On the Town* and *Wonderful Town.* Enoch Light directs the orchestra and Ray Charles Singers. Command LP. **1988 The Bernstein Songbook.** *The Bernstein Songbook* features selections from Bernstein musicals and operas including the 1956 Broadway *Candide,* the 1972 Kennedy Center *Mass* and the 1973 London Weekend Television production of *Trouble in Tahiti.* CBS CD. **1990 The Essential Bernstein.** This album includes fourteen numbers by Bernstein from *Mass, West Wide Story* and *On the Town* sung by Peter Hoffman and Deborah Sasson. Michael Tilson Thomas conducts members of the Los Angeles Philharmonic. Sony Classics CD. **1993 The Gift of Music.** *The Gift of Music* is a documentary about Bernstein with TV material, performance extracts, archival footage and comments from colleagues. Lauren Bacall narrates, Horant Hohlfeld directed. DG DVD/VHS. **1994 Bernstein on Broadway.** *Bernstein on Broadway* is a video featuring highlights from Broadway productions performed by opera singers: *On The Town* has Tyne Daly, Frederica von Stade, Thomas Hampson and Samuel Ramey; *Candide* has Jerry Hadley, June Anderson, Christa Ludwig, Kurt Ollmann and Adolph Green; *West Side Story* has Kiri Te

Kanawa, José Carreras and Tatiana Troyanos. DG VHS/LD. **1997 Blackwell Sings Bernstein.** Harolyn Blackwell performs arias from Bernstein's stage works on the album *Blackwell Sings Bernstein.* They include numbers from *Candide, Mass, West Side Story, Wonderful Town* and *I Hate Music.* RCA CD. **1997 Leonard Bernstein's New York.** *Leonard Bernstein's New York* is a documentary about Bernstein musicals set in New York City: *On the Town, Wonderful Town,* and *West Side Story.* The performers are Dawn Upshaw, Audra McDonald, Mandy Patinkin, Judy Blazer, Richard Muenz, and Donna Murphy, Eric Stern conducts the Orchestra of St. Luke's. Hart Perry directed. Warner Vision/NVC Arts VHS. **1998 Bernstein Arias, Barcarolles, Songs and Duets.** Judy Kaye, William Sharp and Michael Barrett sing numbers from Bernstein vocal works on the album *Leonard Bernstein: Arias and Barcarolles Songs and Duets.* Steven Blier plays piano. Koch International CD. **1998 Bernstein: Reaching for the Note.** *Bernstein: Reaching for the Note* is a documentary about Bernstein's career. It includes interviews with friends and family and scenes from *Candide, Trouble in Tahiti, A Quiet Place* and *Mass.* Susan Lacy directed. DVD has a discography. Winstar DVD/DG VHS/DG CD. **2000 A White House Cantata.** June Anderson is the First Lady, Barbara Hendricks is Seena and Thomas Hampson is the President in this recording of a concert version of Bernstein's *1600 Pennsylvania Avenue.* Victor Acquah is Little Lud, Kenneth Tarver is Lud, Neil Nenkins is Admiral Cockburn and Keel Watson is Henry. Kent Nagano leads the London Voice and London Symphony Orchestra. DG CD.

BERTHA   *1973 opera by Rorem*

Crazy Queen Bertha of Norway repels barbarians with a flashy attack, beheads a Teacher who questions her and abolishes learning, starts a war with Scotland because there is peace, dismisses her Council when they object to war, has young lovers shot and gives her country away. She is hailed by her subjects as a great queen. Ned Rorem's satirical 25-minute chamber opera *Bertha,* libretto by the composer based on a play by Kenneth Koch, premiered at Alice Tully Hall in New York on November 26, 1973. Beverly Wolff sang the role of Bertha and Grayson Hirst was Teacher and Barbarian Chief. The opera has also been produced by Golden Fleece and Wolf Trap.

"BESS, YOU IS MY WOMAN"   *Baritone/soprano duet: Porgy and Bess (1935). Words: Ira Gershwin and DuBose Heyward. Music: George Gershwin.*

Porgy tells Bess that she is his woman now that Crown has run off, she says she agrees and the passion in the music in this duet shows it is true. One of the finest duets in American opera, "Bess, you is my woman" was introduced on stage in 1935 in George Gershwin's PORGY AND BESS by Todd Duncan as Porgy and Anne Brown as Bess. It was first recorded in 1935 by Metropolitan Opera singers Lawrence Tibbett and Helen Jepson. Duncan and Brown recorded it in 1940 when the opera returned to Broadway. Other notable recordings were made by Robert McFerrin and Adele Addison for the 1959 film, Willard White and Leona Mitchell for the Cleveland Orchestra in 1976, Donnie Ray Albert and Clamma Dale as Bess for Houston Grand Opera in 1976 and Willard White and Cynthia Haymon for Glyndebourne Opera in 1987. There are fascinating jazz versions by Louis Armstrong and Ella Fitzgerald and by Ray Charles and Cleo Laine.

BETWEEN TWO WORLDS   *1997 opera by Ran.*
See *THE DYBBUK*

THE BEWITCHED   *1957 "dance-satire" by Partch*

Harry Partch's experimental *The Bewitched,* a nearly wordless "dance-satire" opera, premiered at the Festival of Contemporary Art at the University of Illinois in Urbana on March 26, 1957. Freda Schell played the Witch who sings wordlessly in male and female voices, William Olson was the Male Solo Voice and chorus leader and John Garvey conducted the University of Illinois Musical Ensemble. The Lost Musicians, seventeen instrumentalists performing on instruments designed by Partch and including marimbas and cloud-chamber bowls, were seated on stage on risers. Each of the ten scenes of the opera tells a different story include one about a defeated basketball team in their shower room after the game, one about detectives who turn in their badges and one about a lost political soul among the voteless women of paradise.

1957 University of Illinois. The premiere performance of *The Bewitched* at the University of Illinois with Freda Schell as Witch and William Olson as Male Solo Voice was recorded with the performers as above. John Garvey conducts the University of Illinois Musical Ensemble. 75 minutes. It's on Volume 4 of *The Harry Partch Collection.* CRI CD.

BEZANSON, PHILIP   *American composer (1916–1975)*

Philip Bezanson only wrote two operas. *Western Child,* libretto by P. Engel about a baby born on Christmas in a fort in the gold rush eras, was first performed at the State University of Iowa on July 28, 1959; it was then revised for presentation on NBC television in 1960 as GOLDEN CHILD. *Stranger in Eden,* libretto by William Reardon, was completed in 1963 but not staged. Bezanson, who was born in Athol, Massachusetts, studied at Yale and Iowa University and taught at Iowa and Amherst. He is known primarily as a composer of choral and chamber music.

BIANCA   *1918 opera by Hadley*

The setting is Bianca's inn near Florence, Italy, in the 18th century. It is frequented by a count and a marquis who are rivals for her hand but she tries instead to win a woman-hating knight and ignores Fabricio who truly loves her. When a duel starts, Fabricio courageously stops it and wins Bianca's heart. Henry Hadley's one-act opera *Bianca,* libretto by Grant Stewart based on the Goldoni play *The Mistress of the Inn,* was premiered by the Society of American Singers at the Park Theater in New York on October l5, 1918. Maggie Teyte sang the role of Bianca with Carl Formes as Fabricio, Henri Scott as Cavaliere del Ruggio, Howard White as Conte della Terramonte and Craig Campbell as Marchese d'Amalfi. Hadley conducted. *Bianca* was one of the first American operas to be presented on radio. It was broadcast by NBC's National Grand Opera Company on June 13, 1928, with Hadley himself conducting the Grand Opera Orchestra. It was reprised on stage by Chautauqua Opera in New York in 1934.

BIBLE, FRANCES   *American mezzo-soprano (1919–2001)*

Frances Bible created roles in three American operas and is widely identified with a fourth. She played Elizabeth Proctor in the premiere of Robert Ward's THE CRUCIBLE at the New York City Opera in 1961 and is featured on the premiere recording. She played Frade in the premiere of David Tamkin's opera THE DYBBUK at NYCO in 1951 and she had small roles (Mango Vendor/Servant) in the premiere of William Grant Still's opera TROUBLED ISLAND at NYCO. in 1949. She sang Augusta Tabor in the Central City and New York City Opera productions of Douglas Moore's THE BALLAD OF BABY DOE and is identified with the role though she did not actually create it. She played Ma Moss in a videotaped production of Aaron Copland's THE TENDER LAND in 1978 and recorded a highlights version of Rudolf Friml's THE VAGABOND KING with Alfred Drake in 1951. Bible, born in Sacketts Harbor, N.Y., studied with Met soprano Queena Mario at Juilliard before making her debut at the New York City Opera in 1948. She sang many other roles in American operas during her lifetime, including Mrs. Nolan in Gian Carlo Menotti's *The Medium* and Dinah in Leonard Bernstein's *Trouble in Tahiti*.

BIKINI   *2002 multi-media opera by Reich/Korot*

America's test of the atomic bomb on the small Pacific atoll of Bikini is viewed from the air and ships in a series of elaborate video images. Steve Reich's multi-media opera *Bikini,* libretto by the composer created with his wife, video artist Beryl Korot, premiered at the Spoleto Festival USA in Charleston, SC, on May 31, 2002. Reich and Korot presented their "documentary music video theater" THREE TALES incorporating *Bikini* and two other operas in an abandoned Charleston theater, the Memminger Auditorium, with sixteen musicians and singers. Videos in the auditorium showed historical film, interviews, photographs and text as the operas were sung and played. Nick Mangano was the director and Brad Lubman was the conductor.

2002 New York Studios. *Bikini*, performed by the Steve Reich Ensemble and the Synergy Vocals group, was recorded at the Avatar Studios in New York City in June 2002. The singers are Amanda Morrison, Micaela Haslam, Gerard O'Beirne, Andrew Busher and Phillip Conway-Brown. Bradley Lubman conducts. The opera is featured as the second part of the trilogy *Three Tales* on a 2003 Nonesuch DVD/CD.

BILBY'S DOLL   *1976 opera by Floyd*

In 17th century Massachusetts, Jared Bilby adopts Doll after her parents are burned as witches. Bilby's wife Hannah thinks Doll is a witch, too, but the Deacon's son Titus wants to marry her. Unsure what she is, she prays for a sign and the Minister's son Shad pretends he is a demon. They marry secretly in a pagan ceremony and she becomes pregnant. Doll is put in prison and dies giving birth. Carlisle Floyd's three-act opera *Bilby's Doll,* libretto by the composer based on Esther Forbe's novel *A Mirror of Witches*, was premiered by Houston Grand Opera on February 27, 1976. Catherine Malfitano created the role of Doll, Thomas Paul was Jared Bilby, Joy Davidson was Hannah, Jacques Trussel was Shad, Alan Titus was Titus Thumb, Thomas Page was Deacon Thumb, Barrie Smith was Mrs. Thumb, Tom Fox was Mr. Zelley, David Cornell was Increase Mather, Nell Evans was Goody Goochy, Suzanne Reich was Sorrow, Sharon Sanford was Labour, Kim Josephson was First Suitor, Jerry Solomon was Second Suitor, Graydon Vaught was Captain Buzzey, Dale Smith was Town Crier and Nik Jon Kovalesky was the Young Boy. Ming Cho Lee designed the sets, Suzanne Mess designed the costumes, David Poutney directed assisted by David Alden and Christopher Keene conducted. An alternate cast and conductor was featured on the second night, February 28. with Sheri Greenawald as Doll, Fredda Rakusin as Hannah, Charles P. Long as Titus and Chris Nance as conductor. The opera was reprised by Omaha Opera the same year.

BILLY AND ZELDA   *1998 chamber opera by Davidson*

Billy's death in a war is contrasted with Zelda's death from pneumonia while the Neighbor and the Narrator reveal hidden secrets. *Billy* is an opera and *Zelda* is a play but there is music with both as their stories unfold on stage in two separate playing spaces. Tina Davidson's complex *Billy and Zelda,* libretto by her sisters Eva and Lale, was premiered by OperaDelaware in Wilmington on December 11, 1998. For *Billy* Michelle Wright sang the role of the Neighbor, Sara Jane Duffey was Billy's mother in the present, Robin Leigh Massie was Billy's mother as she was in the past, Scott Murphree was Billy, Patrick Evans was Billy's Father and Derek Goodman, Michael Laroche and Jason Scott were the soldiers. For *Zelda* Martha Slater was the Narrator with musical support from cellist Mary Wooten. Ben Levit directed, Leland P. Kimball III designed the set and Alan Johnson conducted the Elixir String Quartet and percussionist Harvey Price.

BIMBONI, ALBERTO   *American composer (1882–1960)*

Alberto Bimboni wrote two of his six operas in his native Florence but is known operatically primarily for his American opera WINONA. He emigrated to America in 1911 as a conductor and worked with opera companies before turning to teaching music at the Curtis Institute, Pennsylvania University and Juilliard. *Winona*, libretto by Perry Williams based on a Sioux Indian legend, was premiered by the American Grand Opera Company at the Civic Auditorium in Portland, Oregon, on November 11, 1926, with Bimboni conducting. It was reprised in Minneapolis in 1928 where it was admired for incorporating elements of Native American music in its score and was awarded the David Bispham Medal. *Karina*, libretto by C. W. Stork, was performed in Minneapolis in 1928. *There Was a Gilded Gate,* libretto by A. Romano, was presented at the National Arts Club in New York on March 11, 1936. *In the Name of Culture*, libretto by N. F. Stolzenbach, premiered at the Eastman School in Rochester on May 9, 1949.

BING, RUDOLF   *Opera house administrator (1902—1999)*

Metropolitan Opera general manager Rudolf Bing was not overly fond of American opera but he did premiere four during his long stewardship: Samuel Barber's VANESSA and ANTONY AND CLEOPATRA. Gian Carlo Menotti's THE LAST SAVAGE and Marvin Levy's MOURNING BECOMES ELECTRA. He also held the American premiere of Igor Stravinsky's THE RAKE'S PROGRESS. Bing was born in Vienna but spent most of his professional life in Great Britain and America. He was in charge of the Glyndebourne Festival from 1936 to 1940, the Edinburgh Festival from 1947 to 1949 and the Met from 1950 to 1972. Bing was an autocrat and had difficult relationships with many singers but he had the courage to open the Met to African American singers beginning with Marian Anderson.

"BIRDIE'S ARIA"   *Soprano aria: Regina (1949). Words and music: Marc Blitzstein*

Birdie's Aria ("Oh, Lionnet, Lionnet") was first sung by Brenda Lewis in Marc Blitzstein's opera REGINA when it premiered at the Shubert Theater in New Haven, CT, on October 6, 1949, before going to Broadway. The opera, based on Lillian Hellman's play *The Little Foxes,* tells the story of the greedy Hubbard family in Alabama in 1900 including brothers Ben and Oscar and sister Regina, married to Horace Giddens. Birdie is the alcoholic aristocratic wife of Oscar Hubbard. In her confessional aria, she remembers the old days on her family estate of Lionnet, tells how Ben married her simply to get control of it and describes how he tries to cover up her drinking by saying she gets headaches. The aria is sung by Elizabeth Carron in a 1953 New York City Opera production on LP, by Carron again in a 1979 Houston Grand Opera production on audiocassette and by Sheri Greenawald in a 1992 Scottish Opera production on CD.

THE BIRDS *1958 musical theater work by Hiller*

Two Athenians in ancient Greece go the kingdom of the birds in search of an easy life. They convince the king and queen to demand tribute for sacrificial smoke that goes through the kingdom. By the end humans flock to the new paradise and Zeus has to surrender his scepter of power. Larjean Hiller's satirical operatic musical *The Birds,* libretto by Walter Kerr based on the play by Aristophanes, premiered at the University of Illinois on March 12, 1958. Most of the singing is for chorus and there is heavy use of dissonance and serial music. Hiller is known for his work with computer music and his 1956 *Illiac Suite* is considered the first composition created by computer.

BIRTH/DAY: THE FRANKENSTEIN MUSICAL *1994 opera by Wolfe*

Dr. Victor Frankenstein creates a monster hated even by its creator. Neil Wolfe's opera *Birth/Day: The Frankenstein Musical,* libretto by Ron Troutman based on Mary Shelley's novel *Frankenstein,* was premiered by the Deep Ellum Opera Company at the Hickory Street Annex in Dallas, Texas, on October 15, 1994. Gaitley Mathew played Dr. Frankenstein, Tim Worley was Igor, Mary Draper and Andi Allen were maids and Brenda Box Bristol sang a variety of roles. David McClinton directed and played the spinet.

BISHOP, ADELAIDE *American soprano/ director (1926–)*

Adelaide Bishop created roles in three American operas as a singer and directed the premiere of a fourth. She portrayed Griffelkin in Lukas Foss's opera GRIF-FELKIN when it was presented on NBC TV in 1955, was the Maid in Stanley Hollingsworth opera LA GRANDE BRETÈCHE when it was telecast by NBC Opera Theatre in 1957 and played the Stepdaughter in Hugo Weisgall's SIX CHARACTERS IN SEARCH OF AN AUTHOR when it premiered at New York City Opera in 1959. She also sang the solo role of Estelle in Hugo Weisgall's THE STRONGER in New York in 1955 and Mary Stone in a New York City Opera revival of Douglas Moore's folk opera THE DEVIL AND DANIEL WEBSTER in 1959. She staged the premiere of David Amram's opera TWELFTH NIGHT at the Lake George Festival in 1968 and she also directed productions of Lee Hoiby's SUMMER AND SMOKE, David Ward's THE CRUCIBLE and Gian Carlo Menotti's AMAHL AND THE NIGHT VISITORS, THE MEDIUM, THE OLD MAID AND THE THIEF and THE TELEPHONE. Bishop, a native of New York, sang at New York City Opera from 1948 to 1960 before turning to directing and producing.

BISPHAM MEMORIAL MEDAL *Award created to honor American operas*

The David Bispham Memorial Medal honoring American operas and their composers was created in 1924 by Eleanor Freer and Edith Rockefeller McCormick. Freer had founded the Opera in

The David Bispham Memorial Medal was created to honor American operas and their composers.

THE ARTISTIC BARITONE
A COLLECTION OF STANDARD SONGS

DAVID S. BISPHAM
THE VERSATILE BARITONE

THE ARTISTIC SERIES
M·WITMARK & SONS

Baritone David Bispham on cover of a 1912 song book.

Our Language Foundation (1921) and the David Bispham Memorial Fund (1922) and merged them into the American Opera Society of Chicago in 1924 when the first medal was presented. It was named after American baritone David Bispham (1857–1921), an ardent promoter of opera in English and a childhood friend of Freer's. The first Bispham Memorial Medal was awarded to Ernest Carter on March 6, 1924, for his opera *The White Bird.* The medal was not always given in the year the opera premiered and it was awarded posthumously to Victor Herbert. The following is a list of composers and operas known to have been awarded the Bispham Medal up to 1946; fifty-three were awarded before Freer's death in 1942. There are separate entries on most of the operas.

1924 Ernest Carter for *The White Bird*. Charles Wakefield Cadman for *Shanewis*. Francesco DeLeone for *Alglala*. Eleanor E. Freer for *The Legend of the Piper*. Victor Herbert for *Natoma* and *Madeleine*. Harriet Ware for *Undine*. **1925** John Lewis Browne for *The Corsican Girl*. Aldo Franchetti for *Namiko-San*. Henry Hadley for *Azora*. W. Franke Harling for *A Light from St. Agnes*. John Adam Hugo for *The Temple Dancer*. Frank Patterson for *The Echo*. Theodore Stearns for *Snowbird*. Humphrey J. Stewart for *The Hound of Heaven*. Isaac Van Grove for *The Music Robber*. **1926** Simon Bucharoff for *Sakahra*. Charles Frederick Carlson for *Phelias*. Frederick Converse for *The Pipe of Desire*. Henry Eames for *Priscilla and John Alden*. Hamilton Forrest for *Yzdra*. F. H. Harwill for *Bella Donna*. William Lester for *Everyman*. Clarence Loomis for *Yolanda of Cyprus*. Ralph Lyford for *Castle Agrazant*. William J. McCoy for *Egypt*. Jane Van Etten for *Guido Ferranti*. **1927** Charles Skilton for *Kalopin*. **1928** Albert Bimboni for *Winona*. **1929** Walter Damrosch for *Cyrano De Bergerac*. Deems Taylor for *The King's Henchman*. **1930** Pietro Floridia for *Paoletta*. Wesley Laviolette for *Shylock*. Mary Carr Moore for *Narcissa*. **1931** Karl Schmidt for *Lady of the Lake*. **1932** George Antheil for *Helen Retires*. Clarence Cameron White for *Ouanga!* Leslie Grossmith for *Uncle Tom's Cabin*. Louis Gruenberg for *The Emperor Jones*. Otto Luening for *Evangeline*. Marx E. Oberndorfer for *Roseanne*. Bernard Rogers for *The Marriage of Aude*. Virgil Thomson for *Four Saints in Three Acts*. **1934** Howard Hanson for *Merry Mount*. **1935** Samuel Barlow for *Mon Ami Pierrot*. Ethel Leginski for *Gale*. **1937** George Gershwin for *Porgy and Bess*. **1938** Julius Osiier for *The Bride of Baghdad*. Beryl Rubinstein for *The Sleeping Princess*. **1945** John L. Seymour for *In the Pasha's Garden*. **1946** Ernst Bacon for *A Tree on the Plains*

BITTER LOVE   *1998 opera by Tan Dun.*   See Peony Pavilion

BJÖRLING, JUSSI   *Swedish tenor (1911–1960)*

Tenor legend Jussi Björling apparently enjoyed singing Victor Herbert's "Neapolitan Love Song" from the comic opera The Princess Pat as he featured it in two *Voice of Firestone* television appearances in 1950, both available on video. Björling, possibly the greatest tenor of the century after Enrico Caruso, made his debut at the Swedish Royal Opera in 1930 and began to sing in America in 1937.

THE BLACK RIDER   *1990 cabaret opera by Waits*

Wilhelm has to win a shooting contest to marry Kätchen. He obtains magic bullets from devilish Pegleg. In the competition the final bullet is controlled by the devil and kills Kätchen. Tom Waits' cabaret opera *The Black Rider*, libretto by William S. Burroughs based on Johann August Apel and Friedrich Laun's German horror story *Gespensterbuch*, premiered at the Thalia Theater in Hamburg in March 1990 and was presented with the same cast at the Brooklyn Academy of Music on November 9, 1994. Stefan Kurt was Wilhelm, Dominque Horwitz was Pegleg and Anne Paulmann was Kätchen. Robert Wilson designed and directed the production. This same story was used by Carl Maria von Weber as the basis for his 1821 opera *Der Freischütz* but Weber gave it a happy ending. Waits' music is somewhat reminiscent of Kurt Weill's *The Threepenny Opera* but it is scored for an unusual chamber orchestra that includes pump organ, slide guitar, banjo, accordion and

musical saw. *The Black Rider* was reprised at the Edmonton Fringe Festival in Canada in 1998.

1993 Tom Waits in San Francisco. Composer Waits recorded his version of the opera in San Francisco in 1993 leading a chamber orchestra that includes a musical saw, accordion, bassoon, banjo, trombones and viola. Waits performs all the roles himself and tells the complete story of the opera in twenty numbers. Island CD.

BLACK RIVER   *1975 opera by Susa*

The people of Black River Falls, Wisconsin, are obsessed with death and dying as the 19th century ends. Clara Gary is full of guilt over the drowning of her infant son in the Black River so she kills herself. Her stepdaughter Lucy Gray marries a man she does not love but he dies soon after the wedding. Coloratura soprano Pauline L'Allemand, the first American to sing the title role in the opera *Lakmé,* is incarcerated in the state mental hospital and mourns the death of her career. Conrad Susa's three-hour opera *Black River: A Wisconsin Idyll*, libretto by Richard Street and the composer, is based on Michael Vesy's book *Wisconsin Death Trip*, a photographic look at the death-obsession that once gripped a small Wisconsin town. Minnesota Opera premiered *Black River* on November 1, 1975, in St. Paul. Janis Hardy sang the role of Clara, Barbara Brandt was Pauline L'Allemand, Margaret Smith was Lucy, Michael Riley was Rev. Woods, John Brandstetter was Ben Holland, Phil Jorgenson was Horace Gray, Daryl Erickson was Dudley Gray, Margaret Johnson was Mrs. Dudley Gray, Christopher Smith was Frank Holland, Linda Wilcox was Mrs. Frank Holland, Vern Sutton was C. C. Pope, Mr. Vaudry and Dr. Krohn and Yale Marshall was P. H. Howell, and Leo Delibes. The opera was reprised by Minnesota Opera in a revised version on February 21, 1981, with added extracts from an operetta that Pauline L'Allemand had composed. It was revised a third time for a production by Linda Brovsky at Opera Theater of St. Louis in 1994 with Robynne Redmon as Clara, Sharon Daniels as Pauline, Mary Dunleavy as Lucy and Randall Behr conducting. The source book *Wisconsin Death Trip* is also the basis of a documentary film by James Marsh.

1981 KVOM broadcast. Composer Conrad Susa talks about his opera *Black River* and presents excerpts in an interview broadcast by Minnesota station KVOM and recorded for use by the Voice of America. The opera was presented by Minnesota Opera for the second time in 1981. Audiocassette at Library of Congress.

"THE BLACK SWAN" (1)   *Soprano aria: The Medium (1946). Words and music: Gian Carlo Menotti*

Sixteen-year-old Monica rocks her mother like a baby and sings a mournful folk song while her mute friend Toby accompanies her on tambourine. This is the "Black Swan" arietta, the most poetic aria in Gian Carlo Menotti's 1946 opera The Medium. Monica sings that the sun has fallen and lies in blood and the moon is weaving bandages of gold. She asks the black swan where her lover has gone and tells him her bridal gown is tattered and torn and her lamp lost. The stars stitch a shroud for the dying sun with silver needles and thread. She had given her lover a kiss of fire and a golden ring but his eyes are now made of glass and his feet of stone. He has shells for teeth and weeds for tongue deep in the river's bed. The sun is buried and the stars weep. She asks the black wave to take her away and says she will share her golden hair and bridal gown. She asks the black wave to take her and her unborn child down to her wandering lover. At the end the mother joins Monica in asking the black wave to take her away. Evelyn Keller introduced the aria on stage and in the first recording but it is best known as sung by Maria Alberghetti in Menotti's 1951 film of the opera and its soundtrack CD. Other singers who sings it on recordings include Maria José de Vine, Elaine Lublin, Judith Blegen with Washington Opera, Anne-Marie Rodde and Patrice Michaels Bedi with Chicago Opera Theater.

THE BLACK SWAN (2)   *1998 opera by Whitman*

German mother Rosalie hires young American Ken to tutor her daughter Anna and then falls passionately in love with him. Thomas Whitman's chamber opera *The Black Swan*, libretto by Nathalie Anderson, is based on a novel by Thomas Mann and a story by Richard Selzer. It premiered at the Lang Performing Arts Center in Swarthmore, Pennsylvania, on September 11, 1998, in a production by Sarah Caldwell. Freda Herseth sang the role of Rosalie, David Kravitz was Ken, Tamara Matthews was Anna. Herbert Senn and Helen Ponds designed the set and James Freeman conducted the Orchestra 2001. This was Whitman's first opera.

BLACK WATER   *1997 opera by Duffy*

Kelly, an idealistic young woman, meets a sexually attractive U.S. Senator at a Fourth of July party and goes off with him in his car. She is drowned in an accident. John Duffy's opera *Black Water* is a thinly-disguised story about the Chappaquiddick tragedy with libretto by Joyce Carol Oates based on her own novella. The opera premiered at the American Music Theatre Festival in Philadelphia in 1997 with Karen Burlingame as Kelly, Patrick Mason as the Senator, Stephanie Buckley as Buffy and Wilbur Pauley as Roy. Alan Johnson played piano and conducted the chamber orchestra and Gordon Edelstein. **1998 L.A. Theatre Works.** This recording by L.A. Theatre Works is taken from performances of the opera staged in Los Angeles in the summer of 1998. Most of the performers are the same as in the Philadelphia premiere. Karen Burlingame sings the role of Kelly, Patrick Mason is the Senator and Alan Johnson plays piano and conducts the chamber orchestra. LA Theatre Works CD box.

THE BLACK WIDOW   *1972 opera by Pasatieri*

Raquel, a childless Spanish woman, is obsessed by an unattainable dream of becoming a mother. She forces her lover Juan to marry Berta and have a child by her. When the baby is born, Raquel takes it from her. Thomas Pasatieri's melodic tonal three-act opera *The Black Widow*, libretto by the composer based on Miguel de Unamuno's novella *Dos Madres* (Two Mothers), was premiered by Seattle Opera on March 2, 1972. Joanna Simon was Raquel, Evelyn Mandac was Berta, Theodore Uppman wad Juan, Jennie Tourel was Berta's mother Doña Marta and David Lloyd was Berta's father Don Pedro. John T. Naccarato designed the sets, Lotfi Mansouri produced the opera and Henry Holt conducted the orchestra. *The Black Widow* was reprised at the Lake George Opera Festival in New York later in 1972 and staged by Atlanta Opera in 1981. **1972 Seattle Opera.** Joanna Simon sings Raquel with Evelyn Mandac as Berta in this recording of the Seattle Opera premiere on March 2, 1972. Theodore Uppman is Juan, Jennie Tourel is Berta's mother and David Lloyd is Berta's father Don Pedro. Henry Holt conducts. Omega Opera Archives CD. **1977 CBS Television.** Joanna Simon, who created the role of Raquel, performs the "Cradle Song" in a semi-staged scene from *The Black Widow* on the CBS Television program *The Operas of Thomas Pasatieri*. Roger Englander directed the 30-minute telecast for Camera Three. Video at MTR.

THE BLACKBERRY VINE   *1969 mini-opera by Sternberg*

Anna Sternberg composed the music for her mini-opera *The Blackberry Vine*, libretto by Gertrude Stein, for the Broadway show *Gertrude Stein's First Reader* which opened at the Astor Place Theater in New York on December 15, 1969. Joy Garrett was the Narrator, Michael Anthony was the Boy, Sandra Thornton was the Girl and Frank Giordano was the Blackberry Vine. *The Gertrude Stein First Reader*, written at the suggestion of Carl Van Vechten, was published in 1946. **1969 Original cast.** Joy Garrett is the Narrator, Michael Anthony is the Boy, Sandra Thornton is the Girl and Frank Giordano is the Blackberry Vine on the original cast album of *Gertrude Stein's First Reader*. Polydor LP.

BLACKSTONE, TSIANINA   *American mezzo-soprano (1882–1985)*

Princess Tsianina Redfeather Blackstone, the first Native American opera singer to achieve national fame, created leading roles in two operas with Native American subject matter and devoted much of her career to promoting Native American music. Charles Wakefield Cadman's opera SHANEWIS was loosely based on her life and she made her operatic debut singing in it in Denver on December 5, 1924. She created the roles of Wildflower in Cadman's *The Sunset Trail* in 1924 and Wiwaste in S. Earle Blakeslee's THE LEGEND OF WIWASTE in 1927 and she introduced arias from Carlos Troyer's opera *Zuniana* in concert. Born in Oklahoma Indian Territory of Cherokee and Creek descent, Blackstone studied voice and piano in Denver and became known nationally through touring and singing with Cadman.

BLACKWELL, HAROLYN   *American soprano (1956–)*

Metropolitan opera soprano Harolyn Blackwell sang in the premiere of John Cage's "non-intentional" non-narrative *Europera 2* in Frankfurt in 1987. She sings the role of Clara and the aria "Summertime" in George Gershwin's PORGY AND BESS in the 1993 Cincinnati recording and 1988 Glyndebourne film. She played Cunegonde in the 1997 Broadway revival of CANDIDE and is featured on the cast album. She included her *Candide* aria "Glitter and Be Gay" on her 1996 album *Blackwell Sings Bernstein* along with "A Simple Song" from MASS and songs from WEST SIDE STORY. Blackwell made her debut on Broadway in 1980 as Maria in *West Side Story* and her debut at the Met the same year as Oscar in Verdi's *Un Ballo in Maschero*.

BLAKE   *1986 opera by Leslie Adams*

African American slave Blake is working on a Southern plantation just before the Civil War. He is married to Miranda but they are separated when he is sent off on a trip. They are reunited in the Great Dismal Swamp but Miranda dies as the Civil War begins. Blake goes off to join the Union Army. Leslie Adams' four-act opera *Blake*, libretto by Daniel Mayers based on Martin R. Daleny's 1959 novel *Blake: or, The Huts of America*, was completed in 1986 and premiered with piano accompaniment at Brown Memorial Woodbrook Presbyterian Church in Baltimore on October 24, 1997. Five arias from *Blake* are featured on the internet ARIA DATABASE website including "Blake's Monologue" and "Miranda's Prayer." Arias from the opera have become known through being sung in concerts in Indianapolis, Virginia Beach, Pittsburgh, Cleveland, Canton, Kansas City, New York and Washington, D.C.

BLAKESLEE, S. EARLE   *American composer (1883–1972)*

Samuel Earle Blakeslee composed the once-popular opera THE

LEGEND OF WIWASTE based on Dakota Sioux legends and musical motifs. It was premiered At Chaffey College in Ontario, California, on April 25, 1924, with Tsianina Redfeather Blackstone, the first Native American opera singer to achieve national fame, in the title role. Blakeslee, who was born in Oberlin, Ohio, studied music in Oberlin, Denver and Claremont College in California and taught music at Chaffey College from 1916 to 1954. *The Legend of Wiwaste* is his only opera.

BLANK, ALLAN   *American composer (1925–)*

Allan Blank is best known for instrumental music, including a duo for bassoon and piano, but he also composed vocal works including four operas. *Aria da capo,* a one-act chamber opera with libretto by the composed based on the play by Edna St. Vincent Millay, was completed in 1960. *Excitement at the Circus,* a children's opera composed to a libretto by Irving Leitner, premiered at Patterson, NJ, in 1969 and has been widely performed. *The Magic Bonbons,* libretto by the composer based on a fantasy story by Oz creator L. Frank Baum, was composed in 1983 with the help of an NEA grant. *The Noise,* libretto by G. C. Hopper based on a surrealistic story by Boris Vian, was premiered at Virginia Commonwealth University in Richmond in April 1986. Blank was born in New York City and studied at Juilliard, NYU, Minnesota and Columbia Teachers College. After teaching in high schools for some years, he became music professor at Virginia Commonwealth University.

BLANKENSHIP, WILLIAM   *American tenor (1928–)*

William Blankenship created the role of the Lover in Avery Claflin's one-act opera LA GRANDE BRETÈCHE recorded in Vienna in 1956 and the role of Roderick II in Paul Hindemith's one-act opera THE LONG CHRISTMAS DINNER in Mannheim 1961. Blankenship, the father of soprano Rebecca Blankenship, was born in Gatesville, Texas, and studied at Juilliard and in Vienna.

BLAZER, JUDITH   *American soprano (1959–)*

Judith Blazer sings the role of Marietta on the only complete recorded version of Victor Herbert's comic opera NAUGHTY MARIETTA; it was issued by the Smithsonian American Musical Theater in 1980. She is also featured on recordings of the musicals *Babes in Arms, Girl Crazy* and *Sitting Pretty.* Blazer is a graduate of the Manhattan School of Music and performed in opera and concerts in Italy before returning to the U.S. for music theater work.

BLEDSOE, JULES   *American bass-baritone (1898–1943)*

When Paul Robeson had to leave for Europe before the scheduled opening of Jerome Kern's SHOW BOAT, bass-baritone Jules Bledsoe took over the role of the stevedore Joe and introduced the great bass aria "Ol' Man River." He also created roles in notable African American musicals. He sang Tizanne in the premiere of William Harling's Broadway opera DEEP RIVER in 1926 and Voodoo Man in the premiere of Shirley Graham Dubois' TOM-TOM in Cleveland in 1932. Although he didn't create the title role in Louis Gruenberg's opera THE EMPEROR JONES at the Met, he often sang the part in post-Met productions. Bledsoe, born in Waco, Texas, sang with several Chicago and Cleveland opera companies, with the Aeolian Opera Association and acted and in the 1942 movie *Drums of the Congo.*

BLEGEN, JUDITH   *American soprano (1941–)*

Lyric coloratura soprano Judith Blegen had a long association with composer Gian Carlo Menotti starring in productions and recordings of four of his operas. She is Miss Pinkerton in the only complete recording of THE OLD MAID AND THE THIEF and Monica in the 1970 Washington Opera recording of THE MEDIUM. She was violin-playing Emily in the American premiere of HELP, HELP, THE GLOBOLINKS! at Santa Fe in 1969 and she starred in the televised premiere of LANDSCAPES AND REMEMBRANCES in Milwaukee in 1976. Blegen, who began to sing for Menotti in Spoleto in 1963, was born in Missoula, Montana, studied at the Curtis Institute and apprenticed at Santa Fe. She made her Met debut in 1970.

BLENNERHASSETT   *1939 opera by Giannini*

1806. Harman Blennerhassett and Aaron Burr plot to conquer the territory of the United States south of the Ohio River. Stephen and other followers arrange to meet them on the island of Blennerhassett near Parkersburg, West Virginia. Stephen's fiancée Madeleine tries to save him by revealing the plot to General Wilkinson but Stephen is wounded in the confrontation and dies in her arms. Vittorio Giannini's historical radio opera *Blennerhassett*, libretto by Philip Roll and Norman Corwin, was commissioned by CBS and broadcast from New York on November 2, 1939. It was given its stage premiere at the Institute of Musical Art in New York on April 12, 1940.

1939 CBS Radio. The premiere of *Blennerhassett* on CBS Radio on November 2, 1939, was recorded off-air and is available on tape. Omega Opera Archives audiocassette.

THE BLIND GIRL OF CASTEL-CUILLÉ   *1914 opera by Drake*

Margaret, a young woman in a French village. goes blind and her engagement to Baptiste is broken off. When he returns to marry her friend Angela, Margaret becomes so distraught she attends the wedding with a concealed knife and kills herself at Baptiste's feet. Earl R. Drake's romantic three-act grand opera *The Blind Girl of Castel-Cuillé*, libretto by L. C. Babarini based on a Longfellow poem inspired by a French poem by Jacques Jasmin, was premiered at the Globe Theater in Chicago on February 19, 1914. Clara Pascoline played Margaret, Arthur Pascoline was Baptiste, Fannie de Tray was Agnela, Harry Lessinger was Count de Cuillé, Marie Zimmerman was Jane, Kinter Berkebile was Paul and N. R. McIntyr was Father Le France. The composer conducted.

BLITZSTEIN, MARC   *American composer (1906–1964)*

Marc Blitzstein's first opera was the one-act *Triple-Sec*, libretto by Ronald Jeans, which premiered at the Bellevue Stratford Hotel on May 6, 1929. Next was the mythological spoof THE HARPIES composed in 1931 but not staged until 1954. His best-known work, THE CRADLE WILL ROCK, was famously staged in 1937 by Orson Welles after attempts were made to ban it. The ban made it so popular it had a long run and continues to be revived. Blitzstein also created a musical work for radio in 1937, I'VE GOT THE TUNE. His three-act music theater piece NO FOR AN ANSWER was staged in 1941 but got little publicity and was barely noticed. REGINA, an impressive large-scale Broadway opera based on Lillian Hellman's play *The Little Foxes*, was staged in 1949. It was followed in 1955 by REUBEN, REUBEN, an allegorical Broadway opera about a would-be suicide. JUNO, a tuneful musical based on Sean O'Casey's play *Juno and the Paycock,* was staged in 1959. Blitzstein's last three operas were left uncompleted when he was killed. The one-act musicals THE MAGIC BARREL and IDIOTS FIRST, based on stories by Bernard Malamud, were intended to form a double-bill titled *Tales of Malamud.* SACCO AND VANZETTI, based on the story of the celebrated anarchists, was to have been a major work.

Blitzstein's stage works often occupy territory halfway between opera and musical so they have not always been considered operas by critics. In his early years he was inspired by the music theater of Bertolt Brecht and Kurt Weill and Brecht encouraged him to complete *The Cradle Will Rock*. He returned the favor by creating the American version of the Brecht/Weill *The Threepenny Opera* (1954) which led to its renewed popularity.

1956 Blitzstein Discusses His Theater Compositions. Blitzstein talks about three of his operas and numbers from them are performed on the album *Marc Blitzstein Discusses His Theater Compositions*. For *The Cradle Will Fall*, Evelyn Lear sings "Nickel Under the Foot" and the trio of Alvin Epstein, Roddy McDowall and Jane Connell perform the Hotel Lobby scene. For *No for an Answer*, Joshua Kelly sings "Penny Candy" and Evelyn Lear and George Gaynes perform the "Francie" scene. For *Regina*, Brenda Lewis sings Birdie's scena from Act III. Blitzstein accompanies on piano. Spoken Arts LP. **1990 Zipperfly and Other Songs.** Karen Hovik and William Sharp sing numbers from Blitzstein's stage works on a recording made in conjunction with the New York Festival of Song. Steven Blier accompanies on piano on pieces from *The Cradle Will Fall, No for an Answer, Regina, Juno, This Is the Garden* and *Reuben, Reuben*. Koch CD. **1990 A Blitzstein Cabaret.** *A Blitzstein Cabaret* features seventeen numbers from Blitzstein musicals sung by Helene Williams, Ronald Edwards and Leonard Lehrman. The recording is based on a stage show produced by Lehrman and includes work from *Reuben, Reuben, Goloopchik, Idiots First, New York Opera, Parade, No for an Answer, Juno* and *Sacco and Vanzetti*. Premier Recordings CD. **1993 Dawn Upshaw.** Dawn Upshaw sings numbers from *Juno, No for an Answer* and *Reuben, Reuben* on her album *I Wish It So*. Eric Stern conducts the orchestra. Elektra Nonesuch CD. **1998 Marc Blitzstein Musical Theatre Premieres.** *Marc Blitzstein Musical Theatre Premieres* is a compilation album featuring transfers from the original 78 recordings of three early Blitzstein works: *The Cradle Will Rock* (1938), *No for an Answer* (1940) and *The Airborne Symphony* (1945). Pearl/Koch 2-CD box. **2001 A Mark Blitzstein Songbook.** *A Mark Blitzstein Songbook* features songs from Blitzstein music theater works performed by soprano Helen Williams, tenor Gregor Mercer and baritone James Sergi with piano accompaniment by Leonard Lehrman. It includes numbers from *The Cradle Will Rock, Regina, Juno Reuben, Reuben, Idiots First*, and *No for an Answer*. Original Cast Records CD.

BLOOD MOON   *1961 opera by Dello Joio*

Mulatto actress Ninette Lafont passes for white in 19th century New Orleans, New York and Paris and has an unsuccessful love affair with a white man. Norman Dello Joio's three-act opera *Blood Moon,* libretto by Gale Hoffman and the composer based on the life of Ada Mencken, premiered at San Francisco Opera September 18, 1961. Its *Traviata*-like story is emphasized by having Alexandre Dumas as a character. Mary Costa sang the role of Ninette, Albert Lance was her lover Raymond Bardac, Keith Engen was Dumas, Irene Dalis was Cleo Lafont, Dorothy Cole was Madame Bardac, Claude Heater was Tom Henney, Marguerite Gignac was Edmee LeBlanc, Joshua Hect was the Blind Wanderer and Janis Martin was Sister Anne. Rouben Ter-Arutunian designed the sets and Leopold Ludwig was the conductor. *Blood Moon* was the first American opera to premiere at San Francisco Opera. It was not well received at the time though Dello Joio believes it is his best opera.

BLOOD ON THE DINING ROOM FLOOR   *2000 opera by Sheffer*

In this surrealistic murder mystery set in a French village in 1933, Gertrude Stein's car and phone are sabotaged, a suicide is found with two bullets in her head and a woman plunges to her death sleep-walking. The core of the story is a writer's block experienced by Stein which is broken by her attempts to solve the mystery. Jonathan Sheffer's chamber opera *Blood on the Dining Room Floor,* libretto by the composer based on Stein's detective story, had two premieres. It was first seen in excerpt form at the Lewis Theatre in the Guggenheim Museum on April 5, 2000. Juliana Gondek was narrator Gertrude Stein, Ruthann Manley was Alice B. Toklas, Robin Leigh Massie was the Englishwoman, Ilana Davidson was Mme. Pernolet, Jennifer Roderer was Lizzie Borden, David Blackburn was the Pastor, Dean Elzinga was the Officer and John Kuether was the Doctor. Sheffer played piano and conducted the EOS Orchestra. The opera was given its full premiere by WPA Theater at the Peter Norton Space in New York on April 16, 2000. Carolann Page was Gertrude Stein, Wendy Hill was Alice B. Toklas, Sandra Joseph was Rose 1, Anna Bergman was Rose 2, Mary Ann Stewart was Rose 3, Patrick Porter was the Tenor, Michael Zegarski was the Baritone and Keith Howard was the Bass. Steven Capone designed the set, Jeremy Dobrish directed and Stephen Osgood conducted. Sheffer's score is lyrical and singable in the Adams/Thomson manner with memorable arias and even a sextet. The passages chosen from Stein's writings are clever and memorable wordplay.

BLOODLINES   *2003 opera by Teason*

Deborah Fischer Teason's opera *Bloodlines*, libretto by students of South High School in Omaha, Nebraska, was premiered at South High School Auditorium on May 2, 2003, under the guidance of Opera Omaha. South High students, a multi-cultural mix of Hispanics, Sudanese, Asians, Italians and Czechs, interviewed community residents to create an oral history of the neighborhood's immigrant evolution. This information was used to create a libretto that would have taken 72 hours to stage. Teason compressed the story into parallel plots set in 1919 and the present. The main characters are an Italian American grandfather (seen as a nine-year-old in 1919) and his 20-year-old grandson, a Sudanese refugee, a 20ish Hispanic woman, a Mexican American woman, and an Italian single mother raising her son in 1919 with the help of an African American who is lynched. Student singers were supplemented by eight professionals for the older roles. The score was performed by musicians from the Omaha Symphony led by Cina Crissare and the production was staged by Kevin Lawyer. Composer/organizer Teason, who teaches composition at the Hartt School of Music, heads the Children's Original Opera Project.

BLOSSOM, HENRY   *American librettist/lyricist (1866–1919)*

Henry Blossom Jr. wrote the librettos and lyrics for eight of Victor Herbert's comic operas beginning with MLLE, MODISTE in 1905 and its enduring aria "Kiss Me Again." He collaborated with Herbert again on THE RED MILL (1905), *The Prima Donna* (1908), THE ONLY GIRL (1914), THE PRINCESS PAT (1915), *The Century Girl* (1916), EILEEN (1917) and *The Velvet Lady* (1919). Blossom, born in St. Louis, began his writing career as a novelist and turned to theater after adapting one of his novels for the stage. His first stage musical was *The Yankee Consul* (1904), written for composer Alfred Robyn, and he also worked with other composers but his finest achievements were his collaborations with Herbert.

BLOSSOM TIME   *1921 operetta by Romberg*

Blossom Time is Sigmund Romberg's American version of *Das Dreimäderlhaus*, a German pastiche operetta about Shubert's love life by Heinrich Berté based on melodies by Franz Schubert. Romberg recomposed the score using a new libretto by Dorothy Donnelly and virtually created a new operetta. It premiered at the Ambassador Theater in New York on December 29, 1921, with Bertram Peacock as Schubert and Olga Cook as his love Mitzi. The hit number was "The Song of Love" based on a theme from the *Unfinished Symphony.*

1922 Lucy Isabelle Marsh. Soprano Lucy Isabelle Marsh sings "The Song of Love" from *Blossom Time.* It was a best-selling recording in 1922. RCA Victor 78. **1922 Reinard Werrenrath.** Metropolitan opera baritone Reinard Werrenrath sings "Tell Me Daisy" from the operetta for a 1922 recording. Victor Red Seal 78. **1923 Hollis Davenny/Gertrude Lang.** Hollis Davenny and Gertrude Lang, who starred in a 1923 New York production, duet on "The Song of Love" for a 78 record. It's on the album *The Ultimate Sigmund Romberg, Vol. 1.* Pearl CD. **1934 Everett Marshall.** Everett Marshall, who starred in the 1938 Broadway revival, recorded "The Song of Love" for a 1934 Decca 78. It's on the album *The Ultimate Sigmund Romberg, Vol. 1.* Pearl CD. **1962 Lehman Engel.** Lehman Engel conducts chorus and orchestra in this highlights recording created for the *Reader's Digest Treasury of Great Operettas* series. Richard Fredricks is Schubert, Mary Ellen Pracht is Mitzi, William Lewis is Schober, Sara Endich is Bella, George Gaynes is Von Schwind, Arthur Rubin is Vogl and Kenneth Smith is Kupelweiser. RCA LP box set.

March 29, 1953. Etta Warren is Vi and Rawn Spearman is Joe with Jimmy Rushing, Lorenzo Fuller, Warren Coleman and Bill Dillard in the supporting roles. This is the 1925 Ferde Grofé orchestrated version titled *135th Street.* Omega Opera Archives audiocassette. **1976 Gregg Smith Singers.** The Gregg Smith Singers led by Gregg Smith perform the opera with Joyce Andrew as Vi, Thomas Bogdan as Joe, Jeffrey Meyer as Tom, Patrick Mason as Mike, Walter Richardson as Sam and Orestea Cybriwsky as pianist Sweetpea. This is the 1925 Grofé version adapted by Gregg Smith and Edmund Najera. Turnabout LP. **1981 Swiss Television.** Marc Andrae conducts the Orchestra della Svizzera Italiana in a soundtrack recording of a Swiss Television production. La Verne Williams sings Vi, Howard Haskin is Joe, Raymond Bazemore is Mike, Daniel Washington is Tom, Ivan Thomas is Sam, and Oswald Russell plays piano and sings the role of Sweetpea. Aura Classics CD. **1981 Barbara Hendricks.** Barbara Hendricks sings "Has Anyone Seen Joe" accompanied by piano duo Katia and Marielle Labèque on her album *Barbara Hendricks Sings Gershwin.* Philips LP/CD. **1993 Marin Alsop.** Marin Alsop conducts the Concordia Orchestra in a recording of the complete opera. Amy Burton sings Vi, Gregory Hopkins is Joe, William Sharp is Tom, Arthur Woodley is Sam and Jamie J. Offenbach is Sam. EMI CD. **1996 Erich Kunzel.** Erich Kunzel conducts the Central State University Chorus and Cincinnati Pops Orchestra in a recording of the original 1922 version of *Blue Monday* orchestrated by Will

BLUE MONDAY *1922 mini-opera by Gershwin*

George Gershwin's first opera *Blue Monday,* libretto by B. G. De Sylva, focuses on jealousy leading to murder in a Harlem bar. Gambler Joe sings of the power of love and passion as this 25-minute mini-opera opens. At the end his sweetheart Vi shoots him because she thinks he's been unfaithful. *Blue Monday* premiered at the Globe Theater in New York on August 28, 1922, as a part of the *George White Scandals of 1922* but it was withdrawn after one night. Coletta Ryan sang Vi, Richard Bold sang Joe and Jack McGowran sang Sam. *Blue Monday,* a worthy predecessor of PORGY AND BESS, has several memorable arias, including Sam's "Blue Monday Blues" Vi's "Has Anyone Seen Joe?" based on a string quartet Gershwin wrote in 1919 and Joe's "I'm Gonna See My Mother." Ferde Grofé re-orchestrated the opera in 1925 for presentation at Carnegie Hall and renamed it *135th Street.*

1945 Rhapsody in Blue. The Gershwin film *Rhapsody in Blue* features an abridged version of *Blue Monday* performed as *135th Street Blues* including the numbers "Blue Monday Blues," "Has Anyone Seen My Joe?" and "135th Street Blues." They're performed by John B. Hughes and a supporting chorus. Irving Rapper directed the movie for Warner Brothers. The sequence can be heard on the Rhino Movie Music CD soundtrack album *George and Ira Gershwin in Hollywood* and the film is on WB VHS and DVD. **1953 CBS Television.** George Bassman conducts the orchestra in this recording of a CBS Television Omnibus production telecast

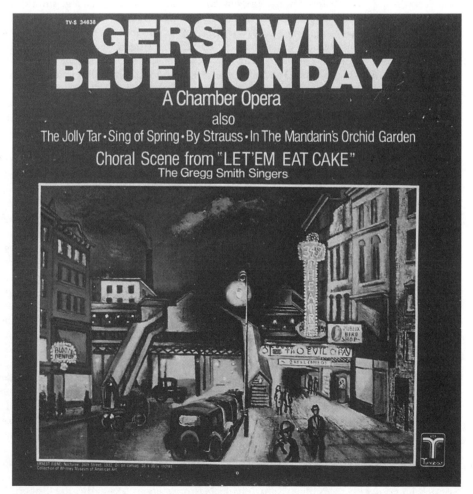

George Gershwin's first opera *Blue Monday* was recorded by the Gregg Smith Singers in 1976.

Vodery. Marquita Lister sings Vi opposite Gregg Baker as Joe with support from William Henry Caldwell, Lawrence Craig, Kirk Walker and Thomas Young. Telarc CD.

BLUE OPERA   *1997 opera by Reed*

Sometime in the future Orpheus and Eurydice live in the Isle of the Blessed but Orpheus has lost his voice. He believes a blue flower will restore it and looks for it in Limbo and seven levels of Hell. Orpheus finds the flower and regains his voice but in the meantime Eurydice has been abducted by Don Giovanni and Medea who want to climb to a higher level. Orpheus sets out to rescue her. Nancy Binns Reed's jazz-influenced two-act *Blue Opera*, libretto by the composer, was premiered by the Reunion Music Society on October 17, 1997. Beverly Cosham was Eurydice, Michael Houston was Orpheus, Peter Ferko was Don Giovanni, Karen Mercedes was Medea, Steve Metzger was Waterman and Ray Dryburgh was Gabriel. Three Spirits were played by Shannon Barnes, Carrie House and Leigh Man and Three Dragons were sung by Meld Downes, Randy Lindgren and Isaac Miller.

THE BLUE PARADISE   *1915 operetta by Romberg*

A young man leaves his sweetheart in Europe to make his fortune in America. Sigmund Romberg's first popular song came from *The Blue Paradise,* a nearly forgotten operetta based on a Viennese operetta by Edmund Eysler titled *Ein Tag im Paradies.* It opened August 5, 1915, at the Casino Theater in New York with Vivienne Segal, Cecil Lean, Cleo Mayfield and Frances Demarest in the principal roles. The hit song was "Auf Wiedersehn," a goodbye number with lyrics by Herbert Reynolds sung by Segal and Lean in the stage production.

1915 Olive Kline/Harry MacDonough. Concert soprano Olive Kline and Canadian tenor Harry MacDonough of the Victor Light Opera Company had a major success in 1915 with their recording of "Auf Wiedersehn." Victor 78. **1916 Julia Culp.** Contralto Julia Culp sings the operetta's popular goodbye song "Auf Wiedersehn" on a 1916 recording. Victor Red Seal 78 **1936 Grace Moore.** Met soprano Grace Moore sings "Auf Wiedersehn" on a radio broadcast in 1936. It was recorded off air and later issued on an LP. EJS LP. **1954 Helen Traubel.** Wagnerian soprano Helen Traubel performs "Auf Wiedersehn" in the Romberg film biography *Deep in My Heart.* MGM-UA VHS/Sony soundtrack CD.

BLUMENFELD, HAROLD   *American composer (1923–)*

Harold Blumenfeld has composed several works based around the life and work of French poet Arthur Rimbaud, including an opera and a cantata. The cantata *La face cendrée* (1982) has been recorded by soprano Christine Schadeberg and is on a CD with three other Rimbaud compositions by Blumenfeld. The opera SEASONS IN HELL, *A Life of Rimbaud* (1996), libretto by Charles Kondek, premiered at Cincinnati College Conservatory of Music and has been recorded. Blumenfeld's first opera *Amphitryon 4* (1962), libretto by the composer based on the Molière play, has only been performed in excerpts. *Gentle Boy* (1968), libretto by the composer based on a story by Nathaniel Hawthorne, and *The Road to Salem* (1969), libretto by the composer, were written for television. Blumenfeld began his fruitful collaboration with librettist Kondek on the 1979 opera *Fritzi,* based on Molnar's *The Witch;* it was premiered by Chicago Opera Theater in 1988 after revisions as BREAKFAST WALTZES. *Fourscore: An Opera of Opposites,* libretto by Kondek based on Austrian playwright Johann Nestroy's *Haus der Temperamente,* was premiered by the University of Cincinnati on March 3, 1989. Borgia, libretto by Kondek, is a two-act opera in

progress. Blumenfeld, born in Seattle, studied at the Eastman School and Yale with Bernard Rogers and Paul Hindemith. He was director of Opera Theater of St. Louis from 1962 to 1966 and of Washington University Opera Studio from 1960 to 1971.

BOATWRIGHT, McHENRY   *American bass-baritone (1931–1994)*

Georgian-born McHenry Boatwright created the central role of Carter Jones in Gunther Schuller's opera THE VISITATION when it was premiered by Hamburg State Opera in 1966 and he made his debut at the Metropolitan Opera in 1967 in the role with the Hamburg company. He portrayed Crown in PORGY AND BESS on stage and is featured in the role on the 1963 Leontyne Price/William Warfield recording and the 1976 Lorin Maazel Cleveland recording. He sang at the Met in the National Negro Opera Foundation's presentation of Clarence Cameron White's OUANGA and he played Kumalo in a stage production of Kurt Weill's LOST IN THE STARS. Boatwright was born in Tennielle, Georgia, and made his professional debut in 1953 at the Tanglewood Festival.

BOCK, JERRY   *American composer (1928–)*

Jerry Bock had great success on Broadway in the 1960s with lyricist partner Sheldon Harnick, especially with FIDDLER ON THE ROOF. Bock, who was born in New Haven, Connecticut, studied at the University of Wisconsin and learned his trade writing for college shows and television. His first stage musical was *Mr. Wonderful* (1956) followed by *The Body Beautiful* (1958). His first show with Harnick was *Fiorello!* (1959), libretto by Jerome Weidman and George Abbott, a musical version of the life of New York Mayor Fiorello La Guardia. It was followed by *Tenderloin* (1960), libretto again by Weidman and Abbott, about vice in old New York. SHE LOVES ME (1963), lyrics by Sheldon Harnick with libretto by Joe Masteroff about a couple who find love via letters, has become popular with regional opera houses. *Fiddler on the Roof* (1964), libretto by Joseph Stein based on stories by Sholom Aleichem about the difficult life of Jewish villagers in old Russia, was a hit around the world on stage and on film and continued to be revived. *The Apple Tree* (1966) and *The Rothschilds* (1970) were the last Harnick-Bock collaborations.

BOK CHOY VARIATIONS   *1995 opera by Chen*

Four young men, including a composer, grow up in Communist China but leave seeking freedom in the U. S. They find American reality more complicated than they supposed and become disillusioned. Evan Chen's opera *Bok Choy Variations,* libretto by Fifi Servoss, was premiered in St. Paul, Minnesota, on June 10, 1995. The composer and the librettist are both first generation Chinese Americans and their opera is romantic as well as satirical. The premiere cast featured Jason Ma as Da Wei, Alan Muraoka as Lee, Edmund Eng as Zhanguo, Scott Watanabe as Fong, Chloe Stewart as May, Linda Balgord as Sophia and Christine Toy as Da Wei's mother. Jeffrey Lewis conducted and Erick Simonson directed.

BOLCOM, WILLIAM   *American composer (1938–)*

William Bolcom was awarded the Pulitzer Prize for Music in 1988 for his piano work *Twelve New Etudes* and soon after began to compose grand opera. MCTEAGUE, libretto by Arnold Weinstein based on the novel that inspired the film *Greed,* was premiered by Lyric Opera of Chicago in 1992. It was staged by film director Robert Altman and starred Ben Heppner and Catherine Malfitano. His second major opera A VIEW FROM THE BRIDGE, libretto by Weinstein based on the play by Arthur Miller, was presented by Lyric Opera of Chicago in 1999. Its success led Chicago to commission two more operas, including *A Wedding* based on Robert Altman's 1978 film. Bolcom's one-act monodrama MEDUSA, based on the Greek legend, was premiered by Cincinnati Opera in 2003 with Catherine Malfitano in the title role. His chamber opera *Idiot's Delight,* libretto by Weinstein based on Robert Sherwood's play, was funded in 2004. The Seattle-born composer began his operatic career after studies in Paris with Milhaud and Messiaen. The "cabaret opera" *Dynamite Tonight,* composed to a libretto by Weinstein who has worked with him on all his later operas, was staged by the Actor's Studio in New York on December 21, 1963. The principal roles were taken by Barbara Harris, Alvin Epstein, George Gaynes and William Redford. Next was the "theater opera" *Greatshot* produced by the Yale Repertory Theater on May 15, 1969. The cabaret opera CASINO PARADISE was produced by the American Musical Theater Festival in Philadelphia in 1990 and recorded. During this time Bolcom also composed music for the film *Hester Street* (1975) and *Songs of Innocence and Experience* (1983), a setting of poems by William Blake. Bolcom is married to soprano Joan Morris, and they have collaborated on several recordings of popular songs.

BOLES, JOHN   *American baritone (1895–1969)*

John Boles created the role of Whitelaw in Kurt Weill's musical ONE TOUCH OF VENUS on Broadway in 1943 after a successful Hollywood career. He played the Red Shadow in the 1929 film of Sigmund Romberg's THE DESERT SONG, the Texas Ranger in the 1929 film of Harry Tierney's RIO RITA and the librettist Bruno in the 1934 film of Jerome Kern's operetta MUSIC IN THE AIR. Boles, who was born in Greenville, Texas, sang opposite Met soprano Gladys Swarthout in the movies *Rose of the Rancho* (1935) and *Romance in the Dark* (1938).

BOMARZO   *1967 opera by Ginastera*

The violent, sexually bizarre life of the evil hunchbacked 16th century Duke of Bomarzo, Pier Francesco Orsini, is portrayed in flashbacks. As he dies of poison, he remembers past events including murdering his brother because of jealousy about his wife. Alberto Ginastera's two-act opera *Bomarzo,* libretto by Manuel Mujico Láinez based on his novel, was commissioned by the Opera Society of Washington which premiered it May 19, 1967, at the Lisner Auditorium in Washington, D. C. Salvador Nova played Pier Francesco Orsini, Claramae Turner was his grandmother Diana Orsini, Brent Ellis was his brother Maerbale, Robert Gregory was his brother Girolamo, Michael Devlin was his father Gian Corrado, Isabel Penagos was his wife Julia, Richard Torigi was the astrologer Silvio de Narni, Joanna Simon was Pantasiliea and Nico Castel was the Messenger. Tito Capobianco staged the opera and Julius Rudel conducted the Washington Opera Chorus and Orchestra. The bizarre Bomarzo Park near Rome, with monstrous statues created by Pier Francesco, was the inspiration for the source novel. The opera was reprised at New York City Opera in March 1968 with virtually the same cast.

1967 Washington Opera. Salvador Nova stars as the evil Bomarzo in this recording of the opera made by the cast of the Washington Opera premiere production. Claramae Turner is his grandmother, Brent Ellis is his brother and Isabel Penagos is his wife. Julius Rudel conducts the Washington Opera Chorus and Orchestra. CBS LP.

BOMHARD, MORITZ VON   *American conductor/director (1908–1995)*

Moritz von Bomhard founded Kentucky Opera in Louisville in 1953 and directed it until 1982. He had a strong interest in American opera and inaugurated the company with productions of Gian Carlo Menotti's *The Telephone* and *The Medium.* He commissioned and conducted premieres of six American operas in the 1950s: Peggy Glanville-Hicks THE TRANSPOSED HEADS in 1954, Richard Mohaupt's DOUBLE TROUBLE in 1954, George Antheil's THE WISH in 1955, Rolf Liebermann's SCHOOL FOR WIVES in 1955, Nicolas Nabokov's THE HOLY DEVIL in 1958 and Lee Hoiby's BEATRICE in 1959. He has also directed/conducted productions of other American operas and including a 1974 Kentucky Opera production of Carlisle Floyd's SUSANNAH. Bomhard began his musical studies in Leipzig but came to New York as a young man and finished his studies at Juilliard and Columbia. He made his debut with New York Lyric Stage in 1948.

BON APPÉTIT!   *1989 opera by Hoiby*

Julia Childs explains to a television audience how to make a French chocolate cake which is fancifully named Le Gateau au Chocolat l'Eminence Brune. Lee Hoiby's brief but delectable monodrama *Bon Appétit!* is based on an episode in Childs' TV cooking program *The French Chef.* It was premiered at the Kennedy Center in Washington, DC, on March 8, 1989, and designed as a curtain-raiser for Hoiby's monodrama THE ITALIAN LESSON. The double bill been popular as performed by Jean Stapleton around the U.S. and continues to be produced in regional theaters.

BONAZZI, ELAINE   *American mezzo-soprano (1938–)*

Coloratura mezzo-soprano Elaine Bonazzi created roles in fifteen American operas on stage, television and record. She even created the first female role in American opera by singing the role of Moll Plackett in the long delayed premiere of the first American opera, Andrew Barton's 1767 THE DISAPPOINTMENT. In the modern era she was Mrs. Linton in Carlisle Floyd's WUTHERING HEIGHTS at Santa Fe in 1958, the Blind Woman in George Thaddeus Jones' BREAK OF DAY on ABC Television in 1961, the Old One in Abraham Ellstein's THE THIEF AND HANGMAN on ABC TV in 1961, Tebell in John LaMontaine's Christmas pageant-opera NOVELLIS NOVELLIS in 1962, the Spy in Gian Carlo Menotti's LABYRINTH on NBC TV in 1963, the cook Christine in Ned Rorem's MISS JULIE at New York City Opera in 1965, the Psychiatrist in Marc Bucci's THE HERO in 1965 on NET television, one of the Three Women in Amram's THE FINAL INGREDIENT in 1965 on ABC TV, and Joan in Henry Humphrey-Rauscher's *Joan of Arc at Reims* in Cincinnati in 1968. She was Mary Todd Lincoln in Thomas Pasatieri's THE TRIAL OF MARY LINCOLN on NET Television in 1972, Lavinia Davenport in Pasatieri's WASHINGTON SQUARE at Michigan Opera Theater in 1976, nanny Grace-Helen Broome in Dominick Argento's MISS HAVISHAM'S FIRE at New York City Opera in 1979, Madame D'Urfe in Argento's CASANOVA'S HOMECOMING in 1985 and Lady Neville in David Carlson's THE MIDNIGHT ANGEL in Saint Louis in 1993, a role written especially for her. She is featured in scenes from Pasatieri's operas THE SEAGULL and *Washington Square* on a 1977 TV program about the composer. Bonazzi, born in Endicott, NY, made her debut in 1959 at the Santa Fe Opera. She has sung in many other American operas on stage including the Baroness in Barber's VANESSA, Dinah in Bernstein's TROUBLE IN TAHITI, the Secretary in Menotti's THE CONSUL, Miss Todd in Menotti's THE OLD MAID AND THE THIEF, Augusta Tabor in Moore's THE BALLAD OF BABY DOE and Baba the Turk in Stravinsky's THE RAKE'S PROGRESS.

BOND, VICTORIA   *American composer/conductor (1945–)*
Victoria Bond, the first woman to get a degree in conducting from Juilliard, is best known as a conductor but she is also a successful composer including several stage works. The most important is TRAVELS, an opera based on Swift's *Gulliver's Travels* but she has attracted interest with her opera MRS. SATAN about the first woman to run for president. Her cabaret work *Power Play*, a mini-drama for mezzo-soprano and chamber ensemble about a woman working out at a health club, was performed by Sequitor in New York in May 18, 2003. Bond, a native of Los Angeles, was music director of Bel Canto Opera in New York from 1983 to 1988 and then became artistic director of Opera Roanoke

BONELLI, RICHARD   *American baritone (1887–1980)*
Richard Bonelli created the role of warrior prince Yiro Danyemon opposite Japanese soprano Tamaki Miuri in Aldo Franchetti's *Namiko-San* premiered by Chicago Opera in 1925. Bonelli, born in Port Byron, NY, studied at Syracuse and in Paris with Jean de Reszke. He made his debut in Brooklyn in 1915 and began to sing at the Metropolitan Opera in 1932.

BONHOEFFER   *2000 opera by Gebuhr*
The life of Dietrich Bonhoeffer, a German Lutheran theologian executed in 1945 for anti-Nazi activities, is shown in a series of scenes, including a failed attempt to kill Hitler. Ann Gebuhr's opera *Bonhoeffer*, libretto by Robert Hatten, premiered at Moore's Opera House at the University of Houston on May 19, 2000. Douglas Yates sang the title role with Houston Baptist University students in the other parts.

BONYNGE, RICHARD   *Australian conductor (1930–)*
Richard Bonynge is known for his interest in early Italian and French operas but he also likes operetta. He conducts the New Philharmonia Orchestra and Ambrosian Light Opera Chorus on the album *The Golden Age of Operetta* while his wife Joan Sutherland sings airs from THE DESERT SONG, THE ONLY GIRL, SHOW BOAT, ROSE-MARIE and THE STUDENT PRINCE.

BOOK OF DAYS   *1988 opera by Monk*
A young Jewish woman in a medieval French village around the year 1350 has visions of life as it is today and attempts to describe them to her grandfather. Fears of the Black Plague of her era and the AIDS plague of the present time are paralleled across time. The young woman dies of the plague but her drawings of airplanes and guns survive and are found in our time. Avant-garde composer Meredith Monk's experimental *Book of Days* is both opera and film. The stage ver-

Baritone Richard Bonelli was promoted in 1936 *Musical America* ad.

sion was produced by Minnesota Opera in 1988 and continues to be reprised including a presentation by the UC Berkeley Chamber Chorus in 2003. The 74-minute operatic film, essentially a meditation on time and history, was premiered at the New York Film Festival and shown on PBS.

1988 *Book of Days* film. *Book of Days,* shot in the preserved medieval town of Cordes, France, centers around the life of a prophetic young Jewish girl who dies of the Black Plague in the year 1350. The film moves obliquely through time from the black-and-white of the medieval story to the color of the present day. The cast includes Monk, Toby Newman, Andrea Goodman and Robert Een. Jerry Pantzer was the cinematographer. 74 minutes. On VHS. **1990 Book of Days CD.** The music of *Book of Days* was recorded by Monk in 1990 and released as a compact disc. ECM New Series CD.

BOOK OF THE DEAD (SEVENTH AVENUE) *2000 multimedia opera by Moran*

The ancient Egyptian underworld meets the modern overworld of New York's Seventh Avenue from gods and mummies to TV and fastfood restaurants. John Moran's experimental multimedia operatic extravaganza *Book of the Dead (Seventh Avenue),* libretto by the composer based on Seventh Avenue dialogue and Egyptian and Tibetan texts, premiered at the Joseph Papp Public Theater in New York on November 20, 2000. Uma Thurman spoke the recorded narration and the on-stage performers included Theo Bleckmann, Patricia R. Floyd, Darryl Gibson, Anthony Henderson, Michael Huston, John Moran, Laine Satterfield, Cabell Tomlinson, David West and M. Drue Williams. Moran designed the sets and video projections, directed the pre-recorded music and staged the production. The "opera," which features an aria built around the phrase "I need a sausage biscuit, Jamal," has been compared by critics to the works of Philip Glass and Laurie Anderson.

THE BOOR *American operas based on Chekhov play*

Widow Popov mourns her husband and is looked after by the old servant Luka. When boorish neighbor Smirnov demands payment for a debt made by her husband, she gets so angry she challenges him to a duel. While he shows her how to use a pistol, they fall in love and decide to get married. Anton Chekhov's short play *The Boor* (aka *The Brute* or *The Bear*) has provided the basis for five American one-act operas.

1949 Mark Bucci. Mark Bucci's one-act opera *The Boor,* libretto by E. Haun based on the Chekhov story, premiered at Finch College in New York on December 29, 1949. **1955 Myron Fink.** Myron Fink's one-act opera *The Boor,* libretto by the composer based on the Chekhov story, was premiered at the Ivory Room in the Jefferson Hotel in St. Louis, Missouri, on February 14, 1955. **1957 Dominick Argento.** Dominick Argento's 48-minute opera *The Boor,* libretto by John Olon-Scrymgeour, premiered at the Eastman School of Music in Rochester on May 6, 1957, in the Festival of American Music. Barbara Altman sang the role of the widow and William Duvall was the boor. Argento's opera has since been staged by many American companies. It was telecast by Germany's Bremerhaven State Theater on July 7, 1964, with Anita Salta as the widow opposite Rudolf Bechtold and Walter Vertrit. Hans Kindler conducted the orchestra and Hans Wachter directed the ZDF telecast. **1961 Lawrence Moss.** Lawrence Moss's 30-minute opera *The Brute,* libretto by Eric Bentley, premiered at the Yale Summer School of Music in Norfolk, CT, July 29, 1961. It has since been staged by SUNY in Buffalo, Washington University in St. Louis and the Southern California Chamber Music Society in Los Angeles. It was telecast in 1966 by the University of Chicago Contemporary Chamber Players with Neva Pilgrim as Widow Popoff, Michael Cousins as Smirnov and Thomas MacBone as Luka. Ralph Shapey conducted the Players Orchestra, and Paul Cahill directed the telecast on May 21, 1966, for Chicago's WBBM-TV. **1968 Ulysses Kay.** Ulysses Kay's 40-minute opera *The Boor,* libretto by the composer based on the Chekhov story, was commissioned by the Koussevitzky Foundation and premiered at the University of Kentucky in Lexington on April 3, 1968.

BORI, LUCREZIA *Spanish-born American soprano (1887–1960)*

Lucrezia Bori created the role of Mary, the Duchess of Towers, in Deem Taylor's opera PETER IBBETSON at the Metropolitan Opera in 1931 and can be heard in a recording of a 1934 broadcast. She had sung Manon with the Met in Paris in 1910 and she came to the Met in New York in 1912 in the role. She continued to sing at the Met until 1936. Bori was one of the most popular sopranos in the world in her time with an extraordinary ability to create characters on stage.

BORKH, INGE *Swiss soprano (1917–)*

Inge Borkh, one of the great modern singing actresses, made her debut in 1940 but became famous singing Magda in the first German-language production of Gian Carlo Menotti's THE CONSUL in Basle in 1951. In the same year she recorded the opera's aria "My Child is Dead" with the Berlin State Opera. Borkh, born in Mannheim, has a voice of great intensity and is noted for her performances in Richard Strauss operas.

BOTTCHER, RON *American baritone (1937–)*

Ron Bottcher created small roles is four American operas at New York City Opera and the Metropolitan Opera. He was Tadeus' Man 2 in Abraham Ellstein's THE GOLEM at NYCO in 1962, the Union Soldier in Carlisle Floyd's THE PASSION OF JONATHAN WADE at NYCO in 1962, Scarus in Samuel Barber's ANTONY AND CLEOPATRA at the Met in 1966 and Peter Niles in Marvin David Levy's MOURNING BECOMES ELECTRA at the Met in 1967.

BOTTONE, BONAVENTURA *English tenor (1950–)*

Bonaventura Bottone plays Sam Kaplan in the 1992 English National Opera recording of Kurt Weill's STREET SCENE, Detlef in the 1989 English recording of Sigmund Romberg's THE STUDENT PRINCE and the Governor in the 1997 Scottish Opera recording of Leonard Bernstein's CANDIDE. He made his debut in 1973 and sings regularly with Scottish Opera, the English National Opera and the Royal Opera House, Covent Garden.

BOURJAILY, VANCE *American librettist/novelist (1922–)*

Vance Bourjaily wrote the libretto for Thomas Turner's opera *Four Thousand Dollars* which was premiered at the University of Iowa in Iowa City on March 6, 1969. Bourjaily, who was a teacher of writing at the University of Iowa, examined aspects of American society in novels like *Now Playing at Canterbury* (1976). Born in Ohio, he first became known through his autobiographical novel *The End of My Life* (1947).

BOWLES, PAUL *American composer (1910–1999)*

Paul Bowles is best known as a writer but he began as a composer and wrote three operas. Born in Jamaica, New York, he studied with Aaron Copland, Virgil Thomson and Nadia Boulanger in Europe during the 1920s and 1930s. After returning to the U.S. in 1936, he wrote the now lost opera *Denmark Vesey*, libretto by Charles-Henri Ford, about an heroic black slave. He married Jane Auer (she was lesbian, he was bisexual) and, despite many affairs, they remained together until her death in 1973. He wrote theater scores for Orson Welles (*Horse Eats Hat*), Tennessee Williams (*The Glass Menagerie, Summer and Smoke*) and William Saroyan (*My Heart's in the Highlands*) and sixteen film scores including *Cyrano De Bergerac, The Tempest* and *The Glass Menagerie*. His major operas were based on plays by the Spanish playwright Federico Garcia Lorca. He received a Guggenheim to compose THE WIND REMAINS and he wrote *Yerma* for blues singer Libby Holman. Bowles lived permanently in Tangier from 1947 and turned from music to writing in 1949 when he received acclaim for his novel *The Sheltering Sky*, filmed by Bernardo Bertolucci. He published his autobiography *Without Stopping* in 1972. Bowles operas are poorly represented on record but three film scores are on disc.

1993 Paul Bowles: The Complete Outsider. Documentary by Catherine Warnow and Regina Weinrich that begins in Tangiers in 1993 and charts Bowles' life, music and writings backwards. Interviews with Bowles, Ned Rorem and Allen Ginsberg. First Run Features VHS. **1999 Night Waltz: The Music of Paul Bowles.** Owsley Browne's documentary about Bowles' music combines recordings with archival footage, new material shot in Tangier, Paris and New York and interviews with Bowles, Allen Ginsberg and William S. Burroughs. On VHS. **1998 Let It Come Down: The Life of Paul Bowles.** Documentary by Jennifer Baichwal and Nick de Pencier centered around an interview with Bowles. William Burroughs, Allen Ginsberg, David Herbert, Mohammed Choukri, Mohammed Mrabet, Phillip Ramey, Ned Rorem and Bowles' wife's lover Cherifa participate. Jonathan Sheffer conducts the EOS Orchestra in the music segments in this film made for Zeitgeist Films. On DVD.

BOWMAN, JOHN S.   *American librettist (1946–)*

John S. Bowman wrote the librettos for three operas composed by Henry Mollicone, including the very popular 1978 THE FACE ON THE BARROOM FLOOR. He began his collaboration with the composer in 1970 with the libretto for YOUNG GOODMAN BROWN, based on a story by Nathaniel Hawthorne. Their other collaboration was the 1981 post-modern EMPEROR NORTON, the story of a 19th century eccentric who claimed to be emperor of the United States.

THE BOY WHO GREW TOO FAST   *1982 children's opera by Menotti*

A boy doesn't fit in at school because he is big. When he is able to save the school from a criminal because he is big, his teacher tells the children they should be glad to be whatever size, shape or color they are. Gian Carlo Menotti's 40-minute children's opera, libretto by the composer, was premiered by Opera Delaware in Wilmington September 24, 1982. Denise Coffey was teacher Miss Hope, Phillip Peterson as big Poponel (the boy who grows too fast), boy soprano Peter Lugar was small Poponel, Sara Hagopian was Mrs. Skosvodmonit, Frank Reynolds was Dr. Shrink, Alan Wagner was the criminal Mad Dog, Joy Vandever was Miss Proctor, Miriam Bennett was Lizzie Spender, Tony Duffy was Ricky and Thomas Littel was the Policeman. Cynthia duPont Tombias designed the sets and Evelyn Swensson conducted the Opera Delaware Orchestra.

1984 Cannes Children's Chorus. The Cannes-Provence-Côte d'Azur Children's Chorus, Orchestra and soloists led by Philippe Bender perform the opera in a French translation at the Cannes Festival Palais in Cannes, France, on January 23, 1984. Auvidis LP. **1987 Royal Opera House.** Menotti produced the opera in London in 1986 and supervised a recording with the Royal Opera House cast in February 1987. Judith Howard is Miss Hope, Graham Godfrey is big Poponel, Daniel Wallder is small Poponel, Maureen Morelle is Mrs. Skosvodmonit, Paul Crook is Dr. Shrink, Eric Garrett is Mad Dog, Elizabeth Bainbridge is Miss Proctor, Alison Machell is Lizzie Spender, Tony Duffy is Ricky and Andrew Plant is the Policeman. David Syrus conducts the Royal Opera House Orchestra. Musical Heritage Society LP/TER Classics CD.

BRADLEY, GWENDOLYN   *American soprano (1952–)*

Metropolitan Opera soprano Gwendolyn Bradley is featured on the 1981 Joel Thome recording of FOUR SAINTS IN THREE ACTS singing the role of St. Settlement. She sang the role of Clara in a 1995 radio broadcast of PORGY AND BESS from the Met. Bradley, who was born in New York, trained at the Curtis Institute of Music and made her debut at the Met in 1981 in Stravinsky's *The Nightingale*.

BRAIN OPERA   *1996 interactive opera by Machover*

Todd Machover's interactive *Brain Opera*, libretto compiled by the composer, was presented at the Juilliard School in New York in 1996 with audience participation part of the performance. The lobby was turned into a "musical arcade" of electronic "hyperinstruments" which attendees were asked to play. The Morse Recital Hall was turned into a kind of sound and light nightclub. The music and voices came from surfing the internet and audience interactivity. Although *Brain Opera* has no narrative, singers or instrumentalists, Machover insists it is an opera with actual dramatic and psychological progression. It is based on MIT Professor Marvin Minsky's theories about the chaotic diversity of the human brain during musical composition.

BRAND, MAX   *American composer (1896–1980)*

Max Brand was a popular opera composer in Austria and Germany before the rise of the Nazis but as he was Jewish, his career was soon curtailed. He left Austria in 1938 and moved to New York, becoming an American citizen in 1944. His scenic oratorio *The Gate*, libretto by J. Chanler, M. A. Sohrab and the composer, premiered at the Metropolitan Opera on May 23, 1944. His next dramatic work was the one-act opera *Stormy Interlude*, libretto by the composer, completed in 1955. *The Wonderful One-Hoss-Shay* was premiered by the Philadelphia Orchestra in 1959. The experimental stage work *The Astronauts: An Epic in Electronics,* which grew out of his interest in technology, was composed in 1962. Brand, who studied with Schrenker in Vienna, is probably best known for his atonal Austrian opera *Machinist Hopkins*.

BRANDSTETTER, JOHN   *American baritone (1949–)*

John Brandstetter created the role of Ben Holland in Conrad Susa's opera BLACK RIVER for Minnesota Opera in 1975, and the roles of Griswold/Captain/Mr. Allen in Dominick Argento's opera THE VOYAGE OF EDGAR ALLAN POE for the Minnesota Opera Studio in 1976. He sings Junior in Leonard Bernstein's 1986 Vienna State Opera recording/video of A QUIET PLACE. Brandstetter, born in Wayne, Nebraska, studied music at the University of Nebraska and made his debut in the Susa opera.

BRANDT, BARBARA   *American soprano (1942–)*

Spinto soprano Barbara Brandt created roles in eight American operas while a resident member of Minnesota Opera. She was the Sphinx in Yale Marshall's *Oedipus and the Sphinx* in 1969, the Lady with a Cake Box in Domenick Argento's POSTCARD FROM MOROCCO in 1971, Margherita in John Gessner's *Faust Counter Faust* in 1971, Ann Sexton in Conrad Susa's TRANSFORMATIONS in 1973, Lois in Philip Brunelle/William Huckaby's *The Newest Opera in the World* in 1974, opera singer Pauline L'Allemand in Susa's BLACK RIVER in 1975, Mrs. Poe in Argento's THE VOYAGE OF EDGAR ALLAN POE in 1976, Claudia Legare in Robert Ward's CLAUDIA LEGARE in 1978 and Mary in William Mayer's A DEATH IN THE FAMILY in 1981. Brandt has also sung leading roles in several other American operas including St. Teresa 1 in Virgil Thomson's FOUR SAINTS IN THREE ACTS. Brandt, who was born in Battle Creek, Michigan, made her debut in Minneapolis in 1966.

BRAXTON, ANTHONY *American composer (1945–)*

Chicago-born Anthony Braxton is an African American composer and saxophone player who moves between experimental avant-garde classical music and cerebral avant-garde jazz. He has composed three operas in a planned twelve-opera cycle titled *Trillium Dialogues. Trillium Dialogues A: After a Period of Change Zaccko Returns to His Place of Birth*, libretto by the composer for six soloists, six instruments, dancers, choir, large orchestra and stage set, was premiered in San Diego in 1985. *Trillium Dialogues M: Joreo's Vision of Forward Motion*, libretto by the composer for six soloists, dancers, choir, piano and large orchestra, was composed in 1986. *Trillium Dialogues R: Shala Fears for the Poor*, libretto by the composer, was completed in 1988. Braxton's recordings are mostly of works called "Compositions" but some features singers.

BRAY, JOHN *English-born American composer (1782–1822)*

John Bray, one of the earliest composers of American operas, lived and worked in Philadelphia and Boston from 1805 to 1822. He came to the U. S. with Warren and Reinagle's New Company and soon began to write musical works for the stage, including eight operas. The most popular one, THE INDIAN PRINCESS, OR LA BELLE SAUVAGE, was premiered at the New Chestnut Street Theater on April 6, 1808, and published with vocal score and instrumental accompaniment. It tells the story of Captain John Smith and Pocahontas and is one of the first American musical theater works with an American subject. The score survives and has been recorded.

BREAK OF DAY *1961 TV opera by Jones*

A Roman soldier is accused of stealing the body of Christ when the tomb is found empty on Easter morning. George Thaddeus Jones' 30-minute opera *Break of Day*, libretto by Leo Brady, was telecast by ABC TV on April 2, 1961. The singers were Elaine Bonazzi, Roald Rutan, Mildred Allen and Loren Driscoll. William Ayres directed, Wiler Hance produced and Glenn Osser conducted.

BREAKFAST WALTZES *1979 opera by Blumenfeld*

Fritz, a married bookkeeper working for an actress, has an affair with her. When he tries to seduce her maid, he is caught by wife and actress before he has had time for breakfast. Harold Blumenfeld's one-act comic opera *Breakfast Waltzes,* libretto by Charles Kondek, is based on Ferenc Molnar's play *The Witch* and includes musical quotes from a number of famous operas. With the title of *Fritzi*, it was staged by Chicago Opera Theater on November 30, 1988. Des Moines Metro Opera revived it in 1997 with Jason Scarcella as the husband, Janara Kellerman as the actress, Andrea Wilkomirski as the Wife and Cheryl Sheneflt as the Maid.

BRECHT, BERTOLT *German librettist (1898–1956)*

German poet-playwright Bertolt Brecht influenced American opera. through two composers. He and Kurt Weill revolutionized music theater in Germany with *The Threepenny Opera* and other collaborations and both fled to America to escape the Nazis. While they never worked together in the U.S., Brecht's influence on Weill's musical style never went away. Brecht had an equally strong influence on Marc Blitzstein, who was inspired to write his agit-prop opera THE CRADLE WILL ROCK by *The Threepenny Opera.* Brecht encouraged him to finish it after hearing its aria "Nickel Under my Foot." Blitzstein repaid the favor by making *The Threepenny Opera* an American success through his brilliant 1954 adaptation.

BREIL, JOSEPH *American composer (1870–1926)*

Joseph Breil is best known for his silent film scores, most notably D. W. Griffith's *The Birth of a Nation* (1915) and *Intolerance* (1916), but he also composed five operas. The most famous was THE LEGEND which premiered at the Metropolitan Opera House in 1919 with Rosa Ponselle in the leading role; it was staged in London the same year. Breil, born in Pittsburgh, began his musical career as a tenor with a German opera company. After he returned to the U. S., he began to write for the stage. His incidental music for Edward Locke's play *The Climax* in 1909 made him a sought-after composer and in 1912 he began to write scores for silent movies starting with Sarah Bernhardt's popular *Queen Elisabeth*. His comic operas include *Love Laughs at Locksmiths*, libretto by the composer, staged in Kingston, New York, and Portland, Maine, in 1910 and *The Seventh Chord*, libretto by the composer and A. Miller, staged in Chicago in 1913. His last opera was *The Asra* premiered at the Gamut Club Theater in Los Angeles in 1925 shortly before his death.

BRICE, CAROL *American contralto (1918–1985)*

Carol Brice made her debut at New York City Opera in 1958 singing Addie in Marc Blitzstein's REGINA and in 1963 she created the role of the Contralto in Jerome Moross's GENTLEMEN, BE SEATED. She sang the role of Maria in the Houston Grand Opera production of PORGY AND BESS and is featured in recordings of *Regina* and *Porgy and Bess.* She played the Voodoo Princess in Clarence Cameron White's opera OUANGA! when it was staged at the Met. Brice made her first public appearance singing in *The Hot Mikado* at the New York World's Fair in 1939 while still a student. She later sang in several musicals including *Showboat* as Queenie and *Finian's Rainbow* as Maude. Brice, a native of Sedalia, North Carolina, completed her music studies at the Juilliard School.

THE BRIDE ELECT *1897 operetta by Sousa*

Princess Minutezza of Capri is the bride-elect who has to marry King of Timberio by her 18th birthday or forfeit her kingdom. Naturally she loves someone else. John Philip Sousa's *The Bride Elect*, for which he wrote an overly-complicated libretto, premiered in New Haven on December 28, 1897, and opened on Broadway at the Knickerbocker Theater on April 11, 1898. Christie MacDonald sang the role of Princess Minutezza, Albert Hart was King Papagallo, Mabella Baker was Queen Bianca and Frank Pollock was Guido. The popular numbers from the show were the lullaby "The Snow Baby" and "The Bride Elect March," based on the second act finale "Unleash the Dogs of War."

1995 Keith Brion/Razumovsky Symphony. Keith Brion and the Razumovsky Symphony Orchestra play eight numbers from

The Bride Elect, including waltzes, "The Dancing Girl" and songs in praise of champagne, wine, cordials and whisky. The music was recorded in Bratislava in October 1995 for the 1998 American Classics album *John Philips Sousa on Stage.* Naxos CD.

A BRIDE FROM PLUTO   *1982 children's opera by Menotti*

An imperious queen from the planet Pluto comes to earth to find a husband and chooses a spoiled boy named Billy. Gian Carlo Menotti's fanciful 40-minute children's opera *A Bride from Pluto,* libretto by the composer, premiered at the Kennedy Center in Washington, D.C., on April 14, 1982. Nicholas Karousatos played Billy, Pamela Hinchman was the Queen, Robert Keefe was Billy's father, Dana Krueger was his mother and Camille Rosso was his girlfriend. Zack Brown designed the sets and costumes and Lorenzo Muti conducted the orchestra.

THE BRIDGE OF SAN LUIS REY   *2002 opera by Kimper*

Brother Juniper witnesses the death of five people when a rope bridge collapses over a gorge in the Peruvian Andes in 1714 and tells their story throuhg the diaries and letters they leave behind. Paula Kimper's opera *The Bridge of San Luis Rey,* libretto by the composer based on the novel by Thornton Wilder, was premiered by American Opera Projects at The Lighthouse in New York City on April 19, 2002. Michael D. Heath was Brother Juniper, Elaine Valby was the Abbess Madre Maria Del Pilar, Ory Brown was the Marquesa de Montemajor, Jody Scheinbaum was Dona Clara, Victoria Weill was Pepita, Sofia Daulatzai was Camila Perichole, Derrick Ballaard was Esteban, Andrew McQuery was Manuel and Burton Green was Uncle Pio.

BRIGADOON   *1947 operetta by Loewe*

American tourists Tommy and Jeff stumble on Brigadoon, a mysterious village in the Scottish highlands that awakens to life only once every hundred years. Tommy falls in love with Brigadoon villager Fiona and decides to stay. Composer Frederick Loewe and librettist Alan Jay Lerner's fantasy operetta *Brigadoon* was their third Broadway musical and first major success. It premiered at the Shubert Theater in New Haven on February 6, 1947, and opened at the Ziegfeld Theater in New York on March 13, 1947. Marion Bell sang the role of Fiona, David Brooks was Tommy, George Keane was Jeff, Pamela Britton was Meg, Lee Sullivan was Charlie and James Mitchell was Harry. Agnes de Mille choreographed the memorable dances, Cheryl Crawford produced, Robert Lewis staged the production and Franz Allers conducted. *Brigadoon* has entered the opera house repertory and was staged by New York City Opera in 1986.

1947 Original Broadway Cast. Marion Bell is Fiona with David Brooks as Tommy in the original Broadway cast recording with Pamela Brooks, Lee Sullivan, Delbert Anderson and Earl Redding. Franz Allers conducts. RCA Victor LP/CD. **1954 MGM film.** Gene Kelly stars as Tommy opposite Cyd Charisse as Fiona (singing dubbed by Carole Richards) and Jimmy Thomson as Charlie (dubbed by John Gustafson) in an MGM film of the musical produced by Arthur Freed and directed by Vincente Minnelli. Lending support are Van Johnson, Elaine Stewart, Barry Jones and. Despite the talented cast and crew, the film is pretty weak. WB VHS and Soundtrack CD. **1957 Shirley Jones/Jack Cassidy.** Shirley Jones sings Fiona opposite Jack Cassidy as Tommy in this excellent studio recording with Lehman Engel conducting the Columbia orchestra and chorus. Frank Porretta is Charlie and Susan Johnson is Meg. Columbia LP/CD. **1960 Jane Powell/ Robert Merrill/Jan Peerce.** Jane Powell as Fiona joins Metropolitan Opera stars Robert Merrill and Jan Peerce in a recording of highlights from *Brigadoon* with support from Phil Harris. Johnny Green leads the RCA Victor Symphony Orchestra and Chorale. RCA Victor LP/CD. **1966 ABC Television.** Sally Anne Howes is Fiona opposite Robert Goulet as Tommy in this soundtrack recording of the television version of the musical directed by Fielder Cook. Peter Falk, Marilyn Mason, Thomas Carlisle and Findlay Currie lend support. Irwin Kostal conducts. Telecast October 15, 1966. Soundtrack on Columbia LP/CD. **1988 London cast.** The cast of the 1988 London stage production perform highlights from the operetta with Stuart Calvert conducting. Jacinta Mulcahy and Robert Meadmore head the cast with support from Lesley Mackie, Maurice Clarke, Donald Jones and Alan Adams. First Night CD.

BRISTOW, GEORGE FREDERICK   *American composer (1825–1898)*

George Frederick Bristow's RIP VAN WINKLE, a "grand romantic opera in three acts" with a libretto by Jonathan Howard Wainwright based on the Washington Irving tale, is the first American grand opera with an American subject. Although there were earlier American musical theater pieces like John Bray's THE INDIAN PRINCESS and many ballad operas, there were no "grand" operas in the Italian style until Henry Fry's LEONORA in 1845. Bristow, born in Brooklyn and named after Handel, came from a musical family and began his career as a violinist with the New York Philharmonic. He felt American orchestras should play music by American composers so he composed a number of symphonies and string quartets. *Rip Van Winkle* is his only completed opera but he started work on two others, *Columbus* and *King of the Mountain.* Librettist Wainwright altered Irving's story considerably so he could include patriotic scenes from the American Revolution The opera premiered in Niblos's Gardens in New York on September 27, 1855, and the libretto and score were reprinted in 1991.

BRITAIN, RADIE   *American composer (1908–)*

Texas-born Radie Britain is best known for atmospheric orchestral compositions reflecting her native state, like *Texas* and *Red Clay,* but she also composed five works for the stage. The musical drama *Ubiquity,* libretto by Lester Luther, was composed in 1937 and the children's operetta *Happyland,* libretto by A. Greenfield, was completed in 1946. The three-act grand opera *Carillon,* libretto by Rupert Hughes, was created in 1952 and the three-act children's operetta *The Spider and the Butterfly,* libretto by Lena Priscilla Hesselberg, was finished in 1953. Her final stage work was the chamber opera *Kuthara,* libretto by Lester Luther, which was premiered in Santa Barbara, California, on June 24 1961. Britain, who was born and grew up on a ranch near Amarillo, Texas, studied at Clarendon College and the American Conservatory in Chicago and in Paris and Munich.

BRITTEN, BENJAMIN   *English composer (1913–1976)*

Benjamin Britten considered his first opera to be American. PAUL BUNYAN, which he composed in New York City in 1940 with W. H. Auden as librettist, has a folkloristic American subject and it was premiered in New York City in 1941. Unfortunately it was shelved after one performance and not revived until 35 years later. Britten and Auden, who had begun collaborating in the 1930s working on films like *Night Mail,* never worked together again after *Paul Bunyan.* The opera remained almost unknown for many years because Britten would not allow it to be produced until after Auden died. In recent years it has been staged, recorded and re-evaluated as a work of genuine merit.

BROOKS, PATRICIA   *American soprano (1937–1993)*

Patricia Brooks, who created roles in five major American operas, mostly at New York City Opera, was noted for her acting ability as well as her singing. She was Abigail Williams in Robert Ward's THE CRUCIBLE AT NYCO in 1961, Amy Pratt in Carlisle Floyd's THE PASSION OF JONATHAN WADE at NYCO in 1962, the governess Lisabetta in Lee Hoiby's NATALIA PETROVNA at NYCO in 1964, Carry Nation's Mother in Douglas Moore's CARRY NATION at the University of Kansas in 1966 and Smeraldina in Vittorio Giannini's THE SERVANT OF TWO MASTERS AT NYCO in 1967. Brooks, a native of New York City, studied at the Manhattan School and worked as an actress before joining New York City Opera in 1960.

THE BROTHERS   *1954 opera by Antheil*

George Antheil's one-act opera *The Brothers*, libretto by the composer, was premiered at the University of Denver in Colorado on July 28, 1954. Susan Downing sang the role of Mary, Anthony Samarzis was Ken and Richard Dvořák was Abe. Waldo Williamson conducted.

BROTONS, SALVADOR   *American composer (1959–)*

Salvador Brotons' 1990 opera REVEREND EVERYMAN is based on Hugo von Hofmannsthal's updating of the medieval morality play *Everyman*. It was staged in Tallahassee, Florida, in the summer of 1990 and taped for television by Florida State Opera in 1991. Brotons, who was born in Barcelona, moved to the U.S. in 1985. His choral and chamber works are on CD but not his opera.

BROWN, ANNE   *American soprano (1912–)*

Anne Brown created the role of Bess in George Gershwin's PORGY AND BESS at the Colonial Theater in Boston in 1935 and sang the part on Broadway. She played the role again when the opera was revived on Broadway in the early 1940s and she recorded much of the opera with Todd Duncan, the original Porgy. She sings "Summertime" in the 1945 Gershwin film biography *Rhapsody in Blue* and is a participant in the 1998 documentary *Porgy and Bess: An American Voice*. She has also directed stage produc-

tions of the opera in France and Norway. Brown, who was born in Baltimore, emigrated to Norway after becoming discouraged by American attitudes to African Americans. She later sang at the Royal Opera House in Copenhagen. Her 1979 autobiography was a best-seller in Scandinavia but remains unpublished in America.

BROWN, DEBRIA   *American mezzo-soprano (1936–2001)*

Debria Brown created the role of Tituba in Robert Ward's Pulitzer Prize-winning *The Crucible* at New York City Opera in 1961 and the role of Grandmother in David Carlson's DREAMKEEPERS in Utah in 1996. She was Naomi in the revised production of Noa Ain's THE OUTCAST at Houston Grand Opera in 1994, was featured in the 1991 New York City Opera and Houston Grand Opera revival of Carlisle Floyd's THE PASSION OF JONATHAN WADE, played Madame Flora in Gian Carlo Menotti's THE MEDIUM, sang Linda in Kurt Weill's LOST IN THE STARS and performed as Bess, Serena and Maria in George Gershwin's PORGY AND BESS. She joined the faculty of the University of Houston's School of Music in 1992 and sang in its production of Domenick Argento's CASANOVA'S HOMECOMING in 2001. Brown, who was born in New Orleans and studied music as Xavier University, had her first major role on stage at New York City Opera in 1958 singing the role of Carmen. She later performed with opera companies around the world, including Vienna, Hamburg, Brussels, Seattle and Boston.

BROWNING, KIRK   *Television opera director (1921–)*

Kirk Browning helped create opera on television, especially American opera, directing such notable works as Gian Carlo Menotti's AMAHL AND THE NIGHT VISITORS, Igor Stravinsky's THE FLOOD, Thomas Pasatieri's THE TRIAL OF MARY LINCOLN and Lukas Foss's GRIFFELKIN. He directed most of the early TV operas and devised the ways in which they could be shot. He was director of NBC OPERA THEATRE working with SAMUEL CHOTZINOFF, he collaborated with PETER HERMAN ADLER at NET OPERA and he worked on the BELL TELEPHONE HOUR. He directed the first *Live from Lincoln Center* and *Live from the Met* telecasts and he worked with regional opera companies from Washington to Dallas. His earlier American operas include ANTONY AND CLEOPATRA, THE ASPERN PAPERS, THE BALLAD OF BABY DOE, THE CONSUL, DESERET, DOWN IN THE VALLEY, GOYA, LA GRANDE BRETÈCHE, LABYRINTH, LIZZIE BORDEN, MARIA GOLOVIN, MARTIN'S LIE, MY HEART'S IN THE HIGHLANDS, NBC OPERA THEATRE, THE OLD MAID AND THE THIEF, RACHEL LA CUBANA, THE SAINT OF BLEECKER STREET, STREET SCENE, SUMMER AND SMOKE, THE TRIAL AT ROUEN, TROUBLE IN TAHITI and VANESSA. His recent productions include A STREETCAR NAMED DESIRE (1998), CENTRAL PARK (1999) and PORGY AND BESS (2002).

BRUCE, NEELY   *American composer/conductor/pianist (1944–)*

Neely Bruce, who founded the American Music/Theater Group in 1978 to perform American music, based most of his earlier compositions on serial techniques but incorporated popular American music styles into later work. He has written three operas: *Pyramus and Thisbe*, libretto by the composer based on Shakespeare's *A Midsummer Night's Dream*, was composed for college opera workshops and premiered at the University of Alabama in Tuscaloosa in 1965. *The Trials of Psyche*, libretto by J. Orr based on the legend as told by Apuleius, premiered at the University of Illinois in Urbana in 1971. *Americana, or A New Tale of the Genii*, libretto by Tony Connor based on an 18th century allegorical masque, was

Soprano Anne Brown

premiered by the American Music/Theater Group in Hartford, CT, in 1985. Bruce, who was born in Memphis, Tennessee, studied music at the universities of Alabama and Illinois. He has composed a good deal of other vocal music including cantatas and choral works.

BRUNELLE, PHILIP   *American conductor (1943–)*

Philip Brunelle, director of the Plymouth Music Series which he founded in 1969, is one of the most adventurous American opera conductors. He has made major contribution to American opera and has conducted the first recordings of Benjamin Britten's PAUL BUNYAN, Aaron Copland's THE TENDER LAND and Dominick Argento's POSTCARD FROM MOROCCO. He was Music Director of Minnesota Opera for seventeen years and conducted the premiere of many American operas there, including four by Argento: POSTCARD FROM MOROCCO (1971), THE VOYAGE OF EDGAR ALLAN POE (1976), A WATER BIRD TALK (1977) and MISS HAVISHAMS'S WEDDING NIGHT(1981). In addition he conducted Argento's THE ASPERN PAPERS for Washington Opera at the Kennedy Center in 1990. His other conducting premieres include Conrad Susa's TRANSFORMATIONS in 1973, Robert Ward's CLAUDIA LEGARE in 1978, Norman Stokes' *The Jealous Cellist* in 1979 and Susa's church opera THE WISE WOMEN in Dallas in 1994. Brunelle was born in Faribault, Minnesota, and studied at the University of Minnesota and St. Olaf College.

THE BRUTE   *1961 opera by Lawrence Moss*   See THE BOOR

BUBBLES, JOHN W.   *American tenor/dancer (1902–1986)*

John W. Bubbles, a self-taught singer and dancer from Louisville, Kentucky, created the role of Sportin' Life in George Gershwin's PORGY AND BESS in 1935 and Gershwin is said to have modeled some aspects of the character on Bubbles. In 1963 he recorded the role with Leontyne Price as Bess and William Warfield as Porgy. Bubbles, who was born John William Sublett, began his career in vaudeville as the dancing half of the duo Buck and Bubbles. The other half of the team was Ford Lee Buck who created the role of Mingo in *Porgy and Bess*. They appear in several films together including *Cabin in the Sky* (1943) and *A Song is Born* (1948). Bubbles was still impressing audiences at the age of 78 when he sang "It Ain't Necessarily So" in the 1980 revue *Black Broadway.*

BUCCI, MARK   *American composer (1924–2002)*

Mark Bucci's first opera was THE BOOR, libretto by E. Haun based on the Chekhov story, which premiered at Finch College in New York on December 29, 1949. It was followed by a version of *The Beggar's Opera* performed in New York in 1950 and *The Adamses* in 1952. His 1953 musical adaptation of James Thurber's THE THIRTEEN CLOCKS premiered on ABC television in 1953 and was warmly received. It was followed by the humorous THE DRESS and the folk opera *Sweet Betsy from Pike,* both premiered at the 92nd Street YMCA in New York on December 8, 1953. His best-known opera is probably the sad TALE FOR A DEAF EAR premiered at the Berkshire Music Festival in 1957 and staged at New York City Opera in 1958. THE HERO, a 1965 television opera commissioned by Lincoln Center and shown on NET, won the Prix Italia in 1966. His one-act opera *Triad* was premiered at Weber State College in Ogden, Utah, in 1970. His musicals include *Cheaper by the Dozen, Ask Any Girl* and *Our Miss Brooks.* Bucci, a native New Yorker, works in a highly singable style and most of operas have been staged.

BUCK, DUDLEY   *American composer/organist (1839–1909)*

Dudley Buck, best known in his time as an organist and composer of church music, created the most controversial American opera of the 19th century. DESERET, OR A SAINT'S AFFLICTION, libretto by journalist William Augustus Croffut about Mormon leader Brigham Young, premiered at Haverley's Fourteenth Street Theater in New York City on October 11, 1880. A polygamous hero was not considered a suitable subject for an opera and the work was condemned by critics for immoral sensationalism. Buck turned to a Christian subject for his second more grandiose opera. *Serapis,* libretto by the composer, is set in Alexandria, Egypt, during the reign of the Emperor Constantine and describes the triumph of Christianity over the cult of Serapis. It was completed in 1888 but never staged. Buck was born in Hartford, CT, studied at Trinity College in Hartford and in France and Germany, and earned his living primarily as an organist. Buck also wrote secular cantatas, including *The Legend of Don Munio* based on a poem by Longfellow.

BUCK, FORD LEE   *American tenor/pianist (1906–1955)*

Ford Lee Buck, a self-taught singer, pianist and dancer from Louisville, Kentucky, created the role of Mingo in George Gershwin's PORGY AND BESS in 1935. Buck (born Ford Lee Washington) began his career in vaudeville as the piano-playing half of the duo Buck and Bubbles with John Bubbles who created the role of Sportin' Life. They appeared in several films together including *Cabin in the Sky* (1943), *Atlantic City* (1944) and *A Song Is Born* (1948).

BUCKLEY, EMERSON   *American conductor (1916–1989)*

Emerson Buckley is one of the leading conductors of American opera. He led the premieres of Douglas Moore's THE BALLAD OF BABY DOE at Central City and GALLANTRY at Columbia University, Robert Ward's THE CRUCIBLE at New York City Opera, THE LADY FROM COLORADO in Central City and MINUTES TILL MIDNIGHT in Miami and Jerome Morass's GENTLEMEN, BE SEATED at NYCO. He has conducted later productions of Dominick Argento's THE BOOR, Carlisle Floyd's OF MICE AND MEN, Gian Carlo Menotti's THE TELEPHONE, Moore's THE WINGS OF THE DOVE and Ward's HE WHO GETS SLAPPED. He leads the New York City Opera Orchestra on cast recordings of *The Ballad of Baby Doe* and *The Crucible.* Buckley made his debut in 1936 conducting *Rigoletto* with the Columbia Grand Opera company in his native New York and has led orchestras around the U.S. including New York City Opera and San Francisco Opera. He was music director of Miami Opera from 1950 to 1973.

BUCKNER, THOMAS   *American baritone (1943–)*

Thomas Buckner, who has been called the "divo of tomorrow's music," is one of the more prominent singers in the avant-garde electronic opera scene. He is especially known for working with composer Robert Ashley and is featured on most of the recordings of his operas. He created principal roles in ATALANTA (ACTS OF GOD) in Chicago in 1982, IMPROVEMENT in New York in 1991, NOW ELEANOR'S IDEA at the Brooklyn Academy of Music in 1994, eL/AFICIONADO in Tokyo in 1995, BALSEROS in Miami Beach in 1997, YOUR MONEY MY LIFE GOODBYE in 1998 and DUST in New York in 1999. He is best known for the roles of Don in *Improvement* and the forgetful spy in *eL/Aficionado.* He also works with other avant-garde composers including Peter Gena and Annea Lockwood. He created the role of the artist Cézanne, which was written for him, in Daniel Rothman's CÉZANNE'S DOUBT in New

York in 1996 and had one of the lead roles in Pauline Oliveros' six-hour *Lunar Opera* in 2000. Buckner, who comes from one of America's wealthiest families (his grandfather founded IBM) began his career specializing in Elizabethan music and became involved with new music in San Francisco. He co-founded the Arch Ensemble for Experimental Music with Robert Hughes.

BUMBRY, GRACE   *American mezzo-soprano/soprano (1937–)*

Grace Bumbry sang the role of Bess in the Metropolitan Opera's first production of George Gershwin's PORGY AND BESS in 1986, the title role in a recording of Oscar Hammerstein's CARMEN JONES in 1967 and Baba the Turk in a recording of Igor Stravinsky's THE RAKE'S PROGRESS in 1996. The St. Louis-born singer won a Met audition in 1958 but didn't make her debut there until 1965. Her career actually took off in Paris and she became the first African American to sing at Bayreuth in 1961. Bumbry began her career as a mezzo and was noted for her performances as Carmen in her early years.

BUOSO'S GHOST   *1997 opera by Ching*

Michael Ching's *Buoso's Ghost,* libretto by the composer, is a one-act sequel to Puccini's *Gianni Schicchi* using the same setting and cast of characters. In the Puccini opera wealthy Buoso Donati dies and leaves nothing to his greedy relatives. Gianni Schicchi devises a scheme to create a new will by pretending to be Buoso and then makes himself the main benefactor. In Ching's opera, which begins with the final chords of Puccini's opera, Schicchi discovers the relatives had poisoned Buoso and now plan to kill him. He scares them away by pretending to be the ghost of Buoso come back to haunt them. Memphis Opera premiered *Buoso's Ghost* on January 25, 1997, at the Orpheus Theater with their production of the Puccini opera. Kristopher Irmiter played Schicchi, Maria Zouves was Lauretta, Mark Duffin was Rinuccio, John Dougherty was Simone, Patti Jo Stevens was Zita and Kent Fleshman was Betto. Ching conducted. The opera was well received and successfully reprised by Indianapolis Opera in 1999.

BURCHINAL, FREDERICK   *American baritone (1948–)*

Frederick Burchinal created the role of Count Gamba in Virgil Thomson's LORD BYRON at the Juilliard American Opera Center in New York in 1972, Aaron Burr in Alvin Carmines' THE DUEL at the Metropolitan Opera Studio in Brooklyn in 1974, Ebenezer Scrooge (a role written for him) in Thea Musgrave's A CHRISTMAS CAROL at Virginia Opera in 1979 and Henry Gatz in John Harbison's THE GREAT GATSBY at the Metropolitan Opera in 1999. On Broadway he sang the role of Tony in Frank Loesser's *The Most Happy Fella.* He has also played Horace Tabor in Douglas Moore's THE BALLAD OF BABY DOE and Nick Shadow in Igor Stravinsky's THE RAKE'S PROGRESS. Burchinal, who was born in Wichita, Kansas, made his European debut in 1976 in Carlisle Floyd's OF MICE AND MEN at Netherlands Opera.

BURNING BRIGHT   *1993 opera by Lewin*

Middle-aged Joe Saul desperately wants a child but seems unable to father one. His young wife Mordeen sleeps with his assistant Victor so she can conceive get pregnant. Saul is outraged until he finds she did so he could have a child. He accepts the baby as his when it is born. The couple appear as circus performers in the first act, farmers in the second and sea folk in the third. Frank Lewin's three-hour opera *Burning Bright,* libretto by the composer based on a play by John Steinbeck, was premiered by the Yale School of Music in New Haven on November 5, 1993. Charles Damsel was Joe Saul, Sherry Overholt was Mordeen, Rinde Ecker was Victor and Julian Rodescu was Joe's friend Ed. Robert Klingelhoefer and Robert Hunsicker designed the sets, Nick Mangano directed and Raymond Harvey conducted the Philharmonia Orchestra of Yale. The opera was given its first professional production by Opera Festival of New Jersey at the McCarter Theatre in Princeton on July 21, 2000. Todd Thomas sang Joe Saul, Indira Mahajan was Mordeen, Adam Klein was Victor and John Marcus was Ed. Kris Stone designed the sets, Karen Tiller directed (he placed the final act in a space ship) and Patrick Hansen conducted.

THE BURNING HOUSE   *1964 opera by Hovhaness*

The opera takes place in the Universe in outer space. Vahaken, after defeating Death and the Demon, turns himself into a burning house which is seen to be one of billions of burning suns. Alan Hovhaness's symbolic mystical 26-minute opera *The Burning House,* libretto by the composer, was premiered in Gatlinburg, Tennessee on August 23, 1964. Vahaken and Death are both baritones, the Demon is a dancer and the chorus is intended to create a sense of mystical mystery.

BURRS, LESLIE SAVOY   *American composer/flautist*

Philadelphia-based African American composer/flautist Leslie Savoy Burrs, joined with novelist/poet John A. Williams to create an opera for Opera/Columbus based on Virginia Hamilton's book *Many Thousands Gone.* VANQUI combines classical, African and contemporary styles of music in the story of two slave ghosts who "ride the air" during the slave era. Burrs, who has played flute with both jazz and classical ensembles, composes what he calls "urban classical music."

BURTON, STEPHEN DOUGLAS   *American composer (1943–)*

Stephen Douglas Burton has composed six operas but the best-known by far is his three-act *The Duchess of Malfi,* libretto by Christopher Keane based on John Webster's revenge tragedy. It was commissioned by the National Opera Institute and was hailed as a masterpiece by the *Washington Post* when it premiered at Wolf Trap in 1978. Burton's other operas are also based on literary works. *No Trifling with Love* (1970) is based on a play by Alfred de Musset, *Dr. Heidegger's Experiment* (1988) on a story by Nathaniel Hawthorne, *Maggie* on a novel by Stephen Crane and *Benito Cereno* on a story by Herman Melville. Burton, head of the music department at George Mason University, was born in Whittier, CA, and studied at Oberlin and Peabody. Most of his compositions are for voice.

BUSSE, BARRY   *American tenor (1946–)*

Barry Busse created the role of the Man with a Shoe Sample Kit in Dominick Argento's POSTCARD FROM MOROCCO in Minneapolis in 1971 and the role of Louis Sullivan in Daren Hagen's SHINING BROW in Madison in 1992. He played James Bothwell in Virginia Opera's American premiere of Thea Musgrave's MARY QUEEN OF SCOTS in 1978 and is featured on the recording.

BUTLER, HENRY   *American librettist/director (1919–1998)*

Henry Butler wrote the libretto for Marvin David Levy's MOURNING BECOMES ELECTRA, based on the Eugene O'Neill trilogy of plays, which premiered at the Metropolitan Opera in 1967. He also wrote the libretto for Robert Cumming's *The Picnic,* premiered by Central City Opera in 1979, and Chester Biscardi's

Tightrope, first performed in New York in 1985. He staged the premiere of Ned Rorem's Three Sisters who are Not Sisters in Philadelphia in 1971. Born in New York City, he began to direct for the Metropolitan Opera in 1961 and worked with the company for ten years.

BUTLER, JOHN   *American dancer/choreographer (1920–1991)*

John Butler, long associated with Gian Carlo Menotti, created the choreography for a number of American operas. He choreographed Menotti's The Consul for Broadway in 1950, Amahl and the Night Visitors for television in 1951 and The Unicorn, The Gorgon and the Manticore for the Library of Congress in 1964. Menotti made him dance director of the Spoleto Festival in Italy in 1958 where he created and performed many dances. He choreographed Alex Wilder's Miss Chicken Little for TV in 1953, Aaron Copland's The Tender Land for New York City Opera in 1954 and Richard Adler's Little Women with Risë Stevens for TV in 1958. He directed Peggy Glanville-Hicks Nausicaa in Greece in 1961 and arranged the dances. He also arranged dances for composer Lee Hoiby, Paul Bowles and Stanley Hollingsworth. Butler was born in Memphis, Tennessee, and has worked at the Metropolitan Opera and many other operas houses.

ary 27, 1945, two months after the her death, when Hugh Hodgson produced it at the Opera Workshop at the University of Georgia, Athens. The professional premiere took place at Lincoln Center on May 13, 1995, under the direction of Hans Nieuwenhus.

1995 Alice Tully Hall. Ransom Wilson conducts a chamber orchestra and chorus in this recording made at a concert performance in Alice Tully Hall, Lincoln Center, on May 13, 1995. Eugene Perry sings the role of Pierre Lafitte, Lauren Flanigan is Lady Valerie, Charlotte Hellekant is Mary, Anthony Dean Griffey is Tom, Paul Groves is Dominque You, Thomas Paul is the Gaoler, Stephen Mo Hanan is the Barker and the New York Concert Singers are the chorus of tourists and prisoners. Delos CD.

CADMAN, CHARLES WAKEFIELD   *American composer (1881–1946)*

Charles Cadman was the first composer to create an opera specifically for radio: The Willow Tree, "a tale of jealous love," premiered on NBC on October 3, 1932. Cadman was also one of the first to base operas around Native American musical motifs. *Daoma, The Land of the Misty Water (1912)* is based on an Omaha legend about friendship and was composed to a libretto by Nelle Richmond Eberhart, who wrote all his librettos. Shanewis, based on the life of Native American opera singer Tsianina Redfeather

C

CABEZA DE VACA   *1959 dramatic cantata by Antheil*

Spanish explorer Álvar Nuñez Cabeza de Vaca sets out in 1527 to colonize Florida but ends up in Texas as the prisoner of Native Americans. He eventually escapes and reaches a Spanish settlement in Mexico. George Antheil's 60-minute dramatic cantata *Cabeza de Vaca,* libretto by Allan Dowling based on letters by Cabeza de Vaca to King Charles V of Spain, was premiered on CBS-TV on June 10, 1962, three years after the death of the composer. Ron Holgate, Rudolf Petrack and Bruce Zaharides were the soloists singing with the AmorArtist Chorale led by Johannes Somary. Drawings by André Girard illustrating the historical events were used as background for the production.

CABILDO   *1932 opera by Beach*

Newlyweds Tom and Mary visit the Cabildo, the old Governor's palace and prison in New Orleans. Mary dreams about what happened there to pirate Pierre Lafitte and his beloved Lady Valerie at the end of the War of 1812. Amy M. Beach's one-act chamber opera *Cabildo,* libretto by Nan Bagby Stephens, was completed in 1932 when she played it for friends. It was not staged, however, until Febru-

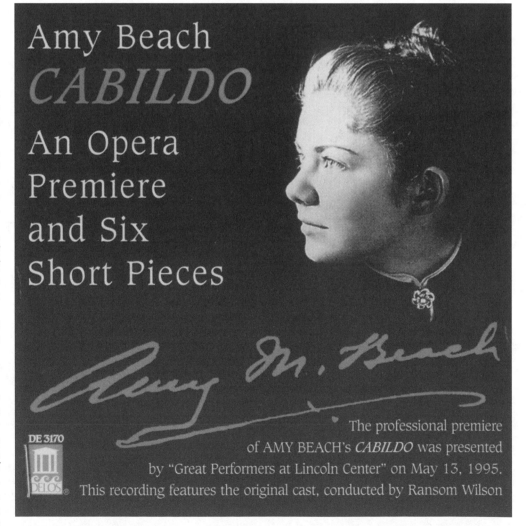

Amy Beach's 1932 opera *Cabildo* was not recorded until 1965 when it was issued as Delos CD.

Blackstone, premiered at the Metropolitan Opera on March 23, 1918. *The Sunset Trail*, featuring Tsianina in the leading role of Wildflower, premiered in Denver on December. 5, 1924. Cadman, born in Johnstown, Pennsylvania, made an intensive study of Native American music and lectured on it. He also toured around the country giving concerts with Princess Tsianina. He had great popular success with songs based around Native American motifs: "At Dawning" was recorded by John McCormack and Paul Robeson while "From the Land of the Sky-Blue Water" was a favorite of singers for many years. His other operas included THE GARDEN OF MYSTERY, based on Nathaniel Hawthorne's macabre story *Rappaccini's Daughter*, which premiered at Carnegie Hall in 1925, and A WITCH OF SALEM, a story about the witch trials in Puritan Salem, that premiered in Chicago in 1926.

THE CAGE *1959 opera by Jones*
An elevator operator dreams of escaping his cage and his demanding mother but changes his mind so his sister can leave the cage to marry. George Thaddeus Jones' one-act opera *The Cage*, libretto by Leo Brady, was previewed at the Catholic University in Washington, DC, in April 1959 and telecast on *The Catholic Hour* on NBC-TV May 10, 1959. One of four short operas commissioned by the National Council of Catholic Men for this TV show, it featured Catholic University students as performers.

CAGE, JOHN *American composer (1912—1992)*
John Cage, who created his own musical system based around *I Ching*-like chance procedures, created operas based on indeterminacy. In fact they are created by their performers who are allowed to sing arias from classic European operas at random. The operas are called simply EUROPERAS 1 AND 2, 3 AND 4 and 5 and combine elements of traditional European opera production in unusual ways. *Europeras 1 and 2,* which has roles for all nineteen of the traditional categories of opera singers, is Cage's equivalent of an elaborate grand opera, while *Europeras 3 and 4* is the equivalent of a chamber opera. They have, to the surprise of many, been staged with success and recorded. Cage, who born in Los Angeles, studied under Arnold Schoenberg and began as an a 12-tone composer,

but he soon went his own way. He first became famous with his "prepared piano" compositions and for his work with dancer/choreographer Merce Cunningham. His ideas have had great influence on contemporary musician and avant-garde artists.

1983 John Cage. This is a documentary centering around a performance held in honor of Cage's 70th birthday. It links a number of his works: *Roaratorio: An Irish Circus on Finnegans Wake, Double Music, Music for Marcel Duchamp, Indeterminacy, Song Books, Branches* and *Inlets.* The 60-minute film was made by Peter Greenaway for his British *4 American Composers* series. Mystic Fire VHS. **1995 From Zero: John Cage.** Cage discusses Zen Buddhism, *Finnegan's Wake,* Marcel Duchamp, music and chance in this 50-minute documentary which includes a performance of Cage's work *Fourteen.* It is performed by the Ives Ensemble with lighting and camera score designed by Andrew Culver. Films for the Humanities and Science VHS.

CAIN, JAMES *American novelist (1992–197?)*
James Cain, who was the son of an opera singer, had hopes for an operatic career but his voice wasn't good enough. He often featured opera in his stories and one of his hard-boiled novels, THE POSTMAN ALWAYS RINGS TWICE, was turned into an opera by composer Stephen Paulus and librettist Colin Graham; it was premiered by Opera Theater of St. Louis in 1982. His novel *Serenade* (1937), about an opera tenor and his troubled rise to stardom, was filmed in 1956 with Mario Lanza as the star. His story *Career in C Major*, about a businessman who has a better voice than his opera-crazy wife, was filmed in 1939 and 1949. Both versions featured specially created "movie operas;" the 1939 film *Wife Husband and Friend* has Sam Pokrass's ARLESIANA and the 1949 film *Everybody Does It* has Mario Castelnuovo-Tedesco's L'AMORE DE FATIMA. Cain, who was born in Annapolis and educated at Washington University, began his writing career as a newspaperman in Baltimore. He found success with his first novel, *The Postman Always Rings Twice* (1934) which has been staged and filmed (twice) and turned into an opera. *Mildred Pierce* (1941) and *Double Indemnity* (1944) were also made into films. Cain moved to Hollywood in 1932 to become a screenwriter but had his greatest success with his novels.

CALDWELL, SARAH *American conductor/director (1924–2006)*
Sarah Caldwell produced and conducted the premieres of four American operas: Robert Middleton's COMMAND PERFORMANCE in November 1961, John La Montaine's BE GLAD THEN AMERICA in 1976, Robert Di Domenica's *The Balcony* in June 1990, and Thomas Whitman's THE BLACK SWAN in 1998. She also conducted the 1976 American premiere of Roger Sessions' MONTEZUMA. Caldwell, born in Maryville, Missouri, studied in Arkansas and Boston and began her musical career as a violinist. She founded the Opera Company of Boston (1959–1990) and won praise for her innovative productions of modern operas. She was the first woman to conduct opera at the Metropolitan Opera.

Conductor/director Sarah Caldwell

CALIFORNIA *American state (1850–)*
California has been involved with creating and presenting American opera since the 19th century, especially in San Francisco and Los Angeles. Two of the first comic operas by American woman composers were staged in San Francisco, Emma Steiner's FLEURETTE in 1889 and Mary Carr Moore's THE ORACLE in 1894. The first American opera to premiere in Los Angeles was Horatio Parker's FAIRYLAND, produced at the Hollywood Bowl in 1915.

Operas set in California include Andrew Imbrie's ANGLE OF

REPOSE (1976), Frederick Converse's THE SACRIFICE (1911), David Conte's opera THE DREAMERS (1996), Harold Farberman's THE LOSERS (1971), Philip Bezanson's GOLDEN CHILD (1960), Lukas Foss's THE JUMPING FROG OF CALAVERAS COUNTY (1950), Jack Beeson's MY HEART'S IN THE HIGHLANDS (1970), Victor Herbert's NATOMA (1911), Carlisle Floyd's OF MICE AND MEN (1970), Nathan Wang's ON GOLD MOUNTAIN (2000), Stephen Paulus's THE POSTMAN ALWAYS RINGS TWICE (1982), Frederick Converse's THE SACRIFICE (1911), and Charles Wakefield Cadman's SHANEWIS (1918).

California-born opera composers include William Bergsma (Oakland), Stephen Douglas Burton (Whittier), John Cage (Los Angeles), David Del Tredici (Cloverdale), Alva Henderson (San Luis Obispo), Harry Partch (Oakland), Joseph Redding (Sacramento) and Morton Subotnick (Los Angeles).

California-born singers include baritone Rodney Gilfry (Covina), tenor Grayson Hirst (Ojai), contralto Claramae Turner (Dinuba), baritone Theodor Uppman (San José), soprano Benita Valente (Delcano) and soprano Carol Wilcox (Antioch).

California opera companies and premieres are listed by city below.

Azusa: Azusa Pacific University's School of Music presents productions of operas by its students.

Berkeley: American operas premiered by Berkeley Opera at UC Berkeley include William J. McCoy's *Egypt* (1921), Roger Sessions' THE TRIAL OF LUCULLUS (1947), Frank Fragale's *Dr. Jekyll and Mr. Hyde* (1958), Arnold Elston's THE LOVE OF DON PERLIMPLIN (1958) and Andrew Imbrie's THREE AGAINST CHRISTMAS (1964). Sessions' cantata WHEN LILACS LAST IN THE DOORYARD BLOOMED was commissioned by UC Berkeley which premiered it in 1971. John Adams' I WAS LOOKING AT THE CEILING AND THEN I SAW THE SKY premiered at the Zellerbach Playhouse in Berkeley in 1995.

Cabrillo: Beth Anderson's oratorio *Joan* was premiered at the Cabrillo Music Festival on August 22, 1974.

Costa Mesa: Opera Pacific, the opera company of Santa Ana, presents productions in the Orange County Performing Arts Center in Costa Mesa. It's first season in 1987 included George Gershwin's PORGY AND BESS and Leonard Bernstein's WEST SIDE STORY. Subsequent seasons featured Forrest/Wright's KISMET in 1988, Frederick Loewe's MY FAIR LADY in 1989, Jerome Kern's SHOW BOAT in 1990, Marc Blitzstein's REGINA in 1996 and Leonard Bernstein's CANDIDE in 2004. Elliot Goldenthal's FIRE WATER PAPER: A VIETNAM ORATORIO was commissioned by the Pacific Symphony Orchestra which premiered it at the Arts Center in 1995.

Davis: Larry Austin's experimental operas *Roma* and *The Maze* were premiered at UC Davis in 1966.

Fairfield: North Bay Opera's productions in the Fairfield Center For Creative Arts Theater have included Gian Carlo Menotti's AMAHL AND THE NIGHT VISITORS, Douglas Moore's THE BALLAD OF BABY DOE and Stephen Sondheim's A LITTLE NIGHT MUSIC.

Idyllwild: Three operas premiered at the Idyllwild School of Music Bowman Art Center Theater. Josef Marais, the composer half of the folk duo Marais and Miranda, premiered his one-act *Tony Beaver* on August 1, 1952, and his two-act *African Heartbeat* on August 28, 1953. James Low premiered his *Moby Dick*, based on the Melville novel, at the School on September 2, 1955.

Long Beach: Long Beach Opera, which performs in the Center Theater, staged Douglas Moore's THE BALLAD OF BABY DOE in 1987 and commissioned and premiered Stewart Wallace's HOPPER'S WIFE in 1997.

Los Angeles: Los Angeles has been a center of American opera since the 1910s, despite not having a major opera company until recently, and has had a large number of premieres. They include Horatio Parker's FAIRYLAND at the Hollywood Bowl in 1915, Joseph Breil's *The Asra* at the Gamut Club Theater in 1925, Mary Carr Moore's *Los Rubios* at the Greek Theater in 1931, Mary Carr Moore's DAVID RIZZIO at the Shrine Auditorium in 1932, Claude Lapham's *Sakura* at the Hollywood Bowl in 1933 in Japanese, Charles Pemberton's *The Painter of Dreams* at USC in 1934, Morris Ruger's *Gettysburg* at the Hollywood Bowl in 1938, Heitor Villa-Lobos' MAGDALENA at the Philharmonic Auditorium in 1948, Ernst Krenek's DARK WATERS at UCLA in 1951, George Antheil's VOLPONE at USC in 1953, Walter Schumann's *John Brown's Body* at Philharmonic Auditorium in 1953, Morris Ruger's THE FALL OF THE HOUSE OF USHER in 1953, Ethel Leginska's *The Rose and the Ring* in 1957, and Ernest Kanitz's *Room No. 12*, *Royal Auction* and *The Lucky Dollar* at UCLA in 1958. Later premieres include Robert Gross's *The Bald Soprano* at Occidental College in 1962, Alan Hovhaness's *Pilate* at Pepperdine College in 1966, Edmund Najera's *The Freeway Opera* at Immaculate Heart College (now the American Film Institute campus) in 1968, Roy Travis's THE PASSION OF OEDIPUS at UCLA in 1968, Ellis Kohs' *Amerika* at Western Opera Theater in 1970, Eugene Zador's YEHU: A CHRISTMAS LEGEND at the Municipal Art Department in 1974, Robert Gross's *Project 1521* at Occidental College in 1974 and Bob Downard's *Celebration of the Angels* in 1980. Los Angeles Opera (formerly Los Angeles Music Center Opera), founded in 1986, provides a home for major productions. It has not favored American opera but it premiered Tobias Picker's FANTASTIC MR. FOX in 1999 and Deborah Drattell's *Nicholas and Alexandra* in 2003 and it staged Maurice Sendak and Oliver Knussen's WHERE THE WILD THINGS ARE in 1990 and George Gershwin's PORGY AND BESS in 1995. Plácido Domingo was named Artistic Director in 2000. UCLA Performing Arts often features American operas like Philip Glass's MONSTERS OF GRACE which premiered there in 1998. Los Angeles Music Theatre Company presents operas regularly at the John Anson Ford Amphitheater in Hollywood. Lyric Opera of Los Angeles performs unusual operas for schoolchildren and their families.

Modesto: Townsend Opera Players (TOP), founded in 1982, presents operas and music theater at the Little Opera House in Modesto. Its American productions include the Wright/Forrest operetta KISMET.

Napa: The Jarvis Conservatory in Napa is famous for presenting Spanish zarzuelas in English, probably the only place in the world where this is being done. Its superb productions are recorded and have been issued on video.

Newport Beach: Mikel Rouse's FUNDING, a video opera about alienated New Yorkers, premiered at the Orange County Art Museum in Newport Beach October 7, 2001.

Oakland: Bertha Weber's *The Mysterious Characters of Mr. Fu* premiered in Oakland in 1932 and Derrick Lehmer's *The Necklace of the Sun* in 1934. Robert Ashley presented a revised version of his experimental THAT MORNING THING at Mills College in Oakland in 1970 and premiered *In Memoriam Kit Carson* in 1971. Oakland Lyric Opera presents productions at the 12th Street City Center Stage in Oakland.

Ojai: The Ojai Music Festival, founded in 1947, presents chamber operas with other classical music works.

Ontario: Samuel Earle Blakeslee's THE LEGEND OF WIWASTE, based on Dakota Sioux legends, premiered at Chaffey College in 1924 with Tsianina Redfeather Blackstone, the first Native American opera singer, in the title role.

Palm Desert: Hubert Bird's *The Powerful Potion of Dr. Dee* was premiered at the College of the Desert October 24, 1971.

Palo Alto: West Bay Opera, founded in 1956 and said to be the second oldest opera company in California, presents productions at the Lucie Stern Theatre. Its American presentations have included Kirke Mechem's TARTUFFE.

Pasadena: Guy Williams' three-act *The Master Thief*, libretto by Frances Tipton, was premiered at the Community Playhouse in Pasadena on November 28, 1933. Four operas by Mary Caldwell have premiered at the Pasadena Civic Auditorium: *Pepito's Golden Flower* in 1955, *A Gift of Song* in 1961, *The Night of the Star* in 1965, and *In the Fullness of Time* in 1978.

Redlands: Three operas premiered at the University of Redlands: Wayne Bohrnstedt's *The Necklace*, libretto by Lucile March, in 1956; Lucille Crews Marsh's *The Concert* in 1958; and Newton Miller's *The Flying Machine* in 1969.

Sacramento: Sacramento Opera, founded in 1947, presents its operas in the Community Center Theater. Most of its repertory is European, but it premiered Monroe Kanouse's *Gambling Jones* in 1987 and co-commissioned David Carlson's THE MIDNIGHT ANGEL, which it staged in 1993.

San Diego: San Diego has a long tradition of opera; its first professional company was formed in 1919 and Charles Wakefield Cadman's *The Sunset Trail* was premiered at the Spreckles Theater on August 23, 1920.

San Diego Opera, founded in 1950, is the major company today and began to stage opera at the Civic Theater in 1966. It presents American operas on a regular basis and has mounted notable premieres: Alva Henderson's MEDEA in 1972, Gian Carlo Menotti's LA LOCA with Beverly Sills in 1979, and Myron Fink's THE CONQUISTADOR in 1997. Its other American opera productions include Carlisle Floyd's COLD SASSY TREE, OF MICE AND MEN, THE PASSION OF JONATHAN WADE and SUSANNAH, George Gershwin's PORGY AND BESS, André Previn's A STREETCAR NAMED DESIRE and Menotti's THE MEDIUM, THE SAINT OF BLEECKER STREET, THE TELEPHONE and HELP, HELP, THE GLOBOLINKS. San Diego Comic Opera, founded in 1979, presents operas and operettas at the Casa del Prado Theater in Balboa Park. Past productions have included Jerry Bock's FIDDLER ON THE ROOF, Cole Porter's KISS ME KATE and Stephen Sondheim's A LITTLE NIGHT MUSIC.

San Francisco: Opera was first staged in San Francisco in 1851 and the city has been enthusiastic about opera ever since. Presentation of American opera began in 1894 at Golden Gate Hall with a production of Mary Carr Moore's comic opera THE ORACLE. Noah Brandt premiered his light opera *Captain Cook* at the Bush Street Theater in 1895, while Victor Herbert premiered his comic opera *The Viceroy* at the Columbia Theater in 1900. Humphrey Stewart's premiered a series of comic and dramatic operas in San Francisco in the following years, including *His Majesty* in 1900, *The Conspirators* in 1900, *Montezuma* in 1903, *The Oracle* in 1910, and *The Hound of Heaven* in 1924. San Francisco Opera, created in 1922, presented Joseph Redding's *Fay-Yen-Fah* at the Columbia Theater in 1926, following its premiere in Monte Carlo. The company did not premiere an American opera until 1961 when it staged Norman Dello Joio's BLOOD MOON. Andrew Imbrie's ANGLE OF REPOSE was premiered in 1976, John Harbison's A WINTER'S TALE in 1979, Conrad Susa's THE DANGEROUS LIAISONS in 1994, Bobby McFerrin's *Gethsemane* in 1995, André Previn's A STREETCAR NAMED DESIRE in 1998 and Jake Heggie's DEAD MAN WALKING in 2000. John Adams' THE DEATH OF KLINGHOFFER was co-commissioned by the company and given its West Coast premiere in 1992. The company's Opera Center premiered Kirke Mechem's TARTUFFE in 1980, Vivien Fine's THE WOMEN IN THE GARDEN in 1982, and John Harbison's FULL MOON IN MARCH in

1982. Pocket Opera, founded in 1976 by Donald Pippin, presents "pocket" versions of operas in English. They are mostly reductions of European operas but have included Igor Stravinsky's THE RAKE'S PROGRESS, George Gershwin's *Oh, Kay!* and Jerome Kern's *Oh, Boy.* Musical Traditions, Inc., presents its productions at various venues. They have included Stephen Mackey's RAVENSHEAD and M. Wold's *A Little Girl Dreams of Taking the Veil.*

San José: Opera in San José developed out of opera workshops at its university. Robert Moran's *Let's Build a Nut House* premiered at San Jose State College in 1969. San José Community Opera Theater, an offshoot of the college founded in 1977, showed a strong interest in American opera; its students staged Virgil Thomson's THE MOTHER OF US ALL in the first season, staged Gian Carlo Menotti's THE TELEPHONE and THE MEDIUM in the second and premiered Alva Henderson's THE LAST LEAF in the third. Opera San José, a professional company that grew out of the student group, was started in 1984 and presents operas at Montgomery Theater. It premiered Henderson's WEST OF WASHINGTON SQUARE in 1988 and Henry Mollicone's HOTEL EDEN in 1989 and staged Carlisle Floyd's OF MICE AND MEN in 1990.

San Luis Obispo: Pacific Repertory Opera presents operas, mostly classic European works, at the Performing Arts Center in San Luis Obispo. Its productions have included Gian Carlo Menotti's AMAHL AND THE NIGHT VISITORS.

Santa Ana: Opera Pacific, based in Santa Ana, presents its operas at Segerstrom Hall in the Orange County Performing Arts Center in Costa Mesa. (See Costa Mesa for its productions.)

Santa Barbara: Vladimir Dukelsky (aka Vernon Duke) premiered his opera *Mistress into Maid* at UC Santa Barbara on December 12, 1958. Radie Britain's *Kuthara*, libretto by Lester Luther, was premiered in Santa Barbara in 1961. Jeffery Babcock premiered his multimedia opera *Mirrors* at UC Santa Barbara on April 6, 1972. The major opera company today is Opera Santa Barbara, founded in 1996 as Santa Barbara Grand Opera; it presents productions in the Lobero Theatre.

Santa Cruz: Lou Harrison's RAPUNZEL was staged and recorded at UC, Santa Cruz, in 1996.

Sonoma: David Conte's *The Dreamers* was commissioned by Sonoma Opera and premiered in 1996 to celebrate the city's sesquicentennial.

Stockton: Two operas were premiered at the College of the Pacific in Stockton. Burdette Fore's *Aria da Capo* was presented in 1951 and Standworth Beckler's THE OUTCASTS OF POKER FLAT in 1960.

Sun Valley: Andrew McClenahan's *The Comedy of Errors*, based on the Shakespeare play, premiered at the Southern California Conservatory on December 15, 1980.

Tiburon: The Marin Opera Company is based in Tiburon.

Walnut Creek: Festival Opera presents operas at the Dean Lesher Regional Center for the Arts in Walnut Creek.

THE CALIPH'S MAGICIAN   *1917 opera by Wayditch*

A Magician performs incredible, often salacious, illusions for the Caliph in an ancient city in the Middle East, but his story about Suh and Sah arouses the Caliph's ire. The Magician disappears before an admiring crowd. Gabriel Von Wayditch's 90-minute one-act opera *The Caliph's Magician*, libretto by the composer in Hungarian, was composed in the South Bronx in 1917 after had Wayditch emigrated to the U.S. It was not performed until 1975 when it was recorded in Hungary.

1975 Budapest National Opera. András Nagy-Soljom sings the role of the Caliph with Zsolt Bende as the Magician in this recording made in Budapest. Sandor Palcso is the Emir, Istvan Rozsos is Nawab, Julia Pászthi is the Eunuch, Csilla Ötvös is Odalisk, and the Djinns are sung by Csaba Otvos and Arpad Kishegi. András Kórody conducts the Budapest National Opera Orchestra and Chorus. Qualiton LP/VAI CD.

CALLOWAY, CAB   *American singer/bandleader (1907–1994)*
Scat singing jazz legend Cab Calloway was George Gershwin's real-life model for the character of Sportin' Life in PORGY AND BESS, and Calloway returned the favor by singing the role on stage and disc. He toured the world in 1952 and 1953 in the Breen production of the opera with Leontyne Price as Bess and William Warfield as Porgy He can be heard singing Sportin' Life's famous aria "It Ain't Necessarily So" on a 1953 recording, on the soundtrack of the 1959 film (replacing Sammy Davis Jr.) and on a 1993 highlights recording. Calloway, born in Rochester, NY, with the full name of Cabell, became famous for scat phrases like "hi di hi di ho" and songs like "Minnie the Moocher." He was the major attraction at the Cotton Club in the early 1930s when Gershwin came to hear him. Calloway also starred in the 1967 all-black stage version of *Hello, Dolly!* opposite Pearl Bailey.

CALVARY   *1971 opera by Pasatieri*
Lazarus and Judas take part in poetic confrontations with Christ. Thomas Pasatieri's one-act chamber opera *Calvary*, using a play by W. B. Yeats as libretto, was premiered at St. Thomas Episcopal Church in the Seattle Opera Festival on April 7, 1971. Clayne Robison was Christ, Archie Drake was Lazarus, Gerald Thorsen was Judas, and Douglas Manning, Winston Cook and Steven Tachell were the Roman soldiers. Angelamaria Ross designed the costumes, Robert De Simone directed the opera and Henry Holt conducted the chamber orchestra. The opera was staged at Wolf Trap in 1974 and has become popular with churches around America.

CAMELOT   *1960 operetta by Loewe*
Frederick Loewe's *Camelot* is one of the great American operettas with a superb score and a bittersweet libretto by Alan Jay Lerner about a love affair that brings ruin to a kingdom. The story is based on T. H. White's magical novel *The Once and Future King*, a retelling of the events surrounding King Arthur and the Knights of the Round Table. The doom-creating love affair between Guenevere and Lancelot is the focus of the story, but there is ample room for idealism, dreams, humor and villainy. *Camelot* was tested in Toronto and Boston before it opened on Broadway at the Majestic Theater on December 3, 1960. Richard Burton played King Arthur, Julie Andrews was Queen Guenevere, Robert Goulet was Sir Lancelot, Roddy McDowell was Mordred, Robert Coote was King Pellinore and M'el Dowd was Morgan Le Fay. Oliver Smith designed the sets, Moss Hart directed the production, and Franz Allers conducted the orchestra.
1960 Broadway cast. Julie Andrews and Richard Burton are Guenevere and Arthur in this fine original cast recording with Franz Allers conducting. Robert Goulet is Lancelot, Roddy McDowell is Mordred, Mary Sue Berry is the spirit Nimuë and Bruce Yarnell, James Gannot and John Cullum are the knights who join Andrews in song. Columbia LP/CD. **1964 London cast.** Elizabeth Larner and Laurence Harvey are Guenevere and Arthur in this London cast recording with Kenneth Alwyn conducting. Barry Kent is Lancelot and the other cast members are Nicky Henson, Josephine Gordon and Kit Williams. HMV and First Night LP/CD. **1967 Warner Brothers film.** Richard Harris is King Arthur with Vanessa Redgrave as Guenevere in the Warner Broth-

ers film version of the operetta written by librettist Alan Jay Lerner. Franco Nero plays Lancelot but his singing is dubbed by Gene Merlino. The film is nicely directly by Joshua Logan but doesn't have nearly the appeal of the stage version. Warner's VHS/Soundtrack LP. **1998 Bryan Terfel.** Baritone Bryan Terfel sings three songs from *Camelot* on his Frederick Loewe tribute album *If Ever I Would Leave You*. Phil Daniel conducts the English Northern Philharmonia. DG CD. **2000 Arlene Auger.** Arlene Auger sings Guenevere's lament "Before I Gaze at You Again" from *Camelot* on her album *Arlene Auger: American Soprano*. Delos CD.

CAMERA THREE   *CBS television series (1953–1979)*
Camera Three devoted programs to the American operas THE ACCUSED, THE CRADLE WILL ROCK, THE FOUR NOTE OPERA and WASHINGTON SQUARE and to American opera composers THOMAS PASATIERI and KURT WEILL. As it presented opera in a low-budget, bare-bones recital format on Sunday mornings, it could do almost anything that didn't cost much money. The series was dropped by CBS in 1978 but revived on PBS in 1979. ROGER ENGLANDER was producer of the series for three years.

CAMILLE   *1930 opera by Forrest*
Courtesan Camille falls in love with a young man in Paris but gives him up for his family's honor and dies after making the sacrifice. Forrest Hamilton's *Camille*, libretto by the composer based on the Alexandre Dumas novel/play that was the basis of Verdi's *La traviata*, was premiered by Chicago Civic Opera on December 10, 1930. It was sung in French at the insistence of Mary Garden who played Marguerite opposite Charles Hackett. Forrest, whose first opera *Yzdra* was dedicated to Garden, was much admired by the diva who persuaded Chicago Civic Opera to premiere *Camille*. It was given six performances and reprised in Boston in 1931. Greta Garbo starred in a 1937 film called *Camille* based on the story, but it used Verdi's music for its soundtrack.

CAMPBELL, PATTON   *American set/costume designer (1926–)*
Omaha-born Patton Campbell designed sets and costumes for a large number of American operas that premiered in New York City, Kansas City, and Santa Fe Opera. After studies at Yale, he made his debut designing the costumes for the premiere of Douglas Moore's THE BALLAD OF BABY DOE at Central City. His other opera premieres include Jack Beeson's LIZZIE BORDEN and CAPTAIN JINKS OF THE HORSE MARINES, Carlisle Floyd's WUTHERING HEIGHTS, Lee Hoiby's NATALIA PETROVNA, Moore's WINGS OF THE DOVE, Ned Rorem's MISS JULIE, Gunther Schuller's THE FISHERMAN AND HIS WIFE and Robert Ward's LADY FROM COLORADO. He also designed new productions of Leonard Bernstein's TROUBLE IN TAHITI and Floyd's SUSANNAH at New York City Opera.

CANDIDE   *1956 operetta by Bernstein*
Candide and Cunegonde believe this is the best of all possible worlds as they have been taught by their mentor Pangloss. After their country is invaded and they are forced to travel around the world undergoing kidnappings, rapes, deaths and similar horrors, they find that such a philosophy has little relevance for them. Leonard Bernstein's *Candide*, an operatic operetta, is based on Voltaire's satirical novel *Candide*. The adaptation for the original 1956 Broadway production was by Lillian Hellman with lyrics by Richard Wilbur, John Latouche, Dorothy Parker, Hellman and Bernstein, but it has been tinkered with many times since. The overture was immediately recognized as a musical marvel and

Des Moines Metro Opera staged Leonard Bernstein's operatic operetta *Candide* in 2002. Photograph courtesy of Des Moines Metro Opera.

entered the concert repertory while the coloratura soprano aria "Glitter and Be Gay" has become a recital standard. The operatic operetta premiered at the Colonial Theater in Boston on October 29, 1956, and opened in New York on December 1, 1956, at the Martin Beck Theater. Barbara Cook played Cunegonde, Robert Rounseville was Candide, Max Adrian was Dr. Pangloss and Martin, Irra Petina was the Old Lady, William Olvis was the Governor of Buenos Aires, Boris Aplon was the Marquis, Louis Edmonds was Maximilian, Joseph Bernard was the Sultan, Conran Raid was the King of Hess and William Chapman was the lawyer Ferone. Oliver Smith designed the sets, Irene Sharaff designed the costumes, Tyrone Guthrie directed and Samuel Krachmalnick conducted. In a 1973 revision by Harold Prince, the character of Paquette was added and the pessimistic Martin was dropped. In a 2004 production at Avery Fisher Hall in New York, Kristin Chenoweth took on the role of Cunegonde opposite Thomas Allen, Paul Groves and Patti Lupone. See also CANDIDE OVERTURE, GLITTER AND BE GAY, MAKE OUR GARDEN GROW.

1956 Original Broadway cast. Barbara Cook is Cunegonde, Robert Rounseville is Candide, and Max Adrian is Dr. Pangloss in this original cast recording. Irra Petina is the Old Lady, William Olvis is the Governor, William Chapman is Ferone, and Robert Mescrobian is the Prince. Samuel Krachmalnick conducts the orchestra. Columbia LP/Sony Broadway CD. **1963 Alfred Drake/Roberta Peters.** Alfred Drake and Roberta Peters perform numbers from *Candide* with the Ray Charles Singers and Enoch Light and his Orchestra on the album *Alfred Drake and Roberta Peters Sing the Popular Music of Leonard Bernstein.* Peters sings "Glitter and Be Gay" and Drake sings "The Best of All Possible Worlds. Command LP. **1974 Chelsea Theater Center.** Maureen Brennan is Cunegonde, Mark Baker is Candide and Leis J. Stadlen is Voltaire/Pangloss in this cast recording of a Harold Prince production at the Chelsea Theater Center of Brooklyn. June Gable is the Old Lady, Deborah St. Darr is Paquette, Sam Freed is Maximilian and Carolann Page has three small roles. The new book was written by Hugh Wheeler with added lyrics by Stephen Sondheim. John Mauceri conducted. Columbia LP. **1985 New York City Opera.** Erie Mills is Cunegonde, David Eisler is Candide and John Langston is Voltaire/Pangloss in this cast recording of a New York City Opera production. Joyce Castle is the Old Lady, Maris Clemente is Paquette, Scott Reeve is Maximilian and Ralph Bassett while Robert Brubaker, Ivy Austin, Rhoda Butler, Don Yule, William Ledbetter, Maria Donaldi, James Billings and Jack Harrold sing the small roles. John Mauceri conducts the New York City Opera Orchestra. New World Records LP/CD. **1989 Barbican Center.** June Anderson is Cunegonde with Jerry Hadley as Candide in an "operatic" concert performance of the operetta videotaped at the Barbican Centre in London on December 13, 1989, with Bernstein conducting the London Symphony Chorus and Orchestra. Adolph Green is Pangloss, Christa Ludwig is the Old Lady, Kurt Ollmann is Maximilian, Nicolai Gedda is the Governor and Della Jones is Paquette while Clive Bayley, Neil Jenkins, Lindsay Benson, Richard Stuart and John Treleaven sing the small roles. Humphrey Burton directed the 147-minute video. Polygram DVD/VHS/LD. A recording featuring the same cast was made at the Abbey Road Studio in London during the same week. DG 2-

CD box. **1991 Roberta Alexander.** Roberta Alexander sings "It Must Be So" and "Is This All Then" on her album *Bernstein: Songs.* Tan Rome provides support. Etcetera CD. **1991 Renée Fleming/Jerry Hadley.** Renée Fleming and Jerry Hadley sing "Make Our Garden Grow" with the Collegiate Chorale at a gala at Lincoln Center. James Conlon conducts the Metropolitan Opera Orchestra in the program *A Salute to American Music.* Telecast by PBS November 10, 1991. RCA Victor CD. **1993 Dawn Upshaw.** awn Upshaw sings the aria "Glitter and Be Gay" from the operetta on her album *I Wish It So.* Eric Stern conducts the orchestra. Elektra Nonesuch CD. **1994 Lyric Opera of Chicago Commentary.** Critical analysis of *Candide* by Alfred Glasser in the Women's Board of Lyric Opera series. It includes musical excerpts, plot summary, composer biography and social and historical background. Lyric Opera Commentaries audiocassette. **1995 Lyric Opera of Chicago.** Elizabeth Futral is Cunegonde with Barry Banks as Candide in a Lyric Opera of Chicago production broadcast May 20, 1995. Timothy Nolen is Voltaire/Pangloss, Phyllis Pancella is the Old Lady, Deborah Darr is Paquette and Dale Travis is Maximilian. George Manahan conducts. On audiocassette. **1996 Boston Brass.** The Boston Brass quintet, based at Boston College, pay homage to Candide in an instrumental version of the aria "Glitter and Be Gay." recorded at Trinity Chapel at Boston College. It's on the album *Stealing the Show.* Summit CD. **1997 Scottish Opera.** Marilyn Hill Smith is Cunegonde and Mark Beudart is Candide with Justine Brown conducting the Scottish Opera Orchestra and Chorus. Nikolas Grace is Voltaire/Pangloss, Ann Howard is the Old Lady, Gayor Miles is Paquette, Mark Tinkler is Maximilian, Bonaventura Bottone is the Captain and Governor and Leon Greene sings the small roles. Jay Records CD. **1997 Hal Prince revival.** Harolyn Blackwell is Cunegonde with Jason Danieley as Candide in this cast recording of a 1997 Broadway revival staged by Hal Prince. Jim Dale is Voltaire/Pangloss, Andrea Martin is the Old Lady, Brent Barrett is Maximilian, Stacey Logan is Paquette, Arte Johnson is Hugo and Mal Z. Lawrence is the Grand Inquisitor. Eric Stern conducts. RCA Victor CD. **1999 Royal National Theatre.** Alex Kelly is Cunegonde opposite Daniel Evans as Candide in this cast recording of a Royal National Theater production in London. Simon Russell Beale is Voltaire/Pangloss, Beverly Klein is the Old Lady, Elizabeth Renihan is Paquette, Simon Day is Maximilian and Clive Rowe is Cacambo. Mark W. Dorrell conducts. First Night Records CD. **1999 Renée Fleming.** Renée Fleming sings "Glitter and Be Gay" on her recital album *I Want Magic* with James Levine conducting the Metropolitan Opera Orchestra. London Classics CD. **2000 Taking a Chance on Love.** This off-Broadway revue, based on the lyrics and life of John Latouche, features two songs written for *Candide,* "Plain Words" and "Ringaroundrosie." The singers are Eddie Korbich, Terry Burrell, Jerry Dixon and Donna English. Original Cast Records CD.

CANDIDE OVERTURE   *Overture: Candide (1956).*
Music: Leonard Bernstein
Leonard Bernstein's overture to *Candide* has become one of the most performed opera/operetta overtures in the repertoire, nearly rivaling the *William Tell* overture. There are a great many recordings. Leonard Bernstein conducts the overture with different orchestras on several albums, including the New York Philharmonic on *The Essential Bernstein* (Sony Classics CD) and the London Symphony Orchestra on the set *Centenary Collection* (DG CD). Skitch Henderson conducts the New York Pops on the album *From Berlin to Bernstein* (Centaur CD). Paul Freeman conducts the Orchestra of the Americas on the album *An American Composers*

Salute (Pro Arte CD). Mariss Jansons conducts the Oslo Philharmonic Orchestra on the *World Encores* (EMI Classics CD). Jacques Delacote conducts the London Arts Orchestra on the album *José Carreras and Friends Sing Operatic Arias and Popular Songs* (Laserlight CD). On the original cast album the Overture is played by the theater orchestra led by Samuel Krachmalnick, on the New York City Opera recording by John Mauceri conducting the New York City Opera Orchestra, on the Barbican concert recording by Bernstein conducting the London Symphony Orchestra, and on the Royal National Theatre recording by Mark W. Dorrell.

THE CANTERBURY PILGRIMS   *1917 opera by De Koven*
English poet Chaucer leads a pilgrimage to Canterbury in 1387 and becomes interested in the Prioress, while the much-married Wife of Bath hatches schemes to snag him as her next husband. Reginald De Koven's four-act folk opera *The Canterbury Pilgrims,* libretto by Percy MacKaye based on Chaucer's *The Canterbury Tales,* premiered at the Metropolitan Opera on March 8, 1917. Johannes Sembach was Chaucer, Margaret Ober was the Wife of Bath, Edith Mason was the Prioress, Paul Althouse was the Squire, Albert Reiss was King Richard, Marie Sundelius was Johanna, Max Block was the Friar, Robert Leonhardt was the Man of Law, Basil Ruuysadael was the Miller, and Giulio Rossi was the Host. Arthur Bodansky conducted the Metropolitan Opera Orchestra and Chorus.

THE CANTOR'S SON   *1937 American "movie opera"*
The Cantor's Son was intended to be the first of six American "movie operas" sung in Yiddish with music by Alexander Olshanetsky produced by Sidney M. Goldin. Goldin died while it was being filmed so this is the only one that was ever made. It tells the story of a cantor's son from Belz in Poland who runs off with a theater troupe and goes to New York where he finds success as a singer and becomes a cantor. He returns home to Belz after fifteen years and is reunited with his family. Moishe Oysher plays the cantor's son Shloimele, Florence Weiss is his singing partner Helen and Judith Abarbanell is his old love Rivkele. Louis Freiman wrote the screenplay, Alexander Olshanetsky conducted the orchestra, Frank Zucker was director of photography and Ilya Motyleff directed the 90-minute film for Eron Pictures.

EL CAPITAN   *1896 comic opera by Sousa*
The Viceroy of Peru is secretly the rebel leader El Capitan and publicly a blowhard. Playing both roles he is easily able to defeat himself as the rebel and solidify his position as Viceroy. John Philip Sousa's famous comic opera *El Capitan,* libretto by Charles Klein, is best known today for its march but it has been staged a number of times recently by opera companies. The opera premiered in New York with DeWolf Hopper as Viceroy Don Errico Medigua, Alfred Klein as Señor Amabile Pozzo, Alice Homser as Princess Marghanza, T. S. Guise as Don Luiz Cazarro, John W. Parr as Scaramba, Edna Wallace-Hopper as Estrelda, and Bertha Waltzingera as Isabel. H.A. Cripps directed and John S. Hillyer conducted. The big hit was the "El Capitan March" which has become part of the brass brand repertory. Sousa created it from the Viceroy's bragging introductory aria which changes into a rousing march as a rebel army advances. *El Capitan* seems to be coming back into fashion. It was staged by the Manhattan School of Music in 1965, Goodspeed Opera House in 1973, Skylight Opera in 1974, Minnesota Opera in 1975, Houston Grand in 1976, Shreveport Opera in 1978, Indiana Opera in 1987 and Opera Americana in Virginia in 1995.

1895 **John Philip Sousa Band.** The first recording of a tune from an American comic opera was "El Capitan March" recorded for Columbia by John Philip Sousa and his Band on June 15, 1895. It was the most popular record of the year and was later re-recorded for Berliner. 1952 **Stars and Stripes Forever.** *Stars and Stripes Forever,* a Hollywood film biography of John Philip Sousa, includes a sequence devoted to *El Capitan.* A theater cast board is shown with DeWolf Hopper's name topping the list as the cast of the operetta rehearse a song and-dance number on stage. Debra Paget leads the singing. Henry Koster directed the film for Twentieth Century Fox. Fox VHS/soundtrack LP. 1981 **Tintypes.** "El Capitan's Song" is featured in the stage revue *Tintypes,* which is built around turn-of-the-century American songs. It's sung on the recording by Trey Wilson as Teddy Roosevelt promoting the Spanish American war against Cuba. Pianist Mel Marvin made the arrangement. DRG CD. 1995 **Keith Brion/Razumovsky Symphony.** Keith Brion leads the Razumovsky Symphony Orchestra in 23 minutes of music from *El Capitan* with an extended version of "O Warrior Grim." The recording was made at the Slovak Radio Concert Hall in Bratislava for the album *John Philip Sousa On Stage.* American Classic Naxos CD. 1997 **University of Illinois Chorale.** Douglas Webster sings the role of El Capitan in this nearly complete recording made by the University of Illinois Chorale and Sinfonia da Camera. Darryl Edwards is Señor Amabile Pozzo, Lucille Beer is Princess Marghanza, Gerald Dolter is Don Luiz Cazarro, Sherri Karam is Isabel, Mary Ann McCormick is Estrelda, Donald Hartmann is Scaramba, Donna Elyashhar is Taciturnez, and Harold Gray Meers is Count Verrarda. Ian Hobson conducts. The opera was restored by Jerrold Fisher and William Bartin. Zephyr CD.

CAPONSACCHI   *1932 opera by Hageman*

Rome in 1698. Cruel, unjust, and mean-spirited Count Guido Franceschini is convicted of murdering his wife Pompilia whom he falsely claimed was having a love affair with the priest Caponsacchi. Richard Hageman's three-act opera *Caponsacchi,* libretto by Arthur Goodrich based on play he wrote with Rose A. Palmer, is derived from Robert Browning's book-length poem *The Ring and the Book.* After winning the David Bispham award as best new American opera, *Caponsacchi* was premiered in Freiburg, Germany, as *Tragödie in Arezzo* on February 18, 1932, in a production by Walter Felsenstein with Hageman conducting and Fritz Neumeyer starring as Count Guido. It reached the Metropolitan Opera in New York on February 4, 1937, with Lawrence Tibbett singing the role of the jealous Count Guido, Helen Jepson as Pompilia, Mario Chamlee as Caponsacchi, and Norman Cordon as Pope Innocent III. Désiré Defrerè staged the opera, George Balanchine arranged the choreography, and Hageman conducted the Metropolitan Opera Orchestra and Chorus. American critics were not particularly fond of the opera despite its success in Germany.

1937 **Helen Jepson.** Metropolitan Opera soprano Helen Jepson recorded two of Pompilia's arias for Victor 78s in 1937 before the opera was staged. "I know you better... This very vivid morn" is her request to Caponsacchi to protect her on a journey to Rome. "Who are you? ... I'll wake him not" is addressed to a sleeping child. Both arias are on the album *Souvenirs from American Operas.* International Record Collectors' Club CD. 1940 **Richard Hageman.** Composer Richard Hageman conducts the San Francisco Symphony Orchestra in the "Overture" and "Carnival Music" from his opera. They're on the album *Carousel of American Music—1940 San Francisco Concerts.* Music and Arts CD box set.

CAPTAIN JINKS OF THE HORSE MARINES
1975 opera by Beeson

Captain Jonathan Jinks bets a friend he can seduce visiting opera singer Aurelia Trentoni. When the two actually fall in love, however, the bet becomes a major problem. Jack Beeson and librettist Sheldon Harnick based their light opera *Captain Jinks of the Horse Marines* on a 1916 play by Clyde Fitch. It was premiered at the Lyric Theater in Kansas City on September 20, 1975, with Carol Wilcox as opera singer Aurelia Trentoni and Robert Owen Jones as Captain Jonathan Jinks. Eugene Green was Colonel Mapleson, Brian Steele was Willie, Ronald Highley was Charlie, Carolyne James was Mrs. Gee, Walter Hook was Papa Belliarti, Nancy Jones was Mary, Linda Sisney was Mrs. Stonington, and Karen Yarmat was Mrs. Jinks. Russell Patterson conducted the Kansas City Phiharmonic Orchestra. The source play was filmed in 1916 by Essanay with Ann Murdock as Aurelia and Richard Travers as Jinks.

1976 **Kansas City Lyric Theater.** Carol Wilcox stars as opera singer Aurelia Trentoni with Robert Owen Jones as Jonathan Jinks in the Kansas City Lyric Theater premiere cast recording of the opera. The other singers are as listed above. Russell Patterson conducts the Kansas City Phiharmonic Orchestra. RCA Red Seal 2-LP box.

CARBONARA, GERARD   *American composer (1896–1959)*

Gerard Carbonara composed the music for the "movie operas" BAL MASQUE and ISABELLE featured in the 1936 Paramount film *Fatal Lady.* He also composed two stage operas in the 1920s, *Armand* and *Nanal,* though neither was produced. Carbonara was born in New York City, but he studied music in Naples and became an opera coach and opera conductor in Italy. After returning to the U. S., he worked at various Hollywood studios writing music for movies, including John Ford's *Stagecoach* (1939*).*

CARD, JUNE   *American soprano (1942–)*

June Card created the role of the Southern Girl in Jerome Moss's GENTLEMEN, BE SEATED! at New York City Opera in 1963 and was one of the ten opera singers in the premiere of John Cage's EUROPERA 1 in Frankfurt in 1987. She has also appeared on stage in Igor Stravinsky's THE RAKE'S PROGRESS. Card, born in Dunkirk, NY, made her debut with Central City Opera in 1966 and later sang in major opera houses in Europe. She has sung in many modern European operas, including works by Henze, Nono and Zimmermann.

CARIAGA, MARVELLEE   *American mezzo-soprano (1940–)*

Dramatic mezzo-soprano Marvellee Cariaga created the role of the Nurse in Alva Henderson's opera MEDEA for San Diego Opera in 1972 and the role of Olga in Thomas Pasatieri's THE THREE SISTERS for Opera/Columbus in 1986. She played Magda in Gian Carlo Menotti's stage production of THE CONSUL when it was telecast from the Spoleto Festival in Charleston in 1977. Cariaga, born in Los Angeles with the maiden name of Moody, began her operatic career with Los Angeles Guild Opera in 1965. She has performed with opera companies in San Francisco, Seattle, Vancouver, and San Diego.

CARLSON, DAVID   *American composer (1952–)*

David Carlson works primarily in the orchestral idiom, but he has composed neo-romantic operas that have had major stage productions. THE MIDNIGHT ANGEL, commissioned by Glimmerglass and Sacramento Opera, is based on a fantasy story about death by

Peter S. Beagle, who also wrote the libretto. It was premiered by Opera Theatre of Saint Louis in 1993 with Elaine Bonazzi in the leading role of Lady Neville. Carlson's second opera DREAMKEEPERS, libretto by Aden Ross about the Ute Indians of Utah, was commissioned by Utah Opera and premiered in 1996 with Juliana Gondek as Ela and Debria Brown as Grandmother; it was reprised by Tulsa Opera in 1998 with Ashley Putnam as Ela and Rosalind Elias as Grandmother. *Anna Karenina*, libretto by Colin Graham based on the Tolstoy novel, was commissioned by Florida Grand Opera in 2004.

CARLSON, LENUS   *American baritone (1945–)*

Lenus Carlson created the role of Thomas Moore in Virgil Thomson's LORD BYRON at Juilliard in 1972 and has sung Nick Shadow on stage in Igor Stravinsky's THE RAKE'S PROGRESS. Carlson, born in Jamestown, North Dakota, studied at Juilliard and made his debut in 1967 in Minneapolis.

CARMEN JONES   *1943 "Americanized opera" by Hammerstein and Bizet*

Oscar Hammerstein II's Americanized version of Georges Bizet's *Carmen* is the best of several semi–American operas based on the music of classic European operas. *Carmen Jones* follows the broad outlines of Henri Meilhac and Ludovic Halevy's libretto and the Prosper Merimée story but is far different. The setting is America during World War II. Carmen the Gypsy is turned into Carmen Jones and the cigarette factory where she works has been transformed into a parachute factory. Don José is now called Joe and he is a corporal in the American Army. Micaëla, his girlfriend from back home, is renamed Cindy Lou and the hulking bullfighter Escamillo is transformed into a boxer called Husky Miller. Mercedes and Frasquita, the gypsy friends of Carmen, are renamed Myrt and Frankie. The basic plot is about the same: Carmen seduces Joe and gets him to desert the Army. When she leaves him for the boxer, Joe stabs her to death. The opera premiered at the Erlanger Theater in Philadelphia on October 19, 1943, and opened in New York at the Broadway Theatre on December 2, 1943, with a double cast because of the operatic demands on the principals. Muriel Smith and Muriel Rahn alternated as Carmen, Luther Saxon and Napoleon Reed sang Joe, Carlotta Franzell and Elton J. Warren were Cindy Lou, Glenn Bryant was Husky Miller, June Hawkins was Frankie and jazz drummer Cozy Cole was Drummer. Charles Friedman directed and Joseph Littau conducted the orchestra. Hammerstein did a superb job of updating the numbers in the opera which have become popular in their own right. The Smugglers' Quintet is called "Whizzin' Away Along de Track," the "Toreador Song" is "Stan' Up and Fight," the "Habanera" is "Dat's Love," the "Seguidilla" is "Dere's a Café on de Corner" and the "Chanson Bohemienne" is "BEAT OUT DAT RHYTHM ON A DRUM." The opera was given 502 performances at the Broadway Theatre and then went on a nationwide tour. It was revived at the Old Vic in London in 1992 to great acclaim and named best

musical of the year in England. It was presented in the *Musicals in Mufti* series in New York in 2001.

1943 Original Broadway cast. Muriel Smith sings Carmen with Luther Saxon as Joe on the original cast album issued in 1943 on a Decca 78 album. Carlotta Franzell is Cindy Lou, Glenn Bryant is Husky Miller, June Hawkins is Frankie, and the other singers are Jessica Russell, Dick Montgomery and Randall Steplight with Cozy Cole as the drum soloist. Joseph Littau conducts the Carmen Jones Orchestra and Robert Shaw directs the Carmen Jones Chorus. Decca LP/Pearl CD. **1944 Kitty Carlisle.** Kitty Carlisle sings "Beat Out Dat Rhythm on a Drum" with Russ Morgan and his orchestra for a 78 record. It's available on her album *The Desert Song.* Box Office CD. **1947 Original cast at Ford Theatre.** Original cast members Muriel Smith (Carmen), Luther Saxon (Joe) and Elton J. Warren (Cindy Lou) are featured on this cast album recorded at the Ford Theater on December 17, 1947, with added narration by Howard Lindsay. Irving Barnes is Husky Miller and the supporting cast includes Valerie Black, Juana Hernandez, Earle Sidnor and Maurice Ellis. Lynn Murray conducts the orchestra. AEI CD. **1954 20th Century-Fox film.** Otto Preminger directed this film version of the opera which is excellent despite having most of the cast dubbed. Dorothy Dandridge is Carmen Jones but her singing voice belongs to Marilyn Horne. Harry Belafonte plays Joe but his singing is by LaVern Hutcherson. Olga James plays Cindy Lou and does her own singing. Joe Adams play Husky Miller but his singing is by Marvin Hayes. Pearl Bailey plays Frankie and does her own singing with a splendid "Beat Out dat Rhythm with a Drum." Diahann Carroll plays Myrt but her singing is by Bernice Peterson. Nick Stewart play Dink but his singing is by Joe Crawford. Brock Peters plays Sgt. Brown and does his own singing. Herschel Burke Gilbert conducts the orchestra. The film was produced by Samuel Goldwyn for 20th Century-Fox in CinemaScope. Soundtrack on RCA Victor LP and Pearl CD.

Scene from the original New York stage production of *Carmen Jones.*

Film on Fox VHS/DVD and Pioneer LD. **1967 London studio recording.** Grace Bumbry sings the role of Carmen Jones opposite George Webb as Joe in this London studio highlights recording of the opera with Kenneth Alwyn conducting the orchestra and chorus. Ena Babb is Cindy Lou, Thomas Baptiste is Husky Miller Elizabeth Welch is Frankie, Ursula Connors is Myrt, Edward Darling is Dink and the Mike Sammes Singers provide solid choral support. World Record Club/Heliodor LP. **1991 London Old Vic.** Wilhelmenia Fernandez and Sharon Benson alternated in the role of Carmen Jones on stage in an award-winning production of the opera at the Old Vic in London, and both are featured on the cast album. Damon Evans, who played Joe to Fernandez and Michael Austin who was Joe to Benson, are also both on the album. Gregg Baker is Husky Miller, Karen Parks is Cindy Lou, Carolyn Sebron is Frankie, Danny John Jules is Dink, Wendy Brown is Myrt, and Clive Rowe is Rum. Henry Lewis conducts. The production, directed by Simon Callow, opened April 8, 1991, and was recorded in June 1991. It was voted best musical of the year by London critics. EMI CD. **1991 Lesley Garrett.** Lesley Garrett sings "Dat's Love" on her album *Diva: A Soprano at the Movies*. Andrew Greenwood conducts the Philharmonia Orchestra. Silva Screen CD.

CARMINES, ALVIN   *American composer (1938–)*

Alvin Carmines has composed nine Gertrude Stein operas/music theater works in collaboration with director Lawrence Kornfeld. The 32-minute WHAT HAPPENED, a play with music for singers, dancers and actors, was staged at the Judson Poets Theater at Judson Memorial Church in New York in 1963 and won five OBIE awards. Carmines was in charge of arts programs at the church when it began to stage opera and drama by parishioners. IN CIRCLES, a full-length work, was staged at the Judson in 1961 and then moved to the Cherry Lane Theater for an extended run. The large-scale opera A MANOIR, based on a Stein play with echoes of Ovid and Rilke, was performed in 1966. LISTEN TO ME, a version of the story of Orpheus and Eurydice, was staged in 1967. The 90-minute THE MAKING OF AMERICANS, libretto by Leon Katz based on the book by Stein, was staged in 1968 and reprised at the Lenox Art Center in 1985. DR. FAUSTUS LIGHTS THE LIGHTS, based on a Stein play, was presented at the Judson Church in 1979. Carmines' non-Stein works include THE DUEL, a one-act opera about a famous duel between Alexander Hamilton and Aaron Burr; it starred Frederick Burchinal as Aaron Burr and Linda Phillips as Theodoria Burr when it premiered at the Metropolitan Opera Studio in Brooklyn in 1974. Carmines, who was born in Hampton, Virginia, studied at Swarthmore and Union Theological Seminary.

CARNIVAL   *1936 "movie opera" by Levant*

Oscar Levant composed the "movie opera" *Carnival*, libretto by William Kernell, for the 1936 film *Charlie Chan at the Opera*. It was essentially created around a Mephistopheles costume used by Lawrence Tibbett in *Metropolitan* which was passed on to the low-budget Chan picture to be worn by a baritone in a stabbing scene. Boris Karloff plays the singer (singing dubbed by Rico Ricardi) suffering from amnesia and a desire for revenge. He is suspected of murdering a woman onstage but detective Charlie Chan (Werner Oland) has doubts. Levant discusses this neglected opera, for which he wrote an overture, prelude, marches and arias, in his autobiography *A Smattering of Ignorance*, and there is an analysis of it by Irene Hahn Atkins in her study *Source Music in Motion Pictures*. This was one of the best of the Chan films based on Earl Derr Biggers' Honolulu detective. H. Bruce Humberstone directed the 66-minute thriller for 20th Century Fox. Key Video VHS.

CAROUSEL   *1945 operatic operetta by Rodgers*

Ne'er-do-well carnival barker Billy Bigelow marries factory worker Julie Jordan but, as they have no money, they have to live with cousin Nettie Fowler. He is killed during a robbery he undertakes to raise money for the baby Julie is expecting, but he is allowed to return to earth to do a good deed and see his daughter. Richard

Boris Karloff was the star of the movie opera *Carnival* created for the 1936 film *Charlie Chan at the Opera*.

Rodgers's *Carousel,* libretto and lyrics by Oscar Hammerstein II, is based on Ferenc Molnar's 1921 play *Liliom* with the setting transferred from Budapest to a New England fishing village. It was premiered by the Theater Guild at the Shubert Theater in New Haven on March 22, 1945, and opened at the Majestic Theater in New York on April 19, 1945. John Raitt was Billy, Jan Clayton was Julie, Jean Darling was Julie's friend Carrie, Eric Mattson was Carrie's husband-to-be Mr. Enoch Snow, Met contralto Christine Johnson was Nettie and Murvyn Vye was Jigger. Jo Mielziner designed the sets, Agnes de Mille arranged the choreography, Rouben Mamoulian directed and Joseph Littau conducted. The role of Nettie, who sings "You'll Never Walk Alone," is usually performed by an opera contralto beginning an RandH tradition of having a big mezzo aria in their musicals. *Carousel* is often performed by opera singers and seems likely to enter the opera house repertory.

1945 Original Broadway cast. John Raitt sings Billy Bigelow opposite Jan Clayton as Julie in the original cast album. Jean Darling is Carrie, Eric Mattson is Mr. Snow and Met contralto Christine Johnson is Nettie. Joseph Littau conducts. Angel LP/MCA CD. **1947 Original London cast.** Stephen Douglass is Billy Bigelow opposite Iva Withers as Julie in this recording with the cast of the first London production. Marion Ross is Nettie, Margo Moser is Carrie and Eric Mattson is Mr. Snow. Reginald Burston conducts. Box Office Recordings CD. **1955 Lehman Engel.** Lehman Engel conducts this operatic studio recording made in New York in 1955. Robert Merrill is Billy, Patrice Munsel is Julie, Florence Henderson is Carrie, Gloria Lane is Nettie and Herbert Banke is Mr. Snow. RCA Victor LP. **1956 20th Century-Fox film.** Gordon MacRae is the swaggering carousel barker Billy who marries factory girl Shirley Jones as Julie in the classic film version of *Carousel.* Claramae Turner is Nettie, Barbara Ruick is Carrie and Robert Rounseville is Mr. Snow. The musical was shot on location by Charles G. Clarke and directed by Henry King for Twentieth Century-Fox. Alfred Newman conducted the chorus and orchestra while Ken Darby made the vocal arrangements. Fox DVD and VHS with soundtrack on Capitol LP and Angel CD. **1956 Jerome Hines.** Jerome Hines sings "You'll Never Walk Alone"" on the *Voice of Firestone* TV program on October 22, 1956. Howard Barlow conducts the Firestone Orchestra. *Jerome Hines in Opera and Song.* VAI VHS. **1960 New York studio recording.** Harry Snow is Billy Bigelow opposite Lois Hunt as Julie Jordan in this New York studio recording. Charmaine Harma is Carrie, Charles Green is Mr. Snow. and Clifford Young is Jigger. Helena Seymour sings Nettie's aria "You'll Never Walk Alone." The orchestra conductor is not identified. Epic LP. **1962 Jay Blackton.** Jay Blackton conducts the chorus and orchestra in this operatic recording made in a New York studio. Alfred Drake is Billy, Roberta Peters is Julie, Claramae Turner is Nettie, Lee Venora is Carrie, Norman Treigle is Jigger and Jon Crain is Mr. Snow. Command LP. **1965 Lincoln Center.** John Raitt returned to play Billy in one of the first Broadway musical revivals staged at Lincoln Center. Eileen Christy is Julie, Katherine Hilgenberg is Nettie, Susan Watson is Carrie and Reid Shelton is Mr. Snow. Franz Allers conducts. BMG/RCA Victor CD. **1967 ABC Television.** Robert Goulet is Billy Bigelow with Mary Grover as Julie Jordan in this ABC television production produced by Norman Rosemont. Patricia Neway is Nettie, Marlyn Mason is Carrie and Jack De Lon is Mr. Snow. Jack Elliott conducts and Paul Bogart directed. Telecast May 7, 1967. Soundtrack on Columbia LP. **1987 Paul Gemignani.** Paul Gemignani conducts the Royal Philharmonic Orchestra and Ambrosian Singers in this London studio recording. Samuel Ramey is Billy, Barbara Cook is Julie, Maureen For-

rester is Nettie, Sarah Brightman is Carrie, and David Rendall is Mr. Snow. MCA Classics CD. **1993 Royal National Theatre.** This recording is based on a Royal National Theatre revival in London staged by Nicholas Hytner. Michael Hayden is Billy Bigelow, Joanna Riding is Julie Jordan, Katrina Murphy is Carrie, Meg Johnson is Nettie, and Clive Rowe is Mr. Snow. William Brohm conducts. BMG/RCA Victor CD. **1994 Lincoln Center.** Nicholas Hytner's London production was brought to Lincoln Center in 1994 and recorded in April with a mostly different cast. Michael Hayden repeats as Billy Bigelow, Sally Murphy is Julie, Audra McDonald is Carrie, Shirley Verrett is Nettie and Eddie Korbich is Mr. Snow. Eric Stern conducts. The show won five Tonys, including one for Best Revival and one for Audra McDonald. Angel CD. **1994 Kiri Te Kanawa.** Kiri Te Kanawa sings "You'll Never Walk Alone" on her album *Kiri! Her Greatest Hits.* Stephen Barlow conducts the London Symphony Orchestra. London Classics CD/VHS/DVD. **1996 Bryan Terfel.** Welsh opera baritone Bryan Terfel sings three songs from *Carousel* on his album *Something Wonderful: Bryan Terfel Sings Rodgers and Hammerstein.* Paul Daniel conducts the English Northern Philharmonic and Opera North Chorus. DG CD. **2000 Lesley Garrett.** Lesley Garrett sings "You'll Never Walk Alone" with the Grimthorpe Colliery Band on the album *Lesley Garrett—I Will Wait for You.* RCA Victor CD.

CARR, BENJAMIN   *English-born American composer (1768–1831)*

Benjamin Carr, one of the earliest American opera composers, emigrated to the U. S. in 1793 from London where his first opera had been staged. He was a singer, pianist, organist, and publisher as well as composer, but he is remembered today primarily for his American ballad operas. The most successful were based on the legend of William Tell: THE ARCHERS: OR, MOUNTAINEERS OF SWITZERLAND, which premiered at the John Street Theater in New York City on April 18, 1796; and *The Patriot: or, Liberty Obtained,* which premiered at the New Chestnut Street Theater in Philadelphia on May 16, 1796. William Dunlop's libretto for *The Archers,* which has survived, is said to be the first American opera libretto of a serious nature written by an American. Carr's *Bourville Castle, or The Gallic Orphans* was premiered at the John Street Theater on January 16, 1797, but it is lost as are his other operas. His appealing ballad opera style can be heard in a recording of his song cycle *The Lady of the Lake.*

1978 The Lady of the Lake. Rossini based an opera on Sir Walter Scott's 1810 narrative poem *The Lady of the Lake,* but Carr preferred to use it for a song cycle. Carr's music, published a few months after the poem was issued, is in the style of ballad opera, but there is no narrative. Six of its songs were recorded by the Recorded Anthology of American Music group in 1978 for the album *The Flowering of Vocal Music in America, Vol. 2:* they are "Mary," "Soldier Rest," "Hymn to the Virgin," "Blanche of Devan," "Alice Brand" and "Coronach." The singers are tenor Charles Bressler, sopranos Cynthia Clarey and Barbara Wallace and baritone Richard Anderson with accompaniment by pianist Harriet Wingreen and harpist Cynthia Otis. New World LP.

CARRERAS, JOSÉ   *Spanish tenor (1946–)*

José Carreras created the role of Christopher Columbus in American composer Leonardo Balada's CRISTÓBAL COLÓN in 1989. He sings opposite Kiri Te Kanawa in operatic recordings of two American operettas: as Tony in Leonard Bernstein's 1985 version of WEST SIDE STORY, and as Emile de Becque in a 1986 version

The New York City Opera
Julius Rudel, General Manager
Presents
CARRY NATION
an Opera in Two Acts
Music by Douglas Moore
Libretto by William North Jayme
Samuel Krachmalnick, Conductor
Staged by Frank Corsaro
Settings by Will Steven Armstrong
Costumes by Paton Campbell
with
Beverly Wolff, Ellen Faull
Julian Patrick
Arnold Voketaitis

Carry Nation **was recorded by New York City Opera in 1968 with Beverly Wolff performing the title role.**

of SOUTH PACIFIC with the music transposed up. He sings "Serenade" from Sigmund Romberg's THE STUDENT PRINCE in a videotaped tribute to Mario Lanza at the Royal Albert Hall in London in 1991. Carreras, born in Barcelona where he made his debut in 1970, is one of the most popular tenors of our time but American operetta, to put it kindly, is not his strong point.

CARRY NATION *1966 opera by Moore*
   Naïve young Carry Nation marries a seemingly respectable doctor who he turns out to be an alcoholic. When he is unable to change his ways, she leaves him and devotes herself to the cause of Prohibition. She begins her famous axe-wielding saloon-smashing campaign in Topeka, Kansas, at the age of 53. Douglas Moore's two-act opera *Carry Nation,* libretto by William North Jayme based on her early life, was commissioned by the University of Kansas and premiered in Lawrence, Kansas, on April 28, 1966. Beverly Wolff created the role of Carry Nation, John Reardon was her husband Charles, Patricia Brooks was her mother, Kenneth Smith was her father, Kenneth Marsolais was Ben, Roger Winell was the preacher, Ed Ellis was the caretaker and Cecil Cole was the saloon

boy. Doris Peterson alternated as Carry, David Holloway as Charles, Norma Sharp as Mother and Michael Riley as Father. Lewis Goff directed and Robert Baustian conducted. The opera was reprised at the San Francisco Spring Opera in June 1966 and reached New York City Opera on March 18, 1968. It was Moore's last opera.

1968 New York City Opera. Beverly Wolff sings Carry Nation in this recording by the cast of the 1968 New York City Opera production. Julian Patrick is Charles, Ellen Faull is Mother, Arnold Voketaitis is Father, Don Yule is the City Marshall, Kellis Miller is Ben, Edward Pierson is the Preacher, and Jack Bittner is the Caretaker. Samuel Krachmalnick conducts the New York City Opera Orchestra. Desto 3-LP set/Bay Cities 2-CD box.

CARTER, ELLIOT   *American composer (1908–)*

Elliot Carter, long ranked among the greatest American composers, came late to opera. WHAT NEXT? was composed in 1999 when he was 91. Although Carter had written for the voice at various times, including an early opera he destroyed and setting poems by John Ashberry and Robert Lowell, *What Next?* was a surprise to his many admirers. Composed to a libretto by Paul Griffiths, it premiered in Berlin in September 1999 and was presented at Carnegie Hall in New York in March 2000. Carter, who was born in New York and educated at Harvard, won the Pulitzer Prize for Music in 1960 for his *Second String Quartet* and won it a second time in 1973 for his *Third String Quartet.*

1999 Elliot Carter: A Labyrinth of Time. Frank Scheffer's film about the composer includes interviews with Carter, John Cage, Oliver Knussen and Pierre Boulez and film of performances of his works by the Arditti Quartet, the Ensemble Intercontemporain, and the Royal Concertgebouw Orchestra. The 110-minute film was shot in New York, London, Paris Madrid and Amsterdam from 1984 to 1999.

CARTER, ERNEST   *American composer (1866–1953)*

Ernest Carter was one of the first American composers to have an opera staged in Europe. THE WHITE BIRD, libretto by Brian Hooker about a jealous husband who arranges his wife's death, was presented in Osnabrück, Germany, in 1927 following its premiere in Chicago in 1924. His first opera, *The Blonde Donna,* libretto by the composer about a love triangle in a Spanish mission in Santa Barbara, premiered in concert form in New York in 1912 and was staged in New York in 1931. Carter, who was born in Orange, NJ, studied music at Princeton and Columbia and in Berlin.

CASANOVA'S HOMECOMING   *1985 opera by Argento*

Italy's most famous lover is allowed to return to Venice from exile when he promises to reform. He is not able to. He seduces a soprano who has disguised herself as a castrato and devises a scheme to swindle a rich widow. Dominick Argento's three-act comic opera *Casanova's Homecoming,* libretto by the composer, is based on the memoirs of the 17th century rake. It was commissioned by Minnesota Opera and premiered in St. Paul on April 12, 1985, with Julian Patrick as Casanova, Vern Sutton as his librettist friend Lorenzo Da Ponte, Elaine Bonazzi as rich widow Madame D'Urfe, Douglas Perry as her nephew Marquis de Lisle, Susanne Marsee as the fake castrato Bellino/Teresa, Carol Kutnik as Giulietta Croce, Michelle McBride as her daughter Barbara, Chris Root as Casanova's serving boy Marcantonio, Stanley Wexler as Businello and Mark Jacobson as Gabrielle. Scott Bergeson conducted the St. Paul Chamber Orchestra. The opera was staged by New York City Opera later the same year. Cincinnati Opera School staged it in an Italian translation at the Teatro del Giglio in Lucca, Italy, in

2003 with Sean Anderson as Casanova and LaToya Lain as Madame D'Urfe.

1985 Minnesota Opera. Julian Patrick sings Casanova with Vern Sutton as Lorenzo in this recording of the Minnesota Opera premiere in St. Paul as broadcast on Minnesota Radio. Elaine Bonazzi is Madame D'Urfe, Douglas Perry is Marquis de Lisle, Susanne Marsee is Bellino/Teresa, Carol Kutnik is Giulietta Croce, Michelle McBride is Barbara, Chris Root is Marcantonio, Stanley Wexler is Businello and Mark Jacobson is Gabrielle. Scott Bergeson conducts the St. Paul Chamber Orchestra. Classic Opera audiocassette.

CASINO PARADISE   *1987 "cabaret opera" by Bolcom*

Millionaire developer Ferguson plans to transform a rundown seaside resort into a gambling center called Casino Paradise. His son Stanley is opposed to the idea, his daughter Cis falls in love with sleazy drifter McCoy and a mysterious Nurse seems to have plans of her own And then Ferguson is shot. William Bolcom's *Casino Paradise,* libretto by Arnold Weinstein and Thomas Babe with lyrics by Weinstein, is an cabaret-style opera that he describes as an "opera for singing actors." It was commissioned by the American Music Theater Festival which premiered it in Philadelphia on April 4, 1990. Timothy Nolen was Ferguson, Eddie Korbich was Stanley, Janet Metz was Cis, Walter Hudson was McCoy, Joan Morris was Nurse, and Keith Curran was Sunny. David Alden directed and Michael Barrett conducted. The opera was reprised at The Ballroom in New York City in June 1992 in a shortened version.

1990 American Music Theater Festival. The American Music Theater Festival cast recorded the opera at Sigma Sound in Philadelphia on April 16, 1990, the day after the production closed. Timothy Nolen Is Ferguson, with the rest of the cast as listed above. Michael Barrett conducts the American Music Theater Festival Orchestra. Koch CD.

THE CASK OF AMONTILLADO   *American operas based on Poe story*

Montresor takes revenge on Fortunato for an old insult to his family by tempting him to taste a fine amontillado from a cask in his cellar. He then walls him in with the wine and is unrepentant when he talks about it fifty years later. EDGAR ALLAN POE's famous story *The Cask of Amontillado,* first published in 1846, has inspired eight American one-act operas.

1953 Charles Hamm. Charles Hamm's one-act opera *The Cask of Amontillado,* libretto by the composer based on the Poe story, was premiered at the Cincinnati Conservatory in Cincinnati, Ohio, on March 1, 1953. **1954 Julia Perry.** Julia Perry's one-act opera *The Cask of Amontillado,* libretto by the composer based on the Poe story, was premiered in New York on November 20, 1955. **1968 Aldo Provenzano.** Aldo Provenzano's one-act opera *The Cask of Amontillado,* libretto by the composer based on the Poe story, was premiered at the Eastman School of Music in Rochester, New York, on April 26, 1968. **1968 Robert James Haskins.** Robert James Haskins' one-act opera *The Cask of Amontillado,* libretto by John Koppenhaver, was first performed in 1968. **1979 Donald Para.** Donald Para's one-act opera *The Cask of Amontillado,* libretto by the composer based on the Poe story, was premiered in Kalamazoo, Michigan, in May 1979. The performance was videotaped. **1982 Russell Currie.** Russell Currie's opera *The Cask of Amontillado,* libretto by Carl Laanes based on the Poe story, was commissioned by the Bronx Historical Society and the Bronx Art Ensemble and premiered by the Ensemble at Fordham University in New York on April 3, 1982. **1997 Bryan Stanley.** Bryan Stanley's one-act opera *The Cask of Amontillado*, libretto by Patrick Buckley based on the Poet story, was premiered by Metro Opera in Des Moines, Iowa, in 1997. **2003 Daniel Pinkham.** Daniel Pinkham's *The Cask of Amontillado*, libretto by the composer based on the Poe story, was premiered by Opera Boston at the Tower Auditorium, Massachusetts College of Art, on June 8, 2003. Richard Conrad sang the role of Montresor and staged the opera with Alan Schneider as the unfortunate Fortunato. John Finney conducted the chamber orchestra.

CASSEL, WALTER *American baritone (1910— 2000)*

Dramatic baritone Walter Cassel created the role of Horace Tabor in Douglas Moore's THE BALLAD OF BABY DOE when it premiered in Central City in 1956, reprised the role at New York City Opera opposite Beverly Sills, and is featured on the NYCO recording. He played Petruchio in Vittorio Giannini's THE TAMING OF THE SHREW when it received its first stage production at New York City Opera in 1958. He also starred in two 1949 New York City Opera productions, as the husband in Gian Carlo Menotti's AMELIA GOES TO THE BALL and Daniel Webster in Moore's THE DEVIL AND DANIEL WEBSTER. Cassel, who was born in Council Bluffs, Iowa, made his stage debut at the Metropolitan Opera in 1942 as Brétigny in Massenet's *Manon* but left the company in 1945. He has also sung in American operettas, including a long run in Romberg's THE DESERT SONG.

CASSILLY, RICHARD *American tenor (1937–1998)*

Heldentenor Richard Cassilly, who created roles in two American operas, made his debut on Broadway in 1955 singing a small part in Gian Carlo Menotti's THE SAINT OF BLEECKER STREET and taking over the role of Michele for an NBC Opera telecast. He created the German Soldier in Mark Bucci's TALE FOR A DEAF EAR at New York City Opera in 1958 and the egocentric tenor Gerardo in Hugo Weisgall's THE TENOR in Baltimore in 1952. He sang Sam opposite Phyllis Curtin in the 1962 New Orleans recording of Carlisle Floyd's SUSANNAH and played the role at New York City Opera in 1965. He sings the drifter Martin in the 1965 recording of Aaron Copland's THE TENDER LAND. Cassilly, who was born in Washington, D. C., studied at the Peabody Conservatory He made his European debut in 1965 and his Met debut in 1970 and had a major international career; he was a resident member of the Hamburg Staatsoper for many years.

CASTEL, NICO *American tenor (1931–)*

Character tenor Nico Castel created roles in five American operas. He was Joseph in Carlisle Floyd's WUTHERING HEIGHTS in 1958, the Young Boy in Ned Rorem's MISS JULIE in 1965, Brighella in Vittorio Giannini's THE SERVANT OF TWO MASTERS in 1967, Tom Tosser in Hugo Weisgall's NINE RIVER FROM JORDAN in 1968, and Diaghilev in Stanley Silverman's MADAME ADARE in 1980. He created the role of the Messenger in Alberto Ginastera's BOMARZO at Washington Opera in 1967. For Gian Carlo Menotti he sang the role of the Magician in 1972 Spoleto Festival and 1974 New York City Opera recordings of THE CONSUL, and the role of Kaspar in the 1979 film of AMAHL AND THE NIGHT VISITORS. Castel, who was born in Lisbon, studied in Venezuela and New York before making his debut with Santa Fe Opera in 1958.

CASTELNUOVO-TEDESCO, MARIO *American composer (1895–1968)*

Mario Castelnuovo-Tedesco left Italy in 1939 and moved to Los Angeles where he became an American citizen and began to com-

pose movie music and operas. He created two "movie operas" in Hollywood, THE LOVES OF FATIMA (1949) composed for the film *Everybody Does It*, and IL RITORNO DE CESARE (1951), composed for the film *Strictly Dishonorable*. Two of his stage operas were based on Shakespeare: THE MERCHANT OF VENICE (1956), produced at the Shrine Auditorium in Los Angeles in 1966, and *All's Well That Ends Well* (1958). His most popular opera THE IMPORTANCE OF BEING EARNEST, based on the Oscar Wilde play, was premiered at Hofstra College in Long Island on January 22, 1975, and revived in Italy in 1984. Hofstra College premiered his Biblical oratorio *Tobias and the Angel* on January 22, 1975, His other film scores include *And Then There Were None* (1945) and *The Loves of Carmen* (1948).

CASTLE, JOYCE *American mezzo-soprano (1944–)*

Lyric mezzo-soprano Joyce Castle created the role of Brunelda in Ellis Kohs opera AMERIKA in 1970, Mrs. Heimlich in Stewart Wallace's WHERE'S DICK in 1989, Zeresh in Hugo Weisgall's ESTHER in 1993, movie star Alla Nazimova in Dominick Argento's THE DREAM OF VALENTINO in 1994, the Mother in Deborah Drattell's THE FESTIVAL OF REGRETS in 1999 and the Old Lady in Michael Torke's STRAWBERRY FIELDS in 1999. She sings the role of the Old Lady in the 1985 New York City Opera recording of Leonard Bernstein's CANDIDE, Augusta in the 1992 Cleveland Opera recording of Douglas Moore's THE BALLAD OF BABY DOE, Madame Flora in the 1996 Chicago Opera Theater recording of Gian Carlo Menotti's THE MEDIUM and the Mother in the 1998 Berkshire Opera recording of Menotti's THE CONSUL. She reprised the role of Augusta in *The Ballad of Baby Doe* at New York City Opera in 2001. Castle, who was born in Beaumont, Texas, studied at the Eastman School and made her debut with San Francisco Opera in 1970.

THE CAT AND THE FIDDLE *1931 operetta by Kern*

Romanian composer Victor Florescu is working in Brussels where he has problems with his new opera *The Passionate Pilgrim*. American composer Shirley Sheridan helps him out with her jazzy ideas and together they are able to create a successful operetta. Jerome Kern's operetta *The Cat and the Fiddle*, libretto by Otto Harbach, premiered at the Globe in New York on October 15, 1931. George Metaxa played Victor, Bettie Hall was Shirley, Odette Myrtil was the opera's prima donna Odette and the Metropolitan Opera's George Meader was street singer Pompineau. Max Gordon produced, José Ruben directed and Victor Baravalle was conductor. *The Cat and the Fiddle* seems to have been an attempt to adapt the traditional Viennese-style operetta for a more modern format. The best-known songs are "The Night Was Made for Love" and "She Didn't Say Yes."

1933 Original London cast. George Metaxa, who created the role of Victor in the New York production, recorded two songs in London when the operetta was staged there in 1932 and his co-star Peggy Wood recorded six others. The 78 recordings are on various LPs, including *Jerome Kern in London* World Record Club LP. **1934 MGM film.** Jeanette MacDonald stars opposite Ramon Novarro in the MGM film of the operetta directed by William K. Howard. Screenwriters Sam and Bella Spewack changed the plot but retained the music. The couple are still composers but Novarro is not successful so that causes them to break up. When he needs help on his operetta, she returns and true love takes over as the film changes into color. Herbert Stothart was music director. Video on MGM-UA DVD/VHS and Soundtrack on LP/CD. **1946 Till the Clouds Roll By.** *Till the Clouds Roll By,* an MGM film about

Kern, features Angela Lansbury singing "She Didn't Say Yes" from *The Cat and the Fiddle*. Richard Whorf and Vincente Minnelli directed. MGM/UA DVD/VHS/LD and soundtrack on MG/UA LP/CD. **1948 Risë Stevens/Gordon MacRae.** Risë Stevens and Gordon MacRae sing the roles of Shirley and Victor on a radio broadcast recorded October 18, 1948, with a radio orchestra. Live Opera audiocassette. **1953 Patrica Neway/Stephen Douglass.** Patrica Neway sings Shirley opposite Stephen Douglass as Victor on this American highlights recording with Lehman Engel conducting the orchestra. RCA Victor LP. **1959 Doreen Hume/Dennis Quilley.** Doreen Hume sings Shirley opposite Dennis Quilley in this English recording of the operetta with Johnny Gregory conducting the orchestra. Epic LP.

THE CAT AND THE MOON   *1958 opera by Putsche*

A blind beggar carries a lame beggar as they seek a magic well whose waters they believe will cure them. They encounter a cat and a saint. Thomas Putsche's 31-minute one-act opera *The Cat and the Moon*, libretto by the composer based on a symbolic 1926 play by W. B. Yeats, premiered in Hartford, Connecticut, on May 22, 1960.

1970 Contemporary Chamber Players of Chicago. Thomas MacBone is the Lame Beggar, James Mack is the Blind Beggar, and Elsa Charleston is Saint Colman in this recording by the Contemporary Chamber Players of the University of Chicago. Ralph Shapey conducts the chamber orchestra. CRI LP/CD.

CATÁN, DANIEL   *Mexican composer (1949–)*

Daniel Catán, Latin America's best-known modern opera composer, has strong connections to the American operatic world as his major opera was commissioned and premiered in the United States and the sole recording of his other major opera was made in America. FLORENCIA EN EL AMAZONAS, was commissioned by Houston Grand Opera, jointly with Seattle and Los Angeles, and was premiered by Houston in 1996. Marcela Fuentes-Berain's libretto about opera diva Florencia Grimaldi is based on themes from the works of Gabriel García Márquez. Catán's 1991 opera RAPPACCINI'S DAUGHTER, libretto by Juan Tovar based on the Nathaniel Hawthorne story as dramatized by Octavio Paz, was presented by San Diego Opera in 1994 following its Mexico City premiere. It was recorded at the Manhattan School of Music Opera Theatre in 1997.

CATHER, WILLA   *American writer (1873–1947)*

Nebraska writer Willa Cather who wrote about pioneer days in *O Pioneers!* (1913) and *My Antonia* (1918), was an opera buff and is said to have visited the Metropolitan Opera three times a week for twenty years. There are three operas based on her stories. Robert Beadell's *Out to the Wind*, libretto by the composer, premiered at the University of Nebraska in 1978. Libby Larsen's ERIC HERMANNSON'S SOUL, libretto by Chas. Rader-Shieber, was premiered by Opera Omaha in November 1998. Tyler Goodrich White's *O Pioneers!*, libretto by the composer, was premiered at the University of Nebraska on November 12, 1999.

Cather often featured opera in her stories, so often that Metropolitan Opera mezzo Ariel Bybee was able to produce a program at the University of Nebraska in 2000 based around arias featured in them. Her novel *The Song of the Lark* (1913) is based on the career of Met soprano Olive Fremstad.

CAVALCANTI   *1932 opera by Pound*

An operatic portrait of the life of 13th century Florentine poet Guido Cavalcanti, the most important poet in Italy before Dante. It combines the poet's lyrics sung in Italian with dialogue in English. Ezra Pound's opera *Cavalcanti*, libretto by the composer, was created in 1932 but not staged until March 28, 1983, when it was premiered by the Arch Ensemble for Experimental Music in San Francisco with Robert Hughes conducting.

2004 Ego Scriptor Cantilenae: Music of Ezra Pound. Recordings of excerpts from the opera are performed by the Arch Ensemble for Experimental Music in 1983 and other ensembles in 2000 and 2001 on the compilation CD *Ego Scriptor Cantilenae: Music of Ezra Pound*. It features music by Pound on recordings made over a 30-year period. Other Minds CD.

THE CAVE   *1993 multimedia opera by Reich and Korot*

The Cave of the Patriarchs in Hebron, where the Biblical Abraham is supposedly buried, is a holy site for Jews, Christians and Muslims and has become a major center of conflict. Composer Steve Reich describes his complex opera *The Cave* as "music video theater." with its music based around interviews with Jews, Christians and Muslims talking about Abraham, Sarah, Isaac, and Hagar. His collaborator Beryl Korot uses video imagery to show the underpinnings of the Middle East conflict. Americans interviewed include sculptor Richard Serra, fashion historian Valerie Steele, astronomy guru Carl Sagan, philosopher Jean Houston, and priest Daniel Berrigan.

1994 Steve Reich Ensemble. Sopranos Cheryl Bensman, Rowe,

Steve Reich and Beryl Korot's innovative multi-media opera *The Cave* was recorded in 1996.

soprano Marion Beckenstein, tenor James Bassi and baritone Hugo Munday are the soloists in this recording of the work by the Steve Reich Ensemble made at the Edison Studio in New York December 12–16 1994. Nonesuch CD box.

CBS RADIO OPERA

CBS Radio was the first radio network to broadcast an American opera and premiered nine others. The first was Deems Taylor's THE KING'S HENCHMAN, broadcast in a 60-minute highlights version on September 18, 1927, from WOR in New York. The cast included Rafaelo Diaz, Marie Sundelius, Giovanni Martino, Richard Hale and Henry Scott.

The American opera premieres were: **1931** *The Octaroon* (Harry Lawrence Freeman). **1937** *Green Mansions* (Louis Gruenberg). *I've Got the Tune* (Marc Blitzstein). *Flora* (Vittorio Giannini). **1938** *Beauty and the Beast* (Vittorio Giannini). **1939** *Blennerhassett* (Vittorio Giannini). **1942** *Solomon and Balkis* (Randall Thomson). **1956** *The Toledo War* (David Broekman). **1957** *La Grande Bretèche* (Avery Claflin).

CBS TELEVISION OPERA

CBS Television premiered eleven American operas between 1953 and 1973. *Opera Television Theater*, which began in 1950 under the direction of Lawrence Tibbett and Henry Souvanin, staged the studio productions. The series ended when CBS could not find sponsors though CBS continued to present operas and operettas in other formats.

American operas presented on CBS Television include: **1948** Menotti *The Medium*. **1953** Gershwin *135th Street/Blue Monday*. Menotti *The Telephone*. Wilder *Miss Chicken Little*. **1954** Herrmann *A Christmas Carol*. **1955** Schumann *The Mighty Casey*. Herrmann *A Child Is Born*. **1956** Simone *The Emperor's New Clothes*. **1958** Herbert *The Red Mill*. Laderman *Sara*. **1960** Copland *The Second Hurricane*. **1961** Jones *Break of Day*. Strauss *The Accused*. **1962** Moore *Gallantry*. Stravinsky *The Flood*. **1965** Menotti *Martin's Lie*. **1967** Laderman *The Trials of Galileo*. **1971** Laderman *And David Wept*. **1972** Pasatieri *The Trial of Mary Lincoln*. Johnson *The Four Note Opera*. **1973** Laderman *The Questions of Abraham*. **1974** Lees *Medea in Corinth*.

CEHANOVSKY, GEORGE   *Russian-born American baritone (1892–1986)*

George Cehanovsky created small but important roles in five American operas at the Metropolitan over a thirty-year period. He was Cynric in Deems Taylor's THE KING'S HENCHMEN in 1927, the Prison Governor in Taylor's PETER IBBETSON in 1931, Thomas Morton in Howard Hanson's MERRY MOUNT in 1934, Reeve in Walter Damrosch's THE MAN WITHOUT A COUNTRY in 1937 and the Major-Domo in Samuel Barber's VANESSA in 1958. Cehanovsky was born in St. Petersburg and made his debut there before emigrating to America in 1923. He sang with the De Feo and San Carlo opera companies before joining the Met in 1926 and singing there for forty seasons. He was married to the soprano Elisabeth Rethberg.

CENTRAL PARK   *1999 opera trilogy*

Playwrights Wendy Wasserstein, A. R. Gurney and Terrence McNally were commissioned to create opera librettos using the setting of Central Park in New York City and were then linked with composers. The results were three one-act operas collectively titled *Central Park* that were premiered at Glimmerglass Opera on August 8, 1999, and staged at New York City Opera in November 1999. The operas were Deborah Drattell's THE FESTIVAL OF REGRETS composed to the libretto by Wasserstein, Michael Torke's STRAWBERRY FIELDS composed to the libretto by Gurney and Robert Beaser's THE FOOD OF LOVE composed to the libretto by McNally. Michael Yeargan designed sets, Mark Lamos directed and Stewart Robertson conducted. The operas were videotaped by Kirk Browning and Mark Lamos at Glimmerglass and telecast on PBS on January 19, 2000.

CÉZANNE'S DOUBT   *1996 opera by Rothman*

Artist Cézanne struggles to find a way to express reality rather than just represent it. Daniel Rothman's avant-garde chamber opera *Cézanne's Doubt*, libretto by the composer based on Cézanne's letters and Baudelaire's poem *Une Charogne*, had its world premiere on October 12, 1996, at the Graz Festival in Austria and its American premiere on October 18, 1996, at Merkin Hall in New York. The opera was written for baritone Thomas Buckner, who plays Cézanne, and the Rothman Ensemble chamber group. The composer says his opera is not opera in the traditional sense but grew out of an essay by Maurice Merleau-Ponty exploring Cézanne's attempt to find a way of expressing objects in the act of appearing. Rothman's musical style, with its uses of microtones and electronic sounds, has been compared to that of Luigi Nono.

1997 Rothman Ensemble. Thomas Buckner, who created the role, sings Cézanne in this recording of the opera made in New York with the Rothman Ensemble. The instrumentalists are David Smeyers on clarinet, Wadada Leo Smith on trumpet, Ted Mook on cello and Kent Clelland on electronics. New World CD.

CHADWICK, GEORGE W.   *American composer (1854–1931)*

George Chadwick's 1912 opera THE PADRONE, a contemporary story about poor Italian immigrants, should have been an important moment in American opera history but the Metropolitan Opera turned it down for being too earthy and realistic. Like Scott Joplin's *Treemonisha*, it was ahead of its time and so was not produced until 1995. Chadwick, who was born in Lowell, MA, became fascinated by the musical stage early in his career and began writing operettas at the age of 30. He became widely known for his 1879 concert overture *Rip Van Winkle*, but he never composed an opera around the Washington Irving story. His first stage work was the operetta *The Peer and the Pauper*, composed in 1884 in the style of Gilbert and Sullivan, but it was never performed. The operetta *A Quite Lodging* was created for a private show in Boston in 1892 and staged privately. His next work was the 1894 burlesque opera TABASCO, libretto by R. A. Barnet, which was an instant hit and toured the country after successful runs in Boston and New York. Next was the ambitious *Judith*, libretto by William C. Langdon based on the Biblical story of Judith and Holofernes. As opera companies at the time were not interested in American operas, he had it performed in a concert version by the Worcester Chorale Festival in 1901. In 1911 he composed the music for Walter Browne's play *Everywoman: Her Pilgrimage in Quest of Love*, which was a success in New York and London. After his failure to get *The Padrone* performed, he gave up writing operas until 1923. His last stage work was the pastoral opera *Love's Sacrifice*, libretto by D. K. Stevens, produced at the Playhouse in Chicago in 1923. Chadwick's operas are not available on commercial recordings but the *Rip Van Winkle* and *Melpomene* overtures are on CD.

CHAMLEE, MARIO   *American tenor (1892–1966)*

Mario Chamlee created the title role in the premiere of Richard Hageman's opera CAPONSACCHI at the Metropolitan Opera in 1937 and played the Lover in the Met production of Gian Carlo Menotti's AMELIA GOES TO THE BALL in 1938. Chamlee, who was born in Los Angeles, made his debut there in 1916 before going to New York in 1920 to sing at the Met. He retired in 1939 after a successful international career.

CHANLER, THEODORE *American composer (1902–1961)*

Theodore Chanler, one of the leading composer/critics of his time, wrote only one opera. THE POT OF FAT (1955) based on a Grimm fairy tale, stars a singing cat and a singing mouse and has been recorded. Chanler, who was born in Newport, RI, studied at Oxford and in Paris under Nadia Boulanger. He returned to America in 1933 and became known for his art songs, including settings of poems by De la Mare, Blake, MacLeish, Feeney and others. His writings about music appeared in the *Boston Herald, Modern Music* and many other publications.

CHANTICLEER *American operas based on Chaucer tale*

Chanticleer, the Widow's boastful rooster, has dreams about being hunted by the Fox but his wife Perelote says he is foolish. When his fears are realized and he is trapped by the Fox, it takes a lot of trickery for him to escape. Geoffrey Chaucer's story "The Nun's Priest Tale" in *The Canterbury Tales* contains the best known version of the Chanticleer legend and has been popular with American opera composers.

1956 Seymour Barab. Seymour Barab's one-act opera *Chanticleer*, libretto by Mary Coline Richards, premiered at Aspen Opera in Colorado on August 4, 1956. Thomas Fitzpatrick sang Chanticleer, Adele Addison was Perelote, Anna Julia Hoyt was the Widow, and Carol White was the Fox. Jan Behr conducted the chamber orchestra. Paul Stuart took the role of Chanticleer when the opera was staged in New York. **1965 Ross Lee Finney.** Ross Lee Finney's 18-minute *The Nun's Priests' Tale*, libretto by the composer, premiered at Dartmouth College in Hanover, NH, in August 1965. Finney's opera includes a women's chorus that makes only hen noises, a chamber ensemble that features dog barks and cowbells and a version of the traditional folk song that begins "The fox went out on a chilly night." **1967 Joyce Barthelson.** Joyce Barthelson's one-act opera *Chanticleer*, libretto by the composer, was premiered by the National Federation of Music Clubs in New York on April 15, 1967. In this version Chanticleer is tricked by Mr. Fox into showing off his crowing and Chanticleer's wife persuades the turkey Gobbler to help him escape.

A CHEKHOV TRILOGY *1993 opera trilogy by Wargo*

Richard Wargo's three one-act Chekhov operas were first presented together as *A Chekhov Trilogy* at Chautauqua Opera in New York in 1993. The first opera is the poignant THE SEDUCTION OF A LADY, the second is the bittersweet A VISIT TO THE COUNTRY and the third is the comic THE MUSIC SHOP. Details about each are given under the individual titles. The trilogy was highly acclaimed when it was produced by Dorothy Danner at the Academy of Vocal Arts Opera Theatre in Philadelphia in 1996. It has also been presented by DiCapo Opera Theater and Skylight Opera Theatre.

A CHILD IS BORN *1955 opera by Hermann*

Joseph and his expectant wife Mary arrive in Bethlehem but there is no room for them in the inn which is filled with soldiers. The innkeeper's wife can only offer the couple the stable as shelter. Afterwards the innkeeper and his wife join shepherds and wise men who have arrived bring gifts for the new-born child. Bernard Herrmann's 30-minute opera *A Child Is Born,* libretto by Stephen Vincent Benét with lyrics by Maxwell Anderson, was premiered on General Electric Theater on CBS-TV on December 25, 1955. Ronald Reagan was the Narrator, Theodor Uppman was the Innkeeper, Nadine Conner was the Innkeeper's Wife and the supporting cast included Robert Middleton, Harve Presnell, and the Roger Wagner Chorale. Mort Abrams produced, Don Medford directed, Roger Wagner led his chorale and Herrmann conducted.

1955 CBS Television. The soundtrack of the CBS-TV production of the opera was released as a LP record in 1955. Ronald Reagan is Narrator, Theodore Uppman is the Innkeeper, Nadine Conner is the Innkeeper's Wife and Bernard Herrmann conducts. Temple LP.

A CHILDHOOD MIRACLE *1951 opera by Rorem*

Sisters Violet and Peony make a snowman that comes alive so they treat it as their brother. When their father forces the snowman to come into the house, it melts and disappears. The sisters run off and turn into snow statues. Ned Rorem's 40-minute chamber opera *A Childhood Miracle*, libretto by Elliot Stein based on Nathaniel Hawthorne's story *The Snow Image*, was premiered by Punch Opera with piano accompaniment at Carl Fischer Hall in New York City on May 10, 1955. Lynn Clark sang the role of Violet, Sarah Dubin was Peony, Don Grobe was the Snowman, Jayne Somogy was Mother, Harriet Hill was Aunt Emma and Gordon Myers was Father. The first performance of the opera with an orchestra was arranged by Plato Karayanis for WRCV Television in Philadelphia. The singers and musicians, undergraduates at the Curtis Institute, included Benita Valente, Dorothy Krebill and Wayne Conner. Jaime Laredo was concertmaster and Donald Johanos conducted the orchestra. It was telecast live on February 5, 1956.

1994 Magic Circle Opera Ensemble. Darcy Dunn is Violet with Michelle Couture as Peony in this recording made with the Magic Circle Opera Orchestra and Soloists led by Ray Evans Harrell. Patrick Greene is the Snowman, Madeline Tsingopoulos is Mother, Mary Cidoni is Aunt Emma, and Peter Castaldi is Father. John Ostendorf produced. Newport Classic CD.

CHINCHILLA *1985 opera by Fink*

Chinchilla coats cause marital problems for two couples in jazz-crazed 1920s New York. Four identical coats are bought for wives and lovers, two by each husband, but the lover in each case is the other man's wife. Myron Fink's adulterous light opera *Chinchilla*, libretto by Donald Moreland, was premiered by Tri-Cities Opera at the Forum Theater in Binghamton, NY, on January 18, 1986. The jazzy score reflects the frivolous feelings of the protagonists.

CHING, MICHAEL *American composer (1956–)*

Michael Ching, popular as conductor as well as composer, likes ghost operas. CUE 67, libretto by Sandra Bernard about ghosts and Shakespearean actors, premiered at Virginia Opera in Norfolk in 1992. BUOSO'S GHOST, libretto by the composer featuring a ghost as its central ruse, is a sequel to Puccini's *Gianni Schicchi*; it was staged at Memphis Opera in 1997. Ching, a Chinese American graduate of Duke University, studied music with Robert Ward and Carlisle Floyd. His operas are all in one act. The first was *Levees*, libretto by the composer, presented in Durham, NC, in the summer of 1980. *Leo, Opera in One Cat*, libretto by Fernando Conseca based on Massey's story *Leo Spat*, was staged by Texas Opera Theater in Houston on June 6, 1985. *Cocks Must Crow,* libretto by the composer based on a story by Margery Kinnan Rawlings, was premiered by Greater Miami Opera in Miami on December 12, 1985. He wrote two operas with librettos by singer/songwriter Hugh Moffatt: *King of the Clouds* was premiered by Dayton Opera in Ohio on January 18, 1993, and staged in five other opera houses. *Out of the Rain* was premiered by Opera Delaware in 1998.

CHIP AND HIS DOG *1979 children's opera by Menotti*

Chip is forced to sell his dog to a haughty Princess when she learns it can dance and play music. When the dog refuses to curtsy to her, she threatens him; Chip pleads for mercy saying a dog must be won by love. She relents, asks them both to stay with her and sends for another crown. In Gian Carlo Menotti's charming 30-minute fairy tale opera *Chip and His Dog,* all the roles are sung by children with musical accompaniment by piano and drums. It was commissioned and premiered by the Canadian Children's Opera Chorus at the University of Guelph on May 4, 1979. Boy soprano David Coulter sang Chip, Andrea Kuzmich was the non-singing Dog, girl soprano Laura Zarins was the Princess, Priscilla Heffernan was the Messenger, John Kuzmich was the Page, Valarie Williams was the Doctor, Heidi Hobday was the Courtier, Avril Helbig was the Gardener, and Breffni O'Reilly was the Scribe. The chorus of courtiers were members of the Canadian Children's Opera Chorus. The opera was written in English but for bilingual Canada a French translation was prepared titled *Luc et son Chien.* Antonini Dimitrov designed the sets, Olga Dimitrov devised the costumes, Derek Hollman was music director, Bruce Ubakata played piano, and David Kent and William Winant were the percussionists.

1979 Canadian Children's Opera. David Coulter is Chip and Laura Zarins is the Princess in this original cast recording of the opera by the Canadian Children's Opera Chorus. Andrea Kuzmichis the Dog, Priscilla Heffernan is the Messenger, John Kuzmich is the Page, Valarie Williams is the Doctor, Heidi Hobday is the Courtier, Erica Giesl is the Cook, Avril Helbig is the Gardener and Breffni O'Reilly is the Scribe. Derek Holman conducts the Canadian Children's Opera Orchestra and Chorus. Aquitaine-CBS Records LP.

CHOOKASIAN, LILI *American contralto (1921–)*

Lili Chookasian created the role of the Grandmother in Jack Beeson's opera MY HEART'S IN THE HIGHLANDS on NET Opera Theater in 1970 and Queen Beatrix in Thomas Pasatieri's INEZ DE CASTRO at Baltimore Opera in 1976. She sang the role of Madame Flora in Gian Carlo Menotti's THE MEDIUM at New York City Opera in 1963, the Maharanee in the American premiere of Menotti's THE LAST SAVAGE at the Met in 1964, and the Nun on the recording of Menotti's THE DEATH OF THE BISHOP OF BRINDISI in 1965, Chookasian, who was born in Chicago, studied with Philip Manuel and made her debut with Arkansas Opera in 1959 as Adalgisa in *Norma.*

CHOTZINOFF, SAMUEL *American opera producer (1889–1964)*

NBC music director Samuel Chotzinoff was one of the most important advocates of American opera on radio and television. In 1939 he commissioned Gian Carlo Menotti's radio opera THE OLD MAID AND THE THIEF. In 1951 he commissioned Menotti's television opera AMAHL AND THE NIGHT VISITORS. He ran NBC OPERA THEATRE from 1949 to 1964 with conductor Peter Herman Adler and director Kirk Browning and commissioned many American operas. He was involved with DESERET, DOWN IN THE VALLEY, LA GRANDE BRETÈCHE, GRIFFELKIN, LABYRINTH, MARIA GOLOVIN, MARTIN'S LIE, THE SAINT OF BLEECKER STREET,

SUMMER AND SMOKE, THE TRIAL AT ROUEN, THE TRIAL OF MARY LINCOLN and TROUBLE IN TAHITI. Chotzinoff, who came to America from Russia in 1896 as a child, began his musical career as a pianist and music critic after studies at Columbia University. He was music critic for *The World* from 1925 to 1931 and the New York Post from 1934 to 1941 and began to work at NBC in 1936. His memoir *A Little Night Music* elaborates his ideas about opera.

A CHRISTMAS CAROL (1) *1954 opera by Herrmann*

Victorian miser Ebenezer Scrooge discovers the true meaning of Christmas after seeing what happens in Christmases past, present and future. He befriends nephew Bob Cratchit's family and finds there is joy in giving. Bernard Herrmann's 60-minute television opera *A Christmas Carol,* libretto by Maxwell Anderson based on Charles Dickens' novel, premiered on CBS-TV on December 23, 1954. Marilyn Horne, William Olvis and David Venesty were the singers with Herrmann conducting the orchestra and Roger Wagner Chorale. Fredric March was old Scrooge, Craig Hill was young Scrooge, Basil Rathbone was Marley, Bob Sweeney was Bob Cratchit, Christopher Cook was Tiny Tim, Sally Fraser was the Spirit of Christmas Past, Ray Middleton was the Spirit of Christmas Present and Queenie Leonard was Mrs. Cratchit. Peter Miles, Janine Perreau, Bonnie Franklin and Judy Franklin took the small roles. Donald Saddler arranged the choreography, Edward Boyle designed the sets and Ralph Levy directed the telecast.

1954 CBS Television. Marilyn Horne, William Olvis and David Venesty are the singers with Bernard Herrmann conducting the orchestra and Roger Wagner Chorale. The opera was made available as both video and soundtrack record with narration by Fredric March. Classic TV VHS/Unicorn LP.

A CHRISTMAS CAROL (2) *1979 opera by Musgrave*

Ebenezer Scrooge is taken on a time trip by the ghost of his former partner and discovers the meaning of Christmas. Thea Musgrave's two-act opera *A Christmas Carol,* libretto by the composer, was commissioned by Virginia Opera which premiered it in Norfolk, VA, on December 7, 1979. Frederick Burchinal was Ebenezer Scrooge, Jerold Norman was Bob Cratchit, Carolyne James was Mrs. Cratchit, James Bartlett was Tiny Tim, Howard Bender was young Scrooge and Fred, Mary Brinkley was Harriet Cratchit, Kathryn Montgomery was Belle and Martha Cratchit, Claudette Peterson was Fan and Lucy and Belle Cratchit, Robert Randolph was Mr. Fezziwig and Portly Gentleman, and Howard Scammon was Marley's Ghost. Dancer Rob Besserer portrayed the Spirits of Christmas Past, Present and Future, David Farrar directed and Peter Mark conducted the Virginia Opera Association Orchestra and Chorus. Musgrave added two scenes to the story: young Scrooge's rejection of his first love Belle and a mourning scene for Tiny Tim's death. Granada Television in England telecast the opera in December 1982 using a video recording of a 1981 Royal Opera production at Sadler's Well in London.

1979 Virginia Opera. Frederick Burchinal is Ebenezer Scrooge in this recording of the opera with the Virginia Opera premiere cast taken from tapes of a December 16, 1979, broadcast on National Public Radio from WHRO-FM. Jerold Norman is Bob Cratchit, Carolyne James is Mrs. Cratchit, James Bartlett is Tiny Tim, Howard Bender is young Scrooge and Fred, Mary Brinkley is Harriet Cratchit, Kathryn Montgomery is Belle and Martha Cratchit, Claudette Peterson is Fan and Lucy and Belle Cratchit, Robert Randolph is Mr. Fezziwig and Portly Gentleman, and Howard Scammon is Marley's Ghost. Peter Mark conducts the

Virginia Opera Orchestra and Chorus. Moss Music Group (MMG) 3-LP set.

A CHRISTMAS CAROL (3) *1977*
opera by Sandow

Ebenezer Scrooge discovers the value of Christmas after he takes another look at the past and experiences what the future might hold. Gregory Sandow's 75-minute one-act opera *A Christmas Carol*, libretto by the composer, was commissioned by Eastern Opera Theater which premiered it in Stratford, Connecticut, on February 21, 1977. Sandow's libretto includes poems by Rossetti and Mackay and the score even features recognizable Christmas carols.

A CHRISTMAS CAROL (4) *1981*
"play with music" by Hoiby

Miser Ebenezer Scrooge reforms after a bad night with a ghost and decides that Christmas is a better idea that he had thought. Lee Hoiby describes his version of *A Christmas Carol* as a "play with music." Dennis Powers and Laird Williamson wrote the libretto for the 110-minute work which telecast December 21, 1981. Lawrence Hecht was Narrator and Ghost of Christmas Present, William Paterson was Scrooge, Raye Birk was Marley's Ghost, Markey Murphey was Bob Cratchit, Delores Mitchell was Mrs. Cratchit, Tyson Thomas was Tiny Tim, Janice Hutchins was Belie, Sydney Walker was Fezziwig, Nicholas Kaledin was the Ghost of Christmas Yet To Come and Thomas Oglesby was the Ghost of Christmas Past. Laird Williamson directed. The work staged in San Francisco on December 2, 1987.

1997 John Ayer/Memphis Chamber Choir. John Ayer conducts the Memphis Chamber Choir, Memphis Boy Choir and Memphis Pro Arte Chamber Orchestra in excerpts from *A Christmas Carol* recorded in Memphis in May 1997. It's on the album *Sing Lullaby*. Pro Organo CD.

CHRISTOPHER SLY *1963 opera by Argento*

Tinker debtor Christopher Sly is chased by creditors into the Garter Inn whose hostess turns out to be another creditor. While they go for a policeman, Sly gets drunk and falls asleep. He is found by a rich Lord who decides to play a trick on him. He has him taken to his mansion and dressed in a nobleman's clothes. When Sly wakes, he is told he is a rich man who has been insane for seven years and just recovered. After a time the Lord tires of the game and takes Sly back to the inn. When the creditors appears, he settles Sly's debts While he is doing this, Sly runs off with the Lord's valuables and mistresses. Dominick Argento's 70-minute opera *Christopher Sly*, libretto by John Manlove based on the introduction to Shakespeare's *The Taming of the Shrew*, premiered at the University of Minnesota in Minneapolis on May 31, 1963. The melodic opera has eight principal roles and scored for a 17-piece chamber orchestra.

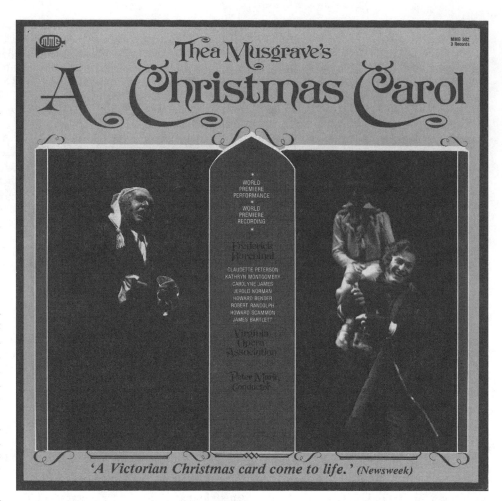

Thea Musgrave's *A Christmas Carol*, based on the Dickens story, was premiered and recorded by Virginia Opera in 1979.

CIESINSKI, KATHERINE   *American mezzo-soprano (1950–)*

Katherine Ciesinski created the role of Sonia in Dominick Argento's THE ASPERN PAPERS in Dallas in 1988, Aunt Cecilia in Mark Adamo's LITTLE WOMEN in Houston in 1998, and Sofia in Tod Machover's RESURRECTION in Houston in 1999. She first became well known singing the role of Erika in a 1978 Spoleto Festival telecast of Samuel Barber's VANESSA. Ciesinski, who was born in Newark, Delaware,, studied at the Curtis Institute and made her debut in Aix-en-Provence in *La traviata* in 1976 and her American debut in Santa Fe in *Lulu* in 1979. She made her first appearance at the Met in 1998.

CIESINSKI, KRISTINE   *American soprano (1952–)*

Kristine Ciesinski, the sister of Katherine Ciesinski, has spent much of her career in Europe. She made her London debut with the English National Opera in 1989 playing Anna Maurrant in Marc Blitzstein's STREET SCENE and she sings the role on the 1992 ENO recording. Like her sister, she was born in Newark, Delaware. After studies in Boston, she won a Swiss singing competition in 1977 and began to sing at Salzburg in 1979. She has also sung with Opera North and Scottish Opera.

CINDERELLA   *1957 operetta by Rodgers*

Cinderella finds her Prince Charming with the help of a Fairy

Godmother despite problems with her stepmother and stepsisters. Richard Rodgers' operetta *Cinderella*, libretto by Oscar Hammerstein II, premiered on CBS Television on March 31, 1957, and then staged, has now entered the opera house repertory. Julie Andrews starred in the CBS premiere as Cinderella with Jon Cypher as Prince Charming, Edith Adams as the Fairy Godmother, Howard Lindsay as the King, Dorothy Stickney as the Queen, Ilka Chase as the Stepmother, Kaye Ballard as stepsister Portia and Alice Ghostley as stepsister Joy. William and Jean Eckart designed the sets, Ralph Nelson directed the 90-minute production and Alfredo Antonini conducted the chorus and orchestra. This was the only musical created for television by Rodgers and Hammerstein.

1957 CBS Television. Julie Andrews sings the role of Cinderella with the cast of the CBS Television production as listed above. Alfredo Antonini conducts the chorus and orchestra and Ralph Nelson directed. The recording was made before the telecast on March 31, 1957. Columbia LP/Sony CD. **1958 London stage show.** Tommy Steele stars in the British stage version of the operetta opposite Bruce Trent, Robin Palmer, Betty Marsden, Enid Lowe and Ted Durante. Bobby Howells conducts the chorus and orchestra. Decca LP. **1965 CBS Television.** Lesley Ann Warren stars as Cinderella in the 1965 CBS Television revival. Stuart Damon is Prince Charming, Celeste Holm is the Fairy Godmother, Walter Pidgeon is the King, Ginger Rogers is the Queen, Pat Carol is stepsister Prunella and Barbara Ruick is stepsister Esmeralda. Eugene Loring designed the choreography, Charles S. Dubin directed the 90-minute production and John Green conducted chorus and orchestra. Telecast February 22, 1965. Soundtrack on Columbia LP/Sony CD; TV show on Columbia Tristar DVD.

CINDERELLA IN SPAIN/CINDERELLA EN ESPAÑA
1998 opera by Warwick

The familiar Cinderella fairytale is told bilingually to demonstrates the universality of the fable. Mary Carol Warwick's opera *Cinderella in Spain/Cinderella en España,* bilingual libretto by Kate Pogue, was premiered by Houston Grand Opera on February 24, 1998, at the Heinen Theater at Houston Community College. The cast was doubled. Cynthia Leforce and Sandra Campbell were Cinderella, Barry Barrios and Billy Hargis were Prince Paul, Shawna Peterson and Kathleen Manley were Stepmother Madrasta and Fairy Godmother Madrina, Deric Rosenblatt and Omari Tau William were stepsister Isabella and the King, Robert Hughes and Kevin Moods were stepsister Margarita and the Town Crier, and Marque Thibodeaux and Laura Chapman were the Puppeteer and voices of Papageno and Huron. Constantinos Kritikos designed the set, Larry Dachslager staged the production and Kim Hupp was music director and pianist.

THE CIVIL WARS *1984 opera/media event by Glass/Wilson*

If it had been completed, *the CIVIL warS: a tree is best measured when it is down* would have been the longest opera ever staged. Designer/director/librettist ROBERT WILSON and composer PHILIP GLASS planned it as a multi-media event for the 1984 Los Angeles Olympics Arts Festival and based it around Matthew Brady's photographs of the American Civil War. Each act was to have been by a different composer. However, it became too expensive to finish and only the sections with music by Glass have been produced.

1984 The Rome Section. *Act V: The Rome Section*, commissioned by Rome Opera, was premiered in Rome on March 26, 1984, with Marcello Panni conducting. The libretto by Wilson and Maita de Niscemi is based on poems by Seneca and letters written during the American Civil War. The chief characters are Abraham Lincoln, Mrs. Lincoln, Mrs. Lincoln as a young woman, Robert E. Lee, Garibaldi (who sings in Italian), Hercules, Hercules' mother Alcmene, Earth Mother and Snow Owl. The singers were Ruby Hinds, Seta Del Grande, Luigi Petroni, Franco Sioli, Luigi Rone and Franco Concilio. **1984 The Cologne Section.** The Cologne section of the opera, based around a play by Heiner Muller, was staged in German by Wilson and telecast by WDR. The singers were Ingrid Andree, Anna Henke, Fred Hospowsky, Hannelore Lübeck, Georg Peter-Pilz, Rainer Philippi and Ilse Ritterl. Jurgen Flimm directed the telecast on June 24, 1984. **1999 The Rome Section.** Mezzo-soprano Denyce Graves sings the roles of Earth Mother and Mrs. Lincoln in this recording of *Act V: The Rome Section.* Soprano Sondra Radvanovsky is Snow Owl and Alcmene, tenor Giuseppe Sabbatini is Garibaldi, baritone Zheng Zhou is Abraham Lincoln, and bass Stephen Morscheck is Hercules. Laurie Anderson speaks the role of young Mrs. Lincoln and Robert Wilson speaks the role of Robert E. Lee. Dennis Russell Davies conducts the American Composers Orchestra and Morgan State University Choir. Electra Nonesuch CD.

CIVILIZATION AND ITS DISCONTENTS *1977*
"theater opera" by Sahl and Salzman

Singer Jill Goodheart and her adman boyfriend Derek Dude have a fight at the Club Bide-a-Wee nightclub and she takes agent Jeremy Jive back to her apartment. Despite his amorous efforts, she won't get off the phone, and he is about to leave when Derek arrives. They begin to discuss an ad campaign when guru Carlos Arachnid arrives and takes Jill back to the club. Eric Salzman and Michael Sahl consider their *Civilization and Its Discontents* as American theater opera in the tradition of Menotti, Gershwin, and Weill. It premiered at the American Musical and Dramatic Academy on May 19, 1977, with Candice Farley as Jill Goodheart, Paul Binotto as Jeremy Jive, Tim Jerome as Derek Dude, and Karl Patrick Krause as Carlos Arachnid. It was broadcast in 1980 on NPR and later by the BBC.

1978 Quog Music Theater. Candice Farley plays Jill Goodheart, Paul Binotto is Jeremy Jive, William Perry is Derek Dude, and Karl Patrick Krause is Carlos Arachnid in this recording made for the Quog Music Theater and National Public Radio. Michael Sahl plays the piano and organ while Cleve Pozar plays drums and percussion. Nonesuch LP.

CLAFLIN, AVERY *American composer (1898–1979)*

Avery Claflin is probably the only bank president to become a successful opera composer and certainly the only one to create a madrigal based on Federal income tax instructions. His work was much praised by Aaron Copland, who selected him a musician of promise in 1926. Virgil Thomson conducted scenes from Claflin's opera *Hester Prynne* in Hartford in 1934; it was based on Nathaniel Hawthorne's THE SCARLET LETTER with libretto by Dorothea Carroll. Claflin's most famous opera, however, is LA GRANDE BRETÈCHE, an operatic version of the Balzac story recorded in 1956 and broadcast on NBC radio in 1957. A native of Keene, NH, and a graduate of Harvard, Claflin worked for the French American Banking Corporation in New York for 35 years, retiring as president in 1954. He composed his first opera in 1921, THE FALL OF THE HOUSE OF USHER based on the story by EDGAR ALLAN POE. His last opera was the 1964 UNCLE TOM'S CABIN, based on the novel by Harriet Beecher Stowe. Claflin's income tax madrigal, a setting of Internal Revenue Service Form 1040 titled *Lament for April 15,* premiered at the Berkshire Music Festival in 1955.

CLARA   *2004 opera by Convery*

Composer/concert pianist Clara Wieck Shumann, wife of composer Robert Schumann, remembers her life from her deathbed. She had tried to balance career and family but it was a near impossible task. Robert Convery's 90-minute chamber opera *Clara*, libretto by Kathleen Cahill based on the life of Clara Schumann, was premiered by Maryland Opera Studio at the Clarice Smith Performng Arts Center in Maryland in 2004. Michelle T. Rice was old Clara, Lee ann Myslewski was young Clara and Ole Hass was Robert Schumann. The singers were all students and alumni of the University of Maryland School of Music. Leon Major staged the opera and Joann Kulesza conducted the student orchestra.

CLAREY, CYNTHIA   *American mezzo-soprano (1949–)*

Cynthia Clarey has been particularly identified with George Gershwin's PORGY AND BESS. She is Serena in the 1987 Glyndebourne Festival Opera recording, the 1988 Glyndebourne Festival Opera video and the 1998 London Proms recording. She has also sung Bess on stage, notably in an historic production of the opera in South Africa. She created the role of Kanaxa in Anthony Davis's impressionistic UNDER THE DOUBLE MOON in St. Louis in 1989, sings Irina in the 1992 recording of Kurt Weill's LOST IN THE STARS and sings one of the main roles in the 1978 recording of BENJAMIN CARR's *The Lady of the Lake*. She played the Countess in the American premiere of Thea Musgrave's THE VOICE OF ARIADNE at New York City Opera in 1977. Clarey was born in Smithfield, Virginia, and studied at Howard and Juilliard. She lives in England.

CLARKE, HENRY   *American composer (1907–1992)*

Henry Clarke wrote two notable operas, both musical discussions about morality. THE LOAFER AND THE LOAF (1954), libretto by the composer based on a play by Evelyn Sharp, centers around the theft of a loaf of bread and focuses on an ethical argument between a Poet's Wife and a Prosperous Citizen. *Lysistrata* (1972), libretto by the composer based on the play by Aristophanes, debates the immorality of war as Athenian and Spartan women join forces to end one. Clark, a native of Dover, New Hampshire, and a graduate of Harvard, studied music under Gustav Holst and Nadia Boulanger. He taught at several American universities before retiring in 1977.

CLAUDIA LEGARE   *1978 opera by Ward*

Claudia Legare, daughter of General Legare and married to George Lowndes, returns to Charleston, South Carolina, after the Civil War with a plan to restore the south to glory by reviving the plantations. Her friend Daphne is working with Claudia's former lover Orlando on a plan to restore it through industrialization. Colonel Blagden, who will choose between the two, has designs on Claudia who has turned bitter. She goads Orlando to his death and later kills herself. Robert Ward's morose four-act opera *Claudia Legare*, libretto by Bernard Stambler loosely based on Henrik Ibsen's play *Hedda Gabler*, was commissioned by New York City Opera but premiered by Minnesota Opera in Minneapolis on April 14, 1978. Barbara Brandt sang the role of Claudia, Vern Sutton was George, John Brandstetter was Orlando, Carl Glaum was Colonel Blagden, Marsha Hunter was Daphne Grayson, Susan Chastain was Aunt Julia and Janis Hardy was Jenny. H. Wesley Balk directed and Philip Brunelle conducted. The opera was reprised at Duke University in 1981.

1991 William Stone. Baritone William Stone sings two arias from *Claudia Legare*, "Lament for Aunt Renie" and "The South Must Industrialize." He is accompanied by pianist Thomas Warburton on the album *Robert Ward: Arias and Songs*. Bay Cities CD.

CLEOPATRA'S NIGHT   *1920 opera by Hadley*

Meiamoun loves Cleopatra and shoots an arrow at her feet declaring his love. She offers to let him have one night with her if he will agree to die the following morning. He does so and the next day takes a cup of poison. Frances Alda starred as Cleopatra in the Metropolitan Opera premiere of Henry Hadley's two-act opera *Cleopatra's Night* on January 21, 1920. Alice L. Pollock wrote the libretto based on Théophile Gautier's story *Une Nuit de Cléopâtre*. Orville Harrold sang the role of Meiamoun opposite Alda, Jeanne Gordon was the servant Mardio who loved Meiamoun and Gennaro Papi was the conductor. The opera was reprised for three more performances in the following season. *Cleopatra's Night* was one of the first American operas to be presented on radio. It was broadcast by NBC's National Grand Opera Company on May 6, 1929, with Astrid Fjelde as Cleopatra and the composer Hadley the National Grand Opera Orchestra.

COAL   *1995 folk opera by Shatin*

Coal and coal miners are the protagonists of Judith Shatin's Appalachian-style opera *Coal: A Blueprint for Understanding Twentieth-Century Music*, libretto by the composer. She based it around West Virginia coal mining songs, sounds and lore and scored it for Appalachian folk instruments and electronics. *Coal* tells the story of the tribulations of coal miners and the importance of their unions. It was premiered at Shepherd College in Shepherdstown, WV, on November 12, 1995, with members of the United Mine Workers as special guests. The principal soloist was country singer Ginny Hawker who sang coal-mining laments backed by a folk instrument quintet while Jan Stengler led the sixty-voice Masterworks Chorale.

COERNE, LOUIS   *American composer (1870–1922)*

Louis Adolphe Coerne's three-act opera ZENOBIA was the first American opera staged in Europe, premiering at the Stadttheater in Bremen, Germany, on December 1, 1905. Coerne was born in Newark, NJ, but he spent some of his childhood in Germany and studied composition in Munich. After working as a conductor and organist in Boston, he went to Leipzig in 1899 to composed *Zenobia* to a libretto by Oskar Stein. It was published in Leipzig in 1903 preceding the Bremen production in 1905 and favorably reviewed by German critics. The opera was never staged in America, however, nor was his later opera *A Woman of Marblehead*. Coerne returned to Harvard for further studies and was the first person to earn a doctorate in music from an American university. He later taught at Connecticut College.

COLD SASSY TREE   *2000 opera by Floyd*

Will Tweedy remembers small town life in Georgia at the beginning of the 20th century when he lived in Cold Sassy Tree. His grandfather Rucker Lattimore marries a young woman named Love Simpson only a few weeks after becoming a widower and the town is scandalized. It turns out Rucker isn't after sex at all, he just wants a cheap housekeeper. Carlisle Floyd's folksy comic opera *Cold Sassy Tree*, libretto by the composer based on the 1984 novel by Olive Ann Burns, was premiered by Houston Grand Opera on April 14, 2000. Dean Peterson was Rucker Lattimore, Patricia Racette was Love Simpson, John McVeigh was Will Tweedy, Judith Christin was Effie Belle Tate, Christopher Schaldenbrand was Clayton, Diane Alexander was Mary Willis Tweedy, Beth Clayton was Lorna

Williams, Chad Shelton was Luther, Joseph Evans was Camp Williams, Matthew A. Kreger was Hosie Roach and Margaret Lloyd was Lightfoot McClendon. Michael Yeargan designed the sets, Bruce Beresford directed and Patrick Summers conducted. Critics said that the opera, co-commissioned by Houston, San Diego, Austin, Carolina and Baltimore opera companies, was in the tradition of Thornton Wilder's *Our Town* and praised its melodious arias It continues to be produced and was staged by Opera Omaha in 2004.

2000 Houston Grand Opera. The Houston Grand Opera production of *Cold Sassy Tree* was broadcast on National Public Radio on November 18, 2000, with the original cast. Dean Peterson was Rucker, Patricia Racette was Love and John McVeigh was Will. Patrick Summers conducted. House of Opera CD.

COLEMAN, CY   *American composer (1929–)*

Cy Coleman was one of the few Broadway musical composers to survive the coming of rock with a chain of successes into the 1990s. Born in New York City and educated as a classical musician, he turned to songwriting for revues and found success in 1960 with his first book musical, *Wildcat*, written for Lucille Ball with lyrics by Carolyn Leigh. They teamed up again in 1962 for *Little Me*, libretto by Neil Simon. With Dorothy Fields as lyricist and Neil Simon again as librettist, he had his biggest stage success with *Sweet Charity* (1966) based on a Fellini movie about a streetwalker. After *Seesaw* (1973) and *I Love My Wife* (1977), he won a Tony for Best Musical for *On the Twentieth Century* (1978) working with Adolph Green and Betty Comden. *Home Again, Home Again* (1979) was followed by *Barnum* (1980), an international hit about showman P. T. Barnum with book by Mark Bramble and lyrics by Michael Stewart. After two minor works he returned to form with *City of Angels* (1989), a Tony award winner about a sleazy private eye in Los Angeles with lyrics by David Zippel and book by Larry Gelbart. *The Will Rogers Follies* (1991), the story of the famous stage and film actor with lyrics by Green and Comden and book by Peter Stone, won a third Tony.

COLEMAN, LEO   *American dancer/mime (1923–)*

Leo Coleman, a dancer studying with Katharine Dunham, created the role of the mute Toby and choreographed Gian Carlo Menotti's opera *The Medium* when it premiered at Columbia University in 1946. Menotti brought him back for the Broadway production in 1947 and he played the role throughout its stage run, in two television versions and in Menotti's 1951 film. Afterwards he went to live in Italy where he performed the role with an Italian cast featuring Gianna Pederzini as Madame Flora and Dora Gatta as Monica. He danced in the premiere of Renzo Rossellini's opera *Il Vortice* in 1958, danced in Federico Fellini's 1960 film *La Dolce Vita* and choreographed Mario Bava's 1961 film *Gli Invasori*.

COLGRASS, MICHAEL   *American composer (1932–)*

Michael Colgrass, who won the Pulitzer Prize for Music in 1978 for *Déjà Vu for Percussion Quartet,* is best known for percussion works but has also written three operas. VIRGIL'S DREAM (1967), libretto by the composer, tells the story of a child prodigy whose future is insured against loss by an insurance company. *Nightingale, Inc* (1971), libretto by the composer, is a comic opera that premiered at the University of Illinois in Urbana. The children's opera *Something's Gonna Happen* (1978) is a modernization of the Jack and the Beanstalk story and premiered in Toronto. Colgrass, who was born in Chicago and graduated from the University of Illinois, studied music under Darius Milhaud and Lukas Foss.

COLLEGES AND UNIVERSITIES   *Venues for American opera premieres*

Many of the most enduring American operas were premiered at colleges and universities and many important composers were able to hone their craft through such productions. Columbia and Indiana University have been especially important. Among the composers who premiered important operas at colleges were George Antheil (VENUS IN AFRICA at Denver, VOLPONE at USC), Jack Beeson (HELLO OUT THERE at Columbia), Carlisle Floyd (SUSANNAH at Florida State), Otto Luening (EVANGELINE at Columbia), Gian Carlo Menotti (AMELIA GOES TO THE BALL at the Curtis Institute, THE MEDIUM at Columbia), Douglas Moore (GIANTS IN THE EARTH at Columbia, CARRY NATION at the University of Kansas), Kurt Weill (DOWN IN THE VALLEY at Indiana), Lukas Foss (THE JUMPING

Cy Coleman's stage musical *Sweet Charity* was made into an excellent film starring Shirley MacLaine.

FROG OF CALAVERAS COUNTY at Indiana)and Virgil Thomson (THE MOTHER OF US ALL at Columbia).

COLONEL JONATHAN THE SAINT   *1961 opera by Argento*

A woman living in post Civil War Maryland cannot forget her dead Confederate soldier lover so she marries a man who resembles him. In her dreams she meets her lover's ghost and pledges her love. Dominick Argento's four-act opera *Colonel Jonathan the Saint*, libretto by John Olon-Scrymgeour, was premiered by Lyric Opera at Loretta Heights College in Denver on December 31, 1971.

COLORADO   *American state (1876–)*

American opera came early to Colorado. The first was W. F. Hunt's *Brittle Silver*, libretto by Stanley Wood, which was premiered at the Tabor Grand Opera House in Denver on January 23, 1882. The opera house was built by Horace Tabor, the silver millionaire whose love affair with Elizabeth "Baby" Doe was the basis of Douglas Moore's opera THE BALLAD OF BABY DOE, premiered in Central City in 1956. Other operas set in Colorado include Robert Ward's THE LADY FROM COLORADO (1964) Henry Mollicone's THE FACE ON THE BARROOM FLOOR (1978), and Ross

Central City — Poster advertising Central City Opera's 2003 season.

Lee Finney's *Weep Torn Land* (1984), which focuses on the violence in Colorado in the 19th century. Opera composers born in Colorado include Cecil Effinger (Colorado Springs), Tom Johnson (Greeley) and Robert Moran (Denver) while African American composer Lawrence Freeman began his career in Denver. Opera premieres and companies are listed under their cities.

Arvada: Pat Mendoza's folk opera *Song of the Plains*, based on his book, premiered in November 1993 at the Center for the Performing Arts in Arvada.

Aspen: Aspen, now a ski resort for the wealthy, is also the home of the Wheeler Opera House built in the glory days of silver mining; it was refurbished and reopened in 1984. Operas premiered in Aspen include Thomas Pasatieri's *The Woman* in 1955, Seymour Barab's CHANTICLEER in 1956, David Del Tredici's *Pop-pourri* in 1970, Pasatieri's *The Penitentes* in 1974, and James Legg's *The Wife of Bath's Tale* in 1986. Opera revivals include Virgil Thomson's FOUR SAINTS IN THREE ACTS in 1991 and Gordon Getty's PLUMP JACK in 1986.

Boulder: Boulder, the home of the University of Colorado, has had a number of premieres. Cecil Effinger's *Pandora's Box*, libretto by Sally Monsour, was staged in 1961; his *Cyrano De Bergerac.* libretto by Donald Sutherland based on the Rostand play, was performed in 1965; and his *The Gentleman Desperado and Miss Bird*, libretto by Sutherland, was staged in 1977 to celebrate the centennial of the University. Mary Davis's *Columbine*, libretto by Joanna Sampson, was premiered by Boulder Civic Opera on April 12, 1973.

Central City: An "American opera" was staged in Central City in 1877 just before the opera house opened but *Pat Casey's Night Hands* was deemed so controversial it closed after one performance. The Central City Opera House was built the following year at the height of the gold mining boom and restored in 1932. It has premiered several notable American operas. Douglas Moore's THE BALLAD OF BABY DOE was premiered on July 7, 1956, and went on to the New York City Opera, television and national success. Robert Ward's THE LADY FROM COLORADO, based on a novel by Homer Croy, was presented in July 1964 but did not get a warm response and was later revised. Henry Mollicone's one-act THE FACE ON THE BARROOM FLOOR was premiered July 22, 1978, and continues to be staged around the U.S. Garland Anderson's *Soyazhe* was premiered July 28, 1979. José Paul Bernardo's *Something for the Palace*, libretto by Bob Joyner about the vaudeville era, was premiered in August 1980. Jonathan Sheffer's *The Mistake*, libretto by Stephen Wadsworth about a soprano during an opera intermission, was premiered by Central City Opera in Denver in 1981. Non-premiere productions include Howard Moss's *The Queen and the Rebels* in 1972, Carlisle Floyd's SUSANNAH in 1997, Robert Ward's THE CRUCIBLE in 1998, Kurt Weill's STREET SCENE in 1999, Leonard Bernstein's CANDIDE in 2000, Mark Adamo's LITTLE WOMEN in 2001, Lee Hoiby's SUMMER AND SMOKE in 2002 and Sigmund Romberg's THE STUDENT PRINCE in 2004.

Colorado Springs: The Colorado Opera Festival, started in 1971, presents operas in the Pikes Peak Center. It staged Igor Stravinsky's THE RAKE'S PROGRESS in 1977 and Douglas Moore's THE BALLAD OF BABY DOE in 1986.

Crested Butte: Alva Henderson's NOSFERATU, based on Murnau's vampire film, was premiered at the Western Slope Summer Music Festival in Crested Butte in 1998.

Denver: W. F. Hunt premiered his *Brittle Silver*, libretto by Stanley Wood, at the Tabor Grand Opera House on January 23, 1882. Henry Houseley premiered his operetta *Native Silver* at the Broadway Theater in 1891, his light opera *The Juggler* at the Broadway Theater in 1895 and his one-act operas *Narcissus and Echo* and *Pygmalion* at El Jebel Temple in 1912. African American composer Lawrence Freeman premiered THE MARTYR at the Deutsche Theater in 1893. After a half century break, George Antheil premiered two operas at the University of Denver, THE BROTHERS in 1954 and VENUS IN AFRICA in 1957. The University was also the site of the premieres of four operas by Normand Lockwood: *Early Dawn* (created to mark the centennial of Denver) in 1961, *The Wizards of Balizar* in 1962 and *The Hanging Judge* and *Requiem for a Rich Young Man* in 1964. Max DiJulio's *Baby Doe*, based on the same historical events as Douglas Moore's opera, premiered at Loretta Heights College on May 22, 1956. Dominick Argento's COLONEL JONATHAN THE SAINT was premiered by Lyric Opera at Loretta Heights College in 1971. Opera Colorado, founded in 1982, is the major Denver opera company of the present day. It premiered Bob Downard's *Martin Avdeich: A Christmas Miracle,* libretto by the composer based on a Tolstoy story, on December 15, 1985, in a double bill with Gian Carlo Menotti's AMAHL AND THE NIGHT VISITORS. Downard's other opera, *One Little Acre,* premiered at Loretto Heights College on May 3, 1988.

Englewood: Colorado Opera Troupe, based in Englewood, presents operas from the European repertory.

Woodland Park: Rocky Mountain Opera is located in Woodland Park.

COLUMBUS   *1945 "movie opera" by Weill*

Kurt Weill wrote the twelve-minute "comic opera" *Columbus* to a libretto by Ira Gershwin for the 1945 film *Where Do We Go from Here?* It is through composed with three arias sung on Christopher Columbus's ship on its way to the New World. Mutineer Benito (Carlos Ramirez) sings about the mutiny saying the world is flat, Columbus (Fortunio Bonanova) defends his voyage for the queen saying the world is round and time traveler Bill Morgan (Fred MacMurray) tells the crew what they are about to discover. In the movie MacMurray plays a 20th Century man with a genie (Gene Sheldon) who lets him to travel backwards into American history. He ends up on Columbus's boat just before land is sighted. Maurice DePackh arranged the music and Gregory Ratoff directed the film for Twentieth Century-Fox.

1944 Kurt Weill/Ira Gershwin. Kurt Weill and Ira Gershwin perform three duets from the film *Where Do We Go from Here?* including the *Columbus* number "The Niña, the Pinta, the Santa Maria." These private recordings made for the producer of the film are on the album *Tryout: A Series of Private Rehearsal Recordings.* Heritage LP/DRG CD.

COMDEN, BETTY   *American librettist/lyricist/singer (1915–)*

Betty Comden collaborated with Adolph Green for six decades years on the lyrics and books of major musicals, many composed by Leonard Bernstein, and was a featured singer in several of them. The threesome worked together creating ON THE TOWN and WONDERFUL TOWN and the duo went on to write *Bells Are Ringing, Applause* and *On the Twentieth Century.* Comden created the role of Claire in *On the Town* in 1944, reprised the role in the recording Bernstein made in 1960 and helps narrate it in the 1992 Barbican Hall recording. Green and Comden won five Tony awards for their musicals and much gratitude from film lovers for their brilliant screenplay for the movie musical *Singin' in the Rain.*

COMMAND PERFORMANCE   *1961 opera by Middleton*

Robert Middleton's four-act opera *Command Performance,* libretto by Harold Wendell Smith, was premiered by the Boston Opera Group at Vassar College at Poughkeepsie, NY, on November 11, 1961. Blanche Thebom played Queen Elizabeth, Ezio Flagello was the Sultan and Robert Trehy was Jack Wilton. Sarah Caldwell staged the opera and conducted the orchestra.

THE CONFIDENCE MAN   *1982 opera by Rochberg*

In a 19th century riverboat town the Confidence Man tells the story of candlemaker China Aster. Aster accepts a loan from Orchis against the advice of his wife Annabella after the Angel of Bright Future gives him a dream of wealth to come. When he is unable to repay it, he is pursued by creditors and dies. George Rochberg's two and one-half hour opera *The Confidence Man,* libretto by his wife Gene Rochberg loosely based on the novel by Herman Melville, was commissioned by Santa Fe Opera which premiered it on July 31, 1982. Brent Ellis was the Confidence Man, Neil Rosenshein was China Aster, Sunny Joy Langton was Annabella, Michael Fiacco was Orchis, Deborah Cook was the Angel, Carolyne James was Mrs. Orchis, and Joseph Frank was the Barber. John Scheffler designed the sets, Richard Pearlman directed and William Harwood conducted. The score is neo-romantic tonal with arias, duets and choruses. Ernst Krenek's 1951 opera DARK WATERS is also based on *The Confidence Man.*

CONLON, JAMES   *American conductor (1950–)*

James Conlon, who made his conducting debut at Menotti's Spoleto Festival in 1971, conducted the first performance of Samuel Barber's revised version of ANTONY AND CLEOPATRA in 1975 at the Juilliard School where he had studied. He made his Met debut in 1976, went on to lead orchestras at major opera houses around the world and became chief conductor at the Cologne Opera in 1989. He conducted the Met orchestra in an American opera concert in 1991 released on CD as *A Salute to American Music.* He has conducted numerous American operas including AMELIA GOES TO THE BALL, CANDIDE, THE DEVIL AND DANIEL WEBSTER, MOURNING BECOMES ELECTRA, PORGY AND BESS, THE RAKE'S PROGRESS, REGINA, STREET SCENE, SUSANNAH and VANESSA. Conlon was named music director of the Ravinia Festival in Illinois in 2004.

CONNECTICUT   *American state (1788–)*

Connecticut has long been a center for operatic activity. One of the first American operas, *Federation Triumphant in the Steady Hearts of Connecticut Alone: or, The Turnpike Road to a Fortune,* was premiered in Hartford in 1801. Hartford was a favorite preview town for Broadway so many Broadway operas and operettas premiered there, including Virgil Thomson's FOUR SAINTS IN THREE ACTS, Marc Blitzstein's REGINA and Richard Rodgers' SOUTH PACIFIC. Connecticut-born opera people include composer Jerry Bock (New Haven), composer Dudley Buck (Hartford), soprano Virginia Copeland, composer Reginald De Koven (Middletown), soprano Eileen Farrell (Willimantic), composer Frederic Gleason (Middletown), composer John Adam Hugo (Bridgeport), composer Ellsworth Phelps (Middletown), soprano Rosa Ponselle (Meriden), soprano Teresa Stich-Randall (West Hartford) and composer Harold Rome (Hartford). Operas set in Connecticut include Ronald Perera's THE YELLOW WALLPAPER (1989) and Paula Kimper's PATIENCE AND SARAH (1998). Connecticut Opera, founded in Hartford in 1942, is the major opera company of the state.

Bridgeport: Neil Slater's *Again D. J.,* libretto by Nick Rossi about Don Juan, was premiered at the University of Bridgeport on May 5, 1972.

East Haddam: Goodspeed Opera House in East Haddam was

opened in 1877, closed at the turn of the century and restored in 1963. It specializes in operettas and musicals and has had considerable success with revivals. Mitch Leigh's MAN OF LA MANCHA (1965) and Charles Strouse's *Annie* (1976) premiered at Goodspeed. It's major revivals include John Philip Sousa's EL CAPITAN (1973), Kurt Weill's ONE TOUCH OF VENUS (1987) and Frank Loesser's THE MOST HAPPY FELLA (1991) .

Elmwood: Arnold Franchetti's *Prelude and Fugue* premiered at the Talcott School of Music on April 21, 1959.

Groton: Sam Dennison's RAPPACCINI'S DAUGHTER premiered at the University of Connecticut in Groton in 1984.

Hartford: Virgil Thomson's FOUR SAINTS IN THREE ACTS premiered at the Wadsworth Athenaeum in 1934 and Kurt Weill's KNICKERBOCKER HOLIDAY at the Horace Bushness Memorial Hall in 1938. The Hartford Opera Workshop produced the first telecast of an American opera in 1943, Gian Carlo Menotti's THE OLD MAID AND THE THIEF. Several operas premiered at the Julius Hartt School of Music: Elie Siegmeister's folk opera *Sing Out, Sweet Land* in 1944, Vittorio Giannini's BEAUTY AND THE BEAST in 1946 (first stage production), Douglas Moore's *White Wings* in 1949, Arnold Franchetti's THE PRINCESS in 1952, William Schuman's THE MIGHTY CASEY in 1953, Elie Siegmeister's *Miranda and the Dark Young Man* in 1956 and Russell Smith's *The Unicorn in the Garden* in 1957. Thomas Putsche's *The Cat and the Moon* premiered at the Avery Memorial Hall in 1960. Bruce Neely's *Americana, or A New Tale of the Genii* was premiered by American Music/Theater Group in 1985. James Sellars' THE WORLD IS ROUND premiered at the Wadsworth Athenaeum in 1993. Connecticut Opera, the sixth oldest opera company in the U.S. (founded in 1942), presents operas at the Bushnell Theater. It premiered Neely Bruce's Hansel and Gretel in 1998 and staged George Gershwin's PORGY AND BESS in 1981, 1988 and 1998 and Leonard Bernstein's TROUBLE IN TAHITI in 1987. The National Lyric Opera, based in Hartford, tours classic operas around New England.

Middletown: Richard Winslow's *Adelaide* was premiered at Wesleyan College in 1957.

New Haven: New Haven's famous Shubert Theater has been a favorite tryout site for Broadway producers for the past century. Its premieres include John Philip Sousa's THE BRIDE ELECT in 1897, Victor Herbert's THE DREAM GIRL in 1924, Irving Berlin's ANNIE GET YOUR GUN in 1946, Richard Rodgers' SOUTH PACIFIC in March 1949 and Marc Blitzstein's REGINA in 1949. The theater was closed from 1976 to 1983 and re-opened as a non-profit performing arts center. It continues to present new productions of music theater from *South Pacific* to *The Music Man*. Lewis Spratlan's three-act opera *Life Is a Dream,* premiered by New Haven Opera Theatre in 1978, was awarded the Pulitzer Prize for Music in 2000 in its concert version. C. Armstrong Gibbs' Christmas opera *The Three Kings* premiered at Prospect High School in New Haven on December 15, 1964. Susan Bingham's THE LAST LEAF was premiered by Chancel Opera in New Haven on December 1, 1984.

New London: Julia Smith's *The Goatherd and the Goblin* was staged with piano accompaniment at Buell Hall in 1949. Arnold Franchetti's *The Lion* premiered at the Williams Memorial Institute on December 16, 1950. Edward Thomas' DESIRE UNDER THE ELMS premiered at Connecticut College on August 10, 1978.

Norfolk: Lawrence Moss's THE BRUTE was premiered at Yale University Summer School on July 15, 1961.

Stamford: Victor Herbert's *My Golden Girl* premiered on December 19, 1919, and his *The Girl in the Spotlight* on July 7, 1920. Efrem Zimbalist's musical *Honeydew* premiered on March 19, 1920, and Ashley Vernon's one-act opera *Gram Slam* on June 25, 1955. Stamford is the home of the Connecticut Grand Opera and Orchestra which presents mostly European opera.

Stratford: Gregory Sandow's A CHRISTMAS CAROL was premiered by Eastern Opera Theater in 1977.

Thomaston: George Chadwick's 1912 opera THE PADRONE received its belated premiere in concert form at the Thomaston Opera House in 1995.

Waterford: Jonathan Sheffer's *Camera Obscura* premiered in Waterford in 1980, Michael Cohen's RAPPACCINI'S DAUGHTER in 1981, Robert Convey *Quince's Dream* and *Pyramus and Thisbe* in 1982, Robert Chauls' THE THIRTEEN CLOCKS in 1983 and Christopher Drobny's LUCY'S LAPSES in 1987.

Westport: Westport's White Barn Theater was the site of four premieres: Arnold Franchetti's *The Maypole* in July 1952, Hugo Weisgall's THE STRONGER in August 1952, Alec Wilder's *The Impossible Forest* in 1958 and Gordon Snell's *Gentleman's Island* in 1959.

Wilton: Peter Whiton's *The Bottle Imp* was premiered at the Wilton Playhouse on April 10, 1958.

THE CONQUISTADOR   *1997 opera by Fink*

The Spanish Inquisition infects Mexico in the 16th century when it is discovered that some of the conquistadors have Jewish ancestors. Provincial governor Don Luis de Carvajal falls from grace, sees his family destroyed and dies in prison. Myron Fink's grand opera *The Conquistador,* libretto by Donald Moreland based on historical events, premiered at San Diego Opera on March 1, 1997. Fink's ambitious four-hour work requires fourteen principal singers and a supporting cast of a hundreds. Jerry Hadley created the role of Don Luis, John Duykers was the Chief Inquisitor, Louis Otey was the Viceroy, Kenneth Cox was the Franciscan monk Bernardino, Adria Firestone was Louis's sister, Kerry O'Brien was his mother, Vivica Genaux was his niece and Elizabeth Hynes was the woman he loves. Kent Dorsey designed the sets, Sharon Ott directed and Karen Keltner conducted.

THE CONSUL   *1950 opera by Menotti*

Somewhere in Europe in the late 1940s. Freedom fighter John Sorel has to flee the country when the secret police try to arrest him. He tell his wife Magda to get a visa from a foreign consulate and follow him with their baby and her mother. She is blocked by a Kafka-esque situation at the consulate where she meets others nearly as desperate. After her mother and baby die, Magda kills herself in a futile attempt to stop her husband from returning. Gian Carlo Menotti's opera *The Consul,* libretto by the composer, premiered at the Schubert Theater in Philadelphia March 1, 1950. Patricia Neway created the role of Magda, Marie Powers was the Mother, Cornell MacNeil was John Sorel, Gloria Lane was the Secretary, Leon Lishner was the Chief Police Agent, Chester Watson was the First Police Agent, Donald Blackey was the Second Police Agent, Andrew McKinley was the magician Nika Magadoff, George Jongeyans was Mr. Kofner, Lydia Summers was Vera Boronel, Maria Marlo was The Foreign Woman, Francis Monachino was Assan and Mabel Mercer was the Voice on the Record. John Butler created the choreography, Menotti directed and Lehman Engel conducted. The opera arrived at the Ethel Barrymore Theater in New York City on March 15 with the same cast. *The Consul* went on to win the New York Drama Critics' Circle award for the best musical of the years and the Pulitzer Prize for Music. It was also popular in Europe and was staged and televised in more than twenty countries. Magda's aria "TO THIS WE'VE COME" is popular as a recital piece for sopranos.

1950 Original cast recording. Patricia Neway is Magda with Marie Powers as Mother and Cornell MacNeil as John Sorel in this original cast recording made under Menotti's direction. Gloria Lane is the Secretary, Leon Lishner is the Chief Police Agent, Andrew McKinley is the Magician, George Jongeyans is Mr. Kofner and Faye Elizabeth Smith takes over the role of Vera Boronel. Lehman Engel conducts. Decca/Brunswick 2-LP set. **1951 Inge Borkh.** Swiss soprano Inge Borkh, who became famous singing the role of Magda in the first German production of the opera, recorded "My Child Is Dead" in 1951 with Arthur Rother leading the Berlin State Opera Orchestra. It's on the 1992 album *The Record of Singing Vol. IV.* EMI CD. **1959 Toronto production.** Patrica Neway, who created the role of Magda, is in wonderful form supported by a fine cast in this excellent Toronto studio production made for pay TV. Evelyn Sachs is the Mother, Chester Ludgin is husband John Sorel, Regina Sarfaty is the Secretary, Leon Lishner is the Secret Agent, Norman Kelley is the Magician and Maria Marlo is the Foreign Woman. Werner Torkanowsky conducts the orchestra. Menotti staged the opera and Jean Dalyrmple directed it for television. It was shown on Toronto Pay TV on March 19, 1959, and released on DVD in 2004. VAI DVD. **1962 ABC TV Australia.** Loris Synan is Magda in an Australian TV production with Morris Williams as Sorel and Justine Rettick as the Mother. Dorothy Deegan is the Secretary, Charles Skase is the Secret Police Agent, Leslie Coe is Mr. Kofner and Lorenzo Nolan is the Magician, Christopher Muir staged the opera and George Tintner conducted. Telecast on ABC December 12, 1962. Premiere Opera VHS. **1963 Vienna Volksoper.** Melita Muszely is Magda in this German-language version of the opera staged by the Vienna Volksoper for Austrian TV. Eberhard Wächter is Sorel, Res Fischer is Mother, Willi Ferenz is the Secret Police Agent, Gloria Lane is the Secretary, Friedrich Nidetzky is Mr. Kofner, Laurence Dutoit is Anna Gomez, Hilde Konetzni is Vera Boronel, Ljuba Welitsch is Foreign Woman and Laszlo Szereme is the Magician. Franz Bauer-Theussl conducts the Vienna Volksoper Orchestra and Werner Gallusser wrote the translation. Telecast on ORF on April 19, 1963. Live Opera audiocassette. **1972 Spoleto Festival.** Virginia Zeani is Magda in this recording made at the Teatro Nuova at the Spoleto Festival in Italy on June 5, 1972. Giovanna Fioroni is the Mother, Gianluigi Golmagro is Sorel, Gianfranco Casarini is the Secret Police Agent, Joy Davidson is the Secretary, Nico Castel is the Magician, Giuliana Matteini is Anna Gomez and Flora Rafanelli is Vera Boronel. Thomas Schippers conducts. Live Opera audiocassette. **1974 New York City Opera.** Olivia Stapp is Magda in this live recording made at New York City Opera on March 27, 1974. John Darrenkamp is John Sorel, Muriel Greenspon is the Mother, Sandra Walker is the Secretary, Edward Pierson is the Secret Police Agent and Nico Castel is the Magician. Christopher Keene conducts. Live Opera audiocassette. **1977 Spoleto Festival USA.** Marvellee Cariaga stars as Magda in this 1977 Spoleto Festival USA production. David Clatworthy is Sorel, Fredda Rakusin is the Mother, Vern Shinall is the Secret Police Agent, Sandra Walker is the Secretary, Gregory Servant is Mr. Kofner, Alice Garrott is Vera Boronel and Jerold Siena is the Magician. Christopher Keene conducts the Spoleto Festival Orchestra and Kirk Browning directed the PBS telecast on March 29, 1978. Live Opera/Music Masters VHS and video at New York Public Library. **1978 Patricia Neway.** Patricia Neway sings the aria "To This We've Come" with orchestra accompanied by Lehman Engel. Her recording is on the album *Toward an American Opera, 1911–1954.* New World Records LP. **1988 Grand Théâtre de Tours.** Martine Surrais is Magda in this recording of the opera sung in French at the

Grand Théâtre de Tours in France on January 24, 1988. Rita Gorr is the Mother, Yves Bisson is Sorel, Bernard Deletre is the Secret Police Agent, Anne Bartelloni is the Secretary, Alain Verhees is Mr. Kofner and Ivan Matiakh is the Magician. Robert Martignon conducts. Live Opera audiocassette. **1996 Eileen Farrell.** Eileen Farrell sings the aria "To this we've come" from *The Consul* on her album *Eileen Farrell Sings Opera Arias and Songs.* Testament CD. **1998 Spoleto Festival.** Susan Bullock is Magda in a Spoleto Festival production recorded in Italy on July 1998. Louis Otey is Sorel, Jacalyn Kreitzer is Mother, Charles Austin is the Secret Agent, Victoria Livengood is the Secretary, Herbert Eckhoff is Mr. Kofner, Giovanna Manci is the Foreign Woman, Robin Blitch is Anna Gomez, Malin Fritz is Vera Boronel, John Horton Murray is the Magician and Greaeme Broadbent is Assan. Richard Hickox conducts the Spoleto Festival Orchestra. Fausto Fiorito designed the sets, Menotti staged the production and Paolo Longobardo directed the video. Opera Dubs/Live Opera VHS and Chandos 2-CD set. **1998 Berkshire Opera.** Beverly O'Regan Thiele is Magda in a Berkshire Opera Company recording made in Lenox, Massachusetts, in July 1998. Michael Chioldi is Sorel, Joyce Castle is Mother, John Cheek is Secret Agent, Emily Golden is Secretary, John Davies is Mr. Kofner, Nathalie Morais is the Foreign Woman, Arianna Zukerman is Anna Gomez, Elisabeth Canis is Vera Boronel, David Cangelosi is Magician and James Demler is Assan. Joel Revzen conducts the Camerata New York Orchestra. Newport Classics 2-CD set. **1999 Washington Opera Commentary.** Saul Lilienstein analyses *The Consul* on this recording in the Washington Opera Commentaries on CD series. The 79-minute commentary is based around musical excerpts from the 1998 Berkshire Opera recording. Washington Opera CD. **1999 Angelika Kirchschlager.** Angelika Kirchschlager sings the Mother's Aria from *The Consul* accompanied by pianist H. Deutsch on her album *When Night Falls.* Sony CD.

CONTE, DAVID   *American composer (1955–)*

Denver native David Conte created his 1996 opera THE DREAMERS, libretto by Philip Little, for the city of Sonoma, California, to help it celebrate its history. His 1997 one-act opera THE GIFT OF THE MAGI, libretto by Nicholas Giardini based on the O. Henry story, was premiered by the San Francisco Conservatory New Music Ensemble. Conte, who studied at Cornell and Bowling Green and with Nadia Boulanger in Paris, has taught composition at the San Francisco Conservatory of Music since 1985. Several of his choral works are on CD.

CONVERSE, FREDERICK S.   *American composer (1871–1940)*

Frederick Converse was the first American composer to have an opera performed at the Metropolitan Opera House. His magical one-act THE PIPE OF DESIRE, libretto by George Edward Burton, was produced at the Met in 1910. He also had success with his California opera THE SACRIFICE, written to his own libretto, which premiered in Boston in 1911. At the time Converse was vice president of the Boston Opera Company, a major rival of the Met. Converse, who was born in Newton, Massachusetts and educated at Harvard, studied with two other American opera composers, George Chadwick and John Knowles Paine. He began to write for the stage in 1905 composing incidental music for Percy MacKaye's play *Jeanne d'Arc* and initiating a long collaboration with him He even wrote the music for a silent film based on a MacKaye play, the 1923 *Puritan Passions* starring Mary Astor.

Converse collaborated on two operas with MacKaye but neither was performed. First was *Beauty and the Beast* (1913), based on tales from the Arabian *Thousand and One Nights.* MacKaye published the libretto in 1917 under the title *Sinbad the Sailor.* Second was *The Immigrants* (1914), which told the story of Italian immigrants to the U.S. in the early years of the century. The Boston Opera Company collapsed before it could be staged. Converse was best known in his time for the 1904 orchestral work *The Mystic Trumpeter* inspired by Walt Whitman. He is also remembered for *Flivver Ten Million,* an epic tone poem celebrating the ten millionth Ford car, which is on CD.

CONVERY, ROBERT   *American composer (1954–)*
Robert Convery, who studied with composers Ned Rorem and Vincent Persichetti, has written operas based on plays by Tennessee Williams and Shakespeare. Convery's first opera *The Lady of Larkspur Lotion,* libretto by the composer based on a play by Tennessee Williams, tells the story of a crazy woman and a failed writer in a New Orleans boarding house. It premiered at the Spoleto Festival in Italy July 15, 1980. The award-winning *Pyramus and Thisbe,* libretto by the composer based on scenes from Shakespeare's *A Midsummer Night's Dream,* identifies each character of this play-within-a-play with a musical instrument. It was performed in workshop at the O'Neill Music Center in Waterford, Connecticut, in May 1982 and premiered at the Curtis Institute in Philadelphia on March 23, 1983. *The Blanket,* libretto by Emmett Robinson, premiered at the Spoleto Festival USA in Charleston, South Carolina, on May 31, 1988.

COOK, BARBARA   *American soprano (1927–)*
Barbara Cook created the role of Cunegonde in the 1956 premiere of Leonard Bernstein's CANDIDE and her original cast recording of its coloratura aria "Glitter and Be Gay" is one of the best. In 1957 she created the role of Marion the librarian in Meredith Willson's classic musical THE MUSIC MAN. She sang Jane Piper on an NBC TV production of Victor Herbert's BABES IN TOYLAND in 1954, Magnolia in recordings of Jerome Kern's SHOW BOAT in 1962 and 1966, Anna in a recording of THE KING AND I in 1964 and Julie in a recording of CAROUSEL with Samuel Ramey in London in 1987. She sang the "Simple Song" from Bernstein's *Mass* in 1980 and her version is on record. Cook, born in Atlanta, Georgia, made her Broadway debut in 1951 as Sandy in the musical *Flahooley.*

COOK, WILL MARION   *American composer (1869–1944)*
Will Marion Cook was a major contributor to the growth of African American musical theater. His 1898 show *Clorindy: or The Origin of the Cakewalk,* book by poet Paul Laurence Dunbar, was the first black musical comedy to succeed on Broadway and it opened the road for other African American musicals. His most famous stage work was *In Dahomey* (1902) with Bert Williams and George Walker. His other shows included *The Cannibal King* (1901) and *The Southerners* (1904). His 1929 *St. Louis 'ooman* is described as a grand opera and his song "Down the Lover's Lane" was recorded by Paul Robeson. Cook, born in Washington, D.C., studied at Oberlin and the National Conservatory and with Anton Dvorák.

COOPER, JAMES FENIMORE   *American novelist (1789–1851)*
James Fenimore Cooper, the first important American novelist, inspired a number of opera composers. THE LAST OF THE MOHICANS (1826) was the basis of three operas: Ellsworth Phelps com-

plete the first in 1890, Paul Hastings Allen composed the second premiered in Florence, Italy, in 1916 and Alva Henderson's version, libretto by Janet Lewis, was staged by Wilmington Opera in 1976. The other Cooper operas are by Europeans. Richard Genée composed an operetta based on *The Last of the Mohicans* in 1878. *The Bravo* (1831) was made into an 1834 opera by M. A. Marliana but Saverio Mercadante's version of 1839 is more famous. *The Spy* (1821) was the source of operas by Angelo Villanis (1850), Fromental Halévy (1855), Luigi Arditi (1856, premiered in New York) and Ivar Hallström (1884).

COPELAND, STEWART   *American composer (1952—)*
Stewart Copeland is better known as rock musician but he has composed two operas. The son of a noted CIA agent, he studied music in California and moved to England to join the group Curved Air and formed the group Police in partnership with Sting in 1977. His first opera, HOLY BLOOD AND CRESCENT MOON, about the Crusades, was commissioned by Cleveland Opera which premiered it in 1989. His second opera, HORSE OPERA, about Old West fantasies, premiered on Channel Four television in England in 1994. Copeland also created the score for Francis Ford Coppola's film *Rumble Fish* and the ballet *King Lear* for San Francisco Ballet.

COPELAND, VIRGINIA   *American soprano (1940–)*
Connecticut-native Virginia Copeland created the role of Annina in THE SAINT OF BLEECKER STREET on Broadway and was featured in three television productions. In January 1955 she appeared in Act Two on CBS on the *Ed Sullivan Show,* in May 1955 she sang the role in the NBC Opera Theatre TV production and in 1956 she reprised it in a BBC TV production., She had made her debut a year earlier in Menotti's THE OLD MAID AND THE THIEF. She sang the role of Baby Doe in the 1957 Omnibus TV production of Douglas Moore's THE BALLAD OF BABY DOE.

COPLAND, AARON   *American composer (1900–1990)*
Aaron Copland wrote only two operas and neither was much of a success in its time. THE SECOND HURRICANE (1937), libretto by Edwin Denby about students who help out after a disaster, was written for a school; Orson Welles directed its premiere. THE TENDER LAND (1954), libretto by Horace Everett, is the story of a young woman in the Midwest who feels it is time to leave home. It was created for television but rejected so it premiered at New York City Opera. Copland, born in Brooklyn, studied music in Paris with Nadia Boulanger, but turned away from European modernistic ideas to become the most "American" of composers. His ballets *Appalachian Spring, Rodeo* and *Billy the Kid* were hugely influential and *Fanfare for the Common Man* and *Lincoln Portrait* are core works of Americana. *Appalachian Spring* won the Pulitzer Prize for Music in 1945. Copland also wrote film scores and was nominated for Oscars for *Of Mice and Men, Our Town, North Star* and *The Heiress* (which won).
1985 Aaron Copland: A Self-Portrait. The composer explains how his style developed in this documentary by Allan Miller. Leonard Bernstein, Ned Rorem, Michael Tilson Thomas, and Agnes de Mille are among the interviewees Vivian Perlis wrote the script for the film telecast on PBS in October 1985. Films for the Humanities and Sciences VHS. **2000 A Copland Celebration.** Compilation of recordings issued for the 100th anniversary of the composer's birth consisting of six CDs in three volumes. Volume 3 has the 1965 concert performance of *The Tender Land* at Lincoln Center with Copland conducting the New York Philharmonic and Choral Art Society. Sony CD set. **2001 Fanfare for**

America: Aaron Copland. Documentary showing how Copland created an American sound in his music. Biographer Howard Pollock talks about important events in Copland's life and Hugh Wolff conducts the Frankfurt Radio Symphony Orchestra in excerpts from Copland works in this 60-minute film. Films for the Humanities and Sciences VHS.

CORIGLIANO, JOHN   *American composer (1938–)*

John Corigliano's truly grand opera THE GHOSTS OF VERSAILLES, an elaborate homage to Beaumarchais and French history composed to a libretto by William M. Hoffman, premiered at the Metropolitan Opera in 1991. It won warm praise from critics, was liked by Met audiences and has already been revived. He also had success with THE NAKED CARMEN (1970), a record based on the Bizet opera featuring unusual instruments and singers. Corigliano, who was born in New York, studied at Columbia and the Manhattan School and with Otto Luening and Vittorio Giannini. He worked as a radio/TV music programmer and then taught composition. He has composed a great deal of instrumental music, especially concertos and he also writes film music; he won a Best Score Oscar for *The Red Violin.*

CORSARO, FRANK   *American director/librettist (1924–)*

Frank Corsaro has been strongly involved with American opera for over thirty years. He made his operatic debut at New York City Opera in 1958 directing Carlisle Floyd's SUSANNAH and staged the premiere of Floyd's OF MICE AND MEN in Seattle in 1970. He directed the premiere of Lee Hoiby's SUMMER AND SMOKE for St. Paul Opera in 1971 and Thomas Pasatieri's THE SEAGULL for Houston Grand Opera in 1974. He wrote the librettos and directed the premieres of Pasatieri's BEFORE BREAKFAST at New York City Opera in 1980, Jay Reise's RASPUTIN at NYCO in 1988 and Pasatieri's HELOISE AND ABELARD at the Juilliard School in 2002. He also directed the influential Houston Grand Opera production of Scott Joplin's TREEMONISHA. His collaborations with author/designer Maurice Sendak included the premieres of WHERE THE WILD THINGS ARE and HIGGLETY PIGGLETY POP! and an awe-inspiring production of THE LOVE FOR THREE ORANGES. Corsaro was born in New York City, studied at Yale and the Actors Studio and worked theater before turning to opera in 1958.

COSTA, MARY   *American soprano (1934–)*

Mary Costa created the role of Ninette in Norman Dello Joio's BLOOD MOON at San Francisco Opera in 1961 and sang in a touring production of Leonard Bernstein's CANDIDE. She made her opera debut at the Met in 1964 as Violetta and sang the title role in a revival of Samuel Barber's VANESSA in 1965. She sings VICTOR HERBERT songs in a 1973 Canadian TV tribute. Costa, born in Knoxville, Tennessee, began her professional career singing in the 1953 film *Marry Me Again* and married its director, Frank Tashlin. She is the voice of the Princess in the 1959 Disney animated movie *Sleeping Beauty.*

COUNTDOWN   *1987 opera by Yavelow*

Jenna and Charlie are soldiers in charge of a NORAD nuclear missile command silo. Jenna reveals that she is pregnant and will be leaving the job. However, they receive a Red Alert and are ordered to launch a missile that will bring a retaliatory strike. Christopher Yavelow's 28-minute opera *Countdown,* libretto by Laura Harrington, was commissioned by the Boston Lyric Opera Company which premiered it February 12, 1987, at the Gardner Museum in Boston. The opera was created with the help of an

Apple Macintosh computer and was performed with its orchestral music played by a Kurzweil 250 Digital Music Workstation. Karen Lykes played Jenna, Mark Aliapoulios was Charlie and Pamela Gailey was Alice, heard as a voice on a loudspeaker. John Balme conducted the electronic orchestra and Anne Ewer was the director. *Countdown* won the Virginia Opera Society's New One-Act Operas competition in 1988 and was staged in Virginia in 1989. In 1994 it became the first opera to be put on the internet with complete audio recording and libretto.

COWELL, HENRY   *American composer (1897–1965)*

Henry Cowell, one of the most prolific and influential modern American composers, wrote a good deal of film, stage and dance music but only two operas. *The Building of Bamba,* "an Irish mythological opera" in 14 scenes, was composed to a libretto by John O. Varian and premiered at the Halycon Sanatorium in California on August 18, 1917. A revised version was presented in Halycon in 1930. *O'Higgins of Chile,* a three-act opera based on the life of South American revolutionary leader General Bernardo O'Higgins, was composed in 1949 to a libretto by Elizabeth Harald Lomax on a commission from the Alice M. Ditson Fund. It is set in the period 1818–1822 when O'Higgins captured Santiago and won independence for Chile. It has not been performed. Cowell was born in Menlo Park, CA, and taught for many years at USC and Peabody.

COWLES, EUGENE   *American bass*

Eugene Cowles created roles in six classic light operas at the turn of the century. He was Will Scarlet in the first performance of Reginald DeKoven's ROBIN HOOD in 1890 and he sang in the premieres of five Victor Herbert operettas, as George LeGrabbe in *Prince Anais* in 1894, Romero in THE SERENADE in 1897, Sandor in THE FORTUNE TELLER in 1898, Duke Rodolph in *The Singing Girl* in 1899 and Mondragon in *Babette* in 1903.

COYOTE TALES   *1998 opera by Mollicone*

Native American folk hero Coyote is alone and lonely in a world of water and asks the Sun to help him create companions. The

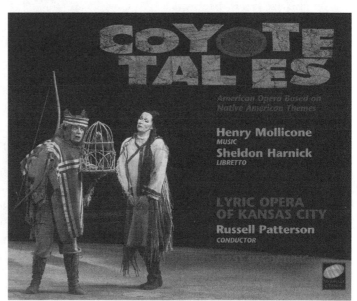

Lyric Opera of Kansas City premiered and recorded Henry Mollicone's opera *Coyote Tales* in 1998.

Great Spirit tells Coyote that when he dies he will be brought back to life so he can continue to learn. Coyote brings fire to people to keep them from freezing. He falls in love with a Star with disastrous consequences. He lusts after a Maiden who is in love with Pavayoykyasi and tricks her into marrying him but is discovered and slain. He is brought to life again so he can continue to learn. Henry Mollicone's opera *Coyote Tales*, libretto by Sheldon Harnick based on native American folk tales about Coyote, was premiered by Lyric Opera of Kansas City on March 7, 1998. Michael Ballam sang the role of Coyote, Brian Steele was the Storyteller, Suzanne Hillis Ackin was Star, Jane Gilbert was the Fox, Suzan Hanson was the Maiden and Gregory Keil was Pavayoykyasi. R. Keith Brumley designed the sets, Baker Smith designed the costumes, Dennis Landsman devised the choreography, Vincent Liotta directed and Russell Patterson conducted the Kansas City Symphony Orchestra.

1998 Lyric Opera of Kansas City. The premiere of *Coyote Tales* by Lyric Opera of Kansas City was recorded live. Michael Ballam sings Coyote, Brian Steele is Storyteller, Suzanne Hillis Ackin is Star, Jane Gilbert is the Fox, Suzan Hanson is the Maiden and Gregory Keil is Pavayoykyasi. Russell Patterson conducts the Kansas City Symphony Orchestra. Newport Classics 2-CD box.

THE CRADLE WILL ROCK   *1937 opera by Blitzstein*

Marc Blitzstein's agit-prop *The Cradle Will Rock* is the closest thing in American opera to the left-wing political operas of Bertolt Brecht and Kurt Weill. *Cradle* was completed after Blitzstein showed Brecht the aria "Nickel Under the Foot" and Brecht expressed his enthusiasm. The story revolves around events at a night court during a strike in the town of Steeltown. Hooker Moll sings of her happiness in finding a nickel under her foot when she had no money and defends her job saying it's easy to be moral when you have plenty to eat. Union organizer Larry Foreman sings the title song as a warning to those who oppose the strike. That opposition includes Steeltown boss Mr. Mister and his family and minions like the press represented by Editor Daily. The first performance was held at the Venice Theater on June 16, 1937, with Blitzstein on stage playing piano. He was the only one on the stage as the performers had to sit with the audience. Their union, under political pressure, had told them they could not perform the work on stage. The Federal Theatre Project had decided the project was a political hot potato, which they didn't want staged, they arranged to lock up the Maxine Elliott Theater where it was to have been produced. But director Orson Welles and producer John Houseman were not about to be stopped from putting on the show. They found another theater, the Venice, and led cast and audience to it. As the actors couldn't go on stage (their union forbid it), Welles told them to sing their parts from their seats while Blitzstein provided piano accompaniment from the stage. When frail young Olive Stanton, playing Moll, stood up and began to sing, the other performers were inspired to follow. They included Howard Da Silva as Larry Foreman, Ralph MacBane as Mr. Mister, Bert Weston as Editor Daily, Blanche Collins as Ella Hammer, Edward Fuller as Yasha, Jules Schmidt as Dauber, Peggy Coudray as Mrs. Mister, Maynard Holmes as Junior Mister, Dulce Fox as Sister Mister,

Howard Bird as Steve, Marian Rudley as Sadie Polock, George Fairchild as Gus Polock, George Fairchild as Gent, Guido Alexander as Dick, Robert Farnsworth as Cop, LeRoi Operti as President Prexy, George Smithfield as Prof. Trixie, George Powers as Bugs and Blitzstein in eight roles substituting for performers who did not show up. *The Cradle Will Rock* was enthusiastically received and became famous overnight. After nineteen sold-out performances at the Venice Theatre with the actors seated in the auditorium, the opera moved to the Windsor Theatre where it opened on January 3, 1938. It had a run of 108 performances, was recorded and published and has been revived many times.

1938 Original Cast album. This is considered the first complete original cast recording of an American opera. Blitzstein plays piano and narrates the story with the cast that performed at the Windsor Theater. They include Olive Stanton as Moll, Howard Da Silva as Larry Foreman, Ralph MacBane as Mr. Mister, Blanche Collins as Ella Hammer, Edward Fuller as Yasha, Jules Schmidt as Dauber, Peggy Coudray as Mrs. Mister, Maynard Holmes as Junior Mister, Dulce Fox as Sister Mister, Charles Niemeyer as Rev. Salvation, Bert Weston as Editor Daily and John Adair as Harry Druggist, The recording, originally issued as eighteen 12" 78 records on the Musicraft label, was later published as an LP and is now on a Pearl CD titled *Marc Blitzstein—Musical Theatre Premieres*. **1960 New York City Opera.** Tammy Grimes sings Moll with David Atkinson as Larry Foreman in this recording of a New York City Opera production by Howard Da Silva broadcast February 21, 1960. Craig Timberlake is Mr. Mister, Jack Harrold is Editor Daily, Kenneth Smith is Reverend Salvation, Jane A Johnston is Ella Hammer, Ruth Kobart is Mrs. Mister, Keith Kaldenberg is Junior Mister, Nancy Dussault is Sister Mister and John Macurdy is President Prexy. Lehman Engel conducted. Omega Opera Archives CD. **1964 Theater Four.** Lauri Peters is Moll with Jerry Orbach as Larry Foreman in this recording of a Theater Four production.

Hank Azaria as Mark Blitzstein in the 1999 film *Cradle Will Rock* which revolves around the staging of his controversial agit-prop opera.

Gordon B. Clarke is Mr. Mister, Dean Dittman is Editor Daily, Micki Grant is Ella Hammer, Nancy Andrews is Mrs. Mister, Joseph Bova is Junior Mister, Rita Gardner is Sister Mister, Hal Buckley is President Prexy, Clifford David is Dauber and Professor Trixie, Nichols Grime is Steve, Karen Cleary is Sadie Polock and Ted Scott is Gus Polock. Gershon Kingsley played piano and Howard Da Silva directed. MGM and CRI LP. **1985 Old Vic.** Patti LuPone recorded the opera with the Acting Company when it was produced at the Old Vic in London. She sings Moll and Sister Mister, Randle Mell is Larry Foreman, David Schramm is Mr. Mister, ,Mary Lou Rosato is Mrs. Mister, Leslie Geraci is Sadie Polock, Norman Snow is Reverend Salvation, Casey Biggs is Gus Polock, and Michele-Denise Woods is Ella Hammer. Michael Barrett plays piano. That's Entertainment LP/Jay Records CD. **1990 Karen Hovik/William Sharp.** Karen Hovik and William Sharp sing arias from the opera on the album *Marc Blitzstein: Zipperfly and Other Songs* recorded for the New York Festival of Song. Steven Blier accompanies them on piano on "Nickel Under the Foot," "The Cradle Will Rock" and the ironic duet "Croon-Spoon." Koch CD. **1994 Blank Theater.** Excellent recording of the opera by the Blank Theater Company of Los Angeles based on a scaled-down stage production. Ron Louis is Narrator, Sandra Terry is Moll, Jeffrey Rockwell is Larry Foreman, Harry S. Murphy is Editor Daily, Peter Van Norden is Mr. Mister, Daniel Henning is Junior Mister and April Dawn is Sister Mister. David Henning produced, directed and designed the set while Stephen Bates provided musical direction and played piano. Lockett Palmer CD. **1999 Cradle Will Rock.** *Cradle Will Rock*, a film written and directed by Tim Robbins for Touchstone, is based around the 1937 premiere of the opera but includes other events of the period, like Mexican artist Diego Riviera's clash with Nelson Rockefeller. Hank Azaria plays Marc Blitzstein, Angus Macfadyen is Orson Welles, Emily Watson is Olive Stanton, Cary Elwes is John Houseman and Cherry Jones is Hallie Flanagan. Watson sings "Moll's Song," Olly Jean Harvey sings "Nickel Under the Foot," Audra McDonald sings "Joe Worker" and Susan Sarandon and Eddie Vedder duet on "Croon-Spoon." Soundtrack album on RCA Victor CD. Disney DVD/VHS.

CRANE, STEPHEN   *American writer (1871–1900)*

Stephen Crane is best known for his great Civil War novel *The Red Badge of Courage* (1895) but it has not yet been turned into an opera. However, there are two based on his novel *Maggie: A Girl of the Streets* (1893), about a woman born in the slums of New York City. They are Stephen Douglas Burton's *Maggie* (1974) and Richard Wernick's *Maggie* (1959) but neither seems to have been staged.

CREECH, PHILIP   *American tenor (1950–)*

Philip Creech, who has sung at the Metropolitan Opera for many years, took the role of Scientist/First Mate in the revival of Philip Glass's THE VOYAGE at the Met in 1996 and was featured in the radio broadcast. He sings the role of Teeboy in the 1986 recording of Joseph Fennimore's EVENTIDE. He has also recorded an album of spirituals by African American composer Harry T. Burleigh. Creech was born in Hempstead, NY.

CRISTÓBAL COLÓN   *1989 opera by Balada*

The story of Christopher Columbus's voyage to America told in flashback. Spanish-born American composer Leonardo Balada's opera *Cristóbal Colón* (Christopher Columbus), libretto by A. Gala, premiered at the Gran Teatre de Liceu in Barcelona September 24,

1989. José Carreras starred as Columbus opposite Montserrat Caballé with support from Victoria Vergara as Beatriz and Carlos Chausson as Pinzon. Theo Alcantara conducted the Liceu Opera Orchestra. The opera was composed to mark the 500th anniversary of Columbus's journey and mixes Catalan and Andalusian themes with Native American elements.

1989 Gran Teatre de Liceu. José Carreras and Montserrat Caballé star in the Spanish telecast premiere of Balada's opera at the Gran Teatre de Liceu in Barcelona September 24, 1989. Theo Alcantara conducts the Liceu Opera Orchestra. Opera Dubs VHS.

CROFT, DWAYNE   *American baritone (1960–)*

Dwayne Croft created the role of Nick Carraway in John Harbison's THE GREAT GATSBY at the Met in 1999 and Roderick Usher in Philip Glass's THE FALL OF THE HOUSE OF USHER in 1988. He sang the role of Figaro in a production of John Corigliano's THE GHOSTS OF VERSAILLES in Chicago and has also sung the role in the Rossini and Mozart operas. Croft began his operatic career as a teenage tenor with the Glimmerglass Opera chorus and did not begin to sing as a baritone until 1989.

CROOKS, RICHARD   *American tenor (1900–1972)*

Lyric tenor Richard Crooks recorded a number of arias from the comic operas of composers Victor Herbert and Sigmund Romberg in the 1920s and these are collected on the Pearl CD *Only a Rose— The Art of Richard Crooks in Song*. They are from THE DESERT SONG, NAUGHTY MARIETTA, THE RED MILL, THE STUDENT PRINCE and THE VAGABOND KING. Crooks, born in Trenton, NJ, made his opera debut in Hamburg in 1927 and became a regular at the Metropolitan Opera in 1933.

Tenor Richard Crooks

CROSS, RICHARD *American bass-baritone (1935–)*

American bass-baritone Richard Cross created roles in nine American operas and sang in recordings of two others. He made his debut at the Spoleto Festival in June 1958 creating the role of the Postman in Lee Hoiby's THE SCARF. He created the role of the blind war veteran Donato in Gian Carlo Menotti's opera MARIA GOLOVIN at the Brussels World Fair in August 1958 and reprised it for NBC Opera Theatre in 1959. He created the Bishop in Menotti's cantata THE DEATH OF THE BISHOP OF BRINDISI (1963), Rakitin in Lee Hoiby's NATALIA PETROVNA/*A Month in the Country* (1964), the Cardinal in Stephen Burton's THE DUCHESS OF MALFI (1975), Dr Sloper in Thomas Pasatieri's WASHINGTON SQUARE (1976), Jaggers in Domenick Argento's MISS HAVISHAMS'S FIRE (1979), Dr. Hoffman in Stanley Silverman's MADAME ADARE (1980) and Amory in Robert Ward's MINUTES TO MIDNIGHT (1982). He was King Melchior in the 1963 NBC Opera Theatre telecast and recording of AMAHL AND THE NIGHT VISITORS and Maurice in the 1958 recording of Hugo Weisgall's THE TENOR and he sang in the 1960 premiere of Hoiby's oratorio *The Hymn of the Nativity.* Cross sang with Frankfurt Opera and New York City Opera from 1966 to 1985.

THE CRUCIBLE *1961 opera by Ward*

A wave of hysteria about witches breaks out in Salem, Massachusetts, in 1692 and nearly destroys the community. Abigail accuses slave Tituba of being a witch, then makes charges against Elizabeth, wife of John Proctor. Witchfinder Rev. Hale extracts confessions and zealous Judge Danforth condemns nineteen men and women to the gallows. Robert Ward's four-act opera *The Crucible,* libretto by Bernard Stambler based on the Pulitzer Prize-winning play by Arthur Miller, won the Pulitzer Prize for Music in 1962. Play and opera were seen as allegorical commentary on the Communist witch hunts of the McCarthy era. The opera premiered at New York City Opera on October 26, 1961, with Patricia Brooks as Abigail Williams, Frances Bible as Elizabeth Proctor, Chester Ludgin as John Proctor, Norman Treigle as the Reverend John Hale and Norman Kelley as the Reverend Samuel Parris. Ken Neate played Judge Danforth, Debria Brown was Tituba, Mary LeSawyer was Ann Putnam, Paul Ukena was Thomas Putnam, Lorna Cenicero was Ruth Putnam, Eunice Alberts was Rebecca Nurse, Joy Clements was Mary Warren, Spiro Malas was Francis Nurse, Maurice Stern was Giles Corey, Harry Theyard was Ezekiel Cheever, Joan Kelm was Sarah Good, Helen Guile was Susanna Walcott, Nancy Roy was Mercy Lewis, Elizabeth Schwering was Martha Sheldon, and Beverly Evans was Bridget. Paul Sylvert designed the sets, Allen Fletcher directed and Emerson Buckley conducted the New York City Opera Orchestra and Chorus. The neo-romantic score is tonal and accessible with echoes of 17th century religious music. *The Crucible* has been reprised many times, including productions in Washington, Chicago, Atlanta, Pittsburgh, Tulsa, Des Moines, Toledo and Kansas City and in Europe and Asia .

1962 New York City Opera. Patricia Brooks stars as Abigail Williams with Norman Treigle as Rev. John Hale and Frances Bible as Elizabeth Proctor in this New York City Opera cast recording. Chester Ludgin is John Proctor, Joyce Ebert is Betty Parris, Norman Kelley is Reverend Samuel Parris, Gloria Wynder is Tituba, Naomi Farr is Ann Putnam, Paul Ukena is Thomas Putnam, Eunice Alberts is Rebecca Nurse, Spiro Malas is Francis Nurse, Maurice Stern is Giles Corey, John Macurdy is Rev. John Hale, Nancy Foster is Mary Warren, Richard Krause is Ezekiel Cheever and Jack DeLon is Judge Danforth. Emerson Buckley conducts the New York City Opera Orchestra and Chorus. Recorded March 25, 1962. CRI LP/Albany CD. **1991 William Stone.** Baritone William Stone sings two arias from *The Crucible* on the album *Robert Ward: Arias and Songs:* "It's a Good Time is Springtime" and "I am John Proctor." He is accompanied by pianist Thomas Warburton. Bay Cities CD.

THE CRY OF CLYTAEMNESTRA *1980 opera by Eaton*

Queen Clytaemnestra cannot forgive her husband King Agamemnon for sacrificing their daughter Iphigenia while on his way to the Trojan War. She decides to kill him when he returns. John Eaton's expressionistic but fiercely dramatic chamber opera *The Cry of Clytaemnestra,* libretto by Patrick Creagh based on Aeschylus's play *Agamemnon,* retells the Greek legend from the point of the view of the murderous queen. It premiered at Indiana University Opera Theater on March 1, 1980, with Nelda Nelson as Clytaemnestra. Timothy Noble sang Agamemnon alternating in the role with Robert Bork while Paula Redd, Eileen Martinez and Sally Wolf alternated Iphigenia, Joseph Levitt was Calchas, Dan Brewer and John Fay alternated Achilles, Michael Johnson and Richard Walker alternated Odysseus, Stanley Springer and Brian Trego alternated Menelaus, Marc Lundberg and Martin Strother alternated Diomedes, Ted Adkins and Kevin Langan alternated Ajax, Richard Cowan and Steven Nelson played Teucer, Colenton Freeman and Larry Paxton played Aegisthus, Victoria Frances Czuba and Edith Diggory played Cassandra, Rebecca Field and Sarah Miller played Electra and Randall Black and Glenn Siebert played Orestes. The harsh but tonal *The Cry of Clytaemnestra,* only 75 minutes long, has become Eaton's most popular opera and has been staged in opera houses around the world from San Francisco to Moscow.

1985 Nelda Nelson. Nelda Nelson, who created Clytaemnestra, sings the Aria and Scena from *The Cry of Clytaemnestra* with the Indiana University New Music Ensemble led by Harvey Sollberg. The excerpts, recorded April 4, 1985, by the Indiana University School of Music Audio Department in Bloomington, are on the 1992 album *The Music of John Eaton.* IUSM CD

CUE 67 *1992 opera by Ching*

Actors playing Ariel and Prospero in a production of Shakespeare's *The Tempest* are killed in a freak accident and the stage director sees their ghosts. Michael Ching's *Cue 67,* libretto by Sandra Bernard, premiered at Virginia Opera in Norfolk on January 24, 1992, in a double bill with Gian Carlo Menotti's *The Medium.* Christine Akre sang the role of Anne/Ariel, Michael Caldwell was Michael/Prospero and David Maze was the stage director Gerry. Librettist Bernard directed and the composer conducted.

CUMMINGS, CONRAD *American composer (1948–)*

Conrad Cummings' TONKIN, one of the few operas to deal with the Vietnam War, was premiered by OperaDelaware in 1994. His first opera, the post-modern neo-Baroque *Eros and Psyche* (1983) derived from a story by Roman writer Apuleius, was commissioned by Oberlin. His chamber opera *Positions* (1988), based on sex instruction manuals of the 1950s, premiered at the Knitting Factory in New York with his chamber opera *Insertions.* Both were written for his Cummings Ensemble of amplified singers and musicians. *Photo-Op* (1989), which he describes as an "imaginary unstaged opera," was also staged by his ensemble at the Knitting Factory. Cummings, who was born in San Francisco, studied music at Yale and Columbia and worked at the Columbia-Princeton Electronic Music Center before teaching at the Oberlin Music Conservatory.

CURRIE, RUSSELL   *American composer (1954–)*

Russell Currie has devoted much of his operatic career to EDGAR ALLAN POE with four operas derived from Poe stories, three commissioned and staged by the Bronx Arts Ensemble. THE CAST OF AMONTILLADO, libretto by Carl Laanes, was premiered at Fordham University in New York on April 3, 1982. *The System of Dr. Tarr and Prof. Fethers* was completed in 1983. *A Dream within a Dream* (1984), libretto by Robert Kornfield based on THE FALL OF THE HOUSE OF USHER, was premiered on April 29, 1984. *Ligeia,* libretto by Kornfield, was performed by the Bronx Arts Ensemble in New York on April 5, 1985. Russell, born in North Arlington, NJ, also composed a musical theater piece about a rock drummer called *Rimshot* (1990).

CURTIN, PHYLLIS   *American soprano (1921–)*

Phyllis Curtin created one of the great heroines of American opera, Carlisle Floyd's SUSANNAH. She first sang the role in February 1955 in Florida, reprised it at the New York City Opera and then recorded it in New Orleans. Curtin went on to create two other notable Floyd opera heroines, Cathy in WUTHERING HEIGHTS at Santa Fe in 1958 and Celia in THE PASSION OF JONATHAN WADE at New York City Opera in 1962. Born in Clarksburg, West Virginia, she studied in Boston, began her career with New England Opera Theater in Boston and made her New York City Opera debut in 1953. Her *Opera Arias (1960–1968)* album includes arias from *Susannah*.

CYRANO   *1913 opera by Damrosch*

Swashbuckling swordsman Cyrano de Bergerac is witty and clever but ashamed of his long nose. He hides his love for his beautiful cousin Roxane but helps handsome soldier Christian to woo her by supplying loving words that win her heart. Walter Damrosch's opera *Cyrano,* which uses Edmund Rostand's 1897 play *Cyrano de Bergerac* as libretto in an adaptation by W. J. Henderson, premiered at the Metropolitan Opera on February 27, 1913. Pasquale Amato was Cyrano, Frances Alda was Roxane, Riccardo Martin was Christian, Albert Reiss was Ragueneau, Vera Curtis was his wife Lise, Marie Mattfeld was the Duenna, Putnam Griswald was the Count de Guiche and William Wade Hinshaw was Le Bret. Jules Speck directed and Alfred Hertz conducted. The opera was well received but was considered overly long and did not stay in the repertory. The music, however, continued to be played; it was used as incidental music for a 1923 New York stage production of the play with Walter Hampden as Cyrano and as the score for a silent Italian film. Augusto Genina's film *Cirano di Bergerac* followed the Rostand play as closely as Damrosch so when the film was shown in New York in 1925, the Damrosch score was used as accompaniment for its screenings at the Colony Theater.

1913 "Prelude" piano roll. Composer Damrosch recorded a piano roll version of the "Prelude" to *Cyrano.* It is available digitally from the Spencer Chase piano roll company. **1942 Balcony Scene.** The balcony scene from the opera featuring the trio "Be silent, all may yet be saved" is performed by Agnes Davies, Earl Wrightson and Felix Knight on a radio broadcast on January 31, 1942. The recording is on the album *Souvenirs from American Operas.* IRRC CD.

CYRANO DE BERGERAC   *American operas based on Rostand play*

Witty master swordsman Cyrano de Bergerac is ashamed of his large nose and hides his love for his beautiful cousin Roxane but he helps young Christian woo and win her. In the final scene Roxane realizes that it was really Cyrano she loved. Edmund Rostand's play *Cyrano de Bergerac,* written in 1897, has been filmed many times and remains one of the most popular French plays.

1899 Victor Herbert. Victor Herbert's comic opera *Cyrano de Bergerac,* libretto by Stuart Reed based on Rostand's play with lyrics by Harry B. Smith, premiered in Montreal at the Academy of Music on September 11, 1899, and opened in New York at the Knickerbocker Theater on September 18, 1899. Francis Wilson was Cyrano, Lulu Glaser was Roxane, Charles H. Bowers was Christian, Peter Lang was Ragueneau, Robert Broderick was the Count de Guiche. A. M. Holbrook staged the opera and John McGhie conducted. Herbert's music won praise from critics and the score is considered one of his best, but the production was not well received as neither Wilson nor Glaser could sing well enough to show the quality of the songs and Wilson tried to mix slapstick with romance. **1913 Walter Damrosch.** See above entry titled CYRANO. **1965 Cecil Effinger.** Cecil Effinger's three-act opera *Cyrano de Bergerac,* libretto by Donald Sutherland based on Edmund Rostand's play, was premiered at the University of Colorado in Boulder on July 21, 1965. **1972 Jack Jarrett.** Jack Jarrett's three-act opera *Cyrano de Bergerac,* libretto by the composer based on Rostand's play, was premiered at the University of North Carolina on April 27, 1972.

CZARITZA   *1937 "movie opera" by Stothart*

Composer Herbert Stothart created *Czaritza,* supposedly a 19th century "French" opera set in Russia, for the 1937 American film MAYTIME. In the film it is composed by a Rossini-like Paris composer named Trentini (Paul Porcasi) for American prima donna Marcia Mornay (Jeanette MacDonald). Stothart based the opera on themes from Tchaikovsky's *Fifth Symphony* and ten minutes of it are fully staged at the climax of the MGM film. Bob Wright and Chet Forrest wrote the libretto and lyrics in English but MGM felt opera shouldn't be in a language that could be understood so it was translated into French by Gilles Guilbert. MacDonald and Nelson Eddy sing the lead roles in *Czarita* with support from Mariska Aldrich, Adia Kuznetzoff and Alex Kandibe. Noel Langley wrote the script and Robert Z. Leonard directed. MGM-UA video/laser/DVD.

D

DAISY   *1973 opera by Smith*

Daisy (Juliette Gordon Lowe) creates the American Girl Scouts after meeting with the founder of the Girl Guides in England. She travels from London to Scotland to Georgia, where the first Girl Scout meeting is held in 1912, and promotes the spread of the organization. Julia Smith's *Daisy,* libretto by Bertita Harding, was commissioned by the Opera Guild of Greater Miami and the Girl Scout Council and premiered by Greater Miami Opera in Miami on November 3, 1973. It has since been staged over forty times around the U.S. The score includes choral ensembles for children and traditional Girl Scout songs.

1973 Charlotte Opera. Highlights from the opera were recorded by the Charlotte Opera company in 1973. The featured soloists are soprano Elizabeth Volkman, baritone David Rae Smith, contralto Linda Smalley, and tenor Larry Gerber. Charles Rosekrans conducts the Charlotte Opera Orchestra and Chorus. The album is titled *Highlights from Daisy.* Orion LP.

Julia Smith's Girl Scout opera *Daisy* was recorded by Charlotte Opera in 1973.

DALE, CLAMMA   *American soprano (1948–)*

Clamma Dale made her debut in 1973 in the role of St. Theresa 1 in a Mini-Met production of Virgil Thomson's FOUR SAINTS IN THREE ACTS. She reprised the role in 1981 for a Carnegie Hall production of the opera and is featured on the recording. She sang Bess in an influential 1976 Houston Grand Opera production of Gershwin's PORGY AND BESS and is featured on the recording. Dale, a featured performer at New York City Opera in the standard repertory roles, has also performed and recorded Leonard Bernstein's "Songfest." She was born in Chester, Pennsylvania, and studied at Settlement Music School and at Juilliard.

DALIS, IRENE   *American mezzo-soprano (1930–)*

Dramatic mezzo-soprano Irene Dalis created the role of Cleo Lafont in Norman Dello Joio's BLOOD MOON for San Francisco Opera in 1961 and the title role in Alva Henderson's MEDEA for San Diego Opera in 1972. Dalis, born in San Jose, CA, made her debut in Berlin and has sung leading roles in European operas with major companies in Germany, France, Spain, England and America. She is noted for performances as tragic Greek heroines in operas by Gluck and Strauss.

DAMROSCH, WALTER   *American composer (1862–1950)*

Walter Damrosch composed five operas, two produced at the Metropolitan. He was born in Germany but he came to America at the age of nine with his father Leopold Damrosch, the conductor who introduced German opera to the Met in 1884. Son Walter, also a popular conductor, founded the Damrosch Opera Company in 1894 and it competed strongly with the Met for five years. Damrosch's first opera was an adaptation of Nathaniel

Hawthorne's THE SCARLET LETTER, libretto by G. P. Lathrop, premiered in Boston in 1896 with a cast headed by Johanna Gadski. Next was the comic opera *The Dove of Peace*, libretto by Wallace Irwin, staged in New York and Philadelphia in 1912. The grandiose four-hour CYRANO, libretto by W. J. Henderson based on the 1897 play *Cyrano De Bergerac* by Edmund Rostand, was premiered at the Met in 1912. THE MAN WITHOUT A COUNTRY, libretto by Arthur Guiterman based on the patriotic story by Edward Everett Hale, was premiered at the Met in 1937. Damrosch's final opera, *The Opera Cloak,* was staged at the Broadway Theater in New York on November 3, 1942.

Composer Walter Damrosch

THE DANGEROUS LIAISONS   *1994 opera by Susa*

Eighteenth century aristocrats Valmont and Madame de Merteuil engage in sexual power games that eventually get out of control. Valmont's seductions of Cécile de Volanges and Madame de Tourvel lead to love and death. Conrad Susa's opera *The Dangerous Liaisons,* libretto by Philip Littell based on the 1782 novel *Les Liaisons dangereuses* by Pierre Choderlos de Laclos, premiered at San Francisco Opera on September 10, 1994. Thomas Hampson sang the role of Valmont opposite Frederica von Stade as Merteuil and Renée Fleming as Tourvel. Judith Forst was Madame de Volanges, Mary Mills was Cécile de Volanges, David Hobson was Chevalier de Danceny and Johanna Meier was Madame de Rosemond. Gerard Howland designed the period sets and costumes, Colin Graham staged the three-hour opera and Donald Runnicles conducted the San Francisco Opera Orchestra. The opera has been reprised a number of times: Washington Opera staged it in March 1998 with Dale Duesing as Valmont, Elisabeth Bishop as Merteuil and Anne Manson conducting. The University of Houston staged it in April 2000 at the Moore Opera Center with Justin White as Valmont, Katherine Korsa as Merteuil and Peter Jacoby conducting.

DANTON AND ROBESPIERRE   *1978 opera by Eaton*

Danton and Robespierre clash over the direction of the French Revolution. Danton is tried and executed when he tries to stop the

Reign of Terror and Robespierre is brought down soon after by a conspiracy. John Eaton's highly dramatic grand opera *Danton and Robespierre,* libretto by Patrick Creagh, premiered at Indiana University Opera Theater on April 21, 1978. Danton was sung by James Anderson who alternated in the role with Michael Ballam, Robespierre was played by Tim Noble who alternated with Robert McFarland, St. Just was played by Kevin Langan who alternated with Rick Pickett, Couthon was played by Randy Hansen who alternated with Kevin Bartley, Marat was Lynn Alan Whaley who alternated with Steve Tickards and Louise Danton was Mary Shearer who alternated with Debra Grodecki. Thomas Baldner led the 102-piece Indiana University Opera Theater Orchestra and the 250-person chorus representing Revolutionary citizens and delegates.

1978 Indiana University Opera. James Anderson sings Danton with Tim Noble as Robespierre in this Indiana University Opera Theater original cast recording supervised by the composer. Kevin Langan is St. Just, Randy Hansen is Couthon, Mary Sherer is Louise, Nelda Nelson is Gabrielle, Grand Wilson is Camille, Edith Vanerette is Lucille, Raul Mattel is Tallien. Paula Rede is the Prostitute, Diane Colton is the Baker's Wife, Debra Dominiak is the Fish Wife and William Parcher is the Drunk. Thomas Baldner leads the orchestra and chorus. CRI 3-LP box.

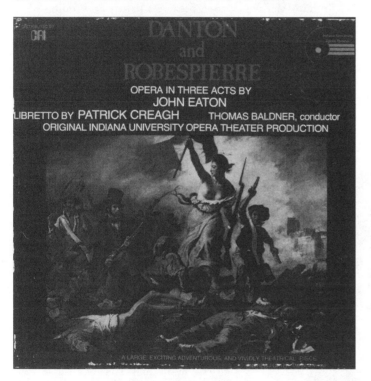

John Eaton's opera *Danton and Robespierre* was premiered and recorded by Indiana University in 1978.

DARK WATERS   *1951 opera by Krenek*

Joe agrees to smuggle diamonds across the border on his boat hoping to meet the leader of the gang. A mysterious Girl, who steals a diamond and is shot by Joe, turns out to be the daughter of the gangster boss. Ernst Krenek's one-act opera *Dark Waters,* libretto by the composer inspired by Herman Melville's novel *The Confidence Man,* premiered at Bovard Auditorium at the University of Southern California in Los Angeles on May 2, 1951. Kalem Kermoyan was Joe, Ava Gjerset was Claire, William Olvis was Phil,

Olive Mae Beach was the Girl, Paul Hinshaw was Tom and Donald Combs and Jerome Zidek were the gangsters. Wolfgang Martin conducted. Krenek invented most of the story and transposed the novel 's setting from the Mississippi to San Pedro Bay. Melville's novel was also the basis of George Rochberg's opera THE CONFIDENCE MAN.

THE DARKENED CITY   *1963 opera by Heiden*

Lazarus, a councillor in a 14th century English city with a holy shrine, dies of the plague. His wife has many suitors but is still unmarried when her husband returns from the dead transformed into a religious zealot. After a confrontation with the city's mayor, Lazarus dies a second time and the light in the shrine goes out. Bernhard Heiden's symbolic opera *The Darkened City,* libretto by Robert Glynn Kelly, premiered at the University of Indiana in Bloomington, Indiana, on February 23, 1963. Heiden was a student of Hindemith and the opera's music is modeled after his style.

DAUGHERTY, MICHAEL   *American composer (1954–)*

Michael Daugherty likes to compose music about pop icons as contemporary folk heroes. He has written pieces about Elvis Presley (*Elvis Everywhere*), Liberace (*Le Tombeau de Liberace*), J. Edgar Hoover (*Sing Sing: J. Edgar Hoover for string quartet and tape*) and Superman (*Metropolis Symphony*) but he is best known for a pop opera about Jacqueline Bouvier Kennedy Onassis. JACKIE O, created with librettist Wayne Koestenbaum, was premiered by Houston Grand Opera as a Houston Opera Studio production on March 14, 1997, and issued on CD. Daugherty, born in Cedar Rapids, Iowa, teaches music at the University of Michigan.

A DAUGHTER OF THE FOREST   *1918 opera by Nevin*

A nature worshipping trapper and his daughter live a life close to nature in western Pennsylvania in the 1860s. When she acquires a lover and becomes pregnant, she kills herself. Her lover dies in battle and her father loses his faith. Arthur Nevin's one-act opera *A Daughter of the Forest,* libretto by Randolph Hartley, was premiered by Chicago Opera at the Auditorium on January 5, 1918. Francesca Peralta sang the Daughter, Forrest Lamont was the Lover and James Goddard was the Father. The composer conducted the Chicago Opera Orchestra.

DAVID RIZZIO   *1932 opera by Mary Carr Moore*

David Rizzio, the trusted Roman Catholic secretary of Mary, Queen of Scots, is murdered by Mary's husband, Lord Darnley and fellow plotters in 1566 at Holyrood Castle in Scotland because. Darnley suspected Rizzio of opposing his plan to become king. Mary Carr Moore's Italianate opera *David Rizzio,* libretto by Emanuel Mapleson Brown, premiered at the Shrine Auditorium in Los Angeles on May 26, 1932. Lutar Hoobyar was David Rizzio, Dorothy Francis was Mary Stuart, Rodolfo Hoyos was Lord Murray, Rosalie Barker Frye was Lady Argyle, William Wheatley was Lord Darnley and Alphonso Pedroza was Douglas. Alberto Conti conducted.

DAVIDSON, TINA   *American composer (1952–)*

Tina Davidson, resident composer with Opera Delaware, premiered her complex chamber opera *Billy and Zelda* in Wilmington in 1998. Composed to a libretto by her sisters Eva and Lale, it combines opera with theater in parallel stories. Davidson, who was born in Stockholm, studied at Bennington with Vivian Fine and has been associated with the New Music Alliance in Philadelphia. Most of her music is for chamber groups and orchestra but she also composes songs. Some of her best known pieces are on the album *I Hear the Mermaids Singing*.

DAVIES, DENNIS RUSSELL   *American conductor* (1944–)

Dennis Russell Davies has conducted the premieres and recordings of operas by Philip Glass, Anthony Davis and William Bolcom. He led the orchestra in Stuttgart State Opera's telecast production of Glass's SATYAGRAHA in 1981, conducted the Stuttgart premiere and recording of Glass's AKHNATEN in 1984, conducted the broadcast production of Glass's THE VOYAGE at the Metropolitan Opera in 1996, conducted the premiere of Glass's WHITE RAVEN (*O Corvo Branco*) in Lisbon in 1998 and conducted the recording of Glass's Rome section of THE CIVIL WARS in 1999. He has conducted three major premieres for Lyric Opera of Chicago: Davis's AMISTAD in 1997, Bolcom's MCTEAGUE in 1992 and Bolcom's A VIEW FROM THE BRIDGE in 1999. Davies, born in Toledo, Ohio, studied at Juilliard and made his debut there in 1968. He was music director of Stuttgart Staatsoper from 1980 to 1987.

DAVIS, ANTHONY   *American composer (1951–)*

Anthony Davis is America's leading living African American opera composer and all his operas have had major stage productions. Davis, who was born in Paterson, NJ, studied at Yale and became known as an avant-garde pianist in the 1970s. His first opera, X, THE LIFE AND TIMES OF MALCOLM X, libretto by his poet cousin Thulani Davis, tells the story of the Black Muslim leader Malcolm X. It was developed by the American Music Theater Festival and had its first full-length production with orchestra in Philadelphia in 1985; it was officially premiered by New York City Opera in 1986. Davis shifted his focus from history to outer space for UNDER THE DOUBLE MOON, libretto by science-fiction writer Deborah Atherton, which was premiered by Opera Theater of St. Louis in 1989. His third opera was TANIA, a controversial work about Patty Hearst, libretto by Michael John LaChiusa, which premiered at the American Music Theater Festival in Philadelphia in 1992. AMISTAD, libretto by Thulani Davis about a famous slave ship rebellion in the 19th century, was premiered by Lyric Opera of Chicago in 1997. *The Trial of Standing Bear*, libretto by Yusef Komunyakaa, was funded by Opera Omaha in 2004.

DAVIS, CARL   *American conductor (1935–)*

British-based American Carl Davis has conducted two Kurt Weill operas, Channel Four's TV version of DOWN IN THE VALLEY in 1984 and English National Opera's recording of STREET SCENE in 1992. He also conducts the Royal Philharmonic Orchestra on the 1989 London concert in which Kiri Te Kanawa sings arias from Victor Herbert's THE ENCHANTRESS and George Gershwin's PORGY AND BESS.

DAVIS, JESSIE BARTLETT   *American contralto* (1860–1905)

Actress-singer Jessie Bartlett Davis created three roles in classic American comic operas and introduced one of the America's most famous songs. She was the first Allan-a-Dale, a trouser role, in Reginald De Koven's 1890 ROBIN HOOD and introduced the song "O Promise Me" which soon became a fixture at weddings. She has starring roles as Idalia in Victor Herbert's *Prince Ananias* in 1894 and as Dolores in Herbert's THE SERENADE in 1897. Davis, born in Morris, Illinois, joined the Old Folks Opera Company in Chicago at the age of fifteen and sang opposite Adelina Patti in Gounod's *Faust* in New York in 1883. She became the principal contralto of the Bostonians in 1888 and spent the rest of her short career with that company.

DEAD MAN WALKING   *2000 opera by Heggie*

A Louisiana nun becomes spiritual advisor to a brutal murderer in jail awaiting execution. She is able to make him understand his crime and repent before he dies. Jake Heggie's opera *Dead Man Walking*, libretto by Terrence McNally based on the story of Sister Helen Prejean, was premiered by San Francisco Opera on October 7, 2000. Susan Graham was Sister Helen, John Packard was condemned killer Joseph de Rocher, Frederica von Stade was his mother, Theresa Hamm-Smith was Sister Rose, Nicolle Foland was the murdered girl's mother, Robert Orth was the murdered girl's father and Gary Rideout was the murdered boy's father. Michael Yeargen designed the sets, Joe Mantello staged the production and Patrick Summers conducted the San Francisco Opera Chorus, San Francisco Girls' Chorus, San Francisco Boys' Chorus, Golden Gate Boys' Chorus and San Francisco Opera Orchestra. Heggie's first full-length opera received an exceptionally favorable welcome. *The Guardian* critic Martin Kettler wrote that "*Dead Man Walking* makes the most concentrated impact of any piece of American music theatre since *West Side Story* more than 40 years ago." The opera has been reprised with great success by other companies including Opera Pacifica, New York City Opera and Cincinnati Opera.

Composer Anthony Davis

Sister Helen Prejean prays as killer Joseph de Rocher is prepared for execution in Opera Pacific's superb production of *Dead Man Walking*. Photograph courtesy of Opera Pacific.

2000 San Francisco Opera. Susan Graham sings the role of Sister Helen Prejean in this live recording of the opera with the San Francisco Opera premiere cast. John Packard is Joseph de Rocher Frederica von Stade is his mother and Theresa Hamm-Smith is Sister Rose. Patrick Summers conducts the San Francisco Opera Chorus, San Francisco Girls' Chorus, San Francisco Boys' Chorus, Golden Gate Boys' Chorus and San Francisco Opera Orchestra. 146 minutes. Erato 2-CD box. **2001 And Then One Night: The Making of Dead Man Walking.** Documentary about the production of the opera in San Francisco including interviews with composer Jake Heggie, librettist Terrence McNally, conductor Patrick Summers, performers Frederica von Stade, Susan Graham and John Packard, author Sister Helen Prejean, SF Opera general director Lotfi Mansouri and Alameda assistant district attorney James Anderson. Angela Bassett is the narrator and Linda Schaller directed the film shown on PBS in 2002. The opera itself was not televised.

A DEATH IN THE FAMILY   *1981 opera by Mayer*

A dysfunctional family is barely able to cope with its many problems in 1915 Knoxville, Tennessee. Jay Follet is a recovering alcoholic, pregnant wife Mary is obsessively religious and son Rufus has persistent nightmares. Jay is killed in a car accident on his way to his father's funeral. William Mayer's three-act opera *A Death in the Family*, libretto by the composer, is based on Tad Mosel's Pulitzer Prize-winning play *All the Way Home*, an adaptation of James Agee's Pulitzer Prize-winning novel *A Death in the Family*. It was commissioned by Minnesota Opera, which previewed it in St. Paul on May 29, 1981, and premiered it March 11, 1983. James

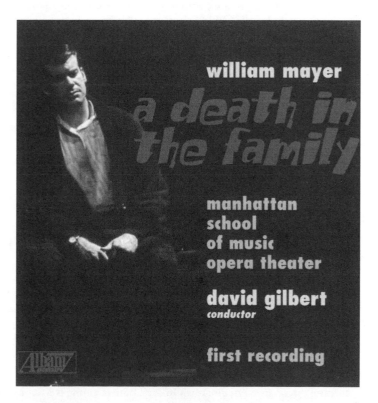

William Mayer's opera *A Death in the Family* was produced and recorded by the Manhattan School of Music in 1999.

E. McKeel, Jr. was Jay, Barbara Brandt was Mary, David Lancaster was Rufus, Mary Boyd Frederickson was Aunt Hannah, Linda Wilcox was Catherine, Gary Briggle was Andrew and Jon Andreason was Ralph. A revised version of the opera starring Dawn Upshaw was produced by St. Louis Opera in 1986 and was broadcast on NPR but the opera was not recorded until 1999 when it was staged by Rhoda Levine at the Manhattan School of Music Opera Theater. Samuel Barber's popular soprano work *Knoxville: Summer of 1915* is based on a poem in the novel.

1994 New Calliope Singers. Excerpts from the opera are performed by the New Calliope Singers and Music Today Ensemble conducted by Gerard Schwarz. Judith Christin sings the last act "Butterfly Aria" with support from Gregory Mercer while Christin and James McKeel sing "How Far We All Come Away." The excerpts are on the album *William Mayer—Voices from the Lost Realms.* Albany CD. **1999 Manhattan School of Music.** Rhoda Levine's production of the opera at the Manhattan School of Music Opera Theater in December 1999 was recorded live. Bert K. Johnson is Jay, Jennifer Goode is Mary, Ian Samplin is Rufus, Deborah Lifton is Catherine and Ted Schmitz is Andrew. David Gilbert conducts the Manhattan School of Music Opera Orchestra. Albany 2-CD set.

THE DEATH OF KLINGHOFFER   *1991 opera by Adams*

The cruise ship Achille Lauro is hijacked in 1985 by Palestinian terrorists and wheelchair passenger Leon Klinghoffer is murdered. John Adams' controversial second opera *The Death of Klinghoffer,* libretto by Alice Goodman, was created by the same team as NIXON IN CHINA with Peter Sellars as director and Mark Morris as choreographer and was also based on real events. It premiered at the Théâtre de la Monnaie in Brussels on March 19, 1991, with Kent Nagano conducting the Lyons Opera Orchestra. James Maddalena was the Captain, Sanford Sylvan was Leon Klinghoffer, Stephanie Friedman was Omar, Thomas Young was Molqi, Eugene Perry was Mamoud, Thomas Hammons was First Officer and Sheila Nader was Marilyn Klinghoffer. Goodman's libretto is different in style from *Nixon,* less declamatory, more compassionate, structured like a Greek tragedy with off-stage violence (Klinghoffer's death is not seen but only spoken about) and choral comment. The opera begins with choruses, one sung by Exiled Palestinians, the other by Exiled Jews, and each scene ends with a chorus reflecting on what has happened. Most of the story is told as reminiscence rather than action; the Captain's opening aria, for example, describes the arrival of the hijackers beginning "It was just after 1:15." The opera received its American premiere at the Brooklyn Academy of Music on September 5, 1991, and then went to San Francisco Opera. It was successfully revived in February 2001 by the Finnish National Opera in Helsinki in a realistic production by Tony Palmer with Hannu Niemela as Klinghoffer, Jaakko Kortekangas as the Captain and Sari Nordqvist as Marilyn Klinghoffer and Sian Edwards conducting. It reached London in January 2002 in a Barbican concert performance by the BBC Symphony Orchestra. It was staged in Prague in May 2003 by the National Opera under the direction of Jiří Nekvasil. The opera has become one of the most controversial in the modern repertory since September 11; a performance of the choruses by the Boston Symphony Orchestra scheduled for October 2001 was cancelled.

1991 Lyons Opera. James Maddalena sings the role of the Captain with Sanford Sylvan as Leon Klinghoffer in this original cast recording. Stephanie Friedman is Omar, Thomas Young is Molqi, Eugene Perry is Mamoud, Thomas Hammons is First Officer, Sheila Nader is Marilyn Klinghoffer and Janice Felty is the Swiss Grandmother. Kent Nagano conducts the Lyons Opera Orchestra and London Opera Chorus. Recorded in Maurice Ravel Auditorium in Lyons. 135 minutes. Elektra Nonesuch 2-CD box. **1999 The John Adams Earbox.** This large anthology of works by Adams includes excerpts from the Lyons performance of *The Death of Klinghoffer.* Nonesuch 10-CD box. **2000 Klinghoffer Choruses.** The seven choruses from *The Death of Klinghoffer* were released on CD in 2000 with Adams' choral work *Harmonium.* They are excerpted from the Lyons Opera recording listed above. Nonesuch CD. **2003 Woolcock film.** Penny Woolcock shot this naturalistic film version of the opera on a cruise ship in the Mediterranean and a ballroom in Malta. The hijacking is presented as a flashback told by the participants after they are back on shore. Sanford Sylvan plays Leon Klinghoffer, Yvonne Howerd is Marilyn Klinghoffer, Chris Maltman is the Captain, Kamel Boutros is Mahmoud, Tom Randle is Molqi, and Emil Marwa is Omar (singing by Susan Bickley). The singers were filmed live performing to a soundtrack pre-recorded by John Adams conducting the London Symphony Orchestra. The film was premiered at the San Francisco Film Festival on Easter Sunday 2003 and telecast in England on Channel Four on May 25. DVD includes documentary on the filming and director's commentary soundtrack. Arthaus/Decca DVD.

THE DEATH OF THE BISHOP OF BRINDISI   *1963 dramatic cantata by Menotti*

A 13th century Italian bishop tells a nun about his tormenting guilt. He once blessed a group of young boys and girls setting off on a children's crusade to the Holy Land and they all drowned when their ship foundered. Gian Carlo Menotti's 30-minute dramatic cantata *The Death of the Bishop of Brindisi,* libretto by the composer, premiered at the Music Hall in Cincinnati on May 18, 1963. Richard Cross was the Bishop and Rosalind Elias was the Nun with support from children's and adult choruses. Max Rudolf conducted.

1965 Erich Leinsdorf. George London sings the role of the Bishop with Lili Chookasian as the Nun on this recording of the cantata. by Erich Leinsdorf who leads the Boston Symphony, New England Conservatory Chorus, Catholic Memorial High School Glee Club and St. Joseph's High School Glee Club. RCA Victor LP/CD.

THE DEATH OF THE VIRGIN   *1983 opera by Owen*

Italian painter Caravaggio uses barmaid Lena as his model for the Virgin Mary in a painting for Cardinal Del Monte. After a disagreement with the Cardinal, Caravaggio is sent to prison for taking back one of his paintings. Lena returns the painting to free him but this angers the painter so much that it causes Lena to drown herself. Caravaggio uses her corpse as the model for his painting "The Death of the Virgin." Richard Owen's one-act opera *The Death of the Virgin,* libretto by Michael Straight based on the Caravaggio painting, was premiered by the New York City Lyric Opera Company on March 31, 1983, in a production by John Haber.

THE DECORATOR   *1959 opera by Woolen*

A family of four move into a suburban home and the wife hires a decorator to spruce it up. He drives the family crazy with descriptions of dozens of different styles they can choose and ways they can be competitive with neighbors. However, a happy solution is finally found. Russell Woolen's 30-minute opera *The Decorator,* libretto by Frank Gelein, premiered at the Catholic University in Washington, DC, in April 1959 and was telecast by NBC on May 24, 1959. The cast were all Catholic University students. This was one of four operas commissioned by the National Council of Catholic Men for the TV series *The Catholic Hour.*

DÉDÉ, EDMOND *African American composer (1827–1901)*

The almost forgotten Edmond Dédé was a New Orleans-born African American Creole composer who spent most of his professional career in France as violinist, conductor and composer. He published his first composition in New Orleans in 1852, the song "Mon pauvre coeur." He moved to France in 1857, studied with Fromental Halévy and became an orchestra conductor in 1960. He married a French woman in 1864 and their son Eugène also became a composer. Dédé composed and published a large quantity of music, including operas and operettas. Portions of his 1877 "saynéte comique" FRANÇOISE ET TORTILLARD have been recorded. He returned to New Orleans in 1893 but racial prejudice soon drove him back to France.

1999 American Classics: Edmond Dédé. Richard Rosenberg's pioneering album of music by Dédé was recorded at the Hot Springs Music Festival after he had carried out research in Paris. It consists of fifteen works including the 1852 song "Mon pauvre coeur," part of the 1865 cantata *Battez aux Champs* and the 1877 "saynéte comique" *Françoise et Tortillard.* Naxos CD.

DEEP RIVER *1926 Broadway opera by Harling*

New Orleans in 1835 at the time of the Quadroon Ball where rich white Creoles look for light-skinned African American mistresses. The villainous Creole Brusard has his eye on beautiful Mugette but she is attracted to Kentucky visitor Hazard. Mugette attends a voodoo séance in the Place Congo to ask for his love but it goes wrong. After duels in which Brusard and Hazard's brother are killed, she is left to whomever will choose her at the Ball. William Franke Harling's Broadway opera *Deep River*, libretto by Lawrence Stalling, is a notable though nearly forgotten predecessor of Gershwin's *Porgy and Bess.* It premiered in Lancaster, PA, on September 18, 1926, was presented in Philadelphia on September 21 and arrived at the Imperial Theater on Broadway on October 4. It was promoted as a "native opera with jazz" and featured a mixed cast of African American and white singers. Jules Bledsoe, who created the role of Joe in *Show Boat* the following year, was Tizanne, Lottice Howell was Mugette, Luis Alberni was Brusard, Roberto Ardelli was Hazard, Charlotte Murray was the Voodoo Queen, David Sage was Jules, Rose McClendon was Octavie, Bessie Allison was Sara, Gladys White was Sara and Louisa Rondstadt was Mugettes's mother. The composer conducted the theater orchestra. Broadway opera lovers didn't support it so it last for only two weeks and has not been recorded.

Rose McClendon in the 1926 production of William Franke Harling's Broadway opera *Deep River*.

DE KOVEN, REGINALD *American composer (1859–1920)*

Reginald De Koven is best remembered for his 1891 comic opera ROBIN HOOD, a huge success in its time and the source of the popular wedding song "Oh, promise me." There was even a sequel in 1902 called *Maid Marian.* His longest running show, however, was ROB ROY, premiered in 1894. De Koven, the most popular American composer of comic operas and operettas at the end of the 19th century, also wrote grand opera. THE CANTERBURY PILGRIMS premiered at the Met in 1917 and RIP VAN WINKLE was staged in Chicago in 1920. De Koven, who was born in Middletown, Connecticut, and studied music in Germany, Italy and Austria, began his music theater career in 1887 with *The Begum.* He created 26 more music theater works in the next 32 years.

DELAWARE *American state (1797–)*

Delaware was late coming to opera because of religious prejudices but this began to change after the opening of the magnificent Grand Opera House in Wilmington in 1871. Two notable American operettas were premiered at the Playhouse in Wilmington on their way to Broadway success, George Gershwin and Herbert Stothart's SONG OF THE FLAME in 1925 and Sigmund Romberg's THE DESERT SONG in 1926. American operas did not begin to be produced until 1969 when OperaDelaware began to commission and stage them. Delaware-born composers include Libby Larsen (Wilmington) and Dorothy Rudd Moore (New Castle).

Wilmington: Wilmington is the only large city in Delaware and the center of most opera activity. OperaDelaware, founded in 1945, has premiered many American operas including Bruce Laird's *The Partisans* in 1969, Alva Henderson's THE LAST OF THE MOHICANS in 1976, Kate Waring's *America Before Columbus* in 1992, Conrad Cumming's TONKIN in 1993, Tina Davidson's BILLY AND ZELDA in 1998 and Michael Ching's *Out of the Rain* in 1998. It's other productions include Ronald Perera's THE YELLOW WALLPAPER in 1993, Thea Musgrave's HARRIET, THE WOMAN CALLED MOSES in 1988 and Gian Carlo Menotti's THE TELEPHONE and THE MEDIUM in 2004. OperaDelaware also commissions operas for children through its Family Opera Theater which has premiered notable works. They include Gian Carlo Menotti's THE BOY WHO GREW TOO FAST in 1982, Charles Strouse's *Charlotte's Web* in 1989, Libby Larsen's A WRINKLE IN TIME in 1992, Evelyn Swensson's *The Enormous Egg* in 1993, Kate Waring's *A.B.C America Before*

Columbus in 1993, Arnold Black's THE PHANTOM TOLLBOOTH in 1995, Swensson's *Redwall* in 1998 and Alan Jay Friedman's *The Hobbit* in 2004. The Family Opera Theater has also presented Victor Herbert's BABES IN TOYLAND and Menotti's HELP, HELP, THE GLOBOLINKS and AMAHL AND THE NIGHT VISITORS. OperaDelaware presents its operas in the splendid Grand Opera House.

DELEONE, FRANCESCO *American composer (1887–1948)*

Ohio native Francesco DeLeone composed the "Buckeye opera" *Alglala: A Romance of the Mesa*, to a libretto by fellow Ohio native Cecil Fanning. It was premiered in Ohio by Cleveland Grand Opera at the Akron Armory on May 24, 1923, reprised in Cleveland in 1924 and then awarded the Bispham Medal. De Leone, born in Ravenna, Ohio, studied music at the Dana Institute in Ohio and the Royal Conservatory of Music in Naples. His three-act operetta *A Millionaire's Caprice* was premiered by the Gravina-Fournier Opera Company in Naples on July 26, 1910. After he returned to Ohio, he established the University of Akron music department and composed several other operettas.

DELLO JOIO, NORMAN *American composer (1913–)*

New Yorker Norman Dello Joio apparently had an obsession about Joan of Arc in the 1950s when he composed three operas about her, plus a symphony and a ballet. *The Trial of Joan*, libretto by Joseph Machlis, premiered at Sarah Lawrence College on May 9, 1950, but was later withdrawn. *The Trial of St. Joan Symphony* (1951) was based on the opera and turned into a ballet by Martha Graham. THE TRIAL AT ROUEN was created for NBC Opera Theatre and telecast on April 8, 1956. THE TRIUMPH OF ST. JOAN was staged by New York City Opera on April 16, 1959. Dello Joio, who won the Pulitzer Prize for music in 1957 for *Meditations on Ecclesiastes* for string orchestra, also found time to write operas on other subjects. THE RUBY, libretto by William Mass based on Dunsany's macabre tale *A Night at the Inn*, premiered at Indiana University on May 13, 1955. BLOOD MOON, libretto by Gale Hoffman and the composer about a 19th century Southern actress with Negro blood who falls in love with a white man, premiered at San Francisco Opera September 18, 1961. *All Is Still* (1971), based on a letter Mozart wrote to his father, was created for television. The Christmas opera-oratorio *Nativity: A Canticle for the Child* was commissioned by the Center for the Arts in Midland, Michigan, which premiered it on December 4, 1987. His many scores for television include the 22 episodes of *Air Power* (1956–57) and *The Louvre* (1965), for which he won an Emmy.

DEL TREDICI, DAVID *American composer (1937–)*

David Del Tredici is not basically an opera composer but his obsession with variations on Lewis Carroll's *Alice in Wonderland* culminated in what he calls "an opera written in concert form." FINAL ALICE, which premiered in Chicago on October 7, 1976, with Barbara Hendricks singing the role of Alice, was supposed to be the last of his Alice compositions but its success led to more commissions. He won the Pulitzer Prize in 1980 for *In Memory of a Summer Day* which is concerned with Alice's childhood. Del Tredici, who was born in Cloverdale, California, and studied at Berkeley, began his career as a pianist.

DEMAIN, JOHN *American conductor (1944–)*

John DeMain has been a notable proponent of American opera and has conducted a large number of premieres, especially for Houston Grand Opera. He conducted the 1976 Houston production of George Gershwin's PORGY AND BESS which went on to Broadway and was the basis of a Grammy-winning recording. His Houston premieres include Carlisle Floyd's WILLIE STARK (1981), Leonard Bernstein's A QUITE PLACE (1983), John Adam's NIXON IN CHINA (1987), Philip Glass's THE MAKING OF REPRESENTATIVE FOR PLANET 8 (1988), Michael Tippett's NEW YEAR (1989), Stewart Wallace's WHERE'S DICK (1989) and Robert Moran's DESERT OF ROSES (1992). Other operas he conducted include Marc Blitzstein's REGINA in 1979, Scott Joplin's TREEMONISHA in 1982, the American premiere of Glass's AKHNATEN in 1985 and the revised version of Carlisle Floyd's THE PASSION OF JONATHAN WADE in 1991. He conducted Virgil Thomson's FOUR SAINT IN THREE ACTS at Aspen in 1991, Gian Carlo Menotti's HELP, HELP, THE GLOBOLINKS at Madison Opera in 1998, Paul Schoenfield's THE MERCHANT AND THE PAUPER at St. Louis in 1999 and the revival of John Philip Sousa's THE GLASS BLOWERS at Glimmerglass in 2000. DeMain, born in Youngstown, Ohio, began his professional career in 1969 as assistant conductor to Peter Herman Adler at NET Opera. In 1972 he joined New York City Opera and in 1975 became music director of Texas Opera Theater. He was made principal conductor for Houston Grand Opera in 1978 and music director in 1980. He is also artistic director of Madison Opera in Wisconsin and Opera Pacific in California.

DEMOCRACY: AN AMERICAN COMEDY *2005 opera by Wheeler*

Love clashes with power in Washington, D.C. in 1875 as corruption envelopes the presidency of Ulysses S. Grant. A woman finds her strict principles under pressure from a charismatic man. Scott Wheeler's opera *Democracy: An American Comedy*, libretto by Romulus Linney based on the novels of Henry Adams, premiered at Lisner Auditorium at George Washington University on January 28, 2005. It was commissioned by Plácido Domingo and performed by members of the Domingo-Cafritz Young Arts Program and The Youth Orchestra of the Americas.

DENNIS CLEVELAND *1996 opera by Rouse*

Dennis Cleveland is the cool host of an American TV talk show. He wanders around the stage, talking and singing, reading from cue cards, listening to the chorus and soliciting confessions from people in the audience. Mikel Rouse's avant-garde talk-show opera *Dennis Cleveland*, libretto by the composer, premiered at The Kitchen in New York on October 29, 1996, with Rouse as Dennis Cleveland. The opera was reprised at the Orange County Performing Arts Center in Costa Mesa, CA, in 1999, with Rouse again in the title role. Rouse dedicated the opera to Robert Ashley who believes the future of American opera is television.

1995 Studio Incontinent. Mikel Rouse plays most of the roles, including host, guests and audience, in this recording made at the Studio Incontinent in New York City. Numbers include "Life in These United States," "Beautiful Murders," "Apparent Money" and "Why Are You Here Today." 74 minutes. New World CD.

DE ORGANIZER *see under* **ORGANIZER**

DE PAUR, LEONARD *American choral director/conductor (1915–1998)*

Leonard De Paur, best known for creating the De Paur Infantry Chorus and De Paur Chorus, was choral director for the 1942 broadcast of Virgil Thomson's FOUR SAINTS IN THREE ACTS, for the 1947 recording of the opera conducted by Thomson and for the 1952 Broadway revival with Leontyne Price. He was also choral director for the Broadway revivals of Oscar Hammerstein's CARMEN JONES in 1956 and George Gershwin's PORGY AND BESS in 1963. He conducted the premiere of James P. Johnson's DE ORGANIZER at Carnegie Hall in 1940 and the premiere of William Grant Still's A BAYOU LEGEND for Opera/South in Mississippi in 1974. Born in Summit, NJ, he studied at Columbia and privately with Hall Johnson and was assistant conductor of Johnson's Choir from 1932 to 1936. He became music director of the Federal Theater Project in New York in 1937 and worked with Orson Welles. He has recorded many works by African American composers.

DESERET (1)   *1880 opera by Buck*

"Deseret," a word taken from the Book of Mormon, meaning "land of the honey bee," was the Mormon's name for their country before it was forced to become the American Territory of Utah in 1850. Brigham Young, the man who led the Mormons to Deseret, became the territorial governor but was deposed in 1857 by President Buchanan because of his advocacy of polygamy (he reputedly married 27 times). Dudley Buck's *Deseret, or A Saint's Affliction*, "an American Opera in Three Acts" with libretto by journalist William Augustus Croffut, was the most controversial American opera of the 19th century. A man with multiple wives was not considered a suitable subject for an opera and the work was condemned by critics for "immoral sensationalism" when it premiered at Haverley's Fourteenth Street Theater in New York City on October 11, 1880. It was reprised in November at the Academy of Music in Baltimore and Pike's Opera House in Cincinnati but moral outrage apparently kept it off the stage after that. Selections from it were published, however. Ironically Buck was best known in his time as a composer of church music.

DESERET (2)   *1961 opera by Kastle*

Sixty-year-old Mormon leader Brigham Young is introduced to eighteen-year-old Anne Louisa Brice in Utah in 1862 and she agrees to become his 25th wife. Before the wedding takes place, however, she falls in love with a young Union Army captain. She decides to go ahead with the wedding anyway as it is her duty. When Young discovers she loves the soldier, he frees her from her promise and sends her off to marry the soldier. Leonard Kastle's opera *Deseret*, libretto by Anne Howard Bailey, was premiered on television by NBC Opera Theatre on January 8, 1961. Kenneth Smith was Brigham Young, Judith Raskin was wife-to-be Anne, John Alexander was Union Army Captain James Lee and Rosemary Kuhlmann was Young's first wife Sarah. The supporting cast included Marjorie McClung and Mae Morgan. Samuel Chotzinoff produced, Jan Scott designed the sets and Peter Herman Adler conducted the orchestra. Kirk Browning directed for television. Kastle later revised *Deseret* for stage production as a three-act opera; it was presented by Memphis Opera Theater in 1967 and by Pasadena Opera Company in 1968.

1961 NBC Opera Theatre. The NBC Opera Theater premiere production was recorded on videotape and can be viewed at the Museum of Television and Radio in New York and Los Angeles.

DESERT OF ROSES   *1992 opera by Moran*

A Civil War officer is transformed into a monster because of war guilt and lives in a prison of thorny roses in the desert. When a visitor picks a rose, the monster threatens to kill him unless he sends his daughter to live in the prison. The daughter agrees but when she becomes homesick, the monster allows her to take a trip home to see her family. When her sisters steal a ring the monster gave her, she realizes she loves him and he is transformed by her love. Robert Moran's two-act opera *Desert of Roses*, libretto by Michael John La Chiusa based on the Beauty and the Beast fairy tale, was premiered by Houston Grand Opera on February 14, 1992. Jayne West was the Girl, John Stephens was the Monster, Stella Zambalis was the Woman, Heidi Jones and Patrica Johnson were the Sisters, Eric Perkins was the Brother and Kelly Anderson was the Father. Heinz Balthes designed the sets, John Dew directed and John DeMain conducted.

1991 Piano Circus Band. Jayne West, who created the role of the Girl, sings two arias in this recording of five sections from *Desert of Roses* recorded in the Barbirolli Hall at St. Clement Danes School with the Piano Circus Band and composer Moran. The arias titled "I can go? I can go to my father?" and "Look into My Eyes" are from Act Two. The recording also includes Movements 1, 3 and 5 of the opera. Argo CD.

THE DESERT SONG   *1926 operetta by Romberg*

The mysterious Red Shadow leads the Moroccan Riffs against the French while singing "The Riff Song." He is actually Pierre Birabeau, son of the French Governor, hidden behind a red cloak. He loves and wins Margot, the fiancée of the Army commander, and gains justice for the Riffs. Sigmund Romberg's *The Desert Song*, libretto by Oscar Hammerstein II, Otto Harbach and Frank Mandel, is pure hokum but wonderfully tuneful as the many recordings and films of this classic operetta demonstrate. It was premiered at the Playhouse in Wilmington, Delaware on October 21, 1925, and opened on Broadway at the Casino Theatre on November 30,

Sigmund Romberg's popular operetta *The Desert Song* was filmed for the third time in 1943, with Dennis Morgan as the Red Shadow.

1926. Robert Halliday played the Red Shadow, Vivienne Segal was Margot, Glen Dale was Paul, Edmund Elton was General Birabeau, Pearl Regay was Azuri, Eddie Buzzell was Bennie and Nellie Breen was Susan. Arthur Hurley directed. *The Desert Song* was the first operetta filmed in the sound era and it seems to entered the light opera repertory. "One Alone" has become its most recorded aria.

1927 Victor Light Opera. The first recording of music from the operetta was a medley of songs performed by the Victor Light Opera Company for a Victor 78. It's on the album *Gems of Broadway.* Vintage Recording LP. **1927 Original London cast.** Harry Welchman is the Red Shadow and Edith Day is Margot on this original London cast highlights recording with Herman Finck conducting. The operetta was staged at the Theater Royal in Drury Lane. World Records LP/Pearl CD. **1929 Richard Crooks.** Met tenor Richard Crooks recorded the aria "One Alone" in 1929 for a 78. It's on the 1998 album *Only a Rose—The Art of Richard Crooks in Song.* Pearl/Koch CD. **1929 Warner Brothers film.** John Boles is the Red Shadow opposite Carlotta King as Margot and Louise Fazenda as Susan in what Warner Brothers promoted as the "first all-singing and talking operetta" with a chorus of 132 voices and 109 musicians. Harvey Gates wrote the adaptation, Bernard McDilled photographed it and Roy del Ruth directed. Premiere Opera VHS. **1932 The Red Shadow.** Warner Brothers made a 20-minute film version of the operetta in 1932 titled *The Red Shadow* with Alexander Gray as the Shadow and Bernice Claire as his Margot. As they had sung the roles opposite each other on stage, they didn't need much rehearsal. **1936 Richard Tauber.** Richard Tauber sings "One Alone" for a 78 recording included on the album *Richard Tauber: Songs of Stage and Screen.* Parlophone LP. **1937 Jussi Björling.** Jussi Björling recorded "The Desert Song" for a 78 record reissued on the 1993 album *Jussi Björling Vol. 2— Operetta and Song (1929–1938).* Pearl/Koch CD. **1943 Warner Brothers film.** Dennis Morgan is the rebel Red Shadow who leads a double life in this Warner Brother color film featuring Irene Manning as Margot. It was made during World War II so the plot was changed to make Germans into the villains. Robert Florey directed. **1944 Wilbur Evans/Kitty Carlisle.** Kitty Carlisle, Wilbur Evans, Felix Knight and Vicki Vola perform a highlights version of the operetta with an orchestra led by Isaac Van Grove. Decca LP/CD and Box Office CD. **1945 Gladys Swarthout.** Met soprano Gladys Swarthout sings "One Alone" on a 1945 radio broadcast. *Gladys Swarthout: Favorites from the Musical Theatre.* Take Two LP. **1945 Lawrence Tibbett.** Met baritone Lawrence Tibbett sings "One Alone" on a *Lucky Strike Hit Parade* radio broadcast. Empire LP. **1952 Earl Wrightson/Frances Greer.** Earl Wrightson, Frances Greer and Jimmy Carroll perform in a highlights version of the operetta with Al Goodman conducting the orchestra. RCA Victor LP. **1952 Nelson Eddy/Doretta Morrow.** Nelson Eddy is the Red Shadow with Doretta Morrow as Margot in this highlights recording produced by Goddard Lieberson. The supporting cast includes Wesley Dalton, Lee Cass and David Atkinson. Lehman Engel conducts. Columbia LP. **1953 Warner Brothers film.** Gordon MacRae is the rebel with a double life in this Warner Brother color film featuring Kathryn Grayson as Margot. This is the best of the film versions, much helped by the musical arrangements made by Max Steiner. Bruce Humberstone directed. WB soundtrack LP/CD and WB VHS/DVD. **1953 Dorothy Warenskjold.** Dorothy Warenskjold sings "Romance" on *The Voice of Firestone* TV program with Howard Barlow leading the Firestone Orchestra. It's on the video *George London in Opera and Song.* VAI VHS. **1954 Gordon MacRae/Marguerite Piazza.** Gordon MacRae sings the role of the Red Shadow oppo-

site Marguerite Piazza and Katherine Hilgenberg in this highlights recording. George Greeley conducts the orchestra. Capitol LP. **1955 NBC Television.** Nelson Eddy stars as the Red Shadow in an NBC Television film directed by Max Liebman. Gale Sherwood is Margo, Met bass Salvatore Baccalone is Ali, Otto Kruger is Birabeau and Rod Alexander and Bambi Lynn are the dancers. Charles Sanford conducts. Video at MTR. **1958 Giorgio Tozzi/ Kathy Barr.** Giorgio Tozzi is the Red Shadow with Kathy Barr as Margot on this highlights recording performed with support from Warren Galjour, Eugene Morgan and Peter Palmer. Lehman Engel conducts. RCA Victor LP. **1959 Mario Lanza/Judith Raskin.** Mario Lanza and Judith Raskin are featured in this highlights recording with support from Donald Arthur and Raymond Murcell. Constantine Callinicos conducts. RCA Victor LP/CD. **1962 Richard Fredricks/Anna Moffo.** Anna Moffo is Margot opposite Richard Fredricks as the Red Shadow in this highlights recording with orchestra and chorus conducted by Lehman Engel. William Lewis is Sid and Kenneth Smith is Ali. It's in the Reader's Digest *Treasury of Great Operettas.* RCA LP. **1963 Gordon MacRae/ Dorothy Kirsten.** Gordon MacRae and Dorothy Kirsten star in this highlights recording with support from Lloyd Bunnell, Gerald Shikey and the Roger Wagner Chorale. Van Alexander conducts. Capitol/Angel LP. **1967 Joan Sutherland.** Joan Sutherland sings "The Desert Song" with the Ambrosian Light Opera Chorus on *The Golden Age of Operetta.* Richard Bonynge conducts the New Philharmonia Orchestra. London LP/CD. **1978 Sherrill Milnes/Beverly Sills.** Beverly Sills and Sherrill Milnes join in duet on "The Desert Song" on their album *Up in Central Park.* Julius Rudel conducts the New York City Opera Orchestra. EMI LP. **1987 Teresa Ringholz/Eastman-Dryden Orchestra.** Soprano Teresa Ringholz and the Eastman-Dryden Orchestra perform excerpts from *The Desert Song* under the direction of Donald Hunsberger on the album *Sigmund Romberg: When I Grow Too Old to Dream.* Arabesque CD. **1993 Jerry Hadley.** Jerry Hadley performs "The Desert Song" and "One Alone" from *The Desert Song* on his album *Golden Days.* Paul Gemignani conducts the American Theatre Orchestra. BMG RCA Victor CD. **1993 Gino Quilico/Barbara Hendricks.** Barbara Hendricks and Gino Quilico join in duet on The Desert Song" on the album *Operetta Duets.* Lawrence Foster conducts the Lyon Opera Orchestra. EMI CD.

DESIRE UNDER THE ELMS *1989 folk opera by Thomas*

Ephraim Cabot, who has already had two wives and three sons, returns to his New England farm with a new young wife named Abbie. Older sons Simeon and Peter leave for California in search of a better life but youngest son Eben stays hoping to inherit the farm. Abbie and Eben fall in love and Abbie has a baby which Ephraim thinks is his. Abbie kills the baby believing it has come between her and Eben but he denounces her to the sheriff. Realizing he still loves her, he tells the sheriff to arrest them both. Edward Thomas's three-act folk opera *Desire Under the Elms,* libretto by Joe Masteroff based on the play by Eugene O'Neill, was first performed at Palmer Auditorium at Connecticut College, New London, CT, on August 10, 1978, and premiered in final form by New York Opera Repertory Theater on January 18, 1989. Judy Kaye sang the role of Abbie, James Schwisow was Eben, Nicholas Solomon was Ephraim, Robert Paul Heimann was Simeon, William Livingston was Peter and Burton Fitzpatrick was the Sheriff.

2002 George Manahan. George Manahan conducts the London Symphony Orchestra. in this studio recording of the opera. Victoria Livengood sings the role of Abbie, Jerry Hadley is Eben,

James Morris is Ephraim, Mel Ulrich is Simeon and Jeffrey Lentz is Peter. 126 minutes. Naxos 2-CD box.

DÉSIRÉE   *1884 comic opera by Sousa*

A romantic tale about musketeers and a mercer's daughter mixes with the intrigues of Louis XIII and Cardinal Richelieu. John Philip Sousa's comic opera *Désirée,* libretto by Edward Taber based on J. M. Morton's *Our Wife,* was premiered at the National Theater in Washington, D. C. by the McCaull Opera Company on May 1, 1884. DeWolf Hopper starred opposite Ida Mosher and Rose Leighton.

1998 Jerrold Fisher. Jerrold Fisher, who restored the score of *Désirée* with Bill Martin, conducts the Pocono Pops Orchestra and Chorus in a live recording of the opera. The singers include Jody Karin Applebaum, Melissa Thorburn, David Price and Richard Lissemore. Amdec CD.

THE DEVIL AND DANIEL WEBSTER   *1939 opera by Moore*

New Hampshire neighbors come to Cross Corner to celebrate the wedding of wealthy Jabez Stone. It turns out he has become wealthy by selling his soul to the Devil who comes to the wedding disguised as Mr. Scratch to collect the debt. Stone's friend Daniel Webster demands a trial. Scratch agrees but forms a jury of traitors and installs a judge from the Salem witch trials. Webster turns the tables on the Devil with his arguments. Douglas Moore's delightful folk opera *The Devil and Daniel Webster,* libretto by Stephen Vincent Benét based on his short story, was premiered by American Lyric Theater at the Martin Beck Theater in New York on May 18, 1939.

Lansing Hatfield was Daniel Webster (alternating in the role with Richard Hale), George Rasely was Mr. Scratch aka the Devil, John Gurney was Jabez Stone, Nancy McCord was Mary Stone (alternating with Bettina Hall), Fred Stewart was the Fiddler, Clair Kramer was Justice Hawthorn and the Voice of Miser Stevens,

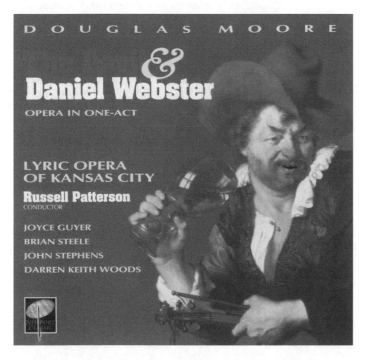

Douglas Moore's folk opera *The Devil and Daniel Webster* was recorded by Lyric Opera of Kansas City in 1995.

Edward Marshall was the Clerk, Don Lee was Walter Butler, Lawrence Siegle was Black Teach, Ernice Marshall was Simon Girry and Philip Whitefield was King Philip. Robert Edmond Jones designed the set, John Houseman directed and Fritz Reiner conducted. Houseman revived the opera at New York City Opera in 1959 with Walter Cassel as Daniel Webster, Norman Kelley as Mr. Scratch, Joshua Hecht as Jabez Stone and Adelaide Bishop as Mary Stone. Rouben Ter-Arutunian designed the sets and Max Goberman conducted.

1957 Armando Aliberti. Armando Aliberti leads the Festival Choir and Orchestra in this recording of the complete opera. Lawrence Winters stars as Daniel Webster, Frederick Weidner is Mr. Scratch, Joe Blankenship is Jabez Stone, Doris Young is Mary Stone, James de Groat is the Fiddler, Nigel Thomas is Simon Girty, Eugene Hartzell is Justice Hawthorne and King Philip, Werner Harms is the Clerk/Walter Butler and James Groat is Miser Stevens. Westminster/Desto LP/Phoenix CD. **1991 Sherrill Milnes.** Sherrill Milnes sings Daniel Webster's aria "I've Got a Ram, Goliath" at a Richard Tucker Foundation gala at Avery Fisher Hall on November 10, 1991. James Conlon conducts members of the Metropolitan Opera Orchestra on *A Salute to American Music.* RCA Victor CD. **1995 Lyric Opera of Kansas City.** Brian Steele is Daniel Webster in this recording of the opera by Lyric Opera of Kansas City. Darren Keith Woods is Mr. Scratch, John Stephens is Jabez Stone, Joyce Guyer is Mary Stone, Robert Gibby Brand is the Fiddler, Cary Miller is Justice Hawthorne, David Soxman is the Clerk, Michael Philip Davis is Simon Girty, Andrew Stuckey is King Philip, Michael Lanman is Blackbeard, Benjamin Bongers is Walter Butler and Matt Foerschler is Miser Stevens. Russell Paterson conducts the Lyric Opera of Kansas City Orchestra and Chorus. 57 minutes. Newport Classic CD.

DIAMOND, DAVID   *American composer (1915–)*

David Diamond has had success with songs and orchestral works but less luck with his operas. He began his opera career with *David* (1935), based on a D. H. Lawrence story, and continued with *Twisting of the Rope* (1940), based on a W. B. Yeats play. Neither was produced. After a long pause, he composed the four-act musical comedy *Mirandolina* (1958), libretto by P. Brown based on a play by Carlo Goldoni, but it was not staged. His "musical folk play" *The Golden Slippers,* libretto by S. Citron based on a Spanish play by Perez Galdos, was staged in New York in 1965. *The Noblest Game,* libretto by Katie Loucheim about a war widow in Washington, D.C., was finished in 1975 and scheduled for production at New York City Opera but postponed. Juliana Gondek sang six arias from it in a Seattle Symphony Orchestra showcase in 1998 and reprised them for a NYCO show in 1999. Diamond, born in Rochester, NY, studied and taught in France, Germany and Italy and was a pupil of Roger Sessions and Nadia Boulanger.

DIARY OF A MADMAN   *1981 monodrama by White*

Office worker Ivanovitch wakes up in his shabby room and begins to write in his diary. He remembers the beautiful Sophie and how she was to wed another. He imagines them dancing together at a ball but falls down as he dances. After he get ups and begins to write in his diary again, he imagines that he is the King of Spain and marches out of the room as king. In the final scene he is seen writing an imaginary diary. Michael White's monodrama DIARY OF A MADMAN, libretto by the composer based on a novella by Nicolai Gogol, was premiered by Opera America in New York in January 1981. It is composed for a baritone with offstage voices provided by a tape recording.

DIARY OF AN AFRICAN AMERICAN   *1994 opera by Peterson*

Avant-garde jazz trumpeter Hannibal Peterson goes to Kenya in 1979 ailing in spirit and body and is revived through the gift of a kalimba (finger piano) from Murasi, a keeper of souls. As it has connected him to his African roots, he decides to pass it on to his son. Peters's autobiographical opera/music theater work *Diary of an African American,* libretto by the composer, was premiered by Minnesota Opera and Music Theater Group at the World Theater in St. Paul on March 8, 1994. Peterson, born in Smithville, Texas in 1948, starred as himself and played trumpet with a cast of singers that included Ann Sinclair, Byron Utley and Brandon Martin. Andy McCloud played bass, Cecil Brooks III played drums and music director Rahn Burton played piano. Diane Wondisford directed.

DICK, PHILIP K   *American writer (1928–1982)*

Todd Machover's multi-media opera VALIS, based on Philip K. Dick's autobiographical tale about a bizarre "pink light experience" that created a split personality, was premiered in Paris in 1987 and presented at MIT in 1988. Dick, who explored ideas of identity and reality in his science fiction, is one of the most prophetic modern American writers. He won the 1962 SF Hugo for *The Man in the High Castle* and several of his stories have been made into films.

DI DOMENICA, ROBERT   *American composer (1927–)*

Robert Di Domenica, an atonal composer from New York who studied at NYU and played flute at the Met and NYCO, has composed two operas. *The Balcony,* libretto by the composer based on the Jean Genet play, was premiered by Sarah Caldwell's adventurous Opera Company of Boston in June 1990 with Mignon Dunn as Madame Irma and reprised at the Bolshoi in Moscow in May 1991. *The Scarlet Letter,* libretto by E. H. Eglin and the composer, was completed in 1986 and scenes from it were presented in the Composer Series at Jordan Hall in Boston in 1997 with Elizabeth Kennedy as Hester Prynne. The trilogy of *Francesco Cenci, Beatrice Cenci* and *The Cenci* is a work in progress. Three of Di Domenica's orchestral works, recorded by Gunther Schuller, are on CD.

DIFFERENT FIELDS   *1996 opera by Reid*

Pro football player Aaron James becomes a pal to teenager Casey whose mother Jenny work for his team's owner. When he is blackmailed into throwing a game to pay gambling debts and found out, the boy's illusions about his role model are crushed. Mike Reid's one-act one-hour chamber opera *Different Fields,* libretto by Sarah Schlesinger, was commissioned by Opera Memphis and the Metropolitan Opera Guild. It was premiered in New York at the New Victory Theater on February 8, 1996, and presented in Memphis on April 25, 1996. Joseph Mahowald sang Aaron, James Harris Wiggins III was Casey, Theresa Hamm-Smith was Jenny, Judith Engel was team owner Doris and Steven Goldstein was Cal. John Michael Deegan and Sarah G. Conly designed the sets, Mel Marvin directed and Joshua Rosenblum conducted. Reid, a popular singer/songwriter, was once a professional football player.

THE DIFFICULTY OF CROSSING A FIELD   *2002 opera by Lang*

Selma, Alabama, in 1854. Mr. Williams is sitting on the verandah of his plantation home with his wife and child. He gets up and walks down a path to a field where he suddenly vanishes. The event is shown seven times with differing reactions from the main characters. Mrs. Williamson goes mad. David Lang's 75-minute chamber opera *The Difficulty of Crossing a Field*, libretto by Mac Wellman subtitled "A New Opera in Seven Tellings," is a Rashomon-style tale based on two stories by Ambrose Bierce. It was premiered by American Conservatory Theater on March 23, 2002, at the Artaud Theater in San Francisco. Julia Migenes was Mrs. Williamson, Anika Noni Rose was Virginia Creeper, Jacob Ming-Trent was Boy Sam and Lianne Marie Dobbs was the Williamson Girl. Carey Perloff staged the opera and the music was performed by the Kronos Quartet who collaborated in its creation.

DI GIACOMO, FRANK   *American composer*

Frank Di Giacomo has composed four operas, three of them performed. BEAUTY AND THE BEAST, libretto by Emul P. Edmon and the composer, was premiered by Opera Theater of Syracuse in 1974 and recorded by the Syracuse company in 1976. The four-act opera *Undine* was composed in 1976 but has not been staged. The Christmas opera *A Journey to Bethlehem* premiered at the Charles W. Baker High School in Baldwinsville, NY, in December 1977. THE DYBBUK, based on the play by Saloman Ansky and Jewish legend, was performed by Opera Theater of Syracuse in 1978.

THE DISAPPOINTMENT   *1767 opera by Barton*

Philadelphia in 1767. A group of Philadelphians, including coopers, tailors, debauchees and loose women, become involved in a hoax involving buried treasure. Andrew Barton's satirical *The Disappointment, or, The Force of Credulity* is the first American opera or, to be exact, the first American ballad opera written by an American for Americans. It also contains the first use of the tune "Yankee Doodle." It was to have premiered in Philadelphia on April 20, 1767, but authorities cancelled the performance saying its satirical elements made it "unfit for the stage." It was published the same year and survives in libretto form but the music was lost and

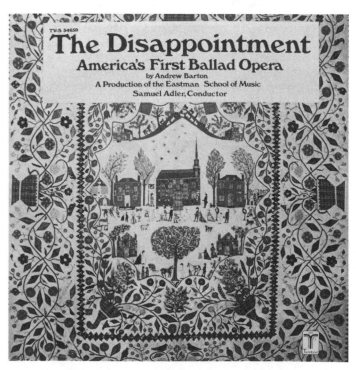

This original cast recording of *The Disappointment* was made in 1976, 200 years after the opera was to have premiered.

the opera was never performed publicly. In 1976 the Library of Congress Music Division and University of Rochester Eastman School of Music sponsored its reconstruction by composer Samuel Adler and scholar Jerald Graue with assistance from Judith Layne. Adler and associates composed music in 18th century style as overture and accompaniment to the original ballads. The reconstructed version was premiered and recorded at the Library of Congress in Washington, D. C., in March 1976 with Elaine Bonazzi as Moll Plackett, Joseph Bias as Raccoon, Ruth Denison as Lucy, Tonio de Paolo as Meanwell, John Denison is Trushoop, William Sharp is Rattletrap, Arden Hopkin as Parchment, Milford Fargo as Quadrant, John Maloy as Washball, Richard Reif as Topinlift and Richard Hudson as McSnip. Adler conducted the Eastman Philharmonia Chamber Ensemble.

1976 Library of Congress. This is an original cast recording made 200 years after the opera was to have been premiered. Samuel Adler conducts the Eastman Philharmonia Chamber Ensemble with Elaine Bonazzi in the role of Moll Plackett, Joseph Bias as Raccoon and Ruth Denison as Lucy. Tonio de Paolo plays Meanwell, John Denison is Trushoop, William Sharp is Rattletrap, Arden Hopkin is Parchment, Milford Fargo is Quadrant, John Maloy is Washball, Richard Reif is Topinlift and Richard Hudson is McSnip. Turnabout LP.

DISTRICT OF COLUMBIA   *American Federal district*

The District of Columbia, essentially the city of Washington, has long been a favorite place to premiere American operas and operettas. Washington Opera has premiered several major works and others have been staged in a variety of venues. Julius Eichberg's THE DOCTOR OF ALCANTARA, the first American opera to be staged by an African American opera company, was presented by the Original Colored American Opera Troupe of Washington in Washington in 1873. The National Negro Opera Company, founded in 1943, presented Clarence Cameron White's OUANGA. Washington-born opera people include soprano Carmen Balthrop, heldentenor Richard Cassilly, composer Duke Ellington, composer John Philip Sousa and composer Andrew Stiller. David Diamond's opera *The Noblest Game* is set in Washington. Listed below are the sites of premieres.

Catholic University. Four 30-minute operas were premiered by students at the Catholic University in Washington in April and May 1959 and then telecast on NBC-TV's *The Catholic Hour*. They were Thaddeus Jones' THE CAGE, William Graves' THE JUGGLER, Emerson Meyers' DOLCEDO and Russell Woolen's THE DECORATOR. **Folger Shakespeare Theatre.** Patrick Kavanaugh's *The Last Supper* was premiered at the Folger Shakespeare Theater in 1983. **Hirschhorn Museum.** Morton Subotnick's *The Last Dream of the Beast*, composed for Joan La Barbara, was premiered at the Hirschhorn in February 1979 and Stephen Dembski's mini-opera *The Show* in 1986. **Kennedy Center for the Performing Arts.** Leonard Bernstein's MASS was created for the opening of the Kennedy Center and premiered there on August 8, 1971. Gian Carlo Menotti's children's opera A BRIDE FROM PLUTO premiered at the Terrace Theater at the Center on April 14, 1982, Lee Hoiby's delectable opera BON APPÉTIT premiered at the Center on March 8, 1989. **Library of Congress.** Gian Carlo Menotti's THE UNICORN, THE GORGON AND THE MANTICORE premiered at the Coolidge Auditorium in the Library of Congress in 1956 and Hugo Weisgall's *Purgatory* was first staged at the Library in 1961. Andrew Barton's THE DISAPPOINTMENT, the first American ballad opera written by an American for Americans, was premiered at the Library of Congress in 1976, 200 years after it was written.

National Cathedral. John La Montaine premiered three one-hour Christmas pageant-opera at the National Cathedral. *Novellis, Novellis* was performed in 1962, THE SHEPHARDES PLAYE was performed and televised in 1967 and *Erode the Great* was presented in 1969. Gian Carlo Menotti's church opera THE EGG premiered at the Cathedral in 1976. **National Theater.** The National Theater premiered a number of notable comic operas and operettas before they moved on to Broadway. They include John Philip Sousa's *The Smugglers* (1882), Sousa's DÉSIRÉE (1884), Sousa's *The Queen of Hearts* (1885), Victor Herbert's BABETTE (1903), Herbert's THE ENCHANTRESS (1911). Victor Jacobi's *Sybil* (1915), Jacobi's *Rambler Rose* (1917), Jerome Kern's SHOW BOAT (1927) and Leonard Bernstein's WEST SIDE STORY (1957). **Smithsonian Institution.** Loran Carrier's one-act *Game Opera* was premiered at the Smithsonian on December 12, 1969. **Summer Opera Theater Company.** Summer Opera, founded in 1978 and based at the Catholic University of America in Washington, presents operas and operettas at the Hartke Theater. Most productions are from the European repertory but it has staged Sigmund Romberg's THE STUDENT PRINCE. **Vocal Arts Society.** The Vocal Arts Society, founded in 1990, presents opera singers in recital, usually the more notable new artists. **Washington Concert Opera.** Washington Concert Opera presents operas with full orchestra but without sets and costumes, usually one or two a year chosen from the classic European repertory. **Washington Opera.** Washington Opera (which changed its name to Washington National Opera in 2004) is the major opera company of Washington. It began in 1956 as the Opera Society of Washington performing in the Lisner Auditorium at George Washington University and moved into its own Opera House at the Kennedy Center in 1971. It has always shown interest in American opera and its first season included Gian Carlo Menotti's THE OLD MAID AND THE THIEF and THE UNICORN, THE GORGON AND THE MANTICORE. It has commissioned and premiered a number of American operas including Alberto Ginastera's BOMARZO in 1967, Ginastera's BEATRIX CENCI in 1971, Menotti's GOYA in 1986 and Dominick Argento's THE DREAM OF VALENTINO in 1994. American operas are staged regularly and have included Dominick Argento's THE ASPERN PAPERS, Samuel Barber's VANESSA, Douglas Moore's THE BALLAD OF BABY DOE, Stephen Paulus's THE POSTMAN ALWAYS RINGS TWICE, André Previn's A STREETCAR NAMED DESIRE Conrad Susa's THE DANGEROUS LIAISONS and Robert Ward's THE CRUCIBLE. Plácido Domingo is currently its artistic director.

LA DIVINA   *1966 opera by Pasatieri*

Coloratura diva Madame Altina is about to give her "farewell" concert to the delight of her maid Cecily and her manager Haemon waiting in her dressing room. After demanding another dress and harassing the conductor, she delights her fans by deciding to give yet another farewell concert. Thomas Pasatieri's one-act opera buffa *La Divina*, libretto by the composer, premiered at the Juilliard School of Music in New York on March 16, 1966. The operas has become a favorite of student groups.

"DO NOT UTTER A WORD"   *Soprano aria: Vanessa (1958). Words: Gian Carlo Menotti. Music: Samuel Barber*

"Do not utter a word, Anatol, do not move." Vanessa has been waiting for her lover for twenty years and when he arrives she tells him he must leave at once if he doesn't still love her. The aria is aimed at the wrong man; the visitor is actually the son of her old lover and a fortune hunter who will seduce her niece on the same night. Eleanor Steber sings the aria in the original 1958 Metropolitan Opera cast recording of VANESSA. Johanna Meier sings it in the 1979 Spoleto Festival telecast of the opera, Leontyne Price sings it on her album *Leontyne Price—The Prima Donna Collection*, Helen-Kay Eberley features it on her album *American Girl* and Renée Fleming includes it on her album *I Want Magic! Vanessa*, once been called "the finest opera written by an American," was inspired by the stories of Danish writer Isak Dinesen and describes a love triangle on an estate in the far north.

DR. FAUSTUS LIGHTS THE LIGHTS   *American operas based on Gertrude Stein play*

Dr. Faustus Lights the Lights is Gertrude Stein's light-hearted three-act retelling of the Faust legend. It starts off with an argument between Faust and Mephisto and is deeply concerned with electric lights, a dog, a boy, a man from overseas and a viper who bites the heroines Marguerite Ida and Helena Annabel. First published in *Last Operas and Plays*, it has been very popular with American composers resulting in seven one-act operas.

1953 Meyer Kupferman. Meyer Kupferman's 20-minute opera *Dr. Faustus Lights the Lights*, libretto by the composer, premiered at Sarah Lawrence College April 5, 1953. **1957 Charles Wuorinen.** Charles Wuorinen's opera Dr. *Dr. Faustus Lights the Lights*, libretto by the composer, was composed in 1957 but apparently not publicly performed. **1979 Alvin Carmines.** Alvin Carmine's *Dr. Faustus Lights the Lights*, libretto by the composer, premiered at the Judson Memorial Church in New York in October 1979 in a production by Lawrence Kornfeld with sets by Ed Lazansky. Jeff Weiss played Faustus, Carmines played Mephistopheles and Sarah Kornfeld played the Girl. **1982 David Ahlstrom.** David Ahlstrom's *Dr. Faustus Lights the Lights*, libretto by the composer, was premiered by VOICES/SF in San Francisco on October 29, 1982. **1987 Vernon Martin.** Vernon Martin's *Dr. Faustus Lights the Lights*, libretto by the composer, was composed in 1987. **1996 Hans Peter Kuhn.** Hans Peter Kuhn's *Dr. Faustus Lights the Lights*, libretto by Robert Wilson based on the Stein play, was premiered at Lincoln Center in New York on July 1992 in a production by Wilson. **2002 Stanley Walden.** Stanley Walden's *Dr. Faustus Lights the Lights*, libretto by the composer, was premiered on March 1, 2202, at the Neighborhood Playhouse in New York City.

DR. HEIDEGGER'S FOUNTAIN OF YOUTH   *1978 opera by Beeson*

Dr. Heidegger invites four elderly friends to test his experimental youth potion. It makes them young but they behave just as badly as they did in their youth. After a time they begin to age once again. Jack Beeson's opera *Dr. Heidegger's Fountain of Youth*, libretto by Sheldon Harnick based on Nathaniel Hawthorne's 1837 story *Dr. Heidegger's Experiment*, premiered at the National Arts Club in New York on November 17, 1978. Carol Wilcox played widow Rachel Lockhart, Judith Christin was spinster Hannah Moody, Grayson Hirst was Reuben Waterford, Robert Shiesley was Colonel Killigrew, Alfred Anderson was Dr. Heidegger and Miranda Beeson was the Maid. Thomas Martin conducted the chamber orchestra. Beeson's opera has since been staged by many companies around the country. It was produced by the Royal Northern College of Music in Manchester, England, in 2004 and well reviewed. Other operatic adaptations of the story are listed under NATHANIEL HAWTHORNE.

1979 National Arts Club. The National Art Club cast recorded the opera at the time of the premiere. Carol Wilcox is Rachel Lockhart, Judith Christin is Hannah Moody, Grayson Hirst is Reuben Waterford, Robert Shiesley is Colonel Killigrew, Alfred Anderson

is Dr. Heidegger and Miranda Beeson is the Maid. Thomas Martin conducts the chamber orchestra. CRI LP.

THE DOCTOR OF ALCANTARA   *1862 opéra bouffe by Eichberg*

Young lovers Isabella and Carlos resist orders from their fathers to marry people they have not seen without realizing the intended partners are each other. Julius Eichberg's opéra bouffe *The Doctor of Alcantara*, libretto by Benjamin E. Woolf, was the most successful early American comic opera and marked the beginning of a truly American style. Following its premiere at the Boston Museum on April 7, 1862, it was produced all over America, Britain and Australia. It was also the first American opera staged by an African American opera company, the Original Colored American Opera Troupe of Washington, D. C., which presented it in Washington and Philadelphia in 1873.

1996 Boston Brass. The quintet Boston Brass, based at Boston College, pay homage to fellow Bostonian Eichberg by playing the Overture from *The Doctor of Alcantara*. It was recorded at Trinity Chapel at Boston College and is featured on their album *Stealing the Show*. Summit CD.

DR. SELAVY'S MAGIC THEATER   *1972 music theater opera by Silverman*

A patient of the surrealist Dr. Selavy is subjected to a series of wacky fantasies and is apparently cured. Stanley Silverman's 65-minute surrealistic music theater opera work *Dr. Selavy's Magic Theater*, libretto by Richard Foreman and lyrics by Tom Hendry inspired by the ideas of artist Marcel Duchamp, premiered at the Berkshire Music Center in Lenox, Massachusetts in August 1972 and opened in New York at the Mercer Arts Center on November 23, 1972. Foreman staged the production and designed the sets while Silverman conducted the chamber orchestra. The cast included Ron Faber, George McGrath, Barry Primus, Jessica Harper, Amy Taubin, Steve Menken, Denise De Lapenha, Robert Schlee and Mary Delson. *Dr. Selavy's Magic Theater*, which is scored for nine singers and four instrumentalists in parodies of musical styles ranging from oratorio to rock, was a huge success and ran for 144 performances, "Selavy" is pronounced like "C'est la vie." The work was reprised at Lake Erie College in 1977 and by Richard Foreman's Music Theater Group in New York in 1984.

1973 Original cast. Composer Silverman conducts the chamber orchestra on this original cast recording with Ron Faber, George McGrath, Barry Primus, Jessica Harper, Amy Taubin, Steve Menken, Denise De Lapenha, Robert Schlee and Mary Delson. United Artist LP.

DOLCEDO   *1959 TV opera by Meyers*

Aging agnostic Dolcedo goes to live in a convent in Rome. He is looked after by Sister Leo and Sister Ursula and has talks with Father Richard. Emerson Meyers' 30-minute opera *Dolcedo*, libretto by Father Dominic Rover, was premiered on *The Catholic Hour* on NBC-TV on May 17, 1959. The singers were students from the Catholic University in Washington, D.C. The opera was one of four commissioned by the National Council of Catholic Men for the Sunday afternoon TV show.

DOLLY   *2002 multi-media opera by Reich/Korot*

The cloning of the sheep Dolly is shown in a series of video images as leading scientists discuss the technological breakthrough. Steve Reich's multi-media opera *Dolly*, libretto by the composer created with his wife, video artist Beryl Korot, premiered at the

Spoleto Festival USA in Charleston, SC, on May 31, 2002. Reich and Korot presented their "documentary music video theater" THREE TALES incorporating *Dolly* and two other operas in an abandoned Charleston theater, the Memminger Auditorium, with sixteen musicians and singers. Videos in the auditorium showed historical film, interviews, photographs and text as the operas were sung and played. Nick Mangano was the director and Brad Lubman was the conductor. The interviewees were James D. Watson, Richard Dawkins, Stephen Jay Gould, Jaron Lanier, Sherry Turkle, Rodney Brooks, Steven Pinker, Robert Pollack, Adin Steinsaltz, Kevin Warwick, Joshua Getzler, Ray Kurzweil, Cynthia Breazeal, Billy Joy, Marvin, Minsky, Henri Atland, Ruth Deech, Gina Kolata and the robot Kismet.

2002 New York Studios. *Dolly,* performed by the Steve Reich Ensemble and the Synergy Vocals group, was recorded at the Avatar Studios in New York City in June 2002. The singers are Amanda Morrison, Micaela Haslam, Gerard O'Beirne, Andrew Busher and Phillip Conway-Brown. Bradley Lubman conducts. The interviewees are James D. Watson, Richard Dawkins, Stephen Jay Gould, Jaron Lanier, Sherry Turkle, Rodney Brooks, Steven Pinker, Robert Pollack, Adin Steinsaltz, Kevin Warwick, Joshua Getzler, Ray Kurzweil, Cynthia Breazeal, Billy Joy, Marvin, Minsky, Henri Atland, Ruth Deech, Gina Kolata and the robot Kismet. The opera is featured as the third part of the trilogy *Three Tales* on a 2003 Nonesuch DVD/CD.

DOMINGO, PLÁCIDO   *Spanish tenor (1941–)*

Plácido (aka Placido) Domingo, the most versatile major tenor of our time, has sung American opera on stage and recorded American music theater works. He created the role of Goya in Gian Carlo Menotti's GOYA in the Washington Opera premiere at the Kennedy Center in 1986. He sings Cervantes/Don Quixote in the 1996 operatic recording of Mitch Leigh's MAN OF LA MANCHA, duets with Denyce Graves on Leonard Bernstein's "Make Our Garden Grow" from CANDIDE on a 1992 concert album, sings Sigmund Romberg's "Overhead the Moon is Beaming" from THE STUDENT PRINCE on a 1993 album and duets with Renée Fleming on Leonard Bernstein's "Tonight" from WEST SIDE STORY on a 1998 album. Born in Madrid but raised in Mexico, Domingo began his career in 1957 singing zarzuelas before making his American debut in Dallas in 1961. He is artistic director of both Washington Opera and Los Angeles Opera.

DON JUAN TRIUMPHANT   *1989 "movie opera" by Segal*

Misha Segal wrote an aria of the Phantom's lost opera *Don Juan Triumphant* for the 1989 film version of *The Phantom of the Opera.* The opera, which is described in Gaston Leroux' 1911 source novel, is sung in the film by Jill Schoelen, the actress playing Christine. Robert Englund portrays the Phantom in the film whose setting is transposed to 19th century Covent Garden. Segal was the music director of the film which Dwight H. Little directed. On VHS/DVD.

DON QUIXOTE   *1996 "theater piece" by Eaton*

John Eaton's *Don Quixote,* which the composer calls a "theater piece for musicians," is an experimental quasi-opera based on the Cervantes novel in which instrumentalists alternate playing their instruments and singing and speaking lines from the libretto. A clarinetist plays/sings/acts the role of Don Quixote, a flutist plays/sings/acts Sancho Panza and a cellist plays/sings/acts Dulcinea. A percussionist and a violinist handle smaller roles and a pianist provides commentary. Eaton created the work for the New

York New Music Ensemble and Eaton Opera Company of Chicago and it was first performed in June 1996. It was reprised at Columbia University in May 2000 with Jean Kopperud as clarinetist, Jayn Rosenfeld as flutist, Theodore Mook as cellist, Pablo Rieppi as percussionist, Linda Quan as violinist and Stephen Gosling as pianist. (The Broadway musical MAN OF LA MANCHA is also based on the Cervantes novel.)

DONNELLY, DOROTHY   *American librettist/lyricist (1880–1928)*

Dorothy Donnelly wrote the librettos for some of the most successful American operettas of the classical era and the lyrics for some of its most popular songs. After starting as an actress, she turned to libretto writing in 1916. She joined forces with Sigmund Romberg for the 1921 BLOSSOM TIME based on a European operetta about Schubert and helped make it a major success. They teamed up again for THE STUDENT PRINCE in 1924, MY MARYLAND in 1926 and *My Princess* in 1927. Her song lyrics include "Deep in My Heart," "Drinking Song" and "Serenade." Donnelly was born in New York City to a theatrical family; her father managed the Grand Opera House and her brother ran a theater company.

DOUBLE TROUBLE   *1954 opera by Mohaupt*

Hocus and Pocus are twin brothers separated since childhood in this Commedia dell'Arte-style opera. Hocus, who has an erotic mistress named Erotia and a nagging wife named Naggia, opposes his daughter Cynthia's desire to marry Lucio. When Pocus arrives looking for his lost brother, multiple confusions abound until all finally ends more or less well. A chorus introduces and comments on the action. Richard Mohaupt's one-act 65-minute opera *Double Trouble,* libretto in English by Roger Maren based on Plautus's play *Menaechmi,* was premiered by Kentucky Opera at Columbia Auditorium in Louisville on December 4, 1954. Richard Dales played Hocus, William Pickett was Pocus, Abby Bierfield was Naggia, Charme Reisley was Cynthia, coloratura soprano Margaret Pulliam was courtesan Erotia, Monas Harlan was Dr. Antibioticus and W. D. Elliott was his son Lucio. Moritz Bomhard conducted the Louisville Orchestra and Kentucky Opera Chorus. The opera was commissioned and recorded by the Louisville Orchestra with Rockefeller Foundation funds.

1954 Kentucky Opera, Moritz Bombard conducts the Louisville Orchestra and Kentucky Opera Chorus in this recording made with the premiere cast. Richard Dales is Hocus, William Pickett is Pocus, Abby Bierfield is Naggia, Charme Reisley is Cynthia, Margaret Pulliam is Erotia, Monas Harlan is Dr. Antibioticus and W. D. Elliott is Lucio. Louisville First Edition Records LP.

DOUGHERTY, CELIUS   *American composer (1902–1986)*

Celius Dougherty, whose art songs were popular with opera divas like Maggie Teyte, Gladys Swarthout and Eileen Farrell, also wrote an opera. MANY MOONS, libretto by the composer based on a story by James Thurber, premiered at Vassar College in 1962. Dougherty, who was born in Glenwood, Minnesota, studied at the University of Minnesota and first became known as a pianist in 1922 performing his own piano concerto. Most of his songs are settings of famous poems by Whitman, Benét, Lowell, etc. but "Love in the Dictionary" has lyrics culled from *Funk and Wagnell;* Cynthia Haymon sings it on a CD.

DOUGLASS, FREDERICK   *1991 opera by Kay*

The final years of African American anti-slavery writer and orator Frederick Douglass as he lectures in the years following the

Civil War. Douglass, who had been a slave himself, became the chief spokesman for former slaves. His autobiography continues to inspire. Ulysses Kay's three-act opera *Frederick Douglass,* libretto by Donald Dorr, was commissioned by the Rockefeller Foundation and the NEA. It was premiered by New Jersey State Opera in Newark on April 14, 1991, with bass Kevin Maynor singing the role of Douglass.

DOUGLASS, JOHN THOMAS　*American composer (1847–1886)*

John Thomas Douglass seems to have been the first African American composer to compose an opera and he was certainly the first to have one staged. His three-act opera *Virginia's Ball* was presented at the Stuyvesant Institute on Broadway in New York in 1868. Douglass, a popular concert violinist, somehow was able to travel to Europe to study music. His opera was copyrighted in 1868 but it is lost and its subject matter is not known. Douglass, born in New York City, was considered one of the finest musicians of his time.

DOW, DOROTHY　*American soprano (1920–)*

Dorothy Dow created the role of Susan B. Anthony in Virgil Thomson's opera THE MOTHER OF US ALL when it premiered at Columbia University in 1947. She had an imposing voice and presence which helped make the opera a success as can be heard on the recording of the premiere Dow, born in Houston, Texas, studied at the Juilliard School and made her debut in 1946 in Buffalo. She went on to sing major roles in classic European operas at La Scala and Glyndebourne but not at the Met.

DOWN IN THE VALLEY　*1945 folk opera by Weill*

Brack Weaver is in jail in Birmingham sentenced to die for killing Thomas Bouché in a fight over Jennie Parsons. On the eve of his execution he escapes to spend the night with Jennie but returns to his death cell at dawn. Kurt Weill's 45-minute folk opera *Down in the Valley,* libretto by Arnold Sundgaard based on the folk ballad "Down in the Valley," was composed in 1945 as a radio opera and recorded but never broadcast. Weill revised it for the stage for amateur singers and premiered it on July 15, 1948, at Indiana University in Bloomington, Indiana. Marion Bell was Jennie, James Welsh was Brack and the other roles were sung by Indiana students. Hans Busch directed and Ernst Hoffman conducted. It was telecast by NBC Opera Theatre on January 25, 1950. The opera begins with the baritone Preacher/Leader singing the folk ballad "Down in the Valley" and four other folk songs are feature in the score. Weill said he wanted to create an opera ordinary people could sing and he succeeded beyond expectation; there were over 6,000 performances in the ten years following its premiere, most by non-professionals. It continues to be staged at colleges and small opera houses around the U.S. *The New York Times* once described it as "the fountainhead of American opera."

1945 Original radio version. The original radio version of the opera was recorded in December 1945 with Maurice Abravanel conducting the orchestra. This audition disc was sent to possible sponsors but as none were interested, the project was abandoned. The recording is available on a rare LP. **1950 NBC Opera Theatre recording.** Marion Bell, who created the role, stars as Jennie with William McGraw as Brack in this NBC Opera Theatre cast recording made January 25, 1950, under Weill's supervision. Kenneth Smith is Leader/Preacher. Ray Jacquemont is Thomas Bouché, Richard Barrows is Jennie's father, Robert Holland is Peters, Roy Johnston is the Prison Guard, Jeanne Privette and Carole O'Hara are the Old Ladies and Ralph Teferteller is Square Dancer Caller. Peter Herman Adler conducts the RCA Victor Orchestra and Chorus. RCA Victor LP. **1950 Alfred Drake/Jane Wilson.** Broadway star Alfred Drake is Brack Weaver opposite Jane Wilson as Jennie in this recording supervised by Kurt Weill. Daniel Slick is Leader/Preacher, Norman Atkins is Thomas Bouché, Leonard Kranendonk is the Guard, Leo Bernache is Peters, John Petterson is Jennie's Father, Herman Hennig is the Man and Dorothy Egens and June McMechon are the Women. Maurice Levine conducts the chorus and orchestra. Decca LP. **1990 Dortmund University** Ilana Davidson is Jennie with Marc Acito as Brack Weaver in this recording made at Dortmund University in Germany in June 1990. Donald Collup is Preacher/Leader, James Mabry is Thomas Bouché and Donald P. Lang is Jennie's Father. Willie Gundlach conducts singers and musicians from Fredonia, Buffalo and Dortmund University. Capriccio CD.

DRACULA　*1999 multimedia music work by Glass*

Count Dracula, an immortal vampire living in a castle in Transylvania, moves to England after he is visited by Jonathan Harker. He turns Lucy into a vampire and becomes enamoured of Mina. After many horrible happenings he is killed by Van Helsing. Bram Stoker's 1897 novel *Dracula* has inspired several American opera composers (see other entries below) and countless movies. The first, Tod Browning's 1931 Universal Studios *Dracula* starring Bela Lugosi, used almost no music. Philip Glass composed a score for it consisting of 27 numbers that can be played live while the film is projected, a variation on the multimedia film opera he created for Jean Cocteau's *La Belle et la Bête.* His 67-minute score was premiered at the Royal Festival Hall in London on October 23, 1999, with Glass performing with the Kronos Quartet.

1999 Kronos Quartet. The Kronos Quartet perform Glass's 67-minute *Dracula* score, 27 named numbers composed to be played with the 1931 movie. Electra Nonesuch CD. **2000 Universal DVD.** Glass's music, performed by the Kronos Quartet, is heard as the soundtrack of the 1931 Universal Studios classic film of *Dracula.* Bela Lugosi play Dracula opposite Edward Van Sloan as Van Helsing under the direction of Tod Browning. Universal DVD.

THE DRACULA DIARY　*1994 opera by Moran*

A vampire becomes an opera diva in the 18th century and creates horrific problems for her jealous impresario. It turns out worse that he could have imagined. Robert Moran's one-act chamber "opera macabre" *The Dracula Diary,* libretto by James Skofield, was produced by Houston Opera Studio for Houston Grand Opera and premiered on March 18, 1994, at the Cullen Theater in Houston. Laura Knoop was opera singer/vampire Angela, James Maddalena was her Impresario, Ray Very was the Tenor, James Scott Sikon was Confessor/Singing Master/Doctor/Apparition, Jill Grove was the Maid/Mother Superior/Courier/Zorina and Michael Chioldi was the Courtier/Photo Crew. Constantinos Kritikos designed sets and costumes, Ross A. Perry directed and Ward Holmquist conducted the Houston Grand Opera Orchestra.

1994 Houston Opera Studio. Laura Knoop stars as opera vampire Angela with James Maddalena as her Impresario in this recording made by the premiere cast at the Cullen Theater on March 21 and 22, 1994. James Scott Sikon is Confessor, Singing Master, Doctor and Apparition, Jill Grove is Mother Superior, Female Courtier, Maid, Zorina and Party Guest, Ray Very is the Monk, Tenor, and Menippuo, and Michael Chioldi is the Male Courtier and Party Guest. Ward Holmquist conducts the Houston Grand Opera Studio Orchestra. 71 minutes. Catalyst 2-CD set.

DRACULA, THE MUSICAL OPERA   *1998 opera by Weidberg*

Count Dracula plunges a stake into the heart of his wife Mina soon after welcoming Renfield to his castle in Transylvania. He goes with him to New York where he attends a party Bella and is attracted to Roberta. After meeting Van Helsing, Dracula who sneaks into Roberta's bedroom, seduces her and takes her away. She is rescued by her lover William who kills Dracula. Ron Weidberg's three-act *Dracula, The Musical Opera,* libretto by Irwin Donald Nier based loosely on the Bram Stoker novel, was premiered by the American Israeli Musical Opera Co. in 1998. Eugene Flam sings the role of Dracula, Del Bach was vampire hunter Van Helsing, Erica Suedberg was Roberta, Dona Cobb was William, Lauren Lipson was Mina and Gloria Aguilar was Bella William Anderson conducted the chamber orchestra and staged the opera.

1998 American Israeli Musical Opera Co. Eugene Flam sings the role of Dracula in this recording of 26 numbers from the opera performed by the American Israeli Musical Opera Company. Del Bach is vampire hunter Van Helsing, Erica Suedberg is Roberta, Dona Cobb is William, Lauren Lipson is Mina and Gloria Aguilar is Bella William Anderson conducts the chamber orchestra. 71 minutes. Company CD.

DRACULA, THE OPERA   *2000 opera by Ziemba*

Paul Ziemba's three act *Dracula, The Opera,* libretto by the composer based on Bram Stoker's novel, premiered at the Harlem Center Theater in Amherst, NY, on April 18, 2000. Thomas Witakowski was Dracula, Richard Bystron was Jonathan Harker, Heide Guay was Mina, Andrea Todaro was Lucy, James Carubba was Dr. Van Helsing, Ian Michaelski was Renfield, Kenneth Schlimgen was Dr. Seward, Alfonzo Tyson was Arthur, Shirley Byczynski and Roberto Gonzales were the gypsies Rupa and Bela and Jillian and Holly Bystron were the brides of Dracula. Ivan Docenko was music director.

DRAKE, ALFRED   *American baritone (1914–1992)*

Alfred Drake created and recorded major roles in major American music theater works and often recorded with opera singers. He created the role of Curly in Rodgers and Hammerstein's OKLAHOMA! (1943/cast album), Macheath in Duke Ellington's BEGGAR'S HOLIDAY (1946/cast album*),* Fred in Cole Porter's KISS ME KATE (1948/two cast albums), Hajj in Forrest/Wright's KISMET (1953/two cast albums) and Marco Polo in Warnick/Paul's THE ADVENTURES OF MARCO POLO (1958/cast album). He even took over the role of the King in Rodgers and Hammerstein's THE KING AND I on Broadway when Yul Brynner went on vacation. He recorded Kurt Weill's DOWN IN THE VALLEY (1950) with Jane Wilson, Rudolf Friml's THE VAGABOND KING (1951) with Frances Bible, Victor Herbert's NAUGHTY MARIETTA (1955 VHS/cast album) with Patrice Munsel and Rodgers and Hammerstein's CAROUSEL (1962) with Roberta Peters. He and Peters also recorded an album of theater songs by LEONARD BERNSTEIN (1963). Drake, whose birth name was Alfredo Capurro, began his career on Broadway in 1935 singing in Gilbert and Sullivan operettas. He sang in only one movie, the forgotten 1945 musical *Tars and Spars,* and most of the roles he created on stage were played in the film versions by Howard Keel.

DRAKE, EARL R.   *American composer (1865–1916)*

Earl R. Drake composed a grand romantic opera complete with ballet, THE BLIND GIRL OF CASTEL-CUILLÉ, and had it staged at the Globe Theater in Chicago in 1914. He followed it with a comic opera, *The Mite and the Mighty,* presented in Chicago the following year. Drake, who was born in Aurora, Illinois, was best known in his time as a master violinist. After studies in Berlin, he returned to Chicago to teach, write articles on violin technique and compose orchestral works two operas.

DRATELL, DEBORAH   *American composer (1956–)*

Brooklyn-born composer Deborah Drattell has created a number of vocal works based on Jewish mysticism, including two operas intended for soprano Lauren Flanigan. LILITH, libretto by David Steven Cohen based on Jewish folk myth about Adam's first wife, was given its concert premiere at Glimmerglass Opera in 1998 and its stage premiere by New York City Opera on November 11, 2001, with Flanigan as Eve. The one-act THE FESTIVAL OF REGRETS, libretto by Wendy Wasserstein, is set at the annual Jewish New Year's ceremony at Central Park's Bethesda Fountain. It was premiered at Glimmerglass Opera on August 8, 1999, as the first part of the trilogy CENTRAL PARK with Flanigan in the leading role and reprised at New York City Opera in November 1999. The chamber opera *Marina: A Captive Spirit,* libretto by Annie Finch based on the life of Marina Tsvetaeva, was premiered at the DR2 Theater in New York in 2003 in a production by Anne Bogard with J. David Jackson as conductor. NICHOLAS AND ALEXANDRA, the story of the tragic last days of the Russian Tsar, was commissioned by Los Angeles Opera which premiered it in 2003.

DREAM GIRL   *1924 operetta by Herbert*

Elspeth dreams herself back to fifteenth century England where she is saved from marriage to a villain by Jack Warren whom she seems to have loved for 500 years. Victor Herbert's final operetta *Dream Girl,* libretto by Rida Johnson Young and Harold Atteridge, premiered in New Haven on April 11, 1924. and opened on Broadway at the Ambassador Theatre on August 20, 1924. Fay Bainter was Elspeth, Walter Woolf was Jack and Billy Van was Jimmie. The hit song was the waltz "My Dream Girl." The libretto was derived from a 1906 play called *The Road to Yesterday* written by Beulah Marie Dix and Evelyn Sutherland.

1924 Reinald Werrenrath. Met baritone Reinald Werrenrath recorded the song "Broad Highway" from the operetta for a Victor Red Seal 78 record in 1924. **1986 Donald Hunsberger/Eastman-Dryden Orchestra.** The Eastman-Dryden Orchestra led by Donald Hunsberger performs eight songs from *The Dream Girl,* including "My Dream Girl," on the album *Victor Herbert: The American Girl.* Arabesque CD.

THE DREAM OF VALENTINO   *1994 opera by Argento*

Rudolph Valentino rises to movie star fame in the 1920s with the help of screenwriter June Mathis and Hollywood publicists. His meteoric rise ends in sudden death. Dominick Argento's opera *The Dream of Valentino,* libretto by Charles Nolte which includes film projection and slides, premiered at Washington Opera on January 15, 1994. Robert Brubaker was Valentino, Suzanne Murphy was June Mathis, Julia Ann Wolf was Natacha Rambova, Joyce Castle was movie star Alla Nazimova, Edrie Means was Valentino's first wife Jean Acker, Julian Patrick was the Mogul and Dan Dressen was the Mogul's nephew Marvin Heeno. Valentino designed the costumes, John Conklin designed the sets, Ann-Margret Pettersson staged the opera and Christopher Keene conducted the Washington Opera Orchestra and Chorus.

1994 Dream of Valentino Tango. The Baltimore Symphony Orchestra, conducted by David Zinman, plays the Tango from *The Dream of Valentino* on the album *Dance Mix.* Argo CD.   **2000**

Valentino Dances. Eiji Oue conducts the Minnesota Orchestra in a ten-minute suite from *The Dream of Valentino* titled "Valentino Dances." William Schimmel is featured on accordion. The album, with other music by Argento, is titled *Valentino Dances.* Reference Recordings CD.

THE DREAMERS   *1996 opera by Conte*

Mexican General Mariano Vallejo founds the city of Sonoma, California, which becomes the center of the Bear Flag Revolt during the 1846 war with Mexico. When Americans capture the General, they declare the city a republic and join it to the U.S. in 1848. David Conte's opera *The Dreamers,* libretto by Philip Littell, was commissioned by Sonoma City Opera to celebrate the 150th anniversary of the city's founding. It premiered in the Sebastiani Theater in August 1996 with Shouvic Mondel as General Vallejo and a large supporting cast that included Karen Connor, Sylvie Braitman, Antoine Garth and Kevin Brackett. Sandra Bernhard staged the opera and John Miner conducted the Sonoma City Opera Orchestra and Chorus.

DREAMKEEPERS   *1996 opera by Carlson*

Ela returns to a Ute reservation in Utah to be with her dying Grandmother, a famous spiritual healer. She is torn between her Native American roots and her new life in the city. When her Anglo doctor lover is injured in a car accident, she has to enter the spirit world to save him and fend off the villain Sloane. David Carlson's neo-romantic opera *Dreamkeepers,* libretto by Aden Ross, was commissioned by Utah Opera to celebrate Utah's centennial and premiered on January 12, 1996, in Salt Lake City. Juliana Gondek created the role of Ela, Debria Brown was Grandmother, Tonio de Paolo was Adam and Brian Montgomery was Sloane. Michael Downs designed the sets, Anne Ewers staged the opera and Stewart Robertson conducted the Utah Symphony. After some revisions, the opera was reprised by Tulsa Opera in March 1998 with Ashley Putnam as Ela, Rosalind Elias as Grandmother, Antonio Nagore as Adam and Jake Gardner as Sloane. Albert Takazauckas directed and Carol Crawford conducted the Tulsa Philharmonic.

1997 Utah Symphony. The Utah Symphony Orchestra plays orchestral music from the opera *Dreamkeepers* under the direction of Stewart Robertson on the album *David Carlson: Symphonic Sequences.* New World CD.

DREISER, THEODORE   *American novelist (1871–1945)*

Theodore Dreiser, the best-known author of the naturalist movement, began his writing career in 1900 with the novel *Sister Carrie.* Two of his works have provided the basis for operas. Earl Robinson's folk opera SANDHOG, libretto by Waldo Salt, is based on Dreiser's story *St. Columba and the River;* it premiered in New York in 1954. Tobias Picker's opera *An American Tragedy,* based on Dreiser's most famous novel, was commissioned by the Metropolitan Opera. Dreiser, who born in Terre Haute, Indiana, studied at Indiana University and earned his living as journalist and magazine editor.

THE DRESS   *1953 opera by Bucci*

Vicki spends the rent money on an expensive dress with a gold collar while husband David is out of town. When he returns unexpectedly, she has problems hiding it from him. Marc Bucci's one-

Movie star Rudolph Valentino, the inspiration for Dominick Argento's opera *The Dream of Valentino,* as he appeared in the 1921 film *The Sheik.*

act comic opera *The Dress,* libretto by the composer, was premiered by the Robert Goss Company at the YMCA in New York on December 8, 1953.

DREW, JAMES   *American composer (1929–)*

James Drew, an eclectic *sui generis* composer who creates diverse kinds of music in his own unique way, has composed a number of operas to his own librettos. *Mysterium* (1975) is a television opera. *Suspense Opera* (1975) is an improvised open form work which was premiered by his New York/New Orleans-based MMT Theater in 1982. *Dr. Cincinnati* (1977) has not yet been performed. *Live from the Black Eagle* was presented by MMT Theater in 1987. *Rats Teeth* was staged by MMT Theater in 1989. Drew, born in St. Paul, Minnesota, has also composed other vocal music including the oratorio *The Fading of the Visible World* (1976) and the soprano aria "Orangethorpe Aria" (1978).

DROBNY, CHRISTOPHER   *American composer (1960–)*

Christopher Drobny began his operatic career with *Koch's Postulate,* libretto by Joan Schenkar, which was staged by the New Dramatists in New York on October 2, 1985. *Fire in the Future, The Heroic Life and Tragic Death of Joan the Maid,* libretto by Schenkar about Joan of Arc, was premiered by Minnesota Opera in St. Paul on April 2, 1987, and reprised by the New Dramatists in New York on February 25, 1988. His best-known opera, LUCY'S LAPSES, libretto by Laura Harrington about a suicidal old woman, was first performed in Waterford, Connecticut, in 1987. Drobny's other operas include *Touch and Go* (1988), performed in Memphis, *Kissing and Horrid Strife* (1997) and *The Kafka Project* (1998).

A DRUMLIN LEGEND   *1949 folk opera by Bacon*

An adventurous pilot is helped to settle down to ordinary life by supernatural creatures who teach him to fly in his imagination. Ernst Bacon's Celtic folk opera *A Drumlin Legend,* libretto by Helene Carus, was premiered at Columbia University in New York City on May 4, 1949.

THE DUCHESS OF MALFI   *1978 opera by Burton*

The Duchess of Malfi loves her steward Antonio and marries him secretly despite opposition from her powerful brothers, Duke Ferdinand and the Cardinal. She has three children by Antonio and loses the respect of the people but won't name their father. Ferdinand finally has her strangled along with her two youngest children but Antonio and the eldest child escape. Ferdinand goes mad with guilt. After wreaking revenge, Antonio become the ruler of Malfi. Stephen Douglas Burton's three-act opera *The Duchess of Malfi,* libretto by Christopher Keane based on John Webster's Jacobean revenge tragedy, was commissioned by the National Opera Institute. It premiered at the Wolf Trap Festival

Baritone Todd Duncan as Porgy in *Porgy and Bess*.

in Vienna, Virginia, on August 18, 1978. Richard Cross played the Cardinal.

THE DUEL   *1974 opera by Carmines*

Alexander Hamilton and Aaron Burr were bitter rivals at the beginning of the 19th century leading opposing political parties. As Hamilton wouldn't stop attacking him, Burr challenged him to a duel in Weehawken, New Jersey, on July 11, 1804. Hamilton was killed and Burr's reputation was destroyed. Alvin Carmines' one-act opera *The Duel*, libretto by the composer based on real events, premiered at the Metropolitan Opera Studio in Brooklyn in 1974. Frederick Burchinal played Aaron Burr and Linda Phillips played his daughter Theodosia, who remained loyal despite all.

DUFFY, JOHN   *American composer (1928–)*

John Duffy has composed over 300 musical works including four operas. The best known is BLACK WATER, libretto by Joyce Carol Oates, a thinly-disguised portrayal of the Chappaquiddick tragedy. Commissioned by the American Music Theater Festival, it premiered in Philadelphia in 1997 and has been recorded. Duffy's first opera was *The Eve of Adam* performed in Interlochen in 1955. It was followed by *Everyman Absurd,* a music drama created for ABC Television. In 2000 he composed *Muhammed Ali,* an opera about the heavyweight boxing champ to a libretto by *New York Times* sports columnist Robert Lipstye. Duffy, who was born in New York and brought up in the Bronx, studied with Aaron Copland and Solomon Rosowsky. He has worked with many theaters and festivals on and off Broadway and is the founder of the *Meet the Composer* series.

DUKE, VERNON   *American composer (1903–1969)*

Vernon Duke is known for songs like "April in Paris" and Broadway musicals like *Cabin in the Sky* but he also composed operas under his real name, Vladimir Dukelsky. *Mistress into Maid,* libretto by the composer based on a Pushkin story, was premiered in Santa Barbara on December 12, 1958. *Zenda,* based on the novel *The Prisoner of Zenda,* was staged in San Francisco in August 1963. Duke, who was born in Russia, came to America. in 1922 and began writing for Broadway revues in the 1930s. He collaborated with John Latouche, librettist of *The Ballad of Baby Doe,* on three musicals including *Cabin in the Sky* and *Banjo Eyes.*

DUNCAN, TODD   *American baritone (1903–1998)*

Todd Duncan created the role of Porgy in George Gershwin's PORGY AND BESS in 1935 at the Colonial Theater in Boston and played the part on Broadway. He sang the role again in later revivals and recorded it with Anne Brown, the original Bess. Duncan, who made his stage debut in 1934 in *Cavalleria Rusticana* with the black Aeolian Opera company, also created the role of Lord's General in Vernon Duke's *Cabin in the Sky* in 1940 and Stephen Kumalo in Kurt Weill's 1949 "musical tragedy" LOST IN THE STARS. Duncan, who was born in Danville, Kentucky, studied at Butler University in Indiana and Columbia University Teacher's College and taught voice at Howard University from 1932 to 1945. He was the first black member of New York City Opera where he made his debut there as Tonio in *Cavalleria Rusticana* on

September 28, 1945. He sang in two movies, the jazz film *Syncopation* (1942) and the prison film *Unchained* (1955), and appears in documentary films about *Porgy and Bess* and Marian Anderson.

DUNN, MIGNON   *American mezzo-soprano (1931–)*

Mignon Dunn created Mehitabel in George Kleinsinger's chamber opera *Archy and Mehitabel* in New York in 1954, the Statue in Lukas Foss's GRIFFELKIN on television in 1955, Katie in Robert Ward's THE LADY FROM COLORADO in Central City in 1964 and Madame Irma in Robert Di Domenica's *The Balcony* in Boston in 1990. She sings the role of Susan B. Anthony in the only recording of Virgil Thomson's opera THE MOTHER OF US ALL, played Baba the Turk in a San Francisco Opera production of Igor Stravinsky's THE RAKE'S PROGRESS and sang the role of Desideria on stage in Gian Carlo Menotti's THE SAINT OF BLEECKER STREET. Dunn, born in Memphis, Tennessee, made her debut in New Orleans in 1955 and began to sing at the Met in 1958.

DUST   *1999 electronic opera by Ashley*

Homeless people sing their life stories while standing behind screens showing images related to the stories. Robert Ashley's opera *Dust*, libretto by the composer, was premiered in Japan in a collaboration with Japanese video artist Yukihiro Yoshihara. It had its American premiere at The Kitchen in New York City on April 14, 1999. The singers were Robert and Sam Ashley, Thomas Buckner, Jacqueline Humbert and Joan LaBarbara and the electronic score was played by Robert Ashley on electronics, "Blue" Gene Tyranny on synthesizers and Tom Hamilton at the mixing board.

1999 The Kitchen. The American premiere of the opera at The Kitchen was recorded live. It features Robert Ashley, Sam Ashley, Thomas Buckner, Jacqueline Humbert. Joan LaBarbara, "Blue" Gene Tyranny and Tom Hamilton. 90 minutes. Lovely Music 2-CD box.

DUVAL, FRANCA   *American soprano (1933–)*

Franca Duval created the title role in Gian Carlo Menotti's opera MARIA GOLOVIN when it premiered in Brussels in 1958. She reprised her performance on Broadway, on the original cast recording and on the 1959 NBC Opera Theatre television production. She played Tosca opposite Franco Corelli in a 1956 film of the Puccini opera.

DUYKERS, JOHN   *American tenor (1942–)*

John Duykers. one of the leading tenors of American opera, has created roles in eight operas and recorded two others. He is best known for creating the role of Mao in John Adams' NIXON IN CHINA at Houston Grand Opera in 1987 and is featured in the telecast and recording. He created fisherman Krillig in Anthony Davis's UNDER THE DOUBLE MOON at Opera Theater of St. Louis in 1989, Dad and Fidel Castro in Davis's TANIA in Philadelphia in 1992, the Chief Inquisitor in Myron Fink's THE CONQUISTADOR in San Diego in 1997, a lead role in Philip Glass's WHITE RAVEN in Lisbon in 1998, a lead role in Erling Wold's *Sub Pontio Pilato* in Seattle in 1999, the Blind King and Krishna in Tony Prabowo and Jarrad Powell's *Kali* in Seattle in 2000 and the Visitor (a role composed for him) in Glass's IN THE PENAL COLONY in Seattle in 2000. He sings principal roles in unique recordings of Ezra Pound's THE TESTAMENT OF FRANÇOIS VILLON made by Western Opera Theater in San Francisco in 1971 and Lou Harrison's RAPUNZEL made at UC, Santa Cruz. in 1996. On stage he has sung Bégears in John Corigliano's THE GHOSTS OF VERSAILLES, the Doctor in Dominick Argento's THE VOYAGE OF EDGAR ALLAN POE, Enoch Pratt in Carlisle Floyd's THE PASSION OF JONATHAN WADE, Lennie in

Floyd's OF MICE AND MEN and Sellem in Igor Stravinsky's THE RAKE'S PROGRESS. Duykers made his debut in Seattle in 1966 and has sung in 56 contemporary operas and 31 world premieres.

THE DYBBUK (1)   *1931 opera by Tamkin*

Leah is possessed by a dybbuk on her wedding day. A dybbuk, according to Hasidic folklore, is a disembodied human spirit that must wander through the world because of its sins looking for haven in a living person. Leah is possessed by the spirit of the Hasidic scholar Channon fell in love with her but killed himself when he learned she was to marry another. Only exorcism can free her. Saloman Ansky's popular 1920 Yiddish play *The Dybbuk (Between Two Worlds)* has been translated into many languages. David Tamkin's three-act opera *The Dybbuk*, libretto by his brother Alex Tamkin based on the Ansky play, was completed in 1931 but not premiered by New York City Opera until October 4, 1951. Patricia Neway was Leah, Robert Rounseville was Channon, Frances Bible was Frade, Mack Harrell was Rabbi Azrael, Lawrence Winters was the Messenger, Emile Renan was Meyer, Michael Pollock was a Wedding Guest and Eunice Alberts was the Elderly Woman. Mstislav Doboujinsky designed the sets, Irving Pichel staged the opera and Joseph Rosenstock conducted the NYCO Orchestra. The opera was broadcast by New York City Opera on October 4, 1951.

New York City Opera. Joseph Rosenstock conducts the New York City Opera Orchestra in this recording of *The Dybbuk* Patricia Neway is Leah, Robert Rounseville is Channon, Frances Bible is Frade, Mack Harrell is Rabbi Azrael, Lawrence Winters is the Messenger, Emile Renan is Meyer and Eunice Alberts is the Elderly Woman. Phoenix LP box/Omega Opera Archives CD.

THE DYBBUK (2)   *Three American operas based on Ansky play*

Saloman Ansky's popular 1920 Yiddish play *The Dybbuk (Between Two Worlds)* has been the basis of three other American operas following the success of the 1931 version by David Tamkin. The plots are more or less the same.

1971 Joel Mandelbaum. Joel Mandelbaum's microtonal four-act opera *The Dybbuk*, libretto by the composer based on the play by Ansky, was premiered in New York City on May 24, 1972. Mandelbaum was well known at the time for his theories on microtonal tunings. **1978 Frank Di Giacomo.** Frank Di Giacomo's opera *The Dybbuk,* libretto by the composer based on Jewish legend and the play by Ansky, was performed by Opera Theater of Syracuse, New York, on May 19, 1978. **1997 Shulamit Ran.** Israeli-born Chicago composer Shulamit Ran's opera *Between Two Worlds (The Dybbuk)*, libretto by Charles Kondek based on the play by Ansky, was premiered by Lyric Opera Center for American Artists in Chicago on June 20, 1997, after being commissioned by Center director Richard Pearlman. Mary Jane Kania was Leya, Matthew Polenzani was Khonnon, Jessie Raven was Leya's nurse, Robin Blitch Wiper was Gittel and Mark McCrory was Reb Azriel. Danila Korogodsky designed sets and costumes, Jonathan Eaton directed and Arthur Fagen conducted. Ran won considerable acclaim for the opera which incorporates klezmer folk music and Hassidic laments in its score.

E

EAMES, EMMA   *American soprano (1865–1952)*

John Knowles Paine wrote his 1898 opera *Azara* for the Metropolitan Opera diva Emma Eames. Paine was one of the most respected composers in America at the time and Eames was one of the Met's biggest stars but that was not enough to convince the Met; it refused to stage any American operas until 1910. Eames, who was born in Shanghai, made her debut in Paris in 1889 and began to sing at the Met in 1891. She remained one of its leading singers until 1909.

EARTH AND THE GREAT WEATHER *1995 "natural opera" by Adams*

John Luther Adams' "natural opera" *Earth and the Great Weather*, staged by Alaska's Anchorage Opera at the Discovery Theater on May l2, 1995, has no plot and no singing. The libretto consists of the names of places, animals and seasons recited on stage by four guides in Inupiaq Eskimo, Gwich'in Athabaskan English and Latin. The premiere featured Arctic Natives James Nageak, Doreen Simmonds, Adeline Peter Raboff and Lincoln Tritt as the guides and incorporated dances and rituals under the direction of Wendy Rogers. Vicki Smith designed the set. The ninety-minute opera is composed for eight players, strings and percussion, and the music is counterpointed by recorded natural Arctic sounds, mixed by Oriolo Galofre for the premiere.

1995 Anchorage Opera. The cast and musicians that presented the work on stage in Anchorage recorded a version of it earlier the same year. Arctic Natives James Nageak, Doreen Simmonds, Adeline Peter Raboff and Lincoln Tritt took the roles of the guides with the recorded natural Arctic sounds mixed by Oriolo Galofre. New World CD.

EASTON, FLORENCE *English-born American soprano (1882–1955)*

Florence Easton created the role of the Temple Dancer in John Adam Hugo's THE TEMPLE DANCER at the Metropolitan Opera in 1919 and Aelfrida in Deems Taylor's THE KING'S HENCHMAN at the Met in 1927. She recorded "Kiss Me Again" from Victor Herbert's MLLE. MODISTE in 1928. Easton made her debut in her native England in 1903, toured the U.S. with H. W. Savage's grand Opera Company and then married American tenor Francis Maclennan. She made her Met debut in 1917 and sang there until 1936 and during this time she made many records.

EATON, JOHN *American composer (1935–)*

John Eaton's best known opera THE TEMPEST, libretto by Andrew Porter based on the Shakespeare play, was premiered by Santa Fe Opera in 1985 but most of his expressionistic operas have been staged in Indiana. He was appointed professor of music at the University of Indiana School of Music in Bloomington in 1970 and his opera HERACLES, libretto by Michael Fried based on plays by Sophocles and Seneca, was the opening event at Indiana University's new Music Center in 1972. MYSHKIN, libretto by Patrick Creagh based on Dostoevsky's novel *The Idiot,* was premiered and telecast by Indiana University Opera Theatre in 1973. THE LION AND ANDROCLES, libretto by D. Anderson, was premiered by Indiana University Opera Theatre at Public School 47 in Indianapolis in 1974 and then telecast. DANTON AND ROBES-PIERRE, libretto by Patrick Creagh about the opposing leaders of the French Revolution, was premiered at Indiana University Opera Theater in 1978. THE CRY OF CLYTAEM-NESTRA, libretto by Creagh based on Aeschylus's play *Agamemnon,* was premiered at Indiana University Opera Theater in 1980. The composer created the Eaton Opera Company of

Chicago in 1993 as a collaboration with the New York New Music Ensemble. It has premiered his operas *Peer Gynt, Let's Get This Show on the Road* and DON QUIXOTE, a work in which the orchestra's musicians do the singing. Two operas have apparently not been performed: *Ma Barker* (1957), libretto by Arthur Gold about the female gangster, and *The Reverend Jim Jones* (1989), libretto by James Reston Jr. about the cult in Guyana. Eaton, who was born in Bryn Mawr, PA, began composing while studying at Princeton.

EBERHART, NELLE *American librettist/lyricist (1871–1944)*

Nelle Richmond Eberhart wrote the librettos for Charles Wakefield Cadman's operas as well as the lyrics for his songs. Her opera SHANEWIS (a.k.a. *The Robin Woman*), based on the life of Native American opera singer Tsianina Redfeather Blackstone, premiered at the Metropolitan Opera on March 23, 1918. Detroit-born Eberhart was one of the first writers to base libretto's around Native American themes. Her first opera with Cadman was the 1912 *Daoma (The Land of the Misty Water)*, based on an Omaha legend about friendship. Second was THE GARDEN OF MYSTERY, based on Nathaniel Hawthorne's story *Rappaccini's Daughter*, written in 1915 but not premiered until 1925 at Carnegie Hall. A WITCH OF SALEM, a story about the witch trials in Puritan Salem, WAS premiered in Chicago in 1926. THE WILLOW TREE, a story about jealousy and slighted love broadcast on NBC in 1932, was the first opera specifically commissioned for radio. Eberhart and Cadman are best known today for their Indian-themed songs including "From the Land of Sky-Blue Waters (now famous for its use as a beer commercial) and "At Dawning."

EBERLEY, HELEN-KAY *American soprano (1958–)*

Soprano Helen-Kay Eberley was ahead of her time in devoting an entire recital album to arias from American operas. Her 1983

Soprano Helen-Kay Eberley on the cover of her pioneering LP album of American opera arias.

LP *American Girl* is an enjoyable compendium of notable arias from Samuel Barber's VANESSA, Aaron Copland's THE TENDER LAND, Carlisle Floyd's SUSANNAH, Lee Hoiby's SUMMER AND SMOKE, Gian Carlo Menotti's THE MEDIUM and THE OLD MAID AND THE THIEF and Douglas Moore's THE BALLAD OF BABY DOE. She is accompanied on them by pianist Donald Isaak.

THE ECHO   *1925 opera by Patterson*

Lawrence Tibbett created the role of Cunnan in the premiere of Frank Patterson's chamber opera *The Echo* in 1925, the first of seven American operas the Met tenor premiered. The plot is minimal. Acantha and Theudas are shipwrecked and take refuge in a cave. Cave dwellers Cunnan and Yfel evoke spirits to try to control them but they escape. Patterson's opera, composed to his own libretto, premiered at the Auditorium in Portland, Oregon, on June 9, 1925, before the Conference of the National Federation of Music Clubs. Marjorie Dodge was Yfel, Forrest Lamont was Theudas and Marie Rappold was Acantha. Walter Henry Rothwell conducted the Portland Symphony Orchestra and Chorus. The opera was awarded the David Bispham Medal the same year.

EDDY, NELSON   *American baritone (1901–1967)*

Nelson Eddy starred in seven films based on American operettas and four "movie operas" created for American films. In the 1937 film *Maytime* he sings in Herbert Stothart's movie opera CZARITZA based on Tchaikovsky themes. In the 1939 film *Balalaika* he sings in Stothart's opera BALALAIKA based on Rimsky-Korsakov themes. In the 1943 film *The Phantom of the Opera* he performs in Edward Ward's operas AMOUR ET GLOIRE, based on Chopin themes, and LE PRINCE MASQUE DE LA CAUCASIE, based on Tchaikovsky themes.

Eddy first teamed with Jeanette MacDonald in 1935 in a movie based on Victor Herbert's NAUGHTY MARIETTA and they were co-stars in film versions of the American operettas ROSE-MARIE (1935), MAYTIME (1937), SWEETHEARTS (1938) and NEW MOON (1940). and the operetta film THE GIRL OF THE GOLDEN WEST (1938). Eddy also sang in a movie version of KNICKERBOCKER HOLIDAY (1944) and a TV version of THE DESERT SONG (1955). His recordings of highlights from operettas and musicals include THE STUDENT PRINCE with Risë Stevens in 1947, THE DESERT SONG with Doretta Morrow in 1952 and *The Desert Song* again with Virginia Haskins in 1952.

Eddy, born in Providence, Rhode Island, began his stage career with the Savoy Opera Company and made his debut with Philadelphia Civic Opera in 1924. He appeared in films until 1947 when he switched to television and touring. He can be heard on many LP and CD albums including *Nelson Eddy's Greatest Hits* (Columbia/1965), *Jeanette MacDonald/Nelson Eddy* (RCA Victor/1966), *MacDonald/Eddy Favorites* (RCA Victor/1975), *MacDonald/Eddy Soundtracks* (Sandy Hook/1976) and *America's Singing Sweethearts* (RCA Victor/1978). There is a 1992 documentary about the pair titled *America's Singing Sweethearts.*

EDISON, THOMAS ALVA   *American inventor (1847–1931)*

Thomas Alva Edison, inventor of the phonograph and godfather of the cinema, featured arias from American comic operas on many of his early records. They include numbers from THE FORTUNE TELLER in 1899, THE RED MILL and OLD DUTCH in 1909, NAUGHTY MARIETTA in 1911 and ORANGE BLOSSOMS in 1924; Victor Herbert was a regular performer. Edison was a prophetic visionary who imagined the DVD long before it's time. In 1893 he described what he called "Kinetoscope operas with phono" and told *The New York Times* there would one day be "such a happy combination of photography and electricity that a man can sit in his own parlor, see depicted upon a curtain the forms of the players in opera upon a distant stage and hear the voices of the singers."

EDUCATION OF THE GIRLCHILD   *1973 experimental opera by Monk*

Meredith Monk's avant-garde "opera" *Education of the Girlchild* is scored for six women's voices, electric organ and piano. The women sing a kind of textless vocalese that can stretch over four octaves. The aria "The Tale" from the opera is one of the few Monk vocal works with actual if rather weird lyrics

1981 Meredith Monk. *The Tale* from *Education of the Girlchild* is performed by Monk, Steve Lockwood and Collin Walcott on the album *Dolmen Music* ECM CD. **1983 Peter Greenaway.** Excerpts from *Education of the Girlchild* are featured in the documentary *Meredith Monk,* a film made in London by Peter Greenaway It also has excerpts from the operas *Quarry* and *Dolmen Music.* Mystic Fire VHS. **1997 Anthony de Mare.** An excerpt from *Education of the Girlchild* titled *The Tale* is performed by Anthony de Mare on the album *Cage/Monk—Pianos and Voices.* Koch CD.

EDWARDS, JOHN OWEN   *English conductor (1950–)*

John Owen Edwards has conducted notable recordings of a number of American operettas and musicals in London, often based on stage productions and sometimes the most complete on disc. For details see ANNIE GET YOUR GUN (1995), THE KING AND I (1994/2000), KISMET (1989), A LITTLE NIGHT MUSIC (1989), THE MOST HAPPY FELLA (1999), MY FAIR LADY (1994), OKLAHOMA! (1980/1998), ON THE TOWN (1995), SHOW BOAT (1993), SONG OF NORWAY (1990), THE STUDENT PRINCE (1989), SOUTH PACIFIC (1996), WEST SIDE STORY (1993), WEST SIDE STORY. Edwards, who was born in Cumbria, has also conducted many traditional operas.

EDWARDS, JULIAN   *American composer (1855–1910)*

Julian Edwards composed over thirty light operas, including one starring Wagnerian contralto Ernestine Schumann-Heink. *Love's Lottery,* which opened at the Broadway Theater in 1904, was Schumann-Heink's only attempt to sing comic opera. She played a German laundry woman who wins a lottery. Edwards also composed dramatic operas and cantatas. The cantata *Lazarus,* libretto by G. Newman based on the Bible story, was presented at the Metropolitan Opera House in 1910 as a Sunday concert. The one-act opera *King René's Daughter,* libretto by the composer, was staged in New York in 1892. The one-act *The Patriot,* libretto by Stanislaus Strange about an attempt to assassinate George Washington, was staged in Boston and New York in 1907 and 1908. Most of Edward's comic operas were created in collaboration with librettist Strange. *Brian Boru,* presented at the Broadway Theater in 1896 was compared to Michael Balfe's *The Bohemian Girl. Dolly Varden,* based on David Garrick's *The Country Girl,* was staged the Herald Square Theater in 1902 and taken to London. *When Johnny Comes Marching Home,* a musical about the American Civil War, opened on Broadway in December 1902. Edwards, born in Manchester, England, started his music career as an opera conductor and emigrated to America in 1888. His other popular comic operas, all with Strange and all staged in New York, include *Friend Fritz* (1893), *Madeleine* (1895), *The Goddess of Truth* (1896) and *The Belle of London Town* (1907).

EFFINGER, CECIL   *American composer (1914–)*

Colorado composer Cecil Effinger, who invented a once popular "musicwriter" typewriter, also created operas and music theater. The three-act opera CYRANO DE BERGERAC, libretto by Donald Sutherland based on the play by Edmund Rostand, was premiered by the University of Colorado in Boulder in 1965. *The Gentleman Desperado and Miss Bird*, libretto by Sutherland, created to celebrate the centennial of the University of Colorado, was presented October 6, 1976. The children's opera *Pandora's Box*, libretto by Sally Monsour, was staged in Boulder in 1961. Effinger, born in Colorado Springs, studied in Colorado colleges and with Nadia Boulanger in France. He is best known for his choral works.

THE EGG   *1976 church opera by Menotti*

In the Byzantine Empire in the fifth century a young boy seeks the meaning of life. His uncle, Saint Simeon the Stylite, says it is contained in the riddle of the egg. Gian Carlo Menotti's 60-minute church opera, libretto by the composer, premiered at the National Cathedral in Washington, D. C. on June 17, 1976. Matthew Murray was the boy Manuel, Anastasios Vrenios was Saint Simeon, Esther Hinds was the Empress of Byzantium, Sigmund Cowan was her courtier Aerobindus, Gimi Beni was the cook Gormantus, boy alto Peter Fish was the cook's assistant Priscus, Gene Tucker was the Eunuch of the Sacred Cubicle, Richard S. Dirksen was the treasurer Pachomius, Dana Krueger was the Empress's sister, Regina McConnell was the beggar woman and Frank Phelan was the guard captain Julian. Paul Calloway conducted. The opera was reprised at the Spoleto Festival USA in 1978, at BAM in 1980 and in Chicago in 1981.

EICHBERG, JULIUS   *American composer (1824–1893)*

Julius Eichberg's opéra bouffe THE DOCTOR OF ALCANTARA, libretto by Benjamin E. Woolf, was the most successful early American comic opera and marked the beginning of an American stage musical style. Following its premiere at the Boston Museum on April 7, 1862, it was presented in other America cities and in Britain and Australia. It was the first American opera staged by an African American opera company; the Original Colored American Opera Troupe of Washington, D. C., presented it in Washington and Philadelphia in 1873. Eichberg's other comic operas, all first performed in Boston with librettos by Woolf and all quite popular, were *A Night in Rome* (1864), *The Rose of Tyrol* (1865) and *The Two Cadis* (1868). Eichberg moved to America from Europe in 1856 and was well known in his time for his violin compositions. Librettist Woolf, a successful poet, wrote librettos for over thirty Boston stage shows.

EILEEN   *1917 operetta by Herbert*

The west coast of Ireland in 1798 during the rebellion against England. The title character is the niece of an English landowner who falls in love with Barry O'Day, a rebel leader. Smugglers, informers and the English army get involved but all ends happily. Irish-born Victor Herbert's operetta *Eileen*, romantic libretto by Henry Blossom, premiered at the Colonial Theater in Cleveland on January 1, 1917, as *Hearts of Erin*. Vernon Stiles played rebel Captain Barry O'Day, Grace Breen was Eileen Mulvaney, Greek Evans was smuggler chieftain Shaun Dhu and Scott Welsh was

lovesick Dinny Doyle. It opened at the Shubert Theater in New York on March 19, 1917, with a new title (*Eileen*) and new leading man (Walter Scanlan) The hit song was "Thine Alone" though "Eileen" and "The Irish Have a Great Day Tonight" also became popular. This is the most Irish of Herbert's operettas and was his favorite.

1917 Original cast. Original cast members recorded four songs from the operetta for 78s. Greek Evans sings "Free Trade and a Misty Moon" and Scott Welsh performs "The Irish Have a Great Day Tonight" on a Columbia 78. Vernon Stiles sings "Ireland, My Sireland" and "The Irish Have a Great Day Tonight" on a Victor 78. They're on the album *Music from the New York Stage 1890–1920*. Pearl CD box set. **1917 Victor Light Opera.** Victor Herbert leads the Victor Light Opera Company in a medley of tunes from his operetta for a Victor 78. They're on the album *The Operetta World of Victor Herbert*. JJA LP. **1917 John McCormack.** Irish tenor John McCormack recorded two songs from *Eileen* for Victor Red Seal, "Ireland My Sireland" and "Eileen Alanna Asthore." They're on several albums, including *The Songs of Victor Herbert*. ASV Living Era CD. **1931 Victor Light Opera.** Nat Shilkret leads the Victor Light Opera Company singers and orchestra in "Vocal Gems" from the operetta for a Victor 78 record. The songs are "Jig," "Erin's Isle," "Eileen" and "The Irish Have a Great Day Tonight." On the album *A Victor Herbert Showcase*. Flapper Past CD. **1938 Charles Kullman.** Met tenor Charles Kullman sings "Thine Alone" with orchestra conducted by Walter Goehr for a 78. It's on several albums, including *Charles Kullman, 20 Unforgettable Classics*. Javelin CD. **1946 Earl Wrightson/Frances Greer.** Earl Wrightson, Frances Greer and Jimmy Carroll perform a highlights version of the operetta with orchestra led by Al Goodman. RCA Victor LP. **1948 Kathryn Grayson.** Kathryn Grayson sings "Thine Alone" on a 1948 radio broadcast with Miklos Rosza conducting the MGM Orchestra. It was issued as a 78 record. **1950**

Victor Herbert's operetta *Eileen* was produced and recorded by Ohio Light Opera in 1997.

Jan Peerce. Jan Peerce sings "Thine Alone" with Howard Barlow conducting the Firestone Orchestra on *The Voice of Firestone* TV show on January 9, 1950. It's on *Jan Peerce in Opera and Song.* VAI VHS. **1954 Igor Gorin.** Met baritone Igor Gorin sings "Thine Alone" for a radio broadcast in 1954. It's included on the album *Igor Gorin.* MC audiocassette. **1955 Robert Merrill.** Robert Merrill sings "Thine Alone" on *The Voice of Firestone* TV show on January 10, 1955, with Howard Barlow conducting the Firestone Orchestra. Its on *Robert Merrill in Opera and Song, Vol. 2.* VAI VHS. **1956 Mario Lanza.** Mario Lanza sings "Thine Alone" with Henri René's Orchestra and The Jeff Alexander Choir. It's on the albums *Cavalcade of Show Tunes* (RCA Victor LP) and *Mario Lanza Collection* (RCA Victor CD). **1961 Robert Shaw Chorale.** The Robert Shaw Chorale and Orchestra perform "Thine Alone" on the album *The Immortal Victor Herbert.* RCA Victor LP. **1975 Beverly Sills.** Beverly Sills sings "Thine Alone" supported by André Kostelanetz and the London Symphony Orchestra on the album *Music of Victor Herbert.* Angel LP. **1978 Beverly Sills/Sherrill Milnes.** Beverly Sills and Sherrill Milnes join in duet on "'Thine Alone" on the album *Up in Central Park.* Julius Rudel conducts the New York City Opera. EMI Angel LP. **1991 Lorin Maazel/Pittsburgh Symphony.** The Pittsburgh Symphony Orchestra led by Lorin Maazel play "The Irish Have a Great Night Tonight" on the album *Popular American Music.* Sony CD. **1997 Ohio Light Opera.** The first complete recording of *Eileen,* based on an Ohio Light Opera stage production by James Stuart at Wooster College in Ohio, was recorded live with complete dialogue. Suzanne Woods stars as Eileen, John Pickle is the rebel Capt. Barry, Catherine Robison is Lady Maude, Alan Payne is Shaun Dhu, Christopher Norton is Dinny Doyle, Cassandra Norville is Rosie Flynn, Boyd Mackus is Sir Reggie, Caroline Taylor is Biddy Flynn, Damian Savarino is Colonel Lester, Patrick Yaeger is Lanty Hackett, Zanna Fredland is Marie, Kiel Klaphake is Humpy Grogan, Robert Daniel Goulet is Mickey O'Brien, Ted Christopher is the Sergeant, Jonathan Dahlke is the Corporal, Thomas Oesterling is Myles and Buck Hujabre is the Messenger. Michael Butterman conducts the Ohio Light Opera Orchestra and Chorus. 106 minutes. Newport Classics 2-CD box. **1999 Virginia Croskery.** Virginia Croskery sings "Thine Alone" with the Slovak Radio Symphony Orchestra led by Keith Brion on the album *Victor Herbert: Beloved Songs and Classic Miniatures.* Naxos CD. **2000 Steven White.** Steven White sings "Thine Alone" with the Rudolph Palmer Singers on the album *Sweethearts.* Robert Tweten plays piano Newport Classics CD.

EINHORN, RICHARD   *American composer (1952–)*

Richard Einhorn's VOICES OF LIGHT (1994) is an opera/oratorio inspired by Carl Dreyer's film *The Passion of Joan of Arc* and intended for performance while the film is screened. Einhorn, who studied music with Jack Beeson at Columbia University, produced classical albums for CBS before turning to composing in 1982. In addition to chamber music, ballets and song cycles, he has scored several films. including Arthur Penn's *Dead of Winter* (1987).

EINSTEIN ON THE BEACH   *1976 opera by Glass and Wilson*

Einstein's life as scientist, musician, humanist and atomic bomb theorist are examined musically. Einstein appears as a violinist positioned between stage and orchestra pit. He walks across the stage as another Einstein chalks equations on an imaginary blackboard. There are no incidents or dialogue but there are trains, trials and spaceships in four acts and seven scenes broken up by five "knee plays." *Einstein on the Beach,* the influential experimental opera created by composer Philip Glass and playwright Robert Wilson, is one of the most famous operas of our time though few people have seen it on stage and there is no commercial video. It doesn't even have a libretto in the normal sense as it grew out of drawings by Wilson with Glass writing lyrics while spoken texts were devised by Lucinda Childs, Samuel L. Johnson and an autistic boy, Christopher Knowles. The title was created by attaching Einstein's name to Nevil Chute's nuclear disaster novel *On the Beach.*

The opera premiered with great success at the Avignon Theatre Festival in France on July 25, 1976, and was staged at opera houses around Europe, including the Metropolitan. The music, scored for four soloists and a twelve-person chorus with chamber orchestra, is repetitive but tonal and addictive. The Met cast included soprano Iris Hiskey and tenor Marc Jacobi with actor/speakers Lucinda Childs, Samuel M. Johnson, Paul Mann and Sheryl Sutton plus George Andoniadis, Connie Beckley, Bruce Burroughs, Ritty Ann Burchfield, Frank Conversano, Andrew deGroat, Charles Dennis Grethe Holby, Jeannie Hutchins, Richard Morrison, Dana Reitz, Marie Rice, Ronald Roxbury, Forrest Warren, Robert Wilson and David P. Woodberry. Robert Brown was violinist Einstein. The opera was revived in 1984 by the Brooklyn Academy of Music and in 1989 by Stuttgart State Opera. See also the aria BED.

1976 Avignon Theatre Festival. The premiere of the opera was videotaped at the Avignon Theatre Festival though this video has never been released commercially. The video, like the opera, runs four hours and forty minutes without intervals with four acts connected by knee plays. **1977 Philip Glass Ensemble.** Iris Hiskey is the soprano soloist in this New York studio recording of all the

Composer Philip Glass and playwright Robert Wilson's influential experimental opera *Einstein on the Beach* was recorded in 1997.

music, lyrics and speeches featured in the original 1976 production. Michael Riesman conducts the Philip Glass Ensemble and small and large choruses. The soloists include tenors Marc Jacobi and Philip Gavin Smith and basses David Anchel and Sean Barker while the actor/speakers are Lucinda Childs, Samuel M. Johnson, Paul Mann and Sheryl Sutton. Paul Zukovksy is violinist Einstein. Tomato LP/Sony and CBS CD. **1981 Einstein on the Beach Suite.** Gregory Fulkerson performs a violin suite based on *Einstein on the Beach* on his album *Chamber Works*. New World CD. **1984 The Changing Image of Opera.** Mark Obenhaus's film *Einstein on the Beach: The Changing Image of Opera* is a behind-the-scenes documentary about the revival of the opera at the Brooklyn Academy of Music in 1984. Glass and Wilson are shown at work and there are scenes of the opera in rehearsal and performance. The one-hour color film was telecast on January 31, 1986. Direct Cinema film/VHS. **1985 A Composer's Notes — Philip Glass.** A section of the "Spaceship" episode from *Einstein on the Beach* is performed by the Philip Glass Ensemble in this documentary film by Michael Blackwood. Glass talks about how the opera was conceived but most of the documentary is devoted to *Akhnaten*. VAI VHS. **1989 Songs from the Trilogy.** This compilation album features four numbers from *Einstein on the Beach:* "Trial/Prison," "Bed," "Knee 1" and "Knee 5." Iris Hiskey is the soprano voice on "Bed." CBS CD. **1992 Jon Gibson.** The soprano aria "Bed," transcribed for organ and saxophone, is played as a saxophone solo by Jon Gibson on the album *Jon Gibson — In Good Company*. Point Music/Polygram CD. **1993 Philip Glass Ensemble.** Patricia Schuman is the soprano soloist in this second complete recording of the opera with Michael Riesman again leading the Philip Glass Ensemble. The other singers are sopranos Marion Beckenstein, Lisa Bielawa, Michele A. Eaton and Kristin Norderval; mezzos Katie Geissinger, Margo Gezairlian Grib and Elsa Higby; tenors Jeffrey Johnson, John Koch and Eric W. Lamp; and baritones Jeff Kensmoe, Gregory Purnhagen and Peter Stewart. The speakers are Lucinda Childs, Gregory Dolbashian, Jasper McGruder and Sheryl Sutton. Electra/Nonesuch CD. **1994 Janice Pendarvis.** The soprano aria "Bed" is sung by Janice Pendarvis on the album *The Essential Philip Glass*. Sony Classics CD.

EKSTROM, PETER   *American composer (1952–)*

Cleveland-born composer Peter Ekstrom calls his stage works "musicals" but his popular versions of O. Henry are virtually chamber operas. THE GIFT OF THE MAGI was created in 1981 for the Actors Theatre of Louisville, and is performed every year there at Christmas. THE LAST LEAF was composed in 1994 for the Barter Theater as a companion piece. Both have been issued on commercial recordings. Ekstrom, who graduated from Antioch College in 1973. wrote many other musicals for the Actors Theater including *Doctors and Diseases* and *Wild Nights*.

EL/AFICIONADO   *1995 opera by Ashley*

Robert Ashley's electronic opera *eL/Aficionado* is a Graham Greene–like spy story describing incidents in the life of a person who believes he is an agent of the "department." Baritone Thomas Buckner stars as the agent with support form soprano Jacqueline Humbert, countertenor Sam Ashley and Robert Ashley as his interrogators. Thomas Hamilton handles the electronics. This is the fourth opera in Ashley's *Now Eleanors Idea* series.

1995 Original cast. Thomas Buckner is the agent in this original cast recording with Jacqueline Humbert, Sam Ashley and Robert Ashley as interrogators. Thomas Hamilton plays the electronic instrumentals. Lovely CD.

ELEPHANT STEPS   *1968 opera by Silverman*

Hartman dreams of gaining enlightenment through the help of his mysterious guru Reinhardt but his wife Hannah, Dr. Worms and his friends are against it. After a visit to a radio station and a return to childhood, he climbs a ladder at Reinhardt's house and is illuminated. Stanley Silverman's surrealist avant-garde opera *Elephant Steps*, libretto by Richard Foreman, was commissioned by the Fromm Foundation and premiered at the Berkshire Festival in Lenox, MA, on August 7, 1968. Linn Maxwell was the Ragtime Lady and Michael Tilson Thomas conducted.

1974 Michael Tilson Thomas. This recording is described on its cover as a "A multi-media pop-opera extravaganza, a fearful radio show with pop singers, opera singers, rock band, electronic tape, raga group tape recorder, gypsy ensemble and elephants all under the direction of Michael Tilson Thomas." Philip Steele is Hartman, Susan Belling is wife Hannah, Roland Gagnon is the Doctor, Luther Enstad is Max, Larry Marshall is Otto, Karen Altman is the Scrubwoman, Marilyn Soko is the Ragtime Lady, Luther Rix is the Rock Singer and Michael Tilson Thomas is Archangel. Patti Austin, Jane Gunther, Dianne Higginbotham, Jane Magruder, Patricia Price, Albertine Robinson, Maeretha Stewart and Rose Taylor form the chorus. Michael Tilson Thomas conducts. Columbia LP.

ELIAS, ROSALIND   *American mezzo-soprano (1929–)*

Lyric mezzo-soprano Rosalind Elias created five roles in American operas. She sang young Erika in the Metropolitan Opera premiere of Samuel Barber's VANESSA IN 1958 and on the recording, the Nun in Gian Carlo Menotti's operatic cantata THE DEATH OF THE BISHOP OF BRINDISI in Cincinnati in 1963, Charmian in the Met premiere of Barber's ANTONY AND CLEOPATRA in 1966, Bathsheba in Ezra Laderman's AND DAVID WEPT on television in 1971 and Arthur's Mother in Mark Houston's HAZEL KIRKE at the Lake George Festival in 1987. She is Desideria in the 1956 BBC television production of Menotti's THE SAINT OF BLEECKER STREET, the Narrator in the 1961 ABC television production of Abraham Ellstein's THE THIEF AND THE HANGMAN, Medea in the 1974 CBS TV production of Benjamin Lees' MEDEA IN CORINTH and Baba the Turk in the 1977 televised Glyndebourne production of Igor Stravinsky's THE RAKE'S PROGRESS.

She joined Anna Moffo and other opera singers in 1962 for a series of Reader's Digest operetta recordings singing Adah in Victor Herbert's NAUGHTY MARIETTA, Wanda in Rudolf Friml's ROSE MARIE, Huguette in Friml's THE VAGABOND KING and Queenie in Jerome Kern's SHOW BOAT. She also sings on Plácido Domingo's 1996 operatic recording of Mitch Leigh's MAN OF LA MANCHA. On stage she sang Grandmother in the 1998 Tulsa Opera revival of David Carlson's DREAMKEEPERS. In 2001 she returned to the opera *Vanessa* taking the role of the old Baroness in a production by Opéra de Monte Carlo. Elias, born in Lowell, Massachusetts, began her career in 1948 the New England Opera, built her reputation at La Scala and San Carlo and sang at the Met from 1954 in over 400 performances.

ELIOT, T. S.   *Anglo American poet/playwright (1888–1965)*

Two American operas are based on the writings of St. Louis-born poet and playwright T. S. Eliot but both are based on the same poetic play, the music hall drama *Sweeney Agonistes: Fragment of an Aristophanic Melodrama* (1932). Arnold Elston's *Sweeney Agonistes*, a chamber opera, was first performed with piano accompaniment at Berkeley on May 1, 1957, with Joseph Kerman directing. It was presented with orchestra in Oakland on January 16, 1967.

Richard Winslow's opera *Sweeney Agonistes* was premiered at Brander Matthews Hall at Columbia University in New York on May 20, 1953. Eliot's 1935 play *Murder in the Cathedral* was the turned into an opera by Italian composer Ildebrando Pizzetti in 1958.

ELKUS, JONATHAN   *American composer (1931–)*

Jonathan Elkus has composed six one-act operas/musicals based on literary works and all have been performed. *The Outcasts of Poker Flat*, libretto by Robert G. Bander based on the Bret Harte story, was premiered at Lehigh University in Bethlehem, PA, April 16, 1960. *Medea*, libretto by the composer based on the Euripides play, and *Helen of Egypt,* libretto by J. Knight based on a play by the poet H.D., were staged together by University of Wisconsin Opera Theater in Milwaukee on November 13, 1970. Elkus's best known stage works are two musicals for children, *Tom Sawyer*, libretto by the composer based on the Mark Twain novel, premiered at Everett J. High School in San Francisco on May 22, 1953, and *Treasure Island,* libretto by B. M. Snyder based on the Robert Louis Stevenson novel, was premiered in San Francisco in 1967. Elkus, who was born in San Francisco, studied at Berkeley, Stanford and Mills and taught at Lehigh University for many years.

ELLINGTON, DUKE   *American composer/conductor/pianist (1899–1974)*

Edward ("Duke") Ellington's compositions are featured in classical as well as jazz catalogs and include operas as well as tone poems, piano works and a ballet. BEGGARS HOLIDAY (1946), is an updated version of *The Beggar's Opera* with librettist John Latouche's keeping the cynical edge of the original. The "street opera buffa" QUEENIE PIE was not completed at the time of Ellington's death but was finished by associates and premiered by his son Mercer in 1986. Ellington's music was featured in revues as early as 1929 including *Hot Chocolates* (1929), *Blackberries of 1930* (1930), *Sweet and Low* (1930) and *Cotton Club Parade* (1937). He wrote all the music for the influential Los Angeles revue *Jump for Joy* (1941), which introduced the term "zoot suit." *Sugar City,* presented in Detroit in 1965, was followed by *Pousse-Café* in 1966. This was an adaptation of the Marlene Dietrich film *The Blue Angel* relocated to New Orleans by librettist Jerome Weidman with lyrics by Marshall Barer and Fred Tobias. It was staged with Lilo, Theodore Bikel, Charles Durning and Ellis Larkins. Ironically Ellington's most successful musical was created after his death by Donald McKayle who pieced together thirty-six Ellington songs to make the 1981 theatrical hit *Sophisticated Ladies.*

ELLIS, BRENT   *American baritone (1946–)*

Brent Ellis created the role of Maerbale in Alberto Ginastera's BOMARZO at Washington Opera in 1967, Morris Townsend in Thomas Pasatieri's WASHINGTON SQUARE at Michigan Opera in 1976 and the Confidence Man in George Rochberg's *The Confidence Man* at Santa Fe Opera in 1982. He played Cortez in the American premiere of Roger Sessions' MONTEZUMA at Boston Opera in 1976 and has sung George Milton in Carlisle Floyd's OF MICE AND MEN and Konstantin in Pasatieri's THE SEAGULL. Ellis, who was born in Kansas City, Missouri, studied in New York and Rome before making his debut in 1967 in *Bomarzo.*

ELLIS, MARY   *American soprano (1900–2003)*

Mary Ellis created the title role in Rudolf Friml's ROSE MARIE on Broadway in 1924 and starred in Jerome Kern's MUSIC IN THE AIR in London's West End in 1933. She is the featured singer in two "movie operas" composed for the 1936 Paramount film *Fatal Lady,* ISABELLE with music by Gerard Carbonara and BAL MASQUE with music by Carbonara and Victor Young. In the film she plays an opera diva who runs away after accusations of murder. *The New York Times* called it "a prima donna's vehicle affording Miss Ellis opportunities of singing choice bravura passages." Ellis, who was born in New York City, was only 18 when she made her debut at the Metropolitan Opera in 1918 as the Novice in the world premiere of Puccini's *Suor Angelica.* After singing opposite Caruso and Chaliapin, she switched from opera to operetta and moved to London where her stage shows included Ivor Novello's *Glamorous Night* and *The Dancing Years.* She continued to perform until 1994.

ELLSTEIN, ABRAHAM   *American composer/conductor (1907–1963)*

New Yorker Abraham Ellstein composed two operas, both of which were staged. THE THIEF AND THE HANGMAN, libretto by Morton Wishengrad about a thief more honest than his judge, premiered in Athens, Ohio, in 1959 and was telecast in 1961; it reprised on stage in Salzberg in November 1965. THE GOLEM, libretto by Sylvia Regan based on the Jewish legend about a Rabbi's Frankenstein-like creation, previewed in Boston in 1961 and was premiered by New York City Opera in 1962 with Chester Ludgin as the Golem. Ellstein was also a conductor and led the orchestra on a number of recordings made by Jan Peerce.

ELMSLIE, KENWARD   *American librettist (1929–)*

Kenward Elmslie is one of the most successful American opera librettists with seven notable operas created in collaboration with composers Jack Beeson, Thomas Pasatieri and Ned Rorem. His first opera libretto was for Beeson, the 1954 one-act HELLO OUT THERE based on a William Saroyan story. Next was the 1957 THE SWEET BYE AND BYE about a female tent show evangelist. In 1965 he wrote LIZZIE BORDEN for Beeson, based on the famous axe-murder trial, and MISS JULIE for Ned Rorem, based on the Strindberg play. His collaboration with Thomas Pasatieri began in 1974 with THE SEAGULL based on the Chekhov play, and continued with WASHINGTON SQUARE in 1976 based on the Henry James novel. His final libretto for Pasatieri was THE THREE SISTERS in 1986, again based on a Chekhov play. Elmslie also wrote two musicals in collaboration with composer Claibe Richardson: *The Grass Harp,* based on Truman Capote's novel, opened in 1971 and *Lola,* dealing with the life of Lola Montez, premiered in 1982; both are on record. There is also a concept album of the musical *Postcards on Parade*, music by Steven Taylor, and a Painted Smiles' album titled *Kenward Elmslie Visited*, which is focused on his lyrics. Elmslie is well known outside the opera world as poet, playwright and performance artist.

ELSTON, ARNOLD   *American composer (1907–1971)*

Arnold Elston composed two one-act operas based on plays by 20th century writers and both premiered at the University of California at Berkeley where Elston taught. *Sweeney Agonistes.* based on the poetic music hall play by T. S. ELIOT, was performed with piano accompaniment at Berkeley on May 1, 1957, with Joseph Kerman directing; it was reprised with orchestra in Oakland on January 16, 1967. *The Love of Don Perlimplin,* based on a play by Federico Garcia Lorca, was premiered at Berkeley on May 16, 1958. Elston, who was born in New York and studied privately, also taught at the University of Oregon.

EMMELINE   *1996 opera by Picker*

New England in the 19th century. Mill worker Emmeline falls in love with and marries a much younger man but is horrified when she finds out who he really is. She had been seduced and made pregnant at the age of thirteen and forced to give up the baby for adoption. Her husband is her own son. Tobias Picker's opera *Emmeline,* libretto by J. D. McClatchy based on a novel by Judith Rossner, was premiered by Santa Fe Opera on July 27, 1996. Patricia Racette created the role of Emmeline, Curt Peterson was her son-husband Matthew Gurney, Victor Ledbetter was her seducer Mr. Maguire, Anne-Marie Owens was Aunt Hannah, Josepha Gayer was Mrs. Bass, Herbert Perry was Pastor Avery, Kevin Langan was Henry Mosher, Melanie Sarakatsannis was Sophie, Wright Moore was Hooker, Michelle Bradley was Harriet Mosher, Gregory Keil was Simon Fenton and Mary Jane Kania was Ella Burling. Robert Israel designed the sets, Francesca Zambello staged the production and George Manahan conducted the Santa Fe Opera Orchestra. New York City Opera also staged the opera with Patrica Racette in the title role. The Santa Fe Opera production was telecast in the PBS *Great Performances* series.

1996 Santa Fe Opera. Patricia Racette stars as Emmeline in the Santa Fe Opera production recorded on July 27, 1996. Curt Peterson is her son-husband, Victor Ledbetter is Mr. Maguire, Anne-Marie Owen is Aunt Hannah, Kevin Langan is Henry Mosher, Melanie Sarakatsannis is Sophie, Joseph Gayer is Mrs. Bass, Herbert Perry is Pastor Avery, Kevin Langan is Henry Mosher, Melanie Sarakatsannis is Sophie, Wright Moore is Hooker, Michelle Bradley is Harriet Mosher, Gregory Keil is Simon Fenton and Mary Jane Kania is Ella Burling. George Manahan conducts the Santa Fe Opera Orchestra and Chorus. 113 minutes. Albany 2-CD box.

THE EMPEROR JONES   *1933 opera by Gruenberg*

African American Brutus Jones had made himself the tyrannical emperor of a West Indian island but he is now being hunted down by his unhappy subjects. After begging God's mercy, he shoots himself. Louis Gruenberg's opera *The Emperor Jones,* libretto by Kathleen de Jaffis, is based on a 1920 Eugene O'Neill play which was made into a film starring Paul Robeson. Robeson would have been ideal for the opera, but the Metropolitan Opera would not open its doors to African American singers until 1955. Instead the Met cast Lawrence Tibbett who played the role in its premiere on January 7, 1933. Marek Windheim was the emperor's Cockney follower Smithers, Pearl Besuner was the Old Native Woman and Hemsley Winfield was the Congo Witch Doctor. Jo Mielziner designed the sets, Armando Agnini directed and Tullio Serafin conducted the Metropolitan Opera Orchestra. "Standin' in the Need of Prayer" is the only real aria in the opera (the singers speak-sing the other vocals) and has become part of the operatic repertory, especially through Tibbett recordings. African American bass-baritone Jules Bledsoe, who created the role of Joe in *Show Boat,* often sang the title role in post-Met productions. *The Emperor Jones* has been successfully revived in recent years with productions by American Music Theater Festival (1984), Michigan Opera Theater (1979), Torino Opera (1976) and Operaworks (2001) with Fredrick Redd in the title role.

1934 Lawrence Tibbett broadcast. Lawrence Tibbett stars in a 30-minute version broadcast October 16, 1934, on *The Packard Hour* radio show. John B. Kennedy introduces scenes from the opera and Wilfred Pelletier conducts. The broadcast was issued on EJS LP in 1958 and the aria "Standin' in the Need of Prayer" is on the album *Souvenirs from American Opera.* IRRC CD. **1934 Lawrence Tibbett recording.** Lawrence Tibbett sings the aria "Standin' in the Need of Prayer" with the Metropolitan Opera Orchestra led by Wilfred Pelletier. This famous recording was made on January 19, 1934, and is on several albums including *Lawrence*

Tibbett: From Broadway to Hollywood. (Nimbus CD) and *Towards an American Opera 1911–1954* (New World LP). **1955 George London.** Met bass-baritone George London recorded "Standin' in the Need of Prayer" in 1955 with the Columbia Symphony Orchestra conducted by Jean Paul Morel. It's on his 1997 album *George London: Of Gods and Demons.* Sony Classics CD. **1999 William Powers.** Baritone William Powers sings "Standin' in the Need of Prayer" on his recital album *Rogues and Villains,* recorded in Czechoslovakia. Dennis Burkh conducts the Janáček Philharmonic Orchestra. Centaur CD.

EMPEROR NORTON   *1981 opera by Mollicone*

Playwright Marla is trying to write a play about Joshua Norton, a 19th century eccentric who had claimed to be Emperor of the United States. Actors Diana and Michael attempt to understand what he is doing as they audition for the unfinished play. Emperor Norton himself appears on stage protesting that they are not telling his story correctly. Henry Mollicone's one-act opera *Emperor Norton,* libretto by John S. Bowman based on episodes in the life of the real life Joshua Norton, was premiered by San Francisco Opera's Brown Bag Opera on May 14, 1981. Thomas Woodman was Norton, Evelyn de la Rosa was Diana, William Pell was Michael and Leslie Richards was Marla. The popular opera has been staged by several other companies.

EMPTY BOTTLE   *1991 opera by Kalmanoff*

Three women describe the final days and death of Silvio, an Italian immigrant who became a gangster in New York's Little Italy in the 1930s. Martin Kalmanoff's three-act opera *Empty Bottles,* libretto by the composer, was premiered by the small but innovative Amato Opera Company in New York on July 19, 1991. Garth Taylor played the gangster Silvio, Helen Van Tine was Silvio's Mother, Alicia Alexander was Maria, Sarah Hill was Antonia and David Kantey was Vincenzo. Richard Leighton staged the opera and Elizabeth La Torre conducted the small orchestra.

THE ENCHANTED KISS   *1945 radio opera by Bennett*

Shy young clerk Samuel Tansey falls asleep on a staircase and dreams of wild adventures culminating in kisses from Katie Peep, the secret love of his life. When he arrives home late, it seems his dream may become a reality. Robert Russell Bennett's radio opera *The Enchanted Kiss,* libretto by Robert A. Simon based on O. Henry's short story, was premiered in abridged form on the Mutual Broadcasting System on December 30, 1945.

THE ENCHANTRESS   *1911 comic opera by Herbert*

The Enchantress is a neglected comic opera by Victor Herbert with a coloratura aria which has become a recital staple for sopranos. The aria, "Art Is Calling for Me" ("I Want to be a Prima Donna"), was introduced on stage by Louise Bliss as a would-be coloratura opera singer who tells us she wants to be a "peachy, screechy cantatrice" like Luisa Tetrazzini. In the opera, set in the usual Ruritanian kingdom, the prima donna Vivien is hired by evil minister Ozir to seduce Prince Ivan so he will marry a commoner and have to abdicate. She falls in love with him, however, and saves his crown. Harry B. Smith wrote the lyrics and co-authored the libretto with Fred de Grésac who gave it an operatic tinge. (Fred was the nom de plume of Mrs. Victor Maurel, wife of the baritone who created Iago, Falstaff and Canio.) The operetta premiered at the National Theater in Washington, D.C., on October 9, 1911. and opened on Broadway at the New York Theater on October 19, 1911. Kitty Gordon played Vivien, Hal Forde was the

Prince and Arthur Forrest was the villain Ozir. Gordon's big aria was the popular "The Land of My Own Romance."

1912 Lucy Isabelle Marsh. Soprano Lucy Isabelle Marsh recorded Vivien's aria "The Land of My Own Romance" (I Have a Dream, by Night, by Day) for a Victor 78 in 1912. **1912 Victor Herbert Orchestra.** Victor Herbert leads his orchestra in a selection of tunes from his operetta for a Victor 78. It's on the album *And Then We Wrote.* New World LP. **1975 Beverly Sills.** Beverly Sills sings two arias from *The Enchantress* accompanied by André Kostelanetz and the London Symphony Orchestra: "Art Is Calling for Me" (I Want to Be a Prima Donna) and "The Land of My Own Romance." They're both on the album *Music of Victor Herbert.* Angel EMI LP/CD. **1992 Lesley Garrett.** Lesley Garrett sings "Art Is Calling for Me" (I Want to Be a Prima Donna) with the Philharmonia Orchestra led by Ivor Bolton on her album *Lesley Garrett–Prima Donna.* Silva America CD **1989/1994 Kiri Te Kanawa.** Kiri Te Kanawa sings "Art Is Calling for Me (I Want to Be a Prima Donna)" in two concerts. On *Kiri in Concert* filmed at the Barbican in London in 1989, Carl Davis leads the Royal Philharmonic Orchestra, EMI VHS/DVD. On *Kiri: Her Greatest Hits Live* filmed at the Royal Albert Hall in 1994, Stephen Barlow conducts the London Symphony. London VHS/DVD and London Classics CD. **1999 Virginia Croskery.** Virginia Croskery sings "Art Is Calling for Me (I Want to Be a Prima Donna)" with the Slovak Radio Symphony Orchestra led by Keith Brion on the album *Victor Herbert: Beloved Songs and Classic Miniatures.* American Classics Naxos CD.

THE END OF THE AFFAIR   *2004 opera by Heggie*

In World War II in London during the Blitz, Sarah has a torrid affair with Maurice, a writer friend of her husband, but gives him up suddenly and completely after a bombing. He can't understand why and makes a great effort to discover what happened after her husband asks for his help. A hired detective called Mr. Parkis steals her diary which explains her reasoning. Jake Heggie's opera *The End of the Affair,* libretto by Heather McDonald based on the novel by Graham Greene, was premiered by Houston Grand Opera on March 3, 2004, in the Cullen Theater. Cheryl Barker was Sarah, Teddy Tahu Rhodes was her lover Maurice Bendrix, Peter Coleman Wright was Sarah's husband Henry, Robert Orth was the detective Mr. Parkis, Katherine Ciesinski was Sarah's mother and Joseph Evan's was rationalist Richard Smythe. Michael McGarty designed the sets, Jess Goldstein designed the costumes, Leonard Foglia directed and Patrick Summers conducted the Houston Grand Opera Orchestra.

LES ENFANTS TERRIBLES   *1996 dance-opera by Glass*

The overly-close relationship between adolescents Lise and Paul, who are sister and brother, lead to game playing and tragedy. Philip Glass's *Les Enfants Terribles,* libretto by the composer and choreographer Susan Marshall based on a 1929 novel by Jean Cocteau and a 1952 film adaptation, tells their story through a combination of song, dance and dialogue. It was premiered by the Brooklyn Academy of Music on November 20, 1996, in a production by Marshall. Lise was sung by Christine Arand and danced by Kristen Hollingsworth, Krista Langberg and Eileen Thomas while Paul was sung by Philip Cutlip and danced by Hans Beenhakker, Mark DeChiazza and John Higginbotham. Valerie Komar sang the roles of Dargelos and Agathe, danced by Susan Blankensop, and Hal Cazalet was the Narrator. Douglas Stein designed the sets and Kasia Walicka Maimone created the costumes. This was the third opera by Glass based on a work by Jean Cocteau.

ENGEL, LEHMAN   *American composer/conductor (1910–1982)*

Lehman Engel has made many contributions to American opera as conductor and composer. He led the orchestra in premieres of Gian Carlo Menotti's THE CONSUL, Aaron Copland's THE SECOND HURRICANE and Kurt Weill's JOHNNY JOHNSON and conducted recordings of several operettas including NAUGHTY MARIETTA, ROSE-MARIE and THE DESERT SONG. Engel, who was born in Jackson, Mississippi, studied music in Cincinnati and his first opera was produced there. *Pierrot of the Minute,* libretto by the composer inspired by Ernest Dowson, premiered in Cincinnati on April 3, 1929. He followed it with *Medea* in 1935 but then composed no more operas until 1953 when he began to collaborate with librettist Lewis Allen. *Golden Ladder,* libretto by Allen, W. A. King and J. Ross, premiered in Cleveland May 28, 1953, with *Brother Joe.* MALADY OF LOVE, a comedy about a psychoanalyst and the patient who seduces him, was presented at Columbia University on May 27, 1954. THE SOLDIER, based on a Roald Dahl story about a crazed soldier who finds civilian life too difficult, premiered at Carnegie Hall on November 25, 1956.

ENGLANDER, ROGER   *American TV director/producer (1935–)*

TV opera pioneer Roger Englander produced two of the first American operas to be shown on television, Gian Carlo Menotti's THE MEDIUM and THE TELEPHONE in 1948 and THE OLD MAID AND THE THIEF in 1953, all three on NBC. He also produced programs for the BELL TELEPHONE HOUR, CAMERA THREE, OMNIBUS and the LEONARD BERNSTEIN series, including Aaron Copland's THE SECOND HURRICANE. His book *Opera, What's All the Screaming About?* includes photographs of these productions.

ERIC HERMANNSON'S SOUL   *1998 opera by Larsen*

Nebraska in the early 1900s. New York socialite Margaret and her brother Wyllis return to their home town to sell their late father's farm. Margaret falls in love with Norwegian farmer Eric Hermannson who has given up playing the violin and dancing and because a hell-fire preacher said they were sinful. Margaret plays him the "Intermezzo" from *Cavalleria Rusticana* and Mascagni's music restores his soul. Libby Larsen's two-act opera *Eric Hermannson's Soul,* libretto by Chas. Rader-Shieber, based on the story by Willa Cather, was commissioned by Opera Omaha which premiered it on November 11, 1998. Jennifer Casey Abbot was Margaret, Theodore Green was Eric, Steven Goldstein was the preacher Asa Skinner, Juline Barol-Gilmore was Lena Hanson, Gustav Andreassen was Jerry Lockhart, Michael Zegarski was Wyllis and Anne DeVriese, Teresa Buchhold, Scott Miller and Jeremy Ayer were the Greek chorus-like quartet. Judy Gailen designed the sets and Hal France staged the production and conducted the Omaha Symphony Orchestra.

ERICKSON, KAAREN   *American soprano (1953–1997)*

Seattle native Kaaren Erickson created the role of Ship's Doctor/Space Twin #1 in the premiere of Glass's THE VOYAGE at the Metropolitan Opera in 1992. She made her debut at New York City Opera in 1984 and her Met debut in 1985.

ERICKSON, ROBERT   *American composer (1917–)*

Robert Erickson, an influential figure in avant-garde music as author and teacher, composed the experimental opera *Cardenitas 68,* libretto by the composer, presented at UC San Diego on June 5. 1968. There is only one singing role and the microtonal music is played by a small ensemble with specially created percussion instruments. Erickson, born in Marquette, Michigan, studied in St. Paul with Ernst Krenek and then moved to California. Some of his vocal compositions are on the CRI album *Music of Robert Erickson.*

ERSKINE, JOHN *American librettist/novelist (1879–1951)*

John Erskine is best known as the author of the popular novel *The Private Life of Helen of Troy* (1925). After its success in hardback in the 1920s, it became one of the most popular paperbacks of the 1950s with a famous cover painting. Erskine adapted it as an opera for composer George Antheil and it was staged as HELEN RETIRES in 1934 at the Juilliard School of Music in New York. He also wrote the librettos for two other operas premiered at Juilliard, Louis Gruenberg's children's opera JACK AND THE BEANSTALK (November 19, 1931) and Beryl Rubenstein's *The Sleeping Princess* (January 19, 1938). Erskine was president of the school at the time. Erskine, born in New York City, wrote many other books, including the popular *Adam and Eve* (1927), but music was his chief interest in later life. All three of his librettos were published.

ESCORIAL *1958 opera by Levy*

The King, who appears to be going mad, orders court jester Folial to entertain him. The jester tells the story of a beggar and a king who switched places. Gradually we discover that the King has poisoned his Queen for having a love affair with the Jester. When it is announced that the Queen is dead, the King has the jester executed. Marvin Davy Levy's grim one-act opera *Escorial*, libretto by Lionel Abel based on a play by Michel de Ghelderode, was commissioned for the Music in our Time series and premiered at the 92nd Street YMCA in New York on May 4, 1958. Robert Rue played the King, Lorne Driscoll was the Jester and Roy Lazarus was the Monk. Margaret Hillis conducted.

ESHAM, FAITH *American soprano (1950–)*

Faith Esham created the role of Rosina in Anton Coppola's opera *Sacco and Vanzetti*, when it was premiered by Opera Tampa in 2001. Esham, born in Vanceburg, KY, studied in Kentucky and at Juilliard, began her career at Santa Fe Opera and joined New York City Opera in the fall of 1977. On stage she has sung the title roles in Douglas Moore's THE BALLAD OF BABY DOE and Carlisle Floyd's SUSANNAH.

ESPERANZA *2000 opera by Bishop*

Immigrant Mexican mine-workers in New Mexico stage a strike to obtain better working conditions. David Bishop's two-act opera *Esperanza*, libretto by Carlos Morton based on Michael Wilson's screenplay for the 1953 film *Salt of the Earth*, premiered at the University of Wisconsin Music Hall in Madison August 25, 2000. The leading roles were sung by Theresa Santiago as Esperanza and William Alvarado as her husband Ramon Quintero. Norma Saldivar directed, Joseph Varga designed the set and Karlos Moser conducted the chamber ensemble. *Salt of the Earth* was made by blacklisted filmmakers including writer Wilson, director Herbert Biberman and actor Will Geer and sponsored by the International Union of Mine, Mill and Smelter Workers. The opera was sponsored by the Wisconsin State AFL-CIO and Wisconsin Labor History Society.

ESSWOOD, PAUL *English countertenor (1942–)*

Paul Esswood, one of the best-known countertenors in the world, created the title role in Philip Glass's opera AKHNATEN in Stuttgart in 1997 and sings the role on the CD produced by Stuttgart State Opera in 1987. He made his stage debut in 1968 and has sung around the world in modern and baroque operas.

ESTES, SIMON *American bass-baritone (1939–)*

Simon Estes created the role of Uncle Albert in Gunther Schuller's *The Visitation* at Hamburg Staatsoper in 1966 and was the first person to sing Porgy at the Metropolitan Opera when George Gershwin's PORGY AND BESS was finally staged there in 1985. He can be heard in the role in a highlights recording made in Berlin in 1986. He was also one of the singers in the first modern performance of Scott Joplin's TREEMONISHA when it was premiered in concert form in Atlanta in 1972. Born in Ames, Iowa, he began his career with Deutsche Oper in Berlin and won praise for Wagnerian roles. He was the first African American man to sing at Bayreuth.

ESTHER *American operas based on Book of Esther*

Persian King Xerxes (called Ahaseurus in the Book of Esther in the Bible) adds Esther to his harem but is not aware that she is Jewish. When Esther's uncle Mordecai warns the King of a plot on his life, the King makes Mordecai one of his favorites. Jealous Prime Minister Haman gets Xerxes to agree to a plot against the captive Hebrews and the King agrees not knowing Mordecai is Jewish. Esther tells the King she and Mordecai are both Hebrews and pleads for mercy for her people. Xerxes arms the Hebrews and they defeat Haman and his ten sons. Mordecai becomes Prime Minister. Two American operas are based on the story.

1957 Jan Meyerowitz. Jan Meyerowitz's three-act opera *Esther*, libretto by Langston Hughes based on the Book of Esther and a play by Racine, premiered at the University of Illinois on March 17, 1957. It was revived in Massachusetts in 1958 and in New York in 1960. **1993 Hugo Weisgall.** Hugo Weisgall's three-act opera *Esther*, libretto by Charles Kondek based on the Book of Esther, was commissioned by San Francisco Opera but premiered by New York City Opera on October 3, 1993. Lauren Flanigan was Esther, Eugene Perry was Xerxes, Allan Glassman was Haman, Joyce Castle was his wife Zeresh, Robynne Redmon was Vashti, Joseph Corteggiano was Mordecai and Thomas Mark Fallson was the harem-keeper eunuch Hegai. Jerome Sirlin designed the sets, Christopher Mattaliano staged the opera and Joseph Colaneri conducted the NYCO Orchestra and Chorus. The opera was hailed as a masterpiece by critics when it premiered but it has not been recorded.

THE ETERNAL ROAD *1937 pageant opera by Weill*

Kurt Weill's pageant opera *The Eternal Road*, libretto by Ludwig Lewisohn based on the Franz Werfel play *Der Weg der Verheissung* with lyrics by Charles Alan, premiered at the Manhattan Opera House in New York City on January 4, 1937. Lotte Lenya played Miriam and the Witch of Endor, Thomas Chalmers was Abraham, Samuel Goldenberg was Moses, Noel Cravat was Aaron, Florence Meyer was Priestess of the Golden Calf, Sarah Osnath-Halevy was Rachel, Bertha Kunz-Baker was Sarah/Naomi, Ralph Jameson was Jacob/Boaz, Walter Gilbert was Saul, Katherine Carrington was Ruth. Earl Weatherford was Joseph/David, Myron Taylor was the Rabbi, Sam Jaffe was the Adversary, Harold Johnsrud was Estranged One, Sidney Lumet was Estranged One's Son, John Uppman was White Angel/Solomon, Edward Cane was First Dark Angel, Ben Cutler was Voice of God/Second Dark Angel and Joseph Macauley was Angel of Death. Meyer W. Weisgall and Crosby Gaige produced, Norman Bel Geddes designed the sets and costumes, Max Reinhardt directed and Isaac Van Grove and Leo Kopp conducted the orchestra. The opera grew out of a collaboration between Weill and Werfel on a German play of the same title but is not at all the same differing in scale and operatic intention. *The Eternal Road* was popular with audiences and was given 153 performances but it was so costly to produce that it lost money and was never revived. The next production was mounted in 1999 by Chemnitz Opera in Germany with Theo Adam, Siegfried Vogel and Peter Schmidt as the principal singers. Michael Heinicke staged it and John Mauceri conducted the Robert Schumann Philharmonie and a chorus of singers from Chemnitz Opera, Cracow Opera and the Leipzig Synagogue. This production was reprised at the Brooklyn Academy of Music in February 2000 with a cast of 130 and an 80-piece orchestra, the largest performing arts production ever staged at BAM.

2004 Jesus Christ Church, Berlin. Gerard Schwarz conducts the Ernest Senff Chorus, the Berlin Radio-Television Children's Chorus and the Berlin Radio-Television Symphony Orchestra in a 73-minute recording of highlights from *The Eternal Road*. The singers, who play 20 different roles, are Ted Christopher, Ian DeNolfo, Karl Dent, Constance Hauman, James Maddalena, Barbara Rearick, Vale Rideout and Hannah Wollschläger. Naxos American Classics CD.

THE ETHIOP   *1814 opera by Taylor*

Raynor Taylor's opera *The Ethiop or The Child of the Desert* was one of the earliest American operas to be staged. It premiered at the New Chestnut Street Theater in Philadelphia on January 1, 1814, using a libretto by William Dimond which had already been set in England by Henry Bishop. The complicated plot concerns a caliph in disguise and a Christian couple trying to make a living in Baghdad where the wife has to repel lecherous magistrates. The opera was reprised in Philadelphia in 1817.

1978 Federal Music Society. Debra Vanderlinde, R. Sebastian Russ, Charles Long and a chorus perform arias, trios and other numbers from *The Ethiop* with the Federal Music Society Opera Company. The restoration by scholar Victor Fell Yellin was recorded at the Columbia Recording Studio in New York with John Baldon conducting. New World Record LP.

EUROPERAS 1 AND 2   *1987 operas by Cage*

Arias from seventy traditional European operas are performed by singers of different vocal types with start and stop times controlled by watches. The arias, dancers and projected images are as random as the tempos, sets, costumes, action and lighting. John Cage's "non-intentional" non-narrative *Europeras 1 and 2*, really a single opera in two parts, was premiered in Frankfurt, Germany, on December 12, 1987. The ten singers who premiered the 90-minute *Europera 1* were Christina Andreou, June Card, Eliane Coelho, Marianne Rørholm, Michal Shamir, Anny Schlemm, Rodney Gilfrey, Heinz Hagenau, Willy Müller and Seppo Ruohonen. The nine singers who introduced the 45-minute *Europera 2* were Harolyn Blackwell, Ilse Gramatzki, Margit Neubauer, Tom Fox, Michael Glücksmann, Valentin Jar, Keith Mikelson, William Workman and Jurij Zinovenko. The operas were first staged in the U.S. at the Pepsico Summerfare Festival in Purchase, New York, on July 14, 1988. *Europeras 1–5* were produced by Hannover Staatsopera in 2001.

EUROPERAS 3 AND 4   *1990 operas by Cage*

Like John Cage's first two non-narrative operas, *Europeras 3 and 4* use arias and music from older non-copyright European operas and combine them into something new and strange. *Europeras 3 and 4* were considered chamber operas by Cage and have much smaller requirements that *Europeras 1 and 2*. The 75-minute *Europera 1* features six singers, two pianists and twelve record players. The 30-minute *Europera 2* requires two singers, a pianist and a wind-up record player. Both operas premiered at the Almeida Theatre in London on June 17, 1990, and were presented by Hannover Staatsopera in 2001.

1993 Long Beach Opera. *Europeras 3 and 4* were recorded by Long Beach Opera at the Center Theater in Long Beach, CA, on November 13, 1993, under the direction of conductor Andrew Culver. *Europera 3* singers are mezzo-sopranos Ruby Hinds and Patricia McAfee, tenors Michael Lyon and Richard Powell, soprano Suzan Hanson and bass Kevin Bell. Vicki Ray and Brian Pezzone are the pianists, Scott Fraser plays the "Truckera" tape of operatic excerpts and the record players are operated by Hannes Geiger, Joseph Giri, William Houston, Dren McDonald, Ronda Rindone and Clarice Ross. *Europera 4* singers are sopranos Anne-Marie Ketchum and Daisetta Kim with Brian Pezzone as pianist. Jerry Wheeler operates the 78 rpm Victrola and Scott Fraser operates the Truckera tape. Mode 2-CD box.

EUROPERA 5   *1991 opera by Cage*

John Cage's *Europera 5* is the most stylized of his non-narrative operas with masks for the singers, a precise stage area divided into 68 squares and utilization of a local radio station. The music again comes from out-of-copyright European operas. Two singers choose five arias which they perform on pre-determined squares. The pianist plays old opera transcriptions and the record player operator plays old opera records. The one-hour opera premiered at the State University of New York in Buffalo in 1991 and was staged in London in 1992. It was reprised in Santa Fe in 2000 using only Wagner opera excerpts and presented by Hannover Staatsopera in 2001.

EVANGELINE   *American music dramas based on Longfellow poem*

British officials evict French Acadians from Nova Scotia in 1755 and Acadian lovers Evangeline and Gabriel are separated. They are not reunited until many years later when Gabriel is dying. Henry Wadsworth Longfellow's 1847 epic narrative poem *Evangeline* was hugely popular in its time and remains so today in Nova Scotia. It inspired a popular 19th century opera-bouffe burlesque and a 20th century grand opera.

1874 Edward E. Rice. Edward E. Rice's *Evangeline*, an extravagant American opéra-bouffe (according to its sheet music) burlesque of Longfellow's poem with libretto by J. Cheever Goodwin, was previewed in Boston and Cambridge and opened in New York's Niblo's Gardens on July 27, 1874. It was one of the most popular music theater works of its time, launching Rice on a long career as a theater composer. Ione Burke played Evangeline and Connie Thomson was her lover Gabriel; unlike the lovers in the poem, they live happily ever after. The most popular character in the stage production was a dancing cow. **1932 Otto Luening.** Otto Luening's four-act grand opera *Evangeline*, libretto by the composer based on Longfellow's poem, was commissioned by the American Opera Company in Rochester. Luening retraced the wanderings of the exiled Acadians while researching the opera and incorporated Acadian music in the score. The American Opera Company folded before it could stage the work but it was presented in excerpt form at the Arts Club of Chicago in 1932 and was awarded a Bispham Medal. It received its stage premiere at Columbia University on May 5, 1948, with Teresa Stich-Randall in the title role and Luening conducting. A revised version with narration was presented by After Dinner Theater in New York on February 8, 1985.

EVANS, DAMON *American tenor*

Damon Evans created the role of Benjie in Thea Musgrave's HARRIET, THE WOMAN CALLED MOSES at Virginia Opera in 1985. He sang Sporting Life in the Glyndebourne Opera production of George Gershwin's PORGY AND BESS and is featured in the 1987 recording and 1988 film. He sang Joe in the London Old Vic revival of Oscar Hammerstein's CARMEN JONES and is featured in the 1991 recording. Evans, born in Baltimore, Maryland, a noted Mozart tenor, is known to television audiences for playing Lionel on the series *The Jeffersons.*

EVENTIDE *1975 opera by Fennimore*

A cottage in the American South during the Depression era. Mahala's seventeen-year-old son Teeboy is missing and her sister Plumy has gone to find him. She returns to say he is living with a woman in the red light district. Plumy had lost an infant son years ago so she understands Mahala's unhappiness. When Teeboy comes back to the cottage, Mahala sends him away. Joseph Fennimore's one-act chamber opera *Eventide*, libretto by the composer based on a story by James Purdy, premiered at Carnegie Recital Hall in New York City on October 1, 1975, with the composer conducting. It was revived by After Dinner Opera in New York on October 3, 1983.

1986 Chelsea Chamber Ensemble. Karen Williams is Mahala, Hilary Johnsson is Plumy and Philip Creech is Teeboy with Timm Rolek conducting the Chelsea Chamber Ensemble. The opera was recorded at the Center for the Performing Arts at SUNY Purchaser in August/September 1986. It's on the album *Music of Joseph Fennimore.* 17 minutes. Albany CD.

F

FABLES *American operas based on Aesop/La Fontaine fables*

Aesop's allegorical animal *Fables* are among the most widely known works of oral literature. They were first heard in Greece in the fifth century BC, when Aesop was supposed to have lived, and were written down by Greek poet Babrius around the second century BC. Jean de La Fontaine revised and adapted them in the late 17th century and wrote many of his own. Several fables have been turned into American chamber operas and there is one about Aesop himself.

1969 Martin Kalmanoff. Martin Kalmanoff's chamber opera *Aesop, the Fabulous Fabulist*, libretto by the composer, was premiered at Camp Pemigewasset in Wentworth, New Hampshire, on August 21, 1969. **1971 Ned Rorem.** Ned Rorem's chamber opera *Fables*, libretto by the composer based on Marianne Moore's translations of fables by Jean de La Fontaine, was premiered at the University of Tennessee in Martin on May 21, 1971. It includes five fables: "The Lion in Love," "The Sun and the Frog," "The Bird Wounded by an Arrow," "The Fox and the Grapes" and "The Animals Sick of the Plague." **1975 Hugh Aitken.** Travelling players act out fables including "The Cicada and the Ant" and "The Raven and the Fox." Hugh Aitken's *Fables*, libretto by the composer based on Aesop's *Fables* as retold by Jean de la Fontaine, was premiered at the Library of Congress by the New York Chamber Solists on November 1, 1997. Grayson Hirst played the First Tenor. The

Famous "Face on the Bar Room Floor" Central City Colorado

The face on the barroom floor in Central City, Colorado, that inspired Henry Mollicone's opera *The Face on the Barroom Floor.*

opera, commissioned by the Elizabeth Sprague Coolidge Foundation, was reprised at the Caramoor Festival in Katonah, NY, in 1976.

THE FACE ON THE BARROOM FLOOR *1978 opera by Mollicone*

In contemporary Central City, Colorado, opera chorus member Isabelle and her boyfriend Larry visit a bar. He asks the bartender Tom about a woman's face painted on the floor. The scene changes to the 19th century. Tom is now barman John who tells bargirl Madeline (played by Isabelle) to sing. Matt (played by Larry) enters the bar and is given whiskey in exchange for painting a picture of a woman he loves. It turns out to be Madeline and the men begin to quarrel and fight. John draws a gun and shoots at Matt but kills Madeline instead. The scenes changes back to the 20th century where Tom reveals he loves Isabelle and the men fight over her. Isabelle is shot and falls onto the face on the barroom floor.

Henry Mollicone's popular one-act chamber opera *The Face on the Barroom Floor,* libretto by John S. Bowman, premiered at Central City Opera House in Colorado on July 22, 1978. It's based on a poem about the portrait of a woman painted on the floor of the Teller House Saloon in Central City where it is set. The face was actually painted in 1936 by Herndon Davis though the saloon itself dates back to 1872. The opera is one of the most often performed American operas and its honky-tonk lyricism never fails to please.

1980 Central City Opera. Leanne McGiffin sings the role of Isabelle/Madeline, Barry McCauley is Larry/Matt and David Holloway is Tom/John in this recording made at the Central City Opera House in Colorado. Composer Henry Mollicone is the pianist, Alice Weir is the flautist and George Banks is the cellist. CRI LP/CD.

FAILING KANSAS *1994 opera by Rouse*

A robbery goes wrong in a Holcomb, Kansas, house in 1959 and two deranged young men murder the entire Clutter family in cold blood. Dennis Rouse's one-man 75-minute post-modern avant-garde opera *Failing Kansas*, libretto by the composer based on Truman Capote's *In Cold Blood*, was premiered at The Kitchen in 1994. Rouse played all the roles and staged the production which uses an electronic score and includes film shot by Cliff Baldwin.

A grandiose scene from the 1915 Hollywood Bowl premiere of Horatio Parker's allegorical opera *Fairyland*.

Failing Kansas has been presented around the world with considerable success.

1995 Mikel Rouse. Mikel Rouse recorded the opera in Italy in 1995, performing all the roles to electronic accompaniment. New Tone/WB Italy CD.

FAIRYLAND   *1915 opera by Parker*

An unnamed European country in the thirteenth century. Corvain seizes the throne of his dreamer brother King Auburn so Auburn decides to become the king of Fairyland with a novice nun named Rosamund as his queen. In the real world both are seized and bound to stakes to be burned alive. At the last moment fairies appear on stage, roses bloom and the couple appear in royal robes as the rightful rulers of Fairyland. Horatio Parker's allegorical three-act opera *Fairyland*, libretto by Brian Hooker, won a $10,000 prize and was premiered at the Hollywood Bowl on July 1, 1915. Ralph Errolle was King Auburn, Marcella Craft was Rosamund, William Wade Hinshaw was Corvain, Kathleen Howard was Abbess Myriel and Albert Reiss was woodsman Robin. Alfred Hertz conducted the orchestra and chorus.

THE FALL OF THE HOUSE OF USHER   *American operas based on story by Edgar Allan Poe*

Roderick Usher invites his childhood friend William to his decaying mansion, the House of Usher. Roderick and his twin sister Madeleine demonstrate an obsessive attachment for each other. When she apparently dies, her body is put in the family vault but she breaks out to search for Roderick. They embrace and fall dead as the house collapses in ruins. Six American operas have been based on EDGAR ALLAN POE's story *The Fall of the House of Usher* first published in 1839 in *Burton's Gentleman's* magazine.

1921 Avery Claflin. Avery Claflin composed three scenes of the one-act opera *The Fall of the House of Usher* in 1921 using his own libretto based on the story. It was never performed. **1941 Clarence Loomis.** Clarence Loomis's one-act opera *The Fall of the House of Usher,* libretto by E. Ferguson, was premiered in concert form at Block's Auditorium in Indianapolis, Indiana, on January 11, 1941. **1952 Morris H. Ruger.** Morris H. Ruger's one-act opera *The Fall of the House of Usher,* libretto by the composer, was premiered in Los Angeles on April 15, 1952. **1975 Gregory Sandow.** Gregory Sandow's one-act opera, libretto by the science-fiction writer

Thomas N. Disch, was premiered in New York in 1975 and reprised in New York on February 3, 1979. **1984 Russell Currie.** Russell Currie's 60-minute opera *A Dream within a Dream*, libretto by Robert Kornfield based on *The Fall of the House of Usher*, was commissioned by the Bronx Art Ensemble which premiered it in concert form at Wave Hill in New York on April 29, 1984. It was staged at the Lehman Center for the Performing Arts on June 15, 1985, and reprised in concert form at Merkin Concert Hall on May 11, 1986. It was presented by Jersey Lyric Opera on June 5, 1985, in a double bill with Currie's other Poe opera *The Cask of Amontillado*. **1988 Philip Glass.** Philip Glass's two-act opera *The Fall of the House of Usher*, libretto by Arthur Yorinks, is the best-known of the American operas based on the Poe story. It was premiered by American Repertory Theater in Cambridge, MA, on May 18, 1988, as a joint commission with Kentucky Opera which presented it on May 31, 1988. The premiere production featured Dwayne Croft and William Hite alternating as Roderick Usher, Sharon Baker and Suzan Hanson alternating as Madeline, David Trombley and Steven Paul Aiken alternating as William, Pawel Izdebski as the Servant and Thomas Oesterling as the Physician.

THE FAN   *1989 opera by Goldstein*

The gift of a fan causes a series of amatory misunderstandings. Lee Goldstein's two-act opera *The Fan*, libretto by Charles Kondek based on Carlo Goldoni's play *Il Ventaglio*, was commissioned by Lyric Opera of Chicago. A workshop performance of Act One was staged in 1988 and the complete opera was premiered on June 17, 1989, at the Blackstone Theater. Pamela Menas played Candida, Carol Madalin was Nina, Phyllis Pancella was Aunt Gertrude, Donn Cook was Count Rocca Marina, Mark Calkins was Evarist, Gary Lehman was Crispino, Susan Foster was Susanna, Stephen Gould was Tomoteo, Joseph Wiggett was Coronato, Henry Runey was Baron del Cedro and Michael Wadsworth was Morracchio. James Morgan designed the set, Charles Kondek staged the opera and Lee Schaenen conducted the Lyric Opera Orchestra.

FANTASTIC MR. FOX   *1998 children's opera by Picker*

Farmers Boggis, Bunce and Bean conspire to get rid of Mr. Fox and his family with the help of Mavis the Tractor and Agnes the Digger. Fox outwits them and gets his revenge. Tobias Picker's children's opera *Fantastic Mr. Fox*, libretto by Donald Sturrock based on Roald Dahl's story of the same name, was premiered by Los Angeles Opera at the Music Center Opera on December 9, 1998, with elaborate sets and costumes by Gerald Scarfe. Gerald Finley was Mr. Fox, Suzanna Guzmán was Mrs. Fox, Louis Lebherz was Farmer Boggis, Doug Jones was Farmer Bunce, Jamie Offenbach was Farmer Bean, Jill Jones was Agnes the Digger, Josepha Gayer was Rita the Rat, Sari Gruber was Miss Hedgehog, Malcolm MacKenzie was Badger the Miner, Jorge Garza was Burrowing Mole and Charles Castronovo was Porcupine. Librettist Donald Sturrock directed and Peter Ash conducted.

FARBERMAN, HAROLD   *American composer/conductor (1912–)*

New Yorker Harold Farberman has composed three operas. *Medea*, libretto by W. Van Lennep, is an expressionist retelling of the Greek myth and was premiered on March 26, 1961, at the Boston Conservatory. THE LOSERS, libretto by Barbara Fried, is the tale of a California motorbike gang and was commissioned by Juilliard American Opera Theatre which premiered it March 26, 1971. *If Music Be* is a multi-media opera requiring four conductors.

Farberman studied at the Juilliard School and has worked as percussionist and conductor with various orchestras.

FARLEY, CAROLE   *American soprano (1946–)*

American coloratura soprano Carole Farley stars as Lucy in the 1992 BBC Scotland film of Gian Carlo Menotti's THE TELEPHONE. She performs songs from Kurt Weill's LADY IN THE DARK, LOVE LIFE and ONE TOUCH OF VENUS on her 1992 album *Kurt Weill Songs*. Farley, born in Le Mars, Iowa, studied at Indiana University and in Munich. She made her debut in Germany in 1969 and her American debut in 1976 with New York City Opera.

FARRELL, EILEEN   *American soprano(1920–)*

Eileen Farrell sings the role of the Abbess on the 1987 operatic recording of Richard Rodgers' THE SOUND OF MUSIC and the aria "To This We've Come" from Gian Carlo Menotti's THE CONSUL on her 1958 album *Opera Arias and Songs*. She is featured on a 1945 recording of Sigmund Romberg's UP IN CENTRAL PARK and a 1946 recording of Victor Herbert's THE RED MILL. Farrell, born in Willimantic, CT, studied privately and sang mainly in concert until her stage opera debut in 1956. She was the voice of opera singer Marjorie Lawrence in the 1955 film biography *Interrupted Melody*.

THE FASHIONABLE LADY   *1730 opera by Ralph*

James Ralph's ballad opera *The Fashionable Lady; or, Harlequin's Opera* is the earliest known opera created by an American though it was actually written and staged in London. Ralph, born in Pennsylvania in 1695, left Philadelphia for London in 1724 and became popular in England as poet and playwright. *The Fashionable Lady* which premiered at Goodman's Fields Theater on April 1, 1730, is a satire about the fashionable foibles of the era. One of the characters is actually called Mrs. Foible (she represents Fashion) and one of the satirical targets is ballad opera itself. Despite its popularity in London, the opera was never staged in America.

FAULKNER, WILLIAM   *American novelist (1897–1962)*

William Faulkner won the Nobel Prize for Literature in 1950 but his stories have not inspired opera composers. The one exception was created by Opera Memphis which commissioned folk operas based on the novels *As I Lay Dying* and *Light in August* from Tommy Goldsmith, Tom House, Karen Pell and David Olney. Olney's *Light in August* was premiered on February 12, 1993.

FAULL, ELLEN   *American soprano (1918–)*

Ellen Faull created the role of the stepmother Abigail Borden in Jack Beeson's LIZZIE BORDEN at New York City Opera in 1965 and is featured on the recording. She sang Miss Pinkerton in New York City Opera's 1948 production of Gian Carlo Menotti's THE OLD MAID AND THE THIEF and reprised the role for a 1949 NBC television production. She is Carry's mother in the 1968 New York City Opera production and recording of Douglas Moore's CARRY NATION. Faull, born in Pittsburgh, made her debut at New York City Opera in 1947 and can be heard in recital on the album *Ellen Faull: An American Soprano* (VAI CD).

FAY-YEN-FAH   *1925 opera by Redding*

The Chinese couple Fay-Yen-Fah and Shiunin destroy the evil power of Fox-God Hou through the strength of their love for each other. Joseph Redding's three-act opera *Fay-Yen-Fah*, libretto by Charles Templeton Crocker based on his play *The Land of Happiness*, became the first American opera to be produced in France when it was premiered at Monte Carlo Opera House February 2, 1925. Fanny Heldy sang Fay-Yen-Fah, René Masion was Shiunin, Julien Lafont was Hou, Henri Fabert was Wang-Loo and Edmond Warney was Tin-Loi. Victor de Sabata conducted the Monte Carlo Opera Orchestra. The opera was sung in a French translation in Monte Carlo and, strangely, the French translation was used when the opera was given its American premiere by the San Francisco Grand Opera Company. It was staged at the Columbia Theater in San Francisco on January 11, 1926, with Lucy Bertrand in the leading role. The opera's music was said by contemporary critics to have pleasant echoes of Debussy and Puccini.

FELDMAN, MORTON *American composer (1926–1987)*

Avant-garde composer Morton Feldman wrote the music for two unusual collaborations with writer Samuel Beckett. Their 1977 opera NEITHER, a monodrama for soprano, has a non-narrative 87-word libretto and almost no plot. It was premiered at the Rome Opera House on May 13, 1977. Their 1987 radio play *Words and Music* features words by Beckett and music by Feldman and almost no plot. Feldman, a native of Buffalo, New York, started composing at the age of nine and attended New York High School for Music and Art. He became part of a New York School of musicians and taught at SUNY in Buffalo in the 1970s. His musical style is atonal, abstract and experimental but recognizably his own.

FENNIMORE, JOSEPH *American composer/pianist (1940–)*

Joseph Fennimore is best known for his piano compositions but he also wrote four operas. *Apache Dance*, libretto by the composer based on a story by James Purdy, was presented at Lincoln Center on April 1 1975. EVENTIDE, libretto by the composer based on another Purdy story, and *Don't Call Me By My Right Name* were performed together at Carnegie Recital Hall on October 1, 1975. *Eventide* was reprised by After Dinner Opera in 1983 and recorded by the Chelsea Chamber Ensemble in 1986. *Isadora*, libretto by the composer based on the life of dancer Isadora Duncan, was presented at Carnegie Recital Hall on March 11, 1978. Fennimore, who was born in New York City, studied at Eastman and Juilliard and often performed his own piano works.

THE FESTIVAL OF REGRETS *1999 opera by Drattell*

Greta and her mother meet Greta's ex-husband and his new girlfriend at a New Year's ceremony at Central Park's Bethesda Fountain. It does not go well. Deborah Drattell's one-act opera *The Festival of Regrets*, libretto by Wendy Wasserstein, is the first opera in the CENTRAL PARK trilogy that premiered at Glimmerglass Opera on August 8, 1999. Joyce Castle played Mother, Lauren Flanigan was Greta, Matthew Dibattista was Wesley, John Hancock was Frank, Margaret Lloyd was Jessica and Joshua Winograde was the Rabbi. Michael Yeargan designed the sets, Mark Lamos directed and Stewart Robertson conducted. When the opera was reprised at New York City Opera in November 1999, Mimi Lerner took over the role of Mother. The trilogy was telecast on PBS in 2000.

FIDDLER ON THE ROOF *1965 musical by Bock*

Jerry Bock's downbeat Jewish musical *Fiddler on the Roof,* has attracted considerable interest from opera singers, including Julia Migenes and Jan Peerce. It's tells the story of Tevye, a poor dairyman who lives in a Jewish village in Russia in 1905 with his wife Golda and five daughters. Daughter Tzeitel marries a poor tailor instead of the rich butcher her father had selected, Hodel falls in love with a revolutionary scholar and Chava gets involved with a Gentile. Cossacks destroy the village and Tevye and family emigrate to America. Joseph Stein wrote the libretto based on stories by Sholem Aleichem in collaboration with Sheldon who Harnick wrote the songs lyrics. *Fiddler* opened at the Imperial Theater in New York, on September 22, 1964, with Zero Mostel as Tevye, Maria Karnilova as Golda, opera star-to-be be Julia Migenes as Hodel (the most vocally demanding role), Bert Convy as her revolutionary lover, Joanna Merlin as Tzeitel, Austin Pendleton as the tailor she loves and Tany Everette as Chava. Harold Prince produced the musical which Harold Robbins choreographed and directed. Metropolitan Opera tenor Jan Peerce took over the lead role of Tevye in 1961 and is often identified with it. Topol, who sang the role in the London production, starred in the movie adaptation.

1964 Original cast. Zero Mostel sings Teyve with, Julia Migenes as his daughter Hodel and Maria Karnilova as Golda in this original cast recording. The rest of the cast are as above. Milton Greene conducts. RCA LP/CD. **1968 Robert Merrill.** Robert Merrill sings the role of Tevye with support from Molly Picon as Golda, Mary Thomas, Andy Cole, James Tullett, Robert Bowman, Sylvia King, Barbara Moore and Patrica Whitmore. Decca/London LP. **1971 Norman Jewison film.** Norman Jewison directed Topol as a realistic Tevye in a film of the musical shot on gritty authentic locations with a script by librettist Joseph Stein. Molly Picon plays Golda and the supporting cast includes Paul Mann, Norma Crane, and Leonard Frey. Isaac Stern plays the violin featured on the soundtrack. The movie won Academy Awards for cinematography (Oswald Morris) and score (John Williams). The film is on DVD/VHS/LD and the soundtrack is on UA LP/CD. **1992 Jan Peerce.** Met tenor is shown singing in *Fiddler on the Roof* in the 1992 documentary *Jan Peerce: If I Were a Rich Man.* Peerce took over the role on Broadway in 1971. Bel Canto Society/Proscenium VHS.

FIELDS, DOROTHY *American librettist/lyricist (1904–1974)*

Dorothy Fields wrote the libretto and lyrics for the last traditional operetta to reach Broadway, Sigmund Romberg's delightfully retro UP IN CENTRAL PARK (1945). In a remarkable career that lasted 45 years, Fields collaborated on many major Broadway musicals including Irving Berlin's ANNIE GET YOUR GUN (1946), Arthur Schwartz's *A Tree Grows in Brooklyn* (1951) and Cy Coleman's *Sweet Charity* (1966). Fields, who was born in Allenhurst, NJ, as the daughter of producer Lew Fields, began her songwriting career in 1928.

FILM AND AMERICAN OPERA

Few American stage operas have been filmed, though the movie of Gian Carlo Menotti's THE MEDIUM is considered one of the best in the genre and George Gershwin's PORGY AND BESS has been filmed twice. Most of the videos of American operas are of taped stage performances. There are also American "movie operas," operas specially created for films. They are discussed in the entry on MOVIE OPERAS.

Operas on Film: 1945 Two Gershwin operas are featured in the Gershwin film biography *Rhapsody in Blue.* BLUE MONDAY is staged in an abridged format and a sequence from *Porgy and Bess* is shown with Anne Brown, the original Bess, singing "Summertime." **1951** Gian Carlo Menotti filmed *The Medium* on location in Rome with its stage star Marie Powers. This is the only opera film produced and directed by a composer. **1954** Oscar Hammerstein's CARMEN JONES filmed by Otto Preminger with Dorothy Dandridge playing Carmen but her singing dubbed by Marilyn Horne. **1959** *Porgy and Bess* filmed by Otto Preminger with Sidney Poitier playing Porgy (sung by Robert McFerrin) and Dorothy Dandridge playing Bess (sung by Adele Addison). **1989** *Porgy and Bess* filmed in England by Trevor Nunn with Willard White as Porgy and Cynthia Haymon as Bess. They do their own singing. **1979** Menotti's AMAHL AND THE NIGHT VISITORS filmed in Israel with Teresa Stratas starring as the Mother of Amahl.

Operettas on film: American comic operas and operettas have been popular with Hollywood filmmakers but have not usually been treated with respect. The first adaptations were made in the silent era with the music from the operetta played live as the films were screened. The first American operetta to be filmed was Victor Herbert's OLD DUTCH in 1915 although he sued in an attempt to prevent it. The first American operetta to be filmed with its music was Sigmund Romberg's THE DESERT SONG, advertised in June 1929 as the "first all-singing and talking operetta." Most of the American-style operettas of Jerome Kern and Richard Rodgers have been filmed. Listed below are the principal film versions. The title is followed by the name of the composer and the star. **Silent Films: 1915** *Old Dutch* (Herbert) Lew Fields. **1923** *Maytime* (Romberg) Clara Bow. **1926** *Mademoiselle Modiste* (Herbert) C. Griffith. **1927** *The Red Mill* (Herbert) Marion Davies. **1927** *The Student Prince* (Romberg) R. Navarro. **1927** *Maytime* (Romberg) John Charles Thomas. **1928** *Rose-Marie* (Friml) Joan Crawford. **Sound Films: 1929** *The Desert Song* (Romberg) John Boles. **1929** *Show Boat* (Kern) Laura La Plante. **1930** *Mlle. Modiste* (*Kiss Me Again*) Bernice Claire. **1930** *The New Moon* (Romberg) Moore and Tibbett. **1930** *The Vagabond King* (Friml) Dennis King. **1932** *The Desert Song* as *The Red Shadow* (Romberg). **1932** *Music in the Air* (Kern) John Boles. **1934** *Babes in Toyland* (Herbert) Laurel and Hardy. **1934** *The Cat and the Fiddle* (Kern) MacDonald. **1934** *The Fortune Teller/La Buenaventura* (Herbert). **1935** *Naughty Marietta* (Herbert) MacDonald and Eddy. **1936** *Rose-Marie* (Friml) MacDonald and Eddy. **1936** *Show Boat* (Kern) Paul Robeson. **1937** *The Firefly* (Friml) MacDonald and Jones. **1937** *Maytime* (Romberg) MacDonald and Eddy. **1938** *Sweethearts* (Herbert) MacDonald and Eddy. **1940** *The New Moon* (Romberg) MacDonald and Eddy. **1943** *The Desert Song* (Romberg) Dennis Morgan. **1946** *Show Boat* in *Till the Clouds Roll By* (Kern). **1948** *Up in Central Park* (Romberg) D. Durbin. **1951** *Show Boat* (Kern) William Warfield. **1953** *The Desert Song* (Romberg) Gordon MacRae. **1954** *Rose-Marie* (Friml) Howard Keel. **1954** *The Student Prince* (Romberg) Mario Lanza. **1955** *Oklahoma!* (Rodgers) Gordon MacRae. **1955** *Kismet* (Wright/Forrest/Borodin) H. Keel. **1956** *Carousel* (Rodgers) Clara Mae Turner. **1956** *The Vagabond King* (Friml) Oreste. **1956** *The King and I* (Rodgers) Yul Brynner. **1958** *South Pacific* (Rodgers) Giorgio Tozzi. **1961** *Babes in Toyland* (Herbert) Ray Bolger. **1961** *West Side Story* (Bernstein) Natalie Wood. **1964** *My Fair Lady* (Loewe) Audrey Hepburn. **1965** *The Sound of Music* (Rodgers) Julie Andrews. **1970** *Song of Norway* (Wright/Forrest/Grieg). **1972** *Man of La Mancha* (Leigh) Peter O'Toole

FINAL ALICE   *1976 "opera in concert form" by Del Tredici*

David Del Teredici's obsession with Lewis Carroll's Alice culminated in what he calls "an opera written in concert form." Based around the last two chapters of *Alice in Wonderland*, it features an amplified soprano narrator, a group of folk instruments and a large orchestra. Arias are interspersed with dramatic episodes ending in pandemonium and Alice's awakening. *Final Alice* was commissioned for the Chicago Symphony Orchestra which premiered it

on October 7, 1976, with Barbara Hendricks singing the role of Alice and Sir Georg Solti conducting. It was such a success it led to many other Alice commissions.

1980 Barbara Hendricks/Chicago Symphony. Barbara Hendricks sings the role of Alice in this recording made at the Medinah Temple in Chicago with Sir Georg Solti conducting the Chicago Symphony. The instrumental folk group consists of soprano saxophones, mandolin, tenor banjo and accordion. London/Decca LP and CD.

THE FINAL INGREDIENT   *1965 opera by Amram*

Jews in a German concentration camp during the second World War need one more ingredient to complete their forbidden Passover supper so they stage a breakout to get an egg. David Amram's opera *The Final Ingredient,* libretto by Arnold Weinstein based on a television play by Reginald Rose, was commissioned for Passover by ABC Television and screened on April 11, 1965, with Amram conducting. William Covington played Aaron, Joseph Sopher was Aaron's Father, Ezio Flagello was Walter, Malcolm Smith was Eli, Richard Frisch was Felix, Alan Baker was Max, Thomas Motto was the Rabbi, Brown Bradley was Sigmund, John Fiorito was Herr Fedwebel, Robert Lancaster was the Corporal, James Olesen was the Private and Sara Mae Endich, Elaine Bonazzi and Marija Kova were the Three Women. Amram interviewed Holocaust survivors to make the opera as authentic as possible.

1965 ABC Television. The opera was so popular it was telecast annually for years and the soundtrack was finally released on record in 1996. The cast is as above with William Covington as Aaron, Alan Baker as Max and Thomas Motto as the Rabbi. Amram conducts. Premiere CD.

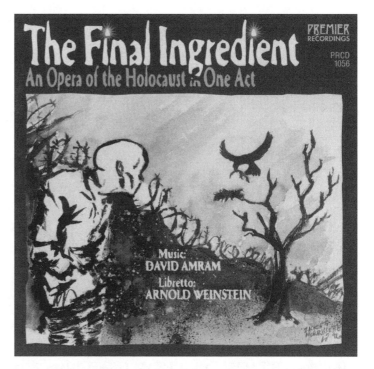

David Amram's TV opera *The Final Ingredient* became so popular that the soundtrack was eventually issued on CD.

FINE, VIVIEN   *American composer (1914–2000)*

Vivian Fine attracted a good deal of attention in 1978 for her feminist opera THE WOMEN IN THE GARDEN which features

Gertrude Stein, Isadora Duncan, Virginia Woolf and Emily Dickinson in discussion. The prelude to *Women in the Garden* was Fine's 1976 oratorio *Meeting for Equal Rights 1866*, a work based on the writings of 19th century suffrage leaders. Her 1994 multimedia opera THE MEMOIRS OF ULIANA ROONEY, libretto by Sonya Friedman, is the semi-autobiographical story of a modern woman composer during eight decades of the twentieth century. Chicago-born Fine was a child prodigy pianist and studied composition with Ruth Crawford-Seeger and Roger Sessions. She began her opera career in 1956 with the humorous *A Guide to the Life Expectancy of the Rose* using a libretto based on a gardening article; it premiered at the Donnell Library Center in New York on February 7, 1956. Fine, who received an NEA grant to write an opera based on James Joyce's *Finnegans Wake*, has composed ballet scores for Martha Graham, Doris Humphrey, and José Limón as well as other vocal, chamber and symphonic works.

FINK, MYRON   *American composer (1932–)*

Myron Fink has been a composer for nearly half a century but his major opera did not premiere until 1997 when his grandiose four-hour THE CONQUISTADOR, libretto by Donald Moreland, was staged by San Diego Opera. Fink, born in Chicago, studied at Juilliard and Illinois University and composed his first opera in 1955 while studying at Cornell; THE BOOR was premiered at the Jefferson Hotel in St. Louis on February 14, 1955. He began working with librettist Moreland the same year on *Susannah and the Elders* and they became regular collaborator. Excerpts from this Biblical tale, which was also the inspiration for Carlisle Floyd's opera SUSANNAH, were staged in Vienna in 1956. Fink's third opera was JEREMIAH, libretto by P. Fink and E. Hawley about a religious fanatic who seduces his son's girlfriend and kills his son using Biblical justification. It was premiered by Tri-Cities Opera at Harpur College in Binghampton, NY, on April 25, 1962.

Judith and Holofernes, libretto by Moreland based on Giraudoux's play *Judith*, was premiered in concert form at SUNY in Purchase, NY, on February 4, 1978. The operetta-like CHINCHILLA, libretto by Moreland and set in New York in the 1920s, was premiered by Tri-Cities Opera at the Forum Theater on January 18, 1986. The one-act operas *The Island of Tomorrow*, libretto by Lou Rodgers about immigrants at Ellis Island, and *The Trojan Women* were staged together by Golden Fleece Opera in 1988.

FINNEY, ROSS LEE   *American composer (1906–)*

Ross Lee Finney wrote three operas to his own librettos, two of them after he retired from teaching in 1971. The first was *The Nun's Priests' Tale,* an eighteen-minute chamber work about CHANTICLEER, the rooster featured in Chaucer's *Canterbury Tales*. It premiered at Dartmouth College in 1965. *Weep Torn Land* (1984) looks at three kinds of violence in Colorado in the 19th century including Indian massacres and Civil War rivalries. *Computer Marriage* (1989) is a comic opera about an bizarre attempt to create a perfect wife by using computers. Finney, born in Wells, Minnesota, spent twenty years teaching at Smith College and another twenty as composer-in-residence at Michigan University.

FIRE WATER PAPER: A VIETNAM ORATORIO   *1995 oratorio by Goldenthal*

The horrors of the Vietnam war are recalled through texts from Vietnamese and American sources. Elliot Goldenthal's grand-scale bilingual choral work *Fire Water Paper: A Vietnam Oratorio*, libretto by the composer, is composed for soprano, baritone, cello, three choruses and large orchestra. It was commissioned by the Pacific Symphony Orchestra which premiered it April 29, 1995, at the Orange County Performing Arts Center in Costa Mesa, California. James Maddalena was the baritone, Ann Panagulias was the soprano and Yo-Yo Ma was the cellist. Carl St. Clair conducted the Pacific Symphony Orchestra, Pacific Chorale, Pacific Chorale Children's Chorus and Ngan-Khoi Vietnamese Children's Chorus.

1995 Pacific Symphony. The oratorio was recorded at the Orange County Performing Arts Center performances on April 29 and 30, 1995, and at the Seiji Ozawa Hall, Tanglewood, performance on July 19, 1995. Carl St. Clair leads the Pacific Symphony Orchestra, Pacific Chorale, Pacific Chorale Children's Chorus and Ngan-Khoi Vietnamese Children's Chorus with soloists James Maddalena (baritone), Ann Panagulias (soprano) and Yo-Yo Ma (cello). Sony Classical CD.

THE FIREBRAND OF FLORENCE   *1945 Broadway opera by Weill*

Renaissance artist Benvenuto Cellini has problems with model Angela, whom he loves, and the Duke of Florence, who suspects him of political conspiracy. Kurt Weill's neglected Broadway opera *The Firebrand of Florence,* lyrics by Ira Gershwin and libretto by Edwin Justus Mayer, based on his 1924 play *The Firebrand*, premiered at the Colonial Theater in Boston on February 23, 1945, with the title *Much Ado About Love* and opened at the Alvin Theater in New York on March 22, 1945, with the present title. Earl Wrightson played Cellini, Beverly Tyler was Angela, Melville Cooper was the Duke, Lotte Lenya was the Duchess, Randolph Symonette was the Hangman, James Dobson was Ascanio, Don Marshall was Tartman and Ferdie Hoffman was Ottaviano. Jo Mielziner designed the sets, John Murray Anderson directed and Maurice Abravanel conducted. The most popular aria was "Sing Me Not a Ballad." Weill called this work his "first Broadway opera" but it not well received. It was revived by Ohio Light Opera in 1999 and presented in concert form in London in 2000. Mayer's play *The Firebrand* had been filmed by 20th Century Fox in 1934 with Fredric March as Cellini.

1942 Kurt Weill. Composer Kurt Weill rehearses seven numbers from the opera, including "Sing Me Not a Ballad" and "You're Far Too Near Me," on the album *Tryout: A Series of Private Rehearsal Recordings.* Heritage LP/DRG CD. **1957 Lotte Lenya.** Original cast member Lotte Lenya performs "Sing Me Not a Ballad" on a recording made New York in August 1957. Maurice Levine conducts the orchestra and chorus. It's on the album *Lotte Lenya Sings Kurt Weill: American Theater Songs.* Sony Classics CD. **1992 Angelina Réaux.** Angelina Réaux performs "Sing Me Not a Ballad" accompanied by pianist Robert Kapilow on the album *Songs of Kurt Weill.* Koch CD. **1996 Sarah Musinovski.** Sarah Musinovski performs "Sing Me Not a Ballad" with support from Hans-Joachim Tinnefeld and Stefan Weinzierl on the album *Weill: Vom Broadway nach Berlin.* Signum CD. **1996 Steve Kimbrough.** Steve Kimbrough performs three arias from the opera on the album *Kurt Weill on Broadway* with the Cologne West German Radio Orchestra led by Victor Symonette. Koch Swann CD. **1997 Thomas Hampson/Elizabeth Futral.** Thomas Hampson as Cellini, Elizabeth Futral as Angela and Jerry Hadley as the Duke perform scenes from the opera on the album *Kurt Weill on Broadway.* John McGlinn conducts the London Sinfonietta. Program notes by Miles Kreuger. EMI Classics CD. **2000 Barbican Hall.** Sir Anthony Davis conducts the BBC Singers and BBC Symphony Orchestra in a concert performance of the opera at the Barbican Hall in London on January 16, 2000. Rodney Gilfrey is Cellini, Lori Ann Fuller is Angela, Felicity Palmer is the Duchess, George

Dvorsky is the Duke, Lucy Schaufer is Emilia, Stephen Charlesworth is Ascanio, Roger Heath is Ottaviano, Robert Johnston is the Marquis Pierre, Henry Waddington is the Hangman and Stuart Macintyre is Maffio. Simon Russell Beale narrates the 118-minute show using linking material written by Sam Brookes. Capriccio CD.

THE FIREFLY   *1912 operetta by Friml*

Italian street singer Nina disguises herself as a boy to get a job on millionaire Jack Travers' yacht and sails to Bermuda from New York as his cabin boy. When she becomes famous as the opera diva Giannini, she marries him. Rudolf Friml's tuneful operetta *The Firefly*, libretto by Otto Harbach, premiered at the Wieting Opera House in Syracuse on October 14, 1912, and opened on Broadway at the Lyric Theater on December 2, 1912. Emma Trentini sang the role of Nina, Craig Campbell was Jack, Katherine Stewart was Mrs. van Dare, Henry Vogel was Professor Franz, Audrey Maple was Geraldine, Melville Steward was John, Ruby Norton was Suzette and Sammy Lee was Pietro. Friml was hired to write the operetta after Victor Herbert refused to work with Trentini again after NAUGHTY MARIETTA. His stage score includes the arias "Giannina Mia," "Love Is Like a Firefly" and "Sympathy" but not the famous "Donkey Song." It was created for the 1937 film version by pastiche masters George Forrest and Robert Wright using an old Friml song called "Chanson" as the melody.

Jeannette MacDonald in the 1937 film of Rudolf Friml's tuneful operetta *The Firefly*.

1913 Craig Campbell. Craig Campbell, who created the role of millionaire Jack Travers in the premiere, made the first recording of music from the operetta singing "A Woman's Smile" for a Columbia 78. It's on the box set *Music from the New York Stage 1890–1920.* Pearl CD **1913 Helen Clark/Walter van Brunt.** Helen Clark and Walter van Brunt recorded the song "Sympathy" and it became a best-selling Victor 78. **1929 Victor Salon Group.** Nathaniel Shilkret leads orchestra and the Victor Salon Group in songs from *The Firefly.* The 78 recordings were reissued on the album *The Music of Rudolf Friml.* RCA Victor LP. **1936 Richard Tauber.** Richard Tauber recorded "Sympathy" for a 78 It's on the album *Richard Tauber: Songs of Stage and Screen.* Parlophone LP. **1937 MGM film.** Jeanette MacDonald stars in an MGM film of the operetta which uses a different plot but retains the songs. including "Giannina Mia," "Love Is Like a Firefly" and "Sympathy." MacDonald plays The Firefly, a Spanish singer recruited to be a spy during the Napoleonic War. Allan Jones gets to sing "The Donkey Serenade" during a trip over a mountain and it made him famous. The supporting cast includes Henry Daniell, Warren William, George Zucco and Billy Gilbert. Frances Goodrich, Albert Hackett and Ogden Nash wrote the screenplay, Herbert Stothart conducted the music and Robert Z. Leonard directed. The film is on MGM-UA VHS/DVD and the soundtrack is on a Chansonette LP. **1938 Allan Jones.** Alan Jones recorded his hit song "The Donkey Serenade" for a 78 in 1938 It's on several albums, including *Allen Jones: The Donkey Serenade.* Camden LP. **1939 Rudolf Friml.** Rudolf Friml played four songs from *The*

Firefly on piano for 78s records in 1939. "Giannina Mia," "When a Maid Comes Knocking," "Sympathy" and "The Donkey Serenade" are on several albums including *The Genius of Rudolf Friml.* Golden Crest LP. **1946 Jeanette MacDonald.** Jeanette MacDonald recorded "Giannina Mia" and "The Donkey Serenade" for a 78 in 1946. They're on various albums including *Jeanette MacDonald's Operetta Favorites.* RCA Victor LP. **1951 Allen Jones/Elaine Malbin.** Allen Jones and Elaine Malbin star in a highlights version of the operetta with an orchestra led by Al Goodman. The supporting cast includes Martha Wright and Hayes Gordon. RCA Victor LP. **1952/1956 Mario Lanza.** Mario Lanza recorded "The Donkey Serenade" with orchestra led by Ray Sinatra for the 1952 album *Mario Lanza: Be My Love* (RCA Victor LP). He recorded "The Donkey Serenade" and "Giannina Mia" with Henri René's Orchestra and the Jeff Alexander Choir for the 1956 album *A Cavalcade of Show Tunes* (RCA Victor LP), reissued on *The Mario Lanza Collection* (RCA Victor CD). **1960 Earl Wrightson/Lois Hunt.** Baritone Earl Wrightson and soprano Lois Hunt perform "Sympathy," "Giannina Mia" and "The Donkey Serenade" with an orchestra led by Frank DeVol on the album *A Night with Rudolf Friml.* Columbia LP. **1963 Stephanie Voss/Laurie Payne.** Stephanie Voss and Laurie Payne star in a highlights version of the operetta with orchestra conducted by Alan Braden. World Record Club LP. **1964 Rudolf Friml/Ivo Zidek.** Rudolf Friml plays piano while Czech tenor Ivo Zidek sings numbers from the operetta on a recording made during a visit to Prague by Friml. They're on the album *Friml Plays Friml.* Supraphon CD. **1986 Teresa Ringholz.** Teresa Ringholz performs "Giannina Mia" with the Eastman-Dryden Orchestra conducted by Donald Hunsberger on the album

Rudolf Friml: Chansonette. Arabesque LP/CD. **1993 Jerry Hadley.** Jerry Hadley performs "Donkey Serenade" on his album *Golden Days.* Paul Gemignani conducts the American Theatre Orchestra. BMG RCA Victor CD.

FIRST AMERICAN OPERAS   *Earliest American operas published and staged*

The first opera presented in America was an English ballad opera, Colley Cibber's *Flora, or Hob in the Well.* It was staged in Charleston, SC, on February 18, 1735, in the Courtroom above Shepheard's Tavern.

First opera written and staged by an American was James Ralph's ballad opera THE FASHIONABLE LADY; *or, Harlequin's Opera* but it was written in London and staged there on April 1, 1730.

First opera-like music drama by an American presented in America was William Smith's masque ALFRED, *An Oratorial Exercise,* an adaptation of a masque by Thomas Arne. It was staged at the College of Philadelphia in December 1756

First American comic opera and the first with an American subject was Thomas Barton's satirical ballad opera THE DISAPPOINTMENT: *or, The Force of Credulity* published in Philadelphia in 1767. The opera was to have premiered in Philadelphia in April 1867 but was forbidden by the censor and was not staged until 1976.

Second American opera/oratorio to be performed was Francis Hopkinson's patriotic AMERICA INDEPENDENT: *or, The Temple of Minerva* presented in Philadelphia in 1781.

Other early American operas include Royall Tyler's *May Day in Town: or, New York in an Uproar* premiered in New York on May 18, 1787; William Dunlap's *Darby's Return* premiered in New York November 24, 1789; *The Better Sort:, or, The Girl of Spirit* published in Boston in 1789; Peter Markoe's *The Reconciliation: or the Triumph of Nature* published in Philadelphia in 1790; James Hewitt's TAMMANY; OR THE INDIAN CHIEF premiered in New York in 1794 and Benjamin Carr's THE ARCHERS; *or The Mountaineers of Switzerland,* premiered in New York in 1796.

First American opera based on American literature was Charles E. Horn's *Ahmed al Kamel; or, The Pilgrim of Love,* libretto by Henry J. Finn, based on Washington Irving's *Tales of the Alhambra.* It premiered at New National Theater in New York on October 12, 1840

First American "grand opera" was William Henry Fry's LEONORA, libretto by the composer based on an Edward Bulwer-Lytton play. It premiered at the Chestnut Street Theater in Philadelphia on June 4, 1845.

First American grand opera with an American subject was George Frederick Bristow's 1855 RIP VAN WINKLE, based on the story by Washington Irving. It was premiered by the Pyne-Harrison opera company in Niblo's Gardens in New York on September 27, 1855.

First American opera presented in Europe was Louis Adolphe Coerne's ZENOBIA which premiered at the Stadttheater in Bremen, Germany, on December 1, 1905.

First American opera presented at the Metropolitan Opera House was Frederick Converse's THE PIPE OF DESIRE staged on March 18, 1910, but it had premiered in Boston in 1906.

First American opera premiered at the Metropolitan Opera House was Horatio Parker's MONA presented on March 14, 1912. It was the winner of a $10,000 Metropolitan Opera competition for an American Opera.

FIRST U.S. OPERA RECORDINGS   *Earliest records of American operas*

The first American operas were recorded in 1911 and 1912 soon after American operas had been accepted at the Metropolitan Opera. Victor Herbert's 1911 NATOMA aroused the greatest interest in the recording industry with four recordings in 1912 and three more in 1913. It was the most recorded American opera before PORGY AND BESS. Alice Nielsen, who played Chonita in Frederick S. Converse's 1911 opera THE SACRIFICE, recorded "Chonita's Prayer" ("Almighty Father") for a Columbia 78 in 1911. John McCormack, who created the role of Lt. Paul Merrill in *Natoma,* recorded "Paul's Address" ("No country can my own outvie") for Victor on April 3, 1912. Reinald Werrenrath recorded "Alvarado's Serenade" ("When the sunlight dies") from *Natoma* for Victor on April 3, 1912. Alma Gluck recorded Barbara's "Spring Song" ("I List the Trill in Golden Throat") from *Natoma* for a Victor Red Seal record in 1912. Victor Herbert and his orchestra recorded the "Dagger Dance" from *Natoma* for Victor in 1912. Caroline White, who sang Barbara in the Chicago premiere of *Natoma,* recorded her aria "Spring Song" for Columbia in 1913. Earl Cartwright and the Victor Light Opera Company recorded "Vaquero's Song" ("Who Dares the Bronco Wild Defy") from *Natoma* for a Victor 78 in 1913. Cecil Fanning recorded "Vaquero's Song" ("Who Dares the Bronco Wild Defy") from *Natoma* for a Columbia 78 in 1913. Frances Alda, who starred in Victor Herbert's second opera MADELEINE, recorded her aria "A Perfect Day" for Victor on February 8, 1914. First American opera to be recorded complete with its original cast was Marc Blitzstein's THE CRADLE WILL ROCK in 1938. It was released on eighteen 12 inch 78 records on the Musicraft label.

FIRST U. S. OPERAS ON RADIO   *Earliest radio broadcasts of American operas*

American operas first began to be presented on radio in 1927. By 1928 the NBC National Grand Opera Company was broadcasting them on a regular basis. Below are firsts in various categories.

First American opera broadcast on radio was Deems Taylor's THE KING'S HENCHMAN presented in 60-minute highlights form by CBS on September 18, 1927, only six months after its premiere at the Met.

First American opera premiered on radio was Harry Lawrence Freeman's VOODOO, broadcast in a 30-minute highlights version on WGBS on May 28, 1928.

First American opera premiered in complete form on radio was Cesare Sodera's OMBRE RUSSE, broadcast in two parts on NBC on May 27 and June 3, 1929.

First American opera commissioned for radio was Charles Wakefield Cadman's THE WILLOW TREE presented on NBC on October 3, 1932.

American operas broadcast from 1927–1932: **1927** Taylor *The King's Henchman* (CBS). **1928** Cadman *Shanewis* (NBC). Freeman *Voodoo* (WGBS). Hadley *Bianca* (NBC). Herbert *Natoma* (NBC). Harling *A Light from St. Agnes* (NBC). **1929** De Leone *Alglala* (NBC). Hadley *Cleopatra's Night* (NBC). Sodero *Ombre Russe* (NBC). Cadman *A Witch of Salem* (NBC). **1930** Skilton *The Sun Bride* (NBC). **1932** Cadman *The Willow Tree* (NBC). Graham *Tom-Tom* (NBC).

FIRST U.S. OPERAS ON TV   *Earliest television productions of American operas*

Gian Carlo Menotti dominated television opera in the early years. The first four American operas on TV were by Menotti, he wrote the first opera commissioned for television and he was the first American composer to have an opera televised in Europe. For more on the subject of television, see TELEVISION AND AMERICAN OPERA.

First American opera on television was Menotti's THE OLD MAID AND THE THIEF telecast by General Electric's Schenectady station WRGB-TV in May 1943. It was a Hartford Opera Workshop studio production with sets and costumes but only piano accompaniment.

Second American opera on television was Menotti's THE TELEPHONE telecast by NBC in May 28, 1948. It featured students from the Curtis Institute of Music.

First American opera televised with a professional cast was Menotti's THE MEDIUM which had two productions in 1948. An NBC version with Mary Davenport was shown in October and a CBS version with Marie Powers was shown in December.

First telecast of an American opera with a New York City Opera cast was Menotti's *The Old Maid and the Thief* shown on NBC on March 16, 1949.

First NBC Opera Theater production was Kurt Weill's DOWN IN THE VALLEY telecast on January 25, 1950.

First original opera premiered on television was Menotti's AMAHL AND THE NIGHT VISITORS telecast by NBC on December 24, 1951.

First American opera shown on television outside the U.S. was Menotti's THE CONSUL televised in May 1951 by BBC in England.

First American opera shown on ABC Television was Mark Bucci's THE THIRTEEN CLOCKS telecast in December 1953

First American opera shown on NET was Jack Beeson's LIZZIE BORDEN telecast in January 1967 with its New York City Opera cast.

First American opera telecast from the New York City Opera stage was Douglas Moore's THE BALLAD OF BABY DOE shown in May 1976. It was the first opera in the *Live from Lincoln Center* series.

First American opera telecast from the Houston Grand Opera stage was Carlisle Floyd's WILLIE STARK in 1981.

First American opera telecast from Chicago was Chicago Opera Theater's production of Lee Hoiby's SUMMER AND SMOKE shown June 1982.

First American opera telecast from the Metropolitan Opera was John Corigliano's THE GHOSTS OF VERSAILLES shown in September 1992.

First American opera telecast from San Francisco Opera was Conrad Susa's THE DANGEROUS LIAISONS shown in October 1994.

FIRST U.S. OPERETTA RECORDS   *Earliest recordings of American comic operas*

Popular numbers from American comic operas were recorded soon after the birth of the record industry. The first was, appropriately, the first hit tune to emerge from a comic opera, "Oh, Promise Me," introduced on stage in 1890 in Reginald De Koven's comic opera ROBIN HOOD. Seven songs were recorded before the turn of the century.

George J. Gaskin, the "Silver-Voice Irish Tenor," recorded "Oh, Promise Me," from *Robin Hood* on March 4, 1893, for the New Jersey recording company. It was one of the most popular records of the year. John Philip Sousa and his Band recorded the title tune from his comic opera EL CAPITAN on June 15, 1895, for Columbia. The "El Capitan March" is still popular. Jessie Bartlett Davis, who played the trouser role of Alan-a-Dale in *Robin Hood* and introduced "Oh Promise Me" on stage, recorded it for Berliner on March 5, 1898. Jessie Bartlett Davis joined W. H. Macdonald, her

co-star in Victor Herbert's comic opera THE SERENADE, in the duet "Don Jose of Sevilla," recorded on March 5, 1898, for Berliner. Alice Nielson, who became famous in Herbert's THE FORTUNE TELLER, recorded her hit tune "Always Do as People Say You Should" for Berliner in October 1898 and joined other cast members in the "Opening Chorus of Schoolgirls" and "Second Act Finale." Haydn Quartet bass William F. Hooley rounded out the century by recording the "Gypsy Love Song" from *The Fortune Teller* for Edison on July 15, 1899.

FISHER, GARRETT   *American composer (1970–)*

Garrett Fisher has completed a number of unusual operas, all written to his own librettos and all staged in Seattle. *The Passion of Saint Sebastian* was staged at the Bumbershoot Festival in Seattle in 1996. *The Passion of Saint Thomas More*, which examines the saint's possible choices before his execution, was staged at the Medieval in Seattle in 1997. *Moon in the Bucket*, based on a Noh play about ghost sisters who turn into a moon, was presented at the Nippon Kan Theatre in Seattle in 1997. *Agamemnon*, about the king who sacrificed her daughter so he could lead his army to Troy, was staged in Seattle in 1997 and 1998. It was later expanded into the *Dream of Zeus* featuring other members of the doomed house of Atreus. *Riverrun*, a choral work based on James Joyce's *Finnegans Wake*, was performed by Esoterics in Seattle in 2000. *Sally Hemings*, about Thomas Jefferson's slave/mistress, was presented in excerpt form in 2000 and then filmed. Fisher, who was born in Michigan, studied music at Oberlin and then moved permanently to Seattle.

THE FISHERMAN AND HIS WIFE   *1970 opera by Schuller*

A fisherman's wife makes increasing demands on a magic fish caught and released by her husband. She asks for a fancy cottage and a palace and decides she wants to be King and Pope. When she asks to be made God, the fish sends her back to her old lifestyle. Gunther Schuller's "fairy tale opera for all ages" *The Fisherman and His Wife*, libretto by John Updike based on a Grimm Brothers story, was commissioned by the Junior League of Boston and premiered by the Boston Opera Company in Boston on May 7, 1970, with sets and costumes by Patton Campbell. The one-hour thirteen-scene opera is scored for four principal singers (Fish, Fisherman, Wife and Cat) in musical styles ranging from jazz and rock to twelve-tone elements.

A FISHERMAN CALLED PETER   *1965 church opera by Owens*

The story of Simon, the fisherman whom Jesus renamed Peter after he became the first to recognize Jesus as the Christ, the expected Messiah. Richard Owen's church opera *A Fisherman Called Peter*, libretto by the composer based in part on the Bible, was commissioned by the Drew Church in Carmel, NY, and premiered there on March 14, 1965. The premiere cast included Metropolitan Opera soprano Lynn Owen, the composer's wife, as Simon's wife Deborah, The opera was reprised in New York in 1967 with Adele Addison as Deborah and staged by Zurich Opera in Switzerland in June 1969.

1969 Zurich recording. Howard Nelson sings the role of Simon/Peter in this recording of the opera in Zurich, Switzerland. Lynn Owen is his wife Deborah, Richard Van Vrooman is his brother Andrew, Lorraine Dogget is Deborah's mother and Roland Hermann is John the Baptist. John Reardon, the Voice of God in Igor Stravinsky's opera THE FLOOD, has the speaking role of Jesus of Nazareth. Frank Egerman conducts the 14-piece chamber orchestra and Gretchen Stein directs the chorus. 51 minutes. Serenus LP.

FITCH, CLYDE   *American dramatist (1865–1909)*

Clyde Fitch is not well known as a playwright today but at the turn of the century he was hugely popular and two of his plays were turned into operas. The 1899 play *Barbara Frietchie*, a dramatization of John Greenleaf Whittier's poem, was the basis of Eugene MacDonald Bonner's 1917 opera *Barbara Frietchie* and Sigmund Romberg's 1927 operetta MY MARYLAND. Fitch's 1901 play CAPTAIN JINKS OF THE HORSE MARINES, about a bet to seduce an opera singer, was adapted by librettist Sheldon Harnick for an opera by Jack Beeson premiered by Lyric Opera of Kansas City in 1975.

FITZGERALD, F. SCOTT   *American writer (1896–1940)*

John Harbison's THE GREAT GATSBY, which premiered at the Metropolitan Opera on December 20, 1999, seems to be the only opera based on a novel or story by F. Scott Fitzgerald. *The Great Gatsby*, considered by some to be the great American novel, was an appropriate choice for the end of the Millenium. Fitzgerald, born in St. Paul, Minnesota, became famous with his first novel *This Side of Paradise* and came to symbolize the jazz age of the 1920s with wife Zelda.

FLAGELLO, EZIO   *American bass (1931–)*

Ezio Flagello created the role of Enobarbus in Samuel Barber's ANTONY AND CLEOPATRA at the Metropolitan Opera in 1966. Earlier he had created the role of the Sultan in Robert Middleton's opera COMMAND PERFORMANCE in Poughkeepsie in 1961 and Walter in David Amram's THE FINAL INGREDIENT on television in 1965. He also played the Maharajah in the American premiere of Gian Carlo Menotti's THE LAST SAVAGE at the Met in 1964. His other stage roles in American operas include the Doctor in Barber's VANESSA, the Husband in Menotti's AMELIA GOES TO THE BALL, and Bull in Norman Dello Joio's THE RUBY. Flagello, born in New York City, studied at the Manhattan School of Music and made his debut in 1955. He began singing at the Met in 1957.

FLAGELLO, NICOLAS   *American composer 1928–)*

Nicolas Flagello wrote seven operas, three premiered at Manhattan School of Music where he taught from 1950 to 1970. *The Sisters,* libretto by Dean Mundy about sisters in 1820 New England, was staged on February 22, 1961, with Johanna Meier in the lead role of Hester. THE JUDGMENT OF ST. FRANCIS, libretto by Armand Aulicino about St. Francis of Assisi, premiered on March 18, 1966. The children's opera THE PIPER OF HAMELIN (1970), libretto by the composer based on Robert Browning's poem, was presented on April 18, 1970. Flagello's other opera for children is RIP VAN WINKLE (1957), libretto by C. Fiore based on the Washington Irving story. He also wrote operas based on stories by Pirandello (*The Wig,* 1953) and Eugene O'Neill (*Beyond the Horizon,* 1983). Flagello, a New York native, studied under Vittorio Giannini and composes in a similar neo-romantic style.

FLANAGAN, WILLIAM   *American composer (1923–1969)*

Detroit-born composer/critic William Flanagan composed the music for two plays by Edward Albee, *The Sandbox* (1961) and *The Ballad of the Sad Café* (1963), and the playwright wrote the librettos for his two operas. BARTLEBY (1961), adapted from the novella by Herman Melville about a man who withdraws from life, was written by Albee in collaboration with I. J. Hinton and premiered at the York Playhouse in New York City on January 24, 1961. *The Ice Age* was commissioned by New York City Opera in 1967 but never completed. Flanagan studied with Barber and Copland and composes in a similar melodious conservative style.

FLANIGAN, LAUREN   *American soprano (1958–)*

Lauren Flanigan has created roles in four American operas and recorded many others. She was only a Ghost singing "dead... bored" in John Corigliano's THE GHOSTS OF VERSAILLES at the Met in 1992 but she had the title role in Hugo Weisgall's ESTHER at New York City Opera in 1993 and major roles in the CENTRAL PARK trilogy at Glimmerglass in 1999, Greta in Deborah Drattell's THE FESTIVAL OF REGRETS and the Woman in Robert Beaser's THE FOOD OF LOVE. She sings Lady Valerie in a 1995 recording of Amy M. Beach's chamber opera CABILDO, Lady Marigold in a 1996 recording of Howard Hanson's opera MERRY MOUNT in Seattle and Mary in a 1999 recording of Deems Taylor's PETER IBBETSON in Seattle. She played the adulterous Christine in Lyric Opera of Chicago's revival of Marvin David Levy's MOURNING BECOME ELECTRA in 1999, stepmother Abigail Borden in New York City Opera's revival of Jack Beeson's LIZZIE BORDEN in 1999 and Susan B. Anthony in New York City Opera's revival of Virgil Thomson's THE MOTHER OF US ALL at in 2000. Flanigan, born in San Francisco, made her stage debut at thirteen singing Flora in *The Turn of the Screw* for Western Opera Theater. She began to sing with New York City Opera in 1991.

FLEMING, RENÉE   *American soprano (1960–)*

Renée Fleming has been identified with American opera in recent years, creating roles in three operas and devoting a recital album to American opera arias. She created the roles of Rosina in John Corigliano's THE GHOSTS OF VERSAILLES at the Metropolitan Opera in 1991, Mme. De Tourvel in Conrad Susa's THE DANGEROUS LIAISONS at San Francisco Opera in 1994 and Blanche Dubois in André Previn's A STREETCAR NAMED DESIRE at San Francisco Opera in 1998. She sang the title role in the Metropolitan Opera production of Carlisle Floyd's classic SUSANNAH. Her 1999 album *I Want Magic* features arias from THE BALLAD OF BABY DOE, CANDIDE, THE MEDIUM, PORGY AND BESS, THE RAKE'S PROGRESS, *A Streetcar Named Desire, Susannah,* VANESSA and WUTHERING HEIGHTS. Her 1998 recital album *Prelude to a Kiss,* recorded with Placido Domingo, includes songs from WEST SIDE STORY and she sings a CANDIDE duet with Jerry Hadley on the 1991 concert album *A Salute to American Music.* She also help promote the career of composer Jake Heggie and is featured on his album of songs. Fleming, born in Rochester, NY, studied at SUNY Potsdam and the Eastman School and made her professional debut in Salzburg in 1986. There is an excellent film about her life and career on a 2002 DVD titled *Ladies and Gentlemen, Miss Renée Fleming...*

FLETCHER, GRANT   *American composer/conductor (1913–)*

Grant Fletcher wrote two somewhat folksy operas. The one-act *The Carrion Crow,* libretto by the composer based on a radio play by John Jacob Niles, tells a tall tale about a tailor who tries to shoot a crow and hits his pet sow. It premiered at Illinois Wesleyan University in Bloomington in 1953. *The Sack of Calabasas,* libretto by the composer based on a story by J. M. Myers about a preacher who swindles people expecting to get rich when the railroad arrives, is a four-act drama set in Calabasas, Arizona, in 1882. It premiered in Phoenix in 1964. Grant, born in Hartsburg,

Illinois, studied at Eastman School and taught music at several universities including Arizona State.

FLETCHER, LUCILLE   *American librettist/playwright (1912–2000)*

Suspense novelist Lucille Fletcher wrote the libretto for husband Bernard Herrmann's 1951 opera WUTHERING HEIGHTS based on the novel by Emily Bronte. Her famous 1944 radio play SORRY, WRONG NUMBER! inspired two American operas, a stage play and two movies. It was first heard on the CBS *Suspense* program in 1943 with Agnes Moorehead as star. Jerome Moross's one-act *Sorry, Wrong Number!*, libretto by the composer, was composed in 1977. Jack Beeson's *Sorry, Wrong Number,* libretto by the composer, premiered at the Center for Contemporary Opera in New York in 1999. Fletcher, a native of Brooklyn, studied at Vassar. Her other famous radio play was *The Hitchhiker* narrated by Orson Welles.

FLEURETTE   *1889 comic opera by Steiner*

Emma Steiner's comic opera *Fleurette* was one of the first by an American woman composer to be to produced on stage. The two-act *Fleurette*, libretto by Edgar Smith and Mrs. B. W. Doremus, was premiered in San Francisco in 1889 and opened at the Standard Theater in New York on August 24, 1891. It has an typical operetta story. Rich handsome aristocrat Marcel falls in love with poor but beautiful flower girl Fleurette and wins her heart at a masked students' ball. Mamie Smith sang the role of Fleurette, Edward Webb was Marcel and Steiner conducted. *Fleurette* was not a big success but its overture was performed at the Metropolitan Opera House on November 17, 1925, when Steiner was honored for her career.

THE FLOATING BOX   *2001 opera by Hwang*

The experiences of a Chinese immigrant family in Chinatown in New York. The father, now dead and seen only as a ghost, had given up his career as a musician to support his child; the mother is an agoraphobic afraid of public places who refuses to learn English; the daughter attempts to create a more American life. Jason Kao Hwang's opera *The Floating Box,* libretto by Catherine Filloux, was premiered by the Asia Society in New York in 2001. The performers were soprano Sanida Ang, mezzo-contralto Ryu-Kyung Kim and baritone Zheng. Alexander Dogde designed the set, Jean Randich directed and Juan Carlo Rivas conducted the orchestra which included Chinese and Western instruments. Hwang was composer-in-residence at the Asia Society when he composed the opera on a Composer/New Residencies grant in collaboration with Chinese organizations in New York.

THE FLOOD   *1962 "musical drama" by Stravinsky*

The Biblical story of mankind from Adam and Eve to Noah and the Flood told by singers, dancers, actors and orchestra. Igor Stravinsky's *The Flood,* libretto by Robert Craft based on Bible tales and English Miracle plays, was premiered on CBS Television on June 14, 1962. The singers were Richard Robinson as Lucifer and John Reardon and Robert Oliver as God. The actors were Laurence Harvey as Narrator, Sebastian Cabot as Noah, Elsa Lancaster as Noah's wife and Paul Tripp as The Caller. The dancers were Jacques D'Amboise as Adam, Suzanne Farrell as Eve, Edward Villella, Ramon Segarra, Joysann Sidimu and the New York City Ballet. Stravinsky devised the production of his "musical play" with choreographer George Balanchine, designer Rouben Ter-Arutunian, director Kirk Browning and Robert Craft who conducted the Columbia Symphony Orchestra and Chorus. The opera was given its stage premiere by Santa Fe Opera on August 21, 1962

1962 CBS Television. Laurence Harvey is the Narrator in the CBS TV premiere production with cast as listed above including Jacques D'Amboise as Adam, Suzanne Farrell as Eve, Sebastian Cabot as Noah, Richard Robinson as Lucifer and John Reardon and Robert Oliver are God. Robert Craft conducts the Columbia Symphony Orchestra and Chorus. The 25-minute opera was telecast June 14, 1962. Video is at MTR, soundtrack is on Sony CD. **1985 Dutch Television.** Dutch director Jaap Drupsteen used the soundtrack of the CBS production to create a new visual version with different actors and elaborate special effects. As in the original, the opera is narrated by Laurence Harvey with the same singers and orchestra conducted by Robert Craft. The visuals are quite different, including Adam and Eve in the nude. Rudi Van Vlaanderen plays Noah, Kitty Courbois is Noah's wife, Pauline Daniels is Lucifer, Rudolf Grasman, Emile Linssen and Carel Willink are God, Silvia Millecam is Eve, Julian Beusker is Adam, Fried Keestulst is Noah's Son and Liesbeth Coops and Annet Malherbe are the Wives. Home Vision video.

FLORENCIA EN EL AMAZONAS   *1996 opera by Catán*

Opera diva Florencia Grimaldi takes a melancholy river journey to scenes of happier times. Mexican composer Daniel Catán's opera *Florencia en el Amazonas*, libretto by Marcela Fuentes-Berain based on themes from the works of Gabriel García Márquez, was premiered by Houston Grand Opera on October 25, 1996. Sheri Greenawald created the role of Florencia, Greg Fedderly was Arcadio, Frank Hernadez was Riolobo, Suzanna Guzmán was Paula, Hector Vasquez was Alvaro, Gabor Andrasy was the Capitán, and Yvonne Gonzalez was Rosalba. Robert Israel designed the sets, Francesca Zambello directed and Vjekoslav Sutej conducted the Houston Symphony. The opera was commissioned by the Houston, Seattle and Los Angeles operas and Opera de Colombia. Catán, who is Latin America's best-known modern opera composer, has close connections to the American opera world.

2001 Houston Grand Opera. Patrica Schumann takes over the role of Florencia in this recording of a revival of the opera produced by Houston Grand Opera in 2001. Chad Shelton is Arcadio, Mark S. Doss is Riolobo, Suzanna Guzmán is Paula, Hector Vasquez is Alvaro, Oren Gradus is the Capitán, and Anna Maria Martinez is Rosalba. Patrick Summers conducts the Houston Grand Opera Orchestra and Chorus. Albany Troy 2-CD set.

FLORIDA   *American state (1845–)*

Saratoga Opera has staged several unusual American operas, Florida Grand Opera has commissioned and premiered three more and Orlando Opera presents American operas on a regular basis. Florida universities have also been welcoming to American opera with Florida State University in Tallahassee premiering six. Florida-born opera people include soprano Cynthia Haymon (Jacksonville), tenor Curtis Rayam (Belleville), composer Lewis Spratlan (Miami), composer Robert Wright (Daytona Beach) and composer Ellen Taaffe Zwilich (Miami). Operas set in Florida include George Antheil's *Cabeza de Vaca* (1959) and Robert Ashley's BALSEROS (1997). Opera and operetta premieres and companies are listed below by city.

Boca Raton: Bruce Pomahac's *Huck and Jim on the Mississippi* premiered at Florida Atlantic University in Boca Raton on November 11, 1983.

Coral Gables: University of Miami Opera premiered Jacques Wolfe's *The Trysting Place* on November 6, 1957, and William Grant Still's HIGHWAY 1, U.S.A., on May 11, 1963.

Fort Lauderdale: Fort Lauderdale Opera performs in the Broward Center for the Performing Arts. Composer Marvin David Levy became its artistic director in 1990 and staged Gian Carlo Menotti's THE SAINT OF BLEECKER STREET in 1991.

Fort Pierce: Treasure Coast Opera, which presents productions in the St. Lucie County Civic Center, staged Sigmund Romberg's THE STUDENT PRINCE.

Gainsville: Jack Jarrett's three-act *Cinderella* was premiered at the University of Florida in Gainsville 1956.

Jacksonville: Carlisle Floyd's monodrama FLOWER AND HAWK premiered at the Civic Auditorium on May 16, 1972.

Miami: Florida Grand Opera (formerly Greater Miami Opera) was founded in 1942 and is the oldest and best-funded opera company in Florida, presenting productions in both Miami and Fort Lauderdale. The company has commissioned and premiered three American operas, Julia Smith's DAISY in 1973, Robert Ward's MINUTES TILL MIDNIGHT in 1982 and Robert Ashley's BALSEROS in 1997. It staged a revised version of Carlisle Floyd's THE PASSION OF JONATHAN WADE in 1991. Its other American opera productions include Marc Blitzstein's REGINA, Floyd's OF MICE AND MEN, Robert Ward's THE CRUCIBLE and Stephen Paulus's THE POSTMAN ALWAYS RINGS TWICE.

Orlando: Orlando Opera, founded in 1963, presented its first American opera in 1991, Carlisle Floyd's SUSANNAH. It has continued to explore the American repertory with productions of George Gershwin's PORGY AND BESS, Gian Carlo Menotti's AMAHL AND THE NIGHT VISITORS, Leonard Bernstein's CANDIDE, Sigmund Romberg's THE STUDENT PRINCE, Mitch Leigh's MAN OF LA MANCHA and Floyd's OF MICE AND MEN

Palm Beach: Palm Beach Opera, which dates from 1962, has staged Carlisle Floyd's SUSANNAH and two operas by Gian Carlo Menotti, AMELIA GOES TO THE BALL and THE MEDIUM.

Pensacola: Pensacola Opera produces operas at the Stanger Theatre.

Pompano Beach: Gold Coast Opera, founded in 1980, has staged a number of American operettas and musicals. They include Forrest/Wright's KISMET, Rudolf Friml's THE VAGABOND KING, Jerome Kern's SHOW BOAT, Frederick Loewe's CAMELOT, Mitch Leigh's MAN OF LA MANCHA, Richard Rodgers' OKLAHOMA!, SOUTH PACIFIC and CAROUSEL and Sigmund Romberg's THE DESERT SONG, THE NEW MOON and THE STUDENT PRINCE,

St. Petersburg: Lee Ahlin's *Charlotte's Web* was premiered by the American Stage company in St. Petersburg on October 20, 1988.

Sarasota: Sarasota prides itself on being the most cultural city in Florida and this is reflected in the adventurous programming of Sarasota Opera. The company, founded in 1960, has staged a number of American operas. They include Raffaelo de Banfield's LORD BYRON'S LOVE LETTER, Seymour Barab's CHANTICLEER, Jerry Bock's SHE LOVES ME, Leonard Bernstein's TROUBLE IN TAHITI, Carlisle Floyd's SUSANNAH, Lee Hoiby's THE SCARF, Gian Carlo Menotti's AMAHL AND THE NIGHT VISITORS and THE MEDIUM, Vittorio Rieti's DON PERLIMPLIN, John Philip Sousa's EL CAPITAN and Igor Stravinsky's THE RAKE'S PROGRESS. John Kennedy's children's opera THE LANGUAGE OF BIRDS, libretto by Peter Krask, was commissioned by Sarasota and premiered on May 8, 2004.

Tallahassee: Florida State University in Tallahassee premiered six American operas, including Carlisle Floyd's classic SUSANNAH in 1955. Floyd's withdrawn opera *The Fugitives* was premiered there in 1951. The other premieres were Walter Kaufmann's *The Research* in 1953, William Presser's *The Belgian Doll* in 1962, Carl Vollrath's *The Quest* in 1966 and Salvador Brotons' REVEREND EVERYMAN in

1990. The second performance of Richard Wargo's THE SEDUCTION OF A LADY was presented in 1985.

Tampa: Opera Tampa, founded in 1995, premiered Anton Coppola's SACCO AND VANZETTI at the Tampa Bay Performing Arts Center on March 17, 2001. Steven Park's *Storm Gathering* and *Sally Back and Forth* were premiered at the University of South Florida in Tampa on October 6, 1959. A series called "Basically Bernstein" featured productions of CANDIDE, TROUBLE IN TAHITI and WEST SIDE STORY.

West Palm Beach: The Raymond F. Kravis Center for the Performing Arts in downtown West Palm Beach has hosted a number of operas in its three performance venues.

Winter Park: Central Florida Lyric Opera is headquartered in Winter Park north of Orlando.

FLORIDIA, PIETRO   *American composer (1860–1932)*

Pietro Floridia, born Baron Napolino di San Silvestro in Sicily, emigrated to America in 1904. His biggest success was the opera PAOLETTA, libretto by Paul Jones, which premiered in Cincinnati in 1910 and was repeated many times. It later won the BISPHAM MEMORIAL MEDAL for an American opera. His opera *The Scarlet Letter,* based on the Nathaniel Hawthorne novel, was submitted to the Metropolitan Opera but rejected. Floridia wrote three operas in Italy. *Carlotta Clepier,* was produced at Naples in 1882 and *Maruzza* was staged in Venice. His third opera, *La Colonia,* based on Bret Harte's story *M'Liss,* premiered in Rome in 1899.

FLOWER AND HAWK   *1972 opera by Floyd*

A flower and a hawk are the symbols of Eleanor of Aquitaine who has been in prison for sixteen years. She reminisces about her former life. She had been the Queen of France while she married to King Louis VII but this marriage was annulled in 1152. She became the Queen of England after wedding Henry Plantagenet who became King Henry II in 1154. When she supported her son Richard the Lionhearted against his father, Henry has her put into prison. She is despondent and ready to take poison when news arrives that Henry has died. She is free, a Queen once again. Carlisle Floyd's monodrama *Flower and Hawk,* libretto by the composer, premiered at the Civic Auditorium in Jacksonville, Florida, on May 16, 1972, with Phyllis Curtain as Eleanor of Aquitaine. Mississippi Opera reprised the opera and telecast it in 1979.

THE FLOWER QUEEN   *1852 "operatic cantata" by Root*

George F. Root's *The Flower Queen, or The Coronation of the Rose* is considered America's first theatrical cantata. Blind gospel songwriter Fannie J. Crosby wrote the libretto for what is an opera in everything but name; operas were frowned on in Root's Protestant milieu. The cantata was used by Root while teaching classes of young women at the Normal Musical Institute in New York and became quite popular. It was the first American cantata published in England.

1982 Isaiah Thomas Singers. The Isaiah Thomas Singers sing the "Hymn to Night" from *The Flower Queen,* a charming trio in which three women portraying Flowers tell a Recluse (bass) about the importance of love and duty. David P. McKay directs the singers and Stephen Long accompanies on organ. The trio is on the album *The Cantata in Early American Music.* Folkways Records LP.

FLOYD, CARLISLE   *American composer (1926–)*

Carlisle Floyd, like George Gershwin, Jack Beeson and Douglas Moore, has helped define the modern American opera through the use of regional settings and folk-influenced styles in audience-friendly works with real arias and memorable melodies Like Gershwin's PORGY AND BESS, Floyd's masterpiece SUSANNAH took half a century to reach the Met but by that time it was already one of the most performed operas in America. Floyd, born in Latta, SC, began his music studies in South Carolina studying piano with Ernst Bacon. He began teaching at Florida State University in 1947 and wrote his first opera, the one-act SLOW DUSK, in 1949. It was followed by *The Fugitives* in 1951, an opera he withdrew after a single performance. His third opera was *Susannah* and it made his reputation. An Appalachian version of the Biblical story of Susannah,, it uses folk idioms in a classical opera style and its soprano aria, AIN'T IT A PRETTY NIGHT, has entered the recital repertory. After its premiere at Florida State in 1955, *Susannah* was presented by New York City Opera with Phyllis Curtin reprising the title role. Next was WUTHERING HEIGHTS, based on the Emily Bronte novel, produced at Santa Fe Opera in 1958 and presented in a revised version at New York City Opera in 1959. THE PASSION OF JONATHAN WADE was staged at New York City Opera in 1962. THE SOJOURNER AND MOLLIE SINCLAIR was created for television but premiered on stage in South Carolina in 1963. MARKHEIM, based on a story by Robert Louis Stevenson, was premiered by New Orleans Opera in 1966. OF MICE AND MEN, based on the John Steinbeck novel and first staged in Seattle in 1970, is Floyd's most popular opera after *Susannah*. FLOWER AND HAWK, an opera about Eleanor of Aquitaine for solo soprano, premiered at Florida State in 1972. Floyd left Florida in 1975 to teach at Houston University and work with Houston Opera Studio. BILBY'S DOLL, based on Esther Forbes' novel *A Mirror for Witches*, was premiered in Houston in 1976. WILLIE STARK, based on Robert Penn Warren's novel *All the King's Men,* was presented in Houston in 1981. COLD SASSY TREE, based on Olive Ann Burns' novel, was premiered in Houston in 2000. Floyd, who writes his own librettos, is loved by producers and audiences who aren't concerned about his critical neglect. It is hard to understand why none of his operas are on DVD.

FLOYD COLLINS *1994 operatic musical by Guettel*

Kentucky in 1925. Cave explorer Floyd Collins becomes trapped in an underground cavern where he is pinned down by an immovable rock. A newspaper man descends to the cave to talk to him and the published interview makes Collins nationally famous. A media circus is born and thrill-seekers come to gawk. After two weeks living underground, Collins dies. Adam Guettel's operatic musical *Floyd Collins*, libretto by Tina Landau and the composer based on real events, premiered at the American Music Theater Festival in Philadelphia on April 9. 1994, under Landau's direction. Jim Morlino was Floyd Collins, Stephen Lee Anderson was Johnnie Gerald, Jason Danieley was Homer Collins, Teresa McCarthy was Nellie Collins, Michael Malone was Jewell Estes, Martin Moran was Skeets Miller, Mary Beth Peil was Miss Jane, Scott Wakefield was Bee Doyle and Nick Plakias was Lee Collins.

The opera was revised and staged off-Broadway by Playwrights Horizons in March 1996 and presented by Skylight Opera Theatre in Milwaukee in 20000. Guettel, one of the new American composers who are breaking down the barriers between opera and musical, incorporates bluegrass and other popular musical forms into his dense musical style. "The Riddle Song" and the climactic "How Glory Goes" were particularly admired by critics. The Floyd Collins story was the basis of the 1951 Billy Wilder movie *Ace in the Hole* starring Kirk Douglas.

1996 Playwrights Horizon. Christopher Innvar sings Floyd Collins in this cast recording of the 1996 Playwrights Horizon off-Broadway production. Stephen Lee Anderson is Bee Doyle, Rudy Roberson is Ed Bishop, Jesse Lenat is Jewell Estes, Don Chastain is Lee Collins, Cass Morgan is Miss Jane, Teresa McCarthy is Nellie Collins, Jason Danieley is Homer Collins, Martin Moran is Skeets Miller and Michael Mulheren is H. T. Carmichael. Ted Sperling conducts an orchestra which includes banjo, harmonica and fiddle. Nonesuch CD.

THE FOOD OF LOVE *1999 opera by Beaser*

A homeless woman in Central Park tries to give away her baby but no one will take it. Robert Beaser's one-act opera *The Food of Love*, libretto by Terrence McNally, the third opera in the CENTRAL PARK trilogy, premiered at Glimmerglass Opera on August 8, 1999. Lauren Flanigan was the Woman, Troy Cook was the Policeman, Jennifer Anne Cooper was the Au Pair, Maggie G. Kuch was the Little Girl, Matthew Dibattista was the Hot Dog Vendor, Kelly E. Kaduce was the Rich Lady, Derrick L. Parker and Torrance Blaisdell were the Frisbee Players, Joshua Winograde was the Painter, Enrique Abadala was the Man with Sun Reflectors, Margaret Lloyd was the Woman with Sun Reflector, Jeffrey Lentz was the Man with Cell Phone, Stephen Gaertner was the Zookeeper, John Hancock was the Elderly Man, and Cynthia Jansen was the Elderly Woman. Michael Yeargan designed the sets, Mark Lamos directed and Stewart Robertson conducted. The trilogy was reprised at New York City Opera in November 1999 and telecast in 2000.

FORD, BRUCE *American tenor (1956–)*

Bruce Ford, now internationally famous as a Rossini tenor, created roles in two American operas at the beginning of his career and sang in the American premiere of another. He created the role of Jeff in Carlisle Floyd's WILLIE STARK at Houston Grand Opera in 1981 and the role of Peccadillo in Peter Schickele's THE ABDUCTION OF FIGARO at Minnesota Opera in 1984. He sang in the American premiere of Philip Glass's *The Madrigal Opera* at the Houston Opera Studio in 1981. Ford, a native of Lubbock, Texas, graduated from Houston Opera Studio in 1982.

FORREST AND WRIGHT *American pastiche masters*

George Forrest and Robert Wright created some of America's most popular operettas but they have never had much respect from music critics because their major successes are pastiches based on music by classical composers. Their first big stage success was SONG OF NORWAY in 1944, a highly romanticized version of the life of Norwegian composer Edvard Greig told to his own melodies. Even more popular was KISMET in 1953, the romantic story of a vagabond poet in old Baghdad based on melodies by Russian composer Alexander Borodin. Forrest (1915–1999), born in Brooklyn, and Wright (1914), born in Daytona Beach, began to work together as teenagers and came to prominence collaborating on MGM musicals in the late 1930s. They created the hit song "The Donkey Serenade" for the film of *The Firefly* from an old Friml melody and received three Oscar nomination for their film work. Their first stage musical was *Thank You, Columbus* produced at Hollywood Playhouse in 1940. Their other pastiche operettas include *Gypsy Lady* (1946, music by Victor Herbert), *The Great Waltz* (1949 and 1965, music by Johann Strauss), *Anya* (1965, music by Rachmaninoff) and *Dumas and Son* (1967, music by Saint-Saens). They wrote the lyrics for Hector Villa Lobos' operatic musical MAGDALENA (1948) and original scores for *The Carefree Heart* (1957), *Kean* (1961) and *Grand Hotel* (1989).

FORREST, HAMILTON   *American composer (1901–1963)*

Forrest Hamilton was much admired by diva Mary Garden who persuaded the Chicago Civic Opera to premiere his grand opera *Camille* with her in the starring role. His earlier opera *Yzdra*, libretto by the composer based on Louis Ledoux's play *Alexander the Great*, was dedicated to her and won the Bispham Medal in 1926. *Camille*, libretto by the composer based on the Alexandre Dumas *fils* novel and play used by Verdi for *La Traviata*, was premiered by Chicago Civic Opera on December 10, 1930. It was sung in French, at the insistence, of Garden who played Marguerite opposite Charles Hackett and Chase Baromeo. It was not well received and has not been revived. Forrest wrote no more operas until the 1950s when he created three one-act works for the Interlochen National Music Camp in Michigan. *Don Fortunio* was staged on July 22, 1952, *Daelia* on July 21, 1954, and *A Matinee Idyll* on August 17, 1954. Forrest, who was born in Chicago, began his musical career as a boy soprano and studied composition with Adolf Weidig.

THE FORTUNE TELLER   *1898 comic opera by Herbert*

Gypsy fortune teller Musette bears a striking resemble to heiress Irma so she is hired to pretend to be her. Naturally this causes great confusion and leads to complications in their lives. Both roles were created on stage by soprano Alice Nielsen who went on to become an international opera diva. Victor Herbert's operetta *The Fortune Teller*, libretto by Harry B. Smith, is full of tuneful Hungarian gypsy music including the popular "Gypsy Love Song" (Herbert's first big hit) and "Romany Life." It premiered at the Grand Opera House in Toronto on September 14, 1898, with Marguerita Sylva (later a famous Carmen) as opera singer Mlle. Pompon, Eugene Cowles as gypsy musician Sandor who loves Musette, Frank Rushworth as Hungarian Capt. Ladislas who loves Irma and Joseph Cawthron as Musette's father. Paul Steindorf was the conductor. The opera opened in New York at Wallack's Theater on September 26, 1998, with the same cast. The Hungarian songs remain popular and there was recently a production by Light Opera of Manhattan.

1898 Alice Nielson. Alice Nielson, who made her name in *The Fortune Teller*, recorded her hit "Always Do as People Say You Should" for Berliner. The company also recorded the "Opening Chorus of Schoolgirls" and "Second Act Finale." All three are on the album *Music from the New York Stage 1890–1920*. Pearl CD box set. **1899 William Hooley.** Haydn Quartet bass William F. Hooley recorded the "Gypsy Love Song" for Edison in 1899 and it became one of the most popular recordings of the year. **1903 Victor Herbert.** Victor Herbert leads his orchestra in a medley titled "Fantasy from *The Fortune Teller*" on a 1903 Edison recordings. It's on the Smithsonian album *The Early Victor Herbert*. Smithsonian LP. **1906 Eugene Cowles.** Eugene Cowles, who played Sandor in the premiere production, recorded the "Gypsy Love Song" for Victor in 1906. It's on *Music from the New York Stage 1890–1920*. Pearl CD box set. **1911 Victor Light Opera.** The Victor Light Opera Company singers perform a medley for a Victor 78 titled *Gems from The Fortune Teller*. It's on the album *The Early Victor Herbert*. Smithsonian LP box. **1920 Reinard Werrenrath.** Met baritone Reinard Werrenrath recorded the "Gypsy Love Song" in 1920 for a Victor Red Seal 78. **1934 La Buenaventura.** Anita Campillo plays Irma/Elvira with Enrico Caruso Jr. as Enrico Baroni in *La Buenaventura,* a Spanish-language film of the operetta made by Warner Brothers in Hollywood. It includes most of Herbert's songs with translated Spanish lyrics. Luis Alberni plays Fresco and Alfonso Pedroza is Sandor. William McGann

directed. **1938 Charles Kullman.** Met tenor Charles Kullman sings the "Gypsy Love Song" with orchestra conducted by Walter Goehr. It on various albums including *Charles Kullman, 20 Unforgettable Classics* (Javelin CD). **1939 The Great Victor Herbert.** Susanna Foster stars in a revival of *The Fortune Teller* in this romantic film which masquerades as a biography of Victor Herbert but is really the story of a couple who sing his music. Mary Martin and Allan Jones star in several Herbert operettas and Foster plays their daughter who carries on the tradition. Andrew L. Stone directed for Paramount. On VHS. **1946 Jeanette MacDonald.** Jeanette MacDonald performs "Romany Life" on the anthology album *The Songs of Victor Herbert*. ASV Living Era CD. **1954 Patrice Munsel.** Met soprano Patrice Munsel sings "Romany Life" on *The Voice of Firestone* TV show with Howard Barlow conducting the Firestone Orchestra. It's on the video *Patrice Munsel in Opera and Song*. VAI VHS. **1956 Mario Lanza.** Mario Lanza sings "Gypsy Love Song" with Henri René's Orchestra and the Jeff Alexander Choir. It's on the RCA Victor LP *A Cavalcade of Show Tunes* and RCA Victor CD *The Mario Lanza Collection*. **1961 Robert Shaw Chorale.** The Robert Shaw Chorale and Orchestra perform "Gypsy Love Song" on the album *The Immortal Victor Herbert*. RCA Victor LP. **1962 Eugene Ormandy.** Eugene Ormandy leads the Philadelphia Orchestra in melodies from *The Fortune Teller*, including "Gypsy Love Song," "Czardas" and "Romany Life," on the album *The Philadelphia Orchestra plays Victor Herbert*. Columbia LP. **1975 Beverly Sills.** Beverly Sills sings "Romany Life" with André Kostelanetz leading the London Symphony Orchestra on the album *Music of Victor Herbert*. Angel LP/CD. **1985 Donald Hunsberger.** The Eastman-Dryden Orchestra under conductor Donald Hunsberger perform seven numbers from the operetta on the album *Victor Herbert: Souvenir*. Arabesque LP/CD. **1989 Marilyn Hill Smith.** Marilyn Hill Smith performs "Romany Life" with the Chandos Concert Orchestra and Chandos Singers conducted by Stuart Barry. It's on the album *Treasures of Operetta III*. Chandos CD. **1991 Lorin Maazel.** The Pittsburgh Symphony Orchestra led by Lorin Maazel plays "Gypsy Love Song" on the album *Popular American Music*. Sony CD. **1993 Jerry Hadley.** Met tenor Jerry Hadley sings ""Romany Life" with Paul Gemignani conducting the American Theatre Orchestra on his album *Golden Days*. RCA Victor CD. **1999 Virginia Croskery.** American soprano Virginia Croskery sings "Romany Life" with the Slovak Radio Symphony Orchestra led by Keith Brion on the album *Victor Herbert: Beloved Songs and Classic Miniatures*. American Classics Naxos CD. **2000 Elizabeth Futral.** Elizabeth Futral sings "Romany Life" with the Rudolph Palmer Singers and pianist Robert Tweten on the album *Sweethearts*. Newport Classics CD.

FORTUNE'S FAVORITES   *1981 chamber opera by Barab*

Former lovers Richard and Emily meet in a restaurant and feel it must be destiny as their spouses have both died. They fall in love again and plan to marry but are worried about their thirteen children. Luckily a solution is found. Seymour Barab's two-character chamber opera *Fortune's Favorites*, libretto by the composer based on H. H. Munro's story "Baker's Dozen," was premiered by The Singer's Theater on August 9, 1981. It has been staged by a number of opera companies but not recorded.

FOSS, LUKAS   *American composer (1922–)*

Lukas Foss has only written three operas but all three have been successful. The folksy tall tale THE JUMPING FROG OF CALAVERAS COUNTY (1950), libretto by Jean Karsavina, is based on a Mark Twain story about crooked behavior during a frog competition.

The nearly nonsensical INTRODUCTIONS AND GOODBYES (1960), libretto by Gian Carlo Menotti, is a delightful piece of fluff created for the Spoleto Festival. The folk tale GRIFFELKIN, libretto by Alastair Reid about a little devil on holiday, was composed for NBC Opera Theatre and premiered in 1955. It has also been put on stage, including a popular 1993 production by New York City Opera. Foss, a child prodigy, started composing at seven and studied with Randall Thompson, Hindemith and Fritz Reiner. He established his reputation at age 22 with his cantata *The Prairie* based on a poem by Carl Sandburg. His later experimental electronic work and does not include opera. Foss is depicted musically in Leonard Bernstein's composition "For Lukas Foss," a section of the work *Five Anniversaries*.

1996 Lukas Foss: Vocal Chamber Works. This is an album of vocal works by Foss with Foss himself conducting. It includes "Lulu's Song" from *The Jumping Frog of Calaveras County* performed by Judith Kellock and Cornell Contemporary Singers. Koch CD.

FOSTER, SUSANNA   *American soprano (1924–)*

Susanna Foster began her film career singing Victor Herbert and

Soprano Susanna Foster in the movie opera *The Magic Voice.*

starred in three "movie operas." In the 1939 Paramount film *The Great Victor Herbert*), she sings "Kiss Me Again," hitting a B above high C, and is pictured in a revival of Herbert's THE FORTUNE TELLER. In the 1943 MGM film *The Phantom of the Opera,* she shows off her high notes to Nelson Eddy in Edward Ward's movie operas AMOUR ET GLOIRE and LE PRINCE MASQUE DE LA CAUCASIE. In the 1944 Universal film *The Climax,* she upsets Boris Karloff when she sings arias from Edward Ward's movie opera THE MAGIC VOICE. Chicago-born Foster was signed for a film by MGM as a child prodigy who could sing F above high C. Although she made twelve films, she never quite made it as a movie star. In 1948 she quit filmmaking and began to work on stage. She sang in a West Coast production of Victor Herbert's NAUGHTY MARIETTA and toured in Jerome Kern's SHOW BOAT and Frederick Loewe's BRIGADOON.

THE FOUR NOTE OPERA   *1972 opera by Johnson*

Five singers (soprano, contralto, tenor, baritone, bass) sing about the music they are singing. They know their destiny is to be obedient to the score as written. Their opening lines are "There are three choruses in this opera. This is the first one." At the end the Baritone sings " Now the Third Chorus has ended, and we must take our positions for the Final Scene." Tom Johnson's amusing minimalist *The Four Note Opera*, libretto by Robert Kushner and the composer, uses only the four notes A, B, D and E. It premiered at the Cubiculo theater in New York on May 5, 1972, to an audience of fifteen delighted friends. It received warm reviews, the audiences grew larger and the opera was eventually telecast by CBS. A dozen American universities staged it, Netherlands Opera mounted a European premiere and opera companies in Vienna and Paris had fun with it. *The Four Note Opera* continues to be revived and enjoyed and has been published but there is no recording.

FOUR SAINTS IN THREE ACTS   *1934 opera by Thomson*

The four saints are St. Teresa of Avila and St. Ignatius Loyola and their confidants St. Settlement and St. Chavez, but there are a dozen others and St. Teresa is represented by two singers. There are also a Compère and a Commère who speak directly to the audience and sing the stage directions. Virgil Thomson's opera *Four Saints in Three Acts,* libretto by Gertrude Stein with a scenario devised by Maurice Grosser, premiered at the Wadsworth Atheneum in Hartford on February 6, 1934. Florine Stettheimer's costume and set designs were based on cellophane and black Americans sang the roles of the white sixteenth century Spanish saints. The music wasn't Spanish either, just down-home American, a potpourri of nineteenth century church and popular music synthesized out of the composer's Kansas City youth. Thomson wanted an African American cast because he liked the clear diction of black singers and because the hymn-like quality of his music gained enormously from their experience with spirituals. Beatrice Robinson-Wayne sang St. Teresa I, Bruce Howard was St. Teresa II, Altonell Hines was Commère, Abner Dorsey was Compère, Bertha Fitzhugh Baker was St. Settlement, Edward Matthews was St. Ignatius, David Bethe was St. Stephen, George Timber was St. Plan, Randolph Robinson was St. Eustace, Embry Bonner was St. Chavez, Leonard Franklin was St. Ferdinand, Kitty Mason was St. Cecilia, Thomas Anderson was St. Giuseppe, Charles Spinnard was St. Anselmo, Marguerite Perry was St. Sara, Flossie Roberts was St. Bernadine, Edward Batten was St. Absalon and Forace Hester was St. Answers. The Eva Jessye Choir performed as the chorus, Frederick Ashton staged the opera and arranged the choreography and Alexander Smallens conducted the orchestra. The opera was produced with funds raised by The Friends and Enemies of Modern Music.

The premiere was a huge success and the opera went on to Broadway where it opened at the 44th Street Theater on February 2, 1935. Stein's libretto became infamous, Stein became a media darling and the aria PIGEONS ON THE GRASS, ALAS was constantly quoted by humorists. *Four Saints* has been revived many times, including another Broadway production in 1952, and is often considered the true beginning of modern American opera. Robert Wilson's production for Houston Grand Opera in 1996 was particularly well received with Ashley Putnam as St. Theresa I, Suzanna Guzmán as St. Theresa II, Sanford Sylvan as St. Ignatius, Eric Owens as St. Plan, Nicole Heaston as St. Settlement, Marietta Simpson as Commère and Wilbur Pauley as Compère; Dennis Russell Davies conducted. Steven Watson's 1999 book *Prepare for Saints* is a fascinating study of how the opera was created.

1934 Premiere film. Julien Levy filmed scenes of the 1934 premiere with a 16mm Bell and Howell camera, including the "Pigeon on the Grass" aria and the finale, and they provide a good idea of the style of the production. Three minutes of his film are seen in the documentary *Virgil Thomson at 90*. FilmAmerica VHS. **1942 Original cast broadcast.** An abridged 49-minute radio version of *Four Saints* was broadcast in New York on June 4, 1942, with members of the original cast and the Leonard De Paur Chorus. The original cast singers are Beatrice Robinson-Wayne as St. Teresa I, Edward Matthews as St. Ignatius, David Bethea as St. Stephen, Altonell Hines as

Virgil Thomson and Gertrude Stein's innovative opera *Four Saints in Three Acts* astounded critics when it premiered in 1934 with its cellophane sets.

Commère and Randolph Robinson as St. Plan. Joining them are Ruby Green as St. Teresa II and Inez Matthews as St. Settlement. Alfred Wallenstein conducts. A recording was made off-air. Omega Opera Archives CD. **1947 Original cast recording.** The abridged 1947 recording of *Four Saints* features a cast similar to the 1942 broadcast but this time conducted by the composer. The original cast singers are Beatrice Robinson-Wayne as St. Teresa I, Edward Matthews as St. Ignatius, David Bethea as St. Stephen, Randolph Robinson as St. Plan, Altonell Hines as Commère and Abner Dorsey as Compère. New singers are Ruby Green as St. Teresa II, Inez Matthews as St. Settlement and Charles Holland as St. Chavez. Thomson abridged the opera to half its original length for this recording made at Town Hall in New York on June 25, 1947. RCA Victor LP/RCA Victor BMG CD. **1970 Gertrude Stein: When This You See, Remember Me.** Virgil Thomson plays piano and rehearses Edward J. Pierson in the "Pigeon on the Grass, Alas" aria and Pierson joins Claudia Lindsey and Betty Allen performing excerpts from the opera. The scenes are in Perry Miller Adato's documentary *Gertrude Stein: When This You See, Remember Me.* Thomson is photographed at Stein's house in France talk-

ing about the opera and his relationship with Stein. "When this you see, remember me"" is sung by the chorus in the final scene of *Saints*. Meridian VHS. **1981 Carnegie Hall.** Joel Thome conducts the Orchestra of Our Time and Lawrence Weller Chorus in a complete recording of the opera based on a 1981 performance at Carnegie Hall. Betty Allen is Commère, Benjamin Matthews is Compère, Arthur Thompson is St. Ignatius, Clamma Dale is St. Teresa I and Florence Quivar is St. Teresa II with William Brown as St. Chavez, Gwendolyn Bradley as St. Settlement, William Penn as St. Plan, Joseph de Vaughn as St. Stephen, Ella Eure-Easton as St. Sara, Denise Lock as St. Cecilia, Maeretha Stewart as St. Celestine, Lloyd Thompkins as St. Lawrence, Clifford Townsend as St. Jan and St. Placide, Leon Wheeler as St. Absalon, Kevin Elliott as St. Eustace, Cheryl Kirk as St. Anne and Louis Tucker as St. Answers. Lawrence Weller was chorus master. The recording was made at Rutgers Church in November 1981. Electra Nonesuch CD box. **1986 Virgil Thomson at 90.** Thomson discusses the opera and sings an aria from it while playing piano in John Huszar's excellent documentary *Virgil Thomson at 90*. The aria is afterwards performed by Betty Allen. FilmAmerica VHS.

FRACKER, RICHARD   *American tenor (1962–)*

Tenor Richard Fracker, who made his debut at the Met in 1989, created the role of Iliodor in Jay Riese's RASPUTIN at New York City Opera in 1988 and has sung in five Philip Glass music theater works. He was one of the main singers in the premiere and recording of HYDROGEN JUKEBOX, he sang the lead tenor role in the premiere of ORPHÉE, he sang the role of Scientist/First Mate in the Metropolitan Opera revival of Glass's THE VOYAGE, he made his Carnegie Hall debut in the lead tenor role of Glass's THE CIVIL WARS and he sang the title role in the Grand Rapids Opera production of THE FALL OF THE HOUSE OF USHER. He has performed on stage in Gian Carlo Menotti's AMAHL AND THE NIGHT VISITORS, Stephen Sondheim's A LITTLE NIGHT MUSIC, Igor Stravinsky's The Rake's Progress (at the University of Michigan under the direction of Robert Altman) and Kurt Weill's STREET SCENE. He has also sung in operetta, playing the Prince in Sigmund Romberg's THE STUDENT PRINCE in a Central City Opera production.

FRANCHETTI, ALDO   *American composer (1883–?)*

Italian-born Aldo Franchetti had been living in the United States for 25 years when he composed his opera *Namiko-San* which premiered at the Chicago Auditorium on December 11, 1925. It was created for the soprano Tamaki Miuri, who wanted another role like Cio-Cio-San in *Madama Butterfly*, and was based on a play by Leo Duran derived from a Japanese tragedy. Franchetti, who was born in Mantua, was accompanist and coach of Alessandro Bonci in the early days of Chicago Opera. He was awarded the Davis Bispham Memorial Medal for American operas for *Namiko-San*.

FRANÇOIS VILLON   *1940 radio opera by Baron*

A musical portrait of 15th century French poet-thief-adventurer-brawler François Villon who was condemned to death for one of his escapades. French-born American composer Maurice Baron's three-act opera *François Villon*, libretto by the composer, was premiered in an abridged form on NBC Radio through WJZ in New York on April 14, 1940.

FRANÇOISE ET TORTILLARD   *1877 "saynéte comique" by Dédé*

Maid Françoise wants soldier boyfriend Tortillard to become the chef at a restaurant she dreams of owning. Although he can't cook, he will inherit a restaurant so it seems they will have a happy marriage. *Françoise et Tortillard*, libretto by E. Duhem, is a brief comic operetta by New Orleans-born African American Creole composer Edmond Dédé who spent most of his career in France. A "saynéte comique" was a popular format for music theater in Spain and France in the 19th century.

1999 Hot Springs Music Festival. Richard Rosenberg leads vocalists and orchestra in four numbers from the "saynéte comique" *Françoise et Tortillard* at the Hot Springs Music Festival. They are Françoise's rondeau sung by soprano Jennifer Foster, a duet sung by Foster and Brandon Brack, the overture and the final quadrille and gallop. They're on the album *American Classics: Edmond Dédé*. Naxos CD.

FRANKENSTEIN: THE MODERN PROMETHEUS   *1990 opera by Larsen*

Dr. Victor Frankenstein creates human life but it seems monstrous to him so he rejects it. When he refuses to make a mate for the Monster, it murders his fiancée Elizabeth, his brother William and other friends. The crazed doctor pursues the monster for revenge. Libby Larsen's 85-minute multimedia opera *Frankenstein: The Modern Prometheus*, libretto by the composer based on the novel by Mary Shelley, was commissioned by Minnesota Opera which premiered it on May 25, 1990. Steven Tharp portrayed Frankenstein, Christian Swenson was his Monster, Elisabeth Comeaux was his fiancée Elizabeth, Andrew Ashcroft was his brother William, Mary Laymon was Justine, Bradley Greenawald was Henry Clerval, Gordon Holleman was Walton and Tom Schumacher was the Man. Nick Muni staged the production with Terry Simpson as videographer. Larsen, who says she borrowed many ideas for the ideas from rock concerts, based it on a 1987 orchestral work, *What the Monster Saw*, which was used as a flashback scene. The opera is scored for woodwind, brass, strings, percussion, piano plus computer, synthesizer and sound system.

FRATERNITY OF DECEIT   *1998 chamber opera by Kowalski*

Wheeling and dealing relationships between three people at the office, at a hotel and at a bar in a large city. Michael Kowalski's avant-garde chamber opera *Fraternity of Deceit*, a postmodern meditation on the American way of work with libretto by the composer, was premiered by the Postindustrial Players in New York in 1998. The performers were baritone Peter Stewart as Jim, baritone Gregory Purnhagen as Sandy and soprano Karen Grahn as Linda. Francesca Vanasco played cello and Kowalski played synthesizer and designed the set.

1998 Postindustrial Players. The Postindustrial Players premiered cast recorded the opera in New York. Peter Stewart is Jim, Gregory Purnhagen is Sandy and Karen Grahn is Linda. Francesca Vanasco plays cello and Kowalski plays synthesizer. Equilibrium CD.

FREDERICK DOUGLASS (1)   *1985 opera by Moore*

Frederick Douglass (1817–1895) escapes slavery in Maryland and becomes famous as an abolitionist, orator and writer. He campaigns for Abraham Lincoln and his autobiography is widely read and quite influential. Dorothy Rudd Moore's biographical three-hour opera *Frederick Douglass*, libretto by the composer, was commissioned by Opera Ebony which premiered it in New York on June 17, 1985. James Butler played Frederick Douglass, Hilda Harris was Anna Douglass, Timothy Allen was Ned, William Drake was the Reverend Butler and Lawrence K. Bakst was the Mayor.

FREDERICK DOUGLASS (2)   *1991 opera by Kay*

Former slave and abolitionist Frederick Douglass, one of the most famous people in America after the Civil War, becomes the spokesperson for former slaves. He marries a white woman, is involved in a bank collapse and creates a diplomatic incident in Haiti. Ulysses Kay's three-act opera *Frederick Douglass*, libretto by Douglas Dorr, was premiered by New Jersey State Opera in Newark on April 14, 1991. Kevin Maynor sang the role of Frederick Douglass, Klara Barlow was his wife Helen, Ronald Daldi was his secretary Aubrey and Gregory Rahming was Douglass' son Howard. Salvatore Tagliarino designed the sets. Louis Johnson directed and Alfredo Silipigni conducted the NJSO Orchestra.

FREDRICKS, RICHARD   *American baritone (1933–)*

Richard Fredricks created the role of Captain Jason McFarland in Jack Beeson's opera LIZZIE BORDEN at New York City Opera in 1965 and is featured on the recording and video. He sings Top in Aaron Copland's 1965 recording of his opera THE TENDER LAND

and plays Horace Tabor in the 1975 NYCO telecast of Douglas Moore's THE BALLAD OF BABY DOE. He has leading roles on five of the 1962 Reader's Digest recordings of American operettas featuring opera singers: he is Schubert in Sigmund Romberg's BLOSSOM TIME, the Red Shadow in Romberg's THE DESERT SONG, Capt. Doris in Herbert's THE RED MILL, Jim Kenyon in Rudolf Friml's ROSE MARIE and Ravenal in Jerome Kern's SHOW BOAT. On stage he sang the Husband in Gian Carlo Menotti's *Amelia Goes to the Ball*, John Sorel in Menotti's *The Consul* and Charles in Douglas Moore's *Carry Nation*. Fredricks, born in Los Angeles, made his debut at New York City Opera in 1960 and became a resident member of the company.

FREEMAN, HARRY LAWRENCE   *American composer (1869–1954)*

Harry Lawrence Freeman, who wrote fourteen operas to his own librettos, was the first African American opera composer to create a substantial body of work. VOODOO, a three-act opera set in Louisiana, was the first American opera premiered on radio. It was broadcast in a 30-minute highlights version on WGBS in New York on May 20, 1928, and staged by the Negro Grand Opera Company at the 52nd Street Theater in New York on September 10, 1928, with Freeman's wife Carlotta in the leading role. *The Octaroon*, based on a novel by English novelist Mary Bradden, was broadcast on CBS Radio in 1931. Freeman, a classically trained musician, worked as an organist in his native Cleveland before moving to Denver where he was inspired to compose opera by seeing a production of Wagner's *Tannhäuser* in 1892.

His first opera was THE MARTYR, staged at the Deutsche Theater in Denver in September 1893 by the Freeman Grand Opera Company and toured to Chicago and Cleveland. His other operas include *Nada* (scenes performed by Cleveland Symphony in 1900, staged in New York in 1930), *Valdo* (staged at Weisgerber's Hall in Cleveland in May 1906), *The Tryst* (premiered by the Freeman Operatic Duo at the Crescent Theater in New York in May 1911), *Vendetta* (premiered at the Lafayette Theater in New York by the Negro Grand Opera Company on November 12, 1923) and *The Plantation* (performed in New York in 1930). Freeman's music was said to be a melodious mixture of folk, jazz, classical and choral elements but there are no recordings.

FREER, ELEANOR EVEREST   *American composer (1864–1942)*

Philadelphian Eleanor Everest Freer created the Opera in Our Language Foundation and David Bispham Memorial Medal to honor composers of American operas. She began to write operas herself after studying in Europe and eight of them were staged. *The Legend of the Piper,* libretto by the composer based on a Josephine Preston Peabody play about the pied piper of Hamelin, premiered in South Bend, Indiana, on February 24, 1925, and was awarded a Bispham Medal. *Massimiliano, the Court Jester,* libretto by Elia W. Peattie, was staged at the University of Nebraska in Lincoln on January 19, 1926. *A Christmas Tale,* based on a play by Maurice Boucher, premiered in Houston on December 27, 1929. *Frithiof,* based on a poem by Esias Tegner, was premiered in Chicago on April 11, 1929. *Joan of Arc,* about the martyred French heroine, premiered in Chicago on December 3, 1929. *A Legend of Spain,* based on a Washington Irving tale, was premiered at Marwood Studios in Milwaukee on June 19, 1931. LITTLE WOMEN, libretto by the composer based on the novel by Louisa May Alcott, was staged in Chicago in 1934. *The Brownings Go to Italy,* libretto by G. A. Hawkins-Ambler, was staged in Chicago on March 11, 1938.

FRIDA: THE STORY OF FRIDA KAHLO   *1991 opera by Rodriguez*

A collage-like musical portrait of Mexican painter Frida Kahlo (1907–1954), whose reputation has soared in recent years. Kahlo, the life companion of muralist Diego Rivera, bared her soul in paintings that reflect the damage inflicted on her body by a childhood accident. The opera traces her life from the accident through her marriage and divorce to her death. Robert X. Rodriguez's two-and-a-half-hour opera *Frida: The Story of Frida Kahlo,* libretto by Hilary Blecher with lyrics and monologues by Migdalia Cruz, premiered in 1991 at Philadelphia's American Music Theater Festival. Angelina Réaux was Frida, William Rhodes was Diego Rivera and Alba Quezada was Kahlo's sister Cristina. Andrew Jackness designed the sets, librettist Blecher directed and Ward Holmquist conducted. The production used masks, puppets, *calaveras*-style skeletons and Kahlo's paintings for atmosphere and the score included Mexican mariachi music, jazzy rhythms and quotations from classical music. *Frida* was praised by John Rockwell in *The New York Times* as "The best opera/music theater of 1991." It was reprised by Houston Grand Opera in June 1993.

1999 Voices of Change. Soprano Angelina Réaux stars as Frida Kahlo in a concert version of the opera performed by the eleven-piece Voices of Change chamber orchestra conducted by the composer. It includes 32 minutes of excerpts from the opera ranging from Frida's childhood and accident to her divorce, remarriage and death. CRI Exchange CD.

FRIEDMAN, CHARLES   *American librettist/director (1903–1984)*

Charles Friedman staged the original productions of Oscar Hammerstein's CARMEN JONES in 1943 and Kurt Weill's STREET SCENE in 1947. He also conceived, wrote and directed the lesser-known Verdi-based Broadway opera MY DARLIN' AIDA in 1952. Friedman was born in Russia but he grew up in Manhattan, and he worked in Hollywood and television as well as theater. He first became known through staging Harold Rome's ground-breaking musicals *Pins and Needles* and *Sing Out the News* in the late 1930s.

FRIML, RUDOLF   *American composer (1879–1972)*

Rudolf Friml, one of the big three American composers of European-style operettas, began his career in Prague but moved to New York in 1904. He was asked to create a comic opera for soprano Emma Trentini in 1912 after Victor Herbert refused to go on working with her. THE FIREFLY was a major hit and it made Friml famous. He continued to have success with European-style operettas like ROSE MARIE, KATINKA, THE VAGABOND KING and THE THREE MUSKETEERS but was not so successful when he tried his hand at American-style musicals. SOMETIME premiered with Mae West and Ed Wynn in the starring roles while THE WHITE EAGLE was based on the play that was filmed as *The Squaw Man*. Friml also wrote music for films when sound arrived, including Jeanette MacDonald's operetta *The Lottery Bride* and Nelson Eddy's western *Northwest Outpost*.

1920s Rudolf Friml. A compilation of recordings made in England with the London casts of Friml operettas. It includes numbers from *Rose-Marie, The Vagabond King, The Three Musketeers, The Blue Kitten* and *Katinka*. World Record Club LP. **1940 Rudolf Friml in Person.** Friml plays piano versions of songs from his operettas for an album of 12 inch 78 records titled *Rudolf Friml in Person*. It was reissued as a long-playing record album with the title *Rudolf Friml Plays His Own Unforgettable Melodies*. Decca LP.

1945 Jarmila Novotná. Friml wrote the charming song "L'Amour, Toujours L'Amour" for the 1916 stage show *The Amber Express* but it was forgotten until Jarmila Novotna revived it in 1945. It's on the album *Jarmila Novotna on Radio.* Radio Years CD. **1960 A Night with Rudolf Friml.** Earl Wrightson and Lois Hunt perform numbers from Friml operettas including *The Firefly, Rose-Marie, The Three Musketeers, The Vagabond King* and *White Eagle.* Frank DeVol conducts the orchestra. Columbia LP. **1961 Rudolf Friml Selects Personal Favorites.** Friml introduces songs from his operettas which are performed by the Singing Choraliers and Longine Symphonette. Longine Symphonette Society LP. **1964 Friml Plays Friml.** Friml and tenor Ivo Zidek perform songs from his operettas. including *The Firefly, Katinka* and *Rose-Marie,* in a recording made in Prague. Supraphon CD. **1986 Rudolf Friml: Chansonette.** Teresa Ringholz and the Eastman-Dryden Orchestra led by Donald Hunsberger perform numbers from the Friml operettas *The Firefly, The Vagabond King, Katinka, Sometime, High Jinks* and *Gloriana.* Arabesque LP/CD.

FROM THE TOWERS OF THE MOON   *1992 opera by Moran*

A girl who is actually a moon goddess is given to a childless peasant couple to heal their grief. Robert Moran's opera *From the Towers of the Moon,* libretto by John Michael LaChiusa based on a Japanese legend, premiered at Minnesota Opera on March 27, 1992. Elizabeth Comeaux was the Girl/Moon Goddess, John Andreasen was the Peasant, Miriam Langsjoen was the Peasant's Wife, Peter Halverson was the Emperor, Antonia Fusaro was the Emperor's Mother, Hugh Givens was the Minister of War and Thomas Schumacher sang the role of the Grand Consul acted by John Whittier. Derek McLane designed the sets, Nicholas Muni staged the production and Jack Gaughan conducted the orchestra.

FROST, ROBERT   *American poet (1874–1963)*

Robert Frost, the most quoted modern American poet, has inspired two operas. Nancy Hayes Van de Vate's chamber opera *The Death of the Hired Man,* based on the Frost poem, was completed in 1960. Ada Belle Gross Marcus's chamber opera *Snow* is based on the Robert Frost poem "Stopping by the Woods on a Snowy Evening." Frost, who was born in San Francisco, posed as a simple New England country tale teller but was actually one of America's most sophisticated poets.

FRY, WILLIAM HENRY   *American composer (1813–1864)*

William Henry Fry's LEONORA is considered the first American "grand" opera. Composed in the Italian continental style and based on Edward Bulwer-Lytton's play *The Lady of Lyons,* it was premiered at the New Chestnut Street Theater in Philadelphia in 1845 by the Seguin company. Fry, who was born in Philadelphia to a rich family, composed two operas before *Leonora* but there is no record of their performance. His fourth and final opera was *Notre Dame of Paris,* based on the Victor Hugo novel. It was premiered in Philadelphia on May 8, 1864, with Edward Seguin as Quasimodo and Mrs. Compte Bouchard as Esmeralda. Both operas were well received but neither entered the repertory. Little of Fry's music is available on record but there is a Naxos CD of short orchestral works, including his *Macbeth* overture and *Santa Claus* symphony.

FUGUE FOR TWO VOICES   *1975 monodrama by Constantinides*

A man has mysteriously died of poisoning in an old blind woman's house. The blind woman, Miss Ellen, tells how it happened. Her friend Celeste helps get rid of the body. A third person arrives. Dinos Constantinides' monodrama *Fugue for Two Voices,* libretto by David Madden, was premiered in Baton Rouge, Louisiana, on February 23, 1975. Miss Ellen, a soprano, is the only singer; Celeste is a speaking role.

FULL MOON IN MARCH   *1979 opera by Harbison*

A queen says she will marry any man whose song pleases her but all who try fail and are beheaded. A swineherd dares to sing for her though he feels she is cold and cruel and he is unworthy. She finds his song insulting, has him beheaded, and then dances with his head. The action is ritualistic and the music is dissonant. John Harbison's one-act opera *Full Moon in March,* libretto by the composer based on a symbolist play by William Butler Yeats, was premiered by Boston Musica Viva at the Sanders Theatre in Cambridge, MA, on April 30, 1979. D'Anna Fortunato sang the role of the Queen with David Arnold as the Swineherd, Cheryl Cobb as the First Attendant and Kim Scown as the Second Attendant. Campbell Baird designed the sets and costumes Nicolas Deutsch was stage director and Richard Pittman conducted the Boston Musica Viva chamber orchestra. *Full Moon in March* was revived in June 2003 by Opera Boston with Lorraine DiSimone as the Queen and James Maddalena as the Swineherd.

1979 Boston Music Viva. D'Anna Fortunato sings the role of the Queen with David Arnold as the Swineherd in this original cast recording of the opera by Boston Music Viva. Richard Pittman conducts the Musica Viva chamber orchestra. CRI LP

FUNDING   *2001 video opera by Rouse*

Five alienated New Yorkers find themselves left out of the economic and cultural successes of the 1990s. They had come to New York to find something they haven't found yet and we see and hear their despair and loneliness. Mikel Rouse's experimental video opera *Funding,* libretto by the composer, premiered at the Orange County Art Museum in Newport Beach, CA, on October 7, 2001. Rouse sings choral lines over complex contrapuntal imagery as the five lives are explored.

FUTRAL, ELIZABETH   *American soprano (1964–)*

Elizabeth Futral, one of the most popular American sopranos of our time, has shown a great interest in American opera and operetta. She created the role of Stella in André Previn's A STREETCAR NAMED DESIRE in San Francisco in 1998 and sang the title role in Douglas Moore's THE BALLAD OF BABY DOE for New York City Opera in 2001. She is one of the principal singers on the recording of Philip Glass's 1990 HYDROGEN JUKE-BOX. She sang Cunegonde in Leonard Bernstein's CANDIDE for Lyric Opera of Chicago and the Coloratura in Hugo Weisgall's SIX CHARACTERS IN SEARCH OF AN AUTHOR for the same company and both were recorded. She has also recorded music from Kurt Weill music theater works, including THE FIREBRAND OF FLORENCE, KNICKERBOCKER HOLIDAY, LOVE LIFE and ONE TOUCH OF VENUS, and music from Herbert/Romberg/Friml operettas, including BABETTE, EILEEN, THE FORTUNE TELLER, MLLE. MODISTE, NAUGHTY MARIETTA, THE NEW MOON and SWEETHEARTS. Futral, born in Smithfield, N.C., studied at Indiana University and began her professional career with Lyric Opera of Chicago in 1989. She has starred in a number of New York City Opera productions.

G

GABRIEL'S DAUGHTER   *2004 opera by Mollicone*

Former Kentucky slave Clara Brown leaves the South after the Civil War and goes to Colorado in 1859 during the gold rush era. She becomes a successful businessman and community leader in Central City and tries to find her lost daughter Eliza Jane from whom she was separated when they were sold at auction to different slave owners. Henry Mollicone's opera *Gabriel's Daughter*, libretto by William Luce, premiered at Central City Opera on July 12, 2003. Lori Brown Mirabal sang the role of Clara, Chad Shelton was evil Colonel Chivington who arranged the Sand Creek Massacre, Alfred Walker was civil rights pioneer Barney Ford, Raymond Diaz was Colonel Wadsworth and Christina Carr was brothel owner Jane Gordon. Michael Lasswell designed the sets, Michael Ehrman staged the production and John Moriarty conducted the Central City Opera Orchestra and Chorus.

GALILEO GALILEI (1)   *1967 opera by Laderman*

Italian astronomer Galileo is accused of heresy by the Catholic Church in 1632 for saying the earth revolves around the sun. Cardinals Barberini defends him until he becomes Pope Urban VIII when changes his mind and has Galileo condemned to prison. The trial is remembered in flashbacks by Galileo while women friends sing about their feelings. Ezra Laderman's 90-minute opera *Galileo Galilei (aka The Trails of Galileo)*, libretto by Joseph Darion, was premiered on television on May 14, 1967, in the CBS series *Look Up and Live*. Ara Berberian portrayed Galileo with David Clatworthy as Cardinal Bellarmine, Ray de Voll as the Interrogator, Joanna Simon as the Friend, Fred Mayer and Vahan Khanzadian. Bruce Minnix directed and Alfredo Antonini conducted the CBS Orchestra and Camerata Singers. The opera was staged in a revised three-act version by Tri-Cities Opera at SUNY in Binghamton, on February 3, 1979.

1967 CBS Television. Ara Berberian portrays Galileo in the CBS Television premiere of the opera commissioned by CBS and listed at the time as an oratorio. Cast and credits as above. The opera was taped at Riverside Church in New York City and telecast on May 14, 1967. Video at MTR.

GALILEO GALILEI (2)   *2002 opera by Glass*

Italian astronomer Galileo, now old and blind, remembers events from his past moving backward in time to his childhood when he saw a production of an opera by his father Vincenzo. He is recants his theory that earth revolves around the sun, is accused of heresy by the Catholic Church, discovers laws of motion, and makes his pendulum observations. Philip Glass's 90-minute opera *Galileo Galilei*, a documentary biography in ten tableaux with libretto by Mary Zimmerman, Arnold Weinstein and the composer, premiered at the Goodman Theater in Chicago on June 24, 2002. John Duykers played the older Galileo, Eugene Perry was young Galileo, Andrew Funk was the Pope, Mark Crayonton was the Inquisitor, Alicia Berneche and Elizabeth Reiter played Galileo's daughter Maria Celeste young and older, Mary Wilson was Grand Duchess Christina, Sarah Shepherd was the Scribe and Andrew McQuery was the Priest. Daniel Ostling designed the sets, Mary Zimmerman directed and Beatrice Jona Affron conducted the chamber orchestra. The opera was reprised at the Brooklyn Academy of Music in October and at the Barbican Theatre in London in November.

Soprano Mary Garden, pictured on a 1913 song sheet, created leading roles in two American operas.

GALLANTRY   *1958 opera by Moore*

A tangled tale of romantic involvements and satiric commercials in a parody of a TV soap opera. Dr. Gregg flirts with Nurse Lola who is engaged to Donald who arrives on a stretcher and asks about the doctor's wife. Douglas Moore's 35-minute opera *Gallantry*, libretto by Arnold Sundgaard, premiered at Brander Matthews Theater at Columbia University on March 19, 1958. Cecila Ward was the Announcer, David Atkinson was Dr. Gregg, Bonnie Murray was Nurse Lola and Joseph Sopher was Donald. The dancing Billy Boy Girls were Debra Joyce Herman, Reni Cooper and Paula Abrams. Don Jensen designed the sets and costumes, Day Tuttle directed and Emerson Buckley was musical director. Critics thought the opera was jazzy and tuneful and it has become popular with small opera companies.

1962 CBS Television. Martha Wright narrates the story and sings the operatic commercials in this CBS Television production. Ronald Holgate is Dr. Gregg, Laurel Hurley is Lola and Charles Anthony is Donald. Martin Carr directs, Alfredo Antonini conducts the CBS Symphony Orchestra and Jan Peerce introduces the opera in a program titled *Arias and Arabesques*. Telecast August 8, 1962. Live Opera audiocassette. **1994 New York Chamber Ensemble.**

Julia Parks is the Announcer in this recording of the opera in May 1994 made at LeFrak Concert Hall, Queens College, New York City. Richard Holmes is Dr Gregg, Margaret Bishop is Lola, and Carl Halvorson is Donald. Stephen Rogers Radcliffe conducts the New York Chamber Ensemble. It's on the album *Happy Endings: Comic Chamber Operas*. 25 minutes. Albany CD.

GALLI-CURCI, AMELITA   *Italian soprano (1882–1963)*

Legendary diva Amelita Galli-Curci, who sang opera at both Chicago and the Met in the early years of the century, also enjoyed operetta. She recorded two Victor Herbert songs for Victor Red Seal in the early 1920s, "Kiss Me Again" from MLLE. MODISTE and "A Kiss in the Dark" from ORANGE BLOSSOMS. She became so well known that pop songs were written about her including Sigmund Romberg's "Galli-Curci Rag" featured in the Broadway musical *The Passing Show of 1918*.

GAME OF CHANCE   *1957 opera by Barab*

The Representative grants three women their dearest wish but the wealth, fame and love they receive are not enough to make them happy. Even the Representative seems dissatisfied with his lot. Seymour Barab's one-act comic opera *A Game of Chance*, libretto by Evelyn Manacher, is based on the play *All on a Summer's Day* by Florence Ryerson and Colin Clements. It premiered at Augustana College in Rock Island, Illinois, on January 11, 1957.

GARDEN, MARY   *Scottish-born U.S. soprano (1874–1967)*

Legendary prima donna Mary Garden created the title role in Victor Herbert's opera NATOMA at the Metropolitan Opera in 1911 and Marguerite in Forrest Hamilton's *Camille* at Chicago Civic Opera in 1930. At the time she was considered the greatest singing actress in the world. Although she lived in America as a child, she made her opera debut in Paris in 1900. She made her American debut in 1907 in *Thais* at the Manhattan Opera House and in 1910 began a twenty-year association with Chicago Grand Opera. She was its director when Sergey Prokofiev's THE LOVE FOR THREE ORANGES was premiered in 1921 and at her insistence it was sung in French.

THE GARDEN OF MYSTERY   *1925 opera by Cadman*
See *RAPPACCINI'S DAUGHTER*

GARDEN PARTY   *2003 opera by Pinkham*

Daniel Pinkham's one-act opera *Garden Party*, libretto by the composer, was completed in 1984 but apparently first staged by Opera Boston on June 7, 2003. It is a retelling of the Garden of Eden story with Adam and Eve deciding that sin is not such a bad thing. Joe Dan Harper played Adam with Emily Browder as Eve in a production by Richard Conrad. John Finney conducted the chamber orchestra. The high point of the opera is a barbershop quartet number about reading the Bible.

THE GARDENS OF ADONIS   *1992 opera by Weisgall*

Goddess Venus falls in love with handsome mortal Adonis but Death claims him from her. Venus takes her revenge on lovers. Hugo Weisgall's opera *The Gardens of Adonis*, libretto by John Olon-Scrymgeour based on André Obey's play and Shakespeare's poem *Venus and Adonis*, was begun in 1959 but not premiered until September 12, 1992, when it was staged by Opera/Omaha in Nebraska. Melanie Helton was Venus, Jon Garrison was Adonis, Eric McCluskey was his friend Martial, Malcolm Rivers was Venus's gardener Tydeus, Kristine Jepson was Death, Jayne West was Zoë and Rebecca Privitera was Cupid. Keith Warner designed the sets and staged the opera and Hal France conducted the orchestra. The music is atonal and based on twelve-tone principles.

GARDINER, JOHN ELIOT   *English conductor (1943–)*

John Eliot Gardiner conducts the Monteverdi Choir and London Symphony Orchestra on the 1999 Best Opera Grammy recording of Igor Stravinsky's THE RAKE'S PROGRESS and the North German Radio Symphony Orchestra on Anne Sofie von Otter's 1995 album *Speak Low—Songs by Kurt Weill*. Gardiner is best known for early music and period performances of Mozart operas.

GARDNER, JAKE   *American baritone (1947–)*

Jake Gardner created the role of James Stuart in Thea Musgrave's MARY, QUEEN OF SCOTS in Edinburgh in 1977 and sings the role on the 1978 Virginia Opera recording. He created Peyton (the only singing role) in Musgrave's radio opera AN OCCURRENCE AT OWL CREEK BRIDGE for BBC in 1982 and the role of Gaxulta in Anthony Davis's science-fiction opera UNDER THE DOUBLE MOON for Opera Theater of St. Louis in 1989. He sang the role of the villain Sloane in the revised version of David Carlson's *Dreamkeepers* at Tulsa Opera in 1998. Gardner was born in Oneonta, NY, and made his debut at Houston Grand Opera in 1975.

GARRETT, LESLEY   *English soprano (1955–)*

Lesley Garrett has become one of the leading performers of American opera and operetta in England. She sang the role of the Secretary in Gian Carlo Menotti's THE CONSUL at English National Opera in 1977, the character Alsi in Philip Glass's THE MAKING OF THE REPRESENTATIVE FOR PLANET 8 at ENO in 1990 and Rose in the telecast ENO production of Kurt Weill's STREET SCENE in 1992. She usually features American arias and songs on her recital albums. On *Diva: A Soprano at the Movies* (1991), she performs arias from Oscar Hammerstein's CARMEN JONES; on *Prima Donna* (1992) she has arias from Weill's STREET SCENE, George Gershwin's PORGY AND BESS and Victor Herbert's THE ENCHANTRESS; on *Lesley Garrett, Soprano in Red* (1995) there are songs from Sigmund Romberg's NEW MOON; and on *Lesley Garrett—I Will Wait for You* (2000) she includes songs from Weill's KNICKERBOCKER HOLIDAY and Richard Rodger's CAROUSEL. Garrett was born in Yorkshire and made her debut with ENO in 1980.

GARRICK   *1937 opera by Stoessel*

Events in the life of British stage actor David Garrick (1971–1779), considered the greatest actor of his era and especially known for promoting Shakespeare's plays. Albert Stoessel's three-act biographical opera *Garrick*, libretto by Robert Simon, premiered at the Juilliard School on February 24, 1937, and was awarded the Bispham Medal as the best American opera of the year. Stoessel, who was director of the opera department at Juilliard, was also music director of Chautauqua Opera where the operas was reprised that summer.

GARRISON, JON   *American tenor (1944–)*

Jon Garrison created the role of Edmund in Stewart Copeland's HOLY BLOOD, CRESCENT MOON in Cleveland in 1988, Nicolas in Jay Reise's RASPUTIN at New York City Opera in 1988 and Adonis in Hugo Weisgall's THE GARDENS OF ADONIS FOR Opera/Omaha in Nebraska in 1992. He sings the role of Lord Darney in the 1978 Virginia Opera recording of Thea Musgrave's MARY QUEEN OF SCOTS and Tom in the 1993 Gregg Smith Singers recording of Igor Stravinsky's THE RAKE'S PROGRESS. Garrison, born in Higginsville, Missouri, made his debut at the Metropolitan Opera in 1975.

GARRISON, MABEL   *American soprano*

Metropolitan Opera soprano Mabel Garrison created the role of Chippewa maiden Alglala in Francesco DeLeone's opera *Alglala: A Romance of the Mesa* for Cleveland Grand Opera in 1923. She made early 78 recordings of songs from Victor Herbert operettas including "When You're Away" from *The Only Girl* in 1915 and "Kiss Me Again" from *Mlle. Modiste* in 1918.

GARWOOD, MARGARET   *American composer (1927–)*

Margaret Garwood composed four operas, all premiered in Pennsylvania. *The Trojan Women*, libretto by Howard Wiley based on the Euripides play, was commissioned by Suburban Opera of Chester, PA, which premiered it October 22, 1967. THE NIGHTINGALE AND THE ROSE, libretto by the composer based on the Oscar Wilde fairy tale, was premiered by Pennsylvania Opera in Chester on October 21, 1973. RAPPACCINI'S DAUGHTER, libretto by the composer based on the story by Nathaniel Hawthorne, was premiered by Pennsylvania Opera in 1983. *Joringel and the Songflowers*, libretto by the composer based on a Grimm fairytale, was premiered in Roxborough, PA, on February 25, 1987. Garwood was born in Haddonfield, NJ, and studied at the Philadelphia Music Academy. She began her music career as a pianist and teacher and began composing after marrying composer Romeo Cascarino.

GATTI-CASAZZA, GIULIO   *Italian opera impresario (1869–1940)*

Giulio Gatti-Casazza initiated the presentation of American operas at the Metropolitan Opera while he was general manager from 1908 to 1935. He began with Frederick S. Converse's THE PIPE OF DESIRE in 1910 and followed with the prize-winning world premiere of Horatio Parker's MONA in 1912. During his tenure he presented fourteen American operas at the Met and most were well received though none entered the repertory. Nevertheless the encouragement of Gatti-Casazza and the Met imprimatur was very important to the development of modern American opera and encourage recording of it. Below is a chronological list of operas presented at the Met in Gatti-Casazza's era.
1910 THE PIPE OF DESIRE (Converse). **1912** MONA (Parker). **1913** CYRANO (Damrosch). **1914** MADELEINE (Herbert). **1917** THE CANTERBURY PILGRIMS (De Koven). **1918** SHANEWIS (Cadman). **1919** THE LEGEND (Breil), THE TEMPLE DANCER (Hugo). **1920** CLEOPATRA'S NIGHT (Hadley). **1927** THE KING'S HENCHMAN (Taylor). **1931** PETER IBBETSON (Taylor). **1933** THE EMPEROR JONES (Gruenberg). **1934** MERRY MOUNT (Hanson). **1935** IN THE PASHA'S GARDEN (Seymour).

GEDDA, NICOLAI   *Swedish tenor (1925–)*

Nicolai Gedda created the role of Anatol in Samuel Barber's opera VANESSA at the Metropolitan Opera in 1958 and is featured on the recording. He sang the role of Kodana in the American premiere of Gian Carlo Menotti's THE LAST SAVAGE at the Met in 1964 and is featured on the recording. He sings Horace in the 1957 Salzburg recording of Rolf Liebermann's SCHOOL FOR WIVES and the Governor in the operatic 1989 London recording/video of Leonard Bernstein's CANDIDE. Gedda made his debut in Stockholm in 1951 and sang at the Met for 22 seasons from 1957 on.

GENTLE, ALICE   *American mezzo soprano (1889–1958)*

Metropolitan Opera mezzo soprano Alice Gentle created the lead role in the first grand opera by an American woman composer, Narcissa in Mary Carr Moore's NARCISSA: *or, The Cost of Empire* premiered in Seattle in 1912. She played Natasha in the Hollywood film of George Gershwin's "romantic opera" SONG OF THE FLAME (1930) and Mooda in the film of Herbert Stothart and Emmerich Kálmán's bizarre operetta GOLDEN DAWN (1930). Gentle made her debut at La Scala in 1916 and at the Metropolitan in 1918. She was brought to Hollywood in 1930 during the first musical boom and made her final movie appearance in *Flying Down to Rio*.

GENTLEMEN, BE SEATED!   *1963 opera/musical by Moross*

The American Civil War portrayed as a minstrel show with four dramatic sequences. "Picnic at Manassas" focuses on the Battle of Bull Run, "The Ballad of Belle Boyd" concerns an actress's experiences while touring, "Mr. Brady Takes a Photograph" is about a Civil War photographer and "Atlanta to the Sea" deals with General Sherman's army in Savannah. The sequences are interspersed with popular songs, jokes of the period and soft shoe dances. Jerome Moross's opera/musical *Gentlemen, Be Seated!*, libretto by Edward Eager, premiered at New York City Opera on October 10, 1963. Dick Shawn was Mr. Interlocutor, Avon Long was Mister Tambo, Charles Atkins was Mister Bones, Carol Brice was the Contralto, Alice Ghostly was the Comedienne, William McDonald was Johnny Reb, Richard Fredericks was Bill Yank, June Card was Southern Girl, Mary Burges was Northern Girl, Bernard Addison was Mister Banjo, Richard Krause was Character Actor, Paul Draper was Mister Taps, Charlotte Povia was Ermyntrude, David Smith was Farmer McLean and Michele Hardy was Florida Cotton. William Pitkin designed the sets, Robert Turoff directed and Emerson Buckley conducted the NYCO Orchestra.

GEORGIA   *American state (1788–)*

Atlanta Symphony Orchestra under the direction of Robert Shaw presented the premiere of a lost American masterpiece in 1972, Scott Joplin's TREEMONISHA. Georgia-born opera people include bass-baritone McHenry Boatwright (Tennielle), soprano Barbara Cook (Atlanta), composer Hall Johnson (Athens), tenor Felix Knight (Macon) and soprano Jessye Norman(Augusta) and mezzo-soprano Beverly Wolff. Operas set in Georgia include Jan Meyerowitz's THE BARRIER (1950) and Carlisle Floyd's COLD SASSY TREE (2000).

Athens: Amy M. Beach's 1932 opera CABILDO was given its belated premiere on February 27, 1945, at the University of Georgia's Opera Workshop.

Atlanta: Atlanta Opera, formed in 1979 by the merger of the Atlanta Lyric Opera and Georgia Opera, has been important in the career of composer Thomas Pasatieri, its artistic director from 1979 to 1985. His opera THE SEAGULL was the company's debut production on March 14, 1980, and his THE BLACK WIDOW was staged in 1981. The company has also staged Gian Carlo Menotti's THE CONSUL and THE MEDIUM and Robert Ward's THE CRUCIBLE. Alicia Blisa's *The Music Club* was premiered by the Contemporary Opera Company on April 22, 1966. Scott Joplin's TREEMONISHA was premiered in concert form on January 28, 1972, by the Atlanta Symphony at Morehouse College with Robert Shaw conducting an orchestration by Thomas J. Anderson.

Augusta: Jerome Moross's opera *Susannah and the Elders* was premiered by the Civic Orchestra in Augusta on January 21, 1961. Augusta Opera, started in 1967, presents American operas and operettas on a regular basis at the Imperial Community Theater. They have included Samuel Barber's A HAND OF BRIDGE, Leonard Bernstein's TROUBLE IN TAHITI, Irving Berlin's ANNIE GET YOUR

GUN, Marc Blitzstein's REGINA, Carlisle Floyd's SUSANNAH, George Gershwin's PORGY AND BESS, Gian Carlo Menotti's THE MEDIUM, THE OLD MAID AND THE THIEF and THE TELEPHONE. and Richard Rodgers' SOUTH PACIFIC.

GERRISH-JONES, ABBIE *American composer (1863–1929)*

Abbie Gerrish-Jones, one of the earliest and most active American women composers, wrote words and music for eight operas Her four-act romantic opera PRISCILLA, a story of love and witchcraft in New England, composed in 1887, is believed to be the first opera written and composed by an American woman. Her "fairy music drama" *The Snow Queen*, libretto by Gerda Wismer Hofmann based on the story by Hans Christian Anderson, was her most successful theater work. It premiered in San Francisco on February 9, 1917, with Margaret Wismer Nicholls in the leading role and ran for twelve weeks. It was then staged in Fresno, Los Angeles, Cleveland and New York. Jones' other operas include *Two Roses*, libretto by the composer based on a Grimm fairy tale; *Abon Hassan or The Sleeper Awakened*, based on an Arabian Nights tale; *The Milkman's Fair*, libretto by Pauline Turner Gregory and the composer; *The Andalusians*, libretto by Percy Friars Valentine; *Sakura-San*, libretto by Gerda Wismer Hofmann; and *The Aztec Princess*, libretto by the composer. Gerrish-Jones, who began to compose at the age of twelve, was born in Vallejo, California, and studied in Sacramento. She also worked as music critic for several California publications.

GERSHWIN, GEORGE *American composer (1898–1937)*

George Gershwin, one of America's finest music theater composers and songwriters, was involved with four "operas." First was the brief BLUE MONDAY (1922), created for a revue and almost a sketch of what was to come. Second was the "romantic opera" SONG

Self-portrait of composer George Gershwin.

OF THE FLAME (1925), really a Broadway operetta. Third was the "Jewish opera" *The Dybbuk* commissioned by the Metropolitan Opera in 1929 but never completed. Last was the magnificent PORGY AND BESS (1935), probably the greatest opera yet produced in America. Gershwin's success in importing jazz and blues idioms into other forms of music has been widely copied and his stage and film scores are among the best of their kind. Born in Brooklyn as Jacob Gershvin, he studied classical piano and harmony but soon turned to popular music and was writing hits as early as 1919. His concerto *Rhapsody in Blue* made him famous and his tone poem *An American in Paris* consolidated his reputation in the classical world. He composed 22 musical comedies and his musical satire *Of Thee I Sing* won the Pulitzer Prize in 1931. He died tragically young while working in Hollywood on the movie *The Goldwyn Follies*.

1937 George Gershwin Memorial Concert. Memorial tribute to Gershwin broadcast on CBS in September 1937, two months after the composer's death. The 2 1/2 hour broadcast includes excerpts from a variety of his compositions including shows like *Girl Crazy, Lady Be Good* and *Show Girl* with singers like Gladys Swarthout, Fred Astaire and Al Jolson; orchestral works like *Rhapsody in Blue* and the *Concerto in F* conducted by Charles Previn, Victor Young and Otto Klemperer; and the opera *Porgy and Bess* (eight numbers with Alexander Steiner conducting the Los Angeles Philharmonic Orchestra in performances by members of the original cast and Lily Pons, who sings "Summertime." Astaire gives a moving spoken tribute to Gershwin. North American Classics 2-CD set. **1938 Magic Key Program: Gems from Gershwin.** The RCA Magic Key Gershwin Memorial Program broadcast on July 10, 1938, has been released on CD as *Gems from Gershwin*. It features highlights from Gershwin's career with Nathaniel Shilkret conducting the Victor Salon Group, Jane Froman, Felix Knight and Sonny Schuyler performs numbers from *Porgy and Bess, Of Thee I Sing, Girl Crazy, Lady Be Good, Oh, Kay!* and other musicals. 42 minutes. RCA Victor CD. **1945 Rhapsody in Blue.** Robert Alda plays Gershwin in this romantic Hollywood film about the composer with Herbert Rudley playing brother Ira. The film includes scenes from *Blue Monday* and *Porgy and Bess*. Irving Rapper directed for Warner Brothers. On video. **1998 Carnegie Hall Tribute.** Gershwin's 100th birthday is celebrated at Carnegie Hall with an evening of music by the composer including excerpts from *Porgy and Bess*. The singers are Audra McDonald, Brian Stokes Mitchell and Frederica von Stade. Michael Tilson Thomas conducts the San Francisco Symphony Orchestra. Brian Large directed the 87-minute video on September 23, 1998. It was shown on PBS on September 30, 1998. **1999 Historic Gershwin.** This anthology of Gershwin recording includes the *Porgy and Bess* suite with Helen Jepson and Lawrence Tibbett, Gershwin playing *Rhapsody in Blue* and contributions from Paul Whiteman, Morton Gould and Leonard Bernstein. RCA Victor CD set. **2000 It's Wonderful: A Tribute to George Gershwin.** Barbara Hendricks pays homage to the composer on the album *It's Wonderful: A Tribute to George Gershwin* which includes numbers from *Porgy and Bess* and songs from his musicals. It was recorded in London with the Guildhall Strings and other musicians. EMI Classics CD.

GERSHWIN, IRA *American lyricist (1896–1983)*

Ira Gershwin, the lyricist for most of brother George's songs. wrote the lyrics of America's best-known opera aria, "Summertime" featured in PORGY AND BESS (1935). He also wrote lyrics for Jerome Kern, Vernon Duke, Harold Arlen and Kurt Weill, including Weill's LADY IN THE DARK (1941), THE FIREBRAND OF FLO-

RENCE (1945) and COLUMBUS (1945). Gershwin was born in New York and shared a Pulitzer Prize in 1932 for the lyrics for Gershwin's *Of Thee I Sing*. He can be heard, with Weill, singing duets from the film *Where Do We Go from Here?* on the CD *Tryout*.

GERTRUDE STEIN'S FIRST READER   *1969 revue by Sternberg with operas*

Anna Sternberg's revue *Gertrude Stein's First Reader,* based on a 1946 book by Gertrude Stein, features three mini-operas with Stein librettos, THREE SISTERS WHO ARE NOT SISTERS, IN A GARDEN and THE BLACKBERRY VINE. The revue opened off-Broadway at the Astor Place Theater in New York on December 15, 1969, in a production by Herbert Machiz. The premiere cast included Sandra Thornton. Joy Garrett, Frank Giordano, Michael Anthony and the composer who also played piano. Kendall Shaw designed the sets.

1969 Original cast album. The original Astor Place Theater cast recorded the revue at the Media Sound studio. The singers are Sandra Thornton. Joy Garrett, Frank Giordano, Michael Anthony and the composer who also plays piano. Polydor LP.

GETTY, GORDON   *American composer (1933–)*

Gordon Getty's opera PLUMP JACK, libretto by the composer based on Shakespeare' *Henry IV* and *Henry V*, was first performed at the Cathedral of St. John the Divine in New York in 1985 and has since had productions around the world. Getty, who was born in Los Angeles, is the brother of opera-loving English philanthropist Sir Paul Getty. He is also a major supporter of the arts and helped finance the recording of Jake Heggie's songs which led to his commission to write the opera *Dead Man Walking*.

GHOSTLY, ALICE   *American soprano (1926–)*

Alice Ghostly created the role of The Comedienne in Jerome Moross's GENTLEMEN, BE SEATED! at New York City Opera in 1963 and sang the role of Dinah in the first New York stage production of Leonard Bernstein's TROUBLE IN TAHITI in 1955. Ghostly, born in Eve, Missouri, is best known for her performance in the stage show *New Faces of 1952*.

THE GHOSTS OF VERSAILLES   *1991 opera by Corigliano*

The Ghosts of Versailles is set beyond time where history and theater mingle with ghosts. French playwright Beaumarchais is in love with Marie Antoinette who feels her trial and execution were unfair. Beaumarchais tries to change history by rewriting his plays but his characters will no longer take his orders. Marie Antoinette finally decides she has to accept her fate.

John Corigliano's grand opera, commissioned by the Metropolitan Opera, premiered with great success on December 19, 1991, and was telecast in 1992. William M. Hoffman's libretto borrows characters from *La mére coupable,* the third play in the Beaumarchais Figaro trilogy.

Teresa Stratas sang Marie Antoinette, Håkan Hagegård was Beaumarchais, Gino Quilico was Figaro, Marilyn Horne was Samira, Renée Fleming was Rosina, Judith Christin was Susanna, Peter Kazaras was Almaviva, Stella Zambalis was Cherubino, Tracy Dahl was Florestine, Graham Clark was the villainous Bégears, Neil Rosenshein was Leon, Richard Drews was the Marquis, James Courtney was Louis XVI, Ara Berberian was Suleyman Pasha, Wilbur Pauley was Wilhelm, Philip Cokorinos was the English Ambassador, Jane Shaulis was the Woman in a Hat, Dean Badolato was the Page and Midhat Sergabi was the Egyptian Violinist. The Gossips were sung by Betsy Norden, Kitt Reuter-Foss and Wendy Hoffman while the Ghosts were Lauren Flanigan, Sondra Kelly, Michael Best and Kevin Short.

John Conklin designed the magnificent sets and costumes, Colin Graham staged the opera with style and James Levine conducted the Metropolitan Opera Orchestra. *The Ghosts of Versailles* is a delightful mixture of Mozart, Rossini, Strauss, Turkish dance, twelve tone and sheer spectacle. It was presented in Chicago by Lyric Opera in 1995 and premiered in Europe in 1999 in a Jerome Sirlin production in Hannover, Germany.

1992 Metropolitan Opera. Teresa Stratas stars as Marie Antoinette in the Met production that was telecast September 14, 1992, on PBS. The rest of the cast is as above with Håkan Hagegård as Beaumarchais, Gino Quilico as Figaro, Marilyn Horne as Samira, Renée Fleming as Rosina, Judith Christin as Susanna, Peter Kazaras as Almaviva, Stella Zambalis as Cherubino. and Graham Clark as Bégears. Levine conducts the Metropolitan Opera Orchestra. Video director Brian Large not only captures the three-hour minute spectacle but enhances it. DG VHS/LD. **2000 Phantasmagoria.** "Phantasmagoria" is a cello and piano work based on *The Ghosts of Versailles*. It is performed by Yo-Yo Ma and Emanuel Ax on the 2000 Sony CD *Phantasmagoria* and by Norman Fischer on the 2002 Gasparo CD *Born in America 1938*.

GIANNINI, DUSOLINA   *American soprano (1902–1986)*

Dusolina Giannini created the role of Hester Prynne in her brother Vittorio Giannini's opera THE SCARLET LETTER at the Hamburg State Opera in 1938. She was born in Philadelphia, studied with Marcella Sembrich and made her debut in Hamburg in 1925. She began to sing at Metropolitan Opera in 1936 and performed there for five years.

GIANNINI, VITTORIO   *American composer (1903–1966)*

Vittorio Giannini came from a family of musicians and opera singers and his soprano sister Dusolina helped him get his first two

Composer Vittorio Giannini

operas staged. *Lucedia*, libretto by·Karl Flaster, was presented in Munich in 1934. THE SCARLET LETTER, libretto by Karl Flaster based on the Hawthorne novel, was premiered in Hamburg in 1938 with Dusolina starring as Hester Prynne. Giannini, who was born in Philadelphia and studied music in Milan and Juilliard, also wrote radio operas for CBS at this time: *Flora* (1937) was followed by BEAUTY AND THE BEAST (1938), libretto by Robert Simon, and BLENNERHASSETT (1939), libretto by Philip Roll and Norman Corwin. They were later staged. Giannini's best-known opera is THE TAMING OF THE SHREW, libretto by the composer and Dorothy Fee based on the Shakespeare play. It captured national attention when it premiered on NBC Opera Theatre in 1954. *The Harvest,* libretto by Karl Flaster about a family in the American Southwest, was staged by Chicago Lyric Opera in 1961 with Marilyn Horne as Laura. *Rehearsal Call,* libretto by F. Swann and Robert Simon, was performed at the Juilliard School in 1962. THE SERVANT OF TWO MASTERS, libretto by Bernard Stambler based on the Goldoni play, was premiered at New York City Opera in 1967. Giannini's operas are in a melodious accessible style once considered old-fashioned but now more often considered singer friendly.

GIANTS IN THE EARTH   *1949 opera by Douglas Moore*

Norwegian emigrants Per and Beret Hansa become homesteaders in unfriendly Dakota Territory in 1873 joining Norwegian friends. Per enjoys the pioneer life but Beret finds it savage and godless. She is driven to madness by the rigorous life and eventually causes her husband's death. Douglas Moore's stark three-act opera *Giants in the Earth,* libretto by Arnold Sundgaard based on the novel by O. E. Rölvaag about pioneers in South Dakota, premiered on March 28, 1951, at Columbia University in New York. Chester Ludgin was Per Hansa. The opera won the Pulitzer Prize for Music in 1951.

THE GIFT OF THE MAGI   *American operas/musicals based on O. Henry story*

Young lovers Jim and Della have no money at Christmas so they sacrifice their most precious possessions to buy each other a gift. He pawns his watch to buy combs for her glorious hair while she cuts and sells her hair to buy a chain for his watch. There are eleven American operas or music theatre pieces based on O. Henry's famous story *The Gift of the Magi*, mostly with librettos by the composers.

The earliest is Richard Adler's musical *The Gift of the Magi* presented on CBS TV in 1958. Next was Ruth Taylor Magney's *The Gift of the Magi* which premiered in Minneapolis on April 15, 1964. Don Gillis's *The Gift of the Magi* was presented at Texas Wesleyan College in Fort Worth on December 7, 1965. Joyce Barthelson's *Greenwich Village, 1910* was staged in Scarsdale, NY, in 1970. Lora Aborn's *The Gift of the Magi* premiered in Oak Park, Illinois, in 1975. Fred Tobias's musical *The Gift of the Magi* premiered on NBC television in 1978.

Peter Ekstrom's *The Gift of the Magi* was staged in Louisville, Kentucky, in 1981. Susan Bingham's *The Gift of the Magi* was presented at the Chancel Opera in 1984. Richard Earl Brown's *The Gift of the Magi*, libretto by Nancy Grobe, was completed in 1985 and Dan Welcher's *Della's Gift*, libretto by Paul Woodruff, was premiered by University of Texas Opera in Austin in 1987. David Conte's *The Gift of the Magi*, libretto by Nicholas Giardini, was presented by Conservatory Cantata Singers in 1997. Recorded and televised versions are described below.

1958 Richard Adler. Richard Adler, the composer of *Pajama Game* and *Damn Yankees*, wrote the music and lyrics for this TV musical version of the story with libretto by Wilson Lehr. Sally

Ann Howes and Gordon MacRae play the young lovers Della and Jim with a supporting cast of Allen Case, Bibi Osterwald, Howard St. Johnson and the Jersey Quartet. Eli Wallach is the narrator, George Schaefer directed for television and Hal Hasting conducted the orchestra. It was telecast by CBS December 9, 1958, and released as a record album. UA LP. **1975 Lora Aborn.** Lora Aborn's one-act opera *The Gift of the Magi* based on the story by O. Henry, premiered in Oak Park, Illinois, in 1975. **1978 Fred Tobias.** Fred Tobias's version of the story, created for NBC TV, stars Debby Boone and John Rubenstein as young lovers Della and Jim and uses a background of immigrant experience. Sidney Michaels wrote the book and Stanley Lebowsky the lyrics. It was telecast by NBC on December 21, 1978. **1981 Peter Ekstrom.** Emily Loesser and Don Stephenson star as the young lovers in this 1999 recording of Peter Ekstrom's version of the story created in 1981 for the Actors' Theatre of Louisville, Kentucky. While described as a musical,, it is virtually through sung. Pianist Albert Ahronheim orchestrated the work and leads the four-piece orchestra. It is performed every year at Christmas in Louisville. Harbinger Records CD. **1998 David Conte.** David Conte's one-act operatic version of the O. Henry story, libretto by Nicholas Giardini, was premiered and recorded by the San Francisco Conservatory New Music Ensemble conducted by Nicole Paiement. Aimée Puentes sings the role of Della, Tim Krol is Jim, Elena Bocharova is Maggie, Chad Runyon is Henry and the Magi are Brandon Smith, Aaron DiPiazza and Gary Sorenson. Arsis CD.

GILBERT, DAVID   *American conductor (1948–)*

David Gilbert has conducted the Manhattan School of Music Opera Theater Orchestra in productions and recordings of American operas. He conducted the premiere of Scott Eyerly's THE HOUSE OF THE SEVEN GABLES in 2000, a production of Dominick Argento's POSTCARD FROM MOROCCO in 1997 and a production of Ronald Perera's THE YELLOW WALLPAPER in 1992. He made a recording of William Mayer's A DEATH IN THE FAMILY in 1999 Ned Rorem's MISS JULIE in 1994 and excerpts from his own opera *The Shadowy Waters* in 1996. Gilbert, who was born in Pennsylvania, studied at the Eastman School. He is a faculty member of the Manhattan School of Music and has been music director and conductor of the Greenwich Symphony since 1975.

GILBERT, HENRY F.   *American composer (1868–1928)*

Henry F. Gilbert, the first composer to incorporate spirituals and ragtime into concert works, created an opera based on the Uncle Remus stories. *Uncle Remus*, libretto by Charles Johnston based on the stories by Joel Chandler Harris, was begun in 1906 but not finished because Harris refused to grant rights. Gilbert used it as the basis of his 1906 orchestral concert piece *Comedy Overture on Negro Themes* which made him known. *Fantasy in Delft* (1919), a one-act comic opera with a libretto by Thomas P. Robinson about two clever young women in 17th century Holland, was rejected by the Met and never performed. Gilbert, born in Somerville, MA, studied at the New England Conservatory of Music and then went to Paris to see Charpentier's opera *Louise* which made him decide to be a composer. He had one work performed at the Met, the symphonic-ballet *Dance in the Place Congo* based on a story by George W. Cable, which premiered March 23, 1918, to considerable acclaim. It is on CD.

GILFRY, RODNEY   *American baritone (1959–)*

Rodney Gilfry created the role of Stanley Kowalski in André Previn's A STREETCAR NAMED DESIRE at San Francisco in 1988 and is featured on the telecast, video and DVD. He played Curly in the Los Angeles Opera production of Richard Rodgers' *Oklahoma!* Gilfrey was born in Covina, California, began as a concert singer, first sang in San Francisco in 1995 and made his Met debut in 1996. He has specialized in Mozart roles and recorded several Mozart operas.

GILLIS, DON   *American composer (1912–1978)*

Don Gillis created seven American vernacular pop-style operas, usually with elements of whimsy, including a popular adaptation of O. Henry's THE GIFT OF THE MAGI performed in Fort Worth, Texas, in 1965. His other operas, composed to his own librettos, include *The Park Avenue Kids* staged in Elkhart, Indiana, in 1957; *Pep Rally* presented at the Interlochen Music Camp in Michigan in 1957; *The Libretto,* presented at the National Opera Convention in Dallas in 1961; and *The Legend of Star Valley Junction* performed by the Metropolitan Opera Studio in New York in 1969. Gillis, born in Cameron, Missouri, studied at Texas Christian University and North Texas State and became a producer for NBC in New York. He worked with Toscanini on his radio broadcasts and helped found the Symphony of the Air orchestra. He was involved with Interlochen Music Camp and taught at Southern Methodist, Dallas Baptist College and South Carolina University.

GIMPEL THE FOOL   *1976 opera by Schiff*

Gimpel lives in a shtetl in Eastern Europe at the turn of the century. He is a gullible fellow constantly deceived and betrayed but he accepts everything that happens with complete faith. David Schiff's operas *Gimpel the Fool,* libretto in Yiddish by Isaac Bashevis Singer based on his popular 1945 story, was created in 1976 as a vaudeville with piano accompaniment. It was revised for a klezmer-style orchestra and staged in Yiddish with English narration in New York on May 20, 1979. It was translated and performed in English in 1985. The story was the basis of a 1998 film by Eric Schwartz.

1985 Divertimento from Gimpel the Fool. Schiff created a chamber work based on his opera. *Divertimento from Gimpel the Fool* for Clarinet, Violin, Cello and Piano was recorded by Chamber Music Northwest. Delos CD.

GINASTERA, ALBERTO   *Argentine composer (1916–1983)*

Alberto Ginastera was commissioned to compose two operas by Washington and both premiered with essentially American casts and production teams. It is difficult to think of them as "American" operas but BOMARZO and BEATRIX CENCI form part of the American opera world. Ginastera, the most important modern Argentine composer, lived for various periods in the U.S. and was a permanent resident for two years in the 1940s. He first became widely known for his ballet *Estancia* commissioned by American Ballet Caravan in 1941 but not staged in Argentina until 1952. His first opera was *Don Rodrigo* which premiered in Buenos Aires in 1964. It was followed by the controversial but hugely successful *Bomarzo* in Washington in 1967 and *Beatrix Cenci* in 1971. Both were reprised by New York City Opera with similar casts. Ginastera's operas feature "sex, violence and hallucination" (his words) and take advantage of disturbing modern music techniques but they are grand in concept and fascinating to experience. All the same *Bomarzo* was initially banned in Argentina because of its "immoral" subject matter.

THE GIRL IN PINK TIGHTS   *1954 musical by Romberg*

A French ballet troupe is added to a Niblo's Garden melodrama after the Academy of Music catches fire and the dancers are left without a theater. The resulting melange, renamed *The Black Crook,* is a huge hit in 1866 and the American musical comedy is born. Sigmund Romberg's *The Girl in the Pink Tights,* lyrics by Leo Robin and libretto by Herbert Fields and Jerome Chodorov based on real events, was Romberg's last Broadway score, produced three years after his death. It opened at the Hellinger Theater in New York on March 5, 1954, with Metropolitan Opera soprano Brenda Lewis as Lotte Leslie, the producer of the melodrama, and French dancer Jeanmaire as Lisette Gervais, the star of the ballet troupe. New York City Opera tenor David Atkinson was playwright Clyde Hallam, Charles Goldner played Maestro Gallo, the head of the ballet company, and Paris Opéra Ballet star Alexander Kalioujny was Lisette's dancing partner. Agnes de Mille created the dances, Eldon Elder designed sets and lighting, Miles White created the costumes, Shepard Traube staged the production and Sylvan Levin conducted the orchestra and chorus. Lewis has good fun with the final numbers "Love is the Funniest Thing" and "The Cardinal's Guard Are We."

1954 Original Broadway Cast. Brenda Lewis stars in the original Broadway cast recording with Jeanmaire as Lisette, Charles Goldner as Maestro Gallo and David Atkinson as Clyde. Lydia Fredericks, Kalem Kermoyan and John Stamford add their support to the ensemble numbers. Sylvan Levin conducts the orchestra and chorus. Columbia LP/DRG CD.

THE GIRL OF THE GOLDEN WEST   *1938 operetta film by Romberg*

Mary, who runs the Polka Saloon in 19th-century gold-rush California, falls in love with bandit Ramerez who takes her to a dance pretending to be Lt. Johnson. He is betrayed to Sheriff Jack Rance by an old girlfriend and gets shot but Mary hides him in the loft of her cabin and plays poker with Rance for his life. When he finds out she cheated, she agrees to marry Rance if he will let Ramerez go. Rance finally realizes how much Mary loves the bandit and lets her go. Sigmund Romberg's operetta film *The Girl of the Golden West,* screenplay by Isabel Dawn and Boyce DeGaw based on David Belasco's 1905 play, has the same source as Puccini's opera *La fanciulla del West.* Jeanette MacDonald plays Mary, Nelson Eddy is Ramerez and Walter Pidgeon is Rance. None of Romberg's songs for the operetta, lyrics by Gus Kahn, became popular. Herbert Stothart conducted the music, Oliver T. Marsh photographed the film and Robert Z. Leonard directed. for MGM. On VHS/DVD.

GITECK, JANICE   *American composer (1946–)*

Janice Giteck created a series of ritual operas based on myths and tales by Native Americans of the Northwest. The "ceremonial opera" *A'Agita,* libretto by R. Gitech based on Pima and Papago Native American tales, was premiered at the Cornish Institute in Seattle, Washington, in the Spring of 1983 and performed around the world by the Port Costa Players. *Breathing Songs from a Turning Sky, Thunder Like a White Bear Dancin'* and *Callin' Home Coyote,* libretto by L. MacAdams, were performed at the Cornish Institute in Seattle in November of 1983. Her operas were featured in Paul Dresher's *Floating Opera: A Treading of Steps,* an "environmental event" performed on waterways around Seattle on September 20, 1987. Gitech, who was born in Brooklyn, studied at Mills, Antioch and the Paris Conservatoire and began to teach at the Cornish College of the Arts in Seattle in 1979. She was a founder of the Port Costa Players.

GIVE ME MY ROBE   *Soprano aria: Antony and Cleopatra (1966). Words: William Shakespeare. Music: Samuel Barber*

Leontyne Price brought down the house with her great Act 3 suicide monologue when Samuel Barber's ANTONY AND CLEOPATRA opened the new Metropolitan Opera September 16, 1966. The words are familiar from the play: "Give me my robe, put on my crown, I have immortal longings in me," and Barber's music intensifies it. Price can be seen performing it on a 1966 video about the premiere and there is a recording of the premiere at the New York Public Library for the Performing Arts. The aria was expanded into a concert scene and recorded by Price in 1968 with Thomas Schippers conducting the New Philharmonia Orchestra for her album *Barber: Two Scenes from Antony and Cleopatra*. Esther Hinds sings it on a video of 1977 telecast and the 1983 Spoleto complete recording. Catherine Malfitano sings it on a recording of the 1991 Lyric Opera of Chicago production and Carol Vaness sings it a recorded Lincoln Center gala in 1991.

"GIVE ME SOME MUSIC" *Soprano aria: Antony and Cleopatra (1966). Words: William Shakespeare. Music: Samuel Barber*

Leontyne Price introduced two great arias when Samuel Barber's ANTONY AND CLEOPATRA opened the new Metropolitan Opera on September 16, 1966. She sings "Give me some music, moody food of us that trade in love" is from Scene 3, Act 1, as Cleopatra waits with her entourage for word of Antony in Rome. Price's original stage version can be heard in a recording at the New York Public Library for the Performing Arts and she recorded a concert version with Thomas Schippers conducting the New Philharmonia Orchestra for her 1968 album *Barber: Two Scenes from Antony and Cleopatra*. Esther Hinds sings it on the 1983 Spoleto recording of the opera, Robert Alexander performs it on her 1992 album *Barber—Scenes and Arias* and Dawn Upshaw features it on her 1995 recital album *The World So Wide*.

GLANVILLE-HICKS, PEGGY *Australian American composer (1912–1990)*

Peggy Glanville-Hicks, who moved to the US in 1942 and became an American citizen in 1948, was an important contributor to American opera as critic and promoter as well as composer. She founded the Artists' Company in 1958 to produce American operas and wrote the section on American music for the fifth edition of *Grove's Dictionary of Music*. Her first major opera THE TRANSPOSED HEADS, based on a Thomas Mann story and commissioned by the Louisville Philharmonic Society, was premiered by Kentucky Opera in 1954 and recorded. THE GLITTERING GATE, a short opera based on a story by Lord Dunsany, premiered in New York in 1959. Her final operas were influenced by living in Greece. NAUSICAA, based on Robert Graves' novel *Homer's Daughter*, premiered in Athens in 1961 with Teresa Stratas in the title role. SAPPHO, written as a vehicle for Maria Callas and based on a Lawrence Durrell play, was composed in 1965 as a commission for the San Francisco Opera but has not been performed. Glanville-Hicks was born in Melbourne and studied with Fritz Hart, Vaughan Williams, Arthur Benjamin and Nadia Boulanger before settling in New York City.

GLASS, PHILIP *American composer (1937–)*

Philip Glass is America's best-known opera composer with world-wide influence. After studies at Juilliard and with Milhaud in America, Boulanger in Europe and Ravi Shankar in India, the prolific Baltimore-born minimalist formed the Philip Glass Ensemble and began to forge his unique style. After becoming a cult favorite in New York, he won international acceptance with his first opera, EINSTEIN ON THE BEACH, created with Robert Wilson and staged in 1976 at the Avignon Festival and the Met. He followed it with two other operas in what he called a "portrait trilogy." SATYAGRAHA, which focuses on Gandhi in South Africa, was premiered by Netherlands Opera in 1980. AKHNATEN, the story of the pharaoh who tried to introduce monotheism to ancient Egypt, premiered in Stuttgart in 1984. His growing popularity led the Metropolitan Opera to commission the elaborate Columbus/spaceship opera THE VOYAGE staged at the Met in 1992. He has also had success transmuting classic films by Jean Cocteau into operas with ORPHÉE (1993), LA BELLE ET LA BÊTE (1994) and LES ENFANTS TERRIBLES (1996).

Other operas and music theatre works have many admirers but have not been so popular. *Madrigal Opera* was premiered in Amsterdam in 1980 and has since emerged in many forms. THE PHOTOGRAPHER, based on the life of 19th century motion picture pioneer Eadweard Muybridge, was first staged by Netherlands Opera in 1982. THE CIVIL WARS, based around Matthew Brady's photographs of the American Civil War, had production problems but Glass's Rome section was presented by Rome Opera in 1984. THE JUNIPER TREE, a collaboration with Robert Moran based on a grim fairytale by the Brothers Grimm, was staged in Cambridge, MA, in 1985. THE FALL OF THE HOUSE OF USHER, his version of the Poe story, premiered in Cambridge in 1988.

THE MAKING OF THE REPRESENTATIVE FOR PLANET 8, a collaboration with novelist Doris Lessing based on her symbolic science-fiction novel, was presented by Houston Grand Opera in 1988. 1000 AIRPLANES ON THE ROOF, another science-fiction opera, premiered in a hangar at Vienna Airport in 1988. HYDROGEN JUKE-BOX, a collaboration with Allen Ginsberg about the "American Empire," was staged at Spoleto Festival USA in 1990. THE MARRIAGES BETWEEN ZONES THREE, FOUR AND FIVE, the second SF opera Glass created with novelist/librettist Doris Lessing, was premiered at the Theater der Stadt in Heidelberg on May 10, 1997.

WHITE RAVEN (*O Corvo Branco*), libretto by Luísa Costa Gomes about the adventures of explorers through history, premiered at the Teatro Camões in Lisbon on September 26, 1998, with

Composer Philip Glass

Dennis Russell Davies conducting, and came to New York in 2001. MONSTERS OF GRACE, a digital film opera created with Robert Wilson, was unveiled in 1998 at UCLA's Melnitz Hall in Los Angeles. IN THE PENAL COLONY, libretto by Rudolph Wurlitzer based on the Franz Kafka story and directed by JoAnne Akalaitis, premiered in September 2000 at Seattle's Falls Theatre. GALILEO GALILEI, libretto by Mary Zimmerman and Arnold Weinstein about the Italian astronomer, was premiered in Chicago in June 2002. THE SOUND OF A VOICE, two interconnected operas based on plays by David Henry Hwang, was premiered at the American Repertory Theater in Cambridge, MA, in May 2003. DRACULA, which premiered at the Brooklyn Academy of Music in 1999, is a film score composed to be played with Tod Browning's 1931 film about the famous vampire. He has also written a score for the 1916 Italian film *Cenere* starring Eleanora Duse. His many scores for contemporary films including new age works like Godfrey Reggio's *Koyaanisqatsi* (1983) and *Powaqqatsi* (1988), documentaries like *The Thin Blue Line* (1988), *A Brief History of Time* (1992) and *The Fog of War* (2003), and Hollywood movies like Martin Scorsese's *Kundun* (1997) for which he got an Oscar nomination, *The Truman Show* (1998), and *The Hours* (2002).

1976 Music with Roots in the Aether. Glass talks about his work and performs a scene from *Einstein on the Beach* and parts of *Music in 12 Parts: Part 2* with the Philip Glass Ensemble on this video made by composer Robert Ashley. **1979 Skyline: Philip Glass.** Television series portrait of the composer with excerpts from various compositions and portions of the opera *Einstein on the Beach*. Program produced by Peggy Daniel and directed by John Merl. **1983 Philip Glass: 4 American Composers.** Peter Greenaway based this film portrait of Glass around performances at London's Sadler Wells Theatre. Glass talks about his work and the Philip Glass Ensemble performs passages from *Einstein on the Beach* and *Glassworks*. Transatlantic Films/Mystic Fire VHS. **1985 Philip Glass: A Composer's Notes.** Most of the film is devoted to productions of *Akhnaten* in Stuttgart and Houston but the Spaceship episode from *Einstein on the Beach* is also performed by the Philip Glass Ensemble, Michael Blackwood directed. VAI VHS.

THE GLASS BLOWERS *1913 comic opera by Sousa*

Manhattan in 1898. Glass manufacturer Silas Pompton wants daughter Geraldine to marry the Duke of Branford while playboy Jack Bartlett is interested in Colonel Vandeveer's daughter Annabelle. All four end up in Cuba during the Spanish American War where Jack becomes a hero and everyone switches partners. John Philip Sousa's comic opera *The Glass Blowers*, libretto by Leonard Liebling, was composed in 1893 but not produced until 1913 in a revised version. After a tryout in Rochester in January 1913, it opened in New York at the Broadway Theater on March 3, 1913, renamed *The American Maid*. Louise Gunning starred as Geraldine, John Park was Jack and Charles Brown was the Duke. The operetta was successfully revived by Glimmerglass Opera in July 2000 as *The Glass Blowers* in a restored version by Jerrold Fisher and William Martin. Jennifer Dudley played Geraldine, Maria Kanyova was Annabelle Vandeveer, Jeffrey Lentz was Jack, and Richard Whitehouse was the Duke. John Conklin's sets were highly praised as was John Alden's innovative staging and John DeMain's lively conducting. It was reprised by New York City Opera in April 2002 with much the same cast but with Anna Christy as Annabelle.

1995 Keith Brion. Keith Brion conducts the Razumovsky Symphony Orchestra in music for the ballet *People Who Live in Glass Houses* from *The Glass Blowers*. It was recorded in Bratislava in 1995 for the American Classics album *John Philips Sousa On Stage*. Naxos CD.

GLEASON, FREDERIC GRANT   *American composer (1848–1903)*

Frederick Grant Gleason wrote two grand operas in the Wagnerian mode and one was performed. The three-act *Otho Visconti*, libretto by the composer about the Milanese duke, was completed in 1877; its overture was performed in Leipzig in 1892 and the complete opera was staged in 1907 at the College Theater in Chicago. *Montezuma* (1885), libretto by the composer about the Aztec leader, has not been staged though title and subject matter were used by Roger Sessions for a 1964 opera. Gleason, whose work was championed by conductor Theodore Thomas, was born in Middletown, Connecticut, and studied in Germany and England. He returned to the US. to teach and run the Chicago Conservatory work and had considerable influence as a music critic and editor.

"GLITTER AND BE GAY"   *Soprano aria: Candide (1956). Words: Richard Wilbur. Music: Leonard Bernstein*

Cunegonde's aria "Glitter and Be Gay," a sparkling homage to 19th century coloratura arias, is sung by a once virginal heroine who is now making a good living by sleeping with wealthy men in Paris. She starts out singing about her shame but gradually becomes deliriously happy thinking of the money she's earned. The aria was created for the operatic operetta *Candide* with music by Leonard Bernstein and lyrics by Richard Wilbur. Sopranos enjoy demonstrating their skill with the dazzling pyrotechnics of the aria which is sometimes compared to *Faust*'s "Jewel Song" but is stylistically more like *La Traviata*'s "Sempre Libera," On the original Broadway cast album, it is sung by Barbara Cook. On subsequent cast albums it is performed by Maureen Brennan, Erie Mills, June Anderson, Elizabeth Futral, Marilyn Hill Smith, Harolyn Blackwell and Alex Kelly. It is featured on many recital discs. Tracy Dahl made it the title number of her album *Glitter and Be Gay*, Dawn Upshaw sings it on her collection *I Wish It So*, Renée Fleming performs it on *I Want Magic*, Sumi Jo features it on her album *Virtuoso Arias*, Harolyn Blackwell includes it on her album *Blackwell Sings Bernstein*, Kathleen Battle performs it on a recital album and Roberta Peters sings it on the 1963 album *Alfred Drake and Roberta Peters Sing the Popular Music of Leonard Bernstein*. Broadway favorite Kristin Chenoweth sang it in a 2004 production at Avery Fisher Hall.

THE GLITTERING GATE   *1959 opera by Glanville-Hicks*

Burglars Bill and Jim decide to break open the Gates of Heaven to see mother and girlfriend. Using their trusty "Old Nutcracker" they finally get in but discover nothing but empty space. There is no heaven. Peggy Glanville-Hicks one-act opera *The Glittering Gate*, libretto by the composer based on a story by Lord Dunsany, was premiered at the 92nd Street YMCA in New York on May 14, 1959. Robert Price sang Bill and David Smith was Jim. James Price staged the opera, Robert Mitchell designed it and Newell Jenkins conducted. This unusual chamber orchestra requires a glockenspiel and an electronic tape of "unearthly laughter."

GLUCK, ALMA   *Romanian-born American soprano (1884–1938)*

Diva Alma Gluck, one of the operatic legends of the early years of the century, made a recording of an aria from an American opera. She recorded Barbara's aria "I List the Trill in Golden Throat" from Victor Herbert's NATOMA for Victor in 1912 and it is available on CD. Gluck, who was born in Bucharest, came to the U.S. as a child and was one of the glories of the Metropolitan Opera from 1909 to 1918.

THE GOATHERD AND THE GOBLIN   *1947 opera by Smith*

Julia Smith's one-act opera *The Goatherd and the Goblin*, libretto by Josephine F. Roule based on a play by C. D. Mackay, premiered on radio on February 22, 1947, when it was broadcast by WNYC for the Mutual Broadcasting System. It was staged with piano accompaniment at Buell Hall in New London, CT, on November 10, 1949, and with full orchestra at the Julius Hartt School of Music in Hartford on November 28, 1949.

GOEKE, LEO
American tenor (1936–)

Leo Goeke sings Tom on the 1977 Glyndebourne Festival video of Igor Stravinsky's THE RAKE'S PROGRESS and Ghandi in the 1982 Stuttgart Opera telecast and video of Philip Glass's SATYAGRAHA. Goeke was born in Kirksville, Missouri, studied in Missouri, Louisiana and Iowa and made his debut at the Met in 1971.

THE GOLDEN APPLE   *1954 comic opera by Moross*

Incidents from *The Iliad* and *The Odyssey* transposed to a small town in the state of Washington at the beginning of the 20th century. Helen is the floozy wife of Sheriff Menelaus and Paris is a traveling salesman who takes her off to the big city of Rhododendron on a hot-air balloon. Ulysses, a soldier back from the Spanish American War, gets an army together to rescue her and the Gods behave like meddling villagers. Jerome Morass's two-act comic opera *The Golden Apple*, libretto by John Latouche, opened in New York at the Phoenix Theater on March 11, 1954.

Kaye Ballard played Helen, Jonathan Lucas was Paris, Dean Michener was Menelaus, Stephen Douglass was Ulysses, Priscilla Gillette was Penelope, Jack Whiting was Hector and Charybdis, Bibi Osterwald was matchmaker Lovey Mars, Portia Nelson was schoolmarm Minerva Oliver, Martha Larrimore was the mystic Mother Hare, Hanya Holm staged the musical numbers, William and Jean Eckart designed the sets, Norman Lloyd was director and Hugh Ross was musical director. The opera, though sometimes called a musical, is through-sung even though it incorporates marches, folk tunes and music hall numbers in its comic pastiche. The most popular aria is Helen's easy-going "Lazy Afternoon" introduced by Ballard The opera was reprised by Oklahoma Symphony Orchestra in 1976 and by New York University Opera Theater in 1988 and 1990.

1954 Original cast. This original cast recorded highlights from the opera with narration by Jack Whiting. Kaye Ballard is Helen, Priscilla Gillette is Penelope, Stephen Douglass is Ulysses, Jack Whiting is Hector and Charybdis, Jonathan Lucas is Paris, Bibi Osterwald is Lovey Mars and Portia Nelson is Minerva. Hugh Ross conducts. RCA LP/CD. **1984 Richard Rodney Bennett.** Richard Rodney Bennett sings and plays "Lazy Afternoon" and "It's the Going Home Together" from *The Golden Apple* on the recital album *Take Love Easy: The Lyrics of John Latouche.* Audiophile LP/CD. **1985 Barbra Streisand.** Barbra Streisand features *The Golden Apple* song "Lazy Afternoon" on her album *Lazy Afternoon.* Sony CD. **2000 Eddie Korbich/Jerry Dixon.** Eddie Korbich and Jerry Dixon perform "Nothing Ever Happens in Angel Roost" and "Lazy Afternoon" from *The Golden Apple* in the off-Broadway revue *Taking a Chance on Love.* The show is based around the lyrics of John Latouche. Original Cast Records CD.

GOLDEN CHILD   *1960 opera by Bezanson*

Christmas Eve, 1849, at Sutter's Fort in California during the gold rush. A pregnant woman, Martha, arrives in a covered wagon with her husband and daughter while the drunken miners celebrate. Captain Sutter protects the family from the hostile miners and the birth of a baby boy creates new harmony. Philip Bezanson's 60-minute opera *Golden Child*, libretto by Paul Engle, was telecast December 16, 1960, on the *Hallmark Hall of Fame* series. Jerome Hines was Captain Sutter, Patricia Neway was Martha, Brenda Lewis was Sara, Stephen Douglass was Martin and Patrica Brooks was Annabelle. Warren Clymer designed the set, Peter Herman Adler was the musical director, Robert Hartung was the TV director and Herman Grossman conducted the orchestra. *Golden Child*, based on Bezanson's earlier opera *Western Child* staged at Iowa State University on July 28, 1959, was publicized as an "original Christmas folk opera."

1960 NBC Television. Jerome Hines sings the role of Captain Sutter with Patricia Neway as Martha in the NBC television premiere on December 16, 1960. The rest of the cast as above with Herman Grossman as the conductor. Video at MTR.

GOLDEN DAWN   *1927 operetta by Stothart and Kálmán*

Dawn, a blonde who believes she is an African princess, falls in love with British officer Steve held prisoner by Germans is East Africa during World War I. A jealous overseer causes problems but finally has to confess that Dawn in a white woman. Herbert Stothart and Emmerich Kálmán's bizarre operetta *Golden Dawn*, libretto by Oscar Hammerstein II and Otto Harbach, opened on Broadway at the Hammerstein Theater on November 30, 1927. Louise Hunter played Dawn, Paul Gregory was Steve, Robert Chisholm was the overseer Shep. Joseph Urban designed the sets, Arthur Hammerstein produced, Reginald Hammerstein directed and Stothart conducted. This Hammerstein family show was a rather dubious achievement. Although the setting is Africa, the music was Viennese. white actors played the Africans and the hit song was a hymn to a whip sung by the black overseer. The score was liked so the operetta ran for half a year and was filmed. The film version, needless to say, is a cult classic.

1928/1930 Whip Song. The only recordings of the operetta were of the evil overseer's bizarre "Whip Song." Robert Chisholm of the original cast recorded it for Brunswick in 1928 and Noah Beery recorded it for Brunswick in 1930. **1930 Warner Bros. film.** Some critics consider this the most offensive operetta film ever made. Metropolitan Opera mezzo-soprano Alice Gentle portrays Mooda, the African woman who rears Dawn, and sings two songs rather well. Broadway star Vivienne Segal does her best with the embarrassing heroine sarong role, Walter Woolf copes bravely with the British officer hero role and Noah Beery (in unconvincing blackface) is the villainous hammy overseer who sings the unbelievable whip song. Ray Enright directed for Warner Brothers in two-color Technicolor but the version on laserdisc is in black and white. Warner LD.

THE GOLDEN LION   *1959 opera by Kechley*

Political intrigue in the Eastern Roman Empire in the 9th century as factions struggle to control choice of a new Empress. Emperor Theophilus at first favors beautiful young Casia, the candidate of the Patriarch, but eventually chooses Theodora after manipulations by the monk Amos. After further changes and developments, the Emperor decides Theodora really is the best choice. Gerald Kechley's two-act opera *The Golden Lion*, libretto by Elwyn Kechley, was premiered at the University of Washington in Seattle on April 28, 1959, and reprised there in 1968.

GOLDENTHAL, ELLIOT *American composer (1954–)*

Composer Elliot Goldenthal and producer/librettist Julie Taymor (who staged Disney's *The Lion King*), collaborated on two innovative music theater works. *The Transposed Heads* (1986), libretto by Taymor and Sidney Goldfarb, was based on the Thomas Mann novel also turned into an opera by Glanville-Hicks. Next was the Obie-winning theatrical oratorio JUAN DARIEN: A CARNIVAL MASS premiered in New York in 1988 and revived at Lincoln Center in 1996. Goldenthal's large-scale oratorio FIRE WATER PAPER: A VIETNAM ORATORIO, libretto by the composer, was premiered by the Pacific Symphony Orchestra in 1996. Goldenthal, born in Brooklyn, has also written for ballet, the concert stage and film including Hollywood movies like *Batman Forever.*

GOLDMAN, WILLIAM *American novelist/screenwriter (1931–)*

William Goldman's novel *No Way to Treat a Lady*, filmed in 1967 with Rod Steiger, was turned into an opera by Douglas Cohen that premiered at the Hudson Guild Theater in New York on June 11, 1987. Goldman, who wrote the screenplays for such notable films as *All the President's Men* and *Butch Cassidy and the Sundance Kid*, is most famous for his dictum on the Hollywood film business: "Nobody knows anything."

GOLDSTEIN, LEE *American composer (1952–1990)*

Lee Goldstein, a native of Woodbury, NJ, and composer-in-residence at Lyric Opera of Chicago in 1987–1988, composed three operas in his short career. First was the one-act *An Idiot Dance*, libretto by the composer, presented at Baldwin-Wallace College in Ohio in 1976. *Marian and the Angel of Death*, libretto by the composer, was first performed in 1984. Goldstein's biggest success was THE FAN, libretto by Charles Kondek based on the Italian play by Carlo Goldoni, which was premiered by Lyric Opera of Chicago in 1989.

THE GOLEM *American operas based on Jewish legend*

A mystical rabbi living in medieval Prague creates a giant creature from clay to protect the Jewish people. The Golem becomes the Rabbi's servant but eventually become uncontrollable and wreaks havoc. The legend is based on folklore about Rabbi Lowe, said to have created the Golem in 1580.

1957 Lazar Weiner. Lazar Weiner's *The Golem*, libretto by R. Smolover, was premiered at the Jewish Community Center in White Plains, NY, on January 13, 1957, and reprised in New York City at the 92nd Street Y in 1981. Weiner was a specialist in Jewish and Yiddish music and lore. **1961 Abraham Ellstein.** Abraham Ellstein's *The Golem*, libretto by Sylvia Regan and the composer, previewed in Boston in November 1961 and was premiered by New York City Opera on March 22, 1962. Chester Ludgin was the Golem, Jon Crain was Rabbi Levi, Lee Venora was his daughter Deborah, William Dupree was Yacov, Dominic Cossa was Isaac, Gladys Kriese was the Rabbi's wife, Maurice Stern was Tanchumm David Bender was Tadeus' Man 1, Ron Bottcher was Tadeus' Man 2 and Ara Berberian was Citizen 2. Allan Fletcher staged the opera, Lester Polakov designed the sets and Julius Rudel conducted the NYCO Orchestra. **1989 Richard Teitelbaum.** Richard Teitelbaum's interactive electronic opera *Golem*, libretto by the composer, was premiered by the Heritage Chamber Orchestra in New York on March 14, 1989. Teitelbaum says he became interested in the legend of the Golem while visiting the tomb of Rabbi Lowe in Prague in 1984. A recording of a performance in Amsterdam, Holland, was made on February 24, 1994. The performers are Shelley Hirsch (voice), David Moss (voice/percussion/electronics), Richard Teitelbaum (synthesizer keyboard/interactive computer), Carlos Zingaro (violin/electronics) and George Lewis (trombone/computer/electronics). Videos, visuals, slides and projections were designed by Ben Rubin, Fred Pommerehn and Cecile Bouchier. Tzadik CD.

GONDEK, JULIANA *American soprano (1967–)*

Juliana Gondek has created roles in four modern American operas and sung in several others. She sang Diane Feinstein in Stewart Wallace's HARVEY MILK at Houston Grand Opera in 1995 and on the San Francisco Opera recording, Ela in David Carlson's DREAMKEEPERS at Utah Opera in 1996, Hedda Hopper in Stewart Wallace's HOPPER'S WIFE at Long Beach Opera in 1997 and Gertrude Stein in Jonathan Sheffer's BLOOD ON THE DINING ROOM FLOOR at the Guggenheim Museum in New York in 2000. She previewed arias from David Diamond's new opera *The Noblest Game* in Seattle and NYCO in 1998 and 1999 and has sung on stage as Pat Nixon in NIXON IN CHINA, Paquette in CANDIDE, Dede in A QUITE PLACE and Marsinah in KISMET. She was Teresa Stratas cover as Marie Antoinette in the premiere of The Ghosts of Versailles at the Met in 1992. Gondek, who was born in Pasadena, CA, studied at USC in Los Angeles.

THE GOOD SOLDIER SCHWEIK *1958 opera by Kurka*

Joseph Schweik, a good-hearted but simple-minded Czech, gets caught up in the madness of World War I. After a series of misadventures, including a stay in an insane asylum, he ends up at the front where he abandons his gun and heads the other way. Robert Kurka's two-act opera *The Good Soldier Schweik*, libretto by Lewis Allan based on Czech writer Jaroslav Hašek's anti-war novel, premiered at New York City Opera on April 23, 1958. Norman Kelley was Joseph Schweik, Mary LeSawyer was Mrs. Muller, David Atkinson was Lt. Lukash, Chester Watson was Palivec/General von Schwarzburg, Jack DeLon was Bretschneider/Army Chaplain, Chester Ludgin was Psychiatrist/Doctor/Voditchka, Emile Renan was Army Doctor, Naomi Collier was Mme. Kakonyi and Helen Baisley was Katy Wendler. Andreas Nomikos designed the sets, Carmen Capalbo was stage director and Julius Rudel was the conductor. Kurka was primarily an orchestral composer but the success of his 1956 suite *The Good Soldier Schweik* convinced him to turn it into an opera. Kurka died before finishing the orchestration completed by Hershy Kay. The opera, somewhat in the *Threepenny Opera* style with plentiful use of popular music and Czech folk melodies, was very well received by audiences and critics and continues to be performed around the world. It was staged by Walter Felsenstein at Komische Oper in East Berlin with Werner Enders as the anti-hero, telecast by ZDF in Germany in 1963, produced and recorded by Chicago Opera Theater in 2001 and staged by Glimmerglass Opera in 2003 with Anthony Dean Griffey as Schweik and Rhoda Levine directing.

2001 Chicago Opera Theater. Alexander Platt conducts the Chicago Opera Theater Ensemble in a recording based on a Chicago Opera Theater production. Jason Collins is Schweik, Marce Embree is Lt. Lukash, Army Doctor and Gentleman of Bohemia, Kelli Harrington is Mrs. Muller and Kathy, Buffy Baggott is Baroness von Botzenheim and Mme. Kakonyi, Timothy Sharp is Palivec and Voditchka, Mark Calvert is Psychiatrist 1 and Chaplin, Wayne Alan Behr is Bretschneider, Vanek and Malingerer 1, Robert Boldin is Doctor 1, Malingerer 2 and Dog, Stephen Noon is Mr., Wendler, Guard, Sergeant and Mr. Kakonyi, Aaron Judisch is Psychiatrist 2 and Doctor 2, Christian Elser is General von

Schwarzburg and Malingerer 3, Alvaro Ramirez is Police Officer, Psychiatrist 3, Malingerer 4 and Colonel von Zillergut. 104 minutes. Cedille 2-CD set. **Good Soldier Schweik Suite.** There are four CD versions of *The Good Soldier Schweik* Suite, the 20-minute prototype for the opera. They are performed by the Louisville Orchestra with Robert Whitney conducting (Albany CD), Westchester Symphony Orchestra with Siegfried Landau conducting (Allegretto CD), Cincinnati College Conservatory of Music Wind Symphony with Eugene Corporan conducting (Klavier CD) and Atlantic Sinfonietta with Andrew Schenck conducting (Koch Classics CD).

GOODMAN, ALICE   *American librettist/poet*

Alice Goodman essentially created what became known as the "CNN opera" based on recent historical events. She wrote the librettos for John Adams most successful operas, NIXON IN CHINA (1987) and THE DEATH OF KLINGHOFFER (1991). While the concept was producer Peter Sellars (he originally asked for "rhyming couplets"), it was Goodman who turned headlines into operatic poetry by forging two of the most notable librettos in modern American opera.

THE GOOSE GIRL   *1981 opera by Pasatieri*

A Princess is tricked by her maid on her way to wed a Prince and forced to switch places. She becomes a goose girl in the castle of the Prince but eventually all is revealed and she is restored to glory. Thomas Pasatieri's children's opera *The Goose Girl,* libretto by the composer based on a fairytale by the Grimm brothers, was premiered by Fort Worth Opera on February 15, 1981. Maryanne Telese played the Goose Girl, Karl Dent was goose boy Conrad and Sue Burrato was the maid. Fritz Berens conducted. The Goose Girl's aria "Bubbles, beautiful bubbles" has become a popular recital piece for sopranos.

1982 Fort Worth Opera. The Fort Worth Opera premiere on February 15, 1981, was recorded live. Maryanne Telese is the Goose Girl, Karl Dent is Conrad, the goose boy and Sue Burrato is the maid. Fritz Berens conducts. Live Opera audiocassette.

Jason Collin as Schweik in Chicago Opera Theater's 2001 production of *The Good Soldier Schweik.* Photograph by Liz Lauren, courtesy of Chicago Opera Theater.

GORIN, IGOR   *Ukrainian-born American baritone (1908–1982)*

Igor Gorin recorded a number of songs from American operettas. After making his debut at the Vienna Volksoper in 1930, he emigrated to the U.S. in 1933, began to sing on radio and played an operatic barber in the 1937 MGM movie *Broadway Melody of 1938.* He sings songs from Sigmund Romberg's THE STUDENT PRINCE with Jan Peerce on a recorded 1940 radio broadcast, "Song of the Flame" from George Gershwin's SONG OF THE FLAME and "March of the Musketeers" from Rudolf Friml's THE THREE MUSKETEERS on a 1951 Voice of Firestone telecast now on video and "Thine Alone" from Victor Herbert's EILEEN on a 1954 recording. He was a regular guest on the *Voice of Firestone* opera TV series in the 1950, starred in NBC Opera Theatre productions and made his debut at the Met in 1964.

THE GOSPEL AT COLONUS   *1983 oratorio by Telson*

The story of Oedipus and his suffering retold as an oratorio in a Black Pentecostal church with actors, gospel groups and gospel chorus. After years of wandering with daughter Antigone, Oedipus finds death and redemption in Colonus. Bob Telson's *The Gospel at Colonus,* conception and libretto by Lee Breuer based on Sophocles' play *Oedipus at Colonus,* premiered at the Brooklyn Academy of Music on November 8, 1983. Gospel singer Clarence Fountain (who inspired the work) played Oedipus, Morgan Freeman was the Minister and Messenger, Isabell Monk was Antigone, Jevetta Steele was Ismene, Robert Earl Jones was King Creon, Carl Lumbley was Theseus, Kevin Davis was Polynices and the gospel groups were the Five Blind Boys of Alabama, J. J. Farley and the Original Soul Stirrers, the J. D. Steele Singers, the Colonus Messengers and Wesley Boyd's Gospel Music Workshop Choir. Breuer staged the production which toured around the world.

1985 American Music Theater Festival. *The Gospel at Colonus* was staged by Breuer at the American Music Theater Festival in Philadelphia in 1985 where it was videotaped and recorded. The featured performers are Clarence Fountain and the Five Blind Boys of Alabama, Morgan Freeman, Isabell Monk, Carl Lumbley, Carl Williams Jr., Robert Earl Jones, Kevin Davis. J. J. Farley and the Original Soul Stirrers, the J. D. Steele Singers with Jevetta Steele, Kevin Davis Sam Butler, Martin Jacob, Carolyn Johnson-White and Willie Rogers. Kirk Browning directed the video telecast in the PBS *Great Performances* series on November 8, 1985. Warner's Home Video and WB LP/Electra CD.

GOTTSCHALK, LOUIS MOREAU
American composer/pianist (1829–1969)

New Orleans-born Creole composer/pianist Louis Gottschalk studied in Paris with Hector Berlioz and became very popular touring and performing the 300 piano pieces he composed. He also wrote four little-known operas: *Isaura di Salerno* (1859), *Charles IX* (1860), *Amalia Warden* (1860) and *Escenas Campestres* (1860). The one-act *Escenas Campestres,* libretto by M. Ramirez about rural life in Cuba, premiered in the Teatro de Tacon in Havana on February 17, 1860, and was presented in New York in 1869. Excerpts from it titled "Cuban Country scenes") are includes on the album *A Gottschalk Festival.* Jose Alberto Esteves, Pablo Garcia and Trinidad Panigua are the performers and Igor Buketoff conducts the Vienna State Orchestra. VoxBox CD.

GOYA   *1986 opera by Menotti*

Spanish painter Francisco Goya (1746–1828) has difficulties in his relationships with the Duchess of Alba and the Queen of Spain who are vicious rivals. Gian Carlo Menotti's three-act opera *Goya*, libretto by the composer, was created for Placido Domingo and Washington Opera and premiered at the Kennedy Center. November 15, 1986. Domingo was Goya, Victoria Vergara was the Duchess of Alba, Karen Huffstodt was the Queen of Spain, Howard Bender was Prime Minister Godoy, Louis Otey was Martin and Suzanna Guzmán was Leocadia. Baayark Lee did the choreography, Pasquale Grossi designed the sets and costumes, Menotti directed and Rafael Frühbeck de Burgos conducted. *Goya* attracted national attention to Washington Opera and was the first to be telecast from the Kennedy Center. It was received politely by the premiere audience but was a critical failure and no further productions were planned. Menotti later revised the opera and relaunched it at the Spoleto Festival in 1991.

1986 Washington Opera. Placido Domingo stars as Goya in this televised Washington Opera production with the premiere cast at the Kennedy Center. Karen Huffstodt is the Queen of Spain, Victoria Vergara is the Duchess of Alba and Raphael Frühbeck de Burgos conducts. Kirk Browning directed the 129-minute telecast on PBS on November 28, 1986. House of Opera VHS/DVD. **1991 Spoleto Festival.** Cesar Hernandez stars as Goya in a live recording of the opera made in June/July 1991 at the Teatro Nuovo in Spoleto, Italy. Suzanna Guzmán is the Duchess of Alba, Penelope Daner is the Queen of Spain, Andrew Wentzel is Manuel Godoy, Howard Bender is the King of Spain, Boaz Senator is Martin Zapater, Karen Nickell is Leocadia, Daniele Tonini is Oste, Angela Adams is the Maid and Dominic Inferrera is the Major-Domo. Steven Mercurio conducts the Spoleto Festival Orchestra and Westminster Choir. Nuevo Era 2-CD set.

GRAHAM, COLIN   *English director/librettist (1931–)*

Colin Graham has written librettos for two American operas and directed premieres of seven. He wrote the libretto for Stephen Paulus's THE POSTMAN ALWAYS RINGS TWICE and staged it for Opera Theater of St. Louis in 1982. He wrote the libretto for Paulus's THE WOODLANDERS which he staged for Opera Theater of St. Louis in 1986. He also staged the premiere of Paulus' THE WOMAN AT OTOWI CROSSING for Opera Theater of St. Louis in 1995 but did not write its libretto. He directed the premieres of Thea Musgrave's MARY QUEEN OF SCOTS for Scottish Opera in 1977, John Corigliano's THE GHOSTS OF VERSAILLES for Metropolitan Opera in 1991, Conrad Susa's THE DANGEROUS LIAISONS for San Francisco Opera in 1994 and Bright Sheng's THE SONG OF MAJNUN for Lyric Opera of Chicago in 1997. Graham, who made his debut as director at Aldeburgh in 1958, now lives in the U.S. and was appointed artistic director of Opera Theater of St. Louis in 1978.

GRAHAM, SHIRLEY DUBOIS   *American composer (1906–1977)*

Placido Domingo starred in Washington Opera's 1986 premiere of Gian Carlo Menotti's opera *Goya*.

Shirley Graham appears to have been the first African American woman to have a dramatic opera produced on stage. Her grandiose three-act pageant opera TOM-TOM, libretto by the composer based on her one-act play, was previewed in excerpt form on NBC radio on June 26, 1932, and premiered on stage by the Cleveland Opera Company at Cleveland Stadium on June 30, 1932. It was a massive production requiring 500 singers, dancers and musicians and starred Jules Bledsoe, who had created Joe in *Show Boat.* Graham also composed an opera for children, a musical version of Helen Bannerman's story *Little Black Sambo* (1937), as well as the once popular *The Swing Mikado* (1938), based on the Gilbert and Sullivan operetta. She wrote many plays including *It's Morning,* directed by Otto Preminger at Yale in 1940, and *Track Thirteen,* produced on Yale's radio station the same years. She is best-known, however, for writing biographies of thirteen famous African Americans, most famously that of Paul Robeson. Graham, born in Indianapolis, Indiana, studied at the Sorbonne in Paris, where she learned about African music, and at Oberlin College and Yale. She headed the Negro unit of the Federal Theatre Project in Chicago in the late 1930s. In 1951 she married W. E. B. Dubois, author of *The Souls of Black Folk* and co-founder of the NAACP.

GRAHAM, SUSAN   *American mezzo-soprano (1960–)*

Susan Graham created major roles in three of the most notable modern American operas. She played Jordan in John Harbison's F. Scott Fitzgerald opera *The Great Gatsby* at the Metropolitan Opera in 1999, Sister Helen Prejean in Jake Heggie's first opera *Dead Man Walking* at San Francisco Opera in 2000, and Sondra in Tobias Picker's *An American Tragedy* at the Met in 2005.

Graham studied at Texas Tech University and Manhattan School of Music and won 9 Met Opera Auditions.

GRAMM, DONALD   *American bass-baritone (1927–1983)*

Donald Gramm created the lead role of Podkolyossin in Bohuslav Martinů's television opera THE MARRIAGE on NBC Opera Theater in 1953 and the role of the valet John in Ned Rorem's MISS JULIE at New York City Opera on November 4, 1965. He played Hortensio in Vittorio Giannini's THE TAMING OF THE SHREW on NBC Opera Theatre in 1954 and the older Diaz in the American premiere of Roger Sessions' MONTEZUMA at Boston Opera Company in 1976. Gramm, born in Milwaukee, Wisconsin, made his debut at the age of 17 in Chicago. He joined New York City Opera in 1952 and began working regularly with Sara Caldwell's Opera Company of Boston in 1958.

LA GRANDE BRETÈCHE   *American operas based on Balzac story*

"La Grande Bretèche" is a mansion in the Loire Valley, site of a drama of intense jealousy in a story by the French writer Honoré Balzac. A husband believes his wife's lover is hiding in a closet which he has walled up as she watches. When she attempts to free the lover, the husband kills her. Balzac's grim story, published in 1832, has been the basis of five operas, three of them by Americans.

1954 Boris Koutzen. Boris Koutzen's opera *The Fatal Oath,* libretto by the composer based on Balzac's *La Grande Bretèche,* was premiered at Hunter College in New York City on May 25, 1955. **1956 Avery Claflin.** Avery Claflin's one-act radio opera *La Grande Bretèche,* libretto by George R. Mills based on the Balzac story, was composed in 1947, recorded in 1956 and premiered on CBS Radio on February 3, 1957. Patricia Brinton is the Wife, Richard Owens is the Husband, William Blankenship is the Lover, Sheila Jones is the Maid, Earl Gilmore is Pierre and Werner Harms, Karis Nurmala and Eugene Hartzell are the Male Trio. F. Charles Adler conducts the Vienna Orchestra. Claflin's opera was recorded at the Columbia Studio in Vienna, Austria, in January 1956. This was the version broadcast on CBS in 1957 with Patricia Brinton as the Wife, Richard Owens as the Husband and William Blankenship as the Lover. F. Charles Adler conducts the Vienna Orchestra. CRI LP. **1957 Stanley Hollingsworth.** Stanley Hollingsworth's 45-minute opera *La Grande Bretèche,* libretto by Harry Duncan and the composer based on the Balzac story, was commissioned by NBC Opera Theatre which telecast it February 10, 1957. Gloria Lane is wife Countess Marie, Hugh Thompson is husband Count Robert, Davis Cunningham is the Spanish prisoner who loves the countess, Adelaide Bishop is the maid and Kimi Beni is handyman Gorenflot. Samuel Chotzinoff produced, John Schwartz directed and Gerald Ritholz designed the sets. Samuel Chotzinoff produced, Peter Herman Adler conducts the Symphony of the Air Orchestra. John Schwartz directed the color telecast.

GRAVES, DENYCE   *American mezzo soprano (1964–)*

Denyce Graves sings the roles of Earth Mother and Mrs. Lincoln in the recording of Philip Glass's THE CIVIL WARS, and performs Erika's aria "Must the winter come so soon" from Samuel Barber's VANESSA on her recital album *Voce di Donna.* On stage

Kathryn Grayson as she appeared in the 1953 film *The Grace Moore Story.*

she has sung Baba the Turk in Igor Stravinsky's THE RAKE'S PROGRESS, Nelly in Carlisle Floyd's THE PASSION OF JONATHAN WADE and the Mother in Gian Carlo Menotti's THE CONSUL. Graves made her debut in 1991 at the Ravinia Festival and then sang at the Metropolitan. She has won acclaim around the world as Carmen

GRAYSON, KATHRYN   *American soprano (1922–)*

Kathryn Grayson was the successor to Jeanette McDonald at MGM in the 1940s and 1950s singing the soprano roles in films based on operettas. Her first operetta film was Harry Tierney's RIO RITA in 1941 but the best were her partnerships with Howard Keel in Jerome Kern's SHOW BOAT in 1951 and Cole Porter's KISS ME KATE in 1953. She also starred in THE DESERT SONG (1953) opposite Gordon MacRae and Rudolf Friml's The VAGABOND KING (1956) opposite Oreste. In 1961, after the movie musical's demise, she turned to operettas on stage including Victor Herbert's *Naughty Marietta.* Grayson was born Zelma Kathryn Hedrick in Winston-Salem, North Carolina, and grew up wanting to be an opera diva. She had a florid coloratura soprano voice, photographed well and was a popular star. She made an adequate operatic partner for Mario Lanza and Lauritz Melchior in semi-operatic films and was able to sing well enough to play Grace Moore in the 1953 biopic *So This Is Love.*

THE GREAT GATSBY   *1999 opera by Harbison*

Mysterious millionaire Jay Gatsby loves his youthful sweetheart Daisy Buchanan, now married to Long Island neighbor Tom Buchanan. In his attempt to win her back, he throws lavish jazz-age style parties and becomes friends with Daisy's cousin Nick Carraway. Buchanan's mistress Myrtle Wilson is killed by Gatsby's car and her husband shoots Gatsby thinking he was driving. The real driver was Daisy. John Harbison's opera *The Great Gatsby*, libretto by the composer based on the 1925 novel by the F. Scott Fitzgerald with song lyrics by Murray Horwitz, premiered at the Metropolitan Opera on December 20, 1999. Jerry Hadley was Gatsby, Dawn Upshaw was Daisy, Mark Baker was Buchanan, Dwayne Croft was Nick, Susan Graham was Daisy's friend Jordan, Lorraine Hunt Lieberson was Myrtle, Richard Paul Fink was her husband George, William Powers was shady businessman Meyer Wolfshiem, Frederick Burchinal was Henry Gatz, Jennifer Dudley was the Tango Singer and Leroy Lehr was the Minister. Michael Yeargan designed the sets, Mark Lamos directed and James Levine conducted the Metropolitan Opera Orchestra. *The Great Gatsby* was reprised by Lyric Opera of Chicago in 2000 with Hadley as Gatsby opposite Alicia Berneche as Daisy.

1994 Remembering Gatsby. The Baltimore Symphony Orchestra conducted by David Zinman plays Harbison's instrumental interlude "Remembering Gatsby" on the album *Dance Mix*. The 1920s-style was composed before the opera but it was incorporated into it. Argo CD. **2000 Metropolitan Opera.** Metropolitan Opera broadcast the opera nationally on January 5, 2000, with the premiere cast as above. Jerry Hadley was Gatsby and Dawn Upshaw was Daisy. James Levine conducted. **2000 Lyric Opera of Chicago Commentary.** Critical analysis of *The Great Gatsby* by Roger Pines in the Women's Board of Lyric Opera series. It includes musical excerpts, plot summary, composer biography and social and historical background. Lyric Opera Commentaries audiocassette. **2001 Lyric Opera of Chicago.** Lyric Opera of Chicago broadcast its production of the opera nationally on May 19, 2001. Jerry Hadley sang Gatsby opposite Alicia Berneche as Daisy, Clifton Forbis was Tom Buchanan, Russell Braun was Nick Carraway, Patricia Risley was Jordan Baker, Jennifer Dudley was Myrtle Wilson and Andrew Shore was George Wilson.

GREEN, ADOLPH   *American librettist/lyricist/singer (1914–2002)*

Adolph Green collaborated with Betty Comden for six decades years on the lyrics and books of major musicals, many composed by Leonard Bernstein, and was a featured singer in several of them. The threesome worked together creating ON THE TOWN and WONDERFUL TOWN, the duo went on to write *Bells Are Ringing, Applause* and *On the Twentieth Century* and Green was a featured performer in a recorded concert of CANDIDE. He created the role of the sailor Ozzie in *On the Town* in 1944, reprised the role in the recording Bernstein made in 1963 and narrated the story with Comden in the 1992 Barbican Hall production which is on DVD and CD He sings the role of Pangloss in Bernstein's production of *Candide* at the Barbican Center in 1989, also on DVD and CD. In addition he can be heard in the role Russell opposite Risë Stevens in the 1963 recording of Kurt Weill's musical LADY IN THE DARK. Green and Comden won five Tony awards for their musicals and much praise for their screenplay for the movie musical *Singin' in the Rain*.

GREEN MANSIONS   *1937 radio opera by Gruenberg*

Abel is living with a tribe in a South American jungle when he meets and falls in love with Rima the bird girl. When she is killed by the tribe, he has them all destroyed. Louis Gruenberg's radio opera *Green Mansions*, libretto by the composer based on the novel by W. H. Hudson, premiered on CBS on November 17, 1937. Gruenberg described it as "a non-visual opera" and experimented with sound effects on it. Rima's voice was represented by a musical saw and live recordings of jungle sounds were part of the score.

GREENAWALD, SHERI   *American soprano (1947–)*

Sheri Greenawald created Marian Harrington in Thomas Pasatieri's WASHINGTON SQUARE for Michigan Opera Theater in 1976 and Dede in Leonard Bernstein's A QUIET PLACE for Houston Grand Opera in 1983. She sang Doll in the premiere performances of Carlisle Floyd's BILBY'S DOLL in Houston in 1976, Birdie in the 1992 Scottish Opera recording of Marc Blitzstein's REGINA, Anne Sexton in the 1997 Opera Theater of St. Louis production of Conrad Susa's TRANSFORMATIONS and Vanessa in the 1999 Seattle Opera broadcast of Samuel Barber's VANESSA. Greenawald was born in Iowa City, Iowa, and made her debut in 1974 at the Manhattan Theater Club.

GREENAWAY, PETER   *English film director (1942–)*

Peter Greenaway, a cutting edge experimental film and opera director, has made four unusual documentaries about experimental American opera composers. The 60-minute films, which explores the work of ROBERT ASHLEY, JOHN CAGE, PHILIP GLASS and MEREDITH MONK, were filmed for the British *4 American Composers* series. They are all on video.

GREENLEAF, ROBERT   *American composer*

Robert Greenleaf, a music professor at Auburn University in Alabama for more than 26 years, succeeded in having his first opera nationally televised. UNDER THE ARBOR, libretto by Marian Carcache about young lovers in 1943 Alabama, was premiered by Auburn University and the Alabama Symphony Orchestra in Birmingham in 1992. It was nationally telecast in 1994.

GRIFFELKIN   *1955 opera by Foss*

Griffelkin is a little devil whose birthday present is a day in the human world to create as much mischief as he wants. The experience changes him because he finds he likes non-devilish things, especially a little girl. He is finally so corrupted he commits a good deed and is expelled from hell and forced to become human. Lukas Foss's opera *Griffelkin*, libretto by Alastair Reid based on the fairy tale *The Little Devil's Birthday* told to Foss by his mother when he was a boy, was commissioned by NBC Opera Theatre which premiered it on November 6, 1955, on television.

Adelaide Bishop played Griffelkin, Mary Kreste was his Grandmother, Mignon Dunn was the Statue, Andrew McKinley was the Letterbox, Paul Ukena was Uncle Skelter, Alice Richmond was the Mother whose life he saves, Rose Geringer was the Little Girl he loves and Lee Cass was the bewildered Policeman. Samuel Chotzinoff produced, Robert Jouffrey choreographed, Rouben Ter-Arutunian designed the sets and Peter Herman Adler conducted the Symphony of the Air.

The opera was premiered on stage at the Tanglewood Festival in Lenox, MA, on August 6, 1956. Mildred Allen was Griffelkin, Regina Sarfaty was the Grandmother, Boris Goldovsky was stage director and the composer conducted. *Griffelkin* was revived in a production by Jonathan Pape at New York City Opera on October 7, 1993, with Robin Tabachnik as Griffelkin and Diana Daniele as the Grandmother.

1955 NBC Opera Theater. Adelaide Bishop stars as Griffelkin in the televised NBC Opera Theatre production by Samuel Chotzinoff with cast as listed above. Peter Herman Adler conducts the Symphony of the Air and Kirk Browning directed the black-and-white telecast November 6, 1955. Video at MTR. **2002 Boston Modern Opera Project.** Kendra Colton stars as Griffelkin in this recording of the opera with Gil Rose conducting the Boston Modern Opera Project Orchestra, Boston's Children's Opera and the Back Bay Chorus. The supporting cast includes Marion Dry, Elizabeth Keusch and Yeghishe Manucharyan. Chandos 2-CD box. **2003 Rosemary Alvino.** Mezzo-soprano Rosemary Alvino sings arias from *Griffelkin* accompanied by Philippe Quint on violin and the composer on piano. They are the Grandmother's "Aria of the Devils," Griffelkin's Act 2 aria and Act 3 arioso and the "Song of the Fountain Statue." Elysium CD.

GRIFFEY, ANTHONY DEAN   *American tenor (1969–)*

Anthony Dean Griffey created the role of Mitch in André Previn's opera A STREETCAR NAMED DESIRE at San Francisco Opera in 1998 and is featured on the CD, telecast and DVD. He sings the role of Tom in the 1995 concert performance (on CD) of Amy M. Beach's CABILDO in Athens, Georgia, and the role of Peter Ibbetson in the recorded 1999 concert performance of Deems Taylor's PETER IBBETSON in Seattle. He played Lennie in Francesca Zambello's productions of Carlisle Floyd's OF MICE AND MEN at Bregenz and Houston Grand Opera (on CD). He sang Sam in Carlisle Floyd's SUSANNAH at the Met opposite Renée Fleming and at Lyric Opera of Chicago. He sang the title role in Robert Kurka's THE GOOD SOLDIER SCHWEIK at Glimmerglass opera in 2003. Griffey, born in High Point, North Carolina, graduated from Wingate University in North Carolina in 1990. He made his debut at the Metropolitan in 1995 and won critical renown in 1997 as Peter Grimes.

GRIFFITH, DAVID   *American tenor (1939–)*

David Griffith created the role of Jonathan in Seymour Barab's *Philip Marshall* at Chautauqua Opera in New York in 1974 and David/Demetrius in Elie Siegmeister's NIGHT OF THE MOONSPELL in Shreveport, LA, in 1976. Griffith, a native of Eugene, Oregon, studied in New York, made his debut with Dallas Civic Opera in 1970 and later joined New York City Opera.

GRIFFITHS, PAUL   *Welsh librettist/music critic (1947–)*

Paul Griffiths wrote the libretto for two notable American operas: Tan Dun's MARCO POLO, based on his novel *Myself and Marco Polo*, which premiered at the Munich Biennale in 1996; and Elliott Carter's WHAT NEXT?, inspired by Jacques Tati's car crash comedy film *Traffic*, which was first performed in Berlin 1999. His own pastiche opera *The Jewel Box*, music by Mozart, was premiered by Opera North in 1991 and staged by Skylight Opera in 1993 and Wolf Trap Opera in 1994. He has also translated a number of libretto. Griffiths, who was born in Bridgend, Wales, is one of the most respected music critics in America and England and has written for *The Financial Times, The Times* of London and *The New Yorker.*

GRIST, RERI   *American soprano (1932–)*

Reri Grist created leading roles in Broadway musicals before she became an opera singer. She was a student when she sang in Jan Meyerowitz's THE BARRIER at Columbia University and on Broadway in 1950. She was still studying when she created the role of Consuela in Leonard Bernstein's WEST SIDE STORY at the National Theater in Washington, DC, and on Broadway in 1957. It is Grist who sings the memorable "Somewhere" on the original cast album. A native New Yorker, she made her opera debut at Santa Fe in 1959, built her reputation in Europe and began to sing at the Metropolitan Opera in 1966.

GRUENBERG, LOUIS   *American composer (1884–1964)*

Louis Gruenberg wrote sixteen operas and operettas and was nominated three times for Oscars for film scores but is remembered primarily for THE EMPEROR JONES which premiered at the Met in 1933. His children's opera JACK AND THE BEANSTALK ran on Broadway for two weeks in 1931 and his radio opera GREEN MANSIONS was broadcast by CBS in 1937. Gruenberg was a child when his parents moved to America but he returned to Europe to study music. He was encouraged to compose in an American rather than European style by Italian composer Ferruccio Busoni. and began to feature jazz, spirituals and other African American music in his compositions. His first stage works were the operettas *Signor Formica* (1910) and *The Witch of Brocken* (1912). His first opera was *The Bride of the Gods*, libretto by Ferruccio Busoni, composed in 1913 but never staged. After returning to the U.S. he earned a living composing musicals and operettas like *Roly-Boly Eyes* and *Lady X* though his main interest was always opera. *Jack and the Beanstalk* (1931), libretto by John Erskine, was his first operatic success but his greatest achievement came in 1933 when the Met staged *The Emperor Jones* based on the play by Eugene O'Neill. Gruenberg moved to Los Angeles in 1937 where he began to compose music for films. He received Oscar nominations for three scores, including *The Commandos Strike at Dawn* (1942), and contributed music to classics like *Stagecoach* (1939) and *All the King's Men* (1949). Gruenberg continued to compose operas but the ones he wrote after 1937 were never performed. They included large-scale adaptations of *Volpone* (1958) and *Antony and Cleopatra* (1961), which he considered his finest work, and three television operas, *The Miracle of Flanders* (1954), *One Night of Cleopatra* (1954) and *The Delicate King* (1955).

A GUEST OF HONOR   *1903 "ragtime opera" by Joplin*

Scott Joplin's one-act "ragtime opera" *A Guest of Honor*, libretto by the composer, was premiered in St. Louis, Missouri, in 1903 by the Scott Joplin Ragtime Opera Company and then taken on tour to five cities. It's composition followed his quasi-operatic *Ragtime Dance of 1899*, a six-minute dance piece for the stage with sung narration and orchestral score. A *Guest of Honor* included twelve ragtime numbers but it was not published and is presently considered lost. A 1989 opera titled *A Guest of Honor: Scott Joplin* was named in honor of Joplin's lost work. It was composed by Steve Weisberg to a libretto by Howard Pflanzer, and uses Joplin's music to tell the story of his life.

GUETTEL, ADAM   *American composer (1965–)*

Adam Guettel. one of the new composers breaking down the barriers between opera and musical, is the grandson of Richard Rodgers and son of Mary Rodgers. His breakthrough success was FLOYD COLLINS, libretto by Tina Landau and the composer, which premiered at the American Music Theater Festival in 1994 with Landau directing. The story of a Kentucky man who became a national celebrity while trapped underground in 1925, it incorporates bluegrass and popular music into a dense musical style. He then received acclaim for *Myths and Hymns* (aka *Saturn Returns*), an oratorio premiered at the Joseph Papp Public Theater in New York in 1998 and performed on CD by Audra McDonald, Mandy Patinkin and Vivian Cherry. It was then staged by Grand Valley

State University Opera Theatre in Allendale, Michigan, as the sequel to Leonard Bernstein's opera *Trouble in Tahiti*. Dinah and Sam, the unhappy suburban couple in Bernstein's opera, reappear in Guettel's work with new hopes and aspirations. Guettel's other operas include *A Christmas Carol* (1989/created with Tina Landau), *The Inverted World of Medusa Gorgon* (1988), and *The Fourth Woman* (1991). His musical LIGHT IN THE PIAZZA premiered in Chicago in 1904. Guettel, a graduate of Yale, began his professional musical career as a boy soprano, played bass with rock and jazz groups and wrote scores for PBS and CBS television documentaries before turning to the state.

GUIDO FERRANTI   *1914 opera by Van Etten*

Jane Van Etten's *Guido Ferranti* was one of the first operas by an American woman composer to be produced by a regular opera company. It was premiered by the Aborn Brothers' Century Opera Company at the 4000-seat Auditorium in Chicago on December 29, 1914. Elsie M. Wilbor based the libretto on Oscar Wilde's play *The Duchess of Padua*. Beatrice is married to the elderly Duke of Padua whom she kills so she can marry her lover, Guido Ferranti. Guido, who had planned to kill the Duke himself, is ashamed and rejects her. She, in turn, is outraged and denounces him as the murderer. Hazel Eden starred as Beatrice with Worthe Faulkner as Guido. Agide Jacchia conducted. The opera, tuneful in the Puccini mode, was awarded the David Bispham Memorial Medal in 1926.

THE GUILT OF LILLIAN SLOAN   *1985 opera by Neil*

Lillian Sloan and her lover are found guilty of murdering her husband at a trial in England in 1922 and both are hanged. What actually happened is gradually revealed during the trial. William Neil's two-act opera *The Guilt of Lillian Sloan*, libretto by Frank Galati, was commissioned by Lyric Opera of Chicago and premiered on June 22, 1985, by the Lyric Opera Center for American Artists. Joan Gibbons was Lillian Sloan, Richard Drew was the Attorney for the Defense, Patrick Wroblewski was the Solicitor General, Stefan Szafarowsky was Howard Sloan, Lisa Bonenfant was Lillian's mother, Joseph Wolverton was the Clerk of the Court and Bonita Hyman was the Prison Matron. The opera was reprised at the University of Illinois in Evanston in June 1986.

GUZMÁN, SUZANNA   *American soprano (1961–)*

Suzanna Guzmán, a native of East Lost Angeles, created the role of Loecadia in Gian Carlo Menotti's GOYA at Washington Opera in 1986 and sings the role of the Duchess of Alba in the live recording of the 1991 Spoleto Festival production. She created the role of Marie Laveau in William Grant Still's MINETTE FONTAINE for Baton Rouge Opera in 1984, La Gitana in Ian Krouse's *Lorca, Child of the Moon* at the Bilingual Foundation in Los Angeles in 1987, the embittered wife Paula in Daniel Catán's FLORENCIA EN EL AMAZONAS at Houston Grand Opera in 1996 and Mrs. Fox in Tobias Picker's FANTASTIC MR. FOX at Los Angeles Opera in 1998. She played Saint Teresa II in Robert Wilson's production of Thomson's FOUR SAINTS IN THREE ACTS at Houston Grand Opera in 1996 and Eunice in San Diego Opera's production of André Previn's A STREETCAR NAMED DESIRE. In addition to *Goya*, she has sung roles in four other Menotti operas, the Mother in AMAHL AND THE NIGHT VISITORS, Madame Flora in THE MEDIUM, Desideria in THE SAINT OF BLEECKER STREET and Miss Todd in THE OLD MAID AND THE THIEF. She has also sung roles in four Richard Rodgers operettas, Nettie in CAROUSEL, Mother Abbess in THE SOUND OF MUSIC, Lady Thiang in THE KING AND I and Bloody Mary in SOUTH PACIFIC. In addition she has played Augusta in Douglas Moore's THE BALLAD OF BABY DOE, Julie in Jerome Kern's SHOW BOAT and Aldonza in MAN OF LA MANCHA.

H

HACKETT, CHARLES   *American tenor (1889–1942)*

Charles Hackett created two operatic roles while singing for Mary Garden's Chicago Civic Opera. He was Arnold in Charles Cadman's A WITCH OF SALEM in 1926 and Armand opposite Mary Garden's Marguerite in Forrest Hamilton's *Camille* in 1930, based on the same story as *La Traviata*. Hackett, born in Worcester, MA, made his debut in Genoa in Italy in 1914, began to sing at Met in 1919 and performed with Chicago Opera from 1922 to 1935. He continued singing professionally until 1939.

HADLEY, HENRY   *American composer/conductor (1871–1937)*

Henry Kimball Hadley's operas were introduced by legendary divas Maggie Teyte and Frances Alda and were well received but they did not enter the repertory. BIANCA, libretto by Grant Stewart based on a Goldoni play, premiered in New York in 1918 with Maggie Teyte in the title role as an 18th century Italian innkeeper. CLEOPATRA'S NIGHT premiered at the Metropolitan Opera in 1920 with Frances Alda as a hard-hearted Cleopatra who will allow a man to spend the night with her if he agrees to die the next morning. Hadley, born in Somerville, MA, studied music in Germany and was greatly influenced by Wagner and Strauss. His first opera, the one-act *Safie*, libretto by Edward Oxenford, was premiered at the Mainz Stadtheater on April 4, 1909, with Hadley conducting. After he built his reputation in Europe, Hadley returned to the U.S. as a highly regarded conductor and was engaged by the Metropolitan Opera, San Francisco Opera and Seattle Symphony Orchestra. AZORA, his opera about an Aztec princess who becomes a Christian, was premiered by Chicago Opera in 1917. He composed several operettas including *Nancy Brown*, produced in New York in 1903, and *The Fire Prince*, staged in Schenectady in 1924. He also wrote the music for Joseph Redding's 1912 masque *The Atonement of Pan*, staged in San Francisco, and the score for one of the first sound films, Vitaphone's 1927 *When a Man Loves* starring John Barrymore. He began to conduct on NBC Radio in the 1920s and his opera *A Night in Old Paris* was premiered on NBC on February 22, 1933. He founded the Berkshire Music Festival in 1934.

HADLEY, JERRY   *American tenor (1952–)*

Jerry Hadley, one of the most popular tenors in American opera, created the role of Jay Gatsby in John Harbison's THE GREAT GATSBY for the Metropolitan Opera in 1999 and the role of Don Luis in Myron Fink's THE CONQUISTADOR for San Diego Opera in 1997. He sings Ravenal in the 1988 operatic recording of Jerome Kern's SHOW BOAT, Candide in the 1989 operatic recording of Leonard Bernstein's CANDIDE, Sam in the 1991 Scottish Opera recording of Kurt Weill's STREET SCENE, Caliph in the 1991 operatic recording of Wright/Forrest's KISMET, Sam Polk in the 1994 Lyons recording of Carlisle Floyd's SUSANNAH, Padre in the 1996 operatic recording of Mitch Leigh's MAN OF LA MANCHA, Duke in the 1997 recording of Kurt Weill's THE FIREBRAND OF FLORENCE and Tom in 1992 Aix-en-Provence, 1996 Salzburg and 1996 Lyons recordings of Igor Stravinsky's THE RAKE'S PROGRESS. He also recorded a splendid album of classic American operetta arias, *Golden Days*, which includes arias from ANGEL FACE, THE DESERT SONG, THE FIREFLY, NAUGHTY MARIETTA, THE NEW MOON, PRINCESS PAT, THE RED MILL THE STUDENT PRINCE and THE VAGABOND KING. Hadley, born in Princeton, NJ, made his debut in Sarasota in 1978, began to sing at New York City Opera in 1979 and made his Metropolitan Opera debut in 1987.

HÅGEGARD, HÅKAN   *Swedish baritone (1945–)*

Håkan Hagegård created the role of Beaumarchais in John Corigliano's THE GHOSTS OF VERSAILLES at the Met in 1991 and he sings the role of Nick Shadow in a 1995 film of Igor Stravinsky's THE RAKE'S PROGRESS. Hagegård, who made his debut at Sweden's Royal Opera in 1968 as Papageno, was introduced to international audiences in when he played the role in Ingmar Bergman's 1974 film *The Magic Flute*.

HAGEMAN, RICHARD   *American composer/conductor (1882–1966)*

Richard Hageman's opera CAPONSACCHI was staged at the Metropolitan Opera in 1937 with Lawrence Tibbett in the title role and the composer conducting but this was not the premiere; it had already been staged in Germany and awarded the David Bispham prize for an American opera. *Caponsacchi* was Hageman's only opera but he also wrote an oratorio, *The Crucible,* presented in Los Angeles in 1943. Hageman, born in Holland, was conductor at Netherlands Opera before coming to the U.S. in 1906. He conducted regularly at the Met from 1908 to 1921 and then with opera companies in Chicago and Los Angeles before becoming director of the opera department at the Curtis Institute in Philadelphia. In 1938 he moved to Hollywood and began to write scores for movies, including the John Ford films *Stagecoach* (for which he won an Oscar), *The Long Voyage Home* and *She Wore a Yellow Ribbon.* He also conducted at the Hollywood Bowl for six seasons. His art song "Do Not Go, My Love" has been recorded by many opera singers including Kiri Te Kanawa, Zinka Milanov, Thomas Hampson and Theodor Uppman.

HAGEN, DARON   *American composer (1961–)*

Daron Eric Hagen won wide praise for his innovative opera SHINING BROW which explored the darker side of architect Frank Lloyd Wright's creativity. Created in collaboration with librettist Paul Muldoon, it was premiered by Madison Opera in Wisconsin in 1993. Next was the children's opera *The Elephant's Child* (1994), libretto by the composer based on a Rudyard Kipling story. VERA OF LAS VEGAS, a "nightmare cabaret opera" with libretto by Muldoon about two fugitives with weird problems in Las Vegas, was premiered by the University of Nevada Las Vegas Opera Theater on March 8, 1996. The monodrama *Madness and Sorrow*, libretto by the composer, premiered in Tacoma on January 31, 1997, with Paul Sperry as the tenor. BANDANA, an *Otello*-like story with libretto by Muldoon set in the contemporary Southwest, was premiered by the University of Texas in Austin in 1999. Hagen, born in Milwaukee, studied at the University of Wisconsin in Madison, at the Curtis Institute in Philadelphia and with Ned Rorem.

HALE, EDWARD EVERETT   *America writer (1822–1909)*

Clergyman/writer Edward Everett Hale is remembered primarily for one story, the highly patriotic 1863 "The Man Without a Country." Written to inspire patriotism in the Civil War, it was turned into an opera in 1937 just before the start of another war. Walter Damrosch's THE MAN WITHOUT A COUNTRY, libretto by

Arthur Guiterman, premiered at the Metropolitan Opera on May 12, 1937, with Arthur Carron as the countryless man and Helen Traubel as the woman who loves him.

HALLMARK HALL OF FAME   *American TV series (1951–)*

Gian Carlo Menotti's AMAHL AND THE NIGHT VISITORS, the first television opera, was the first production in the Hallmark Hall of Fame television series which was initiated with its premiere on December 24, 1951. Most of its productions were plays but it also presented Cole Porter's KISS ME KATE in 1958, Philip Bezanson's GOLDEN CHILD in 1960 and Richard Rodger's CAROUSEL in 1967. Hallmark programs are preserved at the UCLA Film and Television Archive.

HAMM, CHARLES   *American composer/critic (1925–)*

Charles Hamm, who has written highly informative books on opera and popular song, also wrote and composed one-act operas based on literary works. *The Monkey's Paw,* based on a famous story by W. W. Jacobs, was presented at the Cincinnati Conservatory of Music on May 2, 1952. *The Cask of Amontillado,* based on a story by EDGAR ALLAN POE, was performed at the Cincinnati Conservatory on March 1, 1953. *The Secret Life of Walter Mitty,* based on a story by James Thurber, premiered at Ohio University in Athens, Ohio, on July 30, 1953. His last opera was *The Box* presented at Tulane University in New Orleans on February 4, 1961. Hamm, born in Charlottesville, VA, studied at Virginia and Princeton universities and became the professor of music at Dartmouth College in 1976.

HAMMERSTEIN, OSCAR   *American librettist (1895–1960)*

Oscar Hammerstein II, who transformed Bizet's *Carmen* into the American opera CARMEN JONES, is best known for his hugely successful partnerships with composers Jerome Kern (SHOW BOAT, MUSIC IN THE AIR) and Richard Rodgers (OKLAHOMA!, CAROUSEL, THE KING AND I, SOUTH PACIFIC, THE SOUND OF MUSIC). Not only did he help create the modern American musical, he forged its links with the traditional European-style operetta. He wrote traditional operetta librettos for Sigmund Romberg (THE DESERT SONG, THE NEW MOON, VIENNESE NIGHTS), Rudolph Friml (ROSE-MARIE), Emmerich Kálmán (GOLDEN DAWN) and George Gershwin (SONG OF THE FLAME) and helped create what has been called the "American operetta" with Rodgers. He also a wrote the libretto for the 1936 "movie opera" ROMEO AND JULIET with composer Eric Wolfgang Korngold. Oscar II was the grandson of Oscar Hammerstein I, the turn-of-the century opera impresario who created the Manhattan Opera House.

HAMPSON, THOMAS   *American baritone (1955–)*

Thomas Hampson created the leading role of Valmont in Conrad Susa's THE DANGEROUS LIAISONS for San Francisco Opera in 1994. He is sharpshooter Frank in a 1990 recording of Irving Berlin's ANNIE GET YOUR GUN, sailor Gaby in a 1992 London operatic recording of Leonard Bernstein's ON THE TOWN, artist Cellini in a 1997 recording of Kurt Weill's THE FIREBRAND OF FLORENCE and the President in a 2000 recording of Bernstein's *A White House Cantata.* He performs Sigmund Romberg songs on his 1990 recital album *An Old Song Re-Sung* and Weill songs on his 1997 album *Kurt Weill on Broadway.* Hampson, born in Elkhart, Indiana, studied in Los Angeles, made his debut in Dusseldorf in 1981 and began to sing at the Metropolitan Opera in 1986.

A HAND OF BRIDGE   *1959 chamber opera by Barber*

Two couples get together for a game of bridge as they usually do every evening. They begin by singing their bids to make hearts trump and then make small bridge talk secretly revealing they are bored with their mates and with each other. Each sings an aria expressing inner thoughts. Gian Carlo Menotti wrote the clever libretto for this light-hearted nine-minute satiric opera composed by Samuel Barber for the Spoleto *Autumn Leaves* "intellectual cabaret" series. It premiered at the Festival of Two Worlds in Spoleto, Italy, on June 17, 1959, with Patricia Neway as Geraldine, Ellen Miville as Sally, William Lewis as Bill and René Miville as David. Jac Venza designed the set, Menotti directed and Robert Feist conducted the orchestra.

1960 Original cast. Patricia Neway and William Lewis, who originated the roles, sing Geraldine and Bill opposite Eunice Alberts as Sally and Philip Maero as David. Vladimir Golschmann conducts the Symphony of the Air Orchestra. The opera is on the album *Music of Samuel Barber*. Vanguard Classics CD. **1991 Gregg Smith Singers.** Catherine Aks is Geraldine, Fay Kittelson is Sally, William Carney is Bill and Richard Muenz is David in a performance of the opera by the Gregg Smith Singers. It's on the album *3 American One-Act Operas*. Gregg Smith conducts the Adirondack Chamber Orchestra. Premier CD.

HANDT, HERBERT   *American tenor/conductor (1926–)*

Herbert Handt originated the role of tutor Dr. Zuckertanz in Gian Carlo Menotti's MARIA GOLOVIN in Brussels in 1958, is on the original cast recording and reprised the role in a 1959 NBC Opera Theatre production. He sang the role of Father Cornelius in a 1966 Italian television production of Menotti's MARTIN'S LIE. Handt, who was born in Philadelphia and studied at Juilliard, made his debut as singer in Vienna in 1949 and began to conduct in Rome in 1960.

HANGMAN, HANGMAN!   *1982 opera by Balada*

Leonardo Balada's one-act chamber opera *Hangman, Hangman!* is based on a traditional cowboy ballad. Johnny is about to be hanged for stealing a horse but can be freed if a ransom of silver is paid. His parents come to watch but won't pay. His sweetheart arrives but has no money so she begs the townspeople for mercy. They say no, hang him, but another arrival, an rich Irishman who has just bought the whole town, pays the money and hires Johnny to be his deputy. Now everybody wants to be Johnny's friend. The opera was premiered October 10, 1982, by Chamber Opera of Catalonia in Barcelona, and staged at Carnegie Mellon University in Pittsburgh on October 8, 1983. Balada created a sequel called THE TOWN OF GREED in 1997 showing the same characters twenty years later.

2001 Carnegie Mellon Opera Theater. Colman Pierce conducts the Carnegie Mellon University Contemporary Ensemble and Pittsburgh Camerata in a recording made at Kresge Recital Hall at Carnegie Mellon University in April 2001. Anthony McKay is Narrator, James Longmire is Johnny, Stephen Neely is Hangman, Patrick Jacobs is Sheriff, Elizabeth Sederburg is Mother, Robert Fire is Father, Natalya Kraevsky is Sweetheart and Colman Pearce is the rich Irishman. 44 minutes. Naxos CD.

HANNAY, ROGER   *American composer (1930–)*

Roger Hannay moved musically from electronic music and 12-tone dissonance to neo-Romantic lyricism in his three operas. The one-act *Two Tickets to Omaha*, libretto by Jerome Lamb, was premiered by Concordia College Opera Theater in Moorhead,

Minnesota, in 1960. The one-act *The Fortune of St. Macabre*, libretto by R. Bonnard, was presented by Concordia College Opera Theater on March 21, 1964. The two-act "opera-biographica" *The Journey of Edith Wharton*, libretto by the composer based on a play by Russell Graves about the author and her associates, was premiered by the North Carolina University Opera Workshop in Chapel Hill on March 30 1988. Hannay, born in Plattsburgh, NY, studied at Syracuse, Boston, Eastman, Berkshire and Princeton under Howard Hanson and Bernard Rogers and taught at the University of North Carolina.

HANSON, HOWARD   *American composer (1896–1981)*

Howard Hanson's grand opera MERRY MOUNT, libretto by Richard L. Stokes based on Nathaniel Hawthorne's *The Maypole of Merry Mount*, premiered at the Metropolitan Opera in 1934 with Lawrence Tibbett and Gladys Swarthout in leading roles. Set in New England in the 17th century, it centers around a doomed love affair between a Puritan pastor and a Cavalier lady. It was extremely well received by critics and audiences but did not remain in the repertory and was not revived until 1964 when it was staged in San Antonio with Brian Sullivan and Beverly Sills. Hanson, a native of Wahoo, Nebraska became director of the Eastman School of Music in Rochester, NY, in 1924 and remained there until 1964 when he left to found the Institute of American Music.

HANSON, WILLIAM F.   *American composer (1887–?)*

William F. Hanson was one of the first composers to base operas around Native American themes and his operas were premiered in Utah where he was born and brought up near the homes of the Sioux and Ute nations. The five-act *The Sun Dance,* libretto by the composer and a Sioux woman named Zitkala Sa, was premiered by Uintah Academy's music department at Orpheus Hall, Vernal, on February 20 1913. It was reprised on a grand scale at Brigham Young University in Provo the following year and then presented at the University of Utah in Salt Lake City. The three-act *Täm-Män-Näcup,* libretto by the composer based on an Ute ritual, was presented at Brigham Young University in Provo on May 3, 1928, and by the Los Angeles Philharmonic at the University of Utah in Salt Lake City on May 22, 1929. The three-act *The Bleeding Heart of Timpanogas,* libretto by the composer, was produced at Brigham Young University in 1937. Hanson, who was born in Vernal, studied music at Brigham Young University.

HARBACH, OTTO   *American lyricist/librettist (1873–1963)*

Otto Harbach wrote librettos and lyrics for some of America's best-known operettas and musicals. They include Sigmund Romberg's THE DESERT SONG and NINA ROSA, Jerome Kern's ROBERTA and THE CAT AND THE FIDDLE, Rudolf Friml THE FIREFLY and ROSE-MARIE, Vincent Youmans' NO NO NANETTE, George Gershwin's SONG OF THE FLAME and Emmerich Kálmán's GOLDEN DAWN. His famous songs include "Indian Love Call," "Tea For Two" and Smoke Gets in Your Eyes." Harbach, who was born in Salt Lake City and studied at Knox College, began to write for the stage in 1908 when he created lyrics for the Broadway show *Three Twins*.

HARBISON, JOHN   *American composer (1938–)*

John Harbison, who writes his own librettos, has composed three operas but most of the attention has been focused on THE GREAT GATSBY. Based on the novel by F. Scott Fitzgerald, it was commissioned by the Metropolitan Opera to close the millennium and premiered in December 1999 to wide media attention. Harbison's other two operas were premiered in 1979. A WINTER'S TALE, based on the Shakespeare play, was composed in 1974 but not staged until August 1979 when it was produced by San Francisco Opera. FULL MOON IN MARCH, based on a symbolist play by W. B. Yeats, was staged by Musica Viva in Cambridge, Massachusetts, in April 1979. Harbison, a native of Orange, NJ, studied at Harvard and Princeton and with Walter Piston, Roger Sessions and Boris Blacher. He was awarded the Pulitzer Prize for Music in 1987 for his cantata *The Flight into Egypt*. Most of his compositions are for voice and include settings of poems as well as choral works.

HARLING, W. FRANKE *American composer (1887–1958)*

William Franke Harling's 1926 Broadway opera DEEP RIVER, libretto by Lawrence Stalling, is an often overlooked predecessor of Gershwin's PORGY AND BESS. Described as a "native opera with jazz," it featured a mixed cast of African Americans and white Creoles in 19th century New Orleans. Harling's A LIGHT FROM ST. AGNES, staged by Chicago Civic Opera the previous year, is also a jazz opera set in Creole New Orleans. Harling came to America from England as a child but returned there to study music. After teaching at West Point, where he also wrote hymns and marches, he became a fulltime composer and published over a hundred works. He turned to Hollywood movies in 1930 beginning brilliantly with Ernest Lubitsch's innovative *Monte Carlo*. He created an imaginary opera called MONSIEUR BEAUCAIRE for that climax of the film as well as the memorable song "Beyond the Blue Horizon." Harling's successful Hollywood career included scores for classic films like *The Scarlet Empress, Penny Serenade* and *Stagecoach*.

HARNICK, SHELDON *American librettist/lyricist (1924–)*

Sheldon Harnick wrote librettos and lyrics for operas but is best known for musicals he created with composer Jerry Bock, especially FIDDLER ON THE ROOF (1964). His operas, however, are also notable and most have been recorded. Jack Beeson's CAPTAIN JINKS OF THE HORSE MARINES, based on a 1916 play by Clyde Fitch, was premiered by Kansas City Lyric Theater in 1975. Beeson's DR. HEIDEGGER'S FOUNTAIN OF YOUTH, based on a Nathaniel Hawthorne story, was premiered in New York in 1978. Arnold Black's THE PHANTOM TOLLBOOTH, a children's opera based on a novel by Norton Juster, was premiered by OperaDelaware Family Opera Theater in 1995. Henry Mollicone's COYOTE TALES, based on native American folk tales, was premiered by Lyric Opera of Kansas City in 1998. His other opera librettos include two for Thomas Z. Shephard, *That Pig of a Molette* and *A Question of Faith*, an English-language version of Peter Brooks' *La Tragédie de Carmen* and a spoof of Debussy's *Pelléas and Mélisande* called *Frustration*. Harnick, born in Chicago, began to write for the musical stage in 1952 and started to collaborate with Bock in 1958. They had their first big success with the Pulitzer Prize-winning *Fiorello!* in 1959 and won critical acclaim for SHE LOVES ME in 1963 but *Fiddler on the Roof* remains their major achievement.

THE HARPIES *1931 opera by Blitzstein*

In ancient Greece blind oracle Phineus tries to eat but the Harpies won't allow it. The Argonauts led by Jason say they will fight off the Harpies if Phineus assures them of the favor of the gods. Messenger of the gods Iris arrives to send the Harpies away forever. Marc Blitzstein's satirical one-act opera *The Harpies*, libretto by the composer, spoofs Greek mythology while mixing operatic musical jokes with barbershop harmonies. It was written

in 1931 for the League of Composers but not performed through lack of funds. It was finally premiered on May 25, 1953, at the Manhattan School of Music with a student cast and Hugh Ross conducting.

1991 Gregg Smith Singers. Patricia Price, Priscilla Magdamo and Fay Kittelson are the Harpies opposed by Argonauts Edmund Najera, Walter Richardson and Henry Niemann in this recording of the opera made by the Gregg Smith Singers. Thomas Bogdan sings Phineus, and Rosalind Rees is Iris. Gregg Smith conducts the Adirondack Chamber Orchestra on the album *3 American One-Act Operas*. Premier CD.

HARRIET, THE WOMAN CALLED MOSES *1985 opera by Musgrave*

African American slave Harriet Tubman escapes and finds refuge in the North with Quaker Thomas Garrett. She returns to the South to help other slaves escape and a reward is offered for her capture. During her rescue of her mother, father and brother, her lover Josiah is killed by slave owner Preston. Thea Musgrave's two-act opera *Harriet, the Woman Called Moses*, libretto by the composer based on Sarah Bradford's books *Harriet, the Moses of Her People* and *Scenes in the Life of Harriet Tubman*, was co-commissioned by Virginia Opera and the Royal Opera House and premiered by Virginia Opera in Norfolk on March 1, 1985. Cynthia Haymon was Harriet Tubman, Alteouise De Vaughn was her mother Rit, Damon Evans was her brother Benjie, Ben Holt was Josiah, Peter von Derrick was Thomas Garrett, Michael Musico was overseer McLeod, Jay Willoughby was the Old Master, Barry Craft was his son Preston, Anthony Bresnie was Covey and Raymond Bazemore was Ben. Peter Mark conducted the Virginia Opera Orchestra and Chorus. Musgrave incorporates African American gospel music and spirituals into the score.

HARRINGTON, LAURA *American librettist (1964—)*

Laura Harrington wrote the libretto for Tod Machover's RESURRECTION, based on the epic Tolstoy novel, which was premiered at Houston Grand Opera in 1999. She has also written librettos for other American opera composers. She began with Christopher Yavelow's COUNTDOWN, created with the help of a computer, which premiered in Boston in 1987; it was called the first "cyber-opera" as it was made available on the internet. Next was Christopher Drobny's popular LUCY'S LAPSES, which premiered in Hartford in 1987. She collaborated with Roger Ames on three operas: *Angel Face* was premiered in St. Paul in 1988, *Martin Guerre* was first staged in New York in 1989 and HEARTS ON FIRE was premiered in Minneapolis in 1995. She also wrote a new libretto for Victor Herbert's BABES IN TOYLAND for a production by Houston Grand Opera in 1991. Harrington, who began writing while a student at Radcliffe, teaches at MIT.

HARRIS, HILDA *American mezzo-soprano (1950–)*

Metropolitan Opera and New York City Opera mezzo-soprano Hilda Harris created the role of Anna Douglass in Dorothy Rudd Moore's opera FREDERICK DOUGLASS in 1985 and she sings the role of Ella in the 1992 recording of Anthony Davis's opera X, THE LIFE AND TIMES OF MALCOLM X. She sang in the premiere of Ulysses Kay's opera JUBILEE in 1976 and in Ezra Laderman's TV opera THE QUESTIONS OF ABRAHAM in 1973. She played St. Teresa II in Virgil Thomson's FOUR SAINTS IN THREE ACTS in Alan Ailey's production of the opera for the Met in 1973 and she has also played the role of Tituba in Robert Ward's THE CRUCIBLE. Harris, who was born in Warrenton, North Carolina, studied at the University of North Carolina and has taught at Manhattan School of Music and Sarah Lawrence College.

HARRISON, LOU   *American composer (1917–2003)*

Lou Harrison was associated for many years with John Cage and his ideas about music, especially those regarding percussion and pitch. One of Harrison's creations was the famous "tack piano" with a metallic sound created by putting thumb tacks in the piano hammers. He also experimented with Asian instruments and many of his operas feature unusual instrumentation. The fairy tale RAPUNZEL, libretto by the composer based on the fairytale as told by William Morris, was premiered in Rome in 1954 with Leontyne Price in the title role. The "theatre kit" opera *Jephtha's Daughter* was presented at Cabrillo College in Seattle on March 9, 1963. The puppet opera YOUNG CAESER, libretto by Robert Gordon about a gay love affair by young Julius Caesar, was premiered at Pasadena, CA, in 1971. Harrison, who was born in Portland, Oregon, studied with Henry Cowell in San Francisco and Arnold Schoenberg in Paris.

HARRISON LOVES HIS UMBRELLA   *1981 opera by Hollingsworth*

Harrison loves his umbrella so much he carries it everywhere, even when it's not raining. The other kids in town insist they want to carry umbrellas as well. One day Harrison turns up with something new, a red yo-yo. Stanley Hollingsworth's one-act opera *Harrison Loves His Umbrella,* libretto by Rhoda Levine based on her book, was premiered at the Spoleto Festival in Charleston, SC, on May 24, 1981; it was performed by students of Oakland University in Rochester, Minnesota with Levine directing. Hollingsworth's THE SELFISH GIANT was premiered in the same program.

HARROLD, ORVILLE   *American tenor (1878–1933)*

Harrold Orville was principal tenor at Oscar Hammerstein's Manhattan Opera when it was sold to the Metropolitan Opera in 1910. Hammerstein took the comic opera by Victor Herbert he had commissioned for it to Broadway with his star Manhattan Opera singers Harrold and Emma Trentini. Harrold created the role of Captain Dick in NAUGHTY MARIETTA opposite Trentini and was greatly admired. Ten years later he created the role of Meiamoun opposite Frances Alda in Henry Hadley's CLEOPATRA'S NIGHT at the Met where he was singing by that time. Harrold, who was born in Muncie, Indiana, began his singing career in vaudeville and sang with Chicago Opera from 1912 to 1922 and the Metropolitan Opera for five seasons from 1919.

HART, LORENZ   *American lyricist (1895–1943)*

Songwriter Lorenz Hart is not normally associated with opera but he and Richard Rodgers created a "jazz opera" called THE JOY SPREADER for their 1925 show *The Garrick Gaieties.* A saleswoman is locked in a department store overnight with a shipping clerk and both are fired but love wins out. It was not as well done as it should have been and so was dropped from the show. Hart never wrote another American opera but he and Herbert Fields wrote a brilliant parody of American operetta called ROSE OF ARIZONA which was presented in the *Garrick Gaities of 1926.* It was so popular that operetta composers apparently used it as a model. Hart also wrote American words for two European operettas, *The Lady in Ermine* and *The Merry Widow.* His partnership with Rodgers resulted in classic musicals like *On Your Toes, Babes in Arms The Boys from Syracuse* and *Pal Joey* and some of the best songs of the century.

HARTE, BRET   *American writer (1836–1902)*

Bret Harte virtually created the "local color" genre of American fiction while editing his San Francisco magazine *The Overland Monthly.* His most famous story, the romantic-tragic THE OUTCASTS OF POKER FLAT published in 1869, has inspired three American opera composers. Jonathan Elkus's version premiered at Lehigh University in April 1960. Stanworth Beckler's version at Stockton, CA, in December 1960 and Samuel Adler's at North Texas State University in 1962. A lesser known story by Harte, the 1864 *M'liss,* was the basis for American composer Pietro Floridia's 1899 opera *La Colonia* but it was written before he emigrated to the U.S.

HARVEY MILK   *1995 opera by Wallace*

San Francisco City Supervisor Harvey Milk, the first openly gay elected public official in America, is murdered by homophobe ex-supervisor Dan White. The city mourns. Stewart Wallace's three-act opera *Harvey Milk,* libretto by Michael Korie, was commissioned by Houston Grand Opera, New York City Opera and San Francisco Opera and premiered in Houston on January 21, 1995. Robert Orth created the role of Harvey Milk with Raymond Very as Dan White, Gidon Saks as Mayor George Moscone, Bradley Williams as Scott, Juliana Gondek as Diane Feinstein, James Maddalena as Mintz, Jill Grove as Anne Kronenberg, Randall Wong as Henry Wong, Kathryn H. Cavenaugh as Medora and Matthew Cavenaugh as Young Harvey. Most of the cast had multiple roles. Paul Steinberg designed the sets, Christopher Alden directed and Ward Holmquist conducted. *Harvey Milk* was reprised by New York City and San Francisco operas and later staged in Dortmund.

1996 San Francisco Opera. Robert Orth, who created the role, sings Harvey Milk in this recording based on a revised San Francisco Opera production. Elizabeth Bishop is Mama, Juliana Gondek is Diane Feinstein, Jill Grove is Dyke, James Maddalena is Mintz, Gidon Saks is George Moscone, Raymond Very is Dan White, Bradley Williams is Scott Smith, Randall Wong is Joe, Lilly Akseth is Medora, and Adam Jacobs is Young Harvey. Donald Runnicles conducts the San Francisco Opera Orchestra and Chorus. 126 minutes. Teldec 2-CD box.

HATTON, ANN JULIA KEMBLE   *American librettist (1764–1838)*

Ann Julia Kemble Hatton was the first woman librettist in America. A member of the famous Kemble theater family and sister of tragic actress Sarah Siddons, she came to New York in 1893 with husband William. She collaborated with singer/composer/actress Mary Ann Pownall on the ballad opera *Needs Must: or, The Ballad Singers* which was premiered in New York in December 1793. Pownall also collaborated with composer James Hewitt for whom Hatton wrote the libretto of TAMMANY, OR THE INDIAN CHIEF. The first serious American opera with an American story, it tells how Indian chief Tammany rescues his lover from one of Columbus's explorers who then takes revenge by burning them alive. The opera premiered at the John Street Theater in New York on March 3, 1794. Hatton also published novels and poems but is best remembered for the libretto of *Tammany* which has survived.

HAWAII   *American state (1959–)*

Jerry Tanner created four Hawaiian operas: *The Naupaka Floret* was composed in 1974. *Ka lei no kane* (A Lei for Kane), libretto by Harvey Hess based on an Hawaiian legend, was premiered by Opera Players of Hawaii in Honolulu on May 6, 1977, and taken on tour around the islands. *Pupu-Kani-Oe* was premiered at St.

Francis High School in Honolulu on December 12, 1980. *The Kona Coffee Cantata*, described as an Hawaiian baroque chamber opera homage to Bach's *Coffee Cantata*, was premiered by Uptown Opera in Spokane, Washington, on November 13, 1986. Neil McKay premiered two operas at the University of Hawaii in Honolulu: *Ring Around Harlequin* was premiered on April 24, 1967, and *Planting a Pear Tree* was staged on May 17, 1970.

Honolulu: Hawaii Opera Theater, created in 1964, staged Igor Stravinsky's THE RAKE'S PROGRESS at Blaisdell Hall in 1986. While it usually presents classical European operas, they are sometimes produced in unusual local adaptations. *Così fan tutte,* for example, was set during the Hawaiian monarchy and sung in Hawaiian as *Pela no ho'i na wahine.* Mozart would have loved it.

HAWTHORNE, NATHANIEL *American author (1804–1864)*

Thirty-five American operas/music theater works have been based on the novels and stories of Nathaniel Hawthorne. The most popular is the 1850 novel THE SCARLET LETTER which has provided the basis for ten American operas. None of the operas have become famous but the best-known is probably Howard Hanson's MERRY MOUNT produced at the Metropolitan Opera in 1934. The following list is alphabetical by story with date of its publication. Title of opera is same as story and libretto is by composer unless other indicated.

The Birthmark (1843). **1982** Jean Eichelberg Ivey. **Dr. Heidegger's Experiment (1837).** **1956** Paul Schwartz (Kathryn Schwartz) as *The Experiment.* Kenyon College, Gambier, Ohio, January 27, 1956. **1956** Samuel Raphling. New York February 18, 1956. **1978** Jack Beeson (Sheldon Harnick) as *Dr. Heidegger's Fountain of Youth.* National Arts Club, New York, November 17, 1978. **1978** Leo Smith as *Magic Water.* **1979** Richard Wargo as *The Crystal Mirror.* Rochester, NY, April 28, 1979. **1988** Stephen Douglas Burton.

Feathertop (1852). **1945** Normand Lockwood as *The Scarecrow* based on 1908 play adaptation by Percy MacKaye. Columbia University, May 19, 1945. **1955?** Dika Newlin as *Feather Top: An American Folk Tale.* **1959** Lionel Novak as *The Clarkstown Witch.* Piermont, NY, July 11, 1959. **1961** Mary Rodgers (Martin Charnin).Telecast on October 19, 1961. **1965** Joyce Barthelson. Published. **1976** Joseph Turrin (Bernard Stambler). **1980** Edward Barnes (Maurice Valency). Juilliard School, New York, February 7, 1980.

The Gentle Boy (1837). **1950** Harold Blumenfeld. **1999** David Bernstein (Charles Kondek) as *Ibrahim.* Akron University, Ohio, November 6, 1999.

The Great Stone Face (1851). **1968** Martin Kalmanoff. Ball State University, Muncie, Indiana, November 14, 1968.

The Hollow of the Three Hills (1830). **1988** Keith Gates (Susan E. Kelso) as *The Hollow.* Lake Charles, LA, February 4, 1988.

The House of the Seven Gables (1851). **2000** Scott Eyerly. Manhattan School of Music, December 6, 2000.

The Maypole of Merry Mount (1836). **1911** David Smith (Lee Wilson Dodd) as *Merry Mount.* **1927** Rosseter G. Cole (C. Ranck) as *The Maypole Lovers.* **1933** Howard Hanson (Richard L. Stokes) as *Merry Mount.* Metropolitan Opera, February 10, 1934.

My Kinsman, Major Molineux (1832). **1976** Bruce Saylor (Cary Plotkin). Opera Workshop, Pittsburgh, PA, August 28, 1976.

Rappaccini's Daughter (1844). **1925** Charles W. Cadman (N. R. Eberhardt) as *The Garden of Mystery.* Carnegie Hall, March 20, 1925. **1981** Michael Cohen (Linsey Abrams). Waterford, Connecti-

cut, August 12, 1981. **1983** Margaret Garwood. Pennsylvania Opera Theater, Philadelphia, May 6, 1983. **1984** Sam Dennison (Karen Campbell). University of Connecticut, August 18, 1984. **1992** Ellen S. Bender (Robert Di Domenica), New England Conservatory, Boston, October 28, 1992.

The Scarlet Letter (1850). **1855** Lucien H. Southard. Boston, July 1855. **1896** Walter Damrosch (George P. Lathrop). Damrosch Opera, Boston, February 10, 1896. **1902** Pietro Floridia. Rejected by the Metropolitan Opera. **1913** Charles F. Carlson as *Hester, or The Scarlet Letter* (unproduced). **1934** Avery Claflin (Dorothea Claflin) as *Hester Prynne,* Hartford, CT, December 15, 1934. **1938** Vittorio Giannini (Karl Flaster). Hamburg State Opera, Hamburg, June 2, 1938. **1961** Walter Kaufmann. University of Indiana, Bloomington, Indiana, May 6, 1961. **1965** Hugh Mullins. **1970** Robert W. Mann. **1970** Lewis Rosen as *Hester.* **1979** Michael P. Gehlen. **1986** Robert Di Domenica (E. H Eglin). Jordan Hall, Boston, 1997. **1992** Martin Herman (Tom Curley). Berkeley Contemporary Opera, Berkeley, April 1, 1992.

The Snow Image (1851). **1952** Ned Rorem (E. Stein) as *A Childhood Miracle.* Punch Opera, New York, May 10, 1955.

Tanglewood Tales (1837). **1984** Richard Peaslee (Kenneth Cavander). All Children's Theatre, New York, December 23, 1984.

The Wedding Knell (1837). **1952** John Verrall, University of Washington, Seattle. December 5, 1952.

Young Goodman Brown (1835). **1962** Ludwig Lenel. Muhlenberg College, Allentown, PA, April 25, 1963. **1970** Henry Mollicone. Glens Falls, NY, July 1970. **1971** Robert James Haskins (John Koppenhaver). **1988** Alan Stringer. St. Thomas of Canterbury Church, Albuquerque, New Mexico, 1988.

HAYES, SORREL *American composer (1941–)*

Sorrel (née Doris) Hayes, a leading proponent of America's new music, has composed three operas. *The Glass Woman,* libretto by Sally Ordway and the composer, was commissioned by Chattanooga Opera and premiered by Encompass Theater in New York on August 1, 1989. *Love in Space* was premiered on WDR radio in Cologne, Germany, in June 1986. *Touch of Touch,* a video opera, has not been performed. Hays, born in Memphis, Tennessee, combines avant-garde technological ideas with ideas taken from traditional music styles of the American South.

THE HAYMAKERS *1857 "operatic cantata" by Root*

George F. Root's "operatic cantata" *The Haymakers* is an opera in everything but name. As Italian opera was suspected of being "decadent" in Root's Protestant community, Root used the secular cantata format so the work could be given in concert form rather than staged. It deals with the work, companionship and rituals surrounding rural haymaking in Massachusetts. Root had worked on his father's farm as a youth so most of the incidents were derived from experience. *The Haymakers* has been compared to Haydn's oratorio *The Seasons.*

1979 North Texas State University Chorus. The North Texas State University Grand Chorus perform the second part of *The Haymakers* under the leadership of Frank McKinley. The soloists are Mark Myers, Linda Brannon, Gary Petersen. Carolyn Finley, Chris Hodges, Burr Phillips, Patti Abasolo, Phyllis Bush, Marc Much and Mark Jones. Erma Rose accompanies on piano. The 40-minute recording was made in the Recital Hall at North Texas State University for the Recorded Anthology of American Music series. New World Records LP/CD. **1982 Isaiah Thomas Singers.** The Isaiah Thomas Singers sing their version of the rousing choral number "Yes! To the Work" from *The Haymakers,* a number also performed by the North Texas State University chorus. It's on the album *The Cantata in Early American Music*. Folkways LP.

HAYMON, CYNTHIA   *American soprano (1958–)*

Cynthia Haymon created the role of slave leader Harriet Tubman in Thea Musgrave's HARRIET, THE WOMAN CALLED MOSES at Virginia Opera in 1985 and sings Bess in the Glyndebourne Festival production of George Gershwin's PORGY AND BESS recorded in 1987. She also sings Bess in 1998 London Proms radio broadcast which is on tape. Haymon, who was born in Jacksonville, Florida, began her singing career at Santa Fe Opera in 1984.

HAYWOOD, LORNA   *English soprano (1939—)*

Lorna Haywood sings the role of Carmen Ghia in the 1970 Hoople Heavy Opera recording of Peter Schickele's THE STONED GUEST and the role of Mother in the 1986 Royal Opera House recording of Gian Carlo Menotti's AMAHL AND THE NIGHT VISITORS. She has also sung the role of Annina in Menotti's THE SAINT OF BLEECKER STREET at San Diego Opera. Haywood made her debut in New York in 1964 and has sung widely in the U.S.

HAZEL KIRK   *1987 opera by Houston*

Mark Houston's two-act opera *Hazel Kirk*, libretto by Francis Cullinan and the composer based on a 19th century play by Steele Mac-Kaye, was premiered at the Lake George Opera Festival in New York on August 7, 1987. Karen Hunt sang the role of Hazel Kirk, Victoria Livengood was Hazel's mother, David Eisler was Arthur, Rosalind Elias was Arthur's mother and Harlan Foss was Dunstan. Hal France conducted the orchestra.

HE WHO GETS SLAPPED   *1956 opera by Ward*

An unhappy aristocrat becomes the clown Pantaloon, "he who gets slapped," in a provincial circus in pre–World War One France. He falls in love with bareback rider Consuelo and resolves various love and marital problems by his actions, though not his own. Robert Ward's opera *He Who Gets Slapped*, libretto by Bernard Stambler based on Leonid Andreyev's play, was premiered as a Columbia University workshop production at the Juilliard School of Music on May 17, 1956,. Paul Ukena played Pantaloon, Ewan Harbrecht was Consuelo, Regina Sarfaty was the lion-tamer Zinida, Norman Myrvik and Edward Graham were Mancini, James Norbert was circus owner Briquet, Richard Ballard was Bezano, Stephen Harbachick was the Baron, Fred Swanson was Tilly and Charles C. Welch was Polly. Frederick Kiesler designed the sets, Felix Brantano staged the opera and Rudolph Thomas conducted the orchestra. *He Who Gets Slapped* was premiered professionally by New York City Opera on April 12, 1959. David Atkinson was Pantaloon, Regina Sarfaty was Zinida, Chester Ludgin was Briquet, Norman Kelley was Mancini, Lee Venora was his daughter Consuelo, Frank Porretta was Bezano and Emile Renan was Baron

The North Texas State University Grand Chorus recorded George F. Root's "operatic cantata" *The Haymakers* in 1979.

Regnard. Andreas Nomikos designed the sets, Michael Pollock staged the opera and Emerson Buckley conducted. The opera was reprised in Cleveland in 1961, in Winston-Salme in 1973, in New York in 1978 and in Bethesda in 1979. The play was filmed in 1924 with Lon Chaney as Pantaloon.

1977 William Parker. Baritone William Parker sings "Pantaloon's Ballad" accompanied by Dalton Baldwin on piano on the 1977 New World album *Nine Songs*. It is reprised on the 1995 New World anthology CD *The Listeners*. **1991 William Stone.** Baritone William Stone sings "Pantaloon's Ballad" from *He Who Gets Slapped* accompanied by pianist Thomas Warburton. It's on the album *Robert Ward: Arias and Songs*. Bay Cities CD.

THE HEADLESS HORSEMAN   *1937 operetta by Moore*

Yankee schoolteacher Ichabod Crane lives in the 18th century Dutch settlement of Sleepy Hollow on the Hudson River and hears scary stories about a headless horseman who haunts the neighborhood. Abraham von Brunt, his rival for the hand of Katrina van Tassel, likes to play tricks on the schoolmaster. One night a headless horseman pursues Crane and throws his head at him. The is merely a pumpkin but Crane never learns this as he leaves the village that night and never returns. Douglas Moore's 90-minute "school operetta" *The Headless Horseman*, libretto by Stephen Vincent Benét based on Washington Irving's 1820 story *A Legend of Sleepy Hollow*, was premiered at Bronxville High School in

Bronxville, NY, on March 5, 1937. It was composed for performance by schoolchildren and was popular in schools for many years. For other operas based on the story, see list in entry on WASHINGTON IRVING.

HEARING   1976 chamber opera by Rorer

The action takes place in a park with a pond and a tree. A young man fancies a flighty woman but she fancies a more mature gentleman. The woman and the gentleman pair off but the gentleman's lady eventually wins him back and the young woman returns to the young man. Ned Rorem's 50-minute chamber opera *Hearing*, libretto by James Holmes based on poems by Kenneth Koch, was premiered by Rosalind Rees and the Gregg Smith Singers at St. Stephens Church in New York on March 15, 1977. *Hearing* originated in 1966 as a six-movement cycle for soprano and piano; it was orchestrated in 1976 when Holmes turned the poems into a libretto and Rorer used his music to create a mini-opera.

1982 Gregg Smith Ensemble. Rosalind Rees is featured as the young lady in lilac on this recording of the opera made at St. Agnes Catholic Church in Lake Placid in 1982. Max Galloway is the jealous gentleman, Kimball Wheeler is the poetic lady and Ron Hilley is the man with a French horn. Gregg Smith leads the eight-piece chamber orchestra. The opera is on the album *Hearing—32 Songs of Ned Rorem* which features Rees performing Rorem's songs with the composer accompanying her on piano. Premiere CD.

HEARTS ON FIRE   1995 opera by Ames

Despite her mother's anti-sexual attitudes, seventeen-year-old Claire becomes involved with a boy named Tommy and a man named Simon. Roger Ames opera, libretto by Laura Harrington, was premiered by New Music Theater Ensemble in Minneapolis on May 11, 1995. Susan Lamberg created the role of Claire, Ruth MacKenzie was her mother Mae, Bradley Greenwald was Tommy and James Bohn was Simon. Ben Krywosz staged the opera and Thomas Linker was music director.

HECKSCHER, CÉLESTE DE LONGPRÉ   American composer (1860–1928)

Céleste de Longpré Heckscher premiered her opera *The Rose of Destiny* at the Metropolitan Opera House in Philadelphia on May 2, 1918, to raise funds for the Red Cross. Born in Philadelphia (maiden name Massey), she began composing at the age of ten. After marrying Austin Steven Heckscher in 1883, she studied composition and orchestration and wrote two operas, an orchestral suite, a ballet, chamber music, piano pieces and songs. She gave a concert of her compositions at the Aeolian Hall in New York City in 1913.

HEGGIE, JAKE   American composer (1962–)

Jake Heggie, who first attracted attention by writing songs recorded by noted opera singers, composed his first opera in 2000 but it was only ten minutes long. *Again* was premiered in New York May 4, 2000, in the program *Six Ten-Minute Operas II* presented by the EOS Orchestra at the Society for Ethical Culture Auditorium. Heggie's first full-length opera became a major media event. DEAD MAN WALKING, libretto by Terrence McNally about a nun and a condemned killer based on the story of Sister Helen Prejean, was premiered by San Francisco Opera on October 7, 2000, with Susan Graham as Sister Helen and John Packard as the condemned man. *The Guardian* critic wrote that "*Dead Man Walking* makes the most concentrated impact of any piece of American music theatre since *West Side Story* more than 40 years ago." Heggie's second full-length opera was THE END OF THE AFFAIR, libretto by Heather McDonald based on the novel by Graham Greene. It was commissioned by Houston Grand Opera which premiered it on March 4, 2004, with Cheryl Barker as Sarah and Teddy Tahu Rhodes as her lover Maurice.

1999 The Faces of Love. This famous recording of songs by Heggie helped make him nationally known and showed the interest singers had in his work even before he wrote an opera. It features 26 of the 125 songs Heggie has composed, including settings of poems by Emily Dickinson and Edna St. Vincent Millay. The singers are Renée Fleming, Sylvia McNair, Jennifer Larmore, Frederica von Stade, Nicolle Foland, Zheng Cao, Kristin Clayton, Carol Vaness and Brian Asawa. Heggie accompanies on piano with Emil Miland on cello. RCA Victor CD.

HEIDEN, BERNHARD   American composer (1910–)

Bernhard Heiden, who studied with Hindemith in Berlin before moving to America in 1935, has composed many chamber works and sonatas but only one opera. THE DARKENED CITY, libretto by Robert Glynn Kelly, was premiered at the University of Indiana in Bloomington, Indiana, on February 23, 1963. Heiden, who was born in Frankfurt, taught at Indiana University from 1946 to 1981.

HELEN RETIRES   1931 opera by Antheil

George Antheil's much-anticipated second opera *Helen Retires*, which focuses on Helen of Troy, was composed to a libretto by John Erskine in 1931. Antheil considered it a failure when it premiered at the Juilliard Opera School in New York on May 25, 1934. Marvel Biddle and Martha Dwyer alternated in the role of Helen, Julius Huehn and George Briton alternated as Achilles, Gean Greenwell and Roderic Cross played the Old Fisherman and Arthur Mahoney was the Young Fisherman. Albert Stoessel, director of the Juilliard School opera department, conducted. Erskine later published the libretto as a book-length poem. His 1925 novel *The Private Life of Helen of Troy* was a best-seller for many years.

HELLMAN, LILLIAN   American writer (1905–1984)

Marc Blitzstein's REGINA, based on Lillian Hellman's 1939 play *The Little Foxes,* was staged on Broadway in 1949 and is now recognized as a classic. Hellman was not involved in that production but she wrote the libretto and some of the lyrics for Leonard Bernstein's CANDIDE which opened on Broadway in 1956. There were fourteen rewrites and Hellman was blamed for the operetta's failure. She rewrote it once more for its London premiere but reviews were again unfavorable. It kept on being rewritten with each new production until Hellman finally asked that her name be removed. Hellman, who was born in New Orleans, is known primarily as a playwright but she was also a successful screenwriter and essayist. Her much publicized relationship with Dashiell Hammett continues to fascinate the public.

HELLO, OUT THERE   1954 chamber opera by Beeson

A young man is being held in prison in a small Texas town for supposedly raping a woman. He becomes friendly with a young girl who works in the prison but is killed by her jealous husband before she can help him escape. Jack Beeson's 50-minute chamber opera *Hello Out There* is based on a William Saroyan short story adapted by librettist Kenward Elmslie. The opera was first performed by the Columbia University Opera Workshop in New York on May 27, 1954.

1954 Desto recording. John Reardon stars as the Young Man with Leyna Gabriele as the Girl and Marvin Worden as the jealous Husband in this Desto recording of the opera. Frederick Waldman conducts the Columbia Chamber Orchestra. Desto LP/Bay Cities CD.

HELOISE AND ABELARD   *2002 opera by Pasatieri*

French scholar-monk Peter Abelard, aged 38 falls in love with his student Heloise, aged 16. She becomes pregnant and they marry in secret but their relationship creates a scandal in twelfth century France. Canon Fulbert, Heloise's uncle and guardian, has Abelard castrated and Heloise placed in a nunnery. Thomas Pasatieri's three-act opera *Heloise and Abelard,* libretto by Frank Corsaro based on letters written by the couple, was premiered at the Juilliard School in New York on April 24, 2002. Lauren Skuce sang the role of Heloise opposite John Hancock as Abelard, Richard Cox was Fulbert and Matt Burns was William of Champeaux. Frank Colavecchia designed the sets, Christiane Meyers created the costumes, Frank Corsaro staged the production and Miguel Harth-Bedoya conducted the orchestra.

HELP, HELP, THE GLOBOLINKS!   *1968 opera by Menotti*

Globolinks are weird green aliens who invade earth with flashing lights and wispy smoke and the only way to get rid of them is to play music. Music student Emily uses her violin to frighten them off and goes to get help for a bus full of other students. The non-musical dean Dr. Stone is taken over by the aliens but music teacher Madame Euterpova and other teachers use musical instruments to rescue the children. Gian Carlo Menotti's one-act children's opera *Help, Help, The Globolinks!,* libretto by the composer, was commissioned by Hamburg Opera which premiered it December 21, 1968. Edith Mathis was Emily, Arlene Saunders was Madame Euterpova, Raymond Wolansky was Dr. Stone, William Workman was Tony, Kurt Marschner was Timothy, Ursula Boese was Miss Newkirk, Franz Grundheber was Mr. Lavander-Gas and Noel Mangis was Dr. Turtlespit. The children were played by members of the NDR Children's Choir. Alwin Nikolais arranged the choreography, Nicolas Schoffer designed the sets and costumes and Matthias Kuntzsch conducted the Hamburg Philharmonic State Orchestra. Menotti, who says he created his charming opera "for children and those who like children," was inspired by the dance theater of Alwin Nikolais who helped him create the Globolinks.

1970 Hamburg Opera. Edith Mathis plays Emily in a film of the Hamburg Opera premiere production. Arlene Saunders is Madame Euterpova, Raymond Wolansky is Dr. Stone, and the other cast members are as listed above. Matthias Kuntzsch conducts the Hamburg Philharmonic State Orchestra. Joachim Hess filmed the production which was telecast on NDR on December 7, 1970. Video at New York Public Library for the Performing Arts. **1979 University of Michigan.** Gian Carlo Menotti staged *Help, Help, The Globolinks!* with students at the University of Michigan in 1979. The 30-minute documentary *Gian Carlo Menotti* includes excerpts from the opera and shows Menotti discussing the opera with Professor John McCollum. UMI VHS. **1998 Madison Opera.** Erin Windle sings Emily in a Madison Opera production by John Ostendorf recorded live at the Oscar Mayer Theater in Madison, Wisconsin, on November 2, 1998. Rachel Joselson is Madame Euterpova, Paul Radulescu is Dr. Stone, Tony Small is Tony, Mark Schmandt is Timothy, Terry Kiss Frank is Miss Newkirk, Bert Adams is Mr. Lavander-Gas and Kenneth Church

is Dr. Turtlespit. John DeMain conducts the Madison Symphony Orchestra. 63 minutes. Newport Classic CD.

HEMINGWAY, ERNEST   *American writer (1899–1961)*

Ernest Hemingway, despite his critical acclaim and Nobel Prize, has not been popular with composers. The only opera based on a Hemingway work is Mary Warwick's two-act *Lealista,* libretto by the composer, based on Hemingway's play *The Fifth Column.* It premiered on March 29, 1985, at Southwest Texas State University in San Marcos.

HENDERSON, ALVA   *American composer (1940–)*

Alva Henderson has composed eight operas, three based on O. Henry stories. THE LAST LEAF, libretto by the composer based on the O. Henry story *The Last Leaf,* was premiered in San Jose on June 17, 1979. *Mulberry Street,* libretto by Janet Lewis based on the O. Henry story *The Third Ingredient,* was premiered in San Jose on June 17, 1979. WEST OF WASHINGTON SQUARE, libretto by Janet Lewis and the composer, is based on two O. Henry stories, *The Last Leaf* and *Room Across the Hall.* MEDEA, libretto by the composer based on Robinson Jeffers' poetic adaptation of Euripides' tragedy, was premiered by San Diego Opera on November 29, 1972. THE LAST OF THE MOHICANS, libretto by Janet Lewis based on the James Fenimore Cooper novel, was premiered by Wilmington Opera in 1976. NOSFERATU, libretto by Dana Gioia based on F. W. Murnau's 1922 vampire film, was premiered at the Western Slope Summer Music Festival in Crested Butte, Colorado, in June 1998. Henderson has also written operas based on Homer's *The Iliad* and Shakespeare's THE TEMPEST. Henderson, who was born in San Luis Obispo, California, studied music at San Francisco State College.

HENDRICKS, BARBARA   *American soprano (1948–)*

Barbara Hendricks created the role of Lady Charlotte in Virgil Thomson's LORD BYRON in New York in 1972 and Alice in David Del Tredici's FINAL ALICE in 1976. She sings the part of Clara in the famous 1975 Cleveland Opera recording of George Gershwin's PORGY AND BESS, plays Anne in the 1994 Swedish film of Igor Stravinsky's THE RAKE'S PROGRESS and sings Seena in the 2000 recording of LEONARD BERNSTEIN's *A White House Cantata.* She has also made several recital albums featuring American musical theater. She performs arias from Gershwin's *Porgy and Bess* and BLUE MONDAY on her 1981 album *Barbara Hendricks Sings Gershwin* and her 2002 album *It's Wonderful,* and songs from Victor Herbert's NAUGHTY MARIETTA and Rudolf Friml's ROSE MARIE on her 1992 album *Operetta Arias.* She performs a duet from Sigmund Romberg's THE STUDENT PRINCE with Gino Quilico on the 1993 album *Operetta Duets* and is a featured singer on the 1988 TV program *Leonard Bernstein at 70.* Hendricks, born in Stephens, Arkansas, made her opera debut in San Francisco in 1974 and was first heard at the Met in 1986.

HENRY, O.   *American story writer (1862–1910)*

O. Henry, the penname of William Sydney Porter, was noted for his entertaining short stories with surprising final twists. In the early 1900s he was the most popular storyteller in America, Five of his stories were featured in the 1952 movie *O. Henry's Full House* and four of those stories in that film have since been turned into operas: THE COP AND THE ANTHEM, THE GIFT OF THE MAGI, THE LAST LEAF and THE RANSOM OF RED CHIEF. O. Henry stories that have been turned into operas are listed below, opera titles same as story unless otherwise indicated. The composer's name is followed by that of the librettist and the date and place of the opera's premiere.

Alias Jimmy Valentine. 1980 Mary Boylan (Robert Dahdah). Theatre for the New City, New York, September 25, 1980.

The Cop and the Anthem. 1982 Steve Cohen (Alison Hubbard). New York University Opera Theater, June 11, 1982.

The Gift of the Magi. 1958 Richard Adler (Wilson Lehr) CBS TV, December 9, 1958 (musical). **1964** Ruth Taylor Magney (composer). Minneapolis, April 15, 1964. **1965** Don Gillis (composer). Fort Worth, December 7. **1968** Joyce Barthelson (composer) as *Greenwich Village, 1910*. Scarsdale, NY, December 20, 1968. **1975** Lora Aborn (composer). Oak Park, Illinois. **1978** Fred Tobias (Sidney Michaels) NBC TV, December 21, 1978 (musical). **1980** Peter Ekstrom (composer). Actors' Theater, Louisville, KY. **1984** Susan Bingham (composer). Chancel Opera, December 1, 1984. **1985** Richard Earl Brown (Nancy Grobe). **1987** Dan Welcher (Paul Woodruff) as *Della's Gift,* University of Texas Opera, Austin, February 26, 1987. **1997** David Conte (Nicholas Giardini). Conservatory Cantata Singers, 1997.

The Hypo-Thesis of Failure. 1990 Morrie Bobrow as *Love and Money.* Climat Theater, San Francisco, February l5, 1990.

The Last Leaf. 1979 Alva Henderson (composer). San José Community Opera Theater, June 17, 1979. **1984** Susan Bingham (composer). Chancel Opera December 1, 1984. **1988** Alva Henderson (Janet Louis/composer) as *West of Washington Square.* Opera

San José, November 26, 1988. **1988** Mary Warwick (composer). University of Houston, Texas, April 27, 1988. **1994** Peter Ekstrom *(composer.)* Actors' Theater, Louisville, KY, 1994.

The Ransom of Red Chief. 1964 Seymour Barab. Newark, NJ, 1964. **1986** Robert Rodriguez (Daniel Dibbern). Lyric Opera of Dallas, Mesquite, Texas, October 10, 1986.

The Third Ingredient. 1980 Alva Henderson (Janet Lewis) as *Mulberry Street.* San Jose, CA, June l7, 1980.

The Whirligig of Life. 1997 Heskel Brisman (Jerome Greenfield). Ball State University, Muncie, October 25, 1997. **1982** Stanley Fletcher (Frank Fletcher) as *The Five Dollar Opera.* El Paso, Texas, March 5, 1982.

Various. 1988 Milton Granger's *O. Henry's Christmas Carol* is based on several O. Henry stories. Roanoke, VA, December 9, 1988.

HENZE, HANS WERNER *German composer (1926–)*

Hans Werner Henze created an English-language opera for American television in 1974. RACHEL LA CUBAN is a Brecht/Weill-like memory piece about a Cuban cabaret singer during the last days of the Battista regime. Commissioned by Peter Herman Adler for NET Opera and telecast on March 4, 1974, it was well received but its cost overruns led to the demise of original American operas on NET.

HEPPNER, BEN *Canadian tenor (1956–)*

Dramatic tenor Ben Heppner, one of the most sought-after tenors in the world, created the role of McTeague in William Bolcom's MCTEAGUE in 1992 at Lyric Opera of Chicago. After studies at the University of British Columbia, he made his debut in Vancouver in 1981 and became widely known when he began singing at the Royal Swedish Opera in 1989.

HERACLES *1964 opera by Eaton*

Greek hero Heracles (Hercules) wins a great victory over King Eurytus and receives praise from his people but three oracular prophesies block the path to happiness. He wants Iole to be the mother of his sons but she hates him for killing her father. He is betrayed by his friend Lichas. He dies after his wife Deianira gives him a robe impregnated with poison that she thinks is a love potion. John Eaton's epic opera *Heracles,* libretto by Michael Fried, is based on Sophocles' *The Women of Trachis* and Seneca's *Hercules Oetaeus*. It premiered on RAI radio in Turin, Italy, as *Eracle* on February 12, 1970. Renato Cesari sang the role of Heracles and Luisella Ciaffi-Ricagno was Deianira, Liliana Poli was Iole, Gino Sinimberghi was Lichas and Pietro Munteanu was Hyllus. Ferruccio Scaglia conducted the RAI Torino Orchestra. The opera, composed while Eaton was studying in Rome in 1964, received its stage premiere on April 15, 1972, when it was produced as the opening event of the new Indiana University Music Center.

HERBERT, VICTOR *American composer (1859–1924)*

Victor Herbert occupies a place in American music theater rather like that of his contemporary Puccini in Italian opera and both had a wondrous gift for melody. While Herbert actually did compose dramatic operas produced at the Metropolitan Opera House, he is best known for his comic operas that dominated Broadway at the turn of the century. All the same the dramatic opera NATOMA, which premiered at the Met in 1911 with Mary Garden and John McCormack in the main roles, was the most performed and recorded American opera before PORGY AND BESS. MADELEINE, which premiered at the Met in 1914 with Frances Alda in the title

VICTOR HERBERT'S MASTERPIECE
AH! SWEET MYSTERY of LIFE
Lyric by Rida Johnson Young
The Dream Melody from Naughty Marietta
M. WITMARK & SONS NEW YORK

Composer Victor Herbert was so well known that he was even featured on sheet music.

role, continues to be revived. Herbert, who was born in Dublin and brought up in Germany, came to the U.S. in 1886 as a cellist when his wife was engaged to sing at the Met. His first staged comic opera was *Prince Ananias,* premiered in New York in 1894. Over the next twenty years he wrote forty more comic operas and operettas and became one of the most popular composers of the era. His second comic opera, the 1895 THE WIZARD OF THE NILE, is on CD so one can hear how early Herbert music sounded. He went on to compose such music theater classics as THE SERENADE (1897), THE FORTUNE TELLER (1898), BABES IN TOYLAND (1903), MLLE. MODISTE (1905), THE RED MILL (1906), OLD DUTCH (1909), NAUGHTY MARIETTA (1910), THE ENCHANTRESS (1911), SWEETHEARTS (1913), THE ONLY GIRL (1914), THE PRINCESS PAT (1915), EILEEN (1917), ANGEL FACE (1919), ORANGE BLOSSOMS (1922) and DREAM GIRL (1924). European-style American operettas are not as fashionable as they were and their librettos have dated badly, but Herbert's comic operas are still admired and staged and seem likely to survive. Seven Herbert operettas were filmed but they rarely did justice to the music so it is fortunate that some have been recorded in complete form. Herbert wrote for the movies as well as the stage and his score for *The Fall of a Nation* (1916) was one of the earliest original movie scores. There are a great many albums of his songs so only a selection is listed below.

1939 Victor Herbert Salute. *Victor Herbert Salute* is an RCA-sponsored "Magic Key" radio show broadcast on January 29, 1939. Songs from his operettas are performed by Jan Peerce, Anne Jamison and Thomas L. Thomas with the Victor Light Opera Company and Orchestra led by Nat Shilkret. The broadcast was issued on 78 by RCA and on LP by JJA as *The Operetta World of Victor Herbert.* Opera Classics audiotape. **1939 The Great Victor Herbert.** Walter Connolly portrays Herbert in the film *The Great Victor Herbert* which masquerades as a biography but is really the story of a couple who perform his music. Mary Martin and Allan Jones star in various Herbert's operettas and their daughter (Susanna Foster) stars in a revival of *The Fortune Teller* singing "Kiss Me Again." The film features performances of songs from "Ah, Sweet Mystery of Life" to the "March of the Toys." Andrew L. Stone directed for Paramount. Paramount VHS. **1945 Jarmila Novotna on Radio.** Jarmila Novotna sings a pot-pourri of Victor Herbert melodies including "Kiss Me Again" on a 1945 radio broadcast. The medley is on the 1995 album *Jarmila Novotna on Radio.* Radio Years CD. **1946 Bing Crosby Sings Victor Herbert.** Bing Crosby performs eight songs from Herbert operettas with Victor Young and his Orchestra on the album *Bing Crosby Sings Victor Herbert.* Frances Langford joins him on "Sweethearts." This four-record 78 album was reissued in 1951. Decca LP. **1946 Till the Clouds Roll By.** Paul Maxey portrays Victor Herbert in this film biography of Jerome Kern. Richard Whorf directed this movie for MGM. MGM VHS/DVD. **1947 Dorothy Kirsten Sings Victor Herbert Melodies.** Met soprano Dorothy Kirsten sings six songs from Herbert operettas on the album *Dorothy Kirsten Sings Victor Herbert Melodies.* RCA Victor 78 album. **1961 The Immortal Victor Herbert.** The Robert Shaw Chorale, Orchestra and soloists perform songs from eight Victor Herbert operettas on the album *The Immortal Victor Herbert.* Saramae Endich, Florence Kopleff, Mallory Walker and Calvin Marsh perform songs from *Babes in Toyland, Eileen, The Fortune Teller, Mlle. Modiste, Naughty Marietta, Orange Blossoms, The Red Mill* and *Sweethearts.* RCA Victor LP. **1962 Philadelphia Orchestra plays Victor Herbert.** Eugene Ormandy leads the Philadelphia Orchestra in a selection of melodies from *The Fortune Teller* and *Naughty Marietta* on the album *The Philadelphia Orchestra plays Victor Herbert.* Columbia

LP. **1963 Music of Victor Herbert.** André Kostelanetz leads his orchestra in Herbert arias and songs on the album *Music of Victor Herbert.* The selections are from *Babes in Toyland, Dream Girl, Eileen, The Fortune Teller, Mlle. Modiste, Natoma, Naughty Marietta, The Only Girl, Orange Blossoms, The Red Mill* and *Sweethearts.* Columbia LP. **1973 The Music of Victor Herbert.** *The Music of Victor Herbert* is a Canadian TV tribute to Herbert featuring performances by Mary Costa, Anna Shuttleworth, Judith Forst and Robert Jeffrey. Richard Bonynge accompanies on piano. Opera Dubs VHS. **1975 Music of Victor Herbert.** Beverly Sills and André Kostelanetz perform music from Herbert operettas on the album *Music of Victor Herbert.* Sills sings arias from *Eileen, The Enchantress, The Fortune Teller, Mlle. Modiste, Naughty Marietta, The Only Girl, Orange Blossoms* and *The Red Mill.* Kostelanetz conducts the London Symphony Orchestra in medleys from *Babes in Arms, Natoma, Naughty Marietta, The Red Mill* and *Sweethearts.* The album won a Classical Grammy. Angel LP/CD. **1985 Victor Herbert: Souvenir.** Soprano Teresa Ringholz and the Eastman Dryden Orchestra led by Donald Hunsberger perform selections from the Herbert operettas *The Fortune Teller, Mlle. Modiste* and *Naughty Marietta* on the album *Victor Herbert: Souvenir.* Arabesque CD. **1986 Victor Herbert: L'Encore.** Soprano Teresa Ringholz and the Eastman Dryden Orchestra led by Donald Hunsberger perform selections from the Herbert operettas *Babes in Toyland, The Only Girl, The Red Mill* and *Sweethearts* on album *Victor Herbert: L'Encore.* Arabesque CD. **1986 Victor Herbert: The American Girl.** Soprano Teresa Ringholz and the Eastman Dryden Orchestra led by Donald Hunsberger perform stage music by Herbert on the album *Victor Herbert: The American Girl.* There are selections from the opera *Natoma* and the operettas *The Dream Girl, Orange Blossoms* and *The Princess Pat.* Arabesque CD. **1998 Victor Herbert Showcase.** British anthology album of recordings of songs from Herbert operettas dating from 1916 to 1939 copied from the collection of Stuart Upton. The twenty-one numbers feature singers from Reinald Werrenrath to Richard Crooks. Flapper Past CD. **1999 Beloved Songs and Classic Miniatures.** Virginia Croskery and the Slovak Radio Symphony Orchestra led by Keith Brion perform Victor Herbert operetta music on the album *Beloved Songs and Classic Miniatures.* Included are *Babes in Toyland, Eileen, The Enchantress, The Fortune Teller, Mlle. Modiste, Naughty Marietta, The Only Girl, Orange Blossoms* and *The Red Mill.* American Classics Naxos CD. **2000 Sweethearts.** Elizabeth Futral and Steven White perform songs from Herbert (and Romberg) operettas on the album *Sweethearts.* Included are arias and duets from *Eileen, Babette, The Fortune Teller, Mlle. Modiste, Naughty Marietta* and *Sweethearts.* They are accompanied by Robert Tweten on piano with the Palmer Chamber Chorus. Newport Classics CD. **2000 The Songs of Victor Herbert.** *The Songs of Victor Herbert* is a British anthology album featuring 32 recordings made over a 34-year period beginning with Alma Gluck's 1912 recording of the *Natoma* aria "I List the Trill in Golden Throat." ASV Living Era CD.

HERBERT, WALTER   *American conductor (1902–1975)*

Walter Herbert played a major role in the development of modern American opera. He was director of Opera in English in San Francisco in 1942, became the first general director of New Orleans Opera in 1943 and founded Houston Grand Opera in 1955 directing it until 1972. He was also music director of Opera/South and helped found San Diego Opera in 1965 where was general director and conductor from 1969. He conducted the premiere of Alva Henderson's opera MEDEA for San Diego Opera in 1972. Herbert, who studied with Schoenberg in Vienna, left Austria in 1938 and became an American citizen in 1944.

HERMAN, JERRY   *American composer (1933–)*

Jerry Herman is best known for hugely popular Broadway musicals like *Hello Dolly!* (matchmaking in old New York) and *Mame* (uninhibited woman teaches nephew how to live) but he also created fascinating off-beat works like *Mack and Mabel* (moviemaking in the early years) and *La Cage aux Folles* (gay couple deceive straight visitors). Herman, a New York-native who studied drama in Miami, began his career writing songs for off-Broadway revues.

THE HERO (1)   *1965 television opera by Bucci*

Home Sagrin shoots a murderer on a beach and the public make him a hero though he can't remember doing it. When he starts having nightmares, he goes to a psychiatrist who helps him recover his memory. He remembers that he found the murderer lying helpless on the beach so there was no need to shoot him. Sagrin tells the police and others what really happened but no one will blame him. He returns to the beach and drowns himself. Marc Bucci's one-act opera *The Hero*, libretto by David Rogers based on Frank Gilroy's story "Far Rockaway," premiered on NET Television on September 24, 1965. Arthur Rubin was Home Sagrin, Anita Darian was Evelyn Sagrin, Elaine Bonazzi was the Psychiatrist, John Thomas was the Announcer, Kirsten Falke was the Girl, Keith Kaldenberg was the Policeman, Chester Watson was the Minister, Gordon B. Clarke was the Mayor, Jack Dabdoud was the Boss and William Glassman was the Murderer. Producer Jac Venza commissioned the opera directed for TV by Kirk Browning. It won the Prix Italia in 1966.

THE HERO (2)   *1976 opera by Menotti*

David Murphy has been asleep for ten years and has become a tourist attraction. His wife and doctor have become involved and are not happy when he wakes up. However his cousin Barbara loves him and is glad he is back. Gian Carlo Menotti's three-act comic opera *The Hero*, libretto by the composer, was commissioned by the Opera Company of Philadelphia which premiered it at the Academy of Music on June 1, 1976. Dominic Cossas was David Murphy, Nancy Shade was Barbara, Diane Curry was wife Mildred, David Griffin was the doctor, Gary Kendall was the Mayor and Richard Shapp was the Guide. Eugene Barth designed the sets and Christopher Keene conducted the Philadelphia Opera Orchestra. *The Hero* was staged in Brussels in 1979, at Juilliard in 1980 and at North Texas State University in Denton in 1987.

1976 Opera Company of Philadelphia. Dominic Cossas is sleeper David with Nancy Shade as Barbara in this live recording of the Opera Company of Philadelphia premiere on June 1, 1976. Diane Curry is wife Mildred, David Griffin is the Doctor and Christopher Keene conducts the Philadelphia Opera Orchestra. Live Opera audiocassette. **1979 Théâtre Royal de la Monnaie.** Julian Patrick is David Murphy with Nancy Shade as Barbara in this production by the Théâtre Royal de la Monnaie in Brussels. Ira D'Ares is Mildred, Graeme Matheson-Bruce is Dr. Brainkoff and Eric Garrett is the Mayor. Pasquale Grossi designed the costumes and sets, Gian Carlo Menotti directed and Christian Badea conducted the Monnaie orchestra and chorus. Joseph Benedek directed for TV. Premiere Opera VHS.

HERRMANN, BERNARD   *American composer (1911–1975)*

Bernard Herrmann is best known as a movie composer but he also wrote operas. His three-act WUTHERING HEIGHTS, libretto by Lucille Fletcher based on Emily Brontë's novel, was recorded in England in 1966 and staged in America in 1982. His Christmas operas A CHILD IS BORN and A CHRISTMAS CAROL were premiered on television in the 1950s. His epic cantata MOBY DICK, based on the Herman Melville novel, was premiered in 1940. An aria composed for the "movie opera" SALAMMBÔ was used in a key scene in the 1941 film CITIZEN KANE and has been recorded by Kiri Te Kanawa. Herrmann, a New York native, studied with Percy Grainger and Philip James and was brought to Hollywood by Orson Welles with whom he had worked in radio. He wrote scores for over forty films including Alfred Hitchcock's *Psycho*, *North by Northwest* and *Vertigo*. His scores often contain operatic tributes.

HERSTORY III   *1986 monodrama by Vercoe*

Joan of Arc recalls her amazing life which includes leading a French army to victory over the English and then being burned at the stake as a heretic. Elizabeth Vercoe's *Herstory III — Jeanne de Lorraine* is a monodrama for a mezzo-soprano using as libretto the records of the trial of Joan of Arc and poems by her contemporary Christine de Pisan and others. The opera was commissioned by Austin Peay State University in Clarksville, Tennessee, for mezzo-soprano Sharon Mabry, who premiered it 1986. It has been performed many times, broadcast and recorded.

1991 Sharon Mabry. Mezzo-soprano Sharon Mabry, music professor at Austin Peay State University in Clarksville, Tennessee, performs the monodrama created for her accompanied by pianist Rosemary Platt. The album also include Vercoe's song cycle *Irreveries from Sappho*. Owl CD.

HEWITT, JAMES   *American composer (1770–1827)*

James Hewitt composed one of the first American operas, TAMMANY, OR THE INDIAN CHIEF, libretto by Anne Julia Hatton. It was a serious ballad opera about the mistreatment of native Americans by Columbus's men and premiered at the John Street Theater in New York on March 3, 1794. The libretto and one song survive. Hewitt, who came to America from England in 1792, wrote and published over 160 musical works including twenty ballad operas on subjects ranging from Columbus to Robin Hood. The one that has survived complete with libretto and music is *The Tars from Tripoli* (1806).

HEYWARD, DUBOSE   *American librettist/novelist (1885–1940)*

DuBose Heyward wrote the libretto for George Gershwin's opera PORGY AND BESS about poor African Americans living in a tenement on the Charleston, SC, waterfront. It was based on his 1925 novel *Porgy* about a cripple who moved around the city in a goat cart. It was the first novel to feature Gullah, a Creole language spoken by the blacks of the area. Heyward turned *Porgy* into a play with the help of his wife Dorothy and it was staged in New York in 1927 and seen by Gershwin Heyward's other novels include *Angel* (1926), *Mamba's Daughters* (1929) and *Lost Morning* (1936). *Mamba's Daughters* was also turned into a play and staged in New York City in 1939. Heyward was born in Charleston and he wrote about the people he had observed in the city.

HIGGLETY PIGGLETY POP!   *1984 opera by Sendak and Knussen*

The dog Jennie is not satisfied with her life so she sets out to see what else there is. She meet a publicist Pig and a milkman Cat and saves a Baby from a Lion. Because of these experiences, she is hired to star in the Mother Goose Theater where the animals perform the nursery rhyme of the title. American author/illustrator Maurice Sendak and composer Oliver Knussen collaborated on the delightful *Higglety Pigglety Pop!* which premiered in an incomplete form at Glyndebourne on October 13, 1984. It received a full production in 1985 on with colorful costumes and sets created by Sendak. Cynthia Buchan played Jennie, Andrew Gallacher was the Pig, Neil Jenkins was the Cat, Deborah Rees was the Baby, Stephen Richardson was the Lion and Rosemary Hardy was the Maid. Frank Corsaro directed and choreographed and Knussen conducted the London Sinfonietta. A final version was staged at the Music Center in Los Angeles on June 5, 1990. *Higglety Pigglety Pop!* is often paired with the other Sendak/Knussen children's opera WHERE THE WILD THINGS ARE.

1985 Glyndebourne Festival. Cynthia Buchan plays the dog Jennie in the 1985 Glyndebourne production by Frank Corsaro with costumes and sets by Sendak. Andrew Gallacher is the Pig, Neil Jenkins is the Cat, Deborah Rees is the Baby, Stephen Richardson is the Lion and Rosemary Hardy is the Maid. Knussen conducts the London Sinfonietta, Christopher Swann directed the video. 60 minutes. Home Vision VHS/Pioneer Artists LD. **1999 Glyndebourne Festival.** Cynthia Buchan is the dog Jennie in this Glyndebourne Festival cast recording made at the EMI Abbey Road Studios in London in March 1999. Lisa Saffer is the Potted Plant, Baby and Mother Goose, Rosemary Hardy is the Rhoda and the Voice of Baby's Mother, Christopher Gillett is the Cat-Milkman and High Voice of Ash-Tree, David Wilson-Johnson is Pig-in-Sandwich-Boards and Low Voice of Ash Tree Stephen Richardson is the Lion. Oliver Knussen conducts the London Sinfonietta. 62 minutes. DG 2-CD set. (With *Where the Wild Things Are.*)

HIGHWAY 1, U.S.A.   *1963 opera by Still*

Southern gas station owner Bob and his wife Mary make sacrifices to help Bob's no-good brother Nate through college. Mary despises Nate and rejects him when he tries to make love to her. He stabs her but she survives and Nate is arrested. William Grant Still's opera *Highway 1, U.S.A.*, libretto by Verna Arvey, was premiered by University of Miami Opera in Coral Gables, Florida, on May 11, 1963. Cheryl Claiborne was Mary, Patrick Mathews was Bob, Ben Laney was Nate, Frances Maddaford Whitney was Aunt Lou, Nicholas Shipskie was the Sheriff and Donald Smith was the Doctor. Clayton Charles and Robert Stoetzer designed the sets, Gordon Bennett directed and Fabien Sevitsky led the University of Miami Orchestra. The opera was reprised by West Virginia State College in 1967, by Citrus College in 1968, by Jackson State College in 1972, by Virginia Union University in 1974, by Norfolk State College in 1975, by National Opera/Ebony in New York in 1977 and by Gateway Theater in Washington, D.C., in 1979.

1963 University of Miami Opera. The University of Miami Opera premiere was recorded with the cast as above. Fabien Sevitsky conducts. Audiocassettes available from Still Music, 4 South San Francisco Street, Suite 422, Flagstaff, Arizona. **1974 William A. Brown.** William A. Brown performs the tenor arias "What Does He Know of Dreams" and "You're Wonderful, Mary" from *Highway 1, U.S.A.* with the London Symphony Orchestra led by Paul Freeman. They're on the album *Columbia Black Composers Series: William Grant Still/Samuel Coleridge Taylor.* Columbia LP.

HIGHWAY ULYSSES   *2003 music theater by Eckert*

Rinde Eckert's 85-minute music theatre work *Highway Ulysses,* libretto by the composer inspired by Homer's *Odyssey,* was premiered by American Repertory Theater in Cambridge, MA, on March 5, 2003. A modern Ulysses (Thomas Derrah), traveling across America to get his young son (Dana Marks) following the death of his wife, is involved in a car crash. He is rescued by the Bride (Nora Cole) who narrates his story in flashback. His adventures correspond more or less to incidents in the *Odyssey.* Cole, who played the Muse in Eckert's *And God Created Whales,* has the most vocally demanding role as the Bride and she also portrays the ghost of Ulysses' wife. Other roles are played Heather Benton, Karen MacDonald, Will elbow, Michael Potts, Dianne Chalifiore, Alison Clear, Holly Vanesse, Seth Reich and the composer. The production was staged by Robert Woodruff with sets and costumes by David Zinn and lighting by David Weiner. Peter Foley conducted the Empty House Cooperative orchestra which included theremin, singing saw, and handmade instruments.

HILLER, LEJAREN   *American composer (1924–)*

Lejaren Hiller was a pioneer in the field of computer music and his 1956 *Illiac Suite* is believed to be the first composition created by computer. He also created a *Computer Cantata* and music theater works that are close to being operas. They include THE BIRDS, based on the Aristophanes play, which premiered at the University of Illinois in 1958; and *A Rage over the Lost Beethoven,* a three-act work performed at SUNY in Buffalo in 1972. Hiller, born in New York City, studied music with Milton Babbitt and Roger Sessions and taught electronic music at the University of Illinois and at SUNY in Buffalo.

HINDEMITH, PAUL   *German/American composer (1895–1963)*

Paul Hindemith, who emigrated to the U.S. from Germany in 1940, composed a famous opera after settling in America. THE LONG CHRISTMAS DINNER, libretto by Thornton Wilder based on Wilder's play, is the story of an American family having dinner for ninety years. It was premiered in Mannheim in 1961 with Hindemith conducting and was staged at the Juilliard School in New York on March 13, 1963. Hindemith, who began his musical career as a violinist in the Frankfurt Opera Orchestra, began writing operas in 1919.

HINDENBURG   *1998 multi-media opera by Reich/Korot*

The German zeppelin Hindenburg catches fire and crashes on a flight in New Jersey on May 6, 1937, in one of the most famous disasters in aviation history. Scenes showing the zeppelin's construction and earlier successful flights are shown on video while singers describe what is happening. Composer Steve Reich and video artist Beryl Korot's multi-media opera *Hindenburg* was premiered at the Spoleto Festival in Charleston, SC, on May 23, 1998. Reich's music was performed by Micaëla Haslam, Olive Simpson, Gerard O'Beirne, Steve Trowell and Robert Kearnley to video images created by Korot. *Hindenburg* was reprised at the Brooklyn Academy of Music in October 1998 and incorporated into THREE TALES, presented at the Spoleto Festival in 2002.

1998 New York Studios. *Hindenburg,* performed by the Steve Reich Ensemble and the Synergy Vocals group, was recorded at the Kampo Studios in New York City in May 1998 and the Avatar Studios in October 1998. The singers are Olive Simpson, Micaela Haslam, Ashley Catlin, Stephen Trowell and Rob Kearley. Todd Reynolds conducts. The opera is featured as the first part of the trilogy *Three Tales* on a 2003 Nonesuch DVD/CD.

HINDS, ESTHER   *American soprano (1943–)*

Esther Hinds, who starred in Gian Carlo Menotti's revised version of Samuel Barber's ANTONY AND CLEOPATRA at Juilliard and the Spoleto Festival, is also featured on the only complete recording. She created the role of the Empress of Byzantium in Menotti's church opera THE EGG, sings on the Tanglewood recording of Roger Sessions' cantata WHEN LILACS LAST IN THE DOORYARD BLOOMED and sang Barber's *Knoxville: Summer of 1915* at the Spoleto Festival. Hinds, who was born in the Barbados, made her American debut with New York City Opera in 1970 and has sung in opera houses around the world including Berlin, Toronto, San Diego, Houston and Cincinnati.

HINES, JEROME   *American bass/composer (1921–2003)*

Metropolitan Opera basso Jerome Hines (born Heinz) created the role of Captain Sutter in Philip Bezanson's television opera GOLDEN CHILD on NBC in 1960 and the role of Christ in his self-penned opera I AM THE WAY. He became a born-again Christian while composing this sacred opera and sang the title role 93 times; he can be seen performing in it on a 1963 VOICE OF FIRESTONE television program which is on video On other Firestone programs he can be seen singing "I've Got Plenty O' Nuttin" from George Gershwin's PORGY AND BESS and "This Nearly Was Mine"" from Richard Rodger's SOUTH PACIFIC. Hines usually sang European operas on stage but he was Nick Shadow in the 1953 British premiere of Igor Stravinsky's THE RAKE'S PROGRESS. Hines, who was born in Hollywood, made his debut in San Francisco in 1941 and joined the Met in 1946, singing there for a record-setting 41 years. He published an autobiography in 1968 called *This Is My Story, This Is My Song.*

HINSHAW, WILLIAM WADE   *American baritone (1867–1947)*

William Wade Hinshaw, a leading baritone at the Metropolitan from 1910 to 1913 who was known for his interest in opera in English, created roles in three American operas. He was the Druid Gloom in the first American opera to premiere at the Met, Horatio Parker's MONA in 1912. He was Le Bret in Walter Damrosch's CYRANO DE BERGERAC at the Met in 1913 and he was Corvain in Parker's FAIRYLAND at the Hollywood Bowl in 1915. Hinshaw, born in Union, Iowa, made his debut in St. Louis in 1899 and later formed a touring company to present operas sung in English.

HIRST, GRAYSON   *American tenor (1939–)*

Grayson Hirst created roles in nine American operas, including the title role in Virgil Thomson's LORD BYRON when it premiered at Juilliard American Opera Center in New York in 1972. He was the Young Conductor in Thomas Pasatieri's *La Divina* at Juilliard Opera Theater in 1966, Guiscardo in Pasatieri's *Padrevia* at Brooklyn College Opera in 1967, Alfons in Eugen Zador's *The Scarlet Mill* at Brooklyn College Opera in 1968, Orsino in Alberto Ginastera's BEATRIX CENCI at Washington Opera in 1971, the title character in Robert Starer's PANTAGLEIZE at Brooklyn College in 1973, Teacher and Barbarian Chief in Ned Rorem's BERTHA at Lincoln Center in 1973, First Tenor in Hugh Aitken's FABLES at the Library of Congress in 1975 and Reuben Waterford in Jack Beeson's DR. HEIDEGGER'S FOUNTAIN OF YOUTH at the National Arts Club in New York in 1978. He sings the part of Curley in a live recording of a 1971 Cincinnati Opera production of Carlisle Floyd's OF MICE AND MEN. Hirst, born in Ojai, California, studied at Juilliard and UCLA and made his official debut in Washington in 1969.

HOFFMAN, WILLIAM M.   *American librettist/playwright (1938–)*

William H. Hoffman wrote the libretto for John Corigliano's grandiose opera, THE GHOSTS OF VERSAILLES, an elaborate homage to Beaumarchais and French history that premiered at the Metropolitan Opera in 1991. It was the first opera for Hoffman whose primary career has been as a playwright. Born in New York City and educated at City College, he has also written two musicals, *Etiquette* and *Uptight.*

HOIBY, LEE   *American composer (1926–)*

Lee Hoiby's most popular operas are SUMMER AND SMOKE (1971), based on the Tennessee Williams play and staged by St. Paul and New York City Opera; the humorous monodrama THE ITALIAN LESSON (1980), based on a Ruth Draper monologue; THE TEMPEST (1986), based on the Shakespeare play and staged by Des Moines and Kansas City Opera; and BON APPÉTIT! (1988) based on a Julia Childs recipe. Hoiby, one of the best-known American opera composer, first attracted attention with his Chekhov opera THE SCARF, presented at the Spoleto Festival in 1958 and then at New York City Opera. BEATRICE (1959), a somewhat mystical opera fashioned from a Maeterlinck play, premiered on television in Kentucky. NATALIA PETROVNA, based on the Turgenev novel *A Month in the Country*, was staged by New York City Opera in 1964. A CHRISTMAS CAROL, a musical version of the story by Charles Dickens, premiered in San Francisco in 1981. ROMEO AND JULIET, a work-in-progress based on the Shakespeare play, was previewed in March 2000. Hoiby, who was born in Madison, WI, studied composition with Gian Carlo Menotti and his melodic, tonal operas have a kinship with Menotti's.

HOLLAND, CHARLES   *American tenor (1909–1987)*

Charles Holland sings the role of St. Chavez in Virgil Thomson's 1947 recording of his opera FOUR SAINTS IN THREE ACTS. As he was unable to create an opera career in America, he made his debut in 1954 at the Paris Opera and in 1955 became the first black singer to perform at the Opéra-Comique. He had wide success all over Europe.

HOLLANDER, JOHN   *American poet (1929–)*

John Hollander wrote the libretto for Hugo Weisgall's opera *Jenny, or The Hundred Nights* which he based on a Noh play translated by Yuko Mishima. It premiered at the Juilliard American Opera Center in 1976. He also wrote the libretto for British composer Alexander Goehr's 1992 *The Death of Moses*. Hollander, born in New York City, has published seventeen books of poetry.

HOLLINGSWORTH, STANLEY   *American composer (1924–)*

Stanley Hollingsworth had his first success with an opera based on a Hans Christian Andersen fairy tale; THE MOTHER was premiered by the Curtis Institute in Philadelphia in 1954 when he was twenty. His television opera LA GRANDE BRETÈCHE was presented on NBC television in 1957 when he was twenty-three. THE SELFISH GIANT, based on a fairy tale by Oscar Wilde, and HARRISON LOVED HIS UMBRELLA, based on a story by Rhoda Levine, were staged at the Spoleto Festival USA in 1981 in a trilogy with *The Mother*. Hollingsworth, who studied with Darius Milhaud at Mills and Gian Carlo Menotti at the Curtis Institute, has taught at San Jose College and Oakland University in Michigan.

HOLLYWOOD BOWL   *Los Angeles music venue*

The first opera presented at the Hollywood Bowl was an American opera, Horatio Parker's prize-winning FAIRYLAND, premiered in 1915. Samuel Earle Blakeslee's THE LEGEND OF WIWASTE was staged in 1927 with Tsianina Redfeather Blackstone, the first Native American opera singer, in the starring role. Leonard Bernstein's TROUBLE IN TAHITI was presented in 1973 with Evelyn Lear as Dinah. Richard Einhorn's cinematic opera VOICES OF LIGHT had its Los Angeles premiere there in 1984. Composers Richard Hageman and William Grant Still worked there as conductors in the 1930s.

HOLMES, EUGENE   *American baritone (1934–)*

Eugene Holmes created the role of Toimé Ukamba in Gian Carlo Menotti's THE MOST IMPORTANT MAN at New York City Opera in 1971 and he sings Stephen Kumalo in a Mississippi production of Kurt Weill's LOST IN THE STARS recorded in 1968. Born in Brownsville, Tennessee, he made his debut with the Goldovsky Opera Theater in 1963 singing John Proctor in Robert Ward's THE CRUCIBLE. He sang the role of Uncle Alfred in Gunther Schuller's THE VISITATION in San Francisco in 1967 and Porgy in George Gershwin's PORGY AND BESS in Düsseldorf where he was principal baritone from 1971 to 1985.

HOLMES, RICHARD   *American baritone (1970–)*

Richard Holmes created the role of Police Sergeant Duffy in Jack Beeson's chamber opera SORRY, WRONG NUMBER at the Center for Contemporary Opera in New York in 1999. He sings Ben in Gian Carlo Menotti's THE TELEPHONE and Dr. Gregg in Douglas Moore's GALLANTRY on 1994 recordings made by the New York Chamber Ensemble. Holmes, who made his debut at the Lake George Opera Festival, has also sung in Douglas Moore's CARRY NATION and Carlisle Floyd's SUSANNAH.

HOLY BLOOD AND CRESCENT MOON   *1989 opera by Copeland*

Incidents in the lives of the Crusaders and the Muslims in Jerusalem in the l2th century at the time of First Crusade. Stewart Copeland's two-act opera *Holy Blood and Crescent Moon*, libretto by Susan Shirwen, was commissioned by Cleveland Opera which premiered it on October 10, 1988. Edward J. Crafts was the Grand Wazir, Gloria Parker was Dahlia, Douglas Stevens, was Abdulla, Diane Eberts was Fadilla, Jon Garrison was Edmund, Marla Berg was Eleanor, James Rensink was King Tancred, William Powers was the Monk, Jeff Mattsey was Lamarak, Gene Allen was Peter, Paul Groves was Denis and Harold MacKintosh was Herce. Imre Pallo conducted the Cleveland Orchestra and Chorus.

HOLY DEVIL   *1958 opera by Nabokov*

Russian monk Rasputin, the "Holy Devil" who exerts enormous influence over the Russian royal family in the years before the Revolution, is poisoned on December 29, 1916, by conspirators headed by the Prince. He recalls his life in flashbacks and seems about to shake off the effects of the poison so the conspirators shoot him and he dies. Nicolas Nabokov's two-act opera *The Holy Devil*, libretto by poet Stephen Spender, was commissioned by Louisville Orchestra and premiered by Kentucky Opera on April 18, 1958. Robert Fischer played Rasputin, Audrey Nossaman was the Empress, Audrey Sanborn was the Countess Marina, William Pickett was the Prince, Russell Hammar was the Grand Duke, Joel

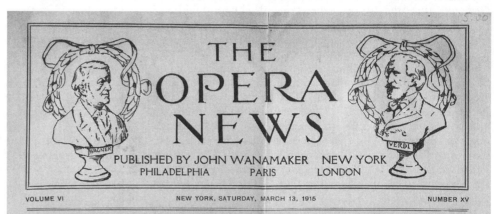

"*Copyright, Underwood & Underwood*"

MADAM LOUISE HOMER IS FIRST A MOTHER—THEN A GREAT SINGER
Left to Right:—Catherine, Mme. Homer, Hester, Ann and Louise

DON'T force distasteful careers upon your children is the epigram of Mme. Louise Homer, famous prima donna and also most famous mother of the operatic stage. Mme. Homer's belief is that after a mother has familiarized herself with her children's ideas and ideals, she must most solicitously look toward the development of their particular talents, but she must be careful not to endeavor to cultivate those gifts as she would have them but according to the child's conception of facts. In other words, a mother must train her offspring to specialize in order to be effective and efficient is the watchword of modern progress. Mothers frequently make the great mistake of trying to rear their children along the lines which they themselves have determined upon. This is always disastrous and frequently terminates in the wrecking of the child's life.

Opera diva Louise Homer and her family were featured on a 1915 magazine cover.

Ebersole was the Doctor, Richard Dales was the Deputy, Lynn Axton was Masha, Elizabeth Johnson was Anna, Larry St. Clair was the Czarevich, Wilma Harrell was the Gypsy, Catherine Cohen was Rasputin's daughter and Carole Jordan, Elizabeth Hill, Virginia Stanford and Grace Wieck were the Empress's daughters. Moritz Bomhard conducted the Louisville Orchestra and Kentucky Opera Chorus. *The Holy Devil* was later expanded to three acts and presented in a German translation in Cologne in 1959.

1958 Kentucky Opera. Robert Fischer sings the role of Rasputin in this recording of the opera made by the Kentucky Opera premiere cast in 1958. Audrey Nossaman is the Empress, Audrey Sanborn is Countess Marina, William Pickett is the Prince, Russell Hammar is the Grand Duke, Joel Ebersole is the Doctor, Richard Dales is the Deputy, Lynn Axton is Masha and the rest of the cast are as listed above. Moritz Bomhard conducts the Louisville Orchestra and Kentucky Opera Chorus. Louisville First Edition LP.

HOMER, LOUISE   *American contralto (1871–1947)*

Legendary diva Louise Homer sang leading roles in the first two American operas presented at the Metropolitan Opera. She was Naoia in Frederick Converse's THE PIPE OF DESIRE in 1910 and she created the title role in Horatio Parker's MONA in 1912. She did not make recordings of her arias in these operas but did record a famous aria from Reginald De Koven's comic opera ROBIN HOOD in 1913. Homer, born in Shadyside, Pittsburgh, was a mainstay of the Met from 1900 on singing opposite Enrico Caruso, and the other great singers of the period. Composer Samuel Barber was her nephew.

HOOK, WALTER   *American baritone (1941–)*

Walter E. Hook created the role of John Hobhouse in Virgil Thomson's LORD BYRON at the Juilliard American Opera Center in 1972 and the role of Papa Belliart in Jack Beeson's CAPTAIN JINKS OF THE HORSE MARINES at Kansas City Lyric in 1975. He sings the role of Hortensio in the 1969 Kansas City Lyric recording of Vittorio Giannini's THE TAMING OF THE SHREW and Brother Smiley in the 1974 Kansas City Lyric recording of Jack Beeson's THE SWEET BYE AND BYE. He has also sung Olin Blitch in Carlisle Floyd's SUSANNAH, Bob in Gian Carlo Menotti's THE OLD MAID AND THE THIEF and the Postman in Lee Hoiby's THE SCARF. He was born in Kansas City, Missouri, studied at the University of Missouri Conservatory of Music and made his debut at Kansas City Lyric in 1958.

HOOKER, BRIAN   *American librettist/playwright (1880–1946)*

Brian Hooker is not much remembered today but he made a considerable contribution to American opera and operetta in its early years and won large amounts of money with his librettos. He wrote the libretto for the first American opera premiered at the Metropolitan Opera, Horatio Parker's MONA, which won a $10,000 competition and was staged in 1912. He then wrote the libretto for Parker's FAIRYLAND which won another $10,000 prize; it was the first opera presented at the Hollywood Bowl where it premiered in 1915. He wrote the libretto for Ernest Carter's THE WHITE BIRD, first heard at Carnegie Hall in 1922 and then produced in Germany in 1927, one of the first American operas to be staged in Europe. He had considerable success on collaborations with operetta composer Rudolf Friml writing THE VAGABOND KING (1925) and WHITE EAGLE (1927). Hooker, a native of New York City, was a university English professor before turning to plays and librettos.

HOPKINSON, FRANCIS   *American composer (1737–1791)*

Philadelphia-born Francis Hopkinson, one of the signers of the Declaration of Independence, claimed to be America's first native composer. His patriotic AMERICA INDEPENDENT: OR, THE TEMPLE OF MINERVA, was the first American opera/oratorio staged when it premiered in Philadelphia on March 21, 1781. Described as an "oratorial entertainment" and through sung, it was created to celebrate the American victory over the British. Hopkinson, who began to play the harpsichord when he was seventeen, was composing songs by the age of twenty-two. His 1759 song "My days Have Been so Wondrous Free" is the earliest surviving American secular composition. He also published a number of song collections.

Composer Francis Hopkinson

HOPPER'S WIFE   *1997 opera by Wallace*

Artist Edward Hopper marries gossip columnist Hedda Hopper and actress Ava Gardner becomes his model. These imaginary happenings are central to fantasy adventures in Hollywood in the 1940s with plenty of guns and nudity. Stewart Wallace's chamber opera *Hopper's Wife*, libretto by Michel Korie, was premiered by Long Beach Opera at the Knoebel Dance Theater in Long Beach, CA, on June 14, 1997. Chris Pedro Trakas was Edward Hopper, Lucy Schaufer was Ava Gardner and Juliana Gondek was Hedda Hopper. Allen Moyer designed the set, Christopher Alden directed and Michael Barrett conducted.

HORNE, MARILYN   *American mezzo-soprano (1934–)*

Marilyn Horne sang her first American opera at the age of twenty, providing the voice of CARMEN JONES in the 1954 film of the opera. She sang in Bernard Herrmann's A CHRISTMAS CAROL on CBS-TV in 1954, created the role of Laura in Vittorio Giannini's *Harvest* at Chicago Lyric Opera in 1961 and created the role of Samira in John Corigliano's THE GHOSTS OF VERSAILLES at the Met in 1991. She sings "Somewhere" on Leonard Bernstein's 1985 operatic recording of WEST SIDE STORY and "Something Wonderful" on the 1992 recording of Rodgers and Hammerstein's THE KING AND I. She dubbed the torch song "Love, Look Away" in the 1961 film of Rodgers and Hammerstein's *Flower Drum Song.* Horne, born in Bradford, PA, studied with Lotte Lehmann at USC and made her stage debut in Los Angeles in 1954. Her career blossomed in Europe, especially in partnership with Joan Sutherland.

HORNSMOKE   *1975 horse opera by Schickele*
Hornsmoke ("a horse opera for brass quintet") is an opera without singers in which musical instruments play the characters in a parody of the cliches and characteristics of movie Westerns. Humorist composer Peter Schickele, writing as his alter-ego P.D.Q. Bach, created this one-act non-vocal opera which features a narrator who sets the scene and introduces the characters.

2000 Chestnut Brass Company. The Chestnut Brass Company, which began as a Philadelphia street band in 1977 and had a hit with the album *Tippecanoe and Tyler, Too,* recorded Schickele's non-vocal opera. The composer narrates the story on the album which won a Grammy in 2000 for Best Classical Crossover album. Newport Classic CD.

HORSE OPERA   *1994 opera by Copeland*
An Englishman fantasizes being a cowboy and models his home after a Western ranch. After a hit on the head, he wakes up in the real 19th century west. He meets his hero Wyatt Earp, who plans to go to Hollywood, and discovers that Jesse James and Billy the Kid are illiterate oafs. Stewart Copeland's TV opera *Horse Opera,* libretto by Jonathan Moore based on Anne Caulfield's play *Cowboys,* premiered on Britain's Channel 4 February 13, 1994. Philip Guy-Bromley played the would-be cowboy, Gina Bellman was his wife, Rich Mayall was Jesse James, librettist Moore was Billy the Kid and composer Copland was Jesse James. Bob Baldwin directed.

HORSPFAL   *1969 opera by Stokes*
The action takes place in a bed which is the home of the American Indian. Betsy Ross and the Daughter of American Revolution invade it, archeologist John Eliot looks for ruins in it, Wild Bill Hickok shoots it up, Frederick Remington paints it, a Real Estate Agent sells it and a Folk Singer sings about it. The bed/home goes up in flames. Eric Stokes' multi-media opera *Horspfal,* libretto by Alvin Greenburg, was premiered by Minnesota Opera in Minneapolis on February 15, 1969. Howard Balk staged the complicated production involving film projection and large crowds and Thomas Nee conducted. The opera was presented with revised orchestration in New York in 1971.

HOTEL EDEN   *1987 opera by Mollicone*
Updated Biblical tales set in a modern hotel. In *Lilith* young Adam and Eve are on their honeymoon when former wife Lilith turns up. In *Mrs. Noah* middle-aged Noah gets drunk in a spa and his wandering wife has to rescue him and turn off the flooding water. In *Sarah* elderly couple Sarah and Abraham discover she is pregnant and wonder how the new child will fit in with a child he has had by their maid Hagar. Henry Mollicone's three-act opera *Hotel Eden,* libretto by Judith Fein based on stories in the Book of Genesis, was commissioned by Hidden Valley Opera, Carmel Valley, California, which premiered it in 1987. It was reprised by Opera San José on November 25, 1989, with Dan Montez as Adam, Julia Wade as Eve, Rachel Louis as Lilith, Gundunas as Mrs. Noah, D'Anna Fortunato as Rachel, Susan Kathleen Nit as Hagar and David Cox-Crewel as the Bellhop.

HOTEL FOR CRIMINALS   *1974 opera by Silverman*
Fantomas, Judex and Irma Vep, the protagonists of Louis Feuillade's surrealistic silent serials of the 1910s, are portrayed in their criminal and heroic adventures. Fantomas is a masked master criminal, Irma Vep (anagram of "vampire") is a sexy vamp in a tight-fitting costume and Judex fights for justice against the Vampire Gang. After complicated feats of derring-do, the audience is asked to return for more of the same the following week. Stanley Silverman's 90-minute opera *Hotel for Criminals,* libretto by Richard Foreman based on Louis Feuillade's silent French films, was commissioned by the National Opera Institute and premiered at the Lenox Arts Center in Stockbridge, MA, on August 14, 1974. It was reprised by the Music Theater Performing Group at the Exchange Theater in Wesbeth, NY, in December 1974. Richard Foreman designed the sets and directed. The music is tuneful in the Kurt Weill manner.

THE HOUSE OF THE SEVEN GABLES   *2000 opera by Eyerly*
The House of the Seven Gables, home of the Pyncheon family, has been cursed for generations. A final conflict between evil Judge Jaffrey, unjustly imprisoned Clifford and protective sister Hepzibah ends in a strange victory for love and righteousness. Scott Eyerly's opera *The House of the Seven Gables,* libretto by the composer based on the Nathaniel Hawthorne novel, was premiered by Manhattan School of Music on December 6, 2000. James Schaffner was the suffering Clifford Pyncheon, Christianne Rushton was frightened sister Hepzibah, Dominic Aquilino was villainous Jaffrey Pyncheon, Bert Johnson was artist boarder Holgrave and Kelly Smith was charming cousin Phoebe. There were also seven non-singing ghosts. Notable numbers were the "Garden Quartet" and Phoebe's aria "Song of the Rose." Dipu Gupta designed the sets, Linda Brovsky was stage director and David Gilbert conducted.

2000 Manhattan School of Music. James Schaffner is Clifford with Christianne Rushton as sister Hepzibah and Dominic Aquilino as Jaffrey, in this recording by the Manhattan School of Music premiere cast. Bert Johnson is Holgrave and Kelly Smith is Phoebe. David Gilbert conducts. Albany Records CD.

HOVHANESS, ALAN   *American composer (1911–2000)*
Armenian American Alan Hovhaness, one of the most prolific composers of the century, won admiration from a range of critics including John Cage. He created over 500 works including hundreds of orchestral works and symphonies and a dozen operas, almost all religious or mystical in nature. None of his operas, composed to his own librettos, are well known. While his music has been extensively recorded, the only operas on CD are LADY OF LIGHT (1968), featuring Patricia Clark and Lesie Fyson, and TALE OF THE SUN GODDESS GOING INTO THE STONE HOUSE (1978), featuring Hinako Fujihara. Hovhaness's first opera was *Etchmiadzin,* premiered at the Armenian St. Vartan's Cathedral in New York in 1945. *Avak the Healer,* a 1946 cantata for soprano, trumpet and strings, has been recorded with Marni Nixon as the singer. The chamber opera *Blue Flame* was performed in San Antonio, Texas on December 15, 1959. *Spirit of the Avalanche,* a 1964 chamber opera, has not been staged. THE BURNING HOUSE, a fiery opera

set in outer space, premiered in Gatlinburg, Tennessee, on August 23, 1964, in a double bill with his dance-drama *Wind Drum*. The ballet-opera PILATE, about the suicide of Pontius Pilate, premiered at Pepperdine College, Los Angeles, on June 26, 1966. THE TRAVELLERS was staged at Foothill College in Los Altos, California, on April 22, 1967. *Pericles*, his operatic version of Shakespeare's play for which he received an NEA grant, was presented in excerpt form in Shippensburg, Pennsylvania, in 1979. Hovhaness, who was born in Somerville, Massachusetts, as Alan Vaness Chamakjian, wrote operas as a teenager but destroyed them along with a thousand other early works.

HOWARD, KATHLEEN *American mezzo-soprano (1880–1956)*

Kathleen Howard created the role of the Abbess in Horatio Parker's FAIRYLAND at the Hollywood Bowl in 1915, Mrs. Everton in Charles Cadman's SHANEWIS at the Metropolitan Opera in 1918 and Marta in Joseph Breil's THE LEGEND at the Met in 1919. Although she had a major career as an opera singer, Howard is best known today as a movie actress, especially through playing W. C. Fields' wife in three films. Howard, who was born in Canada, began her opera career in 1907 and sang with the Met from 1916 to 1928. After leaving the Met she worked as fashion editor before moving to Hollywood in 1934. She worked in movies until she was seventy.

HUGHES, LANGSTON *American poet/librettist (1902–1967)*

Langston Hughes, one of the great African American poets, also made a major contribution to American opera. He wrote the memorable lyrics for Kurt Weill's 1947 STREET SCENE and the librettos for three other opera composers. James P. Johnson's blues opera DE ORGANIZER, about organizing a union, premiered at Carnegie Hall in 1940. William Grant Still's TROUBLED ISLAND, about a Haitian revolutionary, was completed in 1941 and premiered by New York City Opera in 1949, the first African American opera staged by a major company. Hughes wrote librettos for three operas by German American composer Jan Meyerowitz. THE BARRIER was staged in New York in 1950 with Lawrence Tibbett in the leading role, ESTHER was premiered at the University of Illinois in 1957 and *Port Town* was performed at Tanglewood in 1960. Hughes, who was born in Joplin, Missouri, and studied at Columbia and Lincoln universities, also wrote gospel song-plays, including *Black Nativity*, and the Christmas cantata *The Ballad of the Brown King*.

HUGHES, ROBERT *American conductor (1950—)*

Robert Hughes has conducted notable productions and recordings of operas by Ezra Pound. THE TESTAMENT OF FRANÇOIS VILLON was presented on stage in America for the first time in 1971 by the Western Opera Theater of San Francisco Opera and was recorded with Hughes conducting. Pound's second opera CAVALCANTI was composed in 1932 but not given its stage premiere until 1983 when it was presented by the Arch Ensemble for Experimental Music in San Francisco with Hughes conducting. Hughes, music director of the Ensemble, has conducted with the Oakland Symphony, San Francisco Ballet, the Cabrillo Music Festival and orchestras in Alaska, California, Italy and Switzerland. In 1980 he received an award for adventuresome programming of contemporary music.

HUGO, JOHN ADAM *American composer (1873–1945)*

John Adam Hugo had only one of his three operas staged but it got a major production. THE TEMPLE DANCER premiered at the Metropolitan Opera in 1919 with Florence Easton as the Temple Dancer and Morgan Kingston as the Temple Guard, was warmly received and was awarded the David Bispham Medal. His other two operas were apparently not performed. *The Hero of Byzanze* was a student work composed to his own libretto. *The Sun God*, libretto by Bartlett B. James, is a story about Pizzaro and his conflict with the Incas. Hugo, born in Bridgeport, Connecticut, began his musical career in Europe as a pianist and turned to composing after returning to the U.S. in 1906.

HUMPHREYS-RAUSCHER, HENRY *American composer (1909–1991)*

Henry Humphreys-Rauscher composed five operas based on history and literature to his own librettos. MAYERLING, a three-act opera about the Austrian prince who loved a commoner, was presented in Cincinnati on November 16, 1957. *Joan of Arc at Reims*, a one-act opera about the French heroine, premiered in Cincinnati on March 17 1968 with Elaine Bonazzi as Joan. *Sea-Thorn, an American Phaedra,* a two-act opera about a woman who falls in love with her stepson, was presented in Covington, KY, in 1981 in a production by Charles H. Parson with Paul J. Zappa conducting. *Quo Vadis Domine* (Where Are You Going, Lord?) a church opera based on the novel *Quo Vadis* by Henryk Sienkiewicz, was premiered at St. Williams Church in Cincinnati in November 1984. He also worked on an opera based on Charles Laughton's film *Night of the Hunter*. Although Humphreys-Rauscher was born in Vienna, his father was an American and he was American from birth.

HWANG, DAVID HENRY *American librettist (1957–)*

David Henry Hwang has written librettos for operas by Philip Glass, Bright Sheng and Osvaldo Golijov. For Glass he wrote THE VOYAGE, which premiered at the Metropolitan Opera in 1992; co-wrote (with Jerome Serlin); 1000 AIRPLANES ON THE ROOF which premiered in Hangar No. 3 at Vienna International Airport in 1988; and wrote *The Sound of Voice,* premiered in Cambridge, MA, in 2003. For Sheng he wrote THE SILVER RIVER which premiered at the Santa Fe Chamber Music Festival in 1997. For Golijov he wrote AINADAMAR which premiered at the Tanglewood Festival in 2003. Hwang, born in Los Angeles, won the 1981 Obie for his first play. He is best-known for his Tony award-winning 1988 play *M. Butterfly* loosely derived from the Puccini opera.

HYDROGEN JUKEBOX *1990 "music theatre" by Glass*

Theatrical portrait of the "American Empire" as viewed through songs about the Vietnam war, sexual politics, the environmental movement, Eastern mysticism and other events of the past four decades. Philip Glass's music theater work *Hydrogen Jukebox* has a libretto by Alan Ginsberg based on his poems, including "Howl." It premiered in concert format in Philadelphia on April 22, 1990, and was staged at the Spoleto Festival USA in Charleston on May 26, 1990. Jerome Sirlin designed the visual accompaniment for the words and music. It was later revived at the Brooklyn Academy of Music.

1993 Philip Glass Ensemble. Sopranos Elizabeth Futral and Michèle Eaton, baritones Gregory Purnhagen and Nathaniel Watson, mezzo Mary Ann Hart and tenor Richard Fracker are the featured singers with Allen Ginsberg as narrator on this recording produced by Michael Riesman and Kurt Munkacs with the Philip Glass Ensemble. The instrumental performers include Carol Wincene on flute, Richard Peck on tenor sax, Andrew Sterman on soprano sax, Frank Cassara and James Pugliese on percussion,

Philip Glass on piano and Martin Goldray on keyboards while conducting. Electra Nonesuch CD.

"HYMN TO THE SUN" *Counter tenor aria: Akhnaten (1984). Music and lyrics: Philip Glass*

"Hymn to the Sun" from Philip Glass's opera AKHNATEN is the most famous counter tenor aria in American opera. It is sung by the Egyptian Pharaoh Akhnaten, a visionary leader ahead of his time, who creates a religion in 1875 BC based around a single all-powerful god, the Sun. The aria is his colorful 13-minute chant-like hymn to that god who he calls Aten. It is the only aria in the opera in English, the others are sung in Akkadian, Egyptian and Hebrew. "Hymn to the Sun" was introduced by Paul Esswood in the premiere of the opera on March 24, 1984, and was sung in the Houston Grand Opera production by Christopher Robson. It can be heard sung by Esswood on the 1987 Stuttgart Opera recording and on the anthology CD *Songs from the Trilogy.*

I

I AM THE WAY *1956 opera by Hines*

Metropolitan bass Jerome Hines composed the sacred opera *I Am the Way* to his own libretto and toured it around the U.S. playing the lead role of Christus. The opera, a respectful presentation of the life of Jesus, had its first work-in-progress presentation at the 14th Street Salvation Army Temple on 14th Street in New York in 1956. Hines said he became a born-again Christian while composing the opera and he sang the title role 93 times; An excerpt was presented on TV in 1963 but its official stage premiere was in Philadelphia in 1969.

1963 Voice of Firestone. Hines performs a ten-minute scene from his sacred opera *I Am the Way* on *The Voice of Firestone* television program on March 31, 1963. He sings the role of Christus, Mildred Miller is Mother Mary, William Walker is St. Peter and David Starkey is St. John. Walter Hendl conducts the Firestone Orchestra. The excerpt is on the video *Jerome Hines in Opera and Song.* VAI VHS.

"I GOT PLENTY O' NUTTIN'" *Baritone aria: Porgy and Bess (1935). Words: Ira Gershwin and DuBose Heyward. Music: George Gershwin.*

Porgy sings of his new joyful life in the banjo-style baritone aria "I got plenty o' nuttin'" after Bess has become his woman in George Gershwin's PORGY AND BESS. Not only does he have plenty of nothing, he says, but nothing is all he needs. The words were created

Porgy sings of his new life in the baritone aria "I got plenty o' nuttin" in *Porgy and Bess.*

jointly by lyricist Ira Gershwin and librettist DuBose Heyward and were introduced on stage in 1935 by the first Porgy, Todd Duncan. Presumably because he was an unknown black singer, the aria was first recorded by a popular white opera star, the Metropolitan Opera baritone Lawrence Tibbett. Duncan, however, did record in 1940 during the run of another Broadway production. In the 1959 movie version it is sung by Robert McFerrin dubbing for Sidney Poitier. Among the many others who have recorded it are William Warfield, Willard White, Jerome Hines, Donnie Ray Albert, Simon Estes, Gregg Baker, Samuel Ramey and Louis Armstrong.

"I HAVE DREAMT" *Soprano aria: Wuthering Heights (1951). Words: Lucille Fletcher. Music: Bernard Herrmann*

Cathy sings of the dreams she has had that have stayed with her and altered the color of her mind. Cathy's love-hate relationship with Wuthering Heights itself is the basis of the aria "I have dreamt." It was introduced by Morag Beaton in a 1966 recording of Bernard Herrmann's opera WUTHERING HEIGHTS conducted by Herrmann in London. It was sung in its stage premiere at Portland Opera in 1982 by Barrie Smith. Renée Fleming brought it back to prominence when she featured it on her 1999 album *I Want Magic!* Lucille Fletcher, who wrote the lyrics for the aria and the libretto for the opera based on Emily Brontë's novel, was married to Herrmann.

"I WANT MAGIC!"   *Soprano aria: A Streetcar Named Desire (1998). Words: Philip Littell. Music: André Previn*

Faded southern belle Blanche DuBois comes to stay with sister Stella in New Orleans and tells us that she doesn't like the real world. She prefers magic to reality and says that what she tells people ought to be the truth. The aria was introduced by Renée Fleming at the San Francisco Opera premiere of André Previn's A STREETCAR NAMED DESIRE on September 19, 1998. Philip Littell's lyrics reflect the moment of confrontation between Blanche and her brutish brother-in-law Stanley Kowalski in the original Tennessee Williams play and in the opera. It is the title track on Fleming's 1998 album of American opera arias *I Want Magic!*

I WAS LOOKING AT THE CEILING AND THEN I SAW THE SKY   *1995 opera by Adams*

Los Angeles before and after the 1994 Northridge earthquake. Black minister David, who has had many love affairs, is currently involved with Laila, a student who works in an abortion clinic. Dewain, a former gang leader, is arrested by community-oriented white cop Mike. Consuelo, an illegal immigrant from El Salvador, is Dewain's woman and the mother of his baby. Tiffany, a TV news reporter, fancies Mike. Rick, a Vietnamese lawyer, is trying to do good work. They are seen interacting before and after the earthquake which changes them. John Adams' third opera (he called it an "earthquake-romance") *I Was Looking at the Ceiling and Then I Saw the Sky*, libretto by poet June Jordan, premiered at the Zellerbach Playhouse in Berkeley, California, on May 12, 1995. Sophia Salguero was Consuelo, Kennya Ramsey was Laila, Harold Perrineau Jr. was Dewain, Kaitlin Hopkins was Tiffany, Jesse Means was David, Michael Ness was Mike and Welly Yang was Rick. The eight-piece Paul Dresh Ensemble played the music. The opera is Brechtian in style with a strong pop/jazz element and Peter Sellars was staged in collaboration with director. *Ceiling/Sky* was not well received at its premiere or in later stagings in New York and Europe.

Adams worked with a different librettist than on his first two operas and the story is not so highly focused.

1996 Helsinki recording. Adams used mostly different singers for this recording of a shorter version of the opera taped at the Arabian Studios in Helsinki, Finland, in December 1996. Audra McDonald takes the role of Consuelo, Marin Mazzie is Tiffany, Michael McElroy is Dewain, Angela Teek is Leila, Richard Muenz is Mike, Darius De Haas is David and Welly Jang is Rick. Adams conducts the eight-person Finnish musical ensemble. The singing is impressive, especially McDonald performing "Consuelo's Dream" and McDonald, Mazzie and Teek joining voices on "Song about the Bad Boys and the News." Nonesuch CD. **1999 The John Adams Earbox.** This large anthology of works by Adams includes excerpts from the Helsinki recording of *I Was Looking at the Ceiling and Then I Saw the Sky*. Nonesuch 10-CD box.

IBRAHIM   *1999 opera by Bernstein*

Ibrahim is a five-year-old Quaker boy who has been left in a Puritan village. The townspeople are unable to accept his gentle timidity and kindness and he is left to die. David Bernstein's opera *Ibrahim*, libretto by Charles Kondek based on Nathaniel Hawthorne's 1837 story *The Gentle Boy*, was premiered at the University of Akron School of Music in Akron, Ohio, on November 6, 1999.

IDAHO   *American state (1890–)*

Opera Idaho! in Boise is the leading opera company in the state.

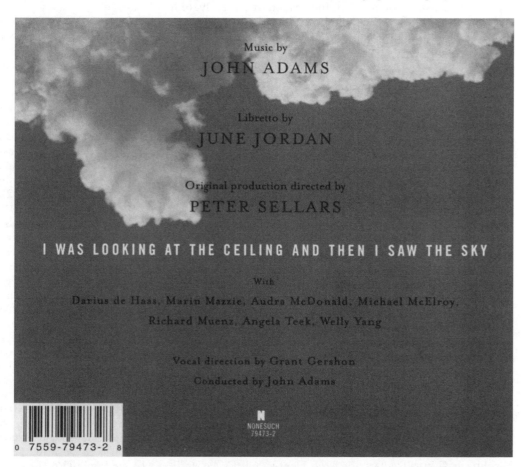

John Adams' "earthquake-romance" *I Was Looking at the Ceiling and Then I Saw the Sky* is set in Los Angeles but it was recorded in Finland.

Idaho's leading opera composer is poet Ezra Pound, born in Hailey, who composed two operas while leading an avant-garde life in Europe.

Boise: Eugene Adrian Farner premiered his one-act opera *The White Buffalo Maiden* at Boise High School Auditorium on April 26, 1923. Opera Idaho! presents opera and operetta at the Shakespeare Festival Amphitheater and the Morrison Center in Boise. Its American productions include Leonard Bernstein's CANDIDE, Aaron Copland's THE TENDER LAND and Douglas Moore's THE BALLAD OF BABY DOE.

Idaho Falls: Idaho Falls Opera Theater is a community opera company founded in 1978 and based in Idaho Falls. All participants are volunteers.

Paris: Alex Gelman premiered *First Cast a Stone,* an Adam and Eve story set in the West, at the Great West Music Festival in Paris, Idaho, in 1998.

IDIOTS FIRST   *1964 opera by Blitzstein/Lehrman*

Death's envoy advises Mendel he will die at midnight. Mendel tries desperately to raise money to send his mentally-handicapped son Itzak to a relative before his time runs out. Marc Blitzstein's one-act blackly comic opera *Idiots First,* libretto by the composer based on a story by Bernard Malamud, was unfinished at the time of the composer's death in 1964 but was intended to be half of the double bill *Tales of Malamud.* It was completed by Leonard Lehrman and previewed in concert form at Cornell University in August 1974. It was given its stage premiere by the Marc Blitzstein Opera Company in Bloomington, Indiana, on March 14, 1976. It was reprised by Bel Canto Opera in New York in January 1978 with Ronald Edwards singing the role of Mendel.

1990 Ronald Edwards. Baritone Ronald Edwards performs two of Mendel's arias from *Idiots First,* "Who Will Close the Door on a Neighbor's Misfortune?" (Mendel's desperate plea for $35 from a neighbor) and "How I Met my New Grandfather." Leonard Lehrman plays piano accompaniment on the album *A Blitzstein Cabaret.* Premiere Recordings CD.

ILLINOIS   *American state (1818–)*

Chicago has been a major center of opera since the 19th century and has held the premieres of many American operas. Silas Pratt premiered *Antonio* at the Farwell Hall in 1874, *Zenobia, Queen of Palmyra* at Central Music Hall in 1882 and *Lucille* at the Columbia Theater in 1882. Frederick Gleason's *Otho Viconti* was premiered at the College Theater in 1907. After Reginald De Koven premiered ROBIN HOOD at the Grand Opera House in 1890, comic operas became enormously popular. Gustav Luders started his career in Chicago and premiered six of his comic operas in the Windy City: *Little Robinson Crusoe* at the Schiller Theater in 1895, *The Burgomaster* at the Dearborn in 1900, *King Dodo* at the Manhattan in 1902, *The Sho-Gun* at the Studebaker in 1904, *The Grand Mogul* at the Colonial in 1906, *Marcelle* at the Casino in 1907 and *The Old Town* at the Studebaker in 1909. Victor Herbert premiered three of his comic operas in Chicago: BABES IN TOYLAND at the Opera House in 1903, *The Prima Donna* at the Studebaker in 1908 and ANGEL FACE at the Colonial in 1919.

The Chicago Grand Opera Company was founded in 1910 and its various permutations and successors, in including Chicago Civic Opera, welcomed many American operas at the 4000-seat Chicago Auditorium. They included Victor Herbert's NATOMA and Jane Van Etten's GUIDO FERRANTI in 1914, Henry Hadley's AZORA in 1917, Arthur Nevin's A DAUGHTER OF THE FOREST in 1918, Reginald De Koven's RIP VAN WINKLE in 1920, Sergey Prokofiev's THE

LOVE FOR THREE ORANGES in 1921, Theodore Stearns' SNOWBIRD in 1919, Aldo Franchetti's NAMIKO-SAN in 1925, William Franke Harling's A LIGHT FROM ST. AGNES in 1925 and Charles Cadman's A WITCH OF SALEM in 1926. The Chicago opera companies began to premiere operas in the New Civic Opera House in 1930 starting with Hamilton Forrest's CAMILLE in 1930 and Ethel Leginska's *Gale* in 1935.

Other notable early Chicago premieres include Earl R. Drake's grand romantic opera THE BLIND GIRL OF CASTEL-CUILLÉ, premiered at the Globe Theater in 1914, and Drake's comic opera *The Mite and the Mighty,* staged in 1915. George W. Chadwick's *Love's Sacrifice* and John Lewis Browne's *The Corsican Girl* were premiered at the Playhouse in 1923. Eleanor Freer premiered four operas in Chicago: *Frithiof* at the Studebaker Theater in 1931, LITTLE WOMEN at the Musician's Club of Women in 1934, *A Christmas Tale* at the Women's Club in 1936 and *The Brownings Go to Italy* at the Arts Club in 1938.

Illinois-born opera composers include Laurie Anderson (Chicago), Jan Bach (Forrest), Ernest Bacon (Chicago), Seymour Barab (Chicago), David Burge (Evanston), Earl R. Drake (Aurora), Grant Fletcher (Hartsburg), Robert Kurka (Cicero), Polly Pen (Chicago), Vivian Fine (Chicago), Kim Sherman (Elgin) and Peter Westergaard (Champaign).

Illinois-born singers include soprano Erie Mills (Granite City), baritone Sherrill Milnes (Hinsdale), baritones Eugene and Herbert Perry, bass-baritone William Powers (Chicago) and soprano Nancy Shade (Rockford). Modern opera premieres are listed below by city.

Bloomington: Grant Fletcher's *The Carrion Crow* premiered at Illinois Wesleyan University in Bloomington in 1953.

Carbondale: Will Gay Bottje's three-act *Algeld* was premiered at Southern Illinois University in Carbondale in 1969.

Chicago: Lyric Opera of Chicago, founded in 1954, is Chicago's major company today and has always shown a strong interest in American opera. It presented Vittorio Giannini's THE TAMING OF THE SHREW in its first season, Raffaelo de Banfield's LORD BYRON'S LOVE LETTER in 1955 and Giannini's *The Harvest* in 196. Composers-in-residence who have premiered new work include William Neil with THE GUILT OF LILLIAN SLOAN (1985) and Lee Goldstein with THE FAN (1989). Commissioned and premiered were William Bolcom's MCTEAGUE (1992), Anthony Davis's AMISTAD (1997) and Bolcom's A VIEW FROM THE BRIDGE (1999). Lyric Opera has also staged Dominick Argento's THE VOYAGE AROUND EDGAR ALLAN POE, Samuel Barber's ANTONY AND CLEOPATRA, John Corigliano's THE GHOSTS OF VERSAILLES, Gian Carlo Menotti's THE CONSUL, Marvin David Levy's MOURNING BECOMES ELECTRA and Hugo Weisgall's ESTHER. Chicago Opera Theater, founded in 1974 to present operas in English, has emphasized American opera. Its productions have include Dominick Argento's POSTCARD FROM MOROCCO, Marc Blitzstein's REGINA, Carlisle Floyd's OF MICE AND MEN and SUSANNAH, Philip Glass's AKHNATEN, Lee Hoiby's SUMMER AND SMOKE (nationally televised) and BON APPÉTIT, Daron Hagen's SHINING BROW, Robert Kurka's THE GOOD SOLDIER SCHWEIK, Mollicone's The Face on the Barroom Floor, Gian Carlo Menotti's THE CONSUL, Conrad Susa's TRANSFORMATIONS, Virgil Thomson's THE MOTHER OF US ALL and FOUR SAINTS IN THREE ACTS and Robert Ward's THE CRUCIBLE. Other modern premieres in Chicago include Charles Garland's *If Men Played Cards Like Women Do* at the American Conservatory of Music in 1952, Lazare Saminsky's *The Vision of Ariel* at the University of Chicago in 1954, Jeanellen McKee's *Collector's Piece* at the Lyon and Healy Recital Hall in 1958, Donald Jenni's *The Emperor Clothed Anew* at

De Paul University in 1965, John Austin's rock opera *Orpheus* at the First Presbyterian Church in 1967, Gian Carlo Menotti's TAMU TAMU at the Studebaker Theater in 1973, Robert Ashley's ATALANTA at the Museum of Contemporary Art in 1982 and Mark Adamczyk's *The Prairie* at Theatre Building Chicago in 2004.

De Kalb: T. J. Anderson's *Thomas Jefferson's Orbiting Minstrels and Contraband* premiered at Northern Illinois University on February 12, 1986.

Evanston: Northwestern University was the site of four premieres: David Burge's *Intervals* in 1962, Anthony Donato's *The Walker-Through-Walls* in 1965, Robert Beadell's *The Number of Fools* in 1966 and Ronald Combs' *The Three Visitors* in 1968.

Galesburg: H. Murray Baylor's comic opera *By Gemini* premiered at Knox College on March 2, 1949.

Highland Park: Ravinia Park, summer home of the Chicago Symphony Orchestra, began to present opera in 1912 and became the home of the Ravinia Festival. It had a major success in 1931 with Deems Taylor's PETER IBBETSON soon after the opera's premiere at the Met. The festival continues today with James Conlon as its music director.

Lincoln: Martin Kalmanoff's *Videomania* premiered at Lincoln College on May 8, 1958.

Oak Park: Lora Aborn's *The Gift of the Magi* premiered in Oak Park, Illinois, in 1975.

Rock Island: Seymour Barab's A GAME OF CHANCE premiered at Augustana College on January 11, 1957.

Skokie: Light Opera Works in Skokie staged Sigmund Romberg's THE STUDENT PRINCE in the Centre East in 1994.

Urbana: The University of Illinois in Urbana has premiered of a number of operas by major composers including three avantgarde works by Harry Partch. They include Victor Rieti's *Don Perlimplin* in 1952, Ben Johnston's *Gertrude: or, Would She Be Pleased to Receive It* in 1956, Ernst Krenek's THE BELL TOWER in 1957, Jan Meyerowitz's *Esther* in 1957, Harry Partch's THE BEWITCHED in 1957, Larjean Hiller's THE BIRDS in 1958, H. Gottlieb's *Sonata Allegro* in 1958, Kenneth Gaburo's *The Widow* in 1961, Partch's REVELATION IN THE COURTHOUSE PARK in 1961, Partch's WATER! WATER!, in 1962, Robert Kelly's *The White Gods* in 1966, Neely Bruce's *The Trials of Psyche* in 1971, Ulysses Kay's *The Capitoline Venus* in 1971 and Michael Colgrass's *Nightingale, Inc* in 1971. John Philip Sousa's comic opera EL CAPITAN was recorded at the University in 1997 by the University of Illinois Chorale.

Waukegan: The Bowen Park Opera Company is located in Waukegan.

IMBRIE, ANDREW   *American composer (1921–)*

Andrew Imbrie has composed a large number of vocal and instrumental works and two operas. The best known is the three-act ANGLE OF REPOSE, libretto by Oakley Hall based on a novel by Wallace Stegner about events in California in 1870, which premiered at San Francisco Opera on November 6, 1976. His comic opera THREE AGAINST CHRISTMAS (aka *Christmas in Peebles Town),* libretto by Richard Wincor about an attempt to ban Christmas, was premiered at the University of California at Berkeley on December 3, 1964, with Robert Commanday conducting. New York native Imbrie was a child prodigy who began his piano studies at the age of four. He studied with Roger Sessions at Princeton and at Berkeley and taught music at Berkeley for over forty years.

THE IMPORTANCE OF BEING EARNEST   *1962 opera by Castelnuovo-Tedesco*

Jack Worthing, found in a handbag in Victoria Station as a baby,

has to prove his parentage before Lady Bracknell will allow him to marry her daughter. All ends well after some complicated genealogy is sorted out. Mario Castelnuovo-Tedesco's comic opera *The Importance of Being Earnest,* libretto by the composer based on the 1895 play by Oscar Wilde, was premiered in an Italian translation on RAI Italian radio on February 1, 1973, with Angelo Campori conducting. Alvino Misciano was John, Florindo Andreolli was Algernon, Edda Vincenzi was Gwendolen, Mariella Adani was Cecile and Laura Zanini was Lady Bracknell. The opera was premiered on stage in English at La Guardia Theater in New York on February 22, 1975, and revived in Florence, Italy, in 1984. Quotations from Bach to Wagner are used by Castelnuovo-Tedesco as musical jokes in the opera to complement Wilde's wit.

IMPROVEMENT   *1991 opera by Ashley*

Don leaves Linda at a roadside in the American West. Don stands symbolically for Spain in 1492, Linda represents the Jews thrown out of Spain that year and Now Eleanor represents America. The settings and happenings are contemporary and include arguments and interrogations at an airline ticket counter and cities from Rome to Berlin. Robert Ashley's *Improvement (Don Leaves Linda), An Opera for Television,* is part of his larger project for voice and electronic orchestra called *Now Eleanor's Idea.* Jacqueline Humbert sang Linda with Thomas Buckner as Don in the first performance in 1991 with Joan la Barbara as Now Eleanor, Sam Ashley as Junior, Jr., Adam Klein as the Doctor, Amy X. Neuburg as Mr. Payne's Mother and Robert Ashley as narrator. The electronic music was arranged by Tom Erbe and Tom Hamilton and performed by Ashley and David Rosenboom.

1992 Original cast. Jacqueline Humbert is Linda, Thomas Buckner is Don and Joan la Barbara is Now Eleanor in this original cast recording. Sam Ashley plays Junior, Jr., Adam Klein is the Doctor, Amy X. Neuburg is Mr. Payne's Mother and Robert Ashley is narrator. The music is performed by Ashley and David Rosenboom. The opera was recorded in Mills College in Oakland and in New York City. Elektra Nonesuch CD box.

Robert Ashley's experimental opera *Improvement* was recorded in 1992.

IN A GARDEN   *American operas with Gertrude Stein libretto*

Young Lucy Willow says she is a queen so her friends Philip Hall and Kit Raccoon say they are kings and want her to be their queen. When she doubts their royalty, they put crowns on their heads as proof. When she can't choose between them, they fight for her and both are killed. She is left with only their crowns. Gertrude Stein's libretto was published in 1946 in *The Gertrude Stein First Reader and Three Plays*. It has been set to music by two American composers.

1949 Meyer Kupferman. Meyer Kupferman's popular 15-minute chamber opera *In a Garden,* libretto by Gertrude Stein, was premiered by After Dinner Opera Company at Finch Junior College in New York on December 29, 1949. The opera, which has become a favorite of colleges, was published with Stein's libretto in 1951. **1969 Anna Sternberg.** Anna Sternberg composed the music for her mini-opera *In a Garden* for the Broadway show GERTRUDE STEIN'S FIRST READER which opened at the Astor Place Theater in New York on December 15, 1969. Michael Anthony played Philip Hall, Joy Garrett was Lucy Willow and Frank Giordano was Kit Raccoon. Polydor LP.

IN CIRCLES   *1961 music theater by Carmines*

Gertrude Stein spins fantastic word webs that whirl in delightful circles around a group of people in a country house garden, each person revealing various degrees of vulnerability. Al Carmines' *In Circles*, libretto by Gertrude Stein, was premiered at the Judson Poets Theater at Judson Memorial Church in New York in 1964 in a production by Lawrence Kornfeld. It opened at the Cherry Lane Theater on November 5, 1967, with Carmines as Stein playing piano and performing with Theo Barnes, Jacque Lynn Colton, Lee Crespi, Julie Kurnitz, Lee Guilliatt. James Hilbrandt, George McGrath, Arlene Rothlein, Elaine Summers, David Tice, David Vaughan, Arthur Williams and Nancy Zala. Johnnie Jones and Roland Turner designed the sets. *In Circles* has been revived several times, including a highly praised production by John Sowle at the Olio Theater in Los Angeles in 1986 with singers said to be worthy of singing at the Met.

1967 Cherry Lane Theater. Carmines impersonates Gertrude Stein and plays piano for the original cast recording of the Cherry Lane Theater production. The other performers are Theo Barnes, Jacque Lynn Colton, Lee Crespi, Julie Kurnitz, Lee Guilliatt. James Hilbrandt, George McGrath, Arlene Rothlein, Elaine Summers, David Tice, David Vaughan, Arthur Williams and Nancy Zala. Avant Garde Records LP.

IN THE PASHA'S GARDEN   *1935 opera by Seymour*

Constantinople at the turn of the century. Hélène, the wife of the Pasha, hides her lover Étienne in a chest when her jealous husband arrives unexpectedly. The Pasha has the chest buried in the palace garden. John Laurence Seymour's one-act opera *In the Pasha's Garden,* libretto by H. C. Tracy based on a story by H. G. Wright, was premiered at the Metropolitan Opera on January 24, 1935. Laurence Tibbett was the Pasha, Helen Jepson was Hélène, Frederick Jagel was Étienne, Marek Windheim was Zümbül Agha and Arthur Anderson was Shaban. Frederick J. Kiesler designed the set, Wilhelm von Wymetal Jr. directed the production and Ettore Panizza conducted the Met orchestra. The opera, composed in a conservative tonal style, was presented three times at the Met but never revived. It received the David Bispham Memorial Award in the year of its production.

IN THE PENAL COLONY   *2000 opera by Glass*

A visitor to a penal colony on an African prison island in 1907 is shown a bizarre punishment machine. The officer in charge explains what is happening as a condemned man has his death sentence written on his body with needles and dies after 12 hours of torment. Philip Glass's 90-minute "pocket opera" *In the Penal Colony*, libretto by Rudolph Wurlitzer based on the story by Franz Kafka, premiered at Seattle's A Contemporary Theatre on September 28, 2000. John Duykers was the Visitor while Herbert and Eugene Perry alternated as the Officer. Kafka, an on-stage character who acts as narrator and speaks words taken from Kafka's diaries, was played by Jose J. Gonzalez. John Conklin designed the set and punishment machine while JoAnne Akalaitis staged the production. The Metropolitan String Ensemble of Seattle played the melodic music whose repetitive rhythms propel the action. The opera was developed with Chicago's Court Theatre, where it was reprised in December with the same cast. It was staged in New York in June 2001 by Manhattan's Classic Stage Company with Tony Boutté alternating with Duykers as the Visitor, the Perry brothers alternating as the Officer, Jessie J. Perez as Kafka, Steven Rishard as the Prisoner and Sterling K. Brown as the Guard.

L'INCANTESIMO   *1942 radio opera by Montemezzi*

Italian composer Italo Montemezzi's American radio opera *L'incantesimo* (Enchantment), libretto by Sem Benelli, premiered on NBC Radio in New York City on October 9, 1942. Vivian Della Chiesa sang the role of Giselda, Mario Berini was Rinaldo, Alexander Sved was Folco and Virgilio Lazzari was Salomone. The composer conducted the NBC Symphony Orchestra. Montemezzi lived in the United States from 1939 to 1949 but this was the only opera he wrote while in America. It was staged in 1952 in Verona, Italy.

THE INDIAN PRINCESS   *1808 opera by Bray*

The Indian Princess is Pocahontas, daughter of Native American chief Powhatan, who according to legend, saved the life of Captain John Smith in 1608 by holding his head in her arms as he was about to be clubbed to death by her father's warriors. She later married a colonist and went to England. John Bray's "operatic melo-drame" *The Indian Princess, or La belle sauvage,* libretto by James Nelson Barker, was first performed at the New Chestnut Street Theater in Philadelphia on April 6, 1808, and published the same year with vocal score and instrumental accompaniment. It was one of the first American music theater works on an American subject.

1978 Federal Music Society. Judith Otten, Joseph Porrello. Richard Anderson, John Mack Ousley, Michael Best, Susan Belling and Debra Vanderlinde perform twelve numbers from *The Indian Princess* for the Federal Music Society Opera Company with John Baldon conducting. The restoration of the score was made by Victor Fell Yellin and the recording was made at the Columbia Studio in New York City. New World Records LP/CD.

INDIANA   *American state (1816–)*

Indiana has two principal venues for the presentation of America operas, the University of Indiana in Bloomington and Indianapolis Opera in Indianapolis. Indiana-born opera composers include William Albright (Gary), Jack Beeson (Muncie), Shirley Graham Dubois (Indianapolis), Cole Porter (Peru), Ned Rorem (Richmond). Indiana-born singers include baritone Thomas Hampson (Elkhart), tenor Orville Harrold (Muncie) and tenor George Shirley (Indianapolis).

Bloomington: Indiana University's School of Music has premiered an impressive number of well-known American operas. Kurt Weill's DOWN IN THE VALLEY was premiered on July 15, 1948, while Lukas Foss's THE JUMPING FROG OF CALAVERAS COUNTY and Bernard Roger's THE VEIL were both premiered on May 18, 1950. The first stage performance of Gian Carlo Menotti's TV opera AMAHL AND THE NIGHT VISITORS was held on February 21, 1952, and Walter Kaufmann's *A Parfait for Irene* was premiered the same night. Norman Dello Joio's THE RUBY premiered in 1955, Carl Van Buskirk's *The Land Between the Rivers* in 1956, Kaufmann's *The Scarlet Letter* in 1961, Bernhard Heiden's THE DARKENED CITY in 1963, Buskirk's *Christmas Doll* in 1966, Kaufmann's *A Hoosier Tale* in 1966 and Bruce Grant's *The Women of Troy* in 1973. The university's Musical Arts Center opened in January 1972 with the American premiere of John Eaton's HERACLES. Three other Eaton operas were premiered: MYSHKIN in 1973, DANTON AND ROBESPIERRE in 1978 and THE CRY OF CLYTEMNESTRA in 1980. Operas at the university are mostly sung by students from the music school, but Marion Bell was brought in for *Down in the Valley* and Walter Cassel, who was teaching at the school, recreated his role of Horace in a 1976 production of THE BALLAD OF BABY DOE. Other faculty members have included Charles Kullman, Martha Lipton, Nancy Shade and Richard Stillwell. Marc Blitzstein's IDIOTS FIRST, completed by Leonard Lehrman, was premiered in Bloomington by the Marc Blitzstein Opera Company on March 14, 1976.

Elkhart: Don Gillis's *Park Avenue Kids* was premiered at Elkhart High School in 1957.

Fort Wayne: J. A. Butterfield's *The Romance of a Summer* was premiered in Fort Wayne in 1881.

Greencastle: Ronald Ray Williams' *The Introduction* was premiered at De Paw University in 1951

Indianapolis: Clarence Loomis's *A Night in Avignon* premiered at the Claypool Hotel in 1932 and his *The Fall of the House of Usher* at Block's Auditorium in January 1941. John Eaton's children's opera *The Lion and Androcles* premiered at Public School 47 in Indianapolis on May 1, 1974. Indianapolis Opera opened in 1976 with two American operas, Gian Carlo Menotti's THE TELEPHONE and Douglas Moore's THE DEVIL AND DANIEL WEBSTER. It has continued to present American works including Leonard Bernstein's CANDIDE, Mitch Leigh's MAN OF LA MANCHA, Moore's THE BALLAD OF BABY DOE and Igor Stravinsky's THE RAKE'S PROGRESS.

Muncie: Ball State University held the premieres of William Mayer's *One Christmas Long Ago* in 1962, Morris Wright's *The Legend* in 1965, Martin Kalmanoff's *The Great Stone Face* in 1968 and Heskel Brisman's *Whirligig* in 1978.

Richmond: The Whitewater Opera Company stages operas in the Civic Hall Performing Arts Center.

South Bend: Eleanor Everest Freer's *The Legend of the Piper* was presented at the Progress Club in 1925 following its premiere in Boston.

INES DE CASTRO   *1976 opera by Pasatieri*

Portuguese Prince Pedro marries Spanish Princess Ines de Castro against the wishes of King Alfonso so the King has her killed. When Pedro becomes King, he has her body exhumed and crowned Queen. Thomas Pasatieri's three-act opera *Ines de Castro*, libretto by Bernard Stambler, was commissioned by Baltimore Lyric Opera which premiered it on April 1, 1976. Evelyn Mandac played Ines de Castro, Richard Stilwell was Pedro, James Morris was King Alfonso, Lili Chookasian was Queen Beatrix, Lou Ann Lee was Doña Constanza, Sheila Nadler was Doña Blanca, William Neill was Dom Goncalo Pereira, James Atherton was Pacheco, Glenn Strand was Coelho, Claire Frances was Joao, Becky Smith was Dinn and Joseph De Cara was Pedro's Servant. Tito Capobianco staged the opera and Christopher Keene conducted. The music is tonal

and melodic in the manner of Menotti and Puccini. The story of Ines de Castro has fascinated composers and been the inspiration of more than twenty operas.

THE INSECT COMEDY   *1977 opera by Kalmanoff*

A disillusioned Vagrant drinks too much and imagines the world as it would be if it was taken over by insects. Martin Kalmanoff's three-act opera *The Insect Comedy*, libretto by Lewis Allen based on the Karel and Josef Capek play, was composed in 1977 and premiered by the Center for Contemporary Opera at Hunter College in New York on May 20, 1993. Stephen Kechulius played the Vagrant with a cast that include Steven Tharp, Amy Goldstein, Karen Burlingame, Paul Houghtalin and James Blanton. Peter Harrison designed the sets, Martha Hally designed the insect costumes, Louis Galterio directed and Richard Marshall conducted the thirty-five piece orchestra.

INTO THE WOODS   *1987 musical by Sondheim*

Stephen Sondheim's *Into the Woods*, a modern examination of the meaning of fairy tales, has been staged by Lyric Opera Cleveland and by Long Beach Civic Light Opera.

INTRODUCTIONS AND GOODBYES   *1960 opera by Foss*

Mr. McC hosts a cocktail party for nine guests including exotic creatures like Dr. Lavender Gas, Miss Addington-Stitch and General Ortega y Guadalupe. They exchange pleasantries for nine minutes. Lukas Foss's mini-opera *Introductions and Goodbyes*, libretto by Gian Carlo Menotti, was created for presentation in *Autumn Leaves*, an intellectual cabaret devised for the Spoleto Festival by Menotti. It premiered at Carnegie Hall on May 6, 1960, with baritone John Reardon as Mr. McC and singers from the Choral Arts Society as the guests. Walter Rosenberger played xylophone and Leonard Bernstein conducted the New York Philharmonic. When the opera was staged in Spoleto in June 1960, the guests mimed their roles and their lines were sung from the orchestra pit.

1976 Gregg Smith Singers. Baritone Jay Willoughby takes the role of Mr. McC in the mini-opera sung by the Gregg Smith Singers led by Gregg Smith. The opera is on the 2001 album *I Build a House: Vocal Music of Lukas Foss*. CRI CD.

IOLAN   *1906 opera by Converse.*   See THE PIPE OF DESIRE

IOWA   *American state (1846–)*

The only permanent opera company in Iowa is Des Moines Metro Opera located in Indianola, 12 miles from the state capital of Des Moines. Founded by Robert Larsen in 1973, it presents its operas in English. Iowa-born opera people include baritone Walter Cassell (Council Bluffs), composer Michael Daugherty (Cedar Rapids), bass-baritone Simone Estes (Ames), soprano Carole Farley (Le Mars), soprano Sheri Greenawald (Iowa City), William Wade Hinshaw (Union), soprano Margaret Lloyd (Ames), soprano Eleanor Painter (Davenport), composer Peter Schickele (Ames), composer John Verrall (Britt), bass-baritone Clarence Whitehill (Parnell) and Meredith Willson (Mason City). Wilson's THE MUSIC MAN is set in River City, an imaginary town based on his native Mason City.

Des Moines: Martin Kalmanoff's *Lizzie Strotter: or, The Women War on War,* based on *Lysistrata,* premiered at Drake University in Des Moines on March 6, 1958.

Indianola: Des Moines Metro Opera commissioned and premiered two American operas, Lee Hoiby's THE TEMPEST in 1986 and Stephen Paulus's children's opera *Harmoonia* in 1991. The company usually presents an American opera every season at the Pote Theater in the Blank Performing Arts Center. They have included Jack Beeson's THE BALLAD OF BABY DOE (televised in Iowa in 1995), Leonard Bernstein's CANDIDE, Carlisle Floyd's OF MICE AND MEN and SUSANNAH, Lee Hoiby's SUMMER AND SMOKE, Gian Carlo Menotti's THE CONSUL, THE MEDIUM and THE SAINT OF BLEECKER STREET, Igor Stravinsky's THE RAKE'S PROGRESS and Robert Ward's THE CRUCIBLE.

Iowa City: The University of Iowa in Iowa City has been presenting opera regularly since 1950 and has had an active Opera Workshop since 1981. Premieres have included Philip Bezanson's *Western Child* in 1959 (revised and presented on TV as GOLDEN CHILD), William J. Fisher's *The Happy Prince* in 1962, Carl Johnson's *Escorial* in 1966 and Thomas Turner's *Four Thousand Dollars*, libretto by novelist Vance Bourjaily, on March 6, 1969. The Opera Workshop has produced Seymour Barab's A GAME OF CHANCE and *Little Red Riding Hood*, Mark Bucci's *Sweet Betsy from Pike*, Elaine Erickson's *Daylight Dreams*, Lee Hoiby's *Something New for the Zoo*, Gian Carlo Menotti's THE TELEPHONE and Thomas Pasatieri's THE GOOSE GIRL.

Sioux City: D. Morrison's *The Merchant's Moon* was premiered at Morningside College on October 29, 1954.

IRVING, WASHINGTON   *American writer (1783–1859)*

Washington Irving has been popular with opera composers for more than 160 years. *The Legends of the Alhambra* (1832) was the basis of C. E. Horn's AHMED AL KAMEL; *or, The Pilgrim of Love* (1840), the first American ballad opera based on an American literary work. *Rip van Winkle* (1819) was the basis of the first American grand opera on an American subject, George Frederick Bristow's RIP VAN WINKLE (1855). Five more adaptations followed, including one by Reginald De Koven premiered by the Chicago Opera Company in 1920. Kurt Weill used *The History of New York* (1809), as the basis for his 1938 musical KNICKERBOCKER HOLIDAY and Douglas Moore began his exploration of Americana with THE HEADLESS HORSEMAN based on *The Legend of Sleepy Hollow* (1820). In the list below, the title of opera is the same as the story and libretto is by composer unless otherwise indicated. Place and date of premiere listed if known.

The Devil and Tom Walker (1824). 1926 John Laurence Seymour (Henry C. Tracy).

The History of New York (1809). 1938 Kurt Weill (Maxwell Anderson) as *Knickerbocker Holiday*. Hartford, September 24, 1938.

History of Life and Voyages of Columbus (1828). 1844 James G. Maeder (S. J. Burr) as *The Peri; or, The Enchanted Fountain*. Boston, February 10, 1844.

The Legend of Sleepy Hollow (1820). 1879 Max Maretzek (Charles Gaynor) as *Sleepy Hollow: or, The Headless Horseman*. Academy of Music, NY, November 19, 1879. **1937** Douglas Moore (Stephen Vincent Benét) as *The Headless Horseman*. Bronxville, NY, March 4, 1937. **1962** John D. White (Martin Nurmi). Kent State University, February 28, 1962. **1968** David Gooding (Paul Lee). Cleveland Opera Children's Theatre, December 1, 1988. **1976** Robert James Haskins (John Koppenhaver). **1986** Robert Carlson (Fred Gaines). Louisville, Kentucky, October 26, 1986.

Rip Van Winkle (1820). 1855 George Frederick Bristow (Jonathan Wainwright). Niblo's Gardens, New York, September 27, 1855. **1897** Jules Jordan. Providence Opera House, Rhode Island, May 25, 1897. **1920** Reginald de Koven (Percy MacKaye). Chicago Opera, January 2, 1920. **1932** Edward B. Manning. Char-

lotte Lund Opera, Town Hall, New York, Feb 12, 1932. **1957** Nicholas Flagello (C. Fiore) (operetta).

The Legends of the Alhambra (1832). 1840 C. E. Horn (Henry J. Finn) as *Ahmed al Kamel; or, The Pilgrim of Love*, New York, October 12, 1840. **1875** Alfred Arthur as *The Water Carrier*. **1927** Eleanor Freer as *A Legend of Spain*, Milwaukee, June 19, 1931.

ISABELLE   *1936 "movie opera" by Carbonara*

The 1936 Paramount movie *Fatal Lady* starring Mary Ellis features two imaginary operas. The first to be seen is *Isabelle* with music by Gerard Carbonara and libretto by David Ormont, Leo Robin and Max Terr. Ellis plays an opera diva who runs away after being accused of a murder and has to sing under a false name. The film includes a second imaginary opera by Carbonara called BAL MASQUE.

THE ISLAND GOD   *1942 opera by Menotti*

On a Mediterranean island in ancient times, Ilo brings a Greek god back into existence by worshipping him. He later destroys the god and himself when he loses Telea, the woman he loves. Menotti's one-act opera *The Island God*, libretto in Italian by the composer as *Ilo e Zeus*, premiered at the Metropolitan Opera House in New York on February 20, 1942, in an English translation by Fleming McLeish. Leonard Warren sang the role of Ilo, Astrid Varnay was Telea, Raoul Jobin was Luca, Norman Cordon was the Greek God and John Carter was the Voice of the Fisherman. Richard Rychtarik designed the sets and costumes and Ettore Panizza conducted the Metropolitan Opera Orchestra. This mythological opera, was Menotti's biggest failure. It was published by G. Ricordi in 1942 but later withdrawn by Menotti.

ISRAEL, ROBERT   *American set/costume designer (1939–)*

Robert Israel made his operatic debut designing sets and costumes for Minnesota Opera's production of Robert Kurka's THE GOOD SOLDIER SCHWEIK in Minneapolis in 1967. Also for Minnesota he created the designs for Marc Blitzstein's THE HARPIES in 1968, the premiere of Conrad Susa's TRANSFORMATIONS in 1973 and the premiere of Easley Blackwood's *Gulliver* in 1975. For Kansas City Lyric he created the designs for the Jack Beeson's THE SWEET BYE AND BYE in 1973. Israel, born in Detroit, has had exhibitions of his designs, paintings and sculptures in several countries.

"IT AIN'T NECESSARILY SO"   *Tenor aria: Porgy and Bess (1935). Words: Ira Gershwin. Music: George Gershwin.*

Sportin' Life, a cynical drug-dealing gambler with no morals, sings the tenor aria "It ain't necessarily so" at a church picnic telling the parishioners that the things that they read in the Bible may not be true. Ira Gershwin's mocking lyrics take irreverent aim at Biblical tall tales about Jonah, Moses, Methuselah and David and Goliath. It was introduced on stage in George Gershwin's PORGY AND BESS by John W. Bubbles. The first version on record was by Metropolitan Opera star tenor Lawrence Tibbett in 1935. Later recordings were made by Bubbles, Paul Robeson, Todd Duncan, Avon Long, Damon Evans, McHenry Boatwright, Sammy Davis Jr. (who sings it in the 1959 movie of the opera), Cab Calloway, François Clemmons, Larry Marshall and Louis Armstrong. The tune became popular with jazz musicians after the film was released and there is a memorable instrumental version by Miles Davis.

IT HAPPENED IN NORDLAND   *1904 operetta by Herbert*

Katherine Peepfoogle, the American ambassador to Nordland,

looks so much like the Queen of the country that she is asked to impersonate her when the Queen disappears just before a marriage she doesn't want. Victor Herbert's comic opera *It Happened in Nordland,* libretto by Glen MacDonough, premiered at the New Lyceum Theater in Harrisburg, Pennsylvania, on November 21, 1904, and opened in New York at the Lew Fields Theater on December 5. Marie Cahill was Katherine, Lew Fields was her brother Herbert and Frank O'Neill was Prince Karl. Julian Mitchell directed. The hit number was the intermezzo "Al Fresco."

1911 Victor Herbert. Victor Herbert leads his orchestra in a recording of "Al Fresco," the intermezzo from *It Happened in Nordland.* It was recorded for Victor on June 19, 1911, and is on he album *The Early Victor Herbert.* Smithsonian LP box. **1991 Pittsburgh Symphony.** "Absinthe Frappe," considered the most sophisticated number in *It Happened in Nordland,* is performed by the Pittsburgh Symphony Orchestra led by Lorin Maazel It's on the album *Popular American Music.* Sony CD.

THE ITALIAN LESSON   *1980 opera by Hoiby*

A Manhattan matron juggles telephone calls, family business, her cook, her son's teacher, a new puppy, her children, a manicurist and her lover while having a lesson in Italian. She discovers she can read Dante's *Divine Comedy* and is fascinated by the lines describing life's complexities as the poet enters Hell. Lee Hoiby's 30-minute one-woman comic opera *The Italian Lesson* is based on a classic monologue by Ruth Draper. Soprano Joan Morris and her pianist/composer husband William Bolcom premiered it at the Aspen Festival on July 6, 1980. It is often performed with Hoiby's brief BON APPÉTIT as a curtain raiser and this double bill was toured by Jean Stapleton with great success.

1998 Dora Ohrenstein. Soprano Dora Ohrenstein sings four numbers (19 minutes) from *The Italian Lesson*: "Signorina," "Jane," "Miss Pounder" and "Puppy." She is accompanied by pianist Philip Bush on the album *Restless Spirits.* Koch International CD.

"ITALIAN STREET SONG"   *Soprano aria: Naughty Marietta (1910). Words: Rida Johnson Young. Music: Victor Herbert.*

Victor Herbert wrote his comic opera NAUGHTY MARIETTA for coloratura opera soprano Emma Trentini so he had no qualms about providing this fiendishly difficult aria for her to demonstrate her vocal skills. The "Italian Street Song" is sung in the opera by Countess Marietta disguised as a boy and hiding out in a puppet theater to keep from being forcibly wed. Rida Johnson Young's lyrics describe her supposed early years in Naples and feature a zesty repeated "zing, zing, ziz-zy ziz-zy, zing, zing boom, boom aye." In the 1935 movie of the operetta it's sung by Jeanette MacDonald while Jane Powell sings it in the 1946 movie *Holiday in Mexico.* Among the sopranos who have recorded it are Roberta Peters, Eleanor Steber, Patrice Munsel, Beverly Sills, Barbara Hendricks, Judith Blazer and Virginia Croskery.

I'VE GOT THE TUNE   *1937 radio "song-play" by Blitzstein*

Composer Mr. Musiker has a melody he likes but he can't find the right lyrics for it. He goes looking for the words with his secretary Beetzie, meets society lady Mrs. Arbutus, observes a meeting of the fascist-like Purple Shirts led by Captain Bristlepunkt, saves a young woman from suicide and finally allows radical marchers to put May Day words to his tune. Marc Blitzstein's autobiographical radio opera *I've Got the Tune,* libretto by the composer, was commissioned by CBS Radio which premiered it October 24, 1937, soon after the premiere of *The Cradle Will Rock.*

Orson Welles was to have played Mr. Musiker but had to cancel so Blitzstein took the role, Shirley Booth was Beetzie, Adelaide Klein was Mrs. Arbutus, Kenneth Delmar was Captain Bristlepunkt, Norman Lloyd was Private Schnook, Hiram Sherman was the Choral Director and Lotte Lenya was the Suicidal Woman. Bernard Herrmann conducted. The work was well received and was put on stage in February 1938 with Blitzstein as Mr. Musiker, Peggy Coudray as Beetzie, Love Stanton as the Suicidal Woman and Count Basie creating swing music for the fascist section.

1937 Original cast album. The left-wing record company Musicraft recorded the production with the original cast and released it as an album on seven 78 records. Musicraft GM 212–118.

IVEY, JEAN EICHELBERG   *American composer (1923–)*

Jean Eichelberg Ivey's opera TESTAMENT OF EVE, libretto by the composer about a argument between Eve and Lucifer, attracted a good deal of critical attention when it was presented in Baltimore on April 21, 1976, and reprised at Columbia University the same year. *The Birthmark,* libretto by the composer based on a story by Nathaniel Hawthorne about a scientist who succeeds in removing a birthmark from his wife's face but kills her doing it, was completed in 1982. Ivey, who was born in Washington, D.C., and studied at Peabody and Eastman, was founding director of the electronic music studio at Eastman House. She has written considerable vocal music, including settings for poems by Teasdale, Arnold, Whitman, Emerson, Rossetti and Shakespeare.

J

JACK AND THE BEANSTALK   *1930 children's opera by Gruenberg*

Jack's mother tells him the Giant killed his father and stole his treasures including a bag of gold, a magic hen and a singing harp. Jack doesn't believe her and sets out to sell their cow. An old woman tells him that if he exchanges the cow for a handful of beans he will recover the family treasures — and a princess. He does as she says and it all happens. Louis Gruenberg's charming children's opera *Jack and the Beanstalk,* libretto by John Erskine, was commissioned by the Juilliard School which premiered November 30, 1931. Albert Stoessel, director of the Juilliard School opera department, conducted. Described as a "a fairy opera for the childlike," *Jack and the Beanstalk,* proved so popular that it was presented on Broadway for two weeks at the 44th Street Theater. Erskine, then president of the Juilliard, published the libretto in book form.

JACKIE O   *1997 opera by Daugherty*

Jackie Kennedy meets Aristotle Onassis, Elizabeth Taylor and Grace Kelly at a party at Andy Warhol's Factory, sings a duet with Maria Callas and remembers her life with John F. Kennedy. Michael Daugherty's pop opera *Jackie O,* libretto by Wayne Koestenbaum, was premiered by Houston Grand Opera as a Houston Opera Studio production at the Cullen Theater on March 14, 1997. It was described as an opera "in which the events are based on history but are largely imaginary or metaphorical." Nicole Heaston sang the role of Jackie, Paul LeGros danced the role of Jackie, Eric Owens was Onassis, Stephanie Novacek was Callas, Joyce DiDonato was Grace Kelly, Jonita Lattimore was Elizabeth Taylor, Daniel Belcher was Andy Warhol, Bruce Brown was Papparazzo and John McVeigh was the voice of JFK. Peter Werner designed the sets and costumes, Nicholas Muni directed and Christopher Larkin conducted the Houston Grand Opera Orchestra and Chorus. The opera was commissioned by Houston and the Banff Center for the Arts. Iowa-born composer Daugherty, who teaches at the University of Michigan, has written concert works about Elvis Presley, Liberace, J. Edgar Hoover and Superman while lyricist Koestenbaum, who teaches at Yale, has written a number of essays about Jackie. *Jackie O* was one of the most controversial operatic works of recent years but it won warm praise from some critical journals, including the influential *Opera Quarterly*.

1997 Houston Grand Opera. Nicole Heaston is Jackie, Eric Owens is Onassis, Stephanie Novacek is Callas, Joyce DiDonato is Grace Kelly, Jonita Lattimore is Elizabeth Taylor, Daniel Belcher is Andy Warhol, Bruce Brown is Papparazzo and John McVeigh is JFK's voice in this live recording based on performances by the Houston Opera Studio in March 1997. Christopher Larkin conducts the Houston Grand Opera Orchestra and Chorus. 79 minutes. Argo CD.

JACOBI, FREDERICK   *American composer (1891–1952)*

Frederick Jacobi composed a good deal of choral, chamber and orchestra music but only one opera, a somewhat unusual folk-style work that won the Bispham Medal in 1945. *The Prodigal Son*, libretto by Herman Voaden, was written with patriotic fervor during World War II and retells the Biblical story of the prodigal son as an American event. The libretto is based on early 19th century American prints showing the characters in contemporary costumes with Johnny Appleseed as an added extra. It premiered in concert form in Chicago in 1947 and was staged in Toronto in 1952. Jacobi, who was born in San Francisco, studied in New York and Berlin and became an expert on Native American music.

JAMES, HENRY   *American writer (1843–1916)*

Henry James apparently like female opera singers but wasn't especially fond of opera. As he was equally at home in America and England, it is not surprising that his works have been popular with opera composers in both countries. The first American opera based on a work by James was Douglas Moore's 1961 WINGS OF THE DOVE. The best-known is probably Dominick Argento's 1988 THE ASPERN PAPERS which was telecast. The most famous James adaptations, however, are English, Benjamin Britten's *The Turn of the Screw* (1954) and *Owen Wingrave* (1970). The list below is alphabetical by story. Title of opera is same as story and libretto is by composer unless indicated Place/date of premiere given if known.

The Aspern Papers (1888). 1980 Philip Hagemann. Bloomington, Indiana, December 4, 1980. **1988** Dominick Argento. Dallas Opera, November 19, 1988.

The Last of the Valerii (1874). 1974 Thea Musgrave (Amalia Elguera) as *The Voice of Ariadne*. English Opera Group, Snape Maltings, June 11, 1974.

Portrait of a Lady (1881). 2004 Oakley Hall (NEA commission).

Washington Square (1880). 1976 Thomas Pasatieri (Kenward Elmslie). Michigan Opera Theater, Detroit, October 1, 1976. **1977** Michael G. Cunningham as *Catherine Sloper* of Washington Square. University of Wisconsin-Eau Claire, March 31, 1978.

Wings of the Dove (1902). 1961 Douglas Moore (Ethan Ayer). New York City Opera, October 12, 1961.

JAZZ OPERAS   *American opera genre*

Operas featuring jazz, blues, ragtime and similar American music

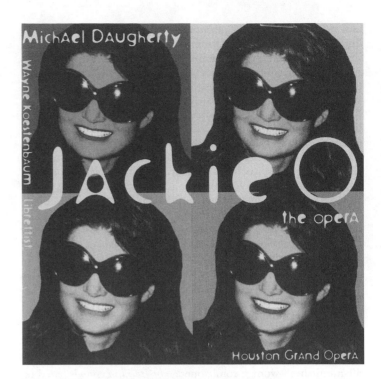

Michael Daugherty's pop opera *Jackie O* was premiered and recorded by Houston Grand Opera in 1997.

styles began to be composed soon after the turn of the century as these styles started to become better known. Some called themselves "jazz operas," others simply used jazz for atmosphere and mood. The following is a partial list of some of these operas.

1903 A Guest of Honor (Scott Joplin). **1906** Uncle Remus (Henry F. Gilbert). **1911** Treemonisha (Scott Joplin). **1922** Blue Monday (George Gershwin). **1924** A Light from St. Agnes (William F. Harling). **1926** Deep River (William Franke Harling). **1928** Voodoo (Harry Lawrence Freeman). **1933** The Emperor Jones (Louis Gruenberg). Run, Little Chillen (Hall Johnson). **1935** Porgy and Bess (George Gershwin). **1940** De Organizer (James P. Johnson). **1946** Beggars Holiday (Duke Ellington). **1966** The Visitation (Gunther Schuller). **1981** Sister Suzie Cinema (Bob Telson). **1983** The Gospel at Colonus (Bob Telson). Thomas Jefferson's Minstrels (T. J. Anderson). **1985** Trillium Dialogues (Anthony Braxton). Chinchilla (Myron Fink). **1986** Queenie Pie (Duke Ellington). **1988** The Outcast (Noa Ain). **1989** A Guest of Honor (Steve Weisberg). **1990** The Mother of Three Sons (Leroy Jenkins). **1993** Vanqui (Leslie Savoy Burrs). **1994** Diary of an African American (H. Peterson). **1997** Blue Opera (Nancy Binns Reed).

JEFFERS, ROBINSON   *American poet (1887–1962)*

Robinson Jeffer's powerful adaptation and translation of Euripides' play *Medea*, first staged in 1946, has provided the basis for two American operas. Benjamin Lees' MEDEA IN CORINTH, libretto by the composer, premiered in concert form in London in 1971, was staged in Antwerp in 1973 and was telecast by CBS in 1974. Alva Henderson's opera MEDEA, libretto by the composer, was premiered by San Diego Opera in 1972. Jeffers, born in Pittsburgh, lived most of his life in Carmel, CA, where he wrote poetry reflecting his view of life as a difficult struggle.

JENNY, OR THE HUNDRED NIGHTS   *1976 opera by Weisgall*

Kensington Gardens, London, in 1899. Ninety-nine-year-old Jenny is scavenging when she meets photographer George. She tells him that when she was young she promised herself to a man if he would court her for a hundred nights. George falls in love with her younger self as Jenny warns that he will die if he does. He does die but tells her they will meet again in a hundred years. Hugo Weisgall's one-act opera *Jenny, or The Hundred Nights,* libretto by poet John Hollander based on a Japanese Noh play by Yukio Mishima, was commissioned by Juilliard and premiered at the Juilliard American Opera Center on April 22, 1976. The premiere was recorded but is not available commercially.

JEPSON, HELEN   *American soprano (1904–1997)*

Metropolitan Opera lyric soprano Helen Jepson was the first person to record American opera's greatest aria, "Summertime." She and Lawrence Tibbett recorded nine numbers from George Gershwin's PORGY AND BESS in October 1935 with the Broadway production orchestra. She also sang in two American operas at the Met with Tibbett. She created the role of Hélène in her Met debut in John Seymour's IN THE PASHA'S GARDEN in 1935. She sang the role of Pompilia in Richard Hageman's CAPONSACCHI in 1937 and recorded two of its arias. Jepson, who was born in Titusville, PA, and grew up in Akron, studied at the Curtis Institute and made her debut with the Philadelphia Grand Opera Company in 1930. Paramount put her under contract in 1935 during the opera movie boom but didn't use her. Her only film was Samuel Goldwyn's *The Goldwyn Follies* (1938), the film on which Gershwin was working when he died.

JEREMIAH   *1962 opera by Fink*

Jeremiah alienates his wife with his religious fanaticism but his passionate nature enables him to seduce a woman who is loved by his son. When his congregation finds out, he cites the Biblical story of Abraham and Isaac as justification for killing his son. Myron Fink's four-act opera *Jeremiah,* libretto by E. Hawley and the composer, was premiered by Tri-Cities Opera in Binghampton on May 25, 1962.

JERRY SPRINGER: THE OPERA   *2002 opera by Thomas*

Richard Thomas's "junk opera" *Jerry Springer: The Opera,* libretto

by Stewart Lee and the composer based on the "trash TV" of Springer's television show, premiered at the Edinburgh Festival in August 2002 after a workshop production. It then moved to the National Theatre in London winning critical acclaim and audience amazement for its extraordinary vulgarity and odd humor. Opera arias will never seem the same after one has heard arias by a Lesbian dwarf diaper fetishist and an aging overweight diva who wants to become a lap dancer. English critics compared it to *The Threepenny Opera* because of its ability to show that low life can be high art pointing out the Bach and Handel style chorales accompanying the bizarre happenings on stage. After exposing the odd lives of his TV guests in the first part of the opera, Springer is killed in a studio fight and taken to hell where he sees what happened to

Soprano Helen Jepson featured in a 1936 advertisement.

them after the show. There were 21 singers in the show at the National Theatre, many taking multiple roles: Michael Brandon played Springer, David Bedella was the Devil, Benjamin Lake was God, and the guests included Wills Morgan, Alison Jierar, Lore Lixenberg and Valda Avika. Librettist Lee staged the opera. The opera began to be staged in America in 2005.

2003 Jerry Springer the Opera Live. This live recording of the stage show features the cast as above with Michael Brandon as Jerry Springer David Bedella as the Devil, Benjamin Lake as God, and guests Wills Morgan, Alison Jierar, Lore Lixenberg and Valda Avika. Sony 2-CD box.

JESSYE, EVA   *American choral conductor/composer* (1895–1992)

African American Eve Jessye made a major contribution to American opera through her choirs featured in the premieres of America's two most innovative operas. She was choral director of Virgil Thomson's FOUR SAINTS IN THREE ACTS in 1934 and George Gershwin's PORGY AND BESS in 1935. Jessye, born in Coffeyville, Kansas, studied music in Kansas and Oklahoma and then moved to New York in 1926 to work with African American composer Will Marion Cook. She formed her own choir, the Original Dixie Jubilee Singers which became the Eva Jessye Choir, to tour and sing on radio. She had her first major success directing the chorus in King Vidor's 1929 film *Hallelujah*. Jessye's many choral compositions include the folk oratorios *Paradise Lost and Regained* and *The Book of Job*. Her original choir can be heard on the 1940 original cast recording of *Porgy and Bess*.

JESUS BEFORE HEROD   *1918 opera by Wayditch*

Evangelist Luke, seated in a cave writing his Gospel, has visions of debauchery and orgies in an Arabian palace garden. They are followed by redeeming visions of Jesus with Herod and on his way to Golgotha and Crucifixion. Gabriel Von Wayditch's one-act opera *Jesus Before Herod,* libretto by the composer in Hungarian, was composed in the South Bronx after Wayditch emigrated to America. It was premiered in English in concert form in San Diego on April 5, 1979. Stephen A. Scot-Shepherd sang the part of Luke, Vincent Russo sang Pabo, Eileen Moss sang Pabula, Michael Best sang Jappeticus, Christopher Lindbloom sang Herod and Pauline Tweed sang the two Girls. Anthony Coggi narrated Luke's spoken dialogue Peter Erös conducted the San Diego Symphony Orchestra and Charles Ketcham directed the San Diego Master Chorale. The English translation was made by Wayditch's son Ivan Walter.

1979 San Diego Symphony. Stephen A. Scot-Shepherd is Luke with Christopher Lindbloom as Herod in this recording of the San Diego premiere with other singers as listed above. Peter Erös conducts the San Diego Symphony Orchestra and Charles Ketcham directs the San Diego Master Chorale. Musical Heritage Society LP/VAI CD.

JOHN BROWN'S BODY   *1953 choral work by Schumann*

Harper's Ferry is seized by abolitionist John Brown in 1859 as the North-South conflict over slavery reaches boiling point and Civil War seems eminent. Jack Ellyat puts the point of the view of the North while Clay Wingate defends the position of the South. Famous figures of the period join in the discussion. Walter Schumann's choral work *John Brown's Body,* libretto by Charles Laughton based on the Pulitzer Prize verse novel by Steven Vincent Benét, features music of the Civil War period. It was premiered in Los Angeles on September 21, 1953, with Stephen Considine and Betty Benson as the soloists supported by the on-

Richard Thomas's "junk opera" *Jerry Springer: The Opera* was recorded in England in 2003.

stage Voices of Walter Schumann chorus led by Richard White. Tyrone Power, Judith Anderson and Raymond Massey were the featured performers under the direction of Charles Laughton in a production conceived by Paul Gregory. *John Brown's Body* is often listed as an opera but is really a musical play with a choral group.

1953 Original Cast Album. Betty Benson, Roger Miller and the choral group Voices of Walter Schumann are the singers on this recording made at Columbia Record's Thirtieth Street Studio in New York City in 1953. Tyrone Power, Judith Anderson and Raymond Massey are the actors and narrators and Richard White leads the chorus. Columbia 2-LP box.

JOHNNY JOHNSON   *1936 cabaret opera by Weill*

Small town America in 1917. Stonemason Johnny Johnson is anti-war but he goes off to war all the same at the urging of his girlfriend Minny Belle. When he tries to promote peace in the trenches, he is sent back home and put in a mental institution. Kurt Weill's anti-war theater piece *Johnny Johnson,* libretto by Paul Green, is a direct descendent of his German cabaret opera *The Threepenny Opera*. It premiered at the Group Theater in New York on November 19, 1936, with a notable cast. Russell Collins was Johnny, Phoebe Brand was Minny Belle, Lee J. Cobb was Dr. McBray, Elia Kazan was Private Kearns, John Garfield was Johann Lang, Bob Lewis was the Mayor, Roman Bohnen was Grandpa Jo, Grover Burgess was Anguish, Sanford Meisner was Captain Valentine, and Morris Carnovsky was Chief of the Allied High Command. Donald Oenslager designed the sets, Lee Strasburg directed and Lehman Engel conducted. The songs include the peace-promoting "Johnny's Song" and the satirical "Democracy's Call," sung by the people of the town as they shift from peace sentiments to war fervor. *Johnny Johnson* was reprised in New York in 1956 and 1971 and continues to be revived.

1956 Off-Broadway cast. Burgess Meredith is Johnny in this recording based on a famous 1956 off-Broadway production. Met soprano Evelyn Lear is Minny Belle, Met baritone Thomas Stewart is the Mayor, Lotte Lenya is the French Nurse, Hiram Sherman is Grandpa Jo, Scott Merrill is Captain Valentine, Jane Connell is Aggie, Jean Sanders is the Goddess, Bob Shaver is Private Hardwood and William Malten is the German Priest. Samuel Matlowsky conducts the orchestra. MGM/Heliodor LP/Polydor CD. **1972 Hal Watters.** Hal Watters sings "A Hymn to Peace" and "Johnny's Song" and joins the cast performing "Songs of Peace and War" in the off-Broadway revue *Berlin to Broadway with Kurt Weill, A Musical Voyage.* Paramount LP. **1985 Van Dyke Parks.** Van Dyke Parks performs a medley of songs from *Johnny Johnson* on the album *The Music of Kurt Weill* A and M LP. **1996 Steve Kimbrough.** Steve Kimbrough performs "Cowboy Song" on the album *Kurt Weill on Broadway* with the Cologne West German Radio Orchestra led by Victor Symonette. Koch Swann CD. **1996 Sarah Musinovski.** Sarah Musinovski performs "Mon Ami, My Friend" and "Listen to My Song" with support from Hans-Joachim Tinnefeld and Stefan Weinzierl on the album *Weill—Vom Broadway nach Berlin.* Signum CD. **1997 Thomas Hampson.** Thomas Hampson performs "Johnny's Song" on the album *Kurt Weill on Broadway.* John McGlinn conducts the London Sinfonietta. Program notes by Miles Kreuger. EMI Classics CD. **1997 Otaré Pit Band.** Donald Wilkinson is Johnny with Ellen Santaniello as Minny Bell in this complete recording of the opera made with the Otaré Pit Band led by Joel Cohen. René de la Garza is the Mayor, Richard Lalli is Capt. Valentine, John Delorey is Grandpa Joe, Lynne Torgove is Aggie, Anne Azema is the French Nurse, D'Anna Fortunato is the Goddess, Mark McSweeney is the West Pointer, Bruce Fithian is the English Sergeant, Paul Cummings is the British Commander and Paul Guttry is Dr. Mahodan. Erato CD.

JOHNS, ERIK   *American librettist (1927–2001)*

Poet Erik Johns, who wrote the libretto for Aaron Copland's only full-length opera THE TENDER LAND using the pseudonym Horace Everett, was born as Horace Eugene Johnson in Los Angeles. He was Copland's close companion from 1946 to 1954 and they were inspired to write the opera by the Walker Evans photographs featured in James Agee's book *Let Us Now Praise Famous Men. The Tender Land* was commissioned as a television opera by Rodgers and Hammerstein but NBC turned it down so they adapted it for the stage and premiered it at New York City Opera on April 1, 1954. Johns also wrote the libretto for Jack Gottlieb's opera *Tea Party* and for John Schlenck's oratorio *Mission to the World.*

JOHNSON, EDWARD   *Canadian tenor/Met manager (1879–1958)*

Edward Johnson created three roles in American operas at the Metropolitan Opera before beginning his reign as the Met's general manager in 1935. He was Aethelwold in Deem's Taylor's THE KING'S HENCHMAN in 1927, Peter Ibbetson in Taylor's PETER IBBETSON in 1931 and Sir Gower in Howard Hanson's MERRY MOUNT in 1934. After becoming the head of the Met, he presented three American operas: Gian Carlo Menotti's AMELIA GOES TO THE BALL in 1938, Menotti's THE ISLAND GOD in 1942 and Bernard Rogers' THE WARRIOR in 1947. Johnson, born in Guelph, Ontario, studied singing in New York and made his professional debut in Reginald DeKoven's operetta *Maid Marion* in Boston. He made his operatic debut in Padua in 1912, was the leading tenor at Chicago Opera from 1919 to 1922 and began to sing at the Met in 1922. During his time as general manager (1935–1950), he emphasized the discovery of American singers.

JOHNSON, HALL   *American composer/choral conductor (1888–1970)*

Hall Johnson, who organized, conducted, wrote and arranged songs for the Hall Johnson Choir, created music for four notable theater works. His folk opera *Run, Little Chillen* ran on Broadway for four months in 1933 and has been revived many times. He arranged the music and his choir was featured in Marc Connelly's Pulitzer Prize-winning play *The Green Pastures* which ran on Broadway for five years and was made into a film. His other dramatic compositions include the cantata *Son of Man* (1946) and the operetta *Fi-Yer* (1959). Johnson, born in Athens, Georgia, studied at Pennsylvania University, Juilliard and USC. He began his professional career as violinist but turned to choral conducting and composing in 1925.

JOHNSON, JAMES P.   *American composer/pianist (1894–1955)*

James P. Johnson is best known as one of the great jazz pianists and the king of the stride style but he was also a notable composer, including one opera. After his success with the 1923 Broadway musical *Runnin' Wild,* he became interested in mixing jazz with classical forms. He wrote *Harlem Symphony* in 1932, the piano concerto *Jassamine* in 1935 and the blues opera DE ORGANIZER in 1940. This opera, composed to a libretto by Langston Hughes about organizing a union in the South, premiered at Carnegie Hall in 1940. Johnson recorded its tenor aria "Hungry Blues" in 1939, the libretto was published in 1996 and the vocal score was rediscovered in 1997. Johnson, who was born in New Brunswick, NJ, and self-taught, had a major influence on Duke Ellington and Fats Waller. A few of his classical compositions, including *Harlem Symphony,* are performed by the Concordia Orchestra on the CD album *Victory Stride.*

JOHNSON, LOCKREM   *American composer (1924–1977)*

Lockrem Johnson had a successful career as composer, publisher, pianist and teacher and his piano sonatas were popular but he is best known for a one-act chamber opera. A LETTER TO EMILY, libretto by the composer based on Robert Hupton's play *Consider the Lilies* about an incident in Emily Dickinson's life, was premiered at the Cornish School of Music in Seattle on April 24, 1951. It was much liked and was staged more than fifty times in the years. Johnson, who was born in Seattle and studied music at the University of Washington, spent most of his career in the Pacific Northwest.

JOHNSON, TOM   *American composer (1939–)*

Tom Johnson's amusing minimalist THE FOUR NOTE OPERA, libretto by Robert Kushner, is the most popular post-modern American opera. Five singers (soprano, contralto, tenor, baritone, bass) sing about the music they are singing using only the notes A, B, D and E. It premiered at the Cubiculo Theater in New York in 1972, was shown on television, intrigued American university opera groups and soon got staged by Vienna, Paris and Dutch opera companies. *Masque of Clouds,* libretto by Kushner, was staged at The Kitchen on October 10, 1976. It was more ambitious with twelve performers including a tenor as the Sun, a mezzo as a Lake, a baritone as a Forest and coloratura sopranos as Clouds. Next came *Five Shaggy-Dog Operas: Door-Window-Drawer-Dryer-Box* which premiered in New York on September 15, 1978. Johnson moved to Europe after that and began to write operas with French and German librettos like *Riemannoper,* a 90-minute opera based on definitions from the German music dictionary *Riemann Musik Lexikon* that premiered in Berlin in 1986. Johnson, born in Greeley, Colorado, studied composing with Morton Feldman in

1968–69. Johnson first became known as a music critic for the *Village Voice* where he praised experimental composers like Robert Ashley, Steve Reich and Philip Glass.

JOHNSTON, BEN   *American composer (1926–)*

Microtonal music theorist Ben Johnston was a student of John Cage and Harry Partch and a pioneer of post-modern music theater. His chamber opera *Gertrude: or, Would She Be Pleased to Receive It*, libretto by Wilford Leach, is a satirical jab at the Gertrude Stein style of opera. It premiered in 1956 at the University of Illinois, where Johnston was teaching. *Carmilla: A Vampire Tale*, libretto by Leach based on a novel by Sheridan Le Fanu, was premiered by La Mama Theater in New York January 16, 1972. Described as a post-modern rock opera, it was issued on LP by Vanguard in 1972.

JOLAS, BETSY   *French/American composer (1926–)*

Betsy Jolas divides her time between America and France and presents her operas in both countries. She was born in Paris but came to America as a teenager and studied with Paul Boepple. Her first opera was the chamber work *Le Pavilion au bord de la rivière*, libretto by Michele Raoul-Davas based on a 13th century Chinese play by Kua Han Chin. It premiered at the Avignon Festival in France in July 1975 and was presented in the U.S. in 1976. *Le Cyclope*, using Euripides' satyr play *Cyclops* as libretto, was premiered in Avigon on July 1986. SCHLIEMANN, libretto by the composer and Bruno Bayen based on a play by Bayen about the German archeologist who found and excavated ancient Troy, was performed in concert form in Paris in 1990 and staged at the Opéra de Lyon on May 3, 1995.

JONAH AND THE WHALE   *1973 oratorio by Argento*

Domenick Argento's *Jonah and the Whale* is a dramatic oratorio with a libretto by the composer based on the 14th century poem *Patience, or Jonah and the Whale*. Argento tells the tale with an eclectic mix of music from whaling songs and Protestant hymns to 12-tone rows. The oratorio premiered in Minneapolis on March 9, 1974, with tenor Vern Sutton as Jonah.

1982 Plymouth Music. Vern Sutton sings the role of Jonah with bass-baritone LeRoy Lehr as the Voice of God in this recording made for the Plymouth Music Series. The other singers are soprano Linda Wilcox and baritone John Brandsetter with Arnold Walker as narrator. Philip Brunelle conducts the Plymouth Festival Choir. The recording was made at the Plymouth Congregational Church in Minneapolis. 52 minutes. PMS LP.

JONES, GEORGE THADDEUS   *American composer (1917–)*

George Thaddeus Jones composed only two operas but both of them were televised. THE CAGE, libretto by Leo Brady about an elevator operator, was telecast on *The Catholic Hour* on NBC-TV on May 10, 1959. BREAK OF DAY, libretto by Leo Brady about a Roman soldier on the first Easter Sunday, was telecast by ABC-TV April 2, 1961. Jones, born in Asheville, NC, was primarily an educator. He taught music at the Eastman School of Music before becoming Professor of Music at Catholic University.

JONES, ROBERT EDMOND   *American designer (1887–1954)*

Robert Jones was one of the most influential set designers in America in the 1920s and 1930s and introduced what became known as the "new stagecraft." He did not often work in Ameri-can opera but he did design the sets for the premiere production of Douglas Moore's THE DEVIL AND DANIEL WEBSTER in 1938.

JOPLIN, SCOTT   *American composer (1868–1917)*

Scott Joplin was almost forgotten until 1970 when he was rediscovered by musicologist Vera Brodsky Lawrence. Her two-volume edition of *The Collected Works of Scott Joplin*, published in 1971 by the New York Public Library, began the Joplin revival. Recordings by Joshua Rifkin and the Joplin rags featured in the 1973 film *The Sting* made him famous again. Recognition as an opera composer soon followed. Joplin's first opera, A *Guest of Honor*, was premiered in St. Louis in 1903 by the Scott Joplin Ragtime Opera Company and taken on tour to five cities. It was a one-act opera with twelve ragtime numbers and seems to have been well liked but it was not published and is considered lost. Joplin's second opera, the three-act TREEMONISHA, was more ambitious. It was composed in the 1908–1911 period, its piano score was published in 1911 and its orchestration (now lost) was completed in 1915. As no one else would take a chance on it despite his fame as a rag composer, Joplin produced the opera himself. A single concert performance in Harlem in 1915 with only piano accompaniment was a failure. Joplin became depressed and died in 1917. *Treemonisha* was virtually forgotten for fifty years and did not win the acclaim it deserved until it was presented professionally in Atlanta in 1972 and given a full production by Houston Grand Opera in 1975. It won a posthumous Pulitzer Prize for the composer. Joplin, who was born in Texarkana, Texas, was not a self-taught genius but rather a trained musician with enormous talent. He studied with German classical musician Julius Weiss in Texarkana and at George Smith College in Sedalia, Missouri, in 1894. He began to play piano for a living in St. Louis in 1885. The publication of "The Maple Leaf Rag" by John Stark in 1889 made him famous and marked the beginning of the ragtime era. Joplin has been the subject of both a biographical film and a biographical opera.

1977 Jeremy Paul Kagan film. The Hollywood film *Scott Joplin* covers many aspects of the composer's life and career but focuses on his ambition to write the opera *Treemonisha*. Billy Dee Williams portrays Joplin, Margaret Avery is Belle Joplin, Eubie Blake is William Williams, Godfrey Cambridge is Tom Turpin, Seymour Casel is Dr. Jaelki, Art Carney is publisher John Stark and Sam Fuller is the Impresario. Christopher Knopf wrote the screenplay and Jeremy Paul Kagan directed the 96-minute film. **1989 Steve Weisberg opera.** The two-act opera *A Guest of Honor: Scott Joplin*, named after Joplin's lost first opera, was composed by Steve Weisberg to a libretto by Howard Pflanzer. It incorporates music by Joplin into scenes picturing his life with its triumphs and despairs. *A Guest of Honor* was premiered in New York City on February 26, 1989, by the Jewish Association for Services to the Aged.

JŌRURI   *1985 opera by Miki*

A Japanese puppet show owner learns that his wife is having an affair with his assistant. He lets them know that he has found out by writing a play that suggests they could culminate their romance with a joint suicide. Minoru Miki's 160-minute opera *Jōruri*, libretto by Colin Graham based on a puppet play by Monzaemon Chikamatsu, was commissioned by Opera Theater of St. Louis and premiered in St. Louis in 1985 with Graham directing. Andrew Wentzel played Shōjo, Faith Esham was Otane, John Brandstetter was Yosuke, Mallory Walker played the Three Visitors and John M. Sullivan, Gordon Holleman and Stephan Kirchgraber were the Assistants. Joseph Rescigno conducted the Opera Theater of St. Louis Orchestra and Chorus. The opera is scored for a Western-style orchestra but features uses some Japanese instruments. "Jōruri" is a kabuki singing style.

1988 Opera Theater of St. Louis. Andrew Wentzel is Shōjo, Faith Esham is Otane, John Brandstetter is Yosuke and Carol Freeman is the Visitor in this Opera Theater of St. Louis production staged by Colin Graham at the Nissei Theater in Tokyo on November 15, 1988. Joseph Rescigno conducts the Opera Theater of St. Louis Orchestra and Chorus. Japanese DVD/VHS/LD.

THE JOY SPREADER   *1925 "American jazz opera" by Rodgers*

In a 1925 New York department store, young saleswomen serve constantly complaining customers. At the end of the day Mary Brown is ready for a date with shipping clerk Tom Jones. Employer Jeremiah Price holds a pep rally staff meeting and gives presents to Mary and Tom for their virtue. When they stay behind a little too long to exchange kisses, they get locked in overnight. They are found asleep in the morning by Price who fires them. They go off to get married while the other employees call a strike. Richard Rodgers' "American jazz opera" *The Joy Spreader*, libretto by Lorenz Hart inspired by Gilbert Seldes, was the first-act finale of *The Garrick Gaieties* when it premiered on May 17, 1925, at the Garrick Theater in New York. Betty Starbuck was Mary, Romney Brent was Tom, Edward Hogan was Price and the supporting cast included June Cochrane, Willard Tobias, Lee Strasburg, Starr Jones, Felix Jacoves and Frances Hyde. The mini-opera was dropped from the show after a few performances (apparently it was not done well) but the show itself is remembered for introducing such classic songs as "Manhattan."

JUAN DARIEN   *1988 "theatrical oratorio" by Goldenthal*

Juan Darien is born a jaguar in the South American jungle but transformed into a human child through mother love. When superstitious villagers accuse him of not being human and try to burn him alive, he changes back into a jaguar. Elliot Goldenthal's theatrical oratorio *Juan Darien: A Carnival Mass*, libretto by Julie Taymor and the composer based on a story by Horacio Quiroga, combines elements of the Catholic Mass with its narrative. It was premiered in March 1988 at St. Clement's in New York City by the Music-Theatre Group and revived in November 1996 at the Vivien Beaumont Theatre in Lincoln Center. Juan was sung by boy soprano Devin Provenzano, Mother by Andrea Frierson Toney and the Circus Barker/Streetsinger roles by the composer. The other roles and chorus are sung by mezzo-sopranos who open the oratorio with an Agnus Dei. Keyboard player Richard Cordova conducted the ten-person chamber orchestra which included pre-Columbia flutes, didjeridu, jawharp, ocarinas, prepared piano and marimba. Director Taylor mixed fantastic puppets with live actors in a dramatic production foreshadowing her success with Disney's *The Lion King*.

1996 Lincoln Center Theater. Andrea Frierson Toney sings the role of the Mother with boy soprano Devin Provenzano as Juan and Goldenthal as Circus Barker/Street singer in this recording of the Lincoln Center production. The chorus members are Elizabeth Acosta, Jennifer Arnold, Ariel Ashwell, Keren Bernbaum, Marion Capriotti, Andrea Kane, Irma-Estel LaGuerre, Nancy Mayans, Ogla Merediz, Alexandra Montano, Jeannine Otis, Tonya Plummer, Andrea Saposnik and Irene Wiley. Richard Cordova leads the chamber orchestra and plays keyboards. Sony CD.

JUBILEE   *1976 opera by Kay*

An African American woman progresses from slavery to freedom in the South during the Antebellum, Civil War, and Reconstruc-

tion eras. Vyry Dutton, slave daughter of a white plantation owner, is whipped when she tries to run away with her son before the war but she survives and gains freedom and relative happiness. Ulysses Kay's three-act opera *Jubilee*, libretto by Donald Dorr based on Margaret Walker's 1966 novel about her great grandmother, was commissioned by Opera/South which premiered it at Jackson State University on November 20, 1976. Joy Blackett sang the role of Vyra, Francois Clemmons was Joey, librettist Dorr designed the sets and directed and James De Priest conducted. This was Kay's first full-length opera and the first based on African American life. The music is tonal with some dissonance and incorporates black spirituals in its chorus numbers.

THE JUDGMENT OF ST. FRANCIS   *1966 opera by Flagello*

Young Francis of Assisi has wealth and status but he would rather help the poor and become a servant of God. His father objects to his giving away his clothes and money and locks him up in a cellar. The local bishop finally accepts that he has a vocation. Nicolas Flagello's one-act opera *The Judgment of St. Francis*, libretto by Armand Aulicino, premiered at the Manhattan School of Music on March 18, 1966.

THE JUGGLER   *1959 opera by Graves*

A deaf-mute juggler offers a bouquet of wild flowers to the Virgin Mary on her feast day but is humiliated by the Priest. The statue of the Virgin Mary comes to life to thank the juggler for his gift. William Graves 30-minute opera *The Juggler*, libretto by Jean Lustberg, was telecast by NBC on *The Catholic Hour* program on May 3, 1959. Rudolph Caringi played the juggler with a supporting cast that included William Lowry, Mary Kennedy, Mary Ann Stabile, Jan Nugent, Daniel Tomaselli, Robert Hubbard and Ann Ricardo. Richard J. Walsh was the producer. The opera, commissioned by the National Council of Catholic Men and based on the legend of the juggler of Notre Dame, features madrigal styles in its score to enhance the period atmosphere.

THE JUMPING FROG OF CALAVERAS COUNTY   *1950 opera by Foss*

California during the gold rush days. A Stranger attempt to win a jumping frog competition in Uncle Henry's Bar by feeding lead pellets to champion frog Daniel Webster. He also flirts with Miss Lulu, the lady love of the frog's owner Smiley. When the townspeople discover the trick, they run the Stranger out of town. Lukas Foss's folksy one-act opera *The Jumping Frog of Calaveras County*, libretto by Jean Karsavina based on the famous story by Mark Twain, premiered on May 18, 1950, at the University of Indiana School of Music in Bloomington. The student cast featured Alton E. Wilder, Lou Herbert and Charles Campbell in the main roles. Hans Busch staged the opera and Ernst Hoffman conducted the Indiana University School of Music Orchestra and Chorus. *Jumping Frog* has become popular with small opera groups around the country and has been staged many times.

1953 After Dinner Opera. Paul Ukena is the Stranger, Burton Trimble is Smiley and Ruth Biller is Miss Lulu in this recording by the After Dinner Opera Company. Elvin Campbell is Uncle Henry, Ralph Cavalucci is the Guitar Player and Karl Brock and Ahti Tuuri are the Crapshooters. Frederic Kurzweill plays piano and Richard Flusser directs. Lyrichord LP/CD. **1996 Manhattan Chamber Orchestra.** Julianne Baird is Miss Lulu, Frederick Urrey is Smiley and Kevin Deas is the Stranger in this recording made at the Church of the Epiphany in New York in October 1996. Peter

Castaldi is Uncle Henry, Christopher Arneson is the Guitar Player, and Geoffrey Friedley and Mark Moliterno are the Crapshooters. Richard Alden Clark leads the Manhattan Chamber Orchestra. The CD includes an additional soprano aria, "Lulu's Song" performed by Baird, and excerpts from the Twain story read by Castaldi. Newport Classic CD. **1996 Judith Kellock.** Judith Kellock and the Cornell Contemporary Singers perform "Lulu's Song" from *The Jumping Frog of Calaveras County* on the album *Lukas Foss: Vocal Chamber Works.* Lukas Foss conducts. Koch CD. **1998 Julianne Baird/Kevin Deas.** Julianne Baird and Kevin Deas perform the duet "That was a mighty fine dinner" from *The Jumping Frog of Calaveras County* on the album *The Art of the American Singer.* It is excerpted from the 1996 Manhattan Chamber Orchestra recording of the opera. Newport CD.

THE JUNIPER TREE   *1985 opera by Glass and Moran*

A young man is killed by his jealous stepmother and served as supper to his father. He is buried under a juniper tree but returns as a bird, exacts vengeance on his killer and is restored to life. Philip Glass and Robert Moran's two-act chamber opera *The Juniper Tree,* libretto by Arthur Yorinks based on a grim fairytale by the Brothers Grimm, premiered at the American Repertory Theater in Cambridge, Massachusetts, on December 12, 1985. The premiere cast included Jayne West, Sanford Sylvan and Lyn Torgove. Michael Yeargan designed the sets, André Serban staged the production and Richard Pittman conducted. The opera was later reprised by Houston Grand Opera, Opera Omaha, Minnesota Opera, Tulsa Opera and other companies.

1985 American Repertory Theater. The 1985 American Repertory Theater premiere in Cambridge, Massachusetts, was recorded live. Jayne West, Sanford Sylvan and Lyn Torgove are the singers. Richard Pittman conducts. Live Opera audiocassette.

JUNO   *1959 musical by Blitzstein*

Juno Boyle experiences harsh economic and personal difficulties during the Irish civil war but gets little support from her husband Jack. He spends his time drinking with his pal Joxer. Marc Blitzstein's operatic musical is based on Sean O'Casey's 1924 play *Juno and the Paycock* as adapted by Joseph Stein with lyrics by the composer. It premiered at the Winter Garden on March 9, 1959, with Shirley Booth as Juno, Melvyn Douglas as Jack Boyle, Jack MacGowran as Joxer, Tommy Rall as Johnny and Monte Amundsen as Mary. The music was praised but the downbeat story was not conducive to Broadway success and the show closed after only two weeks. It has been quite successful in revivals.

1958 Marc Blitzstein. Marc Blitzstein plays piano and sings numbers from *Juno* on this demonstration recording that includes some songs dropped from the show. JJA Records LP. **1959 Original Broadway cast.** Shirley Booth stars as Juno in the original Broadway cast album with Melvyn Douglas as Jack Boyle, Jack MacGowran as Joxer, Monte Amundsen as Mary and Tommy Rall as Johnny. Columbia LP/Fynsworth Alley CD. **1986 Judy Kaye.** Judy Kaye sings "I Wish It So," performed in the opera by Juno's daughter Mary, on the album *Where or When: Rare Songs of the American Theater.* Peter Howard provides accompaniment. Premier CD. **1990 Karen Hovik/William Sharp.** Karen Hovik sings "I Wish It So" and duets with William Sharp in "Bird Upon the Tree." Steven Blier accompanies on piano. The songs are on the album *Marc Blitzstein: Zipperfly and Other Songs* recorded for the New York Festival of Song. Koch CD. **1990 Helene Williams/Ronald Edwards.** Helene Williams and Ronald Edwards sing "What is the Stars?" "My True Heart" and "Quarrel Song" on the

Lukas Foss's *The Jumping Frogs of Calaveras County,* based on a story by Mark Twain, was recorded in New York in 1996 for a Newport Classic CD.

album *A Blitzstein Cabaret.* The recording is based on a show conceived by Leonard Lehrman who accompanies the singers on piano. Premiere CD. **1993 Dawn Upshaw.** Dawn Upshaw sings "I Wish It So" on her album *I Wish It So.* Eric Stern conducts the orchestra. Elektra CD.

K

KABBALAH   *1989 opera by Wallace*

The Kabbalah is the mystical side of Judaism, said to date from the time of Abraham, and its ideas are presented in difficult ritualistic texts. Stewart Wallace's post-minimalist opera *Kabbalah,* libretto by Michael Korie for ten performers, is a dramatized ritual consisting of prologue and seven sections mirroring the seven days of Creation. It was commissioned by the Brooklyn Academy of Music Next Wave/New Music America Festival and premiered at Dance Theater Workshop on November 16, 1989. Dee Wolff designed the sets, Ann Carlson choreographed and directed and Joshua Rosenblum conducted. Subsequent concert versions were presented in Pittsburgh and Houston with Michael Barrett as conductor.

1990 Houston concert. *Kabbalah* was presented in concert in Houston, Texas, in June 1990 by DiverseWorks Artspace and the Jewish Community Center and recorded at Sugar Hill Studios. The singers are Robert Osborne as Abraham and Ben Azzal, Edrie Means as Binah, Pamela Warrick-Smith as Ba'al Shem, Randall Wong as Akiva, Evan Bowers as Ben Zoma, Jerry Godfrey as Ben Abuya, Hugo Munday as Samael, Alexandra Muntano as Harav Seraph, Karen Holvik as a Soul and Michael Sokol as Yesod. The instrumentalists are Andrew Sterman, Tom Christensen, Thomas Gilson, Gary Paisner, Ian Crawford and Bill Ruyle. Michael Barrett conducts. Koch CD

KAFKA: LETTER TO MY FATHER   *2000 opera by Walden*

A tortured, confessional letter by Franz Kafka explores a difficult relationship between father and son. Stanley Walden's one-act opera *Kafka: Letter to My Father,* libretto by the composer based on a Kafka letter, was premiered by the Center for Contemporary Opera at the Kaye Playhouse in New York City on June 28, 2000. Dana Watkins was Kafka, David Shapiro was Kafka's father Herman, Tara Venditti, Tracy Bidleman and Mary Ann Stewart were his sisters, Hope Clarke was his mother and Bartholt Clagett was Kafka as a boy. Atkin Pace designed the set, Charles Mizryan directed and Richard Marshall conducted the 17-piece chamber ensemble.

KAGEN, SERGIUS   *American composer (1909–1964)*

Sergius Kagen, who taught singing at Juilliard from 1940 to 1964, wrote two operas based on famous works of literature. The three-act *Hamlet,* libretto by the composer based on the play by Shakespeare, was premiered in Baltimore on November 9, 1962, with mezzo-soprano Shirley Love as Gertrude. *The Suitor,* libretto by the composed based on Molière's *Monsieur de Purceaugnac,* was unfinished at his death. Kagen, who was born in St. Petersburg, Russia, came to the U.S. in 1925 and became an American citizen in 1930. He wrote over 70 songs and two books on singing.

KALLMAN, CHESTER   *American librettist (1921–1975)*

W. H. Auden said that his partner Chester Kallman made him into an "opera addict" and aroused his interest in writing librettos for operas. Their first collaboration was the libretto for Igor Stravinsky's THE RAKE'S PROGRESS (1948), one of the most admired modern librettos. Their others include an adaptation of a Shakespeare play for Nicolas Nabokov, LOVE'S LABOR'S LOST, which premiered in 1973, and two for Hans Werner Henze, *Elegy for Young Lovers* and *The Bassarids.* Kallman and Auden also made English language versions of Kurt Weill's *The Seven Deadly Sins* and *The Rise and Fall of the City of Mahagonny* and Mozart's *The Magic Flute* and *Don Giovanni.* They were to have been librettists for the musical MAN OF LA MANCHA but this did not work out. Kallman, who was born in Brooklyn, also wrote librettos and translations on his own. For Mexican composer Carlos Chavez he wrote *The Tuscan Players,* performed in New York in 1957 as *Panfilo and Loretta* and in Mexico City in 1963 as *The Visitors.* His English translations of operas by Monteverdi, Verdi and Bartók were considered eminently singable.

KALMANOFF, MARTIN   *American composer (1920–)*

Brooklyn-born Harvard-educated Martin Kalmanoff has composed dozens of operas over the past half century, usually one-act chamber works with small casts, often with literary sources and many intended for children. Most have been performed, including six that premiered on radio. His first opera, the one-act *Fit for a King,* libretto by the composer based on the fairytale *The Emperor's New Clothes,* was broadcast on WNYC in New York in 1949 and staged in 1950. *Noah and the Stowaway,* libretto by Atra Baer, premiered at New York College of Music in 1951. OPERA, OPERA, an opera about opera using a play by William Saroyan as libretto, was first performed by After Dinner Theater Opera at Finch College in New York on February 22, 1956. *The Bald Prima Donna,* based on the Ionesco play, premiered in Brooklyn in 1962. *The Great Stone Face,* based on the Nathaniel Hawthorne story, was performed at Ball State University in Indiana in 1968. *Sganerelle,* based on Molière's play *The Doctor in Spite of Himself,* was presented at Manhattan School of Music in 1977. ON THE HARMFULNESS OF TOBACCO, a monodrama with libretto by Eric Bentley based on a Chekhov story, was premiered at Alice Tully Hall in NYC on March 22, 1979. EMPTY BOTTLE, libretto by the composer about an Italian immigrant gangster in Little Italy, was premiered by the Amato Opera Company in New York in 1991. INSECT COMEDY, libretto by Lewis Allen based on the Karel and Josef Capek play, was premiered by the Center for Contemporary Opera in New York in 1993.

KANITZ, ERNEST   *American composer (1894–1978)*

Ernest Kanitz moved to America from Vienna in 1938 after the Nazi takeover but did not begin to write operas until the 1950s. The first was the two-hour *Kumana,* libretto by Jane Marshall about an American girl raised by Pacific islanders, which was completed in 1953. *Room No. 12,* libretto by Richard Thompson about a young man intent on suicide, was premiered at UCLA on February 26, 1958. *Royal Auction,* libretto by Sidney Shrager and Alexander Chorney about a Ruritanian romance, was performed at UCLA on February 26, 1958. *The Lucky Dollar,* libretto by Ann Stanford about a young woman working unwillingly as a waitress in a Nevada café, was performed at UCLA in 1958. Kanitz's most popular opera PERPETUAL, libretto by Ellen Terry about marionettes, premiered at Antelope Valley College in Los Angeles in 1961. His last music theater work was the opera-cantata *Visions at Midnight,* presented at UCLA on February 26, 1964.

KANSAS   *American state (1861–)*

Kansas is the home state of saloon-smasher Carry Nation, who began her campaign in Topeka, and thus the location of Douglas Moore's famous opera about her that premiered at the University of Kansas in Lawrence. It is also the site of Dennis Rouse's avant-garde opera *Failing Kansas* (1994), based on Truman Capote's book *In Cold Blood* about killers in the small town of Holcomb. Vivian Fine's multimedia opera *The Memoirs of Uliana Rooney* (1994), the story of a woman composer, begins with her Kansas childhood.

Kansas-born opera people include choral director Eva Jessye (Coffeyville), composer Leonard Lehrman (Fort Riley) and bass Samuel Ramey (Colby).

Emporia: Vernon Raines' *The Happy Prince* was premiered at Emporia College in 1955

Fort Hayes: Lewis Miller's *The Imaginary Invalid,* based on the Molière play, premiered at Kansas State College in 1970. His *Letters from Spain,* based on a Beaumarchais play, premiered at the College in 1978.

Larned: Kansas was the 34th state to enter the union. G. R Youse's opera *The Thirty-Fourth Star* was premiered by Grass Roots Opera in tourist-oriented Larned in 1961.

Lawrence: Douglas Moore's CARRY NATION was created for the University of Kansas and was premiered in Lawrence in 1966. Carry began her saloon-smashing career in Topeka.

Manhattan: Kansas State University in Manhattan has an active opera program, including many American operas. Productions in the 1960s included Carlisle Floyd's SLOW DUSK and Gian Carlo Menotti's THE CONSUL. The Opera Workshop has produced an opera and a musical every year since 1972. They include Seymour Barab's A GAME OF CHANCE, Samuel Barber's A HAND OF BRIDGE, Leonard Bernstein's TROUBLE IN TAHITI, Carlisle Floyd's SUSANNAH, Vittorio Giannini's BEAUTY AND THE BEAST and Gian Carlo Menotti's AMAHL AND THE NIGHT VISITORS, THE OLD MAID AND THE THIEF, THE SAINT OF BLEECKER STREET and THE TELEPHONE.

McPherson: Edward Barnes' *The Vagabond Queen* was premiered at McPherson College on April 22, 1989.

Winfield: Gerald Humel's *The Proposal* was premiered at Southwestern College in Winfield in 1958.

KASTLE, LEONARD   *American composer (1929–)*

Leonard Kastle studied at the Curtis Institute and Columbia and was taught by Samuel Barber and Gian Carlo Menotti. He was music director of the 1951 Broadway revival of Menotti's *The Medium* and worked at NBC Opera Theatre which commissioned his first two operas. THE SWING, a story about a bride on her wedding day, was televised in 1956. DESERET, an opera about Mormon leader Brigham Young, was telecast on NBC in 1961 and staged by Opera Memphis in 1967. The three-act opera *The Pariahs*, libretto by the composer about early American whalers, was commissioned by Seattle Opera and presented in Albany in 1985. *The Calling of Mother Ann* and *The Journey of Mother Ann*, two sections of a five-part opera about the Shakers, were staged in Albany and Potsdam in 1985 and 1987. Kastle, who was born in New York City, taught at SUNY in Albany from 1977 to 1988.

KATINKA   *1915 operetta by Friml*

Katinka is in love with Ivan, an attaché at the Russian embassy in Vienna. but seems to be stuck with ambassador Boris as probable husband. After she runs away, fate intervenes. Rudolf Friml's Viennese-style operetta *Katinka*, libretto by Otto Hauerbach, has an unlikely story but good music including the classic "Allah's Holiday" and the hit "Rackety Coo" (it's about a pigeon). The operetta premiered at the Park Theater in Morristown, NJ, on December 2, 1915, and opened on Broadway at the 44th Street Theater on December 23 in a production by Arthur Hammerstein. May Naudain was Katinka, Sam Ash was Ivan, Lorrie Grimaldi was Boris, Franklin Ardell was Thaddeus Hopper and Adele Rowland was Mrs. Hopper.

1916 May Naudain/Sam Ash. May Naudain, who created the role of Katinka, recorded her hit pigeon song "Rackety Coo" for Operaphone in 1916. Sam Ash, who played Ivan opposite her, recorded the song for Columbia with Grace Nash. Both versions are on the anthology album *Music from the New York Stage 1890–1920*. Pearl CD box set. **1918 Rudolf Friml.** Rudolf Friml recorded a piano version of "Allah's Holiday" for a 78. It's on several albums including *The Genius of Rudolf Friml*. Golden Crest LP. **1916 Gladys Moncrieff.** Gladys Moncrieff, who starred in a production of the operetta in Australia in 1918, sings "Rackety Coo" on a Columbia 78. It's on the album *Gladys Moncrieff Sings Musical Comedy and Operetta*. EMI LP. **1929 Victor Salon Group.** The Victor Salon Group perform a medley of tunes from the operetta for a Victor 78 with Nat Shilkret conducting the orchestra. The medley is on the album *The Music of Rudolf Friml*. Victor LP. **1986 Teresa Ringholz/Donald Hunsberger.** Teresa Ringholz and the Eastman-Dryden Orchestra led by Donald Hunsberger perform fifteen selections from *Katinka,* including "Allah's Holiday" "Rackety Coo," and "Charms Are Fairest When They're Hidden" on the album *Rudolf Friml: Chansonette*. Arabesque LP/CD.

KAUFMANN, WALTER   *American composer (1907–1984)*

Walter Kaufmann composed eleven operas to his own librettos, mostly based on literary sources. He was a music professor at Indiana University in Bloomington from 1957 to 1977 and several of his operas were performed there. His first opera was *The Cloak*, based on the Gogol story, which he completed in 1950. Next was *The Research*, staged in Tallahassee, Florida, in 1953. *A Parfait for Irene* was performed at Indiana University Opera Theater in Bloomington in 1952. *Sganerelle,* based on the Molière play, was performed by the Metropolitan Opera Studio in 1961. *The Scarlet Letter,* a three-act opera based on the Hawthorne novel, was staged in Bloomington in 1961. *A Hoosier Tale* was presented in Bloomington in 1966. His last stage work was the children's opera *Rip van Winkle,* based on the Washington Irving tale, composed in 1966. Kaufman, who was born in Czechoslovakia, was an expert on Asian music and published studies of Indian, Chinese and Buddhist music.

KAY, ULYSSES   *American composer (1917–1995)*

Ulysses Kay began his opera career writing short works based on works of literature and ended it composing full-length operas about the African American experience. THE BOOR (1955), libretto by the composer based on a Chekhov story, was premiered by the University of Kentucky in Lexington in 1968. *The Juggler of Our Lady*, libretto by Alexander King, premiered at Xavier College in New Orleans on February 3, 1962. *The Capitoline Venus*, libretto by J. Dvorkin based on the Mark Twain story, premiered in Chicago in 1971. *Trials of Psyche* was performed in Urbana in 1971. JUBILEE, his first African American opera, libretto by Donald Dorr based on the Margaret Walker novel, was commissioned by Opera/South which premiered it at Jackson State University in 1976. FREDERICK DOUGLASS, libretto by Dorr about the African American writer and orator, premiered in Newark, New Jersey, in 1991. Kay is a tonal neo-romantic composer and his music has wide appeal. He was born in Tucson, Arizona, to a musical family that included his uncle, jazz legend King Oliver. He studied at Eastman School, Tanglewood, Yale and Columbia with Howard Hanson, Bernard Rogers and Otto Luening and later taught at UCLA and in New York.

KAYE, JUDY   *American soprano (1948–)*

Judy Kaye sang Abbie in the revised version of Edward Thomas's opera DESIRE UNDER THE ELMS when it premiered in New York in 1989. She was Dinah in the 1994 Cabrillo Music Festival production of Leonard Bernstein's TROUBLE IN TAHITI telecast on Bravo and sang the role in New York. She is featured on notable London recordings of three musicals, as Lalume in the 1990 recording of Wright/Forrest's KISMET, Annie in the 1996 recording of Irving Berlin's ANNIE GET YOUR GUN and Claire in the 1996 recording of Bernstein's ON THE TOWN. She teamed with William Sharp and Michael Barrett in a 1990 album of Bernstein arias and duets and with Sharp for a 1990 album of Gershwin songs. She sang Mrs. Lovett in Stephen Sondheim's *Sweeney Todd* in London in 2000. Kaye, who began her stage music career while a student at UCLA, has sung on Broadway in numerous musicals and made many cast recordings. She has appeared in concert versions of such classic operettas as Victor Herbert's SWEETHEARTS and EILEEN and Jerome Kern's THE CAT AND THE FIDDLE and she created the role of Emma Goldman in the musical *Ragtime*.

KEEL, HOWARD   *American baritone (1917–)*

Howard Keel starred in the movie versions of major American operettas and musicals, usually taking over roles Alfred Drake had originated on stage. He began with the role of Curley in the 1947 London stage production of Rodgers and Hammerstein's OKLAHOMA (cast album) and then moved on to Hollywood movies. He was sharpshooter Frank in Irving Berlin's ANNIE GET YOUR GUN (1950/cast album), gambler Ravenal in Jerome Kern's SHOW BOAT

(1951/cast album), Fred/Petruchio in Cole Porter's Kiss Me Kate (1953/cast album), Royal Canadian Mountie Malone in Rudolf Friml's Rose Marie (1954/cast album) and poet Hajj in Forrest/Wright's Kismet (1955/cast album). He also sings in *Deep in My Heart*, the 1954 film about Sigmund Romberg. His many other movie musicals include such classics as *Calamity Jane* (1953) and *Seven Brides for Seven Brothers* (1954). On stage he sang the role of Billy in the 1957 New York City Center's revival of Rodgers and Hammerstein's Carousel.

KEENE, CHRISTOPHER   *American conductor (1946–1995)*

Christopher Keene conducted the premieres of nine American operas, including three by Gian Carlo Menotti: The Most Important Man in New York in 1971, Tamu-Tamu in Chicago in 1973 and The Hero in Philadelphia in 1976. He also led the orchestra for the premieres of Carlisle Floyd's Bilby's Doll in Houston in 1976, Thomas Pasatieri's Ines de Castro in Baltimore in 1976, Anthony Davis's X, The Life and Times of Malcolm X at New York City Opera in 1986, Jay Reise's Rasputin at New York City Opera in 1988 and Dominick Argento's The Dream of Valentino at Washington Opera in 1994. He conducted the American premiere of Philip Glass's Satyagraha in Buffalo in 1981 and leads the orchestra in the 1985 New York City Opera recording. He was the conductor of the televised Spoleto USA productions of Menotti's The Consul and Samuel Barber's Vanessa in 1978. Keene, born in Berkeley, CA, began his association with Menotti in 1968 when he conducted *The Saint of Bleecker Street* at the Spoleto Festival in Italy. He was music director of the Italian Spoleto Festival in the early 1970s, conductor at the American Spoleto Festival from 1977 to 1980 and music director of New York City Opera from 1983.

KELLEY, NORMAN   *American tenor (1917–)*

Norman Kelley created major roles in the premieres of four American operas while singing with New York City Opera. He created the title role of Joseph Schweik in Robert Kurka's The Good Soldier Schweik in 1958, Lord Mark in Douglas Moore's The Wings of the Dove in 1961, Reverend Samuel Parris in Robert Ward's The Crucible in 1961 and Ely Pratt in Carlisle Floyd's The Passion of Jonathan Wade in 1962. He plays the magician Nika Magadoff in a BBC television production of Gian Carlo Menotti's The Consul and the Lover in Menotti's Amelia Goes to the Ball on stage. Kelley, born in Eddington, Maine, studied at New England Conservatory and Eastman School and made his debut in Philadelphia in 1947.

KENTUCKY   *American state (1792–)*

Two of the original stars of George Gershwin's Porgy and Bess are from Kentucky; Todd Duncan, who created Porgy, was born in Danville and John Bubbles, who created Sportin' Life, was born in Louisville. Bubbles' partner Ford Lee Buck, who had the small role of Mingo, is also from Louisville, the largest city in Kentucky and the center of its opera activity. Other Kentucky opera people include composer Beth Anderson (Lexington), soprano Faith Esham (Vanceburg), tenor Riccardo Martin (Hopkinsville) and composer Julia Perry (Lexington), Adam Guettel's operatic 1994 musical *Floyd Collins* take place in Kentucky

Covington: Henry Humphreys-Rauscher's *Sea-Thorn* was premiered at Holmes High School in Covington in 1981.

Lexington: Two operas premiered at the University of Kentucky in Lexington, Kenneth Wright's *Wings of Expectation*, about

Lincoln, in 1965 and Ulysses Kay's The Boor, based on Chekhov, in 1968.

Louisville: Kentucky Opera in Louisville was founded in 1953 by conductor/artistic director Moritz von Bomhard who inaugurated it with Gian Carlo Menotti's The Telephone and The Medium. It became known for its commitment to American opera when it commissioned six new operas in the 1950s, beginning with Peggy Glanville Hicks' The Transposed Heads in 1954. This was followed by Richard Mohaupt's Double Trouble in 1954, George Antheil's The Wish in 1955, Rolf Liebermann's School of Wives in 1955, Nicolas Nabokov's The Holy Devil in 1958 and Lee Hoiby's Beatrice in 1959. All six operas were recorded and released on the Louisville Orchestra First Edition label. The company has continued to present other American operas ranging from Kurt Weill's Down in the Valley and Carlisle Floyd's Susannah to George Gershwin's Porgy and Bess. It co-commissioned Philip Glass's The Fall of the House of Usher in 1988 and commissioned and premiered Daniel Dutton's *The Stone Man* in 1990. Soprano Nancy Shade made her debut at Kentucky Opera in 1969. Peter Ekstrom's The Gift of the Magi was premiered by Actors' Theater in Louisville in 1981 and Robert Carlson's *The Legend of Sleepy Hollow* was premiered in 1986.

KERN, JEROME   *American composer (1885 —1945)*

Jerome Kern, one of the finest American composers of the century, did not write operas but his operatic musical Show Boat (1927) was the first to enter the opera house repertory. Since its presentation by New York City Opera in 1954, it has been staged by many other opera houses and recorded by major opera singers. Kern and librettist Oscar Hammerstein II integrated American music, American setting and American story in an innovative way and virtually created the genre of the American musical. Kern also composed two Viennese-style operettas set in Europe about showbiz folk staging operettas. The Cat and the Fiddle (1931), libretto by Otto Harbach, focuses on two composers in Brussels who fall in love and join forces to write an opera/operetta. Music in the Air (1932), libretto by Hammerstein, is set in Munich where an operetta librettist and prima donna become involved with a couple from Bavaria. Kern, born in New York City, began to write for the stage in 1905 and made his name with the Princess Theatre musicals in the 1910s. His 1914 song "They Didn't Believe Me" exerted a huge influence on American songwriting. In the 1930s Kern began to write for Hollywood musicals, including the Astaire-Rogers classic *Swing Time*. There are a multitude of recordings of Kern musicals and songs and a film biography. Conductor John McGlinn, who produced a superb recording of *Show Boat* in 1988, has also recorded a excellent version of Kern's 1923 musical *Sitting Pretty* with Judith Blazer, Jason Graee and Roberta Peters.

1946 Till the Clouds Roll By. *Till the Clouds Roll By* is an MGM film biography of Kern (played by Robert Walker) featuring career highlights and a potted version of *Show Boat*. Jean Holloway, George Welles and Myles Connolly wrote the screenplay and Richard Whorf and Vincente Minnelli directed. MGM DVD/VHS/LD.

KILL BEAR COMES HOME   *1996 opera by Stuart*

Iroquois brave Kill Bear is killed by a bear while hunting but he also kills the bear. His widow Cold Feet is importuned by Chief Wife Hunter so her sister Hasty Girl asks advice from a Song Bird. She is told how to resurrect the husband with magic spring water but spills some of it and revives both the man and the bear but with their heads switched. Kill Bear returns to the village and frightens everyone. Afterwards he returns to the magic spring and gets his own head back. Paul Stuart's two-act opera *Kill Bear Comes Home*, libretto by Sally M. Gall based on the Iroquois legend *Bear Man*, was premiered by Opera Theater of Rochester at the Hart Theater in Rochester on April 12, 1996. Mark Schmidt sang Kill Bear, Mi-Kyung Hu was Cold Feet, Elana Gizzi was Hasty Girl, Therese Murray was Song Bird and Jason Smith was Chief Wife Hunter. John King designed the sets, Judith Ranaletta staged the opera and the composer conducted the Opera Theater of Rochester Chorus and Orchestra. Stuart uses flute, drum and rattle to evoke a Native American sound but keeps the score lyrical.

1996 Rochester Opera Theater. The original cast of the opera recorded it soon after the premiere. Mark Schmidt is Kill Bear, Mi-kyung Hu is Cold Feet, Elana Gizzi is Hasty Girl and the other singers are as listed above. Paul Stuart conducts the Opera Theater of Rochester Chorus and Orchestra. Dynamic Recording CD.

THE KING AND I   *1951 musical by Rodgers and Hammerstein*

The King is the autocratic semi-barbaric ruler of 19th century Siam. The "I" is a strong-minded English widow who is hired to teach his children. Their clash of wills and eventual understanding of each other is the focus of this superb operetta-like musical based on Margaret Landon's novel *Anna and the King of Siam* and the diaries of the real Anna. It was written at the urging of Gertrude Lawrence, who felt it would make an ideal musical for her, but it was even more ideal for an unknown actor named Yul Brynner who effectively stole the spotlight from her. Richard Rodgers' *The King and I,* libretto by Oscar Hammerstein, premiered at the Shubert Theatre in New Haven on February 26, 1951, and opened at the St. James Theatre in New York on March 29, 1951. Lawrence played Anna, Brynner played the King, John Stewart was the Crown Prince, Doretta Morrow was Tuptim, Larry Douglas was Lun Tha, Dorothy Sarnoff was Lady Thiang and Sandy Kennedy was Anna's son. Jerome Robbins arranged the choreography, John van Druten directed and Frederick Dvonch conducted. Brynner eventually played the role on stage around 5000 times and won an Oscar for his performance in the film version.

1951 Original Broadway cast. Yul Brynner plays the King opposite Gertrude Lawrence as Anna in this original cast recording. John Stewart is Crown Prince, Doretta Morrow is Tuptim, Larry Douglas is Lun Tha and Dorothy Sarnoff is Lady Thiang. Frederick Dvonch conducts. Decca LP/MCA CD. **1951 Robert Merrill/Patrice Munsel.** Robert Merrill sings the role of the King opposite Patrice Munsel as Anna in this operatic studio recording of highlights. Dinah Shore and Tony Martin lend support and Al Goodman and Henri René conduct. RCA Victor LP/MCA CD. **1953 London cast.** Herbert Lom sings the role of the King opposite Valerie Hobson as Anna in this cast recording of the London stage production. Muriel Smith Is Lady Thiang. Reginald Burston conducts. Phillips LP. **1956 20th Century-Fox film.** Yul Brynner plays the King opposite Deborah Kerr as Anna (singing by Marni Nixon) in this excellent 20th Century-Fox film directed by Walter Lang. Rita Moreno is Tuptim, Carlos Rivas is Lun Tha (singing by Reuben Fuentes) and Terry Saunders is Lady Thiang. Brynner won an Academy Award for his performance and the film won Oscars for art direction, costumes and scoring. Alfred Newman conducts the chorus and orchestra. Fox VHS/DVD. Soundtrack on Capitol LP/EMI CD. **1960 Samuel Jones/Lois Hunt.** Lois Hunt is Anna opposite Samuel Jones as the King in this studio recording of highlights from the operetta. Irene Carroll is Lady Thiang, Charmaine Harma is Tuptim and Harry Snow is Lun Tha.

Paul Stuart's *Kill Bear Comes Home*, based on an Iroquois legend was premiered and recorded by Opera Theater of Rochester in 1996.

Epic LP. **1964 Music Theater Lincoln Center.** Met soprano Rise Stevens sings the role of Anna opposite Darren McGavin as the King in this cast recording of the operatic Music Theater of Lincoln Center revival. Patrica Neway is Lady Thiang, Lee Venora is Tuptim and Frank Porretta is Lun Tha. Franz Allers conducts. RCA Victor LP. **1964 Theodore Bikel/Barbara Cook.** Barbara Cook is Anna opposite Theodore Bikel as the King in this studio recording of highlights from the operetta. Anita Darian is Lady Thiang, Jeanette Scovotti is Tuptim and Daniel Ferro is Lun Tha, Lehman Engel conducts chorus and orchestra. Columbia LP/Sony CD. **1977 Broadway revival cast.** Yul Brynner reprises his role as the King in this cast recording of the 1977 Broadway revival with Constance Towers taking over the role of Anna. June Angela is Tuptim, Martin Vidnovic is Lun Tha and Hye-Young Choi is Lady Thiang. Milton Rosenstock conducts. RCA Victor LP/CD. **1992 Ben Kingsley/ Julie Andrews.** Ben Kingsley is the King, Julie Andrews is Anna and in this fine London studio recording of the operetta. Marilyn Horne plays Lady Thiang and sings "Something Wonderful" wonderfully while Lea Salonga and Peabo Bryson are the young lovers. John Mauceri leads the Hollywood Bowl Orchestra and Los Angeles Master Chorale. Phillips CD. **1994 Christopher Lee/Valerie Masterson.** Christopher Lee plays the King with Valerie Masterson as Anna in this London studio recording. The other singers are Tinuke Olafimihan, Sally Burgess, Alec McCowen, Jason Howard, André Mutis, Bea Julakassiun, Cheng Wah and Henry Williams. John Owen Edwards conducts. TER CD. **1996 Broadway revival cast.** Lou Diamond Phillips as the King with Donna Murphy as Anna in this cast recording of the 1996 Broadway revival. Joohee Choi is Tuptim, Jose Llana is Lun Tha and Taewon Kim is Lady Thiang. Michael Rafter conducts. Varese-Sarabande CD. **1996 Bryan Terfel.** Welsh baritone Bryan Terfel sings "Something Wonderful" and "I Have Dreamed" from *The King and I* on his album *Something Wonderful: Bryan Terfel Sings Rodgers and Hammerstein*. Paul Daniel conducts the English Northern Philharmonic and Opera North Chorus. DG CD. **2000**

The King and I was filmed in 1956 with Deborah Kerr in the role of Anna.

London revival cast. Elaine Paige stars as Anna opposite Jason Scott Lee in this London revival cast recording. The other singers are Richard Avery, Aura Deva, Alexander Deng, Miguel Diaz, Sean Ghazi, Benjamin Ghazi, Benjamin Ibbot, Robin Kermode and Taewon Yi Kim. John Owen Edwards conducts. Warner/Elektra/ Atlantic CD. **2000 Sylvia McNair.** Sylvia McNair sings "Hello, Young Lovers" on the album *The Radio 3 Lunchtime Concert* accompanied by Ted Taylor. BBC Music CD.

KING GESAR   *1996 "campfire opera" by Lieberson*

Incidents in the life of the legendary 10th century Tibetan warrior-king King Gesar of Ling following him from his early years to his final enlightenment. Peter Lieberson's *King Gesar*, a chamber opera for narrator and instrumentalists with libretto by Douglas Penick, was commissioned by Hans Werner Henze for the Munich Biennale where it premiered in 1996. Omar Ebrahim was the Narrator, Yo-Yo-Ma was the cellist, Emanuel Ax and Peter Serkin were the pianists, András Adjornján was the flautist, Deb-

orah Marshall played the clarinet, William Purvis played the French horn, David Taylor played the trombone and Stefan Huge was the percussionist. Lieberson, who conducted, wrote the work specifically for these performers and describes it as a "campfire opera" meant to emulate the atmosphere of traditional storytelling around a Tibetan campfire. For Tibetans the tale has the same value as Homer's epics. *King Gesar*, which is the first of a planned cycle of four operatic works about enlightened rulers called *The Cycle of the Ancestral Sovereigns,* was the basis of the Canadian TV production *Warrior Songs: The Legend of King Gesar.*

1996 Munich Biennale. Omar Ebrahim is the Narrator, Yo-Yo-Ma is the cellist and Emanuel Ax and Peter Serkin are the pianists in this Munich Biennale premiere recording with the other instrumentalist as listed above. Lieberson conducts. Sony Classical CD.

THE KINGDOM OF LOVE   *1976 American "movie opera" by Shire*

New York City in the 1890s. Vaudevillians James Caan and Elliott Gould don exotic Arabic costumes and barge onto a stage where a comic opera called *The Kingdom of Love* is being performed. Star Lesley Ann Warren is horrified but bravely carries on for the sake of the audience. What she doesn't know is that they are trying to delay the show so their gang can finish a robbery before Michael Caine's rival gang arrives. There is a secret tunnel to a bank under the theater. The duo improvise songs and dances and improve the show so much (there is nowhere for it to go but up) that they get standing ovations at the end. This movie opera, created for the film *Harry and Walter Go to New York* by David Shire with Alan and Marilyn Bergman, is truly bad, but then it was meant to be as it sends up the conventions of turn-of-the-century comic opera. Carmine Coppola plays the conductor in the film, John Byrum and Robert Kaufman wrote the screenplay, Laszlo Kovacs was

James Caan and Elliott Gould cavort in the comic opera *The Kingdom of Love* created for the 1976 movie *Harry and Walter Go to New York.*

the cinematographer, and Mark Rydell directed the film for Columbia. Sony VHS.

THE KING'S BREAKFAST   *1973 opera by Barthelson*

King Henry VIII of England is having breakfast in his palace and arguing viciously with his sixth wife, Catherine Parr, who is more than a little jealous of his previous wives. They disagree about everything from eggs to Latin but eventually music, including the song "Alexander's Horse" composed by Henry himself, helps them to become reconciled. Joyce Barthelson's one-act comic opera *The King's Breakfast,* libretto by the composer based on Maurice Baring's play *Catherine Parr,* was premiered by Community Opera of New York City on February 26, 1973, and reprised in Atlantic City, New Jersey, on April 6, 1973, for the National Federation of Music Clubs.

THE KING'S HENCHMAN   *1927 opera by Taylor*

England in the 10th century. King Eadgar, who is interested in marrying Princess Aelfrida, sends his friend Aethelwold to propose to her if she is beautiful. Aethelwood falls in love with her and marries her himself after sending word back to Eadgar that she is ugly and unworthy. When the King finds out that he has been deceived, Aethelwold kills himself. Deems Taylor's three-act opera *The King's Henchman,* libretto by poet Edna St. Vincent Millay based on a Saxon legend very like that used in Wagner's *Tristan und Isolde,* premiered at the Metropolitan Opera on February 17 1927. Lawrence Tibbett created the role of King Eadgar, Florence Easton was Aelfrida, Edward Johnson was Aethelwold, Merle

Alcock was Ase, William Gustafson was Maccus, George Meader was Dunstan, Louis d'Angelo was Ordgar, Arnold Gabor was Thored, Max Block was Hwita, Max Altglass was Gunner and George Cehanovsky was Cynric. Joseph Urban designed the sets, Wilhelm von Wymetal directed and Tullio Serafin conducted the Metropolitan Opera and Chorus. The opera was so popular it was presented at the Met fourteen times over several seasons and toured for thirty weeks. It was the first American opera broadcast on radio when CBS transmitted it coast to coast on September 18, 1927, with Howard Barlow conducting. It has been revived several times in recent years, including productions by Mercyhurst College in Pennsylvania in 1965 and Bel Canto Opera in New York in 1976.

1927 Lawrence Tibbett. Lawrence Tibbett recorded two arias from the opera for a Victor 78 record on April 5, 1927, with the Metropolitan Opera Chorus and Orchestra led by Giulio Setti. "O Caesar, great wert Thou" is sung in the opera by Maccus in the first act while "Nay, Maccus, Lay Him Down" is sung by King Eadgar at the end. The first is on *Souvenirs from American Opera* (IRRC CD), the second is on *Lawrence Tibbett Sings Operatic Arias* (RCA Camden LP). **1927 Columbia Phonograph.** *The King's Henchman* became the first American opera broadcast on radio when it was presented in a 60-minute highlights format by the Columbia Phonograph Broadcasting System (later CBS) over WOR in New York on September 18, 1927, just six months after its Met premiere. Howard Barlow conducted and the cast included Rafaelo Diaz, Marie Sundelius, Richard Hale, Henri Scott and Giovanni Martino. The same singers toured the opera for thirty weeks. **1934 Lawrence Tibbett.** Lawrence Tibbett sings arias from the opera on a *Packard Hour* radio broadcast of the opera on November 20, 1934. Three arias from Act III are on a collector's LP (EJS 124 LP) and the Act III Finale, "Eadgar!, Eadgar!," is on the CD album *Souvenirs from American Opera* (IRRC CD). **1942 Lawrence Tibbett/Risë Stevens.** Lawrence Tibbett, Risë Stevens and Charles Kullman sing Acts Two and Three of the opera on a radio broadcast on June 18, 1942. Omega Opera Archives CD and audiocassette. **1942 Jan Peerce/Vivian Della Chiesa.** Jan Peerce sings King Eadgar opposite Vivian Della Chiesa as Princess Aelfrida in an abridged version of the opera broadcast by the Mutual Broadcasting System August 18, 1942. Alfred Wallenstein conducts. The duet "God Willing, We Leave this House Tonight" is on the album *Souvenirs from American Opera* (IRRC CD) and the whole 60-minute broadcast is on a Live Opera audiocassette and an Omega Opera Archives CD.

KIRCHNER, LEON *American composer (1919–)*

Leon Kirchner's opera LILY, based on the first half of Saul Bellow's novel *Henderson the Rain King*, premiered at New York City Opera in 1977. Although he had studied with Arnold Schoenberg and Roger Sessions and was well acquainted with modern musical styles, Kirchner created a complex tonal style unlike that of anyone else. His only opera, considered a summation of his work, incorporates a wide variety of vocal and musical techniques as well as tape, film and electronics. Kirchner, who was born in Brooklyn and brought up in California, is also a pianist and conductor.

KIRSTEN, DOROTHY *American soprano (1915–1992)*

Dorothy Kirsten, who sang at the Met from 1945 to 1975, was an enthusiast of American operetta and made many highlights recordings, usually with Gordon MacRae but also with Robert Merrill and Robert Rounseville. She began in 1947 with a recital album of songs from Victor Herbert operettas and later recorded highlight versions of his PRINCESS PAT (1952) and MLLE. MODISTE (1953). She also made highlights recordings of Jerome Kern's SHOW BOAT (1949), Rudolf Friml's THE VAGABOND KING (1952), Sigmund Romberg's THE STUDENT PRINCE (1952/1953/1962), THE NEW MOON (1952/1963) and THE DESERT SONG (1963) and Forrest/Wright's KISMET (1964). Kirsten, born in Montclair, NJ, made her debut in 1940 with the Chicago Grand Opera Company. A protégé of Grace Moore, she sang with New York City and San Francisco Opera before joining the Met. She was also very popular on radio and TV.

KISMET *1953 operetta by Wright/Forrest/Borodin*

A charismatic Arabian poet pretends to be a sorcerer in ancient Baghdad. He gets rid of a wicked Wazir, wins the Wazir's gorgeous wife for himself and gains a caliph husband for his daughter. Robert Wright and George Forrest's surprisingly effective pastiche operetta *Kismet*, music by Russian composer Alexander Borodin mostly borrowed from the opera *Prince Igor*, has a libretto by Charles Lederer and Luther Davis based on a 1911 play by Edward Knoblock. It premiered at the Philharmonic Auditorium in Los Angeles on August 17, 1953, and opened on Broadway at the Ziegfeld Theater on December 3, 1953. Alfred Drake portrayed the poet conman Hajj, Doretta Morrow was his beautiful daughter Marsinah, Henry Calvin was the wicked Wazir, Richard Kiley was the Caliph and Joan Diener was the Wazir's seductive wife Lalume. Albert Marre staged the operetta, Jack Cole arranged the choreography and Louis Adrian conducted. The operetta has now become part of the repertory of the New York City Opera and other opera.

1953 Original Broadway cast. Alfred Drake stars as poet Hajj in the original cast album with Doretta Morrow as Marsinah, Henry Calvin as the Wazir, Richard Kiley as the Caliph and Joan Diener as Lalume. Louis Adrian conducts. Columbia LP/CD. **1955 MGM film.** Howard Keel plays the singing poet in this entertaining MGM film of the operetta directed by Hollywood musical master Vincente Minnelli. Ann Blyth is the daughter loved by Caliph Vic Damone while Dolores Gray is the flirtatious wife of wicked Wazir Sebastian Cabot. André Previn and Jeff Alexander conduct. Soundtrack on MCA LP/Rhino CD. Film on MGM VHS/DVD. **1959 Dorothy Kirsten/Thomas L. Thomas.** Dorothy Kirstein duets with Thomas L. Thomas on "And This is My Beloved" on the *Voice of Firestone* TV program on May 18, 1959. It's on the video *Dorothy Kirsten in Opera and Song*. VAI VHS. **1964 Gordon MacRae/Dorothy Kirsten.** Gordon MacRae sings the role of Hajj with Dorothy Kirsten as Marsinah in this studio recording of the musical. Bunny Bishop is Lalume and Salli Terri is Princess Zubbediya. Van Alexander conducts the orchestra. Capitol LP. **1965 Broadway revival cast.** Alfred Drake returns as Hajj in this cast recording of the 1965 Broadway revival. Anne Jeffreys is Lalume, Richard Banke is the Caliph, Lee Venora is Marsinah and Henry Calvin is the Wazir. Franz Allers conducts. RCA LP/CD. **1967 ABC Television cast.** José Ferrer plays the tongue-in-cheek poet who deceives Baghdad in this ABC Television production. Anna Maria Alberghetti is daughter Marsinah, Barbara Eden is Lalume, George Chakiris is the Caliph, Hans Conried is the Wazir and Cecil Kellaway is Omar Khayyam. The 90-minute TV show, directed by Bob Henry, was telecast on October 24, 1967. On audiocassette. **1978 Timbuktu!** A black version of Kismet titled *Timbuktu!* was staged on Broadway in 1978 with Eartha Kitt as the main attraction. The setting was changed to the ancient African kingdom of Mali but the music and story were the same. Kitt made an album of the operetta in 1978 with a completely different cast that featured Johnny Mathis, Sarah Vaughan, Lena Horne, Della Reese and Isaac Hayes. Blackwood LP. **1990 Donald Maxwell/Judy Kaye.** Donald Maxwell is Hajj with Judy Kaye as Lalume on this studio recording. Valerie Masterson is Marsinah, David Rendall is the Caliph, Richard Van Allan is the Wazir and Rosemary Ashe is the Marriage Broker. John Owen Edwards conducts the Philharmonia Orchestra and Ambrosian Chorus. TER CD. **1991 Samuel Ramey/Julia Migenes.** Samuel Ramey is Hajj, Julia Migenes is Lalume, Jerry Hadley is the Caliph and Ruth Ann Swenson is Marsinah in this operatic version of the operetta. Dom DeLuise is Wazir and Mandy Patinkin is the Marriage Broker. Paul Gemignani conducts the Ambrosian Singers, Concert Chorale of New York and London Symphony Orchestra. Sony CD.

KISS ME KATE *1948 musical by Porter*

Cole Porter's 1948 musical *Kiss Me Kate,* libretto by Sam and Bella Spewack based around Shakespeare's *The Taming of the Shrew,* has entered the repertory of opera companies in the U. S. and Europe and been recorded by opera singers. It is set at the Ford's Theater in Baltimore during the tryout of a musical based on *The Taming of the Shrew* and takes place both backstage and onstage. Fred Graham, the producer of the show, plays Petruchio in the musical-within-the-musical opposite his former wife Lilli Vanessi as Kate and their backstage relationship is a reflection of their Shakespearean roles. *Kiss Me Kate* premiered at the Shubert Theater in Philadelphia on December 2, 1948, and opened in New York at the New Century Theater on December 30. Alfred Drake was Fred/Petruchio, Patricia Morison was Lili/Kate, Lisa Kirk was

Lois/Bianca and Harold Lang was her gambling boyfriend Bill/Lucentio. Robert Russell Bennett arranged the orchestration. The role of Lilli was offered to opera singers Jarmila Novotná and Lily Pons but both turned it down. Nearly every song in the musical has attained popularity and the show continues to be revived with great success.

1948 Original Broadway cast. Alfred Drake, Patricia Morison, Lisa Kirk and Harold Lang star in the original cast recording with Pembroke Davenport conducting. Columbia LP/CD. **1949 Gordon MacRae/Jo Stafford.** Gordon MacRae and Jo Stafford star in this studio recording of highlights from the musical. Paul Weston conducts. Capitol Records LP. **1953 MGM film.** Howard Keel is Fred opposite Kathryn Grayson as Lili in this excellent film of the musical shot in CinemaScope and 3D. Ann Miller is Lisa, Tommy Rall is Bill, Bobby Van is Gremio, Bob Fosse is Hortensio and Claud Allister is Paul. Keenan Wynn and James Whitemore are the gangsters who sing "Brush Up Your Shakespeare." André Previn conducted orchestra and chorus and George Sidney directed. Soundtrack on MGM LP/Rhino Records CD. Film on MGM/WB VHS/DVD. **1958 NBC Television.** Alfred Drake and Patricia Morison recreate their starring roles in a Hallmark Hall of Fame television production for NBC directed by George Schaefer. Julie Wilson is Lisa and Bill Hayes is Bill. Telecast on November 20, 1958. Video at UCLA Film and Television Archive. **1959 Original Broadway cast redux.** The original Broadway cast and conductor were reunited in 1959 for a stereophonic recording of the musical. Alfred Drake, Patricia Morison, Lisa Kirk and Harold Lang reprise their roles with Pembroke Davenport conducting. Capitol LP/Angel CD. **1952 Earl Wrightson/Lois Hunt.** Earl Wrightson and Lois Hunt star in this studio recording of highlights from the musical. Glenn Osser conducts the orchestra. Columbia LP. **1968 ABC Television.** Robert Goulet and Carol Lawrence star in this Armstrong Circle Theatre production for ABC Television directed by Paul Bogart. Jessica Walter is Lois, Michael Callan is Bill. Jack Elliott conducts. Telecast on March 25, 1968. Soundtrack on Columbia LP. **1990 Thomas Hampson/Josephine Barstow.** Thomas Hampson, Josephine Barstow, Kim Criswell, George Dvorsky and Damon Evans are the featured singers on this London studio recording of the complete score of the musical. John McGlinn conducts the Ambrosian Chorus and London Sinfonietta. EMI CD. **1999 Broadway revival cast.** Brian Stokes Mitchell is Fred with Marin Mazzie as Lili in this recording made in New York by the 1999 Broadway revival cast. The other singers are Amy Spanger as Lois, Michael Berresse as Bill, Ron Holgate and Lee Wilkof. DRG CD. **2003 Broadway cast in London.** Brent Barrett is Fred opposite Rachel York as Lili in this fine DVD of the Michael Blakemore production which moved to London's West End after 9/11. Nancy Anderson is Lois, Michael Berresse is Bill, and Nolan Frederick is Paul. Teddy Kempner and Jack Chissick are the gangsters brushing up their Shakespeare. Kathleen Marshall arranged the choreography and Paul Gemignani conducted orchestra and chorus. 146 minutes. Image/TDK DVD.

KLEINSINGER, GEORGE   *American composer (1914–1982)*

George Kleinsinger and librettist Joe Darion turned Don Marquis's classic tale of a witty cockroach and a sexy cat into the chamber opera *archy and mehitabel*. It premiered in New York City on December 6, 1954, with Mignon Dunn as Mehitabel. It was then revised and turned into the Broadway musical *Shinbone Alley* which opened on April 13, 1957, with Eartha Kitt as Mehitabel. Kleinsinger's opera *The Tree That Found Christmas*, libretto by Darion based on a story by Christopher Morley, was premiered in New York on December 17, 1955. Kleinsinger, born in San Bernardino, CA, studied at New York University and Juilliard and first became known for his 1940 cantata *I Hear America Singing* based on Walt Whitman poems. His most popular work, however, was the 1942 melodrama *Tubby the Tuba*, libretto by P. Tripp, which sold half a million records and was made into a popular animated film.

KNICKERBOCKER HOLIDAY   *1938 musical by Weill*

Peter Stuyvesant arrives in New Amsterdam (Manhattan) in 1647 to become Governor and turns out to be even more crooked that the city's corrupt councilmen. Foiled in his attempt to marry young Tina Tienhoven, who prefers American Brom Broeck, he finally decides to govern democratically. Kurt Weill's satirical but patriotic musical *Knickerbocker Holiday*, libretto by Maxwell Anderson inspired by Washington's Irving's *The History of New York* (1809) using the name Knickerbocker, premiered at the Horace Bushnell Memorial Hall in Hartford on September 24, 1938, and opened on Broadway at the Ethel Barrymore Theater on November 7, 1938. Walter Huston played Peter, Jeanne Madden was Tina, Richard Kollmar was Brom Broeck, Ray Middleton was Washington Irving and Robert Rounseville was a Citizen. Jo Mielziner designed the sets, Joshua Logan directed and Maurice Abravanel conducted. Huston sang the show's biggest hit, "September Song," about an old man wooing a young girl; it was later recorded by Huston, Bing Crosby, Billy Daniels, Tony Martin and Artie Shaw, among others

1938 Walter Huston. Walter Huston recorded two songs from the show for a 78 in 1938, "September Song" and "The Scars." Both are on the album *Kurt Weill — From Berlin to Broadway*. Pearl CD. **1944 United Artists film.** Charles Coburn stars as Peter with Nelson Eddy as Brom and Constance Dowling as Tina in this poor film version of the musical. Only three Weill songs survive, though one is "September Song" sung by Coburn. Shelley Winters plays Tina's mom. Harry Joe Brown wrote the script and directed for United Artists. The three songs are on the Ariel LP soundtrack album *Kurt Weill in Hollywood*. Coburn performs "September Song" and "The One Indispensable Man" and Eddy sings "There's Nowhere to Go But Up." **1945 Walter Huston/David Brooks.** Walter Huston is Peter opposite David Brooks as Brom and Jeanne Madden as Tina in this radio version of the musical. Maurice Abravanel conducts the chorus and orchestra. They're included on the AEI CD/Pearl CD album *Kurt Weill — From Berlin to Broadway II*. **1950 ABC Television.** Dennis King stars as Peter with John Raitt as Brom and Doretta Morrow as Tina in this ABC Television *Pulitzer Prize Playhouse* production. William H. Brown directed and Glen Osser conducted. Telecast November 17, 1950. On audiocassette. **1957 Lotte Lenya.** Lotte Lenya sings "September Song" and "It Never Was You" on the album *Lotte Lenya Sings Kurt Weill: American Theater Songs* Maurice Levine conducts orchestra and chorus. Sony Classics CD. **1967 Burl Ives.** Burl Ives played Peter in a touring production of the musical in 1950 and he sings some of the songs from the show on his album *Burl's Broadway*. Decca LP. **1972 Berlin to Broadway with Kurt Weill.** In the off-Broadway revue *Berlin to Broadway with Kurt Weill, A Musical Voyage*, Jerry Lanning sings "September Song" And the ensemble sings the "How Can You Tell an American." Paramount LP. **1986 Teresa Stratas.** Teresa Stratas sings "It Never Was You" on her album *Stratas Sings Weill* with Gerard Schwarz conducting the Y Chamber Orchestra. Nonesuch LP/CD. **1996 Steven Kimbrough.** Steven Kimbrough sings "The Bachelor Song" on the album *Kurt Weill on Broadway* with Victor Symonteete conducting the Cologne West German Radio Orchestra. Koch Schwann CD. **1997 Thomas Hampson/Elizabeth Futral.** Thomas Hampson and

Elizabeth Futral perform "It Never Was You" and "How Can You Tell an American?" on the album *Kurt Weill on Broadway*. John McGlinn conducts the London Sinfonietta. EMI Classics CD. **1994 Kiri Te Kanawa.** Kiri Te Kanawa sings "It Never Was You" on her album *Kiri!— Her Greatest Hits*. Stephen Barlow conducts the London Symphony Orchestra. London Classics CD/VHS. **2000 Lesley Garrett.** Lesley Garrett sings "September Song" with the John Harle Band on the album *Lesley Garrett: I Will Wait for You*. RCA Victor CD.

KNIGHT, FELIX   *American tenor (1908–1998)*

Felix Knight created a Philistine Lord in Bernard Rogers' opera THE WARRIOR at the Metropolitan Opera in 1947. He is featured on the only recording of Walter Damrosch's opera CYRANO DE BERGERAC, performing with Agnes Davies and Earl Wrightson on a 1942 radio broadcast. He plays Tom Tom the Piper's Son in the famous 1934 Laurel and Hardy version of Victor Herbert's comic opera BABES IN TOYLAND (he gets to rescue Little Bo Peep) and made highlights recordings of three other Herbert operettas, THE RED MILL (1946), MLLE. MODISTE (1952) and NAUGHTY MARIETTA (1953). He recorded Sigmund Romberg's THE DESERT SONG in 1945 and performs on a Magic Key radio tribute to George Gershwin in 1938. Knight, born in Macon, Georgia, began his opera career after he finished his film. He made his opera debut at the Hollywood Bowl in 1935, won a Metropolitan Opera competition in 1938 and make his debut at the Met in 1946. He was also popular on radio.

THE KNIGHT OF THE BURNING PESTLE   *1974 music theater by Schickele*

Peter Schickele's *The Knight of the Burning Pestle,* based on a 17th century play by Beaumont and Fletcher, was created for the Long Wharf Theater in New Haven. He scored it for the same instruments used in Igor Stravinsky's *The Soldier's Tale,* which was the other half of the premiere evening.

1979 Songs from Knight of the Burning Pestle. Nine songs from the work are performed on this recording by soprano Lucy Shelton, alto Margot Rose, tenor Frank Hoffmeister, baritone Robert Kuehn and Peter Schickle. They are accompanied by an eight-piece chamber orchestra featuring harpsichord and recorder conducted by the composer. Vanguard LP

KNUSSEN, OLIVER   *English composer/conductor (1952–)*

Glasgow-born composer/conductor Oliver Knussen became known as an opera composer through his collaborations with American librettist/author/illustrator/set designer Maurice Sendak. Together they created two of the most popular modern children's operas, HIGGLETY PIGGLETY POP! and WHERE THE WILD THINGS ARE. Knussen is one of the leading promoters and conductors of modern music.

KOHS, ELLIS   *American composer (1916–2000)*

Ellis Kohs, a Chicago-born composer who studied at Juilliard and at Harvard with Walter Piston, was a prolific composer but his only real opera was *Amerika,* libretto by the composer based on the novel by Franz Kafka; it was premiered by the Western Opera Theatre in Los Angeles on May 27, 1970. He also created a three-act concert narrative called *Lord of the Ascendant,* based on the Sumerian epic *Gilgamesh*. His most unusual vocal work was setting the text of a U. S. Army weapons manual to be sung by an all-male a cappella choir. Kohs was on the faculty of USC for 38 years and wrote a number of popular books on music theory.

KONDOROSSY, LESLIE   *American composer (1915–1989)*

Leslie Kondorossy seems to have had more operas premiered and broadcast on radio than any other American composer —five premieres and eleven broadcasts. Most are one-act operas composed to librettos by Shawn Hall and broadcast from radio stations in Cleveland, but most also had subsequent stage performances. The first was *A Night in the Puszta* which premiered at the Music Hall in Cleveland on June 28, 1953, and was broadcast by the Voice of America on July 4, 1953. The operas premiered on radio were *The Midnight Duel* on WSRS, Cleveland, on March 20, 1955; *The Two Imposters* on WSRS on April 10, 1955; *The String Quartet* on WSRS on May 8. 1955; *The Mystic Fortress* on WSRS on June 12, 1955; and *Kalamona and the Four Winds* on WBOE (NPR) on January 27, 1971. The children's opera *Shizuka's Dance* was telecast in Tokyo in 1974. His other operas include *The Pumpkin* (1954), *The Voice* (1954), *The Unexpected Visitor* (1956), *The Fox* (1961), *The Poorest Suitor* (1967) and *Ruth and Naomi* (1969). Kondorossy's operas are not on commercial recordings but presumably there are radio transcripts. Five of them are featured in W. Franklin Summers' production guide *Operas in One Act*. Kondorossy, born in what is now Slovakia, emigrated to America after World War II and became a resident of Cleveland.

KORIE, MICHAEL   *American librettist (1964–)*

Michael Korie has written the librettos for four operas composed by Stewart Wallace and one by Ricky Ian Gordon. His partnership with Wallace began with WHERE'S DICK, modeled on the comic strip *Dick Tracy,* which was premiered by Houston Grand Opera in May 1989. KABBALAH, a dramatized ritual about the seven days of Creation, was performed at the Brooklyn Academy of Music in November 1989. HARVEY MILK, about the killing of a gay San Francisco public official by a homophobe, premiered at Houston Grand Opera in 1995. HOPPERS' WIFE, which imagines that artist Edward Hopper married gossip columnist Hedda Hopper and used actress Ava Gardner as his model, was premiered by Long Beach Opera in 1997. His opera libretto for Gordon is an adaptation of John Steinbeck's *The Grapes of Wrath* which is to be premiered by Minnesota Opera in 2005. Korie has also written the books for two musicals with music by Scott Frankel, *Doll* and *Meet Mister Future*.

KORNGOLD, ERICH   *American composer (1897–1957)*

Erich Wolfgang Korngold was a major opera composer in Europe before he came to America to become a major Hollywood film composer and create what he described as "operas without singing" There are certainly few opera scores more memorable than the music for *The Adventures of Robin Hood* and *Anthony Adverse,* both of which won Academy Awards. Korngold did not write stage operas in America but he did write a movie opera, ROMEO AND JULIET for the 1936 film *Give Us This Night,* and he arranged the music for the 1944 stage production *Helen Goes to Troy,* an English-language version of Offenbach's *La Belle Hélène*. Korngold, who was born in Czechoslovakia, was a child prodigy and his first two operas were produced when he was nineteen. His most popular opera today is probably *Die tote Stadt* (1920).

KOSHETZ, NINA   *American soprano (1894–1965)*

Nina Koshetz created the role of Fata Morgana in Sergei Prokofiev's THE LOVE FOR THREE ORANGES when it premiered in Chicago in 1921. She also sings in Sam Pokrass's "movie opera" ARLESIANA dubbing the voice of Binnie Barnes who plays an opera star in the 1939 film *Wife, Husband and Friend*. Koshetz, who was born in the Ukraine, sang in nine other films. She moved to Hollywood and opened a restaurant after she retired.

KOWALSKI, MICHAEL   *American composer (1957–)*

Michael Kowalski's avant-garde music theatre work STILL IN LOVE, libretto by Kier Peters based on his play *Past, Present and Future Tense,* was premiered by the Postindustrial Players at Roulette in New York in January 1996. His meditation on the American way of work FRATERNITY OF DECEIT was staged in New York by the Players in 1998 and recorded in 1999. Kowalski, who founded the Postindustrial Players in 1995, studied composition with Betsy Jolas, Richard Hervig and Ben Johnston and began presenting performance art in New York in 1980.

KRACHMALNICK, SAMUEL   *American conductor (1928–)*

Samuel Krachmalnick conducted the premiere of Leonard Bernstein's CANDIDE in 1956 and is the conductor on the original Broadway cast album. He conducts the New York City Opera orchestra and chorus in a 1953 recording of Marc Blitzstein's REGINA and a 1968 recording of Douglas Moore's CARRY NATION, both NYCO productions. On television he conducted the 1955 NBC Opera Theatre production of Gian Carlo Menotti's THE SAINT OF BLEECKER STREET and the 1955 CBS production of William Schumann's THE MIGHTY CASEY. He has conducted stage productions of BERNSTEIN'S TROUBLE IN TAHITI and Robert Ward's THE CRUCIBLE. Krachmalnick was born in St. Louis, studied at Juilliard and made his operatic debut conducting *The Saint of Bleecker Street* on Broadway.

KRENEK, ERNST   *Austrian/American composer (1900–1991)*

Ernst Krenek is best known for his German operas, especially the jazz-oriented *Jonny Spielt Auf* (1927), but he wrote a number of operas in America after emigrating in 1938. The first was TARQUIN, libretto by playwright Emmett Lavery, premiered in concert format at Vassar College in Poughkeepsie, New York, on May 13, 1941. The first with a libretto by the composer (he usually wrote his own librettos) was the 1945 comic opera WHAT PRICE CONFIDENCE?. His best-known American opera is DARK WATERS, loosely based on Herman Melville's novel *The Confidence Man,* which premiered at UCLA in Los Angeles in 1951. THE BELL TOWER, also based on a Melville story, was performed at the University of Illinois in Urbana in 1957.

KREUTZ, ARTHUR   *American composer (1906–1991)*

Arthur Kreutz composed three full-length operas in folk and ballad style. The two-hour "ballad opera" *Acres of Sky* was premiered in Fayetteville, Arkansas, on November 16, 1951, and reprised at Columbia University in 1952. The two-hour "Civil War ballad opera" *The University Grays* was presented at the University of Mississippi in Oxford on March 15, 1954. The "folk opera" SOURWOOD MOUNTAIN , libretto by Zoë Lund Schiller, was premiered at the University of Mississippi on January 8, 1959, and reprised in Clinton, Mississippi, and Roanoke, Virginia.

KUHLMANN, ROSEMARY   *American soprano (1927–)*

Rosemary Kuhlmann created the role of the Mother in Gian Carlo Menotti's AMAHL AND THE NIGHT VISITORS on NBC television in 1951, sang the role with New York City Opera in 1952 and reprised the part nine times on television. She created the role of Goosey Loosey in Alec Wilder's MISS CHICKEN LITTLE on CBS

television in 1953 and the role of Sarah in Leonard Kastle's DESERET on NBC television in 1961. She was Desideria in the 1955 NBC Opera Theater production of Menotti's THE SAINT OF BLEECKER STREET and she played Magda in Menotti's THE CONSUL on Broadway and on a European tour. She was a member of the New York City Opera Company for four years.

KULLMAN, CHARLES   *American tenor (1903–1993)*

Charles Kullman, who sang with the Metropolitan Opera for 25 seasons, created the role of the Beast in Vittorio Giannini's BEAUTY AND THE BEAST on CBS radio in 1938. He joined Lawrence Tibbett and Risë Stevens to sing two acts of Deems Taylor's THE KING'S HENCHMAN for a radio broadcast in 1942. He starred as Villon in a radio version of Rudolf Friml's THE VAGABOND KING in 1935. He also recorded songs from four Victor Herbert operettas in 1938, EILEEN, THE FORTUNE TELLER, NAUGHTY MARIETTA and THE ONLY GIRL. Kullman, who was born in New Haven, studied at Yale and Juilliard and made his debut in 1929 with the American Opera Company. He built his career in Europe and began his Met career in 1935.

KUPFERMAN, MEYER   *American composer (1926–2003)*

New Yorker Meyer Kupferman, who taught for many years at Sarah Lawrence College, was a prolific composer who liked to experiment and this is reflected in his operas. The first two were based on works by Gertrude Stein. The popular one-act children's opera IN A GARDEN, libretto by the composer from Stein's play, was premiered by the After Dinner Opera Company at Finch Junior College in New York in 1949. The grander three-act DOCTOR FAUSTUS LIGHTS THE LIGHTS, libretto by the composer based on the Stein play and featuring a large cast and chorus, was performed at Sarah Lawrence College in 1951. The one-act operas *Voices for a Mirror* and *The Curious Fern*, both with librettos by A. Reid, were premiered together by the Living Theater company at the Master Theater Institute in 1957. The children's opera *Draagenfut Girl*, libretto by the composer based on the Cinderella story, was premiered at Sarah Lawrence in 1958. Kupferman carried his experimentation a stage further in his 1966 opera *The Judgement*, libretto by P. Freeman, an ambitious three-act choral work meant to be performed without instrumental accompaniment. The experimental multi-media. *Visions and Games* was presented at Sarah Lawrence on May 24, 1971. *Antigonae*, based on Friedrich Hölderin's version of the Sophocles play, was presented at the Lenox Art Center in Stockbridge, MA, in 1973. *Prometheus*, libretto by the composer based on Goethe, was premiered at the Manhattan School of Music in 1978. THE PROSCENIUM...ON THE DEMISE OF GERTRUDE, libretto by the composer, was premiered at Columbia University in 1991 and reprised at the Music in the Mountains Festival in 1993.

KURKA, ROBERT   *American composer (1921–1957)*

Robert Kurka was primarily a composer of orchestral music but he had such success with his 1956 orchestral suite THE GOOD SOLDIER SCHWEIK that he decided to turn it into an opera. It was based on Czech writer Jaroslav Hašek's anti-war novel which Lewis Allan fashioned into a libretto. Kurka died before finishing the orchestration but it was completed by Hershey Kay. The opera was well received at its premiere by New York City Opera on April 23, 1958, and continues to be performed around the world. Kurka, born in Cicero, Illinois, began his studies as a violinist but later studied composition with Otto Luening and Darius Milhaud. He was only 35 when he died of leukemia.

L

LA BARBARA, JOAN *American soprano/composer (1947–)*

Joan La Barbara, the "vocal wizard of the avant-garde," has created roles in experimental and electronic operas by Robert Ashley and Morton Subotnick and composed two operas herself. Her *Prologue to The Book of Knowing...(and) of Overthrowing*, an aria for voice and tape with visual environment by Judy Chicago, is meant to be the prologue to a full-scale opera; it was performed in New York City on July 6, 1988. Her *Events in the Elsewhere*, an interactive media opera inspired by physicist Stephen Hawking, features a computer system that allows a voice to control music, staging and lighting; it premiered in Santa Fe on August 24, 1990. For Subotnick she sang in *The Double Life of Amphibians* (its "aria" *The Last Dream of the Beast* was premiered in Washington in 1979) and *Jacob's Room,* which was premiered in San Francisco in 1985 and was recorded. For Ashley she created the role of Now Eleanor in IMPROVEMENT in 1991 and reprised the role in the complete version premiered at the Brooklyn Academy of Music in 1994. She sang in the premiere of Ashley's BALSEROS in Miami Beach in 1997 and YOUR MONEY MY LIFE GOODBYE in 1998. She also sang in a 1973 production of Stanley Silverman's surrealist opera DR. SELAVY'S MAGIC THEATER. La Barbara was born in Philadelphia, studied music at Syracuse, NYU and Juilliard and taught and lectured at several universities. She married Subotnick in 1979.

Gian Carlo Menotti's 1963 television opera *Labyrinth: An Operatic Riddle* was a puzzle for most viewers.

LABYRINTH *1963 TV opera by Menotti*

A bride (Judith Raskin) and her groom (John Reardon) plan to spend their honeymoon in a grand hotel but their dreams turns into a nightmare when they can't locate the key to their room. Their frustration is increased by the bizarre people they encounter. A frantic bellboy (Nikiforos Naneris) is in such a hurry he has no time to talk. A mysterious woman who says she is a spy (Elaine Bonazzi) and sings in a medley of languages puzzles them. An old man in a wheel chair (Robert White) says he will help if the groom will play chess with him. He does but the old man simply falls asleep. They get no help from the officious Executive Director (Beverly Wolff) or her secretary (Bob Rickner). The bellboy passes by and points at a door. The groom looks through the keyhole and sees an Italian opera singer (Eugene Green) rehearsing with soprano and a chorus. He looks in another room and finds an astronaut (Frank Porretta) floating inside a space ship. In a third is a passenger car train filled with water as well as passengers. The bride drowns and the groom is sucked down into a ballroom. He asks for help from the Desk Clerk (Leon Lishner) and his assistant (John West) who build a coffin around him. Gian Carlo Menotti's baffling hour-long television opera *Labyrinth: An Operatic Riddle*, libretto by the composer, premiered on NBC Opera Theater on March 3, 1963. Menotti directed, Samuel Chotzinoff produced, Warren Clyner designed the sets, Noel Taylor designed costumes, Herbert Grossman conducted the Symphony of the Air Orchestra. And Kirk Browning directed the telecast. A video can be viewed at the Museum of Television and Radio but there is no recording.

LA CHIUSA, MICHAEL JOHN *American composer/librettist (1962–)*

Michael John La Chiusa emerged as one of the shining hopes of music theater/new opera at the end of the century blurring the line between opera and musical. After writing librettos for operas by Anthony Davis and Robert Moran, he composed his own music theater works. MARIE CHRISTINE, a retelling of the Medea legend in 19th century New Orleans starring Audra McDonald, premiered in Lincoln Center in December 1999. THE WILD PARTY, an adaptation of Joseph Moncure March's narrative poem about 1920s flappers, was hailed as a *Threepenny Opera* for the bathtub gin set when it opened in April 2000. LOVERS AND FRIENDS (CHAUTAUQUA VARIATIONS) about the problems of a poet laureate, was premiered by Lyric Opera of Chicago in June 2001. LaChiusa's librettos for Moran were the beauty-and-the-beast opera DESERT OF ROSES, premiered by Houston Grand Opera in 1992, and the Japanese legend-derived FROM THE TOWERS OF THE MOON, premiered by Minnesota Opera in 1992. His libretto for Davis was the surrealistic opera TANIA, about the kidnapping of heiress Patty Hearst, premiered in Philadelphia in 1992. La Chiusa, who was born in upstate New York, studied piano and writing before moving to Manhattan to work as a pianist and compose for off-Broadway groups. His 1994 musical *Hello Again*, an updated version of Schnitzler's *La Ronde*, won an Obie when it was presented at Lincoln Center. In 1995 he won another award for his off-Broadway show *First Lady Suite*. In 1999 he was made composer-in-residence at Lyric Opera of Chicago.

LADERMAN, EZRA　American composer (1924–)

Ezra Laderman has composed ten singer-friendly operas, including three with Biblical themes and a famous one about a movie star. His first was the ambitious three-act *Jacob and the Indians*, libretto by Ernest Kinoy based on a Stephen Vincent Benét story, which premiered at the Byrdcliffe Theater in Woodstock, on July 26, 1957. The one-act *Goodbye to the Clown*, libretto by Ernest Kinoy about a girl and her imaginary clown, was premiered by the Neway Group in New York in 1960 with Alan Baker as the Clown. The jazz-tinged opera-cantata *The Hunting of the Snark*, based on the poem by Lewis Carroll, was presented in concert form at Hunter College in New York in 1962 and staged at Queens College in New York in 1978. Laderman's first opera for television was the 30-minute SARAH, libretto by Clair Roskam, telecast on CBS in 1959. The 1962 musical comedy *Dominque* was followed by the opera *Air Raid* (1965), libretto by Archibald MacLeish. *Shadows Among Us*, libretto by Norman Rosten about life in a refugee camp, was performed at the Academy of Vocal Arts in Philadelphia in 1979. AND DAVID WEPT, dealing with the tragic love affair of David and Bathsheba. was telecast on CBS-TV in 1971. THE QUESTIONS OF ABRAHAM, dealing with the patriarch's religious doubt, was televised by CBS in 1973. GALILEO GALILEI, based around the trial of the Italian astronomer for heresy, was premiered on TV in 1967 and staged by Tri-Cities Opera in Binghamton in 1979. MARILYN, libretto by Norman Rosten about the life and death of Marilyn Monroe, was premiered by New York City Opera in 1993. Laderman, who was born in Brooklyn, studied at Columbia with Douglas Moore and Otto Luening, taught at SUNY in Binghamton and then became dean of the School of Music at Yale.

LADIES' VOICES　1956 opera by Martin

A group of women talk and the sound of ladies' voices is praised. Various comments are made about people and places but there is no narrative. As one line says, "Many words spoken to me have seemed English." Vernon Martin's satirical nine-minute opera *Ladies' Voices*, libretto by Gertrude Stein, premiered at the University of Oklahoma in Norman on June 3, 1956. It was composed for two sopranos and two mezzos but has been reprised with other combinations.

1965 Addison M. Metcalf. Addison M. Metcalf reads the libretto of Gertrude Stein's *Ladies' Voices* on the album *Mother Goose of Montparnasse*, a selection of her writings. Folkways LP.

THE LADY FROM COLORADO　1964 opera by Ward

Elkhorn, Colorado, toward the end of the 19th century. Irish immigrant Katie Lauder meets and marries Cecil Moon who become a peer when his grandfather dies. Lady Kate goes to England with her husband but doesn't fit in with the aristocracy so they return to Colorado. Lord Moon runs for Senator again villainous Jack Spaniard and wins with the help of his butler Rutledge. Robert Ward's opera *The Lady from Colorado*, libretto by Bernard Stambler based on a 1957 novel by Homer Croy, premiered at Central City Opera House in Colorado on July 3, 1964. The cast included Mary Ellen Pracht as Katie, Thomas Paul as evil Jack Spaniard, Mignon Dunn, Jeff Stafford, John Fiorito, Davis Cunningham and Chester Ludgin. Christopher West staged the opera and Emerson Buckley conducted. The score is tuneful and accessible. Ward and Stambler later revised the opera and relaunched it under the title LADY KATE.

1991 William Stone. Baritone William Stone sings arias from *The Lady from Colorado* on the album *Robert Ward: Arias and Songs*. They are "Law and Order," "I Ride Along," "State Senator, Jack Spaniard! Why Not?" and "I Hail This Land." He is accompanied by pianist Thomas Warburton. Bay Cities CD.

LADY IN THE DARK　1940 musical by Weill

Fashion magazine editor Liza Elliott has four suitors but can't decide if she prefers movie star Randy Curtis, publisher Kendall Nesbitt, staff photographer Russell Paxton or colleague Charlie Johnson. She visits psychiatrist Dr. Brooks and tells him of her elaborate dreams called Glamour, Wedding, Circus and Childhood. Most the music is in the dream sequences which are through sung. Kurt Weill's musical play *Lady in the Dark*, libretto by Moss Hart with lyrics by Ira Gershwin, premiered at the Colonial Theater in Boston on December 30, 1940, and opened on Broadway at the Alvin Theater on January 21, 1941. Gertrude Lawrence was Liza, Victor Mature was Randy, Bert Lytell was Kendall, McDonald Carey was Charley, Danny Kaye was Russell, Donald Randolph was Dr. Brooks and Jeanne Shelby was Miss Bowers. Hassard Short directed and Maurice Abravanel conducted. *Lady in the Dark* was Weill's biggest stage success and Danny Kaye's performance of the song "Tchaikovsky" made him famous. An extended score compiled by John Mauceri and David Loud was conducted by Mauceri at the Edinburgh Festival in 1988.

1941 Original Broadway cast. Gertrude Lawrence and Danny Kaye recorded numbers from the musical in 1941 and they're now on the album *Kurt Weill from Berlin to Broadway* (Pearl CD) and a Prism CD. Lawrence's songs with vocal quartet and orchestra led by Leonard Joy are on an RCA Victor LP and AEI CD. Kaye's songs are on Risë Stevens recording of the show on Sony CD. **1944 Paramount film.** Ginger Roger stars as Liza in the Paramount film of the musical which, rather curiously, eliminates most of Weill's music. Her dreams are portrayed in garish colors by director Mitchell Leisen. Lending support are Ray Milland, Jon Hall, Warner Baxter, Mischa Auer and Barry Sullivan. Paramount VHS/DVD. **1950 Theater Guild of the Air.** Gertrude Lawrence stars as Liza in this Theater Guild of the Air radio version of the musical with orchestra conducted by Maurice Abravanel. Hume Cronyn is Dr. Brooks, McDonald Carey is Charley and Gene Crockett is Russell. AEI CD. **1954 NBC Television.** Ann Sothern plays Lisa in an NBC television version of the musical. Shepherd Strudwick is Dr. Brooks, Luella Gear is Maggie, James Daly is Charley and Paul McGrath is Kendall. Charles Sanford conducts. Jeffrey Hayden directed the stage production and Max Liebman and Bill Hobin directed the telecast on September 25, 1954. Video at MTR. Soundtrack on RCA Victor LP/AEI CD. **1957 Lotte Lenya.** Lotte Lenya performs "The Saga of Jenny" on the album *Lotte Lenya Sings Kurt Weill: American Theater Songs*. Maurice Levine conducts orchestra and chorus. Sony CD. **1963 Risë Stevens/John Reardon.** Risë Stevens stars is Liza in this studio recording of the musical with John Reardon as Randy and Adolph Green as Russell who sings "Tchaikovsky." In support are Roger White, Stephanie Augustine and Kenneth Bridges. Lehman Engel conducts. Columbia LP/Sony CD. **1972 Berlin to Broadway with Kurt Weill.** The cast of the off-Broadway revue *Berlin to Broadway with Kurt Weill: A Musical Voyage* perform "Girl of the Moment," "The Saga of Jenny" and "My Ship," Paramount LP. **1977 Royal National Theatre.** Maria Friedman is Lisa in this cast recording of a 1977 Royal National Theatre production in London. Adrian Dunbar is Charley, Paul Shelley is Kendall, Steven Edward Moore is Randy and James Dreyfus is Russell. The recording features the three dream sequences. Jay Records CD. **1986 Teresa Stratas.** Teresa Stratas sings "One Life to Live" on her album *Stratas Sings Weill* with Gerard Schwarz conducting the Y Chamber Orchestra. Nonesuch LP/CD. **1992 Carole Farley.** Carole Farley sings "The Saga of Jenny" and "One Life to Live" on the album *Kurt Weill Songs* accompanied by Roger Vignoles. ASV CD. **1992 Ute Lemper.** German cabaret artist Ute Lemper performs "The Saga of Jenny" in a live performance on the video *Uta Lemper Sings Kurt Weill.* Jeff Cohen plays piano. London VHS. **1995 Anne Sofie von Otter.** Anne Sofie von Otter sings "My Ship" and "One Life to Live" on the album *Speak Low—Songs by Kurt Weill.* John Eliot Gardiner conducts the North Germany Radio Symphony Orchestra. DG CD. **2000 Sylvia McNair.** Sylvia McNair sings "My Ship" on the album *The Radio 3 Lunchtime Concert* accompanied by Ted Taylor. BBC Music CD. **2000 Urs Affolter.** Urs Affolter sings "My Ship" on his album *Stay Well: Urs Affolter Sings Kurt Weill* accompanied by Uli Kofler. Antes CD. **2001 Palermo Opera.** Bulgarian opera soprano Raina Kabaiwanska (aged 68) sings the role of Liza in this live recording of a performance by Palermo Opera on April 24, 2001. Providing support are Gino Quilico, Victor Ledbetter and Paul Wade. Sung in English. 142 minutes. Live Opera Heaven VHS.

LADY KATE   *1994 revision of Ward's The Lady from Colorado*

Robert Ward's *Lady Kate,* libretto by Bernard Stambler, is a revised and lightened version of their 1964 opera THE LADY FROM COLORADO and was premiered by Ohio Light Opera on June 8, 1994. Emily Martin sang Katie, Bradley Howard was Lord Moon, Dennis Jesse was comic villain Jack Spaniard, Patti Jo Stevens was Eve St. John, Stuart Howe was Tom Wade, Jay Lusteck was Jeff Stafford, Ann Marie Wilcox was Sarah Chicken, Dawn Harris was Lola Lopez and Brian Frutiger was Rutledge Blunt. Carol Stavish designed the sets, James Stuart directed and Steven Byess conducted. The opera was reprised by Triangle Opera Theatre in Durham, NC, in January 1995 with the same cast and director but with Scott Tilley conducting.

1995 Terry Rhodes/Ellen Williams. Soprano Terry Rhodes and mezzo-soprano Ellen Williams join in the duet "Eve, I Can't Lie to an Old Friend" from *Lady Kate* with orchestra led by Scott Tiley. Its on the album *To Sun, to Feast and to Converse—American Vocal Duet Music.* Albany CD.

LADY OF LIGHT   *1968 opera/oratorio by Hovhaness*

A young girl becomes possessed and dances out of a temple into the sun as dancing villagers follow her. A war priest fears the dancing, kills the dancers and burns the Mad Dancing Girl alive. She turns into the Lady of Light and helps the village rid itself of the warlike priest. Alan Hovhaness's opera-oratorio *Lady of Light,* libretto by the composer based on a Swiss version of the Pied Piper of Hamelin story, was premiered in concert form in Montana in 1969. The composer said it was composed in grand opera style as a protest against war.

1971 Ambrosian Singers. Soprano Patricia Clark and baritone Leslie Fyson are the soloists with the Ambrosian Singers on this recording of *Lady of Light* made in London in 1971. Hovhaness conducts the Royal Philharmonic Orchestra. Poseidon LP/Crystal CD.

LA LOCA   *1979 opera by Menotti*

Juana, the only surviving child of Queen Isabella of Spain, inherits the kingdom of Castille in 1504 when her mother dies. Juana's father is Fernando (Ferdinand V), the king who sent Columbus to American in 1492, and he wants the kingdom for himself. Juana marries Austrian Felipe (Philip I, the Handsome) and there is conflict between father and husband over Castille. When Felipe dies and Juana still refuses to abdicate in favor of her father, he takes her son Carlos away from her and has her declared insane. She is put in prison and derided with the name Juana La Loca (Juana the Mad). When her father finally dies years later, she is visited in prison by her son, now Charles V, the most powerful monarch in Europe. She thinks he has come to free her but instead he just wants her to give him Castille. When she refuses, he keeps her in prison until she dies in 1555. Gian Carlo Menotti's three-act opera *La Loca,* libretto by the composer, was premiered by San Diego Opera on June 3, 1979, and telecast. It was commissioned for Beverly Sills who sang the soprano role of Juana while John Brocheler sang the triple baritone part of Fernando the father, Felipe the husband and Carlos the son. Robert Hale was Bishop Ximenes, Susanne Marsee was Doña Manuela, Jane Westbrook was the Nurse, Joseph Evans was Miguel de Ferrara, Vincent Russo was the Chaplain, Carlos Chausson was the Marques de Denia, Nancy Coulson was Juana's daughter Catalina and Marcia Cope and Martha Jane Howe were ladies-in-waiting. Mario Vanarelli designed sets and costumes, Tito Capobianco staged the production and Calvin Simmons conducted the San Diego Opera Orchestra. The opera, also known as *Juana La Loca,* was reprised at New York City with Sills again in the title role and John Mauceri conducting. Pamela Myers sang the role of Juana in a revised version staged by Menotti at the Spoleto Festival in July 1982 with Brian Schexnayder in the triple role of Felipe, Fernando and Carlos.

1979 San Diego Opera. Beverly Sills sings Juana with John Brocheler as her father, husband and son in this recording of the San Diego Opera premiere. Robert Hale is Bishop Ximenes, Susanne Marsee is Doña Manuela, Jane Westbrook is Nurse, Joseph Evans is Miguel de Ferrara, Vincent Russo is Chaplain, Carlos Chausson is Marques de Denia and Nancy Coulson is Catalina. Calvin Simmons conducts the San Diego Opera Orchestra. Live Opera VHS/Custom Opera audiocassette.

LA MONTAINE, JOHN   *American composer (1920–)*

John La Montaine is best known for one-hour Christmas pageant-operas based on medieval English miracle plays presented at the National Cathedral in Washington, D.C. in the 1960s. Premiered over a seven-year period, they featured music influenced by 14th century French composer Guillaume de Machaut. The first was *Novellis, Novellis* performed on December 24, 1962, with Chester Ludgin as Joseph. THE SHEPHARDES PLAYE was presented on December 24, 1967, and later telecast. *Erode the Great* was staged on December 31, 1969. La Montaine has also written Christmas cantatas and carols. For the American Bicentennial he created the patriotic choral opera/oratorio BE GLAD THEN AMERICA, *A Decent Entertainment from the Thirteen Colonies.* It was performed by a 200-voice chorus at Pennsylvania State University on February 6, 1976. All four operas have been published. La Montaine, born in Chicago, studied music at the Juilliard and Eastman schools and with Nadia Boulanger in France.

LAMOS, MARK   *American opera director (1946–)*

Mark Lamos has directed the premieres of a number of major modern American operas. They include Tania Leon's SCOURGE OF HYACINTHS in Munich in 1994, Dominick Argento's THE ASPERN PAPERS at Dallas Opera in 1988, Paul Schoenfield's THE MERCHANT AND THE PAUPER at St Louis Opera in 1999, John Harbison's THE GREAT GATSBY at the Metropolitan Opera in 1999 and the three-composer trilogy CENTRAL PARK at Glimmerglass and New York City Opera in 1999. He also directed the New York City Opera production of Benjamin Britten's PAUL BUNYAN telecast in

1998, a production of Harbison's A WINTER'S TALE and a production in Sweden of Argento's THE VOYAGE OF EDGAR ALLAN POE.

LANDSCAPES AND REMEMBRANCES   *1976 cantata by Menotti*

Gian Carlo Menotti's nostalgic cantata *Landscapes and Remembrances*, libretto by the composer, is a nine-part autobiography in the form of musical impressions. The remembrances begin with his arrival in New York when he was sixteen, move around American landscapes from South Carolina and Texas to Chicago and Vermont and ends with his thoughts on leaving America after forty years. Choral singers and four soloists alternate with a 22-piece orchestra in describing his geographical and spiritual journey. It was commissioned by the Bel Canto Chorus of Milwaukee and was premiered by the Chorus on May 14, 1976, in the Milwaukee Performing Arts Center. The soloists were soprano Judith Blegen, mezzo-soprano Ani Yervanian, tenor Vahan Khanzadian and bass Gary Kendall. The music was performed by the Milwaukee Symphony Orchestra under the direction of James A. Keeley. The cantata was reprised at the Spoleto Festival USA in 1981 and at Lincoln Center in 1996.

1976 Milwaukee Bel Canto Chorus. The cantata was filmed when it was premiered by the Bel Canto Chorus at the Milwaukee Performing Arts Center. The soloists are Judith Blegen, Ani Yervanian, Vahan Khanzadian and Gary Kendall. James A. Keeley leads the Milwaukee Symphony Orchestra Telecast November 14, 1976. Video at Library of Congress.

LANE, BURTON   *American composer (1912–1997)*

Burton Lane's most successful stage musical was *Finian's Rainbow* (1947), a whimsical story about racial prejudice and an Irish pot of gold in the American South with witty libretto by E. Y Harburg and several memorable songs. It was filmed by Francis Ford Coppola in 1968 with Fred Astaire. Also popular was *On a Clear Day You Can See Forever* (1965), libretto by Alan Jay Lerner, later filmed with Barbra Streisand. Lane, who was born in New York, began his musical career in 1931 writing songs for revues and movies.

LANE, GLORIA   *American mezzo-soprano (1930–)*

American mezzo-soprano Gloria Lane made her operatic debut creating the role of the Secretary in the premiere of Gian Carlo Menotti's THE CONSUL in Philadelphia in 1950. She reprised the role on Broadway and sings the role on the Broadcast cast recording. She also performed the role on stage in London and Vienna and in TV productions in London (1951) and Vienna (1963). She created the role of Desideria in Menotti's THE SAINT OF BLEECKER STREET on Broadway in 1954, reprised it for CBS TV in 1955 and is featured on the original Broadway cast recording. She also created the role of Countess Marie in Stanley Hollingsworth's *La Grande Bretèche* on NBC television in 1957. She sings with Lauritz Melchior on a 1950 operatic recording of Sigmund Romberg's THE STUDENT PRINCE and sings Netti on a 1955 operatic recording of CAROUSEL with Robert Merrill. On stage she sang Mother in AMAHL AND THE NIGHT VISITORS and Baba the Turk in the Glyndebourne Festival revival of Igor Stravinsky's THE RAKE'S PROGRESS. Lane, born in Trenton, NJ, studied music in Philadelphia where she made her debut.

LANG, DAVID   *American composer (1957–)*

David Lang is best known as an avant-garde minimalist composer and co-founder of the experimental New York Bang on Can

Festival but he has also written three operas. *Judith and Holofernes* (1989) is based on the Biblical tale about a Jewish woman seducing and beheading an Assyrian general besieging her city. MODERN PAINTERS, libretto by Manuela Hoelterhopp based on John Ruskin's critical study *The Seven Lamps of Architecture,* focuses on Ruskin's unsuccessful marriage to his young cousin. It was commissioned by Santa Fe Opera which premiered it in 1995. THE DIFFICULTY OF CROSSING A FIELD, libretto by Mac Wellman, is a Rashomon-style tale based on stories by Ambrose Bierce. It was premiered by American Conservatory Theater in 2002 in San Francisco with Julia Migenes in the leading role.

THE LANGUAGE OF BIRDS   *2004 opera by Kennedy*

Two young Russian brothers are sent out in the world. One brother's kindness brings him the gift of understanding the language of the birds. He uses the gift wisely to overcome difficulties, rescues his brother and wins the love of a princess. John W. Kennedy's children's opera *The Language of Birds,* libretto by Peter M. Krask based on a book by Rafe Martin derived from a Russian folk tale, was commissioned by Sarasota Youth Opera and premiered on May 8, 2004, with Kennedy conducting the orchestra. The opera is intended for audiences aged from 9 to 18.

LANZA, MARIO   *American tenor (1921—1959)*

Mario Lanza starred in an American "movie opera," Charles Previn's THE PRINCESS, created for the 1949 film *The Midnight Kiss.* He sang in the 1954 operetta film THE STUDENT PRINCE, based on the Sigmund Romberg classic. He also helped to rekindle interest in American operettas through his recordings. He recorded a highlights version of Romberg's THE DESERT SONG and recorded songs from Romberg's MAYTIME and THE NEW MOON, Victor Herbert's EILEEN, THE FORTUNE TELLER and NAUGHTY MARIETTA and Rudolf Friml's THE FIREFLY, ROSE MARIE and THE VAGABOND KING. Lanza, born in Philadelphia as Alfred Arnold Coccozza, made his debut at Tanglewood in *The Merry Wives of Windsor.* His movie and recording career began in 1949 and it is estimated that he has sold around 50 million records.

LARDNER, RING   *American author (1885–1933)*

Ring Lardner , who began as a sports writer in Chicago, wrote a number of sport-centered stories and is best known for his baseball collection *You Know Me Al.* His most famous story is *Haircut* which was turned into an opera by composer Sam Morgenstern and librettist Jan Henry. It premiered at the Metropolitan Opera Studio on May 2, 1969.

LARGE, BRIAN   *English TV opera director (1939–)*

Brian Large, one of the masters of directing opera for television, created the TV versions of a number of American operas, including Carlisle Floyd's WILLIE STARK from Houston in 1981, John Adams' NIXON IN CHINA from Houston in 1988, John Corigliano's THE GHOSTS OF VERSAILLES from the Met in 1991 and Igor Stravinsky THE RAKE'S PROGRESS from Salzburg in 1996. He directs most of the Metropolitan Opera telecasts.

LARSEN, LIBBY   *American composer (1950–)*

Libby Larsen has become one of the most successful modern American opera composers with a style described as an "American breath of fresh air." Her seventeen operas include four based on works by women writers. FRANKENSTEIN: THE MODERN PROMETHEUS, based on Mary Shelley's novel, was premiered by Minnesota Opera in 1990. A WRINKLE IN TIME, based on Madeleine L'Engle's novel, was premiered by Opera Delaware in 1992. MRS. DALLOWAY, based on the novel by Virginia Woolf, was premiered by Lyric Opera Cleveland in 1993. ERIC HERMANNSON'S SOUL, based on a story by Willa Cather, was premiered by Omaha Opera in 1999. *Barnum's Bird*, a cabaret opera about opera singer Jenny Lind and her tour of America in the 19th century, was premiered April 19, 2001, in the Plymouth Music Series with Philip Brunelle conducting. Larsen was born in Wilmington, Delaware, but grew up in Minneapolis and studied music at the University of Minnesota with Dominick Argento. Her first opera *Some Pig,* based on E. B. White's children's novel *Charlotte's Web*, was presented at the University of Minnesota on June 3, 1973. *The Words upon the Windowpane*, based on a play by W. B. Yeats, was premiered in Minnesota in 1977. Two children's operas, *The Silver Fox* based on a Louisiana legend, and *The Emperor's New Clothes,* based on the fairy tale, were performed in St Paul in 1979. *Tumbledown Dick or The Taste of the Times*, libretto by Vern Sutton based on a Henry Fielding story, was presented in St. Paul in 1980. Larsen began to turn to women writers and feminist subjects in 1985 with *Claire de Lune,* libretto by Patrica Hampf about a woman aviator, which was commissioned and premiered by Arkansas Opera Theater. *Daytime Moon* in 1986 was a video opera and *Four on the Four* in 1986 was a film opera. *Christina Romana*, libretto by Vern Sutton, was premiered at the University of Minnesota in 1988; it marked a turn towards an experimental multi-media style with electronic effects and the chorus up on a balcony. opera *Frankenstein: The Modern Prometheus* developed these ideas further with offstage chorus, interaction between singer and synthesized sound and expanded use of video. Larsen's music is complex but accessible and she is a strong believer in electronically manipulated sound like that used in rock concerts.

THE LAST LEAF (1)   *American operas based on O. Henry story*

Greenwich Village in 1905. A young woman catches pneumonia and is forced to stay in bed for a long time. She watches all autumn as the leaves fall from the vine outside her window and decides she will die when the last leaf falls. An elder painter friend decides to prevent this and paints his final masterpiece. O. Henry's famous story was published in 1907 in his collection *The Trimmed Lamp and Other Stories*. At least five American operas/music theatre works are based on it.

1979 Alva Henderson. Alva Henderson's opera *The Last Leaf,* libretto by the composer based on the O Henry story, was premiered by Opera San José in San Jose, CA, on June l7, 1979, and reprised at the Lake George Opera Festival in New York in 1980. It has been superseded by his later opera *West of Washington Square* which incorporates it. **1984 Susan Bingham.** Susan Bingham's opera *The Last Leaf,* libretto by the composer based on the O Henry story, was premiered by Chancel Opera in New Haven, CT, on December l, 1984. **1988 Alva Henderson.** Alva Henderson's opera *West of Washington Square,* libretto by Janet Louis and the composer based on O. Henry's stories *The Last Leaf* and *Room Across the Hall,* was premiered by Opera San José on November 26, 1988. Brenda Willner was Cathy, Terri McKay was Helen, Ronald Gerard was Mr. Behrman, David Cox-Crosswell was Edward, Janis Wilcox was O'Hara, Elizabeth Enmann was Kate and Douglas Nagel was Paul. Barbara Day Turner conducted the Opera San José Orchestra. **1988 Mary Warwick.** Mary Warwick's 35-minute opera *The Last Leaf,* libretto by the composer based on the O Henry story, was premiered at the University of Houston in Texas, on April 27, 1988, and reprised at Lumberton, NC, on September 10, 1989.

THE LAST LEAF (2)   *1999 operatic musical by Ekstrom*

Peter Ekstrom's *The Last Leaf,* libretto by the composer based on O Henry's story *The Last Leaf,* is described as a musical though its songs are described as arias. It was commissioned by Jon Jory as a companion to Ekstrom's other O Henry musical *The Gift of the Magi* and was premiered in December 1994 by the Actors Theater of Louisville at the Barter Theatre. Emily Loesser played Johnsy, Theresa McCarthy was Sue, Don Stephenson was the Narrator/Doctor and Bruce Adler was the artist Mr. Behrman. Pianist Albert Ahronheim orchestrated the work and led the four-piece chamber orchestra.

Actors Theater of Louisville. Emily Loesser is Johnsy in this recording of the production by the Actors Theater of Louisville. Theresa McCarthy is Sue, Don Stephenson is Narrator/Doctor and Bruce Adler is Mr. Behrman. Albert Ahronheim plays piano and leads the four-piece chamber orchestra. Harbinger Records CD.

THE LAST LOVER   *1975 opera by Starer*

Antioch in the fourth century. Pelagia and her maid discuss their lovers while the holy man Veronus contemplates God. Pelagia attempts to seduce him but is instead converted by his devotion. She rejects the Seducer (the Devil), becomes a monk and gives advice to a young nun who is taken by the Seducer. Pelagia is wrongfully banished but many consider her a saint. Robert Starer's 40-minute chamber opera *The Last Lover,* libretto by Gail Godwin based on legends about Pelagia, premiered at the Caramoor Festival in Katonah, NY, on August 2, 1975. Joanna Simon was Pelagia, Richard Fredericks was Veronus/Seducer/Voice of Judge and Linda Phillips was Pelagia's Maid/Young Nun. The music was performed by the Dorian Wind Quartet.

THE LAST OF THE MOHICANS (1)   *American operas based on Cooper novel*

In 1857 during the French and Indian War, sisters Cora and Alice Munro and their guardian Major Heyward are betrayed by Huron guide Magua who hates the women's father Colonel Munro. Hawkeye (Natty Bumppo) and his Indian friends Chingachgook and Uncas save them and aid the English at Fort Henry. Uncas, last of the Mohican tribe, falls in love with Cora and is eventually killed trying to save her. James Fenimore Cooper's 1826 novel *The Last of the Mohicans* has inspired operas by three American composers.

1890 Ellsworth Phelps. Connecticut composer Ellsworth Phelps (1827–1913) composed his opera *The Last of the Mohicans,* based on the Cooper novel, in 1890. **1916 Paul Hastings Allen.** Paul Hastings Allen's three-act *L'Ultimo del Moicano,* libretto in Italian by Zangarini based on the Cooper novel, premiered at the Politeamo Fiorentino in Florence, Italy, on February 24, 1916, and was published by Ricordi. Allen was an American but he wrote most of his operas to Italian librettos.

THE LAST OF THE MOHICANS (2)   *1976 opera by Henderson*

Alva Henderson's three-act opera *The Last of the Mohicans,* libretto by Janet Lewis based on the Cooper novel, was premiered by Wilmington Opera in Delaware on June 12, 1976. Peter van Derick sang the role of Uncas, Linda Roark was Cora, Kristine Comendant was Alice, Alan Wagner was Hawkeye, Cary Smith was Chingachgook, Lawrence Cooper was Magua, William Austin was

Heyward, Robert Benton was Colonel Munro and Nicholas Muni was General Montcalm.

1977 Lake George Festival. The opera was reprised and recorded at the Lake George Opera Festival in August 1977. The principal singers are Barbara Hocher, Maryanne Telese, John Carson Sandor, Ronald Hedlund and Sigmund Cowan. Tonu Kalam conducts orchestra and chorus. Live Opera audiocassette.

THE LAST SAVAGE *1963 opera by Menotti*

A handsome peasant in India pretends to be a savage so he can be trapped by a rich American woman. Gian Carlo's three-act comic opera *The Last Savage,* libretto by the composer, was commissioned by Paris Opéra and premiered in French as *Le dernier sauvage* at the Opéra-Comique on October 22, 1963. Gabriel Bacquier starred as supposed savage Abdul, Mady Mesplé was his captor Kitty, Adriana Maliponte was Sardula, Michele Mosel was Kodanda, Charles Clavensy was the Maharajah, Solange Michel was the Maharanee and Xavier Depraz was Mr. Scattergood. Andrew Beaurepaire designed the sets and costumes, Menotti directed and Serge Baudo conducted. *The Last Savage* was premiered in English at the Metropolitan Opera on January 23, 1964, with George London as Abdul, Roberta Peters as Kitty, Teresa Stratas as Sardula, Nicolai Gedda as Kodanda, Ezio Flagello as the Maharajah, Lili Chookasian as the Maharanee and Morley Meredith as Mr. Scattergood. Beni Montresor designed the sets and costumes, Menotti directed and Thomas Schippers conducted.

1964 Metropolitan Opera. George London sings Abdul in this broadcast of *The Last Savage* by the Metropolitan Opera premiere cast. Roberta Peters is Kitty, Teresa Stratas is Sardula, Nicolai Gedda is Kodanda, Ezio Flagello is Maharajah and Lili Chookasian is Maharanee. Thomas Schippers conducts the Metropolitan Opera Orchestra. The opera was broadcast February 8, 1964. Omega Opera Archive CD. **1980 William D. Revelli.** William D. Revelli conducts the University of Michigan Symphonic Band in instrumental excerpts from *The Last Savage.* The Overture and Hunt sequences are on the album *The Revelli Years.* Golden Crest LP.

THE LAST TALE *1962 opera by Toch*

Scheherazade is persuaded by her revolutionary lover Alcazar to distract the Sultan while his group prepares a revolution. On the last night, the night of the revolution, she tells her own story, how she has waited one thousand nights for her lover. As the revolution develops around them, Scheherazade dies. Ernst Toch's *The Last Tale,* libretto by Melchior Lengyel based on the last story Scheherazade tells in the *Arabian Nights,* was completed in Los Angeles in 1962. It was not performed, however, until November 18, 1995, thirty years after Toch's death, when the Deutsch-Sorbische Volkstheater staged it in Bautzen. Toch, who was born in Austria, became known in Europe with his first opera, the 1927 *The Princess and the Pea,* but he wrote only one opera after emigrating to America. Librettist Lengyel is best-known for his collaboration with Béla Bartók on the ballet *The Miraculous Mandarin.*

LATIN AMERICAN OPERA

A number of operas by Latin American and Spanish American composers have been composed and premiered in the USA. Argentine composer Alberto Ginastera was commissioned by Washington Opera to create two operas that they premiered with American casts and production teams. While it is difficult to think of them as "American" operas, BOMARZO and BEATRIX CENCI form part of the American opera world. Mexican composer Daniel Catán also has strong connections to the American opera world. His FLORENCIA EN EL AMAZONAS was commissioned by Houston Grand Opera which premiered it in 1996. His RAPPACCINI'S DAUGHTER based on the Nathaniel Hawthorne story, was staged by San Diego Opera in 1994 and recorded by Manhattan School of Music Opera in 1997. Leonardo Balada came to the U.S. from Barcelona in 1956 as a student and composed all his operas in America. HANGMAN, HANGMAN! (1982) is a satire about the American West. *Zapata* (1984), commissioned by San Diego Opera, tells the story of the Mexican revolutionary. CRISTÓBAL COLÓN (1989) tells the story of Columbus's voyage to America. THE TOWN OF GREED (1997), a sequel to *Hangman, Hangman!,* has been staged in America and Spain. Cuban-born Tania León's SCOURGE OF HYACINTHS, libretto based on a Wolfe Soyinka play, won an international opera competition when it premiered in 1994. *The Golden Windows* was staged in 1982 by Robert Wilson, *I Got Ovah* was presented at Brooklyn College in 1987 and *Rita and Bessie,* about Rita Montaner and Bessie Smith, was performed by Duo Theater in New York in 1988. José Mojica, Mexico's most famous opera singer before Plácido Domingo, sang with Chicago Opera from 1919 to 1930 and created roles in four American operas.

LATOUCHE, JOHN *American lyricist/librettist (1917–1956)*

John Latouche is one of American music theater's great librettists, the wordsmith behind some of the most popular and innovative operas and musicals. His greatest achievement is the libretto for Douglas Moore's THE BALLAD OF BABY DOE (1956) which, since its premiere at Central City in Colorado in, has become a recognized classic and one of the few American operas whose arias have entered the soprano repertory. His imaginative libretto for Jerome Morass's Broadway opera THE GOLDEN APPLE (1954), an transposition of Homer's *Iliad* to Washington state, is also greatly admired. With Morass he broke down genre boundaries with BALLET BALLADS (1948), three ballet-operas that expanded ideas about opera and ballet. With Duke Ellington he created the Broadway opera BEGGAR'S HOLIDAY (1946), updating John Gay's *The Beggar's Opera* to modern New York. He also wrote the librettos for Earl Robinson's anti-Nazi musical *Sing for Your Supper* (1939); Vernon Duke's black cast musical *Cabin in the Sky* (1940), *Banjo Eyes* and *The Lady Comes Across*; and James Mundy's *The Vamp* (1955). He was one of the writers who worked on Leonard Bernstein's CANDIDE (1956), creating lyrics for some of its songs. Latouche, born in Richmond, VA, studied at Columbia and began to write lyrics in 1936.

1984 Take Love Easy: The Lyrics of John Latouche. Richard Rodney Bennett recorded this anthology of songs by Latouche in 1984 for an LP and added five more in 2000 for a CD version. The fifteen selections, sung and played by Bennett, include numbers from *The Golden Apple, Beggar's Holiday, Cabin in the Sky, Banjo Eyes* and *The Lady Comes Across.* Audiophile LP/CD. **2000 Taking a Chance on Love.** The off-Broadway revue *Taking a Chance on Love* is based around the lyrics of John Latouche. The cast album features songs from *The Ballad of Baby Doe, Ballet Ballads, Beggar's Holiday, Cabin in the Sky, Candide, The Golden Apple* and *The Vamp.* The singers are Eddie Korbich, Terry Burrell, Jerry Dixon and Donna English. Original Cast Records CD.

LAUFER, BEATRICE *American composer (1923–)*

Beatrice Laufer had international success with her one-act opera *Ile* based on Eugene O'Neill's 1917 play about an obsessed whaling captain. It was premiered on radio on WNYC on the Mutual Broadcasting System on February 14, 1954, and on stage at the Brooklyn Museum on April 28, 1957. It was presented by the Royal Opera in Stockholm on October 28, 1958, by the Yale School of Music in 1977 and on National Public Radio in 1978. It has even been staged in China. Laufer, a native New Yorker, studied with Rogers Sessions and Vittorio Giannini at Juilliard.

"LAURIE'S SONG" *Soprano aria: The Tender Land (1954). Words: Horace Everett. Music: Aaron Copland*

Laurie, the adolescent heroine of *The Tender Land,* is ready to spread her wings and fly. She expresses her understanding of "the world so wide" in a charming aria called "Laurie's Song" that begins with the words "Once I thought I'd never grow." She says that once she thought she's never go outside her fence but now the line between earth and sky is beckoning her. Aaron Copland's opera *The Tender Land,* libretto by Horace Everett (pseudonym of poet Eric Johns), tells the story of a Midwest farm family in the 1930s and two drifters who arrive looking for work. Copland said he wanted to give young American singers a simple opera that would be natural for them to perform. "Laurie's Song" was introduced at the 1954 New York City Opera premiere by Rosemary Carlos making her debut. It is performed by Joy Clements on a 1965 Lincoln Center recording, Karen Hunt on a 1978 Michigan Opera Theater DVD, Elisabeth Comeaux on a 1990 Plymouth Music recording, Dawn Upshaw on her 1995 recital album *The World So Wide,* Susan Hanson in a 1999 New Music Ensemble recording and Andrea Jones in a 2002 University of Kentucky Opera Theatre recording.

LAVERY, EMMET *American librettist/playwright (1902–1986)*

Emmet Lavery wrote the libretto for Ernst Krenek's first American opera TARQUIN which was premiered in concert form at Vassar College in Poughkeepsie, New York, on May 13, 1941. Lavery was a Poughkeepsie newspaperman turned playwright who had begun to work with the Federal Theater Project in the 1920s. His most successful play was *The Magnificent Yankee* (1946), the story of Supreme Court Justice Oliver Wendell Holmes.

LEAR, EVELYN *American soprano (1926–)*

Evelyn Lear created the role of Nina in Marc Blitzstein's REUBEN, REUBEN in Boston in 1955, Lavinia in Marvin David Levy' MOURNING BECOMES ELECTRA at the Metropolitan Opera in 1967, Irina Arkadina in Thomas Pasatieri's THE SEAGULL at Houston Grand Opera in 1974 and Margo in Robert Ward's MINUTES TILL MIDNIGHT in Miami in 1982. She sings Minny Belle on a 1956 recording of Kurt Weill's JOHNNY JOHNSON, Augusta's best friend on a 1957 TV version of Douglas Moore's THE BALLAD OF BABY DOE, Dinah in a taped 1973 Hollywood Bowl performance of Leonard Bernstein's TROUBLE IN TAHITI and a cameo role on Bernstein's 1992 operatic recording of ON THE TOWN. Lear, who was born in Brooklyn, studied at Juilliard and made her debut in Berlin in 1959.

LEES, BENJAMIN *American composer (1924–)*

Benjamin Lees, a student of George Antheil, has composed three operas and a cantata. The most successful was MEDEA IN CORINTH, libretto by the composer based on Robinson Jeffers harshly poetic version of the Euripides play. It premiered in concert form in London in 1971, was staged in Antwerp in 1973 and was presented on CBS television in America in 1974. Lees' first opera, the one-act

The Oracle, libretto by the composer about a computer, was written for a British television company in 1955 but not performed. The three-act *The Gilded Cage,* libretto by A. Reid, was staged in 1964 but later withdrawn. The cantata-oratorio *Visions of Poets,* libretto by the composer based on the poems of Walt Whitman, was performed in 1961. Lees was born in Harbin, China, of Russian parents but came to the U.S. as a child. He has had his greatest success with chamber and orchestral works.

THE LEGEND *1919 opera by Breil*

Carmelita's father Stackareff is a Balkan bandit sought by her soldier lover Stephen. To prevent her father being captured, Carmelita stabs Stephen. His soldiers shoot and kill her. Joseph Breil's melodramatic one-act opera *The Legend,* libretto by Jacques Byrne, premiered at the Metropolitan Opera on March 12, 1919, with Rosa Ponselle as Carmelita, Paul Althouse as Stephen, Kathleen Howard as Marta and Louis d'Angelo as Count Stackareff. Robert Moranzoni conducted. Librettist Byrne was a screenplay writer and critics felt the opera was rather too much in the style of the silent movie melodrama.

THE LEGEND OF WIWASTE *1924 opera by Blakeslee*

In the American West before the coming of the White Man, Native Americans take part in rituals like the Feast of the Virgins and the Calumet Ceremony before a betrothal and marriage. Samuel Earle Blakeslee's opera *The Legend of Wiwaste,* libretto by the composer based on Dakota Sioux legends and musical motifs, was premiered at Chaffey College in Ontario, California, on April 25, 1924. Princess Tsianina Redfeather Blackstone, the first Native American opera singer to achieve national recognition, sang the lead role of Wiwaste and helped popularize its aria "Far Away in Northland." The opera was reprised at the Hollywood Bowl in 1927 and revived at UCLA in 1966 under the title *Red Cloud.*

LEGENDE PROVENÇALE *1935 opera by Moore*

Mary Carr Moore's demanding three-act opera *Legende provençale,* libretto by Eleanore Flaig based on Flaig's own play, was Moore's last opera. She considered it her best but it has never been staged.

1984 Evelyn De La Rosa. Soprano Evelyn De La Rosa sings an aria from *Legende provençale* in English and then in French accompanied by pianist Adrea Lenz. "The Star at Eve" and "L'étoile du soir" were recorded on May 17, 1984, at the J. E. Church Fine Arts Theater at the University of Nevada in Reno. They're on the album *The Songs of Mary Carr Moore.* Cambria Records LP.

LEHRMAN, LEONARD *American composer (1945–)*

Leonard Lehrman has helped promote the music and operas of Marc Blitzstein since he was a student at Harvard. He staged THE CRADLE WILL ROCK at Harvard in 1969 and followed it in 1970 with productions of I'VE GOT THE TUNE and THE HARPIES. Leonard Bernstein suggested he complete Blitzstein's Bernard Malamud-based opera IDIOT'S FIRST so he did. It was premiered by the Blitzstein Opera Company in Bloomington, Indiana, on March 14, 1976. Lehrman's one-act opera *Karla,* based on Malamud's story *Notes from a Lady at a Dinner Party* which had premiered in concert form at Cornell University in Ithaca, NY, on August 3, 1974, was staged with it. Both operas were reprised by Bel Canto Opera in 1978 in New York. In 1990 Lehrman organized the New York stage show *A Blitzstein Cabaret* with numbers from Blitzstein operas sung by Helene Williams and Ronald Edwards and Lehrman accompanying on piano. The show was recorded and issued on CD. Lehrman, born in Fort Riley, Kansas, has composed other operas. The first was *Beowulf: or, The Great Dane* which he completed in 1970. *Sima,* libretto by the composer, was performed at Cornell University on October 22, 1976. *Hannah,* libretto by Orel Odinov and the composer about Hannah and the Maccabees and the origins of Hanukkah, was premiered in Mannheim, Germany on May 22, 1980, and broadcast on WBAI in New York on December 26, 1989. *The Family Man,* libretto by the composer based on Sholokhov's tale *Semyoniy Chelovek,* was premiered by TOMI in New York on January 8, 1984. *The Birthday of the Bank,* libretto by the composer based on Chekhov's *The Jubilee,* was commissioned by Opera America for the Lake George Festival where it premiered on August 2, 1988.

LEIGH, MITCH   *American composer (1928–)*

Mitch Leigh did not write operas but opera singers seem to like his 1965 musical MAN OF LA MANCHA which has entered the opera house repertory. Indianapolis Opera Company presented it in 1990 and an operatic cast headed by Placido Domingo recorded it in 1995. Leigh, a native of Brooklyn who studied music at Yale with Hindemith, had originally planned to collaborate with opera librettists W. H. Auden and Chester Kallman on *Man of La Mancha.* His other music theater works have not been particularly successful.

LEMPER, UTE   *German soprano (1963–)*

German cabaret artist Ute Lemper features the American and German songs of Kurt Weill in her shows and has made several CDs and videos featuring his music. She included three songs from ONE TOUCH OF VENUS on a 1988 CD and songs from five Weill shows on a video of a show in Paris.

1992 Ute Lemper Sings Kurt Weill Live in Paris. Ute Lemper sings airs from Weill operas and musicals at Les Bouffes du Nord in Paris. There are selections from Weill's American shows THE FIREBRAND OF FLORENCE, LADY IN THE DARK, KNICKERBOCKER HOLIDAY, LOST IN THE STARS and ONE TOUCH OF VENUS plus the European works *The Three Penny Opera, Mahagonny, Happy End* and *Marie Galante,* Jeff Cohen accompanies her on piano. Tony Stavacre directed. Decca/London VHS.

LENYA, LOTTE   *Austrian/American soprano (1898–1981)*

Lotte Lenya, who married Kurt Weill in 1926 and created the role of Jenny in *The Threepenny Opera* in Berlin in 1928, also created roles in two of his American stage works, Miriam in THE ETERNAL ROAD in New York in 1937 and the Duchess in THE FIREBRAND OF FLORENCE in New York in 1945. She sings the French Nurse on the 1956 cast recording of JOHNNY JOHNSON and she has recorded songs from most of his other theater works. She also created the role of the Suicidal Woman in Marc Blitzstein radio opera I'VE GOT THE TUNE on CBS in 1937. Lenya, born as Karoline Blamauer in Vienna, spent most of the period after Weill's death in 1950 promoting and reviving his work on stage and television.

1957 Lotte Lenya Sings American Theater Songs. Lenya recorded songs from most of Weill's American Theater songs for a 1957 album. The songs are from THE ETERNAL ROAD, THE FIREBRAND OF FLORENCE, KNICKERBOCKER HOLIDAY, LADY IN THE DARK, LOST IN THE STARS, LOVE LIFE, ONE TOUCH OF VENUS and STREET SCENE. Columbia LP/Sony Classics CD.

LEÓN, TANIA   *American composer (1944–)*

Tania León's chamber opera *Scourge of Hyacinths,* libretto based on a Wolfe Soyinka radio play, won an international opera competition when it was premiered at the Munich Biennale in 1994 and it gained wide acclaim when it was staged by Robert Wilson in Switzerland, France and Austria in 1999. León had composed earlier operas. *The Golden Windows* was staged in Munich in 1982 by Robert Wilson. *I Got Ovah* was the winner of a Brooklyn College Chamber Opera competition in 1986 and was presented at Brooklyn College in 1987. *Rita and Bessie,* libretto by Manuel Martin Jr. about Rita Montaner and Bessie Smith, was performed by Duo Theater in New York June 2, 1988. León was born in Havana but moved to New York in 1967. She became music director of the Harlem Dance Theater in 1969 and founded its music department. She has adapted many aspects of Cuban rhythm to classical formats and much of her work is on CD.

LEONORA   *1845 opera by Fry*

William Henry Fry's *Leonora,* libretto by the composer based on Edward Bulwer-Lytton's play *The Lady of Lyons,* was the first American "grand" opera staged in the U.S. It was premiered at the Chestnut Street Theater Philadelphia on June 4, 1845, by Arthur Seguin's company. Mrs. Seguin was Leonora, Edward Seguin was Montalvo, Mr. Frazer was Julio, Mr. Richings was Valdor, Mr. Brinton was Alferez and Miss Ince was Marianna. Fry himself conducted the orchestra. The opera was composed in the Italian style then coming into fashion and a revised Italian-language version was staged in New York in 1858 as *Giulio and Leonora. Leonora* was Fry's third opera.

LERNER, ALAN JAY   *American librettist/lyricist (1918–1986)*

Alan Jay Lerner wrote the libretto and lyrics for Kurt Weill's 1948 vaudeville LOVE LIFE and recorded songs from it in 1955 with Kaye Ballard. His biggest success, however, came in working with composer Frederick Loewe. They created four American operetta-style Broadway musicals which have begun to enter the light opera repertory, BRIGADOON (1947), *Paint Your Wagon* (1951), MY FAIR LADY (1956) and CAMELOT (1960). All four have been turned into films. *My Fair Lady* has been especially popular with opera singers from Blanche Thebom to Kiri Te Kanawa. Lerner's last music theater works were Leonard Bernstein's *1600 Pennsylvania Avenue* (1976), Burton Lane's *Carmelina* (1979) and Charles Strouse's *Dance a Little* (1983). Lerner, born in New York and educated at Harvard, first teamed with Loewe in 1942.

LESSING, DORIS   *British writer/librettist (1919–)*

Doris Lessing wrote the librettos for two Philip Glass operas based on her *Canopus in Argos* science fiction series. Glass contacted her in 1983 and they began with THE MAKING OF THE REPRESENTATIVE FOR PLANET 8 based on her 1982 novel about a world doomed to destruction. It was premiered by Houston Grand Opera in 1988. The second was THE MARRIAGES BETWEEN ZONES THREE, FOUR AND FIVE which was premiered in German at the Theater der Stadt in Heidelberg in 1997. Lessing, born in Iran and brought up in Rhodesia, published her first novel *The Grass is Singing* in 1950. She wrote the *Canopus in Argos* series from 1979 to 1983.

LESSNER, GEORGE   *American composer (1904–?)*

George Lessner's only opera is the one-act THE NIGHTINGALE AND THE ROSE, libretto by the composer based on the story by Oscar Wilde, which premiered on NBC Radio on April 25, 1942. Lessner, who was born in Budapest, studied with Bartok and Kodaly at the Budapest Royal Academy before emigrating to the

U.S. He became an American citizen in 1926 and composed eight symphonies in addition to writing music for radio, movies, stage and television. His Broadway musical *Sleepy Hollow* had a short run in 1948.

"THE LETTER SONG" *Soprano aria: The Ballad of Baby Doe. Words: John Latouche. Music: Douglas Moore*

Baby Doe McCourt writes to her mother from Leadville, Colorado, to say she has broken up with the rich man she loves because he is married. John Latouche's lyrics in Douglas Moore's THE BALLAD OF BABY DOE express her anguish and emotional confusion in such a way that we are not too surprised when she changes her mind when the man's angry wife confronts her. "The Letter Song" ("Dearest Mama") was introduced on stage in Central City, Colorado, in 1956 by Dolores Wilson but it became famous when it was sung by Beverly Sills at New York City Opera in 1958. Sills sings it on the NYCO cast recording of the opera, Ruth Welting on a 1976 New York City Opera telecast, Sheryl Woods in a 1992 Cleveland Opera recording, Eileen di Tullio on a 1995 recording, Evelyn del la Rosa on a 1996 Des Moines Metro Opera video and Jan Grissom on a 1996 Central City Opera recording. The aria has become a popular recital piece for sopranos and Renée Fleming features it on her 1999 album of American opera arias. It is included in Richard Walters' collection *Opera American Style: Arias for Soprano.*

A LETTER TO EMILY *1951 opera by Johnson*

Amherst, Massachusetts, in 1870. Emily Dickinson sends some of her poems to Colonel Higginson in Boston and he comes to visit her. He invites her to Boston to meet other writers; her sister urges her to go, her tyrannical father is bitterly opposed and she decides against it when she finds how little the colonel understands her poetry. Lockrem Johnson's one-act chamber opera *A Letter to Emily*, libretto by the composer based on Robert Hupton's play *Consider the Lilies*, was premiered at the Cornish School of Music in Seattle on April 24, 1951, reprised in Interlochen in July and then presented in Los Angeles. It was popular with audiences and was staged more than fifty times in the years that followed.

LEVANT, OSCAR *American composer (1906–1972)*

Oscar Levant is best known as a humorist, actor, writer, radio wit, pianist and interpreter of George Gershwin music but he was also a composer and the creator of a famous "movie opera." CARNIVAL, libretto by William Kernell, was composed for the 1936 film *Charlie Chan at the Opera* and actually constructed around a costume, the Mephistopheles outfit used by Lawrence Tibbett in *Metropolitan* and passed on to the low-budget Chan film. Levant wrote an overture, a prelude, some marches and some arias for this odd opera starring Boris Karloff. He talks about it in his autobiography *A Smattering of Ignorance*. Levant, who was born in Pittsburgh and studied composition with Arnold Schoenberg, also composed a piano concerto, two string quartets, an orchestral nocturne and scores for several films. His most famous film performances feature him playing music by Gershwin in *An American in Paris* and *Rhapsody in Blue*.

LEVINE, JAMES *American conductor (1943–)*

James Levine conducted the premieres of John Corigliano's THE GHOSTS OF VERSAILLES in 1991 and John Harbison's THE GREAT GATSBY in 1999, both at the Metropolitan Opera. He conducted the Met premiere of George Gershwin's PORGY AND BESS in 1985

and forty-two further performances. He leads the orchestra on Renée Fleming's 1999 album of American opera arias, *I Want Magic,* and on a recording of a 1973 production of Leonard Bernstein's TROUBLE IN TAHITI at the Hollywood Bowl. Levine, who was born in Cincinnati and studied at Juilliard, made his debut at San Francisco Opera in 1970 and at the Met in 1971. He became chief conductor at the Met in 1974 and its artistic director in 1986.

LEVINE, RHODA *American director/librettist (1932–)*

Rhoda Levine has been strongly involved with American opera, including the American Opera Projects program, and has directed the premieres of seven operas: Michael White's *The Metamorphosis* in Philadelphia in 1968, Jack Beeson's MY HEART'S IN THE HIGHLANDS for NET Opera Theater in 1970, Robert Ward's ABELARD AND HELOISE for Charlotte Opera in 1982, Anthony Davis's X, THE LIFE AND TIMES OF MALCOLM X for New York City Opera in 1986, Davis's UNDER THE DOUBLE MOON for Opera Theater of St. Louis in 1989 and Bruce Saylor's ORPHEUS DESCENDING for the Chicago Lyric Opera in Evanston in 1994. Her production of William Mayer's A DEATH IN THE FAMILY at the Manhattan School of Music Opera Theater in 1999 is on CD. She directed the first production of George Gershwin's PORGY AND BESS in South Africa, Douglas Moore's THE BALLAD OF BABY DOE and Robert Kurka's THE GOOD SOLDIER SCHWEIK for New York City Opera, Jack Beeson's LIZZIE BORDEN and Carlisle Floyd's OF MICE AND MEN for Glimmerglass Opera and a new production of Scott Joplin's TREEMONISHA for Opera Theater of St. Louis. Levine is also a librettist and author of children's books. Stanley Hollingsworth's HARRISON LOVED HIS UMBRELLA, libretto by Levine based on her book, was premiered at the Spoleto Festival in Charleston, SC, in 1981. Robert Chaul's *The Thirteen Clocks,* libretto by Levine based on James Thurber's fable, was premiered in Waterford, CT, in 1983. Levine, who born in New York, studied at Bard College and made her directing debut in 1965 at the Spoleto Festival.

LEVOWITZ, ADAM *American composer (1968–)*

Texas-based composer Adam Levowitz has created several operas and musicals based on classic American stories and fairytales. Two of his children's operas have been staged: *The Three Princes* in New York in 1995 and *The Brave Little Tailor* in Texas in 2003. *The Lotus and the Elephant* was given a special presentation in Texas in 2003. The 1993 musical *Rip Van Winkle*, based on the Washington Irving story, and the 1999 chamber opera *The Tell-Tale Heart*, based on the EDGAR ALLAN POE story, have not yet been performed.

LEVY, MARVIN DAVY *American composer (1932–)*

Marvin Davy Levy is best known for his highly acclaimed opera MOURNING BECOMES ELECTRA, based on the Eugene O'Neill play trilogy, which was commissioned and premiered by the Metropolitan Opera in 1967. A revised version was produced by Lyric Opera of Chicago in 1999 and presented in Seattle and New York in 2004. *The Balcony*, libretto by the composer based on the Jean Genet play, was also commissioned by the Met but was not performed. Levy, born in Passaic, NJ, studied music at NYU and Columbia and wrote his first opera while still an undergraduate. *Riders to the Sea,* based on the Irish play by John Millington Synge, was withdrawn and has not been performed. THE TOWER, libretto by Townsend Brewster about King Solomon and his daughter, was presented at Santa Fe Opera in 1956. *Sotoba Komachi,* libretto by S. H. Brock based on a Noh play, was premiered at the 92nd Street YMCA in New York on April 7, 1957. ESCORIAL, libretto by Lionel

Abel based on a play by the Belgian Michel de Ghelderode about a jealous king and his jester, was premiered at the 92nd Street YMCA on May 4, 1958. Levy's music is considered expressionist but quite singable.

LEWIN, FRANK   *American composer (1925–)*

Frank Lewin adapted a John Steinbeck play to create his only opera BURNING BRIGHT. The three-hour work about a childless couple takes place in different settings in each act. It was premiered by the Yale School of Music in New Haven in November 5, 1993, and revived by the Opera Festival of New Jersey at Princeton in 2000. Lewin, who was born in Germany in 1925. became an American citizen in 1946.

LEWIS, BRENDA   *American soprano (1930–)*

Brenda Lewis created roles in four American operas and an operetta. Her most important creation is Lizzie Borden in Jack Beeson's LIZZIE BORDEN which premiered at New York City Opera in 1965; she is featured on the NYCO recording and the 1967 NET telecast. Nearly as memorable are her performances in Marc Blitzstein's REGINA on Broadway in 1949; she created the role of Birdie in the premiere and then took over playing the title role; she is the one who sings the role on the cast recording. She created the character called She in Lehman Engel's opera THE SOLDIER at Carnegie Hall in 1956 and that of Sara in Philip Bezanson's opera GOLDEN CHILD on NBC television in 1960. She replaced Eleanor Steber in the title role of Samuel Barber's VANESSA at the Met on February 11, 1958. Her operetta performances are also notable. She created the role of Lotte Leslie in Sigmund Romberg's THE GIRL IN PINK TIGHTS when it premiered on Broadway in 1954 and she sings the part of opera diva Louisa in a recording of a 1958 production of the Wright/Forrest SONG OF NORWAY. She also sang in Albert Hague's musical *Café Crown* on Broadway in 1964. Lewis, who was born in Sunbury, PA, was with New York City Opera from 1945 to 1967 and at the Metropolitan Opera from 1952 to 1960.

LEWIS, WILLIAM   *American tenor (1935–)*

Dramatic tenor William Lewis created the role of Bill in Samuel Barber's A HAND OF BRIDGE at the Spoleto Festival in 1959 and sings it on a 1960 recording. And he created the part of Mattan in Hugo Weisgall's ATHALIAH in New York in 1964. He sings the role of John Adams in a televised and recorded 1976 Santa Fe Opera production of Virgil Thomson's pageant opera THE MOTHER OF US ALL and he played Prince Hal in a 1999 production of Gordon Getty's PLUMP JACK in San Francisco. He recorded highlight versions of three classic American operettas in 1962 singing Captain Dick in Victor Herbert's NAUGHTY MARIETTA, the Prince in Sigmund Romberg's THE STUDENT PRINCE and François Villon in Rudolf Friml's THE VAGABOND KING. Lewis, who was born in Tulsa, Oklahoma, made his debut at Fort Worth Opera in 1953 and at the Met in 1958.

LIEBERMANN, LOWELL   *American composer (1961–)*

Lowell Liebermann had surprising success with his first opera THE PICTURE OF DORIAN GRAY. It was commissioned by John Mordler, director of the Opéra de Monte-Carlo, and premiered in Monte Carlo in 1996 and Florentine Opera in Milwaukee held its American premiere in 1999. Reviews were positive and a documentary was made about its creation. Liebermann, who has a doctorate in music from Juilliard, is able to make a living on commissions and performances of new works. His 1993 flute solo *Soliloquy* is especially popular and is given hundreds of performances a year.

LIEBERMANN, ROLF   *Swiss composer (1910–1999)*

Rolf Liebermann's opera SCHOOL FOR WIVES, based on Molière's play about a lecher and his plans for a young wife, was commissioned by Louisville Orchestra and premiered by Kentucky Opera on December 3, 1955. Liebermann, who was born in Zurich, is best known as an opera administrator (Hamburg and Paris) but he also wrote six operas including *Penelope* in 1954, *La Forêt* in 1987 and *Medea* in 1995. He produced a number of notable opera films at the Hamburg Staatsoper but none of American operas.

LIEBERSON, LORRAINE HUNT   *American mezzo-soprano (1954–)*

Lorraine Hunt Lieberson created Triraksha in Peter Lieberson's ASHOKA'S DREAM at Santa Fe Opera in 1997, Myrtle Wilson in John Harbison's THE GREAT GATSBY at the Metropolitan Opera in 1999 (her Met debut) and Mary in John Adams' Nativity oratorio EL NIÑO in Paris in 2000. She sang in a workshop production of Robert Aldrich's opera *Elmer Gantry* and in the first performance of John Harbison's Pulitzer Prize-winning *The Flight into Egypt*. Lieberson, born in San Francisco as Lorraine Hunt, married composer Peter Lieberson in 1998. A former viola player, she made her operatic debut in *Hansel and Gretel* in San Quentin Prison with Kent Nagano conducting. She works frequently with Peter Sellars and it was her powerful performance as Sesto in his production of Handel's *Giulio Cesare* at the 1985 PepsiCo Summerfare Festival that made her widely known.

LIEBERSON, PETER   *American composer (1946–)*

Peter Lieberson created what he described as a "campfire opera" in 1996. KING GESAR, libretto by Douglas Penick about a 10th century Tibetan ruler and his spiritual quest, premiered at the Munich Biennale that year. His second opera ASHOKA'S DREAM, libretto by Penick about a famous Asian emperor, was commissioned by Santa Fe Opera which premiered it in 1997. These are intended to be the first of four operatic works in his *Cycle of the Ancestral Sovereigns* dealing with enlightened ancient rulers. Lieberson, who comes from a musical family (his father was Columbia Records chief Goddard Lieberson, his mother ballerina Vera Zorina), studied composition with Milton Babbitt at Columbia and Buddhism in Colorado. His music is influenced by serial techniques but is basically lyrical. He is married to soprano Lorraine Hunt Lieberson.

LIFE IS A DREAM   *1978 opera by Spratlan*

Lewis Spratlan's opera *Life Is a Dream*, libretto by James Maraniss based on the 17th century Spanish play *La vida es sueño* by Pedro Calderón, won the Pulitzer Prize for Music in 2000 in a concert version. The original three-act opera, created with an NEA grant, was premiered by New Haven Opera Theatre in February 1978. Spratlan revised the second act for concert use and this version was premiered on January 28, 2000, by Dinosaur Annex in Boston with J. David Jackson conducting. The Pulitzer jury felt Spratlan combined traditional dance, march and madrigal forms with contemporary styles and created a theatrical world in which each character had a distinct musical personality.

THE LIFE WORK OF JUAN DIAZ   *1990 opera by Rapchak*

A Mexican peasant dies leaving his family penniless. By a quirk of fate he is able to provide for his wife and children after death when his mummified body becomes a tourist attraction. Lawrence Rapchak's one-act opera *The Life Work of Juan Diaz*, libretto by Carl Rather, was premiered April 21, 1990, by Chicago Chamber Opera. Robert Hovencamp played the peasant Juan Diaz, Carole Loverde was his wife Maria, Richard Alderson was gravedigger Alejando, Darrell Rowader was Maria's brother Ricardo and Jason Whitmer, Amanda Armato and Joanni Lind played the Diaz Children, Lawrence Rapchak conducted the Chicago Chamber Opera Orchestra. The opera is based on a short story by Ray Bradbury that was dramatized for a 1964 *Alfred Hitchcock Presents* TV play.

1990 Chicago Chamber Opera. Robert Hovencamp is Juan Diaz in this recording made in Chicago on May 8, 1990, with the premiere cast. Carole Loverde is Maria, Richard Alderson is Alejando, Darrell Rowader is Ricardo and Jason Whitmer, Amanda Armato and Joanni Lind are the children, Lawrence Rapchak conducts the Chicago Chamber Opera Orchestra. Albany Records CD.

LIGEIA   *1994 opera by Thomas*

Dark-haired Ligeia is dying but she tries to convince her husband that a strong will can stave off death. She dies all the same. Her husband remarries but is so unhappy with fair-haired Rowena that he begins taking opium. When Rowena dies, Ligeia returns and takes her place. Augusta Thomas's chamber opera *Ligeia*, libretto by Leslie Dunton-Downer based on a story by EDGAR ALLAN POE but changed into a psychobiography of a drug-taking poet, premiered at the Evian Festival in Evian-les-Bains Festival in May 1994. Mstislav Rostropovich, who commissioned it, conducted the premiere which was staged by Roger Brunyate. The opera was reprised at the Spoleto Festival in Italy, won the International Orpheus Prize and was presented at the Aspen Music Festival on July 27, 1995.

A LIGHT FROM ST. AGNES   *1925 opera by Harling*

Beautiful Toinette is the leader of a gang of ne'er-do-wells living in the village of Bon Hilaire near New Orleans. After her drunken followers celebrate the death of the nun Agnes, parish priest Père Bertrand tells Toinette how much Agnes cared for her and even left her a crucifix. Toinette's lover Michel plans to steal a cross of diamonds from the nun's corpse and when she stops him, he stabs her. As she lays dying, the crucifix appears in her hand. William Franke Harling's "jazz opera" *A Light from St. Agnes*, libretto by Minnie Maddern Fiske based on her play, was premiered by Chicago Civic Opera on December 26, 1925. Rosa Raisa sang the role of Toinette, George Baklanoff was Michael Baklanoff and Forrest Lamont was Père Bertrand. Harling conducted the Chicago Civic Opera Orchestra and choruses of nuns and roisterers. The scoring includes banjos, saxophones, and other jazz instruments and features Creole folk tunes. *A Light from St. Agnes* was one of the first American operas to be presented on radio. It was broadcast by NBC's National Grand Opera Company on November 26, 1928, with Cesare Sudaro conducting the orchestra.

Mother and daughter (Olivia de Havilland and Yvette Mimieux) greet Barry Sullivan in film version of *Light in the Piazza* that preceded the 2004 stage musical.

LIGHT IN THE PIAZZA   *2004 musical by Guettel*

An American woman in Florence, Italy, has a lovely 26-year-old daughter who is being courted by an Italian. The trouble is the innocent girl is "slow" because of an accident she had as a child; she has the mental age of a 12-year-old. The mother doesn't know what to do when the couple decide to marry. Adam Guettel's music theater work *Light in the Piazza*, libretto by Craig Lucas based on a novella by Elizabeth Spencer, opened at the Goodman Theater in Chicago on January 20, 2004, in a production by Bartlett Sher following tryouts in Seattle. Victoria Clark played the mother Margaret Johnson, Cecilia Kennan-Bolger was her daughter Clara, Wayne Wilcox was the Italian Fabrizio Naccarelli, Mark Harelik was Fabrizio's father and Patti Cohenour was his mother. Marcela Lorca was the choreographer, Michael Yeargen designed the sets and Ted Sperling conducted. Guettel, the grandson of Richard Rodgers, is one of the new composers breaking down barriers between opera and musical. The Spencer novel was filmed in 1962 with Olivia De Havilland as the mother and Yvette Mimieux as her daughter.

LILITH   *1998 opera by Dratell*

According to Jewish folklore, Lilith was Adam's first wife but she refused to submit to him. She was replaced by Eve who turned out be more pliant. In Deborah Dratell's opera *Lilith*, libretto by David Steven Cohen, Eve is mourning at Adam's funeral when demons appear. Eve tells her son and daughter they are the children of Adam and Lilith. A seer tells Eve that she and Lilith are actually two sides of the same person. The opera was commissioned by DiCapo Opera Theatre which premiered it on June 3, 1997, in a production by Robin Guarino with Ranson Wilson conducting. It was presented in a concert version at Glimmerglass in 1998 and staged in its final form by New York City Opera on November 11,

2001. Lauren Flanigan played Eve, Beth Clayton was Lilith, Dana Beth Miller was Eve's daughter, Marcus DeLoach was Eve's son and Tom Nelis was the Seer. John Conklin designed the set, James Schuette designed the costumes, Anne Bogart directed the production and choreographed the SITI Company dancers and George Manahan conducted the New York City Opera and Chorus.

1995 Lilith Suite. Drattell's *Lilith Suite,* an orchestral work which preceded the opera, was recorded by the Seattle Symphony in 1995 with Gerard Schwartz conducting. Delos CD.

LILY   *1977 opera by Kirchner*

American millionaire Gene Henderson goes to Africa seeking peace of mind while his ex-wife Lily reflects on their life together. He is welcomed by a tribe in the interior and tries to help them rid their water of frogs. Destroying the frogs also destroys the village water supply. Leon Kirchner's opera *Lily,* libretto by the composer based on the first half of Saul Bellow's novel *Henderson the Rain King,* premiered at New York City Opera on April 14, 1977. Ara Berberian was Henderson, Susan Belling was Lily, George Shirley was Henderson's guide Romilayu, Geanie Faulkner was Princess Mtalba, Joy Blackett was Queen Willatale, Benjamin Matthews was Prince Itelo, Lloyd Walser was the Pianist, Victoria McCarty was Frances, Sandra Walker was Lily's Mother and Gertrude Kirchner was the voice on the tape. Bill Stabile designed the sets, Ivan Tcherepnin was the director of electronic sounds, Tom O'Horgan staged the opera and Kirchner conducted. The opera is considered a summation of Kirchner's musical ideas and features a variety of singing styles and musical techniques from pop and aleatory ideas to tape recording, film and electronic sound.

THE LION AND ANDROCLES   *1974 opera by Easton*

Androcles meets a roaring lion while traveling and realizes it is in distress because it has a thorn stuck in its paw. He persuades it to allow him to remove the thorn and they part on a friendly basis. They meet again in the Roman Coliseum when he is thrown to the lions as a Christian. When the lion refuses to attack him, it is considered a miracle and he is freed. John Eaton's 60-minute children's opera *The Lion and Androcles,* libretto by D. Anderson and E. Walter based on a Roman legend, was presented at Public School 47 in Indianapolis on May 1, 1974. Carmon DeLeone conducted the Indiana University Opera Theatre Orchestra and Public School 47 children's chorus. The soloists were William Reeder, William Oberholzer, Linda Anderson, Michael Rocchio, Signe Lando and Nelda Nelson. Ross Allen staged the production and Harold F. Mack designed the sets. It was telecast on PBS on June 16, 1974.

LIPTON, MARTHA   *American mezzo-soprano (1916–)*

Martha Lipton created the role of the wife Augusta in Jack Beeson's THE BALLAD OF BABY DOE at Central City Opera in Colorado in 1956, reprised the part on ABC television in 1957 opposite Virginia Copeland and sang it at New York City Opera in 1958 opposite Beverly Sills. She also created the role of Aunt Maud in Douglas Moore's THE WINGS OF THE DOVE at New York City Opera in 1961. She sang Mother Goose in the American premiere of Igor Stravinsky's THE RAKE'S PROGRESS at the Metropolitan opera in 1953 and this performance is on record. Lipton, born in New York City, studied at Juilliard and made in debut in 1941. She sang at the Met for seventeen seasons.

LISHNER, LEON   *American bass (1913–1995)*

Leon Lishner created roles in four operas by Gian Carlo Menotti's and is heard on the recordings. He was the sinister Chief Police Agent in THE CONSUL on Broadway in 1950, King Balthazar in AMAHL AND THE NIGHT VISITORS on NBC television in 1951, priest Don Marco in THE SAINT OF BLEECKER STREET on Broadway in 1954 and the Desk Clerk in LABYRINTH on NBC television in 1963. He also created a role in Bohuslav Martinů's TV opera THE MARRIAGE on NBC Opera Theater in 1953. He played Baptista in Vittorio Giannini THE TAMING OF THE SHREW on NBC Opera Theater in 1954, Markheim in Carlisle Floyd's MARKHEIM on PBS television in 1974 and the Reverend Hale in Robert Ward's THE CRUCIBLE on stage. Lishner, who was born in New York City and studied at Juilliard, made his debut with Philadelphia Opera in 1942.

LISTEN TO ME   *1967 opera by Carmines*

Two lovers travel through life and death with echoes of the story of Orpheus and Eurydice. Alvin Carmine's *Listen to Me,* libretto by Gertrude Stein, was premiered at the Judson Poets Theatre in the Judson Memorial Church in New York City in 1967 in a production by Lawrence Kornfeld. *The Village Voice* called it a "painstaking lesson in weaving complexities out of simple statements."

LITTELL, PHILIP   *American librettist (1964–)*

Philip Littell has become one of the leading American opera librettists in recent years with commissions from major opera houses. Conrad Susa's THE DANGEROUS LIAISONS, libretto by Littell based on the 1782 novel *Les Liaisons dangereuses* by Pierre Choderlos de Laclos, was premiered by San Francisco Opera in 1994 with Thomas Hampson, Frederica von Stade and Renée Fleming in the leading roles. Susa's Christmas opera THE WISE WOMEN, libretto by Philip Littell about three women traveling with the three wise man to Bethlehem, was premiered by the American Guild of Organists in Dallas in 1994. David Conte's THE DREAMERS, libretto by Littell, commissioned by Sonoma City Opera to celebrate the 150th anniversary of the city's founding, was premiered in 1996. André Previn's A STREETCAR NAMED DESIRE, libretto by Littell based on the play by Tennessee Williams, was premiered by San Francisco Opera in 1998 with Renée Fleming, Rodney Gilfry and Elizabeth Futral in the leading roles. Fleming used an aria from the opera as the title track of her 1998 album of American opera arias *I Want Magic!* Littell and composer Aaron Jay Kernis were commissioned by Santa Fe Opera in 2003 to write an opera based on Ann Patchett's operatic novel *Bel Canto.*

A LITTLE GIRL DREAMS OF TAKING THE VEIL   *1995 opera by Wold*

A young girl has surrealistic dreams of entering the church as a nun. The conflict between her desires and her ordinary personality are personified in the characters of Marceline-Marie and Spontanette and are seen in four stages as Tenebreuse, Hair, Knife and Celestial Bridegroom. Erling Wold's avant-garde one-act opera *A Little Girl Dreams of Taking Her Veil,* libretto by Carla Harrymore based on Max Ernst's *Rêve d'une petite fille qui voulut entrer au Carmel,* was premiered by Intersection for the Arts in San Francisco on January 19, 1995. Jo Vincent Parks was Marceline-Marie, Mary Forcade was Spontanette and Chris Brophy was Narrator. The music is tonal and highly rhythmic.

LITTLE MARY SUNSHINE   *1959 parody operetta by Besoyan*

Little Mary Sunshine, so named because she has such a sunny disposition, is the adopted daughter of Chief Brown Bear and lives in the Colorado mountains where she runs an inn. Captain Jim Warrington arrives with a band of singing forest rangers looking for renegade Indian Yellow Feather and they are soon smitten. The inn is also hosting opera singer Ernestine Von Lieberdich and a group rich young women looking for men to dazzle. Unfortunately Mary has missed a mortage payment and General Fairfax is about to evict her. Rick Besoyan's *Little Mary Sunshine,* libretto by the composer, premiered off Broadway at the Orpheum on November 18, 1959. Eileen Brennan starred as Mary with strong support from William Graham as Captain Jim, Elizabeth Parrish as opera singer Ernestine, John McMartin as Corporal Billy, Elmarie Wendel as Nancy Twinkle and Ray James as Yellow Feather. Besoyan staged the production and Glenn Osser conducted. This witty and melodious parody of Victor Herbert and Rudolf Friml operettas, especially ROSE MARIE, ran for 1,143 performance and has become a favorite of regional theaters.

1949 Original Cast. Eileen Brennan stars as Mary in this original cast recording of the operetta with support from William Graham, John McMartin and Elmarie Wendel. Glenn Osser conducts Capitol LP/CD. **1962 London cast.** Patricia Routledge stars as Mary in this original London cast recording with support from Bernard Cribbins, Joyce Blair, Terence Cooper and Gita Denise. Philip Martel conducts. Pye LP/AEI CD.

A LITTLE NIGHT MUSIC   *1973 operetta-style musical by Sondheim*

Sweden at the turn of the century. Lawyer Fredrik and his young bride Anne spend the weekend at Madame Armfeldt's country estate with his son Henrik who is in love with Anne. Also present are his former mistress Desirée, her current lover Count Carl-Magnus and the Count's desperate wife Charlotte. Stephen Sondheim's operetta-style musical *A Little Night Music* has entered the opera house repertory and was staged by New York City Opera in 1990 and Houston Grand Opera in 1999. The libretto by Hugh Wheeler (lyrics by the composer) is based on Ingmar Bergman's 1955 film *Smiles of a Summer Night.* The musical opened on Broadway at the Shubert Theater on February 25, 1973, with Glynnis Johns as Desirée (she thus became the first person to sing "Send in the Clowns"), Len Cariou as Fredrik, Victoria Mallory as wife Anne, Mark Lambert as son Henrik, Hermione Gingold as Madame Armfeldt, Laurence Guittard as Count Carl-Magnus and Patricia Elliot as his wife Charlotte. Harold Prince staged the production and Harold Hastings conducted. Frederica von Stade and Thomas Allen starred in a production by Houston Grand Opera in 1999.

1973 Original Broadway cast. Glynnis Johns is Desirée opposite Len Cariou as Fredrik in the original Broadcast album of the musical. Hermione Gingold is Madame Armfeldt, Victoria Mallory is Anne, Mark Lambert is Henrik, Laurence Guittard is Carl-Magnus and Patricia Elliot is Charlotte. Harold Hastings conducts. Columbia LP/CD. **1975 Original London cast.** Jean Simmons is Desirée opposite Joss Ackland as Fredrik in the original London cast recording. Hermione Gingold is Madame Armfeldt, Veronica Pages is Anne, Maria Aitken is Charlotte and Terry Mitchell is Henrik. RCA LP/CD. **1977 New World film.** Elizabeth Taylor plays Desirée in this film of the musical directed by Harold Prince for New World Pictures. Len Cariou is Fredrik, Hermione Gingold is Madame Armfeldt, Diana Rigg is Charlotte, Lesley-Ann Down is Anne and Laurence Guittard is Carl-Magnus. On VHS. **1989 John Owen Edwards recording.** John Owen Edwards conducts this British studio recording featuring Elisabeth Welch, Maria Friedman, Sian Phillips, Eric Flynn, Janis Kelly, Jason Howard and Bonaventura Bottone. Jay Records CD. **1990 New York City**

Opera. Regina Resnik is Madame Armfeldt in this New York City Opera production by Scott Ellis. Sally Ann Howes is Desirée, George Lee Andrews is Fredrik, Beverly Lambert is Anne, Michael Maguire is the Count, Maureen Moore is Charlotte, Kevin Anderson is Henrik and Susanne Marsee is Mrs. Segstrom. Paul Gemignani conducts the New York City Opera and Chorus. Kirk Browning directed the PBS telecast on July 11, 1990. Video at MTR. **1996 London revival cast.** Judi Dench is Desiree opposite Laurence Guittard as Fredrik in this cast recording of a London revival production. Sian Phillips is Madame Armfeldt, Joanne Riding is Anne, Brendan O'Head is Henrik, Lambert Wilson is Carl-Magnus and Patricia Hog is Charlotte. Jo Stewart conducts. Tring Records CD.

A LITTLE NIGHTMARE MUSIC   *1982 satirical opera by Schickele*

Salieri is enjoying a Mozart concert and drinking wine served by P.D.Q. Bach. He is interrupted by vain playwright Schlafer who says that Salieri is jealous of Mozart. Salieri is so annoyed he puts poison in Schlafer's wine but Bach stupidly gives Mozart the wine and Mozart dies. Peter Schickele's *A Little Nightmare Music* satirizes Peter Shaffer's play *Amadeus* and legends about Salieri using as basic score Mozart's *Eine Klein Nachtmusik.* Schickele, as his alter-ego P. D. Q. Bach, premiered this one-act parody at Carnegie Hall on December 27, 1982. It was staged by Madison Opera in 1988.

1983 Peter Schickele. *A Little Nightmare Music* is performed by Peter Schickele and his associates on the albums *P.D.Q. Bach: A Little Nightmare Music* (Vanguard LP) and *Portrait of P.D.Q. Bach* (Vanguard CD).

THE LITTLE PRINCE   *2003 opera by Portman*

A pilot crashes in the desert and meets a boy prince from another planet. He is desperate to get back to his small planet to take care of the rose he loves and is disturbed to find so many roses like it on earth. A gentle fox helps him understand. Rachel Portman's opera *The Little Prince,* libretto by Nicolas Wright based on the 1943 French fable *Le Petit Prince* by Antoine de Saint-Exupéry, was premiered by Houston Grand Opera on May 31, 2003, at the Cullen Theater. Eleven-year-old boy soprano Nathaniel Irvin sang the role of the Little Prince, baritone Teddy Tahu Rhodes was the Pilot who narrates the story, Marie Lenormand was the Fox, Jon Kobet was the Snake and the Vain Man, Scott Succly was the Lamplighter and Kirstin Rieresen was the Prince's beloved Rose. Francesca Zambello staged the opera, Maria Bjørnson designed the imaginative sets and costumes, Karen Reeves directed the children's chorus, and Patrick Summers conducted the Houston Grand Opera Orchestra. *The Little Prince* was reprised by Skylight Opera Theater in 2004.

THE LITTLE THIEVES OF BETHLEHEM   *1997 Christmas opera by Stuart*

The Peacekeeper tells the story of a young brother and sister living in Bethlehem 2000 years ago. They steal food and a cloth from an Innkeeper and his Wife and hide out in the inn stable. When they meet Joseph and Mary, they give the cloth to Mary to cover the baby Jesus; it turns to gold. Paul Stuart's one-act Christmas chamber opera *The Little Thieves of Bethlehem,* libretto by Sally M. Gall, was premiered by Opera Theater of Rochester at the Third Presbyterian Church in Rochester on December 7, 1997. Kelly Hamilton was Mary, Bryan Jackson was Joseph, Elana Gizzi was the Brother, Susanna Adams was the Sister, Mark Schmidt was the Innkeeper, Riker Connaughton was his Wife, Vitali Rosynko, Ivan Griffin and Paul Busselberg were the Three Kings and Fred Nuernberg was the Peacekeeper narrator. Barbara Williams designed the costumes, the composer directed the production, Raffaele Ponti conducted the Opera Theater of Rochester Chorus and Orchestra and Karla Krogstad led the Eastman Bach Children's Chorus. The music is tonal and lyrical and incorporates traditional carols.

1997 Rochester Opera Theater. The opera was recorded soon after the premiere with essentially the same cast. Kelly Hamilton is Mary, Bryan Jackson is Joseph, Elana Gizzi is the Brother and Therese Murray is the Sister and Fred Nuernberg is the Narrator. Raffaele Ponti conducts the Opera Theater of Rochester Chorus and Orchestra and Karla Krogstad directs the Eastman Bach Children's Chorus. Dynamic CD.

LITTLE WOMEN (1)   *American music theater works based on Alcott novel*

Sisters Jo, Meg, Amy and Beth March learn about life, love and each other in Civil War–era New England and are watched over by their patient mother Marmee while their father is away at the war. Louisa May Alcott's famous 1969 novel *Little Women* has provided the basis for five movies and four America music theater works. The UK musical *A Girl Called Jo* (1955) is also based on it.

1934 Eleanor Everest Freer. Eleanor Freer's two-act opera *Little Women*, libretto by the composer, was premiered at the Musician's Club of Women in Chicago on April 2, 1934. **1958 Richard Adler.** Met soprano Risë Stevens sang the role of the mother Marmee in Richard Adler's hour-long *Little Women*, libretto by Wilson Lehr, which premiered on CBS television on October l6, 1958. Jeannie Carson was Jo, Florence Henderson was Meg, Zina Bethune was Amy, Margaret O'Brien was Beth, Roland Winters was Mr. Lawrence , Bill Hayes was John Brooks and Joel Grey was Laurie. Albert Selden produced, John Butler arranged the choreography, Hal Hasting conducted the orchestra and William Corrigan directed the telecast. **1964 William Dyer.** William Dyer's musical *Jo*, libretto by Don Parks and the composer, opened at the Orpheum Theatre in New York n February 12, 1964. Karen Wolfe was Jo, Susan Browning was Meg, Judith McCauley was Beth, April Shawhan was Amy, Joy Hodges was Marmee, Myron Odegaard, Don Stewart was Laurie. John Bishop directed Jane Douglass White conducted the orchestra.

LITTLE WOMEN (2)   *1998 opera by Adamo*

Mark Adamo's two-act opera *Little Women*, libretto by the composer, is the most successful musical adaptation of Louisa May Alcott's novel. It was commissioned by Houston Grand Opera for its Opera Studio which premiered it on March 13, 1998. Adamo focuses on Jo's relationship with her sisters and her distress as they marry and their lives begin to change. By the end of the opera she has learned to accept what has to be. Stephanie Novacek sang Jo, Joyce DiDonato was Meg, Laura A. Coker was Beth, Jennifer Aymer was Amy, Daniel Belcher was John Brooke, Chad Shelton was Laurie, Tiffany Jackson was Mother, Christopher Scott Feigum was Father, Katherine Ciesinski was Aunt Cecilia and Edward Scott Hendrick was German professor Friedrich

Bhaer. Constantinos Kritikos designed the costumes and sets, Peter Webster staged the production and Christopher Lark conducted the orchestra. The opera was so well received it revived at the main Houston opera theater in March 2000 with a few cast changes and recorded for radio, video and CD; Stacey Tappan took over as Beth, Margaret Lloyd as Amy, James Maddalena as Father, Kathryn Cowdrick as Mother and Chen-Ye Yuan as the German professor with Patrick Summers conducting. It was broadcast on National Public Radio on October 21, 2000. It was reprised by Central City Opera in July 2000 in a production by Joshua Major with Stacey Rishoi as Jo, Jane Dutton as Meg, Courtenay Budd as Amy and Tina Milborne as Beth. Belcher and Shelton repeated their roles from Houston. It was reprised by New York City Opera in 2003.

2000 Houston Grand Opera. The Houston Grand Opera production of March 2000 starring Stephanie Novacek as Jo was recorded and videotaped. Stacey Tappan is Meg, Margaret Lloyd is Amy, Daniel Belcher is John Brooke, Chad Shelton is Laurie, Kathryn Cowdrick is Mother, James Maddalena is Father, Katherine Ciesinski is Aunt Cecilia Chen-Ye Yuan is Prof. Bhaer. Patrick Summers conducts and Brian Large directed the PBS telecast on August 29, 2001. Ondine CD.

LIZZIE BORDEN   *1965 opera by Beeson*

Lizzie Borden can barely repress her frustration with her father and stepmother who are unwilling to let her live her own life. When they are murdered with an axe, she is accused of the crime. An understanding jury acquits her. Jack Beeson's powerful opera *Lizzie Borden*, subtitled *A Family Portrait in Three Acts,* libretto by Kenward Elmslie and scenario by Richard Plant based on records

Jack Beeson's opera *Lizzie Borden,* based on real events, was premiered and recorded in 1965 by New York City Opera.

of a real trial in Fall River, Massachusetts, in 1892, was premiered by New York City Opera on March 25, 1965. Brenda Lewis played Lizzie, Ellen Faull was her stepmother Abigail Borden, Herbert Beattie was her father Andrew Borden, Ann Elgar was her sister Margaret Borden, Richard Krause was the Reverend Harrington and Richard Fredricks was Captain Jason MacFarlane. Peter Wexler designed the sets, Patton Campbell designed the costumes, Nikos Psacharopoulos staged the opera and Anton Coppola conducted the New York City Opera orchestra and chorus. *Lizzie Borden* is Beeson's most popular opera and has been staged many times, including a recent revival at New York City Opera with Phyllis Pancella as Lizzie and Lauren Flanigan as a powerful stepmother.

1966 New York City Opera. Brenda Lewis stars as Lizzie Borden in this recording by the original cast of the New York City Opera production. Herbert Beattie is Andrew Borden, Ellen Faull is Abigail, Ann Elgar is Margaret, Richard Krause is Rev. Harrington and Richard Fredricks is Capt. Jason MacFarlane. Anton Coppola conducts the New York City Opera orchestra and chorus. Desto 3-LP box/CRI 2-CD box. **1967 NET Opera Theater.** Brenda Lewis and the rest of the New York City Opera cast are featured in an NET Opera Theater television production directed by James Perrin. Herbert Beattie is Andrew, Ellen Faull is Abigail, Ann Elgar is Margaret, Richard Krause is Rev. Harrington and Richard Fredricks is Capt. MacFarlane. Anton Coppola conducts the Cambridge Festival Orchestra. Kirk Browning directed the 115-minute telecast on January 22, 1967. Video at MTR.

LLOYD, MARGARET *American soprano (1972–)*

Margaret Lloyd, a native of Ames, Iowa, appears to be fond of American opera as she has sung in a number of different productions all around the USA. She created three roles in the televised trilogy CENTRAL PARK at Glimmerglass Opera in 1999; she was Jessica in Deborah Drattell's *The Festival of Regrets,* the Daughter in Michael Torke's *Strawberry Fields* and the Woman with Sun Reflectors in Robert Beaser's *Strawberry Fields.* She created the role of Lightfoot McClendon in Carlisle Floyd's COLD SASSY TREE at Houston Grand Opera in 2000 and reprised the role with Austin Lyric Opera in 2001, Opera Carolina in 2003 and Utah Opera in 2003. She created the title role of Sive in a workshop premiere of Richard Wargo's *Sive* with Skylight Opera in 2001 and she sang Juliet in a 1999 workshop presentation of Lee Hoiby's "work in progress" opera *Romeo and Juliet.* She played Amy in Mark Adamo's LITTLE WOMEN in Houston Grand Opera's revival of the opera in March 2000 and she sang in Cunegonde in productions of Leonard Bernstein's CANDIDE by Central City Opera in 2000 and Portland Opera in 2002. She played Margot in Utah Festival Opera's production of Sigmund Romberg's THE DESERT SONG in 2002. Lloyd began to sing in American opera at Glimmerglass, first as Margaret Borden in Jack Beeson's LIZZIE BORDEN in 1996 and then as Curley's Wife in Carlisle Floyd's OF MICE AND MEN in 1997. She was Nadia in Wargo's A CHEKHOV TRILOGY at Skylight Opera in 1998.

THE LOAFER AND THE LOAF *1954 opera by Clarke*

The Loafer steals a loaf of bread from the Baker Boy and is caught by the Prosperous Citizen. The Poet's Wife defends the Loafer who could be a hungry Poet like her husband. She takes the loaf, the Citizen grabs it back and the Baker Boy accuses the Citizen of being the thief. An ethical argument begins. Henry Clarke's one-act opera *The Loafer and the Loaf,* libretto by the composer based on a play by Evelyn Sharp, premiered at Indian Hill Camp in Stockbridge Massachusetts, in July 1954.

LOCKWOOD, NORMAND *American composer (1906–2002)*

Normand Lockwood composed five operas but the best-known is the first, a symbolic tale about a scarecrow that becomes a man. *The Scarecrow,* based on Percy MacKaye's 1908 theatrical adaptation of Nathaniel Hawthorne's story, premiered at Columbia University on May 19, 1945. Lockwood's other four operas were presented at the University of Denver, where he was composer-in-residence from 1961 to 1975. They are *Early Dawn* (1961), *The Wizards of Balizar* (1962), *The Hanging Judge* (1964) and *Requiem for a Rich Young Man* (1964). Lockwood, born in New York to a musical family, studied in Europe with Nadia Boulanger in Paris and Ottorino Respighi in Rome before returning to America to teach and compose. In addition to his operas, he composed a large number of oratorios. cantatas and orchestral works. His music is considered complex but accessible.

LOESSER, FRANK *American composer/librettist (1910–1969)*

Frank Loesser is best known as the composer of one of America's great musicals, *Guys and Dolls,* but he also composed a "quasi-opera" that straddles genres. THE MOST HAPPY FELLA, which requires an operatic baritone for its leading role, premiered in 1956 with Metropolitan Opera baritone Robert Weede in the part. It has begun to enter the opera house repertory and was staged at New York City Opera in 1991 with Giorgio Tozzi as the star. Loesser, who was self-taught, was one of America's greatest songsmiths creating memorable songs for both movies and shows. He first made his name in Hollywood as a lyricist writing the words for classics like "The Boys in the Back Room" (music by Frederick Hollander) and "Two Sleepy People" (music by Hoagy Carmichael). He began to write the music as well with the World War II hit "Praise the Lord and Pass the Ammunition" and found success with songs like "Spring Will be a Little Late this Year" and "Baby, It's Cold Outside." His first Broadway show was *Where's Charley?* (1948) followed by *Guys and Dolls* (1950), *The Most Happy Fella* (1956), *Greenwillow* (1960), and the Pulitzer Prize-winning *How to Succeed in Business Without Really Trying* (1961).

LOEWE, FREDERICK *American composer (1901—1988)*

Frederick Loewe and his librettist/lyricist partner Alan Jay Lerner created four major Broadway musicals which incorporate elements of European operetta and have begun to enter the light opera repertory: BRIGADOON (1947), *Paint Your Wagon* (1951), MY FAIR LADY (1956) and CAMELOT (1960). *My Fair Lady* has been especially popular with opera singers from Blanche Thebom to Kiri Te Kanawa. Loewe was born in Berlin to Austrian parents and studied composition there before emigrating to America in 1924. He began to write for Broadway in the 1930s and teamed up with Lerner in the early 1940s, starting with the musicals *What's Up?* (1943) and *The Day Before Spring* (1945). *Brigadoon* was their first success and *My Fair Lady* was by far the biggest. Most were turned into films and their film musical *Gigi* (1958) was transmuted into a stage show.

LONDON, GEORGE *American bass-baritone (1920–1985)*

George London sang the role of Abdul in the English-language premiere of Gian Carlo's comic opera THE LAST SAVAGE at the Metropolitan Opera in 1964. He sings the Bishop opposite Lili Chookasian on the 1965 recording of Gian Carlo Menotti's dramatic cantata THE DEATH OF THE BISHOP OF BRINDISI and the aria

"Standin' in the Need of Prayer" from Louis Gruenberg's THE EMPEROR JONES on a 1955 recording. He can be seen performing songs from Victor Herbert's operettas MAYTIME and NAUGHTY MARIETTA and Jerome Kern's SHOW BOAT on a 1953 *Voice of Firestone* TV program. London, born in Montreal, Canada,, made his debut at the Hollywood Bowl in 1941 in *La Traviata* but really became known after he began to sing in Europe in 1949. He made his debut at the Met in 1951.

LONELY HOUSE   *Tenor aria: Street Scene (1947). Words: Langston Hughes. Music: Kurt Weill.*

Student Sam Kaplan lives in a crowded New York tenement building but complains he and the house are alone, though surrounded by people. Unhook the stars, he says, take them down, this is a lonely town. "Lonely House" is a melancholy tenor aria that has been kidnapped by sopranos. The aria, with music by Kurt Weill and lyrics by Langston Hughes, was introduced on stage in STREET SCENE in 1947 by Brian Sullivan who performs it on the original cast recording. Jerry Hadley sings it on the Scottish Opera recording, Bonaventura Bottone on the English National Opera recording and Hal Watters in the off-Broadway revue *Berlin to Broadway with Kurt Weill*. Most of the individual recordings, however, are by sopranos including Teresa Stratas, Lotte Lenya, Dawn Upshaw, Betty Carter, Abbey Lincoln, Helen Schneider, Patricia O'Callahan and Jill Gomez. June Christie even recorded a jazz version.

Leslie Caron and Louis Jourdan in composer Frederick Loewe's movie operetta *Gigi*.

THE LONG CHRISTMAS DINNER   *1961 opera by Hindemith*

Members of the Bayard family are born, marry and die over a ninety-year period as a long Christmas dinner unfolds and generation after generation gets together for an annual gathering. We learn particularly about eleven members of the family. Paul Hindemith's *The Long Christmas Dinner*, libretto by Thornton Wilder based on his play, premiered in a German version as *Das lange Weihnachtsmahl* at the National Theater in Mannheim on December 17, 1961, with Hindemith conducting. Thomas Tipton was Roderick Bayard, Jean Cox was Charles, William Blankenship was Roderick II and Frederick Dalberg was Brandon. The original English version was premiered at the Juilliard School in New York on March 13, 1963. The opera was telecast in Germany in 1985 and in America in 1986.

1986 San Francisco Opera Center. Robert Baustian conducts a performance of the opera in English at the San Francisco Opera Center. The singers are David de Haan, Mark Delavan, Kathryn Cowdrick, Susan Patterson, Philip Skinner, Deborah Voigt, Douglas Wunsch and Christiane Young. 50 minutes. Andrew Thompson VHS.

LONGEST AMERICAN OPERA

There are several candidates but Gabriel Von Waydtch's *The Heretics* is certainly the longest traditional American opera. It would run over eight and one-half hours if it was staged and its orchestral score consists of 2870 pages. Waydtch (1888–1969) was born in Hungary but wrote all fourteen of his operas in America while living in the South Bronx. They comprise the largest body of opera music created by a single composer in the 20th century. Robert Wilson also enjoys long music theater pieces. *The Life and Times of Joseph Stalin*, which he once described as an opera, ran thirteen hours when it was staged at the Brooklyn Academy of Music in 1973. His multi-composer quasi-opera THE CIVIL WARS would have run for twelve hours if it had been completed.

LONGFELLOW, HENRY W.   *American poet (1807–1882)*

Henry Wadsworth Longfellow was a best selling author in the 19th century and the most honored literary figure in America. His fame has faded but he left a legacy of poetry that still influences the way Americans perceive their past. A number of American and European operas have been based on his works though none are particularly well known. The American operas are listed below. Title of opera is same as literary work and librettos are by composer unless otherwise noted.

The Courtship of Miles Standish (1858). 1888 Thomas Surette as *Priscilla, or The Pilgrim's Proxy.* Concord, MA, March 6, 1888 (operetta). 1901 Francesco Fanciulli as *Priscilla, The Maid of Plymouth.* Norfolk, Virginia, November 1, 1901. 1910 Charles Carlson as *The Courtship of Miles Standish* (grand opera, unproduced) 1920 Henry Eames (Hartly Alexander) as *Priscilla and John Alden.* Chicago, 1942. 1943 Timothy Spelman. **Evangeline, A Tale of Acadie (1847).** 1874 Edward E. Rice (J. Goodwin). New York, July 27, 1874. 1932 Otto Luening. American Opera Co., New York, 1932. 1992 Donald Sosin. **The Masque of Pandora (1875).** 1928 Eleanor Freer (published 1930). **The Song of Hiawatha (1855).** 1900 Henry Finck as *Hiawatha.* 1988 Davis Ellis (Eugene Jackson) as *Song of Hiawatha.* Mobile, AL, 1988. **The Spanish Student (1843).** 1928 Eleanor Freer as *Preciosa or The Spanish Student.*

LOOMIS, CLARENCE   *American composer(1889–1965)*

Clarence Loomis, a native of Sioux Falls, South Dakota, studied music at the American Conservatory in Chicago and in Vienna before composing his operas. *A Night in Avignon,* libretto by Cole Young Rice about the Italian poet Petrarch, was his first opera but it was not performed until 1932 in Indianapolis. *Yolanda of Cyprus,* libretto again by Rice, was his most popular opera and was awarded the Bispham Medal in 1926; it was first staged by the American Opera Company in London, Ontario, Canada in 1927 and reprised in New York City. His folk opera *Susanna, Don't You Cry,* libretto by E. Ferguson based on the song by Stephen Foster, was staged in New York in 1931. His Poe adaptation, THE FALL OF THE HOUSE OF USHER, libretto by the composer, was produced in Indianapolis in 1941. The one-act *Revival* was premiered on radio by KWFB in Los Angeles on April 3, 1942. Loomis completed other operas

Virgil Thomson's literary opera *Lord Byron* was recorded at the Monadnock Festival in 1991.

but they were never performed. He said that the music in opera should support rather than dominate the text and that was why he preferred to compose in tonal style.

LOPEZ-COBOS, JESUS   *Spanish conductor (1940–)*

Spanish conductor Jesus Lopez-Cobos, who leads the Philharmonia Orchestra and Ambrosian Opera Chorus in the 1979 film and video of Gian Carlo Menotti's *Amahl and the Night Visitors,* began his career at La Fenice in Venice in 1969. He was music director of the Deutsche Oper for ten years and has conducted at the Metropolitan Opera, the Paris Opera and Covent Garden.

LORD BYRON   *1972 opera by Thomson*

Westminster Abby in London in 1824. Friends and enemies of Lord Byron debate whether he should be buried in Poets' Corner. His scandalous sexual behavior is discussed, especially his relationship with wife Annabella, half-sister Augusta Leigh and mistress Countess Teresa Guiccioli. His friends decide to burn the memoirs he sent to Thomas Moore while the Westminster dean refuses to allow his burial in the Abbey. Virgil Thomson's three-act opera *Lord Byron,* libretto by Jack Larson, premiered at the Juilliard American Opera Center in New York on April 20, 1972. Grayston Hirst was Lord Byron, Carolyn Val-Schmidt was Lady Augusta Leigh, Lynne Wickenden was Lady Byron, Hari Katz was Countess Teresa Guiccioli, Barbara Hendricks was Lady Charlotte, Barrie Smith was Lady Melbourne, Lenus Carlson was Thomas Moore, Walter Hook was John Hobhouse, Frederick Schoepflin was John Murray, Frederick Burchinal was Count Gamba, David Wilder was John Ireland, Jonathan Rigs was Thomas Gray, Neil Shicoff was James Thomson, Donald Slonim was Edmund Spenser, Peter Elkus was John Milton, Michael Li-Paz was Samuel Johnson, John Seabury was Percy Shelley, Donald Barnum and Jerome Mann were English Nobleman, Jean Fuersten was Lady Jane and Ann Farr was the Young Lady. David Mitchell designed the sets, Alvin Ailey arranged the choreography (the second scene of the third act was originally a ballet), John Houseman directed and Gerhard Samuel conducted. The music is tonal and lyrical and includes quotations from popular tunes. *Lord Byron* has been revived a number of times, including a production at the Monadnock Music Festival in New Hampshire in 1991.

1986 Virgil Thomson at 90. Librettist Jack Larson talks about working on the opera with Thomson in the documentary *Virgil Thomson at 90.* John Huszar's film was shown on PBS in 1986. FilmAmerica VHS. **1991 Monadnock Festival.** Matthew Lord is Lord Byron in a recording of the opera made during performances at the Monadnock Festival in New Hampshire in 1991. Jeanne Ommerle is Augusta, D'Anna Fortunato is Lady Byron, Adrienne Csengery is Countess Guiccioli, Richard Zeller is Thomas Moore, Richard Johnson is John Hobhouse, Gregory Mercer is John Murray, Thomas Woodman is John Ireland, Louisa Jonason is Lady Melbourne, Debra Vanderlinde is Lady Charlotte and Lady Caroline, Marion Dry is Lady Jane, Martin Kelley is Thomas Gray, Ted Whalen is James Thomson, David Murray is Edmund Spenser, Jorg Westerkemp is John Dryden, John Holyoke is John Milton and Dave Stoneman is Samuel Johnson. James Bolle conducts the Monadnock Festival Orchestra and chorus. The opera was recorded on August 31 and September 2, 1991, at the Pine Hill Waldorf Auditorium in Wilton, New Hampshire. Koch Classics CD box. **1994 Martyn Hill.** Martyn Hill sings five tenor arias from *Lord Byron* with backing from the Budapest Symphony Orchestra conducted by James Bolle. They're on the album *Orchestral Works by Virgil Thomson.* Albany CD.

LORD BYRON'S LOVE LETTER   *1955 opera by Banfield*

An elderly woman in New Orleans has a love letter from Lord Byron which she allows visitors to see for payment. Her spinster granddaughter shows the letter to visitors during Mardi Gras and reads from her grandmother's diary. The old woman had had an affair with Byron who is the grandfather of the spinster. Raffaelo de Banfield's one-act opera *Lord Byron's Love Letter*, libretto by Tennessee Williams, premiered at Tulane University in New Orleans on January 17, 1955. Patricia Neway was the Old Woman, Gertrude Ribla was the Spinster and Paul Stuart was the Husband. The opera was reprised by Chicago Lyric Opera the same year.

1955 Nicola Rescigno recording. Astrid Varnay sings the role of the Old Woman with Gertrude Ribla as the Spinster in this recording Rome of the opera made in Rome, Italy. Nicoletta Carruba is the visiting Matron and Mario Carlin is the Husband. Nicola Rescigno conducts the Academy Symphony Orchestra of Rome. RCA Victor LP. **1957 Canadian Television.** Mary Simmons sings the Old Woman with Sylvia Grant as her Granddaughter, Patricia Rideout as the Matron, André Turp as the Husband, Michel Bonhomme as the Old Woman when young, and Fernande Chiocchio as the Aunt. Ettore Mazzoleni conducts the CBCF Orchestra, Irving Guttman staged the 48-minute production and Jean-Claude Rinfret designed the sets. Telecast on CFBC on January 31, 1957. On VHS. **1991 Gianfranco Masini recording.** Sopranos Elena Zilio and Sylvie Valayre and contralto Gabriella Brancaccio are the singers on this live recording of the opera made in Italy. Gianfranco Masini conducts the orchestra. Ermitage CD.

THE LOSERS   *1971 opera by Farberman*

Buzz, who leads a violent California motorbike gang called The Losers, is loved by young and innocent Donna. The gang rapes Donna in a small-town bar while he is away despite attempts by the hippie Ken to stop them. After a fight, Buzz and Ken are killed. Harold Farberman's percussive avant-garde opera *The Losers*, libretto by Barbara Fried, was commissioned by Juilliard American Opera Theatre which premiered it on March 26, 1971.

LOSS OF EDEN   *2002 opera by Franklin*

In the year 1932 Bruno Hauptmann is accused of kidnapping and murdering the infant son of aviation hero Charles Lindbergh and his wife Anne Morrow. Lindbergh had become famous by flying his plane *The Spirit of St. Louis* solo from New York to Paris in 1927. The troubled marriages of the Lindberghs and the Hauptmanns are contrasted. Cary John Franklin's opera *Loss of Eden*, libretto by Michael Patrick Albano based on real events, was premiered by Opera Theatre of Saint Louis in June 2002. Keith Phares was Lindbergh, Kellie J. Van Horn was his wife Anne, Mark Duffin was Hauptmann and Ann Panagulias was his wife Anna. Karen Teneyck designed the sets, librettist Albano staged the opera and Philippe Brunelle conducted the Opera Theatre of Saint Louis Orchestra and Chorus.

LOST IN THE STARS   *1949 "musical tragedy" by Weill*

A black minister in 1949 South Africa discovers that his son has been involved in the killing of a white liberal and will be executed for the crime. Kurt Weill's *Lost in the Stars*, libretto by Maxwell Anderson based on Alan Paton's novel *Cry the Beloved Country*, is not quite an opera but has been taken up by opera companies and performed by opera singers. It opened at the Music Box Theater in New York on October 30, 1949, with the involvement of two people from the original *Porgy and Bess*, baritone Todd Duncan, who had created Porgy, and Rouben Mamoulian, who had staged it. Duncan played the minister Stephen Kumalo, Leslie Banks was James Jarvis, Julian Mayfield was Absalom, Inez Matthews was his mistress Irina, Warren Coleman was John Kumalo, Herbert Coleman was Alex, Frank Roane was the Leader, Sheila Guyse was Linda and Robert McFerrin had a role as a Villager. George Jenkins designed the sets, Mamoulian directed and Maurice Levine conducted. The song "Lost in the Stars" became quite popular. The musical was revived at New York City Opera in 1958 with Lawrence Winters as Stephen Kumalo and Shirley Verrett as Irina and on Broadway in 1972 with Brock Peters as Kumalo.

1949 Original Broadway cast. Todd Duncan sings Stephen Kumalo on this original cast recording. Inez Matthews is Irina, Frank Roane is the Leader, Julian Mayfield is Absalom, Herbert Coleman is Alex and Sheila Guyse is Linda. Maurice Levine conducts the Broadway orchestra. Decca LP/MCA CD. **1957 Lotte Lenya.** Lotte Lenya recorded "Trouble Man," "Stay Well" and "Lost in the Stars" from *Lost in the Stars* in New York in 1957. Maurice Levine conducts orchestra and chorus on the album *Lotte Lenya/Kurt Weill/American Theater Songs.* CBS CD. **1961 Earl Wrightson.** Baritone Earl Wrightson sings "Lost in the Stars" with orchestra conducted by Norman Paris on the album *An Enchanted Evening on Broadway with Earl Wrightson.* Columbia LP. **1968 Mississippi stage cast.** Eugene Holmes is Stephen Kumalo in a recording of a 1968 production of *Lost in the Stars* in Mississippi with a cast headed by Gladys Scott and Robert Honeysucker. World audiocassette. **1972 Berlin to Broadway with Kurt Weill.** The songs "Trouble Man," "Train to Johannesburg," "Cry the Beloved Country" and "Lost in the Stars" are featured in the off-Broadway revue *Berlin to Broadway with Kurt Weill, A Musical Voyage.* Paramount LP. **1974 American Film Theater.** Brock Peters stars as Stephen Kumalo in a film of the musical directed by Daniel Mann for the American Film Theatre. Melba Moore is Irina, Raymond St. Jacques is John Kumalo, Clifton Davis is Absalom Kumalo, Paul Rogers is James Jarvis, Pauline Myers is Grace, Paula Kelly is Rose and H. B. Barnum III is Alex. Kino DVD. **1992 New York Chorale.** Arthur Woodley is Stephan Kumalo in this recording with the New York Concert Chorale. Cynthia Clarey is Irina, George Hopkins is Leader, Reginald Pindell is Absalom, Carol Woods is Linda, Jamal Howard is Alex and Richard Vogt is the Judge. Julius Rudel conducts St. Luke's Orchestra. Music Masters CD. **1992 Ute Lemper.** German cabaret performed Ute Lemper sings "Trouble Man" on *Uta Lemper Sings Kurt Weill Live at Les Bouffes du Nord, Paris.* Jeff Cohen plays piano. London/Decca VHS. **1993 Samuel Ramey.** Samuel Ramey sings "Lost in the Stars" with the London Studio Symphony Orchestra conducted by Ettore Stratta on the album *Samuel Ramey on Broadway.* Teldec CD. **1993 Dawn Upshaw.** Dawn Upshaw sings "Stay Well" on her album *I Wish It So* accompanied by a studio orchestra led by Eric Stern. Elektra Nonesuch CD. **2000 Urs Affolter.** Urs Affolter sings "Lost in the Stars" and "Stay Well" on the album *Stay Well: Urs Affolter Sings Kurt Weill* accompanied by Uli Kofler. Antes CD.

LOUISIANA   *American state (1812–)*

The first opera was staged in New Orleans in 1796 and there were rival opera houses by the 1820s. Early operas were sung in French and Louisiana's first opera composer was a French speaker, African American Creole Edmond Dédé, who moved to Paris in 1857 where he had success writing light operas. The earliest American comic opera premiered in Louisiana was probably *The Khedive*, staged at the Opera House in New Orleans in 1890 and taken to Broadway in 1891 by Fred Niblo. The major opera companies are New Orleans Opera, founded in 1943, and Shreveport Opera, founded in 1949; both stage American operas and operettas and premiere new works. The usual sites for premieres, however, are universities like Tulane and Louisiana State.

A large number of notable operas and operettas are set in Louisiana including three with stories by Tennessee Williams: Raffaelo de Banfield's LORD BYRON'S LETTER (1955), Robert Convery's THE LADY OF LARKSPUR LOTION (1980) and André Previn's A STREETCAR NAMED DESIRE (1998). Elie Siegmeister's NIGHT OF THE MOONSPELL (1976) is Shakespeare's *A Midsummer Night's Dream* transposed to a Louisiana bayou, Amy M. Beach's CABILDO (1932) is set in the old New Orleans governors palace, Carlisle Floyd's WILLIE STARK (1981) is based on the life of Louisiana Governor Huey Long, Michael John LaChiusa's MARIE CHRISTINE (1999) transposes the Medea story to New Orleans, Jake Heggie's DEAD MAN WALKING (2000) is the story of a Louisiana nun and a condemned murderer and Duke Ellington's *Pousse-Café* (1966) shifts the story of the film *The Blue Angel* to New Orleans. Victor Herbert's NAUGHTY MARIETTA (1910) and Sigmund Romberg's THE NEW MOON (1927) are tuneful love stories set in New Orleans while W. Franke Harling's DEEP RIVER (1926) and Norman Dello Joio's BLOOD MOON (1961) are tragic love stories set in the city. Harry Lawrence Freeman's VOODOO (1928) and W. Franke Harling's A LIGHT FROM ST. AGNES (1925) are jazz operas with Louisiana settings.

Louisiana-born opera people include bass-baritone Donnie Ray Albert (Baton Rouge), composer Edmond Dédé (New Orleans), composer Louis Gottschalk (New Orleans), librettist Lillian Hellman (New Orleans), bass-baritone Norman Treigle (New Orleans), mezzo-soprano Shirley Verrett (New Orleans), composer Kate Waring (Alexandria) and bass-baritone Jeffrey Wells (Baton Rouge).

Baton Rouge: Louisiana State University in Baton Rouge has been the site of several premieres: Noel Sokolov's *The Franklin's Tale* in 1961, Peter Paul Fuchs' *Serenade at Noon* in 1965, Eugene Zador's *The Magic Chair* in 1966 and Elie Siegmeister's THE PLOUGH AND THE STARS in 1969. Dinos Constantinides' monodrama *Fugue for Two Voices* was premiered in 1975. Baton Rouge Opera, founded in 1982, premiered William Grant Still's MINETTE FONTAINE in 1984.

Lake Charles: Kenneth Gaburo's *The Snow Queen* was premiered at McNeese State College in Lake Charles in 1952.

New Orleans: New Orleans Opera, founded in 1943 and presently the major opera company in Louisiana, premiered Carlisle Floyd's MARKHEIM on March 1, 1966. Most of its repertory is classical European but it has staged Rudolf Friml's THE VAGABOND KING, George Gershwin's PORGY AND BESS, Gian Carlo Menotti's AMELIA GOES TO THE BALL, THE MEDIUM and THE OLD MAID AND THE THIEF and Sigmund Romberg's THE STUDENT PRINCE. Its star performer for many years was New Orleans-born bass-baritone Norman Treigle. Soprano Mignon Dunn made her debut with the company. Tulane University premiered Raffaelo de Banfield's LORD BYRON'S LETTER, libretto by Tennessee Williams, in 1955; Cardon Burnham's *Aria da capo* in 1955, Burnham's *The Nitecap* in 1956 and Charles Hamm's *The Box* in 1961. Xavier University premiered Ulysses Kay's *The Juggler of Our Lady* in 1962, John Duncan's *Gideon and Eliza* in 1972 and David Ahlstrom's *america i love you* in 1981. It held the American premiere of Michael Colgrass's VIRGIL'S DREAM in *1972.*

Shreveport: Gian Carlo Menotti's THE OLD MAID AND THE THIEF was staged just before the official inauguration of Shreveport Opera in 1949 and the company has since presented a number of American works. It premiered Carl Zytowski's church opera *The Play of the Three Shepherds* on January 8, 1984. They has staged Carlisle Floyd's WILLIE STARK, Victor Herbert's NAUGHTY MARIETTA, Gian Carlo Menotti's AMAHL AND THE NIGHT VISITORS and THE MEDIUM, Henry Mollicone's THE FACE ON THE BARROOM FLOOR, Richard Rodger's THE KING AND I and Sigmund Romberg's THE DESERT SONG and THE STUDENT PRINCE. Soprano Patricia Wells made her debut with the company. The Shreveport Symphony Society has premiered two literary operas. Gordon Mack's *Nora,* based on Ibsen's *A Doll's House,* was presented in 1967. Elie Siegmeister's NIGHT OF THE MOONSPELL, based on Shakespeare's *A Midsummer Night's Dream,* was staged in 1976.

THE LOVE FOR THREE ORANGES   *1921 opera by Prokofiev*

The Prince of Clubs is dying because he can't laugh despite the efforts of everyone in the court to amuse him. However, when the witch Fata Morgana slips and falls on her behind, he roars with laugher. She tells him he has to take a voyage to find a suitable wife and that he must locate three oranges that contain princesses. One of them will be his true love. Sergei Prokofiev's *The Love for Three Oranges,* libretto by the composer based on a comic fable by Carlo Gozzi, was composed in New York City in 1919 and premiered by Chicago Grand Opera at the Chicago Auditorium on December 30, 1921. Prokofiev was living in New York when he was commissioned to write this opera by Cleofonte Campanini, director of Chicago Grand Opera. It was sung in French as *L'amour des trois oranges* at the insistence of Mary Garden who had become director of the opera company by the time of the premiere. José Mojica was the Prince, Nina Koshetz was Fata Morgana, Edouard Cotreuil was the King, Irene Pavlovska was Clarissa, William Beck was Leander, Octave Dua was Truffaldino, Desire Defrère was Pantaloon, Hector Dugranen was Celio, James Wolf was Farfarello, Jeanne Schneider was Smeraldina, Constantin Nicolay was Creonta, Lodovico Oliviero was the Master of Ceremonies, Jeanne Dusseau was Ninetta, Frances Paperte was Nicoletta, Philipe Falco was Violetta and Jerome Uhl was the Herald. Alexander Smallens conducted the Chicago Grand Opera Orchestra. This was the first Prokofiev opera to be staged and it was the most successful in his lifetime.

1956 Slovenia National Opera. Yanez Lipushchek sings the Prince with Vanda Guerlovich as Fata Morgana in this Slovenian National Opera recording. Latko Koroshetz is the King, Bogdana Stritar is Clarissa, Danilo Merlak is Leandor, Drago Chuden is Truffaldino, Vekoslav Yanko is Pantaloon and Zdravko Kovach is Chelio. Bogo Leskovich conducts the Slovenian National Opera Chorus and Orchestra. Philips/Epic 2-LP set. **1962 Moscow Radio.** Vladimir Markov is the Prince with Nina Poliakova as Fata Morgana in this Moscow Radio recording. Victor Ribinsky is the King, Lyutsia Rashkovetz is Clarissa, Boris Dobrin is Leandor, Yuri Yelnikov is Truffaldino, Ivan Budrin is Pantaloon and Gennady Troitsky is Chelio. Dzhemal Dalgat conducts the Moscow Radio Chorus and Orchestra. Melodiya/Angel 2-LP set. **1980 BBC Television.** Robin Leggate is the Prince in this BBC-TV production by Brian Large. Joseph Rouleau is the King of Clubs, Pauline Tinsley is Fata Morgana, Alexander Oliver is Truffaldino, Dennis Wicks is Celio, Tom McConnell is Leandro and Katharine Pring is Clarissa. Robin Stapleton conducts the London Philharmonic Orchestra and Ambrosian Opera Chorus. Sung in French with English subtitles. Video at MTR. **1982 Glyndebourne Festival.** Director Frank Corsaro's production presents the commedia dell'arte story as if it is being produced during the French

Revolution with Maurice Sendak's imaginative designs and puppets lending a sense of enchantment. Ryland Davies is the Prince who can't be amused, Willard White is the upright King, Nelly Morpurgo is the bewitching Fata Morgana, Richard Van Allan is magician Celio, Ugo Benelli is Truffaldino, Derek Hammond-Stroud is Farfarello, Colette Alliot-Lugaz is Princess Ninetta, Nuccio Condo is Clarissa and John Pringle is Leandro. Bernard Haitink conducts the London Philharmonic and Rodney Greenberg directed the video. Home Vision VHS/on DVD. **1989 Opéra de Lyon.** Louis Erlo's zestful Lyons Opera production by Jean-François Jung stars Gabriel Bacquier as the King of Clubs. Jean-Luc Viala is the Prince, Hélène Penaguin is Princess Clarissa, Catherine Dubosc is Ninetta, Consuelo Caroli is Linetta, Michèle Lagrange is Fata Morgana, Georges Gautier is Truffaldino, Didier Henry is Pantaloon/Farfarello, Jules Bastin is the Cook and Gregory Reinhart is Celio. Jacques Rapp designed the sets and Ferdinando Bruni created the costumes. Kent Nagano conducts the Opéra de Lyon Orchestra and Chorus. Polygram VHS/DVD and Virgin/EMI 2-CD set. **1998 Kirov Opera.** Yevgeny Akimov is the Prince with Larissa Shevchenko as Fata Morgana in this Kirov Opera recording based on performances at the Amsterdam Concertgebouw in 1997 and 1998. Mikhail Kit is the King, Larissa Diadkova is Princess Clarissa, Anna Netrebko is Ninetta, Lia Shevtsova is Nicoletta, Zlata Bulycheva is Linetta, Alexander Morozov is Leandor, Konstantin Pluzhnikov is Truffaldino, Vassily Gerello is Pantaloon and Vladimir Vaneev is Chelio. Valery Gergiev conducts the Kirov Chorus and Orchestra. Philips 2-CD set.

LOVE LIFE *1948 vaudeville by Weill*

Susan and Sam Cooper set up home in New England and experience changes in their marriage and values across seven historical eras to the present day. They do not age but their relationship greatly alters. Kurt Weill's ambitious "vaudeville" *Love Life*, libretto and lyrics by Alan Jay Lerner, premiered at the Shubert Theater in Boston on September 13, 1948, and opened in New York at the 46th Street Theater on October 7. Nanette Fabray was Susan, Ray Middleton was Sam, Cheryl Archer was Elizabeth, Johnny Stewart was Johnny, Jay Marshall was the Magician, Victor Clarke was the Interlocutor, Sylvia Stahlman was Miss Ideal and the dancers included Melissa Hayden and Arthur Parington. Cheryl Crawford produced, Baris Aronson designed the sets, Michael Kidd arranged the choreography, Elia Kazan directed and Joseph Littau conducted. A 1996 revival by Opera North in England helped restore *Love Life* to a prominent position in the Weill canon and it is now considered one of Weill's major music theater works.

1955 Alan Jay Lerner. Lyricist Alan Jay Lerner recorded seven songs from the musical in 1955 with Kaye Ballard and a vocal quartet. Billy Taylor plays piano and Herb Harris conducts. They songs are on the album *Lyrics by Lerner*. Heritage LP. **1957 Lotte Lenya.** Lotte Lenya sings "Green-up Time" on the album *Lotte Lenya Sings Kurt Weill: American Theater Songs*. Maurice Levine conducts orchestra and chorus. Sony Classics CD. **1972 Jerry Lanning/Hal Watters.** Jerry Lanning and Hal Watters sing the duet "Progress" in the off-Broadway revue *Berlin to Broadway with Kurt Weill: A Musical Voyage*. Paramount LP. **1992 Carole Farley.** Carole Farley sings "Is It Him or Is It Me?" from the show accompanied by Roger Vignoles on the album *Kurt Weill Songs*. ASV CD. **1996 Steven Kimbrough.** Steven Kimbrough sings "This is the Life" and "Here I'll Stay" with Victor Symonteete conducting the Cologne Radio Orchestra on the album *Kurt Weill on Broadway*. Koch Schwann CD. **1997 Thomas Hampson/Elizabeth Futral.**

Thomas Hampson and Elizabeth Futral perform four songs from *Love Life* with John McGlinn conducting the London Sinfonietta on the album *Kurt Weill on Broadway*. EMI Classics CD. **1998 Bryan Terfel.** Bryan Terfel sings "Here I'll Stay" and "This is the Life" on his album *If Ever I Would Leave You*. Paul Daniel conducts the English Northern Philharmonia. DG CD. **2000 Urs Affolter.** Urs Affolter sings "Here I'll Stay" on the album *Stay Well: Urs Affolter Sings Kurt Weill* accompanied by Uli Kofler. Antes CD.

THE LOVE OF DON PERLIMPLIN *American operas based on Lorca play*

Wealthy elder Don Perlimplin marries lusty young Belisa but is worried she will take lovers. To avoid this he disguises himself as a young man and seduces her himself. As honor demands that the husband kill the wife's lover. he makes the ultimate sacrifice and kills himself. His wife then realizes what true love really means. Federico García Lorca's 1931 Spanish play *Amor de Don Perlimplin con Belisa in su jardin* has inspired four American operas.

1958 Arnold Elston. Arnold Elston's twelve-tone one-act opera *The Love of Don Perlimplin*, libretto by the composer based on the García Lorca play, was premiered at the University of California at Berkeley on May 16, 1958. Elston features classical dance forms in the score. **1976 Michael Shapiro.** Michael Shapiro's one-hour opera *The Love of Don Perlimplin and Belisa in the Garden*, libretto by the composer based on the García Lorca play, does not appear to have been performed and may not have been completed. **1984 Conrad Susa.** Conrad Susa's 70-minute opera *The Love of Don Perlimplin*, libretto by Richard Street and the composer based on the García Lorca play, premiered at the PepsiCo Summerfare Festival at State University of New York at Purchase on August 2, 1984, in a production by San Francisco Opera Center. David Malis sang Perlimplin, Ruth Ann Swenson was Belisa, Nancy Gustafson was Belisa's mother and Dolora Zajic was Marcolfa. Douglas W. Schmidt designed the sets, David Alden directed and Andrew Meltzer conducted the New Orchestra of Westchester. The opera was reprised in San Francisco and at Florida State University in 1985 and at Maryland University in 1989. Susa says he was inspired by the music of Scarlatti. **1989 Kim Morrill.** Kim Morrill's one-hour opera *Perlimplin,* libretto by the composer based on the play, was premiered at the Curtis Institute of Music in Philadelphia on February 18, 1989.

LOVERS AND FRIENDS *2001 opera by LaChiusa*

America's Poet Laureate Babbitt Cross has problems. His poem for the inauguration of a new president has been rejected as too pessimistic, his wife Lucy is leaving him for a conductor, his daughter Isis is pregnant with twins from a rock star and his publisher has learned he may not have written the poems that made him famous. John LaChiusa's opera *Lovers and Friends (Chautauqua Variations)*, libretto by the composer, was premiered by Lyric Opera of Chicago in Chicago on June 29, 2001. Robert Orth was Babbit Cross, Melina Pyron was Lucy Cross, Stacey Tappan was Isis, Dina Kuznetsova was B. E., Hollis Resnick was Betsy Laughlin, Michael Sommese was Senator Laughlin, Philip Torre was Edgar Montoya and Christopher Dickerson was Nimrod Baruch. Todd Rosenthal designed the sets, David Petrarca directed and Bradley Veith conducted.

LOVE'S LABOR'S LOST *1973 opera by Nabokov*

The King of Navarre declares love illegal so he and his followers can concentrate on higher things. When the Princess of France arrives with three lovely ladies, the absurd law is quietly broken as the King falls in love with the Princess and three nobleman at his court fall for the ladies. Both groups disguise themselves and the game of love is played out as farce. Nicolas Nabokov's three-act opera *Love's Labor's Lost,* libretto by W. H. Auden and Chester Kallman based on the play by Shakespeare, was premiered in a German translation by Deutsche Oper at the Théâtre de la Monnaie in Brussels on February 7, 1973.

LOVE'S LOTTERY   *1904 comic opera by Edwards*

England in 1818. German-born laundress Lina wins a lottery and with it the heart and hand of an Army sergeant. Julian Edwards' comic opera *Love's Lottery,* libretto by Stanislaus Strange, premiered at the Broadway Theater in New York on October 3, 1904. The opera was created especially for 43-year-old Metropolitan Opera contralto Ernestine Schumann-Heink who played Lina opposite English baritone Wallace Brownlow as the soldier she loves (he had earlier created the role of Luis in the Gilbert and Sullivan comic opera *The Gondoliers*). *Love's Lottery* lasted for fifty performances on the strength of the prima donna's reputation rather than her acting ability. Five years later she went to Dresden to create the more suitable role of Clytemnestra in Richard Strauss' opera *Elektra.*

1906 Ernestine Schumann-Heink. In 1906 Ernestine Schumann-Heink recorded for Victor the aria ,"Sweet Thoughts of Love," the most popular tune in the comic opera *Love's Lottery.* It was the much-applauded closing number and is available on the album *Music from the New York Stage 1890–1920.* Pearl CD box.

THE LOVES OF FATIMA   *1949 movie opera by Castelnuovo-Tedesco*

Mario Castelnuovo-Tedesco created an opera called *The Loves of Fatima* for the 1949 film Everybody Does It with over-the-top arias for soprano and baritone. Paul Douglas sings the baritone role with Linda Darnell as the soprano in the premiere of the opera in the film by the American Scala Opera Company. His singing is done by New York City Opera baritone Stephen Kemalyan while Darnell's is by San Francisco Opera soprano Helen Spann. The premiere is a comic disaster as Douglas takes so many stimulants to get up his courage that he falls down on stage knocking over the sets and ending the performance.

"LUCY'S ARIA"   *Soprano aria: The Telephone (1947). Words and music: Gian Carlo Menotti.*

Lucy loves her telephone and uses it incessantly to the despair of her boyfriend Ben who wants to ask her to marry him. Just as he begins his proposal, the phone rings. Lucy picks it up, says "Hello! Hello?" and begins a long chatty conversation with her friend Margaret. "Lucy's Aria," a delightfully frivolous challenge for coloratura sopranos, was introduced in Gian Carlo Menotti's one-act comic opera *The Telephone or L'amour á trois,* libretto by the composer, at the Hecksher Theater in New York City on February 18, 1947, by Marilyn Cotlow as Lucy. She can be heard singing it on an original cast recording. Eleanor Steber sings it on her album *Eleanor Steber in Concert* 1956–1958, Liliane Berton in a recording of the opera made in France in 1962, Paula Seibel on a 1979 Kentucky Opera recording, Anne Victoria Banks in a recording made at the Teatro San Marco in Italy in 1992, Carole Farley in a 1992 BBC TV Scotland production and Jeanne Ommerle on a recording made at Queens College in New York City in 1994. Robert Larsen and Martha Gerhart feature it in their book *Coloratura Arias for Sopranos* (2002/G. Schirmer).

LUCY'S LAPSES   *1987 opera by Drobny*

Lucy, an elderly woman with Alzheimer's disease, has her children worried because she wants to commit suicide. Christopher Drobny's blackly comic one-act opera *Lucy's Lapses,* libretto by Laura Harrington, mixes traditional opera with jazz and lounge music. It premiered in Waterford, Connecticut, on August 20, 1987, was reprised by Playwrights Horizons in New York in 1989 and staged by Portland Opera in 1990. The Portland production featured Meg Bussert as Lucy, John Leslie Wolfe as Biff, Michael Curran as Danny, Rebecca Baxter as Carrie and Donald Bell.

LUDERS, GUSTAV   *American composer (1865–1913)*

Gustav Luder was one of the most successful composers of continental-style American comic operas at the beginning of the 20th century. His most popular operetta was *The Prince of Pilsen,* libretto by Frank Pixley about mistaken identities in Nice, which premiered in Boston at the Tremont Theater and opened at the Broadway Theater in New York on May 17, 1903. Its "Stein Song" ("It's Always Fair Weather When Good Fellows Get Together) became a favorite of barbershop quartets. It was also staged in London and Paris. *The Sho-Gun,* libretto by Pixley set in Korea, premiered at the Studebaker Theater in Chicago in 1903 and opened on Broadway at Wallach's later the same year. Luder, who was born in Germany, began his musical theater career in Chicago with productions of *Little Robinson Crusoe* in 1895, *The Burgomaster* in 1900 and *King Dodo* in 1902.

LUDGIN, CHESTER   *American baritone (1925 — 2003)*

Chester Ludgin, a mainstay of the New York City Opera company for many years, created roles in nine American operas and sang in many more. He created Psychiatrist/Doctor/Voditchka in Robert Kurka's The Good Soldier Schweik at NYCO in 1958, John Procter in Robert Ward's The Crucible at NYCO in 1961 and the Golem in Abraham Ellstein's The Golem at NYCO in 1962 and he played Briquet in Robert Ward's He Who Gets Slapped in its professional premiere at NYCO in 1959. He created Joseph in John LaMontaine's pageant opera *Novellis, Novellis* in Washington in 1962, a leading role in Robert Ward's The Lady from Colorado at Central City Opera House in 1964, Lyman Ward in Andrew Imbrie's Angle of Repose at San Francisco Opera in 1976, Denys in Ward's Abelard and Heloise in North Carolina in 1982, Hindley in the belated stage premiere of Bernard Herrmann's Wuthering Heights at Portland Opera in 1982 and Old Sam in Leonard Bernstein's A Quite Place at Houston Grand Opera in 1983.

He can be seen on video as the Prisoner in 1959 NBC Opera Theater telecast of Gian Carlo Menotti's Maria Golovin and John Sorel in a 1959 Canadian telecast of Menotti's The Consul. He can be heard on record in most of the original cast NYCO productions including as Horace Tabor on the 1958 NYCO recording of Douglas Moore's The Ballad of Baby Doe. He sang the Postman in a production of Lee Hoiby's The Scarf and he played Per Hansa in a revised version of Douglas Moore's Giants in the Earth presented at the University of North Dakota in 1974. He can be heard as the Valet in the 1958 Vienna State Opera recording of Hugo Weisgall's The Tenor, as Olin Blitch in a 1974 Kentucky Opera production of Carlisle Floyd's Susannah and as Wrestling Bradford in Howard Hanson's Merry Mount on a 1974 broadcast. Ludgin, born in New York City, made his debut as Scarpia with New Orleans Experimental Opera Theater in 1956 and first sang at NYCO in 1957.

LUDWIG, CHRISTA
German mezzo-soprano (1928–)

Christa Ludwig sings the role of the Old Lady in the 1989 operatic recording of Leonard Bernstein's CANDIDE. She played Georgette in the European premiere of Rolf Liebermann's SCHOOL FOR WIVES at the Salzburg Festival in 1957. Ludwig, born in Berlin, established her reputation in Vienna and sang at the Met from 1959 to 1990.

LUENING, OTTO   *American composer/conductor (1900–1996)*

Otto Luening premiered forty operas at Columbia University while he was opera director, including Gian Carlo Menotti's THE MEDIUM in 1946, Virgil Thomson's THE MOTHER OF US ALL in 1947 and his own EVANGELINE in 1948. Luening, who was born in Milwaukee, became interested in American opera while studying in Munich and Zurich. He began his conducting career with the American Grand Opera Company in Chicago, and he was involved in a production of Charles Wakefield Cadman's SHANEWIS in 1922. He was made director of the Eastman School Opera Department in 1928 and conducted for the American Opera Company which commissioned his grand opera, the four-act *Evangeline* based on Longfellow's narrative poem. The company folded before the opera was premiered but it was presented in excerpt form at the Arts Club of Chicago in 1932 and won the Bispham Medal. After teaching and conducting at several universities, Luening was made director of opera production at Columbia University in 1944 and began his remarkable run of producing opera premieres. His students included opera composer John Corigliano.

Jeannette MacDonald singing on stage in the film *San Francisco*.

LYSISTRATA (1)   *1981 opera by Barthelson*

Greece in the 5th Century BC. The women of Athens and Sparta join forces to stop the unending war between their cities. They refuse to sleep with their husbands and say this will continue until the war ceases. Joyce Barthelson's 60-minute opera *Lysistrata*, libretto by the composer, is based on the play by Aristophanes. It premiered at New York University on March 27, 1981.

LYSISTRATA (2)   *2003 opera by Adamo*

Mark Adam's opera Lysistrata, based on the play by Aristophanes, was commissioned by Houston Grand Opera and first seen in a workshop production in 2003.

M

MAAZEL, LORIN   *American conductor (1930–)*

Lorin Maazel conducted the first complete recording of PORGY AND BESS in 1976 with the Cleveland Orchestra, a recording that began critical reassessment of the work as opera rather than musical. With the Pittsburgh Symphony he conducted recordings of numbers from seven Victor Herbert operettas for the album *Popular American Music* including BABES IN THE WOOD, EILEEN, THE FORTUNE TELLER, IT HAPPENED IN NORDLAND, MLLE. MODISTE, NAUGHTY MARIETTA and THE ONLY GIRL. Maazel, born in Neuilly-sur-Seine in France, was music director of the Cleveland

Orchestra from 1972 to 1982 and became music director of the Pittsburgh Symphony in 1988.

MAC   See also *Mc*

MacDONALD, JEANETTE   *American soprano (1903–1965)*

Jeanette MacDonald helped popularize American operetta during the early years of sound cinema. Many of these operettas are known to the wider public primarily through her films and recordings, though the movies were rarely faithful to the stage originals. Six were made for MGM in partnership with Nelson Eddy: Victor Herbert's NAUGHTY MARIETTA (1935) and SWEETHEARTS (1938), Sigmund Romberg's MAYTIME (1937), THE GIRL OF THE GOLDEN WEST (1938) and THE NEW MOON (1940) and Rudolf Friml's ROSE MARIE (1936). She also starred in film versions of the Friml operettas THE VAGABOND KING (1930) with Dennis King and THE FIREFLY (1937) with Allan Jones and the Jerome Kern operetta THE CAT AND THE FIDDLE (1934) with Ramon Navarro. She was featured in specially created "movie operas" in two of her films, MONSIEUR BEAUCAIRE in the film *Monte Carlo* and CZARITZA in the film *Maytime*. She recorded songs from several other operettas, including Herbert's THE FORTUNE TELLER (1946) and Romberg's UP IN CENTRAL PARK (1950). MacDonald, born in Philadelphia, made her first film for Paramount, *The Love Parade,* in 1929. She joined MGM in 1933 where she was teamed with Eddy in a highly successful partnership. In addition to her movies, she can be seen on a 1950 *Voice of Firestone* television program singing arias from *Maytime* and *Naughty Marietta* and a 1993 TV documentary *America's Singing Sweethearts*. Her many record albums include *Jeanette MacDonald/Nelson Eddy* (RCA Victor/1966), *MacDonald/Eddy Favorites* (RCA Victor/1975) and *MacDonald/Eddy Soundtracks* (Sandy Hook/1976). Opera soprano Elizabeth Futral recorded a tribute album to her in 1999.

MacDONOUGH, GLEN   *American librettist/lyricist (187–1924)*

Glen MacDonough wrote librettos for twenty-nine music theater works, including six with music by Victor Herbert: *The Gold Bug* (1896), BABES IN TOYLAND (1903), IT HAPPENED IN NORDLAND (1904), *Wonderland* (1905), *Algeria* (1908) and *The Rose of Algeria* (1909). His other American musicals include *Chris and the Wonderful Lamp* (1900) for John Philips Sousa and *Yesterday* (1919) for Reginald De Koven. MacDonough, who was born in Brooklyn, also adapted European operettas for the American stage.

MACHOVER, TOD   *American composer (1953–)*

Tod Machover is one of the most successful proponents of electronic multimedia opera. His extraordinary version of Philip K. Dick's cult SF novel VALIS premiered in Paris at the Pompidou Center in 1987. It was followed by the interactive BRAIN OPERA presented at the Juilliard School in New York in 1996. The more traditional RESURRECTION, based on Tolstoy's last novel, was premiered by Houston Grand Opera in 1999. Machover, born in New York, began his studies UC Santa Cruz, Columbia and Juilliard and then specialized in computer music at MIT and Stanford. He became director of music research at IRCAM (Institut de Recherche et de Coordination Acoustique/Musique) in Paris in 1980 and was made Director of the Experimental Media Facility at MIT in 1985.

MacKAYE, PERCY   *American playwright/librettist (1875–1956)*

Percy MacKaye, though not well remembered today, was a famous poet and playwright in his time and an important contributor to American opera and pageant theater. His 1903 play about Chaucer and Wife of Bath became the libretto for Reginald De Koven's opera THE CANTERBURY PILGRIMS, premiered at the Met in 1917. He wrote the libretto for De Koven's second opera, RIP VAN WINKLE based on the Washington Irving story, premiered in Chicago in 1920, and he had other plays turned into operas. He collaborated with composer Frederick S. Converse on two operas after Converse created the incidental music for MacKaye's 1906 play *Jeanne d'Arc*. The first was the 1913 *Beauty and the Beast*, libretto by MacKaye based on the Arabian *Thousand and One Nights*; the opera was not performed but the libretto was published in 1917 as *Sinbad the Sailor*. Next was the 1914 *The Immigrants*, a realistic story about Italians living in Boston, but the Boston Opera Company collapsed before it could be staged. Converse also composed the music for a 1923 silent film based on a play by MacKaye, *Puritan Passions* starring Mary Astor. MacKaye, a native of New York City, continued to write in the late 1940s. The operas based on his works are listed below.

Beauty and the Beast (1913). 1913 Frederick S. Converse's *Beauty and the Beast*, libretto by Percy MacKaye. Unperformed. Libretto published in 1917 as *Sinbad the Sailor*. **The Immigrants (1914).** 1914 Frederick S. Converse's *The Immigrants* libretto by Percy MacKaye. Unperformed. **The Canterbury Pilgrims (1903).** 1917 Reginald De Koven's *The Canterbury Pilgrims,* libretto by Percy MacKaye. Premiere: Metropolitan Opera, March 8, 1917. **Jeanne d'Arc (1906).** 1923 Lucille Crews *The Call of Jeanne d'Arc,* libretto by the composer. Unperformed. **Rip Van Winkle (1920).** 1920 Reginald De Koven's *Rip Van Winkle,* libretto by Percy MacKaye. Premiere: Chicago Opera Company, January 30, 1920. **The Scarecrow (1908).** 1945 Normand Lockwood's *The Scarecrow,* libretto based on the MacKaye play. Premiere: Columbia University, May 19, 1945.

MacNEIL, CORNELL   *American baritone (1922–)*

Baritone Cornell MacNeil created one of the most memorable roles in modern American opera, the revolutionary John Sorel in Gian Carlo Menotti's THE CONSUL. He sang it first in Philadelphia in 1950 and then on Broadway and he is featured on the original cast recording. MacNeil, born in Minneapolis, made his professional debut in the role and afterwards joined New York City Opera. He made his debut at the Met in 1959 and sang there until 1987.

MacRAE, GORDON   *American tenor (1921–1986)*

Gordon MacRae was the king of the American operetta in the 1950s, the successor to Nelson Eddy in the movies and the partner of Metropolitan Opera sopranos Risë Stevens and Dorothy Kirsten on radio and record. He is the Red Shadow in the 1953 film of Sigmund Romberg's THE DESERT SONG, Curly in the 1955 film of Rodgers and Hammerstein's OKLAHOMA! and Billy Bigelow in the 1956 film of their CAROUSEL. He sings with Stevens in recorded radio versions of Jerome Kern's THE CAT AND THE FIDDLE (1948) and Victor Herbert's THE RED MILL (1951). He sings with Kirsten in Rudolf Friml's THE VAGABOND KING (1952 radio), Victor Herbert's THE PRINCESS PAT (1952 radio), Romberg's THE NEW MOON (1952 radio/1963 recording), Herbert's MLLE MODISTE (1953 radio), Romberg's THE STUDENT PRINCE (1953 radio/1962 recording), *The Desert Song* (1963 recording) and

Wright/Forrest's KISMET (1965 recording). He recorded operettas with Marguerite Piazza (*The Desert Song* in 1954 and Herbert's NAUGHTY MARIETTA in 1954), Lucille Norman (*The Vagabond King* in 1950, *The New Moon* in 1950, *The Red Mill* in 1955), Dorothy Warenskjold (*The Student Prince* in 1953), Margaret Whiting (Rodger's SOUTH PACIFIC in 1950) and Jo Stafford (Cole Porter's KISS ME KATE in 1949). He even created one role on television in 1958, Jim in Richard Adler's THE GIFT OF THE MAGI. MacRae, born in East Orange, NJ, starred in other movie musicals as well and had his own radio and TV shows.

MACURDY, JOHN   *American bass (1929–)*

John Macurdy created roles in five American operas: Earnshaw in Carlisle Floyd's WUTHERING HEIGHTS at Santa Fe in 1958, the Basso Cantante in Hugo Weisgall's SIX CHARACTERS IN SEARCH OF AN AUTHOR at New York City Opera in 1959, Reb Bashevi in Ellstein's THE GOLEM at NYCO n 1962, Agrippa in Samuel Barber's ANTONY AND CLEOPATRA at the Met in 1966 and General Ezra Mannon in Marvin Levy's MOURNING BECOMES ELECTRA at the Met in 1967. He sings the role of the Chamberlain in the 1961 telecast of Abraham Ellstein's THE THIEF AND THE HANGMAN, Rev. John Hale in the 1962 NYCO recording of Robert Ward's THE CRUCIBLE and Anne's father Trulove in the 1992 Aix-en-Provence Festival telecast of Igor Stravinsky's THE RAKE'S PROGRESS. Macurdy, born in Detroit, joined New York City Opera in 1959 and became a resident member of the Metropolitan Opera in 1962.

MC   See also *MAC*

McCOLLUM, JOHN   *American tenor (1922–)*

Lyric tenor John Morris McCollum created the role of the husband Reuel in Lee Hoiby's THE SCARF at the Spoleto Festival in 1958 and the role of Arkady in Hoiby's NATALIA PETROVNA at New York City Opera in 1964. He sings King Kaspar in the 1963 NBC Opera Theater recording/telecast of Gian Carlo Menotti's AMAHL AND THE NIGHT VISITORS and he can be seen talking with Menotti about HELP, HELP, THE GLOBOLINKS! in a 1979 documentary shot at the University of Michigan where he was teaching. McCollum, born in Coalinga, CA, studied in Oakland and New York and made his debut at New England Opera Theater in 1953.

McCORMACK, JOHN   *Irish tenor (1884–1945)*

Irish tenor legend John McCormack created the role of Lt. Paul Merrill in Victor Herbert's opera NATOMA at the Metropolitan Opera House in Philadelphia in 1911, and recorded its famous aria "No country can my own outvie" in 1912. He also recorded songs from comic operas including "I'm Falling in Love With Someone" from Herbert's NAUGHTY MARIETTA in 1911, "O Promise Me" from Reginald De Koven's ROBIN HOOD in 1915, two songs from Herbert's EILEEN in 1917 and "Rose Marie" from Rudolf Friml's ROSE MARIE in 1925. McCormack, studied in Italy where he made his debut in 1906 using an Italian pseudonym. He made his debut at the Metropolitan Opera in New York in 1910 but gave up stage opera for recitals in 1918.

McDONALD, AUDRA   *American soprano (1970–)*

Audra McDonald, who created the role of Marie Christine in Michael John LaChiusa's MARIE CHRISTINE at Lincoln Center in 1999, has helped to blur the line between opera and musical theater with her performances and has already won three Tony Awards. She won the first singing Carrie in Nicholas Hytner's 1994 Lincoln Center production of Richard Rodgers' CAROUSEL. She won

her second playing a young opera singer taught by Maria Callas in Terrence McNally's play *Master Class* and the third for her performance in the musical *Ragtime*. She sings the role of Consuelo in the 1996 recording of John Adams' opera I WAS LOOKING AT THE CEILING AND THEN I SAW THE SKY, Eileen in the 1998 London recording of Leonard Bernstein's WONDERFUL TOWN, Bess in the 1998 recording of the Catfish Row suite based on George Gershwin's PORGY AND BESS and the song "Joe Worker" in the 1999 film *Cradle Will Rock* based on Marc Blitzstein's THE CRADLE WILL ROCK. McDonald, born in Berlin, Germany, when her father was serving in the Army, studied at Juilliard with Ellen Faull.

McFERRIN, ROBERT   *American baritone (1921–)*

African American baritone Robert McFerrin created the role of Mamaloi in William Grant Still's opera TROUBLED ISLAND when it was premiered by New York City Center Opera in 1949 and the role of a Villager in Kurt Weill's LOST IN THE STARS on Broadway in 1949. He sang the role Porgy in the 1959 film of George Gershwin's PORGY AND BESS though Sidney Poitier was the actor seen on screen. He became the first African American man to sing at the Met on January 27, 1955, when he appeared as Amonasro in *Aida*. McFerrin, born in Marianna, Arkansas, began his opera career with the National Negro Opera Company and joined the New England Opera Company in 1950. He is the father of singer/composer Bobby McFerrin.

McKINLEY, ANDREW   *American tenor (1904–1996)*

Andrew McKinley, who created roles in four American operas, is probably best known for singing the deaf King Kaspar in Gian Carlo Menotti's Christmas opera AMAHL AND THE NIGHT VISITORS on NBC television in 1951. He is featured on the cast recording and his aria "This Is My Box" has become a favorite recital piece. Prior to this McKinley has created the magician Nika Magadoff in Menotti's political opera THE CONSUL on stage in Philadelphia and Broadway in 1950. He had a notable role in the premiere of Bohuslav Martinů's THE MARRIAGE on NBC Opera Theater in 1953 and he sang the part of Letterbox in Lukas Foss's GRIFFELKIN on NBC Opera Theatre in 1955. McKinley was a regular on NBC Opera Theatre in the 1950s playing Captain De Vere in *Billy Budd* (1952), Herod in *Salome* (1954), Prince Shuisky in *Boris Godunov* (1954) and Monostatos in *The Magic Flute* (1956).

McCLATCHY, J. D.   *American poet/librettist (1945–)*

J. D. McClatchy, poet and editor of *The Yale Review*, has written librettos for three American operas. William Schuman's A QUESTION OF TASTE, based on a Roald Dahl story, was premiered by Glimmerglass in 1989. Bruce Saylor's ORPHEUS DESCENDING, based on a Tennessee Williams play, was premiered by Chicago Lyric Opera's Center for American Artists in 1994. His critically acclaimed libretto for Tobias Picker's EMMELINE, based on novel by Judith Rossner, was premiered by Santa Fe Opera in 1996 and nationally televised. McClatchy, born in Bryn Mawr, PA, has published several books of poetry.

McNALLY, TERRENCE   *American librettist/playwright (1939–)*

Tony Award-winning playwright Terrence McNally, who wrote the books for the Broadway musicals *Kiss of the Spider Woman*, *Ragtime* and *The Full Monty*, is an opera enthusiast and has written librettos for operas. Robert Beaser's one-act THE FOOD OF LOVE, the third opera in the CENTRAL PARK trilogy, premiered at Glimmerglass in 1999 and was reprised at New York City Opera.

Jake Heggie's three-act DEAD MAN WALKING, based on the life of Sister Helen Prejean, was premiered by San Francisco Opera in 2000 and recorded. McNally has also written plays with opera content, including *Master Class* and *The Lisbon Traviata*.

McTEAGUE   *1992 opera by Bolcom*

Rough-edged dentist McTeague meets and marries shy Trina who had been courted by his best friend Marcus. When she wins a large amount of money in a lottery and turns into a miser. McTeague's desire for her gold causes him to murder her and flee to the desert. He is pursued by Marcus and they battle to the death. William Bolcom's opera *McTeague*, libretto by Arnold Weinstein and filmmaker Robert Altman based on Frank Norris's novel *McTeague* and Erich von Stroheim's 1924 film *Greed* based on it, was premiered by Lyric Opera of Chicago on October 31, 1992. Ben Heppner was McTeague, Catherine Malfitano was Trina, Timothy Nolen was Marcus, Emily Golden was Maria, William Walker was Papa, Martha Jane Howe was Mama, Patrick Dennison was the Sheriff and Wilbur Pauley was the Lottery Agent. Altman staged the opera and Dennis Russell Davies conducted the Lyric Opera of Chicago Orchestra.

1992 Lyric Opera of Chicago Commentary. Critical analysis of *McTeague* by Alfred Glasser in the Women's Board of Lyric Opera series. He talks to composer Bolcom and plays music by him while proving plot summary to the opera and historical background. Lyric Opera Commentaries audiocassette. **1993 The Real McTeague.** Ben Heppner is seen as McTeague, Catherine Malfitano as Trina and Timothy Nolen as Marcus in scenes from the Lyric Opera of Chicago production in this documentary by Robert Altman. The opera is contrasted with the Norris source novel and the film *Greed* while Studs Terkel reads scenes from the novel and Bolcom and Altman talk about the opera. The hour-long film, made by WTTW Chicago, was telecast on PBS.

MADAME ADARE   *1980 opera by Silverman*

Psychiatrist Dr. Hoffman refuses to give Madame Adare further treatment unless she pays her past bills. She becomes angry and tries to shoot him. Diaghilev persuades her of the glory of the stage so she becomes a opera singer. After she has become successful she returns to pay Hoffman but he refuses saying her mental condition is what enables her to sing so well. She becomes angry and shoots him. Stanley Silverman's one-act opera *Madame Adare*, libretto by Richard Foreman, was commissioned by New York City Opera which premiered it October 9, 1980, in the program *An American Trilogy*. Madame Adare was Carol Gutknecht, Richard Cross was Dr. Hoffman, James Billings was the Agent, Harris Poor was the Devil, Nico Castel was Diaghilev, David Rae Smith was the Interviewer and Lewis White was the Director. Lloyd Evans designed the set and costumes, Richard Foreman directed and Brian Salesky conducted. The musical style is akin to Weill-like music theater.

MADAME MAO   *2003 opera by Sheng*

Jiang Ching becomes a movie star and marries Chinese Communist leader Mao Zedung. Following the horrors of the Cultural Revolution and the death of Chairman Mao, she is tried and imprisoned and eventually commits suicide. Bright Sheng's opera *Madame Mao,* libretto by Colin Graham, premiered at Santa Fe Opera in the summer of 2003 in a production directed by Graham. Soprano Anna Christy sang the role of the beautiful ambitious young actress Jiang Ching while mezzo Robynne Redmon played the mature and vengeful Madame Mao; they appear together in many scenes. Chairman Mao was Alan Opie while Mark Duffin and Kelly Kaduce had multiple roles. John Fiore conducted the Santa Fe Opera Orchestra and Chorus.

MADDALENA, JAMES   *American baritone (19??)*

James Maddalena has created notable roles in many modern American operas, especially in collaboration with composer John Adams and director Peter Sellars. He created the role of Richard Nixon in Adams/Sellars' NIXON IN CHINA at Houston Grand Opera in 1987, sings it on the telecast and recording and reprised the role in the acclaimed 2000 revival at English National Opera in London. He created the role of the Captain in Adams/Sellars' THE DEATH OF KLINGHOFFER in Brussels in 1991 and sings it on the Opera de Lyon recording. He created Merlin in the premiere of Michael Tippett's NEW YEAR at Houston Grand Opera in 1989 and reprised the role on the 1991 BBC telecast. He created Captain Compson in David Carlson's THE MIDNIGHT ANGEL at Opera Theatre of Saint Louis in 1993, the Impresario in Robert Moran's "opera macabre" THE DRACULA DIARY at Houston Opera Studio in 1994, the baritone in Elliot Goldenthal's choral work FIRE WATER PAPER: A VIETNAM ORATORIO in Costa Mesa in 1995 and Mintz in Stewart Wallace's HARVEY MILK at Houston Grand Opera in 1995. He sings the part of Oscar Hubbard in the 1992 Scottish Opera recording of Marc Blitzstein's REGINA, the Father in the 2002 broadcast of Mark Adamo's LITTLE WOMEN at Houston Grand Opera, the Swineherd in the 2003 Opera Boston production of John Harbison's *Full Moon in March* and a protagonist in the 2004 Berlin recording of Kurt Weill's THE ETERNAL ROAD. Maddalena, born in Lynn, MA, was also a featured performer in Peter Sellar's updated versions of the three Mozart/Da Ponte operas.

MADELEINE   *1914 opera by Herbert*

Madeleine Fleury is a popular opera diva in 18th century Paris and has many admirers but on New Year's Day she can find no one to dine with her. Her men friends all say they must spend it with their mothers. Madeleine finally puts a portrait of her late mother on her table saying "I, too, will dine with my mother." The Metropolitan Opera commissioned Victor Herbert's opera *Madeleine* and premiered it on January 24, 1914, with Frances Alda in the leading role. Grant Stewart's libretto is based on a French play by Adrien Decourcelles and L. Thibaut called *Je dine chez ma mère.* Leonora Sparkes played the maid Nichette, Paul Althouse was the Duc d'Esterre, Andrés de Segurola was the artist Didier, Antonio Pini-Corsi was the Chevalier de Mauprat and Marcel Reiner was the Coachman. Giorgio Polacco conducted the Metropolitan Opera Orchestra. Herbert is said to have used Debussy as model for the music and the aria "A Perfect Day" was well-received but the opera itself was felt to be too lightweight and impressionistic to be popular and was dropped from the Met repertory after four performances. It has been revived in recent years in Chicago in 1989 with Lisa Kristina as Madeleine and by Opera Theatre of Northern Virginia in 1996 with Amy Van Roekel in the role.

1914 Frances Alda. The most popular piece of music in *Madeleine* was Madeleine's aria "A Perfect Day." Frances Alda, who introduced it on stage, recorded it for Victor on February 8, 1914, with Herbert conducting. It's on several albums including *Frances Alda — Complete Victor Recordings* (RCA Victor CD) and *Souvenirs from American Opera* (IRRC CD). **1989 De Paul University Opera.** *Madeleine* was staged by DePaul University Opera Theatre in Chicago in June 1989 with Arnold Voketaitis producing. Lisa Kristina is Madeleine, David Tethmann is the artist Didier and the other singers are all De Paul students. The performance was videotaped live from the audience. Live Opera Heaven VHS.

MADEMOISELLE MODISTE *see* MLLE. MODISTE

MAGDALENA   *1947 light opera by Villa-Lobos*

1912 in Colombia at the headwaters of the Magdalena River. Devout Christian Maria, leader of the Muzo Indian tribe, is trying to convert her fiancé Pedro, a rebel bus driver, to Christianity. Major Bianco goes to Paris to alert General Carabaña when the Indians stop working in his emerald mines. The general, who has been having a high time with his mistress Madame Teresa at her Little Black Mouse Café, decides to return to quell the rebellion. Heitor Villa-Lobos' light opera *Magdalena,* libretto by Frederick Hazlitt Brennan and Homer Curran, has lyrics by Robert Wright and George Forrest, the creators of *Kismet* and *Song of Norway.* It was premiered by Los Angeles Civic Light Opera at the Philharmonic Auditorium on July 26, 1948, and opened on Broadway at the Ziegfeld Theater on September 20, 1948. Dorothy Sarnoff was Maria, John Raitt was Pedro, Hugo Haas was the General and Irra Petina was Teresa. Howard Bay designed the sets, Jules Dassin directed and Arthur Kay conducted. Brazilian composer Villa-Lobos wrote the opera while he was living in New York. Forrest and Wright had asked to use his music to create an operetta, as they had done with *Kismet,* but he decided to create

new music for it. *The New York Times* called it "the finest, most sophisticated Broadway score in a generation."

1974 André Kostelanetz. André Kostelanetz conducts an orchestral suite based on the Villa-Lobos operetta. It's on the album *André Kostelanetz Plays Music of Villa-Lobos.* Columbia LP. **1987 Lincoln Center.** Faith Esham is Maria opposite Kevin Gray as Pedro in a concert version of *Magdalena* presented at Lincoln Center in New York on November 23, 1987. Judy Kaye Is Teresa, George Rose is General Carabaña, Jerry Hadley is the Old One, Keith Curran is Major Blanco, Charles Damsel is Padre José and Charles Repole is Zoggie. Evans Haile, who conceived and produced the concert, conducts the New Haven Symphony Orchestra. CBS CD.

THE MAGIC BARREL   *1964 opera by Blitzstein*

Finkle hires a marriage broker but rejects all the candidates he is offered. The right woman turns out to be the marriage broker's daughter. Marc Blitzstein's uncompleted one-act opera *The Magic Barrel* is based on the 1954 story by Bernard Malamud and was to have been half of his double-bill *Tales of Malamud.* The climactic aria of the opera, "Then," was Blitzstein's last composed work.

1990 William Sharp. Baritone William Sharp sings the aria "Then," a reflection on the future, with Steven Blier accompanying on piano. It's on the album *Marc Blitzstein: Zipperfly and Other Songs* recorded for the New York Festival of Song. Koch CD.

Heitor Villa-Lobos' *Magdalena* was premiered by Los Angeles Civic Light Opera in 1948 but it was not recorded until 1987.

THE MAGIC CHAIR   *1966 opera by Zador*

Crux brings his latest invention to the Ministry of Commerce but is turned away by the Minister's assistant Polenta. Crux gets his revenge by making adjustments to a chair he has delivered. Whoever sits in the chair has to tell the truth and most of the revelations regard the Minister. Eugene Zador's one-act opera *The Magic Chair,* libretto by George Jellinek based on a play by Frigyes Karinthy, was premiered at Louisiana State University in Baton Rouge on May 14, 1966.

THE MAGIC KNIGHT   *1906 operatic satire by Herbert*

Elsa is "a typical grand operatic maiden in the usual distressing situation." Lohengrin is "a professional rescuer of distressed maidens" who arrives in a cab drawn by a swan singing "Mein Lieber Schwan." He saves Elsa from a plot hatched by evil Ortrud and Frederick. Victor Herbert's operatic satire *The Magic Knight,* libretto by Edgard Smith, is an Americanized version of Wagner's *Lohengrin* which Herbert uses to poke fun at Wagnerian themes. It was originally meant to be an operatic spoof within his comic opera *Dream City* but when it was judged too difficult for ordinary audiences, it was presented in its own right as the second half of the program. *The Magic Knight* opened in New York on December 25, 1906, with Lillian Blauvelt as Elsa, Maurice Farkoa as Lohengrin, Cora Tracy as Ortrud, Otis

Harlan as Frederick, Frank Belcher as the King, W. L. Romaine as the Herald and Lores Grimm as the Swan/Godfrey. Al Holbrook directed and Louis F. Gottschalk conducted. The critics loved its burlesque of the Wagnerian style and lines like the King's brusque order to "Cut out all that orchestral tone coloring and get down to business."

THE MAGIC VOICE   *1944 "movie opera" by Ward*

The "movie opera" *The Magic Voice* is the central focus of the 1944 Universal movie *The Climax* based on a play by Edward Locke. Opera house physician Boris Karloff had killed the woman who sang it ten years before at the Royal Opera and he thinks it is sacred to her memory. When young soprano Susanna Foster is engaged to sing it in a revival, he attempts to stop her. The opera is seen and heard a number of times during the film in stagings by Lester Horton. Edward Ward, who conducted, composed the music based around themes by Chopin and Schubert using libretto and lyrics by producer/director George Waggner. The individual numbers are titled "The Boulevardier," "Some Day I Know," "The Magic Voice" and "Now at Last."

MAINE   *American state (1820–)*

Joseph Breil's comic opera *Love Laughs at Locksmiths*, libretto by the composer, was premiered in Portland on October 27, 1910. Maine-born opera people include tenor Norman Kelley (Eddington), librettist Edna St. Vincent Millay (Rockland), composer Hall Overton (Bangor) and composer John Knowles Paine (Portland). Most of the large cities in Maine have operas companies.

Augusta: Augusta Opera is based in Augusta.

Camden: Maine Grand Opera, which is located in Camden, produced Frederick Loewe's MY FAIR LADY in 2001.

Portland: Portland has two opera companies: Portland Opera and PortOpera (Portland Opera Repertory Theater). Gian Carlo Menotti's THE MEDIUM was staged in Portland in 2000.

Steuben: Opera Maine is headquartered in Steuben.

"MAKE OUR GARDEN GROW"   *Tenor-soprano duet: Candide (1956). Words: Richard Wilbur. Music: Leonard Bernstein.*

Candide and Cunegonde finally decide to settle down and cultivate their own garden and forget Pangloss's teachings in Leonard Bernstein's CANDIDE. Richard Wilbur's words reflect the final thoughts of Voltaire in the source novel. The song was introduced on stage in 1956 by Robert Rounseville as Candide and Barbara Cook as Cunegonde and was then taken up as an inspiring choral statement by the entire cast. Rounseville and Cook sing it on the original cast recording, Mark Baker and Maureen Brennan on the 1974 Chelsea Theater cast recording, David Eisler and Erie Mills on the 1985 New York City Opera recording, Jerry Hadley and June Anderson on the 1989 London Barbican recording, Mark Beudart and Marilyn Hill Smith on the 1997 Scottish Opera recording and Jason Danieley and Harolyn Blackwell on the 1997 Broadway revival recording. Jerry Hadley and Renée Fleming sing it on the 1991 *Salute to American Music* concert CD while Plácido Domingo and Denyce Grave sing it on the 1992 *Concert for Planet Earth* CD.

THE MAKING OF AMERICANS   *1968 opera by Carmines*

Gertrude Stein recalls three generations of her family and how they were made into Americans. Alvin Carmine's *The Making of Americans*, libretto by Leon Katz based on the book by Gertrude Stein, was premiered at the Judson Poets Theatre in the Judson Memorial Church in New York City in 1968 in a production by Lawrence Kornfeld. Carmines, who also played piano, portrayed Stein as she talked about her family history. The opera was reprised at the Lenox Art Center in 1985.

THE MAKING OF REPRESENTATIVE FOR PLANET 8   *1988 opera by Glass*

The people of Planet 8 are on the verge of extinction because their planet is about to enter an Ice Age. Cosmic agent Johor from Canopus attempts to save the race by uniting its knowledge and souls into one "representative." Memory-keeper Doeg and the young couple Alsi and Nooni are among those affected. Philip Glass's three-act science-fiction opera *The Making of the Representative for Planet 8*, libretto by Doris Lessing based on her 1982 novel, was premiered by Houston Grand Opera on July 8, 1988. Timothy Breese was Johor, Harlan Foss was Doeg, Louise Edeiken was Alsi, Jason Alexander was Nonni, Edric Means was Klim, David Langan was Marl, Julia Parks was Bratch, Richard Sutliff was Pedug, Patricia Shockler was Rivalin and Edgar Moore was Masson. Minoru Terada Domberger choreographed and staged the opera and designed sets and costumes with Eiko Ishioka while John DeMain conducted the Houston Grand Opera Orchestra. The opera, co-commissioned by Houston and a European consortium, was reprised at English National Opera in London and then presented in Holland and Germany.

MALADY OF LOVE   *1954 opera by Engel*

A young woman visits a psychoanalyst and tells him about her dreams which consist of sexually symbolic incidents involving the psychoanalyst. Eventually she confesses that she has fallen in love with him. Lehman Engel's one-act comic opera *Malady of Love*, libretto by Lewis Allen, premiered at Columbia University in New York City on May 27, 1954. Engel mocks jazz and dance styles in the score and uses dancers to mime the dream sequences.

MALAMUD, BERNARD   *American writer (1914–1986)*

Brooklyn-born Bernard Malamud based most of his short stories and novels around Jewish life in New York and they have been popular with both filmmakers and opera composers. The novel *The Natural* (1952) was made into a popular movie in 1984 and the Pulitzer Prizewinning *The Fixer* (1966) was filmed in 1968. His fifty-six short stories, however, are perhaps his finest achievement, and they have provided the basis for several operas. Libretto by composer unless otherwise indicated.

Angel Levine (1955). 1985 Elie Siegmeister's *Angel Levine* (Edward Mably). 92nd Street YMCA, New York City, October 5, 1985. **Idiots First (1961).** 1976 Marc Blitzstein's *Idiot's First* (completed by Leonard Lehrman after Blitzstein's death) Bloomington, Indiana, March 14, 1976. **The Lady of the Lake (1958).** 1985 Elie Siegmeister's *The Lady of the Lake* (Edward Mably) 92nd Street YMCA, New York City, October 5, 1985. **The Magic Barrel (1954).** 1964 Marc Blitzstein's *The Magic Barrel* (Malamud and composer). Ithaca, New York, August 1964. **Notes from a Lady at a Dinner Party (1973).** 1992 Leonard Lehrman's *Karla*. New York City, March 19, 1992.

MALAS, SPIRO   *American bass (1933–)*

Spiro Malas created the role of King Alcinous in Peggy Glanville-Hicks NAUSICAA at the Athens Festival in Greece in August 1961, Francis Nurse in Robert Ward's THE CRUCIBLE at New York City Opera in October 1961, the grocer Kosak in Jack

Beeson's MY HEART'S IN THE HIGHLANDS on NET Opera Theatre on PBS in 1970 and the Narrator in Paul Schoenfield's THE MERCHANT AND THE PAUPER at Opera Theater of St. Louis in 1999. He sang the part of Frank Maurrant for Scottish Opera in the British premiere of Kurt Weill's STREET SCENE in 1989. Malas, born in Baltimore, made his stage debut with the Baltimore Civic Opera in 1959, first sang with the New York City Opera in 1961 and made his debut at the Met in 1983.

MALFITANO, CATHERINE   *American soprano (1948–)*

Catherine Malfitano created the Princess in Conrad Susa's TRANSFORMATIONS at Minnesota Opera in 1973, Catherine Sloper in Thomas Pasatieri's WASHINGTON SQUARE at Michigan Opera in 1976, Doll in Carlisle Floyd's BILBY'S DOLL at Houston Grand Opera in 1976, Trina in William Bolcom's MCTEAGUE at Lyric Opera of Chicago in 1992, Beatrice in Bolcom's A VIEW FROM THE BRIDGE at Lyric Opera of Chicago in 1999, the title role in Bolcom's monodrama MEDUSA at Cincinnati Opera in 2003 and Victoria in Bolcom's A WEDDING at Lyric Opera of Chicago in 2004. She sang Masha in Thomas Pasatieri's THE SEAGULL at Houston Grand Opera in 1974 but did not create the role. For New York City Opera she sang Annina in Gian Carlo Menotti's THE SAINT OF BLEECKER STREET (1976) and Rose in Kurt Weill's STREET SCENE (1978). For Lyric Opera of Chicago she sang Cleopatra in Samuel Barber's ANTONY AND CLEOPATRA (1991) and the title role in Marc Blitzstein's REGINA (2004). She has also sung Lady with a Hand Mirror in Domenick Argento's POSTCARD FROM MOROCCO, Berta in Pasatieri's BLACK WIDOW and Abigail in Robert Ward's THE CRUCIBLE. Malfitano, born in New York, made her debut in 1972 at Central City Opera. She was a regular with New York City Opera from 1973 to 1979 and began to sing at the Met in 1979.

1965 Original Broadway cast. Richard Kiley is Cervantes/Quixote on the original Broadway cast album. Irving Jacobson is Sancho, Joan Diener is Aldonza, Robert Rounseville is the Padre and Ray Middleton is the Innkeeper. Neil Warner conducts. RCA Victor LP/MCA CD. **1965 Marilyn Horne/Richard Tucker.** Marilyn Horne sings the role of Aldonza with Richard Tucker as the Padre in this almost operatic recording. Jim Nabor is the not-very-interesting Cervantes/Quixote with Jack Gilford as his Sancho. Paul Weston conducts. RCA Victor LP/CD. **1972 United Artists film.** Peter O'Toole stars as Quixote/Cervantes with Sophia Loren as Aldonza in one of the least interesting screen adaptations of a major American stage musical even though playwright Dale Wasserman did the adaptation. Neither star can sing and the music takes last place. Laurence Rosenthal conducts. Arthur Hiller directed for United Artists. **1996 Placido Domingo/Julia Migenes.** Placido Domingo stars as Cervantes/Quixote in this operatic recording with Julia Migenes as his Aldonza. Mandy Patinkin is Sancho Panza, Jerry Hadley is the Padre and small roles are taken by Samuel Ramey, Rosalind Elias, Robert White and Carolann Page. Paul Gemignani leads the American Theater Orchestra and Concert Chorale of New York. Sony CD. **1998 Théâtre Royal de Liège.** José Van Dam is Quixote/Cervantes in this operatic French-language production by André Bouseiller presented at the Théâtre Royal de Liège in April 1998. Completing the cast are Alexis Yerna, Anne-Catherine Gillet and Georges Gauthier. Patrick Baton conducted the Opera Royal de Wallonie Orchestra and Benoît Vlietinck directed the video. French translation by Jacques Brel. Telecast in Belgium April 26, 1998. On video. **2000 Covent Garden Festival.** Ron Raines sings the role of Cervantes/Quixote in this recording of a May 2000 concert production created for the Covent Garden Festival in London. Kim

MAN OF LA MANCHA   *1965*
musical by Leigh

Spanish novelist Miguel de Cervantes, in jail for debt, tells fellow prisoners the story of knight Don Quixote and his servant Sancho Panza. *Man of La Mancha* is not an opera but it has entered the opera house repertory and has been recorded by opera singers. Composer Mitch Leigh was to have collaborated with opera librettists W. H. Auden and Chester Kallman in adapting Dale Wasserman's television play *I, Don Quixote* for the stage. When that didn't work out, Wasserman wrote the libretto himself and Joe Darion created the lyrics. *Man of La Mancha* was previewed in Goodspeed Opera House in Connecticut before opening at ANTA's Washington Square Theater on November 22, 1965. Richard Kiley sang the double role of Cervantes and Don Quixote with Irving Jacobson as Sancho, Joan Diener as Aldonza, Robert Rounseville as the Padre and Ray Middleton as the Innkeeper. Albert Marre directed and Neil Warner conducted. The show won the Tony for Best Musical. David Atkinson took over the role of Cervantes/Don Quixote when Kiley left. *Man of La Mancha* was staged by the Indianapolis Opera Company in 1990.

Mitch Leigh's *Man of La Mancha* may not be an opera but it has entered the opera house repertory.

Criswell is Aldonza, Avery Salzman is Sancho and David Charles Abell conducts the large orchestra. This is the only complete version of the musical with its dialogue. Jay Productions CD.

THE MAN WITHOUT A COUNTRY *1937 opera by Damrosch*

Philip Nolan is condemned by a court to spent his life on a ship outside the United States because of his treasonous involvement with Aaron Burr and the Blennerhasset conspiracy. His sweetheart Mary Rutledge fights to get him pardoned. Nolan turns into a patriot, fights heroically in the battle of Tripoli and is mortally wounded. Walter Damrosch's opera *The Man Without a Country,* libretto by Arthur Guiterman based on the patriotic story by Edward Everett Hale, premiered at the Metropolitan Opera on May 12, 1937. Arthur Carron was Philip Nolan, Helen Traubel was Mary Rutledge, George Rasely was Blennerhassett, Joseph Royer was Aaron Burr and George Cehanovsky was Reeve. Damrosch conducted the Metropolitan Opera Orchestra.

1937 Metropolitan Opera. The Metropolitan Opera broadcast the opera on May 22, 1937, with the premiere cast. Arthur Carron is Philip Nolan, Helen Traubel is Mary Rutledge, George Rasely is Blennerhassett and Joseph Royer is Aaron Burr. Wilfred Pelletier conducts in place of Damrosch. Edward J. Smith issued the broadcast on two EJS LP records in 1970. The recording is on an Omega Opera Archives tape.

MANDAC, EVELYN *American soprano (1945–)*

Evelyn Mandac created the role of Berta in Thomas Pasatieri's THE BLACK WIDOW at Seattle Opera in 1972 and the title role in Pasatieri's INES DE CASTRO at Baltimore Opera in 1976. Mandac, born in Mindanao, studied in Manila and at Juilliard and made her debut at Washington Opera in 1969. She began to sing at the Metropolitan Opera at 1975.

MANDELBAUM, JOEL *American composer (1932–)*

Joel Mandelbaum, known for his theories about microtonal tunings, completed five operas, the first three to his own librettos. The 1955 one-act *The Man in the Man-made Moon* was followed in 1956 by the one-act *The Four Chaplains.* He moved to four acts with the highly microtonal 1971 THE DYBBUK, libretto based on the 1920 play by Saloman Ansky, which premiered in New York on May 24, 1972. His 1983 opera *As You Dislike It* was composed to a libretto by L. Fichandler. His 1995 opera THE VILLAGE, composed to a libretto by poet Susan Fox, was well received at its Queens College premiere with the microtonality portion much reduced. Mandelbaum, a Queens College, CUNY, music professor, has composed many other vocal and instrumental works.

THE MANSON FAMILY *1990 opera by John Moran*

This collage-style portrait of murderous cult leader Charles Manson and his deadly family incorporates trial speeches. police sirens and other pop elements. Act One is "The Murders." Act Two is "The Family" and Act Three is "The Hall of Justice" John Moran's avant-garde opera *The Manson Family,* libretto by the composer, was commissioned by Jed Wheeler for the 1990 Serious Fun Festival at Lincoln Center and premiered by the Ridge Theater at Alice Tully Hall. Moran played piano and Bob McGrath directed.

1991 Looking Glass Studios. Moran takes the role of Charles Manson aka Jesus Christ in this recording made at The Looking Glass Studios in New York. Terre Roche is Lynette "Squeaky" Fromme, Richard Sortomme is Catherine Share and plays viola, Iggy Pop is "The Prosecutor" Jack Lord, Paige Snell is Susan D. Atkins aka "Sadie-Mae Glutz," Clifford Lane is the Courtroom Host, Bob McGrath is the Judge and Roger Greenawalt is the Voice of Defense. Moran plays piano as accompaniment with Sortomme playing viola. Phillips CD.

MANSOURI, LOTFI *American director/administrator (1929–)*

Lotfi Mansouri staged the premiere of Thomas Pasatieri's THE BLACK WIDOW at Seattle Opera in 1972 and has directed many other American operas including Samuel Barber's VANESSA, Leonard Bernstein's TROUBLE IN TAHITI, Douglas Moore's GALLANTRY and five by Gian Carlo Menotti. While he was general director of San Francisco Opera from 1988 to 2001, he commissioned and staged Conrad Susa's THE DANGEROUS LIAISONS (1994), Stewart Wallace's HARVEY MILK (1995), André Previn's A STREETCAR NAMED DESIRE (1998) and Jake Heggie's DEAD MAN WALKING (2000). Born In Teheran, Mansouri studied at UCLA and was resident stage director for Zurich and Geneva opera companies before becoming general director of the Canadian Opera Company in 1976.

MANY MOONS *1962 children's opera by Dougherty*

Once-upon-a-long-time-ago in a kingdom-by-the-sea, Princess Lenore got ill from eating too many tarts. She told everyone she couldn't get better until someone brought her the moon. After a heated debate, she was given a tiny gold moon on a chain and immediately recovered. Celius Dougherty children's opera *Many Moons,* libretto by the composer based on a delightful fairy tale by James Thurber, premiered at Vassar College in Poughkeepsie, New York, on November 3, 1962.

MARCO POLO *1995 opera by Tan Dun*

Venetian merchant Marco Polo travels to China in 1271 with his father and uncle and stays for two decades acting as agent/advisor to Kublai Khan. The travel book he writes when he returns in 1295 provides Europe with its first authoritative account of the Far East. Tan Dun's opera *Marco Polo,* libretto by Paul Griffiths based on his novel *Myself and Marco Polo,* was commissioned by the Edinburgh Festival and premiered at the Munich Biennale on May 7, 1996. Marco Polo is portrayed by two people in the opera with Marco the young traveler and Polo the older man remembering his past. There is no straight forward narrative and the journey is seen as a spiritual as well as geographic quest. The score mixes medieval and Chinese music and there is a role for a Peking Opera singer. Tenor Thomas Young was Polo, mezzo-soprano Alexandra Montano was Marco, bass Dong-Jian Gong was Kublai Khan, soprano Susan Botti was Marco Polo's lover Water, baritone Stephen Bryant was Dante/Shakespeare, mezzo-soprano Nina Warren was Scheherezade/Mahler/Queen and Peking Opera singer Shizheng Chen was Rustichello/Li Po. Martha Clarke directed and Tan Dun conducted. The opera, reprised in Holland, Vienna and Hong Kong, was given its first American performance by New York City Opera in November 1997 in a production by Martha Clarke with Tan Dun conducting.

1996 Holland Festival. Thomas Young sings the role of Polo with Alexandra Montano as Marco in this live recording by the original cast made on June 20, 1996, at the Holland Festival in Amsterdam. Dong-Jian Gong is Kublai Khan, Susan Botti is Water, Shizheng Chen is Rustichello/Li Po and Stephen Bryant is Dante/Shakespeare. Tan Dun conducts the Netherlands Radio Orchestra and Amsterdam Cappella. Sony Classics CD. **1999 New Opera.**

The opera was reprised by New Opera in Vienna in 1999 in a production by Erwin Piplits. The cast, drawn from the Serapions Ensemble of Vienna, includes Gisela Theisen, Lela Wiche, Ingrid Bendl, Robert Hillebrand, Alexander Kaimbacher, Michael Wilder and Joseph Garcia. Walter Kobert and Peter Sommerer conduct the Amadeus Ensemble and New Opera Chorus. BOA Videofilmkunst DVD.

MARIA GOLOVIN   *1958 opera by Menotti*

Maria Golovin, whose husband has been a prisoner-of-war for four years, moves into an Italian villa just after World War II and meet blind veteran Donato and his mother Agata who live in a different section of the villa. Maria and Donato begin a torrid affair that lasts until Maria learns her husband has been freed and she will have to return to him. Donato becomes violently jealous and attempts to shoot Maria with a gun he got from an escaped Prisoner. His mother arranges for him to shoot in the wrong direction but lets him think he has shot and killed her. Gian Carlo Menotti's opera *Maria Golovin*, libretto by the composer, was commissioned by NBC Opera Theater and premiered at the Brussels World Fair on August 20, 1958. Franca Duval was Maria Golovin, Richard Cross was Donato, Patrica Neway was Donato's Mother, Ruth Kobart was Agata, Herbert Handt was Dr. Zuckertanz, William Chapman was the escaped Prisoner and Lorenzo Muti was Trottoló. Rouben Ter-Arutunian designed the sets and costume and Peter Herman Adler conducted the production by NBC's Samuel Chotzinoff. The opera was given its American premiere at the Martin Beck Theater in New York on November 5, 1958, and televised on March 8, 1959. It was reprised at New York City Opera on March 30, 1959, with Ilona Kormink as Maria, Richard Cross as Donato, Patricia Neway as Mother and Norman Kelley as Dr. Zuckertanz.

1958 Original cast album. The opera was recorded in Rome in 1958 with most of the original cast. Franca Duval is Maria Golovin, Richard Cross is Donato, Patrica Neway is Mother, Genia Las is Agata, Herbert Handt is Dr. Zuckertanz, William Chapman is the Prisoner and Lorenzo Muti is Trottoló. Peter Herman Adler conducts. RCA Victor 3-LP set. **1959 NBC Opera Theater.** *Maria Golovin* was presented on NBC Opera Theatre on March 8, 1959, in the Samuel Chotzinoff production created for the Brussels premiere. Franca Duval is Maria Golovin, Richard Cross is Donato, Ruth Kobart is Agata, Patricia Neway is Mother, Herbert Handt is Dr. Zuckertanz, Chester Ludgin is the Prisoner and Lorenzo Muti is Trottoló. Peter Herman Adler conducts the Symphony of the Air Orchestra. Rouben Ter-Arutunian designed the sets and Kirk Browning directed the two-hour telecast. Video at MTR.

MARIA MALIBRAN   *1935 opera by Bennett*

Spanish mezzo-soprano Maria Garcia, singing in New York City in 1825 with her father's opera troupe, helps her father out of financial problems by agreeing to marry wealthy Eugene Malibran

Opposite: **Franca Duval and Richard Cross play star-crossed lovers in Gian Carlo Menotti's opera** *Maria Golovin.*

Tan Dun's much-traveled opera *Marco Polo* **was recorded at the Holland Festival in Amsterdam in 1996.**

instead of the man she actually loves. Robert Russell Bennett's opera *Maria Malibran*, libretto by Robert Simon, revolves around incidents in the life of the famous diva at the beginning of her career. The score includes period music associated with Malibran including Rossini's "Una voce poco fa" and "Home Sweet Home." The opera was premiered at the Juilliard Opera School April 8, 1935, with alternating casts. Josephine Antoine and Helen Marshall sang the role of Maria while Allan Stewart and Arthur de Voss sang her lover Philip Cartwright. Albert Stoessel, director of the Juilliard School Opera Department, conducted.

MARIE ANTOINETTE   *1946 "movie opera" by Previn*

Marie Antoinette is a "movie opera" created by Charles Previn and supposedly staged at the Met in the finale of the 1946 MGM film *Two Sisters from Boston*. Lauritz Melchior plays the Metropolitan Opera tenor who sings the opera on stage opposite newcomer Kathryn Grayson. He is King Louis XVI, she is Marie Antoinette and they wear elaborate period costumes and perform in a mammoth set filled with extras (MGM built a 500-foot-wide reproduction of the Old Met interior for the scene). The big number in the opera is their duet "Oh Dream of Love," based on music by Liszt like the rest of the score. The film also features Melchior and Grayson in a duet in another movie opera based on music by Mendelssohn but this one is never named. Emil Rameau plays the nervous orchestra conductor and the opera cast members include Helen Dickson, Symona Boniface, Dina Smirnova, Mario Bramucci, Ed Agresti, Daniel DeGonghe, Tom Tomarez and George Calliga. Joseph Pasternak produced the film and Henry Koster directed. MGM/UA VHS/DVD.

MARIE CHRISTINE   *1999 operatic musical by LaChiusa*

The classical Greek myth of Medea transposed to 1899 New Orleans. Marie Christine, an aristocratic Creole woman with voodoo powers, has been condemned to death and is on death row. She explain to the other prisoners the reason for her condemnation: she had fallen in love with a ambitious sea captain who betrayed to better himself so she killed their two small children in revenge. Michael John LaChiusa's *Marie Christine*, libretto by the composer based on the Greek myth, opened at the Vivien Beaumont Theater in Lincoln Center on December 2, 1999, with Audra McDonald playing Marie, a role that was written for her. Anthony Crivello was her faithless lover Dantes Keyes, Mary Testa was entertainer Magdalena, Vivian Reed was Marie's mother and Mary Bond David, Andrea Frierson-Toney and Jennifer Leigh Warren were the Greek chorus-like trio of prisoners. Christopher Barreca designed the sets, Graciela Daniele directed and David Evans conducted. The critics were impressed by *Marie Christine's* stylish blending of Copland-like folksy classicism with blues, jazz and ragtime idioms but could not decide whether it was a musical or an opera. McDonald and LaChiusa won high praise but the work proved difficult for Broadway audiences and had only a short run.

1999 Original cast album. Audra McDonald sings the role of Marie Christine in this recording by the original cast made in a New York studio on May 6, 1999. Anthony Crivello is Dantes Keyes, Mary Testa is Magdalena, Vivian Reed is Marie's mother and Mary Bond David, Andrea Frierson-Toney and Jennifer Leigh Warren are the prisoners. David Evans conducts. RCA Victor CD.

MARILYN   *1993 opera by Laderman*

The life of Hollywood legend Marilyn Monroe portrayed through flashbacks, memories and dreams in the year 1962. Her relationships with a Senator, a Psychiatrist, her Husband and Movie Moguls are explored. Eventually she takes an overdose of pills and dies on the altar of a church. Ezra Laderman's documentary-like opera *Marilyn*, libretto by Norman Rosten, premiered at New York City Opera on October 6, 1993. Kathryn Gamberoni was Marilyn, Michael Rees Davis was the Senator, Ron Baker was the Psychiatrist, Philip Cokorinos was husband Rick, Susanne Marsee was secretary Rose, Michele McBride was sister Vinnie and John Lankston and Jonathan Green were the Moguls. Jerome Sirlin designed and staged the opera, V. Jane Suttell created the costumes and Hal France conducted the New York City Opera Orchestra. Rosten, a close friend of Monroe in her final years and author of a biography, portrays Monroe as an innocent with irresistible sexuality and a need to be protected. Monroe's three husbands (James Dougherty, Joe DiMaggio, Arthur Miller) are combined into the husband Rick, while John and Robert Kennedy are combined into the Senator. Laderman's tonal score uses jazz and other popular music styles to re-create the feeling of the period.

MARK ME TWAIN   *1993 opera by Herbolsheimer*

After silver is discovered in Virginia City, Nevada, in 1859 and the Comstock Lode makes miners millionaires, the city becomes famous. Writer Mark Twain, actress Adah Menken, millionaire miner John Mackay and brothel keeper Julie Bulette make it notorious. Bern Herbolsheimer's 27-scene opera *Mark Me Twain*, libretto by Phil Shallat, was commissioned by Nevada Opera to celebrate its twenty-fifth season and premiered in Reno on April 22, 1993. Jeffrey Francis was Mark Twain, Nancy Shade was Adah Menken, David Small was Twain's sidekick Dan De Quille, Gregory Stapp was millionaire miner John Mackay and Evelyn de la Rosa was the famous madam Julie Bulette. John Bardwell designed the sets and Nevada Opera founder Ted Puffer staged the opera and conducted the Nevada Opera Orchestra and Chorus.

MARKHEIM   *1966 opera by Floyd*

Markheim murders a pawnbroker on Christmas Eve because he

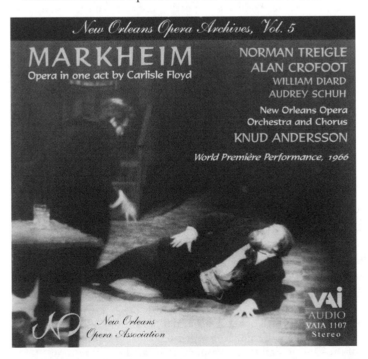

Carlisle Floyd's allegorical opera *Markheim* was premiered and recorded by New Orleans Opera in 1966.

will not loan him money. A Faustian Stranger offers him happiness if he will also kill the pawnbroker's assistant Tess but Markheim refuses and surrenders to the police. Carlisle Floyd's allegorical one-act opera *Markheim,* libretto by the composer based on a Robert Louis Stevenson story, was premiered by New Orleans Opera on March 31, 1966. Norman Treigle starred as Markheim with Alan Crofoot as the pawnbroker Josiah Creach, Audrey Schuh as Tess and William Diard as the Faustian Stranger. The composer staged the opera and Knud Andersson conducted the New Orleans Opera Orchestra and Choir. The opera was given its belated New York premiere in May 2001 by the Center for Contemporary Opera with Richard Marshall conducting.

1966 New Orleans Opera. Norman Treigle is Markheim on this live recording based on the first two performances in 1966. Alan Crofoot is pawnbroker Creach, Audrey Schuh is Tess and William Diard is the Stranger. Knud Andersson conducts the New Orleans Opera Orchestra. VAI CD. **1974 University of Washington.** Leon Lishner is Markheim in a production by the University of Washington School of Music. Robert Julien is Creach, Carol Webber is Tess and Larry Scalf is the Stranger with Samuel Krachmalnick conducting the University of Washington Sinfonietta Dick Kindsman designed the sets, Ralph Rosinbum staged the opera and Ron Ciro directed for KCTS-TV. Telecast on PBS on July 22, 1974. Video at MTR.

THE MARRIAGE   *1953 opera by Martinů*

Young Russian bachelor Podkolyossin thinks it is time he got married so he hires a matchmaker to find the perfect woman. She suggests Agafya but he is reluctant to see her until his friend Kotchkarev makes him go. There are many other suitors but his friend chases them away. The marriage is agreed but then Podkolyossin panics and runs away. Bohuslav Martinů's 60-minute television opera *The Marriage,* libretto by the composer based on a play by Gogol, was premiered by NBC Opera Theatre on February 7, 1953. Donald Gramm was Podkolyossin, Sonia Stollin was Agafya, Michael Pollock was Kotchkarev and the supporting cast included Winifred Heidt, Andrew McKinley, Lloyd Harris, Robert Holland, Ruth Kobart, Leon Lishner and Ann Pitoniak. Samuel Chotzinoff produced, Otis Riggs designed the sets, Peter Herman Adler conducted the orchestra and John Block directed the telecast.

1958 Brno Janáček Opera. Vladimir Bauer is Podkolyossin, Jinkra Pokorná is Agafya and Jaroslav Ulrych is Kotchkarev in this recording made in Czechoslovakia by the Brno Janáček Opera company. Josef Stefl is Stepan, Libuse Lesmanová is Fyokla Ivanovna, Helena Buriánová is Arina, Mila Myslíková is Dunyashka, Jindrich Doubek is Ivan, Václav Nosek conducts the Brno Janáček Opera Orchestra. Supraphon 2-CD set.

THE MARRIAGES BETWEEN ZONES THREE, FOUR AND FIVE   *1997 opera by Glass*

The queen of hedonistic Zone Three is forced to marry the soldier-king of hierarchical Zone Four. After they learn to understand and love each other, the ruling Providers command her to return to her realm while he is ordered to marry the savage ruler of Zone Five. Philip Glass's two-act opera *The Marriages Between Zones Three, Four and Five,* libretto by Doris Lessing, was premiered in German at the Theater der Stadt in Heidelberg on May 10, 1997. Japanese coloratura soprano Akiko Nakajima sang the role of the Queen, Saskia M. Wesnigh. translated the libretto into German, Birgitta Trommler was stage director and Thomas Kalb conducted the orchestra. This second opera collaboration between

Glass and Lessing is based on the second book in her science-fiction series *Canopus in Argos.* Calling for thirty singers and dancers, full symphonic orchestra and a large chorus, it was commissioned by the city of Baden-Württemberg and the Heidelberg Cement Corporation. DePaul Opera Theater staged its American premiere at DePaul University on June 7, 2001.

MARS, LOUISA MELVIN DELOS   *American composer (1860?–?)*

Louisa Melvin Delos Mars was the first African American woman composer to have an operetta staged and published. *Leoni, the Gypsy Queen,* libretto by the composer, was premiered by the Ideal Dramatic Company in Providence, Rhode Island, on December 4, 1889, with the composer singing the role of Leoni and directing the production. Mars (née Melvin) wrote and performed in five operettas presented in the Boston and Providence area in the late 19th century and three were published: *Leoni, the Gypsy Queen, Fun at a Boarding School* and *Love in Disguise.* All five appear to have been lost.

MARSEE, SUSANNE   *American mezzo-soprano (1944–)*

Susan Marsee created important roles in seven American operas. She was Lucile in Hans Werner Henze's TV opera RACHEL LA CUBANA on NET Opera in 1974, Shelly in Andrew Imbrie's ANGLE OF REPOSE at San Francisco Opera in 1976, Estella Drummle in Dominick Argento's MISS HAVISHAM'S FIRE at New York City Opera in March 1979, Doña Manuela in Gian Carlo Menotti's LA LOCA at San Diego Opera in June 1979, beautiful Mariana in Jan Bach's THE STUDENT FROM SALAMANCA at New York City Opera in 1980, fake opera castrato Bellino in Dominick Argento's CASANOVA'S HOMECOMING at Minnesota Opera in St. Paul in 1985 and Marilyn's Monroe's secretary Rose in Ezra Laderman's MARILYN at New York City Opera in 1993. She sang Mrs. Segstrom in the televised 1990 New York City Opera production of Stephen Sondheim's A LITTLE NIGHT MUSIC. Marsee, born in San Diego, made her debut with New York City Opera in 1970.

MARSH, LUCY ISABELLE   *American soprano (1878–1956)*

Lucy Isabelle Marsh was a popular recording artist for Victor records in the early years of the 20th century performing opera arias and duets (including an *Aida* duet with John McCormack) and Broadway operetta and musical songs. She had best-selling records of the "Italian Street Song" from Victor Herbert's NAUGHTY MARIETTA in 1911, "To the Land of My Own Romance" from Herbert's THE ENCHANTRESS in 1912 and "The Song of Love" from Sigmund Romberg's BLOSSOM TIME in 1922. The IRCC CD *American Singers, Volume One* includes "Italian Street Song" and her *Aida* duet with Paul Althouse.

MARTIN, RICCARDO   *American tenor (1874–1952)*

Riccardo Martin created the role of Quintus/Gwynn in Horatio Parker's MONA at the Metropolitan Opera in 1912 and the role of Christian in Walter Damrosch's CYRANO at the Met in 1913. Martin, born as Richard Martin in Hopkinsville, Kentucky, changed his name to Riccardo when he got his start performing opera in Italy and sang at the Metropolitan Opera from 1907 to 1918.

MARTIN, VERNON   *American composer (1929–)*

Vernon Martin likes to include witty word play in his one-act operas and this has helped make them popular with After Dinner

Opera Company in New York, especially those based on work by Gertrude Stein, James Thurber and Constantine Cavafy. He began with the Stein opera LADIES' VOICES performed in Norman, Oklahoma, in 1956. Next was the Cafavy-derived *Waiting for the Barbarians* premiered by After Dinner Opera in 1984. *Fables for Our Time,* based on the Thurber work, was presented by After Dinner Opera in 1984 and 1989. DOCTOR FAUSTUS LIGHTS THE LIGHTS, using the Stein work as libretto, was composed in 1987. Martin was born in Guthrie, Oklahoma.

MARTIN'S LIE   *1964 opera by Menotti*

Martin is a young orphan living in a northern European church during the religious wars of the 16th century. He and other orphans are looked after by the good-hearted housekeeper Naninga and kindly Father Cornelius, the priest in charge of the church. Each night one of the orphans has to stay in the kitchen to frighten the rats away. On Martin's night to guard the kitchen, he opens the door to a Stranger who has been wounded in the stomach and says he will be killed if found. The Stranger convinces Martin that he might be his long lost father, so Martin agrees to hide him under the floor. When the Sheriff arrives looking for the fugitive, Martin refuses to admit he has seen him. The Sheriff attempts to frighten the boy with a hot iron but this causes Martin to collapse and die. The priest takes Martin in his arms and tells him he was right, the Stranger was his father. It is a good lie, he explains. Gian Carlo Menotti's church opera *Martin's Lie,* libretto by the composer, was first performed at Bristol Cathedral in England on June 3, 1964. Michael Wennink sang the role of Martin, Donald McIntyre was the Stranger, William McAlpine was Father Cornelius, Noreen Berry was Naninga, Otakar Kraus was the Sheriff, Keith Collins was Christopher, Roger Nicholas was Timothy and Hugh Smith Marriott was the Executioner. Anthony Powell designed the sets and costumes, Lawrence Leonard conducted the English Chamber Orchestra and St. Mary Redcliffe Secondary School Chorus and Menotti staged the production.

1965 Bristol Cathedral. Michael Wennink is Martin and Donald McIntyre the Stranger in this film of the Bristol Cathedral production shot on June 3, 1964, and telecast by CBS in America on May 30, 1965. William McAlpine is Father Cornelius, Noreen Berry is Naninga, Otakar Kraus is the Sheriff, Keith Collins is Christopher, Roger Nicholas is Timothy and Hugh Smith Marriott is the Executioner. Menotti, who staged the opera, narrates the story as Lawrence Leonard conducts the St. Mary Redcliffe Chorus and English Chamber Orchestra. Kirk Browning directed the 52-minute telecast. Video at MTR. **1996 Newcastle Hospital.** Connor Burrowes is Martin and Alan Opie the Stranger in this recording taped in November 1996 at the Jubilee Theater in St. Nicholas's Hospital, Newcastle, England. Pamela Helen Stephen is Naninga, Robin Leggate is Father Cornelius, Matthew Best is the Sheriff and the Tees Valley Boys' Choir are the orphans. Richard Hickox conducts the Northern Sinfonia Orchestra. 44 minutes. Chandos CD.

MARTINŮ, BOHUSLAV   *Czech composer (1890–1959)*

Bohuslav Martinů, who lived in America from 1940 to 1953, composed two operas with English librettos during this period, both commissioned and premiered by American television companies. THE MARRIAGE, libretto by the composer based on a play by Gogol, was premiered on NBC Opera Theatre on February 7, 1953. WHAT MEN LIVE BY, libretto in English by the composer based on a story by Tolstoy, was premiered in May 1953.

Michael Wennink sang the role of Martin in the 1964 Bristol premiere of *Martin's Lie.*

THE MARTYR   *1893 opera by Freeman*

Egyptian noble Platonus, who has converted to the religion of Jehovah, is condemned to be burned at the stake by the Pharaoh despite the intervention of his beloved Shirah. Harry Lawrence Freeman's *The Martyr,* libretto by the composer, was premiered in September 1893 at the Deutsches Theater in Denver, Colorado, by the Freeman Grand Opera Company. William Carey sang the role of Platonus, Ida Williamson was Shirah, Abram Williamson was the Pharaoh, Adah Roberts was the Queen and Edward Bennett was the High Priest. The same company staged it in Chicago later the same year and in Cleveland in 1894. It was revived in Chicago in 1905 and performed at Carnegie Hall in 1937. This was the first opera by Freeman, the first African American opera composer to create a substantial body of work.

MARY, QUEEN OF SCOTS   *1977 opera by Musgrave*

Intrigues at the court of Mary, Queen of Scots, in the 1560s. The Earl of Moray and James Bothwell contend for Mary's hand but she favors Lord Darnley. After many betrayals, she is forced to flee to England leaving her child behind as king. Thea Musgrave's three-act opera *Mary Queen of Scots,* libretto by the composer based on Amalia Elguera's play *Moray,* was premiered by Scottish Opera in Edinburgh on September 6, 1977. Catherine Wilson was Mary, Queen of Scots, Jake Gardner was James Stuart, David Hillman was Lord Darney, Gregory Dempsey was James Bothwell, Stafford Dean was David Rizzio and Cardinal Beaton, William McCue was Lord Gordon, Ian Comboy was the Earl of Morton, John Robertson was the Earl of Ruthven, Linda Ormiston was Mary Seaton, Eryl Royle was Mary Beaton, Una Buchanan was Mary Livingston and Barbara Barnes was Mary Fleming. Robin Don, Colin Graham and Alex Reid were the designers, Colin Graham directed and the composer conducted. Virginia Opera staged the opera in Norfolk, VA, in March 1978 with Ashley Putnam as Mary, Queen of Scots, and Peter Mark conducting.

1978 Virginia Opera. Ashley Putnam sings the role of Mary, Queen of Scots, in this recording of the opera made in April 1978 with the Virginia Opera cast. Jake Gardner is James Stuart, Barry Busse is James Bothwell, Jon Garrison is Lord Darney, Kenneth Bell is David Riccio, Carlos Serrano is Cardinal Beaton, Francesco Sorianello is Lord Gordon, Robert Randolph is the Earl of Morton, Pietro Pozzo is the Earl of Ruthven, Gloria Capone is Mary Seton, Nancy Boling is Mary Beaton, Ann Scholten is Mary Livingston and Pamela Scott is Mary Fleming. The composer conducts the Virginia Opera Association Orchestra and Chorus. MMG LP box/Novello CD box.

MARY DYER   *1976 opera by Owen*

Quaker Mary Dyer goes to Boston in 1654 to protest the hanging of a Quaker for his beliefs. She is arrested because Massachusetts has a law that excludes Quakers from entering the state on pain of death. Despite strong protests and the reluctance of Governor John Endicott, she is hanged. Richard Owen's three-act opera *Mary Dyer,* libretto by the composer based on the trial transcripts and contemporary letters and diaries, was premiered by the Eastern Opera Company in Suffern, NY, on June 12, 1976.

MARYLAND   *American state (1788–)*

Baltimore heard its first opera in 1752 and had its own opera house by 1782. One of the first American operas, *Columbus: or, The Discovery of America* (composer unknown) was staged in Baltimore on March 18, 1783. Dudley Buck's DESERET, the most controversial American opera of the 19th century (Mormon leader Brigham Young's polygamy,) was staged at the Academy of Music in November 1880. Victor Herbert's comic operas *The Tattooed Man* (1907) and SWEETHEARTS (1913) were premiered at the Academy of Music on their way to Broadway. Another famous comic opera, Victor Jacobi and Fritz Kreisler's *Apple Blossoms* premiered at Ford's Theater in 1919 before going to New York. Ford's Theater is also the setting of Cole Porter's musical KISS ME KATE which takes place in the theater during the tryout of a musical based on *The Taming of the Shrew.* Other operas set in Maryland include Domenick Argento's COLONEL JONATHAN THE SAINT, about a woman in love with a ghost in the post Civil War era, and Sigmund Romberg's MY MARYLAND, set in Frederick and based on Whittier's Civil War poem *Barbara Frietchie.*

Maryland-born opera people include *Porgy and Bess* star Anne Brown (Baltimore), tenor Damon Evans (Baltimore), composer Philip Glass (Baltimore), bass Spiro Malas (Baltimore), composer Christopher Rouse (Baltimore), composer/conductor Emma Steiner (Baltimore), baritone Robert Weede (Baltimore) and librettist Rida Johnson Young (Baltimore). Abolitionist orator FREDERICK DOUGLASS, the subject of two operas, escaped from slavery in Maryland.

Annapolis: Raynor Taylor, who came to America from London in 1791 with an actress, presented three of his ballad operas at the Annapolis Assembly Room in 1793: *Capocchino and Dorinna* and *The Gray Mare's the Best Horse* on January 20 and *The Old Woman of Eighty-Three* on February 28. Annapolis Opera, founded in 1972, presents operas at Maryland Hall for the Creative Arts.

Baltimore: Baltimore (Civic) Opera, founded in 1927, staged operas and operettas by Baltimore composers in the 1930s: Franz

Bornschein's operetta *The Willow Plate* in 1932; Emmanuel Wad's *Swing Low* in 1933; Gustav Strube's *Ramona* (aka *The Captive*) in 1938; and Abram Moses' *Melody in "I"* in 1939. The Baltimore Opera Company, founded in 1950, became nationally known in 1952 when Rosa Ponselle became its artistic director and it began presenting productions at the Lyric Opera House. It premiered Thomas Pasatieri's INES DE CASTRO in 1976 and it co-commissioned Carlisle Floyd's COLD SASSY TREE. It has staged Aaron Copland's THE TENDER LAND, Floyd's SUSANNAH, George Gershwin's PORGY AND BESS, Lee Hoiby's THE ITALIAN LESSON, Pasatieri's LA DIVINA, Hugo Weisgall's THE STRONGER and Virgil Thomson's THE MOTHER OF US ALL. The Peabody Conservatory of Music (now Peabody Opera) saw the premieres of Harriet Ware's *Undine* in 1923, Louis Cheslock's *The Jewel Machine* in 1940, Dominick Argento's *The Sicilian Limes* in 1954, Hugo Weisgall's THE TENOR in 1963, Sergius Kagen's *Hamlet* in 1962 and Douglas Moore's *The Greenfield Christmas Tree* in 1962. Charles Kent's *A Room in Time* was premiered on television on WBAL-TV in Baltimore on January 9, 1966. Jean Eichelberg Ivey's TESTAMENT OF EVE, about a argument between Lucifer and Eve, was premiered in 1976. Leslie Adams' *Blake* was premiered at Brown Memorial Woodbrook Presbyterian Church on October 24, 1997. Opera Vivente, Baltimore's chamber opera company, has presented Aaron Copland's THE TENDER LAND and Gian Carlo Menotti's AMAHL AND THE NIGHT VISITORS.

Chestertown: Gerry E. Clark's *Westchester Limited* premiered at Washington College in Chestertown in 1973.

Cheverley: Three short operas premiered at the Publick Playhouse in Cheverley in January 1981: Thomas Cain's *Jack and Roberta,* David Miller's *Ben* and Lawrence Moss's *Dreamscape.*

Largo: Thomas Czerny-Hydzik's *The Tell-Tale Heart* and Thomas Cain's *The Lesson* were premiered by Prince George's Civic Opera in Largo in 1979.

Lutherville: Hugo Weisgall's THE STRONGER, a soprano tour-de-force based on an August Strindberg play, was created for the Hilltop Opera Company which premiered it in Lutherville on August 6, 1952.

Owing Mills: Maryland Opera recorded Dominick Argento's MISS HAVISHAM'S WEDDING NIGHT and A WATER BIRD TALK at the Gordon Center for the Performing Arts in Owing Mills in 1996. Kirke Mechem's *Newport Rivals* was given a staged reading by Maryland Opera in 2000.

Silver Springs: Alfred Neuman premiered four church operas at the Christ Congregational Church in Silver Spring: *An Opera for Everyone* and *An Opera for Easter* in 1963 and *The Rites of Man* and *An Opera for Christmas* in 1969.

THE MASQUE OF ANGELS   *1964 opera by Argento*

A band of angels led by archangel Metatron get involved with a romance while they are on a church inspection. Dominick Argento's one-act opera *The Masque of Angels,* libretto by John Olon-Scrymgeour, was premiered by the Center Opera Company at the Tyrone Guthrie Theater in Minneapolis on January 9, 1964.

MASS   *1971" theater piece for singers" by Bernstein*

The Roman Catholic Mass is the framework for this music theater work. A path leads from the orchestra pit to the stage to an altar space and then up stairs to a distant summit. There is a pit orchestra of strings, percussion and organ and a stage orchestra of brass, woodwinds, guitars and keyboards with instrumentalists in costume. A chorus of singers and dancers in street clothes performs down stage, a mixed choir in robes sings from upstage pews.

Following loud soprano, bass, soprano/alto and tenor/baritone versions of the *Kyrie Eleison* (Lord, have mercy!), a soft guitar chord introduces a folk singer in blue jeans who performs "A Simple Song" of praise. He puts on vestments and becomes the Celebrant, the central person in *Mass*. The ensemble perform music in a range of styles, including gospel, blues, scat, opera, Broadway musical and Hebrew chant, while asking for peace. The Celebrant, unable to cope with the demand, performs an operatic mad scene and disappears into the orchestra pit. *Mass* ends with the hymn "Secret Songs" performed by boy soprano and ensemble followed by a spoken benediction: "The mass is ended, go in peace." Leonard Bernstein's *Mass,* "A theatre piece for singers, players and dancers," was created for the opening of the John F. Kennedy Center for the Performing Arts in Washington, D.C. and premiered on August 8, 1971. The libretto is taken from the liturgy of the Roman Mass with secular additions by Stephen Schwartz and the composer. Alan Titus was the Celebrant with the chorus ensembles drawn from the Norman Scribner Choir, Berkshire Boy Choir and Alvin Ailey American Dance Theater. Alvin Ailey arranged the choreography, Oliver Smith designed the sets, Frank Thompson designed the costumes, Gordon Davidson staged the production and Leonard Bernstein conducted. *Mass* was savaged by critics but loved by audiences who made the original cast album a best seller. It continues to amaze listeners and some of its numbers have found a recital life on their own.

1971 Kennedy Center. Alan Titus sings the role of the Celebrant with the original cast and choirs of the Kennedy Center production in this recording made soon after the premiere. Leonard Bernstein conducts. Columbia LP/Sony CD. **1973 Vienna Konzerthaus.** John Mauceri leads the Yale Symphony Orchestra and Vienna Singakademie Choir in the European premiere of *Mass* at the Vienna Konzerthaus. Brian Hume and Thomas Whittemore are the soloists, James Schaffer was stage director and Brian Large directed the telecast on November 11 1973. Video at MTR. **1980 Barbara Cook.** Barbara Cook sings "A Simple Song" from *Mass* in a concert at Carnegie Hall on September 14, 1980. It on her album *It's Better with a Band.* MMG CD. **1981 Kennedy Center revival.** John Mauceri conducts the Kennedy Center revival of *Mass* with Joseph Kolinski as the Celebrant, Everett Govan as the Boy Soloist, Stephen Bogardus and Jamie Bernstein. Tom O'Horgan was stage director. Telecast September 19, 1981. Video at MTR. **1990 Peter Hoffman/Deborah Sasson.** Peter Hoffman and Deborah Sasson perform "A Simple Song" and "Secret Songs" from *Mass* on their album *The Essential Bernstein.* Michael Tilson Thomas conducts the Los Angeles Philharmonic. Sony Classics CD. **1991 Roberta Alexander.** Roberta Alexander performs two numbers from *Mass,* "A Simple Song" and "I Go On" the album *Bernstein: Songs* with support from Tan Rome. Etcetera CD. **1997 Harolyn Blackwell.** Harolyn Blackwell sings "A Simple Song" from *Mass* on her album *Blackwell Sings Bernstein.* RCA CD.

MASSACHUSETTS *American state (1788–)*

American opera arrived in Boston in the 18th century. Victor Pelissier's *The Launch, or Huzzah for the Constitution,* premiered at the Haymarket Theater in Boston on September 20, 1897. *The Better Sort: or, The Girl of the Spirit,* an anonymous "operatic, comical farce," was published in Boston in 1789. Lucien Southard's *The Scarlet Letter* was performed in 1855 followed by his *Omano* in 1858. C. D. Blake's *The Electric Spark* and *The Light-Keeper's Daughter* were presented in 1862.

Julius Eichberg premiered three light operas at the Boston Museum: THE DOCTOR OF ALCANTARA in 1862, *A Night in Rome*

in 1864 and *The Rose of Tyrol* in 1865. (*The Doctor of Alcantara* later became the first American opera staged by an African American opera company.) Benjamin Woolf, who wrote the libretto for Eichberg's operas, also composed and he premiered his comic operas *Lawn Tennis* in 1880, *Pounce and Company* in 1883 and *Westward Ho!* in 1894. Owen Wister, author of *The Virginian,* was also a composer and he premiered his opera *La Serenade* in 1883. George Chadwick's popular burlesque opera TABASCO was premiered by the Boston Cadets in 1894. Walter Damrosch's THE SCARLET LETTER was premiered by Boston Opera on February 10, 1896, with Johanna Gadski as Hester Prynne.

Many comic operas premiered at the Tremont Theater before going to Broadway. They included Edgar Kelley's *Puritania: or, The Earl and the Maid of Salem* in 1892, Julian Edwards' *Madeleine: or, The Magic Kiss* in 1894, John Philip Sousa's EL CAPITAN in 1896, Gustav Luders' *The Prince of Pilsen* in 1902 and Alfred Robyn's *The Yankee Consul* in 1903. Victor Herbert's premiered two comic operas at the Schubert Theater, *The Duchess* in 1911 and *The Lady of the Slipper* in 1912.

Massachusetts-born opera composers include John Adams (Worcester), Paul Hastings Allen (Boston), Leonard Bernstein (Lawrence), Philip Bezanson (Athol), George W. Chadwick (Lowell), Frederick Converse (Newton), Henry F. Gilbert (Somerville), Henry K. Hadley (Somerville), Alan Hovhaness (Somerville), Horatio Parker (Auburndale), Edward E. Rice (Brighton), George Frederick Root (Sheffield), Michael Sahl (Boston), Judith Shatin (Brookline), Charles Skilton (Northampton), Richard Wernick (Boston), Frank Wigglesworth (Boston) and Christopher Yavelow (Cambridge).

Massachusetts-born opera singers include contralto Eunice Alberts (Boston), soprano June Anderson (Boston), tenor Michael Bartlett, tenor Charles Hackett (Worcester) and baritone James Maddalena (Lynn).

Operas set in Massachusetts include Richard Owen's MARY DYER (Quaker woman hanged in 1654), Howard Hanson's MERRY MOUNT (Puritan pastor loves Cavalier woman), John La Montaine's patriotic opera/oratorio BE GLAD THEN AMERICA (Boston Tea Party), Carlisle Floyd's BILBY'S DOLL (witchcraft in the 17th century), Robert Ward's THE CRUCIBLE (Salem during the witch trials), Charles Cadman's A WITCH OF SALEM (witchcraft in Salem), George Root's THE HAYMAKERS (farm life in the 19th century), Jack Beeson's LIZZIE BORDEN (axe murders in Fall River), Frank Wigglesworth's *The Police Log of the Chronicle* (Ipswich police tell all), Anton Coppola's SACCO AND VANZETTI (anarchists' trial in 1920s)and Stephen Paulus's SUMMER (unwed mother in village),

Amherst: Richard Rescia's *The Portrait* was premiered by Community Opera in 1964. Ronald Perera's monodrama *The White Whale* was premiered in 1982.

Boston: The first major American opera company to present American operas on a continuing basis was the Boston Opera company, starting in 1896 with Walter Damrosch's THE SCARLET LETTER followed by Frederick Converse's THE PIPE OF DESIRE in 1906 and Converse's THE SACRIFICE in 1911. Julian Edwards's *The Patriot,* about an attempt to assassinate George Washington, premiered in 1907. Owen Wister's prohibition-inspired *Watch Your Thirst: A Dry Opera in Three Acts* was performed in 1924. John Knowles Paine's three-act grand opera AZARA, based on *Aucassin et Nicolette* and written for Emma Eames, was premiered in concert form at Chickering Hall in 1903 after being turned down by the Metropolitan Opera. Jordan Hall saw the premiere of W. Franke Harling's *Alda* on December 7, 1908, and Robert Di Domenica's THE SCARLET LETTER in 1997. Broadway-bound operas and operettas that premiered in Boston include George Gershwin's PORGY AND BESS at the Colonial Theater in 1935; Kurt Weill's LADY IN THE DARK at the Colonial in 1940; Weill's ONE TOUCH OF VENUS at the Schubert in 1943; Weill's LOVE LIFE at the Shubert in 1948; Marc Blitzstein's REUBEN, REUBEN at the Schubert in 1955 (it didn't make it to Broadway); and Leonard Bernstein's CANDIDE at the Colonial in 1956. Sarah Caldwell established her innovative Opera Company of Boston in 1958; it held the American premiere of Roger Session's MONTEZUMA in 1976 and premiered Robert di Domenica's THE BALCONY in 1990. The New England Conservatory was the site of three premieres: Harold Farberman *Medea*, an expressionist version of the Greek myth, in 1961; Alec Wilder's post-modern *The Opening* in 1969; and Ellen Bender's RAPPACCINI'S DAUGHTER, based on the Hawthorne story, in 1992. Gunther Schuller's "fairy tale opera" THE FISHERMAN AND HIS WIFE, libretto by John Updike, was premiered by the Boston Opera Company in 1970. Bruce Adolphe's THE TELL-TALE HEART, based on the Poe story, was premiered by Opera Theatre of Boston in 1982. Boston Lyric Opera, founded in 1976, has shown great interest in American opera. It commissioned Christopher Yavelow's COUNTDOWN and premiered it in 1987. It has staged Leonard Bernstein's CANDIDE, Carlisle Floyd's WUTHERING HEIGHTS, Philip Glass's AKHNATEN, Tod Machover's RESURRECTION, Gian Carlo Menotti's AMAHL AND THE NIGHT VISITORS and THE CONSUL, Douglas Moore's THE BALLAD OF BABY DOE, Stephen Paulus's THE POSTMAN ALWAYS RINGS TWICE, Igor Stravinsky's THE RAKE'S PROGRESS and Kurt Weill's LOST IN THE STARS. Opera Boston staged John Adams' NIXON IN CHINA in 2004. The Boston Academy of Music, based at the Emerson Majestic Theater, is noted for its innovative productions which have included Samuel Barber's VANESSA, Richard Rodgers' SOUTH PACIFIC and Kurt Weill's LADY IN THE DARK. Other Boston companies presenting operas include Boston Festival Opera, Boston Early Music Festival and Exhibition, Opera Aperta and the Handel and Haydn Society.

Brookline: Edith Rowena Noyes' grand opera *Osseo*, based on Indian legends, was premiered at Maud Freschel's Theater in 1917.

Cambridge: Harvard University held the stage premiere of Randall Thompson's light-hearted SOLOMON AND BALKIS in 1942, following its radio premiere. Peter Westergaard's *Charivari* was premiered in 1953 and James Yannatos *The Rocket's Red Blare* in 1971. Theodore Chanler's THE POT OF FAT premiered in concert form at the Longy School of Music in 1955. John Harbison's FULL MOON IN MARCH, based on a Yeats' play, was premiered at the Sanders Theater by Boston Musica Viva in 1979. Philip Glass premiered three operas at the American Repertory Theater in Cambridge: THE JUNIPER TREE in 1985, THE FALL OF THE HOUSE OF USHER IN 1988 and ORPHÉE in 1993.

Concord: Thomas W. Surette's operetta *Priscilla, or The Pilgrim's Proxy* based on Longfellow's *The Courtship of Miles Standish*, was premiered on March 6, 1888. It was said to be so popular it was performed one thousand times.

Duxbury: The Plymouth Rock Center of Music and Drama premiered Alan Davis' *The Ordeal of Osbert* (based on a P. G. Wodehouse story) in 1949, Katherine Davis' *The Unmusical Impresario* in 1955, Alan Davis's *The Sailing of the Nancy Bell* in 1955 and Arnold Black's *The Prince and the Pauper* (based on the Mark Twain novel) in 1955.

Great Barrington: Berkshire Opera, founded in Pittsfield in 1985, moved to Great Barrington in 2000 after purchasing the historic Mahaiwe Theatre. See Pittsfield below for operas.

Interlaken: John Duffy's *The Eve of Adam* was premiered at the Stockbridge School in 1955.

Lenox: Lenox, in the Berkshire Hills, is the site of the Tanglewood country estate, summer home of Boston Symphony Orchestra and America's most important music festival. The Berkshire Music Center became the Tanglewood Music Center in 1985. Its premieres include three by Jan Meyerowitz: *Simoon* in 1949, *Bad Boys in School* in 1953 and *Port Town* (libretto by Langston Hughes) in 1959; Louis Mennini's *The Rope,* based on a Eugene O'Neill play, in 1955; Lukas Foss's GRIFFELKIN, first stage performance in 1956 following its TV debut; and Mark Bucci's TALE FOR A DEAF EAR, based on Elizabeth Enright's *Moment Before the Rain*, in 1957. Stanley Silverman premiered five of his surrealistic music theater works at the festival over a six-year period: ELEPHANT STEPS in 1968, *Dream Tantras* in 1971, DOCTOR SELAVY'S MAGIC THEATER in 1972, *Stage Leers and Love Songs* in 1973 and HOTEL FOR CRIMINALS in 1974. Robert Selig's *Chocorua* was premiered in 1972, John Braswell's *Interior Castle* in 1973 and Noa Ain's *Bring on the Bears* in 1982.

Lexington: G. David Eddleman's *The Cure* was premiered at William Diamond High School in 1964.

Lowell: Edith Rowena Noyes' operetta *Last Summer* was premiered in Lowell in 1896.

Malden: Prism Opera, founded in 1995, is located in Malden.

Medford: T. J. Anderson's *Thomas Jefferson's Minstrels* was premiered in Medford in 1983.

Needham: Longwood Opera, founded in 1886, has staged Gian Carlo Menotti's THE OLD MAID AND THE THIEF and THE TELEPHONE.

Northampton: Ronald Perera's THE YELLOW WALLPAPER, based on the Charlotte Perkins Gilman story, premiered at Smith College in 1989. Richard Einhorn's opera/oratorio VOICES OF LIGHT, created to be shown with Carl Dreyer's film *La Passion de Jeanne d'Arc*, was premiered by the Arcadia Players in 1994. Commonwealth Opera of Western Massachusetts, founded in 1971 as Project Opera, has staged Carlisle Floyd's SUSANNAH and Richard Rodgers' THE KING AND I.

Pittsfield: Berkshire Opera began in Pittsfield (about six miles from Tanglewood) in 1985 and it held the premiere of Stephen Paulus's SUMMER at the Koussevitsky Arts Center there in August 1999. Its other productions have included Carlisle Floyd's SUSANNAH, Gian Carlo Menotti's THE CONSUL and Igor Stravinsky's THE RAKE'S PROGRESS. The company moved to Great Barrington in 2000.

Springfield: The Court Square Theater in Springfield was used a try-out city for comic operas in the early 1900s. John Philip Sousa's popular *The Free Lance* premiered there in 1906 before going on to Broadway success. Victor Herbert premiered *When Sweet Sixteen* there in 1910 and *Her Regiment* in 1917.

Stockbridge: Henry Clarke's THE LOAFER AND THE LOAF premiered at Indian Hill Camp in 1954. Meyer Kupferman's *Antigonae*, based on the Sophocles play, was presented at the Art Center in 1973.

Waltham: Leonard Bernstein's TROUBLE IN TAHITI was first performed at the Ullman Amphitheatre at Brandeis University in 1952.

Weston: Opera Aperta in Weston is Boston's summer opera company and it presents operas in English.

Williamsburg: Alec Wilder's *Nobody's Earnest*, based on Wilde's *The Importance of Being Earnest*, premiered in Williamsburg in 1974.

Worcester: The Salisbury Lyric Opera company is based in Worcester.

MASTERSON, VALERIE   *British soprano (1937–)*

Valerie Masters sings Marsinah in the 1992 London recording of Wright/Forrest's operetta KISMET, Nina in the 1992 London recording of Wright/Forrest's SONG OF NORWAY and Claire in the 1995 London recording of Leonard Bernstein's ON THE TOWN. On the 1990 album *Love Duets from Musicals,* she joins Thomas Allen to sing "Indian Love Song" from Rudolf Friml's ROSE MARIE. Masterson, born in Birkenhead, made her debut in Salzburg in 1963 and has sung regularly at ENO and Covent Garden.

MATA HARI   *1995 opera by McDermott*

Mata Hari, a Dutch housewife named Gertrud Margaretha Zelle married to a soldier in Java, moves to Paris in 1900 and reinvents herself as an exotic dancer borrowing costumes and ideas from Javanese dance and culture She becomes a spy for Germany, obtains military information through sexual liaisons, gets caught and is executed by the French in 1917. Vincent McDermott's chamber opera *Mata Hari,* composed for Javanese gamelan and piano to a libretto by Jan Baross, was premiered by Deep Ellum Opera Theater in Dallas on May 3, 1995, in a production by Gaitley Mathews. Darlene Marks sang the role of the older Mata Hari, Jennifer Roland danced the role of the young Mata Hari, Amy Bell was Javanese goddess Rata Kidul who narrates the story, Jamey Cheek was Misha and Richard Gomez was Henri.

MATTHEWS, EDWARD   *American baritone (1904–1954)*

Edward Matthews created major roles in two important American operas. He sang the role of St. Ignatius in the premiere of Virgil Thomson's FOUR SAINTS IN THREE ACTS in Hartford in 1934 and introduced the famous aria "Pigeons on the Grass Alas"; he can be heard singing it on 1942 and 1947 recordings. He played the villainous Jake in George Gershwin's PORGY AND BESS on Broadway in 1935 and can be heard in the role in various recordings, including the 1940 original cast album.

MAUCERI, JOHN   *American conductor (1945–)*

John Mauceri made his professional debut conducting Gian Carlo Menotti's THE SAINT OF BLEECKER STREET at Wolf Trap in 1973 and has since conducted many other American operas. The following summer he conducted Menotti's anthropological opera TAMU TAMU at the Spoleto Festival in Italy. He worked on many projects with Leonard Bernstein, including productions of CANDIDE on Broadway in 1973 (recorded), at New York City Opera in 1985 (recorded) and Scottish Opera in 1989. He conducted the televised European premiere of Leonard Bernstein's MASS in Vienna in 1973 and its televised revival at the Kennedy Center in 1981. He has also been involved with many of Kurt Weill's music theater works. He conducted the televised 1979 NYCO production of STREET SCENE with Catherine Malfitano and the 1989 British premiere/recording by Scottish Opera. He conducted a revised extended score of LADY IN THE DARK at the Edinburgh Festival in 1988 and leads the orchestra on Ute Lemper's 1988 albums of Weill songs. He conducted the revised version of Weill's pageant opera THE ETERNAL ROAD in Germany in 1999 and its reprise at the Brooklyn Academy of Music in 2000. He conducts the orchestra on the 1987 operatic recording/video of Frederick Loewe's MY FAIR LADY with Kiri te Kanawa in 1987, the Hollywood Bowl Orchestra in Richard Rodgers's THE KING AND I with Julie Andrews in 1992 and the production/recording of Marc Blitzstein's REGINA with Scottish Opera in 1992. He led the orchestra for the premiere of Andrew Imbrie's ANGLE OF REPOSE at San Francisco Opera in 1976 and he conducted the operatic revival of Victor Herbert's NAUGHTY MARIETTA at New York City Opera in 1978. Mauceri, who was born in New York City, studied at Yale and Tanglewood. He was named principal conductor of the Hollywood Bowl

Orchestra in 1991 and music director of Pittsburgh Opera in 2000. He has also been music director of Scottish Opera and Washington Opera.

MAXWELL, LINN   *American mezzo-soprano (1945–)*

Linn Maxwell created the role of Ragtime Lady in Silverman's ELEPHANT STEPS at the Berkshire Festival in 1968. She sings the role of Indiana Elliot on the 1977 recording and telecast of Santa Fe Opera's production of Virgil Thomson's THE MOTHER OF US ALL. Maxwell, born in Washington, DC, studied in Washington and New York. She also performed in a tribute to Ned Rorem and has recorded work by Thomas Pasatieri.

MAYER, WILLIAM   *American composer (1925–)*

William Mayer's best-known opera is A DEATH IN THE FAMILY (1983), based on the novel by James Agee, a powerful evocation of a time and place praised as the best new opera of 1983. He also had success with a sentimental but popular Christmas opera, ONE CHRISTMAS LONG AGO, premiered by the Little Orchestra in New York in 1962. Mayer, born in New York, studied at Yale and Juilliard and with Roger Sessions and Otto Luening. His first opera was the entertaining *Hello World!,* a one-act opera for children with a libretto by S. Otto, premiered by the Little Orchestra in New York in 1959. The micro-opera (three acts in six minutes) *Brief Candle,* libretto by Milton Feist, was premiered at the New School for Social Research in 1967 and presented by After Dinner Opera in 1968. Mayer also composed the dramatic choral work *The Eve of St. Agnes* and the ballets *The Snow Queen.* His style could be described as traditional tonal with influences from American folk styles.

Composer William Mayer

MAYERLING   *1957 opera by Humphreys-Rauscher*

Baroness Marie Vetsera falls in love with Austrian Crown Prince Rudolph, son of Emperor Franz Josef of Austria. The liaison creates a scandal and the lovers decide to die together in a hunting lodge at Mayerling in 1889. Henry Humphreys-Rauscher's three act opera *Mayerling,* libretto by the composer, was premiered in Cincinnati on November 16, 1957, by the Cincinnati Conservatory of Music Opera Department. Carolyn Goodbar and Donnelle Moon sang the role of Marie Vetsera, Samuel Jordan was

Rudolph, George Kirch was Antal/Franz Josef, Miriam Broderick was Countess Marie, John Lankston was Prince Philip, Jon Vian was Count Josef, Barron E. Wilson was Freiherr von Giesl, Arlene Perry was Marta and Will Martin Smith was Ferenc. Vincent Taylor designed the sets, Wilfred Engleman was director and William C. Byrd was the conductor.

MAYTIME   *1917 operetta by Romberg*

True love wins out after sixty years of heartbreak in Sigmund Romberg' *Maytime*, a three-generation romance based on Walter Kollo's German operetta *Wie einst im Mai*. Librettist Rida Johnson Young turned Rudolf Bernauer and Rudolf Schanzer's European story into an American tale set in old New York while Romberg wrote a new score for the show creating nine original songs. The operetta was premiered at the Stamford Theater in Stamford, Connecticut, on August 7, 1917, and opened at the Shubert Theater in New York on August l6, 1917. Peggy Wood and Charles Purcell played the lovers who are thwarted for two-generation but win out in the third. John Charles Thomas, who later sang at the Metropolitan Opera, took over the male role in 1918. The song "Will You Remember" (aka "Sweethearts") was especially successful and been recorded often by many singers.   **1919 Olive Kline/Lambert Murphy.** Soprano Olive Kline and tenor Lambert Murphy, major recording stars of the era, made the first record of "Will You Remember" in 1919 for a Victor 78.   **1922 John Charles Thomas.** Met baritone John Charles Thomas joined the Broadway production in 1918 and recorded "Will You Remember" for a Vocalion 78 in 1922. It's on the Pearl CDs *The Ultimate Sigmund Romberg Volume One* and *Music from the New York Stage, Vol. Four.*   **1923 Preferred Pictures film.** Ethel Shannon and Harrison Ford are the multi-generational lovers in *Maytime*, a silent film based on the operetta and produced by B. P. Schulberg for Preferred Pictures. Clara Bow is third-billed as the girl the hero marries on the rebound. Olga Printzlau wrote the script, Karl Struss photographed it and Louis Gasnier directed. It was usually screened with music from the operetta.   **1927 John Charles Thomas/Vivienne Segal.** "John Charles Thomas, Outstanding American Baritone" duets on "Will You Remember" with soprano Vivienne Segal on a Vitaphone sound short.   **1934 Gladys Swarthout.** Met soprano Gladys Swarthout duets on "Will You Remember" with baritone Frank Chapman on a 1934 radio show. It's on the album *Gladys Swarthout: Favorites from the Musical Theatre.* Take Two LP.   **1935 Nat Shilkret.** Nat Shilkret and his Orchestra perform a medley from *Maytime* with vocals by Fred Kuhnly, Helen Marshall, Milton Watson and Chorus on the album *Gems from Romberg Operettas.* RCA Victor LP.   **1936 Jeanette MacDonald/Nelson Eddy.** Jeanette MacDonald and Nelson Eddy recorded "Will You Remember" and "Farewell to Dreams," with an orchestra led by Nat Shilkret. "Farewell to Dreams" was cut from the film but it's on the albums *Jeanette MacDonald and Nelson Eddy* (RCA LP) and *Great Hits from Sigmund Romberg* (Pearl CD).   **1937 MGM film.** Jeanette MacDonald plays an American opera singer in Paris who falls in love with Nelson Eddy though

Jeanette MacDonald and Nelson Eddy starred in the 1937 film version of Sigmund Romberg's operetta *Maytime.*

she's promised to marry voice teacher John Barrymore. There's not much of the stage *Maytime* left in this MGM film except the song "Will You Remember" and an orchestral version of "Road to Paradise." MacDonald and Eddy perform an original movie opera called CZARITZA which was created for the film by Herbert Stothart. Noel Langley wrote the script and Robert Z. Leonard directed. MGM-UA/Warner VHS.   **1938 Anne Ziegler/Webster Booth.** Anne Ziegler and Webster Booth, the English counterparts of MacDonald and Eddy, duet on "Will You Remember" with backing from Warren Braithwaite and Orchestra on the album *The Golden Age of Anne Ziegler and Webster Booth.* EMI LP and CD.   **1944 Jeanette MacDonald/Nelson Eddy.** Jeanette MacDonald and Nelson Eddy star in an abridged version of *Maytime* on radio and duet once again on "Will You Remember" accompanied by Louis Silver and his Orchestra. Pelican/Sandy Hook LP.   **1949 Leonard Warren/ Eleanor Steber.** Metropolitan opera stars Leonard Warren and Eleanor Steber duet on "Will You Remember" on a *Voice of Firestone* telecast on November 7, 1949. Howard Barlow conducts the Firestone Orchestra. It's on the video *Leonard Warren in Opera and Song Vol. 2.* VAI VHS.   **1950 Jeanette**

MacDonald. Jeanette MacDonald sings "Will You Remember" on November 13, 1950, on *The Voice of Firestone* TV program accompanied by Howard Barlow and the Firestone Orchestra. It's on the video *Jeanette MacDonald in Performance*. VAI VHS. **1953 George London.** George London sings "Will You Remember" on *The Voice of Firestone* TV show on December 28, 1953, accompanied by Howard Barlow and the Firestone Orchestra. It's on the video *George London in Opera and Song*. VAI VHS. **1954 Vic Damone/Jane Powell.** Vic Damone and Jane Powell perform songs from *Maytime* in the MGM film *Deep in My Heart*, a romanticized biography of Sigmund Romberg. Damone sings alone on "Road to Paradise" and they duet on "Will You Remember." Soundtrack on Sony CD and film on Warner VHS. **1956 Mario Lanza.** Mario Lanza sings "Will You Remember" backed by the Jeff Alexander Choir and Henri René and his Orchestra. It's on the RCA Victor LP *A Cavalcade of Show Tunes* and RCA Victor CD *The Mario Lanza Collection*. **1964 Nelson Eddy/Gale Sherwood.** Nelson Eddy recorded "Will You Remember" in 1965 with Gale Sherwood as his singing partner. It's on the album *Helen Morgan and Nelson Eddy: The Torch Singer and the Mountie*. Trisklog LP. **1985 Teresa Ringholz/Donald Hunsberger.** Teresa Ringholz and the Eastman Dryden Orchestra led by Donald Hunsberger perform excerpts from *Maytime* on the album *Sigmund Romberg: When I Grow Too Old to Dream*. Arabesque CD. **1990 Thomas Hampson.** Thomas Hampson sings "Will You Remember" on his album *An Old Song Re-sung: American Concert Songs* accompanied by Armen Guzelimian. EMI Classics CD. **1995 Karita Mattila.** Finnish soprano Karita Mattila, best known for singing in Mozart operas, performs "Will You Remember" with the Tapiola Sinfonietta led by Pekka Savijoki. It's on the album *Karita Mattila: Wonderful*. Ondine CD. **2000 Elizabeth Futral/Steven White.** Elizabeth Futral and Steven White duet on "Will You Remember" on the album *Sweethearts*. Robert Tweten plays the piano. Newport Classics CD.

MECHEM, KIRKE *American composer (1925–)*

Kirke Mechem is best known for his choral works but he has also composed three operas. Best known is the three-act TARTUFFE, libretto by the composer based on the Molière play, which was premiered by San Francisco Opera on May 27, 1980. It has since been performed over a hundred times. *John Brown*, based on the life of the famous anti-slavery campaigner, was completed in 1989 and was to have been premiered by Lyric Opera of Kansas City in 1996 but was postponed. *Newport Rivals*, an Americanized version of Richard Sheridan's play *The Rivals* with libretto by the composer, was given a staged reading by Maryland Opera Theater in December 2000. Mechem has also composed a dramatic cantata that has been staged, *The King's Contest* (1962), libretto by the composer based on a Biblical story.

MEDEA *1972 opera by Henderson*

Medea, who has helped Jason obtain the Golden Fleece and given him two sons, is to be banished from Corinth because ambitious Jason wants to marry King Creon's daughter. The outraged Medea, who has magical powers, decides on total revenge. She causes the death of Creon and his daughter through a poisoned robe and crown and then murders Jason's children. She leaves Corinth with Jason a destroyed man. Alva Henderson's two-act opera *Medea*, libretto by the composer based on Robinson Jeffers' poetic adaptation of Euripides' tragic play, was premiered by San Diego Opera on November 29, 1972. Mezzo-soprano Irene Dalis, noted for her performances as tragic Greek heroines, was Medea,

Marvellee Cariaga was the Nurse and Thomas McKinney was the Tutor. Walter Herbert conducted.

Earlier American operas based on the Euripides play include Rocco DiGiovanni's *Medea*, presented at the Brooklyn Museum in 1955, Harold Farberman's *Medea* staged in Boston in 1961, Jonathan Elkus' *Medea* produced at the University of Wisconsin in Milwaukee and in 1970 and Benjamin Lee's MEDEA IN CORINTH staged in London in 1971.

MEDEA IN CORINTH *1971 opera by Lees*

Medea is to be banished from Corinth because Jason wants to marry King Creon's daughter. Revengeful Medea causes the death of Creon and his daughter and murders Jason's children. Benjamin Lee's 30-minute opera *Medea in Corinth*, based on Robinson Jeffers' adaptation of Euripides' tragedy, was premiered in concert form in London on January 10, 1971, by the Grosvenor Ensemble with Harry Legge conducting. It was staged in Antwerp in 1973 and presented on television in America in 1974.

1974 CBS Television. Rosalind Elias stars as Medea in this CBS Television production of the opera. John Reardon is Jason, Ara Berberian is Creon and Irene Jordan is the Woman. Alfred Antonini conducts the New York Woodwind Orchestra. Jim Drake directed the telecast on May 26, 1974. Video at Museum of Television and Radio.

THE MEDIUM *1946 opera by Menotti*

Madame Flora, who lives in a large apartment with her teenage daughter Monica and mute assistant Toby, makes her living as a medium. With the two as unseen helpers, she is able to make bereaved parents believe they can converse with the spirits of their dead children. During one séance she thinks she feels a hand on her throat and it frightens her so much she can longer continue. She feels Toby is somehow to blame so she banishes him to the streets. When he sneaks back into the apartment to get out of the rain, she thinks he is a ghost and shoots him. Gian Carlo Menotti's chamber opera *The Medium*, libretto by the composer, premiered at Brander Matthews Theater at Columbia University on May 8, 1946. Claramae Turner created the title role of spiritualist Madame Flora/Baba, Evelyn Keller was Monica, Leo Coleman was Toby, Beverly Dame was Mrs. Gobineau, Frank Rogier was Mr. Gobineau and Catherine Mastice was Mrs. Nolan. Oliver Smith designed the sets, Fabio Rieti designed the costumes and Otto Luening conducted. Marie Powers took over the role of Madame Flora when the opera moved to Broadway, opening at the Ethel Barrymore Theatre on May 1, 1947, with Leo Barzin conducting. *The Medium* remains as disturbing as when it premiered, creating a sense of unease unlike that engendered by any other opera. See also the arias THE BLACK SWAN, MONICA'S WALTZ.

1947 Original Broadway cast. Marie Powers is Madame Flora on this recording made with the original Broadway cast. Evelyn Keller is Monica, Beverly Dame is Mrs. Gobineau, Frank Rogier is Mr. Gobineau and Catherine Mastice is Mrs. Nolan. Emanuel Balaban conducts the orchestra. 55 minutes. Columbia 2-LP set and Pearl 2-CD set. **1951 Gian Carlo Menotti film.** Marie Powers is superb as Madame Flora in Menotti's film of his opera. Fourteen-year-old Anna Maria Alberghetti is Monica, Leo Coleman is Toby, Belva Kibler is Mrs. Nolan, Beverly Dame is Mrs. Gobineau and Donald Morgan is Mr. Gobineau. The film was shot in Rome with George Wakhevitch as art director and Enzo Serafin as cinematographer. Thomas Schippers conducts the RAI Symphony Orchestra of Rome. 80 minutes. Soundtrack: Mercury 2-LP set and VAI 2-CD set. Film: VAI VHS/DVD. **1959 NBC Televi-**

sion. Claramae Turner, who created Madame Flora, stars in an Omnibus production staged by Menotti for NBC TV. Lee Venora is Monica, José Perez is Toby, Belva Kibler is Mrs. Nolan, Beverly Dame is Mrs. Gobineau and Donald Morgan is Mr. Gobineau. Werner Torkanowsky leads the Symphony of the Air Orchestra. William A. Graham directed the telecast. Video at MTR. **1961 Vienna Volksoper.** Elisabeth Höngen plays Madame Flora in an Austrian production by Otto Schenk. Maria José de Vine is Monica, Nino Albanese is Toby, Sonja Draksler is Mrs. Gobineau, Norman Foster is Mr. Gobineau and Hilde Konetzni is Mrs. Nolan. Armando Alibert conducts the Vienna Volksoper Orchestra. Telecast on March 22, 1961. Live Opera audiocassette. **1962 Denise Scharley/Elaine Lublin.** Denise Scharley sings Madame Flora in a French recording of the opera. Elaine Lublin is Monica, Nicole Menut is Mrs. Gobineau, Claude Genty is Mr. Gobineau and Solange Michel is Mrs. Nolan. Richard Blareau conducts the orchestra. RCA France LP. **1968 Betty Jane Grimm.** American contralto Betty Jane Grimm sings Madame Flora's accusatory aria "Toby, What Are You Doing" accompanied by pianist Roy Johnson on her album *Betty Jane Grimm in Concert*. Century LP. **1970 Washington Opera.** Regina Resnik is Madame Flora with Judith Blegen as Monica in this Washington Opera production by Richard Pearlman. Emily Derr is Mrs. Gobineau, Julian Patrick is Mr. Gobineau and Claudine Carlson is Mrs. Nolan. Jorge Mester conducts the Washington Opera Orchestra. Columbia LP. **1975 Stratford Ensemble.** Maureen Forrester is Madame Flora in a Stratford Ensemble production filmed by CBC TV. Shawna Farrell is Monica, Stelio Calagias is Toby and Gino Quilico is Mr. Gobineau. Raffi Armenian conducts the Stratford Orchestra. Premiere Opera VHS/video at New York Public Library. **1983 Helen-Kay Eberley.** American soprano Helen-Kay Eberley sings "Monica's Waltz" accompanied by pianist Donald Isaak on her album *American Girl*. Eb-Sko LP. **1985 Paris production with Régine Crespin.** Régine Crespin sings the role of Madame Flora in a French version of the opera recorded live in Paris. Anne-Marie Rodde is Monica and Jerome Kaltenbach conducts. Classic Opera audiocassette/ House of Opera CD. **1993 Jennifer Poffenberger.** Soprano Jennifer Poffenberger sings "Monica's Waltz" accompanied by Lori Piltz on piano. It's on the album *Mostly American*. Enharmonic CD. **1995 Paris production with Rita Gorr.** Mezzo-soprano Rita Gorr sings Madame Flora in a live recording made in Paris on April 25, 1995, with Monique Zanetti as Monica. Cyril Diederich conducts. Live Opera/Opera Classics audiocassette. **1996 Chicago Opera Theater.** Joyce Castle is Madame Flora with Patrice Michaels as Monica in this recording by the Ensemble of Chicago Opera Theater. Diane Ragains is Mrs. Gobineau, Peter Van De Graaf is Mr. Gobineau, Barbara Landis is Mrs. Nolan and Joanna Lind is the Girl's Voice. Lawrence Rapchak conducts. Cedille CD. **1999 Renée Fleming.** Met soprano Renée Fleming sings "Monica's Waltz" from *The Medium* on her recital album *I Want Magic*. She is accompanied by James Levine con-

ducting the Metropolitan Opera Orchestra. London Classics CD. **1999 Torino Opera.** Renata Scotto sings the role of Madame Flora in a live recording of a performance by Torino Opera in Italy in May 1999. House of Opera CD. **2000 Patrice Michaels.** Patrice Michaels sings "Monica's Waltz" from *The Medium* on her recital album *Introducing Patrice Michaels*. Cecille CD.

MEDUSA   *2003 opera by Bolcom*

William Bolcom's one-act monodrama *Medusa*, libretto by Arnold Weinstein, allows the apparently misunderstood female monster of Greek mythology to tell her side of the story in a kind of operatic black comedy. The opera was premiered by Cincinnati Opera in 2003 with Catherine Malfitano in the title role under the direction of Nic Muni. Brian Salesky conducted the all-strings chamber orchestra.

MEIER, JOHANNA   *American soprano (1938–)*

Johanna Meier created the role of Madame de Rosemond in Conrad Susa's THE DANGEROUS LIAISONS at San Francisco Opera

Catherine Lamy and Beverly Evans in Cleveland Opera's 1980 production of Gian Carlo Menotti's *The Medium*. Photograph by Dirk Bakker, courtesy of Cleveland Opera.

in 1994, Blanche in Seymour Barab's *Maladroit Door* at the Manhattan School of Music in New York in 1959 and Hester in Nicolas Flagello's *Sisters* at the Manhattan School in 1960. She sings the role of the actress Estelle in a 1971 recording of Hugo Weisgall's THE STRONGER and the title role of Vanessa in the 1978 Spoleto Festival televised production of Samuel Barber's VANESSA. Meier, who was born in Chicago, began her stage career as an actress in the Black Hills Passion Play and began to sing opera with the Miami Opera Guild. She made her professional opera debut at New York City Opera in 1969.

MELCHIOR, LAURITZ   *American tenor (1890–1973)*

Lauritz Melchior starred in the American "movie opera" *Marie Antoinette,* created by Charles Previn for the 1946 film *Two Sisters from Boston,* and he often performed American operetta songs, especially ones from Sigmund Romberg's THE STUDENT PRINCE. He sings "Serenade" and "Deep in the My Heart" on a 1944 radio show, performs the role of the Prince on a 1950 highlights recording and sings "Serenade" on a 1952 *Voice of Firestone* television show. He sings "I Want What I Want When I Want It" from Victor Herbert's MLLE MODISTE on a 1944 radio show and "The Song is You" from Jerome Kern's MUSIC IN THE AIR and "Some Enchanted Evening" from Richard Rodgers' SOUTH PACIFIC on a 1950 *Voice of Firestone* show. Melchior, born in Copenhagen, made his debut at the Met in 1926 and sang in five American movies.

MELVILLE, HERMAN   *American writer (1819–1891)*

Herman Melville only became popular with American opera composers after his literary reputation had been restored in the 1940s. The best-known American opera based on a Melville story is George Rochberg's 1982 THE CONFIDENCE MAN but the best-known Melville opera is English, Benjamin Britten's *Billy Budd* which premiered with an American in the title role. There are also German and Italian operas based on Melville stories. **Bartleby the Scrivener (1853).** 1961 William Flanagan's opera *Bartleby*, libretto by Edward Albee and I. J. Hinton. Premiere: York Playhouse, New York, Jan 24, 1961. 1964 Walter Aschaffenburg's opera *Bartleby*, libretto by Jay Leyda. Premiere: Oberlin College, Ohio, November 12, 1964. **The Bell Tower (1855).** 1957 Ernst Krenek's opera *The Bell Tower*, libretto by composer. Premiere: University of Illinois, Urbana, Illinois, March 17, 1957. 1974 Stephen Douglas Burton's *The Bell Tower*. 1976 Robert James Haskins' opera *The Bell Tower*, libretto by John Koppenhaver. **Benito Cereno (1855).** 1974 Stephen Douglas Burton's *Benito Cereno*, libretto by composer. Dramatic reading: Opera American Showcase, January 1981. **The Confidence Man (1857).** 1951 Ernst Krenek's *Dark Waters*, libretto by composer. Premiere: USC, Los Angeles, May 2, 1951. 1982 George Rochberg's *The Confidence Man*. libretto by composer. Premiere: Santa Fe Opera, July 31, 1982. **Moby Dick (1851).** 1940 Bernard Herrmann's dramatic cantata *Moby Dick,*, libretto by W. C. Harrington. Premiere: New York City, 1940. 1955 James Low's two-act opera *Moby Dick*, libretto by composer. Premiere: Idyllwild, California, 1955. 1982 Ronald Perera's one-act *The White Whale*, libretto by composer. Premiere: Amherst, MA, April 20, 1982. 1987 Richard Brooks' two-act opera *Moby Dick*, libretto by John Richards. 1999 Laurie Anderson's multi-media opera *Songs and Stories from Moby Dick*, libretto by composer. Premiere: Southern Methodist University, Dallas, April 29, 1999. 2000 Rinde Eckert's semi-opera *And God Created Great Whales*, libretto by composer. Premiere: Culture Project, New York, September 2000. **Norfolk Isle and the Chola Widow (1856).** 1961 Kenneth Gaburo's *The Widow*, libretto by

composer. Premiere: University of Illinois, Urbana, Illinois, February 26, 1961.

THE MEMOIRS OF ULIANA ROONEY   *1994 opera by Fine*

The life of a woman composer is seen through acted and filmed scenes across eight decades of the twentieth century, from her Kansas childhood and four marriages to her final successes. Vivian Fine's 65-minute multimedia opera *The Memoirs of Uliana Rooney*, libretto by Sonya Friedman, is quasi-autobiographical though it also references Fine's teacher Ruth Crawford Seeger and Alma Mahler. It was premiered at Bryant Park in New York in 1994 by American Opera Projects. Melanie Helton created the role of Uliana with James Busterud as her four husbands and David Stoneman as the narrator. Grethe Barrett Holby directed and Fred Cohen conducted. The opera was reprised in 1997 at the Annenberg Center in Philadelphia in collaboration with the Relache Ensemble.

MENOTTI, GIAN CARLO   *Italian American composer (1911–)*

Gian Carlo Menotti helped make opera popular with audiences outside opera houses by presenting his operas on television and Broadway. AMAHL AND THE NIGHT VISITORS (1951) was the first opera created specifically for television and it soon became the most frequently staged American opera. It was preceded by the acclaimed double bill of THE MEDIUM and THE TELEPHONE, produced on Broadway in 1947 and running for an amazing 212 performances. Menotti always wrote his own librettos and he had an extraordinary ability to create dramatic stories that fascinated audiences. He followed *The Medium* with two other Broadway operas, the political THE CONSUL (1950) and the religious THE SAINT OF BLEECKER STREET (1954). Both operas won New York Drama Critics' Circle Awards and Pulitzer Prizes.

Menotti was born in Cadegliano, Italy, but he moved to America at the age of sixteen to study at the Curtis Institute of Music in Philadelphia and most of his professional career was in the U.S. His first success was the light-hearted AMELIA GOES TO THE BALL, premiered in Philadelphia in 1937 and staged at the Metropolitan Opera in 1938. It was followed by the delightful radio opera THE OLD MAID AND THE THIEF (1939), staged in 1941 and televised in 1943. Just when it seemed he couldn't put a note wrong, the symbolic one-act THE ISLAND GOD flopped bigtime at the Metropolitan Opera in 1942 and was withdrawn by the composer. He won his reputation back with *The Medium* in 1947 and he became the first composer to film his own opera when he turned it into a movie in Italy in 1951.

Menotti's many works include THE UNICORN, THE GORGON AND THE MANTICORE (1956 madrigal opera), MARIA GOLOVIN (1958 TV opera), LABYRINTH (1963 TV opera), THE LAST SAVAGE (1963 comic opera created for Paris Opéra), THE DEATH OF THE BISHOP OF BRINDISI (1963 religious cantata), MARTIN'S LIE (1964 church opera), THE MOST IMPORTANT MAN (1971 opera premiered by New York City Opera), TAMU-TAMU (1973 anthropological opera), THE EGG (1976 church opera). THE HERO (1976 comic opera), LANDSCAPES AND REMEMBRANCES (1976 autobiographical cantata), LA LOCA (1979 opera created for Beverly Sills and San Diego Opera) and GOYA (1986 opera created for Plácido Domingo and Washington Opera).

Menotti also wrote operas for children including HELP, HELP, THE GLOBOLINKS! (1968), THE TRIAL OF THE GYPSY (1978), CHIP AND HIS DOG (1979), THE BOY WHO GREW TOO FAST (1982), A BRIDE FROM PLUTO (1982) and THE SINGING CHILD (1993). In addition he wrote librettos for longtime companion Samuel Barber (VANESSA and A HAND OF BRIDGE) and for Lukas Foss (INTRODUCTIONS AND GOOD-BYES). He founded the Festival of Two Worlds in Spoleto, Italy, in 1958 and expanded it to America in 1977. Most of his operas have been recorded and continue to be staged.

There have been a number of documentary films about Menotti which may be available on video. Two of the best are *Gian Carlo Menotti: Musical Magician* (1986) by Tom Bywaters and *Music Master: Gian Carlo Menotti* (2000) by David Thomson.

MERCER, MABEL   *American cabaret singer (1909–1976)*

English-born American cabaret singer Mabel Mercer made a small but notable foray into American opera by recording the mood-setting song which opens Acts One and Two of Gian Carlo Menotti's THE CONSUL. It is sung in French by a cabaret singer in a club across the street from the protagonist's apartment and begins with the words "Tu reviendras." It is a prophetic song telling of a woman waiting for a man to come and how he will never know the truth. It is usually featured in the TV and stage productions of the opera, often using the Mercer recording. The song was never actually finished and Menotti always refused to complete it, even when Mercer asked.

THE MERCHANT AND THE PAUPER
1999 opera by Schoenfield

The Narrator tells how the Pauper's wife was kidnapped by a general and rescued by the Merchant. The Pauper's daughter Beauty becomes engaged to the Merchant's son and the Pauper is made Emperor. He turns evil, causes the Merchant's ruin and arranges for his son to become a castaway and for Beauty to be kidnapped. The Pauper's wife finally restores order and the Pauper is overthrown. Beauty and the Merchant's Son take power and reign in peace. Paul Schoenfield's two-act opera *The Merchant and the Pauper*, libretto by Margaret B. Stearns based on an 1809 parable by Hasidic Rabbi Nachman, was premiered by Opera Theater of St. Louis on June 17, 1999. The parable is said to show how Moses led the Jews out of bondage. Thomas Barrett played the Merchant, Thomas Trotter was the Pauper, Julia Ann Wolf was the Pauper's Wife, Marcus DeLoach was the Merchant's Son, Madeleine Bender was Beauty, Yacov Zamir was the General/Pirate and Spiro Malas was the Narrator. Andrew Liberian designed the sets, Mark Lamos staged the opera and John DeMain conducted. Schoenfield's music is lyrical and singer-friendly with hints of jazz and klezmer music with a sound somewhat similar to Kurt Weill's.

THE MERCHANT OF VENICE   *1956 opera by Castelnuovo-Tedesco*

Venetian merchant Antonio borrows money from Shylock and offers a pound of flesh as surety. When Shylock demands payment, Portia finds a way to defeat him in court. Mario Castelnuovo-Tedesco's neo-romantic opera *The Merchant of Venice*, libretto by the composer based on the play by Shakespeare, was first produced in its original English-language at the Shrine Auditorium version

Composer Gian Carlo Menotti appeared on the cover of the June 1981 *Opera News*.

in Los Angeles on April 12, 1966. It premiered in an Italian translation as *Il mercante di Venezia* at the Teatro Communale in Florence on May 25, 1961, after it won an Italian opera competition. Rosanna Carteri sang the role of Portia, Renato Capecchi was Shylock, Lino Puglisi was Antonio, Aurelio Oppicelli was Bassanio, Jolana Meeguzzer was Jessica and Giuseppe Baratti was Lorenzo. Franco Capuana conducted.

MERCURIO, STEVEN   *American conductor (1956–)*

Steven Mercurio was music director of the Spoleto Festival for five seasons and is often identified with his mentor Gian Carlo Menotti. He conducted a production of GOYA in Spoleto in 1991 that is on CD, *Amelia al ballo* in Monte Carlo, *Vanessa* in Dallas and *The Saint of Bleecker Street* in Philadelphia, Washington and Fort Lauderdale. In 1986 he conducted performances of *The Death of the Bishop of Brindisi* and *Sebastian* for Menotti's 85th birthday celebration. He also conducted on the 1995 recording of Richard Einhorn's opera/oratorio VOICES OF LIGHT. Mercurio, born in Bardonia, NY, studied at Boston University and

Juilliard and began to work as an assistant conductor at the Met in 1987.

MEROLA, GAETANO   *American conductor (1881–1953)*

Gaetano Merola, who founded San Francisco Opera in 1923, conducted the premiere of Victor Herbert's comic opera NAUGHTY MARIETTA in New York in 1910 and Rudolf Friml's THE FIREFLY in New York in 1912. Both featured soprano Emma Trentini. He was general director of San Francisco Opera for thirty years but apparently had no further interest in American opera. Merola was born in Naples but emigrated to America in 1899 and was soon conducting at the Met and at Manhattan Opera.

MERRILL, ROBERT   *American baritone (1917–)*

Metropolitan Opera baritone Robert Merrill enjoyed singing American operetta. He made operatic highlights recordings of Jerome Kern's SHOW BOAT with Dorothy Kirstein in 1949, Richard Rodgers' THE KING AND I with Patrice Munsel in 1951 and Rodgers' CAROUSEL with Munsel in 1955. He recorded the aria "Ma Belle" from Rudolf Friml's THE THREE MUSKETEERS in 1949, arias from George Gershwin's PORGY AND BESS in 1950 and a duet from Sigmund Romberg's UP IN CENTRAL PARK in 1950. He often performed operetta on the *Voice of Firestone* TV show and can be seen on video singing arias from Victor Herbert's EILEEN (1955), NAUGHTY MARIETTA (1955) and THE RED MILL (1957), Romberg's NEW MOON (1955), Frederick Loewe's MY FAIR LADY (1957) and Rodgers' SOUTH PACIFIC (1963). The Brooklyn-born singer made his debut at the Met in 1945 and sang major baritone roles there until 1975.

MERRY MOUNT   *1933 opera by Hanson*

English Cavaliers create Merry Mount as a village of pleasure in 17th century Massachusetts but it is dangerously near a Puritan settlement. The Puritan pastor Wrestling Bradford, who has become obsessed with Cavalier Lady Marigold even though he is betrothed to Puritan Plentiful Tewke, leads an attack on Merry Mount as the Cavaliers celebrate while dancing around a maypole. Bradford carries off Marigold but Indians burn his Puritan village and they both perish in the flames. Howard Hanson's opera *Merry Mount*, libretto by Richard L. Stokes based on Nathaniel Hawthorne's story *The Maypole of Merry Mount*, premiered in concert form in Ann Arbor, Michigan, May 20, 1933, with John Charles Thomas as Bradford, Leonora Corona as Marigold and Frederick Jager as Lackland. It had its fully staged premiere at the Metropolitan Opera, which commissioned it, on February 10, 1934. Lawrence Tibbett was Wrestling Bradford, Göta Ljunberg was Lady Marigold, Gladys Swarthout was Plentiful Tewke, Edward Johnson was Lackland, Alfredo Gandolfi was Myles Brodrib, Giordano Paltrinieri was Jonathan Banks, Marek Windheim was Jack Prence, Arnold Gabor was Faint-Not-Tinker, Irra Petina was Desire Annable, Louis D'Angelo was Praise-God Tewke, Helen Gleason was Peregrine Brodrib, Lillian Clark was Love Brewster and George Cehanovsky was Thomas Morton. Jo Mielziner designed the sets, Wilhelm von Wymetal Jr. directed and Tullio Serafin conducted the Metropolitan Opera Orchestra. The premiere was a huge success and there were fifty curtain calls but the opera did not stay in the repertory. It was revived in 1964 in San Antonio with Brian Sullivan and Beverly Sills in the lead roles and in 1996 in Seattle with Richard Zeller and Lauren Flanigan as the stars. Hanson created a *Merry Mount Suite* based on the music of the opera in 1937.

1934 Lawrence Tibbett. Lawrence Tibbett recorded the *Merry Mount* aria "Oh, 'tis an Earth defiled" for RCA Victor on January 19, 1934, with the orchestra conducted by Wilfrid Pelletier. It's on several albums including *Lawrence Tibbett Sings Operatic Arias* (RCA LP), *Lawrence Tibbett: From Broadway to Hollywood* (Nimbus CD), *Souvenirs from American Opera* (IRCC CD) and *Towards an American Opera* (New World LP). **1934 Metropolitan Opera.** Lawrence Tibbett is Wrestling Bradford with Gladys Swarthout as Plentiful Tewke in a broadcast of the opera from the Met on February 10, 1934. Göta Ljunberg is Lady Marigold, Edward Johnson is Lackland, Irra Petina is Desire Annable, Alfredo Gandolfi is Myles Brodrib, Giordano Paltrinieri is Jonathan Banks, Marek Windheim is Jack Prence, Arnold Gabor is Faint-Not-Tinker, Louis D'Angelo is Praise-God Tewke, Helen Gleason is Peregrine Brodrib, Lillian Clark is Love Brewster and George Cehanovsky is Thomas Morton. Tullio Serafin conducts the Metropolitan Opera Orchestra and Chorus. EJS 2-LP set/Naxos 2-CD set and Omega Opera Archives 2-CD set. **1957 Music as a Language.** Hanson explains how a composer conveys the ideas and emotions of characters in an opera and uses *Merry Mount* for demonstration. This 29-minute film was made for the *Music as a Language* series when Hanson was director of the Eastman School of Music. **1970 Eastman Rochester Symphony.** Hanson conducts the Eastman Rochester Symphony and Eastman Choir in highlights from the opera. Featured are the Prelude and Opening Chorus, Bradford's arias "Woe to the Nation" and "Oh, 'tis an Earth Defiled," the Puritan chorus "It is the House of Gay Carouse" and Bradford's prayer "Almighty Father." The singers are Jerry Crawford, Charlene Chadwick Cullen, Lenita Schadema, William Fleck, Henry Nason, Kerry McDevitt, Janice Shellhammer and Calvin Callen. Mercury and Eastman Rochester Archives LP. **1974 Eastman Rochester Symphony.** Hanson conducts baritone Chester Ludgin and the Eastman Rochester Symphony in excerpts from the opera on a radio broadcast on August 19, 1974. Hanson speaks after an award presentation. Custom Opera audio-cassette. **1978 Warren Jaworski.** Baritone Warren Jaworski sings Wrestling Bradford's aria "Oh, 'tis an Earth Defiled" from *Merry Mount* accompanied by Paul Lee on piano at Indiana University School of Music in 1978. Indiana University audiocassette. **1991 Merry Mount Suite.** Gerard Schwarz conducts the Seattle Symphony Orchestra and Chorale in a performance of the *Merry Mount Suite* which includes the Overture, Children's Dance, Love Duet, Prelude to Act II and Maypole Dances. It's on the album *Howard Hanson: Choral and Orchestra Works*. Delos CD. **1996 Seattle Symphony.** Richard Zeller is Wrestling Bradford, Lauren Flanigan is Lady Marigold and Louise Marley is Plentiful Tewke in this concert performance in Seattle November 28, 1996. Gerard Schwarz, who restored the score, conducts the Seattle Symphony, Seattle Symphony Chorale, Northwest Boys Choir and Seattle Girls' choir. Walter MacNeil is Sir Gower Lackland, Charles Austin is Praise-God Tewke, Paul Gudas is Jack Prence and Barry Johnson is Myles Brodrib. House of Opera CD and Live Opera/Classic Opera audio-cassette. **1996 Boston Pops Orchestra.** The "Maypole Dances" from *Merry Mount* are played by the Boston Pops Orchestra in a concert in Symphony Hall in Boston on November 9, 1996. Keith Lockart conducts on the album *American Visions*. BMG CD. **1999 Merry Mount Suite.** Kenneth Schermerhorn conducts the Nashville Symphony Orchestra in a performance of the *Merry Mount Suite* on the Naxos CD *Howard Hanson: Orchestral Works, Vol. 1*. The "Love Duet" from the suite is included on the Naxos *American Classic Sampler* CD.

A METHOD FOR MADNESS   *1999 opera by Bernstein*

The head of an insane asylum shows off a new treatment in

which the patients act our their fantasies. One woman thinks she is an opera diva performing as Donizetti's Lucia (she sings the Mad Song) and Cherubini's Medea, another thinks he is Napoleon and sings the Marseillaise. Gradually we realize the patients have taken over the asylum. David Bernstein's black comedy opera *A Method for Madness,* libretto by Charles Kondek, is based on the EDGAR ALLAN POE story "The System of Doctor Tarr and Professor Fether." It premiered at the University of Akron School of Music in Akron, Ohio, on November 6, 1999, with Dean Southern as the asylum superintendent, Dina Kuznetsova as the opera diva, Jaret Plasterer as Napoleon, Jennifer Woda as Blue Cheese, Frandal Levin as the Frog and Michael Boley as the Train Engineer. Librettist Kondek staged the opera and Harry Davidson conducted.

MEYEROWITZ, JAN   *American composer (1913–1998)*

Jan Meyerowitz is best known for his 1950 opera THE BARRIER composed to a libretto by Langston Hughes and dealing with racial attitudes in the South. It premiered on Broadway and was later staged and broadcast in Italy and Germany. Meyerowitz composed two further operas with librettos by Hughes, the Biblical ESTHER which premiered at the University of Illinois in 1957 and *Port Town* presented at Tanglewood in 1960. Meyerowitz was born in Breslau (now Wroclaw, Poland) and studied in Berlin and Rome before emigrating to the USA in 1946. His first opera *Simoon,* based on a Strindberg story, premiered at Tanglewood in 1949. *The Barrier,* his second opera, was followed by *Eastward in Eden* (aka *Emily Dickinson*) performed in Detroit in 1951 and *Bad Boys in School* staged at Tanglewood in 1953.

MICHIGAN   *American state (1837–)*

The 2000-seat Detroit Opera House opened in 1869 and survived until 1966. The first American opera premiered in Michigan was Carl Mayer's Indian-themed *The Conspiracy of Pontiac,* staged at Bush Auditorium in Detroit on January 27, 1887. Julian Edwards, one of the leading comic opera composers of his time, premiered *When Johnny Comes Marching Home* in Detroit on October 6, 1902. Michigan Opera Theater in Detroit, founded in 1971, is the major opera company of the state. Michigan-born opera people include composer Robert Ashley (Ann Arbor), soprano Barbara Brandt (Battle Creek), composer Robert Erickson (Marquette), conductor Thomas Schippers (Kalamazoo) and soprano Cheryl Studer (Midland).

Adrian: Opera! Lenawee in Adrian, founded in 1991, presents operas in English with the Adrian Symphony Orchestra.

Albion: Albion College held the premieres of four operas by Anthony Taffs: *The Ten Virgins* in 1960, *Noah* in 1963, *The Summons* in 1964 and *Lilith* in 1967. Taffs was born in London but became an American in 1954.

Allendale: Adam Guettel's oratorio *Myths and Hymns* (aka *Saturn Returns*) was staged by Grand Valley State University Opera Theatre in 1998.

Ann Arbor: Ann Harbor is the home of the University of Michigan. Howard Hanson's MERRY MOUNT was premiered there in concert form on May 20, 1933, the year before its stage premiere at the Metropolitan Opera. Josef Blatt's *Moses on Mount Sinai* was premiered at the University in 1964 and Stanley Silverman's *Up from Paradise,* based on an Arthur Miller play, in 1974. William Albright's *The Magic City* was commissioned in 1978 and Gian Carlo Menotti staged his opera HELP, HELP, THE GLOBOLINKS! with students at the University in 1979. Film director Robert Altman staged Igor Stravinsky's THE RAKE'S PROGRESS for the university in 1989.

Detroit: Detroit Civic Opera, founded in 1928, often presented American operas, including Deems Taylor's three-act PETER IBBETSON soon after its premiere at the Metropolitan. Wayne State University premiered Jan Meyerowitz's *Eastward in Eden,* a story about Emily Dickinson, in 1951. Radie Britain's choral work *Nisan* was premiered at the Sheraton Cadillac Hotel in 1962. Temple Israel was the site of two patriotic Israeli-themed operas, Julius Chajes' *Days of the Desert* in 1966 and Martin Kalmanoff's *The Victory at Masada* in 1968. Michigan Opera Theater, the major Michigan opera company, programs many American operas and operettas. It premiered Thomas Pasatieri's WASHINGTON SQUARE, based on the Henry James novel, at the Music Hall Center in 1976 with Catherine Malfitano and Richard Cross in the main roles. Its other production include Marc Blitzstein's REGINA, Aaron Copland's THE TENDER LAND conducted by Copland and nationally televised, Carlisle Floyd's OF MICE AND MEN, Louis Gruenberg's THE EMPEROR JONES, George Gershwin's PORGY AND BESS with Leona Mitchell, Scott Joplin's TREEMONISHA with Carmen Balthrop, and Douglas Moore's THE BALLAD OF BABY DOE. It has staged three operas by Gian Carlo Menotti: AMAHL AND THE NIGHT VISITORS, THE MEDIUM directed by Sal Mineo, who played Toby, and THE TELEPHONE. It also stages American operettas including Victor Herbert's NAUGHTY MARIETTA, Jerome Kern's SHOW BOAT, Frank Loesser's THE MOST HAPPY FELLA, Richard Rodgers' THE SOUND OF MUSIC and Sigmund Romberg's THE STUDENT PRINCE.

East Lansing: Michigan State University in East Lansing saw the premiere of three dance-operas by H. Owen Reed: *Michigan Dream* in 1955, *Earth-Trapped* in 1962 and *Butterfly Girl and Mirage Boy* in 1980.

Grand Rapids: Opera Grand Rapids presents classic operas and operettas, mostly from the European repertory.

Hancock: The Pine Mountain Music Festival, founded in 1991, regularly presents opera in Calumet, Marquette and Iron Mountain. It commissioned Paul Seitz's *The Children of the Keweenaw,* libretto by Kathleen Masterson based on events surrounding a local disaster involving the children of striking miners, and premiered it on July 11, 2001,

Interlochen: The Interlochen National Music Camp, a center for student musical activity since 1928, became affiliated with the University of Michigan in 1942. It has been the site of a number of opera premieres including Hamilton Forrest's *Don Fortunio* and Edward Chudacoff's *The Circus* in 1952; Alec Wilder's *Sunday Excursion* and Roland Trogan's *The Hat Man* in 1953; Forrest's *Daelia* and *A Matinee Idyll* and Alec Wilder's *Kittiwake Island* in 1954; Don Gillis's *Pep Rally* in 1957 and Jack Williams' *The Hinge Tune* in 1965.

Kalamazoo: Donald Para's THE CASK OF AMONTILLADO, based on the Poe story, was premiered in Kalamazoo in 1979.

Midland: Norman Dello Joio's Christmas opera-oratorio *Nativity: A Canticle for the Child* was premiered at the Midland Center for the Arts in December 1987 by the Music Society which commissioned it.

Saint Joseph: Leon Stein's *The Fisherman's Wife,* based on the Grimm Brothers fairy tale, premiered in Saint Joseph in 1955.

Troy: The Piccolo Opera Company of Troy presents operas from the European repertory.

THE MIDNIGHT ANGEL   *1993 opera by Carlson*

Lady Neville is rich, cynical and bored so she decides to invite Death to be her guest of honor at a gala party. Death turns out to be a young girl who charms the guests. They ask her to stay and she agrees if someone will take over her job. Lady Neville agrees.

David Carlson's opera *The Midnight Angel,* libretto by fantasy writer Peter S. Beagle based on his story "Come, Lady Death," was commissioned by Glimmerglass and Sacramento Opera and premiered by Opera Theatre of Saint Louis on June 1, 1993. Elaine Bonazzi created the role of Lady Neville (it was written for her), Christine Abraham was Death, James Maddalena was Captain Compson, Mary Margaret Sapp was the widow's niece Margaret, Tracey Welborn was her fiancé Henry, Brad Cresswell was the widow's nephew John, Katherine Terrell was Compson's mistress Contessa dei Candini and John Stevens was the knowledgeable Butler. Linda Brovsky directed the production and Stewart Robertson conducted the orchestra. The opera was presented by Sacramento and Glimmerglass operas later the same year.

MIGENES, JULIA   *American soprano (1945–)*

Julie Migenes created the role of rebel daughter Hodel in Jerry Bock's Broadway musical FIDDLER ON THE ROOF in 1964 and began her opera career in 1965 singing Annina in the New York City Opera production of Gian Carlo Menotti's THE SAINT OF BLEECKER STREET. She has recorded operatic versions of two American operettas, singing the role of sexy Lalume opposite Samuel Ramey and Jerry Hadley in the 1991 recording of the Wright/Forrest/Borodin KISMET and Aldonza opposite Placido Domingo in the 1996 recording of Mitch Leigh's MAN OF LA MANCHA. She joins Sherrill Milnes in duet on "Close as Pages in a Book" from Sigmund Romberg's UP IN CENTRAL PARK on a 1985 Berlin TV show and sings "Summertime" from George Gershwin's PORGY AND BESS in a 1991 gala at Seville Stadium in Spain. Migenes, a native New Yorker, sang regularly with the Vienna Volksoper at the beginning of her career and did not come to the Met until 1979. She called herself Migenes-Johnson when she attracted world attention starring in Francesco Rosi's 1984 film *Carmen.*

THE MIGHTY CASEY   *1953 opera by Schuman*

It's the day of the big game with Mudville and Centerville competing for the state baseball championship but it's not going well for the home team. In the words of the poet who immortalized this famous game, "The outlook wasn't brilliant for the Mudville nine that day/The score stood four to two with but one inning left to play." With two men out, the crowd's last hope is that its greatest player, Casey, will get to bat. Big league scouts are watching the game and if Casey does well, his girl Merry knows he will be leaving. Against impossible odds two teammates get hits and Casey gets to bat. The crowd roars with joy but their joy will is short-lived; over-confident Casey strikes out. William Schuman's delightful opera *The Mighty Casey,* libretto by Jeremy Gury based on Ernest L. Thayer's poem "Casey at the Bat," was premiered in Hartford, Connecticut, on May 4, 1953. Casey does not sing (the role is mimed on stage) but his girl Merry does and the score has pleasant echoes of popular 19th century music The opera has been popular with opera organizations around the U.S. but, not surprisingly, has never been performed in Mudville.

1955 CBS Television: Danny Scholl plays Casey with Elise Rhodes as his girl Merry in this *Omnibus* CBS Television production. Rufus Smith is Centerville pitcher Snedeker, Nathaniel Frey is catcher Thatcher, George Irving is the Watchman, David Thomas is Umpire Buttenheiser, Bruce Renshaw is Charlie, Mart Marshall is the Concessionare, Robert Goss is Andy, Del Horstmann is Red, Mark Murphy is Otis, Lee Krieger is Tony, Demy Trevor is Elmer, Loren Welch is Scooter, Van Hawley is Roughhouse Flynn, Donald Clarke is Benny and Albert Linville is the Manager. Elliot Silverstein staged the opera, Samuel Krach-

malnick conducts, and Ted Danielewski directed the 60-minute telecast on March 6, 1955. Video at MTR. **1990 Juilliard Opera Center:** Stacey Robinson is Casey with Catherine Thorpe as Merry in this recording made at the Juilliard Opera Center with the Juilliard Orchestra led by Gerard Schwarz. Russell Cusick is Snedeker, David Corman is Thatcher, Franco Pomponi is the Watchman, Derek Dreyer is Charlie, Carlos Conde is the Umpire, Andrew Parks is the Manager, James Russell is the Concessionaire, Kenn Chester is the Male Fan and Susan Rosenbaum is the Female Fan. Delos CD. **1991 Gregg Smith Singers:** Rosalind Rees sings Merry and Charlie in this abridged recording with composer Schuman reading the final lines of the poem. Thomas Bogdan is pitcher Snedeker, Richard Muenz is Thatcher, Jay Willoughby is Watchman, Brian Phipps is Umpire Buttenheiser and Walter Richardson is the Manager. Gregg Smith conducts the Adirondack Chamber Orchestra, Long Island Choral Association and Gregg Smith Singers. Premier CD.

MIKI, MINORU   *Japanese composer (1930–)*

Opera Theater of St. Louis commissioned and premiered two operas by Minoru Miki, both with English librettos by Colin Graham who staged them in St. Louis. JÕRURI, based on a puppet play by Monzaemon Chikamatsu, was premiered in 1985 and reprised and videotaped in Tokyo in 1988. THE TALE OF GENJI, based on the classic novel by Lady Muraski, was premiered in 2000. Miki writes operas in the European style for a Western-style orchestra but uses Japanese themes, stories, and musical ideas.

THE MILITARY GLORY OF GREAT BRITAIN   *1762 "choral entertainment" by Lyon*

James Lyon's *The Military Glory of Great Britain* is considered to be the first original American dramatic musical work. Described as an "entertainment" with choruses and narrative, it was presented at the College of Jersey (now Princeton) on September 29, 1762, by students and then published. It concerns the heroic deeds of the British Army and leaders like General James Wolfe and General Jeffrey Amherst.

MILLAY, EDNA ST. VINCENT   *American poet/librettist (1892–1950)*

Edna St. Vincent Millay wrote the libretto for Deems Taylor's opera THE KING'S HENCHMAN, which premiered at the Metropolitan Opera in 1927. Her earlier play ARIA DA CAPO is a favorite of American opera composers and has been set at least eleven times. The long poem that first made her famous, *Renascence,* has also been made into an opera and there are more than a hundred setting of her poems. Millay, born in Rockland, Maine, began to write plays for the Provincetown Players in the 1910s after she became famous for her poems. Operas based on her works are listed below, opera title is same as work and libretto is by composer unless indicated.

Aria da Capo (1919). 1951 Burdette Fore. College of the Pacific, Stockton, CA, May 19, 1951. 1955 Cardon Burnham. New Orleans, April 17, 1955. 1960 Alan Blank. First staged in 1960. 1967 John Bilota. Finalist at New York City Opera competition. 1969 Robert Baksa. Lake George Opera, New York, August 1969. 1980 Larry A Smith. Chamber Opera Theatre of Chicago on June 11, 1980. 1981 José-Luis Greco. Encompass Music Theatre, Good Shepherd Faith Church, New York, May 13, 1981. 1990 Brent Weaver. Premiered at Clayton State College in October 1990. 1976 Bern Herbolsheimer. Premiered in Seattle, Washington on November 5, 1976. 1995 Joel E. Naumann. Premiered in 1995. 1997 Lawrence

Axelrod. Premiered on March 25 1997. **The King's Henchman (1927).** 1927 Deems Taylor (Edna St. Vincent Millay). Metropolitan Opera, NY, February 17, 1927. **Renascence (1912).** 1989 Michael Cave. Merkin Hall, November 11, 1989.

MILLER, ARTHUR   *American playwright (1915–)*

Arthur Miller's plays have been adapted for operas and the plays themselves revived to great acclaim in recent years. Robert Ward's version of *The Crucible* (1953) won the Pulitzer Prize in 1962. Miller himself adapted his unsuccessful play *The Creation of the World and Other Business* into the music theater piece *Up from Paradise* for composer Stanley Silverman. William Bolcom's operatic version of *A View from the Bridge* was premiered by Lyric Opera of Chicago. There is also an Italian opera based on *A View from the Bridge* and a French opera based on *Death of a Salesman*. Miller, one of Marilyn Monroe's three husbands, is the basis of a character in Ezra Laderman's opera *Marilyn*. (Titles of works made into operas listed below with composer and premiere. Title of opera is same as work and libretto is by composer unless otherwise indicated.)

The Crucible (1953). 1961 Robert Ward (Bernard Stambler). New York, City Opera, October 25, 1961. **The Creation of the World and Other Business (1972).** 1974 Stanley Silverman as music theater work *Up from Paradise*. Ann Arbor, Summer, 1974. New York, October 1983. **A View from the Bridge (1955).** 1999 William Bolcom (Arnold Weinstein and Arthur Miller). Lyric Opera of Chicago, October 9, 1999.

MILLS, ERIE   *American soprano (1954–)*

Erie Mills sings the role of Cunegonde in Leonard Bernstein's CANDIDE in the 1985 Grammy Award-winning recording and telecast by New York City Opera. She created the role of Sincha in Bruce Adolphe's *Mikhoels the Wise* for Jewish Opera at the Y in New York in 1982. She played the role of Anne Truelove in the New York City Opera production of Igor Stravinsky's *The Rake's Progress* in 1984 and of Sibyl Vane in the American premiere of Lowell Liebermann's opera THE PICTURE OF DORIAN GRAY at Florentine Opera in Milwaukee in 1999. Mills, who was born in Granite City, Illinois, studied at The College of Wooster, Ohio, and the University of Illinois.

MILNES, SHERRILL   *American baritone (1935–)*

Sherrill Milnes created the role of Adam Brant in Marvin Davy Levy's MOURNING BECOMES ELECTRA at the Metropolitan Opera in 1967 and is featured singing Adam's second act aria "Too Weak to Kill the Man I Hate" on the celebratory album *Met 100 Years 100 Singers*. He sings Daniel Webster's aria "I've Got a Ram, Goliath" on a Richard Tucker gala in 1991 and stars as oil baron Ajax in the 1998 Minnesota Opera production of George Antheil's *Transatlantic*. He teamed up with Beverly Sills in 1978 for *Up in Central Park,* an album of American operetta from Sigmund Romberg's UP IN CENTRAL PARK and THE DESERT SONG, Victor Herbert's EILEEN, NAUGHTY MARIETTA and SWEETHEARTS and Rudolf Friml's ROSE MARIE. He duets with Julia Migenes on "Close as Pages in a Book" from *Up in Central Park* in a videotaped 1985 concert in Berlin. Milnes, born in Hinsdale, Illinois, studied with Rosa Ponselle and made his debut with the Boston Opera Company in 1960, He joined the Met in 1965 and sang there for 25 years.

MINETTE FONTAINE   *1984 opera by Still*

Minette Fontaine, prima donna with the New Orleans Opera Company in 1845, makes wealthy plantation owner Diron fall in love with and marry her using voodoo magic. He is horrified when he finds what she has done. William Grant Still's opera *Minette Fontaine,* libretto by Verna Arvey, was premiered by Baton Rouge Opera Company in Baton Rouge, Louisiana, on October 22, 1984. Gail Dobish was Minette, Donald George was Diron, Suzanna Guzmán was Marie Laveau, Nancy Ross Assaf was Claire, Andrew Wentzel was Claude, Stephen Markuson was Lucien, Cynthia Parker was Felice and Terry Patrick Harris was Madame de Noyan. Donald Dorr directed and Charles Rosekrans conducted.

1984 Baton Rouge Opera. The Baton Rouge Opera Company premiere starring Gail Dobish as Minette was recorded with the cast as above. Charles Rosekrans conducts. Cassettes available from William Grant Still Music, 4 South San Francisco St., Suite 422, Flagstaff, AZ.

MINNESOTA   *American state (1858–)*

Minnesota Opera (called Center Opera when it began in 1964) is one of the most important and progressive opera companies in America and has premiered more American operas than any other company at venues in the twin cities of Minneapolis and St. Paul. Composers associated with Minnesota Opera include Dominick Argento and Libby Larsen.

Philip Brunelle, music director of Minnesota Opera for 17 years and founder of Plymouth Music Series, made the first recordings of Benjamin Britten's PAUL BUNYAN, Aaron Copland's THE TENDER LAND and Dominick Argento's POSTCARD FROM MOROCCO.

The first American opera to premiere in Minnesota was a grand opera, tenor/composer Willard Patton's *Pocahontas,* a story about the Native American princess performed in concert at the Radisson Hotel in St, Paul on January 4, 1911. The first resident opera company was Twin Cities opera founded in 1930 while St Paul Opera was begun in 1933.

Minnesota-born opera people include producer/librettist Howard Balk (St. Paul), composer Michael Cunningham (Warren), composer James Drew (St. Paul), composer Ross Lee Finney (Wells), librettist Arnold Sundgaard (St Paul) and composer Jane Van Etten (St Paul).

Bemidji: Bemidji State College premiered Noel S. Steven's *The Enchanted Canary* on March 18, 1961. **Duluth.** Addison Alspach's *Calvario* was premiered at the University of Minnesota in Duluth in May 1958.

Minneapolis: Dominick Argento was a professor at the University of Minnesota Twin Cities Campus in Minneapolis for many years and premiered his Shakespearean opera CHRISTOPHER SLY there in 1967. Libby Larsen's premiered three operas at the university: *Some Pig,* based on E. B. White's *Charlotte's Web,* in 1973; *The Words upon the Windowpane,* based on the Yeats play, in 1977; and *Christina Romana,* libretto by Vern Sutton, in 1988.

Minneapolis/Saint Paul: Minnesota Opera, which presents operas in both of the twin cities, opened in 1964 with Dominick Argento's THE MASQUE OF ANGELS and also premiered his THE SHOEMAKER'S HOLIDAY (1967), POSTCARD FROM MOROCCO (1971), JONAH AND THE WHALE (1974), THE VOYAGE OF EDGAR ALLAN POE (1976), MISS HAVISHAM'S WEDDING NIGHT (1981) and CASANOVA'S HOMECOMING (1985). The company's other premieres, some by its New Music-Theatre Ensemble, include Easley Blackwood's *Gulliver* (1975); Paul and Martha Boessing's *The Wanderer* (1970); Philip Brunelle/William Huckaby's *The Newest Opera in the World* (1974); Christopher Drobny's *Fire in the Future* (1987); John Gessner's *Faust Counter Faust* (1971); William Harper's *Snow Leopard* (1989); Sydney Hodkinson's *Vox Populous* (1973) Libby

Larsen's FRANKENSTEIN: THE MODERN PROMETHEUS (1990); Gunner Madsen's *Cowboy Lips* (1988); Yale Marshall's *The Business of Good Government* (1972), *Christmas Mummeries/Good Government* (1970), *Gallimaufry* (1974) and *Oedipus and the Sphinx* (1969); William Mayer's DEATH IN THE FAMILY (1981/1983); Henry Mollicone's The Mask of Evil (1982); Meredith Monk's *Book of Days* (1988); Robert Moran's FROM THE TOWERS OF THE MOON (1992), Hannibal Peterson's DIARY OF AN AFRICAN AMERICAN (1994), Peter Schickele's THE ABDUCTION OF FIGARO (1984); Kim Sherman's *Femme Fatale* (1986), *A Long Island Dreamer* (1987), *Red Tide* (1989) and *Three Visitations* (1996); Robert Starer's APOLLONIA in 1979; Eric Stokes' HORSPFAL (1969) and *The Jealous Cellist* (1979); Conrad Susa's BLACK RIVER (1975/1981) and TRANSFORMATIONS (1973); Hiram Titus's Rosina (1980); Robert Ward's CLAUDIA ADARE (1978); and Richard Wargo's THE MUSIC SHOP (1984). The Nautilus Music-Theater, formerly The New Music-Theater Ensemble, has staged Carlisle FLOYD'S OF MICE AND MEN and Stephen Sondheim's INTO THE WOODS. Minnesota Opera's many important revivals include George Antheil's TRANSATLANTIC (1998), Argento's THE ASPERN PAPERS (1991), Robert Kurka's THE GOOD SOLDIER SCHWEIK (1967), Stephen Paulus's THE POSTMAN ALWAYS RINGS TWICE (1987), John Philip Sousa's EL CAPITAN (1975) and Stephen Sondheim's PASSION (2004).

Moorhead: Concordia College in Moorhead premiered two operas by Roger Hannay, *Two Tickets to Omaha* in 1960 and *The Fortunes of St. Macabre* in 1964. Fargo-Moorhead Civic Opera, founded in 1969, often stages American operas. They have included Domenick Argento's THE BOOR, Leonard Bernstein's TROUBLE IN TAHITI, Seymour Barab's CHANTICLEER, Carlisle Floyd's SUSANNAH, Victor Herbert's NAUGHTY MARIETTA, Gian Carlo Menotti's AMAHL AND THE NIGHT VISITORS, THE CONSUL and THE OLD MAID AND THE THIEF, Douglas Moore's THE BALLAD OF BABY DOE and Sigmund Romberg's THE DESERT SONG, THE NEW MOON and THE STUDENT PRINCE.

Roseville: Norman Stokes, who founded Minnesota University's electronic music program, premiered *Itaru the Stonecutter,* based on a Japanese folk tale, at the Brimhall School in Roseville on March 25, 1982.

St. Paul: St. Paul Opera, founded in 1933, commissioned and premiered Lee Hoiby's SUMMER AND SMOKE in 1971. It merged with Minnesota Opera in 1975 which has premiered several operas in St. Paul. Libby Larsen's children's operas *The Silver Fox* and *The Emperor's New Clothes* were premiered in 1979 and her *Tumbledown Dick* in 1980. Edward Barnes' *Nezha,* based on a classic Chinese story, premiered in 1986 and Evan Chen's BOK CHOY VARIATIONS, about four Chinese in America, was premiered in 1995. Stephen Paulus' church opera THE THREE HERMITS, based on a Tolstoy story, was commissioned by Motet Choir of House of Hope Presbyterian Church in St. Paul and premiered on April 24, 1997. Philip Brunelle made the first recording of Benjamin Britten's whimsical "American opera" PAUL BUNYAN at the Ordway Music Theatre in St. Paul in 1987.

MINUTES TILL MIDNIGHT   *1982 opera by Ward*

Physicist Emil Roszak was once involved in developing nuclear power but its use made him reject defense work. He and Chris Jessup are working on a way to use cosmic power for peaceful purposes but government minister Amory Dexter wants him to turn it into a bomb. Chris is shot while making an anti-war speech and Emil decides to make the formula available to everyone. Robert Ward's didactic three-act opera *Minutes Till Midnight,* libretto by Daniel Lang, was commissioned by Greater Miami Opera in

Florida which premiered it June 4, 1982. Thomas Stewart was Emil, Richard Cross was Amory, Evelyn Lear was Emil's wife Margo, Henry Price was Chris, Claudia Cummings was Julie and Ralph Renick was the Television Newscaster. Gunther Schneider-Siemssen designed the sets and projections, Nathaniel Merrill directed and Emerson Buckley conducted.

1991 Robert Ward: Arias and Songs. Baritone William Stone sings the aria " Oh Cosmos, with Your Myriad Stars" from *Minutes Till Midnight* accompanied by pianist Thomas Warburton on the album *Robert Ward: Arias and Songs.* Bay Cities CD.

THE MIRACLE OF THE NATIVITY   *1975 lyric drama by Pendleton*

Edmund J. Pendleton's one-act lyric Christmas drama *The Miracle of the Nativity,* libretto by the composer, is based on the Biblical story of the birth of Christ as told in the Gospel of St. Luke. The principal roles are Mary, Joseph, the Angel Gabriel and an Envoy from Caesar.

1978 Michel Piquemal Vocal Ensemble. Susan Bullock sings the role of Mary in this recording by the Michel Piquemal Vocal Ensemble and Ile de France Chamber Orchestra. Stephan Imbodem is Joseph, Douglas Robinson is the Angel Gabriel and Jorge Chamine is Caesar's Envoy. J. W. Audoli conducts. Campion CD.

MISS CHICKEN LITTLE   *1953 opera by Wilder*

Chicken Little is singing "It's a Fine Day for Walkin' Country Style" as she takes a stroll through the forest. When an acorn falls on her head, she thinks a piece of the sky has fallen. She tells her hen friends and Ducky Lucky, Goosey Loosey, and Turkey Lurkey about it and they decide to inform the King. They don't know the way but the wily Fox says he will show them the right road. They follow him to his foxhole where hungry cubs are waiting. Alec Wilder's comic opera *Miss Chicken Little,* libretto by William Engvick based on the folk tale, was first staged in New York in November 1953 with piano accompaniment. At the request of the producers of the *Omnibus* television program, it was orchestrated and telecast on CBS on December 27, 1953. Jo Sullivan played Chicken Little, Rosemary Kuhlmann was Goosey Loosey, Leonore Arnold was Ducky Lucky, Leon Lishner was Turkey Lurkey, Jim Hawthorne was Chocky Locky, George Irving was the Fox, Ruth Kobart, Eleanor Williams, Muriel Shaw and Charlotte Rae were the Singing Hens, Glen Tetley and Felisa Conde were the Dancing Hens and Ian Tucker was the Chick. George Bassman conducted. The 27-minute opera was staged again at Rockland Lyric Theater in Piermont, NY, on August 29, 1958. (Vincent Persichetti also composed an opera based on this fable, *The Sibyl: A Parable of Chicken Little,* premiered by Pennsylvania Opera Theater in 1985.)

MISS HAVISHAM'S FIRE   *1979 opera by Argento*

Rich but eccentric old Miss Havisham dies in a fire and an inquest is held to see how and why it happened. Could it have been because she was jilted on her wedding day? Dominick Argento's 16-scene opera *Miss Havisham's Fire,* libretto by John Olon-Scrymgeour, is based on characters and scenes from Charles Dickens' *Great Expectations.* It premiered at New York City Opera on March 22, 1979, with Rita Shane as old Miss Aurelia Havisham and Gianna Rolandi as her younger self. Susanne Marsee was Estella as a young woman with Lorna Wallach as Estella as a girl, Alan Titus was Pip as a young man and Robert Sapolsky played him as a boy, Elaine Bonazzi was Nanny as a woman and Martha Sheil played her as a girl, Paul Ukena was old Orlick and James Brewer portrayed him a young man, Richard Cross was Jaggers, Ralph Bassett was the inquest Examiner and John Lankston was Bentley Drummle. John Conklin designed the sets, H. Wesley Balk staged the opera and Julius Rudel conducted. The opera was written for Beverly Sills but she withdrew from the project and the premiere production was not well received in its four NYCO performances. Argento revised and shortened the opera for highly acclaimed revival by Opera Theatre of St. Louis in June 2001. Erie Mills sang Miss Havisham both young and old, Keith Phares was the older Pip with treble Jacob Ashworth as his young self and Patricia Risley was the older Estella with Sarah Tannehill as her younger self. James Robinson staged the opera and Beatrice Jona Affron conducted.

1979 New York City Opera. Rita Shane stars as the old Miss Havisham in this live recording of a New York City Opera performance on April 29, 1979. Gianni Rolandi is young Miss Havisham, Susanne Marsee is Estella as a young woman, Alan Titus is Pip as a young man and John Lankston is Bentley Drummle. Julius Rudel conducts. Live Opera audiocassette.

MISS HAVISHAM'S WEDDING NIGHT   *1981 opera by Argento*

Rich elderly Miss Havisham, jilted into madness on her wedding day, vows always to wear her wedding dress and never to leave the house. Dominick Argento's *Miss Havisham's Wedding Night,* libretto by John Olon-Scrymgeour, is one-act one-person opera based on scenes in Charles Dickens' *Great Expectations.* It was premiered by Minnesota Opera at the Tyrone Guthrie Theater in Minneapolis on May 1, 1981, with Rita Shane as Miss Havisham. Philip Brunelle conducted.

1990 Boston Film and Video. Julie Hanson sings the role of Miss Aurelia Havisham with Lynn Philips as Estella and Megan Sullivan as the chambermaid in this production taped by the Boston Film and Video Foundation. Ivan Stolze and Don Sullivan designed the sets, Julie Hanson and Will Graham created the costumes, Will Graham staged the opera and Eric Lindholm conducted. **1996 Maryland Opera.** Linda Mabbs sings the role of Miss Havisham in this recording of the opera made at the Gordon Center for the Performing Arts in Owing Mills, Maryland, in August 1996. She is accompanied by the Sinfonia of St. Cecilia conducted by Sara Watkins. Koch CD.

MISS JULIE   *1965 opera by Rorem*

On Midsummer Eve in a country estate in Sweden in the 1880s, the daughter of the count has become jaded and desperate. Miss Julie breaks her engagement to Niels, seduces her father's valet John even though he is engaged to the cook Christine, steals money for him and then kills herself at his suggestion. Ned Rorem's two-act two-hour opera *Miss Julie,* libretto by Kenward Elmslie is based on the play by August Strindberg, premiered at New York City Opera on November 4, 1965. Marguerite Willauer was Miss Julie, Donald Gramm was the valet John, Elaine Bonazzi was the cook Christine, Richard Krause was Niels, Betsy Hepburn was the Wildcat Boy, Joan Summers was the Young Girl, Nico Castel was the Young Boy and Don Yule was the Stableboy. Will Steven Armstrong designed the sets, Nikos Psacharopoulos staged the opera and Robert Zeller conducted the orchestra. Rorem later reduced the opera to one act and a 90-minute running time. Like his other work it is tonal, lyrical and highly singable. It continues to be staged and was presented at the Curtis Opera Theater in Philadelphia in 2003.

1979 New York Lyric Opera. Judith James, Ronald Madden

Rita Shane in Dominick Argento's *Miss Havisham's Wedding Night* in 1981 Minnesota Opera premiere. Photograph by Dominick Argento, courtesy of Minnesota Opera Company.

Ned Rorem's opera *Miss Julie,* based on a Strindberg play, was recorded by the Manhattan School of Opera in 1994.

and Veronica August star in a 1979 New York Lyric Opera production that was recorded with Peter Leonard conducting. Painted Smiles LP. **1994 Manhattan School of Music.** Theodora Fried sings the role of Miss Julie with Philip Torre as the valet John in this live recording made in December 1994 at a Manhattan School of Music Opera Theater production. Heather Sarris is the cook Christine, David Blackburn is Niels, Mark Mulligan is the Young Boy, Laurelyn Watson is the Young Girl and Judd Ernster is the bass soloist. David Gilbert conducts the Manhattan School of Music Opera Orchestra and Chorus. The recording was produced by John Ostendorf. Newport Classic CD box.

MISSISSIPPI   *American state (1817–)*

Jackson, capital and largest city of Mississippi, is the home of the two major opera companies, Mississippi Opera and Opera/South. Mississippi-born opera people include soprano Leontyne Price (Laurel), composer William Grant Still (Woodville), composer John Luther Adams (Meridian), composer/conductor Lehman Engel (Jackson), baritone Julian Patrick (Meridian) and conductor Russell Patterson (Greenville). Operas set in Mississippi include Lee Hoiby's SUMMER AND SMOKE, William Grant Still's A BAYOU LEGEND and Jerome Kern's SHOW BOAT.

Clinton: Arthur Kreutz presented his folk opera SOURWOOD MOUNTAIN at Mississippi College in Clinton in 1959 following its premiere in Oxford.

Hattiesburg: William Presser's chamber opera *The Whistler* was premiered at the University of Southern Mississippi in Hattiesburg on February 8, 1959.

Jackson: Opera/South, founded in 1970, staged William Grant Still's HIGHWAY 1, U.S.A. and Ulysses Kay's *The Juggler of Our Lady* at Jackson Municipal Auditorium in 1972. It premiered Still's A BAYOU LEGEND at the Auditorium in 1974, reprised it in 1976 and videotaped it in 1979 for a PBS telecast. It commissioned Kay's JUBILEE and premiered it at Jackson State College in 1976. Mississippi Opera, founded in 1945, held the stage premiere of Lehman Engel's THE SOLDIER in Millsaps College Auditorium on November 24, 1958 (Engle was born in Jackson), and its production of Carlisle Floyd's FLOWER AND HAWK was telecast on Mississippi Educational Television in 1979. Other American opera productions by Mississippi Opera include Raffaelo de Banfield's LORD BYRON'S LOVE LETTER, Leonard Bernstein's TROUBLE IN TAHITI, Carlisle Floyd's SLOW DUSK, Victor Herbert's BABES IN TOYLAND, Douglas Moore's GALLANTRY and Gian Carlo Menotti's AMAHL AND THE NIGHT VISITORS, THE CONSUL, HELP, HELP, THE GLOBOLINKS and THE OLD MAID AND THE THIEF.

Oxford: Arthur Kreutz premiered two of his folk-style operas at the University of Mississippi in Oxford, the Civil War ballad opera *The University Grays* (March 15, 1954) and the folk ballad opera *Sourwood Mountain* (January 8, 1959).

Tupelo: Nancy Hayes Van de Vate premiered her chamber opera *In the Shadow of the Glen,* based on the John Millington Synge play, in Tupelo February 8, 1960.

MISSOURI   *American state (1821–)*

The first American opera to premiere in Missouri was William D. Armstrong's *The Spectre Bridegroom,* based on a Washington Irving story, performed at the 14th Street Theater in St. Louis in 1899; Armstrong was a popular St. Louis organist and music professor at the time. Scott Joplin's lost ragtime opera A GUEST OF HONOR was performed in St. Louis in 1903 but its premiere site is unknown. Baritone/music teacher Homer Moore presented three of his historical operas at the Odeon Theater in St. Louis: *The*

Puritans was performed in concert in 1902. *Columbus, or The New World* was presented in concert in 1903. The grandiose *Louis XIV* was staged on February 16, 1917, with a cast of sixty singers and forty dancers and the music performed by the St. Louis Symphony Orchestra conducted by Moore. Julius Osiier's *The Bride of Bagdad* was premiered at the YMHA Auditorium in Kansas City in 1928 and awarded a Bispham Memorial Medal in 1938.

There are an impressive multitude of Missouri-born opera people. They include baritone Alan Baker, soprano Marion Bell (St. Louis), composer Robert Russell Bennett (Kansas City), librettist Henry Blossom (St. Louis), mezzo-soprano Grace Bumbry (St. Louis), author T. S. Eliot (St. Louis), baritone Brent Ellis (Kansas City), tenor John Garrison (Higginsville), soprano Alice Ghostly (Eve), Don Gillis (Cameron), tenor Leo Goeke (Kirksville), composer Milton Granger (Kansas City), baritone Walter Hook (Kansas City), librettist Langston Hughes (Joplin), conductor Samuel Krachmalnick (St. Louis), composer Mikel Rouse (St. Louis), baritone Richard Stilwell (St. Louis), composer Albert Stoessel (St. Louis), contralto Gladys Swarthout (Deepwater), soprano Helen Traubel (St. Louis), composer Edward Ward (St. Louis), librettist Lanford Wilson (Lebanon) and composer Virgil Thomson (Kansas City). Thomson drew upon his memories of the church and pop music he heard while growing up in Kansas City to create the score for FOUR SAINTS IN THREE ACTS.

Bolivar: Alec Wilder's 25-minute "curtain raiser" opera *Sunday Excursion* was produced by the Southwest Baptist Opera Workshop in Bolivar in 1985.

Columbia: Val Patacchi premiered three operas at Stephens College, a private Columbia institution for women: *The Secret* in 1955, *The Bandit* (libretto by William Ashbrook) in 1958 and *The Foundling* in 1959.

Kansas City: Lyric Opera of Kansas City, founded in 1957 by Russell Patterson and originally called Kansas City Lyric Theater, presents its operas in English and has always promoted and highlighted American opera. It premiered Jack Beeson's CAPTAIN JINKS OF THE HORSE MARINES in 1975 and Henry Mollicone's COYOTE TALES in 1998 and issued recordings of these operas. It has also made recordings of productions of Beeson's THE SWEET BYE AND BYE and Vittorio Giannini's THE TAMING OF THE SHREW. In its sixth season (1963–1964), Lyric Opera received a Ford Foundation grant to organize a festival of American opera with the University of Missouri and the Conservatory of Music. The series included Douglas Moore's THE DEVIL AND DANIEL WEBSTER (revived in 1995 and recorded), Samuel Barber's VANESSA and Gian Carlo Menotti's THE MEDIUM. Lyric Opera productions since then have included Leonard Bernstein's CANDIDE, Marc Blitzstein's REGINA, Carlisle Floyd's OF MICE AND MEN and SUSANNAH, Lee Hoiby's THE TEMPEST, Mitch Leigh's MAN OF LA MANCHA, Frank Loesser's THE MOST HAPPY FELLA, Menotti's AMAHL AND THE NIGHT VISITORS and THE SAINT OF BLEECKER STREET, Moore's THE BALLAD OF BABY DOE, Stephen Sondheim's SWEENEY TODD, John Philip Sousa's *The Free Lance,* Igor Stravinsky's THE RAKE'S PROGRESS, Conrad Susa's TRANSFORMATIONS, Virgil Thomson's THE MOTHER OF US ALL, Robert Ward's THE CRUCIBLE and Kurt Weill's DOWN IN THE VALLEY. The Civic Opera Theater of Kansas City produced Conrad Susa's 50-minute church opera THE WISE WOMEN in 1996 and its televised production was issued on video.

Point Lookout: Bert Buhrman's *The Bald Knobbers,* libretto by Karl Bratton based on an Ozarks folk tale, premiered at the College of the Ozarks on May 12, 1968.

St. Louis: The first local opera company was St. Louis Municipal Opera, founded in 1919, which presented light operas, including American operettas, in summer festivals until 1939. It was folded into St. Louis Grand Opera company which mostly presented European operas but did produce a stage version of the film *The Wizard of Oz* in 1942 using Harold Arlen's music. The company folded later the same year. Myron Fink's THE BOOR was premiered in the Ivory Room at the Jefferson Hotel in 1955, Elie Siegmeister's THE PLOUGH AND THE STARS was premiered as *Dublin Song* at Washington University in 1963 and Ronald Arnatt's *The Boy with a Cart* was premiered at the Mary Institute in 1968. Opera Theater of St. Louis, founded in 1976 to present opera at the Loretto-Hilton Center at Webster University, has commissioned and premiered a number of American operas. They include four by Stephen Paulus, including two with librettos by company director Colin Graham: THE VILLAGE SINGER in 1979, THE POSTMAN ALWAYS RINGS TWICE in 1982, THE WOODLANDERS in 1985 and THE WOMAN AT OTOWI CROSSING in 1995. Anthony Davis's UNDER THE DOUBLE MOON was premiered in 1989, David Carlson's THE MIDNIGHT ANGEL in 1993, Paul Schoenfield's THE MERCHANT AND THE PAUPER in 1999, and Cary John Franklin's LOSS OF EDEN in 2002. It also commissioned and premiered two English-language operas by Japanese composer Minoru Miki with librettos written by Colin Graham, JŌRURI in 1985 and THE TALE OF GENJI in 2000. The company is noted for presenting major revivals/revisions of operas: the American professional premiere of Benjamin Britten's BILLY BUDD was held in 1984, a revised version of William Mayer's A DEATH IN THE FAMILY starring Dawn Upshaw was broadcast on NPR in 1986, Samuel Barber's VANESSA starring Susan Graham was presented in 1988, the final revision of Conrad Susa's BLACK RIVER was staged in 1994, the Scottish revision of Leonard Bernstein's CANDIDE was staged in 1994, Susa's TRANSFORMATIONS was staged in 1997, Rhoda Levine's production of Scott Joplin's TREEMONISHA was produced in 2000, James Robinson's production of the revised version of Dominick Argento's MISS HAVISHAM'S FIRE was staged in 2001 and James Robinson's production of John Adams' *Nixon in China* was produced in 2004. The company has also commissioned and premiered children's operas including Claude White's *Love, Death and High Notes* in 1988, James Meyer's *Laclede's Landing* in 1989, Cary John Franklin's *The Very Last Green Thing* in 1992 and *The Thunder of Horses* in 1995 and Adolphus Hailstork's *Joshua's Boots* in 1999.

Springfield: Springfield Regional Opera is located in Springfield.

Warrensburg: Donald Bohlen's opera *Ismene*, libretto by Robert Jones, was premiered at Central Missouri State College in Warrensburg on February 17, 1969

MR. AND MRS. DISCOBBOLOS   *1966 opera by Westergaard*

Mr. and Mrs. Discobbolos climb a wall to have lunch and like it so much they stay for twenty years. One days Mrs. Discobbolos decides it is not advantageous for their twelve children to live on a wall so Mr. Discobbolos blows its up. Peter Westergaard's 17-minute comic chamber opera *Mr. and Mrs. Discobbolos,* libretto by the composer based on a poem by Edward Lear, was premiered at Columbia University on March 21, 1966. It was reprised by Princeton University in 1968, by Washington University in 1969 and by American Chamber Opera in 1987.

MR. AND MRS. OLSEN   *2002 opera by Stein*

A teacher and a taxman try to put some romance back into their failing marriage. Andy Stein's opera *Mr. and Mrs. Olsen,* libretto by humorist Garrison Keiler, was premiered before a sellout crowd in Minneapolis in July 2002. The Minnesota *Star Tribune* critic called it a "triumph of silliness."

MITCHELL, LEONA   *American soprano (1949–)*

Leona Mitchell sings the role of Bess opposite Willard White's Porgy in Lorin Maazel's famous 1976 Cleveland Orchestra recording of George Gershwin's PORGY AND BESS. She sings the role opposite Donnie Ray Albert in a taped 1980 Carnegie Hall program and opposite Simon Estes in a broadcast from the Metropolitan Opera in 1995. Mitchell, born in Enid, Oklahoma, studied at Oklahoma City University and at San Francisco Opera where she made her debut in 1972. She began to sing at the Metropolitan Opera in 1975.

MITROPOULOS, DIMITRI   *Greek-born American conductor (1896–1960)*

Dimitri Mitropoulos conducted the premiere of Samuel Barber's opera VANESSA at the Metropolitan Opera in 1958 and leads the orchestra on the famous recording. Mitropoulos, born in Athens, came to America in 1937 and began to conduct at the Met in 1954. He became an American citizen in 1946.

MLLE. MODISTE   *1905 comic opera by Herbert*

Fifi, an employee in Mme. Cécile's Parisian hat shop, is in love with Captain Étienne de Bouvay. His uncle Count de St. Mar forbids their marriage and Mme. Cécile wants Fifi to marry her son. After Fifi becomes famous as the opera prima donna Madame Bellini, all is happily resolved. Victor Herbert's *Mlle. Modiste,* libretto by Henry Blossom, premiered at the Taylor Opera House in Trenton, NJ, on October 7, 1905, and opened on Broadway at the Knickerbocker Theater on December 25. Fritzi Scheff played Fifi, Walter Percival was Étienne, Josephine Bartlett was Mme. Cécile, William Pruett was the Count, Leo Mars was Cécile's son and Claude Gillingwater was the American millionaire who helps Fifi become an opera singer. *Mlle. Modiste* is one of Herbert's most tuneful comic operas with four hit tunes; Fritzi Scheff, who gave up her career at the Met to sing on Broadway, became famous singing its memorable aria "Kiss Me Again." The aria was liked by other opera sopranos as well and was recorded by Amelita Galli-Curci and Rosa Ponselle while the Count's petulant song "I Want What I Want When I Want It" was recorded by Lauritz Melchior. Three film versions have been made, including one with Scheff, and the operetta continues to be staged. It was revived in 1929 with Scheff as Fifi and staged by the Light Opera Company of Manhattan in 1978 with Georgia McEver as Fifi.

1909/1912 Victor Herbert: Victor Herbert recorded melodies from his operetta twice. In 1909 he led his orchestra in a medley for Edison and in 1912 led the orchestra in "Kiss Me Again" for Victor. *The Early Victor Herbert.* Smithsonian LP. **1910 Victor Light Opera.** The Victor Light Opera Company singers perform a medley of songs from the operetta for a Victor 78 record titled *Gems from Mlle. Modiste.* **1918 Mabel Garrison.** Met soprano Mabel Garrison recorded "Kiss Me Again" for a Victor Red Seal 78 in 1918. **1920 Rosa Ponselle.** Met diva Rosa Ponselle recorded "Kiss Me Again" as a 78 for Columbia with Romano Romani conducting. Album Minerva CD. **1923 Amelita Galli-Curci.** Coloratura legend Amelita Galli-Curci recorded "Kiss Me Again" for Victor with Rosario Bourdon conducting the RCA Victor Symphony Orchestra. Album *Lo! Here the Gentle Lark.* Living Era CD. **1926 First National film.** Corinne Griffith stars as Mlle. Fifi in *Mademoiselle Modiste,* a 70-minute silent feature film of the operetta, screened with Herbert's music played live. Norman Kerry is Étienne, Willard

Louis is Hiram Bent, Dorothy Cumming is Marianne and Rose Dione is Madame Claire. Robert Leonard directed for First National Pictures. **1928 Florence Easton.** Met soprano Florence Easton sings "Kiss Me Again" for a 78 record. On the anthology album *The Songs of Victor Herbert.* ASV Living Era CD. **1931 First National film.** Bernice Clair stars as Mlle. Fifi in *Kiss Me Again,* a sound film of the operetta retaining most of the songs. Walter Pidgeon is Paul de St. Cyr, Edward Everett Horton is René, Judith Vosselli is Mme. Cécile, June Collyer is Marie and Claude Gillingwater is the Count. Erno Rapee was music director and Leo F. Forbstein conducted the Vitaphone Orchestra. William A. Seiter directed and Lee Garmes photographed in two-color Technicolor for First National Pictures. (In England the film was called *Toast of the Legion.*) Live Opera Heaven VHS. **1933 Fifi.** Warner Bros. produced an abbreviated twenty-minute version of the operetta in 1993 called simply *Fifi.* **1936 Fritzi Scheff.** Fritzi Scheff returned to the role that made her famous for a 1936 radio version of the operetta. She is heard on the album *Five Ladies of Song.* Bard LP. **1936 Richard Tauber.** Richard Tauber sings "Kiss Me Again" on a radio broadcast. It's on the album *Richard Tauber.* MC cassette. **1942 Gladys Swarthout.** Gladys Swarthout sings "Kiss Me Again" on a 1945 radio broadcast. *Gladys Swarthout: Favorites from the Musical Theatre.* Take Two LP. **1944 Lauritz Melchior.** Lauritz Melchior sings "I Want What I Want When I Want It" on a 1940s radio broadcast. *The Radio Years: Lauritz Melchior Sings America.* RY CD. **1951 NBC Television.** Fritzi Scheff plays Étienne's mother in NBC's *Musical Comedy Time,* a TV production of the operetta that made her famous, and gets to sing "Kiss Me Again" one last time. Marguerite Piazza is Mlle. Fifi, Brian Sullivan is Étienne, Frank McHugh is Herman Bell and Mary Bell is the hat shop manager. Bernard Schubert produced, Harry Sosnick conducted and William Corrigan directed the 60-minute program telecast on February 5, 1951. **1952 RCA recording.** Doretta Morrow sings Fifi opposite Felix Knight and Robert Roecker in a highlights version of the operetta with orchestra led by Jay Blackton. RCA LP. **1953 Radio adaptation.** Dorothy Kirsten sings Fifi opposite Gordon MacRae in an abridged radio adaptation of the operetta. Demand Performance audiocassette. **1961 Robert Shaw Chorale.** Robert Shaw Chorale performs "Kiss Me Again" and "I Want What I Want When I Want It." *The Immortal Victor Herbert.* RCA Victor LP. **1962 Treasury of Great Operettas.** Jeanette Scovotti is Fifi with Arthur Rubin as Étienne in this highlights version with orchestra and chorus conducted by Lehman Engel. Sara Endich is Fanchette, Patricia Kelly is Nanette, Evelyn Sachs is Mme. Cécile, Robert Nagy is Gaston and Kenneth Smith is the Count. Reader's Digest *Treasury of Great Operettas.* RCA LP box set. **1980 Tintypes.** Two songs from *Mlle. Modiste* were featured in the 1980 stage revue *Tintypes.* Carolyn Mignini, playing Anna Held, sings "Kiss Me Again" with its lead-in "If I Were on the Stage" while Trey Wilson has fun with "I Want What I Want When I Want It." Pianist Mel Marvin made the arrangements. The album was recorded in Los Angeles in April 1981. DRG CD. **1985 Donald Hunsberger.** The Eastman-Dryden Orchestra led by Donald Hunsberger performs eleven numbers from the operetta on *Victor Herbert: Souvenir.* Arabesque CD and cassette. **1991 Lorin Maazel.** Pittsburgh Symphony Orchestra led by Lorin Maazel performs "Kiss Me Again" on album *Popular American Music.* Sony CD. **1999 Virginia Croskery.** Virginia Croskery sings "Kiss Me Again" with Slovak Radio Symphony Orchestra led by Keith Brion on *Victor Herbert: Beloved Songs and Classic Miniatures.* American Classics Naxos CD. **2000 Elizabeth Futral.** Elizabeth Futral sings "Kiss Me Again" with the Rudolph Palmer Singers on album *Sweethearts.* Robert Tweten plays piano. Newport Classics CD.

MOBY DICK *American music theater works based on Melville novel*

Captain Ahab takes his whaling ship Pequod on an obsessive pursuit of a great white whale and brings total destruction to ship and crew. Young Ishmael is the sole survivor. Herman Melville's epic 1851 *Moby Dick,* often ranked as the great American novel, has been filmed twice but seems to have intimidated American opera composers. Bernard Herrmann reduced it to a cantata, Rinde Eckert circled around it and Laurie Anderson tried putting in a multi-media context.

1940 Bernard Herrmann. Bernard Herrmann's dramatic cantata *Moby Dick,* libretto by W. Clark Harrington for soloists, male chorus and orchestra, premiered in New York City in April 1940 with Sir John Barbirolli conducting the New York Philharmonic Symphony. It consists of five sections based on lines from the novel opening with the male chorus singing "And God created great whales." There are also solos by Ishmael, Ahab, Starbuck and two sailors. David Kelly sings the role of Captain Ahab and John Amis is Ishmael in a recording of the cantata by the Aeolian Singers under the direction of Sebastian Forbes with the composer conducting the National Philharmonic Orchestra. Robert Bowman sings Starbuck and Pip and Michael Rippon is First and Second Sailor. The recording was made in May 1967 at the Assembly Hall in Barking, Essex, England. Unicorn/Pye LP/Unicorn/Kanchana CD. **1955 James Low.** James Low's two-act opera *Moby Dick,* libretto by the composer, was premiered in Idyllwild, California, on September 2, 1955. **1982 Ronald Perera.** Ronald Perera's 29-minute monodrama *The White Whale,* libretto by the composer, was premiered at Amherst, Massachusetts, on April 20, 1982. **1987 Richard Brooks.** Richard Brooks' two-act opera *Moby Dick,* libretto by John Richards, is about two and a-half hours in length but has not been staged. The overture has been recorded and is on CD as *Seascape: Overture to Moby Dick.* **1999 Laurie Anderson.** Laurie Anderson's experimental multi-media opera *Songs and Stories from Moby Dick,* libretto by the composer, was commissioned by Spoleto Festival USA and staged there in June 1999 after try-outs in Dallas and Philadelphia. Anderson portrayed the whale in a visually imaginative production that combined projected images and four actor/singers with electronic whale music and haunting songs. **2000 Rinde Eckert.** Rinde Eckert's 75-minute experimental semi-opera *And God Created Whales,* libretto by the composer, was premiered by Foundry Theater at Culture Project Theater in New York on September 15, 2000. A composer (Eckert), is alone in a room trying to write an opera based on *Moby Dick* and is helped by a Muse (Nora Cole). As he is losing his memory, he carries a tape recorder which gives instructions on how to finish the opera. The Muse also plays an opera singer and Pequod sailors including harpooner Queequeg; she ends the piece singing Ishmael's final words. The production was staged by David Schweizer with lighting by Kevin Adams.

MODENOS, JOHN *American baritone (1930–)*

John Philip Modenos created the role of the Odysseus-like Crete nobleman Aethon opposite Teresa Stratas in Peggy Glanville-Hicks' NAUSICAA at the Athens Festival in Greece in 1961. Modenos, born in Cyprus, studied at the Manhattan School of Music and made his debut at New York City Opera in 1956.

MODERN PAINTERS *1995 opera by Lang*

Victorian art critic John Ruskin's life is portrayed in seven scenes paralleling the seven virtues of a work of art. The opera begins with an overture for sledgehammers as an historic church is being destroyed. Ruskin protests the destruction of the church, attends a funeral in Venice and finds on his wedding night that his young bride Effie is not what he imagined. Effie seeks refuge in the arms of Ruskin's best friend, painter John Everett Millais, while Ruskin becomes fascinated by another young girl and involved in another controversy. David Lang's opera *Modern Painters,* libretto by Manuela Hoelterhopp based on John Ruskin's critical study *The Seven Lamps of Architecture,* was commissioned by Santa Fe Opera which premiered it on July 29, 1995. Francois Leroux played John Ruskin, Ana Panagulias was Effie, Mark Thomsen was John Everett Millais, Sheila Nadler was Ruskin's mother, Dale Travis was Ruskin's Father, Judith Christin was Effie's mother and Margaret Mack was Mrs. La Touche. Allison Chitty designed the sets, Francesca Zambella staged the opera and George Manahan conducted the orchestra. Much of the music is strictly minimalist. Lang was co-founder of the Bang on a Can Music Festival in New York.

MOFFO, ANNA   *American soprano (1934–)*

Anna Moffo sang opera on stage but in 1962 she starred in a series of American operetta recordings organized by *The Reader's Digest* for its anthology *Treasury of Great Operettas.* She is Marietta in Victor Herbert's NAUGHTY MARIETTA, Margo in Sigmund Romberg's THE DESERT SONG, Rose Marie in Rudolf Friml's ROSE MARIE, Julie in Jerome Kern's SHOW BOAT and Clara in George Gershwin's PORGY AND BESS. In 1979 she sang the role of Kate in a production of Vittorio Giannini's THE TAMING OF THE SHREW for Wolf Trap Opera in Virginia. Moffo, born in Wayne, Pennsylvania, made her debut at the Spoleto Festival in 1955 and joined the Metropolitan Opera in 1959. She spent much of her career in Italy.

MOHAUPT, RICHARD   *American composer (1904–1957)*

Richard Mohaupt is best known for his Commedia dell'Arte style opera DOUBLE TROUBLE based on a Roman play by Plautus about twin brothers. It was commissioned by the Louisville Orchestra and premiered by Kentucky Opera on December 4, 1954. Mohaupt, who was born in Austria, emigrated to the US in 1939 and wrote most of his music in America. His other compositions include cantatas, ballets, chamber and orchestra pieces.

MOHEGA   *1859 opera by Sobolewski*

Native American Mohega falls in love with Polish nobleman Casimir Pulaski who is fighting on the side of America in the War of Independence. She dies tries to save him during the siege of Savannah in 1779. Edward Sobolewski's three-act grand opera *Mohega, The Flower of the Forest,* libretto in German by the composer, was premiered at Albany Hall in Milwaukee, Wisconsin, on October 11, 1859. Mohega was sung by Malvina Sobolewski, the composer's daughter, with William H. Jacobs as the English Colonel. Emil Neymann as the Indian Chief and a hundred-voice chorus representing soldiers and Native Americans. Sobolewski, a Polish immigrant whose father had fought with Pulaski, was strongly influenced in his musical style by Wagner and chose to present his opera in Milwaukee because of its famous singing societies.

MOJICA, JOSE   *Mexican tenor (1896–1974)*

José Mojica, Mexico's most famous opera singer in the early 20th century, sang with Chicago Opera from 1919 to 1930 and created roles in four American operas. He played the Prince in the premiere of Sergei Prokofiev's THE LOVE FOR THREE ORANGES in 1921, Archer in Theodore Stearns SNOWBIRD in 1923, the Young Lover in Aldo Franchetti's NAMIKO-SAN in 1925 and Deacon Fairfield in Charles Cadman's A WITCH OF SALEM in 1926. In 1930 he left the opera stage to make Hollywood movies for Fox. *One Mad Kiss* was shot in both English and Spanish but his other films were strictly for the Spanish-speaking market. He made ten films for Fox between 1930 and 1934 and a further fifteen in Mexico and Argentina. He entered the priesthood in 1947 and later wrote a famous autobiography *Yo Pecador.*

MOLLICONE, HENRY   *American composer (1946–)*

Henry Mollicone's one-act opera THE FACE ON THE BARROOM FLOOR, libretto by John S. Bowman, premiered in Central City, Colorado, in 1978 and quickly became one of the most popular American operas. The composer also had success with his full-length COYOTE TALES, libretto by Sheldon Harnick, premiered by Lyric Opera of Kansas City in 1998. Mollicone, born in Providence, RI, studied composition with Gunther Schuller and Donald Martino. His first opera was YOUNG GOODMAN BROWN, based on a Hawthorne story; it premiered at the Lake George Festival in New York in 1970. His three one-act operas composed to librettos by Kate Pogue are also popular: the science-fiction-children's opera STARBIRD was premiered by Houston Grand Opera in 1981, the Pirandello-esque EMPEROR NORTON was presented by San Francisco Opera in 1981 and the vampire tale *The Mask of Evil* was staged by Minnesota Opera in Minneapolis in 1982. Mollicone's three-act Biblical opera THE GARDEN OF EDEN, libretto by Judith Fein, was premiered by Opera San José in 1989. GABRIEL'S DAUGHTER, libretto by William Luce about a freed slave who goes to Colorado during the gold rush, was premiered by Central City Opera in 2003.

MON AMI PIERROT   *1935 opera by Barlow*

Samuel Barlow's one-act opera *Mon Ami Pierrot* was the first American opera to premiere at the Opéra-Comique in Paris (January 11, 1935), principally because its librettist was Paris favorite Sacha Guitry. *Mon Ami Pierrot* revolves around incidents in the life of 17th century composer Jean-Baptiste Lully and the possible origin of the popular tune "Au clair de la lune." Victor Pujo played Lully, Lillie Grandval was Ninon, Jeanne Mattio was the Vegetable Seller, Andrée Bernadet was the Fish Seller, Jean Vieuille was the Pastry Cook, Christina Gaudel was the Young Woman, Madeleine Drouot was the Elegant Woman and Jeanne Secondi was the Working Woman. Guitry staged the opera and Gustave Cooez conducted the orchestra.

MONA   *1912 opera by Parker*

Horatio Parker's three-act *Mona* was the first American opera to premiere at the Metropolitan Opera. It won a $10,000 Metropolitan Opera competition and was staged at the Met on March 14, 1912. Brian Hooker's poetic libretto tells a story similar to that of *Norma:* Mona is a British princess during the Roman occupation who has to choose between love for Gwynn (secretly Quintus, son of the Roman Governor) or fighting for freedom for her country. Louise Homer starred as Mona with Riccardo Martin as Gwynn/Quintus, Rita Fornia as Mona's foster mother Enya, Herbert Witherspoon as Enya's husband Arth, William Hinshaw as Arth's son Gloom, Lambert Murphy as chief bard Caradoc, Putnam Griswold as the Roman Governor and Basil Ruuysadael as an Old Man. Loomis Taylor directed and Alfred Hertz conducted the Metropolitan Opera Orchestra. *Mona* was performed four times by the Met but was not revived.

1961 Arlene Saunders/Enrico Di Giuseppe. The *Mona* duet "Thy golden heart wide open" is sung by Arlene Saunders and Enrico Di Giuseppe on a radio broadcast on February 22, 1961. It's on the album *Souvenirs from American Opera.* IRRC CD. **1970 Eastman-Rochester Symphony.** The Prelude to *Mona* is performed by the Eastman-Rochester Symphony Orchestra led by Howard Hanson at the Eastman School of Music on the album *Merry Mount.* Mercury LP.

"MONICA'S WALTZ" *Soprano aria: The Medium (1946) Word and Music: Gian Carlo Menotti*

This is a poignant soprano fantasy by a teenage girl pretending to have an evening out with a mute friend after he stages a puppet show for her. "Bravo!" she says, "and after the theater, supper and dance." Monica is the daughter of a fake medium who has a mental breakdown after feeling a ghostly hand on her throat in the middle of a séance. Gian Carlo Menotti's aria for his opera THE MEDIUM was introduced by Evelyn Keller in the Columbia University premiere and Broadway production and she sings it on the original cast album. Lois Hunt performed it on a 1948 CBS TV production and Lee Ventura on a 1959 NBC show but it's best known as sung by Anna Maria Alberghetti in Menotti's 1951 film of the opera. Judith Blegen performs it on a Washington Opera recording, Patrice Michaels Bedi on a Chicago Opera recording, Renée Fleming on her American opera album *I Want Magic!* and Helen-Kay Eberley on her American opera album *American Girl.* "Monica's Waltz" is one of four American arias analyzed in Martial Singher's 1983 study *An Interpretive Guide to Operatic Arias.*

MONK, MEREDITH *American composer/performer (1943–)*

Avant-garde composer/singer/filmmaker Meredith Monk creates experimental operas that stretch the boundaries of the genre using unusual combinations of performers, instruments and film. A pioneer of what is often called "extended vocal technique," she and her amazing singers perform a kind of textless vocalese that can stretch over four octaves. Her major stage work is the three-hour opera ATLAS, premiered by Houston Grand Opera in 1991, in which nineteen singer/actors tell the story of a woman explorer searches for spiritual values. Monk's first music theater work was *Juice: A Theatre Cantata;* scored for 85 voices, 85 Jews harps and two violins; it was premiered on a runway at the Guggenheim Museum in 1969. Next was the 1970 theatre piece *Needle-brain Lloyd and the Systems Kid,* scored for 150 voices, electric organ, flute and guitar. It was followed by the 1971 "opera epic" *Vessel,* composed for 75 voices, two dulcimers, accordion and electric organ; a condense version was presented in Paris in 1972. The opera EDUCATION OF THE GIRLCHILD, scored for six women's voices, electric organ and piano, was presented in France in 1973. The opera *Quarry,* scored for 38 voices, two harmoniums, two soprano recorders and tape recorder, was performed in Venice and Milan in 1976. The archeological ensemble piece *Dolmen Music,* scored for six voices, cello and percussion, premiered at LaMama in New York in 1979. *Recent Ruins* was performed at Nanterre in France on February 28, 1980. *Specimen Days* was presented at the New York Shakespeare Festival on December 2, 1981. *The Games: Days of Wrath,* libretto by Ping Chong and the composer about a nuclear disaster, is scored for sixteen voices, synthesizer, Chinese horn and several kinds of bagpipes; it was premiered in Berlin on November 28, 1983, and reprised at the Next Wave Festival in Brooklyn in 1984. *Acts from Under and Above,* created in collaboration with composer Lanny Harrison, was premiered at LaMama in New York

on April 3, 1986. *Do You Be?* was presented in Vancouver on April 5, 1988; an excerpt is heard in Jean-Luc Godard's film *Nouvelle Vague* The opera BOOK OF DAYS was staged in St. Paul in May 1988 and the film version was premiered a the New York Film Festival. Monk describes her 1999 *Magic Frequencies* as a "multi-media science fiction chamber opera" while her 2003 *Mercy* is a multi-media work mixing music, dance and video with sets and theater.

1981 Dolmen Music. Twenty minutes of swooping vocals from the opera *Dolmen Music* are performed by Monk, Julius Eastman, Robert Een, Andrea Goodman and Paul Langland on the album *Dolmen Music* ECM CD. **1981 Specimen Days.** "Travel Song" from the 1981 opera *Specimen Days* is performed by Anthony de Mare on the album *Cage/Monk—Pianos and Voices.* Koch CD. **1983 Peter Greenaway film.** *Meredith Monk,* a film about the composer shot in London by Peter Greenaway, includes excerpts from the "operas" *Education of A Girlchild* and *Quarry* and Monk's 1981 short film *Ellis Island.* The composer/singer is seen in performance on *Dolmen Music* and *Turtle Dreams.* Performing with her are Robert Een, Andrea Goodman, Naaz Hosseini, Paul Langland, Steve Lockwood, Ron Roxburg and Gail Turner. the Mystic Fire VHS.

MONKEY SEE, MONKEY DO *1986 opera by Rodriguez*

An *Opera News* survey listed this as the fourth most often-performed contemporary opera in America. Organ grinder Antonio loses his pet monkey and forbids the marriage of his daughter Maria to sombrero salesman Pedrito. When monkeys led by Antonio's pet steal Pedrito's hats, he throws his sombrero onto the ground causing the monkeys to do likewise in "monkey see, monkey do" fashion. The villagers buy the famous hats, Antonio gets his monkey back and gives his blessing to the marriage and the audience joins the cast in the celebration clapping and singing. Robert X. Rodríguez's charming 30-minute children's opera *Monkey See, Monkey Do,* libretto by Mary Duren and the composer based on a Mexican folk tale, was commissioned by Dallas Opera which premiered it January 26, 1987. This is Rodriguez's most popular opera with over one thousand performances.

MONODRAMAS *Operas for one singer*

Some of the most enjoyable American operas are monodramas, short operas for one singer sometimes supported by a mime or a speaker. As they are easily staged, they are popular with small opera companies and touring singers. They are for all voice types, but most often soprano, and can be humorous or dramatic. Dominick Argento's A WATER BIRD TALE (baritone: henpecked husband gets confused lecturing about birds) is based on the same Chekhov story that inspired Martin Kalmanoff's ON THE HARMFULNESS OF TOBACCO (baritone: henpecked husband gets confused lecturing about tobacco). Lee Hoiby's BON APPÉTIT! (soprano: Julia Childs sings a recipe for chocolate cake) was created as a companion piece to Hoiby's THE ITALIAN LESSON (mezzo: woman juggles her problems during language lesson). There are even historical monodramas like Carlisle Floyd's FLOWER AND HAWK (soprano: Eleanor of Aquitaine talks about her distressful life) and Elizabeth Vercoe's HERSTORY III—JEANNE DE LORRAINE (mezzo: Joan of Arc describes her adventurous life). Other notable monodramas include Beth Anderson's *Riot Rot* (soprano: New York street riots); Argento's MISS HAVISHAM'S WEDDING NIGHT (soprano: spinster from *Great Expectations* relives her worst night), Dinos Constantinides' FUGUE FOR TWO VOICES (soprano: blind woman describes man's death), Solomon Epstein's *Water Songs* (soprano: woman remembers her life after taking pills), Daron Hagen's *Madness and Sorrow* (tenor:

man unable to cope with life), Jean Ivey's TESTAMENT OF EVE (mezzo: Eve engages in argument with Lucifer); Marc Neikrug's THROUGH ROSES (actor and eight instruments: violinist survivor of concentration camp finds music discordant); Thomas Pasatieri's BEFORE BREAKFAST (soprano: woman tries to wake non-existent husband), Ronald Perera's *The White Whale* (baritone: the tale of Moby Dick), George Rochberg's PHAEDRA (mezzo: wife of Theseus hangs herself when her stepson rejects her), Roger Sessions' *Idyll of Theocritus*; John Strauss's THE ACCUSED (soprano: woman accused of being a witch in Puritan Salem); Morton Subotnick's *Jacob's Room* (soprano: Jacob's impressions from Virginia Woolf's novel), Hugo Weisgall's THE STRONGER (soprano: actress reveals fears to friend), Morton Feldman's NEITHER (soprano sings Samuel Beckett at the top of her range), and Michael White's DIARY OF A MADMAN (madman in asylum remember his life).

MONSIEUR BEAUCAIRE   *1930 "movie opera" by Harling*

Stage opera composer W. Franke Harling began his Hollywood career by creating an imaginary opera for a Paramount movie. He joined forces with Richard Whiting and Leo Robin to create the opera *Monsieur Beaucaire* for the climactic scene of Ernst Lubitsch's 1930 musical *Monte Carlo*. A rich count (Jack Buchanan) poses as a hairdresser to woo an impoverished countess (Jeanette MacDonald). After many misunderstandings he insists she attend the opera which turns out to be a story about a nobleman who poses as a barber and falls in love with a princess. The countess finally understands and they go off together singing "Beyond the Blue Horizon." In the opera Donald Novis sings the role of Monsieur Beaucaire, Helen Garden is Lady Mary, Erik Bey is Lord Winterset and David Percy is the Herald. Billy Bevan plays the conductor but it is Harling, the music director of the film, who conducts the orchestra we hear. The opera was based on a popular play by Booth Tarkington and Eleanor G. Sutherland filmed by Paramount in 1924 with Rudolf Valentino as Beaucaire.

MONSTERS OF GRACE   *1998 3-D opera by Glass*

Monsters of Grace is the first 3-D opera. It was premiered at Royce Hall in Los Angeles on April 15, 1998, with the audience wearing 3-D glasses in order to see the three-dimensional film images created by Diana Walczak and Jeff Kleiser that were an integral part of the stage performance. As there was no narrative and the premiere was still considered a work-in-progress, the images seemed rather arbitrary as they evolved from polar bears and mutilated hands to soaring helicopters and Chinese chopsticks. It was fascinating all the same as a major component of this

W. Franke Harling's movie opera *Monsieur Beaucaire* was based on a play that was filmed with Rudolf Valentino in 1924.

experimental digital opera by composer Philip Glass and designer/director Robert Wilson. The "libretto" consisted mostly of poems by Persian mystic Jelaluddin Rumi translated into English by Coleman Barks. They were sung by soprano Marie Mascari, mezzo-soprano Alexandra Montano, baritone Gregory Purnhagen and bass Peter Stewart. The music was performed by the Philip Glass Ensemble led by Michael Riesman. The opera was reprised in London and then brought back to UCLA in revised form.

MONTANA   *American state (1889–)*

Eugene Weigel's *The Mountain Child*, libretto by R. O. Bowen, premiered at Montana University in Missoula on July 27, 1959. Alan Hovhaness's opera-oratorio LADY OF LIGHT was premiered in concert form in Montana in 1969. ARTHUR NEVIN lived with the Blackfoot tribe in Montana for two years studying their music and based his opera POIA on what he learned. Soprano JUDITH BLEGEN, who starred in several Gian Carlo Menotti operas, was born in Missoula. Composer William Brandt was born in Butte.

MONTEMEZZI, ITALO   *Italian composer (1875–1952)*

Italian composer Italo Montemezzi lived in the United States from 1939 to 1949 and wrote his last opera in America. L'INCANTESIMO, libretto by Sem Benelli, had its world premiere on NBC Radio on October 9, 1942. Montemezzi is best known for his doleful 1913 opera, *L'Amore dei Tre Re* (The Love of Three Kings), a smash hit at the Met in the early years of the century.

MONTEZUMA   *1964 opera by Sessions*

Spanish explorer Hernando Cortez arrives in the New World and begins the conquest of Mexico. Indian Princess Malinche, converted to Christianity, becomes his mistress and leads the conquistadors to the Aztec city of gold. Aztec chief Montezuma and Cortez want peace but their followers will not accept it and the invasion ends with the death of Montezuma. Roger Sessions' three-act opera *Montezuma*, libretto by Giuseppe Antonio Borgese based on the writings of conquistador Bernal Diaz del Castillo, was premiered in West Berlin by Deutsche Oper Berlin on April 19, 1964. Ernest Krukowski took the role of the narrator Bernal Diaz as an older man, Karl Ernst Mercker was young Diaz, William Dooley was Cortez, Helmut Melchert was Montezuma, Annabella Bernard was Princess Malinche, Loren Driscoll was Alvarado, Manfred Rohrl was Fray Olmedo and Barry McDaniel was Cuauhtemoc. Michael Raffaelli designed the costumes and sets, Rudolf Sellner staged the opera and Heinrich Hollreiser conducted the orchestra. The opera was premiered in the U.S. in 1976 by the Boston Opera Company and reprised by the Juilliard American Opera Center in 1982. The score is complex and atonal with dramatic use of 12-note techniques.

1976 Boston Opera. The opera was presented by the Boston Opera Company on May 31, 1976, broadcast on NPR Radio and recorded. Donald Gramm was Bernal Diaz as an old man, Alexander Stevenson was Diaz as a young man, Brent Ellis was Cortez, Richard Lewis was Montezuma, Phyllis Bryn-Julson was Princess Malinche, William Fleck was Fray Olmedo, Alan Crofoot was Alvarado and David Evitts was Cuauhtemoc. Sarah Caldwell staged the opera and conducted the orchestra. Opera Classics cassette.

MONTH IN THE COUNTRY   *1981 opera by Hoiby*

See *NATALIA PETROVNA*

MONTICELLO   *2000 opera by Paxton*

A scandal breaks out in 1803 when President Thomas Jefferson is rumored to have a mulatto slave mistress named Sally Hemings. Her brother James tries to persuade her to leave him but she refuses and gives birth to five children fathered by Jefferson. Twenty-three years later the dying Jefferson refuses to honor his promise to Sally to free all his slaves. Glenn Paxton's two-act 95-minute opera *Monticello*, libretto by Leroy Aarons based on historical assumptions, was premiered in a concert version by L.A. Theatre Works at the Skirball Cultural Center in Los Angeles on April 26, 2000, and broadcast on KCRW. Shana Blake Hill sang the role of Sally Hemings, Christopher Schuman was Thomas Jefferson, Cynthia Jansen was Jefferson's daughter Patsy, Annette Daniels was Betty Hemings, Haquimai Sharpe was Madison Hemings, Michael Paul Smith was James Hemings, Hakeem Jawanza was Young Madison, and Susan Hull was Narrator. John Rubinstein directed, Susan Albert Loewenberg was the executive producer, Victoria Kirsch was music director and played piano accompaniment, and Richard Rintoul was the conductor.

2000 L.A. Theatre Works. The opera was produced for radio by Raymond Guarna and recorded with the cast as above headed by Shana Blake Hill as Sally Hemings and Christopher Schuman as Thomas Jefferson. Victoria Kirsch is the pianist and Richard Rintoul is the conductor. LA Theatre Works 2-CD box.

"MOON-FACED, STARRY-EYED"   *Soprano/tenor duet: Street Scene (1947). Words: Langston Hughes. Music: Kurt Weill.*

"Moon-faced, starry-eyed" is probably the only operatic duet in the jitterbug genre. Introduced in Kurt Weill's Broadway opera STREET SCENE by a swinging jive-talking young couple, it became the most popular number in the show and was widely recorded. Langston Hughes' lyrics allow Mae Jones and Dick McGann to tell each other how much they dig each other before they start crazily dancing all over the stage. He says she's peaches and cream with nuts on the side and she says he's whiskey straight with beer on the side. The number was originally sung and danced by Sheila Bond and Danny Daniels and they nearly stopped the show. It became a hit song for Benny Goodman and his Orchestra with Johnny Mercer doing the jive singing and for Freddy Martin and his Orchestra with Murray Arnold as singer. It was only used as an orchestral number on the original cast album but is sung by Mary Munger and Philip Gould on the 1991 Scottish Opera recording, by Catherine Zeta Jones and Philip Day on the 1992 English National Opera recording and by Deborah Leamy and Alex Sharp in the 1994 Houston Grand Opera telecast.

MOORE, DOROTHY RUDD   *American composer (1940–)*

Dorothy Rudd Moore was commissioned to write an opera about 19th century abolitionist and orator Frederick Douglass by Opera Ebony. Her three-hour opera FREDERICK DOUGLASS, libretto by the composer, was premiered by Opera Ebony in New York City on June 17, 1985. Moore, who was born in New Castle, Delaware, studied composition at Howard University and with Nadia Boulanger. She has written a large quantity of music, including many songs, but only one opera.

MOORE, DOUGLAS   *American composer (1893–1969)*

Douglas Moore was one of the major creators of the modern American opera and his work has had wide influence, especially through his choice of American subjects. He was encouraged to use American themes by poet Vachel Lindsay whom met in 1923. During the bicentenary celebrations in 1976, Moore romantic opera THE BALLAD OF BABY DOE (1956), was given five major

Composer Douglas Moore

productions around the U.S. and praised as possibly the great American opera. The libretto by John Latouche tells the touching story of a love affair between a 19th century Colorado mining magnate and a young woman, Baby Doe, one of the truly iconic figures of American opera. CARRY NATION (1966), libretto by William North Jayne; focuses on another iconic American woman, the anti-saloon campaigner who became famous by swinging an axe. Moore's folk operas THE HEADLESS HORSEMAN (1936) and THE DEVIL AND DANIEL WEBSTER (1938), both with superb librettos by Stephen Vincent Bénet, are Americana at its best. His soap opera spoof GALLANTRY (1957), libretto by Arnold Sundgaard, was one of the first American operas to satirize television. Moore won the Pulitzer Prize in 1949 for the much more somber GIANTS IN THE EARTH, libretto by Sundgaard based on a novel by O. E. Rölvaag about the pioneer life in 19th century South Dakota, but it has never been popular. Moore, born in Cutchogue, NY, studied at Yale with Horatio Parker and in Paris. From the beginning he showed he was interested in American subjects for his operas. He began in 1928 with the opera *Jesse James*, libretto by J. M. Brown, and then adapted a Philip Barry play for WHITE WINGS (1935). After his Bénet folk operas, he tried his hand at writing for children and composed *The Emperor's New Clothes* (1948) and *Puss in Boots* (1950), both staged in New York City. In 1961 he created an opera based on a Henry James novel, WINGS OF THE DOVE, libretto by Ethan Ayer. In 1962 he composed the Christmas entertainment *The Greenfield Christmas Tree*, libretto by Sundgaard, which was premiered in Baltimore. *Carry Nation* was his last opera.

MOORE, GRACE   *American soprano (1901–1947)*

Met soprano Grace Moore, who became a movie star in the 1930s, starred in a prescient 1922 Broadway musical called ABOVE THE CLOUDS in which she played a movie star for Tom and Will B. Johnstone. In 1930 she starred in a film version of Sigmund Romberg's THE NEW MOON opposite Lawrence Tibbett. On record she can be heard in 1936 singing "Auf Wiedersehn" from Romberg's BLUE PARADISE. Otherwise she was not much involved with American opera and operetta despite beginning her career in musical comedy. Moore, born in Nough, Tennessee, made her operatic debut in Paris in 1928 and got an Oscar nomination in 1934 for her film, *One Night of Love*. She died in a plane crash in Denmark in 1947.

MOORE, MARY CARR   *American composer (1873–1957)*

Mary Carr Moore, America's first notable woman opera composer, began her operatic career at the age of 21 starring in the premiere of her light opera THE ORACLE at Golden Gate Hall in San Francisco on March 19, 1894. She gave up singing to compose and teach and completed nine more operas, most of them performed. Her grand opera NARCISSA: *or, The Cost of Empire*, libretto by Sarah Pratt Carr, premiered at the Moore Theater in Seattle on April 22, 1912, with the composer directing and conducting. It is considered the first grand opera by an American woman composer. It was followed by *The Leper* (1912), *Memories* (1914) and *Harmony* (1917). Her next big success was *The Flaming Arrow: or, The Shaft of Ku'pish-ta-ya*, libretto by Sarah Pratt Moore based on an Indian legend, which premiered at the Century Club in San Francisco on March 27, 1922, with Emilie Lancel, Easton Kent and Marion Vecki as the main singers and the composer conducting; it was reprised by Los Angeles Opera in 1927. *Los Rubios*, libretto by Neeta Marquis, was commissioned by the City of Los Angeles and premiered at the Greek Theater in Los Angeles on September 10, 1931. The grand opera DAVID RIZZIO, libretto by Emanuel Mapleson Brown about Mary Queen of Scots and her secretary, premiered at Shrine Auditorium in Los Angeles on May 26, 1932. Moore's last opera was the 1935 three-act LEGENDE PROVENÇALE, libretto by Eleanore Flaig, considered by some to be her best. Moore, who was born in Memphis, Tennessee, with the maiden name of Carr, moved to California with her family at the age of twelve and began her music studies in San Francisco.

MORAN, JOHN   *American composer (1966–)*

Avant-garde opera composer John Moran's multimedia opera THE MANSON FAMILY was commissioned by Jed Wheeler for the 1990 Serious Fun Festival at Lincoln Center, premiered by Ridge Theater at Alice Tully Hall and recorded. Moran, who grew up in Nebraska where his mother was an opera singer and his father director of a choral group, began his operatic career with an ambitious adaptation of *Parsifal*. As no one was interested, he took samplings from *The Jack Benny Show* TV show and created a multimedia theatrical piece titled *Jack Benny!* using dialogue as music with performers lip-synching to his samples. It was performed by Performance Space 122 in 1988 and *Rules of Nakedness* was staged by LaMama in 1989. His multimedia operatic extravaganza BOOK OF THE DEAD (SEVENTH AVENUE) premiered in New York on November 2000.

MORAN, ROBERT   *American composer (1937–)*

Robert Moran began to acquire renown as an opera composer in 1984 with the success of THE JUNIPER TREE composed in collaboration with Philip Glass but he had already been working in experimental music theater for many years. His first opera was the one-act *Let's Build a Nut House* premiered at San Jose State College in California on April 19, 1969. In 1971 he composed *Divertissement No. 3: A Lunchbag Opera* for BBC Television in England and in 1974 he created the department store window opera *Metamenagerie*. *Durst Wüsten und Woken* (1975) was followed by *Hitler: Geschichten aus der Zukunft*, based on Hitler-era documents. *Erlösung dem Erlöser* is an experimental opera set inside the brain of the dying Wagner. The grim fairytale *The Jupiter Tree* marked a shift to a more romantic style and was followed in 1986 with his *Leipzig Candle Play* in honor of Handel, Bach and Scarlatti. In 1992 he premiered two operas with librettos by Michael John LaChiusa, the beauty-and-the-beast story DESERT OF ROSES which premiered at Houston Grand Opera and the Japanese legend FROM THE

TOWERS OF THE MOON which premiered at Minnesota Opera. In 1995 the short Oscar Wilde opera NIGHT PASSAGE was premiered in Seattle. In 1996 the vampire opera THE DRACULA DIARY, libretto by James Skofield, was premiered in Houston. Moran's 10-minute virtuoso piece for men's chorus REMEMBER HIM TO ME, text by Gertrude Stein, was premiered by Long Beach Opera in 2003. Moran, born in Denver, studied at San Francisco State and Mills colleges and in Vienna. He has been a popular lecturer on contemporary music but now devotes himself to composing.

MORGAN, BEVERLY   *American soprano (1952–)*

Beverly Morgan created the role of Kasturbai in Philip Glass's SATYAGRAHA in Amsterdam in 1980. She sang the role of Dede in Leonard Bernstein's A QUIET PLACE at La Scala in Milan in 1984 and at the Vienna Staatsoper in 1986 and is featured on the Vienna recording. Morgan, who was born in Hanover, NH, studied in Boston and often sings in contemporary operas.

MOROSS, JEROME   *American composer (1913–1983)*

Jerome Moross blurred the boundaries between opera, musical, ballet and folk music in a thoroughly American way. THE GOLDEN APPLE, an updated through-sung version of Homer's *Iliad* and *Odyssey* set in the state of Washington, was thought to be rather operatic when it opened as a Broadway musical in New York in 1954. GENTLEMEN, BE SEATED!, a portrait of the American Civil War as a minstrel show, was considered rather like a musical when it premiered at New York City Opera on October 10, 1963. BALLET BALLADS combined opera with ballet and folk legends when it premiered in 1948 with the triple-bill of *Susanna and the Elders*, *Willie the Weeper* and *The Eccentricities of Davy Crockett*. SORRY, WRONG NUMBER! in 1977 was a one-act thriller based on a radio play by Lucille Fletcher. An American folk-tinged vernacular style links all his work. His first symphony incorporated the prison folk song "Midnight Special" and his ballet *Frankie and Johnnie* was based on a famous folk ballad. When he went to work writing scores for Hollywood movies, it could be heard in films like *The Big Country*. Moross, born in Brooklyn, began his professional career with the 1935 revue *Parade* and then went to work for George Gershwin on a West Coast production of *Porgy and Bess*. The librettos for most of his operas are by John Latouche, librettist of THE BALLAD OF BABY DOE.

2000 Windflower: The Songs of Jerome Moross. This is an expanded cast album based on tributes to the composer held at Joe's Pub in New York City in February/March 2000. It includes numbers from *The Golden Apple* and other lesser known music theater works by Morass. The featured performers are Alice Ripley, Richard Munez, Jessica Molaskey, Henny Giering and Philip Chaffin with musical director Eric Stern accompanying on piano. Ps classics CD.

MORRIS, JAMES   *American bass-baritone (1947–)*

James Morris, who found international success singing Wotan in Wagner's *Ring* cycle, created the role of King Alfonso in Thomas Pasatieri's INES DE CASTRO at Baltimore Lyric Opera in 1976. He was born in Baltimore and made his debut there in 1967 after studying with Rosa Ponselle. He joined the Metropolitan Opera in 1970. He is married to Met mezzo-soprano Susan Quittmeyer.

MORRIS, MARK   *American choreographer (1956–)*

Choreographer/dancer Mark Morris helped create two of the most critically acclaimed and influential recent American operas and helped revitalize a classic. With composer John Adams. director Peter Sellars and librettist Alice Goodman he collaborated on the production of NIXON IN CHINA at Houston Grand opera in 1987 (agitprop ballet) and THE DEATH OF KLINGHOFFER (abstract dances) at the Théâtre de la Monnaie in Brussels in 1991. He won acclaim for his brilliant production of Virgil Thomson's abridged version of FOUR SAINTS IN THREE ACTS which premiered at English National Opera in 2000 in a double-bill with Purcell's *Dido and Aeneas*. He also choreographed a production of Stephen Sondheim's *Sweeney Todd* in Seattle. Morris, who was born in Seattle, was once known as "the big hairy guy of dance." He began to choreograph in 1971 and was quickly acclaimed for his original versions of ballet and opera classics.

MORROW, DORETTA   *American soprano (1927–1965)*

Doretta Morrow created the role of Tuptim in Richard Rodgers' THE KING AND I on Broadway in 1951 (cast album), Marsinah in Wright/Forrest's KISMET on Broadway in 1953 (cast album) and Marco Polo's girlfriend in Warnick/Paul's THE ADVENTURES OF MARCO POLO on NBC television in 1958 (cast album). She played Tina in a 1950 ABC television production of Kurt Weill's KNICKERBOCKER HOLIDAY. Her recordings include highlight albums of three classic operettas: Sigmund Romberg's THE DESERT SONG (1952), Victor Herbert's MLLE. MODISTE (1952) and Herbert's NAUGHTY MARIETTA (1953). She made one film, singing opposite Mario Lanza in *Because You're Mine* (1952).

MOSLEY, ROBERT   *American baritone (1934–)*

Robert Mosley created the role of Leonce in William Grant Still's A BAYOU LEGEND with Opera/South in Jackson, Mississippi in 1974. On stage he sang Porgy in George Gershwin's *Porgy and Bess* and Father in Scott Joplin's *Treemonisha*. Mosley, who was born in Coulder, Pennsylvania, made his debut with New York City Opera in 1966.

MOSS, HOWARD   *American composer (1927–)*

Howard Moss created two operas of note based on literary works and half a dozen music theater works. THE BRUTE, libretto by Eric Bentley based on a play by Chekhov, was staged at Yale in 1961 and televised in 1966. *The Queen and the Rebels*, libretto by the composer based on the Italian play by Ugo Betti, was premiered in New York on November 1, 1962, and staged at Central City Opera in Colorado in 1972. The music theater piece *Unseen Leaves* was based on Walt Whitman's *Leaves of Grass*. Moss, who was born in Los Angeles, studied at UCLA, USC and the Eastman School and taught at Yale, Mills and Maryland.

THE MOST HAPPY FELLA   *1956 "quasi-opera" by Loesser*

Elderly Napa Valley wine grower Tony falls in love with young San Francisco waitress Rosabella and tricks her into coming to marry him by sending her a photo of his handsome young foreman Joe. She is so upset when she discovers this that she allows Joe to seduce her on her wedding night. She becomes pregnant and Tony asks her to leave. After some heart searching, they become reconciled. Frank Loesser's "quasi-opera" *The Most Happy Fella*, libretto by the composer based on Sidney Howard's play *They Knew What They Wanted*, premiered at the Shubert Theater in Boston on March 13, 1956, and opened on Broadway at the Imperial Theater on May 3, 1956. Metropolitan Opera baritone Robert Weede starred as the happy fella of the title and this confused the critics who wondered if this musical was really an opera in disguise. As it has less than fifteen minutes of spoken dialogue and is replete with arias, duets, trios, quartets and choral pieces, the confusion was understandable. Jo Sullivan was Rosabella, Art Lund was Joey, Susan Johnson was Cleo, Shorty Long was Herman, Mona Paulee was Marie and Zina Bethuene was Tessie. Joseph Anthony directed and Herbert Green conducted. The hit song was the very non-operatic but memorable "Standing on the Corner." *The Most Happy Fella* has begun to enter the opera repertory and was revived by New York City Opera in 1991 with Giorgio Tozzi as Tony.

1956 Original Broadway cast. Met baritone Robert Weede sings the role of Tony with Jo Sullivan as Rosabella, Art Lund as Joe, Susan Johnson as Cleo and Shorty Long as Herman. Herbert Green conducts the orchestra. Columbia LP/Sony CD. **199 London cast.** Canadian opera baritone Louis Quilico sings Tony in this complete recording made in London with the National Symphony Orchestra conducted by John Owen Edwards. Emily Loesser is Rosabella, Karen Ziemba is Cleo, Richard Muenz is Joey, Nancy Shade is Marie, Don Stephenson is Herman, William Burden is the Doctor, Georgy Dvorsky is Al, Alfred Boe is Giuseppe and Michael Gruber is Clem. Jay 2-CD set.

THE MOST IMPORTANT MAN   *1971 opera by Menotti*

Toimé Ukamba, black protégé of a famous white scientist working in colonial Africa, discovers a formula that could change the world and make him the most important man. He becomes involved with the scientist's daughter Cora and is killed. Gian Carlo Menotti's controversial three-act opera *The Most Important Man*, libretto by the composer, was premiered by New York City Opera on March 7, 1971. Eugene Holmes was Toimé Ukamba, Harry Theyard was Dr. Arnek, Joanna Bruno was Arnek's daughter Cora, Beverly Wolff was his wife Leona, Richard Stilwell was Eric Rupert, John Lankston was Professor Clement, Joaquin Romaguera was Professor Risselberg, Thomas Jamerson was Professor Bolental and Don Yule was Professor Grippel. Oliver Smith designed the sets, Menotti directed and Christopher Keene conducted.

MOTEN, ETTA   *American mezzo-soprano (1902–2004)*

Mezzo-soprano Etta Moten became a star in *Porgy and Bess* in the 1942 Broadway revival when she replaced Anne Brown as Bess. George Gershwin had considered her for the role in the original production but wanted a soprano rather than a mezzo and wouldn't transpose the role down for her. Moten had been one of the few African Americans allowed to sing in Hollywood films in the 1930s; she sang a solo part in one section of "The Carioca" number in *Flying Down to Rio* and had a solo singing appearance in the "Remember the Forgotten Man" sequence of *Gold Diggers of 1933*. This last appearance impressed First Lady Eleanor Roosevelt who invited her to sing it for President Roosevelt at the White House in 1934. Moten married Claude Barnett, founder of the Associated Negro Press, the same year.

THE MOTHER   *1954 opera by Hollingsworth*

Death disguised as an Old Man takes Anna's sick child. She follows him getting directions from Night by singing her a lullaby, from Blackthorn by warming him in an embrace and from Lake who receives her tears. When she finds Death, he tells her the child is at peace and she must return to the land of the living. Stanley Hollingsworth's one-act opera *The Mother*, libretto by John Fandel and the composer based on a Hans Christian Andersen fairy tale, premiered at the Curtis Institute in Philadelphia on March 29, 1954.

THE MOTHER OF THREE SONS   *1990 dance opera by Jenkins*

A rich woman in an African village yearns for a son but gives birth to a daughter whom she abandons. Her husband dies of grief so she takes up with the River God who gives her three sons. They are imperfect (blind, deaf and dumb) so she rejects them and goes to work in a brothel in the city. After her sons are killed because of her, she drowns herself in the River. Leroy Jenkins's dance opera *The Mother of Three Sons,* based on a Yoruba legend, is a collaboration with librettist Ann T. Green and dancer/choreographer/director Bill T. Jones. It was commissioned by the Munich Biennale, premiered at the Aachen State Theater in May 1990 and was given its American premiere by New York City Opera October 19, 1991. The Munich and New York productions featured Ruby Hinds as the Mother (the role was written for her and she is the only on-stage singer) with Bill Jones as River God and Rhodessa Jones as brothel keeper Djinn. Jenkins, a jazz violinist, combines jazz ideas and African drumming with Stravinsky-style musical ideas in the score.

THE MOTHER OF US ALL   *1947 pageant opera by Thomson*

Susan B. Anthony struggles to obtains rights for women in the 19th century and encounters famous people who support or oppose her work. Virgil Thomson's pageant opera *The Mother of Us All,* libretto by Gertrude Stein with scenario by Maurice Grosser, was rejected by the major New York opera companies despite the fame of composer and librettist and premiered at Brander Matthews Hall at Columbia University on May 7, 1947. Dorothy Dow created the role of Susan B. Anthony with Belva Kibler as Anne, Hazell Gravell as Gertrude S., Robert Grooters as Virgil T., Bertram Rowe as Daniel Webster, William Horne as Jo the Loiterer, Carlton Sunday as Chris the Citizen, Ruth Krug as Indiana Elliott, Carolyn Blakeslee as Angel More, Teresa Stich-Randall as Henrietta M, Jacques La Rochelle as Henry B., James M. Chartrand as Anthony Comstock, Robert Sprecher as John Adams, Alfred Kunz as Thaddeus Stevens, Alice Howland as Constance Fletcher, Michael Therry as Gloster Heming, Shirley Sudock as Isabel Wentworth, Jean Handzlik as Anna Hope, Nancy Reid as Lillian Russell, Diana Herman as Jenny Reefer, Everett Anderson as Ulysses S. Grant, Edward J. Larson as Herman Atlan, Edward Cohen as Donald Gallup, Winston Ross as Andrew J. and Dale Burr, James Clarke, Vernon Van Dutton and Isaah Clarke as A.A. and T.T. Paul du Pont designed the sets, John Taras staged the opera and Otto Luening conducted the orchestra. The music is tonal, tuneful and very American incorporating 19th century songs, folk ballads, gospel hymns and marches. *The Mother of Us All* has been revived many times in recent years with productions by Eastman Opera Theater in 1996, Baltimore Opera in 1997 and Glimmerglass Opera in 1998. When Christopher Alden's Glimmerglass production was staged by New York City Opera in 2000 with Lauren Flanigan as Susan B. Anthony, *The Mother of Us All* was hailed by critics as one of the genuine masterpieces of American opera. In 2004 it became the first American opera in 81 years to be the gala opening program at San Francisco Opera.

1947 Premiere Cast. Dorothy Dow, who created the role of Susan B. Anthony, leads the cast in this live recording of the premiere at Columbia University on May 7, 1947. Belva Kibler is Anne, Hazell Gravell is Gertrude S., Robert Grooters is Virgil T., Bertram Rowe is Daniel Webster and William Horne is Jo the Loiterer with Otto Luening conducting. Premiere Opera 2-CD set. **1976 Chicago Opera Theater.** The Chicago Opera Theater production staged by Frank Galati in 1976 was videotaped and telecast on the Central Education Network in March 1977. Judith Erickson is Susan B. Anthony, Adrienne Passen is Anne, William Martin is Jo the Loiterer, William Eichorn is John Adams, Carol Gutknecht is Constance Fletcher, Warren Fremling is Daniel Webster, Robert Orth is Virgil T, Anne Irving is Gertrude S., Clayton Hochhalter is Thaddeus Stevens, Steven Emanuel is Chris the Citizen, Maria Lagios is Angel More, Dalia Bach is Indiana Elliot, Vittorio Giammarrusco is Andrew Johnson, Douglas Kiddie is Anthony Comstock and Robert Heitzinger is Gloster Heming. Robert Frisbie conducts the Chicago Opera Studio Orchestra. Peter Amster devised the choreography, Mary Griswold designed the sets and David Erdman directed the 64-minute video. **1976 Santa Fe Opera.** The Santa Fe Opera production staged by Peter Wood in 1976 was videotaped and telecast on PBS on July 5, 1977. Mignon Dunn is Susan B. Anthony, Ashley Putnam is Angel More, Batyah Godfrey is Anne, James Atherton is Jo the Loiterer, William Lewis is John Adams, Helen Vanni is Constance Fletcher, Philip Booth is Daniel Webster, Gene Ives is Virgil T, Aviva Orvath is Gertrude S., Douglas Perry is Thaddeus Stevens, Joseph McKee is Chris the Citizen,. Linn Maxwell is Indiana Elliot, Karen Beck is Lillian Russell, Steven Loewengart is Ulysses S. Grant, David W. Fuller is Anthony Comstock, Billie Nash is Henrietta M. and Ronald Raines is Henry B. Raymond Leppard conducts the Santa Fe Opera Orchestra. Robert Indiana designed the sets and David Chesire directed the 90-minute video. **1977 Santa Fe Opera.** Mignon Dunn stars as Susan B. Anthony in this recording based on the 1976 Santa Fe Opera production. James Atherton is Jo the Loiterer, Philip Booth is Daniel Webster, Ashley Putnam is Angel More, Gene Ives is Virgil T, Aviva Orvath is Gertrude S., Batyah Godfrey is Anne, Douglas Perry is Thaddeus Stevens, Joseph McKee is Chris the Citizen, William Lewis is John Adams. Linn Maxwell is Indiana Elliot, Karen Beck is Lillian Russell, Steven Loewengart is Ulysses S. Grant, David W. Fuller is Anthony Comstock, Billie Nash is Henrietta M., Ronald Raines is Henry B. and Helen Vanni is Constance Fletcher. Raymond Leppard conducts the Santa Fe Opera Orchestra. New World Records LP box/CD box. **1986 Virgil Thomson at 90.** John Huszar's documentary *Virgil Thomson at 90* features Thomson talking about the origins of *The Mother of Us All* and includes photographic scenes from productions. The 60-minute color film was telecast on November 30, 1986. Film-America VHS.

MOULSON, ROBERT *American tenor (1932–2003)*

Robert Moulson has sung in three operas by Carlisle Floyd and created roles in two of them. He created the feeble-minded Lennie in Carlisle Floyd's OF MICE AND MEN at Seattle Opera in 1970, and reprised the role at New York City Opera when it was first presented there in 1983; .he can be heard singing the role on a live recording of a 1971 Cincinnati Opera production He also created the role of Sugar Boy in Floyd's WILLIE STARK at Houston Grand Opera on 1981. Moulson, who made his operatic debut singing Sam Polk in Floyd's *Susannah* at New York City Opera in 1958, was born in Rosell, GA, and studied privately in New York.

MOURNING BECOMES ELECTRA *1967 opera by Levy*

In a New England seaport at the end of the American Civil War, the Mannon family awaits the return of General Ezra Mannon. His wife Christine is involved with sea captain Adam Brant but her daughter Lavinia threatens to expose her. When Ezra returns, Christine poisons him and Lavinia tells her brother Orin. Orin kills Brant and Christine shoots herself. Lavinia and Orin become incestuously involved but the guilt-ridden Orin eventually kills himself and Lavinia goes mad. Marvin David Levy's three-act opera *Mourning Becomes Electra,* libretto by Henry Butler based on the Eugene O'Neill trilogy of plays, premiered at the Metropolitan Opera on March 17, 1967. Evelyn Lear was Lavinia, John Reardon was Orin, Marie Collier was Christine, Sherrill Milnes was Adam, John Macurdy was Ezra, Ron Bottcher was Peter Niles, Lilian Sukis was Helen Niles and Raymond Michalski was Jed. Boris Aronson designed the sets and Zubin Mehta conducted the Met orchestra. Greek film director Michael Cacoyannis was chosen to stage the opera as the story derives from Aeschylus's *Oresteia* trilogy of plays about Orestes and Electra. The music is expressionist but tonal. The opera was revived by Lyric Opera of Chicago in 1999 and by Seattle Opera and New York City Opera in 2004.

1967 Metropolitan Opera. Marie Collier is Christine, Sherrill Milnes is Adam, Evelyn Lear is Lavinia and John Reardon is Orin in this PBS broadcast of the Metropolitan Opera premiere on March 17, 1967. The rest of the cast is as above. Zubin Mehta conducts the Met orchestra. On audiocassette. **1968 Met: 100 Years 100 Singers.** Sherrill Milnes, who created the role of Adam Brant, sings Adam's second act aria "Too Weak to Kill the Man I Hate" on the album *Met 100 Years 100 Singers.* Anton Guadagno conducts the New Philharmonic Orchestra. RCA Victor CD. **1991 Sherrill Milnes.** Leontyne Price introduces Sherrill Milnes who sings Adam Brant's aria "Too Weak to Kill the Man I Hate" at a televised *Richard Tucker Foundation Gala* at Avery Fisher Hall November 10, 1991. James Conlon conducts the Metropolitan Opera Orchestra in the televised, recorded performance. PBS telecast/ RCA Victor CD. **1998 Lyric Opera of Chicago Commentary.** Critical analysis of *Mourning Becomes Electra* by Roger Pines with comments by composer Marvin David Levy in the Women's Board of Lyric Opera. series. It includes musical excerpts, plot summary, composer biography and social and historical background. Lyric Opera Commentaries audiocassette. **1999 Lyric Opera of Chicago broadcast.** Lauren Flanigan is Christine, Jason Howard is Adam, Cynthia Lawrence is Lavinia and Randolph Locke is Orin in this June 5 radio broadcast of the Lyric Opera of Chicago production. Richard Buckley conducts. On audiotape. **2003 Seattle Opera.** Lauren Flanigan is Christine, Jason Howard is Adam, Nina Warren is Lavinia, Kurt Ollmann is Orin and Gabor Andrasy is Ezra in this broadcast of Seattle Opera production of a revised version of the opera. Michael Yeargan designed the sets, Bartlett Sher directed and Richard Buckley conducted.

MOVIE OPERAS *American operas created for films*

While there have been no full-scale American operas created as films, there have been a number of partial ones composed and staged for movies and involving opera singers. These movie operas, usually created by the composer of the score for the film, were devised to allow actors to behave or sing in ways required by the plot. The most famous example is the opera SALAMMBÔ created for the movie *Citizen Kane* by Bernard Herrmann because director Orson Welles needed an opera which opens with a soprano in mid-aria singing against a dominant orchestra. As no such opera could be found, Herrmann created one. *Salammbô*, like other movie operas, exists only in fragments so it cannot be staged outside the movie in which it is seen. However, the soprano aria created by Herrmann for *Salammbô* has been recorded by Kiri Te Kanawa and appears to have its own viability. The creators of movie operas include notable stage opera composers Erich Wolfgang Korngold, Kurt Weill and Mario Castelnuovo-Tedesco. The operas listed below have their own entry with further information.

1930 Monsieur Beaucaire (Harling/Paramount). 1936 Romeo and Juliet (Korngold/Paramount). 1936 Bal Masque (Carbonara/Universal). 1936 Isabelle (Carbonara/Universal). 1937 Carnival (Levant/Fox). 1937 Czaritza (Stothart/MGM). 1937 The Cantor's Son (Olshanetsky/Eron). 1939 Arlesiana (Pokrass/Fox). 1939 Balalaika (Stothart/MGM). 1941 Salammbô (Hermann/RKO). 1943 Amour et Gloire (Ward/MGM). 1943 Prince Masque de la Caucasie (Ward/MGM). 1944 The Magic Voice (Ward/Universal). 1945 Columbus (Weill/Fox). 1945 Tillie Tell (Skiles-Rossini/Columbia). 1946 Marie Antoinette (Previn/MGM). 1949 The Princess (Previn/MGM). 1949 Amore di Fatima(Castelnuovo-Tedesco/Fox). 1951 Il Ritorno di Cesare (Castelnuovo-Tedesco/MGM). 1989 Don Juan Triumphant (Segal — UA). 1990 Die Schlumpf (Pasatieri — WB). 2001 Vide Cor Meum (Cassidy-Universal).

MRS. DALLOWAY   *1993 opera by Larsen*

Two stories set in London after World War I are told simultaneously. Mrs. Dalloway, middle-aged wife of a minor MP, is making preparations for a dinner party. She remembers Sally to whom she felt attracted while being wooed by Peter Walsh, whom she rejected. Both turn up at her dinner party. At the same time war veteran Septimus Warren Smith has a nervous breakdown over guilt about what he did in the war. His Italian wife can't help and he kills himself. A doctor friend tells his story at Mrs. Dalloway's party. Libby Larsen's two-act chamber opera *Mrs. Dalloway*, libretto by Bonnie Grice based on the Virginia Woolf novel, was premiered by Lyric Opera Cleveland on July 22, 1993. Mary Elizabeth Poore sang the role of Clarissa Dalloway, Hillary Nicholson was Sally Seton, Richard Lewis was Peter Walsh, Gary Briggle was Septimus Smith, Fontaine Follansbee was Rezia, Quentin Quereau was Richard Dalloway, Peg Cleveland was Lucy, Michy Houlahan was Sir William and Virginia Bruozis was the Old Woman. Michael McConnell staged the opera, Steven Perry designed the abstract set and Benton Hess led the orchestra. The score is tonal and harmonious.

MRS. SATAN   *2000 opera by Bond*

Victoria Woodhull, who ran for the American presidency before women had the vote, was dubbed "Mrs. Satan" by political satirist Thomas Nast. She was a radical publisher, stockbroker and free lover brought down by a sex scandal involving preacher Henry Ward Beecher. Victoria Bond's opera, *Mrs. Satan*, libretto by Hilary Bell, was given a workshop performance by the Center for Contemporary Opera and Music Theatre April 27, 2000, in the Hayden Auditorium at Greenwich House. and the completed opera was performed in concert at the John Drew Theater, East Hampton, NY, on December 22, 2002. The principal singers were Deborah Mayer, Adam Klein, Robert Osborne, Andrew Childs, Heather Sarris, Tami Swartz and Joy Hermalyn. The composer conducted the orchestra and chorus with assistance from chorus master Timothy Mount and assistant conductor David Mayfield.

MUNSEL, PATRICE   *American soprano (1923–)*

Met soprano Patrice Munsel was as popular for her light opera roles as for her coloratura performances in dramatic opera and recorded several of them. She is featured on a recorded radio broadcast of Sigmund Romberg's UP IN CENTRAL PARK in 1945, portrays Anna opposite Robert Merrill's King in a 1951 recording of Richard Rodgers' THE KING AND I, sings Julie opposite Merrill's Billy on a 1955 recording of Rodgers' CAROUSEL, portrays Marietta opposite Alfred Drake's Dick in a 1955 NBC TV production of Victor Herbert's NAUGHTY MARIETTA and sings with Merrill and Risë Stevens on a 1956 recording of Jerome Kern's Show Boat. She also sang comic opera arias on her appearances on the *Voice of Firestone* TV show, "Romany Life" from THE FORTUNE TELLER in January 1954 and the "Italian Street Song" from *Naughty Marietta* in May 1954. Munsel, who was born in Spokane, Washington, made her debut at the Met in 1943 at the age of eighteen, the youngest singer ever signed by the Met. In the 1950s she hosted a TV variety show called *The Patrice Munsel Show.*

THE MURDER OF COMRADE SHARIK   *1973 opera by Bergsma*

In Moscow in 1925 Dr. Danielov carries out an experiment on a dog named Sharik who ends up becoming a Soviet citizen after human organs are implanted. The dog becomes a rigid follower of the party so finally the doctor turns him back into a dog. William Bergsma's comic opera *The Murder of Comrade Sharik*, libretto by the composer based on Mikhail Bulgakov's satirical novel *Heart of a Dog*, premiered at Brooklyn College on April 10, 1986. Bergsma makes the orchestra the voice of Stalin (a patient of the doctor) and uses quotes from classic operas like Carmen for satirical effect.

MUSEUM OF TELEVISION AND RADIO (MTR)

The Museum of Television and Radio (MTR), which has viewing facilities in New York and Los Angles, has over 70,000 videos in its archive including a large number featuring American opera and operetta. These include collections of *CBS Television Opera Theater, NBC Opera Theater, Voice of Firestone, Bell Telephone Hour* and *Cameo Operas*. Many American operas can only be seen at the MTR which is open to anyone for a small fee.

MUSGRAVE, THEA   *American composer (1928–)*

Thea Musgrave, one of the most successful composers in America today, works primarily with the Virginia Opera company where her husband Peter Mark is conductor and general director. MARY,

Composer Thea Musgrave

QUEEN OF SCOTS was staged and recorded by Virginia Opera in 1978. A CHRISTMAS CAROL, based on the Charles Dickens story, was premiered and recorded by Virginia Opera in 1979. AN OCCURRENCE AT OWL CREEK BRIDGE, a radio opera about the American Civil War based on a story by by Ambrose Bierce, was premiered by BBC in 1982. HARRIET, THE WOMAN CALLED MOSES, the story of an African American slave who escapes and helps free other slaves, was premiered by Virginia Opera in 1985. SIMÓN BOLÍVAR, a portrait of the South American liberator, was premiered by Virginia Opera in 1995. PONTALBA, A LOUISIANA LEGACY, based on the life of the Baroness Pontalba, was commissioned by New Orleans Opera and premiered in New Orleans in 2003. Musgrave was born in Scotland but she moved permanently to the U.S. in 1972.

MUSIC IN THE AIR   *1932 operetta by Kern*

A Bavarian village musician writes what he thinks is a hit tune ("I've Told Every Little Star") so his daughter Sieglinde travels to the big city of Munich with a schoolmaster friend to find a publisher. Composer Bruno Mahler hears her sing it and is so impressed that when his temperamental prima donna mistress Frieda walks out of rehearsals of his new operetta, he asks Sieglinde to take over. She tries but isn't good enough so she decides to go back to her village and marry the schoolmaster. Jerome Kern's Viennese-style operetta *Music in the Air,* libretto by Oscar Hammerstein II, premiered at the Garrick Theater in Philadelphia on October 17, 1932, and opened at the Alvin Theater in New York on November 8, 1932. Tullio Carminati was Bruno Mahler, Natalie Hall was prima donna Frieda, Katherine Carrington was country girl Sieglinde, Walter Slezak was her sweetheart Karl and Al Shean was Sieglinde's father. Joseph Urban designed the sets, Kern and Hammerstein directed and Victor Baravalle was the conductor. The operetta was staged in London in 1933 with former Metropolitan Opera soprano Mary Ellis as Frieda and revived on Broadway in 1951 with Jane Pickens as Frieda and Dennis King as Bruno.

1932 Nathaniel Shilkret. Nathaniel Shilkret conducts the

Jerome Kern's Viennese-style operetta *Music in the Air* was filmed in 1934 with Gloria Swanson as a temperamental diva.

orchestra with Marjorie Horton, Robert Simmons, Jack Parker and Conrad Thibault as the principal singers on this early highlights version of the operetta. RCA Victor LP/The Music of Broadway 1930–1936 2-CD set. **1932 Alan Braden.** Alan Braden conducts the orchestra with Marion Grimaldi, Andy Cole and Maggie Fitzgibbon as the featured singers on this early British recording of highlights from the operetta. World LP. **1932 Lawrence Tibbett.** Lawrence Tibbett recorded "And Love Was Born" and "The Song Is You" from *Music in the Air* in December 1932 with an orchestra led by Nathaniel Shilkret. RCA Victor 78s issued on various LPs and CDs. **1933 Mary Ellis.** Mary Ellis, the former Met soprano who starred in the London production, recorded three songs from the operetta with Hyam Greenburg conducting the orchestra: "I've Told Every Little Star," "The Song Is You" and "I'm Alone." They're on Columbia 78s reissued on various LPs. **1934 Fox Film.** Gloria Swanson stars as temperamental diva Frieda quarreling with librettist lover Bruno (John Boles) in this Fox film of the operetta. Swanson takes up with Bavarian songwriter/teacher Karl (Douglas Montgomery) while Boles flirts with the teacher's singer sweetheart Sieglinde (June Lang). Betty Hiestand dubs Lang's singing and James O'Brien does the same for Montgomery. Louis De Francesco was music director, Billy Wilder and Howard Young wrote the script and Joe May directed. Soundtrack on album *Jerome Kern 1934–1938*. JJA/Box Office LP. **1950 Lauritz Melchior.** Lauritz Melchior performs "The Song is You" on *The Voice of Firestone* TV program on February 6, 1950, with Howard Barlow conducting the Firestone Orchestra. Its on the video *Lauritz Melchior in Opera and Song*. VAI VHS. **1951 Jane Pickens.** Jane Pickens, who played Frieda in the 1951 New York revival, performs highlights from the operetta with Al Goodman conducting the orchestra and chorus. RCA Victor LP. **1952 Radio version.** Nancy Carr, Lois Gentille and Thomas L. Thomas star in this recording of a 1952 radio version of the operetta. AEI CD. **1967 Joan Sutherland.** Joan Sutherland sings "And Love Was Born" on the album *The Golden Age of Operetta* with Richard Bonynge conducting the New Philharmonia Orchestra and Ambrosian Light Opera Chorus. Decca/London LP/CD.

THE MUSIC MAN   *1957 musical by Willson*

"Professor" Harold Hill, a fast-talking musical con man, travels around the country selling marching band instruments and uniforms to small Midwestern towns while promising to teach the local kids to perform like professionals. Marian, the Balzac-loving librarian in the town of River City, Iowa, catches him out. Meredith Willson's *The Music Man,* an outpouring of melodic nostalgia for his Iowa childhood, is one of the finest celebrations of Americana ever to grace the stage and has now entered the opera house repertory. From its memorable rhythmic opening of travelling salesmen chanting on a train to its brassy Sousa-evoking "Seven-Six Trombones," there are few more inventive musicals. It opened on Broadway at the Majestic Theater on December 19, 1957, with Robert Preston as Hill, Barbara Cook as Marian, Iggie Wolfington as Hill's former partner Marcellus, David Burns as the Mayor, Helen Raymond as the Mayor's wife Eulalie, Pert Kelton as Marian's mother and Eddie Hodges as little Winthrop. Kermit Bloomgarden produced, Onna White choreographed, Morton Da Costa directed and Herbert Greene conducted the orchestra and chorus.

1957 Original cast. Robert Preston is Harold Hill opposite Barbara Cook as Marian in this original cast recording with David Burns as the Mayor and Pert Kelton as Marian's mother. Herbert Greene conducts. Capitol LP/CD. **1962 Warner Bros. film.**

Robert Preston and Shirley Jones star in this excellent film version. Buddy Hackett is Hill's old partner, Paul Ford is the Mayor, Hermione Gingold is the Mayor's wife, Pert Kelton is Marian's mother and Ron Howard is little Winthrop. Morton Da Costa produced and directed. The DVD version includes a 30-minute documentary *Right Here in River City: The Making of Meredith Willson's The Music Man.* WB DVD/VHS/LD and WB soundtrack CD. **1991 Music Hall, Cincinnati.** Eric Kunzel conducts the Cincinnati Pops Orchestra and Indiana University Singing Hoosiers in this recording made at the Music Hall in Cincinnati. Ohio. Timothy Noble is Professor Harold Hill, Kathleen Brett is Marian, Doc Severinsen is Marcellus, Patsy Meyers is Marian's mother, Janet Burnett is the Mayor's wife and James Thomas Hodges is little Winthrop. Telarc CD. **2000 Broadway revival.** Craig Bierko takes on the role of Professor Harold Hill opposite Rebecca Luker as Marian in this cast recording of the popular 2000 Broadway revival staged by director/choreographer Susan Stroman. WB CD.

THE MUSIC SHOP   *1984 opera by Wargo*

A confused husband goes to a music shop to purchase an aria for his domineering opera singer wife. He has forgotten which aria so the shopkeeper tries to jar his memory. Richard Wargo one-act comic opera *The Music Shop,* libretto by the composer based on the Anton Chekhov story *Forgot,* was first performed by Minnesota Opera in Minneapolis on December 26, 1984, and was staged as the third part of his A CHEKHOV TRILOGY in 1993. In an acclaimed 1996 Philadelphia Academy of Vocal Arts Opera Theater production by Dorothy Danner, Philippe Gendron played the unlucky husband and Melissa Parks was the imperious wife.

MUSIC WITH ROOTS IN THE AETHER   *1976 "opera" by Ashley*

Seven avant-garde composers (Robert Ashley, Philip Glass, David Behrman, Alvin Lucier, Gordon Mumma, Pauline Oliveros and Terry Riley) talk about their ideas and perform some of their work. Robert Ashley premiered this television "opera" at the Paris Festival d'Automne in 1976. Ashley's segment includes excerpts from his operas *What She Thinks* and *Title Withdrawn.* Glass's segment includes an excerpt from his opera EINSTEIN ON THE BEACH. 840 minutes. Lovely Music VHS.

MY COUNTRY   *1946 movie opera by Previn*

My Country is an imaginary opera based on music by Franz Liszt featured in the 1946 film TWO SISTERS FROM BOSTON. Lauritz Melchior plays a Metropolitan Opera tenor who sings some of it on stage with Kathryn Grayson. Charles Previn arranged the music.

MY DARLIN' AIDA   *1952 "Americanized opera" by Friedman/Verdi*

Charles Friedman, who directed *Carmen Jones* and *Street Scene* on Broadway and conceived the show *Pins and Needles,* attempted to do with Verdi what Oscar Hammerstein had successfully done with Bizet. His Americanization of *Aida* as *My Darlin' Aida* is set on General Farrow's plantation near Memphis during the American Civil War. Aida becomes Aida Brown, her father Amonasro is runway slave Amos Brown, her lover Radames is Confederate officer Raymond Demarest, her jealous enemy Amneris is General Farrow's daughter Jessica and the vengeful priests of Isis are now the Ku Klux Klan. Radames aria "Celeste Aida" was transformed into "My Darlin' Aida," Aida's aria "Ritorna vincitor" became "March on for Tennessee and other arias were changed into "Me and Lee" and "Knights of the White Cross." The opera opened at the Winter Garden Theater on October 27, 1952, with Elaine Malbin as Aida, Howard Jarratt as Demarest and Dorothy Sarnoff as Jessica with choral music provided by Robert Shaw's singers. Friedman directed while Hassard Short, his partner from *Carmen Jones,* supervised the lavish production. Franz Allers was the conductor. The critics disliked the show intensely saying Friedman was nowhere near as good a librettist and lyricist as Hammerstein. The show lasted for 89 performances but it was not recorded and it has not been revived.

MY FAIR LADY   *1956 American operetta by Loewe*

Phonetics Professor Henry Higgins teaches Covent Garden flower girl Eliza Doolittle to talk like a lady to win a bet with Colonel Pickering. He succeeds gloriously and Eliza's father Alfred also has his life changed. Frederick Loewe's American operetta *My Fair Lady,* libretto by Alan Jay Lerner based on George Bernard Shaw's play *Pygmalion,* premiered at the Shubert Theater in New Haven on February 4, 1956, and opened at the Mark Hellinger Theater in New York on March 15, 1956. Julie Andrews created the role of Eliza opposite Rex Harrison as Higgins. Stanley Holloway was Eliza's father Alfred Doolittle, John Michael King was Freddy and Robert Coote was Colonel Pickering. Hanya Holm arranged the choreography, Moss Hart directed and Franz Allers conducted.

1956 Original Broadway cast. Julie Andrews is Eliza Doolittle in the original Broadway cast recording with Rex Harrison as Higgins, Stanley Holloway as Doolittle, John Michael King as Freddy and Robert Coote as Pickering. Franz Allers conducts. Columbia LP/Sony CD. **1956 Blanche Thebom.** Blanche Thebom sings "I Could Have Danced All Night" on the *Voice of Firestone* TV program November 5, 1956, with Howard Barlow conducting the Firestone Orchestra. It's on the video *Blanche Thebom in Opera and Song.* VAI VHS. **1957 Robert Merrill.** Robert Merrill sings "On the Street Where You Live" from *My Fair Lady* on May 20, 1957, on the *Voice of Firestone* TV show. Howard Barlow conducts the Firestone Orchestra. It's on the video *Robert Merrill in Opera and Song.* VAI VHS. **1959 London premiere cast.** Julie Andrews is Eliza in this cast recording of the first London production with Rex Harrison as Higgins and Stanley Holloway as Doolittle. Leonard Weir is Freddy and Robert Coote is Pickering. Cyril Ornadel conducts. Columbia LP/Sony CD. **1964 Columbia film.** Audrey Hepburn took over the role of Eliza for the elaborate film version of the operetta with her singing dubbed by Marni Nixon. Rex Harrison is formidable as Professor Higgins, Stanley Holloway exuberant as Eliza's father Alfred, Jeremy Brett excellent as Freddy and Wilfred Hyde-White perfect as Colonel Pickering. André Previn conducts. The film won eight Oscars including Best Picture. Columbia LP/Sony CD and Sony VHS/DVD. **1976 Broadway revival.** Christine Andreas is Eliza in this cast recording of the 1976 Broadway revival. Ian Richardson is Higgins, George Rose is Doolittle. Jerry Lanning is Freddy and Robert Coote is Pickering. Theodore Saidenberg conducts. Columbia LP/Sony CD. **1987 Royal Albert Hall.** Kiri Te Kanawa sings the role of Eliza Doolittle in a concert performance of *My Fair Lady* at London's Royal Albert Hall. Jeremy Irons is Higgins, Warren Mitchell is Alfred and John Gielgud as Pickering. John Mauceri conducts the London Symphony Orchestra in *An Evening with Kiri Te Kanawa.* London VHS/DVD/CD. **1994 John Owen Edwards.** Tinuke Olafimihan is Eliza in this London studio recording opposite Alec McCowen as Higgins and Bob Hoskins as Doolittle. Lending support are Michael Denison, Dulcie Gray, Derek James,

Henry Wickham, Derek James and Diane Langton. John Owen Edwards leads the orchestra, TER CD. **1998 Bryan Terfel.** Bryan Terfel sings "On the Street Where You Live" and "With a Little Bit of Luck" on his album *If Ever I Would Leave You.* Paul Daniel conducts the English Northern Philharmonia. DG CD. **2001 Royal National Theatre.** Martine McCutcheon is Eliza opposite Jonathan Pryce as Higgins in this recording made by the cast of a Royal National Theater production in London. Dennis Waterman is Doolittle and Mark Embers is Freddy. First Night Records CD.

MY HEART'S IN THE HIGHLANDS   *1970 opera by Beeson*

Incidents in the life of an eccentric family in Fresno, California, in 1914. When Johnny hears an old man playing "My Heart's in the Highlands" on the cornet, he invites him into his house to eat. Father Ben writes poetry and Grandmother sings Armenian songs but they have no food or money so Johnny gets some food on credit. The old man turns out to be a fugitive from an old people's home. After he is taken back, the family is evicted from its home. Jack Beeson's opera *My Heart's in the Highlands,* libretto by the composer based on William Saroyan's wistful 1939 play, premiered on NET Opera Theatre on PBS on March 18, 1970. Gerard Harrington III was Johnny, Alan Crofoot was Ben, Lili Chookasian was Grandmother, Kenneth Smith was the old man Jasper MacGregor, Spiro Malas was the grocer Kosak, Michael Ferguson was the Paperboy and composer Beeson played the Young Husband. Rhoda Levine staged the opera, Kirk Brown directed for television, Eldon Elder designed the sets and Peter Herman Adler produced and conducted the orchestra. The 90-minute opera with its melodic accessible music was lengthened to 105 minutes by the composer for its stage premiere by the Center for Contemporary Opera on October 25, 1988.

1970 NET Opera Theatre. Gerard Harrington III is Johnny and Alan Crofoot is Ben in this video recording of the premiere of the opera as telecast on NET Opera Theatre on March 18, 1970. Lili Chookasian is Grandmother, Kenneth Smith is Jasper, Spiro Malas isKosak, Michael Ferguson is the Paperboy and Jack Beeson is the Young Husband. Rhoda Levine staged the opera, Peter Herman Adler conducts the orchestra and Kirk Browning directed for television. Video at MTR.

MY KINSMAN, MAJOR MOLINEUX   *1976 opera by Saylor*

Young Englishman Robin arrives in town just as the American Revolution is about to begin. He expects his kinsman Major Molineux to help him settle in but no one will tell him where he lives. Suddenly the town erupts in rebellion, the townspeople curse the English King and Governor Molineux is apparently out of town. Bruce Saylor's one-act opera *My Kinsman, Major Molineux,* libretto by Cary Plotkin based on an 1851 story by Nathaniel Hawthorne, was commissioned by the Opera Workshop in Pittsburgh, PA, which premiered it on August 28, 1976.

MY MAN'S GONE NOW   *Soprano Aria: Porgy and Bess (1935). Words: DuBose Heyward. Music: George Gershwin.*

Serena sings her anguished lament "My man's gone now" in the first act of George Gershwin's PORGY AND BESS after her husband Robbins has been killed by Crown in a fight during a crap game. She tells us that Ole Man Sorrow is the only one who will be keeping her company from now on. The song was introduced on stage in 1935 by Ruby Elzy as Serena and first recorded by Metropolitan Opera soprano Helen Jepson. Later recording were made by

Anne Brown (the original Bess) with the Eva Jessye Choir, Risë Stevens with the Robert Shaw Chorale, Inez Williams on record and in the film, Florence Quivar in the famous Cleveland recording, Wilma Shakesnider in the Houston Grand Opera recording, Cynthia Clarey in the Glyndebourne Opera recording and Renée Fleming in her 1998 recital album of American opera arias. There are also superb jazz versions performed by Ella Fitzgerald, Sarah Vaughan, Cleo Laine and Miles Davis.

MY MARYLAND   *1927 operetta by Romberg*

Beautiful Barbara Frietchie is caught in the middle of the Civil War torn between Confederate and Union admirers. When she defends the American flag in her Maryland town of Frederick, she is almost shot. Sigmund Romberg's *My Maryland* is an adaptation by Dorothy Donnelly of *Barbara Frietchie,* an 1899 play by Clyde Fitch based on John Greenleaf Whittier's poem. It opened in New York on September 12, 1927, after a successful ten-month stay in Philadelphia, the longest run ever in a Philadelphia theater. Evelyn Herbert played Barbara, Nathaniel Wagner was her Yankee lover and Warren Hull was his Confederate rival.

1927 Evelyn Herbert. Evelyn Herbert of the original Broadcast cast recorded two songs from the operetta, "Mother" and "Silver Moon" for RCA Victor 78s. they're on the anthology album *The Ultimate Sigmund Romberg, Volume 1.* Pearl CD. **1945 Risë Stevens.** Risë Stevens recorded songs from *My Maryland* in 1945 with the Victor Light Opera Company and orchestra conducted by Nathaniel Shilkret. Her versions of "Your Land Is Mine," "Silver Moon," "Mother," "Dixie" and "Boys in Gray" are on the album *Great Hits from Sigmund Romberg.* British Past CD.

MY ROMANCE   *1948 operetta by Romberg*

An opera singer and a bishop fall in love but their romance is doomed from the start. Sigmund Romberg's charming if rather old-fashioned operetta *My Romance,* lyrics and libretto by Rowland Leigh based on Edward Sheldon's play *Romance,* opened at the Shubert Theater on Broadway on October 19, 1948. Anne Jeffreys played opera singer Madame Marguerita Cavallini, Lawrence Brooks was Bishop Armstrong, Luella Gear was Octavia Fotheringham and Gail Adams was Veronica De Witt. Watson Barratt designed the sets, librettist Leigh staged he production and Roland Fiore conducted the orchestra and chorus. *My Romance* was attacked by theater critic Brooks Atkinson in *The New York Times* simply for being an old-fashioned operetta and his vicious review marked the demise for a time of traditional operetta on Broadway.

MYSHKIN   *1971 TV opera by Eaton*

Prince Myshkin is a mentally-fragile Christ-like figure subject to epileptic fits, a holy "idiot" who becomes involved in a complex love intrigue with two women attracted by his innocence. John Eaton's 60-minute television opera *Myshkin,* libretto by Patrick Creagh based on Dostoevsky's novel *The Idiot,* was produced on television by Indiana University Opera Theater and telecast on PBS April 23, 1973. The opera, composed in 1971, is presented from Myshkin's point of view but as he is the camera he is never seen. The music reflects his swings between rationality and unreality in multiple time frames. Linda Anderson played Natasha, William Hartwell was Rogozhin, James Bert Neely was Dr. Schneider and William Oberholzer was Yepanchin. Peter Herman Adler was the executive producer, Andreas Nomikos designed the sets and costumes, John Reeves White conducted the Indiana Opera Theater Orchestra and Herbert Seltz and Ross Allen directed. Video at Museum of Television and Radio.

MYSTERIES OF ELEUSIS   *1986 opera by Feigin*

Demeter, goddess of the harvest, creates a famine after her daughter Persephone is taken to Hades. When her lover dies of starvation, she goes to the underworld and Hades allows Persephone to return to the land of the living for part of the year. Joel Feigin's one-act opera *Mysteries of Eleusis,* libretto by Jaime Manrique and the composer, is based on the ancient Greek poem "Hymn to Demeter" attributed to Homer, It premiered at Cornell University in Ithaca, New York, on April 23 1986. Christine Schadeberg was Demeter, Mimi Fulmer was Persephone Gregory Mercer was Triptolemus, Patrice Pastore was Metainera, Andrea R. Abushada was Iambe/Rhea and Edward Bogusz was Hades. Fred Cohen conducted and David Feldfuh was the stage director. The opera was reprised at the Juilliard School of Music in 1994 and the Moscow Conservatory of Music in Russia in 1999 and 2000. There are no commercial recordings but CDs and videos are available to professionals.

N

NABOKOV, NICOLAS   *American composer (1903–1978)*

Nicolas Nabokov, who moved to the United States from Paris in 1933 after studies in Yalta and Berlin, wrote both of his operas long after becoming an American. THE HOLY DEVIL, libretto by Stephen Spender, tells the story of the Russian monk Rasputin. It was commissioned by the Louisville Orchestra and premiered by Kentucky Opera on April 16, 1958. LOVE'S LABOUR'S LOST, libretto by W. H. Auden and Chester Kallman based on the play by Shakespeare in which love is declared illegal, was premiered by Deutsche Oper at the Théâtre de la Monnaie in Brussels on February 7, 1973.

NAGANO, KENT   *American conductor (1951–)*

Kent Nagano, principal conductor at Opéra de Lyon in France and Los Angeles Opera in America, has been strongly involved in the presentation of American opera. He conducted the premiere and recording of John Adams' THE DEATH OF KLINGHOFFER with the Opéra de Lyon Orchestra in Brussels in 1991 and the premiere of Adams' EL NIÑO in Paris in 2000. He conducted the Opéra de Lyon Orchestra in the first complete recording of Carlisle Floyd's SUSANNAH in 1994. He conducts the 1988 Opéra de Lyon production of Sergei Prokofiev's THE LOVE FOR THREE ORANGES which is on CD and video and the 1992 and 1996 productions of Igor Stravinsky's THE RAKE'S PROGRESS which are also on CD and video. In 2000 he led the London Symphony Orchestra in the first recording of Leonard Bernstein's *A White House Cantata.* Nagano, born in Morro Bay, CA, to a Japanese American family, made his operatic debut in San Francisco in 1976. He took over the Opéra de Lyon orchestra in 1989 from John Eliot Gardiner and became principal conductor of Los Angeles Opera in 2001.

THE NAKED CARMEN   *1970 opera by Corigliano*

John Corigliano's *The Naked Carmen,* which he created in collaboration with record producer-writer David A. Hess, could be described as Bizet's *Carmen* transmuted into an eclectic post-modern electric rock, pop, opera work utilizing synthesizers, kazoo and traditional instruments. It has never been performed live as it was devised to be an LP record.

1970 Original cast album. *The Naked Carmen* on record consists of a number of widely-different components based around arias and music from Bizet's *Carmen* with a cast of performers from around the musical world, including the Metropolitan Opera, the Juilliard School of Music, the musical *Hair* and the Newport Folk Festival. Melba Moore sings Carmen's Habanera as "When Love Is Free," Micaela's Air as "Time" and the Card Song as "The Tarot Dealer." William Walker sings the Toreador Song as "Playin' the Game" Mary Bruce and Her Starbuds perform the Gypsy Song as "This Sick and Hungry World." Symphonic excerpts from *Carmen* are performed by the Detroit Symphony Orchestra led by Paul Paray. Mercury LP.

NAMIKO-SAN   *1925 opera by Franchetti*

Medieval Japan. Sixteen-year-old geisha Namiko-San, who is kept by warrior prince Yiro Danyemon, befriends a young monk named Yasui. Her friendship is discovered by the jealous prince who forces her to betray him. She dies trying to save his life. Aldo Franchetti's *Namiko-San,* libretto by Leo Duran based on his play *The Daymio,* was premiered by Chicago Opera at the Chicago Auditorium on December 11, 1925. Japanese soprano Tamaki Miuri, for whom the opera was composed, played Namiko-San, Richard Bonelli was Prince Yiro, Theodore Ritch was the monk Yasui, José Mojica and Elizabeth Kerr were the Young Lovers, Vittorio Trevisan was the gardener Sato, Lodovic Oliviero was Kajiro, Alice d'Hermanoy was widow Towa-San and Antonio Nicolich was Ashigaro. The composer conducted. Miuri, the first opera singer from Japan to become internationally famous, asked Franchetti to write the opera because she wanted another role like Cio-Cio-San in *Madama Butterfly* in which she was immensely popular After performances in Chicago, Miuri and Franchetti took the opera on tour. Franchetti was awarded a Bispham Memorial Medal for the opera.

NARCISSA   *1912 opera by Moore*

Narcissa is considered the first grand opera by an American woman composer. It takes place in Washington state in 1847. Narcissa Prentiss Whitman, a pioneer missionary and patriot, and her husband Marcus are friendly with the Native Americans who live near their Mission House. Both are killed by a renegade band after the chief's son Elijah is shot by a settler at Sutter's Fort. Mary Carr Moore's historical opera *Narcissa: or, The Cost of Empire.* libretto by her journalist mother Sarah Pratt Carr, is told from the point of view of Narcissa. It was premiered at the Moore Theater in Seattle on April 22, 1912, and given four performances with the composer directing and conducting. It was revived in 1925 in San Francisco for California's Diamond Jubilee celebrations and given nine performances at the Wilkes Theater with the composer conducting. Alice Gentle sang the part of Narcissa, James Gerard was Marcus, Harold Spaulding was Elijah, Frederick Warford was Yellow Serpent, Ruth Scott Laidlaw was Siskadee and Albert Gillette was Delaware Tom. The opera was awarded the Bispham Memorial Medal in 1930 and revived in Los Angeles in 1945 but it has not been recorded.

NATALIA PETROVNA   *1964 opera by Hoiby*

Natalia Petrovna and her elderly husband Arkady live on a provincial estate in 19th century Russia. She falls in love with her son's tutor Belaev but her friend Rakitin becomes jealous as he has long harbored a hopeless love for her. In the end the passionate feelings are revealed, both men have to leave the estate and Natalia is left alone with her aging husband. Lee Hoiby's two-act opera *Natalia Petrovna,* libretto by William Ball based on the Turgenev novel *A Month in the Country,* premiered at New York City Opera on October 8, 1964. Maria Dornya was Natalia, John Reardon was

Belaev, Richard Cross was Rakitin, John McCollum was Arkady, Patricia Brooks was Lisavetta, Sandra Darling was Vera, Muriel Greenspon was Anna, Jack Harrold was the Doctor and Richard Krause was Bolisov. Howard Bay designed the sets, librettist William Ball directed and Julius Rudel conducted the New York City Opera Orchestra. Hoiby and Ball later revised the opera which was staged as *A Month in the Country* in Boston in January 1981.

NATIVE AMERICAN OPERA

There are many operas with Native American subject matter, some based on Indian myths and music, but they have never achieved the popularity of operas based around African American life and music. There do not appear to be any operas actually composed by Native Americans but a Native American opera singer achieved national fame. She was Princess Tsianina Redfeather Blackstone (1882–1985) and Charles Wakefield Cadman's opera SHANEWIS is loosely based on her life. Listed below are some of the better known operas with native American themes or subjects.

1794 James Hewitt's TAMMANY; OR THE INDIAN CHIEF, libretto by Ann Julia Kemble Hatton, was premiered in New York City in 1794. It tells how Indian chief Tammany rescues his lover from one of Columbus's explorers who takes revenge by burning them alive. 1808 John Bray's THE INDIAN PRINCESS, OR LA BELLE SAUVAGE, which tells the story of Captain John Smith and Pocahontas, was premiered at the New Chestnut Street Theater in New York City on April 6, 1808. 1858 Lucien H. Southard's Indian-themed *Omano* was premiered in Boston in 1858. 1859 Edward Sobolewski's MOHEGA, THE FLOWER OF THE FOREST, about a Native American woman who falls in love with a Polish aristocrat during the American Revolution, premiered in Milwaukee in 1859. 1887 Carl Mayer's *The Conspiracy of Pontiac* was premiered in Detroit, Michigan, on January 27, 1887. It concerns the chief of the Ottawa tribe during the Pontiac War of 1763–64. 1910 Arthur Nevin's POIA, libretto by Randolph Hartley about Blackfoot Indians and the coming of sun worship, was premiered by Berlin Opera on April 23, 1910. 1911 Victor Herbert's NATOMA, libretto by Joseph D. Redding about a Native American woman in California in 1820, premiered at the Metropolitan Opera House in Philadelphia on February 25, 1911. 1916 Edith Rowena Noyes' *Osseo,* based on Indian legends, premiered in Brookline, Massachusetts, in 1917. 1918 Charles Wakefield Cadman's SHANEWIS, libretto by Nelle Richmond Eberhart based on the life of Indian Princess Tsianina Redfeather Blackstone, was premiered at the Metropolitan Opera on March 12, 1918. 1922 Mary Carr Moore's *The Flaming Arrow: or, The Shaft of Ku'pish-ta-ya,* libretto by Sarah Pratt Moore based on an Indian legend, was premiered in San Francisco on March 27, 1922. 1926 Alberto Bimboni's WINONA, libretto by Perry Williams based on a Sioux Indian legend, was premiered by the American Grand Opera Company in Portland, Oregon, in 1926. 1927 Earle Blakeslee's THE LEGEND OF WIWASTE, based on Dakota Sioux legends and musical motifs, was premiered in 1927 with Princess Tsianina Redfeather Blackstone in the leading role. 1927 Charles Skilton's *Kalopin,* libretto by Virginia Nelson Palmer, based on a Native American legend. It received a David Bisham Memorial Medal. 1927 Rudolf Friml's operetta *White Eagle,* based on Edwin Milton Royle's play *The Squaw Man,* premiered at the Casino Theater in New York on December 26, 1927. 1928 William F. Hanson's *Tam-Man-Nacup,* about Uintah Indian life in Utah, was staged in Provo in 1928. 1930 Charles Skilton's THE SUN BRIDE, libretto by Lillian White Spencer based on a Pueblo Indian legend about sun worship, was broadcast on NBC in 1930. 1964 Roger Sessions' MONTEZUMA, about the Aztec chief Montezuma and Indian Princess Malinche, was premiered on April 19, 1964. 1965 Morris Wright's *The Legend*, a story about the Aga Aga Indians, was presented at Ball State University in Muncie, Indiana, in 1965. 1966 Robert Kelly's *The White Gods,* about the conquest of Mexico from the Aztec point of view, was presented at the University of Illinois in 1966. 1976 Alva Henderson's THE LAST OF THE MOHICANS, based on the novel by James Fenimore Cooper, was premiered by Wilmington Opera in Delaware in 1976. 1987 John Luther Adams trilogy *Giving Birth to Thunder, Sleeping with His Daughter* and *Coyote Builds North America,* composed to Indian stories dramatized by Barry Lopez, was premiered in Juneau, Alaska, in 1987. 1995 Stephen Paulus' THE WOMAN AT OTOWI CROSSING, libretto by Joan Vail Thorne based on the novel by Frank Waters, was premiered by Opera Theater of Saint Louis in 1995. 1996 Paul Stuart's KILL BEAR COMES HOME, libretto by Sally M. Gall based on an Iroquois legend, was premiered by Opera Theater of Rochester, New York, in 1996. 2000 Jean-Michael Damase's *Ochelata's Wedding,* revolving around the marriage of the daughter of a Cherokee chief in 1878, was premiered in Bartleville, Oklahoma, in 2000.

THE NATIVITY ACCORDING TO ST. LUKE   *1961*
church opera by Thompson

The story of the Nativity of Christ from Annunciation to Birth as described in the Gospel of St. Luke in the Bible. Randall Thompson's opera *The Nativity According to St. Luke,* libretto by R. Rowlands based on the Gospel, was created to celebrate the 200th anniversary of Christ Church in Cambridge, Massachusetts. It was premiered there on December 13, 1961.

1997 Cleveland Sinfonia Sacra. Frances Burmeister conducts a recording of the opera with the Warren First Presbyterian Church Chancel Choir and the Cleveland Sinfonia Sacra. The soloists are mezzo-soprano Judith Hughes, contralto A. J. Abbot, tenor David Root and baritone Ken Kramer. Burmeister plays the organ. Koch CD.

NATOMA   *1911 opera by Herbert*

Spanish California in 1820. Lt. Paul Merrill of the U.S. Navy meets young Indian woman Natoma and there is an immediate attraction. She is a friend of Barbara, daughter of local wealthy rancher Don Francisco, whom Alvarado wants to marry. When she rejects him, he sets out to kidnap her with the help of Castro. Natoma stabs him to prevent the abduction and flees into a church claiming sanctuary. When the truth is discovered, she relinquishes Paul to Barbara and enters a convent. Victor Herbert's *Natoma,* libretto by Joseph D. Redding, premiered at the Metropolitan Opera House in Philadelphia on February 25, 1911. Mary Garden sang Natoma, John McCormack was Paul, Lillian Grenville was Barbara, Mario Sammarco was Alvarado, Frank Preisch was Casto, Gustave Huberdeau was Don Francisco, Hector Dufranne was Ather Peralta, Constantin Nicolay was Kagama and Armand Crabbé was Pico. Cleofante Campanini was the conductor. The opera was presented at the Metropolitan Opera House In New York on February 28 with the same cast and then went on to Chicago. *Natoma* was the most performed and recorded American opera until the arrival of *Porgy and Bess* in 1935. John McCormack recorded his aria "No Country Can my Own Outvie" in 1912 and it remains in print after nearly a century. A ringing patriotic ode to America, it was composed soon after the Spanish American War. Paul presents his captain's compliments to a Spanish rancher and then praises his native land in extravagant terms, saying America's name is stamped in gold on his heart. Other arias from the opera

were recorded by Alma Gluck, Jan Peerce and Earl Cartwright and the "Dagger Dance" remains popular with pianists. Recent recordings demonstrate the opera's melodic strengths.

1912 John McCormack. John McCormack recorded his powerful aria "No Country Can my Own Outvie" in 1912. The 78 rpm Victor recording, titled "Paul's Address," was put on wax in April 3, 1912, and is on several albums including the anthologies *Towards an American Opera* (New World LP), *Souvenirs from American Opera* (IRRC CD) and *The Songs of Victor Herbert* (ASV Living Era CD). **1912 Alma Gluck.** Alma Gluck recorded Barbara's aria "I List the Trill in Golden Throat" as the "Spring Song" for a Victor Red Seal 78 record. It's on several albums including the anthologies *Souvenirs from American Opera* (IRRC CD) and *The Songs of Victor Herbert* (ASV Living Era CD). **1912 Reinald Werrenrath.** Reinald Werrenrath recorded Alvarado's Serenade "When the Sunlight Dies" for a Victor Red Seal 78 record in 1912. It's on the albums *Souvenirs from American Opera* (IRRC CD) and *A Victor Herbert Showcase* (Flapper Past CD). **1912 Victor Herbert.** Victor Herbert led his orchestra in a recording for a Victor 78 record of the music of the "Dagger Dance," performed in the opera by Natoma and Castro. **1913 Earl Cartwright.** Earl Cartwright and the Victor Light Opera Company recorded the Vaquero's Song, "Who Dares the Bronco Wild Defy" for a Victor 78. It's performed in the opera by Pico and the other vaqueros and is on the album *Souvenirs from American Opera.* IRRC CD. **1913 Cecil Fanning.** Cecil Fanning recorded the Vaquero's Song, "Who Dares the Bronco Wild Defy," for a Columbia 78. **1913 Carolina White.** Caroline White, who sang Barbara in the Chicago premiere of the opera, recorded her aria "I List the Trill in Golden Throat" as "Spring Song" for Columbia. It's on the album *American Singers, Volume One.* IRRC CD. **1928 NBC National Grand Opera.** *Natoma.* one of the first American operas presented on radio, was broadcast by NBC's National Grand Opera Company on November 5, 1928, in an abridged format. Cesare Sudaro conducted. It was so popular it was repeated on April 15, 1929, and March 27, 1930. **1935 Jan Peerce.** Jan Peerce sings Paul's aria "Gentle Maiden," addressed to Natoma when Paul first meets her, on a August 30, 1935, radio broadcast. It's on the album *Souvenirs from American Opera.* IRRC CD. **1952 Risë Stevens.** Risë Stevens sings the aria "Beware of a Hawk, My Baby" from *Natoma* on a Bell Telephone Hour program. It's on the video album *Great Stars of Opera.* VAI DVD. **1965 André Kostelanetz.** André Kostelanetz conducts the "Habanera" from *Natoma* on two recordings. On the 1965 *Music of Victor Herbert* (Columbia LP) he leads his own orchestra, on the 1975 *Music of Victor Herbert* (EMI LP) made with Beverly Sills, he leads the London Symphony Orchestra. **1986 Donald Hunsberger.** Donald Hunsberger conducts the Eastman Dryden Orchestra in twelve numbers from *Natoma* including arias and duets by Natoma, Alvarado and Paul, the Habanera and the Dagger Dance. The album is titled *Victor Herbert: The American Girl.* Arabesque LP/CD. **2000 Keith Brion.** Herbert specialist Keith Brion leads the Bratislava Slovak Radio Symphony Orchestra in excerpts from *Natoma* on the American Classics album *Victor Herbert: Columbus Suite.* Naxos CD.

NAUGHTY MARIETTA   *1910 comic opera by Herbert*

In the year 1780 Countess Marietta d'Altena flees to New Orleans on a ship with a group of husband-seeking French casquette girls. She ends up falling in love with ship captain Dick Warrington who wins her through his knowledge of a mysterious melody we know as "Ah, Sweet Mystery of Life." Beautiful quadroon slave Adah loves the governor's son Etienne but he is secretly the pirate Bras-Priqué. Victor Herbert's popular comic opera, libretto by Rida Johnson Young, was commissioned by impresario Oscar Hammerstein for his Manhattan Opera House and its prima donna Emma Trentini who was given coloratura-style arias like the "Italian Street Song." Hammerstein's opera house closed before the comic opera was finished so it was moved to a Broadway theater. It premiered at the Wieting Opera House in Syracuse, NY, on October 24, 1910, and opened on Broadway at the New York Theater on November 7, 1910. Trentini played Marietta, Manhattan Opera House tenor Orville Harrold was Dick, Marie Dechene was Adah and Edward Martindel was Etienne. Gaetano Merola, who founded San Francisco Opera in 1923, was the conductor. Major opera singers who have recorded arias from this tuneful work include John McCormack, Jan Peerce, Richard Crooks, Felix Knight, Charles Kullman, Jerry Hadley, Risë Stevens, Barbara Hendricks and Eleanor Steber. *Naughty Marietta* had an operatic revival at the New York City Opera in 1978 with Gianni Rolandi as Marietta Jacques Trussel as Dick and John Mauceri conducting.

1910 Byron Harlan/Frank Stanley. Byron Harlan and Frank Stanley made the first recording of "Tramp! Tramp! Tramp!" for Victor in 1910. It was one of the most popular records of the year. **1911 John McCormack.** John McCormack sings "I'm Falling in Love With Someone" for a Victor 78. It's can be found on several McCormack anthology LPs and CDs. **1911 Lucy Isabelle Marsh.** Soprano Lucy Isabelle Marsh sings "Italian Street Song" with the Victor Light Opera Company on a best-selling Victor 78. It's on the album *American Singers, Volume One.* IRCC CD. **1911/1912 Victor Herbert.** Victor Herbert and his Orchestra recorded "Dream Melody" and "Intermezzo" for an Edison 78 in 1911 and "Intermezzo" for a Victor 78 in 1912. **1928 Richard Crooks.** Met tenor Richard Crooks sings "Ah! Sweet Mystery of Life" and "I'm Falling in Love with Someone" for a 78. It on the album *The Artistry of Richard Crooks, Volume One.* Pearl CD. **1934 Jan Peerce.** Jan Peerce sings "'I'm Falling in Love With Someone" on WBS radio with Erno Rapee's Orchestra. It's on the album *The Unknown Jan Peerce.* Rockport Records CD. **1935 MGM film.** Nelson Eddy and Jeanette MacDonald were teamed for the first time in the MGM film *Naughty Marietta.* The plot is somewhat different than the stage show with MacDonald transmuted into a French princess falling in love with American rescuer Eddy but the essentials are the same. Five songs were retained but there are new lyrics by Gus Kahn for "Tramp, Tramp, Tramp" and "'Neath the Southern Moon." Frank Morgan is the Governor, Elsa Lanchester is Madame d'Annard and Douglass Dumbrille is Marietta's uncle. W. S. Van Dyke directed from a script by John Lee Mahin, Frances Goodrich and Albert Hackett. Hollywood Soundstage LP and MGM UA VHS/DVD. **1935 Jeanette MacDonald/Nelson Eddy.** Nelson Eddy and Jeanette MacDonald recorded several songs for 78s while making the MGM film. Eddy recorded "Tramp! Tramp! Tramp!," "'Neath the Southern Moon" and "I'm Falling in Love with Someone" with an orchestra led by Nat Shilkret. MacDonald recorded "Italian Street Song" with Herbert Stothart conducting the MGM Orchestra. Together they sing "Ah! Sweet Mystery of Life" with the Nat Shilkret orchestra. The recordings are on several albums includ-

Victor Herbert's operatic operetta *Naughty Marietta* was filmed in 1935 with Nelson Eddy and Jeanette MacDonald.

ing *The Songs of Victor Herbert.* ASV Living Era CD. **1936 Jussi Björling.** Jussi Björling recorded "Ah! Sweet Mystery of Life" from *Naughty Marietta.* It's on the album *Jussi Björling Vol. 2 — Operetta and Song (1929–1938).* Pearl/Koch CD. **1936 Richard Tauber.** Richard Tauber sings Ah! Sweet Mystery of Life" on a radio broadcast. It's ion the album *Richard Tauber.* MC audiocassette. **1938 Charles Kullman.** Met tenor Charles Kullman sings "Ah! Sweet Mystery of Life" and "I'm Falling in Love with Someone" with an orchestra led by Fred Hartley. The songs are on various albums, including *Serenade.* Memoir Classics CD. **1938 Jan Peerce.** Jan Peerce sings "Ah! Sweet Mystery of Life" on a Chevrolet Musical Moments Revue program on WDS radio. It's on the album *The Unknown Jan Peerce.* Rockport Records CD. **1939 RCA Magic Key.** Jan Peerce, Anne Jamison and Thomas L. Thomas perform selections from the operetta for an *RCA Magic Key* radio broadcast with the Victor Light Opera Company and Nat Shilkret and Orchestra. The broadcast was issued as an LP record by RCA titled *The Operetta World of Victor Herbert.* JJA LP/Opera Classics audiocassette. **1945 Jane Powell.** Jane Powell performs the "Italian Street Song" in the MGM movie musical *Holiday in Mexico* directed by George Sidney for MGM. **1949 Risë Stevens.** Met mezzo Risë Stevens recorded "I'm Falling in Love With Someone" with an orchestra conducted by Sylvan Shulman for her album *Love Songs.* Columbia LP. **1949 Eleanor Steber.** Eleanor Steber sings "Italian Street Song" and "I'm Falling in Love with Someone" accompanied by the Firestone Orchestra led by Howard Barlow on the *Voice of Firestone* TV. It's on the video *Eleanor Steber in Opera and Song.* VAI VHS. **1949 Nelson Eddy/ Nadine Conner.** Nelson Eddy and Nadine Conner perform eight songs in a highlights version of the operetta with chorus and orchestra conducted by Robert Armbruster. Columbia LP. **1950 Earl Wrightson/Elaine Malbin.** Earl Wrightson, Elaine Malbin and Jimmy Carroll join forces on a highlights recording with Al Goodman conducting the orchestra. RCA LP. **1950 Jan Peerce.** Jan Peerce recorded two arias from *Naughty Marietta.* in London. "Ah! Sweet Mystery of Life" is on *The Record of Singing, Volume 4* (EMI Classics CD) and "I'm Falling in Love with Someone" is on *Bluebird of Happiness* (Pearl/Koch CD). **1950 Jeanette MacDonald.** Jeanette MacDonald sings "Italian Street Song" on November 13, 1950, on *The Voice of Firestone* TV program accompanied by Howard Barlow and the Firestone Orchestra. It's on the video *Jeanette MacDonald in Performance.* VAI VHS. **1951 Risë Stevens.** Met mezzo Risë Stevens sings "I'm Falling in Love with Someone" on the *Voice of Firestone* television program July 23, 1951, with the Firestone Orchestra led by Howard Barlow. It's on the video *Risë Stevens in Opera and Song, Vol. 2.* VAI VHS. **1952 Mario Lanza.** Mario Lanza recorded "Ah! Sweet Mystery of Life" with an orchestra led by Ray Sinatra for the LP *Mario Lanza — Be My Love,* "Tramp! Tramp! Tramp!" with Henri René's Orchestra for the LP *Mario Lanza in a Cavalcade of Show Tunes* and "It's Pretty Soft for Simon" with an orchestra led by Constantin Callinicos for the LP *Mario Lanza — Live in London.* All three are on *The Mario Lanza Collection.* RCA Victor CD. **1952 Roberta Peters.** Roberta Peters sings "Italian Street Song" accompanied by Howard Barlow and Firestone Orchestra on the *Voice of Firestone* TV show March 24, 1952. It's on *Roberta Peters in Opera and Song Vol. 2.* VAI video. **1953 Felix Knight/Doretta Morrow.** Felix Knight and Doretta Morrow perform songs from the operetta on a highlights recording with Jay Blackstone conducting the orchestra. RCA LP. **1953 George London/Dorothy Warenskjold.** George London joins Dorothy Warenskjold in "I'm Falling in Love with Someone" and "Ah! Sweet Mystery of Life" on the *Voice of Firestone* TV program April 27, 1953. They're accompanied by Howard Barlow and the Firestone Orchestra. It's on the video *George London in Opera and Song.* VAI VHS. **1954 Patrice Munsel.** Met soprano Patrice Munsel sings the "Italian Street Song" on the *Voice of Firestone* TV show on May 17, 1954. Howard Barlow conducts the Firestone Orchestra. It's on the video *Patrice Munsel in Opera and Song.* VAI VHS. **1954 Gordon MacRae/Marguerite Piazza.** Gordon MacRae stars opposite Marguerite Piazza and Katherine Hilgenberg in this highlights recording with an orchestra led by George Greeley. Capitol LP. **1955 NBC Television.** Met soprano Patrice Munsel and Broadway baritone Alfred Drake star as Marietta and Captain Dick in this excellent 90-minute NBC TV color production by Max Liebman. John Conte is Etienne, Gale Sherwood is Yvonne, Donn Driver is Louis, Robert Gallagher is the Ship Captain and William LeMassena is Rudolfo. Bambi Linn and Rod Alexander are the dancers while Charles Dagmar creates the Punch and Judy show. This charming faithful adaptation of the operetta was written by Neil Simon with Fred Saidy, Will Glickman and William Friedberg. Charles Sanford conducts. Telecast live on January 15, 1955. VAI VHS/DVD and Live Opera audiocassette. **1955 Robert Merrill.** Met baritone Robert Merrill sings "I'm Falling in Love with Someone" on January 10, 1955, on the *Voice of Firestone* TV show. Howard Barlow conducts the Firestone Orchestra. It's on the video *Robert Merrill in Opera and Song, Vol. 2.* VAI VHS. **1961 Robert Shaw Chorale.** The Robert

Shaw Chorale and Orchestra perform "Tramp! Tramp! Tramp!," "Ah! Sweet Mystery of Life," "I'm Falling in Love with Someone" and "Italian Street Song" on the album *The Immortal Victor Herbert.* RCA Victor LP. **1962 Eugene Ormandy/Philadelphia Orchestra.** Eugene Ormandy leads the Philadelphia Orchestra in "Italian Street Song," "Tramp, Tramp, Tramp" and "I'm Falling in Love with Someone." The songs are on the album *The Philadelphia Orchestra Plays Victor Herbert.* Columbia LP. **1962 Anna Moffo/William Lewis.** Anna Moffo sings Marietta with William Lewis as Captain Dick and Rosalind Elias as Adah in this highlights recording with orchestra and chorus led by Lehman Engel. It's part of the Reader's Digest *Treasury of Great Operettas.* RCA LP box set. **1974 Madeleine Kahn.** Madeleine Kahn, who once sang Musetta in *La Bohème,* renders a rather unforgettable version of "Ah, Sweet Mystery of Life" in the Mel Brooks' movie *Young Frankenstein.* 20th Century-Fox film. On VHS. **1975 Beverly Sills.** Beverly Sills sings "Italian Street Song," "Ah! Sweet Mystery of Life" and "I'm Falling in Love with Someone" with André Kostelanetz conducting the London Symphony Orchestra. They're on the album *Music of Victor Herbert.* Angel LP/CD. **1978 Beverly Sills/Sherrill Milnes.** Beverly Sills and Sherrill Milnes duet on "'Neath the Summer Moon" and "It Never, Never Can Be Love" on the album *Up in Central Park.* Julius Rudel conducts the New York City Opera. EMI Angel LP. **1978 New York City Opera.** Gianni Rolandi sings Marietta with Jacques Trussel as Captain Dick in a live recording of a New York City Opera production broadcast on September 3, 1978. Joanna Simon is Adah, Alan Titus is Etienne Grandet, Richard McKee is Pierre La Farge and James Billings is the Governor. John Mauceri conducts the NYCO Orchestra. Live Opera audiocassette. **1980 Smithsonian American Musical Theater.** This Smithsonian American Musical Theater recording includes the complete original score. Judith Blazer is Marietta, Leslie Harrington is Captain Dick, Elvira Green is Adah, Wayne Turnage is Etienne Grandet, Steve Liebman is Simon O'Hara, Dana Krueger is Lizette, Harry Winter is Rudolfo, Joseph de Genova is Lt. Governor Grandet and Helen Bickers is Franchon. James R. Morris conducts the Catholic University of America A Capella Choir and Millennium Chamber Orchestra. Smithsonian LP box set. **1985 Teresa Ringholz/ Eastman-Dryden Orchestra.** Soprano Teresa Ringholz and the Eastman-Dryden Orchestra led by Donald Hunsberger perform five songs on the album *Victor Herbert: Souvenir.* Arabesque CD and tape. **1985 Peter Morrison.** Peter Morrison sings "Tramp! Tramp! Tramp!" with the Ambrosian Singers and Chandos Concert Orchestra led by Stuart Barry on the album *Treasures of Operetta.* Chandos CD. **1991 Lorin Maazel' Pittsburgh Symphony.** Lorin Maazel conducts the Pittsburgh Symphony Orchestra in "Italian Street Song" and "I'm Falling in Love with Someone" on the album *Popular American Music.* Sony CD. **1992 Barbara Hendricks.** Barbara Hendricks sings "Italian Street Song" and "Ah! Sweet Mystery of Life" with the Ambrosian Singers and Philharmonic Orchestra led by Lawrence Foster. They on the album *Operetta Arias.* EMI CD. **1993 Jerry Hadley.** Jerry Hadley performs "I'm Falling in Love with Someone" on his album *Golden Days.* Paul Gemignani conducts the American Theatre Orchestra. RCA Victor CD. **1999 Virginia Croskery.** Virginia Croskery sings "Italian Street Song" and "Ah! Sweet Mystery of Life" with the Slovak Radio Symphony Orchestra led by Keith Brion on the album *Victor Herbert: Beloved Songs and Classic Miniatures.* American Classics Naxos CD. **2000 Elizabeth Futral/Steven White.** Elizabeth Futral and Steven White duet on "Ah! Sweet Mystery of Life" and Futral sings "Italian Street Song" on the album *Sweethearts.* They're supported by the Palmer Chamber Chorus and pianist Robert Tweten. Newport Classic CD. **2000 Ohio Light Opera.** Suzanne Woods is Marietta with John Pickle as Captain Dick in this complete Ohio Light Opera production by Steven Daigle featuring the original Rida Johnson Young libretto. Anne Marie Wilcox is Adah, Ted Christopher is Etienne, Stephen Carr is Silas, Zanna Freedland is Lizette, Boyd Mackus is Lt. Governor Grandet, Richard Stevens is Rudolfo, Lucas Meachem is Sir Harry Blake and Nancy Maria Balach is Felice. Steven Byess conducts the Ohio Light Opera Orchestra. and Chorus. Albany 2-CD box.

NAUSICAA   *1961 opera by Glanville-Hicks*

Greece circa 700 BC as Nausicaa remembers how she came to write *The Odyssey.* When her father was gone on a long trip and feared lost, suitors besieged her to marry them. To fight them off, she enlists the help of the shipwrecked Cretan nobleman Aethon who draws the Great Bow of Hercules and shoots them. This incident inspires her to write the story of Odysseus and Penelope. Peggy Glanville-Hicks three-act opera *Nausicaa,* libretto by Robert Graves and Alastair Reid based on Graves' novel *Homer's Daughter,* premiered at the Athens Festival in Greece on August 19, 1961. Teresa Stratas was Nausicaa, John Modenos was Aethon, Edward Ruhl was minstrel Phemius, George Tsantikos was Clytoneus, Sophia Steffan was Queen Arete, Spiro Malas was King Alcinous, Michalis Heliotis was Antinous, George Moutsios was Eurymachus and Vassilis Koundouris was the Messenger. John Butler staged the opera, Dandresa Nomikos designed the sets and costumes and Carlos Surinach conducted the Athens Symphony Orchestra and Chorus. The premiere performance was recorded and broadcast on CBS radio on September 23, 1961.

1961 Athens Festival. Teresa Stratas sings Nausicaa in this recording of the premiere performance at the Athens Festival with Carlos Surinach conducting the Athens Symphony Orchestra and Chorus. John Modenos is Aethon, Edward Ruhl is Phemius,

Peggy Glanville-Hicks' opera *Nausicaa* was premiered and recorded at the Athens Festival in Greece in 1961.

George Tsantikos is Clytoneus, Sophia Steffan is Arete and Spiro Malas is Alcinous. CRI CD.

NBC OPERA THEATRE   *Television opera series (1949–1964)*

Ten American operas were premiered by NBC Opera Theatre between 1951 and 1963 under the guidance of producer Samuel Chotzinoff, artistic director Peter Herman Adler and TV director Kirk Browning. The series premiered on January 14, 1950, with Kurt Weill's DOWN IN THE VALLEY and became nationally known in 1951 with the premiere of the first opera created for television, Gian Carlo Menotti's AMAHL AND THE NIGHT VISITORS. Chotzinoff also commissioned and premiered Bohuslav Martinů's THE MARRIAGE, Lukas Foss's GRIFFELKIN, Norman Dello Joio's THE TRIAL OF ROUEN, Stanley Hollingsworth's LA GRANDE BRETÈCHE, Menotti's MARIA GOLOVIN and Leonard Kastle's DESERET. Leonard Bernstein's TROUBLE IN TAHITI was telecast but was not a premiere. The series ended with the death of Chotzinoff in 1964. Soundtracks of several of the operas were issued on LP and most can be viewed at the Museum of Television and Radio.

NBC RADIO

NBC pioneered opera on radio from 1925 to 1930 through the NBC National Grand Opera Company, organized by conductor Cesare Sudaro, and presented a number of American operas. They included the premieres of Sudan's own OMBRE RUSSE in 1929 and Charles Skilton's THE SUN BRIDE in 1930. The following list includes all the American operas known to have been broadcast by NBC Radio.

1928 Charles Wakefield Cadman, SHANEWIS; Aldo Franchetti, NAMIKO-SAN; Henry Hadley, *Bianca;* Victor Herbert, NATOMA; W. Franke Harling, A LIGHT FROM ST. AGNES. 1929 Charles W. Cadman, A WITCH OF SALEM; Francesco De Leone, ALGLALA; Henry Hadley, CLEOPATRA'S NIGHT; Cesare Sodero, OMBRE RUSSE. 1930 Charles Skilton, THE SUN BRIDE. 1932 Charles W. Cadman, THE WILLOW TREE; Shirley Graham, TOM-TOM. 1933 Henry Hadley, *A Night in Old Paris.* 1939 G. C. Menotti, THE OLD MAID AND THE THIEF. 1939 Eugene Zador, *Christopher Columbus.* 1940 Maurice Baron, FRANÇOIS VILLON. 1942 George Lessner, THE NIGHTINGALE AND THE ROSE. 1942 Italo Montemezzi, L'INCANTESIMO.

NEBRASKA   *American state (1867–)*

Opera Omaha is the major opera company in Nebraska and there are several operas based on stories by Willa Cather including Libby Larsen's ERIC HERMANNSON'S SOUL, Tyler Goodrich White's O PIONEERS! and Robert Beadell's *Out to the Wind.* Cather's novel *The Song of the Lark is* one of the great fictional portraits of an opera singer. John G. Neihardt, the Poet Laureate of Nebraska who wrote *Black Elk Speaks,* wrote the libretto for Lucille Crews 1926 grand opera *Eight Hundred Rubles.* Nebraska-born opera people include baritone John Brandstetter (Wayne), soprano Annunciata Garrotto, composer Howard Hanson (Wahoo), composer George Hufsmith (Omaha), composer John Moran (Lincoln), music critic Conrad L. Osborne, composer Burrill Phillips (Omaha), soprano Linda Phillips (Hastings), opera critic Ken Wlaschin (Scottsbluff) and composer Paul Stuart (Omaha). Soprano Barbara Hendricks studied at Nebraska University.

Lincoln: Most of the premieres in Lincoln were held at the University of Nebraska. Howard Kirkpatrick's grand opera *Olaf* premiered at the University in 1912 and his light opera *La Menuette* at the Orpheum Theater in 1924. Henry Eames' *The Sacred Tree*

of the Omaha. libretto by Nebraskan Hartley Alexander, was staged at the University in 1916 and Eleanor Everett Freer's *Massimiliano or the Court Jester* was premiered in 1926. Robert Beadell presented four operas at the University: *The Sweetwater Affair* in 1961, *The Number of Fools* in 1976, *Napoleon* in 1973 and *Out to the Wind* in 1978. Dan Locklair's church opera *Good Tidings from the Holy Beast,* based on a miracle play, premiered at Plymouth Congregational Church in 1978.

Omaha: Henry Eames collaborated with Nebraskan librettist Hartley Alexander on several pageant operas: *Prairie Vespers* and *Coronado* were presented by Ak-Sar-Ben in Omaha in 1922. Opera Omaha, the major opera company in Nebraska founded in 1959 as the Omaha Civic Opera Company, has premiered several American operas. Stewart Wallace's WHERE'S DICK? was commissioned and premiered in workshop format in 1987. Hugo Weisgall's THE GARDENS OF ADONIS was premiered in 1992 and Libby Larsen's ERIC HERMANNSON'S SOUL in 1998. Anthony Davis's *The Trial of Standing Bear,* libretto by Yusef Komunyakaa, was commissioned by the company in 2004. Opera Omaha's first season featured Richard Rodgers' OKLAHOMA! and it has since staged Carlisle Floyd's BILBY'S DOLL, COLD SASSY TREE and SUSANNAH, George Gershwin's PORGY AND BESS, Philip Glass's THE JUNIPER TREE, Jerome Kern's SHOW BOAT, Frederick Loewe's MY FAIR LADY, Douglas Moore's THE BALLAD OF BABY DOE and Rodgers' CAROUSEL. Jan Bach's *The Happy Prince* was premiered by the Omaha Symphony in 1980.

NEILL, WILLIAM   *American tenor*

William Neill created the role of Henri Faust in John Gessner's *Faust Counter Faust* at Minneapolis Opera in 1971 and Dom Goncalo Pereira in Thomas Pasatieri's INES DE CASTRO at Baltimore Lyric Opera in 1976. He has also sung the role of Lennie in Carlisle Floyd's OF MICE AND MEN. Neill studied at the University of Texas and made his debut in Essen, Germany, in 1968.

NEITHER   *1977 monodrama by Feldman*

Morton Feldman's one-hour monodrama for soprano *Neither,* composed to an 87-word 16-line libretto by Samuel Beckett, is probably as close to being minimalist as opera can be. Though composed for the stage (it was premiered at the Teatro dell'Opera in Rome on May 13, 1977), it has no plot or events and, in true Beckett manner, moves very slowly indeed. The unnamed protagonist sings in the highest soprano register with little variation in pitch. *Neither* has been compared to Schoenberg's monodrama ERWARTUNG, which is also an interior monologue for soprano.

1977 Teatro dell'Opera. The premiere of the opera at the Teatro dell'Opera in Rome was recorded. Legno CD. **1990 Frankfurt Television.** Sarah Leonard sings the role of the Woman in this German television production directed by Barrie Gavin. Claire-Lise Leisegang-Holy designed the minimalist set and Zoltán Peskó conducted the Frankfurt Radio-Television Symphony Orchestra. It was telecast April 13, 1990, on HR Television and. soundtrack issued on CD. Hat-Hut CD.

NET OPERA COMPANY   *TV opera series (1969–1977)*

The NET Opera Company, created by Peter Herman Adler and Kirk Browning after they left NBC Opera Theater, presented five American operas, four of them premieres: Marc Bucci's THE HERO in 1965, Jack Beeson's LIZZIE BORDEN in 1967, Beeson's MY HEART'S IN THE HIGHLANDS in 1970, Thomas Pasatieri's THE TRIAL OF MARY LINCOLN in 1972 and Hans Werner Henze's RACHEL LA CUBANA in 1974. Henze's opera ran so far over budget that original productions ceased. NET, the National Educational Television network, was a collective network founded in 1957 with the help of Sarah Caldwell.

NEVADA   *American state (1864–)*

Nevada Opera in Reno is the state's principal opera company. Operas set in Nevada include Bern Herbolsheimer's MARK ME TWAIN, premiered by Nevada Opera in Reno in 1993, and Earnest Kanitz's *The Lucky Dollar,* premiered in Los Angeles in 1958.

Las Vegas: Daron Hagen's BANDANNA was recorded by the University of Nevada Opera Theatre in Las Vegas on March 3, 2000.

Reno: Nevada Opera, founded in 1968, presents three to four operas and operettas a year in the Pioneer Center for the Performing Arts. It commissioned and premiered Bern Herbolsheimer's *Mark Me Twain* to celebrate the company's 25th anniversary. Its other productions have included Irving Berlin's ANNIE GET YOUR GUN, Carlisle Floyd's OF MICE AND MEN and SUSANNAH, Jerome Kern's SHOW BOAT, Gian Carlo Menotti's AMAHL AND THE NIGHT VISITORS and THE MEDIUM and Sigmund Romberg's THE DESERT SONG and THE STUDENT PRINCE.

NEVIN, ARTHUR   *American composer (1871—1943)*

Arthur Nevin was the first American composer to have an opera premiered in Germany. His three-act POIA, libretto by Randolph Hartley about Blackfoot Indians and the coming of sun worship, was staged at Berlin Opera on April 23, 1910, with a major cast including Florence Easton and Walter Kirchoff. Nevin's one-act opera A DAUGHTER OF THE FOREST was staged by Chicago Opera in 1918. Nevin, who was born in Edgeworth, PA, studied at the New England Conservatory and in Berlin under Engelbert Humperdinck. He lived with the Blackfoot tribe in Montana for two years studying their myths and music and based his opera *Poia* on what he learned.

NEW HAMPSHIRE   *American state (1788–)*

Operas set in New Hampshire included Douglas Moore's THE DEVIL AND DANIEL WEBSTER, in which New Hampshire native Webster prevents a New Hampshire man from losing his soul to the Devil. New Hampshire-born opera people include composer Amy Cheney Beach (Henniker), composer Avery Claflin (Keene), composer Henry Clarke (Dover), soprano Beverly Morgan (Hanover) and soprano Patricia Racette (Bedford),

Hanover: Ross Lee Finney's 18-minute *The Nun's Priests' Tale,* libretto by the composer based on Chaucer's *The Canterbury Tales,* premiered at Dartmouth College in Hanover in August 1965. Composers who studied or taught at Dartmouth include John Adams, Charles Hamm and Richard Owen,

Lebanon: Opera North, a community opera company founded in 1981 and supported by the adjacent cities of Norwich in Vermont and Lebanon in New Hampshire, produces operas at the Lebanon Opera House. It has staged Domenick ARGENTO's THE BOOR, Carlisle Floyd's SUSANNAH, Henry Mollicone's THE FACE ON THE BARROOM FLOOR and Gian Carlo Menotti's THE MEDIUM.

Manchester: Opera Northeast, founded in 1972 as a professional opera company in residence at Pace University in New York City, later relocated to Manchester. It tours fully-staged operas with piano accompaniment.

Peterborough: Monadnock Music, a festival founded by James Bolle in 1966, regularly presents works by modern American composers in southern New Hampshire towns. Virgil Thomson's opera LORD BYRON was produced at the Festival in 1991 and recorded at Pine Hill Waldorf Auditorium in Wilton.

Wentworth: Martin Kalmanoff's *Aesop, the Fabulous Fabulist,* about the Greek creator of FABLES, was premiered at Camp Pemigewasset in Wentworth on August 21, 1969.

NEW JERSEY   *American state (1787–)*

Atlantic City, long an important preview city for Broadway, has premiered notable comic operas by Victor Herbert and Rudolf Friml. Operas set in New Jersey include Jack Beeson's THE SWEET BYE AND BYE, which takes place in Atlantic City; and Steve Reich's HINDENBURG a multi-media portrait of the German zeppelin which crashed in New Jersey on May 6, 1937.

New Jersey-born opera people include composer George Antheil (Trenton), composer Ernest Carter (Orange), composer Louis Adolphe Coerne (Newark), tenor Richard Crooks (Trenton), composer Russell Currie (North Arlington) composer Anthony David (Paterson), choral director Leonard De Paur (Summit), librettist Dorothy Fields (Allenhurst), composer Margaret Garwood (Haddonfield), composer Lee Goldstein (Woodbury), tenor Jerry Hadley (Princeton), composer John Harbison (Orange), composer James P. Johnson (New Brunswick), soprano Dorothy Kirsten (Montclair), mezzo-soprano Gloria Lane (Trenton), composer Marvin Davy Levy (Passaic), tenor Gordon MacRae (East Orange), composer Stephen Paulus (Summit), bass-baritone Paul Robeson (Princeton), composer George Rochberg (Paterson), composer Norman Stokes (Haddon Heights), composer Harry Tierney (Perth Amboy), composer Nancy Van de Vate (Plainfield), mezzo-soprano Frederica von Stade (Somerville) and poet/playwright William Carlos Williams (Rutherford).

Atlantic City: Victor Herbert premiered four of his comic operas in Atlantic City: *Algeria* at the Apollo Theater on August 24, 1908; *The Debutante* at the New Nixon Theater on September 21, 1914; THE ONLY GIRL at the New Nixon Theater on October 1, 1914; and THE PRINCESS PAT at the Cort Theater on August 23, 1915. Rudolf Friml's *Some Time* was premiered at the Globe Theater on August 26, 1918, and his classic ROSE MARIE at the New Nixon Theater on August 18, 1924. Joyce Barthelson's comic opera *The King's Breakfast,* based on Maurice Baring's *Catherine Parr,* was premiered on April 6, 1973.

Glassboro: Lloyd Avril's *Heads or Tales* was premiered at Glassboro State College on February 23, 1968.

Lawrenceville: Opera Festival of New Jersey, founded in 1984, presents three or four operas in English every summer. It was held in the Arts Center at the Lawrenceville School until 1998 when it moved to Princeton's McCarter Theatre. The festival premiered Peter Westergaard's THE TEMPEST in 1994 (Westergaard helped found the festival) and it staged Dominick Argento's POSTCARD FROM MOROCCO in 1999.

Montclair: Montclair State College has been the site of four premieres: Alec Wilder's *The Lowland Sea* on May 8, 1952, and *Cumberland Fair* on May 22, 1953; Jean Berger's *Yiphth and His Daughter* on May 11, 1972; and Paul Knudson's *The Actress* on May 11, 1976. Emil Kahn's *The Ribbon* premiered at Hillside Junior High School on May 8, 1952.

Morristown: Rudolf Friml's operetta KATINKA premiered at the Park Theater in Morristown on December 2, 1915, before it opened on Broadway

New Brunswick: Alan Schmitz' four-act opera *Julius Caesar,* libretto based on the play by Shakespeare, premiered at Rutgers College in New Brunswick on April 7, 1978.

Newark: Tenor/composer Ralph Errolle's *The Messenger* premiered in Newark in 1938, Irving Mopper's *The Door* premiered at the Lauter Auditorium in 1954 and Wheeler Beckett's *The Magic Mirror* premiered at the Mosque Theater in 1955. Seymour Barab's *The Ransom of Red Chief,* based on an O. Henry story, was premiered in Newark in 1964. Ulysses Kay's three-act FREDERICK DOUGLASS, libretto by Douglas Dorr, was premiered by New Jersey State Opera in Newark on April 14, 1991.

Paramus: Ars Musica Chorale presents classic operas in concert in various sites in New Jersey.

Paterson: Allan Blank's *Excitement at the Circus,* a widely-performed children's opera, libretto by Irving Leitner, premiered in Paterson in 1969.

Princeton: Olga Gorelli's *Between the Shadow and the Glen,* libretto based on the John Millington Synge play, was premiered by Princeton Opera on May 28, 1972. Opera Festival of New Jersey moved to Princeton in 1998 so it could stage its productions at the McCarter Theatre. Polly Pen's *The Night Governess*, based on a thriller by Louis May Alcott, premiered at the McCarter in May 2000. Hugo Weisgall's SIX CHARACTERS IN SEARCH OF AN AUTHOR, based on the play by Pirandello, was revived by Opera Festival of New Jersey in 2000 and Frank Lewin's BURNING BRIGHT, based on the play by John Steinbeck, was given its first professional production at the McCarter Theater . Its other productions include Samuel Barber's VANESSA and Carlisle Floyd's SUSANNAH.

Rutherford: Theodore Harris's *The First President,* libretto based on the play about George Washington by Rutherford native William Carlos Williams, was premiered at Fairleigh Dickinson University in 1964.

Sayreville: The Queens Opera Association based in Sayreville has been touring operas around the country since 1961.

Trenton: Victor Herbert's comic opera MLLE. MODISTE, starring Fritzi Scheff, premiered at the Taylor Opera House in Trenton on October 7, 1905, before opening on Broadway to huge acclaim. George Antheil's controversial TRANSATLANTIC was presented in a revised version by Encompass Music Theater in Trenton in 1981. Bohème Opera, founded in Trenton in 1993, presents operas from the classic repertory.

NEW MEXICO   *American state (1912–)*

New Mexico is the home of one of America's most famous regional opera companies, Santa Fe Opera, founded by John Crosby in 1957. It has premiered many important American operas and helped launch the career of an exceptional number of singers. Those making their debut at Santa Fe include soprano Judith Blegen, mezzo-soprano Elaine Bonazzi, tenor Nico Castel, soprano Katherine Ciesinski, soprano Faith Esham, soprano Reri Grist, soprano Cynthia Haymon and mezzo-soprano Regina Sarfaty. Operas set in New Mexico include David Bishop's ESPERANZA, about New Mexican mine-workers holding a strike to obtain better working conditions, and Stephen Paulus' THE WOMAN AT OTOWI CROSSING, about a woman involved with scientists of the Manhattan Project and the local Native Americans.

Albuquerque: Opera Southwest is headquartered in Albuquerque. John Donald Robb's *Little Jo* was premiered at the Little Theater in Albuquerque on January 18, 1950.

Santa Fe: Santa Fe Opera's first season in the summer of 1957 included the premiere of Marvin David Levy's *The Tower* and an acclaimed production of Igor Stravinsky's THE RAKE'S PROGRESS. The company has continued to present new American operas on a regular basis. Premieres have included Carlisle Floyd's WUTHERING HEIGHTS in 1958, Stravinsky's THE FLOOD (first stage production) in 1962, Heitor Villa-Lobos YERMA in 1971, George Rochberg's THE CONFIDENCE MAN in 1982, John Eaton's THE

TEMPEST in 1985, David Lang's MODERN PAINTERS in 1995, Tobias Picker's EMMELINE in 1996 (televised and issued on video and CD) and Peter Lieberson's ASHOKA'S DREAM in 1997. Santa Fe Opera staged Douglas MOORE's THE BALLAD OF BABY DOE in 1961 and held the American premiere of Gian Carlo Menotti's HELP, HELP, THE GLOBOLINKS! in 1969. Its 1976 production of Virgil Thomson's THE MOTHER OF US ALL was telecast and recorded. Celius Dougherty's *Many Moons* was premiered in Santa Fe in July 1962. Joan La Barbara's *Events in the Elsewhere*, an interactive opera inspired by physicist Stephen Hawking, premiered in Santa Fe in 1990. Bright Sheng's THE SILVER RIVER premiered at the Santa Fe Chamber Music Festival in 1997. John Cage's EUROPERA 5 was staged in Santa Fe in 2000 using excerpts from Wagner operas.

THE NEW MOON   *1927 operetta by Romberg*

French rebel aristocrat Robert Misson, in 18th century New Orleans to recruit freedom fighters, falls in love with haughty Marianne. Taken prisoner by the French policeman Ribaud, he is put on the ship New Moon to be returned to France. It is captured by his followers and they set up a colony of free men on an island where he slowly wins Marianne's love. Sigmund Romberg's tuneful operetta *The New Moon*, libretto and lyrics by Oscar Hammerstein II, Laurence Schwab and Frank Mandel, premiered at the Chestnut Street Opera House in Philadelphia on December 22, 1927. Robert Halliday played Misson and Desirée Tabor was Marianne. It was not well received and after many revisions was re-staged by Edgar MacGregor in Cleveland on August 27, 1928, with Evelyn Herbert taking over the role of Marianne. This version opened at the Imperial Theater on Broadway on September 19, 1928, and was a huge success going on to London and Paris afterwards. Its famous songs include "Softly as in a Morning Sunrise," "One Kiss," "Stouthearted Men," "Wanting You" and "Lover Come Back to Me." A New York City Center Encores! concert staging of the operetta in March 2003 featured opera singers Rodney Gilfrey and Christiane Noll in the leading roles. The operetta has been filmed twice, most successfully by Jeanette MacDonald and Nelson Eddy in 1940, though, oddly, both films drop the article and are called simply *New Moon*.

1929 Original London cast. Evelyn Laye is Marianne, Howett Worster is Misson and Ben Williams is Ribaud in this London cast highlights recording. Delores Farris and Gene Gerrard sing "Gorgeous Alexander" and "Try Her Out at Dances." World LP/Pearl CD. **1929 London Theatre Orchestra.** Sigmund Romberg conducts the London Theatre Orchestra in a medley of nine tunes from his operetta for a 78 record. It's on the British Pearl CD *Great Hits from Sigmund Romberg*. **1929 Evelyn Herbert/ William O'Neal.** Broadway cast star Evelyn Herbert sings "One Kiss" and "Lover, Come Back to Me" in a London recording and William O'Neal sings "Softly, as in a Morning Sunrise" and "Stouthearted Men." *Music of Broadway: The Twenties, Volume 3.* JJA Records LP. **1930 MGM film.** Grace Moore and Lawrence Tibbett star in an MGM film of the operetta titled *New Moon* but with a different plot. The couple meet on the ship New Moon on the Caspian Sea where Moore is a Slavic princess fought

over by Russian officer Tibbett and his superior Adolphe Menjou. Tibbett sings "Stouthearted Men," Moore sings "Softly as in a Morning Sunrise" and "One Kiss" and they duet on "Wanting You" and "Lover Come Back to Me." Jack Conway directed. Soundtrack extracts on various CDs. Premiere Opera VHS. **1931 Lawrence Tibbett.** Lawrence Tibbett recorded "Lover, Come Back to Me" and "Wanting You" for RCA Victor 78 records in March 1931. They're on various albums including *Lawrence Tibbett: The Song Is You.* RCA CD. **1936 Richard Tauber.** Richard Tauber sings "Lover, Come Back to Me" for a 78 record included on the album *Richard Tauber: Songs of Stage and Screen.* Parlophone LP. **1939 Jeanette MacDonald.** Jeanette MacDonald recorded "Lover, Come Back to Me" and "One Kiss" in 1939 with orchestra conducted by Giuseppe Bamboschek. The songs are on RCA Victor LP and CD albums including *Jeanette MacDonald and Nelson Eddy* and *Jeanette MacDonald* (Chansophone CD). **1940 MGM film.** The 1940 MGM film *New Moon* with Jeanette MacDonald and Nelson Eddy sticks fairly close to the original plot of the operetta. Eddy is a fugitive French freedom-loving aristocrat in New Orleans and MacDonald is the haughty woman he loves. Most of the famous songs are used including "One Kiss," "Softly as in a Morning Sunrise," "Lover Come Back to Me" and "Stout-Hearted Men." William Daniels was cinematographer and Robert Z. Leonard

Original sheet music issued for the 1929 English premiere of Sigmund Romberg's operetta *The New Moon*.

directed. Soundtrack on Pelican LP. MGM-UA VHS/DVD. **1940 Josephine Antoine.** Metropolitan Opera soprano Josephine Antoine sings "One Kiss" on the radio show *Concert Hall* conducted by Donald Voorhees. It's on the 1995 album *The American Prima Donna.* Eklipse CD. **1940 Nelson Eddy.** Nelson Eddy recorded "Lover, Come Back to Me," "Stout-Hearted Men," "Softly, as in a Morning Sunrise" and "Wanting You" for 78 records in 1940. The songs are on various Columbia LP and CD albums including *Nelson Eddy's Greatest Hits.* **1940 Helen Traubel.** Met soprano Helen Traubel sings "Stout-Hearted Men" on a radio broadcast. It's on the album *The Radio Years: Helen Traubel Rarities.* Radio Years (Italy) CD. **1949 Risë Stevens.** Met mezzo Risë Stevens recorded "Lover, Come Back to Me" with orchestra conducted by Sylvan Shuman for her album *Love Songs.* Columbia LP. **1950 Eleanor Steber/Nelson Eddy.** Met soprano Eleanor Steber and Nelson Eddy perform a highlights version of the operetta with Leon Arnaud leading the orchestra and chorus. The album includes nine numbers. Columbia LP. **1950 Lucille Norman/Gordon MacRae.** Lucille Norman and Gordon MacRae star in an abridged highlights version of the opera recorded in 1950 with Paul Weston and His Orchestra. Capitol LP. **1950 Jan Peerce.** Jan Peerce recorded "Softly, as in a Morning Sunrise" in London in 1950. It's on the album *Great Voices of the Century.* Everest/Scala LP. **1951 Richard Tucker.** Richard Tucker recorded "Softly, as in a Morning Sunrise" with orchestra led by Skitch Henderson. It's on the album *Essential Operetta.* Sony Classics CD. **1952 Dorothy Kirsten/Gordon MacRae.** Dorothy Kirsten and Gordon MacRae perform an abridged version of the operetta on the radio. Demand Performance audiocassette. **1953 Thomas Hayward/Jane Wilson.** Thomas Hayward, Jane Wilson and Lee Sweetland perform seven numbers from the opera with Victor Young conducting the orchestra and chorus. Decca CD. **1953 Frances Greer/Earl Wrightson.** Frances Greer and Earl Wrightson star on this highlights recording with support from Donald Dame and Earl Oxford. Al Goodman conducts. RCA Victor LP. **1954 Deep in My Heart.** Three songs from *The New Moon* are featured in MGM's film *Deep in My Heart,* a highly fictional biography of Romberg. Helen Traubel sings "Stouthearted Men," and "Softly as in a Morning Sunrise," Tony Martin and Joan Weldson perform "Lover, Come Back to Me" and Tamara Toumanova sings and dances "Softly as in a Morning Sunrise." Sony soundtrack CD. MGM-UA VHS/DVD. **1955 Robert Merrill.** Robert Merrill sings "Stout-hearted Men" on the *Voice of Firestone* TV show on September 18, 1955. Howard Barlow conducts the Firestone Orchestra. *Robert Merrill in Opera and Song, Vol. 2.* VAI VHS. **1956 Mario Lanza.** Mario Lanza sings "Lover, Come Back to Me" with Henri René's Orchestra and the Jeff Alexander Choir on the albums *Mario Lanza in a Cavalcade of Show Tunes* (RCA Victor LP) and *The Mario Lanza Collection* (RCA Victor CD). He sings "Softly, as in a Morning Sunrise" with Constantin Callinicos orchestra on the album *Mario Lanza Live from London* (RCA Victor LP/CD). **1957 Jeanette MacDonald/Nelson Eddy.** Jeanette MacDonald and Nelson Eddy recorded together in 1957 for the first time since 1938 (they had contracts with different record companies) and created a new version of the duet "Wanting You." It's on the album *Jeanette MacDonald and Nelson Eddy: Favorites in Hi-Fi.* RCA Victor LP. **1962 Jeanette Scotti/Peter Palmer.** Jeanette Scotti is Marianne with Peter Palmer as Robert in this highlights version of the operetta with Arthur Rubin as Philippe. Lehman Engel conducts the orchestra and chorus while Henri Rene created the arrangements for the Reader's Digest *Treasury of Great Operettas* collection. RCA 10-LP box set. **1963 Dorothy Kirsten/Gordon MacRae.** Dorothy

Kirsten is Marianne with Gordon MacRae as Misson in this highlights recording. Richard Robinson is Alexander, Jeannine Wagner is Julie, Earle Wilkie is Besace and James Tippey is Philippe. Van Alexander leads the Roger Wagner Chorale and Orchestra. Capitol/Angel LP. **1967 John Hanson/ Patricia Michael.** England's touring operetta specialist John Hanson performs highlights from *The New Moon* partnered with Patricia Michael. Johnny Arthey conducts the orchestra. Phillips LP. **1985 Teresa Ringholz/Eastman Dryden Orchestra.** Soprano Teresa Ringholz and the Eastman Dryden Orchestra perform excerpts from the operetta under the direction of Donald Hunsberger on the album *Sigmund Romberg: When I Grow Too Old to Dream.* Arabesque CD. **1988 New York City Opera.** Leigh Munro is Marianne with Richard White as Misson and David Rae Smith as Ribaud in this TV film of a New York City Opera production. It was staged at Wolf Trap by Robert Johanson and filmed with Beverly Sills as host. James Coleman conducts the New York City Opera Orchestra. Kirk Browning directed the video telecast on April 7, 1989. On VHS. **1991 Texas stage production.** Tanya Rodgers stars as Marianne opposite Royce Blackburn as Misson in this video of a rather amateurish production staged in Texas on July 15, 1991. Charles Sims is Philipe, Jane Guitar is Julie and Michael Wheeler is Alexander. Scott Mathers conducts the Rose Rosa Orchestra. Premiere Opera VHS. **1993 Jerry Hadley.** Met tenor Jerry Hadley sings "Stout-hearted Men" "Marianne" and "Softly as in a Morning Sunrise" on his album *Golden Days.* Paul Gemignani conducts the American Theatre Orchestra. BMG RCA Victor CD. **1993 Barbara Hendricks/Gino Quilico.** Soprano Barbara Hendricks and baritone Gino Quilico join in duet on "Wanting You" on the album *Operetta Duets.* Lawrence Foster conducts the Lyon Opera Orchestra. EMI CD. **1995 Lesley Garrett.** Soprano Lesley Garret sings "Lover Come Back to Me" and "Softly, as in a Morning Sunrise" on her album *Lesley Garrett, Soprano in Red.* James Holmes conducts the Royal Philharmonic Concert Orchestra. Silva Classics CD. **2000 Elizabeth Futral/Steven White.** Elizabeth Futral and Steven White perform five songs from the operetta on the album *Sweethearts.* Robert Tweten accompanies on piano. Newport Classics CD. **2001 The New Moon anthology.** This anthology CD features vintage recordings of the operetta, including a 1950s radio version, songs recorded by members of the original Broadway and London casts and Sigmund Romberg playing his piano version of "Lover, Come Back to Me." AEI CD.

NEW YEAR *1989 opera by Tippett*

A spaceship from Nowhere Tomorrow lands in the world of Somewhere Today. Pelegrin, the ship's pilot, has been attracted by the anguished face of child psychologist Jo Ann whose foster brother Donny is causing her grief. Pelegrin finds Jo Ann at midnight in a crowd awaiting the New Year in Times Square. Donny, it seems, could be the bad old year. Michael Tippett's 90-minute opera *New Year,* libretto by the composer, was premiered October 27, 1989, by Houston Grand Opera which commissioned it in collaboration with the Glyndebourne Festival and BBC Television. Helen Field was Jo Ann, Peter Kazaras was Pelegrin, Krister St. Hill was Donny, James Maddalena was Merlin, Richetta Manager was Regan, Jane Shaulis was Nan and John Schiappa was the Presenter. Alison Chitty designed the costumes and sets, Peter Hall directed and John DeMain conducted the Houston Symphony. Much of the opera's musical inspiration is American, especially the Broadway musical style. The spaceship music is taped and there is strong use of saxophones and electric guitars for Donny's numbers.

NEW YORK   *American State (1788–)*

New York state has a multitude of opera centers outside New York City with major summer festivals in Glimmerglass, Chautauqua and Lake George and year round activity in Binghamton, Buffalo, Rochester and Syracuse. The Eastman House of Music in Rochester has been a major contributor to the growth of America opera and the site of a number of premieres.

Among the many operas set in New York state are George Frederick Bristow's RIP VAN WINKLE, John Harbison's THE GREAT GATSBY, Douglas Moore's THE HEADLESS HORSEMAN and Walter Schumann's THE MIGHTY CASEY.

New York-born opera people include: composer David Ahlstrom (Lancaster), composer Roger Ames (Cooperstown), mezzo-soprano Elaine Bonazzi (Endicott), baritone Richard Bonelli (Port Byron), Paul Bowles (Jamaica), tenor Cab Calloway (Rochester), soprano June Card (Dunkirk), tenor Philip Creech (Hempstead), David Diamond (Rochester), soprano Renée Fleming (Rochester), baritone Jake Gardner (Oneonta), composer Roger Hannay (Plattsburgh), composer Marvin Davy Levy (Passaic), conductor Steven Mercurio (Bardonia), Douglas Moore (Cutchogue), librettist Joyce Carol Oates (Millerport), mezzo-soprano Regina Sarfaty (Rochester), librettist Harry B. Smith (Buffalo), soprano Ruth Ann Swenson (Commack), librettist Stephen Wadsworth (Mt. Kisko), author E. B. White (Mt. Vernon), composer Alec Wilder (Rochester) and bass Herbert Witherspoon (Buffalo).

Albany: José Paul Bernardo's *The Child* premiered at the St. George Opera Festival at the University in Albany on August 8, 1974. James Sellars' *Beulah in Chicago*, based on poems by Frank O'Hara, premiered at the Art Institute of Albany on March 28, 1982. Leonard Kastle's *The Pariahs*, about early American whalers, premiered in Albany in 1985.

Amherst: Paul Ziemba's DRACULA, THE OPERA premiered at the Harlem Center Theater in Amherst April 18, 2000.

Baldwinsville: Frank Di Giacomo's Christmas opera *A Journey to Bethlehem* premiered at the Charles W. Baker High School in Baldwinsville in December 1977.

Binghamton: Tri-Cities Opera, founded in 1949, has premiered a number of American operas including two by Myron Fink. His four-act *Jeremiah* premiered at Harpur College on May 25, 1962, and his jazzy operetta CHINCHILLA was staged at the Forum Theater on January 18, 1986. Richard Brooks' RAPUNZEL was premiered on January 22, 1971. Ezra Laderman's GALILEO GALILEI, a revised three-act version of the television version, was presented at SUNY on February 3, 1979. Tri-Cities Opera has also staged Victor Herbert's NAUGHTY MARIETTA, Gian Carlo Menotti's AMAHL AND THE NIGHT VISITORS, THE MEDIUM, THE OLD MAID AND THE THIEF and THE TELEPHONE, Sigmund Romberg's THE STUDENT PRINCE, Robert Ward's THE CRUCIBLE and Wright/Forrest's KISMET.

Bronxville: Douglas Moore's folk opera THE HEADLESS HORSEMAN, libretto by Stephen Vincent Benét based on Washington Irving's *A Legend of Sleepy Hollow*, premiered at Bronxville High School on March 5, 1937. Sarah Lawrence College in Bronxville has hosted several premieres. Norman Dello Joio's *The Trial of Joan* was presented on May 9, 1950, Meyer Kupferman, who taught at Sarah Lawrence, premiered three operas there: DR. FAUSTUS LIGHTS THE LIGHTS, based on the Gertrude Stein play, in 1951; *Draagenfut Girl*, based on the Cinderella fairytale, in 1958; and the multi-media *Visions and Games* in 1971.

Buffalo: Buffalo was an important site for Broadway tryouts at the turn of the century. The Star Theater held the premiere of Louis A Coerne's *A Woman of Marblehead* in 1897, Victor Herbert's *Wonderland* in 1905 and Herbert's THE RED MILL in 1906.

The University of Buffalo hosted the premiere of Susan La Mothe's *The Kitchen Sink*, libretto by David Posner, on February 19, 1965. Philip Glass's SATYAGRAHA had its American premiere at Art Park outside Buffalo in 1981. Greater Buffalo Opera, formed by the merger of Buffalo Lyric Opera and Western New York Opera Theater in 1988, presents three operas every season at the Buffalo Center for the Performing Arts. The company staged George Gershwin's PORGY AND BESS In 1989 and Gian Carlo Menotti's AMAHL AND THE NIGHT VISITORS in 1990.

Carmel: Florence Wickham's operetta *Rosalind*, based on Shakespeare's *As You Like It*, premiered at the Rockridge Theater on August 5, 1938. Richard Owen's religious opera A FISHERMAN CALLED PETER premiered at Drew Church on March 14, 1965.

Chautauqua: Chautauqua Opera was founded as a summer festival in 1929 in the birthplace of the 19th century Chautauqua movement and American opera and operetta has been integral to its repertory. Albert Stoessel, its first musical director, was also head of the opera department at Juilliard and brought several of its premieres to Chautauqua, including Luis Gruenberg's JACK AND THE BEANSTALK, Robert Russell Bennett's MARIA MALIBRAN and his own GARRICK. Other American presentations during this early period included Henry Hadley's BIANCA in 1934, Reginald De Koven's ROBIN HOOD in 1935, Victor Herbert's NAUGHTY MARIETTA in 1939 and Douglas Moore's THE DEVIL AND DANIEL WEBSTER in 1940. After his death in 1943, American operas and operettas continued to be staged regularly. They have included Marc Blitzstein's REGINA, Jerry Bock's SHE LOVES ME, Carlisle Floyd's OF MICE AND MEN, SUSANNAH and WUTHERING HEIGHTS, Lukas Foss's THE JUMPING FROG OF CALAVERAS COUNTY, Vittorio Giannini's THE TAMING OF THE SHREW, Mitch Leigh's MAN OF LA MANCHA, Frederick Loewe's BRIGADOON and MY FAIR LADY, Gian Carlo Menotti's AMAHL AND THE NIGHT VISITORS and THE OLD MAID AND THE THIEF, Douglas Moore's THE BALLAD OF BABY DOE, Cole Porter's KISS ME KATE, Richard Rodgers' THE KING AND I, OKLAHOMA and SOUTH PACIFIC, Sigmund Romberg's THE DESERT SONG and THE STUDENT PRINCE, Robert Ward's THE CRUCIBLE and Kurt Weill's STREET SCENE. Operas premiered by Chautauqua Opera in recent years include Seymour Barab's PHILIP MARSHALL on July 12, 1974, and Richard Wargo's three-part A CHEKHOV TRILOGY on August 13, 1993.

Chichester: Herbert Hausfrecht's "pantomime opera" *Boney Quillen* premiered at the American Legion Hall on August 18, 1951.

Cooperstown: Glimmerglass Opera, a prestigious summer festival begun in 1975, presents American opera on a regular basis and many of its productions are reprised by New York City Opera. William Schuman's A QUESTION OF TASTE was commissioned by the company and premiered June 24, 1989, in a double-bill with his baseball opera THE MIGHTY CASEY. The trilogy CENTRAL PARK, co-commissioned by Glimmerglass and NYCO, premiered on August 8, 1999, and was presented in New York in November. Highly praised revivals of Jack Beeson's LIZZIE BORDEN, Benjamin Britten's PAUL BUNYAN, John Philip Sousa's THE GLASS BLOWERS and Virgil Thomson's THE MOTHER OF US ALL also went to New York. Other American productions include Leonard Bernstein's TROUBLE IN TAHITI, David Carlson's MIDNIGHT ANGEL (co-commissioned by Glimmerglass), Carlisle Floyd's OF MICE AND MEN, Gian Carlo Menotti's THE MEDIUM and THE TELEPHONE, Douglas Moore's GALLANTRY and Sigmund Romberg's THE STUDENT PRINCE.

Glen Falls/Saratoga Springs: Lake George Opera Festival, a summer event founded in 1961, has premiered several American operas: David Amram's TWELFTH NIGHT, libretto by Joseph Papp based on the Shakespeare play, was staged July 28, 1968; Henry Mollicone's YOUNG GOODMAN BROWN, based on the Hawthorne story, was presented in July 1970; Robert Convey's *Pyramus and Thisbee*, based on Shakespeare's *A Midsummer Night's Dream*, was produced in July 1982; Mark Houston's HAZEL KIRKE was staged on August 7, 1987; and Leonard Lehrman's *The Birthday of the Bank*, based on Chekhov's *The Jubilee*, premiered August 2, 1988. Alva Henderson's THE LAST OF THE MOHICANS, based on the James Fenimore Cooper novel, was staged and recorded in August 1977; parts of the novel are set in the Lake George area.

Hempstead: Elie Siegmeister premiered his folk opera *Darling Corie*, libretto by Lewis Allen, at Hofstra College in Hempstead in February 1954 and presented his *The Mermaid in Lock Number 7* there in May 1962.

Islip: Walter Schadd's three-act *Plango* was premiered in Islip in 1938.

Ithaca: Charles F. Hackett's *Donna Rosita*, libretto by William Oliver based on a Lorca play, was premiered by Ithaca Opera on April 6, 1973. Leonard Lehrman premiered two operas at Cornell University: *Karla*, based on Bernard Malamud's story *Notes from a Lady at a Dinner Party*, was presented in concert form on August 3, 1974, while *Sima* was produced on October 22, 1976.

Katonah: Three operas premiered at the Caramoor Festival in Katonah: Robert Starer's THE LAST LOVER, based on legends about Pelagia, on August 2, 1975; Dennis Arlan's *The Ballad of the Bremen Band*, based on a Grimm Brothers tale, on June 25, 1977; and Arlan's *The Daughter of the Double Duke of Single* on June 17, 1978. Hugh Aitken's FABLES, based on Aesop/La Fontaine, was presented at the festival June 6, 1976, following its premiere at the Library of Congress.

Kingston: Two one-act operas premiered at Kingston Opera House on October 26, 1910: Irenee Berge's *Corsica* and Joseph Carl Breil's *Love Laughs at Locksmiths*.

Lake Placid: After Dinner Opera premiered two short operas based on plays by Gertrude Stein on July 27, 1971, Martin Kalmanoff's *Photograph 1920* and Marvin Schwartz's *Look and Long.*

Lindenhurst: Paul Hasting Allen's *Mamzelle Figaro (La piccola Figaro)* premiered in Lindenhurst on May 20, 1948.

Long Island: William Mayer's "trip around the world" *Hello World* was presented at Hofstra College in January 1960. Mario Castelnuovo-Tedesco presented two of his stage works at La Guardia Community College on January 22, 1975: the three-act opera THE IMPORTANT OF BEING ERNEST, based on the Oscar Wilde play (later staged in Italy), and the Biblical oratorio *Tobias and the Angel.*

New York City: See separate entry below.

Nyack: Alec Wilder's *The Long Way*, libretto by Arnold Sundgaard, premiered in Nyack on June 3, 1955.

Piermont: Rockland Lyric Theater has hosted several premieres: Alec Wilder's MISS CHICKEN LITTLE received its first stage production on August 29, 1958, following its premiere on TV. Lionel Novak's *The Clarkstown Witch* was staged on July 11, 1959; Herbert Haslum's *Postlogue* and H. D, Brandt's *Grand Universal Circus* were presented in August 1960; and Novak's *Katydids* was premiered on July 26, 1962.

Pottersville: Alfred D. Geto's one-act *The Treasure* was premiered at Schroon Crest on August 22, 1953.

Poughkeepsie: Vassar College in Poughkeepsie has hosted several premieres. Ernst Krenek's first American opera, TARQUIN, was staged there in concert form on May 13, 1941. Dorothy Lamb's THE NIGHTINGALE, based on the Hans Christian Anderson tale,

was presented April 27, 1954. Robert Middleton's COMMAND PERFORMANCE, libretto by Harold Wendell Smith, was premiered by Boston Opera Group November 11, 1961. Celius DOUGHERTY'S MANY MOONS, based on the James Thurber story, was presented November 3, 1962, following its premiere in Santa Fe. A festival devoted to the music of Victor Herbert is held in Poughkeepsie.

Purchase: Conrad Susa's THE LOVE OF DON PERLIMPLIN was premiered at the PepsiCo Festival at Purchase SUNY in 1984.

Rochester: The Lyceum Theater in Rochester was a Broadway musical tryout site and held the premieres of Victor Herbert's comic operas *Miss Dolly Dollars* (August 30, 1905) and *The Madcap Duchess* (October 13, 1913) and John Philip Sousa's THE GLASS BLOWERS in January 1913. The Eastman School of Music in Rochester, one of the most important music centers in America, is associated with many American opera composers and premieres. Howard Hanson headed the School from 1924 to 1964, Richard Pearlman ran it after him and Otto Luening was director of the Opera Department for many years. The Eastman School premieres include Bernard Rogers' *The Marriage of Aude* based on the *Chanson de Roland* (May 22, 1932), Robert Russell Bennett's *Endymion* (April 5, 1935), Alberto Bimboni's *In the Name of Culture* (May 9, 1949), Burrill Phillips' *Don't We All* (May 9, 1949), Louis Mennini's *The Well* (May 8, 1951), Thomas Canning's *Beyond Belief* (May 14, 1956), Dominick Argento's THE BOOR (May 6, 1957), Martin Mailman's *The Hunted* (April 27, 1959), Geoffrey Gibbs' *Dolphin Off Hippo* (May 9, 1965), Aldo Provenzano's THE CASK OF AMONTILLADO (April 26, 1968), Alec Wilder's *The Truth About Windmills* (October 14, 1973) and Richard Wargo's *The Crystal Mirror* (April 28, 1979). Andrew Barton's 1767 THE DISAPPOINTMENT, the first American ballad opera written by an American for Americans, was premiered by Eastman School in a reconstruction by Samuel Adler at the Library of Congress in March 1976. Virgil Thomson's THE MOTHER OF US ALL was staged in 1996 to mark the 75th anniversary of women's suffrage in Rochester. Leonard Bernstein's CANDIDE was staged in 1998. Opera Theater of Rochester premiered Paul Stuart's Native American opera KILL BEAR COMES HOME on April 12, 1996, and his Christmas opera THE LITTLE THIEVES OF BETHLEHEM on December 7, 1997, Both were recorded and issued on CD. The Eastman-Dryden Orchestra, under the direction of Donald Hunsberger, has made a number of recording of highlights from the comic operas of Rudolf Friml, Victor Herbert and Sigmund Romberg.

Saratoga Springs: See Glen Falls for Lake George Opera Festival.

Scarsdale: Siegfried Landau's *The Sons of Aaron* premiered at Scarsdale Junior High School on February 28, 1959. Joyce Barthelson *Greenwich Village, 1910*, based on O Henry's story THE GIFT OF THE MAGI, was premiered in Scarsdale on December 20, 1968.

Schroon Lake: John Duke premiered three music theater works with librettos by Dorothy Duke at festivals at the Oscar Seagle Colony at Schroon Lake in the Adirondacks: the chamber opera *Captain Lovelock* on August 18, 1953; the chamber opera *The Sire de Maladroit* on August 15, 1958; and the operetta *A Yankee Pedlar* on August 17, 1962.

Suffern: Richard Owen's MARY DYER, based on transcripts of her trial and her letters, was premiered by Eastern Opera Company in Suffern on June 12, 1976.

Syracuse: The Wieting Opera House in Syracuse premiered two of America's most popular comic operas before they went to Broadway: Victor Herbert's NAUGHTY MARIETTA on October 24, 1910, and Rudolf Friml's THE FIREFLY on October 14, 1912. Both starred coloratura opera soprano Emma Trentini. The University of Syracuse has held several premieres including Carlisle Floyd's first opera *Slow Dusk* (May 2, 1949) while he was a student there, Franklin Morris's *The Postponement* (May 7, 1959), Lonnie Liggett's *The Hermits* (April 23, 1964) and Earl George's bicentennial double bill *Birthdays* (*Another Fourth of July* and *Pursuing Happiness*) on April 23, 1976. George Rochberg's monodrama PHAEDRA, based on Robert Lowell's version of Racine's play *Phèdre*, premiered in Syracuse on January 9, 1976. Syracuse Opera, founded in 1974, has hosted four American premieres: Frank DiGiacomo's BEAUTY AND THE BEAST, libretto by Emul P. Edmon, was premiered in 1974 and recorded in 1976. DiGiacomo's THE DYBBUK, based on the play by Saloman Ansky and Jewish legend, was performed on May 19, 1978. Joseph Israel's children's opera *Winnie the Pooh,* based on the A. A. Milne stories, was first performed on June 1, 1979, and reprised in October 1989. Ross Dabrusin's *The Night Harry Stopped Smoking*, libretto by John Davies, was performed on April 28, 1983. Michael Mautner's *Carazan: An Original Musical Fantasy*, libretto by Diane Bostick, was presented on May 17, 1988. Syracuse Opera has also performed Dominick Argento's A WATERBIRD TALK, George Gershwin's PORGY AND BESS, Victor Herbert's BABES IN TOYLAND, Gian Carlo Menotti's THE MEDIUM, Richard Rodgers' CAROUSEL and Julia Smith's Christmas opera *The Shepherdess and the Chimney Sweep.*

Troy: Victor Herbert's comic opera *The Idol's Eyes* premiered at Rand's Opera House in Troy on September 20, 1897, before going to Broadway

Wesbeth: Stanley Silverman's *Hotel for Criminals,* based on Louis Feuillade's silent films, was presented by the Music-Theater Performing Group at the Exchange Theater in Wesbeth in December 1974.

Westbury: Florence Du Page premiered three religious operas with librettos by Sister Jean at the Advent Tuller School in Westbury: *Trial Universelle* (May 17, 1963), *Whither* (May 15, 1964) and *New World for Nellie* (June 11, 1965).

White Plains: The Jewish Community Center in Westchester has hosted three Jewish-themed operas: Robert Strassburg's *Chelm* and Frederick Piket's *Isaac Levi,* both on December 11, 1955; and Lazar Weiner's THE GOLEM on January 13, 1957.

Woodstock: Three premieres were held at the Byrdville Theater: Ashley Vernon's *Cupid and Psyche* (July 6, 1956), Ezra Laderman's *Jacob and the Indians,* based on Stephen Vincent Benét's story (July 26, 1957), and Saul Honigman's *The Tickets* (July 11, 1958).

NEW YORK CITY   *American metropolis (1609–)*

New York City is one of the most important centers of American opera with hundreds of premieres and dozens of companies and opera sites. One of the first American operas, the patriotic *The Blockheads: or, Fortunate Contractor,* premiered in New York in 1782. Royall Tyler's *May Day in Town: or, New York in an Uproar,* premiered on May 18, 1787, and William Dunlap's *Darby's Return* on November 24, 1789. The most important study of early opera in the city is Julius Mattfeld's fascinating book *A Hundred Years of Grand Opera in New York 1825–1925, A Record of Performances.*

Among the many American operas using New York City as locale are Gian Carlo Menotti's THE SAINT OF BLEECKER STREET (possibly the only opera with a scene set in a New York subway station), George Antheil's TRANSATLANTIC, Kurt Weill's STREET SCENE, George Gershwin's BLUE MONDAY, the three composer trilogy CENTRAL PARK and Leonard Bernstein's WEST SIDE STORY.

New York City-born composers include Richard Adler, Bruce Adolphe, Hugh Aitken, George Frederick Bristow, Elliot Carter, Aaron Copland, John Corigliano Norman Dello Joio, George Gershwin, Bernard Herrmann, Andrew Imbrie, Leon Kirchner, Tod Machover, William Mayer, Steve Reich, Bernard Rogers, Jerry Ross, Gunther Schuller, William Schuman, Roger Sessions, Elie Siegmeister, Deems Taylor and Randall Thompson.

Most of the Broadway operas and comic operas by Victor Herbert, Sigmund Romberg, George Gershwin, Kurt Weill, et al were premiered in other cities in tryout runs before they opened on Broadway.

Academy of Music: The New York Academy of Music, New York's leading opera house in the years before the Met, introduced several Verdi operas to America and premiered two American operas: Charles Hopkin's operatic oratorio *Samuel* was presented on May 3, 1877, and Max Maretzek's' *Sleepy Hollow: or, The Headless Horseman,* based on the Washington Irving tale, on September 25, 1879.

Actor's Studio: William Bolcom's *Dynamite Tonight,* libretto by Arnold Weinstein, premiered at the Actor's Studio on December 21, 1963.

Adelphi Theatre: Kurt Weill's "American opera" STREET SCENE opened at the Adelphi Theater in New York on January 9, 1947, following its premiere at the Shubert Theatre in Philadelphia.

Alice Tully Hall: Alice Tully Hall in Lincoln Center is primarily a concert hall but it has also hosted operas. Ned Rorem's BERTHA was premiered there on November 25, 1973. Gian Carlo Menotti's dramatic cantata THE TRIAL OF THE GYPSY was premiered May 24, 1978. Martin Kalmanoff's ON THE HARMFULNESS OF TOBACCO was premiered by the Manhattan Opera Singers on March 22, 1979. John Moran's THE MANSON FAMILY, commissioned for the Serious Fun Festival, was premiered by Ridge Theater in 1990. Amy M. Beach's CABILDO was performed by the New York Concert Singers on May 13, 1995, and the performance issued on CD.

Alvin Theatre: Jerome Kern's MUSIC IN THE AIR opened at the Alvin Theater on November 8, 1932, following its premiere in Philadelphia. George Gershwin's PORGY AND BESS opened at the Alvin on October 10, 1935, following its premiere in Boston. Kurt Weill's LADY IN THE DARK opened at the Alvin January 21, 1941, following its premiere in Boston. Kurt Weill's THE FIREBRAND OF FLORENCE premiered at the Alvin on March 22, 1945.

Amato Opera Theater: Amato Opera Theatre, founded in 1948 by Anthony Amato, presents operas in a 107-seat theater in the Bowery. Most are European but it has premiered three American operas: George Wehner's *Three Days After* in 1965, Stelio Dubbiosi's *The Pied Piper* in 1965 and Martin Kalmanoff's EMPTY BOTTLES in 1991. Stephen Ives's documentary *Amato: A Love Affair with Opera* is a portrait of this remarkable theater and its founder.

Ambassador Theater: Sigmund Romberg's *Blossom Time* opened at the Ambassador Theater on December 29, 1921.

American Chamber Opera: American Chamber Opera held the stage premiere of Charles Wakefield Cadman's 1925 opera *The Garden of Mystery (*RAPPACCINI'S DAUGHTER) on February 16, 1966, at the Kate Murphy Theater in the garment district. It also staged Vittorio Giannini's radio opera BLENNERHASSETT.

American Opera Projects: American Opera Projects premiered Vivian Fine's THE MEMOIRS OF ULIANA ROONEY in 1994, Paula Kimper's PATIENCE AND SARAH in 1998, a revised version of Rusty Magee's *Flurry Tale,* libretto by Billy Aronson, in 1998 and Lenny Pickett's WELFARE: THE OPERA in 2004.

Broadway Theater: Victor Herbert's first comic opera *Prince Ananias* premiered at the Broadway on November 20, 1984. Met soprano Ernestine Schumann-Heinck starred in Julian Edwards'

Love's Lottery at the Broadway in 1904. John Philip Sousa's THE GLASS BLOWERS was performed at the theater as *The American Maid* in 1913. Walter Damrosch's *The Opera Cloak* premiered on November 3, 1942. Oscar Hammerstein's Bizet-based CARMEN JONES opened on December 2, 1943, following its premiere in Philadelphia. Duke Ellington's ballad opera BEGGAR'S HOLIDAY opened on December 26, 1946. Gian Carlo Menotti's Pulitzer Prize-winning THE SAINT OF BLEECKER STREET opened on December 27, 1954. Leonard Bernstein's CANDIDE was revived at the theater in 1974.

Bronx Opera: The Bronx Opera Company, founded in 1967 by Michael Spierman, staged Carlisle Floyd's SUSANNAH in 1992.

Brooklyn Academy of Music: The Brooklyn Academy of Music (BAM) is on the cutting edge of American opera. John Adams' THE DEATH OF KLINGHOFFER received its American premiere there on September 5, 1991, and his NIXON IN CHINA was staged there in 1999. Philip Glass's EINSTEIN ON THE BEACH was staged in 1984, HYDROGEN JUKEBOX in 1991, MONSTERS OF GRACE in 1998 and DRACULA in 1999. Meredith Monk's ATLAS was staged in 1993 following its Houston premiere. Tom Wait's THE BLACK RIDER had its American premiere on November 9, 1994. Robert Ashley's electronic opera NOW ELEANOR'S IDEA was presented in 1995. Steve Reich's video opera HINDENBURG was presented in 1998. Earlier operas premiered at BAM include Camillo's Bonsignore's *I miserabili* in 1925 and Rodolfo Martinelli's *Alone I Stand* in 1951.

Brooklyn Atheneum: Frederick Bechtel's *Alfred the Great* was premiered in concert format at the Brooklyn Atheneum on November 16, 1880.

Brooklyn College: Brooklyn College premieres include Jan Meyerowitz's *Godfather Death* (June 2, 1961); Thomas Pasatieri's *Padrevia,* based on a Boccaccio tale (November 18, 1967); and Eugene Zador's *The Scarlet Mill,* based on Molnar (October 26, 1968).

Brooklyn Lyceum: John M Loretz's *The Pearl of Bagdad* was premiered at the Brooklyn Lyceum in May 1872.

Brooklyn Museum: Rocco DiGiovanni's *Medea*, based on the Euripides play, premiered at the Museum February 12, 1955.

Carl Fischer Hall: Ned Rorem's A CHILDHOOD MIRACLE, based on a Hawthorne story, was premiered by Punch Opera at Carl Fischer Hall on May 10, 1955. Karl Newbern's *The Armour of Life* was premiered February 26, 1957, and Robert L Milano's *The Hired Hand* on March 23, 1959.

Carnegie Hall: Carnegie Hall, the most famous concert hall in America, has not only crowned the reputation of opera singers from Caruso to Callas but hosted a number of opera productions and premieres. They include: 1922 THE WHITE BIRD (Ernest Carter). 1925 135TH STREET (George Gershwin). 1925 THE GARDEN OF MYSTERY (C. W. Cadman). 1937 THE MARTYR (Harry Lawrence Freeman). 1940 DE ORGANIZER (James P. Johnson). 1944 *US Highball* (Harry Partch). 1949 *The Emperor's New Clothes* (Douglas Moore). 1955 *Hopitu* (Lois Albright). 1956 THE SOLDIER (Lehman Engel). 1960 INTRODUCTIONS AND GOODBYES (Lukas Foss). 1967 THE STONED GUEST (Peter Schickele). 1969 *The Broker's Opera* (George Mead). 1970 *The Fool* (Ray Crabtree). 1975 EVENTIDE (Joseph Fennimore); *Don't Call Me By My Right Name* (Fennimore). 1981 THREE SISTERS (Andrew Rudin); FOUR SAINTS IN THREE ACTS (Virgil Thomson). 1982 A LITTLE NIGHTMARE MUSIC (Peter Schickele). 2000 WHITE RAVEN (Philip Glass) US premiere; WHAT NEXT? (Elliot Carter) US premiere.

Casino Theater: Sigmund Romberg's THE BLUE PARADISE opened at the Casino Theater on August 5, 1915. Rudolf Friml's THE VAGABOND KING opened September 21, 1925. Sigmund

Romberg's THE DESERT SONG opened November 30, 1926, following its premiere in Wilmington.

Columbia University: Columbia University has been an important center for American opera for more than seventy years and had many notable premieres. Otto Luening, its opera director for many years, premiered forty operas during his tenure, including Gian Carlo Menotti's THE MEDIUM and Virgil Thomson's THE MOTHER OF US ALL. Columbia is also the home of the Pulitzer Prize which has been awarded to a number of operas. American operas premiered at the university, mostly at Brander Matthews Hall, include: 1941 PAUL BUNYAN (Benjamin Britten). 1944 *Pieces of Eight* (Bernard Wagenaar). 1945 *The Scarecrow* (Norman Lockwood). 1946 THE MEDIUM (Gian Carlo Menotti). 1947 THE MOTHER OF US ALL (Virgil Thomson). 1948 EVANGELINE (Otto Luening). 1949 DRUMLIN LEGEND (Ernst Bacon). 1950 THE BARRIER (Jan Meyerowitz). 1951 GIANTS IN THE EARTH (Douglas Moore). 1953 *Sweeny Agonistes* (Richard Winslow). 1954 HELLO OUT THERE (Jack Beeson); MALADY OF LOVE (Lehman Engel); THE CASK OF AMONTILLADO (Julia Perry). 1957 *Panfilo and Lauretta* (Carlos Chavez). 1958 GALLANTRY (Douglas Moore). 1966 MR. AND MRS. DISCOBBOLOS (Peter Westergaard). 1990 APOCALYPSE (Alice Shields).

CoOPERAtive: CoOPERAtive, a cooperative venture founded in 1995, presents opera twice a year at the Little Theater at the YMCA on West 63rd Street. Its productions have included Vittorio Giannini's BEAUTY AND THE BEAST and Henry Mollicone's THE FACE ON THE BARROOM FLOOR.

Crescent Theater: African American composer Harry Lawrence Freeman's *The Tryst* was premiered by the Freeman Operatic Duo at the Crescent Theater in May 1911.

Criterion Theater: Maurice Arnold-Strothotte's comic opera *The Merry Benedicts* premiered at the Criterion Theater in Brooklyn in 1894.

Cubiculo Theater: Premieres at the Cubiculo Theater include Norman Siegel's *Who Stole the Crown Jewels?* (1970), Tom Johnson's THE FOUR NOTE OPERA (1972) for an audience of fifteen friends, John H McDowell's *After the Ball* (1973), Paul Reif's *The Curse of Mauvais-Air* (1974) and Eric Salzman's STAUF (1976).

DiCapo Opera Theater: The intimate Di Capo Opera Theatre, founded in 1981, commissioned Deborah Drattell's LILITH and premiered it June 3, 1997. It has also presented Carlisle Floyd's SUSANNAH, Gian Carlo Menotti's THE SAINT OF BLEECKER STREET, Richard Wargo's A CHEKHOV TRILOGY and Kurt Weill's STREET SCENE.

Donnell Library Center: Vivian Fine's humorous *A Guide to the Life Expectancy of the Rose,* based on a gardening article, premiered at the Donnell Library Center on February 7, 1956.

Encompass Music Theatre: Encompass Music Theater, based in Brooklyn, premiered George Quincy's *Home and the River* on June 10, 1997.

52nd Street Theater: African American composer Harry Lawrence Freeman's VOODOO, the first American opera premiered on radio, was broadcast in a highlights version on WGBS in New York on May 20, 1928, and staged by the Negro Grand Opera Company at the 52nd Street Theater on September 10, 1928.

Finch College: After Dinner Opera has premiered three operas at Finch College: Mark Bucci's THE BOOR, based on the Chekhov story, and Meyer Kupferman's IN A GARDEN, based on the play by Gertrude Stein, were both staged on December 29, 1949. Martin Kalmanoff's OPERA, OPERA, libretto by William Saroyan, was presented on February 26, 1956.

Fordham University: Russell Currie's THE CASK OF AMONTIL-

LADO, based on the Poe story, was premiered at Fordham University on April 3, 1982.

44th Street Theater: George Gershwin and Herbert Stothart's SONG OF THE FLAME opened at the 44th Street Theater on December 30, 1925, following its premiere in Wilmington, Delaware.

46th Street Theater: Kurt Weill's "vaudeville" LOVE LIFE opened at the 46th Street Theater on October 7, 1948, following its premiere at the Shubert Theater in Boston.

Globe Theater: George Gershwin's BLUE MONDAY was premiered at the Globe Theater on August 28, 1922, as a part of the *George White Scandals of 1922*. Jerome Kern's light opera THE CAT AND THE FIDDLE opened at the Globe on October 15, 1931. Ivan Caryll's musicals *Chin Chin* and *Jack O'Lantern* premiered at the Globe in 1914 and 1917.

Golden Fleece: Golden Fleece, the Composer's Chamber Theatre, has produced and premiered many American chamber operas. They include Seymour Barab's NOT A SPANISH KISS (1981), Lor Crane's *The Pearl* (1984 premiere), Myron Fink's *The Island of Tomorrow* and *The Trojan Women* (both 1988), Thomas Flanagan's *I Rise in Flame, Cried the Phoenix* (1980 premiere), Ned Rorem's BERTHA, Judith Shatin's *Carreño* (1990 premiere) and Alice Shields' *Wraecca* (1989 premiere).

Grand Street Playhouse: Aaron Copland's THE SECOND HURRICANE, a "play opera" for high school students, was premiered by the Music School of the Henry Street Settlement at the Grand Street Playhouse on April 21, 1937, with Orson Welles directing.

Guggenheim Museum: Jonathan Sheffer's BLOOD ON THE DINING ROOM FLOOR, based on Gertrude Stein's detective story, was first seen in excerpt form at the Lewis Theatre in the Guggenheim Museum on April 5, 2000. It was given its full premiere at the WPA Theater at the Peter Norton Space on April 16.

Haverley's Fourteenth Street Theater: Dudley Buck's DESERET, the most controversial American opera of the 19th century, premiered at Haverley's Fourteenth Street Theater on October 11, 1880. It was about Brigham Young and was condemned by critics for immoral sensationalism.

Hunter College: Hunter College has hosted a number of premieres. They include Emile Anders' *King Harald* (January 7, 1948), Baldwin Bergerson's *Far Harbour* (January 30, 1948), Paul Berl's *Judgement Day* (May 28, 1951), Nicolai Berezovsky's *Babar the Elephant*, based on the children's tale (February 21, 1953), Ashley Vernon's *The Barber of New York* (May 26, 1953), Boris Koutzen's *The Fatal Oath* based on Balzac's LA GRANDE BRETÈCHE (May 25, 1955), George Kleinsinger's *The Tree That Found Christmas* based on a story by Christopher Morley (December 17, 1955) and Mary Johnson's THE THIRTEEN CLOCKS based on the James Thurber fable (March 18, 1958).

Imperial Theatre: Rudolf Friml's ROSE MARIE opened at the Imperial Theater September 2, 1924, following its premiere in Atlantic City. Sigmund Romberg's THE NEW MOON opened on September 19, 1928, after its premiere in Philadelphia and revised staging in Cleveland. Kurt Weill's ONE TOUCH OF VENUS opened on October 7, 1943, following its premiere in Boston. Robert Wright and George Forrest's SONG OF NORWAY opened August 21, 1944, following presentations in San Francisco and Los Angeles. Irving Berlin's ANNIE GET YOUR GUN opened on May 16, 1946, following its premiere in New Haven. Frank Loesser's THE MOST HAPPY FELLA opened on May 3, 1956, following its premiere in Boston. Jerry Bock's FIDDLER ON THE ROOF opened on September 22, 1964.

James Street Theater: Royall Tyler's two-act comic opera *May Day in Town: or, New York in an Uproar* was premiered by the Old American Company on May 18, 1787.

John Street Theater: The John Street Theater, built by impresario David Douglas in 1767, hosted a number of early American opera premieres. James Hewitt's TAMMANY, OR THE INDIAN CHIEF, on March 3, 1794; Hewitt's *The Patriot, or Liberty Asserted* on June 5, 1794; Benjamin Carr's THE ARCHERS OR THE MOUNTAINEERS OF SWITZERLAND on April 18, 1796; Victor Pelissier's *Edwin and Angelina* on December 19, 1796; Benjamin Carr's *Bourville Castle, or The Gallic Orphans* on January 16, 1797; and Pelissier's *The Fourth of July, or The Temple of American Independence* on July 4, 1799

Jolson Theatre: Sigmund Romberg's operetta THE STUDENT PRINCE opened at the Jolson Theater on December 2, 1924, following its premiere in Atlantic City.

Juilliard School of Music: The Juilliard School, which has trained many of America's finest composers and singers, has also hosted a number of notable American opera premieres. 1931 Louis Gruenberg's JACK AND THE BEANSTALK. 1934 George Antheil's HELEN RETIRES. 1935 Robert Russell Bennett's MARIA MALIBRAN. 1937 Albert Stoessel's GARRICK. 1938 Beryl Rubenstein's *The Sleeping Princess*. 1942 Joseph Wood's *The Mother*. 1950 Hall Overton's *The Enchanted Pear Tree*. 1956 W Bergsma's THE WIFE OF MARTIN GUERRE; Robert Ward's PANTALOON. 1957 Jack Beeson's THE SWEET BYE AND BYE. 1962 Vittorio Giannini's *Rehearsal Call*; Gordon Richmond's *The Wild Beasts*. 1966 Thomas Pasatieri's LA DIVINA. 1971 Alan Leichtling's *A White Butterfly*; Harold Farberman's THE LOSERS; Hall Overton's *Huckleberry Finn*. 1972 Virgil Thomson's LORD BYRON. 1976 H. Weisgall's JENNY OR THE HUNDRED KNIGHTS. 1980 Edward Barnes' *Feathertop*. 1989 Milton Babbitt's *Fabulous Voyage*. 1996 Todd Machover's BRAIN OPERA. 2002 Stephen Paulus' HELOISE AND ABELARD. Other important productions include Paul Hindemith's THE LONG CHRISTMAS DINNER (American premiere) in 1963, Samuel Barber's ANTHONY AND CLEOPATRA (revised version) in 1975, Gian Carlo Menotti's THE HERO in 1980, Roger Sessions' MONTEZUMA in 1982, William Schuman's A QUESTION OF TASTE in 1990, Samuel Barber's VANESSA in 1991 and Joel Feigin's MYSTERIES OF ELEUSIS in 1994.

Knickerbocker Theater: Victor Herbert's comic opera MLLE. MODISTE opened at the Knickerbocker Theater on December 25, 1905, following its premiere in Trenton. Herbert's THE RED MILL opened at the Knickerbocker on September 24, 1906, after its premiere in Buffalo.

Lafayette Theater: African American composer Harry Lawrence Freeman's *Vendetta* was premiered by the Negro Grand Opera Company at the Lafayette Theater on November 12, 1923.

Lunt-Fontanne Theater: Richard Rodgers' THE SOUND OF MUSIC opened at the Lunt-Fontanne Theater on November 16, 1959, following its premiere in New Haven.

Lyric Theater: Rudolf Friml's THE FIREFLY opened at the Lyric Theater on December 2, 1912, following its premiere at the Wieting Opera House in Syracuse.

Majestic Theater (Columbus Circle): Victor Herbert's BABES IN TOYLAND opened at the Majestic Theater on October 13, 1903, following its premiere at the Grand Opera House in Chicago.

Majestic Theater (West 44th Street): Richard Rodgers's CAROUSEL opened at the Majestic Theater on April 19, 1945, following its premiere in New Haven. Rodgers' SOUTH PACIFIC opened at the Majestic on April 7, 1949, following its premiere in New Haven. Frederick Loewe's CAMELOT opened at the Majestic on December 3, 1960, following tryouts in Toronto and Boston.

Manhattan Opera House: Kurt Weill's pageant opera THE ETERNAL ROAD, libretto by Ludwig Lewisohn based on Franz

Werfel's play, premiered at the Manhattan Opera House on January 4, 1937.

Manhattan School of Music: The Manhattan School of Music is an important venue for modern opera. Marc Blitzstein's THE HARPIES was premiered there in 1953 and Seymour Barab's *The Maladroit Door* in 1959. Nicolas Flagello taught at the school from 1950 to 1970 and premiered three of his operas there: *The Sisters* in 1961, THE JUDGMENT OF ST. FRANCIS IN 1966 and THE PIPER OF HAMELIN IN 1970 (recorded in 1999). It's many other productions include John Philip Sousa's EL CAPITAN (1965), Charles Wuorinen's THE W. OF BABYLON (1975/premiere), Martin Kalmanoff's *Sganerelle* (1977/premiere), Meyer Kupferman's *Prometheus* (1978/premiere), Richard Owen's TOM SAWYER (1989/premiere), Ronald Perera's THE YELLOW WALLPAPER (1992), Ned Rorem's MISS JULIE (1994/CD), Hugo Weisgall's SIX CHARACTERS IN SEARCH OF AN AUTHOR (1996), Dominick Argento's POSTCARD FROM MOROCCO (1997), Daniel Catán's RAPPACCINI'S DAUGHTER (1997/CD), Leonard Bernstein's TROUBLE IN TAHITI (1998/CD), William Mayer's A DEATH IN THE FAMILY (1999/CD) and Scott Eyerly's THE HOUSE OF THE SEVEN GABLES (2000/premiere/CD).

Mannes College of Music: A number of modern opera composers studied at Mannes College and several operas were premiered there. They include Ned Rorem's *The Robbers* based on Chaucer's *The Pardoner's Tale* (April 14, 1958), Menachem Zur's *The Affairs* (1970), Jan Bach's THE SYSTEM based on an Edgar Allan Poe story (March 5, 1974) and Frank Stewart's *To Let the Captives Go* (March 5, 1974).

Mark Hellinger Theater: Frederick Loewe's American operetta MY FAIR LADY opened at the Mark Hellinger Theater on March 15, 1956, following its premiere in New Haven.

Martin Beck Theater: Douglas Moore's THE DEVIL AND DANIEL WEBSTER was premiered by American Lyric Theater at the Martin Beck Theater on May 18, 1939. Vernon Duke's *Cabin in the Sky* opened at the theater on October 25, 1940, and Leonard Bernstein's CANDIDE opened on December 1, 1956, following its Boston premiere. Gian Carlo Menotti's MARIA GOLOVIN had its American premiere at the theater on November 5, 1958.

Mecca Auditorium: Marc Blitzstein's Broadway opera NO FOR AN ANSWER, the agitprop sequel to THE CRADLE WILL ROCK, premiered at the Mecca Auditorium on January 5, 1941. Jacob Weinberg's *The Pioneers of Israel* was presented at the Mecca on November 25, 1934.

Metropolitan Opera: The Metropolitan Opera has been America's best-known opera house for over a hundred years and remains one of the best in the world. It is also of great importance in the history of American opera as it was the first major company to present American operas on a continuing basis. Giulio Gatti-Casazza, who became general manager in 1908, initiated the policy in 1910 with the presentation of Frederick Converse's THE PIPE OF DESIRE. American opera premieres at the Met include: 1912 Horatio Parker's MONA. 1913 Walter Damrosch's CYRANO DE BERGERAC. 1914 Victor Herbert's MADELEINE. 1917 Reginald De Koven's THE CANTERBURY TALES. 1918 Charles W. Cadman's SHANEWIS. 1919 Joseph Breil's THE LEGEND; John Adam Hugo's THE TEMPLE DANCER. 1921 Henry Hadley's CLEOPATRA'S NIGHT. 1927 Deems Taylor's THE KING'S HENCHMAN. 1931 Deems Taylor's PETER IBBETSON. 1933 Louis Gruenberg's THE EMPEROR JONES. 1934 Howard Hanson's MERRY MOUNT. 1935 John L Seymour's IN THE PASHA'S GARDEN. 1937 W. Damrosch's THE MAN WITHOUT A COUNTRY. 1942 Gian Carlo Menotti's THE ISLAND GOD. 1947 Bernard Rogers' THE WARRIOR. 1958 Samuel Barber's VANESSA. 1966 Samuel Barber's ANTONY AND CLEOPATRA. 1967

Marvin Levy's MOURNING BECOMES ELECTRA. 1991 John Corigliano's THE GHOSTS OF VERSAILLES. 1992 Philip Glass's THE VOYAGE. 1999 John Harbison's THE GREAT GATSBY. American operas presented at the Met, but not premiered there, include George Gershwin's PORGY AND BESS, Victor Herbert's NATOMA and Gian Carlo Menotti's AMELIA GOES TO THE BALL and THE LAST SAVAGE.

Metropolitan Opera Studio: The Metropolitan Opera Studio in Lincoln Center has premiered several chamber operas including Walter Kaufmann's *Sganerelle* in 1961, Sam Morgenstern's *The Big Black Box* in 1968, Don Gillis's *The Legend of Star Valley Junction* in 1969, Sam Morgenstern's *Haircut* in 1969, Alvin Carmines' *The Duel* in 1974 and Joseph Fennimore's *Apache Dance* in 1975

Museum of Modern Art: In addition to being a major art museum and influential film archive and theater, MOMA has also contributed to opera. Its premieres include Paul Bowles' THE WIND REMAINS in 1943 with Leonard Bernstein conducting, Gail Kubik's "opera piccolo" *Boston Baked Beans* in 1952 and Benjamin Lees' *The Gilded Cage* in 1964.

Music Box Theater: Kurt Weill's LOST IN THE STARS opened at the Music Box Theater on October 30, 1949.

Music-Theatre Group: Music-Theatre Group, which presents productions at various New York City venues, including the Cooper Union and the Actors Studio Free Theater, premiered Deirdre Murray's *Running Man*, libretto by Cornelius Easy, in 1998. It has also staged Tan Dun's MARCO POLO.

New Amsterdam Theatre: Victor Herbert's comic opera SWEETHEARTS opened at the New Amsterdam Theater on September 8, 1913, following its premiere in Baltimore.

New Century Theater: Sigmund Romberg's *Princess Flavia* opened at the Century Theater on November 2, 1925. Romberg's vintage New York-based operetta UP IN CENTRAL PARK opened at the Theatre on January 27, 1945. Cole Porter's KISS ME KATE opened at the theater on December 30, 1948, after its Philadelphia premiere.

New National Theater: Charles E. Horn's AHMED AL KAMEL, the first American opera based on a work of American literature (Washington Irving's *Tales of the Alhambra*), premiered at the New National Theater October 12, 1840.

New School for Social Research: Domenick Argento's *Sicilian Limes* was premiered at the New School in October 1954. Ned Rorem's *The Last Days* was premiered there on May 22, 1967.

New York City Opera: The New York City Opera, one of the main showcases for American opera, was started as a lower priced alternative to the Met in 1944 and was often more adventurous than its rival. Beverly Sills, its resident diva, was helped on her way to stardom by starring in Douglas Moore's THE BALLAD OF BABY DOE in 1958. The company has premiered many major American operas and popularized many others, most notably Carlisle Floyd's SUSANNAH, Leonard Bernstein's TROUBLE IN TAHITI, Jerome Kern's SHOW BOAT (first American operetta to enter the opera house repertory) and *The Ballad of Baby Doe*. Its American premieres include: 1949 William Grant Still's TROUBLED ISLAND. 1951 David Tamkin's THE DYBBUK. 1954 Aaron Copland's THE TENDER LAND. 1958 Robert Kurka's THE GOOD SOLDIER SCHWEIK. 1959 Hugo Weisgall's SIX CHARACTERS IN SEARCH OF AN AUTHOR; Norman Dello Joio's THE TRIUMPH OF ST. JOAN. 1961 Douglas Moore's THE WINGS OF THE DOVE; Robert Ward's THE CRUCIBLE. 1962 Abraham Ellstein's THE GOLEM; Carlisle Floyd's THE PASSION OF JONATHAN WADE. 1963 Jerome Morass's GENTLEMEN, BE SEATED! 1964 Lee Hoiby's NATALIA PETRONOVNA. 1965 Jack Beeson's LIZZIE BORDEN; Ned Rorem's MISS JULIE. 1967 Vittorio Giannini's THE SERVANT OF

TWO MASTERS. 1968 Hugo Weisgall's NINE RIVERS FROM JORDAN. 1971 Gian Carlo Menotti's THE MOST IMPORTANT MAN. 1977 Leon Kirchner's LILY. 1979 Domenick Argento's MISS HAVISHAM'S FIRE. 1980 Jan Bach's THE STUDENT FROM SALAMANCA; Thomas Pasatieri's BEFORE BREAKFAST; Stanley Silverman's MADAME ADARE. 1986 Anthony Davis's X, THE LIFE AND TIMES OF MALCOLM X. 1988 Jay Reise's RASPUTIN. 1993 Ezra Laderman's MARILYN; Lukas Foss's GRIFFELKIN (stage version); Hugo Weisgall's ESTHER. 2001 Deborah Dratell's LILITH. Other American operas and operettas whose reputations have been enhanced by NYCO productions: Mark Adamo's LITTLE WOMEN, Dominick Argento's CASANOVA'S HOMECOMING, Leonard Bernstein's CANDIDE and WONDERFUL TOWN, Marc Blitzstein's THE CRADLE WILL ROCK and REGINA, Benjamin Britten's PAUL BUNYAN, Drattell/Torke/Beaser's three-opera CENTRAL PARK, Tan Dun's MARCO POLO, Carlisle Floyd's OF MICE AND MEN, George Gershwin's PORGY AND BESS, Philip Glass's AKHNATEN and SATYAGRAHA, Jake Heggie's DEAD MAN WALKING, Victor Herbert's NAUGHTY MARIETTA, Marvin David Levy's MOURNING BECOMES ELECTRA, Frank Loesser's THE MOST HAPPY FELLA, Gian Carlo Menotti's AMAHL AND THE NIGHT VISITORS (first professional stage performance), THE CONSUL, MARIA GOLOVIN, THE MEDIUM, THE OLD MAID AND THE THIEF and THE SAINT OF BLEECKER STREEt, Douglas Moore's CARRY NATION, Tobias Picker's EMMELINE, Richard Rodger's CINDERELLA, THE SOUND OF MUSIC and SOUTH PACIFIC, Sigmund Romberg's THE DESERT SONG and THE STUDENT PRINCE, Stephen Sondheim's A LITTLE NIGHT MUSIC and SWEENEY TODD, John Philip Sousa's THE GLASSBLOWERS, Tan Dun's MARCO POLO, Virgil Thomson's THE MOTHER OF US ALL, Stewart Wallace's HARVEY MILK, Kurt Weill's STREET SCENE, Meredith Willson's THE MUSIC MAN and Wright and Forrest's KISMET. Many of NYCO's American productions have been televised. The first was Menotti's *The Old Maid and the Thief* which was shown on NBC TV on March 16, 1949. The first to be telecast by NET was Jack Beeson's *Lizzie Borden* in 1967. The first televised opera in the *Live from Lincoln Center* series was the New York City Opera production of Douglas Moore's *The Ballad of Baby Doe* in May 1976. NYCO began a program in 1999 to promote new American operas called "Showcasing American Composers." The series has included new work by Mark Adamo, Victoria Bond, Anton Coppola, John Duffy, Manley Romero, Sheila Silver and Charles Wuorinen.

New York Grand Opera: New York Grand Opera, which presents fully-staged operas in Central Park at no charge, staged Gian Carlo Menotti's THE SAINT OF BLEECKER STREET in 1961.

New York Lyric Opera: Richard Owen's ABIGAIL ADAMS, based on her letters, was premiered by New York Lyric Opera in 1987 as part of the Bicentennial celebrations. Thomas Pasatieri's WASHINGTON SQUARE was staged in 1977 and Ned Rorem's MISS JULIE was staged and recorded in 1989.

New York Public Library for the Performing Arts: The New York Public Library for the Performing Arts at Lincoln Center (NYPL) has a division for music hosting the Rodgers and Hammerstein Archives of Recorded Sound. It's large collection of opera recordings and videos, many unavailable elsewhere, includes radio broadcasts of the Metropolitan Opera and Bell Telephone Hour from the 1930s to the present day.

New York Theater: William Dunlap's *Darby's Return* was premiered by the Old American Company at the New York Theater on November 24, 1789. Victor Herbert's NAUGHTY MARIETTA opened at the New York Theater on November 7, 1910, following its premiere at the Wieting Opera House in Syracuse.

New York University: New York University has hosted several premieres: Deem Taylor's *The Dragon,* based on a Lady Gregory play, in 1958; Thomas Wagner's *The Crocodile,* based on a Dostoyevsky story, in 1963; Joel Mandelbaum's microtonal THE DYBBUK, based on the Ansky play, in 1972; Vincent Zito's *Sganarelle,* based on the play by Molière. in 1972; and Timothy Lloyd's *The Witch Boy,* based on Howard Richardson's play *Dark of the Moon,* in 1991.

Niblo's Gardens: George Frederick Bristow's RIP VAN WINKLE, the first American grand opera with an American subject, was premiered by the Pyne-Harrison opera company at Niblo's Gardens on September 27, 1855. Edward E. Rice's EVANGELINE, an opéra-bouffe burlesque of Longfellow's poem, opened in Niblo's Gardens on July 27, 1874.

92nd Street Y: The venerable 92nd Street YMCA, one of New York's cutting edge cultural centers, has premiered a remarkable number of operas at its Kaufmann Concert Hall. They include: 1951 *The Wise and the Foolish* (Kurt List). 1953 *Sweet Betsy from Pike* (Mark Bucci); THE DRESS (Mark Bucci). 1954 *Barbara Allen* (David Broekman. 1957 *Stoba Komachi* (Marvin David Levy). 1958 *The Pet Shop* (Vittorio Rieti); ESCORIAL—(Marvin Levy). 1959 THE GLITTERING GATE (Peggy Glanville-Hicks); RAPUNZEL (Lou Harrison). 1960 *A Goat in Chelm* (Abraham Binder); *Stacked Deck* (Richard Maxfield); *Shilappadikaram* (Harold Schramm). 1969 *Street Scene* (Joel Chadabe). 1980 AND DAVID WEPT (Ezra Laderman). 1981 THE GOLEM (Lazar Weiner)—reprise. 1982 *Mikhoels the Wise* (Bruce Adolphe). 1983 *The False Messiah* (Bruce Adolphe). 1985 ANGEL LEVINE (Ellie Siegmeister). 1985 *The Lady of the Lake* (Ellie Siegmeister).

Opera Company of Brooklyn: Opera Company of Brooklyn has presented Aaron Copland's THE TENDER LAND.

Opera Ebony: Opera Ebony, America's leading opera company for African American artists, was founded by Benjamin Matthews, Wayne Sanders and Sister Mary Elise in New York in 1973. Its projects have included Dorothy Rudd Moore's FREDERICK DOUGLASS, commissioned by Opera Ebony and staged in 1985; Valerie Capers' *Sojourner Truth,* staged in 1986; Noa Ain's THE OUTCAST, premiered in 1990; Lena McLin's *Oh Freedom* and Benjamin Matthews' *Journin.'* It has also staged Carlisle Floyd's SUSANNAH.

Opera Ensemble of New York: The Opera Ensemble of New York, founded on a shoestring in 1978, had its greatest success with a production of Virgil Thomson FOUR SAINTS IN THREE ACTS in 1986. It premiered Hugo Weisgall's *Will You Marry Me?* on October 5, 1988, and it has also staged Marc Blitzstein's REGINA. It presented operas at the Lillie Blake Elementary School on 81st Street until it closed in 1990.

Operaworks: Operaworks presents opera in English at the Raw Space Theater on West 43rd Street. It's productions have included Douglas Moore's THE BALLAD OF BABY DOE and Thomas Pasatieri's THE SEAGULL.

Park Theater: The Park Theater, which opened in 1798 and became known for introducing classic European operas to America, also premiered American operas. James Hewitt premiered five of his operas there: *The Mysterious Marriage* (1799), *The Wild Goose Chase* (1800), *The Spanish Castle* (1800), Robin Hood (1800) and *The Cottagers* (1801). Victor Pelissier premiered four: *Sterne's Maria* (1799), *Fourth of July* (1799), *The Good Neighbor* (1893) and *The Wife of Two Husbands* (1804). Charles E. Horn premiered three: *Dido* (1828), *Nadir and Zuleika* (1832) and *The Maid of Saxony* (1842). Also premiered were F. H. F. Berkeley's *Rokeby* in 1830, John Jones' *The Enchanted Horse* in 1844 and Henry Hadley's *Bianca* in 1918.

Piccolo Teatro dell'Opera: Il Piccolo Teatro dell'Opera, based in Brooklyn, presents operas in various venues. Its productions have included Gian Carlo Menotti's AMAHL AND THE NIGHT VISITORS.

St. James Theatre: Richard Rodgers' OKLAHOMA opened at the St. James Theater on March 31, 1943, following its premiere in New Haven. Rodgers' THE KING AND I opened at the St. James Theatre in New York on March 29, 1951, after its premiere in New Haven.

Shubert Theater: Sigmund Romberg' MAYTIME opened at the Shubert Theater on August 16, 1917, following its premiere in Stamford, Connecticut. Victor Herbert's SWEETHEARTS was revived at the Shubert in 1947. Stephen Sondheim's operetta A LITTLE NIGHT MUSIC opened on February 25, 1973,

Standard Theatre: Reginald De Koven's comic opera ROBIN HOOD opened at the Standard Theater on September 22, 1891, following its premiere at the Chicago Opera House

Venice Theater: Marc Blitzstein's THE CRADLE WILL ROCK premiered at the Venice Theater on June 16, 1937, in one of the most exciting premieres in New York theatrical history. Orson Welles led the cast and audience to the Venice after the Maxine Elliott Theater was closed by Federal officials.

Wallack's Theatre: Victor Herbert's THE FORTUNE TELLER opened at Wallack's Theater on September 26, 1998, following its premiere at the Grand Opera House in Toronto.

Washington Square Theater: Mitch Leigh's *Man of La Mancha* opened at ANTA's Washington Square Theater on November 22, 1965, after being previewed at the Goodspeed Opera House in Connecticut.

Winter Garden: Leonard Bernstein's musical WONDERFUL TOWN opened at the Winter Garden on February 25, 1953. Bernstein's WEST SIDE STORY opened at the Winter Garden on September 26, 1957, following its premiere in Washington.

Ziegfeld Theatre: Jerome Kern's SHOW BOAT opened at the Ziegfeld Theater on December 27, 1927, following its Washington premiere. Victor Herbert's THE RED MILL was successfully revived at the Ziegfeld in 1945. Frederick Loewe's BRIGADOON opened on March 13, 1947, following its premiere in New Haven. George Gershwin's PORGY AND BESS, starring Leontyne Price as Bess, was revived at the Ziegfeld on March 10, 1953. Robert Wright and George Forrest's KISMET opened December 3, 1953, following its premiere in Los Angeles.

NEWAY, PATRICIA *American soprano (1919–)*

Patricia Neway created major roles in eleven American operas. She played Magda in the premiere of Gian Carlo Menotti's THE CONSUL (1950) in Philadelphia, Leah in David Tamkin's THE DYBBUK (1951) at New York City Opera, the Old Woman in Rafael De Banfield's LORD BYRON'S LOVE LETTER (1955) in New Orleans, Miriam in Hoiby's THE SCARF (1958) at the Spoleto Festival, the Mother in Menotti's MARIA GOLOVIN (1958) at the Brussels World Fair, Sarah in Ezra Laderman's SARAH (1958) on CBS Television, the Mother in Hugo Weisgall's SIX CHARACTERS IN SEARCH OF AN AUTHOR (1959) at New York City Opera, Geraldine in Samuel Barber's A HAND OF BRIDGE (1959) at the Spoleto Festival, Martha in Philip Bezanson's GOLDEN CHILD (1960) on NBC Television, the Woman in John Strauss's THE ACCUSED (1961) on CBS Television and Molly Sinclair in Carlisle Floyd's THE SOJOURNER AND MOLLIE SINCLAIR (1963) in North Carolina. She had a long association with Menotti and sang in or directed productions of AMAHL AND THE NIGHT VISITORS, THE DEATH OF THE BISHOP OF BRINDISI, THE OLD MAID AND THE THIEF and THE TELEPHONE. She appeared in many other American music theater works, including singing Nettie in a 1967 television version of Richard Rodgers' CAROUSEL. Neway, who was born in Brooklyn, made her debut in 1946 and joined New York City Opera in 1948.

"NEWS HAS A KIND OF MYSTERY" *Tenor aria: Nixon in China (1987). Words: Alice Goodman. Music: John Adams.*

The spectacle of President Nixon and Chairman Mao exchanging arias in John Adams' NIXON IN CHINA was one of the best things that happened to modern American opera and helped change ideas about opera subject matter. Nixon's innocent aria "News has a kind of mystery" is especially memorable. *Nixon in China*, libretto by Alice Goodman, which originated what became known as the "CNN opera," revolves around President Nixon's 1972 visit to China and meeting with Chairman Mao. It premiered at the Houston Opera, was televised and is on CD. James Maddalena as Nixon introduced the aria and has continued to perform it in new productions.

NICHOLAS AND ALEXANDRA *2003 opera by Drattell*

Class struggle in Russia in the early 20th century leads to violent revolution and the overthrow of Czar Nicholas and his wife Alexandra. Deborah Drattell's two-and-one-half hour historical opera *Nicholas and Alexandra*, libretto by Nicholas von Hoffman, was premiered by Los Angeles Opera on September 14, 2003. It begins and ends with the imperial family in prison in 1918 just before they are to be killed. Rodney Gilfry was Nicholas, Nancy Gustafson was Alexandra, Plácido Domingo was the religious mystic Rasputin and Jessica Rivera was daughter Anastasia. Anne Bogart staged the opera and Mstislav Rostropovich conducted the Los Angeles Opera Orchestra. Drattell wrote music in a Russian liturgical style for part of the opera.

2003 Los Angeles Opera. Rodney Gilfry is Nicholas, Nancy Gustafson is Alexandra and Plácido Domingo is Rasputin in the premiere production of *Nicholas and Alexandra* taped at Los Angeles Opera on September 14, 2003. Mstislav Rostropovich conducts the Los Angeles Opera Orchestra. Brian Large directed the video with Moshe Barkat of Modern VideoFilm as producer. Los Angeles Opera DVD.

"NICKEL UNDER THE FOOT" *Soprano aria: The Cradle Will Rock (1937). Words and music: Marc Blitzstein.*

"Nickel Under the Foot" is the most popular left-wing aria in American opera. Moll, a prostitute at a night court, sings of her joy of finding a nickel when she had no money for food. "Mister, you don't know what it felt like thinking that was a nickel under my foot." She condemns those that condemn her saying it's easy to be moralistic when you have plenty to eat. The verbal and musical style used by Marc Blitzstein in his opera *The Cradle Will Rock* is similar to that used by Bertolt Brecht and Kurt Weill in *The Three Penny Opera* and Brecht encouraged Blitzstein to compose the opera after hearing "Nickel." Olive Stanton, who introduced "Nickel," was the heroine of the tumultuous censored premiere where the actors were forbidden to perform on stage by their union. She was the first to sing from her seat in the auditorium and got the show off to a magnificent start. She is heard on the 1938 original cast album, the first complete recording ever made of a Broadway musical show. Tammy Grimes sings it on a 1960 New York City Opera recording, Lauri Peters on a 1964 Theater Four recording, Patti LuPone on a 1985 Old Vic recording in London, Karen Hovik on a 1990 album of Blitzstein music, Sandra Terry on a

1994 Blank Theater recording in Los Angeles and Emily Watson in the 1999 film *Cradle Will Rock*.

NICOLE AND THE TRIAL OF THE CENTURY *1999 opera by Newman*

Football star O. J. Simpson meets and marries Nicole Brown but their marriage has many problems. In 1995 he is tried for her murder and acquitted after a controversial trial. Anthony Newman's opera *Nicole and the Trial of the Century*, libretto by Raoul Cansino and the composer, was completed in 1999. Newman says: "The work is dedicated to the memory of Nicole Brown Simpson, and written as a statement against the spousal abuse of women. From the mountain of trial transcripts, as well as books and articles written about Nicole and O. J. Simpson, Raoul Cansino and I wrote a libretto in two acts: the first tragic, the second comic. The songs are introduced by a speaker/reciter, accompanied by timpani, much in the manner of Stravinsky's *Oedipus Rex*." One critic wrote: "Listening to Kato the Dog sing a florid aria about how he witnessed Mona's murder but can't speak (because he is a dog) is so outrageous that it can't but amuse. Skillful, postmodern parody."

1999 Musica Antiqua. A chamber version of the work with the trial scene trimmed to accommodate a single CD. Melissa Fathman, Malinda Haslett and Susan Lewis play Nicole Brown Simpson, Joel Frederickson and Paul Houghtalin play O. J. Simpson, Mark Heller is Kato the Dog and Robert Kardarshian, Davis Ossenfort is the Director, Ronald Goldman and Dennis Fung, Amy Butler is Rosa Lopez and Connie Chung, Stephen Tharp is Barry Sheck and the Commentator and Lee Winston is the Speaker. Anthony and Mary Jane Newman conduct Musica Antiqua New York. Albany CD.

NIELSEN, ALICE *American soprano (1876–1943)*

Alice Nielson began her career with the light opera troupe the Bostonians singing American comic operas before going on to grand opera fame singing Mimi opposite Enrico Caruso. She played Maid Marian in Reginald De Koven's ROBIN HOOD, though she did not create the role, but she did create the role of Yvonne in Victor Herbert's 1897 THE SERENADE. Herbert was impressed and composed two comic opera especially for her, THE FORTUNE TELLER in 1898, in which she created the double role of Musette/Irma, and *The Singing Girl* in 1899. She recorded her *Fortune Teller* hit, "Always Do as People Say You Should," for Berliner. In 1911 she recorded "Chonita's Prayer" from Frederick Converse's opera THE SACRIFICE for a Columbia 78. Her last Broadway musical was Rudolf Friml's *Kitty Darlin'* in 1917.

NIGHT OF THE MOONSPELL *1976 opera by Siegmeister*

Shakespeare's *A Midsummer Night's Dream* is retold as if set in the bayou country of Louisiana at the turn of the 20th century during Carnival time. Shakespeare's nobles are transmuted into plantation owners, the rustics are Cajun workmen and the King and Queen are African Americans ruling over Mardi Gras. The narrative remains more or less the same with runaway lovers getting mixed up while the rustic members of the French Opera, Choral and Pastry Society try to stage *Pyramus and Thisbe*. Elie Siegmeister's three-act opera *Night of the Moonspell*, libretto by Edward Mabley based on Shakespeare's play, was premiered by the Shreveport Symphony Society in Shreveport, Louisiana, on November 14, 1976. Elizabeth Kirkpatrick played Margaret (Hermia in the Shakespeare play), Forrest Lorey was Anthony (Lysander), Mary Beth Armes was Holly (Helena), David Griffith was David (Demetrius), Horace English was the Colonel (Theseus), Nita Renshaw was Josephine (Hippolyte), Edward Pearson was the Mardi Gras King (Oberon), Joy Blackett was the Mardi Gras Queen (Titania), Eugene Edwards was Robin (Puck), Emile Renan was Nic Bazette (Bottom), Will Andress was François Flute (Flute), David Casteel was Jean Bienadroit (Snug), Brian Schexnayder was Robert Faimdeloup (Starveling), Richard Cage was Pierre Marteau (Quince) and Gianni Zeno was Matthew (Hermia's father). Each group of characters has its own musical identity with a Cajun folk style for the rustics, a dissonant modern style for the nobility and jazz for the African American royal couple and their fairy troupe.

NIGHT PASSAGE *1995 opera by Moran*

After the imprisonment of Oscar Wilde in 1895, six hundred gay men flee England fearing they too may be arrested for the crime of homosexuality. Robert Moran's 35-minute opera *Night Passage*, libretto by the composer based on actual events, was commissioned by the Seattle Men's Chorus. It was premiered on April 17, 1995, at the Meany Theatre at the University of Washington in Seattle.

NIGHTINGALE *1980 children's opera by Strouse*

A Storyteller sings of a sad Emperor in ancient China who is given a Nightingale by his Maid. Its song makes him and everyone else happy. After a time, a Mechanical Nightingale becomes more popular and the real Nightingale leaves. The Palace becomes sad again and the Emperor nearly dies before the Nightingale returns to restore happiness and love. Charles Strouse's children's opera *Nightingale*, libretto by the composer based on the story by Hans Christian Andersen, was premiered at First All Children's Theater in New York in March 1980 in a production by Meridee Stein. The score is melodic and singable and the lyrics full of multiple rhymes. The opera was staged by Central City Opera in 1981, by Wolf Trap in 1982, in London in 1982 and in Milwaukee in 1997. (An earlier opera based on the same tale, Dorothy Lamb's *The Nightingale*, was premiered in Poughkeepsie, New York, on April 27, 1954.)

1983 Original London cast. Sarah Brightman is the Nightingale in this recording of the opera based on a 1982 production by Peter James at the Lyric Theatre, Hammersmith, in London. Gordon Sandison is the Emperor, Susannah Fellows is the Maid, Andrew Shore is the Narrator, Dinah Harris and Jill Pert are Peacocks, Bruce Ogston and Grant Smith are Aides, Michael Heath is Death, Carole Brooke is the Mechanical Nightingale, Debbie Goodman is the Court Choreographer and Roy Skelton and Michael Heath are the Doctors and Scientists. David Firman conducts the orchestra. The opera was recorded at the Abbey Road Studios in January 1983. That's Entertainment LP.

THE NIGHTINGALE AND THE ROSE *American operas based on Oscar Wilde story*

Oscar Wilde's fairy tale *The Nightingale and the Rose* (1888) is an anti-romantic allegory about the meaninglessness of sacrifices made for love. A poor student loves a girl who says she might care for him if he gave her a red rose. A nightingale who loves the student goes to get him one but discovers the red rose bush will only bloom if she sings with its thorn piercing her heart. She sacrifices herself for love but the fickle girl rejects the rose and the disillusioned student throws the rose away. The story has inspired operas by two American composers.

1942 George Lessner. George Lessner's one-act opera *The Nightingale and the Rose*, libretto by the composer, was premiered on NBC Radio on April 25, 1942. It follows the Wilde story fairly closely, as was possible on radio, but it is the composer's only opera. **1973 Margaret Garwood.** Margaret Garwood one-act opera *The Nightingale and the Rose,* libretto by the composer, personifies the nightingale for the stage as Rossignol, a young girl living in the 14th century. She loves Stefan but he loves Narcissa who wants a red rose. As no roses have bloomed for fifteen years, Rossignol offers to help. When she discovers that she was found under a rose bush that will bloom again when a thorn pierces her heart, she sacrifices her life for love of Stefan. He gives the rose to Narcissa but she rejects it and Stefan finds, too late, that he really loves Rossignol. The opera, commissioned by Franklin Concerts, was premiered by Pennsylvania Opera in Chester, PA, on October 21, 1973, and praised by critics for its Strauss-like musical style. It was revived in 1978 for presentation by the National Federation of Women's Clubs.

NINA ROSA   *1930 operetta by Romberg*

American mining engineer Jack Haines falls in love with Nina Rosa while working in Peru and wins her despite opposition from the villainous Pablo. Sigmund Romberg's operetta *Nina Rosa,* libretto by Otto Harbach with lyrics by Irving Caesar, opened in New York at the Majestic Theater on August 20, 1930, with Ethelind Terry as Nina Rosa, Guy Robertson as Jack and Leonard Ceeley as Pablo. The show was also popular in London and Paris. **1931 Original London cast.** The original cast of the London production of *Nina Rosa* recorded highlights from the operetta for release on 78 records. Geoffrey Gwyther sings "Adored One" and "Nina Rosa." Helen Gilliland, who replaced Ethelind Terry, sings "My First Love, My Last Love." Gilliland and Robert Chisholm sing "The Gaucho's March." The songs are on the album *Great Hits from Sigmund Romberg.* Pearl CD. **1931 André Baugé.** French baritone André Baugé, who starred in the hugely successful Paris production of the operetta, performs two of its songs with orchestral backing. "La march de Nina Rosa" and "Ah! Combien perfides son les femmes" are on the album *Les Grand Messieurs de Operette.* EPM CD. **1956 Irving Caesar.** Lyricist Irving Caesar who wrote the words for the songs for *Nina Rosa,* sings "My First Love, My Last Love" on the album *Irving Caesar: And Then I Wrote.* Coral LP.

NINE RIVERS FROM JORDAN   *1968 opera by Weisgall*

British soldier Don Hanwell is shown sitting on his grave in May 1945 while flashbacks portray his spiritual journey from the River Jordan in the Middle East to Italy during World War II. In Rome Michelangelo's statue Pieta comes to life and shows him a concentration camp. He eventually kills German camp guard Otto Suder with a grenade. Hugo Weisgall's symbolic opera *Nine River from Jordan,* libretto by Denis Johnston, premiered at New York City Opera on October 9, 1968. Julian Patrick was Don Hanwell, Nico Castel was Tom Tosser, Ronald Bentley was Bartolomeo, William Brown was Lieut. Jean l'Aiglon, David Clements was Otto Suder, Irene Schauler was the Salt Woman, and Don Yule was the Leader of the Bedouins. Will Steven Armstrong designed the sets, Vlado Habunek directed and Gustav Meier conducted the NYCO Orchestra. The music is atonal but there are still arias, duets and other classic vocal numbers.

EL NIÑO   *2000 opera/oratorio by Adams*

The story of the birth of Jesus as described in *The Bible* the Infancy Gospels and poems by Sor Juan Ines de la Cruz and Rosario Castellanos. John Adams' *El Niño,* a Nativity opera/oratorio cre-

ated in collaboration with director Peter Sellars and incorporating film and dance, was premiered at the Theatre de Châtelet in Paris on December 15, 2000. Dawn Upshaw and Lorraine Hunt Lieberson played the two Marys, Willard White was both Joseph and Herod, and the supporting singers included Daniel Bubeck, Brian Cummings, Steven Rickhards, the Maîtrise de Paris Children's Choir, the Theatre of Voices and the London Voices. Kent Nagano conducted the Berlin Deutsches Symphonie Orchester. *El Niño* was reprised in the U.S. in 2001.

2000 Théâtre du Châtelet. Dawn Upshaw and Lorraine Hunt Lieberson sing the two Marys with Willard White as Joseph and Herod in live audio and video recordings of Peter Sellars' premiere production at the Théâtre du Châtelet in Paris. Kent Nagano conducts the Deutsches Symphonie Orchester Berlin, Maîtrise de Paris Children's Choir, Theatre of Voices and London Voices choruses. Nonesuch CD (119 minutes) and Arthaus Musik DVD (147 minutes with documentary).

NISKA, MARALIN   *American soprano (1930–)*

Maralin Niska has sung the role of Susannah in Carlisle Floyd's Susannah at both the Metropolitan Opera (1965) and New York City Opera (1971) and there is a recording of her 1971 performance. She sang the title role in a 1979 Houston Grand Opera production of Marc Blitzstein's Regina and there is a recording of this performance. Niska, born in San Pedro, California, studied at UCLA and USC and made her debut with Los Angeles Opera in 1959. She sang at the Met and NYCO from 1965 to 1978.

NIXON IN CHINA   *1987 opera by Adams*

President Nixon makes an historic visit to China accompanied by his wife Pat and his Secretary of State Henry Kissinger. They land in Beijing in February 1972 and have friendly but formal meetings with Chairman Mao, Madame Mao and Premier Chou En-lai but relax more during a banquet. The personality of each of the participants is revealed in unusual but highly effective arias. These include Richard Nixon's "News has a kind of mystery," Pat Nixon's "This is prophetic," coloratura Madame Mao's "I am the wife of Mao-Tse-tung," and Chou-En-lai's final summing up "I am old and I cannot sleep." John Adams *Nixon in China*, libretto by Alice Goodman, was premiered by Houston Grand Opera on October 22, 1987. James Maddalena played Richard Nixon, Carolann Page was Pat Nixon, Sanford Sylvan was Chou en-Lai, John Duykers was Mao, Trudy Ellen Craney was Madame Mao, Thomas Hammons was Henry Kissinger, Mari Opatz was Mao's First Secretary Nancy T'ang, Stephanie Friedman was Second Secretary, Marion Dry was Third Secretary, Stephen Ochoa was Hung Ch'ang-ch'ing and Hether Tomas was Wu Ching-hua. John DeMain conducted the Houston Grand Opera Orchestra and Chorus. *Nixon in China* was conceived by director Peter Sellars who wanted to stage an opera based on a current news event; a genre later christened the "CNN opera." Adams, Sellers, Goodman and choreographer Mark Morris created the opera on a commission from Houston Grand Opera, the Brooklyn Academy of Music and the Kennedy Center. Sellars and set designer Adrianne Lobel produced a number of startling visual effects, including the landing of the presidential airplane at the airport. The music is minimalist but listener-friendly. After Houston the opera was recorded and staged in Washington, Brooklyn and the Netherlands. In 1998 Adams presented a one-hour concert version of the opera at the Aspen Music Festival titled *The Nixon Tapes.* The opera was revived at the Brooklyn Academy of Music in 1999 with minimal staging.

When it was staged by English National Opera in London in June 2000, it was hailed as one of the classics of modern opera. Opera Theatre of Saint Louis and Boston Opera presented new interpretations in 2004 productions. Arias from the opera have become recital pieces.

1987 Houston Grand Opera. The Houston Grand Opera premiere production was videotaped in October/November 1987 with the cast as above. James Maddalena is Richard Nixon, Carolann Page is Pat Nixon, Sanford Sylvan is Chou en-Lai, John Duykers is Mao, Trudy Ellen Craney is Madame Mao and Thomas Hammons is Kissinger. John DeMain conducts the Houston Grand Opera Orchestra. The telecast is introduced by Walter Cronkite, who talks about the real events on which it is based, and Adams is interviewed during the interval. Brian Large directed the telecast on April 15, 1988. Video at MTR. **1987 Brooklyn Academy of Music.** The opera was recorded in New York City in December 1987 while it was being performed at the Brooklyn Academy of Music. The original cast is featured but there is a different orchestra. James Maddalena is Nixon, Carolann Page is Pat Nixon, Sanford Sylvan is Chou en-Lai, John Duykers is Mao, Trudy Ellen Craney is Madame Mao and Thomas Hammons is Kissinger. Edo de Waart conducts the Orchestra of St. Luke's. Nonesuch 2-CD box. **1995 Dawn Upshaw.** Met soprano Dawn Upshaw sings Pat Nixon's aria "This is prophetic" accompanied by pianist David Zinman on her album *The World So Wide*. Nonesuch CD. **1995 Elin Carlson.** Elin Carlson sings Madame Mao's aria "I am the wife of Mao-Tse-tung" on her debut album *And What of Love*. She is accompanied by Alan Steinberg and William Vendice. Singularity Records CD.

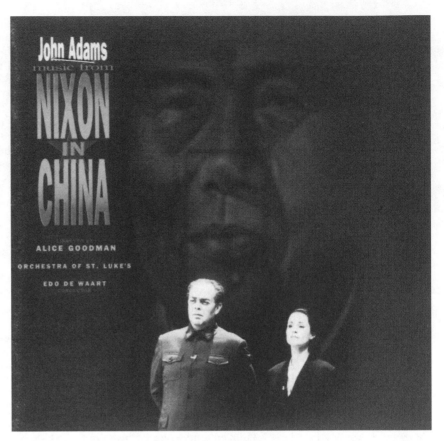

John Adam's *Nixon in China*, considered the first CNN opera, was recorded in Brooklyn in 1987.

"NO COUNTRY CAN MY OWN OUTVIE" *Tenor aria: Natoma (1911). Words: Joseph D. Redding. Music: Victor Herbert.*

Irish tenor John McCormack introduced this aria at the Philadelphia premiere of the opera and it has been closely identified with him ever since. His 1912 recording is a marvel and has remained in print in various editions for nearly a century. The opera is set in Spanish-controlled California in 1820 and the aria, a ringing patriotic ode to America, was composed not long after the Spanish American War. U.S. naval officer Paul Merrill presents his ship's captain's compliments to a festival crowd and then goes on to praise his native land in extravagant terms. It's name, he says, is stamped in gold on his heart. *Natoma* was the most performed and most recorded American opera until *Porgy and Bess* arrived in 1935 and was staged at the Met in New York and in the Chicago Opera soon after its premiere with McCormack singing opposite Mary Garden. There are other arias from it on disc by several notable singers including Alma Gluck, Jan Peerce and Earl Cartwright.

NO FOR AN ANSWER   *1940 opera by Blitzstein*

Radical ideas are emerging from the Diogenes Social Club which discusses the exploitation of the working class during meetings in the back of a lunch counter owned by Nick. Most of the members are hotel workers but intellectuals Paul and Clara belong and sympathize. Then Nick's union organizer son Joe is killed by goons. Marc Blitzstein's Broadway opera *No for an Answer* was the agit-prop sequel to his smash hit *The Cradle Will Rock*, but it never achieved the same kind of notoriety. It premiered at the Mecca Auditorium in New York on January 5, 1941, and had only a three-night run but was recorded by the original cast was recorded. Martin Wolfson was Nick Kyriakos, Michael Loring was his son Joe, Norma Green was his girlfriend Francie, Lloyd Gough was intellectual Paul Chase, Olive Deering was his wife Clara, Alfred Ryder was the lawyer Max Kraus, Carol Channing was nightclub entertainer Bobbie (making her Broadway debut), Coby Ruskin was her singing partner Jimmy for the song "Fraught," Charles Polacheck was Cutch, Curt Conway was Bulge, Bert Conway was Mike. Hester Sondergaard was Gina and Martin Ritt was a member of the Diogenes Club. Marc Blitzstein accompanied the singers on piano.

1940 Original cast album. The tiny Keynote label recorded the original cast of the opera for one of the first American musical theater cast albums. Martin Wolfson is Nick, Michael Loring is Joe, Charles Polacheck is Cutch, Norma Green is Francie, Lloyd Gough is Paul, Olive Deering is Clara, Carol Channing is Bobby, Coby Ruskin is Jimmy, Curt Conway is Bulge, Bert Conway is Mike and Hester Sondergaard is Gina. Marc Blitzstein accompanies the singers on piano. AEI LP/CD and Pearl CD *Marc Blitzstein — Musical Theatre Premieres.* **1942 Paul Robeson.** Paul Robeson sings "The Purest Kind of Guy" from the opera accompanied by pianist Lawrence Brown. Originally a Columbia 78 recorded in January 1942, it's on the album *Songs of Free Men*. Sony Classical CD. **1955 Charlotte Rae.** Charlotte Rae sings "Fraught" from *No for an Answer* on her album *Songs I Taught My Mother* with backing from husband John Strauss and his Baroque Bearcats combo. The album also features the Blitzstein cabaret song "Modest Maid." Vanguard LP. **1956 Joshua Kelly/Evelyn Lear/George Gaynes.** Joshua Kelly sings "Penny Candy" and Evelyn Lear and George Gaynes perform the "Francie" scene from *No for an Answer* on the album *Marc Blitzstein Discusses His Theater Compositions* Blitzstein talks about the opera and plays piano. Spoken Arts LP. **1990 Karen Hovik/William Sharp.** Karen Hovik and William Sharp sing "In the Clear" and "Penny Candy" from the opera on the album *Marc Blitzstein: Zipperfly and Other Songs* recorded for the New York Festival of Song. Steven Blier accompanies on piano. Koch CD. **1990 Helen Williams/Leonard Lehrman.** Helene Williams sings "Fraught" and pianist Leonard Lehrman plays "Penny Candy" on the album *A Blitzstein Cabaret*. Premiere CD. **1993 Dawn Upshaw.** Dawn Upshaw sings "In the Clear" from the opera on her album *I Wish It So* with Eric Stern conducting the orchestra. Elektra Nonesuch CD.

"NO, I HAVEN'T BEEN WELL" *Soprano aria: Summer and Smoke, 1971. Words: Lanford Wilson. Music: Lee Hoiby.*

Alma's revealing aria "No, I haven't been well" was introduced by soprano Mary Jane Peil in Lee Hoiby's opera *Summer and Smoke*, libretto by Lanford Wilson, when it was premiered by St. Paul Opera on June 19, 1971. Alma, a lonely, unmarried and sexually repressed minister's daughter living in Mississippi at the turn of the century, is in the office of Dr. John Buchanan where she confesses her love for him. The character of Alma was created by playwright Tennessee Williams in the 1948 play on which the opera was based and he describes her as "suffocated in smoke from something on fire inside her." Piel can be seen and heard singing "No, I haven't been well" in the 1982 Chicago Opera Theater television version of the opera. Helen-Kay Eberley sings it on her 1983 album *American Girl*, accompanied by pianist Donald Isaak.

NO WORD FROM TOM *Soprano aria: The Rake's Progress (1951). Words: W. H Auden and Chester Kallman. Music: Igor Stravinsky.*

Anne Trulove sings sadly of her despair waiting for her lover Tom Rakewell to return from London to her country home. "No word from Tom. Has love no voice?" she asks. Weeping is not enough, she decides, he needs her help, Love hears, knows and answers across the silent miles. She sets off for London to find him. Not all American opera arias sound particularly American though Igor Stravinsky composed this opera twelve years after he emigrated to the U.S. Stravinsky was inspired to write the opera by an exhibition of Hogarth etchings in Chicago and asked W. H. Auden to write the libretto with Chester Kallman. They created a brilliant amalgam of past and present in the story of a man in 18th century England led into dissolute ways by the Devil. Elizabeth Schwarzkopf introduced the aria at the opera's premiere in Venice in 1951 and her version is on record. Helde Gueden sings it in a studio recording based on the 1953 Met production with Stravinsky conducting. Other complete recordings feature Judith Raskin, Felicity Lott, Cecilia Gasdia, Cathryn Pope, Jayne West, Barbara Hendricks, Sylvia McNair, Dawn Upshaw and Deborah York. Renée Fleming features it on her American opera recital album *I Want Magic* and Upshaw sings it again on her recital album *Knoxville: Summer of 1915.*

NOBLE, TIMOTHY *American baritone (1946–)*

Timothy Noble created the role of Agamemnon in John Eaton's

THE CRY OF CLYTAEMNESTRA at Indiana University Opera in 1980, Prospero in Eaton's THE TEMPEST at Santa Fe Opera in 1985 and Columbus in Philip Glass's THE VOYAGE at the Metropolitan Opera in 1992. He sings Prof. Harold Hill in the 1991 Cincinnati Music Hall recording of Meredith Willson's THE MUSIC MAN and Benjamin Hubbard in the 1992 Scottish Opera recording of Marc Blitzstein's REGINA. Noble, who sang in the major opera houses of the world for 22 years, was born in Peru, Indiana, hometown of Cole Porter, and he has recorded an album of Porter songs titled *Simply Cole*. He is current Professor of Music at Indiana University in Bloomington.

NOLEN, TIMOTHY *American baritone (1941–)*

Timothy Nolen created the title role in Carlisle Floyd's WILLIE STARK at Houston Grand Opera in 1981, Junior in Leonard Bernstein's A QUIET PLACE at Houston Grand Opera in 1983, Ferguson in William Bolcom's CASINO PARADISE at the American Music Theater Festival in Philadelphia in 1990, Marcus in Bolcom's MCTEAGUE at Lyric Opera of Chicago in 1992 and Alfieri in Bolcom's A VIEW FROM THE BRIDGE at Lyric Opera of Chicago in 1999. He sang in the premiere of Robert Selig's *Chocurua* at Tanglewood in 1972 and he sings Voltaire/Pangloss in a recording of the 1995 Lyric Opera of Chicago production of Leonard Bernstein's CANDIDE. On stage he has sung the title roles in Dominick Argento's CHRISTOPHER SLY and Stephen Sondheim's SWEENEY TODD and Bob in Gian Carlo Menotti's THE OLD MAID AND THE THIEF. Nolen, born in Rotan, Texas, studied at the Manhattan School of Music and made his debut at San Francisco Opera in 1968.

NOLTE, CHARLES *American librettist/playwright (1920–)*

Charles Nolte wrote the librettos for two operas composed by Dominick Argento, THE VOYAGE OF EDGAR ALLAN POE, which premiered at Minnesota Opera in 1976 and THE DREAM OF VALENTINO, which premiered as Washington Opera in 1994. Nolte, a playwright, director and actor, has been a teacher for 35 years and is a professor in the Department of Theater Arts at the University of Minnesota.

NORMAN, JEROLD *American tenor (1950–)*

Jerold Norman created three roles in Thea Musgrave's A CHRISTMAS CAROL when it was premiered by Virginia Opera in 1979: Bob Cratchit, Mr. Dorritt and the Man with a Snuff Box. He created the leading role of Abelard in Robert Ward's three-act opera ABELARD AND HELOISE when it was premiered by Charlotte Opera in 1982. He has also sung the role of Sam on stage in Carlisle Floyd's SUSANNAH. He made his debut at the Met in 1979 in the title role of *Werther* and has sung with many other companies.

NORRIS, FRANK *American novelist (1870–1902)*

Frank Norris, the first great American naturalist novelist, is best known for two books, *McTeague* (1899) and *The Octopus* (1901). *McTeague,* the story of a brutal California dentist and his miserly wife, inspired one of the masterpieces of silent cinema, Erich von Stroheim's *Greed*. The film and the novel were the inspiration for William Bolcom's opera MCTEAGUE which premiered at Lyric Opera of Chicago in 1992. A 1993 documentary film by Robert Altman compares the book with the film and the opera.

NORTH CAROLINA *American state (1789–)*

Opera Carolina in Charlotte, the oldest opera company in North

Carolina, regularly features American operas and operettas. Long Leaf Opera and Triangle Opera in Durham also present American works. North Carolina-born opera people include contralto Carol Brice (Sedalia), soprano Kathryn Grayson (Winston-Salem), tenor Anthony Dean Griffey (High Point), composer Lamar Stringfield (Raleigh) and tenor Ray Yeates.

Boone: Wilton Mason's one-act *Kingdom Come* was premiered at Appalachian State Teacher's College on April 26, 1923.

Chapel Hill: Roger Hannay's "opera-biographica" *The Journey of Edith Wharton,* based on a Russell Graves play, was premiered by North Carolina University Opera Workshop in Chapel Hill on March 30. 1988.

Charlotte: Opera Carolina, founded in 1949, has presented many American operas and operettas. It commissioned Robert Ward's ABELARD AND HELOISE and premiered it at Ovens Auditorium on February 19, 1982. It premiered Charles Haubiel's folk opera *Sunday Costs Five Pesos,* libretto by Josephine Niggli, at Piedmont Junior College on November 6, 1950. Other productions have included Irving Berlin's ANNIE GET YOUR GUN, Leonard Bernstein's TROUBLE IN TAHITI, Carlisle Floyd's SUSANNAH, George Gershwin's PORGY AND BESS, Frank Loesser's THE MOST HAPPY FELLA, Gian Carlo Menotti's AMELIA GOES TO THE BALL and THE MEDIUM, Cole Porter's KISS ME KATE, Richard Rodgers' CAROUSEL and THE KING AND I, Sigmund Romberg's THE DESERT SONG and THE STUDENT PRINCE, Julia Smith's DAISY, Stephen Sondheim's A LITTLE NIGHT MUSIC, Robert WARD's THE CRUCIBLE, Kurt Weill's DOWN IN THE VALLEY and Wright/Forrest's KISMET.

Davidson: Wilmer Hayden Welsh's *Waiting for Lila Sinclair,* based on Clifford Odets' *Waiting for Lefty,* was commissioned by Davidson College and premiered by its Opera Workshop on May 10, 1985.

Durham: Triangle Opera, founded by composer Robert Ward, began its presentations in 1984 with a street production of Gian Carlo Menotti's THE MEDIUM. It moved indoors to the Carolina Theater in 1985 but has continued to present American operas on a regular basis. Ward's THE CRUCIBLE was staged in 1985, his ROMAN FEVER was premiered on June 9, 1993, and his LADY KATE was staged at Page Auditorium at Duke University in January 1995. Other Triangle productions have included Richard Wargo's THE SEDUCTION OF A LADY, based on a Neil Simon play, and James Legg's *The Informer,* libretto by Sandra Russell. Long Leaf Opera, founded in 1999 to present small-scale English-language musical works, has staged a number of American operas. They include Carlisle Floyd's SUSANNAH, Tom Johnson's FOUR NOTE OPERA, Gian Carlo Menotti's AMAHL AND THE NIGHT VISITORS, THE CONSUL and THE MEDIUM, Ned Rorem's THREE SISTERS WHO ARE NOT SISTERS, William Grant Still's HIGHWAY 1, USA, Kurt Weill's DOWN IN THE VALLEY and Alec Wilder's SUNDAY EXCURSION.

Greensboro: Jack Jarrett's three-act CYRANO DE BERGERAC, based on the play by Edmund de Rostand, premiered at the University of North Carolina on April 27, 1972. Greensboro Opera, founded in 1981, presents an opera every year at the War Memorial Auditorium. Peter Paul Fuchs' *The White Agony,* based on a play by Karel Capek, was presented in a shortened version in 1992.

Raleigh: Carlisle Floyd's comic opera THE SOJOURNER AND MOLLIE SINCLAIR was commissioned for the Carolina Tercentenary and premiered at East Carolina College in Raleigh on December 2, 1963, with Norman Treigle in the leading role. The National Opera Company is based at the Fletcher School of Performing Arts.

Winston-Salem: Robert Mayer's *The Porter at the Door* premiered at Salem College on February 2, 1954. Keith Gates'

chamber opera *Migle and the Bugs* premiered at North Carolina School of the Arts in February 1968. Charles Fussell's *Julian,* based on a Flaubert story, premiered at Reynolds Memorial Stadium on April 15, 1972. Piedmont Opera Theater, founded in 1978, presented Gian Carlo Menotti's AMAHL AND THE NIGHT VISITORS in 1984 and George Gershwin's PORGY AND BESS in 2004.

NORTH DAKOTA   *American state (1889–)*

North Dakota split off from South Dakota when the two states entered the union in 1889. Its principal city is Fargo, population 13,000, which has given a surprising welcome to American opera.

Fargo: The Fargo-Moorhead Civic Opera, launched in April 1969 at North Dakota State University in Fargo, has staged many American operas. (Moorhead is across the Red River in Minnesota.) The company has staged Domenick Argento's THE BOOR, Leonard Bernstein's TROUBLE IN TAHITI, Seymour Barab's CHANTICLEER, Carlisle Floyd's SUSANNAH, Victor Herbert's NAUGHTY MARIETTA, Gian Carlo Menotti's AMAHL AND THE NIGHT VISITORS, THE CONSUL and THE OLD MAID AND THE THIEF, Douglas Moore's THE BALLAD OF BABY DOE and Sigmund Romberg's THE DESERT SONG, THE NEW MOON and THE STUDENT PRINCE.

Minot: Two American operas were premiered at Minot State College. Ira Schwartz's *All in Black My Love Went Riding* was staged on November 11, 1965, and Cardon Burnham's *Ceremony of Strangers* was presented on December 13, 1972.

NOSFERATU   *1998 opera by Henderson*

Count Orloch, actually the vampire Nosferatu, lusts after the lovely Ellen. He leaves his Transylvanian home to pursue her and she has to make the ultimate self-sacrifice. Alva Henderson's opera *Nosferatu,* libretto by Dana Gioia based on F. W. Murnau's 1922 German vampire film, was premiered at the Western Slope Summer Music Festival in Crested Butte, Colorado, in June 1998. Baritone Douglas Nagel sang the role of the vampire count, soprano Susan Gundunas was Ellen and Robert McPherson was her husband Eric. Imre Pallio of the University of Indiana conducted the 40-piece orchestra. (*Nosferatu* is based on Bram Stoker's novel *Dracula* but screenwriter Henrik Galeen changed the names of the characters for copyright reasons.)

NOT A SPANISH KISS   *1977 opera by Barab*

A young poet offers to buy a kiss from the wife of a merchant and they haggle over the price. Seymour Barab's pleasant Spanish-themed comic opera *Not a Spanish Kiss,* libretto by the composer, was premiered by the New York Singing Teachers Association in 1977, revived by Golden Fleece in 1981 and reprised by the Association for Opera Awareness in 1982.

NOVOTNÁ, JARMILA   *American soprano (1907–1994)*

Czech-born soprano Jarmila Novotná, who sang at the Met from 1940 to 1956, did not sing in American operas on stage but she did perform songs from American operettas on radio. She sings a pot-pourri of Victor Herbert melodies, including "Kiss Me Again" from MLLE. MODISTE, on one recorded radio show and she revived Rudolf Friml's charming "L'Amour, Toujours L'Amour" from *The Amber Express* on another. She was offered the role of Lilli in Cole Porter's KISS ME KATE in 1948 but turned it down. She can be seen in two Hollywood movies, *The Great Caruso* and *The Search.*

NOW ELEANOR'S IDEA   *1994 electronic opera by Ashley*

Robert Ashley's opera *Now Eleanor's Idea,* a four-part work for live and pre-recorded electronics and solo voices, was premiered in its final form at the Brooklyn Academy of Music in 1994 with soprano Joan La Barbara and baritone Thomas Buckner in leading roles. Much of the singing is improvised and the narrative is multi-linear. Parts of the opera had been performed before, including IMPROVEMENT in 1991.

O

O PIONEERS!   *1999 opera by White*

Alexandra Bergson struggles to save the family homestead in Nebraska in the late 19th century and is heartened by the return of her old love Carl Linstrum. Her beloved brother Emil becomes involved with married neighbor Marie Shabata and both are killed by Marie's husband. Tyler Goodrich White's opera *O Pioneers!*, libretto by the composer based on a 1913 novel by Willa Cather, was premiered at Kimball Hall in the University of Nebraska School of Music in Lincoln on November 12, 1999. Karen Hughes was Alexandra, Dawn Pawlewski was Marie, Philip Sulzberger was Emil, Leo Skeffington was Carl, Harold Barnard II was Oscar and Jeff Keele was Frank. Richard Durst designed the set, William Shomos staged the production and the composer conducted. The tonal score was in the American mode of Aaron Copland and Nebraskan Howard Hanson.

OATES, JOYCE CAROL   *American writer/librettist 1938–)*

Joyce Carol Oates wrote the libretto for John Duffy's opera *Black Water* which premiered at the American Music Theatre Festival in Philadelphia in 1997. It is a thinly-disguised story about the Chappaquiddick tragedy based on her own novella. Oates, who was born in Millerport, NY, and studied at Syracuse and Wisconsin, has won many awards for her stories which often focus on aspects of self-destruction and violence.

AN OCCURRENCE AT OWL CREEK BRIDGE   *1982 radio opera by Musgrave*

Southern plantation owner Peyton Farquhar is caught trying to burn a bridge during the American Civil War and is condemned to be hanged by Northern soldiers. At the moment of his execution the rope breaks and he is able to escape and go home. At the end of the opera we learn the escape is a final-second fantasy before he dies. A woman, who turns out to be his wife, narrates the story but the hanged man is the only singer. Thea Musgrave's radio opera *An Occurrence at Owl Creek Bridge*, libretto by the composer based on the story by Ambrose Bierce, premiered on BBC Radio on September 14, 1982. Jake Gardner sang the role of Peyton, Gayle Hunnicut was the narrator and the composer conducted the London Sinfonietta.

OCHELATA'S WEDDING   *2000 opera by Damase*

André La Font is sent to Indian Territory in 1878 to compose music for the daughter of Ochelata, Chief of the Cherokee nation. His spinet is put in a crate on a riverboat but it used by outlaws to hide their loot from a robbery and rangers are in hot pursuit. Jean-Michael Damase's comic opera/operetta *Ochelata's Wedding*, libretto by Joe Sears and Jaston Williams, was premiered by the OK Mozart Festival, which commissioned it, on June 10, 2000, in Bartleville, Oklahoma. Soprano Arianna Zukerman was the bride Wilma, tenor James Burritt was her bridegroom Tito, tenor Robert Swensen was composer André La Font, bass Bradley Garvin was Ochelata and Charles Robert Stephen, Shon Sim and Jonathan

Hayes played the Outlaws and the Rangers. Leon Major staged the opera and Ransom Wilson conducted the Solisti New York Orchestra. Librettists Sears and Williams are the creators of a series of comic dramas about Tuna, Texas.

ODE TO PHAEDRA   *1995 opera by Roumanis*

Athens, Greece, in pre-historic times. Phaedra is a young woman married to a much older man, King Theseus. She falls in love with young Hippolytus, his son from a previous marriage, and attempts to seduce him. He rejects her with tragic results. George Roumanis's three-act opera *Ode to Phaedra*, libretto by Frank Zajaczkowski based on Euripides's tragedy *Hippolytus*, was premiered on PBS on August 26, 1995, as a presentation of Opera San José and KTEH Public TV. Cynthia Clayton was Phaedra, Carlo Scibelli was Hippolytus and Douglas Nagel was Theseus. Daniel Helfgot was the artistic director and Barbara Day Turner conducted the Opera San José Orchestra and Chorus. Daniel L. McGuire and Roi Peers directed for television. (George Rochberg's 1976 opera PHAEDRA is based on the same story.)

1995 Opera San José. Cynthia Clayton is Phaedra, Carlo Scibelli is Hippolytus and Douglas Nagel is Theseus in this video recording of the Opera San José premiere production. Barbara Day Turner conducts the Opera San José Orchestra and Chorus. Daniel Helfgot was artistic director and Daniel L. McGuire directed for television. KTEH-TV VHS.

ODETS, CLIFFORD   *American playwright (1906–1963)*

Clifford Odets, the leading leftist playwright of the 1930s, made his reputation with his radical plays *Waiting for Lefty* and *Awake and Sing* while more mainstream plays like *Golden Boy*, *The Country Girl* and *The Big Knife* were turned into films. Three of his plays have inspired music theater works. The most famous is the 1964 Broadway musical *Golden Boy*, libretto by Odets and William Gibson with lyrics by Lee Adams and music by Charles Strouse, which starred Sammy Davis Jr. when it opened on Broadway. Less successful was the 1970 musical *Two by Two* based on Odets' play *The Flowering Peach*, libretto by Peter Stone and lyrics by Martin Charnin with music by Richard Rodgers, which starred Danny Kaye. Wilmer Hayden Welsh's opera *Waiting for Lila Sinclair*, a revised and updated version of *Waiting for Lefty,* was commissioned by Davidson College in North Carolina which premiered it on May 10, 1985.

OEDIPUS   *1951 opera by Partch*

King Oedipus of Thebes bring a plague on his land because years before, without knowing it, he had killed his father and married his mother. When this is discovered, she hangs herself and he puts out his own eyes. He is sent into exile. Harry Partch's opera *Oedipus*, libretto by the composer based on William Butler Yeats' translation of Sophocles's play *Oedipus Rex*, was premiered as *King Oedipus,* on March 14, 1951, at Mills College in Oakland, CA. It was later revised by Partch and staged in 1954 with the new title *Oedipus*. (Roy Travis's 1968 opera THE PASSION OF OEDIPUS is also based on the Sophocles play.)

OEDIPUS TEX   *1988 spoof opera by Schickele*

Oedipus Tex is the cowboy brother of Oedipus Rex and has a similar fate. He shoots a man on his way into a town and then marries the dead man's wife, Billie Jo Casta, Queen of the Rodeo When the town fortune teller Madame Peep says he is responsible for a plague, Billie Joe kills herself and Oedipus puts out his eyes. Peter Schickele, composing and writing as his alter-ego P.D.Q.

Bach, premiered his one-act "spoof" chamber opera *Oedipus Tex* at the Plymouth Music Series in Minneapolis in on March 15, 1988. It is scored for a fourteen-piece orchestra, four soloists and chorus.

1990 Greater Hoople Area Off-Season Orchestra. Newton Wayland leads the Greater Hoople Area Off-Season Philharmonic Orchestra and Okay Chorale in a production of the opera. It's on the album *P. D. Q. Bach: Oedipus Tex and Other Choral Calamities.* Telarc CD.

OF MICE AND MEN   *1970 opera by Floyd*

Lennie and George are migratory California farmhands. Lennie is a giant with a child's mind so George looks after him. They find work at a farm where Lennie accidentally kills ranchowner Curley's wife when she tries to seduce him. George realizes that he will have to take care of Lennie one last time. Carlisle Floyd's three-act opera *Of Mice and Men*, libretto by the composer based on John Steinbeck's novel and play, was premiered by Seattle Opera on January 22, 1970. Robert Moulson was Lennie, Julian Patrick was George, Harry Theyard was Curley, Carol Bayard was Curley's wife, Archie Drake was the old ranchhand Candy, Kerry McDevitt was his sidekick Slim, Erik Townsend was Carlson and Gerald Thorsen was the ballad singer. Allen Charles Klein designed the sets, Frank Corsaro directed and Anton Coppola conducted the orchestra. *Of Mice and Men* is one of Floyd's most popular operas and has been staged around the world with productions in Nantes, Augsberg, Wexford, New York, Chicago, Cincinnati, Cleveland and Washington, DC. It was presented at the Bregenz Festival in Austria in 2001 in a much-praised production by Francesca Zambello with Anthony Dean Griffey as Lennie, Nancy Allen Lundy as Curley's wife and Gordon Hawkins as George. Rhoda Levine's 2004 production at New York City Opera also featured Griffey as Lennie and Lundy as Curly's wife with Rod Nelman as George.

1971 Cincinnati Opera. Robert Moulson is Lennie, Julian Patrick is George, Grayson Hirst is Curley and Andrew Harry Foldi is Candy in this production staged by Cincinnati Opera with most of the premiere cast. Emerson Buckley conducts the Cincinnati Opera Orchestra. The opera was recorded live on July 9, 1971. Live Opera audiocassette. **2002 Houston Grand Opera.** Francesca Zambello's much-praised 2001 production of the opera in Bregenz was reprised by Houston Grand Opera in 2002. Anthony Dean Griffey is superb as Lennie, Gordon Hawkins is George, Elizabeth Futral is Curley's wife, Julian Patrick (who created the role of George) is Candy and James Maddalena is Slim. Patrick Summers conducts the Houston Grand Opera Orchestra and Chorus. 113 minutes. Albany 2-CD box.

"OH, SWEET JESUS, SPARE ME THIS AGONY"   *Soprano aria: The Saint of Bleecker Street (1954). Words and Music: Gian Carlo Menotti.*

Annina has religious visions and stigmata but is desperately ill and praying to become a nun before she dies. Her Catholic neighbors in Greenwich Village demand to see her because they want miracles. She is brought out from her bedroom to the waiting crowd, wakes in pain and sings "Oh, sweet Jesus, spare me this agony. Too great a pain is this for one so weak." Gian Carlo Menotti's opera *The Saint of Bleecker Street*, libretto by the composer, opened at the Broadway Theatre in New York on December 27, 1954. The aria was introduced by Virginia Copeland and Gabrielle Ruggiero alternating as Annina with Ruggiero singing it on the original cast recording and Copeland singing it in the 1955 NBC telecast. Catherine Malfitano sings the aria in 1976 and 1978 New York City Opera productions while Julia Melinek sings it in the 2001 Spoleto Festival production.

OHIO   *American state (1803–)*

Ohio, which has notable opera companies in Cincinnati, Cleveland, Dayton and Toledo, began to present American operas in the 19th century. Dudley Buck's DESERET, the most controversial American opera of the 19th century, was presented at Pike's Opera House in Cincinnati in November 1880 and George Whiting's *Leonora* was premiered there in 1893. Cincinnati Music Hall, opened in 1878 and now the home of Cincinnati Opera, was the site of several early premieres: Pier Tirindelli's *Blanc et Noir* in 1897, Frank Van der Stucken's *William Ratcliffe* in 1899, John Van Broekoven's *A Colonial Wedding* in 1905 and Pietro Floridia's popular Bispham Medal winner PAOLETTA in 1910. Ralph Lyford's *Castle Agrazant,* premiered on April 29, 1926, was also awarded a Bispham Medal.

Meanwhile in Cleveland Alfred Arthur premiered three operas: *The Water Carrier* in 1877, *The Roundheads and the Cavaliers* in 1878 and *Adaline* in 1879. African American Harry Lawrence Freeman's first opera THE MARTYR was presented at Weisgerber's Hall by Freeman Grand Opera Company in 1984 and his *Valdo* was premiered there in May 1906. Victor Herbert's THE SERENADE was premiered by the Bostonians at the Colonial Theater on February 17, 1897, before going to Broadway and his Irish comic opera

Candy (Ryan Allen), Lennie (David Pomeroy), and George (John Packard) sing a trio in Lyric Opera of Kansas City's much-praised production *Of Mice and Men*. Photograph by Doug Hamer, courtesy of Lyric Opera of Kansas City.

An impressive set was featured in Cincinnati Opera's 2002 production of *Dead Man Walking*. Photograph by Philip Groshong, courtesy of Cincinnati Opera.

EILEEN was premiered there on January 1, 1917. Mary Williams Belcher's *The Legend of Ronsard and Madelon* premiered at the Art Museum in June 1918.

Ohio-born opera people include composer Leslie Adams (Cleveland), mezzo-soprano Bette Allen (Campbell), soprano Kathleen Battle (Portsmouth), composer S. Earle Blakesee (Oberlin), author Vance Bourjaily, conductor Dennis Russell Davies (Toledo), composer Francesco De Leone (Ravenna), conductor John DeMain (Youngstown), composer Peter Ekstrom (Cleveland), librettist Cecil Fanning, composer Harry Lawrence Freeman (Cleveland), conductor James Levine (Cincinnati), tenor Robert Moulson (Cleveland), soprano Mary Ellen Pracht (Bellaire), soprano Arlene Saunders (Cleveland), composer Theodore Stearns (Berea), soprano Nell Tangeman (Columbus), composer Robert Ward (Cleveland), mezzo-soprano Nancy Williams (Cleveland) and tenor Thomas J. Young (Cleveland).

Akron: Ohio native Francesco De Leone's ALGLALA: *A Romance of the Mesa*, libretto by Ohio native Cecil Fanning, was premiered by Cleveland Grand Opera at the Akron Armory on May 24, 1923, with Mabel Garrison and Edward Johnson in the leading roles. Three one-act operas by David Bernstein, librettos by Charles Kondek based on classic American stories, premiered at Akron University on November 6, 1999: IBRAHIM, based on Hawthorne's *The Gentle Boy*; A METHOD FOR MADNESS, based on Poe's *The System of Doctor Tarr and Professor Fether*; and THE TELL-TALE HEART, based on the Poe story.

Athens: Ohio University has been the site of a number of premieres: Max Wald's *A Provincial Episode* on July 17, 1952; Charles Hamm's *The Secret Life of Walter Mitty* on July 30, 1953; Alfred Grant Goodman's *The Audition* on July 27, 1954; Philip Slates' *The Bargain* on July 29, 1955; Slates' *The Candle* on July 27, 1956; and Abraham Ellstein's THE THIEF AND HANGMAN on January 17, 1959.

Berea: Lee Goldstein's one-act *An Idiot Dance* was premiered at Baldwin-Wallace College in 1976.

Bethel: John Eaton's children's opera *Androcles and the Lion* was performed by the Cincinnati Pops Orchestra on June 22, 1973.

Bowling Green: Robert Wykes' one-act chamber opera *The Prankster* was premiered at Bowling Green State University on January 12, 1952.

Cincinnati: Cincinnati Opera, founded in 1920, is the second oldest opera company in the USA. It started as the Zoological Gardens Opera (it was then located in the Cincinnati Zoo) and presented American operas almost from its beginning. Isaac van Grove, director of the company, premiered his two-act *The Music Robber*, libretto by Richard L. Stokes about Mozart and his Requiem Mass, on July 4, 1926. *Enter Pauline,* an operetta by Cincinnati composers Clark B. Firestone and Joseph Surdo, was premiered in July 1929. Two operas by Deems Taylor from the Met were staged at the Zoo in 1936: THE KING'S HENCHMAN and PETER IBBETSON. Carlisle Floyd's SUSANNAH has been staged by the company four times (1959, 1964, 1979, 1988) and Floyd's OF MICE AND MEN was produced in 1971. Cincinnati Opera moved from the Zoo's

Opera Pavilion to the renovated Cincinnati Music Hall in 1972 and began to include light opera in its repertory. Recent productions have included Jake Heggie's DEAD MAN WALKING, Jerome Kern's SHOW BOAT and *Roberta*, Frank Loesser's THE MOST HAPPY FELLA, Meredith Willson's THE MUSIC MAN, Douglas Moore's THE BALLAD OF BABY DOE, and Richard Rodger's CAROUSEL, THE SOUND OF MUSIC and SOUTH PACIFIC. Vittorio Giannini's popular opera THE TAMING OF THE SHREW, libretto by Dorothy Fee based on Shakespeare's play, was premiered in a concert version by the Music Drama Guild at the Music Hall on January 31, 1953. Lehman Engel, who studied at Cincinnati College of Music, premiered his one-act *Pierrot of the Minute* at the college on April 3, 1929. Three one-act operas were premiered at the college on April 1, 1953: William C. Byrd's *The Scandal at Mulford Inn*, Karl Magnuson's *Adam and Eve and the Devil* and Ronald Ray Williams' *Oleander Road*. Charles Hamm premiered two operas at the Conservatory of Music: *The Monkey's Paw,* based on the W. W. Jacobs story, on May 2, 1952; and *The Cask of Amontillado,* based on the Poe story, on March 1, 1953. David Ahlstrom premiered three operas in Cincinnati: THREE SISTERS WHO ARE NOT SISTERS, libretto by Gertrude Stein, and *The Open Window* at the Conservatory on March 1, 1953; and *Charlie's Uncle* at the Music Hall for the Music Drama Guild on April 23, 1954. Henry Humphreys-Rauscher premiered his opera MAYERLING on November 16, 1957, at Taft High School in a production by the Conservatory of Music. He premiered *Joan of Arc at Reims* at Christ Church on March 17, 1968, with Elaine Bonazzi as Joan; and *Quo Vadis Domine,* based on the novel *Quo Vadis*, at St. Williams Church in November 1984. Gian Carlo Menotti's dramatic cantata THE DEATH OF THE BISHOP OF BRINDISI premiered at the Music Hall on May 18, 1963. Harold Blumenfeld's SEASONS IN HELL was premiered and recorded at the Conservatory of Music on February 8, 1996, and his *Fourscore: An Opera of Opposites* was premiered at the University of Cincinnati on March 3, 1989. William C. Byrd's *Lyneia* premiered at the University of Cincinnati on January 20, 1949. Scott Huston's *The Giggling Goblin* was premiered there on June 2, 1974. his *Land Rights* in 1976 and his video opera *Blind Girl* in 1987 (it was telecast on February 13, 1988).

Cleveland: Shirley Graham's three-act sixteen-scene pageant opera TOM-TOM, the first dramatic opera by an African American woman to be staged, was commissioned by Lawrence Higgins for a Cleveland summer program and premiered by the Cleveland Opera Company at Cleveland Stadium on June 30, 1932. Clarence Metcalf's *The Town Musicians of Bremen* was presented by Cafarelli Opera in 1953. Leslie Kondorossy premiered twelve operas in Cleveland: *A Night in the Puszta* premiered at the Music Hall on June 28, 1953; *The Voice* and *The Pumpkin* at Severence Chamber Music Hall on May 15, 1955; *The Unexpected Visitor* at the Little Theater on October 21, 1956; and *Ruth and Naomi* at the Cleveland Baptist Church on April 28, 1974. Cleveland radio station WSRS premiered Kondorossy's *The Midnight Duel* on March 20, 1955; *The Two Imposters* on April 10, 1955; *The String Quartet* on May 8. 1955; and *The Mystic Fortress* on June 12, 1955. WBOE premiered his *Kalamona and the Four Winds* on January 27, 1971. Other Kondorossy operas premiered in Cleveland include *The Fox* on January 28, 1961; *The Poorest Suitor* on May 24, 1967; and *Shizuka's Dance* on April 22, 1969. Lehman Engel premiered his one-act operas *Brother Joe* and *Golden Ladder* at Karamu House May 28, 1953. Other operas premiered at Karamu House include J. Harold Brown's *King Solomon* (1951), Hale Smith's *Blood Wedding* (1953), Raymond W. White's *The Selfish Giant* (1965) and Harold Fink's *The Bridegroom* (1966). The modern Cleveland

Opera company, founded in 1976 and presenting productions at the restored State Theater since 1984, stages American opera on a regular basis. It premiered David Gooding's *The Legend of Sleepy Hollow* on December 1, 1988, and Stewart Copeland's HOLY BLOOD AND CRESCENT MOON on October 10, 1989. It has also staged Leonard Bernstein's WEST SIDE STORY, Carlisle Floyd's OF MICE AND MEN, George Gershwin's PORGY AND BESS, Victor Herbert's NAUGHTY MARIETTA, Jerome Kern's SHOW BOAT, Frederick Loewe's MY FAIR LADY, Gian Carlo Menotti's THE CONSUL and THE MEDIUM, Douglas Moore's THE BALLAD OF BABY DOE, Cole Porter's KISS ME KATE, Richard Rodgers' CAROUSEL and THE SOUND OF MUSIC and Virgil Thomson's THE MOTHER OF US ALL. Lyric Opera Cleveland, founded in 1974, has premiered two American operas: Larry Baker's *Haydn's Head* on July 30, 1987, and Libby Larsen's MRS. DALLOWAY on July 22 1993. Its other American presentations include Leonard Bernstein's CANDIDE, Jan Bach's THE STUDENT FROM SALAMANCA, Jerry Bock's SHE LOVES ME, Carlisle Floyd's OF MICE AND MEN, Gian Carlo Menotti's AMAHL AND THE NIGHT VISITORS and THE OLD MAID AND THE THIEF; Stephen Sondheim's A LITTLE NIGHT MUSIC and INTO THE WOODS and Conrad Susa's TRANSFORMATIONS. Lorin Maazel conducted the Cleveland Orchestra in the first complete recording of PORGY AND BESS in 1976, a recording that began critical reassessment of the work as opera rather than musical. Maazel was music director of the orchestra from 1972 to 1982 and added opera to its repertory.

Columbus: Ohio State University in Columbus has hosted three premieres: Daniel Sable's one-act *The Informer* in 1955, Paul Marshall's one-act *The Mink Stockings* in 1961 and Gerald Seager's one-act *The Marriage of the Grocer of Seville* in 1971. Opera/Columbus, an outgrowth of the Columbus Symphony Orchestra, was founded in 1981. It held the premiere of Thomas Pasatieri's THREE SISTERS, libretto by Kenward Elmslie based on the Chekhov play, on March 13, 1986, and then recorded it. Opera/Columbus commissioned African American composer Leslie Savoy Burrs opera VANQUI, based on Virginia Hamilton's book *Many Thousands Gone*, and premiered it on February 27, 1999. It has also staged George Gershwin's PORGY AND BESS, Victor Herbert's BABES IN TOYLAND and Mitch Leigh's MAN OF LA MANCHA.

Dayton: Dayton Opera, founded in 1961 and presenting operas at Memorial Hall, premiered Michael Ching's *King of the Clouds,* libretto by singer/songwriter Hugh Moffatt, on January 18, 1993. Adolphus Hailstork's one-act opera PAUL LAWRENCE DUNBAR: COMMON GROUND, libretto by Herbert Woodward Martin, was premiered on February 10, 1995, as a collaboration with local African American groups. Its other American presentations have included Carlisle Floyd's SUSANNAH, George Gershwin's PORGY AND BESS. Gian Carlo Menotti's AMAHL AND THE NIGHT VISITORS, Douglas Moore's THE BALLAD OF BABY DOE and Wright/Forrest's KISMET.

Gambier: Paul Schwartz's *The Experiment,* based on Nathaniel Hawthorne's story *Dr. Heidegger's Experiment,* premiered at Kenyon College on January 27, 1956.

Kent: Kent Stage University has hosted two premieres: John D White's *The Legend of Sleepy Hollow,* based on the Washington Irving story, in 1962; and Paul Koplow's *The Brick House* in 1965.

Middletown: Sorg Opera is located in Middletown.

Oberlin: Aaron Copland's revised version of THE TENDER LAND was presented at Oberlin College on May 20, 1955. The College premiered Gerald Humel's two-act *The Triangle,* libretto by Roger Brucker, on November 14, 1958; and Walter Aschaffenburg's BARTLEBY, libretto by Jay Leyda based on the Herman Melville story, on November 12, 1964.

Oxford: Joseph W Clokely premiered an oratorio and two operas at Miami University in Oxford while he was teaching there: the oratorio *Isaiah LV* on June 4, 1916; the three-act opera *The Pied Piper of Hamelin,* libretto by Anna J. Beiswenger based on the Robert Browning poem, on May 14, 1920; and the three-act opera *The Nightingale,* libretto by Willis Knapp Jones based on the Hans Christian Anderson tale, on December 12, 1925.

Springfield: Robert Haskin's one-act *Cassandra Southwick,* libretto by John Koppenhaver based on a Whittier story, was premiered by Springfield Civic Opera on January 24, 1964. Koppenhaver's *A Piano Comes to Arkansas,* libretto by Haskins based on a story by Thomas Thorpe, was premiered by Springfield Lyric Opera in 1977

Toledo: Toledo Opera, founded in 1959 and presenting its productions in the venerable Valentine Theater, has staged several American works. They include Jerry Bock's FIDDLER ON THE ROOF, George Gershwin's PORGY AND BESS, Victor Herbert's BABES IN TOYLAND, Frank Loesser's GUYS AND DOLLS, Sigmund Romberg's THE STUDENT PRINCE and Robert Ward's THE CRUCIBLE.

Wooster: Ohio Light Opera, the resident professional company of the College of Wooster founded by James Stuart and the College in 1979, is famous for its revival of classic light operas at the Freelander Theater and has been called the "Bayreuth of operetta." It has staged more than 85 operettas by 35 composers. Robert Ward's *Lady Kate,* libretto by Bernard Stambler, a revised and lightened version of THE LADY FROM COLORADO, was premiered on June 8, 1994. It has staged and released live recordings of four comic operas by Victor Herbert: EILEEN (1997), Herbert's ROSE-MARIE (2000), Herbert's THE RED MILL (2001) and SWEETHEARTS (2001). It's other productions include Frederick Loewe's MY FAIR LADY, Sigmund Romberg's THE STUDENT PRINCE and Kurt Weill's THE FIREBRAND OF FLORENCE and STREET SCENE. Soprano Erie Mills was a student at Wooster prior to the founding of Ohio Light Opera.

OKLAHOMA (1) *American state (1907–)*

Tulsa has had a Grand Opera House since 1906 and an opera company since 1948. The first American opera presented in the state was Deems Taylor's THE KING'S HENCHMAN which arrived on tour in Tulsa with the Metropolitan Opera in 1928.

Oklahoma-born opera people include composer Larry Austin (Duncan), mezzo-soprano Tsianina Redfeather Blackstone (Oklahoma Indian Territory), composer Gail Kubik (South Coffeyville), tenor William Lewis (Tulsa), composer Vernon Martin (Guthrie), soprano Leona Mitchell (Enid) and tenor Vern Sutton (Oklahoma City).

Richard Rodgers' OKLAHOMA!, the "first American vernacular opera," is set in Oklahoma and its famous aria has become the state anthem. Charles Wakefield Cadman's opera SHANEWIS, libretto by Nelle Richmond Eberhart based on the life of Oklahoma Territory native Tsianina Redfeather Blackstone, is partially set in Oklahoma as is Ellis Kohs' opera AMERIKA, based on the novel by Franz Kafka.

Bartlesville: Ruth Brush's *The Fair* premiered in Bartlesville in February 1965. Jean-Michael Damase's OCHELATA'S WEDDING, libretto by Joe Sears and Jaston Williams, was commissioned by the OK Mozart Festival which premiered it in Bartlesville on June 10, 2000.

Norman: The University of Oklahoma in Norman has hosted three premieres: Vernon Martin's one-act LADIES' VOICES, based on a Gertrude Stein play, on June 3, 1956; Don Gillis's one-act

The Libretto in December 1960; and Charle Eakin's one-act *The Box* on April 15, 1966.

Tulsa: Tulsa Opera, founded in 1948, presented Victor Herbert's THE RED MILL in 1949, Sigmund Romberg's THE NEW MOON in 1950 and Romberg's THE DESERT SONG in 1951. Douglas Moore's THE BALLAD OF BABY DOE was staged in 1976 and followed by Leonard Bernstein's TROUBLE IN TAHITI, Carlisle Floyd's SUSANNAH, George Gershwin's PORGY AND BESS, Philip Glass's THE JUNIPER TREE, Gian Carlo Menotti's AMAHL AND THE NIGHT VISITORS, Henry Mollicone's THE FACE ON THE BARROOM FLOOR and Robert Ward's THE CRUCIBLE. David Carlson's DREAMKEEPERS was staged in 1998 soon after its premiere in Utah.

James Sellars' first opera, *The Family,* libretto by W. Giorda, was created for Tulsa television; it was premiered on the Educational Television Network in 1963.

OKLAHOMA! (2) *1943" vernacular opera" by Rodgers and Hammerstein*

Composer Richard Rodgers and librettist Oscar Hammerstein's *Oklahoma!* is usually described as a musical or an operetta but it has also been called the "first American vernacular opera" combining music, drama and ballet in its storytelling. The story takes place when the state of Oklahoma is about to be born. Cowboy Curly wants to take farm girl Laurey to a box social and has problems with menacing hired hand Jud. Overly-friendly Ado Annie gets overly involved with two men at the same time, cowboy Will and peddler Ali. *Oklahoma,* based on the play *Green Grow the Lilacs* by Lynn Riggs, was premiered at the Shubert Theater in New Haven on February 26, 1951, and opened at the St. James Theater in New York on March 31, 1943. Alfred Drake was Curly, Joan Roberts was Laurey, Howard de Silva was Jud, Celeste Holm was Ado Annie, Bette Garde was Aunt Eller, Lee Dixon was Will Parker and Joseph Buloff was Ali. Agnes de Mille did the choreography, Rouben Mamoulian directed and Jay Blackton conducted.

1943 Original Broadway cast. Alfred Drake is Curley, Joan Roberts is Laurey, Howard de Silva is Jud, Celeste Holm is Ado Annie, Lee Dixon is Will and Bette Garde is Aunt Eller. Jay Blackton conducts the chorus and orchestra. It is often called the first original cast album of a Broadway musical though the recording of Marc Blitzstein's *The Cradle Will Rock* preceded it. Decca LP/MCA CD. **1947 London stage cast.** Howard Keel is Curley with Betty Jane Watson as Laurey in this recording made with the original London stage cast. Henry Clarke is Jud, Walter Donahue is Will and Dorothea MacFarland is Ado Annie. Reginald Burston conducts. Laserlight/Box Office Recordings CD. **1951 Risë Stevens.** Met mezzo Risë Stevens sings "People Will Say We're in Love" on *The Voice of Firestone* television program July 23, 1951, with the Firestone Orchestra led by Howard Barlow. It's on the video *Risë Stevens in Opera and Song, Vol. 2.* VAI VHS. **1952 Nelson Eddy/Virginia Haskins.** Nelson Eddy is Curley opposite Virginia Haskins as Laurey in this Columbia recording made in a New York studio. Kaye Ballard is Ado Annie, Wilton Clary is Will, Portia Nelson is Aunt Eller and Lee Cass is Jud. Lehman Engel conducts. Sony CD/Columbia LP. **1953 George London.** Canadian bass-baritone George London sings "Oh, What a Beautiful Morning" on *The Voice of Firestone* TV program on December 28, 1953, accompanied by Howard Barlow and the Firestone Orchestra. It's on the video *George London in Opera and Song.* VAI VHS. **1955 Twentieth Century-Fox film.** Gordon MacRae is Curly with Shirley Jones as Laurey in this film of the musical directed by Fred Zinnemann for Twentieth Century-Fox. Rod Steiger is Jud, Gloria Graham is Ado Annie, Charlotte Greenwood is Aunt Eller and

Gene Nelson is Will. Jay Blackton conducts. Soundtrack is on Capitol LP/Angel CD. Fox VHS/DVD. **1980 Broadway revival.** Laurence Guittard is Curley and Christine Andreas is Laurey in a recording by the cast of a 1979 Broadway revival staged by Oscar's son William. Martin Vidnovic is Jud, Christine Ebersole is Ado Annie and Mary Wickes is Aunt Eller. Jay Blackton conducts. BMG/RCA Victor CD. **1980 London revival.** John Deidrich is Curly with Rosamund Shelley as Laurey in a recording by the 1980 London stage revival cast. Jillian Mack is Ado Annie, Madge Ryan is Aunt Eller and Alfred Molina is Jud. John Owen Edwards conducts. Laserlight CD. **1996 Bryan Terfel.** Bryan Terfel sings "Oh, What a Beautiful Mornin'" and "The Surrey with the Fringe on Top" from *Oklahoma!* on his album *Something Wonderful: Bryan Terfel Sings Rodgers and Hammerstein.* Paul Daniel conducts the English Northern Philharmonic and Opera North Chorus. DG CD. **1998 Royal National Theatre.** Hugh Jackman is Curly with Josefina Gabrielle as Laurey in a recording by the cast of the 1998 London Royal National Theatre production. Maureen Lipman is Aunt Eller, Jimmy Johnston is Will, Vicki Simon is Ado Annie and Shuler Hensley is Jud. John Owen Edwards conducts. It was staged by Trevor Nunn in a much darker mode than the Hollywood movie. The stage show was videotaped and shown on American television in 2003. First Night Cast CD.

Gordon MacRae (Curly) and Shirley Jones (Laurey) in the film version of Richard Rodgers' *Oklahoma!,* the "first American vernacular opera."

"OL' MAN RIVER"   *Bass aria: Show Boat (1927). Words: Oscar Hammerstein II. Music: Jerome Kern.*

"Ol' Man River" is the best known bass aria in American music theater and the highpoint of America's greatest operatic musical. In the show it is a passionate cry of pain by a black stevedore summing up the horrors of being black in turn-of-the-century Mississippi but it has since become more universal, an heroic expression of man's inhumanity to man. It was introduced in Jerome Kern's SHOW BOAT, libretto by Oscar Hammerstein II based on Edna Ferber's novel, at the National Theater in Washington, D. C., on November 25, 1927. It is often identified with Paul Robeson, who was to have introduced it on stage, but production delays required a change of cast as he had to leave for Europe to honor other commitments. Bass-baritone Jules Bledsoe took over the role of the stevedore Joe and introduced "Ol' Man River" on stage at the end of the first scene of act one. Robeson, however, played the role in the 1928 London production and 1932 Broadway revival and was cast as Joe in the 1936 movie version. He recorded it seven times (three times by 1930) while Bledsoe only recorded it once in 1931. Met baritone Lawrence Tibbett made recordings of it in 1932 and

1955 but the aria was mainly identified with black singers until Frank Sinatra began to sing it, recording it in 1944 and performing it in a white tuxedo in the 1946 film *Till the Clouds Roll By.* Todd Duncan, the original Porgy, sang the aria in a 1944 Los Angeles production and recorded it in 1947. William Warfield, famous for portraying Porgy on stage, sang it in the 1951 MGM film of *Show Boat,* on a 1962 album with Franz Allers conducting and in a 1966 Lincoln Center production. There have been many other notable modern recordings of the aria, including versions by Robert Merrill, Valentine Pringle, Imia Te Watia, Thomas Carey, Bruce Hubbard, Willard White and Michael Bell. Will Friedwald's *Stardust Melodies* contains a fascinating history of song's creation and performance history.

OLD DUTCH   *1909 operetta by Herbert*

"Old Dutch" is a nickname for Ludwig Streuss and, a famous inventor who wants to have an incognito holiday in the Tyrol with his daughter. He runs into problems when he loses his identity papers. Victor Herbert's operetta *Old Dutch,* libretto by Edgar Smith with lyrics by George V. Hobart, premiered at the Grand Opera House in Wilkes-Barre, PA, on November 6, 1909, and opened at the Herald Square Theater in New York on November 22. Comedian Lew Fields was Old Dutch (a non-singing role) with Alice Dovey as his daughter, William Raymond as her beau Alfred and John E. Henshaw as a man who pretends to be Old Dutch. This is one of Herbert's weaker stage works but he recorded music from it and it was filmed. Its songs included "My Gypsy Sweetheart" and the duet "You, Dearie." The supporting cast was remarkable as it included Helen Hayes (making her debut), John Bunny (just before he be came a major movie star) and Vernon Castle (dancing without Irene).

1909 Victor Herbert. Composer Victor Herbert led his orchestra in a medley of tunes from his operetta for an Edison cylinder recording in 1909. The medley is included on the album *Victor Herbert and His Orchestra.* March LP. **1915 Shubert film.** The Shubert Film company turned *Old Dutch* into a silent film in 1915 with comedian Lew Fields reprising his stage role. Vivian Martin plays his daughter Violet and George Hassell is the man who pretends to be Old Dutch. Frank Crane directed. Herbert sued to block the film but was unsuccessful and it was screened in cinemas with his music performed live.

THE OLD MAID AND THE THIEF *1939 opera by Menotti*

Spinster Miss Todd and her young servant Laetitia give shelter to beggar Bob even after they discover he is an escaped thief. They rob a liquor store when he wants gin and cater to all his wishes. When Miss Todd threatens to turn him over to the police, he steals her car and elopes with Laetitia. Gian Carlo Menotti's opera *The Old Maid and the Thief,* libretto by the composer, was commissioned by Samuel Chotzinoff for NBC and was one of the first operas composed especially for radio. It was broadcast April 22, 1939, with Joseph Curtin as Narrator, Mary Hoppel as Miss Todd, Margaret Down as Laetitia, Dorothy Sarnoff as Miss Pinkerton, Robert Weede as Bob and Dorothy Sarnoff as Miss Pinkerton. Alberto Erede conducted. It was premiered on stage by Philadelphia Opera at the Academy of Music on February 11, 1941. In May 1943 the Hartford Opera Workshop presented the opera with scenery, costumes and piano accompaniment on General Electric's Schenectady station WRGB-TV, one of the first American opera telecasts. *The Old Maid and the Thief* was revived on stage by New York City Opera in 1948 with Marie Powers at Miss Todd and it continues to be staged today by regional opera companies. See also the aria STEAL ME, SWEET THIEF.

1939 NBC Radio. The NBC Radio premiere on April 22, 1939, was recorded off-air. Mary Hoppel is Miss Todd, Margaret Down is Laetitia, Dorothy Sarnoff is Miss Pinkerton and Robert Weede is Bob. Alberto Erede conducts. Unique Opera Records LP/Omega Opera Archive CD. **1949 NBC Opera Theatre.** Marie Powers stars as Miss Todd in an early NBC TV Opera Theatre production based on a 1948 New York City Opera production and featuring the same cast. Norman Young is Bob, Virginia MacWatters is Laetitia and Ellen Faull is Miss Pinkerton. Peter Herman Adler conducts the Symphony of the Air Orchestra. Roger Englander produced, Menotti directed and Kirk Browning directed the telecast on March 16, 1949. Live Opera audiocassette. **1964 ORF Austrian Television.** Elisabeth Höngen is Miss Todd in a German-language TV production by Otto Schenk. Eberhard Wächter is Bob, Olive Moorefield is Laetitia and Hilde Konetzni is Miss Pinkerton. Telecast on ORF on June 26, 1964. Premiere Opera VHS. **1970 Teatro Communale, Trieste.** Judith Blegen is Miss Pinkerton in a recording of the opera made at the Teatro Communale in Trieste, Italy. Margaret Baker is Laetitia, Anna Reynolds is Miss Todd and John Reardon is Bob. Jorge Mester conducts the Trieste Teatro Verdi Orchestra. Mercury/Turnabout LP. **1983**

Helen-Kay Eberley. Helen-Kay Eberley features Laetitia's aria, "Steal me, sweet thief" accompanied by pianist Donald Isaak, on her 1983 album *American Girl.* Eb-Sko LP. **1989 Dawn Upshaw.** Dawn Upshaw sings the aria "Steal me, sweet thief" with its preceding recitative "What a curse for a woman is a timid man" on her album *Knoxville: Summer of 1915.* David Zinman conducts the Orchestra of St. Luke's. Electra/Nonesuch CD.

OLLMANN, KURT *American baritone (1957–)*

Kurt Ollmann created the title role in Peter Lieberson's ASHOKA at Santa Fe Opera in 1997. He is Riff in the 1985 operatic recording of Leonard Bernstein's WEST SIDE STORY, one of the Trio in the TROUBLE IN TAHITI section of A QUIET PLACE in the 1986 Vienna State Opera production, Maximilian in the 1989 operatic video and CD of Bernstein's CANDIDE, Harry Easter in the 1991 Scottish Opera recording of Kurt Weill's STREET SCENE and Chip in the 1992 operatic video and recording of Bernstein's ON THE TOWN. He sings the role of the father Eddie in Carly Simon's ROMULUS HUNT in the 1993 cast recording but he did not create the role. Ollmann, who was born in Racine, Wisconsin, began his career at Skylight Opera in Milwaukee.

OLON-SCRYMGEOUR, JOHN *American librettist (1926–)*

John Olon-Scrymgeour, the professional name of John Scrymgeour, wrote the librettos for seven operas composed by Dominick Argento. *The Sicilian Limes* was premiered at the Peabody Conservatory in Baltimore in 1954, THE BOOR at the Eastman School of Music in Rochester in 1957, THE MASQUE OF ANGELS by the Center Opera Company in Minneapolis in 1964, THE SHOEMAKER'S HOLIDAY by Minnesota Opera in 1967, COLONEL JONATHAN THE SAINT at Loretta Heights College in Denver in 1971, MISS HAVISHAM'S FIRE by New York City Opera in 1979 and MISS HAVISHAM'S WEDDING NIGHT by Minnesota Opera in 1981. He also wrote the libretto for Hugo Weisgall's opera THE GARDENS OF ADONIS premiered by Opera/Omaha in 1992. Scrymgeour was stage director of the Hilltop Musical Company at Peabody when Argento became its musical director in 1954 and their partnership grew out this collaboration.

OMBRE RUSSE *1929 opera by Sodero*

Russian Nihilist student Ivan Korschkoff becomes involved with revolutionary activity in Moscow in 1907 and causes the death of Varvara, the woman he loves. Cesare Sodero's three-act opera *Ombre Russe* (Russian Shadows), libretto by Silvio Picchianti, became the first opera to be premiered complete on radio when it was broadcast on NBC in 1929 on May 27 (acts one and two) and June 3 (act three). It was sung in English (libretto translated by Alice Mattulath) and featured Julian Oliver as Ivan, Astrid Fjelde as Varvara, Fred Patton as the police chief and Nihilist leader and Grace Leslie as Lida, Ivan's revengeful former lover. The cast also included Paula Heminghuas, Frederic Baer, Joe Cavador and Walter Preston. Sodero conducted the NBC National Grand Opera Orchestra. The opera was given its stage premiere at La Fenice Opera House in Venice on June 19, 1930. It was sung in Italian with a cast headed by Antonio Melandri as Ivan, Pia Tassinari as Varvara, Vera De Cristoff as Lida, Luigi Sardi as Tromensky, and Carlo Morelli as Nikita Petrowich. Giulio Falcone conducted the La Fenice Opera Orchestra and Chorus.

OMNIBUS *American TV series (1952–1959)*

Omnibus presented a number American operas during its eight years of cultural programming. They included Gian Carlo Menotti's THE TELEPHONE in 1952, George Gershwin's BLUE MONDAY (as *135th Street*) in 1953, William Schuman's THE MIGHTY CASEY in 1955, Douglas Moore's THE BALLAD OF BABY DOE in 1957 and Menotti's THE MEDIUM in 1959. *Omnibus* began on CBS and later moved to ABC and NBC.

ON GOLD MOUNTAIN   *2000 opera by Wang*

Chinese immigrant Fong See arrives in California in 1871 at the age of fourteen, marries a white American woman who helps him becomes a success and then betrays her by taking a Chinese wife. Nathan Wang's one-act opera *On Gold Mountain*, libretto by Lisa See based on her book about her grandfather, was premiered by Los Angeles Opera at the Japan America Theater in Los Angeles on June 10, 2000. Ge-Gun Wang sang the role of Fong See, Shana Blake Hill was his wife Ticie, Judy J. Hur was Fong See as a juvenile, Duk Hee Cho was Fong See's wastrel father, Kristin Rothfuss was Madame Matilde. Karen TenEyck designed the set, Andrew Tsao directed and Leland Sun conducted the orchestra and Los Angeles Chinese Chorale. The score is accessible and tonal.

ON THE HARMFULNESS OF TOBACCO   *1979 monodrama by Kalmanoff*

A man lecturing on the evils of tobacco begins to wander away from the subject as he reveals his unhappy life and the dominance of his wife. He fantasizes about running away but when his wife appears in the wings, he meekly returns to describing the evils of tobacco. Martin Kalmanoff's monodrama *On the Harmfulness of Tobacco*, libretto by Eric Bentley based on Anton Chekhov's story with the same title, was premiered by the Manhattan Opera Singers at Alice Hall in New York City on March 22, 1979. The only singer is the lecturer, a baritone, whose music becomes more dissonant as his lecture progresses.

ON THE TOWN   *1944 musical by Bernstein*

Three sailors set out to discover New York during a 24-hour leave and meet three compatible women. Leonard Bernstein's musical *On the Town*, book and lyrics by Betty Comden and Adolph Green, was premiered at the Adelphi Theater in New York City on December 12, 1944. The three sailors were John Battles (Gaby), Adolph Green (Ozzie) and Cris Alexander (Chip). The three women were Nancy walker (Hildy), Betty Comden (Claire) and Sono Osato (Ivy). Jerome Robbins created the choreography, including the famous ballet "Miss Turnstiles,{ and George Abbott staged the musical. There is no original cast album though a Victor 78 album was released in 1945 with Bernstein conducting some of the ballet music and four of the cast were reunited for a 1960 recording. The sailor's introductory trio "New York, New York" has become virtually the theme song of the city. *On the Town* has been revived many times and has even been recorded by opera singers.

1944 Leonard Bernstein/Robert Shaw. Leonard Bernstein conducts the original production orchestra in ballet music from *On the Town* including "Lonely Town," Times Square" and "Dream in the Subway." Robert Shaw conducts the Victor Chorale in five numbers including "New York, New York" and Luck to be Me. The numbers were recorded for a Victor 78 album later released on LP. **1949 MGM film.** *On the Town* became an excellent MGM film musical in 1949 under the direction of Gene Kelly and Stanley Donen using a screenplay by bookwriters Betty Comden and Adolph Green. Kelly, Frank Sinatra and Jules Munshin star as the sailors and Vera Allen, Ann Miller and Betty Garrett are the girl-

friends. The 98-minute color movie was shot on location in New York but it features only four songs from the original musical. MGM-UA VHS/DVD. Soundtrack is on an LP. **1960 Original cast members.** Leonard Bernstein conducts an abridged version of the musical with four members of the original cast including sailors Adolph Green and Cris Alexander and girlfriends Nancy Walker, and Betty Comden. John Reardon takes over the role of Gaby. Columbia/Sony CD. **1992 Barbican Hall.** *On the Town* was performed with opera singers in the principal roles at a concert performance in 1992 at London's Barbican Hall. Thomas Hampson is Gaby, Samuel Ramey is Pitkin, Frederica von Stade is Claire, Kurt Ollmann is Chip, David Garrison is Ozzie and Tyne Daly is Hildy. Marie McLaughlin, Evelyn Lear and Cleo Laine make cameo appearances while Adolph Green and Betty Comden narrate the story. Michael Tilson Thomas conducts the London Symphony Orchestra and Christopher Swann directs. DG VHS/DVD/CD. **1995 John Yap.** Producer John Yap used the original stage orchestrations for what he said was the first complete recording of the musical. The singers are Gregg Edelman, Tim Flavin, Ethan Freeman, Kim Criswell, Judy Kaye, Valerie Masterson, Tinuke Olafimihan, Louise Gold, David Green and Nicolas Colicos. John Owen Edwards conducts the National Symphony Orchestra. Jay/TER CD box.

ONE CHRISTMAS LONG AGO   *1962 opera by Mayer*

Bells in a high church tower ring only when a good deed is done. They do not ring when the Countess gives away her jewels nor when the Rich Man gives away his gold. They do not ring for the Artist who gives up his portrait nor even for the King when he gives up his crown. But when a little boy stays up all night in bitter cold weather taking care of an Old Beggar Woman and sings a carol to cheer her up, the bells begin to ring. William Mayer's one-act opera *One Christmas Long Ago*, libretto by the composer based on Raymond MacDonald Alden's *Why the Chimes Rang*, was premiered by the Little Orchestra Society at Ball State University in Muncie, Indiana, on November 9, 1962.

1994 Florilegium Chamber Choir. The "Alleluia" from *One Christmas Long Ago* is performed by the Florilegium Chamber Choir and the New Calliope Singers led by Peter Schubert on the album *William Mayer—Voices from the Lost Realms*. Albany CD.

135TH STREET   See *BLUE MONDAY*

1000 AIRPLANES ON THE ROOF   *1988 music drama by Glass*

Philip Glass's "science fiction music drama" *1000 Airplanes on the Roof*, libretto by David Henry Hwang and Jerome Serlin, premiered in Hangar No. 3 at Vienna International Airport on July l5, 1988. It was the third science-fiction opera by Glass and its title derives from a description of the sound of a UFO approaching. It received its American premiere at the American Music Theatre Festival in Philadelpha on September 21, 1988.

1989 Philip Glass Ensemble. Linda Ronstadt is the vocalist with the Philip Glass Ensemble on this recording of *1000 Airplanes on the Roof* made at the Living Room in New York City. Martin Goldray conducts the Ensemble featuring Jon Gibson, Jack Kripl, Richard Peck and himself. The recording features 13 numbers from the work. Virgin Records CD.

ONE TOUCH OF VENUS   *1943 musical by Weill*

Whitelaw Savory unearths a statue of Venus and puts it on display in his New York museum. When Ozone Heights barber

Rodney Hatch puts an engagement ring on its finger, it comes to life and attempts to seduce the barber. Kurt Weill's risqué musical *One Touch of Venus*, libretto by S. J. Perlman and Ogden Nash based on the 19th century novel *The Tinted Venus* by F. J. Anstey, premiered at the Shubert Theater in Boston on September 17, 1943, and opened in New York at the Imperial Theater on October 7, 1943. Mary Martin played Venus, Kenny Baker was Rodney and John Boles was Whitelaw. Agnes de Mille arranged the choreography, Elia Kazan directed and Maurice Abravanel conducted the chorus and orchestra. The musical includes such memorable songs as "Speak Low" and "Foolish Heart." Goodspeed Opera revived the musical with great success in 1987.

1942 Kurt Weill. Kurt Weill sings seven songs from *One Touch of Venus* accompanying himself on piano on the albums *Tryout: Kurt Weill and Ira Gershwin* (Heritage LP/CD) and *Kurt Weill—*

Mary Martin as she appeared in the Broadway premiere of Kurt Weill's risqué *One Touch of Venus*.

From Berlin to Broadway II (Pearl CD). **1943 Original Broadway cast.** Mary Martin and Kenny Baker perform ten songs from the musical with Maurice Abravanel conducting Chorus and Orchestra. Decca LP/AEI CD and anthology *Kurt Weill— From Berlin to Broadway* (Pearl CD). **1948 Universal film.** Ava Gardner stars as Venus in this poor version of the musical. Robert Walker is Rodney, Tom Conway is museum owner Whitfield Savory, Dick Haymes is Rodney's friend Joe Grant, Eve Arden is Whitfield's secretary Molly and Olga San Juan is Rodney's girlfriend Gloria. Only three songs were used: "Speak Low," "Don't Look Now But My Heart Is Showing" and "That's Him." Leo Arnaud conducted the orchestra and William A. Seiter directed for Universal. **1955 NBC Television.** Janet Blair stars as Venus in a NBC television version of the musical. Russell Nype is Rodney, George Gaynes is Whitfield Savory and Laurel Shelby is Molly. Gino Smart conducts chorus and orchestra. George Schaefer directed the telecast on August 27, 1955. Video at MTR. **1957 Lotte Lenya.** Lotte Lenya sings "Foolish Heart" and "Speak Low" on the album *Lotte Lenya Sings Kurt Weill: American Theater Songs* Maurice Levine conducts the orchestra and chorus. Sony Classics CD. **1972 Berlin to Broadway with Kurt Weill.** The cast of the off-Broadway revue *Berlin to Broadway with Kurt Weill* perform "Speak Low" and "That's Him." Paramount LP. **1986 Teresa Stratas.** Teresa Stratas sings "I'm a Stranger Here Myself" and "Foolish Heart" on her album *Stratas Sings Weill* with Gerard Schwarz conducting the Y Chamber Orchestra. Nonesuch LP/CD. **1981 Kurt Weill Revisited.** Paula Lawrence, Ann Miller, John Reardon, Chita Rivera, Arthur Siegel and Jo Sullivan perform songs from *One Touch of Venus* in this Ben Bagley recording: "Vive La Difference," "One Touch of Venus," "That's How Much I Love You" and "Very Very Very." Painted Smiles LP/CD. **1988 Ute Lemper.** Ute Lemper sings "I'm a Stranger Here Myself," "Westwind" and "Speak Low" on the album *Ute Lemper Sings Kurt Weill*. John Mauceri conducts the RIAS Berlin Kammerensemble. London CD. **1992 Carole Farley.** Carole Farley sings "Speak Low," "That's Him" and "Foolish Heart" on the album *Kurt Weill Songs* accompanied by Roger Vignoles. ASV CD. **1992 Ute Lemper.** Ute Lemper sings "I'm a Stranger Here Myself," on the video *Ute Lemper Sings Kurt Weill*. Jeff Cohen plays the piano. London VHS. **1995 Anne Sofie von Otter.** Anne Sofie von Otter sings "Speak Low," "Foolish Heart" and "I'm a Stranger Here Myself" on the album *Speak Low—Songs by Kurt Weill*. John Eliot Gardiner conducts the North Germany Radio Symphony Orchestra. DG CD. **1996 Steven Kimbrough.** Steven Kimbrough sings "Westwind," "Who Am I?" and "The Moritat of Dr. Crippen" on the album *Kurt Weill on Broadway*. Victor Symonteete conducts the Cologne West German Radio Orchestra. Koch Schwann CD. **1997 Thomas Hampson/Elizabeth Futral.** Thomas Hampson, Elizabeth Futral, Jerry Hadley and Jeanne Lehman perform "Westwind" on the album *Kurt Weill on Broadway*. John McGlinn conducts the London Sinfonietta. EMI Classics CD. **2000 Urs Affolter.** Urs Affolter sings "Speak Low" on the album *Urs Affolter Sings Kurt Weill* accompanied by Uli Kofler. Antes CD.

O'NEILL, EUGENE   *American playwright (1888–1953)*

Eugene O'Neill is considered the Great American Playwright and he certainly tried hard to write the Great American Play. *A Long Day's Journey into Night* is the top contender with *Desire Under the Elms* and *Mourning Becomes Electra* as runners-up. American operas and musicals based on his plays have achieved considerable status, including two that premiered at the Metropolitan Opera and one at New York City Opera. O'Neill's plays have also been popular with filmmakers and Italian opera composers.

Ah, Wilderness! (1933). 1959 Bob Merrill's musical *Take Me Along,* libretto by Robert Russell and Joseph Stein. Premiere: Shubert Theater, October 22, 1959. **Anna Christie (1921).** 1957 Bob Merrill's musical *New Girl in Town,* libretto by George Abbott. Premiere: 46th Street Theater, May 14, 1957. **Before Breakfast (1916).** 1980 Thomas Pasatieri's opera BEFORE BREAKFAST, libretto by Frank Corsaro. Premiere: New York City Opera, October 9, 1980. **Beyond the Horizon (1920).** 1983 Nicolas Flagello's opera *Beyond the Horizon,* libretto by the composer. **Desire Under the Elms (1924).** 1978 Edward Thomas's opera DESIRE UNDER THE ELMS, libretto by Joe Masteroff. Premiere: New London, CT, August 10, 1978. **The Emperor Jones (1920).** 1933 Louis Gruenberg's opera THE EMPEROR JONES, libretto by K. de Jaffa and the composer. Premiere: Metropolitan Opera, January 7, 1933. **Ile (1917).** 1958 Beatrice Laufer's opera *Ile,* libretto by the composer. Radio premiere: WNYC, Municipal Broadcasting System, February 14, 1954. Stage premiere: Brooklyn Museum, April 18, 1957; European premiere: Royal Swedish Opera, Stockholm, October 28, 1958. **Mourning Becomes Electra (1931).** 1967 Marvin Levy's opera MOURNING BECOMES ELECTRA, libretto by Henry Butler. Premiere: Metropolitan Opera, March 17, 1967. **The Rope (1918).** 1955 Louis Mennini's opera *The Rope,* libretto by the composer. Premiere: Berkshire Musical Festival, August 8, 1955.

THE ONLY GIRL *1914 operetta by Herbert*

Three confirmed bachelors get married and their friend, a librettist, finds the only girl for him is his composer partner. Victor Herbert's operetta *The Only Girl,* libretto by Henry Blossom based on the play *Our Wives* by Helen Craft and Frank Mandel, premiered at the 39th Street Theater in New York November 2, 1914. Thurston Hall played the librettist Kim who finds true love with composer Ruth (Wilda Bennett) The other failed bachelors were played by Richard Bartlett, Jed Prouty and Ernest Torrence. Bennett sang the operetta's hit "When You're Away," the only song that has really survived, but it has been recorded by a large number of opera singers.

1915 Mabel Garrison. Metropolitan Opera soprano Mabel Garrison sings "When You're Away" from *The Only Girl* on a Victor Red Seal 78. **1915 Olive Kline.** Soprano Olive Kline of the Victor Light Opera Company sings "When You're Away" on a Victor 78. **1915 Columbia Light Opera.** The Columbia Light Opera Company performs a medley of tunes for a Columbia 78 record. **1929 Richard Crooks.** Met tenor Richard Crooks sings "When You're Away" for a 78. It's on the CD *Only a Rose—The Art of Richard Crooks in Song.* Pearl/Koch CD. **1931 Victor Salon Group.** The Victor Salon Group led by Nat Shilkret perform a medley of tunes for a Victor 78. It's on the album *The Music of Victor Herbert, Vol. 2.* RCA Victor LP. **1938 Charles Kullman.** Met tenor Charles Kullman sings "When You're Away" accompanied by orchestra led by Walter Goehr. It's on the 1997 album *Charles Kullman, 20 Unforgettable Classics.* Javelin (UK) CD. **1938 Richard Tauber.** Richard Tauber sings "When You're Away" with orchestra conducted by Henry Geehl. It's on the anthology album *The Songs of Victor Herbert.* ASV Living Era CD. **1967 Joan Sutherland.** Joan Sutherland sings "When You're Away" with Richard Bonynge leading the New Philharmonia Orchestra and Ambrosian Light Opera Chorus. It's on her album *The Golden Age of Operetta.* Decca/London LP. **1961 Robert Shaw Chorale.** The Robert Shaw Chorale and Orchestra perform "When You're Away" on the album *The Immortal Victor Herbert.* RCA Victor LP. **1975 Beverly Sills.** Beverly Sills sings "When You're Away" with André Kostelanetz leading the London Symphony Orchestra on the album

Music of Victor Herbert. Angel LP/CD. **1986 Teresa Ringholz.** Teresa Ringholz sings "When You're Away" with the Eastman Dryden Orchestra conducted by Donald Hunsberger. It's on the album *Victor Herbert: L'Encore.* Arabesque CD. **1991 Pittsburgh Symphony.** The Pittsburgh Symphony Orchestra led by Lorin Maazel performs "When You're Away" on the album *Popular American Music.* Sony CD. **1993 Jerry Hadley.** Met tenor Jerry Hadley sings "When You're Away" on his album *Golden Days.* Paul Gemignani conducts the American Theatre Orchestra. BMG RCA Victor CD. **1999 Virginia Croskery.** Virginia Croskery sings "When You're Away" with the Slovak Radio Symphony Orchestra led by Keith Brion on the album *Victor Herbert: Beloved Songs and Classic Miniatures.* Naxos CD.

THE OPENING *1969 opera by Wilder*

The curtain goes up on the front row of a theater. Gerald's play *The Reason Why* is about to premiere as he arrives with his wife Antoinette along with critic Alastair and his wife Trudi. Leading man Prince Charming comes out and tells the audience that leading lady Marcia has broken her leg. He tries a glass slipper on various women in the audience and finds it fits the Usher. Marcia arrives on stage in a cast and is told the play is over. Alec Wilder's one-act comic opera *The Opening,* libretto by Arnold Sundgaard, was premiered at the New England Conservatory in Boston on May 19, 1969. It was written for workshop productions with minimal set and vocal requirements.

OPERA AMERICA *American opera organization (1970–)*

Opera America, based in Washington, D.C., was started in 1970 to promote opera in America and has been particularly valuable in promoting and encouraging the creation and production of American operas. Its magazine *Encore* is an invaluable resource.

OPERA, OPERA *1956 opera by Kalmanoff*

This surrealistic opera about opera grew out of William Saroyan's longstanding desire to write a libretto for an opera. He wrote this one without a composer in mind, describing it as an "old all-time never-ending never-making-sense opera." A narrator comes on stage to sell candy, argue with a woman who wants to hear *Tristan* and tell the audience they are part of the opera as he has written the intermissions into the libretto. Men with candy appear in the aisles and a woman comes on stage and sings the numbers "one, two, three," etc. A man joins her and they sing numbers together. After a gorilla boy with a revolver shoots the man, the couple sing a mournful dying duet of numbers. The narrator explains that in opera everybody kills everybody else before the opera is over. Martin Kalmanoff's one-act opera *Opera, Opera,* using Saroyan's 1942 play as libretto, was first performed by After Dinner Theater Opera at Finch College in New York on February 22, 1956.

OPERAS BASED ON MOVIES *American operas derived from movies*

American composers have only recently begun to use movies as the basis for operas but a Frenchman pioneered the idea over 80 years ago. Cecil B. De Mille's popular 1915 film *The Cheat* was the inspiration for composer Camille Erlanger's 1921 opera *La Forfaiture.* Returning the favor in recent years, Philip Glass has found inspiration in French films. His operas ORPHÉE, LA BELLE ET LA BÊTE and LES ENFANTS TERRIBLES are based on films by Jean Cocteau and *Belle* is actually sung while the movie is projected. The only American film that has inspired him so far is Tod Browning's 1931 DRACULA for which he has written a score. David

Bishop's opera ESPERANZA is based on Michael Wilson's screenplay for the 1953 American film *Salt of the Earth*. William Bolcom's opera MCTEAGUE is based on Erich Von Stroheim's silent film *Greed* and Frank Norris's novel *McTeague*. Polly Pen composed an opera based on Abraham Room's silent Soviet film BED AND SOFA. Dominick Argento composed the movie-oriented THE DREAM OF VALENTINO about silent star Rudolph Valentino and intends to use the screenplay of Luchino Visconti's *The Leopard* as libretto for an opera. Stephen Sondheim's operatic musical PASSION is based on an Italian film. Conrad Susa's opera THE DANGEROUS LIAISONS is based on the French novel but was said to be influenced by the three films of the novel that preceded it. André Previn's A STREET-CAR NAMED DESIRE is based on the play by Tennessee Williams but critics could not avoid comparing it to the Marlon Brando/Vivien Leigh film.

OPERETTA!   *1979 operetta by Sharkey and Reiser*

High-born beauty Princess Beatrix of Butania disguises herself as a poor peasant woman to escape marriage to Duke Rorick and run off with "The Chocolate Shadow" who is really Sir Cuthbert of Craven in disguise. Her handmaiden Gwen is the beloved of Godfrey, a member of the Shadow's outland band. Jack Sharkey and Dave Reiser's operetta *Operetta!*, which they describe as a "stampede through nostalgia," is dedicated "to Sigmund Romberg, Oscar Straus, Franz Lehar, Victor Herbert, Rudolph Friml, and all other creators of the countless warmly recalled and well beloved predecessor of our emulative opus." It ends with a grandiose waltz finale.

THE ORACLE   *1894 comic opera by Moore*

Mary Carr Moore's three-act comic opera *The Oracle,* libretto by the composer, premiered at Golden Gate Hall in San Francisco on March 19, 1894. Moore, who was 21 at time, sang the leading role. It was the first American opera to be staged in San Francisco. It was reprised in Seattle in January 1902.

ORANGE BLOSSOMS   *1922 operetta by Herbert*

Kitty agrees to help Baron Roger Belmont overcome a trouble-some legacy problem with an arranged phony marriage and immediate divorce. Not surprisingly, the marriage works out for real. Victor Herbert's *Orange Blossoms,* libretto by Fred de Gresac (Mrs. Victor Maurel) based on her play, opened on September 19, 1922, at the Fulton Theater with Irene Day as Kitty, Robert Michaels as the Baron and Pat Somerset as the lawyer Brossac. It was the last Herbert operetta to be staged in its lifetime and its classic waltz, "A Kiss in the Dark," has been recorded by many opera sopranos.

1923 Amelita Galli-Curci. Coloratura legend Amelita Galli-Curci sings "A Kiss in the Dark" for a Victor Red Seal 78 with Rosario Bourdon conducting the RCA Victor Symphony Orchestra. It's on the album *Lo! Here the Gentle Lark.* Living Era CD. **1924 Claudia Muzio.** Soprano Claudia Muzio sings "A Kiss in the Dark" for an Edison 78. It's on various albums including *Claudia Muzio—The Published Edisons.* Biographies in Music CD. **1924 Fritz Kreisler.** Violinist Fritz Kreisler plays "A Kiss in the Dark" with pianist Carl Lamson for a 78 recording. It's on the album *The Kreisler Collection: 1921–25.* Biddulph CD. **1942 Gladys Swarthout.** Metropolitan Opera soprano Gladys Swarthout sings "A Kiss in the Dark" on a 1945 radio broadcast. It's on the album *Gladys Swarthout: Favorites from the Musical Theatre.* Take Two LP. **1951 Eleanor Steber.** Eleanor Steber sings "A Kiss in the Dark" with orchestra conducted by Howard Barlow on *The Voice of*

Firestone television show September 7, 1951. It's on *Eleanor Steber in Opera and Song.* VAI video. **1961 Robert Shaw Chorale.** The Robert Shaw Chorale and Orchestra perform "A Kiss in the Dark" on the album *The Immortal Victor Herbert.* RCA Victor LP. **1975 Beverly Sills.** Beverly Sills sings "A Kiss in the Dark" with the London Symphony Orchestra led by André Kostelanetz on the album *Music of Victor Herbert.* Angel LP/CD. **1986 Teresa Ringholz.** Teresa Ringholz sings "A Kiss in the Dark" with the Eastman-Dryden Orchestra led by Donald Hunsberger on album *Victor Herbert: The American Girl.* Arabesque LP/CD. **1999 Virginia Croskery.** Virginia Croskery sings "A Kiss in the Dark" with the Slovak Radio Symphony Orchestra led by Keith Brion on album *Victor Herbert: Beloved Songs and Classic Miniatures.* American Classics Naxos CD.

ORATORIOS   *Religious musical dramas (1600–)*

The oratorio and the opera are closely related and originated at almost the same time. An oratorio, in essence, is a religious opera presented without scenery, costumes or action but with story and vocal parts for soloists and ensembles. Some American oratorios are not traditionally religious and it is not always easy to distinguish between the genres. Among the American opera/oratorios with entries in this book are John Adams' EL NIÑO, Domenick Argento's JONAH AND THE WHALE, Richard Einhorn's VOICES OF LIGHT, Crawford Gates' THE PROMISED VALLEY, Alan Hovhaness's LADY OF LIGHT, Elliot Goldenthal's JUAN DARIEN and FIRE WATER PAPER, Francis Hopkinson's AMERICAN INDEPENDENT, John La Montaine's BE GLAD THEN AMERICA and Bob Telson's THE GOSPEL AT COLONUS.

OREGON   *American state (1859–)*

Oregon, has been enjoying opera since the 19th century and has hosted many American opera premieres. The earliest seems to have been Emil Enna's four-act *The Dawn of the West* premiered in Portland in 1915. Portland's 3000-seat Civic Auditorium was the site of a number of early premieres. Frank Patterson's opera THE ECHO, with young Lawrence Tibbett in the cast, premiered there on June 9, 1925, at a convention held by the National Federation of Music Clubs. Charles Wakefield Cadman's allegorical pageant *Rosaria*, libretto by Doris Smith of Portland, was presented there on June 15, 1925. Alberto Bimboni's grand opera WINONA, libretto by Perry Williams based on a Sioux Indian legend, was premiered by the American Grand Opera Company at the Auditorium on November 11, 1926. E. Bruce Knowlton, who founded the American Grand Opera Company in 1925, premiered six operas in Portland, most at the Auditorium: *The Monk of Toledo* on May 10, 1926; *Wakuta* on October 14, 1928; *The Woodsman* on April 4, 1929; *Charlotte* on December 11, 1929; *Antonio* on October 27, 1931; and *Montana* in 1933. Oregon-born opera people include tenor David Griffith (Eugene), composer Lou Harrison (Portland). Composer David Tamkin was brought up in Portland.

Eugene: Gail Kubik's one-act folk opera *Mirror in the Sky,* libretto by the composer about John James Audubon, was premiered at the University of Oregon on May 23, 1938. Eugene Opera, founded in 1982 and presenting operas at the Hult Center, has staged Leonard Bernstein's CANDIDE, George Gershwin's PORGY AND BESS, Gian Carlo Menotti's THE MEDIUM and THE TELEPHONE and Henry Mollicone's THE FACE ON THE BARROOM FLOOR.

Portland: Portland Opera, founded in 1965, presents productions in the venerable 3,000-seat Civic Auditorium. The company premiered Bernard Herrmann's WUTHERING HEIGHTS on November 6, 1982, and mounted a notable production of Christopher Drobny's LUCY'S LAPSES on April 27, 1990. Other American presentations have included Leonard Bernstein's CANDIDE, William Bolcom's A VIEW FROM THE BRIDGE, George Gershwin's PORGY AND BESS, Jerome Kern's SHOW BOAT, Mitch Leigh's MAN OF LA MANCHA, Frederick Loewe's MY FAIR LADY, Gian Carlo Menotti's THE CONSUL, Sergei Prokofiev's THE LOVE FOR THREE ORANGES, Richard Rodgers' CAROUSEL, Sigmund Romberg's THE STUDENT PRINCE and Kurt Weill's STREET SCENE. Its general director is Christopher Mattaliano.

DE ORGANIZER   *1940 opera by Johnson*

Black sharecroppers on a poor plantation in the American South in the 1930s meet to organize a union and wait for the Organizer to arrive. Brothers Dosher and Bates (tenors) talk about him and union activity and his Woman (contralto) arrives carrying leaflets. The Organizer (baritone) arrives and explains why they need to unite. The Overseer (bass) breaks in and stop the meeting but fails. A union is organized. James P. Johnson's 40-minute *De Organizer, A Blues Opera in One Act,* libretto by Langston Hughes, premiered at Carnegie Hall on May 31, 1940, with Leonard De Paur conducting the International Ladies' Garment Works Union Negro Chorus and Symphony Orchestra. There were no further productions until 2002 as it was considered too controversial. The work includes arias, duets, trios, quartets and choruses but all of the music disappeared except "Hungry Blues" which had been recorded by Johnson. Langston's libretto was finally published in 1996 in *Lost Plays of the Harlem Renaissance 1920–1940* (Wayne State University Press) and the lost vocal score was re-discovered in 1997 in the Eva Jessye Collection at the Center for African and Afro-American Studies at the University of Michigan by Prof. James Dapogney. He reconstructed the orchestration with Johnson's grandson Barry Glover and helped arrange two semi-staged performances, one at Detroit's Orchestra Hall on December 3, 2002, and one at the Power Center in Ann Arbor on December 11. Daniel Washington sang the role of the Organizer, Kimberly Hayes was the Organizer's Woman, Dorian Payton Hall was Brother Dosher, Frederick A. Peterbark was Brother Bates, Jaunelle Roberta Celair was the Old Woman, Silas Norman Jr. was the Old Man, Arianna Wadkins was the Sharecropper and Darnell Ishmel was the Overseer. Kenneth Kiesler conducted the University Symphony Orchestra and Chamber Choir with James Dapogney playing stride piano.

1939 Hungry Blues. James P Johnson recorded the bittersweet lament "Hungry Blues" in 1939, the only piece of music from the opera that known before the rediscovery of the vocal score. It is sung in the opera by Brother Dosher. Johnson's recording is available on several albums including *James P Johnson 1938–1942* (Melodie Jazz Classic CD).

ORMANDY, EUGENE   *American conductor (1899–1985)*

Eugene Ormandy leads the Philadelphia Orchestra in recordings of music from four American operas and operettas. He conducts the "Overture" to Gian Carlo Menotti's AMELIA GOES TO THE BALL in 1939, accompanies Paul Robeson on a 1940 abridged radio version of Louis Gruenberg's THE EMPEROR JONES and conducts songs from Victor Herbert's THE FORTUNE TELLER and NAUGHTY MARIETTA on an album of Herbert melodies in 1962. Ormandy, who was born in Budapest, came to New York in 1921 and became an American citizen in 1927. He began working with the Philadelphia Orchestra in 1930. He conducted few operas but he had great success with operettas in the 1950s.

ORPHÉE   *1993 opera by Glass*

The Orpheus myth retold in 1940s Paris. Death is a princess who falls in love with the poet Orpheus and helps him get to Hell to retrieve his lost love Eurydice. Death's messengers are portrayed as black leather-garbed motorcyclists. Philip Glass took the libretto for his opera directly from the screenplay of the 1949 French film *Orphée* written and directed by Jean Cocteau. Francesca Zambello directed the premiere of the Glass opera at the American Repertory Theater in Cambridge, Massachusetts, on May 14, 1993. Eugene Perry sang the role of Orpheus, Lynn Torgove was Eurydice, Wendy Hill was the Princess and Richard Fracker had the lead tenor role. Martin Goldray conducted the Philip Glass Ensemble and Robert Israel designed the moveable sets.

ORPHEUS DESCENDING   *1994 opera by Saylor*

Handsome guitar-playing drifter Val arrives in a small Southern town in his showy snakeskin jacket, goes to work in a store owned by mean, crippled Jabe Torrance and begins a steamy love affair with Jabe's neurotic Italian wife Lady. Other women become interested in Val including Vee, the pathetic wife of the sheriff, and seductive Carol, who covets the snakeskin jacket. Jabe learns of the affair and shoots Lady who is pregnant by Val while the sheriff and his friends hunt down Val and burn him to death. Bruce Saylor's two-act opera *Orpheus Descending*, libretto by J. D. McClatchy based on Tennessee Williams' 1957 play inspired by the Orpheus and Eurydice myth, was premiered by Chicago Lyric Opera's Center for American Artists at Northwestern University's Cahn Auditorium in Evanston on June 10, 1994. Victor Benedetti was Val, Juliana Rambaldi was Lady, Stephen Morscheck was Jabe, Terese Fedea was Carol Cutrere, Emily Magee was Vee, Natalie Arduino was Beulah, Kimberly Jones was Dolly, Stephen Powell was Sheriff Talbott, Gary Martin was David Cutrere and Gwendolyn Brown was the Nurse. Marie Anne Chicment designed the sets, Rhoda Levine staged the opera and Stewart Robinson conducted. Saylor's musical style is tonal, lyrical and American verismo in the mode of Beeson and Floyd. Williams' play was the basis for the 1959 film *The Fugitive Kind* starring Marlon Brando and Anna Magnani scripted by Williams; librettist McClatchy says he based his adaptation on Williams' ideas for the film. The play was also the basis of the 1980 TV film *Orpheus Descending* with Vanessa Redgrave and Kevin Anderson.

OUANGA   *1932 opera by White*

Witchcraft in Haiti at the beginning of the 19th century as Jean Jacques Dessalines leads the black slaves in a revolution. Clarence Cameron White's three-act opera, *Ouanga,* libretto by John F. Matheus based on Haitian history, won the David Bispham Medal when it was presented in concert form at the Three Arts Club in Chicago on November 12, 1931. It was reprised in concert form at the Studio Theater at the New School of Social Research in New York on June 18, 1941, with Lawrence Winters as Dessalines, staged at Central High School Auditorium in South Bend, Indiana on June 19, 1949, staged at the Metropolitan Opera in New York in May 1956 by the National Negro Opera Company and revived by the African American Dra Mu Opera Company. Among those who have sung the opera in its various permutations are Lawrence Winters as Dessalines, Carol Brice as Voodoo Princess, Evelyn Green as Licite, Roy O'Laughlin as Michel and Melbourne Reid as El Bossol. Larl Beechum created the choreography for the Met production. White began working on the opera while living in France but did not finish it until he was teaching at the Hampton Institute in Virginia. Carl G. Harris, Jr. has written that the opera is "characterized by jolting rhythms, athletic movement, and extreme dynamics." The title comes from a Haitian Creole word of Bantu origin meaning voodoo sorcery. (The 1936 black cast film *Ouanga*, which also deals with voodoo in Haiti, has no apparent connection with the opera.)

THE OUTCAST   *1988 opera by Ain*

Noa Ain based her opera *The Outcast* on the story of the Biblical Ruth who follows her mother-in-law Naomi into an intolerant foreign land where she ends up in tears amidst the alien corn, In Ain's opera, Ruth is called Ruta and the music is a blend of operatic style with gospel, jazz, African folk and New Age. It was developed by Opera Ebony and given an initial reading on December 11, 1988, and staged on June 17, 1990. On June 3, 1994, a longer revised version was given a major production by Houston Grand Opera and was made the focus of an intensive outreach program. All the Houston cast members were African Americans except Gail Hadani as Ruta. Debria Brown was Naomi, Ann Duquesnay was Ar, Eugene Perry was Gideon, Jose Garcia was Ain's husband Boaz, Roslyn Burrough was Judith, Felicia Coleman Evans was Inanna, Lionel Bracksins was King, Hope Shiver was Queen and Joan Hubert and Linda Thompson were Handmaidens. Christopher Barreca designed the sets, George Faison choreographed and directed and Ward Holmquist conducted the Houston Grand Opera Orchestra. The opera was restaged by Opera Ebony and New Jersey State Opera in Brooklyn in 1995 with Clare Gormley as Ruta, Elvira Green as Naomi, Lawrence Craig as Gideon and Kevin Deas as Boas.

1994 Houston Grand Opera. William Howze created a 30-minute video around Houston Grand Opera's 1994 production of the opera. It shows the development of the opera as it was used for audience outreach to the local community. The video is available from the Houston Grand Opera Education and Outreach Department.

THE OUTCASTS OF POKER FLAT   *American operas based on Bret Harte story*

Gambler Oakhurst, brothel keeper Duchess and town drunk Uncle Billy are driven out of the small Western town of Poker Flat during a clean-up campaign in mid-19th century. A snowstorm forces them to take refuge in a shack where they are joined by eloping couple Piney and Innocent. There is little food or heat and even less chance of survival. Bret Harte's famous 1869 story *The Outcasts of Poker Flat* has inspired four American opera composers.

1960 Jonathan Elkus. Jonathan Elkus's one-act opera *The Outcasts of Poker Flat*, libretto by Robert G. Bander, was premiered at Lehigh University in Bethlehem, PA, on April 16, 1960. **1960 Stanworth Beckler.** Stanworth Beckler's opera *The Outcasts of Poker Flat*, libretto by Jon Pearce, won an opera competition and was premiered at the College of the Pacific in Stockton, CA, on December 16, 1960. **1962 Samuel Adler.** Samuel Adler's popular one-act opera *The Outcasts of Poker Flat*, libretto by Judah Stampfer, premiered at North Texas State University in Denton on June 8, 1962. Edward Bailey sang the role of Uncle Billy. Adler uses folk elements in the colorful score. **1979 Michael P. Gehlen.** Michael P. Gehlen's three-act opera *The Outcasts of Poker Flat*, libretto by the composer, does not appear to have been staged.

OVERTON, HALL   *American composer (1920–1972)*

Hall Overton, who composed three operas, was an important figure in the jazz world and a respected teacher at Juilliard, the New School and Yale. After studies at Juilliard and with Darius Milhaud, the Maine-born composer began to play with jazz musicians like Stan Getz and Oscar Pettiford and write arrangement for Thelonius Monk. His first opera was *The Enchanted Pear Tree*, libretto by J. Thompson based on a story in Boccaccio's *Decameron*, which was premiered at the Juilliard School of Music on February 7, 1950. The one-act chamber opera *Pietro's Petard*, libretto by R. DeMaria, was premiered by the After Dinner Opera Company in New York in June 1963. *Huckleberry Finn*, libretto by J. Stampfer and the composer based on the novel by Mark Twain, premiered at the Juilliard American Opera Center in New York on May 20, 1971. Overton's other classical works includes ballets, chamber and orchestral pieces.

OWEN, RICHARD   *American composer (1922–)*

Richard Owen composed six operas that have been staged, three centering around the lives of notable women. *A Moment of War*, libretto by the composer, was premiered in Buenos Aires in 1964 and presented in Houston in 1985. The church opera A FISHERMAN CALLED PETER, libretto by the composer based on incidents in the Bible, was staged in Carmel, NY, on March 14, 1965, with Howard Nelson as Peter. MARY DYER, libretto by the composer based on the trial of a Quaker woman hanged in Boston on 1600, was premiered by the Eastern Opera Company in Suffern, NY, in 1976. THE DEATH OF THE VIRGIN, libretto by Michael Straight about the model for a famous painting by Caravaggio, premiered in New York in 1983. ABIGAIL ADAMS, libretto by the composer based on the letters of a woman whose husband and son were American presidents, premiered in New York in 1987. The children's opera TOM SAWYER, libretto by the composer based on the novel by Mark Twain, was premiered at the Manhattan School of Music in New York on April 9, 1989. Owen, a New York native and a graduate of Dartmouth College, studied composition with Vittorio Giannini and Robert Starer.

OZAWA, SEIJI   *Chinese-born American conductor (1935–)*

Seiji Ozawa conducts the Saito Kinen Orchestra and Tokyo Opera Singers in a 1995 Saito Kinen Festival recording of Igor Stravinsky's THE RAKE'S PROGRESS and the Boston Symphony Orchestra in a 1997 Tanglewood Festival recording of Roger Sessions' cantata WHEN LILACS LAST IN THE DOORYARD BLOOMED. Ozawa, who was born in Fenytien, China, studied in Tokyo and first came to the U.S. in 1960. He became music director of the Boston Symphony Orchestra in 1973.

P

THE PADRONE   *1912 opera by Chadwick*

A penniless Italian immigrant has his passage to America paid by a benefactor, the Padrone, but is forced to work for many years to pay off his debt. George Chadwick's opera *The Padrone*, libretto by D. K. Stevens and the composer, was completed in 1912 and offered to Giulio Gatti-Casazza at the Met. Gatti-Casazza was looking for American operas but he rejected Chadwick's opera, possibly because of its explosive subject and earthy realism. It was shelved and not produced until September 29, 1995, when conductor Leif Bjaland resurrected it for the American Music Festival in Connecticut. It premiered in concert format at the Thomaston Opera House in Thomaston with the leading roles sung by Alexandra Gruber-Malkin, Jacqueline Pierce, Jane Dutton,

Barton Green, Chad Shelton and Thomas Woodman. Bjaland led the Waterbury Symphony Orchestra, Waterbury Chorale, Naugatuck Valley College Chorus and Concora chorus.

1995 American Music Festival. The premiere performance conducted by Leif Bjaland with cast as above was recorded for the New England Conservatory of Music archive, which holds the original score, but it has not been released commercially.

PAGE, CAROLANN   *American soprano (1961–)*

Carolann Page created the role of Pat Nixon in John Adams' NIXON IN CHINA at Houston Grand Opera in 1987 and is featured on the telecast and recording. She created the role of Frank Lloyd Wright's lover Mamah Cheney in Daron Hagen's SHINING BROW at Madison Opera in 1993, Doll in Hagen's VERA OF LAS VEGAS at the University of Nevada in 1996 and Gertrude Stein in Jonathan Sheffer's BLOOD ON THE DINING ROOM FLOOR at the Peter Norton Space in New York in 2000. She sings on the 1974 recording of Leonard Bernstein's CANDIDE and on Placido Domingo's 1996 operatic recording of Mitch Leigh's MAN OF LA Mancha. On stage she has performed in many other American operas and operettas including Celia in Carlisle Floyd's THE PASSION OF JONATHAN WADE, Rose in Kurt Weill's STREET SCENE, Rosabella in Frank Loesser's THE MOST HAPPY FELLA, Ado Annie in Richard Rodgers' OKLAHOMA, Maria in THE SOUND OF MUSIC and Isabel in John Philip Sousa's EL CAPITAN. Page, who comes from a musical family (father, mother, sister, son) is a founding member of the Professional Musical Theatre Workshop at the Manhattan School of Music.

PAINE, JOHN KNOWLES   *American composer (1839–1906)*

John Knowles Paine was one of the most respected composers in America at the end of the 19th century but that was not enough to convince the Metropolitan Opera to stage his 1898 three-act grand opera AZARA. Emma Eames, for whom it was written, wanted to sing it, too, but the Met resisted and did not present any American operas until 1910. Paine's only other opera was an 1862 comic pastiche called *Il pesceballo,* libretto by F. J. Child and J. R. Lowell, created for a Civil War benefit. Paine, who was born in Portland, Maine, and studied music in Berlin, was also one of the great organists of his time. He was the founder of the music department at Harvard University.

PAINTER, ELEANOR   *American soprano (1886–1947)*

Eleanor Painter created roles in several American operettas and musicals on Broadway in the early 20th century, most famously Victor Herbert's Princess in PRINCESS PAT in 1915. Her recording of its hit song, "Love is the Best of All," was so popular that she featured it a 1929 Vitaphone film called *Eleanor Painter, The Lyric Soprano.* She also created the title role in Rudolf Friml's *Glorianna* in 1918 and Jenny Lind in Armand Vecsey's *The Nightingale* in 1927. Her other Broadway musicals included *Florodora, The Lilac Domino, The Last Waltz* and *The Chiffon Girl.* Painter, who born in Davenport, Iowa, began her stage career an opera and operetta singer in Germany.

PANTAGLEIZE   *1967 opera by Starer*

Pantagleize is a somewhat naïve philosopher living in a European city that has just finished a nasty war. He makes a casual remark in public that is mistaken for the signal to start a revolution. It is eventually crushed after much loss of life. Robert Starer's three-act opera *Pantagleize,* libretto by the composer based on a 1929 play by Belgian Michel de Ghelderode, was premiered at Brooklyn College Opera on April 8, 1973. Grayson Hirst sang Pantagleize and Edward Pierson was Bamboola. The opera requires a cast of fourteen plus chorus and dancers.

PANTALOON   *1961 opera by Ward*   See HE WHO GETS SLAPPED.

PAOLETTA   *1910 opera by Floridia*

Princess Paoletta of Castille is offered in marriage to the prince who performs the greatest deed of valor against the enemy kingdom of Aragon. Gomarez, an evil Moorish magician, wins the contest with the help of an evil spirit while masquerading as be his cousin Prince Muza. He is unmasked by a Sacred Mirror and Paoletta is able to marry her real love Don Pedro. Pietro Floridia's four-act opera *Paoletta,* libretto by Paul Jones, was commissioned for the Ohio Valley Exposition and premiered at the Music Hall in Cincinnati on August 29, 1910. Bernice de Pasquali and Edna Showalter alternated the role of Princess Paoletta, Tom Daniel was her father the King of Castille, David Bispham and Carl Gantvoort alternated Gomarez, Humbert Duffrey and Hougard Nielson alternated Don Pedro and Cecelia Hoffman and Mary Conrey alternated Jacinta. Castle and Harvey created the sets, Ben Teal staged the production and the composer conducted John C. Weber's Grand Orchestra. *Paoletta* was performed 29 times at the Music Hall and Act One was reprised at the Capitol Theater in New York City in March 1920. It was awarded the BISPHAM MEMORIAL MEDAL in 1930.

PARKER, HORATIO   *American composer (1863–1919)*

Horatio Parker was the first American composer to have an opera premiered at the Metropolitan Opera. When the Met announced a $10,000 competition in 1908 for an American opera, Parker linked up with popular playwright Brian Hooker to create the winning entry MONA. It was staged at the Met on March 14, 1912, with Louise Homer as Mona and given four performances. Parker's second opera, again with a libretto by Hooker, was the three-act FAIRYLAND, which won another $10,000 competition. It premiered at Clune's Auditorium in Los Angeles on July 1, 1915. Parker, born in Auburndale, Massachusetts, became dean of the Yale School of Music in 1904 and his pupils included Charles Ives and Roger Sessions. During his lifetime he was best known for the oratorio *Hora novissima.*

PARKER, WILLIAM   *American baritone (1943–1993)*

William Parker sings the Doctor's aria "Anatomy Lesson" from Lee Hoiby's SUMMER AND SMOKE and "Pantaloon's Ballad" from Robert Ward's HE WHO GETS SLAPPED on his recital album *The Listeners.* Parker, born in Butler, Pennsylvania, studied at Princeton and with Rosa Ponselle. He was best known for his interpretations of American art songs, premiering Ned Rorem's *Santa Fe Songs* and Ernest Bacon's *Last Invocation.* He devoted his final years to raising awareness about AIDS.

THE PARROT   *1953 TV opera by Peter*

An eccentric old lady with a large fortune dies and leaves everything to her parrot. Darrell Peter's 30-minute TV opera *The Parrot,* libretto by Frank P. De Felitta, was the first television opera commissioned by a commercial sponsor. It was premiered on Armstrong Circle Theater on NBC television on March 24, 1953, with Josephine Schillig, Shannon Bolin and Chester Watson in the main roles. It was composed for piano accompaniment.

PARTCH, HARRY   *American composer (1901–1974)*

Harry Partch is probably the most unusual opera composer America has produced and one of the most influential, though he is barely known to the wider public. While he has sometimes been dismissed as an eccentric who devised odd musical theories, he has many admirers and much of his music is on CD. Partch, who was largely self-taught, created musical instruments capable of such tiny intervals that he had to invent a 43-tone scale for them. He composed six experimental operas ("music-dance dramas") to his own librettos. They are not often seen as they are difficult to stage and require a wide array of special instruments. *US Highball*, a 25-minute drama about a cross-country hobo trip, premiered in Carnegie Chamber Hall on April 22, 1944, and was recorded in Evanston, Illinois, in 1958 by the Gate 5 Ensemble (it's on *Harry Partch Collection, Volume 2.* CRI CD); it was turned into a string quartet and recorded by the Kronos Quartet in 2003. *Oedipus*, based on William Butler Yeats' version of the Sophocles tragedy, premiered at Mills College in Oakland, CA, on March 14, 1952. THE BEWITCHED, a compendium of tales about forms of defeat, was premiered in Urbana, Illinois, in 1957, with John Garvey leading the University of Illinois Music Ensemble. REVELATION IN THE COURTHOUSE PARK, which contrasts rock star adulation with similarly behavior in ancient Greece, is loosely based on Euripides' *The Bacchae*. It premiered at the University of Illinois in 1961, and was recorded in Philadelphia in 1987. WATER! WATER!, about the problems caused by both too little and too much water, premiered at the University of Illinois in Urbana in 1962. *Delusion of the Fury*, a dream ritual opera, was premiered at UCLA on January 9, 1969.

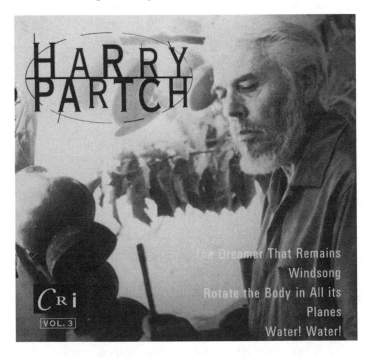

Composer Harry Partch

PASATIERI, THOMAS   *American composer (1945–)*

Thomas Pasatieri has had considerable success with his operas which are popular with performers because of their singable qualities. The first to be staged was *The Women*, libretto by the composer, presented in Aspen, Colorado, on August 20, 1965. The opera buffa LA DIVINA, about an aging coloratura giving a farewell recital who decides to give another show, premiered at the Juilliard School in 1966. *Padrevia* was performed at Brooklyn College in 1967. CALVARY, a setting of a play by W. B. Yeats, won national acclaim in 1971. It was followed by the 1972 TV opera THE TRIAL OF MARY LINCOLN, a harrowing portrait of President Lincoln's widow who is put on trial for her sanity. BLACK WIDOW, based on an Unamuno novella about a desperate childless Spanish woman, was presented by Seattle Opera in 1972. THE SEAGULL, libretto by Kenward Elmslie based on the Chekhov play, was commissioned by Houston Grand Opera which premiered it on March 5, 1974. SIGNORE DELUSO, based on a Molière play in which lovers falsely suspect each other of infidelity, was premiered at Wolf Trap in Virginia on July 27, 1974. *The Penitentes,* libretto by A. H. Bailey, was premiered in Aspen on August 3, 1974. INES DE CASTRO, the tragic story of a Portuguese woman involved with a prince, was premiered by Baltimore Opera on April 1, 1976. WASHINGTON SQUARE, based on the Henry James novel about a woman betrayed by her lover, was premiered by Michigan Opera on October 1, 1976. THE THREE SISTERS, libretto by Elmslie based on the Chekhov play, was staged by Opera/Columbia in 1986. BEFORE BREAKFAST, based on a Eugene O'Neill play about a crazed woman trying to wake her husband, was staged by New York City Opera in 1980. THE GOOSE GIRL, based on a Grimm Brothers tale, was first performed in Forth Worth in 1981. *Maria Elena,* based on a Mexican story, was premiered by the University of Arizona in Tucson on April 6, 1983. DIE SCHLUMPF, a "movie opera" created for the 1990 film *Dick Tracy,* is a brief Wagnerian pastiche. Pasatieri, a New York native who began composing at the age of fifteen, studied with Nadia Boulanger and Vittorio Giannini and at Juilliard. He has taught at a number of music schools and was director of Atlanta Opera in the early 1980s.

PASSION   *1994 operatic musical by Sondheim*

Italian Army officer Giorgio Bachetti is posted to a remote military base and separated from his married mistress Clara. He becomes involved with sickly and mentally disturbed Fosca who schemes to make him fall in love with her. She succeeds through emotional blackmail and eventually causes his death. Stephen Sondheim's operatic musical *Passion* has been promoted by some enthusiastic admirers as the most important American opera of the past half century. James Lapine's libretto and Sondheim's lyrics are based on Ettore Scola's 1981 film *Passione d'Amore* which in turn was based on Igino Tarchetti's 1869 novel *Fosca*. *Passion* premiered at the Plymouth Theater in New York on May 9, 1994, with Donna Murphy as Fosca, Jere Shea as Giorgio, Marin Mazzie as Clara, Gregg Edelman as Colonel Ricci and Tom Aldredge as Dr. Tambourri. Adrianne Lobel designed the sets, James Lapine directed and Paul Gemignani conducted. *Passion* won four Tonys, including Best Musical, and was later staged in London and televised. Minnesota Opera presented a much praised new production in 2004 with Patrica Racette as Fosca, William Burden as Giorgio and Evelyn Pollack as Clara. Tim Albery produced and Dean Williams conducted.

1995 Original Broadway Cast. Donna Murphy sings Fosca opposite Jere Shea as Giorgio in the original cast album of the musical. Marin Mazzie is Clara, Gregg Edelman is Colonel Ricci and Tom Aldredge is Dr. Tambourri and Paul Gemignani conducts. The album won the Grammy for Best Musical Show of the year. Angel CD. **1997 London Cast.** Maria Friedman is Fosca opposite Michael Ball as Giorgio and Helen Hobson as Clara in the original London cast album recorded live during a concert performance at the Hippodrome Theater in Golders

Green. First Night Records CD. **1997 American Playhouse.** The original Broadway cast was brought together for an American Playhouse television production of the musical. Donna Murphy is Fosca, Jere Shea is Giorgio and Marin Mazzie is Clara. Image VHS/LD.

Stephen Sondheim's operatic musical *Passion* has been described by admirers as the most important American opera of the past half century.

THE PASSION OF JONATHAN WADE   *1962 opera by Floyd*

Union Army Colonel Jonathan Wade, in charge of occupation forces in Columbia, South Carolina, following the Civil War, marries Celia, daughter of Judge Townsend. Northern extremists led by Radical Republican Ely Pratt and Southern extremists led by KKK chief Lucas Wardlaw create conflicts leading to Wade's murder. Carlisle Floyd's ambitious grand opera *The Passion of Jonathan Wade,* libretto by the composer, premiered at New York City Opera on October 11, 1962. Theodore Uppman was Jonathan Wade, Norman Treigle was Judge Townsend, Phyllis Curtin was his daughter Celia, Norman Kelley was Ely Pratt, Frank Porretta was Lucas Wardlaw, Patricia Brooks was Amy Pratt, Harry Theyard was Lt. Patrick, Miriam Burton was Nicey, Eugene Brice was the Senator, Richard Fredericks was the Confederate Soldier and Ron Bottcher was the Union Soldier. Will Steven Armstrong designed the sets, Allen Fletcher directed and Julius Rudel conducted the NYCO Orchestra. Like Verdi's *Don Carlo, The Passion of Jonathan Wade* features six major singing roles and requires over one hundred performers and sixty musicians. It was well received at its premiere but Floyd radically revised it for a new production by Houston Grand Opera in January 1991; Dale Duesing was Jonathan Wade, Julian Patrick was Judge Townsend, Sheryl Wood was Celia, the composer directed and John DeMain conducted. The revised version was staged by San Diego Opera in 1996.

1961 New York City Opera. The New York City Opera premiere performance on October 11, 1962, was recorded live. Theodore Uppman is Jonathan Wade, Norman Treigle is Judge Townsend, Phyllis Curtin is Celia, Norman Kelley is Ely Pratt, Frank Porretta us Lucas Wardlaw, Patricia Brooks is Amy Pratt, Harry Theyard is Lt. Patrick, Miriam Burton is Nicey and Eugene Brice is the Senator. Julius Rudel conducts the NYCO Orchestra. Live Opera audiocassette.

THE PASSION OF OEDIPUS   *1965 opera by Travis*

Thebes is devastated by a plague that the oracle says will continue until the murderer of old king Laios is discovered. Oedipus, the present king, has a phobia about oracles. His wife Jocasta's attempt to reassure him recalls a forgotten confrontation with an old man at a triple crossroads. He is the cause of the plague; the stranger he killed was his father and the woman he married was his mother. She hangs herself after which he puts out his eyes and goes into exile. Roy Travis's two-act opera *The Passion of Oedipus,* libretto by the composer loosely based on Sophocles' play *Oedipus Rex,* was premiered by UCLA Opera Theater in Los Angeles on November 8, 1968. William Du Pré sang the role of Oedipus, Christina Krooskos was Jocasta, John Robert Dunlap was Creon, William Farrell was Tiresias, Anna Levistki was the Sphinx, Cary Archer Smith was the Stranger/Laios, James Johnson was the Corinthian Envoy and Richard Hale was the Old Shepherd. Jan Popper staged the opera and conducted the UCLA Opera Theater Orchestra and Chorus. (Harry Partch's 1951 opera OEDIPUS is also based on the Sophocles play.)

1968 St. Giles Church, London. William Du Pré sings the role of Oedipus opposite Maureen Lehane as Jocasta in this recording of scenes from the opera performed at St. Giles Church in London, England. Joy Mammen is the Oracle, John Robert Dunlap is the Stranger/Laios, Robert Lloyd is the Corinthian Envoy, Richard Hale is the Old Shepherd and the Chorus plays the citizens of Thebes. Jan Popper conducts the Royal Philharmonic Orchestra and Chorus. Orion LP.

THE PASSION OF SAINT THOMAS MORE   *2000 opera by Fisher*

England in 1535. The last days of Sir Thomas More after he refuses to sanction King Henry VIII's divorce from Catherine of Aragon. More is given a paper to sign by the King; if he signs, he will live, if he doesn't, he will die. His daughter Margaret urges him to sign. A Dancer acts as a silent narrator of the story and three Dark Angels describe what is about to happen. More is executed and goes to Heaven. Garrett Fisher's *The Passion of Saint Thomas More,* libretto by the composer based on historical events, was staged and recorded in Sweden in July 2000. Anna Vinten-Johansen was Thomas More and Dark Angel No. 2, Christina Högman was Margaret and Dark Angel No. 1 and Olle Persson was King Henry VIII and Dark Angel No. 3.

2000 Lånna Church, Sweden. Anna Vinten-Johansen is Thomas More/Dark Angel No. 2, Christina Högman is Margaret/Dark Angel No. 1 and Olle Persson is King Henry VIII/Dark Angel No. 3 in this recording of the opera made at the Lånna Church in Sweden in July 2000. Taina Karr plays the cor anglais, Sven Åberg plays the guitar, Garrett Fisher plays the Indian harmonium and Göran Månsson plays percussion. 64 minutes. BIS CD.

PATIENCE AND SARAH   *1998 opera by Kimper*

In 1816 Connecticut painter Patience White falls in love with Sarah Dowling, the breeches-wearing woman who delivers wood to the house where Patience lives with her brother. When he disapproves, she breaks off the relationship but it makes her miserable. The women are reunited and decide to live together away from society in the wilds of the Catskills. Paula M. Kimper's chamber opera *Patience and Sarah*, libretto by Wende Persons based on the novel by Isabel Miller, was premiered by American Opera Projects at the Lincoln Center Festival on July 8, 1998. Lori Ann Phillips was Patience, Elaine Valby was Sarah and Barton Green was Parson Peel. Doug Moser staged the opera and Steven Osgood conducted the orchestra. *Patience and Sarah*, hailed as the first Lesbian opera, is based on the lives of real people. The composer calls it an "American folk opera" and says gay composers Aaron Copland and Samuel Barber were her musical models.

1998 Lori Phillips/Elaine Valby. Lori Phillips and Elaine Valby, who created the roles of Patience and Sarah, sing the duet "I want to live" from *Patience and Sarah*. It's on the album *Lesbian American Composers*. CRI CD.

PATRICK, JULIAN   *American baritone (1927–)*

Julian Patrick has been a major presence in modern American opera on stage, TV and record and has created six roles. He created the Troll in Andrew Imbrie's THREE AGAINST CHRISTMAS at the University of California at Berkeley in 1964, Don Hanwell in Hugo Weisgall's NINE RIVERS TO JORDAN at New York City Opera in 1969, George in Carlisle Floyd's OF MICE AND MEN at Seattle Opera in 1970, Lincoln's clerk in Thomas Pasatieri's THE TRIAL OF MARY LINCOLN on NET Opera in 1972, Casanova in Dominick Argento's CASANOVA'S HOMECOMING at Minnesota Opera in 1985 and the Mogul in Argento's THE DREAM OF VALENTINO at Washington Opera in 1994. He plays the Page in the 1963 NBC Opera telecast/recording of Gian Carlo Menotti's AMAHL AND THE NIGHT VISITORS, Carry's husband Charles in the 1968 New York City Opera production/recording of Douglas Moore's CARRY NATION, Mr. Gobineau in the 1970 Washington Opera production/recording of Menotti's THE MEDIUM and Sam in the 1973 London Weekend Television telecast/recording of Leonard Bernstein's TROUBLE IN TAHITI. He sang Judge Townsend in the premiere of the revised version of Floyd's THE PASSION OF JONATHAN WADE at Houston Grand Opera in 1991 and Prospero in the 1997 Dallas Opera revival of Lee Hoiby's THE TEMPEST. Patrick, who was born in Meridian, Mississippi, made his debut with the Mobile Opera Company in Alabama in 1950.

PATTERSON, FRANK   *American composer (1871–1966)*

Lawrence Tibbett sang a leading role in Franklin Peale Patterson's chamber opera THE ECHO when it premiered in Portland, Oregon, in 1925; the opera later won the David Bispham Medal. Patterson composed seven operas but only two seem to have been staged. The other was his one-act *Beggar's Love*, a revision of his *A Little Girl at Play*, which was presented in New York in 1930. Patterson, who was born in Philadelphia and studied in Munich, founded the Pasadena Orchestra and Choral Society. His style was apparently conservative and melodic but there are no recordings of his operas.

PATTERSON, RUSSELL   *American conductor (1928–)*

Russell Patterson founded Lyric Opera of Kansas City in 1957 and made American opera a central part of its repertory; all operas are sung in English. He conducted many of its American operas including two premieres and four recordings. He conducted the recording of Vittorio Giannini's THE TAMING OF THE SHREW in 1969, the recording of Jack Beeson's THE SWEET BYE AND BYE in 1974, the premiere and recording of Jack Beeson's CAPTAIN JINKS OF THE HORSE MARINES in 1975 and the premiere and recording of Henry Mollicone's COYOTE TALES in 1998. Other operas he conducted for the company include Carlisle Floyd's OF MICE AND MEN, Douglas Moore's THE DEVIL AND DANIEL WEBSTER, Robert Ward's THE CRUCIBLE, Kurt Weill's DOWN IN THE VALLEY and Gian Carlo Menotti's AMAHL AND THE NIGHT VISITORS, THE MEDIUM, THE SAINT OF BLEECKER STREET and THE TELEPHONE. Patterson, born in Greenville, Mississippi, studied at several universities and trained to be a conductor in Europe. He made his debut conducting opera at Kansas City Lyric in 1958.

PAUL, THOMAS   *American bass (1934–)*

Thomas Paul created the role of the villainous Jack Spaniard in Robert Ward's THE LADY FROM COLORADO at Central City Opera in 1964 and Jared Bilby in Carlisle Floyd's BILBY'S DOLL at Houston Grand Opera in 1976. He sings the Gaoler in the 1995 concert recording of Amy M. Beach's CABILDO at Lincoln Center and he played Don Marco in the New York City Opera production of Gian Carlo Menotti's THE SAINT OF BLEECKER STREET in 1954. Paul, who was born in Chicago, studied at Juilliard and made his debut at New York City Opera in 1962.

PAUL BUNYAN   *1941 "American opera" by Britten*

Paul Bunyan organizes lumberjacks to clear the virgin forest and persuades them to become farmers when America becomes settled. The mythical giant logger Paul is only an off-stage speaker but he is the one who makes things happen. The on-stage cast includes the ballad-singer Narrator, Bunyan's daughter Tiny, the cook Slim, two bad cooks, accountant Johnny Inkslinger, rebellious Hel

Benjamin Britten's 1941 "American opera" *Paul Bunyan* was not recorded until 1987.

Helson, four Swedes, a dog named Fido and cats called Moppet and Poppet. Benjamin Britten's whimsical "American opera" *Paul Bunyan*, composed to a brilliant libretto by W. H. Auden, premiered at Brander Matthews Hall at Columbia University on May 5, 1941. Milton Warchoff was Paul, Mordecai Baumann was the Narrator, Helen Marshall was Tiny, William Hess was Johnny Inkslinger, Charles Cammock was Slim, Pauline Kleinhesselink was Fido, Harriet Greene was Moppet, Augusta Dorn was Poppet, Walter Graf was Cross Crosshaulson, Leonard Stalker was John Shears, Clifford Jackson was Sam Sharkey, Eugene Bauman was Ben Benny, Ernest Holecombe was Jen Jensen, Lewis Pierce was Peter Peterson, Ben Carpens was Andy Anderson, Bliss Woodward was Hel Helson and Henry Bauman was the Western Union Boy. Hugh Ross conducted the orchestra. Auden and Britten had come to New York in 1939 and their publisher suggested they write a music theater piece for high school students following their success in films and song cycles. *Paul Bunyan* was first referred to as an operetta, then an "opera for Broadway" and eventually just as an opera but there is no designation for it on the opening night program. There are musical influences from Gershwin and Weill in this tuneful work but it was not well produced at Columbia and was considered a failure. Britten returned to England and, as he was estranged from Auden, the opera was not staged again until after Auden's death. It was well received this time and its reputation has risen sharply in recent years following major productions by St. Louis Opera in 1984, Glimmerglass Opera in 1996, New York City Opera in 1998 and the Royal Opera, Covent Garden, in 1999.

1987 Plymouth Music. Philip Brunelle leads soloists, chorus and orchestra of the Plymouth Music Series in this recording of the opera made at the Ordway Music Theatre in St. Paul, Minnesota. James Lawless is the voice of Paul Bunyan, Pop Wagner is the Narrator, Dan Dressen is Johnny Inkslinger, Elisabeth Comeaux Nelson is Tiny, Clifton Ware is Slim, Vern Sutton is bad cook Sam Sharkey, Merle Fristad is bad cook Ben Benny, James Bohn is Hel Helson, Phil Jordenson is Andy Anderson, Tim Dahl is Pete Peterson, Thomas Shaffer is Jen Jensen, Lawrence Weller is Cross Crosshaulson, James McKeel is John Shears, James Westbrook is Western Union Boy, Marie Jette is Fido, Sue Herber is Moppet, Janis Hardy is Poppet and Richard Allison, Benjamin Allen, Stanford Felix and Jay Ramos are the Four Cronies. Virgin Classics CD box. **1998 New York City Opera.** John McDonough is Paul Bunyan with David Lutken as Narrator in a telecast New York City Opera production by Mark Lamos. Elisabeth Comeaux is Tiny, Jeffrey Lentz is Johnny Inkslinger, John McVeigh is Slim, Jami Rogers is Fido, Indira Mahajan is Moppet, Leah Creek is Poppet and Erin Caves is Hel Helson. Kate Egan, Leah Summers and Beverly O'Regan Thiel are the Wild Geese; Timothy Truschel, Darren Keith Woods, Eric Dillner and Judd Ernester are the Swedes; James Bobick is John Shears, David Cangelosi is Sam Sharkey, Don Yule is Ben Benny and James Ruff is the Western Union Boy. Stewart Robertson conducted. Live from Lincoln Center program telecast on PBS April 22, 1998. Video at MTR. **1999 Royal Opera House.** Richard Hickox conducts a Royal Opera House production by Francesca Zambello. Kenneth Cranham is Paul Bunyan, Peter Coleman-Wright is Narrator, Susan Gritton is Tiny, Kurt Streit is Johnny Inkslinger, Lilian Watson is Fido, Timothy Robinson is Slim and Jeremy White is Hel Helson. The smaller roles are sung by Francis Egerton, Graeme Broadbent, Neil Gillespie, Neil Griffiths, Christopher Lackner, Jonathan Coad, Roderick Erle, Henry Moss, Pamela Helen Stephen and Leah-Marian Jones. Recorded live. Chandos CD box.

PAUL LAWRENCE DUNBAR: COMMON GROUND
1995 opera by Hailstork

Highlights in the life of Paul Lawrence Dunbar, the first African American to achieve national success as an author. Adolphus Hailstork's one-act opera *Paul Lawrence Dunbar: Common Ground*, libretto by Herbert Woodward Martin featuring poems by Dunbar, was premiered by Dayton Opera February 10, 1995, as a collaboration with local African American groups. The premiere cast featured soprano Marcia D. Porter and Angela Powell, tenor Ray M Wade Jr. and baritone Kirk A. Walker. Mikell Pinkney staged it and Jeffrey Powell conducted the chamber orchestra.

PAULUS, STEVEN   *America composer (1949–)*

Stephen Paulus built his reputation with operas based on works of literature, especially those commissioned by Opera Theatre of St. Louis. THE VILLAGE SINGER (1979), libretto by Michael Dennis Browne based on a Mary Wilkins Freeman story, concerns an elderly woman church singer in a Vermont village who does not want to be replaced. THE POSTMAN ALWAYS RINGS TWICE (1982), libretto by Colin Graham based on the James Cain novel about murderous lovers in rural California, was acclaimed at the Edinburgh Festival after its St. Louis premiere. THE WOODLANDERS (1985), libretto by Graham based on a Thomas Hardy novel, concern events in the lives of people in an English hamlet. *Harmoonia* (1991), a children's opera with libretto by Michael Dennis Browne, was commissioned and premiered by Des Moines Metro Opera. THE WOMAN AT OTOWI CROSSING (1995), libretto by Joan Vail Thorne based on a Frank Waters novel about an woman involved with the Manhattan Project, was premiered by Opera Theater of St. Louis. THE THREE HERMITS (1998), a church opera with libretto by Michael Dennis Browne based on a story by Tolstoy, was premiered in a St. Paul church. SUMMER (1999), libretto by Joan Vail Thorne based on an Edith Wharton novella, was premiered by Berkshire Opera in Massachusetts. HELOISE AND ABELARD, libretto by Frank Corsaro based on the story of the medieval lovers, was premiered by the Juilliard School in New York on April 24, 2002. Paulus, a native of Summit, NJ, studied with Dominick Argento and Paul Fetler at the University of Minnesota where he co-founded the Composers Forum.

PEARLMAN, RICHARD   *American director (1937–)*

Richard Pearlman favors opera in English and has staged a number of American operas. He became director of the Lyric Opera Center for American Artists in 1995 after eighteen years heading the Eastman School of Music Opera Theatre. He commissioned Shulamit Ran's opera BETWEEN TWO WORLDS (THE DYBBUK), premiered by the Center in 1997. He directed the premiere of George Rochberg's opera THE CONFIDENCE MAN at Santa Fe Opera in 1982 and the premiere of the Kurt Weill revue *There Once Was a Girl Named Jenny* at Eastman Opera Theatre in 1995. He staged the 1970 Washington Opera production of Gian Carlo Menotti's THE MEDIUM with Regina Resnik, which was recorded, and has also staged, Menotti's THE MEDIUM (with Jan Degaetani in an Aspen cafeteria), Dominick Argento's A WATERBIRD TALK, Samuel Barber's VANESSA, Lee Hoiby's NATALIA PETROVNA, Conrad Susa's TRANSFORMATIONS and Robert Ward's THE CRUCIBLE. Pearlman was born in Norfolk, Connecticut, and learned to direct working as assistant to Menotti, Luchino Visconti and Franco Zeffirelli. He made his debut directed opera in Washington in 1964.

PEERCE, JAN   *American tenor (1904–1984)*

Jan Peerce sings Paul's aria "Gentle Maiden" from Victor Herbert's opera NATOMA on a record of a 1935 radio broadcast and King Eadgar on a record of a 1942 radio version of Deems Taylor's THE KING'S HENCHMAN. Peerce, who was popular on radio before he began to sing at the Metropolitan Opera, often featured American operetta tunes in his radio and TV appearances and on his recordings. He recorded songs from Reginald De Koven's ROBIN HOOD in 1948, Victor Herbert's NAUGHTY MARIETTA in 1950 and Sigmund Romberg's THE NEW MOON in 1950. He performs songs from Herbert's operettas on a 1939 RCA Magic Key radio broadcast issued on disc as *The Operetta World of Victor Herbert*. He sings numbers from Romberg's THE STUDENT PRINCE on a 1940 radio broadcast and recorded the operetta with Roberta Peters and Giorgio Tozzi in 1962. He sings Herbert's EILEEN on a *Voice of Firestone* TV show in 1950. Peerce, a New York native, began his professional career at Radio City Music Hall and sang at the Met from 1941 to 1968. He move to Broadway in 1971 taking over the role of Tevye in FIDDLER ON THE ROOF; the documentary *Jan Peerce: If I Were a Rich Man* shows him singing in it.

PEN, POLLY   *American composer (1953–)*

Polly Pen has had success with offbeat music theater works on the edge between opera and musical and derived from unusual sources. Her 1996 "silent movie opera" BED AND SOFA, based on a 1926 silent Soviet film by Abram Room, premiered at the off-Broadway Vineyard Theater on February 1, 1996. It tells the story of a love triangle in a one-room apartment in Communist Moscow. Her 1985 operetta *Goblin Market*, libretto by Peggy Harmon based on an 1859 narrative poem by Christina Rossetti about the sexual temptations of two young women, premiered at the Vineyard Theater on Oct 17, 1985. The musical *The Night Governess*, libretto by the composer based on a thriller by Louis May Alcott about a governess with a secret past, premiered in May 2000 at the McCarter Theatre in Princeton, NJ. Her other works include *Her Lightness* presented by Sarasota Opera, *The Dumb Cake* premiered on NPR radio and *Christina Alberta's Father* staged by Vineyard Theater. Pen, a Chicago native, studied at Ithaca College and was an actress before devoting herself to composing.

PENNSYLVANIA   *American state (1787–)*

Pennsylvania is the birthplace of American opera. William Smith's masque ALFRED was the first opera-like music drama by an American presented in America. Smith adapted Thomas Arne's *The Masque of Alfred,* about Alfred the Great, for presentation at the College of Philadelphia in December 1756. The first truly American opera, Thomas Barton's satirical comic ballad opera THE DISAPPOINTMENT, published in Philadelphia in 1767 and set in Philadelphia, was to premiere in Philadelphia on April 20, 1767, but was blocked by the censor. Francis Hopkinson's AMERICA INDEPENDENT, one of the first American oratorios to be staged, premiered in Philadelphia on March 17, 1781, at the home of the French ambassador to the Continental Congress.

Prolific composer Alexander Reinagle premiered fourteen music theater works and operas in Philadelphia at his New Theater on Chestnut Street, beginning with the pantomime *La forêt noire* on April 26, 1794. His comic opera *The Volunteers,* premiered in 1795, is the only one that has survived in part (fourteen songs); the others were burned in a fire that destroyed the New Theater in 1820.

The New Chestnut Street Theater also hosted the premieres of Benjamin Carr's *The Patriot* (May 16, 1796), John Bray's THE INDIAN PRINCESS (April 6, 1808), Raynor Taylor's THE ETHIOP (January 1, 1814) and the first American "grand opera," William Henry Fry's LEONORA (June 4, 1845).

The Walnut Street Theater hosted two early premieres: Anthony P. Heinrich's *The Child of the Mountain: or, The Deserted Mother*, libretto by J. McMurtie (February 10, 1821) and John Clemens' *Justina* (May 18, 1830).

The oldest opera house still in regular use in the United State is Philadelphia's Academy of Music, opened in 1851, and it has hosted many premieres. They include William Henry Fry's *Notre Dame de Paris* (May 4, 1864), Johann H Bonawitz's *The Bride of Messina* (April 22, 1874), Bonawitz's *Ostrolenka* (December 3, 1974) and Wassili Leps' *Andron* (December 22, 1905).

The Music Fund Hall premiered Natale Parelli's *Belshazzar* (January 3, 1850), L. La Grassa's *Anne of Austria* (May 1856) and Parelli's *Clarisss Harlow* (English-language version, 1866).

John Philip Sousa premiered *Our Flirtations* at the Abbey Theater in Philadelphia in August 1880 before taking it on tour. Caryl Florio premiered *Uncle Tom's Cabin*, based on the novel by Harriet Beecher Stowe, in Philadelphia in 1882. Francis Sully premiered *Fortunio and His Seven Gifted Sons* at the Lyceum Theater in 1883. Gustav Hinrichs premiered *Onti-Ori* at the Grand Opera House on July 28, 1890.

Victor Herbert's grand opera NATOMA was premiered at the Metropolitan Opera House in Philadelphia on February 25, 1911, with Mary Garden and John McCormack in the leading roles. Victor Herbert premiered five of his comic operas in Philadelphia before taking them to New York: *Little Nemo* at the Forrest Theater (September 28, 1908), *The Lady of the Slipper* at the Chestnut Street Theater (January 8, 1912); *The Velvet Lady* at the Forrest Theater (December 23, 1918), *Oui, Madame* at the Philadelphia Theater (March 23, 1920) and ORANGE BLOSSOMS at the Garrick Theater (September 4, 1922).

Sigmund Romberg's MY MARYLAND premiered in Philadelphia in December 1926 on its way to Broadway but was so popular it stayed for ten months, the longest run ever by a musical in a Philadelphia theater. Romberg's next operetta THE NEW MOON was premiered at the Chestnut Street Opera House on December 22, 1927.

Attilio Parelli's one-act *I dispettosi amanti* was premiered at the Metropolitan Opera House on March 6, 1912. Céleste de Longpré Heckscher premiered her opera *The Rose of Destiny* at the Metropolitan Opera House on May 2, 1918, to raise funds for the Red Cross.

Pennsylvania-born opera people include tenor Paul Althouse (Reading), composer David Amram (Philadelphia), composer T. J. Anderson (Coatesville), composer Dominick Argento (York), composer Milton Babbitt (Philadelphia), composer Samuel Barber (Westchester), composer Marc Blitzstein (Philadelphia), composer Joseph Breil (Pittsburgh), composer Charles Wakefield Cadman (Johnstown), composer John Eaton (Bryn Mawr), soprano Ellen Faull (Pittsburgh), composer Eleanor Everest Freer (Philadelphia), composer William Henry Fry (Philadelphia), soprano Dusolina Giannini (Philadelphia), composer Vittorio Giannini (Philadelphia), tenor Herbert Handt (Philadelphia), composer Céleste de Longpré Heckscher (Philadelphia), contralto Louise Homer (Pittsburgh), composer Francis Hopkinson (Philadelphia), mezzo-soprano Marilyn Horne (Bradford), poet Robinson Jeffers (Pittsburgh), soprano Helen Jepson (Titusville), soprano Joan LaBarbara (Philadelphia), tenor Mario Lanza (Philadelphia), composer Oscar Levant (Pittsburgh), soprano Brenda Lewis (Sunbury), librettist J. D. McClatchy (Bryn Mawr), soprano Jeanette MacDonald (Philadelphia), composer Arthur Nevin (Edgeworth), baritone William Parker (Butler), composer Frank Patterson (Philadelphia), composer Vincent Persichetti (Philadelphia), tenor David

Poleri (Chestnut Hill), contralto Marie Powers (Mount Carmel), mezzo-soprano Florence Quivar (Philadelphia), composer James Ralph (Philadelphia), composer Michael Reid (Altoona), composer Bruce Saylor (Philadelphia), director Peter Sellars (Pittsburgh), composer Leo Smit (Philadelphia), composer Conrad Susa (Springdale), mezzo-soprano Blanche Thebom (Monessen), composer Isaac Van Grove (Philadelphia), composer Stewart Wallace (Philadelphia) and soprano Juanita Waller (Pittsburgh).

Allentown: Two operas by Ludwig Lenel were premiered at Muhlenberg College: *Young Goodman Brown*, based on the Hawthorne story, on April 25, 1963, and *The Rose* on May 13, 1965.

Bethlehem: Jonathan Elkus's THE OUTCASTS OF POKER FLAT, based on the Bret Harte story, premiered at Lehigh University in Bethlehem on April 16, 1960.

Chester: Margaret Garwood premiered two operas in Chester. *The Trojan Women*, based on the Euripides play, was commissioned by Suburban Opera which presented it on October 10, 1967. THE NIGHTINGALE AND THE ROSE, based on the Oscar Wilde story, was staged by Pennsylvania Opera on October 21, 1973.

Edinboro: William Alexander's *The Monkey's Paw*, based on the story by W. W. Jacobs, was premiered at Edinboro State College (now Edinboro University of Pennsylvania) on November 13, 1972.

Harrisburg: Victor Herbert's comic opera IT HAPPENED IN NORDLAND premiered at the New Lyceum Theater on November 21, 1904, before going to Broadway.

Lancaster: William Franke Harling's Broadway opera DEEP RIVER, a predecessor of George Gershwin's PORGY AND BESS, premiered in Lancaster on September 18, 1926, before opening in New York. The Lancaster Opera Company presented Douglas Moore's THE BALLAD OF BABY DOE at the Fulton Theater in 1992 and the production was videotaped.

Philadelphia: Philadelphia Lyric Opera was founded in 1923 and Philadelphia Grand Opera in 1927 but neither seemed to be interested in American opera. Lyric Opera's music director Alexander Smallens conducted premieres of four important American operas but not in Philadelphia. Gabriel Von Wayditch four-hour opera *Horus* was staged by Philadelphia's La Scala Opera Company on January 5, 1939, with Fritz Mahler conducting. Marc Blitzstein's first opera TRIPLE-SEC, in which the audience supposedly gets drunk and sees everything in triplicate, premiered at the Bellevue Stratford Hotel on May 6, 1929. Robert Elmore's one-act *It Happened at Breakfast* was premiered at the same hotel on February 18, 1941. Philadelphia Opera premiered Deems Taylor's *Ramuntcho* at the Academy on February 8, 1942. Kurt Weill's "American opera" STREET SCENE premiered at the Shubert Theatre on December 16, 1946, before going to Broadway. Gian Carlo Menotti's opera career began in Philadelphia and four of his operas were premiered in the city. The Curtis Institute of Music, where he studied, premiered AMELIA GOES TO THE BALL on April 1, 1937. Philadelphia Opera, created in 1938 to present operas in English at the Academy of Music, mounted the stage premiere of Menotti's THE OLD MAID AND THE THIEF on February 11, 1941. The Opera Company of Philadelphia, created in 1975 through merging the Grand Opera and Lyric Opera companies, premiered Menotti's THE HERO on June 1, 1976. Later seasons featured Menotti's THE MEDIUM and THE SAINT OF BLEECKER STREET. THE CONSUL was premiered at the Schubert Theater in Philadelphia on March 1, 1950, before going on to Broadway. The Opera Company premiered Joseph Baber's *Rumpelstilskin* at the Walnut Street Theater on December 26, 1978, and revived John Philip Sousa's *The Free Lance* in 1979. The Curtis Institute of Music premiered Stanley

Hollingsworth's THE MOTHER, based on a Hans Christian Anderson tale, on March 29, 1954; Robert Convery's *Pyramus and Thisbe*, based on Shakespeare's *A Midsummer Night's Dream*, on March 23, 1983; and Kim Morrill's *Perlimplin*, libretto by the composer based on a García Lorca play, on February 18, 1989. The Community Opera company premiered Martin Kalmanoff's *The Delinquents* on April 26, 1955. Michael White's *Metamorphosis*, based on the Kafka story, was premiered in 1968. Ned Rorem's THREE SISTERS WHO ARE NOT SISTERS, libretto from the play by Gertrude Stein, was premiered at Temple University in 1971. Jerome Hines' religious opera I AM THE WAY was staged in 1969. The American Music Theater Festival has made a major contribution to American opera in recent years through its commissions and productions. They include Noa Ain's gospel-style *Trio* in 1984, Anthony Davis's biographical X THE LIFE AND TIMES OF MALCOLM X in 1985, Duke Ellington's "street opera" QUEENIE PIE in 1986, Harry Partch's REVELATION IN THE COURTHOUSE PARK in 1987, Michael Sahl and Eric Salzman's STAUF in 1987, William Bolcom's cabaret opera CASINO PARADISE in 1990, Meredith Monk's grandiose ATLAS in 1991, Anthony Davis's controversial TANIA in 1992, Milton Subotnick's multi-media *Jacob's Room* in 1993, Adam Guettel's operatic musical FLOYD COLLINS in 1994, Richard X. Rodriguez's biographical FRIDA: THE STORY OF FRIDA KAHLO in 1991 and John Duffy's controversial BLACK WATER in 1997. The Academy of Vocal Arts Opera Theatre premiered Robert Baksa's ARIA DA CAPO, based on the Edna St. Vincent Millay play, on May on 11, 1981, and presented a notable production of Richard Wargo's A CHEKHOV TRILOGY in 1996. The Opera Company of Philadelphia co-commissioned Wargo's 1999 BALLYMORE. Pennsylvania Opera Theater, founded in 1975 to present alternative operatic works in English, has premiered three American operas: Margaret Garwood's RAPPACCINI'S DAUGHTER, based on the Hawthorne story, was presented with piano on November 21, 1980, and staged with orchestra on May 6, 1983. Vincent Persichetti's *The Sibyl: A Parable of Chicken Little* was staged on April 13, 1985. Greg Pliska's *The Secret Garden*, libretto by David Ives based on the children's novel by Frances Hodgson Burnett, was presented December 16, 1988, and March 2, 1991. Other Opera Theater productions have included Leonard Bernstein's CANDIDE, Stephen Sondheim's SWEENEY TODD and Robert Ward's THE CRUCIBLE. Maurice Wright's electronic opera *The Trojan Conflict* was commissioned by the Philadelphia Network of Music and premiered at the Painted Bride Arts Center on April 2, 1989. Eugene Ormandy leads the Philadelphia Orchestra in recordings of music from four American operas and operettas including Gian Carlo Menotti's AMELIA GOES TO THE BALL.

Pittsburgh: Thomas Surette's *Cascabel: or, The Broken Tryst* was premiered in Philadelphia in 1899. Arthur Nevin's POIA, the first American grand opera to premiere in Germany, was presented in concert format in Pittsburgh on January 15, 1906, with singers and the Pittsburgh Symphony Orchestra conducted by the composer. Matthew Frey's *The Violin Maker of Cremona* was premiered at the Carnegie Institute of Technology on March 24, 1922. Elie Siegmeister's *The Mermaid in Lock No. 7*, libretto by Edward Eager, was premiered at Point State Park in Pittsburgh on July 20, 1958. Bruce Saylor's MY KINSMAN, MAJOR MOLINEUX, libretto by Cary Plotkin based on a Hawthorne story, was commissioned by the Opera Workshop which premiered it on August 28, 1976. Stewart Wallace's post-minimalist opera KABBALAH, libretto by Michael Korie, was presented in Pittsburgh in 1990 with Michael Barrett conducting. Pittsburgh Opera, founded in 1940 and now performing in the Benedum Center for the Performing Arts, concentrates on European works but has also presented American operas including Carlisle Floyd's SUSANNAH, Robert Ward's THE CRUCIBLE and Kurt Weill's STREET SCENE. Opera Theater of Pittsburgh, which produces its operas at the Byham Theater, has staged Gian Carlo Menotti's THE SAINT OF BLEECKER STREET. Nikolai Lopatnikoff's *Danton*, based on Büchner's play *Danton's Death*, was presented in concert form by the Pittsburgh Symphony Orchestra on March 25, 1967. The orchestra, now led by Lorin Maazel, made a recording of excerpts from Victor Herbert comic operas in 1991.

Roxborough: Margaret Garwood's *Joringel and the Songflowers*, based on a Grimm fairytale, was premiered in Roxborough, PA, on February 25, 1987.

Scranton: Victor Herbert's comic opera *The Ameer* premiered at the Lyceum Theater on October 9, 1899, before opening on Broadway at Wallack's on December 4.

Shippensburg: Armenian American composer Alan Hovhaness's *Pericles*, based on the Shakespeare play, was performed in excerpt form in Shippensburg in 1979.

Tamiment: Sol Berkovitz's jazz opera *Fat Tuesday* premiered at the Playhouse in Tamiment on August 11, 1956.

Wilkes-Barre: Victor Herbert premiered two of his comic operas at the Grand Opera House in Wilkes-Barre before taking them to Broadway. THE WIZARD OF THE NILE was staged on September 26, 1895, and OLD DUTCH was presented on November 6, 1909. Jerome Moross's *The Eccentricities of Davy Crockett*, one of the components of his BALLET BALLADS, was presented at Wilkes College on April 16, 1971.

Williamsport: Thomas Canning's one-act *Albert and Tiberius* was presented at Lycoming College in May 1956

Visually powerful scene from Pittsburgh Opera's fine production of *Dead Man Walking*. Photograph by David Bachman, courtesy of Pittsburgh Opera.

PEONY PAVILION   1998
adaptation of Chinese opera by Tan

A young Chinese woman dies of love, descends into hell and is brought back to life by love. *Peony Pavilion* is a modern adaptation of a 16th century Chinese Kunqu opera created by Chinese American composer Tan Dun and American producer Peter Sellars. It was premiered at the Vienna Festival on May 12, 1998, in a production that operated on three levels. The original play, written by Tang Xianzu and considered China's greatest drama, was performed in Chinese with Hua Wenyi as the woman. On the second level Cyril Birch's translation of the play was performed in English with Donna Leichenko as the heroine. On the third level Tan Dun's music was added and sung by soprano Ying Huang and tenor Lin Quiang Xu with Steven R. Osgood conducting an ensemble of Chinese and western instruments. The music is a blend of disparate styles ranging from Tibetan and Chinese music to synthesizers and electric guitars that Tan has described as "Gregorian chant meets rock'n'roll meeting ancient Chinese Kunqu Opera." The opera later toured Europe and was staged in California in 1998.

1999 Bitter Love. *Bitter Love* is a 60-minute version *of Peony Pavilion* rearranged for soprano, vocalists and small ensemble by Tan Dun and recorded in New York. Soprano Ying Huang is the featured singer and tells the story of the opera through her arias. Tan conducts the New York Virtuoso Singers and instrumental ensemble. Sony CD.

PERFECT LIVES   *1980 opera by Ashley*

A football star, a piano player and an adventurous woman in a small Midwest town decide to "borrow" money from a bank for a day as a prank. Their story is told in seven half-hour scenes set in different places in the town: a park, a supermarket, a bank, a bar, a living room, a church and a backyard. Robert Ashley's video opera *Perfect Lives,* libretto by the composer, was created for and premiered at The Kitchen in New York City in 1980. David Van Tieghem played football star D, Jill Kroesen was Isolde, "Blue" Gene Tyranny was piano player Buddy and composer Ashley was the narrator. John Sanborn created the video imagery and Peter Gordon produced the music

1983 Original cast. Jill Kroesen is Isolde, David Van Tieghem is football team captain D, "Blue" Gene Tyranny is piano player Buddy and Robert Ashley is the narrator in this production of the opera. John Sanborn directed the video. Lovely Music VHS and CD. **1983 London production.** Ashley employs video monitors and multiple images in a performance of the opera in a theater in London, England, with Jill Kroesen (Isolde) and David Van Tieghem (D) as the singers, "Blue" Gene Tyranny playing keyboards and Ashley as narrator. Scenes from the production are featured in Peter Greenaway's documentary *Robert Ashley* in his *4 American Composers* series. Mystic Fire VHS. **1984 Music Word Fire: The Lessons.** *Music Word Fire and I Would Do It Again: The Lessons* consists of variations on themes from *Private Lives* with brief portraits of Buddy, Isolde, NoZhay, and Donnie. Lovely Music VHS.

PERPETUAL   *1961 opera by Kanitz*

Three commedia dell'arte marionettes in an 18th century mechanical music theater spin around and sing when they stop. Colombina and Arlecchino face each and sing a love duet as Scaramuccio expresses his cynicism. Colombina and Scaramuccio face each other and sing a light-hearted duet as Arlecchino expresses his jealousy. Finally all three face the audience and complain about being alone. Ernest Kanitz's one-act sixteen-minute chamber opera *Perpetual,* libretto by Ellen Terry, was premiered at Antelope Valley College in Los Angeles on April 26, 1961. It is Kanitz's most popular opera, especially with colleges, and was commissioned by After Dinner Opera which presented it in New York for a week.

PERRY, DOUGLAS   *American tenor (1947–)*

Douglas Perry created the role of the Doctor in Gian Carlo Menotti's TAMU-TAMU in Chicago in 1973, Gandhi in Philip Glass's SATYAGRAHA for Netherlands Opera in Rotterdam in 1980, the Analyst in Leonard Bernstein's A QUIET PLACE at Houston Grand Opera in 1983, the Marquis de Lisle in Dominick Argento's CASANOVA'S HOMECOMING for Minnesota Opera in 1985, the Scientist/First Mate in Philip Glass's THE VOYAGE for the Metropolitan Opera in 1992 and a leading role in Susan Botti's 1994 chamber

opera *Wonderland* He sings the role of Thaddeus Stevens in the 1977 Santa Fe Opera production and recording of Virgil Thomson's THE MOTHER OF US ALL.

PERRY, EUGENE   *American baritone (1956–)*

Eugene Perry, the twin brother of Herbert Perry, often works with composers Anthony Davis and Philip Glass and director Peter Sellars, and has created roles in six American operas. He played Tarj in Davis's UNDER THE DOUBLE MOON in 1989, Mamoud in John Adams' THE DEATH OF KLINGHOFFER when it was staged by Sellars in Brussels in 1991, Orpheus in Glass's ORPHÉE at the American Repertory Theater in Cambridge in 1993, the Persian King Xerses in Hugo Weisgall's ESTHER at New York City Opera in 1993, Antonio in Davis's AMISTAD at Lyric Theater of Chicago in 1997 and the Officer in Philip Glass's IN THE PENAL COLONY in Seattle in 2000 (jointly with brother Herbert). He sings Malcolm X in the 1992 cast recording of Davis's X, THE LIFE AND TIMES OF MALCOLM X (but did not create the role), Gideon in Noa Ain's THE OUTCAST in the 1994 Houston Grand Opera production and Pierre Lafitte in the 1995 Lincoln Center production and recording of Amy M. Beach's CABILDO. Perry, who was born in Illinois, made his debut at Arizona Opera in 1980.

PERRY, HERBERT   *American bass-baritone (1956–)*

Herbert Perry, twin brother of Eugene Perry, created the role of Pastor Avery in Tobias Picker's EMMELINE at Santa Fe Opera in 1991 and is featured on the telecast and CD. He played the Officer in the premiered of Philip Glass's IN THE PENAL COLONY in Seattle in 2000 (jointly with his brother Eugene). He sings Reginald in the 1992 cast recording of X, THE LIFE AND TIMES OF MALCOLM X. Perry was born in Illinois and made his debut at Arizona Opera in 1979.

PERRY, JULIA   *American composer (1924–1979)*

Julia Perry created three operas based on stories by Edgar Allan Poe and Oscar Wilde. *The Bottle,* libretto by the composer based on Poe's story *The Cask of Amontillado,* was written in 1953 but not staged. She revisited the story for *The Cask of Amontillado,* this time collaborating on the libretto with V. Card. It was presented at Columbia University on November 24, 1954. Both operas were published. The three-act opera-ballet *The Selfish Giant,* libretto by the composer based on the Oscar Wilde fairy tale, was completed in 1964 and published but not staged. Perry, an African American, was born in Lexington, Kentucky, and studied at Princeton and Juilliard and in Europe with Nadia Boulanger. She won two Guggenheim fellowships and two of her compositions have been recorded including a *Stabat Mater.*

PERSICHETTI, VINCENT   *American composer (1915–1987)*

Vincent Persichetti wrote a great deal of music but only one opera, a dark atonal version of the fable of Chicken Little who believes the sky is falling. *The Sibyl: A Parable of Chicken Little,* composed in 1976 to his own libretto, was commissioned by Pennsylvania Opera Theater which premiered it in Philadelphia on April 13, 1985. Persichetti, who was born in Philadelphia, became a professional musician at the age of eleven, and studied at the Philadelphia Conservatory and at Juilliard. His other compositions include *Harmonium,* a setting for soprano of Wallace Stevens' poem, and *A Lincoln Address,* a setting of excerpts from Lincoln's second inaugural address. His manual *Twentieth Century Harmony* has become a standard text.

PETER IBBETSON *1931 opera by Taylor*

Peter Ibbetson rediscovers his lost childhood sweetheart Mary who is now the Duchess of Towers. After accidentally killing his father Colonel Ibbetson, Peter is sentenced to death but saved by Mary's intervention. The couple escape from the impossibilities of reality into a shared dream world. Deems Taylor's three-act opera *Peter Ibbetson*, libretto by Constance Collier and the composer based on Gerald Du Maurier's 1891 novel and John Nathaniel Raphael's l915 stage adaptation, premiered at the Metropolitan Opera on February 7, 1931. Edward Johnson was Peter Ibbetson, Lucrezia Bori was Mary, Lawrence Tibbett was Colonel Ibbetson, Marion Telva was Mrs. Deane, Ina Bourskaya was Mrs. Glyn, Angelo Bada was Achille, Leon Rothier was Duquesnois, Louis d'Angelo was the Chaplain, Grace Divine was Madge and George Cehanovsky was the Prison Governor. Joseph Urban designed the sets, Wilhelm von Wymetal directed and Tullio Serafin conducted the Metropolitan Opera Orchestra and Chorus. The opera received thirty-six curtain calls at its premiere and was staged twenty more times in following seasons. It was revived in 1960 at the Empire State Music Festival and in 1999 by the Seattle Symphony.

1934 Metropolitan Opera. Edward Johnson is Peter Ibbetson, Lucrezia Bori is Mary, Lawrence Tibbett is Colonel Ibbetson and Gladys Swarthout is Mrs. Deane in a recording of a Metropolitan Opera broadcast on March 17, 1934. Tullio Serafin conducts the Metropolitan Opera Orchestra. Unique Opera Records LP/Omega Opera Archives CD. **1935 Paramount film.** *Peter Ibbetson* was adapted for the screen in 1935 by the opera's librettist Constance Collier, but Taylor's music was not used. Ernst Toch wrote a different score which was nominated for an Oscar. Gary Cooper plays Peter Ibbetson opposite Ann Harding as Mary with opera soprano Marguerite Namara in a small role. Henry Hathaway directed the 88-minute film for Paramount. Luis Buñuel called it "one of the world's ten best films." **1960 Licia Albanese.** Licia Albanese sings Mary's aria "I could never dedicate my days" on a recording of a radio broadcast on June 29, 1960. It's on the album *Souvenirs from American Opera.* International Record Collectors' Club CD. **1999 Seattle Symphony.** Anthony Griffey sings the role of Peter Ibbetson with Lauren Flanigan as Mary in this recording of a Seattle Symphony concert version of the opera broadcast on April 30, 1999. The reprise was arranged by Gerard Schwartz who conducts the Seattle Symphony Orchestra. Richard Zeller is Colonel Ibbetson, Lori Summers is Mrs. Deane, Charles Austin is Major Duquesnois, Emily Lunde is Mrs. Glyn, Carolyn Gronlund is Madge Plunkett, Terri Richter is Pasquier and Paul Gudas is Charlie Plunkett. Opera Classics audiocassette.

PETERS, ROBERTA *American soprano (1930–)*

Roberta Peters created the role of the Princess in Mark Bucci's TV opera THE THIRTEEN CLOCKS on ABC Television in 1953 and played Kitty in the American premiere of Gian Carl Menotti's THE LAST SAVAGE at the Met in 1964. Peters, a New York native who made her debut at the Met in 1950 at the age of 19, can be heard several recordings of American operettas. She sings Kathie in a 1962 recording of Sigmund Romberg's THE STUDENT PRINCE opposite Jan Peerce and Giorgio Tozzi and Julie in a 1962 recording of Richard Rodgers' CAROUSEL opposite Alfred Drake. Her 1963 album with Drake of Leonard Bernstein songs includes "Glitter and Be Gay" from CANDIDE. She can be seen on videos of *Voice of Firestone* television programs singing "Italian Street Song from Victor Herbert's NAUGHTY MARIETTA in 1952 and "Indian Love Call" from Rudolf Friml's ROSE MARIE in 1954.

PHAEDRA *1976 opera by Rochberg*

Athens, Greece, in pre-historic times. Phaedra is now married to Theseus who had earlier killed her half-brother the Minotaur and abandoned her sister Ariadne. She falls desperately in love with her stepson Hippolytus but he rejects her. She angrily accuses him of raping her and then hangs herself. George Rochberg's seven-act, one character opera *Phaedra,* based on Robert Lowell's version of Jean Racine's play *Phèdre* derived from a Greek myth, was premiered in Syracuse, NY, on January 9, 1976. Mezzo-soprano Neva Pilgrim sang the role of Phaedra and D. Loebel conducted the orchestra. (George Roumanis's 1995 opera ODE TO PHAEDRA is based on the same story.)

THE PHANTOM TOLLBOOTH *1995 children's opera by Black*

Young Milo drives through a magic tollbooth into the kingdoms of Dictionopolis and Digitopolis who are at war about the importance of words versus numbers. He jumps to a place called Conclusion and visits the silent Valley of Sound. Finally he saves Princesses Rhyme and Reason from the beasts Gross Exaggeration and Threadbare Excuse. Arnold Black's children's opera *The Phantom Tollbooth*, libretto by Broadway lyricist Sheldon Harnick based on the novel by Norton Juster, was premiered by OperaDelaware's Family Opera Theater in Wilmington on March 4, 1995. Matthew Williams was young Milo, Cal Brackin was Tock the Watchdog, Anne DiFernando and Sara Jane Duffey were Princesses Rhyme and Reason and Alan Wagner and John Dennison were the rival monarchs. Leland Kimball directed and designed the sets and Evelyn Swenson conducted the 36-piece orchestra.

PHILIP MARSHALL *1974 opera by Barab*

Philip Marshall returns home after fighting for the Confederacy during the American Civil War. His attempts to do the right thing for his friends have tragic results. Seymour Barab's opera *Philip Marshall,* libretto by the composer based on Dostoevsky's novel *The Idiot* but transposed to Virginia in 1866, was premiered by Chautauqua Opera in New York on July 12, 1974. It was revived by California State College in Hayward in 1979.

PHILLIPS, LINDA *American soprano (1946–)*

Linda Phillips created the role of Theodoria Burr in Carmines' THE DUEL at the Metropolitan Opera Studio in Brooklyn in 1974 and the role of Pelagia's Maid in Robert Starer's THE LAST LOVER at the Caramoor Festival in Katonah, NY, in 1975. On stage she has sung the role of Monica in Gian Carlo Menotti's THE MEDIUM. Phillips, who was born in Hastings, Nebraska, studied at Indiana University and made her debut at Kansas City Lyric in 1968.

THE PHOTOGRAPHER *1982 music theater work by Glass*

A dramatic portrayal of the life of 19th century motion picture pioneer Eadweard Muybridge who photographed horses and people in motion, invented the zoopraxiscope and murdered his wife's lover. The first act is a play with music, the second act a concert with a photographic slide show and the third act a dance piece. Philip Glass's music theatre work *The Photographer,* libretto by Dutch director/designer Rob Malasch and the composer, was premiered by Netherlands Opera in Amsterdam May 30, 1982. Composed for solo vocalist, chorus, and chamber orchestra, it was performed by DeGroep with set designs by Rein Jansma and Joost Eiffers. Michael Riesman conducted. The work was reprised at the Brooklyn Academy of Music in October 1983 with a new text by

Robert Coe under the direction of JoAnne Akalaitis with choreography by David Gordon.

1983 Philip Glass Ensemble. *The Photographer* was recorded at the Greene Street Recording Studio in New York in 1983 with Michael Riesman conducting the Philip Glass Ensemble and Chorus. Paul Zukovsky is the solo violinist and Maeretha Stewart and Marlene VerPlanck are the lead vocalists on "A Gentlemen's Honor." Glass began to experiment with extensive overdubbing with this studio recording. Sony Classics CD.

PICKER, TOBIAS   *American composer (1954–)*

Tobias Picker emerged at the end of the 20th century as one of the most promising new American opera composers. He received considerable praise for EMMELINE, a reworking of the Oedipus myth transposed to 19th century New England by librettist J. D. McClatchy, which was premiered by Santa Fe Opera in 1996. It was followed by the visually dazzling but less well-received FANTASTIC MR. FOX, libretto by Donald Sturrock based on the story by Roald Dahl, which premiered at Los Angeles Opera in 1999. THÉRÈSE RAQUIN, libretto by Gene Scheer based on the novel by Emil Zola, was commissioned by Dallas Opera which premiered it on November 30, 2001, with Sara Fulgoni in the title role. *An American Tragedy,* based on the Theodore Dreiser novel, was commissioned by the Metropolitan Opera. Tobias Picker, who was born in New York City, studied at Juilliard, Manhattan School of Music and Princeton. He has composed a wide spectrum of works including symphonies, concertos and song-cycles.

PICKETT, WILLIAM   *American baritone (1929–)*

William Pickett created and recorded roles in five operas at Kentucky Opera in the 1950s. He was Nanda in Peggy Glanville-Hicks chamber opera *The Transposed Heads,* based on the Thomas Mann novel, in April 1954; twin brother Pocus in Richard Mohaupt's *Double Trouble,* based on Plautus's play *Menaechmi,* in December 1954; husband Josh dining with a ghostly wife in George Antheil's macabre *The Wish* in April 1955; Arnolphe in Rolf Liebermann's *School for Wives,* based on Molière's play *L'école des femmes,* in December 1955, and the Prince conspiring against Rasputin in Nicolas Nabokov's *The Holy Devil* in April 1958.

THE PICTURE OF DORIAN GRAY   *1996 opera by Liebermann*

Dorian Gray gives away his soul so he can stay young and handsome while a portrait of him grows old and ugly. After he causes the death of an actress friend, the portrait reflects his growing cruelty and is hidden in the attic. Many years later Dorian shows the changes in the portrait to the horrified painter and kills him after an argument. After more crimes, Dorian stabs the portrait and dies. Lowell Liebermann's two-act opera *The Picture of Dorian Gray,* libretto by the composer based on the novel by Oscar Wilde, was commissioned by Monte Carlo Opera and Opera Pacific and premiered in Monte Carlo on May 8, 1996. It was the first American opera premiered there. Jeffrey Lentz sang the tenor role of Dorian Gray, John Hancock was his friend Lord Henry Wotton, Gregory Reinhart was the painter Basil Hallward, Korliss Uecker was the actress friend Sibyl Vane, Ron Baker was her brother James Vane, Vivian Tierney was the Whore, Stephen Chanundy was Lord Geoffrey and Bryan Jones was the Gamekeeper. Stephen Brimson Lewis designed the sets, John Cox directed and Steuart Bedford conducted the Monte Carlo Orchestra. Florentine Opera in Milwaukee mounted the American premiere of *The Picture of Dorian Gray* on February 5, 1999, using sets and costumes from the Monte Carlo production with Bedford again conducting. Mark Thomsen took over the role of Dorian, John Hancock was Wotton, Erie Mills was Sibyl and Nancy Shade was the Whore. Linda Brodsky directed.

2001 Florentine Opera. Mark Thomsen is Dorian Gray in this recording of a production of the opera by Florentine Opera in Milwaukee on November 8, 2001. Erie Mills is Sibyl, John Hancock is Wotton, Nancy Shade is the Whore and J. Anderson is Basil. House of Opera CD.

PIERSON, EDWARD   *American bass-baritone (1931–)*

Edward Pierson created the role of El Cimarron in Hans Werner Henze's RACHEL, LA CUBANA on NET TV in 1973 and the role of Bamboola in Robert Starer's PANTAGLEIZE at Brooklyn College the same year. He sang Parson Alltalk in the 1975 Houston Grand Opera production/recording of TREEMONISHA. He can be seen rehearsing the aria "Pigeon on the Grass, Alas" from FOUR SAINTS IN THREE ACTS with composer Virgil Thomson in the documentary film *Gertrude Stein: When This You See, Remember Me.* On stage he has sung Olin Blitch in Carlisle Floyd's SUSANNAH, Porgy and Crown in George Gershwin's PORGY AND BESS and Count Cenci in Alberto Ginastera's BEATRIX CENCI. Pierson, who was born in Chicago, made his debut at New York City Opera in 1966.

PIGEONS ON THE GRASS, ALAS   *Aria/Ensemble: Four Saints in Three Acts (1934). Words: Gertrude Stein. Music: Virgil Thomson*

"Pigeons on the Grass Alas," though rarely performed, remains one of the most famous numbers in American opera, known more for its words than for its music. Gertrude Stein's "nonsense" lyrics to Virgil Thomson's music were the weapon humorists used to show the supposed silliness of this avant-garde opera and their attacks make the phrase nationally famous. "Pigeons" is actually a hymn-like baritone aria performed by St. Ignatius with the ensemble after he has a miraculous vision of the Holy Ghost. The dove or pigeon is the symbol in religious art for the Holy Spirit which is why he sings "Pigeon on the grass alas." A men's chorus repeats the phrase and Ignatius asks "If they were not pigeons on the grass alas what were they?" The Compere suggests Ignatius has "heard of a third" (the Holy Ghost is the third part of the Holy Trinity) and the experience is examined in repetitive phrases. The pigeon on the grass is eventually transmogrified into a magpie in the sky. It's quite fun verbally and religious in an odd way but hardly nonsense. In the 1947 recording of the opera conducted by the composer, the aria is beautifully sung by Edward Matthews as St. Ignatius while on the 1981 recording conducted by Joe Thome it's nicely sung by Arthur Thompson.

PILATE   *1966 ballet-opera by Hovhaness*

Pontius Pilate is suffering remorse for condemning Jesus Christ even though he had washed his hands of responsibility for his Crucifixion. He climbs to the top of Mt. Pilatus as the bird-like figure Silent Wings dances around him and he sees visions of a saint and a murderer. A Chorus tells him what he should have done. He throws himself off the mountain in atonement. Alan Hovhaness's 30-minute ballet-opera *Pilate,* libretto by the composer based on folk legend, premiered at Pepperdine College in Los Angeles, on June 26, 1966. Pilate and the Chorus are both bass roles, Silent Wings is a contralto and the saint and the murderer are dancers.

PINKHAM, DANIEL   *American composer (1923–)*

Daniel Pinkham, born in Lynn, Massachusetts, has composed half a dozen operas to his own librettos and most of them have been produced. *The Passion of Judas* was staged in Montreal in 1979. *The Dreadful Dining Car*, based on a story by Mark Twain, was completed in 1982. *The Left-Behind Beasts* was commissioned by the Children's Opera Program and James Otis School of Boston and staged in Boston in 1985. THE CASK OF AMONTILLADO, based on the story by EDGAR ALLAN POE, was staged by Opera Boston in 2003 together with his opera GARDEN PARTY, which takes place in the Garden of Eden.

PINZA, EZIO   *American bass (1892–1957)*

Ezio Pinza created leading roles in two notable Broadway musicals and sang in a memorable movie opera. He left the Metropolitan Opera in 1949 after twenty-two years to play French planter Emile de Becque in SOUTH PACIFIC, a part created for him by composer Richard Rodgers and librettist Oscar Hammerstein. He was a huge success and went on to create the role of César in Harold Rome's *Fanny* in 1954. In Mario Castelnuovo-Tedesco's movie opera IL RITORNO DI CESARE, created for the 1951 film *Strictly Dishonorable*, he sings the aria "Il Ritorno de Cesare" on a Met-like stage. Pinza, born in Rome, began his career in Italy and came to the Met in 1926. In addition to Hollywood films, he also had his own TV series.

THE PIPE OF DESIRE   *1906 opera by Converse*

The pipe of desire is a magic pipe owned by the Old One, leader of the elves. Young Iolan uses it wrongly and causes the death of his lover Naoia and himself. Frederick Converse's "romantic grand opera in one act" *Iolan or The Pipe of Desire*, libretto by George Edward Burton, was the first American opera presented at the Metropolitan Opera in New York. It was staged March 18, 1910, with Louise Homer as Naoia, Ricardo Martin as Iolan, Clarence Whitehill as the Old One, Leonora Sparkes as First Sylph, Lillia Snelling as Undine, Glenn Hall as Salamander and Herbert Witherspoon as Gnome. Kurt Stern directed and Alfred Herz conducted. It was presented at the Met as the first half of a double bill with *Pagliacci* but it was not a premiere. *The Pipe of Desire* was first performed by the Boston Opera Company in Boston on January 31, 1906, with Bertha Cushing Child as Naoia, George Dean as Iolan, Stephen Townsend as the Old One and Alice Bates Rice as First Sylph. Wallace Goodrich conducted. The opera was reprised by Boston Opera in 1911 and Chatterton Opera in Bloomington, Illinois, in 1915.

THE PIPER OF HAMELIN   *1970 children's opera by Flagello*

The town of Hamelin in northern Germany is overrun by rats and mice until a Piper appears and offers to lure them away for payment. After he does so, the greedy town leaders refuse to pay saying it is no longer necessary. In response the Piper lures away the children of the town. The town pays up and the children are returned. Nicholas Flagello's children's opera *The Piper of Hamelin*, libretto by the composer based on Robert Browning's poem *The Pied Piper of Hamelin*, was premiered April 18, 1970, by students at the Manhattan School of Music in New York. Flagello created the happy ending; in the poem the children are never seen again. **1999 Manhattan School of Music.** The Manhattan School of Music reprised the opera in March 1999 and recorded it live. Bob McGrath is the narrator, Brace Negron is the Piper, Troy Doney is the Mayor of Hamelin, Nicole McQuade is First Woman, Alek-

sei Archer is Second Woman, Jessica Dawer is Third Woman, Andrew Wolinsky is First Man, Anthony Jimenez is Second Man and José-Manuel Fernandez is Third Man. Gordon Ostrowski staged the opera and Jonathan Strasser conducted. Newport Classic CD.

A PLACE TO CALL HOME   *1992 opera by Barnes*

Asian, Latin American, Middle Eastern and Native American students, all recent arrivals in Los Angeles, struggle to make the new city their home. Edward Barnes multi-ethnic one-act opera *A Place to Call Home,* libretto by the composer, was premiered by Los Angeles Opera on March 2, 1992, with a cast of students from Birmingham High School in Van Nuys. Barnes wrote the libretto based on interviews with students who had recently come to Los Angeles from Mexico, El Salvador, Vietnam, Cambodia and other countries.

PLISHKA, PAUL   *American bass (1941–)*

Metropolitan bass Paul Plishka has not sung American opera at the Met but he is featured on recordings of two American music theatre works. He sings the role of Nick Shadow in a recording if Igor Stravinsky's THE RAKE'S PROGRESS, based on Graham Vick's 1995 production at the Saito Kinen Festival in Japan, and Judge Turpin in a 1999 New York concert performance of Stephen Sondheim's SWEENEY TODD. Plishka was born and raised in a Ukrainian community in Old Forge, Pennsylvania.

THE PLOUGH AND THE STARS   *1969 opera by Siegmeister*

Dublin, Ireland, at the time of the Easter Uprising in 1916. Nora Clitheroe is pregnant but her husband Jack goes off anyway to join the Irish Citizen Army. In a pub he sings of the Plough and the Stars, the flag symbolizing the revolution. Nora's baby dies during the fighting when she goes out to look for her husband. Protestant Bessie takes care of Nora until she is shot by a sniper. Jack is shot dead in the street. Elie Siegmeister's tragic three-act opera *The Plough and the Stars,* libretto by Edward Mabley based on Sean O'Casey's play, was first staged as *Dublin Song* at Washington University in St. Louis May 15, 1963, and revised for presentation with the play title at Louisiana State University in Baton Rouge on March 16, 1969. It was reprised at the opera house in Bordeaux, France, in 1970. The score is mostly melodic and tonal, incorporating various styles of popular music from pub songs to hymns.

PLUMP JACK   *1985 opera by Getty*

Plump Jack is Shakespeare's Falstaff, the bragging companion of Prince Hall and would-be suitor of Dame Quickly. Gordon Getty's opera *Plump Jack*, libretto by the composer based on Shakespeare's plays *Henry IV* and *Henry V*, was first performed at the Cathedral of St. John the Divine in New York on December 31, 1985. It was reprised in Aspen, Colorado, in 1986; Graz in Austria and San Francisco in 1987; Incline Village in New York and Marin Opera in 1988; Dartmouth College and the Spoleto Festival in 1989; and Larkspur, California, in 1990. In the production by Golden Gate Opera at the Florence Gould Theater in San Francisco on March 6, 1999, Macatee Hollie played Falstaff, Diane Kehrig was Dame Quickly, William Lewis sang the Prince Hal from the pit with Mark Hernandez on stage, Tom Hart was Bardolph, David Newman was Pistol, Joseph Meyers was Snare and Shallow, Lisa Elan was Boy and Clifton Roming sang four small roles. Peter Crompton designed the sets, Callie Floor designed the costumes, Janet

Bookspan directed, Kristin Pankonin played piano and Charles Kecham conducted.

POE, EDGAR ALLAN   *American writer (1809–1849)*

Edgar Allan Poe, who had world-wide influence through his poems and stories and virtually created the detective story, has been very popular with musicians. Over 150 composers around the world have used his work as the basis of compositions ranging from operas and ballets to choral works and chamber pieces. There are at least 26 American operas based on his stories and even one based on his life, Dominick Argento's 1976 THE VOYAGE OF EDGAR ALLAN POE. The most popular stories with American composers are THE CASK OF AMONTILLADO, THE FALL OF THE HOUSE OF USHER. and THE TELL-TALE HEART. In the list below titles of the operas are same as the story unless other indicated. Composer name is given first, libretto by composer unless other indicated. Place and date of premiere given if known.

The Cask of Amontillado (1846). 1953 Charles Hamm. Cincinnati Conservatory, March 1, 1953. 1954 Julia Perry as *The Bottle.* New York, November 20, 1955. 1968 Aldo Provenzano. Eastman School of Music, Rochester, New York, April 26, 1968; Robert James Haskins (John Koppenhaver). 1979 Donald Para. Kalamazoo, Michigan, May 1979. 1982 Russell Currie (Carl Laanes). Bronx Art Ensemble, New York, April 3, 1982. 1997 Bryan Stanley (Patrick Buckley). Des Moines Metro Opera, 1997. 2003 Daniel Pinkham. Opera Boston, Massachusetts College of Art, June 8, 2003.

The Devil in the Belfry (1839). 1984 David McKay. Performed for the Modern Language Association.

The Fall of the House of Usher (1839). 1921 Avery Claflin. 1941 Clarence Loomis (E Ferguson). Indianapolis, Indiana, January 11, 1941. 1952 Morris H. Ruger. Los Angeles, CA. April 15, 1952. 1975 Gregory Sandow (Thomas N. Disch). New York, 1975. 1984 Russell Currie's *A Dream within a Dream* (Robert Kornfield). Bronx Art Ensemble, NY, April 29, 1984. 1988 Philip Glass (Arthur Yorinks). Cambridge, MA, May 18, 1988.

Ligeia (1838). 1987 Russell Currie (Robert Kornfield). Bronx Art Ensemble, New York, April 5, 1987. 1994 Augusta Read Thomas (Leslie Dunton Downer). Evian-les-Bains Festival, May 1994.

The Masque of the Red Death (1842). 1925 Lazare Saminsky's *The Gagliarda of a Merry Plague.* New York, February 22, 1925. 1976 Robert James Haskins (John Koppenhaver).

The Raven (1845). 1895 Charles Sanford Skilton's cantata *Lenore.* Boston, 1895.

The System of Doctor Tarr and Professor Fether (1845). 1974 Jan Bach's *The System.* Mannes College of Music, New York, March 5, 1974. 1983 Russell Currie. 1999 David Bernstein *A Method for Madness* (Charles Kondek). Akron, Ohio, November 6, 1999.

The Tell-Tale Heart (1843). 1968 Leo Horácek (Joseph Golz). Morgantown, West Virginia, August 7, 1968. 1979 Thomas Czerny-Hydzik. Prince George's Civic Opera, Largo, MD, December 27, 1979. 1982 Bruce Adolphe. Opera Theatre of Boston, January 22, 1982. 1982 Daniel Kessner. Utrecht, The Netherlands, March 12, 1982. 1999 David Bernstein (Charles Kondek). Akron University School of Music, Ohio, November 6, 1999.

Biographical. 1976 Dominick Argento's *The Voyage of Edgar Allan Poe* (Charles Nolte). Minnesota Opera, Minneapolis, April 24, 1976.

POIA   *1910 opera by Nevin*

Poia, a prophet of the Blackfoot tribe, competes with evil warrior Sumatsi for the hand of the beautiful Natoya. Noia undertakes a dangerous journey to the court of the Sun God, returns a hero and is awarded Natoya but she is killed. Arthur Nevin's three-act opera *Poia,* libretto by Randolph Hartley based on a Blackfoot myth about the coming of sun worship, was the first American grand opera to premiere in Germany. It was staged by Berlin Opera at the Royal Opera House on April 23, 1910, with a notable cast. Walter Kirchoff was Poia, Florence Easton was Natoya, Johannes Bischoff was Sumatsi, Margarete Ober was Nenahu, and Putnam Griswold was the Sun God Natosi. Karl Much conducted. The opera had four performances in Berlin but it caused a good deal of patriotic controversy. Prior to the Berlin premiere, selections were presented in concert in Pittsburgh with the Pittsburgh Symphony Orchestra and soloists conducted by the composer. Blackfoot musical themes are featured in the score, including a hymn to the sun.

POLERI, DAVID   *American tenor (1921–1967)*

David Poleri created the role of the incestuous brother Michele in Gian Carlo Menotti's THE SAINT OF BLEECKER STREET on Broadway in 1954, sang it in the Italian premiere at Teatro alla Scala and is featured on the original cast recording. He sings the role of Alan in a recorded 1949 radio version of Victor Herbert's BABES IN TOYLAND and Robin Hood in a recorded 1952 radio version of Reginald De Koven's ROBIN HOOD. Poleri, born in Chestnut Hill, PA, studied in Philadelphia and New York. He made his debut in Chicago in 1949 with the touring San Carlo Opera Company and later sang at New York City and around the world. He sang in four NBC television operas in the 1950s and dubbed Caruso's singing voice in the 1960 film *Pay or Die.*

THE POLITICS OF HARMONY   *1968 opera by Wuorinen*

A monarch pays a ceremonial visit to the palace of another monarch and plays part of an attractive melody for him. The host's music master warns that the complete tune is evil but his employer insists on hearing it. When the music finishes, a storm arises and the palace collapses killing the host while his malevolent visitor escapes. Charles Wuorinen's masque *The Politics of Harmony,* libretto by Richard Monaco based on a story by Chinese writer Su-ma Ch'ien, was premiered in New York October 28, 1968. The music, for alto, tenor, bass and chamber orchestra, is serial-derived and highly programmatic.

POLLOCK, MICHAEL   *American tenor (1921–2003)*

New York native Michael Pollock was associated with a number of American operas during his long career at New York City Opera following his debut there in 1949. He created the role of the Wedding Guest in David Tamkin's THE DYBBUK in 1951, played King Kaspar in the stage premiere of Gian Carlo Menotti's AMAHL AND THE NIGHT VISITORS in 1952 and created the role of the postman Mr. Splinters in Aaron Copland's THE TENDER LAND in 1954. He also created the role of Kotchkarev in Bohuslav Martinů's television opera *The Marriage* when it was premiered by NBC Opera Theatre in 1953. He became a stage director for NYCO in 1957 and staged Leonard Bernstein's TROUBLE IN TAHITI and Mark Bucci's TALE FOR A DEAF EAR in 1958 and Robert Ward's HE WHO GETS SLAPPED in 1959.

PONSELLE, ROSA   *American soprano (1897–1981)*

Rosa Ponselle created the lead role of Carmelita in Joseph Breil's opera THE LEGEND at the Metropolitan Opera in 1919. She recorded Victor Herbert's aria "Kiss Me Again" from MLLE. MODISTE in 1920, a tune she had often sung on stage in vaudeville before she became an opera diva. She was named Ponzillo when she was born in Meriden, Connecticut, and began her career touring with sister Carmela as the "Tailored Italian Girls. She made her debut at the Met in 1918 at the age of 21 opposite Enrico Caruso and stayed a Met favorite until her retirement to Baltimore in 1937. She helped the Baltimore Opera Company to became nationally known in the 1950s when she became its artistic director.

PONTALBA *2003 opera by Musgrave*

New Orleans architect Micaela Almonester marries Célestin de Pontalba, the weak son of an avaricious baron, in 1811 and moves to France. The Pontalba family attempts to take control of her inheritance and she spends twenty years fighting them. After she wins the long struggle, she returns to New Orleans and helps beautify the city. Thea Musgrave's opera *Pontalba*, libretto by the composer, is based on Christina Vella's biography *Intimate Enemies* which describes the life of Baroness Micaela de Pontalba. It was commissioned by New Orleans Opera which premiered it on October 2, 2003, reportedly at a cost of a million dollars. Yali-Marie Williams sang the role of Micaela, Robert Breault was her husband Célestin, Jake Gardner was Baron Pontalba, Kathryn Day was the Baroness, Jane Gilbert was Mme. Almonester, Ray Fellman was Mr. Monroe and Fahnlohnee Harris was Cassie. Ehard Rom designed the sets, Jay Lesgner staged the production and Robert Lyall conducted the New Orleans Opera Chorus and Orchestra.

POPPER, FELIX *American conductor (1908–2000)*

Felix Popper was music administrator at New York City Opera from 1958 to 1980 and conducted performances of many American operas in the 19060s including Douglas Moore's THE BALLAD OF BABY DOE, Carlisle Floyd's SUSANNAH and Gian Carlo Menotti's operas AMAHL AND THE NIGHT VISITORS, AMELIA GOES TO THE BALL and THE CONSUL Popper, who was born in Vienna and emigrated to America in 19490. He began working with New York City Opera in 1949 and was also associated with NBC Television Opera from 1954 to 1974.

POPPER, JAN *American conductor (1907–1987)*

Jan Popper conducted the premieres of two American operas: Roy Travis's THE PASSION OF OEDIPUS at UCLA Opera Theater in Los Angeles in 1968 and Jerome William Rosen's *Calisto and Melibea* at the University of California, Davis, in 1979. While he director of UCLA Opera Theater, he conducted the West Coast premieres of William Schuman's THE MIGHTY CASEY, Robert Ward's THE CRUCIBLE, Virgil Thomson's THE MOTHER OF US ALL and Eugene Zador's *The Scarlet Mill*.

He also conducted the premiere of George Gershwin's PORGY AND BESS in Japan. Popper was born in Czechoslovakia and emigrated to America in 1940. He is credited with helping to raise awareness of opera in California; UCLA named one of its performance halls after him in 1981.

PORGY AND BESS *1935 opera by Gershwin*

Love, death and betrayal in the African American ghetto of Catfish Row in Charleston, South Carolina, in 1920. Crippled Porgy becomes involved with beautiful Bess after her dangerous man Crown kills a man and flees the police. Porgy kills Crown when he returns but Bess goes off to New York with drug dealer Sportin' Life. George Gershwin's *Porgy and Bess* is the great American opera and one of the first to achieve international fame. It took a long time to win respect. When first staged on Broadway, it was considered too popular to be high art and there was doubt of whether a trio of white men could or should create an African American opera. DuBose Heyward wrote the libretto based on his 1925 novel and play and Ira Gershwin helped with the lyrics. George Gershwin composed music for their words that is likely to live as long as anything by Mozart or Verdi. The unforgettable arias of what Gershwin called a "folk opera" include "Summertime," "It ain't necessarily so" and "I got plenty o' nuttin'." The opera premiered in Boston at the Colonial Theater on September 30, 1935, and arrived on Broadway at the Alvin Theater on Octo-

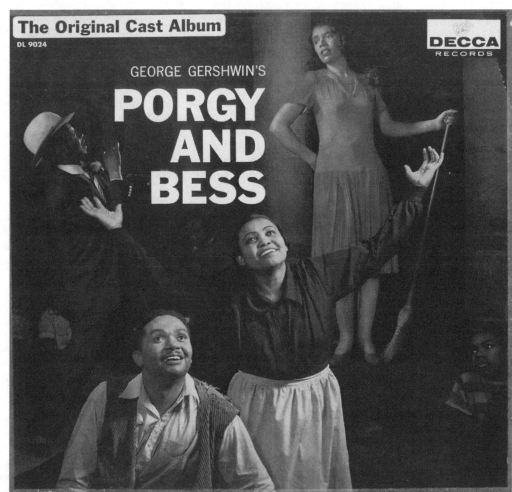

The original cast album of George Gershwin's *Porgy and Bess.*

ber 10. Todd Duncan created the role of Porgy, Anne Brown was the first Bess, John W. Bubbles was Sportin' Life, Abbie Mitchell was Clara, Warren Coleman was Crown, Ruby Elzy was Serena, Georgette Harvey was Maria, Edward Matthews was Jake, Ford L. Buck was Mingo, Henry David was Robbins, Gun Simons was Peter, J. Rosamond Johnson was Frazier, Olive Ball was Annie, Helen Dowdy was Strawberry Woman and Lily, Jack Carr was Jim, John Garth was the Undertaker, Ray Yeates was Nelson and Crab Man, George Leesy was the Detective, Aldander Campbell was the Policeman and Harold Woolf was the Coroner. They were supported by the Eva Jessye Choir and the Charleston Orphans' Band. Rouben Mamoulian staged the opera, Sergei Soudeikine designed the sets and Alexander Smallens conducted the orchestra. The opera was revived on Broadway a number of times, beginning in 1940 with Todd Duncan and Anne Brown re-creating their roles as Porgy and Bess. When Brown left the show, Etta Moten took over the role of Bess and was just as popular. The 1953 revival at the Ziegfeld Theater starring Leontyne Price as Bess gained new respect for the opera; many consider Price the best ever in the role. New York City Opera staged the opera in 1962 with Lawrence Winters as Porgy, Leesa Foster as Bess, Rawn Spearman as Sportin' Life and Carol Brice as Maria but *Porgy and Bess* did not receive full critical recognition as an opera until 1976. That was the year Lorin Maazel made the first complete operatic recording with the Cleveland Symphony and Houston Grand Opera produced a truly memorable production. Shamefully the opera was not staged at the Metropolitan Opera House until 1985, fifty years after its premiere. It was staged in Cape Town, South Africa, in 1991 with Rhoda Levine directing a mostly American cast and revived by Cape Town Opera in 2001 with Americans Alvy Powell and Roberta Laws as Porgy and Bess under the direction of Angelo Gobbato.

The following listings include the most important audio and visual recordings of the opera and its arias, mainly those by opera singers, but there are many more with over 500 recordings of "Summertime" alone, many by jazz musicians. Will Friedwald's splendid book *Stardust Melodies* (2002/Pantheon Books) includes a useful history of the various recordings. See also listings under the arias "BESS, YOU IS MY WOMAN," "I GOT PLENTY O' NOTHIN'," IT AIN'T NECESSARILY SO and SUMMERTIME.

1935 Porgy and Bess rehearsal. The earliest recording of music from the opera was made on July 19, 1935, three months before the opera opened, and has been issued on various albums. It was recorded during a rehearsal with the composer conducting and playing piano as members of the cast performed: Abbie Mitchell sings "Summertime"; Edward Matthews sings "A woman is a sometime thing"; Ruby Elzy sings "My man's gone now"; Todd Duncan and Anne Brown duet on "Bess, you is my woman" and the orchestra plays the Finale of Scene 1, Act 1. The numbers are on *Gershwin Performs Gershwin: Rare Recordings 1931–1935* (Music Masters Jazz CD), *Gershwin — Porgy and Bess* (Naxos Historical CD) and *George Gershwin Conducts Excerpts from Porgy and Bess* (Mark 56 Records LP). **1935 Lawrence Tibbett/Helen Jepson.** The first commercial recordings of *Porgy and Bess* were made by Metropolitan Opera stars Lawrence Tibbett and Helen Jepson. They recorded nine arias and duets for Victor in October 1935 with the Broadway production orchestra and chorus led by Alexander Smallens. Jepson sings "Summertime" and "My man's gone now," Tibbett sings on "A woman is a sometime thing," "I got plenty o' nuttin'," "The Buzzard Song," "It ain't necessarily so" and "Where is my Bess" and they duet on "Summertime," "The Crap Game" and "Bess, you is my woman." These recordings, originally

in a four-record 12" 78rpm album, have been reissued on several albums including *Lawrence Tibbett: From Broadway to Hollywood* (Nimbus CD), *Dear Rogue* (Pearl CD) and *A Collector's Porgy and Bess* (RCA LP). **1937 George Gershwin Memorial Concert.** This radio tribute to Gershwin broadcast on CBS in September 1937 includes eight numbers from *Porgy and Bess.* Alexander Smallens (using the name Steinert) conducts the Los Angeles Philharmonic Orchestra in performances by Lily Pons and members of the original cast. Pons sings "Summertime," Ruby Elzy sings "My man's gone now," Todd Duncan sings "The Buzzard's Song," "I got plenty o'nuttin'," and "I'm on my way," Anne Brown sings "The Train Song" and Duncan and Brown duet on "Bess, you is my woman." 150 minutes. North American Classics 2-CD set. **1938 Magic Key Program.** The RCA Magic Key Gershwin Memorial Program broadcast on July 10, 1938, features seven numbers from *Porgy and Bess* performed by Jane Froman and Felix Knight with Nathaniel Shilkret conducting the Victor Salon Group. RCA Victor CD. **1940 Original cast album.** Jack Kapp of Decca recorded members of the original cast in 1940 and 1942 for a two-part 78 highlights album. Todd Duncan sings Porgy, Anne Brown is Bess, Edward Matthews is Jake, Helen Dowdy is Strawberry Woman and Georgette Harvey is Maria with Alexander Smallens conducting the Decca Symphony Orchestra and Eva Jessye Choir. Added to the cast are Avon Long as Sportin' Life, Harriet Jackson, Gladys Goode and William Woolfolk. The 78s eventually became two 10" LPs and are now an MCA CD. **1945 Rhapsody in Blue.** Anne Brown, who created the role, plays Bess in the *Porgy and Bess* sequence of the 1945 film *Rhapsody in Blue* and sings "Summertime," William Gillespie is Porgy and Robert Johnson is Sporting Life. Irving Rapper directed the movie for Warner Brother. The aria is on the Rhino Movie Music CD box set soundtrack album *George and Ira Gershwin in Hollywood* and the film is on WB VHS/DVD. **1946 Eleanor Steber.** Met soprano Eleanor Steber recorded her version of "Summertime" for RCA Victor on January 15, 1946, with orchestra conducted by Jay Blackton. It's on *A Collector's Porgy and Bess.* RCA LP. **1947 Paul Robeson.** Paul Robeson recorded "It ain't necessarily so" in November 1947 for a Columbia 78 album with Emanuel Balaban conducting the Columbia Concert Orchestra. It's on the album *Songs of Free Men.* Sony Classics CD. **1950 Risë Stevens and Robert Merrill.** Met soprano Risë Stevens recorded "My man's gone now" on September 13, 1950, with the Robert Shaw Chorale and orchestra conducted by Robert Russell Bennett. Met baritone Robert Merrill recorded "A woman is a sometime thing" and "Oh Lawd, I'm on my way" on the same day with the same backing. They're on various albums including *A Collector's Porgy and Bess.* RCA LP. **1951 Jerome Hines.** Met bass Jerome Hines sings the aria "I got plenty o' nuttin'" on the *Voice of Firestone* television program on August 27, 1951. Howard Barlow conducts the Firestone Orchestra. It's on the video *Jerome Hines in Opera and Song.* VAI VHS. **1951 Columbia "complete" recording.** Lawrence Winters sings Porgy with Camilla Williams as Bess in a famous Columbia recording issued on three 12-inch LPs that claimed to be complete. They're supported by Avon Long as Sportin' Life singing "It ain't necessarily so," June McMechen as Clara singing "Summertime," Inez Matthew as Serena singing "My man's gone now," Warren Coleman as Crown, Eddie Matthew as Jake and Helen Dowdy as Maria, Lily and Strawberry Woman. Lehman Engel conducts the orchestra and the John Rosamond Johnson Chorus. Columbia LP box/Sony Classic 2-CD box. **1953 Cab Calloway.** Cab Calloway as Sportin' Life recorded his famous version of "It ain't necessarily so" on May 5, 1953. It's on various albums including *A Collector's*

Porgy and Bess. RCA LP. **1954 Eleanor Steber.** Eleanor Steber sings "Summertime" on *The Voice of Firestone* television program August 2, 1954, with orchestra conducted by Howard Barlow. It's on the video *Eleanor Steber in Opera and Song, Vol. 2.* VAI VHS. **1955 Lawrence Tibbett.** Lawrence Tibbett made studio recordings in 1955 of the arias "I got plenty o' nuttin'" and "It ain't necessarily so." They're on various albums including an Allegro-Royale LP. **1956 Mel Tormé/Frances Faye.** Mel Tormé sings Porgy with Frances Faye as Bess in this cool jazz highlights version of the opera recorded in 1956 with narration by Al "Jazzbo" Collins. The other singers are Joe Derise, Sallie Blair, Frank Rosolino, Betty Roche, George Kirby, Johnny Hartman, Bob Dorough and Loulie Jean Norman. Russ Garcia leads the cool jazz orchestra. Bethlehem Archives/Avenue Jazz CD. **1958 Ella Fitzgerald/Louis Armstrong.** Ella Fitzgerald as Bess and Louis Armstrong as Porgy recorded fifteen numbers from the opera in this delightful highlights album with backing from an orchestra conducted by Russell Garcia. Verve LP/CD. **1958 Miles Davis.** The filming of *Porgy and Bess* sparked several jazz albums based on the opera. Trumpet genius Miles Davis recorded fifteen numbers from the opera for his classic album *Porgy and Bess.* Columbia LP/CD. **1959 Samuel Goldwyn film.** Sidney Poitier plays Porgy with Dorothy Dandridge as Bess in Otto Preminger's controversial film of the opera produced by Samuel Goldwyn. Robert McFerrin is the singing voice of Porgy and Adele Addison sings Bess. Sammy Davis Jr. is Sporting Life, Pearl Bailey is Maria, Diahann Carroll is Clara (sung by Loulie Jean Norman), Ruth Attaway is Serena (sung by Inez Matthews), Brock Peters is Crown and Maya Angelou has a small role as a dancer. André Previn and Ken Darby's arrangements of the music won an Academy Award and the film was nominated for three other Oscars. This was Goldwyn's final and most expensive film. Ira Gershwin said he liked it at the time and *The New York Times* listed it as one of the Ten Best Films of the Year but it was not a commercial success. It has been withdrawn from circulation by the Gershwin/Hammerstein heirs but there is a print at the Library of Congress and it is occasionally screened at film festivals. **1959 Samuel Goldwyn film soundtrack.** The soundtrack of the Otto Preminger film of the opera was issued as an album but it's a rather peculiar artifact. Most of the stars are dubbed and Sammy Davis Jr.'s voice couldn't be used as he was under contract to another record company. Robert McFerrin sings Porgy, Adele Addison sings Bess, Cab Calloway sings Sportin' Life replacing Davis, Pearl Bailey sings Maria as she did in the film (a superb "Beat Out Dat Rhythm with a Drum"), Loulie Jean Norman sings Clara, Inez Matthews sings Serena and Brock Peters sings Crown as he did in the film. André Previn conducts. Columbia LP. **1962 Anna Moffo/Avon Long.** Anna Moffo as Clara and Avon Long as Sporting Life dominate this highlights recording for the Reader's Digest *Treasury of Great Operettas* series. Valentine Pringle is Porgy, Urylee Leonardos is Bess, Billie Daniels is Serena and Andrew Frierson is Jake. Lehman Engel conducts the orchestra and chorus RCA LP box set. **1963 Leontyne Price/William Warfield.** Leontyne Price is Bess opposite William Warfield as Porgy in this highlights recording featuring the stars of the famous 1952 touring stage production. John W. Bubbles, who created the role, sings Sporting Life and McHenry Boatwright is Crown. Skitch Henderson conducts. The album is titled *Great Scenes from Gershwin's Porgy and Bess.* RCA Victor LP and BMG/RCA CD. **1976 A Collector's Porgy and Bess.** *A Collector's Porgy and Bess* is an anthology of arias recorded by opera singers between 1935 and 1953. Eleanor Steber sings "Summertime," Robert Merrill sings "A woman is a sometime thing" and "Oh Lawd, I'm on my way," Risë Stevens sings

"My man's gone now," Lawrence Tibbett sings "I got plenty o' nuttin'" and "The Buzzard Song," Helen Jepson and Tibbett duet on "Bess, you is my woman now" and Cab Calloway sings "It ain't necessarily so." RCA Victor Victrola America LP. **1976 Lorin Maazel recording.** Lorin Maazel leads the Cleveland Orchestra and Chorus in this famous complete recording that began critical reappraisal of *Porgy and Bess* as opera rather than musical. Willard White sings Porgy, Leona Mitchell is Bess, Francois Clemmons is Sportin' Life, Barbara Hendricks is Clara, Florence Quivar is Serena, McHenry Boatwright is Crown, Arthur Thompson is Jake, Barbara Conrad is Maria/Strawberry Woman, Isola Jones is Lily, James Vincent Pickens is Mingo/Undertaker, Samuel Hagen is Robbins/Crab Man, William Brown is Peter/Nelson, Christopher Deane is Frazier/Jim, Alpha Floyd is Annie, John Buck is Mr. Archdale, Robert Snook is the Detective, Ralph Neely is the Policeman, Alan Leatherman is the Coroner and Donald Zucco is Scipio. Decca/London LP/CD. **1976 Houston Grand Opera.** The 1976 Houston Grand Opera stage production continued the reappraisal of *Porgy and Bess* as opera rather than musical. John DeMain conducts the Houston Grand Opera Orchestra in this cast recording with Donnie Ray Albert as Porgy and Clamma Dale as Bess. Andrew Smith is Crown, Larry Marshall is Sportin' Life, Wilma Shakesnider is Serena, Betty Lane is Clara, Carol Brice is Maria Alexander B. Smalls is Jake, Bernard Thacker is Mingo, Glover Parham is Robbins, Mervin Wallace is Peter, Raymond Bazemore is Frazier, Shirley Baines is Annie, Myra Merritt, is Lily, Phyllis Bash is Strawberry Woman, Hartwell Mace is Jim, Cornel Richie is Undertaker, Steven Alex-Colle is Nelson and Crab Man, Kenneth Barry is Mr. Archdale, Hansford Rowe is Detective, William Gammon is Policeman, John B. Ross is Coroner, Alexander Carrington is Scipio and Dick Hyman is Jasbo Brown, RCA Victor LP/CD. **1980 Donnie Ray Albert/Leonie Mitchell.** Leona Mitchell as Bess and Donnie Ray Albert as Porgy perform excerpts from the opera at Carnegie Hall in the program *Tribute to André Kostelanetz.* Live Opera audio-cassette. **1981 Barbara Hendricks.** Barbara Hendricks sings "Summertime" and "I loves you, Porgy" accompanied by piano duo Katia and Marielle Labèque on her Paris album *Barbara Hendricks Sings Gershwin.* Philips LP. **1983/1987/1994 Michael Tilson Thomas.** Michael Tilson Thomas has conducted five albums devoted to Gershwin music, including three with excerpts from *Porgy and Bess: Gershwin Live* (1983), *Classic Gershwin* (1987) and *Greatest Hits: Gershwin* (1994). **1986 Roberta Alexander/Simon Estes.** Robert Alexander sings Bess with Simon Estes as Porgy in a highlights recording of the opera. Leonard Slatkin conducts the Berlin Radio Symphony Orchestra. On CD. **1987 Roberta Alexander/Gregg Baker.** Roberta Alexander and Gregg Baker perform arias and duets from the opera in this highlights recording. Zubin Mehta conducts the New York Choral Artists and Philharmonic Orchestra. Teldec CD. **1987 Glyndebourne Festival Opera.** Willard White stars as Porgy with Cynthia Haymon as Bess in this recording based on a famous Glyndebourne stage production by Trevor Nunn. Damon Evans is Sporting Life, Gregg Baker is Crown, Cynthia Clarey is Serena and Marietta Simpson is Maria. Simon Rattle conducts the London Philharmonic Orchestra and Glyndebourne Festival Chorus. EMI Classics CD. **1989/1991 Kiri Te Kanawa.** Kiri Te Kanawa can be seen performing "Summertime" on two British videos: *Kiri in Concert* (1989 EMI VHS/DVD) filmed at the Barbican in London with Carl Davis leading the Royal Philharmonic Orchestra and *Kiri Te Kanawa* (1991 EMI VHS/DVD), a program filmed for the South Bank Show. **1990/1991 Kathleen Battle.** Kathleen Battle sings "Summertime" on video and CD. She accompanied by pianist

Warren Jones at the Egyptian Temple in the 1990 PolyGram VHS *Kathleen Battle at the Metropolitan Museum* and by pianist Margo Garrett at Carnegie Hall on the 1991 DG CD *Kathleen Battle at Carnegie Hall.* **1991 Denise Woods.** Denise Woods as Bess leads the Collegiate Choir in "Leavin' for the Promised Land" at a televised gala at Avery Fisher Hall on November 10, 1991. James Conlon conducts members of the Metropolitan Opera Orchestra on the PBS telecast titled *A Salute to American Music.* RCA Victor CD. **1991 Julia Migenes.** Julia Migenes sings "Summertime" at the Seville Stadium in Spain at a televised gala with backing from the National Symphonic Orchestra of Spain led by Eugene Kohn. It's on the video *Plácido Grandisimo: Plácido Domingo and Julia Migenes.* Kultur VHS. **1992 Trevor Nunn film.** Willard White stars as Porgy with Cynthia Haymon as Bess in this superb Trevor Nunn production filmed in London's Shepperton Studios. The performers are from his Covent Garden revival, essentially the same as in his 1986 Glyndebourne Festival production, but the soundtrack is the 1988 Glyndebourne cast recording. Damon Evans is Sportin' Life, Gregg Baker is Crown, Cynthia Clarey is Serena, Marietta Simpson is Maria, Paula Ingram is Clara (with the voice of Harolyn Blackwell), Bruce Hubbard is Jake, Barrington Coleman is Mingo, Johnny Worthy is Robbins, Curtis Watson is Jim, Mervyn Wallace is Peter, Maureen Brathwaite is Lily, Autris Paige is the Undertaker, William Johnson is Frazier, Paula Ingram is Annie, Colenton Freeman is Nelson and the Crab Man, Camelia Johnson is Strawberry Woman, Alan Tilvern is the Detective, Billy J. Mitchell is the Coroner, Ted Maynard is Mr. Archdale, Ron Travis is the Policeman and Wayne Marshall is Jasbo. John Gunter designed the sets, Sir Simon Rattle conducted the London Philharmonic Orchestra and Glyndebourne Festival Chorus and Greg Smith directed the 184-minute video. EMI Classics DVD/VHS/LD. **1992 Kathleen Kuhlmann.** Kathleen Kuhlmann sings "Summertime" in the Red Square in Moscow at a televised opera gala. It's on the video *José Carreras Opera Gala in Moscow.* Kultur VHS. **1992 Lesley Garrett.** Lesley Garrett sings "Summertime" with backing from the Philharmonia Orchestra led by Ivor Bolton on the album *Lesley Garrett, Prima Donna.* Silva America CD. **1992 Melanie Marshall.** Mezzo-soprano Melanie Marshall sings "I loves you, Porgy," "Summertime" and "There's a boat dat's leavin'" accompanied by pianist Wayne Marshall on the album *Soirée at Snape.* Mel CD. **1993 Erich Kunzel.** Erich Kunzel leads the Cincinnati Pops Orchestra and Central State University Chorus in this recording of highlights from the opera. Gregg Baker is Porgy, Marquita Lister is Bess, Cab Calloway is Sporting Life, Harolyn Blackwell is Clara (singing "Summertime"), Sebronette Barnes is Maria and Angela Brown is Serena joining Lister in the Act III lullaby "Lonely Boy" (cut from the original production). Telarc CD. **1993 Samuel Ramey.** Samuel Ramey sings "I got plenty o' nuttin'" with the London Studio Symphony Orchestra conducted by Ettore Stratta. It's on the album *Samuel Ramey on Broadway.* Teldec CD. **1995 Metropolitan Opera.** Simon Estes sings Porgy opposite Leona Mitchell as Bess in a Metropolitan Opera Texaco broadcast on January 27, 1990. Ben Holt is Sporting Life, Gwendolyn Bradley is Clara, Camellia Johnson is Serena, Marjorie Wharton is Maria and Gregg Baker is Crown. James Levine conducts. Opera audiocassette. **1998 Porgy and Bess: An American Voice.** *Porgy and Bess: An American Voice* is a documentary film tracing the history of the opera. Todd Duncan and Anne Brown, who created the title roles, are featured along with Leontyne Price, William Warfield, Grace Bumbry, Cab Calloway, Diahann Carroll and Willard White. Ruby Dee narrates, Gloria Naylor and Ed Apfel wrote the script and James A. Standifer produced the documen-

tary telecast on PBS February 4, 1998, in the *Great Performances* series. PBS VHS. **1998 London Proms.** Cynthia Haymon is Bess, Willard White is Porgy, Michael Forest is Sportin' Life and Cynthia Clarey is Serena in this recording of the opera as it was broadcast from the London Proms on August 1, 1998. House of Opera CD. **1998 Catfish Row suite.** Audra McDonald and Brian Stokes Mitchell perform the major songs from the opera in this live recording of Gershwin's *Catfish Row* suite from *Porgy and Bess.* Michael Tilson Thomas conducts the San Francisco Symphony Orchestra. It's on the concert album *Gershwin 100th Birthday Celebration.* BMG/RCA Victor CD. **1999 Renée Fleming.** Renée Fleming sings "Summertime" and "My man's gone now" with backing from James Levine conducting the Metropolitan Opera Orchestra. It's on her album *I Want Magic.* London Classics CD. **1999 Charlotte Church.** British teenage soprano Charlotte Church features the aria "Summertime" on her 1999 recital album *Charlotte Church.* On CD. **2000 Barbara Hendricks.** Barbara Hendricks performs several numbers from *Porgy and Bess* on her London album *It's Wonderful: A Tribute to George Gershwin.* Backing is from the Guildhall Strings and other musicians. EMI Classics CD. **2000 Sylvia McNair.** Sylvia McNair sings "Summertime" on the album *The Radio 3 Lunchtime Concert,* accompanied by Ted Taylor. BBC Music CD. **2002 New York City Opera.** Alvy Powell is Porgy with Marquita Lister as Bess in this New York City Opera production by Tazewell Thomson. Dwayne Clark is Sportin' Life, Angela Simpson is Serena, Timothy Robert Blevins is Crown, Sabrina Elayne Carten is Maria, Adina Aaron is Clara and David Aron Damane is Jake. Douglas Schmidt designed the sets, John Demain conducted the NYCO Orchestra and Chorus and Kirk Browning directed the live telecast on PBS on March 20, 2002. Video at MTR. **2003 Gershwin — Porgy and Bess.** This 137-minute anthology put together by David Lennick features recordings of *Porgy and Bess* made within ten years of its premiere. It includes the 1935 Tibbett-Jepson recordings, the 1940–1942 original cast recordings with the Decca Symphony, 1935–1942 recordings by members of the original cast with Leo Reisman's orchestra, "Porgy and Bess: A Symphonic Picture" arranged by Robert Russell Bennett and selections by Edward Matthews, Paul Robeson and Jascha Heifetz. Naxos Historical 2-CD box.

PORRETTA, FRANK *American tenor (1932–)*

Frank Porretta, lead tenor for New York City Opera for many years, created roles in many American operas. He began with the small role of the Steward in William Bergsma's THE WIFE OF MARTIN GUERRE at Juilliard in 1956. At New York City Opera he created the role of the English Sentry in Norman Dello Joio's THE TRIUMPH OF ST. JOAN in 1959, Lucas Wardlaw in Carlisle Floyd's THE PASSION OF JONATHAN WADE in 1962 and Florindo in Vittorio Giannini's THE SERVANT OF TWO MASTERS in 1967. He sang but did not create Bezano in Robert Ward's HE WHO GETS SLAPPED (1956) and Edgar Linton in Floyd's WUTHERING HEIGHTS (1959). On television he sang the role of the Thief in Abraham Ellstein's THE THIEF AND THE HANGMAN on ABC in 1961 and created the role of the Astronaut in Gian Carlo Menotti's LABYRINTH on NBC in 1963. He sang Lun Tha in the 1964 Lincoln Center production of Richard Rodger's THE KING AND I, the poet Nordraak in the 1970 film of the Wright/Forrest operetta SONG OF NORWAY and the title role in Leonard Bernstein's CANDIDE at San Francisco Light Opera in 1971, His recordings include *The Wife of Martin Guerre* (1956), *Brigadoon* (1957), *The King and I* (1964) and *Song of Norway* (1970). Porretta was Frank Jr., his son Frank III is also an opera singer.

PORTER, ANDREW *British librettist/critic (1928–)*

Andrew Porter wrote the libretto for John Eaton's THE TEMPEST, premiered at Santa Fe Opera in 1985, and for Bright Sheng's THE SONG OF MAJNUN, premiered at Lyric Opera of Chicago in 1992. He also wrote the libretto for Roger Session's *The Emperor's New Clothes* which was uncompleted when the composer died. Porter, born in Cape Town, South Africa, has written about opera for *The Financial Times, The Observer, Opera* and *Gramophone* in England and *The New Yorker* in America.

PORTER, COLE *American composer/lyricist (1891–1964)*

Cole Porter's 1948 musical KISS ME KATE, based on Shakespeare's *The Taming of the Shrew,* has entered the repertory of opera companies in the U.S. and Europe and been recorded by opera singers. Porter, born in Peru, Indiana, wrote the words and music for 23 Broadway musicals beginning in 1916 with the *See American First* and ending in 1955 with *Silk Stocking.* His other notable musicals include *Gay Divorce* (1932), *Anything Goes* (1934), *Mexican Hayride* (1944) and *Can-Can* (1953). His melodies are memorable and his lyrics are among the most literate in the genre so it is not surprising that many of his songs have become standards. Twenty-one films have been based around Porter music and musicals from *The Battle of Paris* in 1929 to *De-Lovely* in 2004. The 1946 movie biography *Night and Day* stars Cary Grant as Porter.

PORTMAN, RACHEL *English composer (1960–)*

Rachel Portman's opera THE LITTLE PRINCE, libretto by Nicolas Wright based on the book by Antoine de Saint-Exupéry, was premiered by Houston Grand Opera in June 2003 in a production by Francesca Zambello. Her score for the 1996 film *The Adventures of Pinocchio* has been called a miniature opera with Pinocchio as the hero and arias sung by Jerry Hadley. Portman is the only female composer ever to win an Oscar for best music score (it was for the 1995 film *Emma).*

POSTCARD FROM MOROCCO *1971 opera by Argento*

An odd group of travelers meet at a mysterious train station and try to ferret out each other's secrets. Dominick Argento's popular opera *Postcard from Morocco,* libretto by John Donahue, was premiered by Minnesota Opera at the Cedar Village Theater in Minneapolis on October 14, 1971. Sarita Roche was the Lady with a Hand Mirror and the Operetta Singer; Barbara Brandt was the Lady with a Cake Box; Janis Hardy was the Lady with a Hat Box and the Foreign Singer; Yale Marshall was the Man with Old Luggage, First Puppet and Operetta Singer; Vern Sutton was the Man with a Paint Box (Mr. Owen); Barry Busse was the Man with a Shoe Sample Kit and Second Puppet; and

Michael Foreman was the Man with a Cornet Case and Puppet Maker. The non-singing Mimes were played by Wendy Lehr and Bain Boehlke. John Donahue was stage director, Jon Barkla designed the sets and costumes and Philip Brunelle conducted the Minnesota Opera Orchestra. The opera was Argento's first major success and has since been presented by a number of opera companies around the U.S. including Chicago, Manhattan, New Jersey and Washington Opera.

1971 Minnesota Opera. The Minnesota Opera original cast recorded the opera in Minneapolis at the time of the premiere. The singers are as above including Sarita Roche, Barbara Brandt, Janis Hardy, Vern Sutton, Yale Marshall, Barry Busse and Michael Foreman. Composer Philip Brunelle conducts the Minnesota Opera Orchestra. The 95-minute performance was also videotaped but the video is not available commercially. Desto LP/CRI CD.

THE POSTMAN ALWAYS RINGS TWICE *1982 opera by Paulus*

Depression era hobo Frank goes to work for gas station-restaurant owner Nick Papadakis in rural California. He falls in lust and love with Nick's wife Cora and they conspire to murder her husband. Cora is later accidentally killed in a car accident and Nick is sentenced to death for her murder. Stephen Paulus's two-hour opera *The Postman Always Rings Twice,* libretto by Colin Graham based on the novel by James M. Cain, was the first American opera to be presented at the Edinburgh Festival. It was commissioned by Opera Theater of St. Louis which premiered it on June 17, 1982. Kathryn Bouleyn played Cora, David Parson was Frank, Michael Myers was Nick, Carroll Freeman was Katz, Daniel Sullivan was Sackett, David Everts was Cop One and Kennedy and Stephen Morton was Cop Two. John Conklin designed the sets, Colin Graham directed and C. William Harwood conducted the orchestra. The opera was presented by Opera Theater of St. Louis at the

A scene from Dominick Argento's *Postcard from Morocco.* Courtesy of Minnesota Opera.

Edinburgh Festival in 1983 and has since been produced by many companies, including Fort Worth Opera (1985), Minnesota Opera (1987), Greater Miami Opera (1988), Washington Opera (1989) and Boston Lyric Opera (1994).

THE POT OF FAT   *1955 chamber opera by Chanler*

Cat marries Mouse but they have a falling out over a pot of fat when times get tough. Theodore Chanler's chamber opera *The Pot of Fat*, libretto by Hester Packman, is based on a Grimm fairy tale. It was first performed in concert at the Longy School of Music in Cambridge, MA, on May 9, 1955, and first staged in New York on February 22, 1956. by the After Dinner Opera Company. Richard Flusser produced it in New York and at the Edinburgh Festival.

1956 After Dinner Opera. Soprano Dixie Stewart sings the role of Mouse with baritone Arthur Burrows as Cat in this recording of the opera by the After Dinner Opera Company in New York. Bruce Abel is the Narrator and Jorge Mester conducts the CRI Chamber Orchestra. CRI LP.

POUND, EZRA   *American poet/composer (1885–1972)*

Ezra Pound is best known as a poet with major influence on modern literature but he also wrote two operas, both about poets. THE TESTAMENT OF FRANÇOIS VILLON, based on the autobiographical poem by the 15th century French poet, was composed with the assistance of George Antheil. It reflects Pound's interest in the music of the French troubadours and its libretto combines lyrics by Villon with English dialogue. It was premiered in Paris in 1926 in concert form and has since been produced a number of times on stage and radio. Pound's second opera CAVALCANTI, composed in 1932 and based on the life of 13th century Florentine poet Guido Cavalcanti, the most important poet in Italy before Dante, also incorporates lyrics by the poet into the libretto. It was belatedly premiered by the Arch Ensemble for Experimental Music in San Francisco on March 28, 1983. Pound, born in Hailey, Idaho, had a strong interest in music. He wrote a book on harmony, worked as a music critic in London in the 1910s, had a preference for early opera and helped organize the first modern presentation of a Vivaldi opera. He was accused of broadcasting Fascist propaganda from Rome during World War II and was confined in a mental hospital in Washington, DC, from 1945 to 1958. After he was released, he returned to Italy and died in Venice. Pound's own work has also inspired an opera: Francesco Pennies one-act opera *Tristan*, based on a play by Pound, was staged in Bologna in 1996.

2003 Ego Scriptor Cantilenae: The Music of Ezra Pound. Excerpts from Pound operas recorded over a 30-year period are featured on this compilation CD. The six from *Testament* were recorded in 1971, 1980 and 1992 and the seven from *Cavalcanti* come from performances in 1983, 2000 and 2001. The CD also includes an excerpt from Pound's third unfinished opera *Collia O Heliconii* recorded in 2001. The linking factor is conductor/researcher Robert Hughes. Other Minds CD.

POUNTNEY, DAVID   *English director (1947–)*

David Pountney staged the premieres of two major operas by Philip Glass, the Netherlands Opera production of SATYAGRAHA in 1980 and the Metropolitan Opera's production of THE VOYAGE in 1992. He also staged a notable production of Kurt Weill's STREET SCENE for Scottish Opera in 1992.

POWERS, MARIE   *American contralto (1910–1973)*

Marie Powers is forever identified with Gian Carlo Menotti and the role of the fake medium Madame Flora in his opera THE MEDIUM. She did not create the role but she took it over from Claramae Turner when the opera moved to Broadway in 1947 and she sings the role in the 1947 cast recording, 1948 television production and 1951 film. She created the role of the Mother in Menotti's THE CONSUL in Philadelphia and New York in 1950 and sings on the cast recording and telecast. She sings Miss Todd in productions of Menotti's THE OLD MAID AND THE THIEF at New York City Opera in 1948, on NBC television in 1949 and on BBC television in 1954. She also created a role in a non-Menotti opera, Azelia in William Grant Still's TROUBLED ISLAND which premiered at New York City Center Opera in 1949. Powers, born in Mount Carmel, Pennsylvania, toured with the San Carlo Opera company before finding fame in *The Medium*.

POWERS, WILLIAM   *American bass-baritone (1941–)*

William Powers, known for his "villain" roles, created the shady businessman Meyer Wolfshiem in John Harbison's opera THE GREAT GATSBY at the Metropolitan Opera in 1999 and the dangerous Monk in Stewart Copeland's HOLY BLOOD AND CRESCENT MOON at Cleveland Opera in 1988. He sings Lucentio's father Vincentio in Kansas City Lyric Theater's 1969 recording of Vittorio Giannini's THE TAMING OF THE SHREW. He features two arias from American operas in which villains repent on his 1999 album *Rogues and Villains*, Olin Blitch's "Hear Me O Lord" from Carlisle Floyd's SUSANNAH and Brutus Jones' "Standin' in the Need of Prayer" from Louis Gruenberg's THE EMPEROR JONES. On the concert stage he partnered his soprano wife Jennifer Larmore on "What Good Would the Moon Be" from Kurt Weill's *Street Screen*. His other stage roles include Candy in Floyd's OF MICE AND MEN and the Rev. Hale in Robert Ward's THE CRUCIBLE. Powers, born in Chicago, studied in Illinois and made his debut at Chicago Lyric Opera in 1964.

POWNALL, MARY ANN   *American composer (1751–1793)*

Composer/singer/actress Mary Ann Pownall collaborated with librettist Ann Julia Kemble Hatton on the ballad opera *Needs Must; or, The Ballad Singers,* which was staged in New York City in 1793. It was the first ballad opera created by women in America. Pownall, who had become known playing Lucy Lockit in the ballad opera *The Beggar's Opera* in London, had emigrated to America and joined the Old American Company She soon began to write songs as well as sing them and published the collection *Six Songs for the Harpsichord* in New York in 1794 and *Kisses Sued For* in 1795. She died young before her composing career could develop.

PRACHT, MARY ELLEN   *American soprano (1936–)*

Mary Ellen Pracht created the role of Octavia in Samuel Barber's ANTONY AND CLEOPATRA at the Metropolitan Opera in 1966 and the role of Katie in Robert Ward's THE LADY FROM COLORADO at Central City Opera in 1964. She sings leading roles on four of the 1962 Reader's Digest recordings of American operettas featuring opera singers. She is Jane in Victor Herbert BABES IN TOYLAND and Gretchen in his THE RED MILL, Mitzi in Sigmund Romberg's BLOSSOM TIME and Magnolia in Jerome Kern's SHOW BOAT. Pracht was born in Bellaire, Ohio, studied music in Cincinnati and made her debut at the Met in 1961.

PRATT, SILAS   *American composer (1846–1916)*

Vermont-born Silas Pratt, a notable proponent of American opera, had only reasonable success with his own. The most popular was the four-act *Zenobia, Queen of Palmyra*, libretto by the composer, which was staged in Chicago and New York in 1883; selections from it were performed at the Crystal Palace in London in 1885. *Lucille*, a revision of an earlier opera titled *Antonio*, was staged at the Columbia Theater in Chicago in 1887. The five-act *The Triumph of Columbus* was produced in concert form in New York in 1892.

PREMINGER, OTTO *Austrian-born American director (1906–1986)*

Otto Preminger directed two important film adaptations of American operas. In 1954 he filmed CARMEN JONES based on Oscar Hammerstein's Americanized version of Bizet's *Carmen*, with Dorothy Dandridge as Carmen and her singing by Marilyn Horne. In 1959 he filmed George Gershwin's PORGY AND BESS with Sidney Poitier as Porgy (sung by Robert McFerrin) and Dorothy Dandridge as Bess (sung by Adele Addison). Well received at the time, it later became controversial and has been withdrawn. Preminger's personal relationship with Dandridge has also been controversial. Preminger, who was born in Vienna, began directing films in the 1930s and made his breakthrough in 1944 with *Laura*.

PREVIN, ANDRÉ *American composer/conductor (1929–)*

André Previn's A STREETCAR NAMED DESIRE, libretto by Philip Littell based on the play by Tennessee Williams, was commissioned by San Francisco Opera which premiered it on September 19, 1998. He conducted the orchestra for Otto Preminger's 1959 film of PORGY AND BESS and won an Academy Award for scoring it. His other music theater works include *Coco* (1969), *The Good Companions* (1974), *Every Good Boy Deserves a Favour* (1979) and *Rough Crossing*, the last two with librettos by Tom Stoppard. Previn, who studied composition with opera composer Mario Castelnuovo-Tedesco, began his career as a jazz pianist and movie music orchestrator but is best known today as a conductor. He was a Kennedy Center honoree in 1998.

PREVIN, CHARLES *American composer (1988–)*

Charles Previn created two movie operas, both based on themes from classical composers. The first was MARIE ANTOINETTE, created for Lauritz Melchior as the finale of the 1946 MGM film *Two Sisters from Boston*. It is based on music by Liszt and is supposedly staged at the Met. The second was THE PRINCESS, the opera in which Mario Lanza and Kathryn Grayson make their debut in the 1949 film *The Midnight Kiss*. Previn based the music for this one on themes from Tchaikovsky's *Fifth Symphony*. Previn, who was born in Brooklyn, studied music at Ithaca College and Cornell University. He was head of the Music department at Universal Studios for eight years, was nominated for an Oscar seven times and won in 1937 for *100 Men and a Girl*.

PRICE, LEONTYNE *American soprano (1927–)*

Leontyne Price created the role of Cleopatra in Samuel Barber's ANTONY AND CLEOPATRA when it opened the new Metropolitan Opera in Lincoln Center in 1966. She can be seen rehearsing the role in a TV documentary and she has recorded arias from it. Price made her stage debut in 1952 in an American opera, singing St. Cecilia on Broadway in Virgil Thomson's FOUR SAINTS IN THREE ACTS, and then went on a world tour for two years singing Bess opposite William Warfield in George Gershwin's PORGY AND BESS. She recorded the arias "He has come, he has come!" and "Do not utter a word" from Samuel Barber's VANESSA in 1967 and the aria "While I waste these precious hours" from Gian Carlo Menotti's AMELIA GOES TO THE BALL in 1978. She introduces ARIAS, DUETS

AND ENSEMBLES from twelve American operas in the 1991 Lincoln Center concert *A Salute to American Music,* which is on CD. Price, who was born in Laurel, Mississippi, won a scholarship to Juilliard and made her American opera house debut in San Francisco in 1957. She sang a wide series of roles at the Met before retiring from the stage in 1985.

LE PRINCE MASQUE DE LA CAUCASIE *1943 "movie opera" by Ward*

Edward Ward's "fiery Russian movie opera" *Le Prince Masque de la Caucasie,* libretto by George Waggner, was one of two created for the 1943 Universal film *The Phantom of the Opera* to be sung by Paris Opera stars Nelson Eddy and Susanna Foster. It's based on themes from Tchaikovsky's *Fourth Symphony* and is elaborately staged and sung in a French translation by William Von Wymetal Jr. In this film of the Gaston Leroux tale. Claude Rains plays the crazed Phantom in love with a young Paris Opera soprano. Wilhelm Wymetal Jr. staged the opera sequences, Samuel Hoffenstein and Eric Taylor wrote the script, Hal Mohr was cinematographer and Arthur Lubin directed the 93-minute color movie for Universal. The other opera created for the movie is called AMOUR ET GLOIRE. MCA VHS/DVD.

THE PRINCESS *1949 "movie opera" by Charles Previn*

Mario Lanza and Kathryn Grayson make their cinematic opera debut in Philadelphia in the "movie opera" *The Princess* created for the 1949 film *The Midnight Kiss*. Charles Previn based the music on themes from Tchaikovsky's *Fifth Symphony* working with William Katz who wrote the lyrics. The principal aria is titled "Love is Music." The opera is staged as the climax of the film with a huge Grecian-style garden set, Lanza dressed like a military prince and Grayson as his princess. In the movie plot he is a truck driver with a great voice and Grayson is an heiress who wants to be an opera singer. Norman Taurog directed the film for MGM. MGM/UA VHS/DVD.

THE PRINCESS PAT *1915 comic opera by Herbert*

Irish beauty Pat O'Connor is married to Prince Antonio di Montalo but the relationship seems to be cooling. When she helps her friend Grace try to win a man, she wins back her husband as well. Victor Herbert's *The Princess Pat*, libretto by Henry Blossom, was premiered at the Cort Theater In Atlantic City, NJ, on August 23, 1915, and opened on Broadway on September 29 with Eleanor Painter starring as the Irish heroine. She was supported by Eva Fallon as her friend Grace, Joseph Lertora as the Prince, Angela Palmer as Grace and Al Shean as a man Pat pretends to elope with to help Grace. It was staged by Fred G. Lathem. The most popular songs are "Love is the Best of All" sung by Pat and "Neapolitan Love Song" sung by the Prince.

1915 Eleanor Painter. Eleanor Painter, who originated the role of Princess Pat, recorded her hit song "Love is the Best of All" for Columbia in 1915. It's on the CD box set *Music from the New York Stage 1890–1920*. **1916 Reinard Werrenrath.** Met baritone Reinard Werrenrath recorded "Neapolitan Love Song" in 1916 for a Victor Red Seal 78. **1916 Victor Light Opera.** The Victor Light Opera Company singers perform a medley of tunes from the operetta for a Victor 78. **1929 Eleanor Painter.** Eleanor Painter can be seen as well as heard singing "Love is the Best of All" on a 1929 Vitaphone Warner Brothers sound film called *Eleanor Painter, the Lyric Soprano*. **1931 Victor Light Opera.** Nat Shilkret leads the Victor Light Opera Company in "Vocal Gems" from the operetta. "I Wish I Was an Island on an Ocean of Girls," "All for

You," "Love Is Best of All," "Make Him Guess" and "Neapolitan Love Song" are on album *A Victor Herbert Showcase*. Flapper Past CD. **1932 Richard Crooks.** Richard Crooks sings the "Neapolitan Love Song" with the Victor Orchestra led by William Merrigan Daly. It's on the anthology album *The Songs of Victor Herbert*. ASV Living Era CD. **1950 Jussi Björling.** Jussi Björling sang "Neapolitan Love Song" twice on the TV series *The Voice of Firestone*. The video *Jussi Björling in Opera and Song Volume 1* has the March 6, 1950, performance while the *Volume 2* video shows him on November 20, 1950. He is accompanied by Howard Barlow and the Firestone Orchestra. VAI VHS. **1952 Dorothy Kirsten/Gordon MacRae.** Dorothy Kirsten and Gordon MacRae perform an abridged radio version of the comic opera. Demand Performance audiocassette. **1957 Richard Tucker.** Richard Tucker sings "Neapolitan Love Song" on the TV series *The Voice of Firestone* with Howard Barlow conducting the Firestone Orchestra. It's on *Richard Tucker in Opera and Song*. VAI VHS. **1986 Teresa Ringholz/Eastman-Dryden Orchestra.** Teresa Ringholz and the Eastman Dryden Orchestra led by Donald Hunsberger perform six songs from *The Princess Pat* on the album *Victor Herbert: The American Girl*. Arabesque CD. **1993 Jerry Hadley.** Jerry Hadley sings "Neapolitan Love Song" on his album *Golden Days*. Paul Gemignani conducts the American Theatre Orchestra. BMG RCA Victor CD.

Victor Herbert's comic opera *The Princess Pat* opened on Broadway in 1915 with a fashion plate cast.

PRISCILLA   *1887 opera by Gerrish-Jones*

New England at the time of Revolution. Priscilla loves Robert who has gone to war in a ship that appears to have been lost. Guy attempts to win Priscilla when her lover does not return and asks help from a Witch. When he is unsuccessful, he attacks the Witch and is killed as the Witch vanishes. Priscilla, who lost her mind with longing, regains it when Robert returns the following Halloween. Abbie Gerrish-Jones' four-act romantic opera *Priscilla*, libretto by the composer, was completed in 1887. It is believed to be the first American opera with libretto and score by a woman. It was to have been produced by the American Grand Opera Company in Portland, Oregon, but this does not seem to have happened.

PROKOFIEV, SERGEY   *Russian composer (1891–1953)*

Sergey Prokofiev was living in New York City when he was commissioned to write an opera by Cleofante Campanini, director of the Chicago Grand Opera. THE LOVE FOR THREE ORANGES, libretto by the composer based on a fantasy fable by Venetian playwright Carlo Gozzi, was composed in New York in 1919 and premiered in Chicago at the Auditorium on December 30, 1921. At the insistence of new director Mary Garden, it was sung in French as *L'amour des trois oranges*. José Mojica played the Prince, Nina

Koshetz was Fata Morgana and Alexander Smallens conducted the Chicago Grand Opera Orchestra. This was the first Prokofiev opera to be staged and it was the most successful in his lifetime. Prokofiev made such great demands on the Chicago company there were no further American commissions.

THE PROMISED VALLEY   *1947 oratorio by Gates*

Crawford Gates' oratorio *The Promised Valley*, which he called a "musical play," was premiered in 1947 as part of Utah's centennial celebration. It depicts the Mormon migration from Illinois to the Great Salt Lake in 1847 with soloists representing Mormon travelers making the difficult trip. *The Promised Valley* combines opera, oratorio and musical with extended symphonic sections.

1983 Utah Chorale and Symphony

Soprano JoAnn Ottley, tenor Noel Twitchell and baritone Robert Peterson are the soloists on this recording of *The Promised Valley* made in 1983 with Crawford Gates leading the Utah Chorale, Utah Children's Chorus and the Utah Symphony Orchestra. Citadel CD.

THE PROSCENIUM   *1993 opera by Kupferman*

Meyer Kupferman's one-woman opera The *Proscenium... on the Demise of Gertrude*, libretto by the composer, was premiered at the Miller Theater at Columbia University on November 3, 1991. Barbara Hardgrave played Gertrude and Kupferman conducted the chamber orchestra. The monodrama was reprised at the Music in the Mountains Festival in 1993.

1993 Music in the Mountains Festival. Barbara Hardgrave sings the role of Gertrude in a production of the opera staged at the Music in the Mountains Festival. Meyer Kupferman conducts the Music in the Mountains Festival Chamber Players. Soundspells Productions CD.

PUCCINI, GIACOMO   *Italian composer (1858–1924)*

Giacomo Puccini based two of his operas on American stories

and premiered one of them in the New York. *Madama Butterfly* is based on a play by American David Belasco that Puccini saw in London in 1900. The story, a Japanese girl marries an American naval lieutenant and kills herself when he abandons her, originated as a novella by John Luther Long. *La fanciulla del West* is based on another David Belasco play, *The Girl of the Golden West,* which Puccini saw in New York in 1907. The libretto follows the play fairly closely. Minnie runs a saloon in a gold mining town in California, falls in love with a bandit and saves his life. *Fanciulla* was premiered at the Metropolitan Opera in New York on December 10, 1910, with Enrico Caruso as Dick Johnson and Emmy Destinn as Minnie, and staged in Chicago two weeks later, December 27, with Amadeo Bassi as Dick Johnson. Carolina White as Minnie.

PULITZER PRIZES FOR OPERA

The Pulitzer Prizes, awarded for outstanding achievements in American drama, letters, music, and journalism, were established in 1917 by Joseph Pulitzer. They are presented annually by Columbia University on recommendations from the Pulitzer Prize Board. An award for a musical composition was not established until 1943. Six of the awards have gone to operas, another seventeen have gone to opera composers for non-operatic compositions.

Pulitzer Prize Operas: 1950 *The Consul,* Gian Carlo Menotti. 1951 *Giants in the Earth,* Douglas Moore. 1955 *The Saint of Bleecker Street,* Gian Carlo Menotti. 1958 *Vanessa,* Samuel Barber. 1962 *The Crucible,* Robert Ward. 2000 *Life Is a Dream,* Lewis Spratlan.

Pulitzer Prizes Awarded to Opera Composers: 1943 William Schuman: Secular Cantata No. 2. 1944 Howard Hanson: Symphony No. 4. 1945 Aaron Copland: Appalachian Spring. 1949 Virgil Thomson: Louisiana Story. 1956 Ernst Toch: Symphony No. 3. 1957 Norman Dello Joio: Meditations on Ecclesiastes. 1960 Elliott Carter: String Quartet No. 2. 1963 Samuel Barber: Piano Concerto No. 1. 1967 Leon Kirchner: Quartet No. 3. 1970 Charles Wuorinen: Time's Encomium. 1973 Elliott Carter: String Quartet No. 3. 1975 Dominick Argento: From the Diary of Virginia Woolf. 1976 Ned Rorem: Air Music. 1978 Michael Colgrass: Déjà vu for Percussion Quartet. 1980 David Del Tredici: In Memory of a Summer Day. 1982 Roger Sessions: Concerts for Orchestra. 1987 John Harbison: The Flight into Egypt. 1988 William Bolcom: 12 New Etudes for Piano. 1989 Roger Reynolds: Whispers Out of Time. 1994 Gunther Schuller: Of Reminiscences and Reflections. 2001 John Corigliano: Symphony 2 for String Orchestra.

PUPPY AND THE BIG GUY   *1995 youth opera by Tinsley*

A young woman named Puppy takes a stand against drug use. Sterling Tinsley's youth opera *Puppy and the Big Guy,* libretto by Kate Pogue, was premiered by Houston Grand Opera at Houston City Hall on December 18, 1995. Marsha Thompson played Puppy, Susan Stone was Annie, Nathan White was Ike, Billy Hargis was Mr. Taupe-Baby, Barry Barrios was Shades and Christopher Strane was Officer Lopez and the Voice of the Big Guy. Constinos Kritikos designed the costumes and props, Kate Pogue directed and Kim Hupp was the music director and pianist.

PURDY, JAMES   *American writer (1923–)*

James Purdy made his literary reputation with his 1959 novel *Malcolm,* about a 15-year-old boy in search of himself. Most of his stories deal with small-town life and family relationships. Two have been turned into one-act operas by composer Joseph Fennimore, *Apache Dance,* libretto by the composer, was premiered at the Metropolitan Opera Studio on April 1, 1975. *Eventide,* libretto by the composer, was premiered at Carnegie Recital Hall on October 1, 1975, and revived by After Dinner Opera in 1983.

PURGATORY   *1961 opera by Weisgall*

An old man takes his 16-year-old son to visit the ruins of the family house where he had murdered his own father many years before. The ghosts of the past return and the old man kills his son while trying to exorcise them. Hugo Weisgall's allegorical atonal one-act opera *Purgatory,* libretto by the composer based on the poetic play by William Butler Yeats, was first performed at the Library of Congress in Washington in 1961. Robert Trehy played the Old Man and Loren Driscoll was the Young Boy. The opera was commissioned by BBC Television and the Cheltenham Festival which staged it in 1966.

PUTNAM, ASHLEY   *American soprano (1952–)*

Ashley Putnam has sung leading roles in a number of American operas and there are recordings of many of them. She was Angel More in the 1977 Santa Fe Opera production of Virgil Thomson's THE MOTHER OF US ALL (televised and recorded). She sang the title role in the 1978 Virginia Opera production of Thea Musgrave's MARY QUEEN OF SCOTS (recorded live). She plays Anna Maurrant in the 1994 Houston Grand Opera production of Kurt Weill's STREET SCENE at Berlin's Theater des Western (on DVD). She played Saint Teresa I in Robert Wilson's production of Virgil Thomson's FOUR SAINTS IN THREE ACTS for Houston Grand Opera in 1996 and the lead role of Ela in the reprise of David Carlson's DREAMKEEPERS at Tulsa Opera in 1998. Putnam, born in New York City, studied at Michigan University and made her debut in 1976 at Norfolk, VA.

Q

QUEENIE PIE   *1986 "street opera" by Ellington and Peress*

In the mythical kingdom of Harlem the aging beauty queen Queenie Pie fears her 13-year reign is about to be ended by the younger, livelier Cafe O'Lay. Queenie has desperate dreams of finding eternal youth on a tropical island, but she finally comes to term with growing old and decides to abdicate. Duke Ellington's "street opera" *Queenie Pie* has been compared to *Porgy and Bess* and one critic felt it told what might have happened to Bess after she left Catfish Row. The opera, originally conceived for television, was unfinished when Ellington died. It was completed in 1986 by George C. Wolfe (libretto), George David Weiss (lyrics), Maurice Peress (music) and Barrie Lee Hall (adaptation/orchestration). Ellington's son Mercer conducted its premiere at the American Music Festival at the Zellerback Theater in Philadelphia on September 18, 1986, with Garth Fagan as director and choreographer. Teresa Burrell was Queenie, Patty Lilley was Café O'Lay, Larry Marshall was Lil Daddy, Lillias White was LaVerne, Teresa Bowers was La Grille, Melodee Savage was LaRue, Ken Prymus was Mayor and André Montgomery was Judge Willie Bo Bo Brown. The opera was reprised at the Kennedy Center in Washington in November 1986. Patti LaBelle made a return to the U.S. stage in 1989 playing Queenie in a touring production. Melba Moore and Brian Stokes Mitchell were featured in a 1993 concert production of the original uncomplete opera at the Brooklyn Academy of Music with the Ellington Orchestra. Mitchell reportedly recorded the score of *Queenie Pie* with Cleo Lane and Roberta Flack but no commercial recording is available.

1988 Duke Ellington Orchestra. Mercer Ellington leads the Duke Ellington Orchestra in a performance of "Queenie Pie Reggae" on the 1988 album *Music Is My Mistress*. Musicmasters CD.

A QUESTION OF TASTE   *1989 opera by Schuman*

At a dinner in 1910 a wine expert, asked by his host if he can identify an unusual wine, makes a high-stakes wager. He bets half a million dollars against the hand of the host's daughter in marriage. There is, not surprisingly, an attempt to cheat. William Schuman's one-act opera *A Question of Taste*, libretto by J. D. McClatchy, is based on the story "Taste" by Roald Dahl. It was commissioned by Glimmerglass Opera, tried out at the Juilliard School in August 1988 and premiered by Glimmerglass in Cooperstown, New York, on June 24, 1989. Schuman's score for the opera is based around waltzes meant to evoke the period.

1990 Juilliard Opera Center. Angela Norton sings the role of Louise, object of the bet, in this recording of the opera made with the Juilliard Opera Center and Juilliard Orchestra conducted by Gerard Schwarz. Scott Wilde is the wine expert Phillisto Pratte, Travis Paul Groves is Tom, Elizabeth Bishop is Mrs Schofield, David Corman is Mr. Schofield, Elizabeth Grohowski is Mrs. Hudson and Carolyn Scimone is Sarah. Delos CD.

THE QUESTIONS OF ABRAHAM   *1973 TV opera by Laderman*

Hebrew patriarch Abraham queries God before the destruction of Sodom and Gomorrah asking if he means to destroy the righteous with the wicked. God agrees to spare the cities if ten rightous men can be found in them. Ezra Laderman's 50-minute television opera *The Questions of Abraham*, libretto by Joseph Darion based on Chapter 18 of Genesis in the Bible, was telecast in color by CBS Television on September 30, 1973, with Hilda Harris as Abraham's wife Sarah.

A QUIET PLACE   *1983 opera by Bernstein*

An unhappy American family gets together for the first time in twenty years and attempts to resolve disagreements. They have come for the funeral of Dinah, wife of Sam and mother of Junior and Dede, who has been been killed in a car accident. They remember things about her and recall family events before their separation and finally meet in her garden, her "quiet place," to mark a reconciliation. Leonard Bernstein's *A Quiet Place*, libretto by Stephen Wadsworth, is a sequel to his 1952 TROUBLE IN TAHITI and incorporates the earlier opera. It was co-commissioned by Houston Grand Opera, the Kennedy Center and Teatro alla Scala and premiered by Houston on June 17, 1983. Chester Ludgin was Sam, Timothy Nolen was Junior, Sheri Greenawald was Dede, Peter Kazaras was son-in-law François, Theodore Uppman was Bill, Douglas Perry was the Analyst, Peter Harrower was Doc, Carolyne James was Mrs. Doc and Charles Walker was the Funeral Director. *Trouble in Tahiti* was staged as a prologue with Diane Kesling as Dinah, Edward Crafts as Sam and James Michael McGuire, Mark Thomsen and Lee Merrill as the jazz trio chorus. David Gropman designed the sets, Peter Mark Schifter directed and John DeMain conducted. The opera was staged at La Scala the following June in a revised version with John Maurceri conducting. (Bernstein composed a song called "A Quiet Place" for Julian Claman's 1955 play *A Quiet Place* which has a completely different plot.)

1986 Vienna State Opera. Leonard Bernstein conducts the ORF Austrian Radio/Television Symphony Orchestra in a television adaptation of the Vienna State Opera production. Chester Ludgin is old Sam, Edward Crafts is young Sam, Wendy White is Dinah, Beverly Morgan is Dede, Theodore Uppmann is Bill, Peter Kazaras is Francois, Clarity James is Mrs. Doc, Jean Craft is Susie, John Kuether is Doc, John Brandstetter is Junior and the Chorus Trio are Louise Edeiken, Mark Thomsen and Kurt Ollman. Librettist Stephen Wadsworth was stage director and Hugo Kach directed for television. The opera was telecast April 12, 1986. Custom Opera VHS/DG CD.

QUITTMEYER, SUSAN   *American mezzo-soprano (1953–)*

Susan Quittmeyer created the role Hermione in John Harbison's A WINTER'S TALE for San Francisco Opera's American Opera Project in 1979, Elmire in Kirke Mechem's TARTUFFE for San Francisco Opera's American Opera Project in 1980 and Ariel in John Eaton's THE TEMPEST at Santa Fe Opera in 1985. She is married to James Morris.

QUIVAR, FLORENCE   *American mezzo-soprano (1944–)*

Florence Quivar created the role of the Goddess of the Waters in Anthony Davis's *Amistad* at Lyric Theater of Chicago in 1997. She sings Serena in the 1976 Lorin Maazel Cleveland recording of George Gershwin's PORGY AND BESS and reprised the role at the Met. She sings St. Teresa II in Joel Thome's 1981 recording of Virgil Thomson's FOUR SAINTS IN THREE ACTS and is one of the soloists in the 1977 Tanglewood Festival recording of Roger Sessions cantata WHEN LILACS LAST IN THE DOORYARD BLOOMED. She premiered William Bolcom's song cycle *The Diary of Sally Hemings* in Washington, D.C., in 2001. Quivar, born in Philadelphia, studied in Philadelphia and in New York at Juilliard. She made her Metropolitan Opera debut in 1977.

R

RACETTE, PATRICIA   *American soprano (1966–)*

Patricia Racette created the title role in Tobias Picker's EMMELINE at Santa Fe Opera in 1996 and was featured in the telecast, recording and reprise at New York City Opera. She created Love Simpson in Carlisle Floyd's COLD SASSY TREE at Houston Grand Opera in 2000 and reprised the role for San Diego Opera. She sang the title role in a San Francisco Opera workshop production of Hugo Weisgall's ESTHER and Fosca in a Minnesota Opera production of Stephen Sondheim's PASSION Racette, who born in Bedford, New Hampshire, and studied at North Texas State University, made her debut in 1989 and her Met debut in 1992. She has sung leading roles in most of the American and European opera houses.

RACHEL, LA CUBANA   *1974 TV opera by Henze*

Cuban cabaret singer Rachel reminisces about the past in 1959 during the last days of the Battista regime and remembers key moments in her life. Hans Werner Henze's 90-minute "vaudeville with music" *Rachel, La Cubana*, libretto by Hans Magnus Enzenberger based on Miguel Barnet's 1969 novel *La canción de Rachel*, was commissioned by Peter Herman Adler for NET Opera and telecast in an English translation by Mel Mandel on March 4, 1974. Lee Verona played young Rachel, Lili Darvas was the nonsinging older Rachel, Alan Titus played the men in her life, Susanne Marsee was Lucile, Edward Pierson was El Cimarrón and the supporting cast included Robert Rounseville, Ronald Young, David Rae Smith and Olympia Dukakis. David Griffiths produced, Bob

Herger arranged the choreography, Rouben Ter-Arutunian designed the sets and costumes and Henze himself conducted the NET orchestra. Production costs were four times the budget, director Kirk Browning quit over its problems and NET never produced another original opera. Video at Museum of Television and Radio.

RADIO AND AMERICAN OPERA

American operas began to be broadcast soon after radio became popular in the 1920s. The first was Deems Taylor's THE KING'S HENCHMAN. It was presented in a 60-minute highlights format by the Columbia Phonograph Broadcasting System (later CBS) over WOR in New York on September 18, 1927, just six months after its Met premiere. Howard Barlow conducted. It was NBC, however, that pioneered opera on radio through its National Grand Opera Company organized by conductor Cesare Sudaro. Its first American opera was Aldo Franchetti's NAMIKO-SAN presented on March 7, 1928. The first American opera to be premiered on radio was Harry Lawrence Freeman VOODOO, broadcast on WGBS in New York on May 20, 1928, in a 30-minute highlights version. For a list of premieres, see below. For listings of operas broadcast by networks and stations, see CBS RADIO, NBC RADIO, WNYC RADIO.

Original American operas premiered on radio: American composers were the first to present original operas on the radio. The first was by an African American, Harry Lawrence Freeman, whose VOODOO was broadcast on WGBS (CBS) in New York on May 20, 1928, in a 30-minute highlights version. The first complete opera premiered on radio was Cesare Sodera's three-act OMBRE RUSSE broadcast on NBC in two parts in 1929, Acts One and Two on May 27 and Act Three on June 3. It was followed by Charles Sanford Skilton's one-act opera THE SUN BRIDE broadcast on NBC on April 17, 1930. The first opera commissioned for radio was Charles Cadman's THE WILLOW TREE premiered on NBC on October 3, 1932. The most successful American radio operas were composed by Gian Carlo Menotti and Kurt Weill. Menotti's THE OLD MAID AND THIEF, broadcast by NBC in 1939 and staged by Philadelphia Opera in 1941, has entered the operatic repertory. Weill's DOWN IN THE VALLEY was composed for radio and recorded in 1945 but not broadcast; it was finally premiered on stage in 1948 and quickly became one of the most popular American operas.

Listed here by year are American operas known to have premiered on radio. For further details, see composer or opera entry. 1928 Freeman, *Voodoo* (WGBS). 1929 Sodero, *Ombre Russe* (NBC). 1930 Skilton, *The Sun Bride* (NBC). 1932 Cadman, *The Willow Tree* (NBC); Graham, *Tom-Tom* (NBC). 1933 Hadley, *A Night in Old Paris* (NBC). 1937 Giannini, *Flora* (CBS); Gruenberg, *Green Mansions* (CBS); Blitzstein, *I've Got the Tune* (CBS). 1938 Giannini, *Beauty and the Beast* (CBS). 1939 Menotti, *The Old Maid and the Thief* (NBC); Giannini, *Blennerhassett* (CBS); Zador, *Christopher Columbus* (NBC). 1940 Baron, *François Villon* (NBC); Weill, *The Ballad of Magna Carta* (CBS). 1942 Kern, *Lamplighter* (MBS); Lessner, *The Nightingale and the Rose* (NBC); Thompson, *Solomon and Balkis* (CBS); Loomis, *Revival* (KWFB). 1943 Montemezzi, *L'Incantesimo* (NBC). 1945 Weill, *Down in the Valley* (recorded); Bennett, *The Enchanted Kiss* (WNYC-MBS). 1947 Smith, *The Gooseherd and the Goblin* (WYNC). 1948 Virzi, *Sulamita* (WYNC-MBS). 1949 Kalmanoff, *Fit for a King* (WYNC-MBS). 1951 Kalmanoff, *Noah and the Stowaway* (WYNC). 1952 Kalmanoff, *The Empty Bottle* (WYNC-MBS). 1954 Laufer, *Ile* (WYNC-MBS). 1955 Kondorossy, *Midnight Duel* (WSRS); *Mystic Fortress* (WSRS); *The String Quartet* (WSRS); *The Two Imposters* (WSRS). 1956 Helm, *The Siege of Tottenburg* (SDR, Stuttgart); Kalmanoff, *Opera, Opera* (WYNC-MBS); Broekman, *The Toledo War* (CBS). 1957 Claflin, *La Grande Bretèche* (CBS). 1958 Kayden, *Mardi Gras* (WYNC-MBS). 1964 Eaton, *Heracles* (RAI, Italy); Hausfrecht, *A Pot of Broth* (WYNC-MBS). 1971 Kondorossy, *Kalamona and Four Winds* (WPOE). 1982 Musgrave, *An Occurrence at Owl Creek Bridge* (BBC, England). 1986 Hayes, *Love in Space* (WDR, Germany).

RAGE D'AMOURS   *2002 opera by Zuidam*

Spanish Queen Juana, nicknamed La Loca (the mad one), is married to Philip I, the king who created the Habsburg dynasty in Spain. She is so obsessed with her faithless husband, known around Europe as Philip the Handsome, that she even embraces his corpse. Robert Zuidam's chamber opera *Rage d'amours*, libretto by the composer based on the life of Queen Juana of Castille, was premiered at the Tanglewood Festival in August 2003. Sopranos Lucy Shelton, Rochelle Bard and Amy Zynatzke sang the role of Queen Juana while Stefan Asbury conducted the Tanglewood student orchestra. The musical style is Stravinsky-like modern.

RAIN QUARTET   *Quartet: Regina (1949). Words and music: Marc Blitzstein.*

The Mozart-like "Rain Quartet," which begins with the words "make it a quiet day," tells of the falling of friendly rain that nourishes the earth that some people eat. It is sung in Act Three of Marc Blitzstein's *Regina* by Regina's husband Horace, her sister-in-law Birdie, ex-slave Addie and Alexandra and is one of the highlights of the opera. It was introduced on stage in the 1949 premiere by William Wilderman as Horace, Brenda Lewis as Birdie, Priscilla Gillette as Alexandra and Lillyan Brown as Addie. There are three recordings that feature the quartet. In the 1958 New York City Opera recording of the opera with Samuel Krachmalnick conducting, Joshua Hecht sings the role of Horace, Elizabeth Carron is Birdie, Helen Strine is Alexandra and Carol Brice is Addie. In the 1992 Scottish Opera recording of the opera with John Mauceri conducting, Samuel Ramey is Horace, Sheri Greenawald is Birdie, Angelina Réaux is Alexandra and Theresa Merritt is Addie. In the recorded and televised Richard Tucker Foundation gala at Lincoln Center in 1991 with James Conlon conducting, the singers are Samuel Ramey, Renée Fleming, Maureen O'Flynn and Denise Woods.

RAISA, ROSA   *American soprano (1893–1963)*

Chicago Opera soprano Rosa Raisa created a major role in an American opera in 1925 a year before she created the title role in Puccini's *Turandot*. She sang the lead role of Toinette in the premiere of William Franke Harling's "jazz opera" A LIGHT FROM ST. AGNES at Chicago Civic Opera on December 26, 1925. Richard Rodgers and Lorenz Hart paid tribute to her the following year in their spoof operetta ROSE OF ARIZONA which they set in a town called Rosa Raisa (*Turandot* had premiered on April 12 so her name was in the news when *Rose of Arizona* was presented on May 10). Raisa, who was born in Poland as Rose Burchstein, made her debut in Parma in 1913 and began to sing in Philadelphia the same year. She was one of the principal performers in Chicago opera from 1916 to 1936 and opened a singing school in Chicago in 1937 after retiring from the stage.

THE RAKE'S PROGRESS   *1951 opera by Stravinsky*

Tom Rakewell and Anne Trulove are engaged to be married but Nick Shadow persuades him to abandon her and go to London because he has inherited a fortune. Shadow is actually the Devil and he eventually persuades Tom to marry the bearded lady Baba the Turk while leading him down the road to ruin. Anne follows him to London to try to save him but Tom ends up in a madhouse. Igor Stravinsky's opera *The Rake's Progress*, libretto by W. H. Auden and Chester Kallman inspired by Hogarth's series *A Rake's Progress*, premiered at Teatro La Fenice in Venice on September 11, 1951. Robert Rounseville was Tom, Elizabeth Schwarzkopf was Anne, Otakar Krause was Shadow, Jennie Tourel was Baba the Turk, Rafael Arié was Trulove, Hugues Cuénod was Sellem and Nell Tangeman was Mother Goose. Stravinsky conducted the Teatro alla Scala Orchestra and Chorus. The opera was given its American premiere at the Metropolitan Opera on February 14, 1953, with Eugene Conley as Tom, Hilde Gueden as Anne, Mack Harrell as Shadow and Blanche Thebom as Baba while Fritz Reiner conducted. Stravinsky composed the opera twelve years after he had emigrated to the U. S., inspired by a Chicago exhibition of the Hogarth drawings. Anne Truelove's aria "NO WORD FROM TOM" has become a recital piece for sopranos.

1951 Teatro La Fenice. The premiere at Teatro La Fenice in Venice on September 11, 1951, was recorded live with the cast as above. Robert Rounseville is Tom, Elizabeth Schwarzkopf is Anne, Otakar Krause is Shadow and Jennie Tourel is Baba the Turk. Stravinsky conducts. Fonit-Cetra LP/Omega Opera Archives CD. **1953**

Igor Stravinsky's 1951 opera *The Rake's Progress* was inspired by the art of William Hogarth.

Metropolitan Opera. Eugene Conley is Tom, Hilde Gueden is Anne and Mack Harrell is Shadow in this recording based on the production at the Met. Blanche Thebom is Baba the Turk, Martha Lipton is Mother Goose, Norman Scott is Trulove and Paul Franke is Sellem. Stravinsky conducts the Metropolitan Opera Chorus and Orchestra. CBS/Phillips LP. **1964 Sadler Wells Opera.** Alexander Young is Tom, Judith Raskin is Anne and John Reardon is Shadow in this recording based on a Sadler Wells Opera production. Regina Sarfaty is Baba the Turk, Don Garrard is Trulove, Jean Manning is Mother Goose and Kevin Miller plays Sellem. Stravinsky conducts the Royal Philharmonic Orchestra and Sadler Wells Opera Chorus. Columbia LP box/Sony CD box. **1967 Swedish Royal Opera.** Barbro Erickson as Baba the Turk and Ragnar Ulfung as Tom perform Act 2, Scene 3, in Swedish in a recording of an excerpt from a Swedish Royal Opera House production in Montreal. Varviso leads the Royal Opera House Orchestra. EMI LP. **1977 Glyndebourne Festival.** Leo Goeke is Tom, Felicity Lott is Anne and Samuel Ramey is Shadow in this Glyndebourne Festival production with colorful Hogarthian set designs by David Hockney. Rosalind Elias is Baba the Turk and Richard van Allen is Trulove. Bernard Haitink leads the London Philharmonic Orchestra and the Glyndebourne Festival Chorus. The opera was staged by John Cox and directed for video by Dave Heather. VAI VHS/DVD. **1982 Maggio Musicale.** Ken Russell staged this lively production for the Maggio Musicale Festival at

the Teatro della Pergola in Florence with sets and costumes by filmmaker Derek Jarman. Gösta Winbergh is Tom, Cecilia Gasdia is Anne, Istvan Gatti is Shadow, Carlo Del Bosco is Trulove and Michael Aspinall is Mother Goose. Riccardo Chailly conducted the Maggio Musicale Fiorentino Orchestra and Russell directed for Italian TV. Premiere Opera VHS. **1983 Riccardo Chailly.** Philip Langridge is Tom, Cathryn Pope is Anne and Samuel Ramey is Shadow in this recording with Riccardo Chailly conducting the London Sinfonietta Chorus and Orchestra. Sarah Walker is Baba the Turk, Astrid Varnay is Mother Goose, Stafford Dean is Trulove and Kevin Dobson is Sellem. Decca/London LP/CD. **1993 Gregg Smith Singers.** Jon Garrison is Tom, Jayne West is Anne and John Cheek is Shadow in this recording by the Gregg Smith Singers and St. Luke's Orchestra conducted by Robert Craft. Wendy White is Baba the Turk, Melvin Lowery is Sellem, Shirley Love is Mother Goose and Arthur Woodley is Trulove. Music Masters CD. **1994 Inger Aby film.** Inger Aby's film of the opera is based on Ingmar Bergman's 1961 stage production. Greg Fedderly is Tom, Barbara Hendricks is Anne, Håkan Hagegård is Nick Shadow, Arild Hellegard is Sellem, Erk Saeden is Trulove, Gunilla Söderström is Mother Goose and countertenor Brian Asawa is Baba the Turk. Gunnar Kallstrom photographed the film and Esa-Pekka Salonen conducted the Swedish Radio Choir and Symphony Orchestra. Warner Vision/ Premiere Opera VHS. **1994 Lyric Opera of Chicago Commentary.** Critical analysis of *The*

Rake's Progress by Alfred Glasser in the Women's Board of Lyric Opera series. It includes musical excerpts, plot summary, composer biography and social and historical background. Lyric Opera Commentaries audiocassette. **1995 Saito Kinen Festival.** Anthony Rolfe-Johnson is Tom, Sylvia McNair is Anne and Paul Plishka is Shadow in this recording based on Graham Vick's production for the Saito Kinen Festival. Seiji Ozawa conducts the Saito Kinen Orchestra and Tokyo Opera Singers. Philips CD. **1996 Salzburg Festival.** Jerry Hadley is Tom with Dawn Upshaw as Anne and Monte Pederson as Shadow in this Salzburg Festival production by Peter Mussbach. Jane Henschel is Baba the Turk, Linda Ormiston is Mother Goose, Jonathan Best is Trulove, Barry Banks is Sellem and Peter Tuff is Keeper. Sylvain Cambreling conducts the Camerata Academica and Vienna State Opera Chorus. Jorg Immendorff designed sets and costumes and Brian Large directed the video. Image Entertainment/Arthaus DVD. **1996 Opera de Lyon.** Jerry Hadley is Tom, Dawn Upshaw is Anne and Samuel Ramey is Shadow in this Opera de Lyon recording based on an Aix-en-Provence Festival production. Grace Bumbry is Baba the Turk, Robert Lloyd is Trulove, Anne Collins is Mother Goose and Steven Cole is Sellem. Kent Nagano conducts the Opera de Lyon Orchestra and Chorus. Erato CD box. **1999 John Eliot Gardiner.** John Eliot Gardiner conducts the Monteverdi Choir and London Symphony Orchestra.in this Grammy-winning recording of the opera. Ian Bostridge is Tom, Deborah York is Anne, Bryn Terfel is Shadow, Sofie Von Otter is Baba the Turk, Peter Bronders is Sellem, Anne Howells is Mother Goose and Martin Robson is Trulove. DG CD box. **1999 Renée Fleming.** Renée Fleming sings the aria "No Word from Tom" on her American opera recital album *I Want Magic.* James Levine conducts the Metropolitan Opera Orchestra. London Classics CD.

RALPH, JAMES   *American playwright (1695–1764)*

James Ralph, who was born in Philadelphia in 1695, is considered the first American to create an opera. He did not compose the music for the ballad opera *The Fashionable Lady: or Harlequin's Opera,* which premiered in London in 1730, but he wrote the libretto and he chose the tunes and he is the only one credited for it. Ralph went to London with his close friend Benjamin Franklin in 1724 and never returned. He became involved in British theater through working with Henry Fielding and wrote numerous books including a history of England and many poems.

RAMEY, SAMUEL   *American bass (1942–)*

Samuel Ramey sings Shadow in Igor Stravinsky's THE RAKE'S PROGRESS on the 1983 London recording, the 1977 Glyndebourne Festival video, the 1992 Aix-en-Provence Festival video and the 1996 Lyons Opera recording. He sings Frank Maurrant in the 1991 Scottish Opera recording of Kurt Weill's STREET SCENE, Horace Giddens in the 1992 Scottish Opera recording of Marc Blitzstein's REGINA and Owen Blitch in the 1994 Lyons Opera recording of Carlisle Floyd's SUSANNAH. He is Billy in a 1987 London recording of Richard Rodgers' CAROUSEL, poet Hajj in the 1991 operatic recording of the Wright/Forrest operetta KISMET, Pitkin in the 1992 operatic recording/video of Leonard Bernstein's ON THE TOWN and a supporting singer for Placido Domingo in the 1996 operatic recording of Mitch Leigh's MAN OF LA MANCHA. On his 1993 album *Samuel Ramey on Broadway,* he performs arias from Kurt Weill's LOST IN THE STARS and George Gershwin's PORGY AND BESS. Ramey, who was born in Colby, Kansas, made his debut at New York City Opera in 1973 and at the Metropolitan Opera in 1984, and was soon acclaimed as one of the finest basses in the world.

RAN, SHULAMIT   *American composer (1949–)*

Shulamit Ran won considerable critical acclaim for her opera BETWEEN TWO WORLDS (THE DYBBUK), libretto by Charles Kondek based on the Yiddish play by Salomon Ansky, when it was premiered by the Lyric Opera Center for American Artists in Chicago in 1997. Ran, who was born in Israel, studied composition at Mannes College of Music with opera composer Norman Dello Joio and performed her piano composition *Capriccio* with Leonard Bernstein and the New York Philharmonic. She has taught music at the University of Chicago. Her only other stage work was the 1967 television pantomime *The Laughing Man.*

RANDS, BERNARD   *American composer (1934–)*

Bernard Rands, who won the Pulitzer Prize for Music in 1984 for his song cycle *Canti del Sole,* was commissioned to write his first opera by the Aspen Music Festival to celebrate the festival's 50th anniversary. BELLADONNA, libretto by Leslie Dunton-Downer, was premiered by the Aspen Opera Theater Center in the Wheeler Opera House on July 29, 1999. Rands, who was born in Sheffield, England, became an American citizen in 1983. He first attracted attention for his inventive instrumental compositions but he is best known for his ballads and song cycles.

THE RANSOM OF RED CHIEF   *1986 opera by Rodriguez*

Alabama at the beginning of the 20th Century. Northern crooks Sam and Bill kidnap the son of a banker in the small town Summit and demand ransom. The ten-year-old boy, who calls himself Red Chief, terrorizes and humiliates the kidnappers until they finally agree to pay his father to take him back. O. Henry's famous short story *The Ransom of Red Chief,* first published in *Ainslee's Magazine* and included in the 1910 collection *Whirligigs,* has inspired two American operas.

1964 Seymour Barab. Seymour Barab's *The Ransom of Red Chief,* libretto by the composer based on the O. Henry story, was premiered in Newark, New Jersey in 1964. **1986 Robert X. Rodriguez.** Robert X. Rodriguez's *The Ransom of Red Chief,* libretto by Daniel Dibbern based on the O. Henry story, was commissioned by the City of Mesquite, Texas, in celebration of the Texas Sesquicentennial and premiered by Lyric Opera of Dallas in Mesquite on October 10, 1986. The setting of the story was moved from Alabama to Texas for this version of the story. Rodriguez utilizes folk instruments like banjo, harmonica and accordion to play snippets of bluegrass, Dixieland and ragtime music and he also includes quotes from popular songs and other operas.

RAPCHAK, LAWRENCE   *American composer/conductor (1951–)*

Lawrence Rapchak, music director of Chicago Opera Theater, based his 1990 chamber opera THE LIFE WORK OF JUAN DIAZ, libretto by Carl Ratner, on a short story by Ray Bradbury as dramatized in the *Alfred Hitchcock Presents* TV series. It was staged and recorded by Chicago Opera Theater with Rapchak conducting. Rapchak also conducted the 1996 Chicago Opera Theater recording of Gian Carlo Menotti's opera THE MEDIUM and the 1997 Chicago Opera Theater revival of Daron Hagen's opera SHINING BROW.

RAPPACCINI'S DAUGHTER   *American operas based on Hawthorne story*

Rappaccini's daughter Beatrice is brought up in Padua in the 19th century as a poisonous experiment by her scientist father. Any living thing that touches her dies. When Giovanni falls in love with her, she takes an antidote he prepares even though she knows it will kill her. Nathaniel Hawthorne published his symbolic story in the magazine *Democratic Review* in 1844 and in the 1846 collection *Mosses of an Old Manse*. The story has been quite popular with opera composers but the only recording is of Mexican composer Daniel Catán's version as performed by the Manhattan School of Music Opera Theatre.

1925 Charles Cadman. Charles Cadman's *The Garden of Mystery*, libretto by Nelle Richmond Eberhart based on *Rappaccini's Daughter*, was premiered at Carnegie Hall on March 25, 1925. George Walker was Dr. Rappaccini, Helene Cadmus was Beatrice, Ernest Davis was Giovanni, Yvonne de Treville was Bianca and Hubert Linscott was Enrico. Howard Barlow conducted the orchestra. **1982 Michael Cohen.** Michael Cohen's opera *Rappaccini's Daughter,* libretto by Linsey Abrams based on the Hawthorne story, was premiered in Waterford, Connecticut, on August 12, 1981. **1980 Margaret Garwood.** Margaret Garwood's two-act opera *Rappaccini's Daughter,* libretto by composer based on the Hawthorne story, was premiered by Pennsylvania Opera Theater in Philadelphia, on November 21, 1980, with piano and presented with full orchestral score on May 6, 1983. **1984 Sam Dennison.** Sam Dennison's 55-minute opera *Rappaccini's Daughter,* libretto by Karen Campbell based on the Hawthorne story, premiered at the University of Connecticut on August 18, 1984. Georgina Marshall was Beatrice, Edward Randall was Giovanni, William Gleason was Rappaccini, Diane Thornton was Lisabetta and George Randall Mackes was Baglioni. Christopher Whelen designed the set, Howard Zogatt directed and Victor Norman conducted. The opera was reprised by Minikin Opera in Washington, DC, in 1985. **1992 Ellen Bender.** Ellen Bender's opera *Rappaccini's Daughter,* libretto by the composer based on the Hawthorne story, was premiered by the New England Conservatory in Boston in 1992. **1997 Daniel Catán.** Mexican composer Daniel Catán's opera *Rappaccini's Daughter,* libretto by Juan Tovar based on the Hawthorne story as dramatized by Octavio Paz, is the only version of the story that has been recorded. Following a production by San Diego Opera in 1994, the opera was produced and recorded in 1997 by the Manhattan School of Music Opera Theatre and issued on a Newport Classic CD. David Alan Marshall is Rappaccini, Olivia Gorra is Beatriz, Brandon Jovanovich is Giovanni and Julian Rebolledo is Baglioni. Eduard Daizmunoz conducts the Manhattan School of Music Opera Theatre Orchestra.

RAPUNZEL (1)   *1952 opera by Harrison*

Beautiful young Rapunzel has been imprisoned by a Witch in a tower without stairs and the only access is by climbing up Rapunzel's long golden hair. She is rescued by a Prince. Lou Harrison's fairy tale chamber opera *Rapunzel,* libretto by the composer based on William Morris's interpretation of the Grimm fairy tale, was first performed in Rome in May 1954 where one of its arias won a major music award. The opera consists of six short acts and its three soloists sing their arias in a serial manner. Harris says the opera is partially self-analysis. It was given its American premiere at the 92nd Street YMCA in New York May 14, 1959.

1996 UC Santa Cruz. *Rapunzel* was staged and recorded at the University of California, Santa Cruz, in June 1996. The singers are tenor John Duykers as the Prince, soprano Patrice Maginnis as Rapunzel and mezzo Lynne McMurtry as the Witch. Nicole Paiement conducts the Ensemble Paralléle chamber orchestra. New Albion CD.

RAPUNZEL (2)   *1971 opera by Brooks*

Rapunzel's parents are forced to give their golden-haired daughter Rapunzel to a Witch who keeps her imprisoned in a tower without stairs. A Prince hears her singing and tries to get into the tower but cannot. Finally he sees how Rapunzel lets down her long hair as a kind of stairway for the Witch and he climbs up. He wants to marry her but the Witch finds out, exiles Rapunzel to the desert and causes blindness in the Prince. In the end the lovers find each other again, she heals his eyes with her tears and they live happily ever after. Richard Brooks' youth-oriented opera *Rapunzel,* libretto by Harold Mason based on the original Grimm fairy tale, was commissioned by Tri-Cities Opera. It was premiered in Binghamton, New York, on January 22, 1971.

RASPUTIN   *1988 opera by Reise*

Siberian monk Rasputin gains a malignant influence over Tsar Nicholas and Tsarina Alexandra in 1917 Russia after he heals a royal infant. As his power grows he leads a dissolute life keeping a harem and holding nude orgies. He is eventually killed by homosexual Prince Yusopov and a group of conspirators and the Romanov family is murdered by Bolsheviks. Jay Reise's dissonant atonal opera *Rasputin,* libretto by the composer and Frank Corsaro, was commissioned by Beverly Sills for New York City Opera which premiered it on September 17, 1988. Basso John Cheek played Rasputin with John Garrison as Nicolas, Richard Fracker as Iliodor and Margaret Cusack. Franco Colavecchia designed the sets, Christopher Keene conducted and Frank Corsaro directed.

RAVENSHEAD   *1999 opera by Mackey*

Flamboyant businessman Donald Crowhurst attempts to sail around the world single-handed. Unable to cope with failure, he decides to fake his voyage. Stephen Mackey's one-man chamber opera *Ravenshead,* libretto by Rinde Eckert, tells the story of Crowhurst in all his delusional glory. The opera was commissioned by the Paul Dresher Ensemble Electro-Acoustic Band and premiered at Columbia University in New York on November 12, 1998. Eckert, who has a four-octave vocal range, played Crowhurst navigating the world in an imaginative stage boat. Ellen McLaughlin spoke the voiceovers and Jonatha Brooke was the pre-recorded singer. Mackey's high-tech score ranges from classical baroque to Caribbean pop. *USA Today* called it "the best new opera of 1998."

2000 Paul Dresher Ensemble. Rinde Eckert stars as Crowhurst in this recording of the opera made with the Paul Dresher Ensemble Electro-Acoustic Band. Ellen McLaughlin speaks the voiceovers and Jonatha Brooke is the singer. Minmax/Starkland 2-CD box.

RAYAM, CURTIS   *American tenor (1951–)*

Curtis Rayam created the role of Remus in the first full staging of Scott Joplin's *Treemonisha* by Houston Grand Opera in 1975. He sings the role on the recording and reprises it in the 1982 video and telecast. Rayam's other recordings are of European operas but he has sung in George Gershwin's *Porgy and Bess* on stage. He was born in Belleville, Florida, and studied at the University of Miami. He made his debut with Miami Opera in 1971.

A REAL SLOW DRAG   *Soprano aria/ensemble: Treemonisha (1915). Words and music: Scott Joplin.*

"A Real Slow Drag" is the singing, dancing climax of Scott Joplin's ragtime opera *Treemonisha* and virtually a coloratura aria with ensemble support. After Treemonisha has helped her people defeat evil magicians, she tells everyone to salute their partner and do the drag and leads them into the refrain "Marching onward, marching onward, marching to that lovely tune." The stage fills with dancing partners as her voice floats high above the others. It's the high point of the opera and with it Joplin raises ragtime to operatic grandeur. The 1975 Houston Grand Opera performance is on disc and video with Carmen Balthrop superb as Treemonisha. Valerie Stegart sings it on a 1985 recording of a broadcast while Jessye Norman leads the company in a 1986 Royal Gala at the Royal Opera House in London.

REARDON, JOHN   *American baritone (1930–)*

John Reardon is one of the major proponents of modern American opera having created and recorded more roles than any other male singer. He began relatively small in 1954 by creating on record the role of the Young Man in Jack Beeson's HELLO, OUT THERE at Columbia University. He was Second Guest in Gian Carlo Menotti's THE SAINT OF BLEECKER STREET on Broadway in December 1954, the man called simply He in Lehman Engel's THE SOLDIER at Carnegie Hall in 1956 and Mr. McC in Lukas Foss's mini-opera INTRODUCTIONS AND GOODBYES at Carnegie Hall in 1960. Then the roles got bigger. He was Miles Dunster in Douglas Moore's THE WINGS OF THE DOVE at New York City Opera in 1961, the Voice of God in Igor Stravinsky TV opera THE FLOOD on CBS in 1962, the Groom in Menotti's TV opera LABYRINTH on NBC Opera Theater in 1963, the tutor Belaev in Lee Hoiby's NATALIA PETROVNA at New York City Opera in 1964, Yehoyada in Hugo Weisgall's ATHALIAH at Philharmonic Hall in New York in 1964, Carry's husband Charles in Douglas Moore's CARRY NATION at the University of Kansas in Lawrence in 1966, Orin in Marvin David Levy's MOURNING BECOMES ELECTRA at the Met in 1967, John Buchanan in Hoiby's SUMMER AND SMOKE at St Paul Opera in 1971, Boris Trigorin in Thomas Pasatieri's THE SEAGULL at Houston Grand Opera in 1974 and the Poet in Chester Biscardi's *Tight-Rope* at the Musicians Club in New York in 1985. He was also the singer in Fred Rogers' children TV opera WINDSTORM IN BUBBLELAND in 1980. His recording career is equally impressive. He is Grieg in a famous 1958 recording of the Wright/Forrest operetta SONG OF NORWAY, one of the sailors in Leonard Bernstein's 1960 recording of ON THE TOWN, Randy in the 1963 Risë Stevens recording of Kurt Weill's LADY IN THE DARK, Shadow in a 1964 Sadler Wells recording of Igor Stravinsky's THE RAKE'S PROGRESS, Jesus of Nazareth in a 1969 recording of Richard Owen's A FISHERMAN CALLED PETER, Jason in a 1974 CBS television production of Benjamin Lees' MEDEA IN CORINTH, Bob in a 1970

Baritone John Reardon created more roles in American Opera than any other male singer.

Trieste recording of Menotti's THE OLD MAID AND THE THIEF and he sings numbers from Weill's ONE TOUCH OF VENUS on a 1981 album. On stage he has sung Heathcliff in Floyd's WUTHERING HEIGHTS and other roles in Menotti operas including the Husband in AMELIA GOES TO THE BALL, Abdul in THE LAST SAVAGE, Dr Stone in HELP, HELP, THE GLOBOLINKS! and Donato in MARIA GOLOVIN. Reardon, who was born in New York City, made his debut with New York City Opera in 1954.

THE RED MILL   *1906 operetta by Herbert*

Two American tourists end up broke while on a visit to Holland and have to work at an inn to pay off a debt. Kid Conner and Con Kidder rescue Gretchen from a windmill with an acrobatic stunt and then don disguises to help her avoid a forced marriage to the Governor. All ends happily. Victor Herbert's operetta *The Red Mill*, libretto by Henry Blossom, premiered at the Star Theater in Buffalo, NY, on September 3, 1906, and opened in New York on September 24 at the Knickerbocker Theater. Fred Stone played Con, David Montgomery was Kid, Ethel Jackson was Tina, Augusta Greenleaf was Gretchen, Edward Begley was the Burgomaster and Joseph M. Ratliff was Gretchen's soldier. *The Red Mill* was written as a vehicle for comedians Stone and Montgomery but it still has plenty of good tunes like "Every Day Is Ladies Day with Me." It remains one of Herbert's most popular operettas and continues to be staged, including a Broadway revival.

1909 Victor Herbert. Victor Herbert leads his orchestra in a selection of tunes from his operetta for an Edison recording. They're on the album *Victor Herbert and His Orchestra*. Mark LP. **1910 Victor Light Opera.** The Victor Light Opera Company performs a medley of songs including "Because You're You" and "Good-a-Bye John" for the Victor 78 record *Gems from The Red Mill*. **1927 MGM film.** Marion Davies plays Tina who pretends to be Gretchen (Louise Fazenda) to prevent her friend having to marry the Governor. She is imprisoned in a windmill but rescued by her beloved Dennis (Owen Moore). Frances Marion wrote the revised screenplay and William Goodrich (Fatty Arbuckle) directed the film which was silent though Herbert's music was played live in cinemas. **1929 Richard Crooks.** Met tenor Richard Crooks recorded the aria "Moonbeams" in 1929. It's on various albums including *Only a Rose—The Art of Richard Crooks in Song*. Pearl/Koch CD. **1939 Victor Light Opera Company.** Jan Peerce, Anne Jamison and Thomas L. Thomas sings selections with the Victor Light Opera Company and Nat Shilkret and his Orchestra on an RCA Magic Key radio broadcast. It was issued as *The Operetta World of Victor Herbert* on a 78 album by RCA and on LP by JJA. Opera Classics cassette. **1946 Earl Wrightson/Mary Briney.** Earl Wrightson plays The Governor with Mary Martha Briney as Gretchen in this highlights recording with orchestra led by Al Goodman. Donald Dame is Hendrik von Damm and the Mullen Sisters are Luzette, Flaurette and Nanette. The album was based on a Paula Stone/Hunt Stromberg Jr. stage production. RCA Victor LP. **1946 Eileen Farrell/Wilbur Evans/Felix Knight.** Eileen Farrell, Wilbur Evans and Felix Knight are featured in this studio recording of highlights from the operetta. Jay Blackton leads the orchestra and chorus. Decca LP/CD. **1951 Rise Stevens/Gordon MacRae.** Rise Stevens and Gordon MacRae perform an abridged radio version of the opera broadcast on December 10, 1951. Live Opera audiocassette. **1955 Lucille Norman/Gordon MacRae.** Gordon MacRae stars opposite Lucille Norman in this highlights version of the operetta with orchestra conducted by Carmen Dragon. Capitol LP. **1957 Robert Merrill.** Robert Merrill sings "Every Day Is Ladies' Day" on the *Voice of Firestone* TV show on

May 20, 1957. Howard Barlow conducts the Firestone Orchestra. It's on the video *Robert Merrill in Opera and Song.* VAI VHS. **1958 CBS Television.** Shirley Jones is Gretchen opposite Donald O'Connor as Johnny Shaw in this CBS Television production directed by Delbert Mann, Mike Nichols is Red Carter, Elaine May is Candy Carter and Elaine Stritch is the Mayor with Harpo Marx and Evelyn Rudie as narrators. Writer Robert Alan Arthur modernized the story and reset it in Brussels during the World Fair, Fred Coe produced and Don Walker was musical director. Video at MTR. **1961 Robert Shaw Chorale.** The Robert Shaw Chorale and Orchestra perform "The Streets of New York" and "Every Day Is Ladies Day with Me" on the album *The Immortal Victor Herbert.* RCA Victor LP. **1962 Mary Pracht/Richard Fredricks.** Mary Ellen Pracht is Gretchen with Richard Fredricks as Capt. Doris in this highlights version of the operetta with orchestra conducted by Lehman Engel. Jean Sanders is Tina, Evelyn Sachs is Bertha, William Chapman is the Governor and Stanley Grover is Con Kidder. Reader's Digest *Treasury of Great Operettas.* RCA LP box set. **1986 Donald Hunsberger.** The Eastman-Dryden Orchestra led by Donald Hunsberger performs six songs from the operetta on the album *Victor Herbert: L'Encore.* Arabesque CD. **1993 Jerry Hadley.** Met tenor Jerry Hadley performs "Every Day Is Ladies' Day with Me" and "The Streets of New York" with the Harvard Glee Club. Paul Gemignani conducts the American Theatre Orchestra. They're on the album *Golden Days.* BMG RCA Victor CD. **1996 Keith Brion.** Forty minutes of instrumental music from *The Red Mill* are performed by the Razumovsky Symphony Orchestra led by Victor Herbert operetta specialist Keith Brion. American Classics Naxos CD. **1999 Virginia Croskery.** Virginia Croskery sings "Moonbeams" with the Slovak Radio Symphony Orchestra led by Keith Brion on the album *Victor Herbert: Beloved Songs and Classic Miniatures.* American Classics Naxos CD. **2001 Ohio Light Opera.** Anthony Maid is Kid Conner with Cassidy King as Con Kidder in this Ohio Light Opera production at Wooster College. Nancy Maria Balach is Gretchen, Brian Woods is Christian, Megan Loomis is Tina, David Wannen is her father Willem, Lucas Meachem is the Burgomaster, John Sumners is Pennyfeather, Ann Marie Wilcox is Bertha, Jessie Wright Martin is the Contesse, Jonathan Stinson is Alphonse and Wade Woodward is the Governor. J. Lynn Thompson conducts the Ohio Light Opera Orchestra and Chorus in a production directed by Steven Daigle. Recorded live with dialogue. Albany Records 2-CD box.

REDDING, JOSEPH *American composer (1859–1932)*

Joseph Redding made important contributions to American opera both as librettist and composer. He was the librettist for Victor Herbert's 1911 grand opera NATOMA and the composer of the 1925 grand opera FAY-YEN-FAH, the first American opera to be performed in France. Redding, who was born in Sacramento, studied at the California Military Academy and Harvard Law School and then practiced law in San Francisco. He wrote the music for a number of San Francisco plays and the libretto for Henry Hadley's masque *The Atonement of Pan.* His opera music is lyrical with echoes of Puccini and Debussy.

REGINA *1949 opera by Blitzstein*

Cold-hearted Regina Giddens, who makes greed into an art, is a member of a old family in the American South. She destroys all around her, including her husband Horace and her brothers, as she fights to control the family business. Marc Blitzstein's opera *Regina,* libretto by the composer based on Lillian Hellman's play *The Little Foxes,* premiered at the Shubert Theater in New Haven, CT, on October 6, 1949, and opened in New York at the 46th Street Theater on October 31, 1949. Jane Pickens was Regina, Brenda Lewis was Birdie, William Wilderman was Horace, George Lipton was Benjamin, Russell Nype was Leo, Priscilla Gillette was Alexandra, David Thomas was Oscar, William Warfield was Cal, Donald Clarke was William, Bill Dillard was Jazz and Lillyan Brown was Addie. Robert Lewis directed and Emanuel Balaban conducted. Blitzstein uses various pop musical styles to provide a feeling of period including ragtime, blues and spirituals. The best-known numbers are in Act Three, the RAIN QUARTET and BIRDIE'S ARIA. *Regina* has been revived by New York City Opera and other companies and seems to have entered the repertory. Catherine Malfitano had a major success singing the title role in Chicago in 2004.

1956 Brenda Lewis. Brenda Lewis sings Birdie's scena from Act III of *Regina* on the album *Marc Blitzstein Discusses His Theater Compositions.* Blitzstein talks about the opera and plays piano accompaniment. Spoken Arts LP. **1958 New York City Opera.** Brenda Lewis sings Regina in this recording based on a New York City Opera production. Elizabeth Carron is Birdie, Carol Brice is Addie, Joshua Hecht is Horace, Helen Strine is Alexandra, George Irving is Benjamin, Emile Renan is Oscar, Loren Driscoll is Leo, Ernest McChesney is William Marshall and Andrew Frierson is Cal. Samuel Krachmalnick conducts the New York City Opera Orchestra and Chorus. The recording was made on April 28, 1958. Columbia Odyssey LP box. **1979 Houston Grand Opera.** Mar-

Scene from 1994 Des Moines Metro Opera production of *Regina*. Photograph courtesy of Des Moines Metro Opera.

alin Niska is Regina with Elizabeth Carron as Birdie in this live recording of a 1979 Houston Grand Opera production. Also in the cast are Don Garrard and Giorgio Tozzi. John DeMain conducts the Houston Grand Opera Orchestra. Live Opera audiocassette. **1990 William Sharp/Karen Hovik.** William Sharp and Karen Hovik perform arias from the opera on the album *Marc Blitzstein: Zipperfly and Other Songs.* Sharp sings "Blues," composed for Cal but sung by Addie in the final version, while Hovik sings "What Will It Be For Me," performed by Regina's daughter Alexandra. Steven Blier accompanies on piano. Koch CD. **1991 Lincoln Center.** Leontyne Price introduces the Mozart-like "Rain Quartet" from *Regina* at a gala at Lincoln Center on November 10, 1991. The singers are Samuel Ramey, Renée Fleming, Maureen O'Flynn and Denise Woods. James Conlon leads the Metropolitan Opera Orchestra on the PBS telecast *A Salute to American Music.* RCA Victor CD. **1992 Scottish Opera.** Katherine Ciesinski sings the role of Regina with John Mauceri conducting the Scottish Opera Orchestra. Samuel Ramey is Horace Giddens, Sheri Greenawald is Birdie, Angelina Réaux is Alexandra, Theresa Merritt is Addie, James Maddalena is Oscar Hubbard, Timothy Noble is Benjamin Hubbard, David Kuebler is Leo Hubbard and Tim Johnson is Jazz. London CD box. **2004 Lyric Opera of Chicago Commentary.** Critical analysis of *Regina* by William Mason in the Women's Board of Lyric Opera of Chicago series. It includes musical excerpts, plot summary, composer biography and social and historical background. Lyric Opera Commentaries CD.

REICH, STEVE   *American composer (1936–)*

Steve Reich creates experimental multi-media "operas" with his video artist wife Beryl Korot that combine music and images in documentary-like stories based on real people and events. THE CAVE (1993) tells a powerful story about the underpinnings of the Middle East conflict with the video screens providing text as well as images. HINDENBURG (1998) is an audiovisual portrait of the famous German zeppelin which caught fire and crashed in 1937. THREE TALES (2002) incorporates *Hindenburg* with *Bikini* (about the atomic atoll) and *Dolly* (about the cloned sheep). Reich, one of the leaders of the minimalist movement, was born in New York City and studied music around the world from Cornell and Juilliard to the University of Accra in Ghana. He founded his own music group, Steven Reich and Musicians, in 1966.

REID, MICHAEL   *American composer (1947–)*

Michael (Mike) Reid's "football opera" DIFFERENT FIELDS, libretto by Sarah Schlesinger, was commissioned by Opera Memphis and the Metropolitan Opera Guild and premiered in New York and Memphis in 1996. Reid, who was born in Altoona, PA, and studied music at Penn State on a football scholarship, was an All Pro football player with the Cincinnati Bengals in the 1970s. After an injury he became a successful singer/songwriter and wrote over a dozen No. 1 hits for singers like Willie Nelson and Wynona Judd. His songs are romantic while his opera music has been described as Coplandesque.

REINAGLE, ALEXANDER   *American composer (1756–1809)*

Prolific composer Alexander Reinagle premiered at least fourteen comic operas and other music theater works in Philadelphia between 1794 and 1807 and contributed music to many others. They were all staged by his New Company at the New Theater on Chestnut Street. *Slaves in Algiers,* a play by actress Susanna Row-

son with music by Reinagle, was premiered on January 22, 1794. The musical pantomime *La forêt noire* was presented on April 26, 1794. Reinagle's comic opera *The Volunteers,* libretto by Rowson, was premiered on January 21, 1795; and is the only one of his works that has partially survived as the others were burned in a fire that destroyed the New Theater in 1820. Reinagle, born in Portsmouth, England, moved to Philadelphia in 1786 and remained active as a composer until his death. His New Company maintained theaters in Baltimore as well as Philadelphia.

REINER, FRITZ   *American conductor (1888–1963)*

Fritz Reiner conducted the premiere of Gian Carlo Menotti's AMELIA GOES TO THE BALL at the Philadelphia Academy of Music in 1937, the premiere of Douglas Moore's THE DEVIL AND DANIEL WEBSTER at the Martin Beck Theater in New York in 1939 and the American premiere of Igor Stravinsky's THE RAKE'S PROGRESS at the Metropolitan Opera in 1953. Reiner, born in Budapest, began conducting in Europe but then moved to the U. S. and became an American citizen in 1928. After conducting orchestras in Philadelphia and San Francisco, he taught at the Curtis Institute where his pupils included Leonard Bernstein and Lukas Foss. He conducted at the Met from 1948 to 1953.

REISE, JAY   *American composer (1950–)*

Jay Reise's major stage work is the atonal opera RASPUTIN, libretto by the composer, about the monk who dominated the Russian family at the time of the Revolution. It was commissioned by Beverly Sills for the New York City Opera which premiered it September 17, 1988, with attention-attracting nude orgies. His first stage work was the "operatic tableau" *Alice at the End,* presented at Hamilton College in New York on August 1, 1978. *Le Diable au Corps: The Operafilm,* commissioned by Operamovies in London, is a full-length opera written for the cinema in 1998 with music conducted by Steven Mercurio. Reise was a music student at Hamilton College and Pennsylvania University studying with George Crumb and Richard Wernick. He later taught at both colleges.

REMEMBER HIM TO ME   *2003 opera by Moran*

Robert Moran's ten-minute opera *Remember Him to Me,* a plotless virtuoso work for men's chorus, four-hand piano and percussion composed to a text by Gertrude Stein, was premiered at Long Beach Opera on June 8, 2003, in the program "Seven Small Operas." The soloists were James Schaffner, John Duykers, Paul Sabuc and Dennis Rupp and the pianists were Andreas Mitisek and Kristof Van Grysperre.

RENAN, EMILE   *American bass-baritone (1913–2001)*

Emile Renan, who made his debut at New York City Opera in 1944 in the company's first production. soon became one of its stalwarts. He created the role of Meyer in David Tamkin's THE DYBBUK in 1951, Baron Regnard in Robert Ward's HE WHO GETS SLAPPED in 1956 and the Army Doctor in Robert Kurka's THE GOOD SOLDIER SCHWEIK in 1958. He played the Secret Police Agent in Giancarlo Menotti's *The Consul* in 1952, Oscar Hubbard in the 1953 production/recording of Marc Blitzstein's REGINA and Justice Hawthorne in Douglas Moore's *The Devil and Daniel Webster* in 1959. In one of his few excursions outside NYCO, he created the role of Nic Bazette (Bottom) in Elie Siegmeister's NIGHT OF THE MOONSPELL in Shreveport, LA, in 1976. Renan, who was born in Brooklyn, made his debut directing at NYCO in 1965 with *Carmen.*

RENDALL, DAVID   *British tenor (1948–)*

David Rendall has been featured on British recordings of four American operettas. He sings Mr. Snow in a 1987 recording of Richard Rodgers' CAROUSEL opposite Samuel Ramey. Working with conductor John Owen Edwards. he sings the Prince in a complete version of Sigmund Romberg's THE STUDENT PRINCE in 1989, the Caliph in Forrest/Wright's KISMET in 1992 and Noordraak in Forrest/Wright's SONG OF NORWAY in 1992. On stage he has sung Tom in Igor Stravinsky's THE RAKE'S PROGRESS.

RESNIK, REGINA   *American mezzo-soprano (1922–)*

Regina Resnik, who began her singing career as a soprano, created the role of Delilah in Bernard Rogers' THE WARRIOR at the Metropolitan Opera in 1947. After redefining herself as a mezzo-soprano, she create the role of the Old Baroness in Samuel Barber's VANESSA at the Met in 1958; she is featured on the Met recording of the opera and she later sang the part at the Salzburg Festival. She sings Madame Flora in Gian Carlo Menotti's THE MEDIUM in a 1970 Washington Opera recording and Madame Arnfeld in a televised 1990 New York City Opera production of Stephen Sondheim's A LITTLE NIGHT MUSIC. Resnick, who born in New York, made her debut in 1942 and sang with the Metropolitan Opera from 1944 to 1974.

RESURRECTION   *1999 opera by Machover*

In 19th century Russia, the wealthy Prince Dimitry sacrifices everything to help a woman he once knew. She has become a prostitute and is sent to prison in Siberia where he follows to do what he can to resurrect her and himself. Tod Machover's opera *Resurrection,* libretto by Laura Harrington based on Leo Tolstoy's novel, premiered at Houston Grand Opera on April 23, 1999. Scott Hendricks played Prince Dimitry Nekhlyudov, Joyce DiDonato was the prostitute Katerina Maslova, Katherine Ciesinski was Sofia Ivanova, Derrick Parker was the Foreman, James F. Love was the First Judge, David L Paxton was Kulashov, Raymond Very was Peter Simonson and Prince Myagkaya, Jessica Jones was Princess Myagkaya and Nekhlyudov's Sister, Dale Travis was Prince Korchagin, Kerri Marcinko was Princess Missy Korchagin, James C. Holloway was Patinkin and Kriltsov, Daniel Belcher was Baklashov and Prison Inspector and Judith Christin was Princess Sophia Korchagin. Simon Higlet designed the sets and costumes, Graham Murray mounted the elaborate production and Patrick Summers conducted the Houston Grand Opera Orchestra and Chorus. There is continual use of computer-linked keyboard synthesizers in support of the 32-piece orchestra but *Resurrection* is more in the style of *opera seria* than electronic opera.

1999 Houston Grand Opera. Scott Hendricks is Prince Dimitry, Joyce DiDonato is Katerina and Katherine Ciesinski is Sofia in this live recording of the Houston Grand Opera premiere cast. Kerri Marcinko is Princess Missy Korchagin, Raymond Very is Prince Myagkaya and Peter Simonson, Dale Travis is Prince Korchagin, James C. Holloway is Patinkin and Kriltsov, Jessica Jones is Princess Myagkaya and Nekhlyudov's Sister, Derrick Parker is the Foreman and Daniel Belcher is Baklashov and the Prison Inspector. Patrick Summers conducts the Houston Grand Opera Orchestra and Chorus. 129 minutes. Albany 2-CD box.

REUBEN, REUBEN   *1955 Broadway opera by Blitzstein*

Reuben wants to commit suicide so con artist Bart and the greedy Countess persuade him to do it via daredevil trapeze stunts they can use to make money. Nina falls in love with Reuben and convinces him to live. Marc Blitzstein's undervalued Broadway opera *Reuben, Reuben,* libretto by the composer, never got to Broadway after its unsuccessful Boston premiere at the Shubert Theater on October 10, 1955. The complex libretto confused critics and audiences despite a remarkable score. Eddie Albert was Reuben, Kaye Ballard was the Countess, George Gaynes was Bart and Evelyn Lear was Nina. Cheryl Crawford, who produced *Regina* on Broadway, was the producer and Robert Lewis directed. Reuben's aria "The Rose Song" has become popular as a recital piece and one critic said that Mahler would have composed something like it if he had written for Broadway.

1990 William Sharp. Baritone William Sharp sings "The Rose Song" and "Monday Morning Blues" on the album *Marc Blitzstein: Zipperfly and Other Songs.* Steven Blier plays piano. The album was recorded for the New York Festival of Song. Koch CD. **1990 Helene Williams/Ronald Edwards.** Helene Williams and Ronald Edwards sing "The Rose Song," "The Miracle Song," "Be With Me," "Such a Little While" and "Love at First Word" on the album *A Blitzstein Cabaret.* Leonard Lehrman, who conceived the show, plays piano. Premiere CD. **1993 Dawn Upshaw.** Dawn Upshaw sings "Never Get Lost" from the opera on her album *I Wish It So* with Eric Stern conducting the orchestra. Elektra Nonesuch CD.

REVELATION IN THE COURTHOUSE PARK   *1960 opera by Partch*

Parallel stories set in the present and in ancient Greece contrast the crazed worshippers of both eras. Hollywood rock star Sonny is ritually welcomed in Courthouse Park by the cult leader Mom and his fans, but in ancient Thebes King Pentheus denounces the Bacchae cult and their worship of Bacchus. Mom and the Bacchae leader Agave are played by the same woman and Sonny and Pentheus are played by the same man, and there are ritual choruses in both eras. Harry Partch's *Revelation in the Courthouse Park,* libretto by the composer partially based on Euripides's play *The Bacchae,* was premiered at the University of Illinois in Urbana on April 11, 1961. It was the only performance during the composer's lifetime. The required instruments include three types of marimba, two kinds of kithara, two harmonic canons, cloud-chamber bowls, two adapted guitars, two chromelodeons, a "spoils of wars" instrument made of shell casings, an adapted cello and a marching band.

1987 American Music Theater Festival. The American Music Theater Festival production of the opera directred by Jiriz Zizka was recorded at the Great Hall of the University of the Arts in Philadelphia on October 12, 1987. Susanne Costallos is Mom and Agave, Christopher Durham is Sonny and Pentheus, Edward Earle is the Hobo and Teresias, Matthew Kimbrough is the Vendor and the Herdsman, Obba Babatunde is Dion and Dionysus, Casper Roos is the Mayor and Cadmus, Olivia Williams is Korypheus and Rozwill Young is the Cop and the Guard. Danlee Mitchell was the conductor. Tomato CD.

REVEREND EVERYMAN   *1990 opera by Brotons*

Salvador Brotons' opera *Reverend Everyman,* libretto by Gary Corseri based on Hugo von Hofmannsthal's modernization of the medieval morality play *Everyman,* was created for presentation on stage and television. It was premiered by Florida State Opera in Tallahassee in the summer of 1990 with Brotons conducting and taped for television in 1991.

1991 Florida State Opera. Grant Young sings the role of the Reverend Everyman in this Florida State Opera television production at the Florida School of Music in Tallahassee. Roy Delp is Cosmos, Larry Gerber is Buster, Calla Connors is Eveline, Kimber Jorgensen is the Make-up Girl, Heide Holcomb is the Crippled

Girl, Jeannie Zinagle is the Old Woman, Martin Sola is the Veteran, Duane McDevitt is the Wino, Eric Hoven is Thanatos, Juan Jackson is the Young Man, Patricia Pease is Fata Morgana, Alan Kagan is the Marrying Minister and Brian Zwolinski, Perry Baker and Michael Nuestein are the Cameramen. Keven Locke designed the sets, Brian Terrel directed and Brotons conducted the Florida State University Chamber Orchestra. On video.

REYNOLDS, ROGER   *American composer (1934–)*

Roger Reynolds, who won the Pulitzer Prize for Music in 1989 for his symphony *Whispers Out of Time,* has written influential music theater works that are considered avant-garde operas. *The Emperor of Ice Cream,* libretto by the composer based on Wallace Stevens's poem and scored for eight soloists and chamber orchestra, was premiered in New York on March 19, 1965, and reprised at the University of Wisconsin in Milwaukee on November 17, 1965. *I/O: A Ritual for 23 Performers,* libretto by the composer based on a concept by Buckminster Fuller and scored for nine female vocalists, nine male mimes, two performers, slide projector and chamber orchestra, was premiered in Pasadena, California, on January 24, 1971. Many of Reynolds's compositions are based around texts by writers like Borges, Beckett and Joyce. Reynolds, who was born in Detroit, turned to music after studying physics at the University of Michigan and was co-founder with Robert Ashley of the ONCE group in Ann Arbor.

RHODE ISLAND   *American state (1790–)*

The first opera performed in Rhode Island was English composer William Shield's *The Poor Soldier* presented at King's Church in Providence in 1795. Tenor/composer Jules Jordan founded the Arion Club in Providence in 1881 to perform concert versions of operas and premiered his RIP VAN WINKLE at the Providence Opera House in 1897. Wasili Leps, composer of the opera *Hoshi-San,* founded the Providence Symphony Orchestra in 1932. Rhode Island-born opera people include composer Theodore Chanler (Newport), baritone Nelson Eddy (Providence) and composer Henry Mollicone (Providence),

Kingston: Richard Winslow's *Endgame,* based on the play by Samuel Beckett, was premiered at the University of Rhode Island in Kingston on November 6, 1974.

Newport: The Newport Music Festival, inaugurated on July 31, 1969, as an outdoor music event, is now indoors and the main venue for classical music in Rhode Island

Providence: Louisa Melvin De Los Mars, the first African American woman composer to write an operetta and have it staged and published, premiered her *Leoni, the Gypsy Queen* in Providence on December 4, 1889; she sang the main role and staged the operetta for the Ideal Dramatic Company. Jules Jordan's RIP VAN WINKLE, based on the Washington Irving story, premiered at the Providence Opera House on May 25, 1897. Providence had two opera companies for a time in the 1970s and 1980s but both are now closed. Ocean State Lyric Opera in Providence is currently Rhode Island's only professional opera company.

RICE, EDWARD E.   *American composer (1848–1924)*

Edward E. Rice was one of the most popular American composers and directors at the end of the 19th century. His extravagant opéra-bouffe EVANGELINE, a burlesque of Longfellow's epic poem with a clever libretto by J. Cheever Goodwin, opened in New York's Niblo's Gardens in 1874 and was one of the most popular music theater works of its time, partially because it had a completely original score. It launched Rice on a long and success career

as a theater composer and director with his own company. He was involved in the early careers of Will Marion Cook, Jerome Kern, Irving Berlin and Lillian Russell.

RICE, ELMER   *American playwright (1892–1967)*

Elmer Rice attracted a good deal of attention with his expressionist 1923 play *The Adding Machine* but he won the Pulitzer Prize in 1929 for his gritty portrait of tenement life in STREET SCENE. It was turned into one of America's finest operas in 1947 by Kurt Weill with Rice himself writing the libretto and Langston Hughes writing the lyrics. It opened in New York in 1947 and is now part of the world opera repertory.

RIESMAN, MICHAEL   *American conductor (1950–)*

Michael Riesman conducts the Philip Glass Ensemble and plays keyboards in the premieres and recordings of many of Philip Glass's operas. They include EINSTEIN ON THE BEACH in 1976/1977, THE PHOTOGRAPHER in 1982, LA BELLE ET LA BÊTE in 1994, HYDROGEN JUKEBOX in 1990 and MONSTERS OF GRACE in 1998. He is also credited for the synthesizer sound design in Glass operas. Riesman, a New York native, studied at the Mannes College Of Music in New York, and with Roger Sessions and Leon Kirchner at Harvard.

RIO RITA   *1927 operetta by Tierney*

Texas Ranger James Stewart cross the Rio Grande in search of a masked bank robber named Kinkajou and falls in love with beautiful Rio Rita, who he fears may be the outlaw's sister. Harry Tierney's old-fashioned operetta *Rio Rita,* libretto by Guy Bolton and Fred Thompson with lyrics by Joseph McCarthy, opened in New York at the Ziegfeld Theater on February 2, 1927. Ethelind Terry played Rio Rita opposite J. Harold Murray as the Ranger Bert Wheeler and Robert Woolsey providing the commedy. John Harwood directed.

1927 J. Harold Murray. J. Harold Murray, who played the Ranger in the Braodway production, recorded two songs from the show with the Victor Light Opera Company. They're available on various albums including the RCA Victor LP *Originals: Musical Comedy 1909–1935.* **1929 RKO film.** Bebe Daniel stars as Rio Rita opposite John Boles as the Texas Ranger in the "screen operetta" *Rio Rita.* Filmed in color, it was a huge success with the help comedians Bert Wheeler and Robert Woolsey who made their film debuts as Chick and Lovett. Victor Baravalle conducted the music Pietro Cimini was chorus master and Luther Reed directed the film for RKO. **1927 Bebe Daniels.** Bebe Daniels, who played Rio Rita in the RKO film, recorded two songs from the show. They're on a various albums including the RCA Victor LP *Stars of the Silver Screen, 1929–1930.* **1930 Edith Day.** Edith Day, who played Rio Rita in the original London stage production, is featured on this highlights recording singing opposite her stage partner Geoffrey Bwyther. The album is titled *Edith Day: The Queen of Drury Lane.* World LP. **1942 MGM film.** Kathryn Grayson has the Rio Rita role opposite hero John Carroll in this film of the operetta created as a vehicle for comedians Bud Abbott and Lou Costello. Screenwriters Richard Connell and Gladys Lehman updated and completely changed the story which concerns Nazis hiding out on a modern Western ranch. Herbert Stothart conducted the music and S. Sylvan Simon directed the film for MGM. **1952 Earl Wrightson/Elaine Malbin.** Earl Wrightson and Elaine Malbin performs highlights from the operetta on this album with support from the Guild Choristers. Al Goodman conducts the orchestra. RCA Victor LP.

RIP VAN WINKLE   *American operas based on Irving story*

Rip Van Winkle quarrels with his wife and goes off hunting in 1763. He meets and drinks with some amiable ghosts and falls asleep for twenty years. When he wakes up his world has been changed by the American Revolution. Washington Irving's famous story *Rip Van Winkle* was first published in 1819 in *The Sketch Book*. Five American operas have been based on the tale.

1855 George F. Bristow. George Frederick Bristow's *Rip Van Winkle*, a "grand romantic opera in three acts" based on the Irving story, is the first American grand opera with an American subject. Although there were earlier American ballad operas like THE DISAPPOINTMENT and music theater pieces like John Bray's THE INDIAN PRINCESS, there were no American operas in traditional Italian operatic style until Henry Fry's LEONORA in 1845. *Rip Van Winkle* is the second American opera of this type though its dialogue is spoken, not sung. Librettist Jonathan Howard Wainwright altered Irving's story considerably, especially for the second act in which Rip is asleep and Rip's daughter Alice has marital problems during the Revolution. In the third act Rip returns and saves his daughter from a fraudulent marriage. The opera was premiered by the Pyne-Harrison opera company in Niblo's Gardens in New York on September 27, 1855. George Stratton sang the role of Rip, Louisa Pyne was Rip's wife, William Harrison was Edward and Miss Gourley was Alice. Bristow conducted the orchestra. The libretto was later heavily revised by J. W. Shannon. The only recent performance of the opera was by Neely Bruce and his American Music Group at a meeting of the Music Library Association at the University of Illinois on February 2, 1974. Shannon's revised libretto and score were reprinted by Da Capo Press in 1991 with editing and introduction by Steven Ledbetter. **1897 Jules Jordan.** Jules Jordan's three-act opera *Rip Van Winkle* was premiered at the Providence Opera House in Providence, RI, on May 25, 1897. **1920 Reginald De Koven.** Reginald De Koven's romantic opera *Rip Van Winkle*, libretto by Percy MacKaye based on the Irving story, has a somewhat different plot than the Bristow opera. In it Rip Van Winkle is in love with shrewish Katrina who sends him off to get a magic potion from Hendrick Hudson's ghost. He falls asleep for twenty years and wakes to a different world where Katrina's more agreeable little sister Peterkee is waiting for him. De Koven's *Rip Van Winkle* was premiered at the Chicago Opera House on January 2, 1920. George Baklanoff was Rip Van Winkle, Edna Darch was bride-to-be Katrina Vedder, Evelyn Herbert was Katrina's little sister Peterkee Vedder, Gustave Huberdeau was their father Nicholas Vedder, Hector Dufranne was Henrik Hudson and Howard Carroll was Hans Van Bummel. Alexander Smallens conducted. **1932 Edward Manning.** Edward Manning's three-act opera *Rip Van Winkle*, libretto by the composer, was premiered at the Town Hall in New York on February 12, 1932. **1957 Nicolas Flagello.** Nicolas Flagello's children's opera *Rip Van Winkle*, libretto by C. Fiore based on the Washington Irving story, was completed in 1957. **1993 Adam Levowitz.** Adam Levowitz's musical *Rip Van Winkle*, libretto by the composer based on the Irving story, was completed in 1993.

IL RITORNO DI CESARE   *1951 "movie opera" by Castelnuovo-Tedesco*

Mario Castelnuovo-Tedesco created the movie opera *Il Ritorno di Cesare* (The Return of Caesar) for the 1951 MGM film *Strictly Dishonorable*. Ezio Pinza portrays the opera singer who stars in it and sings the aria "Il Ritorno de Cesare" with Janet Leigh on stage as his sword bearer. Off stage he is an operatic Don Juan and she

is an nave innocent who falls in love with him. He has to marry her to save her reputation. Or so he says. The film, based on a 1931 play by Preston Sturges, was directed by Melvin Frank and Norman Panama.

RIVER OF WOMEN/RIO DE MUJERES   *2001 opera by Armienta*

A Mexican American woman living in San Antonio, Texas, struggles to escape from her rural home and make a better life for her and her daughter but she finds it difficult to escape the confines of her culture. Her story parallels that of the magical mythical La Llorona, the Weeping Woman of legend. American American composer Hector Armienta's chamber opera *River of Women/Rio de Mujeres*, libretto by the composer, is partially based on the life of his grandmother. It premiered at the Artaud Theater in San Francisco on May 10, 2001, in a production staged by José Maria Condemi.

ROB ROY   *1895 comic opera by De Koven*

Scotland at the time of Bonnie Prince Charlie. Rob Roy and his woman friend Janet (secretly his wife) help the Prince and his lady Flora MacDonald to escape to France. Janet's father, the Mayor of the Perth, is the comic villain. Reginald De Koven's three-act "romantic opera" *Rob Roy, or The Thistle and the Rose*, libretto by Harry B. Smith, premiered at the Herald Square Theater in New York on October 29, 1894. William Pruette played Rob Roy, Juliet Cordon was Janet, Richard F. Carroll was the Mayor of Perth, Baron Berthald was Prince Charles, Lizzie McNicol was Florrie MacDonald and W. H. McLaughlin was Lochiel. There is little connection between this opera and Sir Walter Scott's novel except the title.

1913 Frank Pollock/Henrietta Wakefield. Frank Pollock and Henrietta Wakefield who starred in the 1913 revival of *Rob Roy*, recorded their hit song "Who Can Tell Me Where She Dwells?" for RCA Victor in 1913. It's on the album *Music from the New York Stage 1890–1920*. GEMM CD box set.

ROBERTSON, STEWART   *Scottish-born conductor (1948–)*

Stewart Robertson, music director at Glimmerglass Opera, conducted the premieres of the three CENTRAL PARK operas at Glimmerglass in 1999: Deborah Drattell's *The Festival of Regrets*, Michael Torke's *Strawberry Fields* and Robert Beaser's *Strawberry Fields*. He conducted the premiere of David Carlson's DREAMKEEPERS, for Utah Opera in Salt Lake City in 1996, and recorded orchestral music from it, and he conducted the premiere of Carlson's THE MIDNIGHT ANGEL at Opera Theatre of Saint Louis in 1993. He led the orchestra in the telecast production of Benjamin Britten's PAUL BUNYAN from New York City Opera in 1998 and has conducted other American operas at Glimmerglass including Carlisle Floyd's OF MICE AND MEN and Jack Beeson's LIZZIE BORDEN. Robertson, who was born in Glasgow, studied and conducted in Europe before moving to the U.S. He was music director of several other American companies before joining Glimmerglass in 1987.

ROBESON, PAUL   *American bass-baritone (1898–1976)*

Paul Robeson starred on stage and film in Eugene O'Neill's play THE EMPEROR JONES but was not allowed to sing in Louis Gruenberg's opera version staged at the Metropolitan Opera in 1934; he broadcast an abridged version in 1940 with Eugene Ormandy conducting. He was cast as Joe in the original Broadway production of Jerome Kern's SHOW BOAT but had to withdraw when it was delayed, though he was able to sing the role on stage in London; he sings the role in the 1936 film version where he performs

Bass-baritone Paul Robeson

the definitive version of "Ol' Man River." George Gershwin's wanted him to sing Porgy in PORGY AND BESS but that did not work out either; he later recorded one of its arias, "It Ain't Necessarily So." He was the soloist when Earl Robinson's cantata *Ballad for Americans* was broadcast in 1938 and he recorded "The Purest Kind of Guy" from Marc Blitzstein's Broadway opera NO FOR AN ANSWER. That was the extent of the opera career of Robeson who was not able to become a professional opera singer because of the bigotry of his time. Robeson, who was born in Princeton, NJ, and eduated at Rutgers and Columbia, had to settle for a concert career.

ROBIN HOOD   *1890 comic opera by De Koven*

The Earl of Huntington becomes the outlaw leader Robin Hood in Sherwood Forrest after his property is illegally seized by the evil Sheriff of Nottingham. He is betrayed by one of his band and sentenced to die but saved by a pardon from King Richard just arrived back from the Crusades. Reginald De Koven's comic opera *Robin Hood*, libretto by Harry B. Smith, marked the emergence of American operetta when it was premiered by the Bostonians at the Chicago Opera House on June 9, 1890. Edwin Hoff played Robin Hood, Marie Stone was Maid Marian, Jessie Bartlett Davis was Alan-a-Dale (she introduced the hit song "O Promise Me"), Henry Clay Barnabee was the Sheriff of Nottingham, Peter Lang was Guy of Gisbourne, Eugene Cowles was Will Scarlet, W. J. MacDonald was Little John, George Frothingham was Friar Tuck, Josephine Bartlett was Dame Durdon and Carlotta Maconda was Annabel. Fred Dixon staged the opera and S. L. Studley conducted. It arrived in New York at the Standard Theater on September 22, 1891, with a slightly different cast and then toured for years. The recording of "Oh, Promise Me" in 1893 is considered the first of a song or aria from an American comic opera.

1893 George J. Gaskin. George J. Gaskin, publicized as the "Silver-Voiced Irish Tenor," recorded "Oh, Promise Me" for the New Jersey record company on March 4, 1993. This was the first recording of an aria from an American comic opera. **1898 Jessie Bartlett Davis.** Jessie Bartlett Davis, who played the trouser role of Alan-a-Dale in *Robin Hood,* introduced "O Promise Me" on stage in 1890 and recorded it in 1898 for Berliner. The original recording is at the Library of Congress and it is featured on the AEI CD *Reginald De Koven's Robin Hood* and the Pearl CD *Music from the New York Stage, Volume One.* **1905 Henry Burr.** Henry Burr, the most popular ballad singer in the early recording era, recorded "Oh, Promise Me" for Edison in 1905 and it was a huge hit for him. **1906 Eugene Cowles.** Eugene Cowles, who created the role of Will Scarlet in *Robin Hood,* recorded "The Armorer's Song" for Victor. It's on the AEI CD *Reginald De Koven's Robin Hood* and Pearl CD *Music from the New York Stage, Volume One.* **1909 Victor Light Opera.** The Victor Light Opera company performs selections from the comic opera on two sides of a 78 made in 1909. They're on the album *Reginald De Koven's Robin Hood.* AEI CD. **1913 Louise Homer.** Metropolitan Opera contralto Louise Homer recorded "Oh Promise Me" for a Victor Red Seal 78 in 1913. **1915 John McCormack.** John McCormack recorded "O Promise Me" in 1915 with accompaniment by pianist Gerald Moore. It's on various albums including *John McCormack, Tenor* (Arabesque LP) and *Count John McCormack: Music of the Night* (Pearl/Koch CD). **1919 New York Revival cast.** Cora Tracey, James Stevens, Herbert Waterous and members of the 1919 New York revival cast are featured in a highlights recording with eight songs including "O Promise Me," "Brown October Ale," "The Legend of the Chimes" and the sextet "O See the Lamkins Play." AEI CD *Reginald De Koven's Robin Hood.* **1920 Reinard Werrenrath.** Metropolitan Opera baritone Reinard Werrenrath recorded "Brown October Ale" for a Victor Red Seal 78 in 1920. **1925 Peter Dawson.** British bass-baritone Peter Dawson recorded "O Promise Me" for Victor in 1925. It's on his album *Peter Dawson Sings On Stage.* EMI LP. **1937 The Adventures of Robin Hood.** De Koven's music was not used in this famous Warner Bros. film because rights had been acquired by a rival studio. However, the screenplay is partially based on the libretto of De Koven's comic

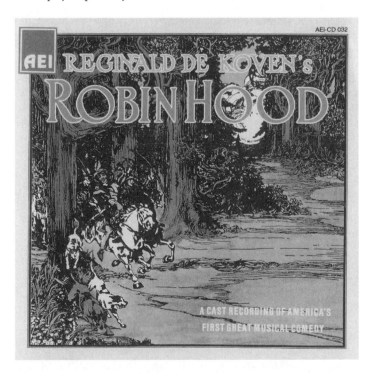

Reginald De Koven's comic opera *Robin Hood* marked the emergence of American operetta when it was premiered in Chicago in 1890.

opera as it is the only version in which Robin and Sir Guy duel over Maid Marian. Errol Flynn plays Robin, Basil Rathbone is Guy and Olivia De Havilland is Marian. Erich Wolfgang Korngold wrote the new score and Michael Curtiz and William Keighley directed. WB VHS. **1945 Robert Merrill.** Robert Merrill sings "O Promise Me" from *Robin Hood* on the album *Robert Merrill on Radio: Unpublished Broadcasts from 1940 to 1946.* Radio Years CD. **1946 Lauritz Melchior.** Lauritz Melchior sings "O Promise Me" from *Robin Hood* on various albums including *Lauritz Melchior: Complete MGM Recordings.* Romophone CD. **1948 Jan Peerce.** Jan Peerce sings "O Promise Me" from *Robin Hood* on a radio broadcast. It's on the album *Bluebird of Happiness.* Pearl/Koch CD. **1952 Radio Version.** Virginia Haskins sings Maid Marian with David Poleri as Robin Hood in a highlights radio version of the comic opera which includes sixteen of its numbers. Arnold Schweig, Bruce Foote and Earle Wilde complete the cast. AEI CD/LP. **1978 Cincinnati University Singers.** Michael Van Engen sings "Brown October Ale" with Cincinnati's University Singers and Theater Orchestra. Earl Rivers conducts on the album *I Wants to Be an Actor Lady.* New World LP/CD. **1981 Julie Andrews.** Julie Andrews sings "O Promise Me" in Blake Edwards' Lorimar movie *S.O.B.* **1986 Reginald de Koven's Robin Hood.** The centerpieces of the historic CD album *Reginald De Koven's Robin Hood* is the 1952 radio version but it also includes recordings made in 1898, 1906, 1908 and 1999. AEI CD.

THE ROBIN WOMAN   *1918 opera by Cadman*
See SHANEWIS

ROBINSON, EARL   *American composer (1910–1991)*
Blacklisted composer Earl Robinson, one of the musical heroes of the old left, first achieved fame for his 1938 cantata *Ballad for Americans* broadcast on radio with Paul Robeson as soloist. Although known for songs like "Joe Hill," he also composed musicals, concertos, ballets and operas. His anti-Nazi musical *Sing for Your Supper,* libretto by John Latouche, was staged in New York in 1939 and has been recorded. His folk opera SANDHOG, libretto by Waldo Salt based on a story by Theodore Dreiser, was premiered in New York in 1954. The folk opera *David of Sassoon,* libretto by the composer about an Armenian folk hero, was presented in Fresco, CA, in 1978. The children's opera *Listen for the Dolphin,* libretto by the composer, was staged at Garden Street Theater in Santa Barbara, CA, in 1981. Robinson won an Academy Award for his music for the 1946 short film *The House I Live In* starring Frank Sinatra. The song, lyrics by opera librettist Lewis Allan, was later recorded by Lauritz Melchior. Robinson, who was born in Seattle, studied music at the University of Washington and with Aaron Copland and Hanns Eisler.

ROBINSON-WAYNE, BEATRICE   *American soprano (1904–1986?)*
Beatrice Robinson-Wayne created the leading role of St Teresa I in Virgil Thomson's FOUR SAINTS IN THREE ACTS at Wadsworth Atheneum in Hartford in 1934. She sings the role on a recording of a 1942 radio broadcast of an abridged version and on the 1947 RCA Victor cast recording with Thomson conducting.

ROCHBERG, GEORGE   *American composer (1918–)*
George Rochberg composed two operas based on major literary works, both to librettos by his wife Gene Rochberg. PHAEDRA, a monodrama based on Robert Lowell's version of Racine's play, was premiered in Syracuse, NY, on January 9, 1976. THE CONFIDENCE MAN, based on the novel by Herman Melville, was commissioned by Santa Fe Opera which premiered it on July 31, 1982. Rochberg, who was born in Paterson, NJ, studied music at the Mannes College of Music in New York and the Curtis Institute and taught at Curtis and the University of Pennsylvania. He has been guest composer at several institutions and has written extensively about 20th Century music. He composes in various modern idioms, especially forms of serialism, but his operas are relatively tonal.

RODGERS, RICHARD   *American composer (1902–1979)*
Richard Rodgers is not usually thought of as opera composer but many of his music theater works are becoming part of the opera house repertory. OKLAHOMA! was once described as the "the first American vernacular opera," and his other collaborations with librettist Oscar Hammerstein II are equally memorable, especially CAROUSEL, SOUTH PACIFIC, THE KING AND I, THE SOUND OF MUSIC and. CINDERELLA. Many of these musicals require trained operatic voices, especially for the mezzo-soprano roles, and *South Pacific* was composed for an opera basso, Ezio Pinza.

Rodgers' earlier stage musicals were created in collaboration with Lorenz Hart and are not so operatic though, surprisingly, the pair featured an "American jazz opera" called THE JOY SPREADERS in their first stage show. In their second, the *Garrick Gaieties of 1926,* they had fun satirizing the American operetta ROSE OF ARIZONA. Their later shows, which features some of the finest songs ever written, include *On Your Toes, Babes in Arms, The Boys from Syracuse* and the mastepiece *Pal Joey,*

Rodgers, with and without his partners, was a major force in American theater music and his reputation is unlikely to diminish in the years to come.

1957 Mary Martin/Richard Rodgers. Mary Martin sings and Rodgers plays piano while they perform twelve songs from his musicals at Webster Hall in New York in 1957. John Lesko conducts. The album is called *Mary Martin Sings, Richard Rodgers Plays.* RCA Victor LP/CD. **1995 Rodgers and Hammerstein: The Sound of Movies.** Mini-history of the screen versions of the Rodgers and Hammerstein musicals, including *Oklahoma!, Carousel, The King and I* and *The Sound of Music.* Shirley Jones is host and there are guest appearances from many singing stars. Image Entertainment DVD. **1996 Bryan Terfel.** Bryan Terfel performs twenty songs from Rodgers musicals on the album *Something Wonderful: Bryan Terfel Sings Rodgers and Hammerstein.* Paul Daniel leads the English Northern Philharmonic and Opera North Chorus. DG CD. **2002 Bernadette Peters.** Bernadette Peters sings a wide selection of songs by Rodgers on her recital album *Bernadette Peters Loves Rodgers and Hammerstein.* Angel CD. **2002 Wall to Wall Richard Rodgers.** Fifteen numbers are performed by theater and cabaret stars in a March 23, 2002, tribute to Rodgers. The singers include Mary Cleer Haran, Judy Kaye, Maureen McGovern, K. T. Sullivan and Steve Ross. Fynsoreth Alley CD.

RODRIGUEZ, ROBERT X.   *American composer (1946–)*
Texas composer Robert Xavier Rodriguez's major opera is FRIDA: THE STORY OF FRIDA KAHLO, a three-act work about the Mexican woman painter which premiered at Philadelphia's American Music Theater Festival in 1991. His first was the one-act *Le Diable amoureux/The Devil in Love,* libretto by the composer and Frans Boerlage after Cazotte, televised by KERA-TV in Dallas on April 11, 1979, and staged in Wichita Falls, Texas, in 1982. It was followed by the one-act *Suor Isabella/Sister Isabella,* libretto by Daniel Dibbern based on a story in Boccaccio's *Decameron,* which premiered at the University of Texas in Dallas on July 7, 1982. The

one-act tango history TANGO, libretto by the composer, was staged in Dallas on January 29, 1986. THE RANSOM OF RED CHIEF, libretto by Daniel Dibbern based on the O. Henry story, was presented by Lyric Opera of Dallas in Mesquite, Texas, on October 10, 1986. The popular children's opera MONKEY SEE, MONKEY DO, libretto by Mary Duren based on a folk tale, was commissioned by Dallas Opera which premiered it January 26, 1987; it is his most performed opera. *The Old Majestic,* libretto by Mary Duren, was premiered at the University of Texas in San Antonio on May 28, 1988. Rodriguez, who was born in San Antonio and studied at the University of Texas in Dallas where he lives and teaches, has created an eclectic style mixing popular music with operatic elements. He could be become a Texas-style Kurt Weill.

ROGERS, BERNARD *American composer (1893–1968)*

Bernard Rogers composed four operas, the best-known being THE WARRIOR, libretto by Norman Corwin based on the Biblical story of Samson and Delilah, which premiered at the Metropolitan Opera in 1947. *The Marriage of Aude*, libretto by Charles Rodde based on the *Chanson de Roland*, was presented at the Festival of American Music at Eastman House in Rochester, NY, on May 22, 1932, and was awarded a David Bispham medal. THE VEIL, libretto by Robert Lawrence about a woman killed by a bridal veil, was staged at Indiana University in Bloomington on May 18, 1950. *The Nightingale*, libretto by the composer based on the fairytale by Hans Christian Anderson, was presented by the Punch Opera Company in New York on May 10, 1955. Rogers, who was born in New York, attended the Cleveland Institute of Music and studied in Europe with Nadia Boulanger and Frank Bridge and then returned to teach at the Eastman School of Music.

ROMAN FEVER *1993 opera by Ward*

Two widows meet in a terrace restaurant in a hotel overlooking the Forum in Rome. As they and their daughters talk, they reveal how they met at the same place twenty years before and were involved in an adulterous triangle. Robert Ward's tuneful, tonal one-act opera *Roman Fever*, libretto by Roger Brunyate based on a 1934 Edith Wharton story, was premiered by Triangle Opera on June 9, 1993, at Duke University in Durham, NC. Katherine Kulas and Melody Morrison were mother and daughter Alida and Jenny Slade, Monica Reinagel and Karie Brown were mother and daughter Grace and Barbara Ansley and Paul Gibson was the singing waiter. Richard Canning designed the set, Charles St. Clair directed and Scott Tiley conducted. The opera was revived in 2001 by the Manhattan School of Music Opera Theatre in a production by Robin Guarino with David Gilbert conducting and was recorded. **1995 Terry Rhodes/Ellen Williams.** Terry Rhodes and Ellen Williams sing the duet "It's still the most beautiful view in the world" from *Roman Fever* with an orchestra led by Scott Tiley. Its on the album *To Sun, to Feast and to Converse — American Vocal Duet Music.* Albany CD. **2001 Manhattan School of Music.** David Gilbert conducts the Manhattan School of Music Opera Theater Orchestra. in this live recording of a Manhattan School of Music Opera Theater production staged by Robin Guarino in December 2001. Dorothy Grimley is Alida, Erin Elizabeth Smith is Grace, Amy Shoremount and Eudora Brown are their daughters, and Maxime Alvarez de Toledo is the singing waiter. Albany Records CD.

ROMBERG, SIGMUND *American composer (1887–1951)*

Sigmund Romberg, who carried on the tradition of Viennese-style American comic opera popularized by Victor Herbert, is best known for THE STUDENT PRINCE (1924), THE DESERT SONG (1926) and THE NEW MOON (1928). He was born in Hungary but all his operettas were composed in America after he emigrated. His other successes include MAYTIME, (1918), BLOSSOM TIME (1926), MY MARYLAND (1927) and NINA ROSA (1930). He also created original operettas for Hollywood movies, notably VIENNESE NIGHTS (1930) and The Girl of the Golden West (1938). His composing career lasted well into the modern era: UP IN CENTRAL PARK (1945) marked a successful return to the old operetta style, MY ROMANCE (1948) was attacked for being an operetta and THE GIRL IN THE PINK TIGHTS (1954) starred Met soprano Brenda Lewis in a story about the birth of the American musical. **1954 Deep in My Heart.** Stanley Donen directed this highly musical and highly fictional MGM film biography of Romberg. José Ferrer is superb as Romberg previewing a show by singing, dancing and acting all the roles and partnering with Helen Traubel and Rosemary Clooney. Traubel plays the jolly woman who runs the restaurant where his career begins, Merle Oberon plays Romberg's wife, Walter Pidgeon is J. J. Shubert and Paul Henried is Florenz Ziegfeld. Guest stars include Cyd Charisse, Gene Kelly, Jane Powell, Ann Miller, Howard Keel and Tony Martin. Soundtrack: Sony CD. Film: MGM VHS/DVD. **1960 A Night with Sigmund Romberg.** Baritone Earl Wrightson and soprano Lois Hunt perform a selection of songs from Romberg operettas with orchestra conducted by Percy Faith on album *A Night with Sigmund Romberg.* Columbia LP. **1985 When I Grow Too Old to Dream.** Soprano Teresa Ringholz and the Eastman-Dryden Orchestra led by Donald Hunsberger perform selections from six Romberg shows including *The New Moon, Maytime, Desert Song, Her Soldier Boy, Doing Our Bit* and *Viennese Nights.* Arabesque LP/CD. **1991 Great Hits from Sigmund Romberg.** *Great Hits from Sigmund Romberg* is a British anthology of early recordings of songs from Romberg operettas including *Blossom Time, The Desert Song, Maytime, My Maryland, The New Moon, Nina Rosa* and *The Student Prince.* Pearl CD. **2001 The Ultimate Sigmund Romberg: Volume I.** *The Ultimate Sigmund Romberg Anthology* is a British anthology of original cast recordings of Romberg operettas beginning with *Maytime* and John Charles Thomas's "Will You Remember?" Pearl CD.

ROME, HAROLD *American composer/lyricist (1908–)*

Metropolitan Opera baritones helped Harold Rome achieve his greatest success on Broadway. His musical *Fanny,* based on the Marcel Pagnol trilogy, starred Ezio Pinza as César when it opened on November 4, 1954, at the Majestic Theater, and the role was taken over by Lawrence Tibbett when he left. Rome, born in Hartford, CT, first found success on Broadway with the help of a swimming pool on stage in the 1952 *Wish You Were Here.* His other popular musicals include *Destry Rides Again* (1959), *I Can Get It for You Wholesale* (1962) and *Gone with the Wind* (1972).

ROMEO AND JULIET *American musicals based on Shakespeare play*

William Shakespeare's play *Romeo and Juliet* has inspired a large number of operas and musical theatre works around the world including half a dozen American versions. The best known is Leonard Bernstein's operatic musical WEST SIDE STORY but Lee Hoiby's work-in-progress was well received. See also SHAKESPEARE OPERAS. **1936 Eric Korngold.** Met soprano Gladys Swarthout sings Juliet to Jan Kiepura's Romeo in Eric Wolfgang Korngold's movie opera *Romeo and Juliet,* libretto by Oscar Hammerstein II. It was created for the 1936 Paramount film *Give Us This Night* and much of the plot revolves around it. Kiepura plays a fisherman who is a gifted tenor but whose mother opposes an operatic career. After trials and tribulations he replaces a bad tenor on stage in the premiere of *Romeo and Juliet* in the climax of the film and wins Swarthout at the same time. Korngold, already a successful opera composer in Europe at this time, was a old friend of Kiepura's. Alexander Hall directed the film written by Edwin Justus Mayer and Lynn Starling. **1957 Leonard Bernstein.** Leonard Bernstein's version of *Romeo and Juliet* set in modern New York is one of the glories of the American stage. For a full description see WEST SIDE STORY. **2000 Lee Hoiby.** Lee Hoiby's three-act opera *Romeo and Juliet*, libretto by Mark Shulgasser, was previewed as a work-in-progress by the Choral Art Society at the Kennedy Center in Washington, D.C. on May 14, 2000. Norman Scriber directed.

ROMULUS HUNT   *1993 "family opera" by Simon*

Twelve-year-old Romulus Hunt, unhappy about his parents' divorce, schemes to get them reunited. His mom is a business-oriented workaholic, his dad a Bohemian choreographer with a live-in artist girlfriend and his best friend is an imaginary reggae singer. Carly Simon's "family opera" *Romulus Hunt,* libretto by Jacob Brackman and the composer, was commissioned by the Metropolitan Opera Guild Education Department and the Kennedy Center. It was premiered at the John Jay Theater in New York on February 25, 1993, and staged in Washington in April. Andrew Leeds played Romulus, Luretta Bybee was his mother Joanna, Greer Grimsley was his father Eddie, Wendy Hill was the girlfriend Mica and Jeff Hairston was the imaginary friend Zoogy. Francesca Zambello directed and Jeff Halbert conducted. Critics felt Simon succeeded in creating an accessible opera for children incorporating operatic conventions like crossed letters and disguised flirting à la *Der Fledermaus.*

1993 New York cast. Andrew Leeds sings the role of Romulus Hunt in this recording of the opera made at the Right Track Studios in New York with most of the original New York cast. Luretta Bybee is mother Joanna, Jeff Hairston is imaginary friend Zoogy, Wendy Hill is artist Mica and Kurt Ollmann takes over the role of father Eddie. Jeff Halbert conducts. Angel CD.

ROOT, GEORGE F.   *American composer (1820–1895)*

George Frederick Root is best known for his Civil War songs, including "The Battle Cry of Freedom," but he also wrote four "operatic cantatas." THE FLOWER QUEEN, OR THE CORONATION OF THE ROSE, libretto by Fannie J. Crosby, which premiered in New York in 1852, is considered the first American theatrical cantata. The second was the Biblical *Daniel or The Captivity and Restoration* (1853) with a libretto by Crosby and C. M. Cady. The third was THE HAYMAKERS, the first American secular cantata, composed in 1857 to Root's own libretto. His final cantata was the religious 1860 *Belshazzar's Feast.* After that he went back to songwriting, which was much more profitable. Root, who was born in Sheffield, Massachusetts to a musical family, spent a year studying music in Paris where he was able to hear famous opera singers like Henriette Sontag and Pauline Viardot in concert. He taught singing in Boston and New York schools and he usually composed the music for his classes, included cantatas.

ROREM, NED   *American composer (1923–)*

Ned Rorem, America's finest art song composer, has written seven operas with tonal lyrical arias and choral ensembles. All have been staged and four have been recorded. Rorem's major operatic work is the full-length MISS JULIE, libretto by Kenward Elmslie based on the play by August Strindberg, which New York City Opera commissioned and premiered in 1965. His other operas are short chamber works. The 40-minute A CHILDHOOD MIRACLE, libretto by Elliot Stein based on a story by Nathaniel Hawthorne about a snowman that comes to life, was composed in 1951 and premiered in 1955 by Punch Opera in New York. The 28-minute *The Robbers*, libretto by the composer revised by Marc Blitzstein and based on Chaucer's *The Pardoner's Tale*, premiered at Mannes College of Music in New York on April 14, 1958. *The Last Days* was premiered on May 22, 1967, at the New School for Social Research in New York. The 25-minute BERTHA, libretto by the composer based on a play by Kenneth Koch about a mad queen, premiered at Alice Tully Hall in New York in 1973. FABLES, four linked short operas based on animal fables by Jean de la Fontaine, premiered at the University of Tennessee in Martin in 1971. THREE SISTERS WHO ARE NOT SISTERS, libretto from the play by Gertrude Stein about children involved in a murder mystery, was composed in 1968 on a grant from the Met and premiered in Philadelphia in 1971. The 50-minute HEARING, libretto by James Holmes based on poems by Kenneth Koch about a love quadrangle, was premiered by the Gregg Smith Singers at St. Stephens Church in New York in 1977. Rorem, born in Richmond, Indiana, studied at the Curtis Institute and Juilliard School and then with Virgil Thomson, his chief influence. He achieved early renown in 1948 when "The Lordly Hudson" won a prize as best song of the year, and he went on to win the Pulitzer Prize in 1976 for the orchestral suite *Air Music.* Rorem has published fourteen books of diaries and notebooks which reveal a great deal about the American musical and literary world of the past half century.

ROSE MARIE   *1924 operetta by Friml and Stothart*

Rose Marie is in love with outlaw Jim Kenyon who is pursued on a murder charge by Mounted Policeman Sergeant Malone. Rudolf Friml and Herbert Stothart's operetta *Rose Marie,* libretto by Otto Harbach and Oscar Hammerstein II, was a worldwide success, especially for it a spectacular "Totem Tom Tom" number. It premiered at the New Nixon/Apollo Theater in Atlantic City, NJ, on August 18, 1924, and opened on Broadway at the Imperial Theater on September 2. Mary Ellis was Rose Marie, Dennis King was Jim Kenyon and Arthur Deagon was Sgt. Malone. The operetta has been recorded on film three times with varying plots and character names and recorded on discs many more times but only in abridged versions. Note: *Rose Marie* without a hyphen is the stage show name, *Rose-Marie* with the hyphen is the film title.

1925 Victor Light Opera. The Victor Light Opera Company made the first recording of songs from the operetta, a medley created for a Victor 78 in 1925. **1925 John McCormack.** Irish tenor John McCormack made a popular recording of the song "Rose Marie" in 1925 for a Victor Red Seal 78. It's on several McCormack albums. **1925 London Cast.** Edith Day is Rose Marie in highlights recordings made by the original London cast. Day sings "Pretty Things, and "Door of My Dreams" and teams with Derek Oldham on "Indian Love Call." The other singers are Billy Merson, Clarice Hardwicke and John Dunsmure. Herman Finck conducts. The 78s were re-issued on several albums, including *Rudolph Friml in London.* World LP. **1928 MGM film.** Joan Crawford stars in the first film version playing trading post woman Rose-Marie who loves outlaw trapper James Murray who is pursued by Mountie House Peters. The film is silent but it was screened with the Friml/Stothart score played live. Lucien Hubbard directed for MGM. **1936 MGM film.** Jeanette MacDonald and Nelson Eddy are the stars of the MGM film *Rose-Marie* with a heavily revised libretto by Frances Goodrich, Albert Hackett and Alice Duer Miller. Jeanette plays an opera singer searching the Pacific northwest for fugitive brother James Stewart who is sought by Canadian Mountie Nelson Eddy. The film retains the stage show "Totem Tom-Tom" number and "Indian Love Call" but drops the other Friml songs and adds opera scenes for MacDonald. William Daniel photographed the story at Lake Tahoe under the direction of W. S. Van Dyke. Herbert Stothart was music director. MGM-UA VHS/ DVD/LD. Soundtrack LP/ CD. **1936 Jeanette Mac-Donald/Nelson Eddy.** Jeanette MacDonald and Nelson Eddy recorded "Indian Love Call" and Eddy recorded "The Mounties" and "Rose Marie"

Oliver Henderson, Amy Pfrimmer and Anthony Maida in Ohio Light Opera's fine staging of Rudolf Friml and Herbert Stothart's operetta *Rose Marie.*

in 1936 with Nat Shilkret conducting. The songs are on several albums including *Jeanette MacDonald and Nelson Eddy.* RCA LP. **1948 Marion Bell/Charles Fredericks.** Marion Bell sings Rose Marie opposite Charles Fredericks in this studio recording of highlights from the operetta. Al Goodman conducts. RCA Victor LP. **1951 Dorothy Kirsten/Nelson Eddy.** Dorothy Kirsten and Nelson Eddy perform a highlights version of the operetta with the Howard Chandler Chorus and Leon Arnaud conducting. Columbia LP. **1954 MGM film.** Howard Keel and Ann Blythe star in this third MGM film of the operetta shot in CinemaScope and color with screenplay by Ronald Millar. Keel is the Mountie, Blythe is Rose-Marie, Fernando Lamas is the fur trapper she loves, Joan Taylor is the Indian girl who loves him and Marjorie Main is Lady Jane. Bert Lahr sings "I'm the Mountie Who Never Got his Man." Mervyn LeRoy directed for MGM. MGM-UA VHS/ DVD. Soundtrack on MGM LP/CD. **1954 Roberta Peters.** Roberta Peters sings "Indian Love Call" with Howard Barlow and the Firestone Orchestra on the *Voice of Firestone* TV show on November 14, 1952. *Roberta Peters in Opera and Song, Vol. 1.* VAI VHS. **1956 Mario Lanza.** Mario Lanza sings "Rose Marie" with Henri René's Orchestra and the Jeff Alexander Choir on the albums *A Cavalcade of Show Tunes* (RCA Victor LP) and *The Mario Lanza Collection* (Victor CD). **1958 Giorgio Tozzi/Julie Andrews.** Julie Andrews is Rose-Marie and Giorgio Tozzi is Jim Kenyon in this highlights recording. Meier Tzelniker is Hard-Boiled Herman, Frances Day is Lady Jane, Marion Keene is Wanda, Frederick Harvey is Sergeant Malone and John Huaxvell is Emile La Flamme. Lehman Engel conducts the Michael Sammes Singers and New Symphony Orchestra of London. RCA Victor LP. **1960 Earl Wrightson/Lois Hunt.** Baritone Earl Wrightson and soprano Lois Hunt sing "Rose Marie" and "Indian Love Song" with the orchestra conducted by Frank DeVol on the album *A Night with Rudolf Friml.* Columbia LP. **1962 Anna Moffo/Rosalind Elias.** Anna Moffo is Rose Marie and Rosalind Elias is Wanda in this highlights

recording with Richard Fredricks as Jim and William Chapman as Malone Lehman Engel conducts the orchestra and chorus for Reader's Digest *Treasury of Great Operettas* recording. RCA LP box set. **1967 Joan Sutherland.** Joan Sutherland sings "Indian Love Call" with the Ambrosian Light Opera Chorus while Richard Bonynge conducts the New Philharmonia Orchestra on *The Golden Age of Operetta.* London/Decca LP/CD. **1974 Beverly Sills/ Johnny Carson.** Beverly Sills plays Jeanette MacDonald to Johnny Carson's Nelson Eddy on the *Johnny Carson Show* on television. He puts on a Mountie costume and they duet on "Indian Love Call." **1978 Beverly Sills/Sherrill Milnes.** Beverly Sills and Sherrill Milnes join in duet on "Indian Love Call" on the album *Up in Central Park.* Julius Rudel conducts the New York City Opera Orchestra. EMI Angel LP. **1990 Valerie Masterson/Thomas Allen.** Soprano Valerie Masterson and baritone Thomas Allen sing "Indian Love Song" with John Owen Edwards leading the Philharmonic Orchestra on the album *If I Loved You — Love Duets from the Musicals.* TER CD. **1992 Sandro Massimini.** Italian operetta king Sandro Massimini and associates perform "Rose Marie," "Indian Love Call" and "Pretty Things" in Italian on the Italian TV program *Operette, Che Passione!* Ricordi VHS. **1993 Barbara Hendricks/Gino Quilico.** Barbara Hendricks and Gino Quilico join in duet on "Indian Love Call" on the album *Operetta Duets.* Lawrence Foster conducts the Lyon Opera Orchestra. EMI CD. **1999 Elizabeth Futral/Steven White.** Elizabeth Futral and Steven White duet on "Indian Love Call" on the album *Sweethearts* with Robert Tweten on piano. Newport Classics CD.

ROSE OF ARIZONA *1926 operetta parody by Rodgers*

In the Arizona town of Rose Raisa, Gloria has fallen in love with police Captain Allan. When she is kidnapped by the dastardly bandit Caramba, he has to rescue her. Richard Rodgers spoof operetta *Rose of Arizona,* libretto by Herbert Fields with lyrics by Lorenz Hart, was premiered on May 10, 1926, as part of the revue

Garrick Gaieties of 1926. Blanche Fleming was Gloria, Jack Edwards was Allan, Romney Brent was Caramba, Philip Loeb was Gloria's father and Eleanor Shaler was Rosabelle. *Rose of Arizona,* a parody of American operettas like ROSE MARIE as devised by Rudolf Friml and Victor Herbert, was hugely popular with critics and audiences. Rose Raisa, of course, is the name of the famous opera soprano who created the role of Turandot.

ROSS, JERRY   *American composer (1926–1955)*

Jerry Ross had major successes on Broadway in partnership with Richard Adler. *The Pajama Game* (1954), libretto by George Abbott and Richard Bissell about romance and union activity in a factory, had memorable songs and kick-started the careers of Shirley MacLaine, Jerome Robbins and Bob Foss. *Damn Yankees* (1956), libretto by Abbot and George Wallop, about a Washington baseball fan who sells his soul to the devil to help his team, launched the career of Gwen Verdon. There are original cast albums of both and both were made into excellent films. Ross, born in New York as Jerrold Rosenberg, died from bronchiectasis at the age of 29 just as his career was beginning.

ROUNSEVILLE, ROBERT   *American tenor (1914–1974)*

Robert Rounseville created some of the most important roles in modern American music theater. He created Tom in Igor Stravinsky's THE RAKE'S PROGRESS at La Fenice in Venice 1951 (cast album), Candide in Leonard Bernstein's CANDIDE on Broadway in 1956 (cast album). Channon in David Tamkin's THE DYBBUK at New York City Opera in 1951 (cast album), the Padre in Mitch Leigh's MAN OF LA MANCHA on Broadway in 1956 (cast album), a major character in Hans Werner Henze's RACHEL, LA CUBANA on NBC Television in 1974, a New Amsterdam citizen in Kurt Weill's KNICKERBOCKER HOLIDAY on Broadway in 1938 and a Tweed crony in Sigmund Romberg's UP IN CENTRAL PARK on Broadway in 1945. He was Ravenal in New York City Opera's 1954 production of Jerome Kern's SHOW BOAT, Mr. Snow in the 1956 movie of Rodgers and Hammerstein's CAROUSEL (cast album) and Charlie in the NYCO's production of BRIGADOON in 1957. His other recordings include a 1952 highlights version of Sigmund Romberg's THE STUDENT PRINCE with Dorothy Kirsten.

ROUSE, MIKEL   *American composer (1957–)*

Mikel Rouse writes, composes and stars in post-modern avant-garde operas using words sung and spoken in interlinked rhythmic patterns he calls Counter-poetry ("multiple unpitched voices in strict metric counterpoint"). FAILING KANSAS, inspired by Truman Capote's *In Cold Blood* about a famous Kansas murder case, premiered at The Kitchen in 1994. DENNIS CLEVELAND, an opera staged as if it were a TV talk show, premiered at The Kitchen in 1996. FUNDING, a video opera about five alienated New Yorkers, premiered at the Orange County Art Museum in Newport Beach, CA, on October 7, 2001. *The End of Cinematics,* an opera about corporate-driven entertainment, is to premiere at the Brooklyn Academy of Music. Rouse, born in St. Louis, studied music at the University of Missouri and developed his rhythmic minimalist musical style in New York with his chamber ensemble The Mikel Rouse Broken Consort. His 1984 work *Quorum* was used by choreographer Ulysses Dove for the dance *Vespers* performed by Alvin Ailey's American Theater.

ROWSON, SUSANNA   *American librettist (1762–1824)*

Susanna Rowson wrote the librettos for two early operas/musical plays working in collaboration with composer Alexander Reinagle. *Slaves in Algiers: or, A Struggle for Freedom,* about American prisoners held by the Barbary pirates, was premiered on January 22, 1794, at the New Theater on Chestnut Street in Philadelphia. The libretto survives but not the music. Next was Reinagle's comic opera *The Volunteers,* about the Whiskey Rebellion in Pennsylvania, which premiered on January 21, 1795, at the New Theater. Rowson, who acted in her plays as well, lived in Massachusetts from 1767 to 1778 while her naval lieutenant father was stationed there. She moved back to England with her father and wrote several novels, including the popular 1791 *Charlotte, A Tale of Truth,* before returning to Philadelphia in 1793 with her husband. She continued to write and is said to have acted in over a hundred plays.

THE RUBY   *1955 opera by Dello Joio*

A gang of thieves steal a ruby from a stone idol in a temple in India and hide out in Scott's hunting lodge in turn-of-the-century England. Scott is the leader and dominates gang members Bull, Albert and Sniggers and his wife Laura. Indian priests try to take back the ruby but the gang kills them. Finally the idol itself arrives and takes back the ruby. Norman Dello Joio's *The Ruby,* libretto by William Mass based on Lord Dunsany's macabre play *A Night at the Inn,* premiered at Indiana University in Bloomington on May 13, 1955. Ezio Flagello, just beginning his singing career, played the role of Bull.

RUDEL, JULIUS   *American conductor (1921–)*

Julius Rudel is one of the great architects of modern American opera. He was artistic director of New York City Opera from 1957 to 1979 and obtained a Ford Foundation grant to commission American operas Without him American opera would have been a lesser presence. Ironically it was the relative lack of success of two American operas, Hugo Weisgall's NINE RIVERS TO JORDAN and Dominick Argento's MISS HAVISHAM'S FIRE, which led to his separation from the company. Rudel conducted seven premieres at NYCO, Robert Kurka's THE GOOD SOLDIER SCHWEIK in 1958, Douglas Moore's THE WINGS OF THE DOVE in 1961, Abraham Ellstein's THE GOLEM in 1962, Carlisle Floyd's THE PASSION OF JONATHAN WADE in 1962, Lee Hoiby's NATALIA PETROVNA in 1964, Vittorio Giannini's THE SERVANT OF TWO MASTERs in 1967 and Argento's MISS HAVISHAM'S FIRE in 1979. In addition he conducted the premiere of John Strauss's THE ACCUSED on CBS television in 1961, Carlisle Floyd's THE SOJOURNER AND MOLLIE SINCLAIR at East Carolina College in 1963, Alberto Ginastera's BOMARZO at Washington Opera in 1967 and Ginastera's BEATRIX CENCI at Washington Opera in 1971. He made several recordings with Beverly Sills and he leads the New York City Opera orchestra on her 1978 American operetta album *Up in Central Park.* In 1992 he recorded Kurt Weill's LOST IN THE STARS with St. Luke's Orchestra. Rudel, who was born in Vienna, emigrated to America at the age of seventeen.

RUSSELL, ANNA   *Canadian soprano (1911–)*

Satirist Anna Russell featured a one-woman version of an old-fashioned American operetta, *The Prince of Philadelphia,* in her 1953 Broadway show *Anna Russell's Little Show.* She later recorded its famous aria "Ah, Lover!" which Russell says was composed "For Loud Singers With No Brains." Russell, who was born in London, moved to Canada in 1939 and made her American debut at Carnegie Hall in 1947. She retired back to Canada in 1986 but continues to delight on record and video.

S

SACCO AND VANZETTI (1)   *1964 opera by Blitzstein*

Italian immigrant anarchists Nicola Sacco, a shoemaker, and Bartolomeo Vanzetti, a fish peddler, are charged with murders committed during a theft in Massachusetts in 1920. Their trial and execution are controversial and cause world-wide protests. American celebrities get involved and the trial becomes a rallying call for the left. Marc Blitzstein's opera *Sacco and Vanzetti* was commissioned by the Metropolitan Opera in 1959 but was uncompleted at his death in 1964. Leonard Lehrman created a version of it from Blitzstein's notes and his version was presented in Westport, Connecticut, in 2001.

1990 Ronald Edwards. Ronald Edwards sings Sacco's prison soliloquy "With a Woman to Be" on the album *A Blitzstein Cabaret* accompanied on piano by Leonard Lehrman. The recording is based on a stage show produced by Lehrman and includes music from several Blitzstein operas. Premier Recordings CD.

SACCO AND VANZETTI (2)   *2001 opera by Coppola*

The story of the trial and conviction of Italian immigrant anarchists Nicola Sacco and Bartolomeo Vanzetti charged with murders committed during a theft in Massachusetts in 1920. Anton Coppola's *Sacco and Vanzetti,* libretto by the composer, was premiered by Opera Tampa at the Tampa Bay Performing Arts Center in Florida on March 17, 2001. Jeffrey Springer was Sacco, Emile Fath was Vanzetti, Faith Esham was Sacco's wife Rosina, Vernon Hartman was the pair's attorney Fred Moore, Theodore Lambrinos was Tresca, Hallie Neill was the anarchist Lucia, Diedra Palmore was Mary Donovan, Nan Hughes was Katherine Anne Porter, Charles Robert Stevens was William Thompson, Raul Melo was Bianchini and Rebecca O'Brien was Mrs. Evans. Francis Ford Coppola was artistic supervisor, John Farrell designed the sets, Matthew Lata directed and the 83-year-old composer conducted the Florida Orchestra. The opera was created after filmmaker Francis Ford Coppola decided to make a TV documentary about the famous pair and asked his uncle Anton Coppola to write music for it. The documentary was never made but the composer, then 78, decided to use the music for an opera. It was a major hit and was to have been recorded and made available on the internet but the orchestra would not allow a recording without payment of an upfront fee so it did not happen. *The Opera Quarterly* felt the opera was of such importance that it published a 25-page essay/analysis by Eugene H. Cropsey.

THE SACRED TREE   *Mezzo-soprano aria: Treemonisha (1911). Words and music: Scott Joplin.*

Monisha's aria "The Sacred Tree," sung in Act One of Scott Joplin's ragtime opera TREEMONISHA, tells the story of how the baby Treemonisha was found near a sacred tree and protected from rain and sun by its sheltering leaves. Treemonisha is very surprised to learn that Monisha and Ned are not her parents. It is not known who sang the aria in the 1915 tryout premiere but it is best known as performed by mezzo-sopranos at Houston Grand Opera. It is sung by Betty Allen as Monisha in the 1975 production and audio recording and Delores Ivory as Monisha in the 1983 production and video. Marion Lowe plays Monisha and sings the aria on a 1985 recording of the original piano version of the opera.

THE SACRIFICE   *1911 opera by Converse*

In 1846 California. American Captain Burton and Mexican officer Bernal compete for the love of the beautiful Chonita. She dies as a result of their overly intense rivalry. Frederick S. Converse's opera *The Sacrifice,* libretto by the composer with lyrics by John Albert Macy, was premiered by the Boston Opera Company on March 3, 1911. It is based on the story "Dolores" from the book *Los Gringos* by Lt. Henry Augustus Wise. Alice Nielson sang the role of Chonita at the premiere, Florencio Constantino was Bernal, Roman Bianchart was Burton, Maria Claessens was Tomasa, Bernice Fisher was Magdalena and Grace Fisher was Marianna. Wallace Goodrich conducted the Boston Symphony Orchestra and the Opera School of New England Conservatory of Music Chorus.

1912 Alice Nielsen. Alice Nielsen, who created the role of Chonita, recorded the aria "Almighty Father," known as "Chonita's Prayer," for a Columbia 78 in 1911. It's on the album *Souvenirs from American Opera.* International Record Collectors' Club CD.

THE SAD LAMENT OF PECOS BILL ON THE EVE OF KILLING HIS WIFE   *1976 opera by Stone and Shephard*

Catherine Stone and Sam Shephard's opera *The Sad Lament of Pecos Bill on the Eve of Killing His Wife,* libretto by Sam Shephard, was first staged at the Bay Area Playwrights Festival at the Palace of the Legion of Honor in San Francisco in 1976. Emil Borelli played Pecos Bill, Sigrid Wurschmidt was his wife Sue and Robert Woodruff directed.

SAHL, MICHAEL   *American composer (1934–)*

Michael Sahl is best known for his Prix Italia-winning music theater work CIVILIZATION AND ITS DISCONTENTS which was premiered in New York in 1997, recorded in 1978 and broadcast in 1980. It was created in collaboration with Eric Salzman. Their first joint effort was the "pop opera" *The Conjurer* produced by Joseph Papp at the Public Theater in New York in 1975. It was followed by STAUF, a modern version of the Faust story with a nuclear scientist as protagonist, which premiered in New York in 1976. *Noah* was staged at the Pratt Institute in Brooklyn in 1978, *The Passion of Simple Simon* was premiered by the Theatre for the New City, New York, in 1979 and broadcast on NPR. *Boxes,* a "music theater work for radio," was performed in 1988. Sahl, who was born in Boston, studied at Princeton with Roger Sessions and Milton Babbit and at Tanglewood with Aaron Copland and Lukas Foss. His early work was atonal but he changed to an accessible singable style when he began to compose music theater.

THE SAINT OF BLEECKER STREET   *1954 opera by Menotti*

Annina, who lives in the Italian Bleecker Street area of New York, experiences religious visions and suffers stigmata,. She is quite ill and prays to become a nun before she dies while her Catholic neighbors urge her to perform miracles. Her brother Michele is so obsessively jealous that when his girlfriend Desideria accuses him of loving his sister too much, he goes crazy and kills her. Annina meets him in a subway station for a final farewell and then takes the nun's veil in a ceremony at home before dying. Gian Carlo Menotti's three-act opera *The Saint of Bleecker Street,* libretto by the composer, opened at the Broadway Theatre in New York on December 27, 1954, and ran for 92 performances. Menotti staged the opera with Virginia Copeland and Gabrielle Ruggiero alternating as Annina and David Poleri and Davis Cunningham alternating as Michele. Gloria Lane was Desideria, Leon Lishner was the priest Don Marco, Maria Di Gerlando was Carmela, Maria Marlo was Maria Corona, David Aiken was Salvatore and Lucy

Des Moines Metro Opera staged Gian Carlo Menotti's Pulitzer Prize–winning opera *The Saint of Bleecker Street* in 1993. Photograph courtesy of Des Moines Metro Opera.

Becque was Concettina. Robert Randolph designed the sets and costumes and Thomas Schippers conducted. The opera, which won the composer his second Pulitzer Prize and New York Drama Circle Critic's Award, features a large cast, chorus and orchestra which has kept it from becoming popular with small regional theaters. It was staged by New York City Opera in 1965 and 1972 and by Lyric Opera of Kansas City in 1972 and has been produced internationally. Menotti mounted a production at the Spoleto Festival in Italy in June 2001 to celebrate his 90th birthday.

1955 Original Broadway cast. Gabrielle Ruggiero is Annina opposite David Poleri as Michele in this original cast recording made under Menotti's direction. Gloria Lane is Desideria, Leon Lishner is Don Marco, Maria Di Gerlando is Carmela, David Aiken is Salvatore, Catherine Akos is Assunta, Maria Marlo is Maria Corona, Ernest Gonzales is her son, Lucy Becque is Concettina, Richard Cassilly is a young man, Elizabeth Carron is a young woman, Keith Kaldenberg is first guest, John Reardon is second guest and Russell Goodwin is barman. Thomas Schippers leads the orchestra and chorus. The cover of the LP box is a reproduction of a painting of a nun by Menotti's friend Milena Barilla that was an inspiration for the opera. RCA Victor 2-LP set. **1955 NBC Opera Theater.** Virginia Copeland is Annina in this excellent NBC Opera Theatre production by Samuel Chotzinoff. Richard Cassilly is brother Michele, Leon Lishner is priest Don Marco, David Aiken is Salvatore and Rosemary Kuhlmann is

Desideria. Samuel Krachmalnick conducts the Symphony of the Air Orchestra with Peter Herman Adler as music and artistic director, Trew Hocker designed the sets and Kirk Browning directed the telecast on May 15, 1955. Video at MTR. **1976 New York City Opera.** Catherine Malfitano sings Annina in this audiotape recording of a November 1976 New York City Opera production. Enrico Di Giuseppe is Michele, Jeanne Piland is Desideria, Diane Soviero is Carmela, and Irwin Densen is Don Marco. Cal Stewart Kellogg conducts. Live Opera audiocassette. **1978 New York City Opera.** Catherine Malfitano is Annina in this televised New York City Opera production by Francis Rizzo. Enrico di Giuseppe is brother Michele, Irwin Densen is Don Marco, Sandra Walker is Desideria and Diane Soviero is Carmela. Cal Stewart Kellogg conducts the orchestra. Kirk Browning directed the *Live from Lincoln Center* telecast on April 19, 1978. Classical Video VHS/Live Opera audiocassette. **2001 Spoleto Festival.** Julia Melinek sings the role of Annina opposite Timothy Richards as Michele in this Spoleto Festival, Italy, recording made under Menotti's supervision. Pamela Helen Stephen is Desideria, John Marcus Bindel is Don Marco, Sandra Zeltzer is Carmela, Vitale Rozynko is Salvatore, Yvonne Howard is Assunta, Amelia Farrugia is Maria Corona, Riccardo Bartoli is her son, Veronica Napoleoni is Concettina, Benjamin Harbold is a Young Man, Jennifer Check is a Young Woman, Heather Lockard is an Old Woman, Nejla Hennard is Renata, Mark T. Panuccio is First Guest, Levi Hernandez is Second

Guest, Dennis McVeigh is Third Guest and Paul Fogle is the Bartender. Richard Wilcox conducts the Spoleto Festival Orchestra and Choir. The recording was made at the Teatro Nuovo in Spoleto on July 7, 10 and 14 2001. 125 minutes. Chandos 2-CD set.

SALAMMBÔ   *1941 "movie opera" by Herrmann*

Kiri Te Kanawa has recorded an aria from this movie opera created by Bernard Herrmann for the 1941 RKO film *Citizen Kane*. Herrmann wrote *Salammbô* because director Orson Welles wanted a peculiar kind of opera in which the soprano is on stage as the curtain goes up and has to sing over a powerful orchestra. In the film this is a vocal disaster for Kane's singer wife Susan Alexander whom he has forced into an opera career. The actress is Dorothy Comingore but the singing is by San Francisco Opera soprano Jean Forward who was asked to sing in a key too high for her so she would sound amateurish as she struggled to be heard over the booming orchestra. It's a great scene with many plot ramifications, including the sacking of Kane's critic friend Joseph Cotten. The *Salammbô* aria sung professionally by Te Kanawa and other modern sopranos actually sounds pretty good. Herrmann used material from Racine's play *Phèdre* for his libretto. William Randolph Hearst, one of the prototypes for Kane, did have an opera singer girlfriend, Sibyl Sanderson, but she was successful. A better prototype was Chicago newspaper magnate Harold McCormick who promoted a rather untalented Polish soprano called Ganna Walska. He arranged for her to star in Leoncavallo's opera *Zazà* at the Chicago Opera Company as he was its chief funder. Like Susan Alexander, Walska had a disastrous experience and fled the city before the premiere.

1941 Jean Forward. In *Citizen Kane* the *Salammbô* aria is performed by San Francisco Opera soprano Jean Forward who has to sing in a key too high for her so she will sound amateurish. It is heartbreaking to watch as she (and actress Dorothy Comingore who acts the role) struggle to be heard over the booming orchestra. *Citizen Kane* was voted the best American film of the century in an American Film Institute poll and is available on VHS and DVD. **1989 Kiri Te Kanawa.** Kiri Te Kanawa has recorded the aria from *Salammbô* for several albums. She is accompanied by the National Philharmonic Orchestra led by George Gerhardt on the album *Citizen Kane: The Classic Film Scores of Bernard Herrmann* (RCA Victor CD) and by the London Symphony Orchestra led by Stephen Barlow on *Kiri!— Her Greatest Hits* (London Classics CD/VHS).

SALZMAN, ERIC   *American composer (1933–)*

Eric is best known for his collaborations with Michael Sahl on music theater, most notably CIVILIZATION AND ITS DISCONTENTS which was premiered in New York in 1997, recorded in 1978 and broadcast in 1980. Their first joint effort was the "pop opera" *The Conjurer* produced by Joseph Papp at the Public Theater in New York in 1975 followed by STAUF, a modern version of the Faust story with a nuclear scientist as protagonist, which premiered in New York in 1976. *Noah* was staged at the Pratt Institute in Brooklyn in 1978, *The Passion of Simple Simon* was premiered by the Theater for the New York City in 1979 and broadcast on NPR. *Boxes*, a "music theater work for radio," was performed in 1988. Salzman who was born in New York, studied at Columbia with Jack Beeson and Vladimir Ussachevsky and at Princeton with Roger Sessions and Milton Babbit. He has worked with poets and artists on a number of music theater works beginning in 1967 with *Foxes and Hedgehogs* composed to a libretto by John Ashberry. He founded Quog Music Theater in 1970.

SANDHOG   *1954 folk opera by Robinson*

Johnny O'Sullivan works as a sandhog digging in a tunnel under a New York river during the construction of the Hoboken Bridge. He quits his job after friends are killed in an accident but later returns and miraculously survives a second accident. Earl Robinson's three-act folk opera *Sandhog*, libretto by screenwriter Waldo Salt based on the Theodore Dreiser story *St. Columba and the River*, opened in New York at the Phoenix Theater in New York on November 23, 1954. Jack Cassidy sang the role of Johnny and Betty Oakes was his wife Betty. Robinson uses Wagner-like leitmotifs for his main characters.

1955 Earl Robinson/Waldo Salt. Librettist Waldo Salt narrates this recording of the folk opera with composer Earl Robinson singing the arias and playing the piano. Vanguard LP.

SAPPHO   *1965 opera by Glanville-Hicks*

The story takes place on the Greek island kingdom of Lesbos around 650 BC. King Kreon seeks information about the mysterious birth of his beautiful wife Sappho, who has become involved with the handsome Phaon, and he also quarrels bitterly with his twin brother Pittakos. A letter reveals Sappho is actually Kreon's daughter and they are both banished. *Sappho*, libretto by Lawrence Durrell based on his own play, was composed in 1965 as a commission for the San Francisco Opera. It was written as a vehicle for Maria Callas but was rejected by San Francisco Opera and has not been performed.

SARAH   *1958 TV opera by Laderman*

Sarah is unable to give her husband Abraham a son so she suggests he lie with her handmaiden Hagar. When Hagar conceives, Sarah becomes jealous and drives her away. After Hagar returns and gives birth to Ishmael, Sarah has her own child, Isaac. Ezra Laderman's 30-minute TV opera *Sarah*, libretto by Clair Roskam based on the Biblical story, was premiered on CBS Television on November 30, 1958, in the series *Look Up and Live*. Patrica Neway sang the role of Sarah, Mildred Allen was Hagar, Ara Berberian was Abraham and Alan Baker was the Angel of God. Jack Kuney produced, Roger Englander directed and Laderman conducted the orchestra.

SARFATY, REGINA   *American mezzo-soprano (1932–)*

Regina Sarfaty has been a major presence in American opera creating roles on television and stage and recording others. She began in 1955 by creating the role of the Devil's Grandmother in Lukas Foss's GRIFFELKIN on NBC television. In 1956 she created two roles at the Juilliard School of Music: the servant Catherine in William Bergsma's THE RETURN OF MARTIN GUERRE in February and the lion-tamer Zinida in Robert Ward's HE WHO GETS SLAPPED in May 17. In 1958 she went to Santa Fe Opera to create Nelly in Carlisle Floyd's WUTHERING HEIGHTS. In April 1959 she created two roles at New York City Opera, the Mezzo in Hugo Weisgall's SIX CHARACTERS IN SEARCH OF AN AUTHOR and the Heavenly Voice in Norman Dello Joio's stage version of THE TRIUMPH OF ST. JOAN. In 1961 she created Kate Croy in Douglas Moore's THE WINGS OF THE DOVE at New York City Opera. She was Agata in New York City Opera's 1959 production of Gian Carlo Menotti's MARIA GOLOVIN, the Secretary in Menotti's THE CONSUL in a 1959 Canadian TV production and Baba the Turk in the 1964 Sadler Wells Opera recording of Igor Stravinsky's THE RAKE'S PROGRESS. Sarfaty, who was born in Rochester, NY, studied at Juilliard and made her official debut at Santa Fe Opera in 1957.

SAROYAN, WILLIAM　*American writer (1908–1981)*

The prolific Armenian writer William Saroyan was equally at home in play, story, novel, essay and opera librettos. The one-act OPERA OPERA, a surrealistic opera about how to stage an opera, was written in 1942 without a composer in mind. Martin Kalmanoff set it to music in 1956 and it was premiered by After Dinner Theater Opera at Finch College. Paul Bowles had composed music for Saroyan's play *My Heart's in the Highlands* when it was staged on Broadway in 1939 and Saroyan returned the favor by writing a libretto for Bowles' opera THE WIND REMAINS. Bowles decided not to use it and the opera premiered in 1943 with a libretto by the composer. Jack Beeson turned MY HEART'S IN THE HIGHLANDS into an opera in 1970 and premiered on NET Opera Theatre on PBS. A second opera based on *My Heart's in the Highlands* was composed by David Ahlstrom in 1990. Beeson had earlier turned a short Saroyan play into a one-act opera. HELLO OUT THERE, a bittersweet story about a sad romance in a Texas jail with a libretto by Kenward Elmslie, was premiered by Columbia University Opera Workshop on May 27, 1954. Saroyan, who was born in Fresno, California, the setting of *My Heart's in the Highlands,* won the Pulitzer Prize for his 1939 play *The Time of Your Life.*

SATYAGRAHA　*1980 opera by Glass*

Gandhi develops his technique of peaceful non-resistance in South Africa as he protests discrimination again the black population. He bases it on the concept of Satyagraha ("holding firmly to the truth) which he finds in the sacred Indian epic the *Bhagavad-Gita*. Every word used is taken from a verse in the *Gita* and is sung in the original Sanskrit while the prologue features its protagonists Prince Arjuna and Lord Krishna. The other scenes revolve around Gandhi's activities in South Africa and each act is presided over by an inspirational figures, Leo Tolstoy, Rabindranath Tagore and Martin Luther King, Jr. Philip Glass's opera *Satyagraha*, libretto by Constance De Jong in Sanskrit, was premiered in Rotterdam by Netherlands Opera on September 5, 1980, in a production by David Pountney with set designs by Robert Israel. Douglas Perry was Gandhi, Claudia Cummings was Gandhi's secretary Miss Schlesen, Iris Hiskey was Mrs. Naidoo, Bruce Hall was Mr. Kallenbach, René Claessen was Prince Arjuna and Beverly Morgan was Gandhi's wife Kasturbai. Bruce Ferden conducted the Netherlands Opera Orchestra. *Satyagraha*, the second in Glass's trilogy about men who changed the world, is bit more like a conventional opera that *Einstein on the Beach* but still quite mysterious. It was given its American premiere at Art Park outside Buffalo, NY, in 1981 with Christopher Keene conducting and then staged at Brooklyn Academy of Music, New York City Opera, Lyric Opera of Chicago, Seattle Opera and San Francisco Opera.

1981 Stuttgart State Opera. Gandhi is portrayed by three people in this Stuttgart Opera by Achim Freyer who also wrote the scenario and designed the sets and costumes. Leo Goeke is Gandhi 1 Ralf Harster is Gandhi 2, Helmut Danniger is Gandhi 3, Inga Nielsen is Gandhi's secretary Schlesen, Elke Estlinbaum is Gandhi's wife Kasturbai, Helmut Holzapfel is Prince Arjuna, Karl-Friedrich Dürr is Krishna, George Greiwe is Tolstoy and Tagore, Helga Merkl-Freivogel is Mrs. Alexander, Wolfgang Probst and Kimmo Lappalainen are Gandhi's European aides and Daniel Bonilla and Melinda Liebermann are Gandhi's Indian aides. Dennis Russell Davies conducts the Staatsoper Stuttgart Orchestra and Chorus. Sung in Sanskrit Hugo Kach directed the video for NVC/RM Arts. Image Entertainment and Arthaus DVD. **1985 New York City Opera.** Douglas Perry is Gandhi in this New York Opera recording with Christopher Keene conducting the NYCO Orchestra and Chorus. Claudia Cummings is Miss Schlesen, Rhonda Liss is Gandhi's wife Kasturbai and Mrs. Alexander, Scott Reeve is Lord Krishna and Parsi Rustomji, Robert McFarland is Prince Arjuna and Mr. Kallenbach and Sheryl Wood is Mrs. Naidoo. Sony Classical CD. **1985 A Composer's Notes: Philip Glass.** Excerpts from Achim Freyer's 1981 production of *Satyagraha* for Stuttgart State Opera are featured in Michael Blackwood's documentary film *A Composer's Notes: Philip Glass.* VAI VHS. **1993 Donald Joyce.** Organist Donald Joyce plays the conclusion of Act III of on his album *Glass: Organ Works.* Catalyst CD. **1994 Douglas Perry.** Douglas Perry as Gandhi performs two scenes from the opera with New York City Opera Orchestra and Chorus on the album *The Essential Philip Glass.* The scenes are from the 1985 NYCO recording. Sony Classical CD.

SAUNDERS, ARLENE　*American soprano (1935–)*

Arlene Saunders created the role of the music teacher Mme. Euterpova in Gian Carlo Menotti's HELP, HELP, THE GLOBOLINKS! at Hamburg Opera in 1968 and the title role in Alberto Ginastera's BEATRIX CENCI at Washington Opera in 1971. She sings the duet "Thy golden heart wide open" from Horatio Parker's 1912 opera MONA with Enrico Di Giuseppe on a 1961 radio broadcast. Saunders, born in Cleveland, made her debut at the Teatro Nuovo in Milan in 1961 and later sang at New York City Opera and the Met.

SAYLOR, BRUCE　*American composer (1946–)*

Philadelphia-born composer Bruce Saylor has composed literary operas based on works by Tennessee Williams and Nathaniel Hawthorne. The first was the mysterious one-act MY KINSMAN, MAJOR MOLINEUX, libretto by Cary Plotkin based on a Hawthorne story, in which a young man thinks the people of a town have gone mad. It was commissioned by Opera Workshop in Pittsburgh which premiered it in 1976. ORPHEUS DESCENDING, a two-act opera with libretto by J. D. McClatchy based on the Tennessee Williams play, was premiered by Lyric Opera of Chicago in 1994. Saylor, who studied at Juilliard with Hugo Weisgall and Roger Sessions, was resident composer at Chicago Lyric Opera in the early nineties and professor of music at SUNY Queens College.

THE SCARF　*1958 opera by Hoiby*

Miriam weaves a scarlet scarf in an isolated farmhouse while a blizzard and her elderly husband Reuel accuses her of casting spells to attract young men to stay the night. When a postman arrives and asks to stay, Reuel insists he leave. Miriam gives the postman the scarf and tells him to bring it back later. When her husband returns wearing the scarf, Miriam uses it to strangle him. Lee Hoiby's one-act opera *The Scarf*, libretto by Harry Duncan based on Chekhov's story *The Witch*, premiered at the Spoleto Festival in Italy on June 20, 1958. Patricia Neway created the role of Miriam, Richard Cross was the Postman and John McCollum was the husband. Rouben Ter-Arutunian designed the sets and costumes and Reinhardt Peter conducted. The opera was presented at New York City Opera on April 5, 1959, with Neway and Cross repeating their roles and John Druary playing the husband. Rouben Ter-Arutunian again designed the sets and costumes, Kirk Browning directed and Russell Stanger conducted the orchestra.

THE SCARLET LETTER　*American operas based on Hawthorne novel*

Hester Prynne is condemned as an adulteress in 17th century Puritan Boston and forced to wear a scarlet letter "A" on her dress.

When she refuses to say who is the father of her child Pearl, her elderly husband Roger Chillingsworth attempts to expose him. Young minister Arthur Dimmesdale eventually confesses. Nathaniel Hawthorne said that his popular 1850 novel was based on historical events and the woman who inspired it is identified on a grave in central Boston. *The Scarlet Letter* has inspired many opera composers as the listings below show.

1855 Lucien H. Southard. Lucien H. Southard's operatic adaptation of *The Scarlet Letter* was composed only five years after the novel was published. It premiered in Boston in July 1855 but has never been revived. Southard (1827–1881) had his greatest success with his 1858 Indian opera *Omano*. **1896 Walter Damrosch.** Walter Damrosch's opera *The Scarlet Letter*, libretto by George Parons Lathrop, is the most famous opera based on the story. It was premiered at the Boston Theater by the Damrosch Opera Company on February 10, 1896, and reprised in New York at the Academy of Music on March 2. Johanna Gadski sang the role of Hester Prynne, Banon Berthald was Arthur Dimmesdale, Wilhelm Mertens was Roger Chillingsworth and Konrad Behrens was George Bellingham. Damrosch conducted. **1902 Pietro Floridia.** Pietro Floridia's opera *The Scarlet Letter* was submitted to the Metropolitan Opera in 1902 but rejected as the Met was not yet ready to stage American operas. Sicilian-born Floridia (1860–1917) won the BISPHAM MEMORIAL MEDAL for an American opera in 1930 with PAOLETTA. **1913 Charles F. Carlson.** Charles F. Carlson's opera *Hester, or The Scarlet Letter*, libretto by the composer, was apparently never staged. Carlson (1875–1950) was awarded the BISPHAM MEMORIAL MEDAL in 1926 for his opera *Phelias*. **1934 Avery Claflin.** Avery Claflin's opera *Hester Prynne*, libretto by Dorothea Claflin , was premiered in Hartford, CT, on December l5, 1934. Claflin also composed operas based on works by Edgar Allan Poe (THE FALL OF THE HOUSE OF USHER) and Harriet

Beecher Stowe (UNCLE TOM'S CABIN) but had his greatest success with LA GRANDE BRETÈCHE based on a Balzac story. **1938 Vittorio Giannini.** Vittorio Giannini's two-act opera *The Scarlet Letter*, libretto by Karl Flaster, was premiered by Hamburg State Opera on June 2, 1938. It was sung in a German translation by Julius Kapp titled *Das Brandmal*. Dusolina Giannini, Vittorio's sister, sang the role of Hester, opposite Ferdinand Frantz, Hans Hotter and Joachim Sattler. Eugene Jochum conducted the Hamburg Staatsoper Orchestra. **1961 Walter Kaufmann.** Walter Kaufmann's opera *The Scarlet Letter*, libretto by the composer, was staged at the University of Indiana in Bloomington, Indiana, on May 6, 1961, and reprised in Indianapolis in 1962. Kaufmann (1907–1984) composed 11 operas including a children's opera for based on RIP VAN WINKLE. **1965 Hugh Mullins.** Hugh Mullins' opera *The Scarlet Letter,* libretto by the composer, was completed in 1965. Mullins (1922–) had three of his one-act operas staged in Los Angeles in the 1960s. **1970 Robert W. Mann.** Robert W. Mann's opera *The Scarlet Letter,* libretto by the composer, was completed in 1979. It is apparently his only opera. **1970 Lewis Rosen.** Lewis Rosen's opera *Hester*, libretto by the composer based on *The Scarlet Letter*, was composed in 1970. **1979 Michael P. Gehlen.** Michael P. Gehlen's three-act opera *The Scarlet Letter*, libretto by the composer, was completed in 1979. He also wrote an opera based on Bret Harte's THE OUTCASTS OF POKER FLAT. **1986 Robert Di Domenica.** Robert Di Domenica's opera *The Scarlet Letter,* libretto by E. H. Eglin and the composer, was completed in 1986 but not staged until 1997. Scenes from it were presented that year at Jordan Hall in Boston in the Composer Series with Elizabeth Kennedy in the role of Hester Prynne. **1992 Martin Herman.** Martin Herman's opera *The Scarlet Letter*, libretto by Tom Curley, was premiered in Berkeley on April 1, 1992. by the Berkeley Contemporary Opera company.

SCHAENEN, LEE   *American conductor (1925–)*

Lee Schaenen conducted the Lyric Opera of Chicago Orchestra in the premiere of Lee Goldstein's THE FAN in 1989 and he leads the orchestra in the 1990 live broadcast recording of Hugo Weisgall's SIX CHARACTERS IN SEARCH OF AN AUTHOR. He has also conducted stage productions of George Gershwin's PORGY AND BESS and Gian Carlo Menotti's THE CONSUL and THE MEDIUM. Schaenen, a native of New York, studied at Juilliard and Columbia and made his operatic debut with New York City Opera in 1949.

SCHEFF, FRITZI   *American soprano (1879–1954)*

Met soprano Fritzi Scheff created the lead roles in four comic operas composed by Victor Herbert. Her first appearance on Broadway was in the title role of Herbert's BABETTE in 1903. She won high praise for her performance but the operetta had only a short run. In 1905 she created the title role of Fifi in MLLE. MODISTE and it became the biggest success of her career, especially because of her aria "Kiss Me Again." She played the role again in a 1929 stage revival and 1936 radio production and appeared in a 1951 television version. She had less success with the next two Herbert operettas in the roles of the Paris prima donna Mlle. Athenée in *The Prima Donna* in 1908 and the Paris flower shop girl Mlle. Rosita in *The Duchess* in 1911. Scheff, who was born in Vienna, made her operatic debut in 1897 in Frankfurt as Juliette. She moved to the U.S. in 1900 singing Musetta in Los Angeles in 1900 and Marzelline at the Metropolitan the same year. After three years at the Met, she switched to light opera and was promoted as the "Little Devil of Grand Opera."

Soprano *Fritzi Scheff*

SCHICKELE, PETER   *American composer (1935–)*

Peter Schickele created an alter-ego named P. D. Q. Bach when he began to write parodies of operas. The "half-act opera" THE STONED GUEST was presented in Carnegie Hall in 1967. *Hansel and Gretel and Ted and Alice*, "an opera in one unnatural act for bargain countertenor and beriberitone," was presented in Houston in 1972. A LITTLE NIGHTMARE MUSIC, which satirizes the play *Amadeus*, was performed at Carnegie Hall in 1982. THE ABDUCTION OF FIGARO was staged in Minneapolis in 1984 and reprised in Sweden in 1989. *The Magic Bassoon* was presented in Denver in 1986. The mock Greek tragedy OEDIPUS TEX was premiered at the Plymouth Music Series in Minneapolis in 1988. The "undiscovered opera" *Prelude to Einstein on the Fritz* was presented in Carnegie Hall in 1989. *La Clemenza di Genghis Khan* exists so far only in overture form. HORNSMOKE, "a horse opera for brass quintet," is an opera without singers in which musical instruments are the characters and interact while otherwise mocking the cliches of movie Westerns. It was composed in 1975 and recorded in 2000. Schickele, who was born in Ames, Iowa, studied at Swarthmore, Juilliard and Aspen with Persichetti, Bergsma and Milhaud. He is a prolific composer with over 100 works for voice, choral groups, chamber ensembles, symphony orchestras, film and television as well as being host of a popular classical music program. His one music theatre work using his real name is THE KNIGHT OF BURNING PESTLE (1974).

SCHIFF, DAVID   *American composer (1945–)*

David Schiff's best-known opera is GIMPEL THE FOOL, composed to a Yiddish libretto by Isaac Bashevis Singer, which was performed in Yiddish in 1979 and in English in 1985. He has also composed an opera based on James Joyce's *Dubliners* and chamber works based on other writings by Joyce. Schiff, who was born in the Bronx and studied at Columbia, Cambridge and Juilliard with John Corigliano and Elliot Carter, has published a book-length study of Carter.

SCHIPPERS, THOMAS   *American conductor (1930–1977)*

Thomas Schippers began a long collaboration with Gian Carlo Menotti in 1949 when he took over as conductor of THE CONSUL on Broadway. In 1950 he conducted the Symphony Orchestra of Rome for the soundtrack of Menotti's film of his opera THE MEDIUM. In 1951 he conducted the NBC Television premiere and recording of AMAHL AND THE NIGHT VISITORS. In 1954 he conducted the premiere and recording of THE SAINT OF BLEECKER STREET and led the orchestra in the 1956 BBC television version. In 1957 he conducted the New York City Ballet production and recording of THE UNICORN, THE GORGON AND THE MANTICORE. In 1958 he was made music director of Menotti's Festival of Two Worlds at Spoleto in Italy. In 1964 he conducted the premiere of Menotti's THE LAST SAVAGE at the Met. In 1972 he conducted a new production of THE CONSUL at the Spoleto Festival. Schippers led the orchestra at the opening of the new Met in 1966 with Samuel Barber's ANTONY AND CLEOPATRA and can be seen preparing for the premiere in the TV documentary *The New Met— Countdown to Curtain*. He also conducted the orchestra for Leontyne Price's recording of arias from the opera. Schippers was also a major presence at New York City Opera where he conducted the premiere of Aaron Copland's THE TENDER LAND in 1954. He made recordings of the Intermezzo from Barber's VANESSA in 1960 and the Overture to Menotti's AMELIA GOES TO THE BALL in 1961. Schippers, born in Kalamazoo, Michigan, made his conducting debut in 1948 with the Lemonade Opera Company in New York.

SCHLIEMANN   *1995 opera by Jolas*

Self-taught German archaeologist Heinrich Schliemann makes a fortune in the California gold rush and uses it to dig up Troy and unearth what he considers Trojan King Priam's gold. Schliemann is pictured on a ship on his way to Athens, with his teenage wife Sophia wearing a Trojan diadem and finally on his deathbed. Betsy Jolas' three-act opera *Schliemann*, libretto by the composer based on Bruno Bayen's 1982 play *Schliemann, Épisodes Ignorés*, was premiered by Lyons Opera in France on May 3, 1995. Jean-Marie Fremeau was Schliemann, Virginia Pochon was Sophia, Jean Dupouy was Mr. Haad and Hélène Delavault was Nelly. Carlo Tommasi designed the sets, Alain Francon directed and Kent Nagano conducted. The music is tonal, somewhat in the Debussy mode.

DIE SCHLUMPF   *1990 "movie opera" by Pasatieri*

Wagnerian-like singers perform an exceeding long duet on stage in Thomas Pasatieri's "movie opera" *Die Schlumpf*, created for the 1990 film *Dick Tracy*. The Wagnerian pastiche is only ever shown in long shot from where Dick Tracy (Warren Beatty) and his girlfriend Tess Trueheart (Glenn Headley) are seated in the opera house. The excerpt shown on screen is brief but the duet apparently continues for a very long time as Tracy leaves the opera house for hours and returns to find the duet still in progress. The singers are Marvellee Cariaga and Michael Gallup. *Dick Tracy*, directed by Beatty for Touchstone Pictures and Warner Bros., is based on the comic strip by Chester Gould and is on VHS and DVD.

SCHMIDT, HARVEY   *American composer (1929–)*

Harvey Schmidt's off-Broadway musical *The Fantasticks*, libretto by Tom Jones based on Edmund Rostand's play *Les Romanesques*, was presented as an opera by the Skylight Comic Opera Company in Milwaukee in 1988. It was first staged on May 3, 1960, at the Sullivan Street Playhouse in New York where it became the longest running musical in theater history. *The Fantasticks* was the first musical for the Dallas-born composer and his lyricist partner. Schmidt and Jones' musical *110 in the Shade*, based on Richard Nash's *Rainmakers*, opened at the Broadhurst Theatre in New York on October 24, 1963, and entered the New York City Opera repertory on July 21, 1992. Their other collaborations include *Celebration* (1960), *I Do! I Do!* (1966) and *Philemon* (1975).

SCHOENFELD, PAUL   *American composer (1947–)*

Detroit-born composer Paul Schoenfield's opera THE MERCHANT AND THE PAUPER, libretto by Margaret B. Stearns based on a folk tale by Hasidic Rabbi Nachman, attracted considerable attention when it was premiered by Opera Theater of St. Louis in 1999. It is a parable about Moses leading the Jews out of Egypt and is Schoenfield's only opera. The composer, who now lives in Israel, is best known for his instrumental and vocal works that reflect folk music styles, like "Klezmer Rondos for Baritone, Flute and Orchestra."

SCHOOL FOR WIVES   *1955 opera by Liebermann*

Aging lecher Arnolphe boasts of how easy it is to seduce wives. To protect his own young wife-to-be, he has orphan Agnes educated in a convent far from temptation. His cunning plan goes astray when young neighbor Horace see Agnes over a wall and falls in love with her. Arnolphe is outwitted by a man claiming to be Agnes's father who says she should marry Horace. Playwright

Molière (Jean-Baptiste Poquelin) sits on the stage making comments about what happens and plays three roles himself. Rolf Liebermann's three-act opera *School for Wives,* libretto by Heinrich Strobel based on Molière's play *l'Ecole des femmes,* was commissioned by the Louisville Philharmonic Society and premiered by Kentucky Opera on December 3, 1955. Liebermann is Swiss and his collaborator wrote the libretto in German but it was translated into English by Elizabeth Montague. Robert Fischer played Molière/Poquelin, William Pickett was Arnolphe, Audrey Nossaman was Agnes, Monas Harlan was Horace, Charme Riesley was Georgette and Richard Dales was Oronte. Moritz Bomhard conducted the Louisville Orchestra. *School for Wives* was one of six American operas commissioned by Louisville in the 1950s. It received its European premiere in Salzburg on August 17, 1957, when it was sung in German as *Die Schule der Frauen.*

1955 Kentucky Opera. Robert Fischer is Molière/Poquelin in this recording made by the premiere cast. William Pickett is Arnolphe, Audrey Nossaman is Agnes, Monas Harlan is Horace, Charme Riesley is Georgette and Richard Dales is Oronte. Moritz Bombard conducts the Louisville Orchestra. Sung in English. Louisville First Edition Records 2-LP set. **1957 Salzburg Festival.** Walter Berry sings Molière/Poquelin in the European premiere of *School for Wives* at the Salzburg Festival on August 17, 1957. Kurt Böhme is Arnolphe, Anneliese Rothenberger is Agnes, Christa Ludwig is Georgette, Nicolai Gedda is Horace and Alois Pernerstorfer is Oronte. George Szell conducts the Vienna Philharmonic Orchestra. Recorded live, sung in German. 84 minutes. Orfeo d'Or 2-CD set.

SCHULLER, GUNTHER   *American composer/conductor (1925–)*

Gunther Schuller's major opera is THE VISITATION (1966), loosely based on Franz Kafka's novel *The Trial* transposed to the American South with a Black protagonist. He also had success with the fairy tale opera THE FISHERMAN AND HIS WIFE (1970), libretto by John Updike based on a Grimm fairytale. He revised, orchestrated and conducted the 1911 Scott Joplin opera TREEMONISHA for Houston Grand Opera in 1975. Schuller, a multi-talented self-taught composer, was born in Jackson Heights, New York. He started his music career as a boy soprano, switched to French horn when his voice changed, played horn at the Metropolitan Opera from 1945 to 1959 and then began to conduct and compose. He seems equally comfortable composing in styles from jazz to twelve tone and his scholarly writings about jazz and classical music are highly regarded, especially his study *The Compleat Conductor.*

SCHUMAN, WILLIAM   *American composer (1910–1992)*

William Schuman wrote only two operas but both remain popular The most famous is the jazzy one-act THE MIGHTY CASEY, libretto by Jeremy Gury based on Ernest L. Thayer's 1888 poem "Casey at the Bat, which was premiered in 1953. A QUESTION OF TASTE, libretto by J. D. McClatchy based on a Roald Dahl story about a man willing to wager his own daughter, was commissioned by Glimmerglass Opera which premiered it on June 24, 1989. Schumann, a native New Yorker, studied music at NYU, Juilliard and Columbia University. He was a prolific composer of symphonic, orchestral and vocal works and won the first Pulitzer Prize in Music in 1943 for *A Free Song: Secular Cantata No. 2,* based on a Walt Whitman poem.

SCHUMANN, WALTER   *American composer (1913–1958)*

Walter Schumann wrote music for radio, television and movies and is particularly remembered for creating the syncopated theme of *Dragnet* and the haunting score of *The Night of the Hunter.* He composed a choral work that is often described as an opera but which is really a poetic play with music. JOHN BROWN'S BODY, adapted by Charles Laughton from Stephen Vincent Benét's Pulitzer Prize-winning verse novel, was premiered in Los Angeles on September 21, 1953, in a production organized by Paul Gregory. Schumann's music for the work is based around songs of the Civil War era.

SCHUMANN-HEINK, ERNESTINE   *American contralto (1861–1936)*

Metropolitan prima donna Ernestine Schumann-Heink, who created the role of Clytemnestra in Richard Strauss' opera *Elektra,* also created a leading role in an American comic opera. She portrayed Lina in Julian Edwards' LOVE'S LOTTERY, libretto by Stanislaus Strange, which opened on Broadway on October 3, 1904. It was composed for her and it lasted for 50 performances on the strength of her reputation. The 43-year-old prima donna played a German laundress living in England in 1818 who wins a lottery and the heart of a sergeant, played by English baritone Wallace Brownlow. Schumann-Heink, born in a town near Prague, began her career in Hamburg and Bayreuth but later moved to the U.S. and became an American. She started to sing at the Metropolitan Opera in 1898 and gave her final performance there in 1932.

SCHWARTZ, ARTHUR   *American composer (1900–1984)*

Brooklyn-born composer Arthur Schwartz is best-known as a songwriter working in collaboration with lyricists Howard Dietz, Frank Loesser and Dorothy Fields. He created the music for over twenty stage musicals and a dozen of films. His most successful stage work was the 1931 revue *The Band Wagon* with Dietz, but he also had a fine partnership with Dorothy Fields creating musicals like the 1951 *A Tree Grows in Brooklyn.*

SCHWARTZ, STEPHEN   *American composer/librettist (1948–)*

Stephen Schwartz wrote the secular lyrics for Leonard Bernstein's 1971 MASS but is best known as the composer of the rock opera *Godspell,* based on the Gospel of Matthew. Schwartz's other stage musicals include *Pippin* (1972, *The Magic Show* (1974), *The Baker's Wife* (1976) and *Rags* (1986)

SCIENCE FICTION OPERAS   *American operas with SF elements*

Science fiction has become one of the dominant literary trends in America during the past fifty years and this is reflected in the growing number of American operas with SF elements. The most prolific composers in the genre are Philip Glass with five operas, including two based on SF novels by Doris Lessing, and Gian Carlo Menotti who composed three to his own librettos. The most popular SF writer is, surprisingly, Nathaniel Hawthorne, with nine operas based on his mad scientist tales of SF-style experiments. In *Dr. Heidegger's Experiment* (DR. HEIDEGGER'S FOUNTAIN OF YOUTH), he plays around with the idea of eternal youth and in RAPPACCINI'S DAUGHTER, he considers the dangers of poisons. See NATHANIEL HAWTHORNE for complete lists of operas based on his stories.

Ashley, Robert. 1984 ATALANTA (ACTS OF GOD) features an episode called "The Flying Saucer" with aliens in a space ship discussing humans. **Beeson, Jack.** 1978 DR. HEIDEGGER'S FOUNTAIN OF YOUTH, libretto by Sheldon Harnick based on the Hawthorne story. **Bender, Ellen S.** 1991 RAPPACCINI'S DAUGHTER, libretto by

Robert Di Domenica based on the Hawthorne story. **Cadman, Charles W.** 1925 *The Garden of Mystery*, libretto by N. R. Eberhardt based on Hawthorne's *Rappaccini's Daughter*. **Cohen, Michael.** 1981 RAPPACCINI'S DAUGHTER, libretto by Linsey Abrams based on the Hawthorne story. **Dennison, Sam.** 1984 RAPPACCINI'S DAUGHTER, libretto by Karen Campbell based on the Hawthorne story. **Garwood, Margaret.** 1983 RAPPACCINI'S DAUGHTER, libretto by the composer based on the Hawthorne story. **Glass, Philip.** 1976 EINSTEIN ON THE BEACH, libretto by composer and Robert Wilson with scene on spaceship. 1988 THE MAKING OF THE REPRESENTATIVE FOR PLANET 8, libretto by Doris Lessing based on her SF novel about a doomed world. 1988 1000 AIRPLANES ON THE ROOF, an operatic description of the arrival of a UFO. 1992 THE VOYAGE, libretto by David Henry Hwang about exploration with a spaceship having a crash-landing on earth. 1997 THE MARRIAGES BETWEEN ZONES, THREE, FOUR AND FIVE, libretto by Doris Lessing based on her SF novel about male-female relationships. **Larsen, Libby.** 1992 A WRINKLE IN TIME, libretto by Walter Green based on the SF novel by Madeleine L'Engle about a trip to a parallel universe. **Machover, Tod.** 1987 VALIS, based on a novel by Philip K. Dick about a Vast Active Living Intelligence System. **Menotti, Gian Carlo.** 1963 LABYRINTH, surrealistic television opera with an astronaut sequence. 1968 HELP, HELP, THE GLOBOLINKS!, children's opera about alien invaders who are conquered by music. 1982 A BRIDE FROM PLUTO, children's opera about an alien looking for a mate on earth. **Mollicone, Henry.** 1979 THE STARBIRD, libretto by Kate Pogue about animals on a spaceship learning about life. **Schwartz, Paul.** 1956 *The Experiment*, libretto by Kathryn Schwartz based on Hawthorne's story *Dr. Heidegger's Experiment*. **Smith, Leo.** 1969 *The Alchemy of Love*, libretto by Fred Hoyle about an alien trying to obtain a secret formula. 1978 *Dr. Heidegger's Experiment*, libretto by the composer based on the Hawthorne story. **Stokes, Eric.** 1979 *The Jealous Cellist and Others Acts of Misconduct*, libretto by Alvin Greenburg about couples who are switched in time. 1986 *We're Not Robots, You Know*, libretto by K. Gunderson about marionettes who get robots to do their housework. 1990 *The Future Voyages of the Santa Maria*, libretto by Alvin Greenberg in which the ghost of Columbus joins astronauts on a space ship called Santa Maria. **Tippett, Michael.** 1989 NEW YEAR, libretto by the composer about a spaceship landing in New York on New Year's Eve. **Wargo, Richard.** 1979 *The Crystal Mirror*, libretto by the composer based on Nathaniel Hawthorne's story *Dr. Heidegger's Experiment*. **Weill, Kurt.** 1945 COLUMBUS, libretto by Ira Gershwin about a time traveler who lands on Christopher Columbus's ship as it sails to the New World.

SCOURGE OF HYACINTHS *1994 opera by Leon*

Miguel escapes from jail in an unnamed country and attempts to prove his innocence while his mother Tiatin prays to the goddess Yemanja for help. Hyacinths clog the water in a lagoon as he tries to escape by boat and he is caught and executed. Tania Leon's symbolic opera *Scourge of Hyacinths*, libretto by the composer based on a radio play by Nobel Prize-winning Nigerian writer Wole Soyinka, was premiered at the Munich Biennale on May 1, 1994. Andrew Solomon Glover was Miguel, Vanessa Ayers was Tiatin and Opera Ebony assisted on the production (all seven men in the cast are black). Mark Lamos staged the opera and the composer conducted the orchestra. *Scourge of Hyacinths* was one of six operas commissioned by Hans Werner Henze for the International Festival for New Music Theater competition which it won. It was reprised in 1999 by Robert Wilson and staged in Geneva, France and Austria with Timothy Robert Blevins as Miguel and Bonita Hyman as Tiatin.

1995 Dawn Upshaw. Soprano Dawn Upshaw sings the aria "Oh Yemanja" (Mother's Prayer) from *Scourge of Hyacinths* as Tiatin asks the goddess Yemanja to protect her son as he flees across the lagoon. It's on her album of music from modern American operas *The World So Wide*. She is accompanied by pianist David Zinman. Nonesuch CD.

SCOVOTTI, JEANETTE *American soprano (1936–)*

Coloratura soprano Jeanette Scovotti created the role of Miss Hampton in Gunther Schuller's opera THE VISITATION at Hamburg Opera in 1966. She sings leading roles on four of the 1962 Reader's Digest recordings of American operettas with opera singers: BoPeep in Victor Herbert's BABES IN TOYLAND, Fifi in Herbert's MLLE. MODISTE, Marianne in Sigmund Romberg's THE NEW MOON and Kathie in Romberg's THE STUDENT PRINCE. She also sings on a 1964 recording of Richard Rodgers' THE KING AND I. Scovotti, who was born in New York City, studied at Juilliard and made her debut at the Metropolitan Opera in 1962 before becoming a resident member of Staatsoper Hamburg.

THE SEAGULL *1974 opera by Pasatieri*

Love, despair and death at a country estate in 19th century Russia. Young actress Nina is loved by young writer Constantine who is the son of jealous older actress Irina Arkadina who is having an affair with popular writer Boris Trigorin. Masha loves Constantine while Nina fancies Trigorin. Constantine kills a seagull as a symbolic gesture but Nina continues to reject him so he kills himself. Thomas Pasatieri's three-act opera *The Seagull*, libretto by Kenward Elmslie based on the play by Anton Chekhov, was premiered by Houston Grand Opera on March 5, 1974. Frederica von Stade created the role of Nina, Evelyn Lear was Irina, Richard Stilwell was Constantine, Patricia Wells was Masha, John Reardon was Trigorin, Dana Krueger was Pauline, David Rae Smith was Sorin, Jon Enloe was Shamrayeff, Jack Trussel was Dr. Dorn and Michael Best was Medvedenco. Allen Charles Klein designed the sets and costumes, Emile Ardolino designed the projected media, Frank Corsaro staged the production and Charles Rosenkrans conducted the orchestra. An alternate cast sang four of the roles on March 9 with Evelyn Petros as Nina, Catherine Malfitano as Masha, Dolores Strazicich as Irina and Ronald Hedlund as Trigorin. This highly singable opera has since been produced by many other companies, including Seattle Opera in 1976, Washington Opera in 1978, Atlanta Opera in 1980, Fort Worth Opera in 1982 and the Manhattan School of Music in 2002.

1977 CBS Television. Elaine Bonazzi and Brent Ellis perform the duet "Nina's Good-bye to Constantine" in a semi-staged scene from *The Seagull* on the CBS television program *The Operas of Thomas Pasatieri*. Roger Englander directed the 30-minute color telecast for the Camera Three series. Video at MTR and New York State Education Department. **2002 Manhattan School of Music.** David Gilbert conducts the Manhattan School of Music Opera Orchestra in this recording of a live performance of the opera by the Manhattan School of Music Opera Theater. Amy Shoremount is Nina, Amy Gough is Madame Arkadina, Raymond Ayers is Constantine, Matthew Worth is Trigorin, Keri Behan is Masha and Maxime Alvarez de Toledo is Sorin. Albany Troy CD.

SEASONS IN HELL *1996 opera by Blumenfeld*

French poet Arthur Rimbaud (1854–1891) recalls the revolution he created with his poetry and remembers his love affair with fellow poet Paul Verlaine. The poet's life seesaws backward and forward from his deathbed and from age fifteen as seen by Old and

Young Rimbauds. Harold Blumenfeld's opera *Seasons in Hell*, subtitled *A Life of Rimbaud*, is composed to a libretto by Charles Kondek that paraphrases Rimbaud's poems and letters. The poet's *Une saison en enfer* is seen as an allegorical confession of his affair with Verlaine but the opera's main concern is why a writer of genius gave up his art to become an African trader. *Seasons in Hell* premiered at the Cincinnati College Conservatory of Music on February 8, 1996, with Gerhard Samuel conducting and Malcolm Fraser directing. Michael Kavelhuna sang Young Rimbaud, Craig Phillips was Old Rimbaud, Timothy Swaim was Verlaine, Mary Elizabeth Kures was the Voice of Rimbaud and Elizabeth Saunders was Rimbaud's Mother. On the second night the main roles were taken over by Randall Gremillion, Philip Mark Horst and Chad Smith.

1996 Cincinnati College of Music. This recording of the opera is based on the 1996 premiere stage production but features the second night cast. Randall Gremillion is Young Rimbaud, Philip Mark Horst is Old Rimbaud, Chad Smith is Verlaine, Mary Elizabeth Kures is the Voice of Rimbaud and Elizabeth Saunders is Rimbaud's Mother. Gerhard Samuel conducts the Cincinnati College Conservatory of Music Philharmonia. Albany CD box.

THE SECOND HURRICANE   *1936 opera by Copland*

High school students volunteer to help an aviator take supplies to an area hit by a hurricane but end up stranded on a high hill. Butch, Fat, Queenie and the others have to learn how to cooperate to survive. Aaron Copland's opera *The Second Hurricane*, libretto by Edwin Denby, was created as a "play opera" for high school students and was premiered by the Music School of the Henry Street Settlement at the Grand Street Playhouse in New York on April 21, 1937. It was staged by Orson Welles with Lehman Engel conducting the orchestra. Leonard Bernstein brought the opera back to prominence in 1960 when he telecast and recorded it. Since then there have been a number of performance by opera companies and universities, including one at the Henry Street Settlement's New Federal Theater in 1985.

1942 New York broadcast. *The Second Hurricane* was broadcast on radio from New York on June 11, 1942, and a transcription disc was made. Cast and orchestra not known. Omega Opera Archives audiocassette. **1960 Carnegie Hall.** Leonard Bernstein narrates the story of the opera and conducts the New York Philharmonic in a concert presentation at Carnegie Hall. The singers are students from the New York City High School of Performing Arts with soloists Marion Cowings, Julian Liss, Julie Makis, Omega Melbourne, John Richardson, Steven Wertheimer and Lawrence Willis. The concert was filmed by Roger Englander and telecast April 24, 1960, in the CBS TV series *Young People's Concerts*. Video recording at MTR, audio recording on Columbia LP/Sony CD.

THE SEDUCTION OF A LADY   *1985 opera by Wargo*

Rake Peter Semyonych sets out to seduce the married opera singer Irena but is worried about falling in love. He explains his problem to Nicky who encourages him, not knowing his wife is the woman in question. When Nicky tells Irena of Peter's dilemma, she becomes willing to be seduced but Peter decides against it as he does not want to break up her marriage. Richard Wargo's poignant one-act opera *The Seduction of a Lady*, libretto by the composer based on Neal Simon's play *The Good Doctor* in turn derives from a Chekhov story, was premiered at the National Institute for Music Theater in New York on May 11, 1984. Joseph Evan played Peter Semyonych, Pamela South was the wife Irena and David Barron was the husband Nicky. The opera became the first

part of Wargo's *A Chekhov Trilogy* in 1993. It has been reprised by Florida State Opera, Skylight Opera Theater, DiCapo Opera Theater, Chautauqua Opera, Triangle Opera Theater and the Lake George Opera Festival.

SEGUROLA, ANDRÉS DE   *American bass (1875–1953)*

Andrés de Segurola created the role of the artist Didier in Victor Herbert's opera MADELEINE at the Metropolitan Opera in 1914 though he is better known for creating the role of Jake in Puccini's *La Fanciulla del West* at the Met in 1910. Segurola, one of the great bass singers of his era, made his debut in Barcelona in 1895 and sang at the Met from 1902 until 1913. Later he had a Hollywood movie career and was Deanna Durbin's vocal coach.

THE SELFISH GIANT   *1981 opera by Hollingsworth*

A Giant chases off the children playing in his garden but after they leave, the flowers and birds vanish. When a little boy in white tries to climb a tree, the lonely giant lifts him up and the tree blossoms. The next day the children return and the garden is again a place of joy. Some time later the boy in white returns wounded. The Giant asks to go with him to his garden. The children find the Giant seemingly asleep. Stanley Hollingsworth's one-act opera *The Selfish Giant,* libretto by Herbert Moulton and the composer based on the fairy tale by Oscar Wilde, was premiered at the Spoleto Festival in Charleston, SC, on May 24, 1981, with Hollingsworth's other children's opera *Harrison Loved His Umbrella*.

SELLARS, JAMES   *American composer (1943–)*

James Sellars' first opera *The Family*, libretto by W. Giorda, was presented on the Educational Television network from Tulsa, Oklahoma, in 1963. *Chanson Dada*, libretto by the composer based on poems by Dada founder Tristan Tzara, is a one-person opera for soprano that was presented by the Brooklyn Philharmonic Orchestra in New York on April 26, 1985. *Beulah in Chicago*, libretto by the composer based on poems by Frank O'Hara and structured like a nightclub show, was premiered at the Art Institute of Albany in Albany, NY, on March 28, 1982. THE WORLD IS ROUND, libretto by Juanita Rockwell based on a 1939 children's book by Gertrude Stein, was premiered in Hartford in 1993. Sellars' major work is said to be the uncompleted *The Turing Opera* based on the life of mathematical genius Alan Turing. Sellars was born in Fort Smith, Arkansas, studied at Manhattan School, Southern Methodist and North Texas State and taught at the Hartt School of Music in Hartford.

SELLARS, PETER   *American opera director (1957–)*

Peter Sellars has collaborated with composer John Adams on four operas. The first was NIXON IN CHINA, which was conceived by Sellars who said he wanted to stage an opera that reflected the headlines of the day, This operatic treatment of President Nixon's visit to China, which became the first of the so-called "CNN operas," was premiered by Houston Grand Opera in 1987. Next was THE DEATH OF KLINGHOFFER, based around the 1985 hijacking of the cruise ship Achille Lauro by Palestinian terrorists and the murder of wheelchair passenger Leon Klinghoffer. It was premiered at the Théâtre de la Monnaie in Brussels in 1991. I WAS LOOKING AT THE CEILING AND THEN I SAW THE SKY, a moralist fable about people involved in a California earthquake, premiered at the Zellerbach Playhouse in Berkeley in 1995. The Nativity oratorio EL NIÑO had its premiere at the Theatre du Chatelet in Paris in 2000. Sellars also worked with Chinese American composer Tan Dun on PEONY PAVILION, a modern adaptation of a 16th century

Chinese Kunqu opera, which premiered at the Vienna Festival in 1998. Sellars, born in Pittsburgh, studied at Harvard and began his theatrical career in Cambridge in 1980.

SENDAK, MAURICE   *American designer/librettist (1928–)*

Maurice Sendak co-created two notable children's operas working in collaboration with English composer Oliver Knussen. WHERE THE WILD THINGS ARE, based on his 1963 book, had a preliminary presentation in Brussels in 1980 and achieved final form in 1984 when it was staged by Glyndebourne. HIGGLETY PIGGLETY POP!, based on his 1967 book, followed at Glyndebourne in 1984/1985. Sendak wrote the librettos for both operas and designed their wondrous sets and costumes. He has also created awe-inspiring sets for other operas, most notably for the 1982 Glyndebourne production of Serge Prokofiev's THE LOVE FOR THREE ORANGES. Frank Corsaro worked with him as director on all three productions. Sendak, born in New York City, started writing and illustrating children's books in 1956.

SERAFIN, TULLIO   *Italian conductor (1878–1968)*

Tullio Serafin, one of the most influential conductors of the modern era, conducted the premieres of four American operas at the Met: Deems Taylor's *The King's Henchman* in 1927, Taylor's *Peter Ibbetson* in 1931, Louis Gruenberg's *The Emperor Jones* in 1933 and Howard Hanson's Merry Mount in 1934. Serafin conducted at La Scala from 1908 to 1918 and at the Met from 1924 to 1934. He was associated with the careers of Rosa Ponselle, Maria Callas and Joan Sutherland.

THE SERENADE   *1897 comic opera by Herbert*

Dolores is loved by three men but it's the opera singer who finally wins her. Victor Herbert's comic opera *The Serenade*, libretto and lyrics by Harry B. Smith, was premiered by the Bostonians at the Colonial Theater in Cleveland on February 17, 1897, and opened in New York at the Knickerbocker Theater on March 16, 1997, with the composer conducting. Jesse Bartlett Davis starred as the much-loved Dolores who is wooed by her guardian (Henry Clay Barnabee), by a brigand (Eugene Cowles) and by a Madrid Opera baritone (W. H. MacDonald). Davis sings the popular "The Angelus" when she is locked in a convent by her guardian and watched over by Josephine Bartlett as the Mother Superior. Alice Nielsen, who played the Madrid ballet dancer Yvonne who also fancies the opera singer, won special praise for her performance of the syncopated number "Cupid and I."

1898 Jessie Bartlett Davis/W. H. Macdonald. Jessie Bartlett Davis and W. H. Macdonald, stars of the original production, sing the duet "Don Jose of Sevilla" on a Berliner recording made on March 5, 1898. It's on the anthology album *Music from the New York Stage, Volume One.* Pearl CD box. **1898 Barnabee/Frothingham/Fredricks.** Henry Clay Barnabee and George Frothingham of the original cast join Helena Fredricks in singing three verses of the trio "Dreaming, Dreaming" for Berliner records. It's on the anthology album *Music from the New York Stage, Volume One.* Pearl CD box. **1910 Victor Light Opera.** The Victor Light Opera Company perform a medley of songs from the operetta for a Victor 78 record. **1910 Columbia Light Opera.** The Columbia Light Opera Company performs a medley of songs from the operetta for a Columbia 78 record.

THE SERVANT OF TWO MASTERS   *1967 opera by Giannini*

Venetian servant Truffaldino attempts to serve two masters and collect pay from two sources. One is Beatrice masquerading as her brother Federigo so she can search for her lover Florindo who is actually Truffaldino's other master. Comedic errors abound with two sets of lovers and two impossible fathers. Vittorio Giannini's two-act opera *The Servant of Two Masters*, libretto by Bernard Stambler based on the play by Carlo Goldoni, was premiered by New York City Opera on March 9, 1967. Raymond Myers was Truffaldino, Eileen Schauler was Beatrice, Frank Porretta was Florindo, Patricia Brooks was Smeraldina, Michael Devlin was Pantalone, Donna Jeffrey was Clarissa, Charles Hindsley was Silvio, Nico Castel was Brighella and David Smith was Lombardi. Robert Fletcher designed the sets and costumes, Tito Capobianco directed and Julius Rudel conducted.

SERVICE, ROBERT   *Canadian poet/novelist (1874–1958)*

Robert Service is best known for his Yukon gold rush ballads, most famously *The Shooting of Dan McGrew* and *The Cremation of Sam Magee*, and at least one inspired an American opera. Alan Chapman's *The Lady That's Known as Lou*, libretto by Gordon Duffey about the heroine of *The Shooting of Dan McGrew*, was premiered, quite appropriately, in Douglas, Alaska, on November 12, 1985. Service, who left Scotland for Canada at the age of twenty, spent eight years in gold rush territory. His cabin in Yukon Territory is now a museum.

SESSIONS, ROGER   *American composer (1896–1985)*

Roger Sessions, who was twice awarded the Pulitzer Prize for Music, created influential operas with complex atonal scores based on the dramatic use of 12-note techniques. The one-act opera THE TRIAL OF LUCULLUS, an adaptation by the composer of a radio play by Bertolt Brecht, was premiered by the Drama Department of the University of California at Berkeley on April 18, 1947. MONTEZUMA, libretto by Giuseppe Borghese, was premiered in Berlin on April 19, 1964, and staged in Boston in 1976. Less known is his 42-minute Greek monodrama *Idyll of Theocritus*, composed in 1954. Sessions' last dramatic work was the 1971 cantata WHEN LILACS LAST IN THE DOORYARD BLOOMED, based on the poem by Walt Whitman; it is considered by many to be his greatest work. An opera titled *The Emperor's New Clothes*, libretto by Andrew Porter, was left uncompleted when he died. Sessions was born in Brooklyn and studied at Harvard and with composers Horatio Parker and Ernest Bloch. He lived in Europe from 1926 to 1933 and then taught at Princeton, Berkeley and Juilliard. One of the most important theorists of his era, his ideas have influenced many American opera composers, including John Harbison and Andrew Imbrie.

SEXTON, ANNE   *American poet (1928–1974)*

Anne Sexton, one of the most admired modern American poets, won a Pulitzer Prize in 1967 for *Live or Die.* Her 1971 book of poems *Transformations,* a reworking of Grimm fairy tales into feminist fables, provided the basis for an opera by Conrad Susa. TRANSFORMATIONS. which featured as narrator a character called Anne Sexton, was premiered at Minnesota Opera in 1973. Sexton, born in Newton, MA, was known for the confessional quality of her work but she could also be comic and sexy. She suffered recurring bouts of depression and took her own life in 1974.

SEYMOUR, JOHN LAURENCE   *American composer (1893–1986)*

John Laurence Seymour's opera IN THE PASHA'S GARDEN, libretto by Henry C. Tracy, was premiered at the Metropolitan

Opera on January 24, 1935, with Laurence Tibbett in the title role. Seymour, who composed fifteen operas and operettas over 57 years between 1920 and 1977, also had success with his opera *Ramona*, libretto by Tracy based on the novel by Helen Hunt Jackson, which premiered at Brigham Young University in Provo, Utah, on November 11, 1970. His other music theater works include *The Affected Maids* (1920), based on Molière's play *Les Précieuses Ridicules*; *Antigone* (1920), based on the play by Sophocles; *The Devil and Tom Walker* (1920), libretto by Tracy based on a Washington Irving story; and *Hollywood Madness* (1936), libretto by the composer. His last opera, *Ollanta, el Jefe Kolla*, was composed in 1977 to a libretto in Spanish by F. Diaz de Medina and won a prize in Bolivia. Seymour, a Los Angeles native, studied music in Italy and France with Ildebrando Pizzetti and others before returning to the U.S. to teach at the University of California in Berkeley and Sacramento Junior College.

SHADE, NANCY   *American soprano (1946–)*

Nancy Shade created the role of Susan in Andrew Imbrie's ANGLE OF REPOSE at San Francisco Opera in 1976, Barbara in Gian Carlo Menotti's THE HERO in Philadelpha in 1976, Eloise in Robert Ward's ABELARD AND HELOISE at Charlotte Opera in 1982 and Adah Menken in Bern Herbolsheimer's *Mark Me Twain* in Reno, Nevada, in 1993. She sang the Whore in the American premiere of Lowell Liebermann's THE PICTURE OF DORIAN GRAY in Milwaukee in 1999. She sings the title role in a live recording of a Kentucky Opera production of Carlisle Floyd's opera SUSANNAH in 1974 and Marie on an operatic recording of Frank Loesser's THE MOST HAPPY FELLOW in 2000. Shade, who was born in Rockford, Illinois, and studied at De Pauw and Indiana universities, made her debut at Kentucky Opera in 1969.

SHAKESPEARE OPERAS   *American operas based on Shakespeare plays*

William Shakespeare's plays have inspired many American opera and operetta composers. The best known operas are Samuel Barber's ANTONY AND CLEOPATRA, which opened the new Met in 1966, and John Eaton's THE TEMPEST, which premiered at Santa Fe Opera in 1985. Neither approaches the popularity of Leonard Bernstein's operatic musical WEST SIDE STORY, based loosely on *Romeo and Juliet*. The American composer with the greatest interest in Shakespeare was Mario Castelnuovo-Tedesco with two operas and seven overtures. American operas based on Shakespeare are listed below with further details in the opera or composer entry. Opera titles are the same as the play and libretto is by composer unless other indicated.

All's Well That Ends Well. 1958 Mario Castelnuovo-Tedesco, unperformed. 1979 S. Anderson, Los Angeles. 1987 David Winkler (composer and David Pfeiffer), Delle'Arte Players, New York, January 30, 1987. **Antony and Cleopatra.** 1947 Mario Castelnuovo-Tedesco, Overture only. 1961 Louis Gruenberg, unperformed. 1966 Samuel Barber (Franco Zeffirelli/Gian Carlo Menotti), Metropolitan Opera, NY, September 16, 1966. **As You Like It.** 1876 John Knowles Paine, Overture only. 1953 Mario Castelnuovo-Tedesco, Overture only. 1964 J. Balamos (D. Seitz and T. Seitz), Westport, Connecticut, 1964. **Coriolanus.** 1947 Mario Castelnuovo-Tedesco, Overture only. **Hamlet.** 1952 Edwin S. Lindsey, University of Chattanooga, Tennessee, 1952. 1962 Sergius Kagen, Baltimore, November 9, 1962. **Henry IV.** 1927 Porter Steele (James P Webber and Brian Hooker) as *Falstaff*, New York, December 25, 1927. 1995 Gordon Getty as *Plump Jack*, New York, December 31, 1985. **Henry V.** 1964 Eugene Misterly, Highland

Park Symphony, Los Angeles, 1969. **Julius Caesar.** 1970 Alan Schmitz, Rutgers University, New Brunswick, NJ, April 7, 1978. **King John.** 1941 Mario Castelnuovo-Tedesco, Overture only. **King Lear.** 1976 Russell Smith (Smith), unperformed. **Love's Labour's Lost.** 1953 Mario Castelnuovo-Tedesco, Four Dances. 1973 Nicolas Nabokov (W. H. Auden and Chester Kallman), La Monnaie, Brussels, February 7, 1973. **Macbeth.** 1965 Sidney Halpern, Off-Broadway Opera, New York, April 4, 1965. **Measure for Measure.** 1973 John Laurence Seymour, unperformed. **The Merchant of Venice.** 1956 Mario Castelnuovo-Tedesco, Teatro Communale, Florence, May 25, 1961. **The Merry Wives of Windsor.** 1982 Alan Rea (William Monson) as *Falstaff In and Out of Love*, Fresno, CA. **A Midsummer Night's Dream.** 1940 Mario Castelnuovo-Tedesco, Overture only. 1965 Neely Bruce as *Pyramus and Thisbe*, Alabama University, Tuscaloosa. 1976 Elie Siegmeister (Edward Mabley), as *Night of the Moonspell*, Shreveport, LA. 1972 Robert Convey as *Quince's Dream*, Waterford, CT, 1982. 1982 Robert Convey as *Pyramus and Thisbee*, Glens Falls, NY. 1987 Max Roach (George Ferencz), San Diego Repertory Theater, CA, September 1987. **Much Ado About Nothing.** 1953 Mario Castelnuovo-Tedesco, Overture only. **Otello.** 1919 Henry Hadley, Overture only. **Pericles.** 1983 R. Leslee (Leslee and S. Elkin) as *Americles*, Buffalo, New York. **Richard III.** 1980 Paul Turok, Philadelphia, April 28, 1980. **Romeo and Juliet.** 1901 Harry Roe Shelley, unperformed. 1915 Conrad Schaefer, unperformed. 1957 Leonard Bernstein (Arthur Laurents/Stephen Sondheim), as *West Side Story*, Winter Garden Theater, NY, Sept 26, 1957. 1984 W. E. Black as *Romeo and Juliet: New Wave*, New York City. 2001 Lee Hoiby (Mark Shulgasser), in progress. **The Taming of the Shrew.** 1939 H. Biggs (J. Staton and H. Moore), as *Shrew*, Seattle. 1948 P. G. Clapp, unperformed. 1954 Howard Groth as *Petruchio*, Conway, Arkansas, March 19, 1954. 1954 Victor Giannini (Dorothy Fee and composer), NBC TV, March 13, 1954. 1963 Dominick Argento (John Manlove) as *Christopher Sly*, University of Minnesota, Minneapolis, May 31, 1963. 1977 Richard A. Barbie as *Good King Hal*, Bismarck, ND, 1977. 1982 R. Leslee (S. Elkin and composer), Buffalo, NY. **The Tempest.** 1916 Arthur Farwell (Percy MacKaye), as *Caliban by the Yellow Sands*, New York, May 1916. 1970 Douglas Post, San Antonio, Texas, 1970. 1973 Alva Henderson, unperformed. 1974 Russell Smith, unperformed. 1984 Peter Westergaard, Princeton, June 29, 1984. 1984 J. Petosa, Washington, DC, 1984. 1986 John Eaton (Andrew Porter), Santa Fe Opera, July 27, 1985. 1985 Lee Hoiby (Mark Shulgasser), Des Moines Metro Opera, Indianola, June 21, 1986. **Timon of Athens.** 1971 Jonathan Tunick, New York, 1971. **Twelfth Night.** 1957 C. F. Swier (B Bruestle), Tulsa, OK, 1957. 1968 David Amram (Joseph Papp), Lake George Opera Festival, Glen Falls, NY, July 20, 1968. **The Two Gentlemen of Verona.** 1937 John Laurence Seymour (Henry Chester Tracy), unperformed. 1987 C. Frezza, Pittsburgh, 1987. **The Winter's Tale.** 1979 John Harbison, San Francisco Opera, August 20, 1979. 1979 David Douglas (Dana Axelrod/Kelli James), New Burbank Theatre Guild, Burbank, CA, December 7, 1984. **Various.** 1989 Robert Waldman (Edward West), *The Play's the Thing/Shakespeare: or, What You Will*, Theatreworks/USA, NY, January 1989.

SHANEWIS   *1918 opera by Cadman*

Native American singer Shanewis is educated by the rich matron Mrs. Everton and makes her debut at Everton's California home. She becomes involved with a white man named Lionel and invites him to meet her people in Oklahoma Indian Territory. When she finds he is already engaged to Everton's daughter, she feels betrayed and rejects him. He is killed by her tribal brother. Charles

Wakefield Cadman's one-act opera *Shanewis*, libretto by Nelle Richmond Eberhart based on the life of Cherokee/Creek Indian Tsianina Redfeather Blackstone, was premiered at the Metropolitan Opera on March 12, 1918, in a triple bill as *The Robin Woman: Shanewis*. Sophie Braslau sang the role of Shanewis, Paul Althouse was Lionel, Thomas Chalmers was Philip, Kathleen Howard was Mrs. Everton and Marie Sundelius was Amy. Roberto Moranzoni conducted. The opera was reprised by the Met the following year, the first American opera to survive there for more than one season, and was performed eight more times. It was reprised by the American Grand Opera Company in Chicago on November 9, 1922, and presented there again in 1923 and 1924. It was staged in Denver on December 5 and 6, 1924, with Cadman conducting and Tsianina Redfeather making her operatic debut singing the role written about her; she reprised the role in Los Angeles on June 24, 1926. The vocal score was published with the title *The Robin Woman (Shanewis)*. In recent years it has been staged by Opera in the Ozarks, the summer festival at Inspiration Point Fine Arts Colony in Eureka Springs.

1925 Elsie Baker. Contralto Elsie Baker recorded two arias from *Shanewis* for Victor in 1925. "Once on a Time" (Spring Song of the Robin Woman) and "Out on the Lake" (Ojibway Canoe Song) are on the album *Souvenirs from American Opera*. IRRC CD. **1928 NBC National Grand Opera Company.** *Shanewis* was one of the first American operas to be presented on radio. It was broadcast by NBC's National Grand Opera Company on May 9, 1928, with Cesare Sudaro conducting the orchestra. It was so popular so it was repeated on January 7, 1929.

SHAPIRO, KARL   *American poet/librettist (1913–2000)*

Karl Shapiro wrote the libretto for Hugo Weisgall's opera THE TENOR based on a play by Frank Wedekind. It premiered in Baltimore in 1955 but was not well received so he wrote no more librettos. Shapiro, who was born in Baltimore, won a Pulitzer Prize for a book of his poems in 1945.

SHATIN, JUDITH   *American composer (1949–)*

Judith Shatin's Appalachian-style folk opera COAL, libretto by the composer based on West Virginia coal mining songs and sounds, was premiered at Shepherd College in Shepherdstown, WV, on November 12, 1995. Shatin's first opera was *Follies and Fancies*, libretto by the composer and Gloria Russo based on Molière's *Les Précieuses ridicules,* which premiered at Charlottesville, VA, August 14, 1981. (The Molière play also provided the basis for a 1920 opera by John Laurence Seymour). In 1983 Shatin composed the opera-oratorio *Job* for ten singers and piano. Her one-act opera *Carreño,* about Therese Carreño, was premiered by Golden Fleece in New York in June 1990. Shatin, who was born in Brookline, MA, studied at Princeton and Juilliard before becoming a music professor at the University of Virginia.

LOW VOICE   HIGH VOICE

Produced with Eminent Success at the Metropolitan Opera House, 1918.

SPRING SONG
OF THE
ROBIN WOMAN

RECITATIVE AND SONG

From the American Opera

"SHANEWIS"
[*The Robin Woman*]

BY

NELLE RICHMOND EBERHART

AND

CHARLES WAKEFIELD CADMAN

Price 75 cents

WHITE-SMITH MUSIC PUBLISHING CO.
BOSTON   NEW YORK   CHICAGO

TSIANINA, "SHANEWIS"

Charles Wakefield Cadman's opera *Shanewis* was presented at the Met in 1918.

SHAW, ROBERT   *American chorus leader/conductor (1916–1999)*

Robert Shaw, creator of the famous Robert Shaw Chorale, conducted the Atlanta Symphony Orchestra in the first modern performance of Scott Joplin's TREEMONISHA at Morehouse College in Atlanta on January 28, 1972. He conducted the Carmen Jones Chorus in the Broadway production of the Hammerstein/Bizet opera CARMEN JONES in 1943 and his chorus is featured on the cast album. In a similar way he provided the choral music for the Friedman/Verdi MY DARLIN' AIDA on Broadway in 1952. He conducts the Robert Shaw Chorale in support of Met soprano Risë Stevens on her recording of the PORGY AND BESS aria "My Man's Gone Now" in 1950. He conducts the Robert Shaw Chorale, Orchestra and soloists in performances of songs from eight Victor Herbert operettas on the 1961 album *The Immortal Victor Herbert*.

SHE LOVES ME   *1963 musical by Bock*

Budapest in 1934. Amalia and Georg, who work together in a

perfume shop and don't get on, have formed relationship with anonymous penpals; they don't realize they are writing to each other. Also involved are Ilona, Steven and shop owner Mr. Maracek. Jerry Bock's delightful *She Loves Me*, lyrics by Sheldon Harnick and libretto by Joe Masteroff based on an Hungarian play by Miklos Laszlo, premiered at the Eugene O'Neill Theater on Broadway on April 23, 1963. Barbara Cook was Amalia Balash, Daniel Massey was Georg Nowack, Barbara Baxley was Ilona Ritter, Jack Cassidy was caddish Steven Kodaly, Ralph Williams was Arpad Laszlo, Nathaniel Frey was Ladislav Sipos and Ludwig Donath was Mr. Maracek. William and Jean Ekart designed the sets, Harold Prince directed and Harold Hastings was the music director. *She Loves Me* was revived on Broadway in 1993 and there are cast albums of both productions. It has become quite popular with regional opera houses and has been staged by Chautauqua Opera, Lyric Opera Cleveland and Sarasota Opera The source play has been filmed three times. Ernst Lubitsch was first with *The Shop Around the Corner* in 1940 starring James Stewart and Margaret Sullavan. It was then turned into a semi-musical in 1949 for Judy Garland and Van Johnson and filmed as *In the Good Old Summertime*. Finally it was updated to the e-mail era in 2000 as *You've Got Mail* with Tom Hanks and Meg Ryan.

1963 Broadway Cast. Barbara Cook stars as Amalia in this famous original cast album. Daniel Massey is Georg, Barbara Baxley is Ilona, Jack Cassidy is Kodaly, Ralph Williams as Arpad Laszlo and Ludwig Donath is Mr. Maracek. Harold Hastings conducts. Decca 2-LP set and CD. **1964 London Cast.** Anne Rogers stars opposite Gary Raymond in the 1964 London production of the musical with a supporting cast that includes Rita Morena, Gary Miller, Peter Sallis, and Gregory Phillips. HMV LP/Angel CD. **1993 Broadway Cast.** Diane Fratantoni plays Amalia opposite Boyd Gaines as Georg in the 1993 revival of the musical directed by Scott Ellis. Sally Mayes is Ilona and Howard McGillin is Kodaly. Varese CD. **1994 London Cast.** Ruthie Hensall is Amalia opposite John Gordon in the much-acclaimed 1994 London production of the musical. Tracie Bennett is Ilona, Barry James is Ladislav and Gerard Casey is Steven Gary . First Night Records CD.

SHEFFER, JONATHAN *American composer (1959–)*

Jonathan Sheffer's chamber opera BLOOD ON THE DINING ROOM FLOOR, libretto by the composer based on Gertrude Stein's surrealistic murder mystery premiered in New York in April 2000 and was much liked by critics. Sheffer, the founder and conductor of the Eos Ensemble, is known for his programs of new American music but he has also composed three unusual works of music theater. The first was *Camera Obscura*, libretto by Robert Patrick, a 10-minute opera premiered in Waterford, Connecticut, on July 18, 1980. *The Mistake*, libretto by Stephen Wadsworth focussing on a soprano during the intermission of a concert, was premiered by Central City Opera in Denver on August 16, 1981.

SHENG, BRIGHT *Chinese-born American composer (1955–)*

Bright Sheng had a major success with his first opera THE SONG OF MAJNUN, libretto by Andrew Porter, which was commissioned by Lyric Opera of Chicago and premiered on April 9, 1992. It was reprised in 1995 by the Houston Opera Studio which recorded it. His next opera was the multi-cultural THE SILVER RIVER, libretto by David Henry Hwang based on a Chinese folk tale about the love between a goddess and a cowherd. It premiered at the Santa Fe Chamber Music Festival in July 1997 and was presented at Spoleto Festival USA in May 2000 and Philadelphia in April 2001.

MADAME MAO, libretto by Colin Graham, was premiered at Santa Fe Opera in the summer of 2003. Sheng was born in Shanghai, studied at the Shanghai Conservatory of Music and moved to New York in 1992 to study at Columbia and Queens College. His music has been well received around the world and he has served as composer-in-residence at several institutions.

THE SHEPHARDES PLAYE *1967 Christmas pageant-opera by La Montaine*

Shepherds watch over their flock in the fields on the night of Christ's birth. A lamb is stolen and hidden in a baby cradle. John La Montaine's 60-minute Christmas pageant-opera *The Shephardes Playe*, libretto by the composer based on the medieval English *Second Shepherd's Play*, was premiered on December 24, 1967, at the National Cathedral in Washington, D.C. Robert Trehy was Henkin, Lee Cass was Harvye, David Lloyd was Tudd, Rick Hanson was Trowle, William Brown was the Angel and Mary Ann Brown was May. Robert Delaney directed and Paul Callway conducted. *The Shephardes Playe* was videotaped during its presentation at the National Cathedral and telecast by ABC on December 22, 1968.

SHERMAN, KIM *American composer (1954–)*

Kim D. Sherman has composed five operas since 1983 and four were staged in Minneapolis. *Lenny and the Heartbreakers*, libretto by the composer and Kenneth Robins, was presented at the New York Shakespeare Festival on December 22, 1983. *Femme Fatale*, libretto by Lara Farabough about Greta Garbo and Mata Hari, was staged by Minnesota Opera in Minneapolis on April 11, 1986. *A Long Island Dreamer*, libretto by Paul Selig about a singer trying to record a hit song, was presented by Minnesota Opera in St. Paul on April 9, 1987. *Red Tide*, libretto by Paul Selig about a teenager desperately waiting for a lifeguard, was premiered by Minnesota Opera in Minneapolis on March 23, 1989. *Three Visitations*, staged by the New Music-Theatre Ensemble at the Southern Theater in Minneapolis in June 1996, is a trilogy consisting of three short operas by Sherman and librettist Paul Selig. It combines the earlier *Red Tide* and *A Long Island Dreamer* with a new opera called *Lamentations* about a boy whose father has died, perhaps murdered by his mother. Sherman was born in Elgin, Illinois.

SHICOFF, NEIL *American tenor (1949–)*

Neil Shicoff created the role of poet James Thomson in Virgil Thomson's LORD BYRON at the Juilliard American Opera Center in 1972 while he was a student at the Juilliard School. Shicoff, a native New Yorker, made his Metropolitan Opera debut in 1976 and began to sing at Covent Garden in 1978.

SHIELDS, ALICE *American composer (1943–)*

Alice Shields has composed and written nine operas/music dramas and was one of the first American composers to create electronic operas. The best known is APOCALYPSE, AN ELECTRONIC OPERA (1990) which followed earlier smaller experimental music theater works and vocal experimentation. *Odyssey II* was performed at the Lake George Opera Festival in 1970 and *Odyssey III*, for male soloists, male chorus and orchestra, was completed in 1975. *Shaman*, a full-length electronic opera created in 1978 for singers, tape and amplified chamber orchestra, was premiered by American Chamber Opera in New York in May 1987. The one-act chamber opera *Wraecca*, libretto by the composer based on Anglo-Saxon poems, was premiered by Golden Fleece in New York on June 27, 1989. The electronic opera *Mass for the Dead* was premiered by

American Chamber Opera Company in New York in 1993. Shields recorded a number of vocal electronic pieces at the Columbia-Princeton Electronic Music Center in the 1970s and two are on CD: *Study for Voice and Tape* and *The Transformation of Ani for Electronically Altered Voice*, based on the Egyptian *Book of the Dead*. Shields is also a trained mezzo-soprano and has sung in traditional operas with New York City Opera and Washington Opera. She used her own voice to create electronic music on tape for a 1996 performance of Robert Ward's opera THE CRUCIBLE at the Lake George Opera Festival when she was a composer apprentice.

SHILKRET, NATHANIEL   *American conductor/composer (1895–1982)*

Nathaniel (Nat) Shilkret made an important contribution to American operetta through his broadcasts and recordings. He was music director for Victor for twenty years and organized the Victor Salon Orchestra. He made thousands of broadcasts and his orchestra accompanied performers from Lawrence Tibbett and Rise Stevens to Nelson Eddy and Jeanette MacDonald. His recordings include highlight versions of Rudolf Friml's KATINKA (1929); Victor Herbert's BABES IN TOYLAND (1938), EILEEN (1931), NAUGHTY MARIETTA (1935 and 1939) and PRINCESS PAT (1931); Jerome Kern's MUSIC IN THE AIR (1932) and Sigmund Romberg's MAYTIME (1935 and 1936) and MY MARYLAND (1945). Shilkret, born in New York, played clarinet at the Metropolitan Opera in his early years. He wrote scores for a number of films after moving to Hollywood in 1935, including John Ford's *Mary of Scotland* (1936). In 1947 he commissioned the Biblical cantata *Genesis* from, among others, opera composers Igor Stravinsky, Arnold Schoenberg and Mario Castelnuovo-Tedesco.

Conductor/composer Nathaniel Shilkret

SHINING BROW   *1992 opera by Hagen*

Architect Frank Lloyd Wright's leads a controversial life from 1903 to 1914. He causes a scandal by eloping with client's wife Mamah Cheney, is vilified when his own wife Catherine refuses a divorce, breaks with his mentor Louis Sullivan and builds his monumental home Taliesin (Welsh for Shining Brow). Mamah Cheney is killed by a madman and Taliesen burns down but Wright rebuilds it. Daron Hagen's two-act opera *Shining Brow*, libretto by Paul Muldoon, was premiered by Madison Opera on April 21, 1993. Michael Sokol sang the role of Wright, Carolann Page was

Mamah, Barry Busse was Louis Sullivan, Kitt Reuter Foss was Catherine Wright and Bradley Garvin was Edwin Cheney. Stephen Wadsworth staged the opera, David Birn designed the sets and Roland Johnson conducted the orchestra. It was revived in an acclaimed production by Ken Cazan for Chicago Opera Theater in 1997 with Robert Orth as Wright and Brenda Harris as Mamah and Lawrence Rapchak conducting. *Chicago Tribune* critic John von Rhein described *Shining Brow* as "one of the most important American operas of the past decade." A studio recording of the complete opera is planned.

2000 Paul Kreider. Baritone Paul Kreider sings Frank Lloyd Wright's "Arietta" from *Shining Brow* accompanied by Daron Hagen on piano. It's on the album *Love in a Life*. ARSIS CD.

SHIRLEY, GEORGE   *American tenor (1934–)*

George Shirley created the role of Romilayu, Henderson's African guide, in Leon Kirchner's LILY in the 1997 New York City Opera production. Shirley, who was born in Indianapolis, studied in Washington and New York and made his debut at Woodstock in 1959. He was the first African American tenor to have a major Met career with thirty roles in twelve seasons, starting in 1961. He became director the University of Michigan's Vocal Arts Division in 1987 but continued to sing; he was Sportin' Life in *Porgy and Bess* at the Bregenz Festival in 1999 and Kaspar in a production of *Amahl and the Night Visitors*.

THE SHOEMAKER'S HOLIDAY   *1967 opera by Argento*

Simon tells the story of the young lovers Rose and Roland in 17th century London; they are separated by relatives but reunited when he returns disguised as a shoemaker. Dominick Argento's opera *The Shoemaker's Holiday*, libretto by John Olon-Scrymgeour based on the play by Thomas Dekker, was premiered by Minnesota Opera on June 1, 1967. Helen Carey was Rose, Michael Moriarty was Roland Lacy, Douglas Campbell was Simon Eyre, Nick Savian was Sir Hugh Lacy, Len Cariou was Ralph, Paul Ballantyne was Sir Roger Oteley, Patricia Elliott was Sybil, Earl Boen was Warner and Grace Keagey was Margery. Dahl Delu designed the sets and costumes, Douglas Campbell and John Olon staged the production and Herbert Pilholfer conducted the orchestra.

SHOW BOAT   *1927 operatic musical by Kern*

The traveling show people who live on a turn-of-the-century Mississippi river boat experience love, loss, troubles, tribulation and reconciliation. Magnolia, daughter of showboat owner, falls in love with gambler Gaylord Ravenal and marries him but their marriage runs into difficulties. Singer Julie La Verne has to leave the boat with her white husband when her mulatto origins are revealed. Stevedore Joe tells the world what it means to be a poor black man in Mississippi through the aria "OL' MAN RIVER." Jerome Kern's *Show Boat*, libretto by Oscar Hammerstein II based on the Edna Ferber novel, premiered at the National Theater in Washington, D. C., on November 25, 1927, and opened at the Ziegfeld Theatre in New York on December 17, 1927. Norma Terris was Magnolia, Howard Marsh was Gaylord, Helen Morgan was Julie, Jules Bledsoe was Joe, Charles Winninger was Cap'n Andy, Edna May Oliver was his wife Parthy Ann, Tess Gardella was Queenie and Sammy White and Eva Puck played the singing-dancing partners Frank and Ellie. Joseph Urban designed the sets, Sammy Lee arranged the choreography, Victor Baravalle conducted the orchestra and Hammerstein staged the production with Zeke Colvan. *Show Boat* has now entered the opera repertory. New York City Opera staged it in 1954 with Robert Rounseville as Ravenal and

Laurel Hurley as Magnolia, and Houston Grand Opera mounted a notable production in 1983. An impressive recording was made by opera singers Frederica von Stade, Teresa Stratas and Jerry Hadley in 1988. *Show Boat* has been filmed four times and there are countless audio recordings; the principal ones are listed below. Miles Kreuger's book *Show Boat: The Story of a Classic American Musical* is the definitive study while Will Friedwald's *Stardust Melodies* contains a fascinating history of the aria "Ol' Man River."

1927 Original Broadway cast. Three members of the original Broadway cast made recordings of songs from the show which are on various CD and LP albums. Helen Morgan recorded "Bill" and "Can't Help Lovin' Dat Man," Jules Bledsoe recorded "Ol' Man River" in London 1931 (plus two non-Gershwin songs from the 1929 film) and Tess Gardella, who played Queenie, recorded "Can't Help Lovin' Dat Man."

1928 Original London cast. Paul Robeson played Joe in the 1928 London production at Drury Lane of *Show Boat* and took part in an early original cast album singing a magnificent "Ol' Man River." Edith Day sings Magnolia, Howett Worster is Ravenal and Marie Burke is Julie. Herman Finck conducts the Drury Lane Orchestra. Pearl CD/World Record Club LP.

1928–1933 Paul Robeson. Paul Robeson, the original choice to sing the role of Joe, is often identified with the basso aria "Ol' Man River"; he recorded it three times in 1928 and 1930 and sang it as Joe on the London stage and in the 1936 film. These 78 recordings, re-issued on various LPs and CDs, were made with the Paul Whiteman Orchestra in 1928, with the Drury Lane Orchestra in London led by Herman Finck in 1928, and with Ray Noble and his Orchestra in 1930. **1929 Universal film.** Laura La Plante is Magnolia, Joseph Schildkraut is Ravenal, Alma Rubens is Julie and Stepin Fetchit is Joe in the silent film of *Show Boat*. It was based on the novel rather than the musical but the success of the Kern musical led to Universal acquiring rights to the songs. An 18-minute sound prologue was added featuring five songs by members of the New York stage cast, including Jules Bledsoe (Joe) and Helen Morgan (Julie). Harry Pollard directed the movie and wrote the screenplay with Tom Reed and Charles Kenyon. The film was not seen for many years but has now been restored and is available on laserdisc and DVD but without the sound prologue. **1932 Broadway cast.** Paul Robeson and Helen Morgan of the cast of Florenz Ziegfeld's 1932 Broadway revival production are joined by non-cast singers, including James Melton and Olga Albani, in what was called an original cast album. It was made in a New York studio with Victor Young conducting the Brunswick studio orchestra. Originally a 78 album with eight 12" records, it has been re-issued on CD. Pearl Records 2-CD box. **1932 Lawrence Tibbett.** Lawrence Tibbett made a personal recording of "Ol' Man River" for Victor in December 1932. It is on the album *A Tribute to Tibbett.* OASI LP. **1936 Universal film.** Universal's second film of the musical was a vast improvement over the first. Oscar Hammerstein II wrote the screenplay himself and James Whale directed a first-class cast with great sensitivity. Paul Robeson, who had been the original choice as Joe for the American stage version and had played the role in London. was now seen and heard by American

Paul Robeson as Joe in the 1936 film of *Show Boat*.

audiences. Irene Dunne is Magnolia, Allan Jones is Gaylord, Helen Morgan is Julie, Charles Winninger is Cap'n. Andy, Helen Westley is Parthy, Sammy White is Frank and Hattie McDaniel is Queenie. Victor Baravalle of the original stage production conducts the orchestra. Many consider this the best film version. Soundtrack on LP and CD, film on VHS, DVD and LD. **1940 Universal film cast.** Three cast members from the 1936 Universal film participated in a highlights version broadcast on radio in 1940. Irene Dunne sings Magnolia, Allan Jones is Gaylord and Charles Winninger is Capt. Andy. Louis Silvers conducts the orchestra. Sunbeam Records LP. **1946 Till the Clouds Roll By.** *Till the Clouds Roll By,* MGM's romanticized biography of Jerome Kern, contains a staged highlights version of *Show Boat*. Kathryn Grayson is Magnolia, Tony Martin is Ravenal, Lena Horne is Julie and Caleb Peterson is Joe. Frank Sinatra sings "Ol' Man River" in a resplendent white tuxedo, Lena Horne sings "Can't Help Loving That Man," Virginia O'Brien sings "Life Upon the Wicked Stage" and Kathryn Grayson and Tony Martin duet on "Make Believe." Richard Whorf and Vincente Minnelli directed. MGM DVD/VHS/LD. **1947 Paul Robeson.** Paul Robeson had recorded "Ol' Man River" six times when he recorded it again in November 1947 with "I Still Suits Me." Emanuel Balaban conducts the Columbia Concert Orchestra. It's on the album *Songs of Free Men.* Sony CD. **1949 Dorothy Kirsten/Robert Merrill.** Dorothy Kirsten and Robert Merrill sing highlights from the musical in 1949 with John Scott Trotter conducting the orchestra. RCA Victor LP. **1951 MGM film.** Opera bass William Warfield, known for singing Porgy on stage, portrays Joe in this MGM color film directed by George Sidney and written by John Lee Mahin. Kathryn Grayson is Magnolia, Howard Keel is Ravenal, Ava Gardner is Julie (singing by Annette Warren), Joe E. Brown is Capt. Andy, Agnes Moorehead is Parthy and Marge and Gower Champion are the singing-dancing duo Frank and Elly. Adolf Deutsch conducts the MGM

Studio Orchestra. Soundtrack is on MGM LP/Rhino CD; film is MGM DVD/VHS/LD. **1953 George London/Nadine Conner.** Met regulars George London and Nadine Conner sing "Make Believe" on the *Voice of Firestone* TV program on December 28, 1953, accompanied by Howard Barlow and the Firestone Orchestra. *George London in Opera and Song.* VAI VHS. **1955 Lawrence Tibbett.** Lawrence Tibbett sings "Ol' Man River" on a studio recording made in 1955. Allegro-Royale LP. **1962 Patrice Munsel/Robert Merrill/Risë Stevens.** Patrice Munsel is Magnolia, Robert Merrill is Ravenal and Joe and Risë Stevens is Julie in this operatic recording made with orchestra and chorus conducted by Lehman Engel. Supporting are Katherine Graves, Janet Pavek and Kevin Scott. RCA Victor LP. **1962 Anna Moffo/Rosalind Elias.** Anna Moffo as Julie and Rosalind Elias as Queenie dominate this operatic highlights recording with the orchestra and chorus led by Lehman Engel. Mary Ellen Pracht is Magnolia, Richard Fredricks is Ravenal and Valentine Pringle is Joe. Henri Rene created the arrangements for The Reader's Digest *Treasury of Great Operettas.* RCA LP box set. **1962 Barbara Cook/John Raitt/William Warfield.** Barbara Cook is Magnolia, John Raitt is Gaylord, William Warfield is Joe, and Anita Darian is Julie on this studio recording. Franz Allers conducts. The CD also includes early recordings by Helen Morgan and Tess Gardella (the original Julie and Queenie), Paul Robeson and Jan Clayton. Sony Classics CD. **1966 Lincoln Center.** Barbara Cook is Magnolia with William Warfield as Joe in this cast recording of a 1966 Lincoln Center production. The other singers are Constance Towers, Stephen Douglass, David Wayne, Rosetta LeNoire Allyn McLerie and Eddie Phillips. Franz Allers conducts. BMG/RCA Victor LP/CD. **1967 Joan Sutherland.** Joan Sutherland sings "Make Believe" on the album *The Golden Age of Operetta* with Richard Bonynge conducting the New Philharmonia Orchestra. Decca/London LP. **1972 London revival.** Cleo Laine stars as Julie with Lorna Dallas as Magnolia and André Jobin as Ravenal in this cast recording of a 1971 London production directed by Wendy Toye. Thomas Carey is Joe, Ena Cabayo is Queenie, Jan Hunt is Ellie and Kenneth Nelson is Frank. Ray Cook conducts the orchestra. Stanyan LP/Laserlight CD. **1976 Collector's Show Boat.** This is an anthology album of operatic recordings from *Show Boat.* Robert Merrill sings "Till Good Luck Comes My Way"; Patrice Munsel sings "After the Ball," Merrill and Munsel duet on "Make Believe," "Where's the Mate for Me?" and "You Are Love"; Risë Stevens sings "Dance Away the Night"; Dorothy Kirsten joins Robert Merrill on "Why Do I Love You?" and Paul Robeson sings "Ol' Man River." Victrola America RCA LP. **1987 John McGlinn.** John McGlinn conducts the Ambrosian Chorus and London Sinfonietta in the first complete recording using the original 1927 Robert Russell Bennett orchestrations. Frederica von Stade is Magnolia, Jerry Hadley is Ravenal, Teresa Stratas is Julie, Bruce Hubbard is Joe, Karla Burns is Queenie, David Garrison is Frank, Paige O'Hara is Ellie, Robert Nichols is Cap'n Andy and Nancy Kulp is Parthy. EMI 3-CD box. **1992 John Owen Edwards.** John Owen Edwards conducts this London studio recording with Willard White as Joe, Sally Burgess, Jason Howard, Janis Kelly, Caroline O'Connor, Gareth Snook, Simon Green, Brian Greene, Shezwae Powell, Fran Landesman and James Buller. Jay CD. **1993 Toronto revival.** Rebecca Luker is Magnolia, Mark Jacoby is Ravenal and Lonette McKee is Julie in this cast recording of the 1993 Toronto revival cast; it was directed by Hal Prince and transferred to Broadway in 1994. Michel Bell is Joe, Gretha Boston is Queenie, Joel Blum is Frank, Dorothy Stanley is Ellie, Robert Morse is Cap'n Andy and Elaine Stritch is Parthy. Jeffrey Huard conducts. Quality Records CD.

SIEGMEISTER, ELIE *American composer (1909–1991)*

Elie Siegmeister had a multi-faceted career promoting American folk music and composing operas and musicals for over forty years including works based on Sean O'Casey, Bernard Malamud and Shakespeare. He founded the American Ballad Singers group in 1939 and introduced Broadway to folk music with the 1944 *Sing Out Sweet Land,* an anthology of American folk songs put together by Siegmeister and librettist Walter Kerr and sung by Burl Ives and Alfred Drake. The one-act *Darling Corie,* libretto by Lewis Allen based on the folk ballad, was staged at Hofstra University in Hempstead, NY, in 1954. The one-act comedy *Miranda and the Dark Young Man,* libretto by Edward Eager about a trap to catch a suitor, was staged in Hartford in 1956. Siegmeister then began a fruitful collaboration with Edward Mabley, who wrote the librettos for nearly all his later operas. The first was the one-act fantasy *The Mermaid in Lock 7,* about a mermaid who entices her lover into the water where he drowns; it premiered at Point State Park in Pittsburgh on July 20, 1958. THE PLOUGH AND THE STARS, based on Sean O'Casey's play, was first staged as *Dublin Song* in 1963. and then revised and retitled for presentation at Louisiana State University in 1969. NIGHT OF THE MOONSPELL based on Shakespeare's *A Midsummer Night's Dream* was premiered in Shreveport, LA, in 1976. Siegmeister's last two operas were ANGEL LEVINE and *The Lady of the Lake,* one-act operas based on stories by Bernard Malamud with librettos by Mabley; they were premiered by Jewish Opera at the Y in New York in 1985. Siegmeister, a native New Yorker, studied composition at Columbia and with Nadia Boulanger. His music sounds "American" even when dissonantly modern and all his operas are singer friendly.

SIGNORE DELUSO *1974 opera by Pasatieri*

Spouses and lovers suspect their partners of being unfaithful as a picture locket causes multiple confusions. Thomas Pasatieri's one-act opera buffa *Signore Deluso,* libretto by the composer based on Molière's *Sganarelle,* was premiered by the Wolf Trap Company in Virginia on July 27, 1974. Judith Christin was Rosine, Raeder Anderson was Signore Deluso, Alise Veloze was Celie, Stanley Wexler was Gorgibus, Linda Lane Smith was Clara, Modesto Criser was Leon and J. Scott Brumit was the Magistrate. Holly Cole designed the set, David Bartholomen directed and John Moriarty conducted. The opera was reprised by Opera in the Ozarks, the summer festival at Inspiration Point Fine Arts Colony in Eureka Springs, Arkansas.

SILLS, BEVERLY *American soprano (1929–)*

Beverly Sills became famous singing Baby Doe in the New York City Opera production of Douglas Moore's THE BALLAD OF BABY DOE in 1958 and classic recording. She did not create this role but she did create the role of the Coloratura in Hugo Weisgall's SIX CHARACTER IN SEARCH OF AN AUTHOR at NYCO in 1959 and the Spanish Queen Juana the Mad in Gian Carlo Menotti's LA LOCA at San Diego Opera in 1979. She won a Grammy for her 1975 album *Music of Victor Herbert* made with André Kostelanetz; on it she sings arias from the operettas EILEEN, THE ENCHANTRESS, THE FORTUNE TELLER, MLLE. MODISTE, NAUGHTY MARIETTA, THE ONLY GIRL, ORANGE BLOSSOMS and THE RED MILL. She followed it in 1978 with an album of operetta duets with Sherrill Milnes titled *Up in Central Park.* On stage she has sung the role of Marigold in Howard Hanson's MERRY MOUNT in San Antonio in 1964 and Milly Theale in Douglas Moore's THE WINGS OF THE DOVE at NYCO. Sills, born Belle Miriam Silverman in Brooklyn, made her debut in 1947 with the Philadelphia Civic Opera. She joined NYCO in 1955 and quickly became its prima donna, nick-named "Bubbles." She was general director of NYCO from 1979 to 1989 and then became head of the whole Lincoln Center arts complex.

"THE SILVER ARIA" *Soprano aria: The Ballad of Baby Doe (1956). Words: John Latouche. Music: Douglas Moore.*

Baby Doe Tabor speaks out in defense of silver at her wedding reception in the Willard Hotel in Washington, D.C. in Douglas Moore's THE BALLAD OF BABY DOE. She is there with silver millionaire husband Horace, who has been appointed short-term Senator from Colorado. When guests praise gold and say silver is out of date, Baby Doe charms them by saying she is a child of the moon and silver is the moon metal. John Latouche's clever lyrics allow her to express her love for her husband in terms of the basis of his wealth. "The Silver Aria" ("Gold is a fine thing for those who admire it") was introduced on stage in Central City, Colorado, in 1956 by Dolores Wilson but it became better known sung by Beverly Sills at New York City Opera in 1958. Sills sings it on the NYCO cast recording of the opera, Ruth Welting on a 1976 New York City Opera telecast and Jan Grissom on a 1996 Central City Opera cast recording. It is performed by Helen-Kay Eberley on her album of America opera arias and is included in Richard Walters' compilation *Opera American Style: Arias for Soprano.*

THE SILVER RIVER *1997 opera by Sheng*

An ancient Chinese folk myth describes the forbidden love between a goddess and a mortal. The Silver River is the Milky Way that separates them. Once a year birds create a bridge for the devoted lovers. The mortal is a Cowherd. portrayed by an operatic baritone and a flautist. The Goddess-Weaver is portrayed by a dancer and a Chinese lute player. The Golden Buffalo, who acts as matchmaker, is played by a black American actress, who speaks her lines in English. The Jade Emperor, father of the goddess, is played by a Chinese Opera actor who performs in Mandarin. Bright Sheng's multi-cultural one-act chamber opera *The Silver River,* libretto by David Henry Hwang based on the folk tale, was commissioned by an opera house consortium and premiered at Santa Fe Chamber Music Festival in July 1997. The Cowherd was played by baritone Michael Chioldi and flautist David Fedele, the Goddess was lutist Wu Man and dancer Muna Tseng, the Jade Emperor was Jamie Guan and the Golden Buffalo was Karen Kandel. Ong Keng Sen staged the opera. It was reprised at the Spoleto Festival USA in May 2000 and at the Prince Music Theater in Philadelphia in April 2001.

SILVERMAN, STANLEY *American composer (1938–)*

Stanley Silverman premiered five operas at the Berkshire Music Festival in Lenox, Massachusetts, all with librettos by Richard Foreman. The best-known is the symbolic, surrealistic ELEPHANT STEPS, about a mysterious guru, presented in 1968. It was followed by *Dream Tantras* in 1971; DR. SELAVY'S MAGIC THEATER, about the fantasy cure of an asylum patient, in 1972; *Stage Leers and Love Songs* in 1973; and HOTEL FOR CRIMINALS, based on Louis Feuillade's surrealistic films, in 1974. MADAME ADARE, again with libretto by Foreman, was commissioned by New York City Opera which staged it in 1980. Two of Silverman's musicals have been produced by opera companies, *Superspy!: The S-e-c-r-e-t Musical* by the Center for Contemporary Opera and *E.G.: A Musical Portrait of Emma Goldman* by the National Opera Association. His musical *Up from Paradise,* based on Arthur Miller's play *The Creation of the World and Other Business,* premiered at the University of Michigan in Ann Arbor in 1974 and was then staged in Washington and New York. Silverman, a native New Yorker, studied at Mills and Columbia and with Leon Kirchner.

SIMON, CARLY *American composer/singer (1945–)*

Pop singer-songwriter Carly Simon ("You're So Vain") was commissioned to create a children's opera by the Metropolitan Opera Guild Education Department and Kennedy Center to launch their New Opera for New Ears program. She devised the tuneful pop opera ROMULUS HUNT about a twelve-year-old boy who schemes to reunite his divorced parents; it was premiered in New York and Washington in 1993. Simon, who has won Grammies and Oscars for her composing, was born in New York City and taken to the Met by her parents as a child but says opera never appealed to her. She released her first solo album in 1971 and remains popular after thirty years of pop stardom.

SIMON, NEIL *American playwright (1927–)*

Most of Neil Simon's plays have been turned into successful films but he has not been so popular with opera composers. Only one has so far been turned into an opera. *The Good Doctor,* based on a poignant Chekhov story, was turned into a one-act opera by Richard Wargo. *The Seduction of a Lady* premiered at the National Institute for Music Theater in New York on May 11, 1984, and was reprised at Florida State University and the Lake George Opera Festival. Wargo later used the opera as the first section of his 1993 *A Chekhov Trilogy.*

SIMÓN BOLÍVAR *1995 opera by Musgrave*

Revolutionary leader Simón Bolívar, known as the Liberator, helps five South American countries gain independence in the early years of the 19th century but his idealist idea of a federation of nations is a failure. He dies in exile and is unpopular because of his views but is later acclaimed a hero. Thea Musgrave's two-act

Soprano Beverly Sills

opera *Simón Bolívar,* libretto by the composer based on the life of the Liberator, premiered at Virginia Opera in Norfolk on January 20, 1995. Stephen Guggenheim was Bolivar, Amy Johnson was his great love Manuela Sáenz, Michael Lynn Galanter was General Sucre, Douglas Nagle was General Santander, Russell Cusick was General Páez, Richard Lewis was Rodriguez/El Serrano, Bill Sinclair was O'Leary, Patricia Saunders Nixon was Hipolita, Frank Ward was Pepe, David Pratt was Officer/Aide/Conspirator, Tobin Jones was Pedro, Randall Gregoire was Pablo and Sean Peterson was young Bolívar. John Conklin designed the sets, Lillian Garrett-Groag directed and the composer conducted. The original libretto is in English but the opera premiered in a Spanish version written by director Garrett-Groag. *Simón Bolívar,* which incorporates traditional South American and Spanish melodies in its score, was co-commissioned by Virginia Opera, Los Angeles Music Center Opera and Scottish Opera.

THE SINGING CHILD   *1993 children's opera by Menotti*

A lonely boy imagines a singing child companion because his culture hungry parents leave him alone too much. Gian Carlo Menotti's 40-minute children's opera *The Singing Child,* libretto by the composer, It premiered at the Spoleto Festival USA in Charleston on May 31, 1993. William Cole was the boy Jeremy, Harold Haughton was the Singing Child, Ana Maria Martinez was Jeremy's mother and Eric McClusky was his father. Campbell Baird designed the sets and Federico Cortese conducted. The boy sopranos came from the American Boys Choir of Princeton.

SISTER SUZIE CINEMA   *1983 "doo-wop opera" by Telson and Breuer*

Five teenagers go into an empty movie theater and sing about their cinematic fantasies in 1950s doo-wop style. Their explorations include cinematic ideas about love ('you are my two-shot'), Veronica Lake, Dolores Del Rio, drive-in movies and in-flight films. Composer Bob Telson and librettist Lee Breuer's charming 23-minute "do-wop opera" *Sister Suzie Cinema* was premiered by New Jersey's *a cappella* quintet Fourteen Carat Soul at the Public Theater in New York in 1981 with Ben Halley Jr. as commentator. The quintet is composed of tenors David S Thurmond, Glenn Wright, and Bobby W. Wilson, baritone Russell Fox and bass Reginald Brisbon.

1986 Alive from Off Center. Actor Ben Halley Jr. and the *a cappella* quintet Fourteen Carat Soul are the performers in John Sanborn's video version of *Sister Suzie Cinema.* It was produced by the Women's Interart Center for the TV program *Alive from Off Center* and telecast on July 7, 1986. Video at MTR.

SIX CHARACTERS IN SEARCH OF AN AUTHOR
1959 opera by Weisgall

An opera company is rehearsing a new opera when six characters from an unfinished opera arrive looking for an author to complete their story. Hugo Weisgall's opera *Six Characters in Search of an Author,* libretto by Denis Johnston based on the play by Luigi Pirandello, premiered at New York City Opera on April 26, 1959. The opera company consisted of Beverly Sills as the Coloratura, Regina Sarfaty as the Mezzo, Ernest McChesney as the Director, Grant Williams as the Tenore Buffo, John Macurdy as the Basso Cantante, Craig Timberlake as the Accompanist, Arnold Voketaitis as Stage Manager, Anita Darian as Prompter and Elizabeth Mannion as Wardrobe Mistress. The six opera characters were Patricia Neway as the Mother, Adelaide Bishop as the Stepdaughter, Paul Ukena as the Father, Robert Trehy as the Son, Ruth

Kobart as Madame Pace, Marc Sullivan as the Boy and Barbara Becker as the Child. The Chorus/Seven Deadly Sins were Mary LeSawyer as Pride, Jennie Andrea as Envy, Lou Rodgers as Sloth, Rita Metzger as Lust, William Saxon as Anger, George Del Monte as Avarice, Peter Sliker as Glutton and Anthony Balestrieri as Another Tenor. Gary Smith designed the sets and costumes, William Ball directed and Sylvan Levin conducted the NYCO Orchestra. The opera continues to be revived and seem to be entering the repertory. It was much admired in a revival by Opera Festival of New Jersey in 2000.

1959 New York City Opera. Beverly Sills is the Coloratura in this live recording of the original New York City Opera production. Regina Sarfaty is the Mezzo, Patrica Neway is the Mother, Adelaide Bishop is the stepdaughter and the other cast members are as listed as above. Sylvan Levin conducts. Live Opera audiocassette. **1990 Chicago Lyric Opera Center.** Elizabeth Futral is the Coloratura in this recording of a production by Lyric Opera Center for American Artists in Chicago. The opera company members are Joslyn King as the Mezzo, Kevin Anderson as the Director, Bruce Fowler as the Tenore Buffo, Michael Wadsworth as the Basso Cantante, Andrew Schroeder as the Accompanist, Philip Zawisza as the Stage Manager, Susan Foster as the Prompter and Dianne Pritchett as the Wardrobe Mistress. The six characters are Robert Orth as the Father, Elizabeth Byrne as the Stepdaughter, Nancy Maultsby as the Mother, Gary Lehman as the Son, Paula LoVerne as Madame Pace, Victor Rooney as the Boy and Jenna Hefferman as the Child. Beverly Thiele is a member of the chorus. Lee Schaenen conducts the Lyric Opera of Chicago Orchestra. The opera was recorded live at the Civic Theater in Chicago on June 14 and 16, 1990, by National Public Radio. New World CD box.

SKILTON, CHARLES   *American composer (1868–1941)*

Charles Skilton was one of the first composers to have an opera premiered on radio. His one-act THE SUN BRIDE, libretto by Lillian White Spencer based on a Pueblo Indian legend about sun worship, was broadcast on NBC on April 17, 1930. Skilton, who was born in Northampton, Massachusetts, and studied at Yale and in Berlin, became interested in Native American tales and melodies while teaching at the University of Kansas. He composed two operas based on Indian legends and several other works incorporating Indian dances and rhythms. The first opera was the 1927 three-act *Kalopin,* libretto by Virginia Nelson Palmer, which received a David Bispham Memorial Medal but was never staged. Second was *The Sun Bride.* His third and last opera was the 1936 *The Day of Gayomair,* libretto by Allen. Crafton based on a story by Friedrich Gerstäcker.

SLOW DUSK   *1949 opera by Floyd*

Sadie, who lives on a farm in the South with her Aunt Sue and brother Jess, decides to marry Micah even though they belong to different religious groups. After he proposes and she accepts, Micah goes fishing and drowns. Carlisle Floyd's first opera, the folksy one-act *Slow Dusk,* libretto by the composer, was premiered at Syracuse University on May 2, 1949, while Floyd was a student. It has been staged a number of times since.

SMALLENS, ALEXANDER   *American conductor (1889–1972)*

Alexander Smallens conducted the premieres of the two most influential American operas, Virgil Thomson's FOUR SAINTS IN THREE ACTS in Hartford in 1934 and George Gershwin's PORGY

AND BESS in Boston in 1935. He had earlier conducted two other important premieres in Chicago, Reginald De Koven's RIP VAN WINKLE in 1920 and Sergey Prokofiev's THE LOVE OF THREE ORANGES in 1921. He conducted the first recordings of *Porgy and Bess,* with Lawrence Tibbett and Helen Jepson in 1935 and with original cast members Todd Duncan and Anne Brown in 1940, and he conducted the opera on its European tour in 1952. In 1953 he made a recording of Victor Herbert's BABES IN TOYLAND. Smallens, who was born in Russia, studied in New York and Paris and became an American citizen in 1919, the year he became conductor of the Chicago Opera. He was music director of Philadelphia Civic Opera from 1924 to 1931 and of Radio City Music Hall from 1947 to 1950.

SMIT, LEO   *American composer (1921–)*

Leo Smit's operas are in the science-fiction mode. *The Alchemy of Love* (1969) has a libretto by astronomer/SF writer Fred Hoyle and, not surprisingly, features aliens and thought control. *Magic Water* (1979), libretto by the composer based on NATHANIEL HAWTHORNE's story *Dr. Heidegger's Experiment,* is about water that restores youth and how drinking it affects the scientist's friends. It was staged at the University of Buffalo in New York. Smit, who was born in Philadelphia, is a notable pianist as well as composer and played with Balanchine's American Ballet company in the late 1930s. He studied at the Curtis Institute and has taught at Sarah Lawrence, UCLA and Buffalo. His other compositions include the ballets *Yerma* and *Virginia Sampler.*

SMITH, HARRY B.   *American librettist/lyricist (1860–1936)*

Harry B. Smith is believed to be the most prolific American music theater writer of all time, having reportedly written over 300 librettos and 6000 lyrics. Not all were memorable, of course, but he did help create American comic opera classics in collaboration with Victor Herbert and Reginald De Koven. He wrote sixteen shows for De Koven, including the trend-setting ROBIN HOOD (1891) and ROB ROY (1895); fourteen with Victor Herbert, including THE WIZARD OF THE NILE (1895). THE SERENADE (1897), THE FORTUNE TELLER (1898), CYRANO DE BERGERAC (1899), BABETTE (1903), THE ENCHANTRESS (1911), SWEETHEARTS (1913) and ANGEL FACE (1919); two with Sigmund Romberg, *Princess Flavia* (1925) and *Cherry Blossoms* (1927); one with John Philip Sousa, *The Free Lance* (1906); three with Jerome Kern, *Oh, I Say!* (1913). *90 in the Shade* (1915) and *Love o' Mike* (1917); two with Irving Berlin, *Watch Your Step* (1914) and *Stop! Look! Listen!* (1915); one with Walter Donaldson, *Sweetheart Time* (1925); and others with composers like Julian Edwards, Gustav Kerker and Ludwig Englander. He also wrote material for the early *Ziegfeld Follies* and adapted a large number of European operettas for the American stage. Smith, born in Buffalo, NY, began his stage career in 1884 with *Rosita* and continued until 1932 with *Marching By.* Harry's brother Robert B. Smith also had a successful career in music theater, primarily as a lyricist, including the words for Herbert's famous song "Sweethearts."

SMITH, JULIA   *American composer (1911–1989)*

Julia Smith composed six operas, all performed, but is best known for DAISY, libretto by Bertita Harding, which tells the story of Juliette Gordon Lowe, founder of the Girl Scouts. *Daisy* was premiered by Greater Miami Opera in Miami on November 3, 1973, has since been staged over forty times and has been recorded. Smith, who was born in Denton, Texas, graduated from North

Texas State University in 1930 and went on to study at Juilliard and NYU. After working as a professional pianist for many years, she began to compose. Her first opera was *Cynthia Parker,* libretto by Isabel Fortune based on a Texas legend, staged at North Texas State February 16, 1939, and by the University of Texas at Austin on December 5, 1985. *The Stranger of Manzano,* libretto by J. W. Rogers, was premiered at North Texas State on May 1, 1946. *The Gooseherd and the Goblin,* libretto by Josephine F Roule based on a story by C. D. MacKay, was broadcast on the Mutual Broadcasting System station WNYC on February 22, 1947, and staged in New London (1949) and Amarillo (1977). *Cockcrow,* libretto by C. D. MacKay based on a Grimm fairy tale, premiered in Austin on April 22, 1954. The Christmas opera *The Shepherdess and the Chimney Sweep,* libretto by C. D. MacKay based on a Hans Christian Anderson story, was staged by Fort Worth Opera on December 28, 1966, with Rudolf Kruger conducting. Smith's music is accessible and tuneful and her instrumental works are regularly performed.

SMITH, MARILYN HILL   *English soprano (1952–)*

Marilyn Hill Smith, much admired for her *Treasures of Operetta* recordings, sings Kathie in the 1989 British complete version of Sigmund Romberg's THE STUDENT PRINCE and Cunegonde in the 1997 Scottish Opera recording of CANDIDE. On her 1989 *Treasures of Operetta III* album, she performs "Romany Life" from Victor Herbert's THE FORTUNE TELLER. Smith, who was born in Surrey, studied at the Guildhall School of Music and made her debut with English National Opera in 1978. She became a principal soprano with the company in 1987.

SMITH, WILLIAM   *American librettist (1729–?)*

William Smith wrote the masque ALFRED, *An Oratorial Exercise,* staged in Philadelphia in 1756. It was the first opera-like musical drama created by an American to be presented in America. Smith, at that time Provost of the College of Philadelphia, adapted Thomas Arne's *The Masque of Alfred* about the ninth century English king for presentation at the college during Christmas holidays 1756 and January 1757. It was in three acts, the singers wore costumes and some of the music was original. The libretto was published in the *Pennsylvania Gazette* in January and February 1957.

SNOW LEOPARD   *1989 opera by Harper*

An American engineer, who has built a secret hydroelectric dam in the Tibet mountains, is forced to rethink what he is doing by a Buddhist potter who controls mysterious spirits. He is killed and has a spiritual rebirth. William Harper's opera *Snow Leopard,* libretto by Roger Nieboer and the composer based on Peter Matthiesen's book about his trip through the Himalayas, was premiered by Minnesota Opera's New Music-Theater Ensemble on November 9, 1989. Created to be performed by nine vocalists and computer synthesizers in seven scenes, it was reprised by the Ensemble in 1991 in a revised version. An earlier version titled *Tantracidal Mania* was presented in St. Paul in 1987.

SNOWBIRD   *1923 opera by Stearns*

Siberia around 900 AD A Tartar Prince, who has quarreled with his father the King over an amulet, is living like a hermit in the wilderness. He rescues a Tartar girl from the sea and calls her Snowbird after wrapping her in a white robe. Tartar chieftains, led by the Archer, seek the Prince swearing anyone wearing the amulet must die. When they see Snowbird wearing it, the Archer shoots her. The dying Snowbird tells the Prince he is her father. Theodore

Sterns one-act opera *Snowbird,* libretto by the composer, was premiered by Chicago Civic Opera on January 13, 1923. Mary McCormick was Snowbird, José Mojica was the Archer, Charles Marshall was the Hermit Prince and Edouard Cotreuill and Milo Luka were the Chieftains. Giorgio Ploacco conducted. *Snowbird* was reprised by Chicago Civic Opera in December 1923 and presented at Dresden Staatsoper in November 1928.

SOBOLEWSKI, EDWARD   *American composer (1804–1872)*

Edward Sobelewski's three-act grand opera MOHEGA, *The Flower of the Forest,* libretto in German by the composer, premiered at Albany Hall in Milwaukee, Wisconsin, on October 11, 1859. Sobolewski, a Pole who had had success in Germany with his operas, presented *Mohega* in Milwaukee because of the reputation of its singing societies; his opera required a chorus of one hundred singers. In the opera a native American woman falls in love with Polish nobleman Casimir Pulaski who is fighting on the side of America in the War of Independence. She dies tries to save him during the siege of Savannah in 1779. Sobolewski, whose grandfather had fought with Pulaski, was born in Köningsberg where most of his earlier operas were produced. After presenting *Mohega* in Milwaukee, he moved to St. Louis and became an American, founding the Philharmonic Orchestra which he conducted until 1870.

SODERO, CESARE   *American composer/conductor (1886–1947)*

Metropolitan Opera conductor Cesare Sodero, one of the pioneers of opera on radio, was in charge of NBC's National Grand Opera Company from 1925 to 1930, conducting performances of several American operas and premiering three. His own opera OMBRE RUSSE (Russian Shadows), the first opera to be premiered in complete form on radio, was broadcast on NBC in New York in 1929 before its stage premiere at La Fenice in June 1930. In 1930 he conducted a broadcast of Charles Sanford Skilton's THE SUN BRIDE, the second opera to be premiered complete on radio. The third was Charles Wakefield Cadman's THE WILLOW TREE, broadcast in 1932. After leaving NBC, Sodero conducted for WOR radio in New York until 1942 when he joined the Metropolitan Opera. He conducted the Met Orchestra in 188 performances of operas.

SÖDERSTRÖM, ELISABETH   *Swedish soprano (1927–)*

Elisabeth Söderström created the role of the diva Juliana Bordereau in Dominick Argento's opera *The Aspern Papers* when it premiered at Dallas Opera in 1988 and was telecast. Söderström, who made her debut in Drottningholm in 1947, is a member of the Swedish Royal Opera but sings in opera houses around the world.

THE SOJOURNER AND MOLLIE SINCLAIR   *1963 opera by Floyd*

The Carolinas in 1776 as the America Revolution begins. Dougald MacDougald is the "sojourner," a Scot living in East Carolina who wants to remain loyal to the British crown. His daughter Jenny has been causing him concern, however, and he disapproves of her boyfriend. Mollie Sinclair persuades him to join the revolution after the British blockade Wilmington harbor. Carlisle Floyd's comic opera *The Sojourner and Mollie Sinclair,* libretto by the composer, was commissioned for the Carolina Tercentenary for television and premiered on stage at East Carolina College in Raleigh, NC, on December 2, 1963. Norman Treigle

was sojourner Dougald MacDougald, Patricia Neway was Mollie Sinclair, Alison Herne Moss was Jenny MacDougald, William Newberry was Lachlan Sinclaire and Jerold Teachey was the Spokesman. John A. Sneden designed the sets, Betsy Rose Griffith arranged the choreography, Gene Strassler produced, Edgard R. Losessin directed and Julius Rudel conducted the East Carolina School of Music Orchestra and Chorus.

1963 East Carolina College. Norman Treigle and Patricia Neway star in the premiere of the opera by East Carolina College as it was telecast December l5, 1963. Julius Rudel conducts the East Carolina School of Music Orchestra and Chorus. The video of the telecast has been lost but the audio soundtrack was preserved by Treigle. VAI CD.

THE SOLDIER   *1956 opera by Engel*

Former soldier Robert returns from a war feeling persecuted. He is afraid of everything, even his wife Edna, but able to survive at first by remembering his childhood and happier times. His delusions grow to the point where he threatens his wife with a knife and she has him committed to an asylum. Lehman Engel's dark opera *The Soldier,* libretto by Lewis Allen based on a "psycho drama" by Roald Dahl, premiered at Carnegie Hall November 25, 1956, in concert form. Warren Galjour was the Soldier, Leneen MacGrath was his wife Edna, John Reardon was He and Brenda Lewis was She (friends of the Man) and James Hurst was the Doctor. *The Soldier* was given its stage premiere by Mississippi Opera in Jackson, Mississippi, on November 24, 1958.

SOLOMON AND BALKIS   *1942 radio opera by Thompson*

King Solomon is saved from the constant quarreling of his 999 wives by the wise and beautiful Queen Balkis. She arranges for Solomon to overhear a butterfly in his palace garden threatening to stamp its foot and make the palace vanish unless his wives stops

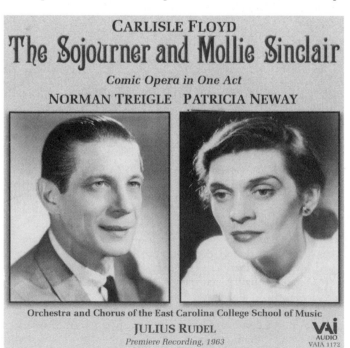

Carlisle Floyd's comic opera *The Sojourner and Mollie Sinclair* was composed in 1963 to celebrate the Carolina Tercentenary.

quarreling. Solomon gets his magic Djinns to allow the butterfly to do as it threatens. Randall Thompson's light-hearted 43-minute opera *Solomon and Balkis*, libretto by the composer based on Rudyard Kipling's fable *The Butterfly That Stamped* from the *Just So Stories*, was created for CBS Radio and broadcast on March 29, 1942. It was staged by Harvard University in Cambridge, Massachusetts, on April 14, 1942, and has been reprised by Opera in the Ozarks, the summer festival at Inspiration Point Fine Arts Colony in Eureka Springs, Arkansas.

"SOME ENCHANTED EVENING"   *Baritone aria: South Pacific (1949). Words: Oscar Hammerstein II. Music: Richard Rodgers.*

Metropolitan Opera bass Ezio Pinza introduced the powerful aria "Some Enchanted Evening" on the first night of SOUTH PACIFIC in 1949 and helped make it one of the most popular songs in American music theater history. In the operetta it is sung by French plantation owner Emile de Becque to American nurse Nellie Forbush (Mary Martin) describing their relationship and, indirectly, proposing marriage. Rodgers and Hammerstein wrote the song specifically for Pinza but it is reprised by Martin in the second act and has become popular with both male and female singers. Pinza's recordings of the song sold a million copies and it was also a pop hit for Perry Como, Frank Sinatra and Jo Stafford. In the film version of *South Pacific* it is sung by Metropolitan Opera baritone Giorgio Tozzi who starred in a revival of the operetta at Lincoln Center in 1967. It is sung by Emil Belcourt in the 1988 London revival recording, by Justino Diaz in the 1996 London recording, by Rade Sherbedgia in the 2001 Disney TV film and by Philip Quast in the 2001 Royal National Theatre recording. It has been recorded by a number of opera baritones, including Lauritz Melchior, Robert Merrill and Bryan Terfel, and even by a tenor, José Carreras, who sings it with the music transposed up.

"SOMEHOW I NEVER COULD BELIEVE"   *Soprano aria: Street Scene (1948). Words: Langston Hughes. Music: Kurt Weill.*

Anna Maurrant's sad aria of lost hopes and faded dreams is one of the most memorable moment in the Broadway opera *Street Scene,* based on the Elmer Rice play. She is unhappily married to Frank and living in a dismal tenement in New York. She finds a lover but the affair ends tragically. The aria, music by Kurt Weill and lyrics by Langston Hughes, is traditionally operatic in the style of Puccini and was introduced on stage and on the cast album by Polyna Stoska. Josephine Barstow sings it on the Scottish Opera recording of the opera and Kristina Ciesinski sings it on the English National Opera recording. It is one of the arias included in Richard Walters' book *Opera American Style: Arias for Soprano.*

SOMETIME   *1918 operetta by Friml*

A vamp gets a man into trouble with his fiancée and it takes five years and a flashback to sort it out. Rudolf Friml's operetta *Sometime,* libretto by Rida Johnson Young, is now forgotten but it was one of the hits of 1918, primarily because of its stars, Mae West as the vamp and Ed Wynn as the comic Loney. It opened on October 4, 1918, at the Shubert Theater with Harrison Brockbank as the man vamped by West and Francine Larrimore as the unhappy fiancée. West's big song was "Any Kind of Man" in which she says she is willing to take on any boob who can walk. She also did a shimmy song titled "Shimmy Schwabble."

1986 Eastman-Dryden Orchestra. The Eastman-Dryden Orchestra conducted by Donald Hunsberger plays three songs from *Sometime:* "Any Kind of Man," "Beautiful Night" and "No One But You." They're on the album *Rudolf Friml: Chansonette.* Arabesque LP/CD.

SOMEWHERE   *Duet and aria: West Side Story (1957). Words: Stephen Sondheim. Music: Leonard Bernstein*

"Somewhere" begins as a duet between doomed lovers Maria and Tony who imagine that somewhere there is a time and place for them. The duet introduces a dream ballet and the song is continued by an offstage voice (that of Consuelo) in the operatic musical WEST SIDE STORY. It is reprised by Maria and sung to Tony as he lies dying at the end of the musical. "Somewhere" was introduced on stage by Carol Lawrence (Maria), Larry Kert (Tony) and Reri Grist (Consuelo) at the premiere at the National Theater in Washington, D.C., on August 19, 1957, and Stephen Sondheim's words and Leonard Bernstein's music made it one of the highlights of the show. It is performed by Marni Nixon and Jim Bryant as the (dubbed) voices of Maria and Tony in the 1961 film of the musical, Marilyn Horne on the 1985 operatic recording by Bernstein, Sally Burgess on the 1993 recording based on a London stage production, Kiri Te Kanawa on her 1994 *Greatest Hits* album and Renée Fleming on her 1998 album *Prelude to a Kiss.* There have been many popular recordings, including versions by Barbra Streisand and P. J. Proby.

SONDHEIM, STEPHEN   *American composer (1930–)*

Stephen Sondheim does not want his musicals to be called Broadway operas, despite evidence to the contrary, but they are entering the opera house repertory all the same. A LITTLE NIGHT MUSIC (1973), a classic operetta in disguise based on a melancholic Ingmar Bergman movie, was staged by New York City Opera in 1990. SWEENEY TODD (1979), which is virtually through sung with operatic motifs and ensembles, has been staged by New York City Opera, Houston Grand Opera, Opera North in Leeds and Finnish Opera. Its story of a barber who gets revenge on society by making people into meat pies is hardly musical comedy territory. INTO THE WOODS (1989), a post-modern re-evaluation of fairy tales, was staged by Lyric Opera Cleveland. PASSION (1994), based on an Italian film about obsessive love, was described by one critic as "the most important modern American opera. Sondheim, a native of New York, became nationally known after writing the brilliant lyrics for Leonard Bernstein's "American opera" WEST SIDE STORY (1957) and Jules Styne's *Gypsy* (1959). His first show as both composer and lyricist was *A Funny Thing Happened on the Way to the Forum* (1962) followed by *Anyone Can Whistle* (1964). His later shows, all stretching the boundaries of music theater, include *Company* (1970), *Follies* (1971), *Pacific Overtures* (1976), *Merrily We Roll Along* (1981), *Sunday in the Park with George* (1984) and *Assassins* (1991).

THE SONG OF MAJNUN   *1997 opera by Sheng*

Majnun is prevented from marrying his love Layla by her father. When she is forced to marry someone else, Majnun goes mad while writing songs about his undying love for her. They meet once again and die of unhappiness. Bright Sheng's chamber opera *The Song of Majnun,* libretto by Andrew Porter based on the epic Persian poem *Layla and Majnun* by Nizami, was commissioned by Lyric Opera of Chicago which premiered it on April 9, 1992. Rodrick Dixon was Majnun, Jan Yan Wang was Layla, Mark Jones was Layla's father, Eleni Matos was Layla's mother, Jonathan Oehler was Majun's father, Elias Mokoe was Ibn Salamm Kimberly Jones was the Bird and Beverly Thiele and Julia Bentley were the tale-telling Gossips. Marie Anne Chimenti designed the set, Colin Graham staged the opera and Richard Buckley conducted.

1995 Houston Opera Studio. The Houston Opera Studio reprised the opera in March 1995 and recorded it live in performance with singer Anna Maria Martinez, Jill Grove, Raymond Very, Patrick Blackwell, Michael Chioldi, Mary Petro, Jonita Lattimore and Grant Youngblood. Ward Holmquist conducts the Houston Opera Studio Chorus and Grand Opera Orchestra. The recording includes an interview with the composer and librettist. Delos CD.

SONG OF NORWAY   1944 pastiche operetta by Wright/Forrest/Grieg

Norwegian composer Edvard Grieg plans to spend his life writing nationalistic music for his country with poet friend Nordraak and sweetheart Nina but is diverted to Rome by seductive opera diva Louisa. When Nordraak dies, Grieg returns home to fulfil his destiny as the great Norwegian composer. Robert Wright and George Forrest's pastiche operetta *Song of Norway,* libretto by Milton Lazarus derived from a play by Homer Curran, is based on the life and music of Grieg. It was performed by opera companies in San Francisco and Los Angeles before it opened in New York at the Imperial Theater on August 21, 1944. Lawrence Brooks was Grieg, Irra Petina was Louisa Giovanni, Robert Schafer was Nordraak and Helena Bliss was Nina. George Balanchine arranged the choreography, Edwin Lester and Charles K. Freeman staged the operetta and Charles Arthur Kay conducted. *Song of Norway* has been revived many times and entered the opera house repertory in 1981 when it was staged by New York City Opera.

1944 Original cast. Lawrence Brooks is Grieg in this recording featuring most of the original cast. Robert Schafer is Nordraak, Helena Bliss is Nina and Kitty Carlisle is Louisa (replacing Irra Petina who was contracted to different record label). Arthur Kays conducts. Decca LP/MCA CD. **1958 Jones Beach Theater.** Opera baritone John Reardon is Grieg in this operatic cast recording of a lavish Jones Beach Marine Theater production. Brenda Lewis is opera diva Louisa, Helena Scott is Nina, William Olvis is Nordraak and Muriel O'Malley is Mother Grieg. Lehman Engel conducts. Columbia LP. **1970 ABC Pictures.** Toralv Maurstad portrays Grieg in this lavish widescreen Super Panavision ABC Pictures movie with Florence Henderson as Nina, Frank Porretta as Nordraak and Robert Morley as Berg. It looks beautiful and the music, played by the London Symphony Orchestra led by Roland Shaw, sounds fine but director Andrew L. Stone's screenplay is rather feeble. ABC Records LP/VHS. **1990 John Owens Edwards.** Donald Maxwell is Grieg with Valerie Masterson as Nina in this London recording. Diana Montague is Louisa, David Rendall is Nordraak, Richard Van Allen is Father Grieg, Elizabeth Bainbridge is Mother Grieg, Jason Howard is Peppi Le Loup and Yitkin Seow is Grieg on piano. John Owens Edwards conducts the Philharmonia Orchestra and Ambrosian Chorus. TER CD.

SONG OF THE FLAME   1925 "romantic opera" by Gershwin and Stothart

Russian aristocrat Aniuta disguises herself as The Flame and sings to incite the downtrodden to rebel against the Czarist government. Handsome Prince Voloyda falls in love with her in this disguise and, after the Revolution turns sour, they find each other and happiness in exile in Paris. George Gershwin and Herbert Stothart's *Song of the Flame,* libretto by Otto Harbach and Oscar Hammerstein II, premiered at the Wilmington Playhouse in Delaware on December 10, 1925, and opened on Broadway at the 44th Street Theater on December 30, 1925, Tessa Kosta was Flame Aniuta, Guy Robertson was the Prince who loves her and the supporting cast included Dorothy Mackaye, Greek Evans and the Russian Art Choir. Frank Retcher directed, Jack Haskell staged the musical numbers and Herbert Stothart conducted. The popular songs were the title number and the "Cossack Love Song." *Song of the Flame* was promoted as a "romantic opera" when it opened on Broadway thought it is actually an old-fashioned Viennese-style operetta

1926 Tessa Costa. Tessa Costa, the original Aniuta, recorded eight numbers from the comic opera for a highlights recording

Bernice Claire as Aniuta the Flame with Alexander Gray as the Prince in the 1930 film of George Gershwin and Herbert Stothart's *Song of the Flame.*

with the Russian Art Choir. They include "Song of the Flame," "Cossack Love Song," "I Was There" and "The Song of Gold." The recordings, originally on Columbia 78s, were reissued on several LPs. **1926 Victor Light Opera.** The Victor Light Opera Company performs "Song of the Flame" from the opera for a Victor 78. **1930 First National.** Met mezzo-soprano Alice Gentle plays Natasha, the Flame's rival, in this First National film of the operetta. Bernice Claire stars as Aniuta the Flame with Alexander Gray as Prince Volodya and Noah Beery as Konstantin, the revolutionary who turns bad guy. Alan Crosland directed this 89-minute film which is apparently lost. **1930 Noah Beery.** Noah Beery, who plays the villain Konstantin in the film of *Song of the Flame*, recorded "One Little Drink" for a 78 in 1930 and it was later re-issued on LP. **1934 Vitaphone.** Bernice Claire stars as Aniuta the Flame in an abridged film version made for Vitaphone in 1934 and retitled *The Flame Song*. J. Harold Murray takes the role of Prince Volodya. The 20-minute movie features four songs from the operetta. **1951 Igor Gorin.** Met baritone Igor Gorin sings "Song of the Flame" with Howard Barlow conducting the Firestone orchestra on a *Voice of Firestone* television program in 1951. It's on the video *Igor Gorin in Opera and Song*. VAI VHS.

SORRY, WRONG NUMBER!   *American operas based on Lucille Fletcher play*

A talkative invalid overhears a conversation on a crossed line and discovers a woman is going to be murdered by a hired killer. She tries fruitlessly to summon help via the telephone and learns, too late, that she is the intended victim. Lucille Fletcher's famous 1943 radio play *Sorry, Wrong Number!* has inspired two American operas. The original radio play, broadcast in the CBS series *Suspense*. starred Agnes Moorehead. was turned into a stage play popular in schools and colleges, a 1948 movie starring Barbara Stanwyck and a 1989 TV movie with Loni Anderson.

1977 Jerome Moross. Jerome Moross's one-act chamber opera *Sorry, Wrong Number!*, libretto by the composer based on the radio play, was composed in 1977. **1999 Jack Beeson.** Jack Beeson's one-act chamber opera *Sorry, Wrong Number!*, libretto by the composer based on the radio play, premiered at the Kaye Playhouse at the Center for Contemporary Opera in New York on May 25, 1999. Patricia Dell was the endangered Mrs. Stevenson. Richard Holmes was police Sergeant Duffy, Charlotte Surkin, Maria Bedo and Patricia Sonego were the telephone operators, Roosevelt André Credit was the hit man and Kimako Trotman was his employer. Charles Maryann directed.

THE SOUND OF A VOICE   *2003 operas by Glass*

Philip Glass's *The Sound of a Voice*, two interconnected operas based on plays by David Henry Hwang, was premiered at the American Repertory Theater in Cambridge, MA, on May 28, 2003. The title play takes place in ancient Japan where a samurai warrior seeks out a witch woman in the forest and falls under her spell. In the second play, *Hotel of Dreams,* which takes place in the present, an elderly novelist visits the madam of a brothel that caters to old men and falls under spell. Both operas are scored for four instruments including the pipa (a Chinese lute played by Wu Man), cello, flute and percussion. Herbert Perry sang the role of the samurai in the first opera with Suzan Hanson as the witch woman while Eugene Perry was the elderly writer in the second opera with Janice Felty as the madam. Robert Israel designed the sets, Robert Woodruff directed and Glass conducted the ensemble.

THE SOUND OF MUSIC   *1959 operetta by Rodgers*

Austria in 1938. Novice nun Maria is sent by the Abbess of her convent to be governess to the seven children of wealthy local landowner Capt. Von Trapp. She teaches the children to sing and marries their father but they have to flee the country when the Nazis arrive. Richard Rodger's operetta *The Sound of Music,* libretto by Howard Lindsay and Russell Crouse based on Maria Von Trapp's autobiography *The Trapp Family Singers* with lyrics by Oscar Hammerstein II, was premiered at the Shubert Theatre in New Haven on October 3, 1959, and opened at the Lunt-Fontanne Theater in New York on November 16, 1959. Mary Martin was Maria, Theodore Bikel was Capt. Von Trapp, opera soprano Patrica Neway was the Abbess who sings the memorable "Climb Ev'ry Mountain." Marion Marlowe was Elsa, Lauri Peters was Liesl, Brian Davies was Rolf, Kurt Kasznar was Max and Met diva-to-be Tatiana Troyanos was in the chorus. Jay Layton arranged the choreography, Oliver Smith designed the sets, Vincent J. Donahue directed and Frederick Dvonch conducted. *The Sound of Music* has now entered the opera house repertory, including a production at New York City Opera in 1990, and was revived on Broadway in 1998.

1959 Original cast. Mary Martin stars as Maria in the original Broadway cast recording, Patricia Neway is the Abbess, Theodore Bikel is Von Trapp, Marion Marlowe is Elsa and Lauri Peters is Liesl. Frederick Dvonch conducts the orchestra. Columbia LP/ Sony CD. **1965 20th Century-Fox.** Julie Andrews soars as Maria in Robert Wise's superb film of the operetta with its famous opening mountaintop sequence. Christopher Plummer is Von Trapp (singing voice of Bill Lee), Peggy Wood is the Abbess (singing voice of Margery McKay), Charmian Carr is Liesl and Eleanor Parker is Elsa. Ernest Lehman wrote the screenplay and Irwin Kostal conducts chorus and orchestra. The film won five Oscars for 20th Century Fox, including Best Picture and Best Director. Soundtrack: RCA LP/CD. Film: Fox VHS/DVD. **1987 Erich Kunzel.** Frederica von Stade is Maria in this operatic studio recording with Erich Kunzel conducting. Håkan Hagegård is Von Trapp, Eileen Farrell is the Abbess, Barbara Daniels is Elsa, Jeanne Menke is Liesl and Neil Jones Is Rolf. Telarc CD. **1994 Kiri Te Kanawa.** Kiri Te Kanawa sings "Climb Ev'ry Mountain" on her album *Kiri! Her Greatest Hits*. Stephen Barlow conducts the London Symphony Orchestra. London Classics CD/VHS. **1996 Bryan Terfel.** Bryan Terfel sings "Edelweiss" on his album *Something Wonderful: Bryan Terfel Sings Rodgers and Hammerstein*. Paul Daniel leads the English Northern Philharmonic and Opera North Chorus. DG CD. **1998 Broadway revival.** Rebecca Luker is Maria in this Broadway revival cast recording. Michael Silbery is Von Trapp, Patti Cohenour is the Abbess, Jan Maxwell is Elsa, Fred Applegate is Max and Sara Zelle is Liesl. Frederick. BMG RCA Victor CD.

SOURWOOD MOUNTAIN   *1959 "folk opera" by Kreutz*

The Porters and the Lowells have been feuding in the Appalachians for years. When Danny Lowell falls in love with Lucy Porter, the feud heats up and the backwoods Romeo and Juliet are forced to flee. When a Porter man mistakenly shoots and wounds Lucy, both sides decide to call it quits and let the lovers marry. Arthur Kreutz's "folk opera" *Sourwood Mountain,* libretto by Zoë Lund Schiller, premiered at the University of Mississippi in Oxford on January 8, 1959, and was reprised the same year in Clinton, MS, and Roanoke, VA.

SOUSA, JOHN PHILIP   *American composer (1854–1932)*

March king John Philip Sousa's reputation as a composer of American comic operas has begun to revive in recent years with recordings and productions of his major stage works. Most notable were a much-praised Glimmerglass production of THE GLASS BLOWERS in 2000 and several stagings of his famous operetta EL CAPITAN. Sousa was greatly influenced in creating music theater by Jacques Offenbach (he played in his orchestra in Philadelphia in 1876) and Arthur Sullivan (he conducted *H.M.S. Pinafore* and *The Contrabandista* in 1879). He wanted to create American comic operas equivalent to the Gilbert and Sullivan masterpieces and his first staged comic opera was based on the story used by Sullivan for *The Contrabandista*. *The Smugglers* was staged in Sousa's hometown, Washington, D.C. in 1882, and was followed in 1884 by DÉSIRÉE, libretto by Edward Taber, a tale of Musketeers and a lady. Sousa's greatest success came with *El Capitan*, libretto by Charles Klein, which was staged on Broadway in 1896 and in London in 1899 with De Wolf Hopper as the bragging Viceroy of Peru. Sousa wrote his own libretto for THE BRIDE ELECT (1897), the story of a princess who has to marry someone she doesn't love. *The Charlatan* (1898), libretto by Charles Klein, concerns a magician mixing up love affairs in Czarist Russia. *Chris and the Wonderful Lamp* (1900) was a fairy tale spectacle with a libretto by Glen MacDonough, the man who wrote *Babes in Toyland* for Victor Herbert. *The Free Lance* (1906), libretto by Harry B. Smith about a royal marital mix-up, was well received on Broadway and revived by the Opera Company of Philadelphia in 1979. Sousa's last comic opera was *The Glass Blowers*, libretto by Leonard Liebling, which opened in 1913 as *The American Maid*. Sousa wrote quite a lot of memorable music but he never found a good permanent librettist so his operettas faded from fashion. Seven of Sousa's operettas were published, however, and they are now being restored by Jerrold Fisher and William Martin.

1995 John Philip Sousa On Stage. Keith Brion conducts the Razumovsky Symphony Orchestra in music from four of Sousa's stage shows, *The Bride Elect, El Capitan, The Glass Blowers* and *Our Flirtations*. The numbers were recorded in Bratislava in for the album *John Philip Sousa On Stage*. Naxos CD. **1952 Stars and Stripes Forever.** Clifton Webb plays John Philip Sousa in this pleasant film biography showing his rise from leader of the Marine Corps Band to international fame. Most of the movie is devoted to marches but there are two stage sequences, one featuring his operetta *El Capitan*. Debra Paget sings in the *El Capitan* scene, Ruth Hussey plays Sousa's wife and Robert Wagner plays sousaphone. Ernest Vajda and Lamar Trotti wrote the story and screenplay and Henry Koster directed the 80-minute film for Twentieth Century Fox. Fox VHS.

SOUTH CAROLINA *American state (1788–)*

South Carolina was the site of the first opera staged in America: English composer Colley Cibber's ballad opera *Flora, or Hob in the Well* presented at the Courtroom Theater in Charleston on February 18, 1735. The first American opera staged there was *Americania and Elutheria: or, A New Tale of the Genii*, a ballad opera presented in Charleston in 1798. Charleston is the locale of America's most famous opera, George Gershwin's PORGY AND BESS based on DuBose Heyward's book *Porgy*. The opera was not staged in Charleston until 1970, thirty-five years after its premiere, but has been revived twice since, and Catfish Row has become a tourist attraction. Other operas set in South Carolina include Carlisle Floyd's THE PASSION OF JONATHAN WADE (Columbia) and Robert Ward's CLAUDIA LEGARE (Charleston). South Carolina-born opera people include Carlisle Floyd (Latta), librettist DuBose Heyward (Charleston), bass-baritone Lawrence Winters (Kings Creek).

Abbeville: Thomas Pasatieri's three-act opera WASHINGTON SQUARE was produced in Abbeville in 1979 and recorded live with Maryanne Telese as Catherine Sloper.

Charleston: The Charleston Opera Company was founded by Vernon Weston in 1965 to stage traditional operas, including a revival of Cibber's *Flora*. Gian Carlo Menotti founded the American version of his Italian Spoleto festival in Charleston in 1977. The first American opera presented there was Menotti's THE CONSUL followed in 1978 by his church operas MARTIN'S LIE and THE EGG and Samuel Barber's VANESSA. Menotti is no longer associated with the event but it continues to be one of the most important arts festivals in America. It has premiered Laurie Anderson's EMPTY PLACES (1989) and SONGS AND STORIES FROM MOBY DICK (1999), Robert Convery's *The Blanket* (1988), Philip Glass's HYDROGEN JUKEBOX (1990), Paul Dresher's *Pioneer* (1990), Stanley Hollingsworth's children's operas HARRISON LOVES HIS UMBRELLA (1981) and THE SELFISH GIANT (1981), Menotti's children's opera THE SINGING CHILD, (1993) and Steve Reich's multimedia HINDENBURG (1998). Over the years most of Menotti's operas were staged there including CHIP AND HIS DOG, LA LOCA, THE LAST SAVAGE, MARIA GOLOVIN, THE MEDIUM, THE SAINT OF BLEECKER STREET and THE UNICORN, THE GORGON AND THE MANTICORE. The festival has also presented revised versions of Barber's ANTONY AND CLEOPATRA, Raffaelo de Banfield's LORD BYRON'S LETTER, Dresher's SLOW FIRE and Hollingsworth's THE MOTHER.

Columbia: The University of South Carolina in Columbia premiered Jack E. Williams *Alexander the Great* on August 8, 1971.

Greenville: Bob Jones University premiered Dwight Gustafson's one-act *The Jailer* on May 27, 1954, and Gustafson's one act *The Hunted* on May 26, 1960. East Carolina University premiered Gregory Kosteck's *Maura,* based on John Millington Synge's Irish play *Riders to the Sea,* on April 24, 1968; and Kosteck's *The Stronger,* based on the Strindberg play, on April 30, 1970.

Myrtle Beach: Jack E. Williams premiered *We Gave Him Piano Lessons* in Myrtle Beach on August 8, 1971.

Newberry: South Carolina Opera presents its productions at the Newberry Opera House.

Spartanburg: Ernst Bacon's A TREE ON THE PLAINS, libretto by Paul Horgan, was premiered at Converse College on May 2, 1942.

SOUTH DAKOTA *American state (1889–)*

Most of South Dakota's operatic activity is centered around its colleges in Aberdeen, Vermillion and Yankton. Douglas Moore's Pulitzer Prize-winning 1951 opera GIANTS IN THE EARTH, libretto by Arnold Sundgaard, is based on a novel by O. E. Rölvaag about a pioneer family in Dakota Territory. Composer Clarence Loomis, who wrote eight operas and was awarded the Bispham Medal in 1926, was born in Sioux Falls. Tenor Jess Thomas, who created the role of Octavius in Samuel Barber's ANTONY AND CLEOPATRA, was born in Hot Springs.

Aberdeen: Paul Ramsier's *The Man on the Bearskin Rug,* libretto by James Edward, was premiered at Northern State Teacher College on April 13, 1969.

Vermillion: Robert Marek's *Arabesque* was premiered at the University of South Dakota on April 14, 1967. H. Owen Reed's dance opera *Living Solid* premiered at the university on November 28, 1976.

Yankton: Three operas/music theater works have been premiered at Yankton College: Felix Vinatieri's *The American Volunteer,* composed in 1889, was premiered on March 4, 1961. Floyd McClain's *The Snack Shop* was presented on June 12, 1958, and his musical *The Princess and the Frog* on June 13, 1959.

SOUTH PACIFIC   *1949 operetta by Rodgers*

Life on a small island in the South Pacific during World War II as cross-cultural love affairs develop. French planter Emile de Becque and Little Rock nurse Nellie Forbush overcome their differences and find love on an enchanted evening. Lt. Joe Cable's romance with Polynesian girlfriend Liat ends tragically. Bloody Mary provides an earthy brand of wisdom. Richard Rodgers' *South Pacific,* libretto by Oscar Hammerstein II Hammerstein and Joshua Logan based on stories in James Michener's *Tales of the South Pacific,* premiered at the Shubert Theater in New Haven, Connecticut, on March 7, 1949, and opened in New York at the Majestic Theater on April 7. Ezio Pinza played Emile de Becque, Mary Martin was Nellie Forbush, William Tabbert was Lt. Joe Cable, Betta St. John was Liat, Juanita Hall was Bloody Mary and Myron McCormick was Luther Billis. Joshua Logan directed and Salvatore dell'Isola conducted the orchestra. The role of de Becque was tailored for Pinza and he was followed into the role by other Metropolitan Opera basses; Giorgio Tozzi sang it in the 1958 film and 1967 Lincoln Center revival and Justino Diaz sang it in the 1998 recording. *South Pacific,* which won eight Tony awards and the Pulitzer Prize for Drama, has now entered the opera house repertory.

1949 Original Broadway cast. Ezio Pinza stars as planter Emile de Becque in this original cast album of the musical. Mary Martin is Nellie, William Tabbert is Cable and Juanita Hall is Bloody Mary. Salvatore dell'Isola conducts the chorus and orchestra. Columbia LP/Sony CD. **1950 Lauritz**

The 1958 film version of *South Pacific,* starring Rossano Brazzi and Mitzi Gaynor, featured the voice of Metropolitan Opera bass Giorgio Tozzi.

Melchior. Lauritz Melchior sings "Some Enchanted Evening" from *South Pacific* on the *Voice of Firestone* TV program on February 6, 1950. Howard Barlow conducts the Firestone Orchestra. It's on the video *Lauritz Melchior in Opera and Song.* VAI VHS. **1950 Jan Peerce.** Jan Peerce sings "Younger Than Springtime" while Howard Barlow conducts the Firestone Orchestra on the *Voice of Firestone* TV show on January 9, 1950. It's on the video *Jan Peerce in Opera and Song.* VAI VHS. **1950 Capitol recording.** Gordon MacRae, Margaret White and Peggy Lee perform highlights from *South Pacific* on a studio recording of the operetta. Capitol LP. **1951 Jerome Hines.** Jerome Hines sings "This Nearly Was Mine"" from *South Pacific* on the *Voice of Firestone* TV program on August 27, 1951. Howard Barlow conducts the Firestone Orchestra. It's on the video *Jerome Hines in Opera and Song.* VAI VHS. **1958 Twentieth Century-Fox film.** Met basso Giorgio Tozzi is the singing voice of Rossano Brazzi, who plays de Beque on screen, in this film of the operetta. Mitzi Gaynor is Nellie, John Kerr is Cable (singing by Bill Lee), France Nuyen is Liat and Juanita Hall is Bloody Mary (singing by Muriel Smith who played the role on stage in London). Paul Osborne wrote the screenplay adaptation and cinematographer Leon Shamroy shot the film in Kauai and Fiji. Joshua Logan, who produced the operetta on Broadway, directed for Twentieth Century-Fox. Soundtrack: RCA Victor LP/CD. Film: Fox VHS/DVD. **1963 Robert Merrill.** Robert Merrill sings "Some Enchanted Evening" from *South Pacific* on January 13, 1963, on the *Voice of Firestone* TV show. Howard Barlow conducts the Firestone Orchestra. It's on the video *Anna Moffo in Opera and Song.* VAI VHS. **1967 Lincoln Center revival.** Giorgio Tozzi sings

the role of Emile de Becque opposite Florence Henderson as Nellie in this recording of the Lincoln Center revival of the musical. The supporting cast includes Irene Byatt as Bloody Mary, Justin McDonough, Eleanor Cables, and David Doyle. Jonathan Anderson conducts. RCA Victor LP/CD. **1986 South Pacific: The London Sessions.** Kiri Te Kanawa and José Carreras star in a concert performance of *South Pacific* that was filmed in rehearsal Tenor Carreras sings the bass role of Emile de Becque with music transposed up, Te Kanawa is Nellie, Sarah Vaughan is Bloody Mary and Mandy Patinkin is Cable. Jonathan Tunich conducts the London Symphony Orchestra. CBS VHS/Sony CD. **1988 London revival.** Emile Belcourt is Emile de Becque opposite Gemma Craven as Nellie in a 1988 recording of the London stage revival. The supporting cast includes Beatrice Reading as Bloody Mary, Andrew C. Wadsworth and Johnny Wade. Alan Bence conducts. First Night CD. **1996 John Owen Edwards.** John Owen Edwards leads the National Symphony Orchestra in this 1988 London studio recording. Justino Diaz is Emile opposite Paige O'Hara as Nellie with Sean McDermott as Lt. Cable and Pat Suzuki as Bloody Mary. Jay Records CD. **1996 Bryan Terfel.** Bryan Terfel sings five songs from *South Pacific* on his album *Something Wonderful: Bryan Terfel Sings Rodgers and Hammerstein.* Paul Daniel conducts the English Northern Philharmonic and Opera North Chorus. DG CD. **2001 Disney TV film.** Glenn Close stars as Nellie with Rade Sherbedgia as Emile in this Disney television version of the musical. Harry Connick, Jr. is Lt. Cable, Lori Tan Chinn is Bloody Mary and Robert Pastorelli is Billis. Richard Pearce directed. Buena Vista DVD. **2001 Royal National Theatre.** Cast recording of a revival of *South Pacific* that opened at the Royal National Theatre in London in December 2001. Philip Quast is Emile, Lauren Kennedy is Nellie, Edward Baker-Duly is Cable, Sheila Francisco is Bloody Mary and Elaine Tan is Liat. First Night Records CD.

SPELMAN, TIMOTHY   *American composer (1891–1970)*

Brooklyn-born Timothy Spelman, who lived much of his life in Florence, Italy, is best known for his orchestral work but he also composed six operas. Three have librettos by his poet wife Leolyn Louise Everett: *La Magnifica* (1924), *The Sea Rovers* (1924) and *Babakan* (1933) and three were composed to his own librettos: *Lizzie Hexam* (1929), *The Sunken City* (1930) and *The Courtship of Miles Standish* (1941) based on the poem by Longfellow. The Spelmans willed their Florence Villa to John Hopkins University.

SPRATLAN, LEWIS   *American composer (1940–)*

Lewis Spratlan won the Pulitzer Prize for Music in 2000 for the concert version of his opera LIFE IS A DREAM. Spratlan, born in Miami, has been teaching music at Amherst College since 1970 and became a professor there in 1980. He has written a good deal of vocal and chamber music but only one opera.

STAMBLER, BERNARD   *American librettist*

Bernard Stambler made a major contribution to modern American opera by writing librettos for eight operas, five in collaboration with composer Robert Ward. Stambler began working with Ward, a colleague at Juilliard School of Music, on HE WHO GETS SLAPPED/PANTALOON, based on a Leonid Andreyev play, which premiered at Juilliard in 1956. Next was THE CRUCIBLE, based on the play by Arthur Miller, which premiered at New York City Opera in 1961 and won a Pulitzer Prize. The collaborators followed with THE LADY FROM COLORADO, based on a novel by Homer Croy, premiered at Central City Opera House in 1964. They later revised it and with the new title LADY KATE it was premiered by Ohio Light Opera in 1994. CLAUDIA LEGARE, based on Ibsen's *Hedda Gabler*, was premiered by Minnesota Opera in 1978. Stambler also created librettos for three other composers. For Vittorio Giannini he wrote THE SERVANT OF TWO MASTERS, based on the Goldoni play, which was premiered by New York City Opera in 1967. For Thomas Pasatieri he wrote INES DE CASTRO, premiered by Baltimore Lyric Opera in 1976. For Joseph Turrin he wrote *Feathertop*, based on the Nathaniel Hawthorne story, which was commissioned by the New Jersey State Council on the Arts in 1976.

"STANDIN' IN THE NEED OF PRAYER"   *Baritone aria: The Emperor Jones (1933). Music and Lyrics: Traditional, arranged by Gruenberg.*

This spiritual has a position in American opera rather like that of "The Last Rose of Summer" as used in Flotow's *Martha*. Both are traditional melodies which have become part of the operatic repertory through their use in an opera. It was discovered by African American singer-composer Henry T. Burleigh and used by composer Luis Gruenberg as an aria in his 1933 opera THE EMPEROR JONES. Lawrence Tibbett sang it at the Met when the opera premiered and it became one of his best known recital pieces. "Standin' in the Need of Prayer" is the climax of the opera and is its only real aria because the singers speak-sing the other vocals. African American Pullman porter Brutus Jones has made himself emperor of a West Indian island but is being hunted down by rebellious subjects. After begging God's mercy, he shoots himself. *The Emperor Jones* is based on a 1920 Eugene O'Neill play made into a film starring Paul Robeson. "Standin' in the Need of Prayer"

remains popular through recordings by Tibbett and George London as well as gospel singers.

STAPLETON, JEAN   *American singing actress (1923–)*

Jean Stapleton, who played Archie Bunker's wife in the series *All in the Family* and had leading roles in several Broadway musicals, isn't usually thought of an opera singer but she had great success touring the U.S. with two American operas. She played the Manhattan matron juggling too many roles in Lee Hoiby's THE ITALIAN LESSON and the TV chef declaiming a recipe for chocolate cake in Hoiby's BON APPÉTIT! Stapleton, a New York native, inherited her talent as her mother was an opera singer.

THE STARBIRD   *1981 children's opera by Mollicone*

Dog, Cat and Donkey are abandoned and homeless after being replaced by mechanical devices. Starbird arrives and tells them that she was once a real bird but was taken to the planet Arcturus and changed into a metal one. When robots take Starbird away, the animals hide out on the spaceship. Starbird tells them how to deactivate the robots and they return to earth with a better understanding of what they are. Henry Mollicone's popular one-act children's opera *Starbird,* libretto by Kate Pogue, was commissioned by Houston Grand Opera and premiered at St. John the Divine School in Houston on April 27, 1981. Kathryn Wright was Starbird, Neil Wilson was Dog, Lynn Yakes was Cat, S. Ray Jacobs was Donkey and Chris Trakas and Dennis Peterson were the Robots. Franco Colavecchia designed the costumes, Maxine Willi Klein designed the sets, Mabel Robinson directed and Louis Salemno conducted.

STARER, ROBERT   *American composer (1924–2001)*

Robert Starer is best known for orchestral and chamber work, including a critically-acclaimed violin concerto, but he also composed six operas, three with librettos by Gail Godwin. THE LAST LOVER, libretto by Godwin about a female saint in ancient Antioch, premiered at Caramoor Festival in Katonah, NY, in 1975. APOLLONIA, libretto by Godwin about a woman with magic powers, was staged by Minnesota Opera in 1979. *Anna Margarita's Will,* libretto by Godwin, was performed in New York in 1981. Starer's first opera was *The Intruder,* libretto by M. A. Pryor about an intruder in a New England farmhouse; it was performed in New York in 1956. PANTAGLEIZE, libretto by the composer based on a Michel de Ghelderode play about an innocent who starts a revolution, premiered at Brooklyn College Opera in 1973. *Mystic Trumpeter,* libretto by the composer based on a Walt Whitman poem, was presented at Brooklyn College in 1983. Starer, who was born in Austria and studied in Vienna, Jerusalem and New York, became an American citizen in 1957. He published an autobiography in 1987 called *Continuo: A Life in Music.*

STAUF   *1976 music theater by Sahl and Salzman*

Idealistic inventor Henry Stauf joins the Goodwerx company and falls in love with receptionist Margarita. The deities Jove and Kali use Stauf and Margarita as pawns in a destructive game they play. When Stauf becomes an executive in a nuclear power corporation and Margarita attempts to get a dangerous plant closed, he has her killed. Michael Sahl and Eric Salzman's *Stauf,* libretto by the composers based on the Faust legend, was premiered by Quog Music Theater at the Cubiculo Theater in New York on May 25, 1976. The score is an eclectic mixture of musical styles ranging from traditional opera and classical serial to gospel, country and Broadway. *Stauf* was reprised at the American Music Theatre Festival in Philadelphia in 1987.

STEAL ME, SWEET THIEF *Soprano aria: The Old Maid and the Thief (1939). Words and music: Gian Carlo Menotti.*

"What a curse for a woman is a timid man!" declaims the maid Laetitia who is upset because the thief she and her old maid employer are hiding won't make any advances. After her recitative, she sings the soprano aria "Steal me, oh steal me, sweet thief" in Gian Carlo Menotti's 1939 opera *The Old Maid and the Thief.* The aria was introduced in its radio premiere by Margaret Down as Laetitia and her version is on CD. Virginia MacWatters sings it in a 1949 NBC Television production, Olive Moorefield in a 1964 Austrian TV production, Margaret Baker in a recording made in Italy in 1970, Helen-Kay Eberley on her 1983 recital album *American Girl* and Dawn Upshaw on her 1989 recital album *Knoxville: Summer of 1915.* "Steal me, sweet thief" is one of four American opera arias analyzed in Martial Singher's superb study *An Interpretive Guide to Operatic Arias.*

STEARNS, THEODORE *American composer (1875–1935)*

Theodore Stearns, awarded the Bispham Memorial Medal in 1925 for his opera SNOWBIRD, was a conductor and music critic in addition to being composer. He wrote two operas that were staged. *Snowbird,* libretto by the composer about a Tartar prince and a girl he rescues, was premiered by Chicago Civic Opera on January 13, 1923, with Mary McCormick as Snowbird and José Mojica as The Archer; it was reprised by Dresden State Opera in Germany in 1928. The two-act *Atlantis,* libretto by the composer about a contemporary couple who discover they were lovers in ancient Atlantis, was also staged by Dresden Opera. Stearns was born in Berea, Ohio, studied at Oberlin College and the Royal Music School in Würzburg, Bavaria, and became head of the music department at UCLA in 1932.

STEBER, ELEANOR *American soprano (1916–1990)*

Eleanor Steber created the role of Vanessa in Samuel Barber's opera VANESSA at the Metropolitan Opera in 1958, is featured on the classic Met recording of the opera and led its famous quintet "To Leave, To Break" in a farewell concert gala at the old Met in 1966. She sings "Summertime" from George Gershwin's PORGY AND BESS on a 1946 recording and "Lucy's Aria" from Gian Carlo Menotti's THE TELEPHONE on a 1992 album of concert performances. She was one of the most popular stars on the *Voice of Firestone* TV series where she sang two arias from Victor Herbert's NAUGHTY MARIETTA (1949), one from Sigmund Romberg's MAYTIME (1949), one from Herbert's ORANGE BLOSSOMS (1951), one from Herbert's SWEETHEARTS (1952) and one from PORGY AND BESS (1954). She recorded a highlights version of Romberg's operetta THE NEW MOON with Nelson Eddy in 1950. Steber, born in Wheeling, West Virginia, began to sing at the Met in 1940 and performed there regularly until 1963. She may be undervalued today but her status as one of the great American sopranos is evident through her recordings.

STEGNER, WALLACE *American writer (1909–1993)*

Wallace Stegner wrote fiction and non-fiction about life in the American West and became widely known with his fifth novel, *The Big Rock Candy Mountain* (1943). He won the Pulitzer Prize for *Angle of Repose* (1971) and this novel became the basis for an opera. Andrew Imbrie's three-act opera ANGLE OF REPOSE, libretto by Oakley Hall, tells the story of a troubled modern historian looking back at the hardships endured by his pioneer grandparents in California. It was premiered at San Francisco Opera in 1976.

STEIN, GERTRUDE *American writer/librettist (1874–1946)*

Gertrude Stein has had a strong influence on American opera through her librettos and plays and has inspired dozens of composers. Her libretto for FOUR SAINTS IN THREE ACTS (1934), created in collaboration with composer Virgil Thomson, changed ideas about what opera librettos could be and is still amazing after all these years. Thomson's THE MOTHER OF US ALL (1947), a pageant opera revolving around 19th American feminist leader Susan B. Anthony, was ahead of it time and is only now beginning to be recognized for its innovations. Lord Berners commissioned a libretto from Stein on the Faust legend which resulted in her 1938 libretto DOCTOR FAUSTUS LIGHTS THE LIGHTS. He never composed music for it but it was later set by five American composers. Her other librettos and plays are equally popular with American composers and many have been set more than once. She also appears in operas. Stein and Alice B. Toklas are the principal characters in Eugene Armour's *We're Back* (1981), set in their Paris apartment; Stein is seen as Gertrude S. in Thomson's *The Mother of Us All*; and Ben Johnston's opera *Gertrude: or, Would She Be Pleased to Receive It* (1956) is a satire on her style. Stein, who was born in Allegheny, Pennsylvania, and studied at Radcliffe, became the center of an artistic salon in Paris with her lifetime companion Alice B. Toklas. Her influence on writers and artists was as important as her involvement in music and opera.

1964 The Making of America. Marian Seldes reads Stein's *The Making of America* and *Lectures in America* in the Poet's Theatre series produced by Scott D'Arcy. Folkways LP. **1965 Mother Goose of Montparnasse.** Addison M. Metcalf reads Stein's opera libretto *Ladies' Voices,* an excerpt from the libretto *What Happened,* the song *Susie Asado* and other Stein works on the record album *Mother Goose of Montparnasse.* Folkways LP. **1970 When This You See, Remember Me.** Perry Miller Adato's documentary film *Gertrude Stein: When This You See, Remember Me* traces her life and career from childhood and includes Virgil Thomson talking about their collaboration."When this you see, remember me" is a line sung by the chorus in their opera *Four Saints in Three Acts.* Meridian VHS. **1987 Waiting for the Moon.** Jill Godmilow's fiction film *Waiting for the Moon,* screenplay by Mark McGill, stars Linda Bassett as Gertrude Stein and Linda Hunt as her life companion Alice B. Toklas. It is mainly concerned with their relationship. Key Video VHS.

Operas: In the following list of Stein operas. the composer's name is followed by place and date of premiere. Librettos by Stein unless otherwise indicated. **The Blackberry Vine.** 1969 Anna Sternberg, Astor Place Theater, New York City, December 15, 1969. **Doctor Faustus Lights the Lights.** 1953 Meyer Kupferman, Sarah Lawrence College, Bronxville, NY, April 5, 1953. 1957 Charles Wuorinen, unperformed. 1979 Alvin Carmines, Judson Memorial Church, New York City, October 1979. 1982 David Ahlstrom, San Francisco, October 29, 1982. 1987 Vernon Martin, unperformed. **Four Saints in Three Acts.** 1934 Virgil Thomson, Hartford, Connecticut, February 6, 1934. **In a Garden.** 1949 Meyer Kupferman, After Dinner Opera, New York City, December 29, 1949. 1969 Anna Sternberg, Astor Place Theater, New York City, December 15, 1969. **In Circles.** 1961 Alvin Carmines, Judson Memorial Church, New York City, October 1961. **Ladies' Voices.** 1956 Vernon Martin, Norman, Oklahoma, June 3, 1956. 1980 Kay Gardner, unperformed. **Listen to Me.** 1967 Alvin Carmines, Judson Memorial Church, New York City, May 1967. **Look and Long.** 1971 Marvin Schwartz, After Dinner Opera, Lake Placid, NY, July 27, 1971. **The Making of America.** 1968 Alvin

Carmines, libretto by Leon Katz based on book by Stein, Judson Memorial Church, New York City, 1968. **A Manoir.** 1966 Alvin Carmines, Judson Memorial Church, New York City, 1966. **A Memoir.** 1977 Alvin Carmines, Judson Memorial Church, New York City, April 22, 1977. **The Mother of Us All.** 1947 Virgil Thomson, Columbia University, New York City, May 7, 1947. **Photograph 1920.** 1971 Martin Kalmanoff, After Dinner Opera, Lake Placid, NY, July 27, 1971. **Remember Him to Me.** 2003 Robert Moran, Long Beach Opera, Long Beach, CA, June 8, 2003. **Three Sisters Who Are Not Sisters.** 1953 David Ahlstrom, Cincinnati, March 1, 1953. 1969 Anna Sternberg, Astor Place Theater, New York City, December 15, 1969. 1971 Ned Rorem, Temple University, Philadelphia, July 24, 1971. **What Happened.** 1963 Alvin Carmine, Judson Memorial Church, New York City, 1963. **The World Is Round.** 1993 James Sellars, libretto by Juanita Rockwell, based on Stein's book, Hartford, 1993.

STEINBECK, JOHN *American writer (1902–1968)*

John Steinbeck. who was born in Salinas, California, received the Nobel Prize for Literature in 1962. He first became known in the 1930s through his California novels *Tortilla Flat* (1935) and *Of Mice and Men* (1937) but it was *The Grapes of Wrath* (1939), his novel about Dust Bowl refugees, that made him a national figure. It has been compared in its effect on public opinion to *Uncle Tom's Cabin* and was awarded the the Pulitzer Prize. It was made into a superb film by John Ford in 1940 and Minnesota Opera has commissioned composer Ricky Ian Gordon and librettist Michael Korie to turn it into an opera. Three other Steinbeck novels have already been made into operas.

Burning Bright. 1993 Frank Lewin's *Burning Bright*, libretto by composer. Premiere: Yale School of Music, New Haven, November 5, 1993. **The Grapes of Wrath.** 2006 Ricky Ian Gordon's *The Grapes of Wrath*, libretto by Michael Korie. To be premiered by Minnesota Opera in 2006–2007 season. **Of Mice and Men.** 1970 Carlisle Floyd's OF MICE AND MEN, libretto by the composer. Premiere: Seattle Opera, Seattle, January 22, 1970. **The Pearl.** 1971 Lor Crane's *The Pearl*, libretto by Seymour Reiter. Premiere: Golden Fleece, New York, June 7, 1984.

STEINER, EMMA *American composer/conductor (1852–1929)*

Emma Steiner was one of the first American women to have a comic opera produced on stage. Her two-act FLEURETTE, libretto by Edgar Smith and B. W. Doremus, was staged in San Francisco in 1889 and in New York in 1891. Its overture was performed at the Metropolitan Opera House on November 17, 1925, when Steiner was honored for her achievements. The Met program also included scenes from two other Steiner operas: the two-act opéra bouffe *The Man from Paris*, libretto by M. I Macdonald and J. W. Castle, and the three-act light opera *The Burra Pundit*, libretto by Katherine Stagg and Joe-Ker. Steiner composed nine light operas in all and reportedly conducted over 6000 performances of operas and operettas with touring companies. She was born in Baltimore, began composing at an early age and learned her trade conducting touring productions of Gilbert and Sullivan operettas.

STERLINGMAN *1957 TV opera by Roy*

In a small town on St. Martin's Eve a stranger visits an elderly couple and makes them an offer they can't refuse. Klaus George Roy's satirical 54-minute opera *Sterlingman, or Generosity Rewarded*, libretto by the composer based on a story by Arkady Averchenko, was premiered on WGFBH-TV in Boston on April 18, 1957, and staged by Western Reserve University in Cleveland on May 26, 1960.

STEVENS, RISË *American mezzo-soprano (1913–)*

Risë Stevens is best known for singing Carmen but she was also interested in American opera and operetta. She performs an abridged version of Deems Taylor's THE KING'S HENCHMAN with Lawrence Tibbett and Charles Kullman on a 1942 radio broadcast, recorded the aria "My Man's Gone Now," from George Gershwin's PORGY AND BESS in 1950 and sings the aria "Beware of a Hawk" from Victor Herbert's NATOMA on a 1952 Bell Telephone Hour program. She created the role of Marsee in Richard Adler's *Little Women* on CBS Television in 1958 and made many recordings of classic operettas. She sings numbers from Sigmund Romberg's MY MARYLAND on a 1945 recording, Kathie in a 1947 highlights recording of Romberg's THE STUDENT PRINCE, Shirley in a 1948 broadcast recording of Jerome Kern's THE CAT AND THE FIDDLE, Gretchen in a 1951 broadcast recording of Herbert's THE RED MILL, Julie in a 1962 operatic recording of Kern's SHOW BOAT, Liza in a 1963 studio recording of Kurt Weill's' LADY IN THE DARK and Anna in a 1964 Lincoln Center revival recording of Richard Rodgers' THE KING AND I. She recorded "Lover, Come Back to Me" from Romberg's THE NEW MOON and "I'm Falling in Love With Someone" from Herbert's NAUGHTY MARIETTA in 1949 and she sang the Herbert aria again on a 1951 *Voice of Firestone* TV program. Stevens, who was born in New York City and studied at Juilliard, made her debut in Prague in 1936 and sang at the Met from 1938 to 1960. She was the most popular guest on the *Voice of Firestone* television series, appearing 47 times, but is best known to the general public for her appearance in the 1944 film *Going My Way*.

STEVENS, WALLACE *American poet (1879–1955)*

Wallace Stevens, the only major poet to be a full-time insurance executive, created some of the most memorable poems and images of the 20th century. While many of his poems have been set to music, there appears to be only one music theater work based on a Stevens' poem. Roger Reynolds, who won the 1989 Pulitzer Prize for Music for *Whispers Out of Time*, used Wallace's poem *The Emperor of Ice Cream* as libretto for his 1962 theatre piece featuring eight soloists, piano, percussion and bass. It was performed in New York City on March 19, 1965, and at the University of Wisconsin in Milwaukee on November 17, 1965.

STICH-RANDALL, TERESA *American soprano (1927–)*

Teresa Stich-Randall created the role of Henrietta M. in Virgil Thomson's THE MOTHER OF US ALL in 1947 at Columbia University while she was still a student. The following year she sang the title role in the first full stage production of Otto Luening's opera EVANGELINE, again at Columbia University. Arturo Toscanini heard her singing on the radio, cast her in his broadcast of *Aida* and launched her on a successful international career. She made her Met debut in 1961 but her greatest popularity was at the Vienna State Opera where she sang for twenty years. Stich-Randall, who was born in West Hartford, CT, and studied at Hartford and Columbia, retired from the stage in 1971.

STILL, WILLIAM GRANT *American composer (1895–1978)*

African American composer William Grant Still began to compose operas in the mid-1930s but only three of his operas were staged in his lifetime. TROUBLED ISLAND (1941), libretto by Langston Hughes about Haitian revolutionary Jean Jacques Dessalines, was produced at New York City Opera in 1949 and was the first African American opera staged by a major company. Still's other operas were composed to librettos by his wife Verna Arvey. HIGHWAY 1 U.S.A. (1962), libretto by Arvey about a man who make sacrifices to put his no-good brother through college, was staged at the University of Miami in 1963. A BAYOU LEGEND (1941), libretto by Arvey based on a Mississippi legend about a spirit lover, was premiered by Opera/South in Jackson, Mississippi. in 1974 and telecast in 1981. MINETTE FONTAINE, libretto by Arvey about an opera diva and her lover in 19th century New Orleans, was premiered by Baton Rouge Opera in Louisiana on October 22, 1985. Still, who was born in Woodville, Mississippi, and studied at Oberlin, first attracted attention with his 1930 *Afro-American Symphony*. His operas are melodious and tonal and continue to be performed.

STILL IN LOVE   *1996 music theater work by Kowalski*

He and She separate and then reunite. Their breakups and sexual dalliances are portrayed in flashback, in the present and in a dream of the future. Michael Kowalski's postmodern music theater piece *Still in Love*, libretto by Kier Peters based on his play *Past, Present and Future Tense*, was premiered by the Postindustrial Players at Roulette in New York in January 1996 after previews at the Context Studio in July 1995. Karen Grahn sang the role of She, Gregory Purnhagen was He and April Greenberg was Betty. Gerhard Schlanzky designed the set, Constance McCord directed and Kowalski conducted and played the synthesizer while Yari Bond played cello.

1996 Postindustrial Players. Karen Grahn is She and Gregory Purnhagen is He in this recording made on February 17 and 28 1996 at Sorcerer Sounds in New York following the premiere at Roulette. Yari Bond plays cello and Michael Kowalski plays synthesizer and leads the group. Equilibrium CD.

STILLER, ANDREW   *American composer (1946–)*

Andrew Stiller is best known as a music critic and composer of instrumental works but he composed one chamber opera. *Lavender*, libretto by the composer based on an underground comic strip by Trina Robbins about a sorceress, was premiered by Opera Antica e Moderna at State University of New York at Buffalo, on May 25, 1978. Stiller, who was born in Washington, D.C., studied composition at SUNY Buffalo where he later taught.

STILWELL, RICHARD   *American baritone (1942–)*

Richard Stilwell created roles in four American operas. He was Eric Rupert in Gian Carlo Menotti's THE MOST IMPORTANT MAN at New York City Opera in 1971, Constantine in Thomas Pasatieri's THE SEAGULL at Houston Grand Opera in 1974, Pedro in Thomas Pasatieri's INES DI CASTRO at Baltimore Opera in 1976 and the Lodger in Dominick Argento's THE ASPERN PAPERS at Dallas Opera in 1988. He sings Horace in a live recording of a 1992 Cleveland Opera production of Douglas Moore's THE BALLAD OF BABY DOE, Griswold in a 1992 Lyric Opera of Chicago broadcast of Dominick Argento's THE VOYAGE OF EDGAR ALLAN POE and the Doctor in a Seattle Opera broadcast of Samuel Barber's VANESSA in 1999. Stilwell, who was born in St. Louis, began his musical career with the US Army Chorus and made his debut with New York City Opera in 1970.

STOESSEL, ALBERT   *American composer/conductor (1894–1943)*

Albert Stoessel became director of the opera and orchestra departments of the Juilliard School in 1927 and conducted the premieres of George Antheil's HELEN RETIRES, Robert Russell

Bennett's MARIA MALIBRAN, Luis Gruenberg's JACK AND THE BEANSTALK and his own GARRICK. This three-act opera, libretto by Robert Simon about the English stage actor David Garrick, premiered at Juilliard on February 24, 1937, and was awarded the Bispham Medal as the best American opera of the year. Stoessel was born in St. Louis and studied there and in Berlin. He began his career as a violinist and learned to conduct while serving in the Army in World War I. He was conducted several music festivals in the 1920s and organized New York University's music department.

STOKES, NORMAN   *American composer (1930–1999)*

Norman Stokes, who founded Minnesota University's electronic music program, composed seven experimental operas. The elaborate multi-media work HORSPFAL, libretto by Alvin Greenburg dealing with the exploitation of native Americans and requiring multiple conductors and film projection, was premiered by Minnesota Opera in Minneapolis February 15, 1969. The jokey birthday celebration micro-opera *HAPP, or Orpheus in Clover*, libretto by the composer of lyrics that spell "Happy Birthday," was premiered in Minneapolis October 11, 1977. *The Jealous Cellist*, libretto by Greenberg, is a science-fiction story about couples switching in time, features barbershop quartets and accordion ensembles; it was premiered by Minnesota Opera on February 2, 1979, with Philip Brunelle conducting. *Itaru the Stonecutter,* an opera for children and adults with libretto by the composer based on a Japanese folk tale, premiered at the Brimhall School in Roseville, Minnesota, on March 25, 1982. The TV opera *We're Not Robots, You Know*, libretto by Keith Gunderson about marionettes who get robots to do their housework, was telecast in Minneapolis in 1986. *Apollonia's Circus* (1994), libretto by Greenberg retelling the Orpheus myth in a modern circus context, was commissioned by University of Minnesota Opera which premiered it on May 13, 1994; tenor Vern Sutton was the principal singer and David Zinman conducted. *The Future Voyages of the Santa Maria*, libretto by Greenberg, allows the spirit of Columbus to join astronauts on a space ship called the Santa Maria. Stokes, who was born in Haddon Heights, New Jersey, studied at Lawrence, New England Conservatory and Minnesota University and was professor of music at Minnesota from 1961 to 1988.

STOKES, RICHARD   *American librettist*

Richard L. Stokes wrote the libretto for Howard Hanson's MERRY MOUNT based on Nathaniel Hawthorne's story *The Maypole of Merry Mount*. It premiered at the Metropolitan Opera in 1934. Earlier he had written the libretto for Isaac's Van Grove's prize-winning opera about Mozart's last days, *The Music Robber*, which premiered at Cincinnati Opera in 1926.

STONE, WILLIAM   *American baritone*

William Stone has recorded arias from six operas by Robert Ward: ABELARD AND HELOISE, CLAUDIA LEGARE, THE CRUCIBLE, HE WHO GETS SLAPPED, THE LADY FROM COLORADO and MINUTES TILL MIDNIGHT. They're on his CD *Robert Ward: Arias and Songs*. Stone, who has sung in European operas at most of the major opera houses including the Met and New York City Opera, made his his debut at Washington Opera playing John Sorel in Gian Carlo Menotti's THE CONSUL. He sang the baritone role in the premiere of Leon Kirchner's *Of Things Exactly as They Are* in Boston in 1997.

THE STONED GUEST   *1967 parody opera by Schickele*

Mezzanine-soprano Donna Ribalda, a high-born lady of the

lowlands, has been abducted and is lost in a forest where she meets off-coloratura Carmen Ghia, a woman of ailing repute. Bargain counter tenor Don Octave arrives and is complaining about his fate when he is recognized by Donna Ribalda as her abductor. Her brother, Houndtenor Dog, a friendly St. Bernard, arrives with an empty liquor cask that was consumed by basso blatto Il Commendatoreador, the Stoned Guest, who is also Carmen's father. P.D.Q. Bach's aka Peter Schickele's "half-act opera" *The Stoned Guest,* libretto by the composer, premiered at Carnegie Hall in New York in December 1967. It features a cast borrowed from Mozart's *Don Giovanni* and Bizet's *Carmen* and a title stolen from Dargomizhsky's Russian opera *The Stone Guest.* It has become popular with small opera companies and there have been more than a dozen productions around the U.S. from Pittsburgh to Santa Cruz.

1970 Hoople Heavy Opera Company. This recording is in the form of an imaginary broadcast of *The Stoned Guest* with a Met-style intermission quiz. Marlene Kleinman is Donna Ribalda, Lorna Haywood is Carmen Ghia, John Ferrante is Don Octave, Bernice is the Dog and Peter Schickele the Commendatoreador Stoned Guest. John Nelson conducts the Orchestra of the University of Southern North Dakota for the Hoople Heavy Opera Company in Hoople. The "broadcast" also includes Will Jordan as Milton Host and Billy Macy as Paul Henry Lung. The recording was produced by Seymour Solomon with supervision from Schickele. Vanguard LP/CD.

STOTHART, HERBERT   *American composer (1895–1949)*

MGM stalwart Herbert Stothart, one of the principal promoters of opera in Hollywood, created the movie operas CZARITZA for MAYTIME (1937) and BALALAIKA for *Balalaika* (1939) and co-composed the stage operettas THE SONG OF THE FLAME with George Gershwin and ROSE MARIE with Rudolf Friml. He worked on all the Jeanette MacDonald/Nelson Eddy films operetta films, including SWEETHEARTS, NEW MOON, THE GIRL OF THE GOLDEN WEST and THE FIREFLY, and won an Oscar for orchestrating *The Wizard of Oz* (1939). Stothart was born in Milwaukee and studied music at the University of Wisconsin where he began to compose and conduct university productions. He began working on Broadway in 1920 and moved to Hollywood in 1929 where he composed, arranged and conducted 110 films for MGM.

STOWE, HARRIET BEECHER   *American novelist (1811–1896)*

Harriet Beecher Stowe's anti-slavery novel UNCLE TOM'S CABIN (1852), inspired by the Fugitive Slave Act of 1850, is one of the most influential novels ever written. It is credited with increasing American resistance to slavery and furthering the move towards Civil War and was equally popular internationally. The first opera based on it was composed in Italy just a year after it was published, Paolo Giorza's *La Capanna dello zio Tom.* It has inspired four American operas, by Caryl Florio (1882), Harrison Millard (1883) Leslie Grossmith (1928) and Avery Claflin (1966), but none were particularly successful. Stowe was the daughter of a clergyman (Lyman Beecher) and the wife of another (Calvin Ellis Stowe) Her other books include non-fiction works like *A Key to Uncle Tom's Cabin* (1853) and novels like *The Minister's Wooing* (1859) and *Oldtown Folks* (1868).

STRATAS, TERESA   *Canadian soprano (1938–)*

Teresa Stratas has created major roles in American operas. She sang the title role in the premiere of Peggy Glanville-Hicks NAUSICAA at the Athens Festival in Greece in 1961 and Marie Antoinette in John Corigliano's THE GHOSTS OF VERSAILLES at the Metropolitan Opera in 1991. She played Mother in the 1979 film of Gian Carlo Menotti's AMAHL AND THE NIGHT VISITORS and sang the role of Sardula in the American premiere of Menotti's THE LAST SAVAGE at the Met in 1963. She sings Julie on a 1988 operatic recording of Jerome Kern's SHOW BOAT and she performs a selection of songs from American music theater works by Kurt Weill on her 1986 album *Stratas Sings Weill,* including numbers from KNICKERBOCKER HOLIDAY, LADY IN THE DARK, ONE TOUCH OF VENUS and STREET SCENE. Stratas, born Anastasia Strataki in Canada, made her debut in 1958 in Toronto and began to sing at the Met in 1959.

STRAVINSKY, IGOR   *American composer (1882–1971)*

Igor Stravinsky, who created operas that broke the boundaries of what operas were expected to be, composed two after he emigrated to America. The most important is THE RAKE'S PROGRESS (1951), his most popular opera, with modern 18th century-like music composed to a brilliant libretto by W. H. Auden and Chester Kallman. He was inspired to write it while visiting an exhibition of Hogarth drawings in Chicago that featured *A Rake's Progress.* His last opera was created for American television. THE FLOOD, libretto by Robert Craft about the Biblical story of humanity from Adam to Noah, was commissioned by CBS and telecast in 1962. Stravinsky, who was born in Russia, spent the last thirty years of his life in the U.S. He even left his mark on Hollywood as composer of one of the memorable episodes in Walt Disney's *Fantasia.*

1968 A Stravinsky Portrait. Richard Leacock's 57-minute documentary film *A Stravinsky Portrait* shows the composer discussing his work with colleagues, conducting a German orchestra and relaxing with his wife in Beverly Hills. On VHS. **1982 "Once, at a border..." Aspects of Stravinsky.** Tony Palmer's three-hour film *"Once, at a border..." Aspects of Stravinsky* consist of three parts: the first about his career in Russia, the second about his work in Europe and the third about his life in the U.S. It includes documents, photographs, film extracts, music and interviews. Kultur VHS.

STRAWBERRY FIELDS   *1999 opera by Torke*

A confused old lady thinks Central Park is the Metropolitan Opera and is enjoying herself until her children take her off to a retirement home. Michael Torke's one-act opera *Strawberry Fields,* libretto by A. R. Gurney, is the second opera in the CENTRAL PARK trilogy premiered at Glimmerglass Opera on August 8, 1999, and staged at New York City Opera in November 1999. Joyce Castle played the Old Lady, Jeffery Lentz was the Student, Daniel Ihasz was the Workman, John Hancock was the Son, Enrique Abdala was the Boy, Kelly E. Kaduce was the Girl, Troy Cook was the Panhandler, Barbara Lemay was the Nurse, and Margaret Lloyd was the daughter. Michael Yeargan designed the sets, Mark Lamos directed and Stewart Robertson conducted. When the opera was reprised at New York City opera, Mimi Lerner played the Old Lady. The trilogy was telecast in 2000.

STREET SCENE   *1946 opera by Weill*

Twenty four hours in the life of Manhattan tenement dwellers on a hot summer day. The loose plot revolves around Anna Maurrant who is having an affair and will be killed over it by her jealous husband Frank. Their daughter Rose is loved by Sam but is tempted to go off with smooth-talking Harry. Kurt Weill's Broadway opera *Street Scene,* libretto by Elmer Rice based on his Pulitzer

Scene from 1999 Des Moines Metro Opera production of *Street Scene.* **Photograph courtesy of Des Moines Metro Opera.**

Prize-winning play with lyrics by poet Langston Hughes, premiered at the Shubert Theatre in Philadelphia on December 16, 1946, and opened at the Adelphi Theater in New York on January 9, 1947. Anne Jeffreys was Rose, Brian Sullivan was Sam, Polyna Stoska was Anna, Norman Cordon was Frank, Hope Emerson was Emma Jones, Remo Lotta was Daniel Buchanan, Beverly Janis was Jennie Hildebrand, Bennett Burrill was Charlie Hildebrand, Creighton Thompson was Henry Davis, Don Saxon was Harry Easter and Norma Chambers was Shirley Kaplan. Jo Mielziner designed the sets, Charles Friedman directed and Maurice Abravanel conducted the orchestra. The opera's many memorable numbers include the opening quartet "Ain't it awful, the heat?" sung by street residents, Anna's tragic "SOMEHOW I NEVER COULD BELIEVE," the street resident's delightful "Ice-Cream Sextet," in praise of one of life's great pleasures, Frank's plea "Let things be like they always was," Sam's sad "LONELY HOUSE," Harry's seductive "Wouldn't you like to be on Broadway?" sung to Rose, Rose's melancholic answer "WHAT GOOD WOULD THE MOON BE?" and Dick and Mae's jitterbug number "MOON-FACED, STARRY EYED." The opera was revived by New York City Opera in 1959 and 1966 and continues to be staged, including recent productions by Scottish Opera, English National Opera, Houston Grand Opera and Lyric Opera of Chicago.

1931 Goldwyn film. Elmer Rice's play *Street Scene,* which is essentially the libretto of the opera, was filmed by Samuel Goldwyn in 1931 in an adaptation made by Rice himself. Sylvia Sidney plays Rose, William Collier Jr. is Sam, Estelle Taylor is Anna, David Landau is Frank and Beulah Bondi as Emma Jones. King Vidor directed. On VHS. **1947 Original Broadway Cast.** Kurt Weill supervised an album of highlights from the opera with the original Broadcast cast. Anne Jeffreys is Rose, Polyna Stoska is Anna, Brian Sullivan is Sam, Norman Cordon is Frank, Hope Emerson is Emma Jones, Remo Lotta is Daniel Buchanan, Beverly Janis is Jennie Hildebrand, Creighton Thompson is Henry Davis and Don Saxon is Harry Easter. Maurice Abravanel conducts. The liner notes are by Weill. Columbia LP/CBS CD. **1957 Lotte Lenya.** Lotte Lenya sings "Lonely House" and "A Boy Like You" with Maurice Levine conducting the orchestra on the album *Lotte Lenya Sings Kurt Weill: American Theater Songs.* Sony Classic CD. **1972 Berlin to Broadway with Kurt Weill.** In the off-Broadway revue *Berlin to Broadway with Kurt Weill, A Musical Voyage,* Hal Watters sings "Lonely House" and the cast perform "Ain't It Awful the Heat?" Paramount LP. **1978 New York City Opera.** Catherine Malfitano is Rose in this recording of a New York City Opera revival production. Eileen Schauler is Anna, Alan Kays is Sam, William Chapman is Frank, Alan Titus is Harry Easter, Rosemarie Freni is Olga Olsen and Dianne Curry is Emma Jones, John Mauceri conducts the ENO Orchestra and Chorus. Recorded November 5, 1978. Live opera audiocassette. **1979 New York City Opera.** Catherine Malfitano is again Rose in this fine New York City Opera production. Eileen Schauler is Anna, Alan Kays is Sam, William Chapman is Frank and Harlan Foss is Harry Easter. John Mauceri conducts the New York City Opera Orchestra and Chorus. Paul Sylvert designed the sets and Jack O'Brien staged the opera. Kirk Browning directed the telecast October 27,

1979, in the *Live from Lincoln Center* series. Music Master VHS. **1986 Teresa Stratas.** Soprano Teresa Stratas sings the tenor aria "Lonely House" on her album *Stratas Sings Weill* with Gerard Schwarz conducting the Y Chamber Orchestra. Nonesuch LP/CD. **1988 Jill Gomez.** Soprano Jill Gomez sings the tenor aria "Lonely House" on her album *Cabaret Classics* accompanied by pianist John Constable. Unicorn-Kanchana CD. **1991 Scottish Opera.** Josephine Barstow is Anna in this Scottish Opera recording of the opera. Angelina Reaux is Rose, Samuel Ramey is Frank, Jerry Hadley is Sam, Kurt Ollmann is Harry Easter, Ryan McBride is Willie Maurrant, Mary Munger is Mae Jones, Philip Gould is Dick McGann, Emile Belcourt is Abraham Kaplan, Elaine Mackillop is Greta Fiorentino, Anthony Mee is Lippo Fiorentino, David Kuebler is Mr. Buchanan, David Marsh is Carl Olsen, Meriel Dickinson is Emma Jones, Barbara Bonney is Jennie Hildebrand, Fiona Kimm is Olga Olsen, Sheila Bond is Mae Jones and Danny Daniels is Dick McGann. John Mauceri conducts the Scottish Opera Orchestra and Chorus. London/Decca CD box. **1991 Lincoln Center.** Leontyne Price introduces the "Ice Cream Sextet" from *Street Scene* at a televised concert at Lincoln Center on November 10, 1991. The singers are Maureen O'Flynn, Phyllis Pancella, Jerry Hadley, Paul Groves, Daniel Smith and Jeff Mattsey. James Conlon conducts members of the Metropolitan Opera Orchestra. The album is called *A Salute to American Music*. RCA Victor CD. **1992 Lesley Garrett.** Leslie Garrett sings Rose's aria "What Good Would the Moon Be?" with the Philharmonia Orchestra conducted by Ivor Bolton on her album *Lesley Garrett, Prima Donna*. Silva America CD. **1992 Melanie Marshall.** Mezzo-soprano Melanie Marshall sings the tenor aria "Lonely House" accompanied by pianist Wayne Marshall on the album *Soirée at Snape*. Mel CD. **1992 Angelina Réaux.** Soprano Angelina Reaux sings the tenor aria "Lonely House" accompanied by pianist Robert Kapilow on the album *Songs of Kurt Weill*. Koch International CD. **1992 English National Opera (recording).** Janis Kelly is Rose with Kristine Ciesinski as Anna in this English National Opera recording. Bonaventura Bottone is Sam, Richard Van Allan is Frank, Timothy Jenkins is Abraham, Claire Daniels is Jenny Hildebrand, Meriel Dickinson is Emma Jones, Susan Bullock is Greta Fiorentino, Peter Bronder is Lippo Fiorentino, Catherine Zeta Jones is Mae Jones, Arwel Huw Morgan is Mr. Olsen and Angela Hickey is Olga Olsen. Carl Davis conducts the ENO Chorus and Orchestra. TER Classics CD box. **1992 English National Opera (telecast).** Lesley Garrett is Rose with Janice Cairns as Anna in this English National Opera production taped for BBC Television. Kevin Anderson is Sam, Mark Richardson is Frank, Terry Jenkins is Abraham Kaplan, Richard Halton is Harry Easter, Sheila Squires is Olga Olsen, Arwel Huw Morgan is Mr. Olsen and Meriel Dickinson is Emma Jones. James Holmes conducts the English National Opera Orchestra and Chorus. This co-production with Scottish Opera, originally produced by David Pountney, was revived at ENO by Nicolette Molnár. David Fielding designed the set and Barrie Gavin directed the telecast on January 1, 1993. Live Opera VHS. **1994 Houston Grand Opera.** Ashley Putnam is Anna in this Houston Grand Opera production staged by Francesca Zambello in partnership with Theater im Pfalzbau and Theater des Westerns in Berlin. Teri Hansen is Rose, Marc Embree is Frank, Kip Wilborn is Sam, Wendy Hill is Mrs. Fiorentino, Anthony Mee is Lippo Fiorentino, Janice Felty is Mrs. Jones, Heidi Eisenberg is Mrs. Olsen, John Kuether is Mr. Olsen, David Rae Smith is Abraham Kaplan, Michael Scarborough is Mr. Easter, Dean Anthony is Mr. Buchanan, Anita Vidovic is Mae Jones, Danny Costello is Dick McGann and Ivan Thomas is Henry Davis. James Holmes con-

ducts the Staatsphilharmonie Rheinland/Pfalz Orchestra, Adrianne Lobel designed the sets, Manfred Bödefeld was cinematographer and José Montes-Baquer directed the video shot in December 1994. The production originated in Houston where it was staged in January 1994. Image Entertainment/Arthaus DVD. **1995 Dawn Upshaw.** Dawn Upshaw sings the tenor aria "Lonely House" accompanied by pianist David Zinman on her album *The World So Wide*. Nonesuch CD. **2000 Urs Affolter.** Urs Affolter sings "Lonely House" from *Street Scene* on the album *Stay Well: Urs Affolter Sings Kurt Weill* accompanied by Uli Kofler on piano. Antes CD. **2002 Lyric Opera of Chicago Commentary.** Critical analysis of *Street Scene* by Roger Pines in the *Women's Board of Lyric Opera* series. It includes musical excerpts, plot summary, composer biography and social and historical background. Lyric Opera Commentaries CD.

A STREETCAR NAMED DESIRE   *1998 opera by Previn*

Blanche DuBois, who says she has always relied on the kindness of strangers, comes to stay with her sister Stella in their New Orleans apartment. Stella is married to the uncouth Stanley Kowalski who is deeply suspicious of Blanche and her old South aristocratic attitudes. He investigates her past, which turns out to be fairly lurid, and tells his friend Mitch, who had wanted to marry her. Stella goes into hospital to have a baby, Stanley rapes Blanche and Blanche retreats into fantasy. André Previn's opera *A Streetcar Named Desire*, libretto by Philip Littell based on the play by Tennessee Williams, was commissioned by San Francisco Opera which premiered it on September 19, 1998. Renée Fleming was Blanche Dubois, Rodney Gilfry was Stanley, Elizabeth Futral was Stella, Anthony Dean Griffey was Mitch, Judith Forst was Eunice, Josepha Gayer was the Flower Seller, Matthew Lord was Steve, Jeffrey Lentz was the Young Collector, Ray Reinhardt was the Doctor, Luis Oropeza was Pablo Gonzales and Lynne Soffer was the Nurse. Michael Yeargan designed the sets, Colin Graham directed and André Previn conducted the orchestra. The opera received mixed reviews but was generally praised for its faithfulness to the play. San Diego Opera reprised the opera in April 2000 with a new Blanche (Sheryl Woods) and Stanley (David Okerlund), Austin Lyric Opera presented it in 2002 with Susannah Glanville as Blanche and Teddy Tahu Rhodes as Stanley and Washington Opera staged it in 2004 with Glanville and Rhodes again in the leading roles.

1998 San Francisco Opera. *A Streetcar Named Desire* was taped live for TV, DVD and CD at the War Memorial Opera House in September 1998 with the premiere cast. Renée Fleming is Blanche Dubois, Rodney Gilfry is Stanley, Elizabeth Futral is Stella, Anthony Dean Griffey is Mitch, Judith Forst is Eunice and the rest of the cast are as above. André Previn conducts. Kirk Browning directed the 166-minute video telecast on December 30, 1998, on PBS. Image Entertainment DVD/Kultur VHS/DG 2-CD box. **1999 Renée Fleming.** Renée Fleming, who created the role of Blanche, sings the aria "I Want Magic" from *A Streetcar Named Desire*, on her recital album *I Want Magic*. She is accompanied by James Levine and the Metropolitan Opera Orchestra. London Classics CD. **2001 André Previn.** Tony Palmer's 90-minute documentary *André Previn: The Kindness of Strangers* was made in connection with the San Francisco premiere of *A Streetcar Named Desire*. "The kindness of strangers" is a phrase used by Blanche in the opera and the play. Arthaus DVD. **2004 Washington Opera commentary.** Saul Lilienstein analyses *A Streetcar Named Desire* on this recording in the *Washington Opera Commentaries on CD* series. The commentary includes background on the opera and its composer with plot description and excerpts from the San Francisco recording with Renée Fleming as Blanche Dubois, Rodney Gilfry as Stanley and Elizabeth Futral as Stella. Washington Opera CD.

STRINGFIELD, LAMAR   *American composer (1897–1959)*

Lamar Stringfield, who founded the Folk Music Institute at the University of North Carolina, is more important to the world of folk music than opera but he composed two interesting folk-influenced stage works, the folk opera *The Mountain Song* (1929) and the folk comedy *Carolina Charcoal* (1953). Stringfield, who was born near Raleigh, NC, and studied at the Institute of Musical Art in New York, pioneered interest in traditional mountain music. He was awarded a Pulitzer Prize Music Scholarship in 1928 for *From the Southern Mountains* and he founded the North Carolina Symphony Orchestra in 1932.

THE STRONGER   *1952 opera by Weisgall*

An actress meets a friend in a cocktail bar on Christmas Eve afternoon and reveals her secret fears as she drinks. Estelle, the actress who can't stop talking about her husband Harold, is gradually revealed in her weakness while her friend Lisa, who never speaks, becomes stronger. Hugo Weisgall's one-act opera *The Stronger*, a soprano tour-de-force with libretto by Richard Hart based on August Strindberg's play *Den starkare*, was written for the Hilltop Opera Company of Baltimore which premiered it in Lutherville on August 6, 1952, with piano accompaniment. Weisgall replaced the original Estelle after the first performances with her understudy Eva Bober. The music is dissonant and atonal reflecting the feelings of Estelle. The opera was reprised with orchestra at Columbia University in New York in 1955 and has been staged a number of times since; it is Weisgall's most frequently performed opera.

Another American opera based on the Strindberg play, Gregory Kosteck's *The Stronger*, was premiered at East Carolina University in Greenville, SC, on April 30, 1970.

1955 Adelaide Bishop. Adelaide Bishop sings the solo soprano role of Estelle in this performance of the opera in New York with an orchestra conducted by Alfredo Antonini. Columbia LP. **1971 Johanna Meier.** Johanna Meier sings the solo soprano role of the opera in this recording with the Aeolian Chamber Players conducted by the composer. CRI LP/CD.

STROUSE, CHARLES   *American composer (1928–)*

Charles Strouse, a Broadway composer with a classical music education, wrote a charming much-performed opera for children. NIGHTINGALE, libretto by the composer based on a story by Hans Christian Andersen, premiered in New York in 1980 and was staged in London in 1982. Strouse's first Broadway musical, *Bye-Bye-Birdie*, lyrics by Lee Adams, was a hit and won the Tony as best musical of the year in 1960. His other Broadway successes include *Applause* (1970), again with Adams, and *Annie* (1977). Strouse, a native New Yorker, studied with Bernard Rogers at the Eastman School, with Aaron Copland at Berkshire Music Center and with Nadia Boulanger in Paris.

STUART, PAUL   *American composer (1956–)*

Paul Stuart has composed two operas, both staged and on record. KILL BEAR COMES HOME, libretto by Sally M. Gall based on an Iroquois legend, was premiered by Opera Theater of Rochester, New York, in April 1996. It tells the story of a man and a bear whose heads are transposed. The Christmas opera THE LITTLE THIEVES OF BETHLEHEM, libretto by Sally M. Gall, was premiered in the Third Presbyterian Church in Rochester on December 7, 1997. Stuart, who was born in Omaha, Nebraska, and studied at the Eastman School with David Diamond, also composes orchestral, chamber and choral music.

THE STUDENT FROM SALAMANCA   *1980 opera by Bach*

A husband is cuckolded by a clever wife. When he goes off on a trip, she invites male friends over for a party. Jan Bach's comic one-act opera *The Student from Salamanca*, libretto by the composer based on a tale by Cervantes, won a New York City Opera competition and was premiered by NYCO on October 9, 1980, in the program *An American Trilogy*. Susanne Marsee played the beautiful wife Mariana, Beverly Evans was her servant Cristina, John Lankston was her middle-aged husband Craccio, David Hall was Gonzalo, Jan Opalach was Nicolas and Allen Glassman was Stephano. Lloyd Evans designed the set, Jack Eddleman directed and Judith Somogi conducted the NYCO orchestra.

THE STUDENT PRINCE   *1924 operetta by Romberg*

Heidelberg in 1860. German Prince Karl-Franz has a bittersweet romance with innkeeper's daughter Kathie while he is a student at the university. They finally learn to accept that it is his duty to marry a princess for the good of the country. Sigmund Romberg's tuneful operetta *The Student Prince*, libretto by Dorothy Donnelly based on the 1902 German play *Alt Heidelberg* by Wilhelm Meyer-Forster, premiered at the Apollo Theater in Atlantic City, NJ, on October 27, 1924, and opened at the Jolson Theater in New York on December 2. Howard Marsh played the Prince, Ilse Marvenga was Kathi, Greek Evans was the Prince's tutor Dr. Engel, George Hassell was his valet Lutz and Roberta Betty was the Princess. This is Romberg's most popular operetta and features many well-known songs, including "Deep in My Heart," "Serenade" and "The Drinking Song." It has been recorded by many opera singers and revived many times.

1925 Victor Light Opera. The first recording from the operetta was a medley of songs performed by the Victor Light Opera Company for a Victor 78 titled *Gems from The Student Prince*. It includes "Deep in My Heart" and "The Drinking Song." **1926 London stage cast.** The stars of the first London stage production recorded a highlights version in 1926. Alan Prior is the Prince opposite Lucyenne Herval as Kathie with support from John Coast, Raymond Marlow and Paul Clemon World LP and *The Ultimate Sigmund Romberg* Pearl CD. **1927 MGM film.** Ernst Lubitsch's silent version of the operetta, *The Student Prince in Old Heidelberg*, stars Ramon Novarro as the Prince with Norma Shearer as Kathie. Lubitsch expands the story to include the early years of the Prince before he goes to university. Hans Kraly wrote the screenplay and John Mescall was the cinematographer. It was screened with a score by David Mendoza and William Axt and is on video with an orchestral soundtrack. MGM/UA VHS/DVD. **1929 Richard Crooks.** Met tenor Richard Crooks recorded "Serenade" in 1929 for a 78. It's on the 1998 album *Only a Rose—The Art of Richard Crooks in Song*. Pearl/Koch CD. **1940 Jan Peerce/Igor Gorin.** Jan Peerce and Igor Gorin perform songs from the operetta on a radio broadcast on May 16, 1940. Live Opera audiocassette. **1943 Lauritz Melchior.** Met tenor Lauritz Melchior sings "Serenade" plus "Deep in My Heart" on a 1940s radio broadcast. They're on the 1995 album of live radio performances *Lauritz Melchior Sings America*. Radio Years CD. **1947 Risë Stevens/Nelson Eddy.** Met soprano Risë Stevens joins Nelson Eddy in this highlights version of the operetta with an orchestra conducted by Robert Armbruster. Columbia LP/Box Office CD titled *Change Partners*. **1947 Earl Wrightson/Frances Greer.** Earl Wrightson and Frances Greer perform a highlights version of the operetta with support from Mary Martha Briney and Donald Dame. Al Goodman conducts the orchestra. RCA Victor/Camden LP. **1948 Sigmund Romberg.** Composer Sigmund Romberg conducts waltzes from *The Student Prince* on the album *Composers Do Their Own Thing*. Pelican LP. **1950 Jan Peerce.** Met tenor Jan Peerce sings "Serenade" from *The Student Prince* on the album *Golden Moments of Song*. RCA LP. **1950 Lauritz Melchior/Gloria Lane.** Met tenor Lauritz Melchior joins Gloria Lane, Jane Wilson and Lee Sweetland in a highlights version of the operetta. Victor Young conducts. Decca LP. **1952 Dorothy Kirsten/Robert Rounseville.** Dorothy Kirsten of the Met and Robert Rounseville of New York City Opera are the stars of this excellent highlights version with the orchestra conducted by Lehman Engel. Met singers Genevieve Warner, Clifford Harvuot and George Gaynes lend support. Goddard Lieberson produced. Columbia Odyssey LP/DRG CD. **1952 Lauritz Melchior.** Danish tenor Lauritz Melchior sings "Serenade" on *The Voice of Firestone* television program on November 17, 1952, with Howard Barlow conducting the Firestone Orchestra. It's on the video *Lauritz Melchior in Opera and Song*. VAI VHS. **1953 Gordon MacRae/Dorothy Warenskjold.** Gordon MacRae and Dorothy Warenskjold star in a studio highlights version of the operetta with support from Harry Stanton. George Greely conducts. Capitol LP. **1953 Dorothy Kirsten/Gordon MacRae.** Dorothy Kirsten, Gordon MacRae, Francis X Bushman and Bobbie Driscoll perform an abridged version of the operetta on a radio broadcast October 5, 1953. Demand Performance/Live Opera Cassette. **1953 Mario Lanza/Elizabeth Doubleday.** Mario Lanza recorded a highlights version of the operetta with Constantine Callinicos conducting. Elizabeth Doubleday joins him on "Summertime in Heidelberg" and "Deep in My Heart." The album is called *Mario Lanza Sings the Hit Songs from The Student Prince and Other Great Musical Comedies*. RCA Victor LP/CD. **1954 MGM film.** Edmund Purdom appears on screen as the Student Prince but he sings with Mario Lanza's voice in this film of the operetta. Lanza recorded the soundtrack before he quit MGM so the studio hired Purdom to replace him on screen and dubbed in the songs. Ann Blyth is the barmaid he loves. Richard Thorpe directed the 107-minute color film. MGM/UA VHS. **1957 Richard Tucker.** Richard Tucker sings "Serenade" on the *Voice of Firestone* TV program. Howard Barlow conducts the Firestone Orchestra on the video *Richard Tucker in Opera and Song*. VAI VHS. **1959 Mario Lanza/Norma Giusti.** Mario Lanza made a second recording of highlights from the operetta with an orchestra led by Paul Baron. Norma Giusti joins Lanza on "Just We Two" and "Deep in My Heart." RCA Victor LP. **1962 Roberta Peters/Jan Peerce/Giorgio Tozzi.** Roberta Peters is Kathie, Jan Peerce is the Prince and Giorgio Tozzi is Engel in this operatic highlights version of the operetta with Anita Darian as Princess Margaret and Lawrence Avery as Tarnitz. Franz Allers conducts the orchestra and the Merrill Staton Choir. Columbia LP. **1962 Dorothy Kirsten/Gordon MacRae.** Met soprano Dorothy Kirsten and Gordon MacRae star in this highlights version with Van Alexander conducting. Lending support are Earle Wilkie, William Felber and Richard Robinson. Capitol LP/EMI CD. **1962 William Lewis/Jeanette Scovotti.** William Lewis is the Prince with Jeanette Scovotti as Kathie in this highlights version of the operetta. William Chapman is Engel, Sara Endich is the Princess, Lee Cass is Lucas, Robert Nagy is Detlef

and Peter Palmer is Von Asterberg. Lehman Engel conducts. Reader's Digest *Treasury of Great Operettas*. RCA LP box set. **1967 Joan Sutherland.** Joan Sutherland sings "The Student Chorus" and "Deep in My Heart, Dear" with the Ambrosian Light Opera Chorus. Richard Bonynge conducts the New Philharmonia Orchestra on her album *The Golden Age of Operetta*. London/Decca LP/CD. **1968 John Hanson.** John Hanson, who presented *The Student Prince* on stage in London in 1968, stars in this British highlights version with his stage cast including Barbara Strathdee and Christine Parker. Johnny Arthey conducts. Philips LP. **1979 Hamburg State Opera.** American tenor Erik Geisen is the Prince in this performance of the operetta by the Hamburg State Opera company. Celia Jeffreys is Kathie with Dieter Hönig as Dr. Engel. Stefan Gyarto conducts the Hamburg State Opera Orchestra and Chorus. Bayer CD. **1989 David Rendall/Marilyn Hill Smith.** David Rendall is the Prince and Marilyn Hill Smith is Kathie in this complete recording of the operetta. Norman Bailey is Dr. Engel, Diana Montague is Princess Margaret, Bonaventura Bottone is Detlef, Donald Maxwell is Lucas, Jason Howard is Ruder and Rosemary Ashe is Gretchen. John Owen Edwards conducts the Philharmonia Orchestra and Ambrosian Chorus. TER Classics CD. **1991 José Carreras.** José Carreras salutes his youthful idol Mario Lanza in a videotaped recital at the Royal Albert Hall in London and sings "Serenade" from *The Student Prince*. Enrique Ricci conducts the BBC Concert Orchestra and English Concert Chorus. The video is titled *Tribute to Mario Lanza, With a Song in My Heart*. Teldec VHS. **1993 Placido Domingo.** Placido Domingo performs "Overhead the Moon Is Beaming" from *The Student Prince* with Jonathan Tunick conducting on his album *Together—Placido Domingo and Itzak Perlman*. EMI Classics CD. **1993 Barbara Hendricks/Gino Quilico.** Soprano Barbara Hendricks and baritone Gino Quilico join in duet on "Deep in My Heart, Dear" on the album *Operetta Duets*. Lawrence Foster conducts the Lyon Opera Orchestra. EMI CD. **1993 Jerry Hadley/Mario Lanza.** Jerry Hadley uses electronic magic to team up with Mario Lanza on his album *Golden Days*. Hadley sings "The Drinking Song" and "Serenade" from *The Student Prince* and duets with Lanza on "Golden Days." Paul Gemignani conducts the American Theatre Orchestra. RCA Victor CD. **1994 Abilene Opera.** Kelly Neil is the Prince opposite Jane Guitar as Kathie in this video of a rather amateurish stage production by Abilene Opera taped at the Paramount Theater in Abilene, Texas, on July 22, 1994. Wendy Mitchell-Humphrey is Gretchen, David Lawrence is Detlef, Andrew LeBlanc is Dr. Engel, Amy James is the Grand Duchess and Lanie Westman is Princess Margaret. Ted Starnes designed the sets, Wyatt Hester directed and Richard Burke conducted. Premiere Opera VHS.

STUDER, CHERYL *American soprano (1955–)*

Cheryl Studer sings the title role in the first complete recording of Carlisle Floyd's SUSANNAH, produced in 1994 in France with Lyons Opera and conductor Kent Nagano in 1994. She has also made a recording of Samuel Barber songs. Studer, who was born in Midland, Michigan, studied in Vienna and made her debut in Munich in 1980. She began to sing in America in 1984.

STYNE, JULES *American composer (1905–1989)*

Hollywood and Broadway composer Jules Styne began his composing career as a songwriter working with lyricist Sammy Kahn on Oscar-winning movie songs like "Three Coins in the Fountain." His first Broadway show was *High Button Shoes* (1947) with Kahn and for the next 25 years he was one of America's most successful music theater composers working with many different partners. His greatest successes include *Gentlemen Prefer Blondes* (1949), *Bells Are Ringing* (1956), *Gypsy* (1959) with Stephen Sondheim as lyricist and *Funny Girl* (1970), all of which were filmed. Styne, who was born in London, came to America as a child and studied at the Chicago College of Music. He was a concert pianist and bandleader before turning to composing.

SUBOTNICK, MORTON   *American composer (1933–)*

Morton Subotnick is usually thought of as a forceful proponent of electronic music rather than an opera composer, but he created a number of interesting avant-garde operas. *The Double Life of Amphibians,* featuring interaction between singers, instrumentalists and computer, was premiered in early form at IRCAM in Paris in 1982 and developed with director Lee Breuer and visual artist Irving Petlin for presentation at the Olympics Arts Festival in Los Angeles on June 20, 1984. An "aria" from it, "The Last Dream of the Beast," was created for Joan La Barbara, who premiered it at the Hirschhorn Museum in Washington, D.C., in February 1979. It was reworked for a 1984 stage version and recorded by Nonesuch with instrumental components of the operas *Ascent in the Air* and *The Fluttering of Wings*. The electronic multimedia opera *Hungers*, libretto and images by filmmaker-artist Ed Emshwiller, was commissioned by the Los Angeles Fringe Festival and premiered in Los Angeles on September 26, 1987. *Jacob's Room*, libretto by the composer based on Virginia Woolf's novel, was created in two versions. The concert version, a monodrama commissioned by Betty Freeman for Joan La Barbara and the Kronos Quartet, was premiered in San Francisco in January 1985 and recorded by La Barbara in 1986. The multimedia version, directed by Herbert Blau with video imagery by Steina and Woody Vasulke, was premiered in the American Music Theater Festival Philadelphia in April 1993, again with La Barbara. It was reprised at the Kitchen in New York and the MANCA Festival in Nice. Subotnick, who was born in Los Angeles, studied at the University of Denver and Mills College with Darius Milhaud and Leon Kirchner and first became known for his synthesizer composition *Silver Apples of the Moon* (1967). He has been music director and composer-in-residence at many universities and institutions, He married avant-garde vocal wizard Joan La Barbara in 1979.

SULLIVAN, BRIAN   *American tenor (1917–1969)*

Brian Sullivan created the role of Sam in Kurt Weill's STREET SCENE in Philadelphia in 1946, reprised it on Broadway in 1947 and is featured on the cast recording. He sings Etienne in a 1951 NBC TV production of Victor Herbert's MLLE. MODISTE and he played Wrestling Bradford opposite Beverly Sills in Howard Hanson's MERRY MOUNT in a 1964 San Antonio revival. Sullivan, born in Oakland, CA, studied at USC and made his debut at Long Beach Opera in 1940. He made his debut at the Met in 1948 and sang there for twelve years.

SUMMER   *1999 opera by Paulus*

The early 1900s in a mountain village in Massachusetts. Eighteen-year-old Charity Royall, the illegitimate child of an unwed mother, has been raised by Lawyer Royall. She has a secret affair with the architect Lucius Harney and becomes pregnant. He wants to marry someone else so she turns for help to her guardian. It turns out he has always secretly loved her so he agrees to marry her. Stephen Paulus' two-act opera *Summer*, libretto by Joan Vail Thorne based on a 1917 novella by Edith Wharton, was commissioned by Berkshire Opera which premiered it on August 28, 1999,

at the Koussevitsky Arts Center in Pittsfield, Massachusetts. Charity Royall was played by Margaret Lattimore, Lawyer Royall by John Cheek, Lucius Harney by Michael Chioldi, Miss Hatchard by Joanna Johnston. Verena Marsh by Marion Pratnicki, the Rev. Miles by Mark Schowalter, Annabel Balch by Michaela Gurevich, Liff Hyatt by Matthew Lau and Ally Hawes by Jane Jennin. David P. Gordon designed the sets, Mary Duncan staged the opera and Joel Revzen conducted. The opera was reprised at the Kaye Playhouse in New York in June 2002.

1999 Berkshire Opera Company. The Berkshire Opera Company premiere was recorded with Margaret Lattimore as Charity Royall, John Cheek as Lawyer Royall, Michael Chioldi as Lucius Harney and the rest of the cast as above. Joel Revzen conducted. The two-CD set is available from Paulus Publications, 1719 Summit Avenue, St. Paul, Minnesota 55105.

SUMMER AND SMOKE   *1971 opera by Hoiby*

Mississippi in 1910. Minister's daughter Alma Winemiller is unable to admit her love for John Buchanan, a doctor she has known since childhood. When he finally loses interest and finds another love, she gives herself in despair to a traveling salesman. Lee Hoiby's two-act opera *Summer and Smoke*, libretto by Lanford Wilson based on the 1948 play by Tennessee Williams, was commissioned by St. Paul Opera which premiered it on June 19, 1971. Mary Jane Peil sang the role of Alma, John Reardon was Dr. Buchanan, Sondra Harnes was Nellie, Nancy Williams was Mrs. Bassett, Alan Titus was the traveling salesman. Gimi Beni was Papa Gonzalez and Zoya Leporska was Alma's mother. Lloyd Evans designed the sets, Frank Corsaro was director and Igor Buketoff conducted the orchestra. *Summer and Smoke* was reprised by New York City Opera in 1972 with Peil and Reardon again in the leading roles and has since been staged by many opera companies around the U.S.

1982 Chicago Opera Theater. Mary Jane Peil, who created the role, sings Alma opposite Robert Orth as Dr. Buchanan in a TV version of the opera based on a Chicago Opera Theatre production. Diane Barclay is Nellie, Joyce Carter is Rosa, Clayton Hochhalter is Roger, Charlotte Gardner is Mrs. Winemiller, Paul Kiesen is Mr. Winemiller and Dennis Marshall is Archie. Robert Frisbie conducted the Chicago Opera Theater Orchestra. Director Kirk Browning brought the cast into the studio to maintain atmosphere. It was telecast in color on PBS on June 23, 1982. Video at New York Public Library and at MTR. **1983 Helen-Kay Eberley.** Soprano Helen-Kay Eberley sings Alma's aria "No, I haven't been well" from *Summer and Smoke* accompanied by pianist Donald Isaak on her album *American Girl*. Eb-Sko LP. **1995 William Parker.** Baritone William Parker sings the Doctor's aria "Anatomy Lesson" from *Summer and Smoke* accompanied by pianist William Huckaby on the anthology album *The Listeners*. New World CD.

SUMMERS, PATRICK   *American conductor (1965–)*

Patrick Summers conducted the revival of Lee Hoiby's THE TEMPEST at Dallas Opera in 1996, some of the premiere performances of André Previn's A STREETCAR NAMED DESIRE at San Francisco Opera in 1998, the premiere of Tod Machover's RESURRECTION at Houston Grand Opera in April 1999, the revival of Mark Adamo's LITTLE WOMEN at Houston in March 2000, the premiere of Carlisle Floyd's COLD SASSY TREE at Houston in April 2000 and the premiere of Jake Heggie's DEAD MAN WALKING at San Francisco in October 2000. Summers, who was born and raised in Indiana and studied at Indiana University, began to conduct at

San Francisco Opera in 1990 and became Houston Grand Opera's music director in 1999.

SUMMERTIME *Soprano aria: Porgy and Bess (1935). Words: DuBose Heyward. Music: George Gershwin.*

"Summertime" is the best known aria from America's greatest opera, PORGY AND BESS, and the most often recorded. It is American opera's equivalent to a Puccini soprano aria, as moving and foreboding as anything in *Madama Butterfly*. It is first sung by Clara to her baby and is a harbinger of violence whenever it is heard. George Gershwin, who wrote the music to lyrics by Du Bose Heyward, said it was the first thing he composed for the opera. Abby Mitchell introduced "Summertime" on stage in 1935 but she was an unknown black singer so it was white Metropolitan Opera soprano Helen Jepson who made the first recording, quickly followed by Billie Holiday. It's sung by Anne Brown (the original Bess) on a 1940 Broadway revival cast recording and in the 1945 film *Rhapsody in Blue*, by Met soprano Eleanor Steber in a 1946 recording and a 1954 video of a TV show, by Loulie Jean Norman dubbing Diahann Carroll in the 1959 film of the opera, by Leontyne Price in a 1963 recording, by Barbara Hendricks in the 1975 Cleveland recording, by Betty Lane in the 1976 Houston Grand Opera recording, by Harolyn Blackwell in the 1987 Glyndebourne recording and by Renée Fleming in her 1998 recital album of American opera arias. "Summertime" has been recorded more than 500 times. There are many other operatic versions and the aria is equally known through memorable recordings by jazz singers like Billie Holiday, Lena Horne, Mildred Bailey, Maxine Sullivan, Helen Humes, Chris Conner and Ella Fitzgerald. A definitive study of the aria is featured in Will Friedwald's splendid book *Stardust Melodies* (2002/Pantheon Books) and it is included in Richard Walters' compilation *Opera American Style: Arias for Soprano*.

THE SUN BRIDE *1930 opera by Skilton*

Navajo brave Bluefeather attempts to force his love on a woman who has been named the bride of the sun and is struck dead for the sacrilege. Charles Sanford Skilton's one-act opera *The Sun Bride*, libretto by Lillian White Spencer, was broadcast on NBC on April 17, 1930, as one of the first operas premiered on radio. Astrid Fjelde took the part of the Sun Bride and Judson House was Bluefeather. Cesare Sudaro conducted the NBCV National Grand Opera Company. Stilton's music for the opera was taken from his 1920 orchestral work *Suite Primeval* which he based on Native American dance music.

SUNDAY EXCURSION *1953 opera by Wilder*

Alice, Veronica, Hilary and Marvin return home on a Sunday excursion coach on the New York, New Haven and Hartford Railroad about 1910. They tell each other their adventures as candy-man Tim tries to sell them his wares. Alec Wilder's 25-minute "curtain raiser" opera *Sunday Excursion*, libretto by Arnold Sundgaard, was premiered in New York City on April 17, 1953. The music is melodic and lightly nostalgic and the opera has become quite popular. It was produced in Chicago and Interlochen later the same year and there were televised productions at Pepperdine University in Los Angeles in 1981 and Southwest Baptist Opera Workshop in Bolivar, Missouri, in 1985. Long Leaf Opera of Durham, North Carolina, reprised it in January 2000.

SUNDGAARD, ARNOLD *American librettist (1909–)*

Arnold Sundgaard wrote the librettos for ten American operas. He began with Kurt Weill's popular folk opera DOWN IN THE VAL-LEY, which premiered at Indiana University in 1948. Next he worked with Douglas Moore on GIANTS IN THE EARTH, an adaptation of an O. E. Rölvaag novel; it premiered at Columbia University in 1951 and won the Pulitzer Prize for Music. He also collaborated with Moore on two slighter works, the "soap opera" GALLANTRY, which premiered at Columbia University in 1958, and the "Christmas entertainment" *The Greenfield Christmas Tree* which premiered in Baltimore in 1962. He began a twenty-year partnership with composer Alec Wilder In 1952 and together they created eight operas and a musical. The first was *The Lowland Seat* which premiered in Montclair, NJ, on May 8, 1952. Next was SUNDAY EXCURSION, a still popular curtain raiser focusing on people travelling on a New York Sunday excursion train in 1910, which was premiered in New York City on April 17, 1953. *Cumberland Fair* was performed in Montclair, NJ, on May 22, 1953. *Kittiwake Island* was presented at Interlochen on August 7, 1954, and was staged off-Broadway in New York in 1960 with Kathleen Murray and Lainie Kazan. *The Long Way* was premiered in Nyack, NY, on June 3, 1955. *The Impossible Forest* was presented at Westport, CT, on July 13, 1958. THE OPENING, a post-modern story about problems on the opening night of a play, premiered at the New England Conservatory in Boston in 1969. *The Truth about Windmills* was performed at the Eastman School of Music in Rochester, NY, on October 14, 1973. Their musical, *Nobody's Earnest* based on Oscar Wilde's play *The Importance of Being Earnest*, was first performed in Williamsburg, MA, in June 1974. Sundgaard also contributed lyrics to the 1961 Broadway musical *Young Abe Lincoln*, music by Victor Ziskin. He was born in St. Paul, Minnesota.

THE SURVIVAL OF ST. JOAN *1970 rock opera by Smoke Rise*

Joan of Arc is secretly released from prison in 1431 and placed in the custody of a widower on a farm. This is organized by the Bishop of Beauvais after she has led the French to victory over the English. He makes her believe survival is the best tactic and arranges for another young woman to be burned at the stake in her place. Joan becomes disillusioned, escapes from the farm, is taken prisoner by religious penitents and is burned at the stake as a witch. Smoke Rise's rock opera *The Survival of St. Joan,* lyrics by James Lindeberg, is a free adaptation of a legend about the Maid of Orleans.

1970 Paramount recording. Smoke Rise integrate the story line with the lyrics on this version of the opera adapted for a record by Chuck Gnys. Hank Ruffin plays keyboards, Stan Ruffin plays drums, Gary Ruffin plays guitar and Rand Bugg plays bass. Paramount 2-LP folder.

SUSA, CONRAD *American composer (1935–)*

Conrad Susa has composed a large number of scores for film, theater and television so it is not surprising that his operas have cinematic qualities. TRANSFORMATIONS, libretto by the composer based on Anne Sexton's poetic versions of Grimm fairy tales, was premiered by Minnesota Opera in Minneapolis in 1973. It references musical styles of the 1940s and 1950s and has become one of the most frequently performed modern American operas. BLACK RIVER, libretto by Richard Street and the composer based on Michael Lesy's disturbing non-fiction book *Wisconsin Death Trip,* was premiered by Minnesota Opera in 1975. It features flashbacks telling the stories of three women suffering from a strange malaise. THE LOVE OF DON PERLIMPLIN, libretto by Street and the composer based on a play by Lorca about an old man's bizarre love for his young wife, was inspired by the music of Scarlatti and premiered at the PepsiCo Summerfare festival at SUNY Purchase in 1984. THE DANGEROUS LIAISONS, libretto by Philip Littell based on the French novel *Les Liaisons Dangereuses* by Pierre Choderlos de Laclos and influenced by film versions of the story, was premiered by San Francisco Opera in 1994. The Christmas church opera THE WISE WOMEN, libretto by Littell about three women who follow the star to Bethlehem with the Three Wise Men, was commissioned by the American Guild of Organists for their Dallas Convention in 1994. Susa, who was born in Springdale, PA, and studied at Juilliard with William Bergsma, has taught in San Diego and San Francisco.

SUSAN B!   *1998 opera by Tierney*

The life and struggles of Susan B. Anthony (1820–1906), the 19th century suffragette leader who campaigned for half a century for voting rights for women. Thomas Tierney's opera *Susan B!*, libretto by Ted Drachman and Jules Tasca, was premiered by Theatreworks/USA in New York on November 19, 1988. Anthony is also the subject of the opera THE MOTHER OF US ALL, composed by Virgil Thomson to a libretto by Gertrude Stein.

SUSANNAH   *1955 opera by Floyd*

Eighteen-year-old Susannah Polk, condemned by Church elders for bathing nude in the river, is seduced by preacher Olin Blitch. When her brother Sam finds out, he shoots Blitch. Carlisle Floyd's three-act opera *Susannah*, libretto by the composer based on the Biblical story of Susanna and the Elders transposed to the mountains of Tennessee and incorporating hymns, folk songs and Appalachian-style square dance music, premiered at Florida State University in Tallahassee on February 24, 1955. Phyllis Curtin created the role of Susannah, Mack Harrell was Blitch, Walter James was Sam, Eb Thomas was Susanna's friend and betrayer Little Bat, Harrison Fisher was Elder McLean, Dayton Smith was Elder Hayes, Lee Liming was Elder Ott, Kenneth Nelson was Elder Gleaton, Martha Kay Willis was Mrs. McLean, Joan Nichly was Mrs. Hayes, Bette Jo Armstrong was Mrs. Ott and Catherine Murphey was Mrs. Gleaton. Franklin Adams designed the sets, Lynn Orr was stage director and Kurt Kuersteiner conducted the orchestra. Curtin reprised the title role she created when *Susannah* arrived at New York City Opera on September 27, 1956, and Eb Thomas returned as Little Bat while Norman Treigle took over the role of Blitch and Jon Crain played Sam. *Susannah* has become one of the most popular American operas with over 250 productions since 1955. New York City Opera has produced it four times and there have been large-scale productions by Lyric Opera of Chicago and Houston Grand Opera. It took half a century for it to reach the Metropolitan Opera but it was a huge success in 1999 with Renée Fleming in the role of Susannah. Some of its arias, like "AIN'T IT A PRETTY NIGHT" and "THE TREES ON THE MOUNTAINS" have entered the soprano recital repertory.

1962 New Orleans Opera. Phyllis Curtin, who created the role, stars as Susannah with Norman Treigle as Blitch in this New Orleans Opera production recorded live on March 31, 1962. Richard Cassilly is Sam Polk, Keith Kaldenberg is Little Bat, Jack Davis is Elder McLean, Marietta Muhs Cosenza is Mrs. McLean, Thomas Carter is Elder Gleaton, Marilyn Davidson is Mrs. Gleaton, Alton Brim is Elder Hayes, Kay Long is Mrs. Hayes, Burton Parker is Elder Ott and Jean Young is Mrs. Ott. Knud Andersson conducts the New Orleans Opera Orchestra and Chorus. VAI CD. **1962 Phyllis Curtin.** Phyllis Curtin sings the aria "Ain't it a pretty night" on the 1999 album *Phyllis Curtin: Opera Arias.* The aria is taken from the New Orleans recording described above. VAI

CD. **1965 New York City Opera.** Joy Clements is Susannah in this live recording made at New York City Opera on April 1, 1965. Norman Treigle is Blitch, Richard Cassilly is Sam Polk and Julian Miller is Little Bat. Felix Popper conducts. Live Opera audiocassette. **1971 New York City Opera.** Maralin Niska is Susannah in this live recording made at New York City Opera on October 31, 1971. Norman Treigle is Blitch, Harry Theyard is Sam Polk and David Hall is Little Bat. Julius Rudel conducts. Live Opera audiocassette. **1974 Kentucky Opera.** Nancy Shade is Susannah in this live recording made on January 11, 1974, at Kentucky Opera in Louisville. Chester Ludgin is Blitch and Moritz von Bomhard conducts. Live Opera audiocassette. **1975 Houston Grand Opera.** Diana Soviero is Susannah in this live recording made in June 1975 at Houston Grand Opera. Ronald Hedlund is Olin Blitch. Live Opera audiocassette. **1979 Indiana Opera.** Jean Herzberg is Susannah in this Indiana Opera Theater production videotaped live at the Musical Arts Center in Bloomington in 1979. William Parcher is Blitch, Jon Fay is Sam and Neil Jones is Little Bat. Brian Falkwill conducts. Allan Ross staged the opera and Mickey Klein directed for WTIV Television. Video at MTR. **1983 Helen-Kay Eberley.** Helen-Kay Eberley sings the arias "Ain't it a pretty night"

Kelly Cae Hogan as Susannah Polk in Hawaii Opera Theatre's excellent 2004 production of Carlisle Floyd's *Susannah*. Photograph by Cory Lum, courtesy of Hawaii Opera Theatre.

and "Come back, oh summer" from *Susannah* accompanied by pianist Donald Isaak on her album *American Girl*. Eb-Sko LP. **1991 Samuel Ramey.** Samuel Ramey sings Blitch's prayer of repentance "Hear me, O Lord" at a Lincoln Center gala on November 10, 1991. James Conlon conducts members of the Metropolitan Opera Orchestra on the PBS telecast. It's on the album *A Salute to American Music*. RCA Victor CD. **1994 Lyons Opera.** Cheryl Studer is Susannah opposite Samuel Ramey as Blitch in this recording of the complete opera. Jerry Hadley is Sam Polk, Kenn Chester is Little Bat, Michael Druiett is Elder McLean, Anne Howells is Mrs. McLean, Steven Cole is Elder Gleaton, Della Jones is Mrs. Gleaton, Stuart Kale is Elder Hayes, Jean Glennon is Mrs. Hayes, David Pittsinger is Elder Ott and Elizabeth Laurence is Mrs. Ott. Kent Nagano conducts the Lyons Opera Orchestra and Chorus. The recording was made at Lyons Opera in August 1993 and Bavarian Music Studios in March 1994. Virgin Classics CD. **1995 Dawn Upshaw.** Dawn Upshaw sings the aria "Ain't it a pretty night" from *Susannah* accompanied by pianist David Zinman on her album *The World So Wide*. Nonesuch CD. **1999 Renée Fleming.** Renée Fleming, who played Susannah in the Met production of the opera, sings "Ain't it a pretty night" and "The trees on the mountains" on her recital album *I Want Magic*. She is accompanied by James Levine and the Metropolitan Opera Orchestra. London Classics CD. **1999 William Powers.** Baritone William Powers sings Blitch's prayer aria "Hear me O Lord" on his recital album *Rogues and Villains* recorded in Czechoslovakia. Dennis Burkh conducts the Janá_ek Philharmonic Orchestra. Centaur CD. **2001 Geneva Opera.** Nancy Gustafson is Susannah opposite Samuel Ramey as Blitch in a recording of the opera broadcast in Geneva, Switzerland, on June 30, 2001. Also in the cast are Gordon Gietz and Beau Palmer. Anne Manson conducts. House of Opera CD. **2002 Lyric Opera of Chicago Commentary.** Jean Keister Kellogg analyzes *Susannah* on this CD in the *Women's Board of Lyric Opera Commentaries* series, with plot description, information on the composer and historical background, The musical excerpts are taken from the 1994 Lyons Opera recording. Lyric Opera Commentaries CD.

SUTHERLAND, JOAN   *Australian soprano (1926–)*

Joan Sutherland recorded some of her favorite American operetta songs for her 1967 recital album *The Golden Age of Operetta* with husband Richard Bonynge conducting the New Philharmonia Orchestra It includes songs from Rudolf Friml's ROSE MARIE, Jerome Kern's MUSIC IN THE AIR and SHOW BOAT and Sigmund Romberg's THE DESERT SONG and THE STUDENT PRINCE. Sydney-born Sutherland, one of the leading sopranos in the world in the 1950s, noted especially for her Italian bel canto roles, continued to sing on stage until 1990. She was made a Dame in 1979.

SUTTON, VERN   *American tenor (1938–)*

Minnesota Opera tenor Vern Sutton has created roles in ten American operas, five composed by Dominick Argento: John in *Masque of Angels* in 1963, Mr. Owen in POSTCARD FROM MOROCCO in 1971, Doctor/Wedding Guest/Passenger in THE VOYAGE OF EDGAR ALLAN POE in 1976, the Lecturer in A WATERBIRD TALK in 1977 and Lorenzo da Ponte in CASANOVA'S HOMECOMING in 1985. In addition he created John Faustus in John Gessner's *Faust Counter Faust* in 1971, the Wizard in Conrad Susa's TRANSFORMATIONS in 1973, C.C. Pope/Mr. Vaudry/Dr. Krohn in Susa's BLACK RIVER in 1975, Fulbert in Robert Ward's ABELARD AND HELOISE in North Carolina in 1982 and the tenor lead in Eric

Stokes' *Apollonia's Circus* in 1994. He wrote the libretto for Libby Larsen's opera *Christina Romana* which was premiered by the University of Minnesota in 1988. Sutton, born in Oklahoma City, studied in Texas and Minneapolis and made his debut in 1963 in Argento's *Masque of Angels* at Center Opera in Minneapolis.

SWARTHOUT, GLADYS   *American contralto*
(1900–1969)

Gladys Swarthout created the role of Plentiful Tewke in Howard Hanson's MERRY MOUNT at the Metropolitan Opera in 1934 and sang the role of Mrs. Deane in a Met broadcast of Deems Taylor's PETER IBBETSON the same year. Both performances are on record. She sings Juliet to Jan Kiepura's Romeo in Eric Wolfgang Korngold's movie opera ROMEO AND JULIET, libretto by Oscar Hammerstein II, created for the 1936 film *Give Us This Night*. She featured American operetta songs on her radio appearances and several broadcasts were recorded. The album *Gladys Swarthout: Favorites from the Musical Theatre* includes radio performances of numbers from Sigmund Romberg's MAYTIME recorded in 1934, Victor Herbert's MLLE. MODISTE in 1942, Herbert's ORANGE BLOSSOMS in 1942, Romberg's THE DESERT SONG in 1945 and Rudolf Friml's THE VAGABOND KING in 1946. She recorded a song from Friml's little known operetta WHITE EAGLE in 1942. Swarthout, who was born in Deepwater, Missouri, studied in Chicago and made her debut with the Chicago Civic Opera in 1924. She began to sing at the Met in 1929 and was a regular until 1945. She starred in five movies for Paramount in the 1930s.

Contralto Gladys Swarthout pictured in 1936 Musical America ad.

SWEENEY TODD   *1979 Broadway opera by Sondheim*

London around 1847. Demon barber Sweeney Todd escapes from prison and sets out to wreak revenge on the judge who jailed him and ravished his wife. Enterprising Mrs. Lovett helps him set up a grisly meat pie business in which barbershop customers become the ingredients for the pies. Business booms. Stephen Sondheim's Grand Guignol Broadway opera *Sweeney Todd, the Demon Barber of Fleet Street*, libretto by Hugh Wheeler based on plays by George Dibdin Pitt and Christopher Bond with lyrics by the composer, opened at the Uris Theater in New York on March 1, 1979. Len Cariou was Sweeney Todd, Angela Lansbury was Mrs. Lovett, Edmund Lyndeck was Judge Turbin, Sarah Rice was Johanna, Victor Garber was Anthony Hall, Ken Jennings was Tobias Ragg, Merle Louise was the Beggar Woman, Joaquin Romaguera was Pirelli and Eric Williams was the Beadle. Eugene and Franne Lee designed the sets, Harold Prince directed and Paul Gemignani conducted. *Sweeney Todd* won eight Tony awards and began to enter the opera house repertory in 1984. It was presented in London in 1980 and 1983, by New York City Opera in 1984, by Opera North in Leeds in 1998 and by Finnish National Opera in Helsinki in 1998. Lyric Opera of Chicago staged it in 2003 with Bryan Terfel as Sweeney and Judith Christin as Mrs. Lovett while NYCO staged it for a second time in 2004 with Mark Delavan as Sweeney and Elaine Paige was Mrs. Lovett. The score is quite operatic; most of it is sung and there are recurring motifs and complex ensembles.

1979 Original Broadway cast. Len Cariou is Sweeney Todd opposite Angela Lansbury as Mrs. Lovett in the original Broadway cast album. Edmund Lyndeck is Judge Turbin, Sarah Rice is Johanna, Victor Garber is Anthony, Ken Jennings is Tobias, Joaquin Romaguera is Pirelli, Merle Louise is the Beggar Woman and Eric Williams is the Beadle. Paul Gemignani conducts. RCA LP/CD. **1982 Los Angeles cast.** George Hearn, who replaced Cariou on Broadway, is Sweeney Todd with Angela Lansbury as Mrs. Lovett in a production taped at the Dorothy Chandler Pavilion in Los Angeles. Edmund Lyndeck is Judge Turpin, Betsy Joslyn is Johanna, Chris Groenendaal is Anthony, Calvin Remsberg is The Beadle, Ken Jennings is Tobias and Sara Woods is the Beggar Woman. Eugene Lee designed the sets, Terry Hughes directed and Paul Gemignani conducted. RKO VHS. **1999 New York concert.** George Hearn sings Sweeney Todd opposite Patti LuPone in this live recording of a semi-staged concert version. Audra McDonald is the Beggar Woman, Paul Plishka is Judge Turpin, John Aler is the Beadle and Stanford Olson is Pirelli. Andrew Litton conducted the New York Philharmonic Special Editions CD. **2001 San Francisco cast.** George Hearn is Sweeney Todd opposite Patti LuPone as Mrs. Lovett in a semi-staged concert version directed by Lonny Price and taped live at Davis Symphony Hall in San Francisco in July 2001. Victoria Clark is the Beggar Woman, Timothy Nolen is Judge Turpin, John Aler is the Beadle, Lisa Vroman is Johanna, David Gaines is Anthony, Stanford Olson is Pirelli and Neal Patrick Harris is Tobias. Image Enter-

Demon barber Sweeney Todd tells his tale to an entranced Mrs. Lovett in Arizona Opera's fine production of *Sweeney Todd*. Photograph by Tim Fuller, courtesy of Arizona Opera.

tainment DVD/VHS. **2003 Lyric Opera of Chicago Commentary.** Critical analysis of *Sweeney Todd* in the *Women's Board of Lyric Opera Commentaries* series with plot summary, composer biography and social and historical background. Lyric Opera Commentaries CD.

THE SWEET BYE AND BYE   *1957 opera by Beeson*

Sister Rose Ora, leader of an evangelical sect based in Atlantic City, is mourned by followers who think she has drowned. Mother Rainey discovers she has actually eloped with her lover Billy and persuades her to return. When Sister Rose changes her mind, Mother Rainey shoots Billy and makes another sister leader. Jack Beeson's two-act opera *The Sweet Bye and Bye*, libretto by Kenward

Elmslie, was suggested by the career of 1920s evangelist Aimee Semple McPherson and features hymns and jazzy flapper music of the period It premiered at the Juilliard School of Music Concert Hall in New York City on November 21, 1957. Shirlee Emmons was Sister Rose Ora, Ruth Kobart was Mother Rainey, William McGrath was Billy, Alice Robiczek was Sister Gladys, Anne Perillo was Sister Rees, Richard Kuelling was Brother Smiley, Alexandra Hunt was Mary Jane Ripley, Clifton Steere was Second Bather and W. Haggin Perry was Third Bather. Frederic Cohen was the producer and Frederick Waldman conducted the orchestra.

1974 Kansas City Lyric Theater. Noel Rogers stars as Sister Rosa Ora with Carolyne James as Mother Rainey in this recording of a Kansas City Lyric Theater production of the opera. Robert Owen Jones is Billy Wilcox, Judith Anthony is Sister Rees, Paul Seibel is Sister Gladys, Walter Hook is Brother Smiley, Elizabeth Green is Mary Jane Riley, Thomas Claffy is Second Bather, Dennis Howell is Third Bather and William Latimer is the Beauty Judge. Russell Patterson conducts the Kansas City Lyric Theater Orchestra and Chorus. Desto 3-LP box/Citadel 2-CD box.

Jack Beeson's evangelical opera *The Sweet Bye and Bye* was produced and recorded by Lyric Opera of Kansas City. Photograph courtesy of Lyric Opera of Kansas City.

SWEETHEARTS   *1913 comic opera by Herbert*

An abandoned infant, found by Mother Goose, is reared as a laundry worker named Sylvia. She is actually a princess, however, so she gets to marry a prince in the end. Victor Herbert's comic opera *Sweethearts* has a ludicrous plot (libretto by Harry B. Smith and Fred de Grésac, lyrics by Robert B. Smith) but great music. It premiered at the Academy of Music in Baltimore on March 24, 1913, and opened on Broadway on September 8, 1913, at the New Amsterdam Theater. Christie MacDonald, who got to sing the best songs, played Sylvia with Thomas Conkey as her prince charming. Ethel Du Fre Houston was Mother Goose, Tom McNaughton was the monk Mikel, Edwin Wilson was Lt. Karl and Hazel Kirke was Liane. Fred Latham directed and John McGhie conducted. The songs include "Sweethearts," "The Cricket on the Hearth," "The Angelus" and "Pretty as a Picture." *Sweethearts* was revived on Broadway in 1947 and by Ohio Light Opera in 2001.

1913 Christie MacDonald/Reinald Werrenrath. Christie MacDonald, who introduced the operetta's hits, recorded them with Met baritone Reinald Werrenrath and the RCA Victor Male Chorus. "The Cricket on the Hearth," "The Angelus" and "Sweethearts," are on *Music from the New York Stage 1890–1920* (Pearl CD box set) and *The Songs of Victor Herbert* (ASV Living Era CD). **1913 Victor Light Opera.** Victor Light Opera Company vocalists perform a medley of songs from the operetta for a Victor 78 record titled *Gems from Sweethearts*. **1914 Victor Herbert.** Composer Victor Herbert and his Orchestra perform "Sweethearts" and a medley of other songs from the operetta for a Victor 78. **1938 MGM film.** Screenwriters Dorothy Parker and Alan Campbell created a new storyline for MGM's lavish Technicolor film of the operetta, and only five songs of the stage production were retained. Nelson Eddy and Jeanette MacDonald play a happily married couple who star in a stage production of *Sweethearts*. Producer Frank Morgan causes them to split up for a time because of his maladroit

interference but they get back together in the end. Some of the songs had new lyrics by Chet Forrest and Bob Wright and the new song "Summer Serenade" was based on Victor Herbert's piano piece "Badinage." W. S. Van Dyke directed. MGM DVD/VHS/LD. **1938 Jan Peerce/Anne Jamison.** Jan Peerce and Ann Jamison sing a medley of songs from the operetta for a 78 with Nathaniel Shilkret conducting his orchestra. It's on the album *The Operetta World of Victor Herbert*. JJA LP. **1938 George Melachrino/Eve Becke.** Louis Levy and his Gaumont British Symphony perform six numbers from the operetta with vocals by George Melachrino and Eve Becke for an HMV 78. They're on the anthology album *A Victor Herbert Showcase*. Flapper Past CD. **1939 Richard Tauber.** Richard Tauber sings "Sweethearts" with an orchestra conducted by Henry Geehl for a 78. It's on the anthology album *The Songs of Victor Herbert*. ASV Living Era CD. **1945 Jeanette MacDonald.** Jeanette MacDonald recorded "Sweetheart Waltz" and "Summer Serenade" for a 78 with orchestra conducted by Maximilian Pilzer. The songs are on various albums including *Jean MacDonald and Nelson Eddy* (RCA LP). **1946 Jeanette MacDonald/Nelson Eddy.** Jeanette MacDonald and Nelson Eddy star in a four-song radio highlights version of the operetta that follows the film rather than the stage plot. Pelican LP/Demand Performance audiocassette. **1947 Earl Wrightson/Frances Greer.** Earl Wrightson and Frances Greer star in this highlights version of the operetta with supported from Jimmy Carroll and Christina Lind. Al Goodman conducts the orchestra RCA Victor LP. **1951 Dorothy Kirstein.** Dorothy Kirstein, who plays Enrico Caruso's Metropolitan Opera stage partner in the biopic *The Great Caruso*, sings "Sweethearts" in the film. It's performed at the home of the woman he wants to marry while he is away performing at a concert. Peter Herman Adler conducted the music and Richard Thorpe directed the film. MGM-UA DVD/VHS. **1952 Eleanor Steber.** Eleanor Steber sings "Sweethearts" on *The Voice of Firestone* TV program

Ohio Light Opera revived Victor Herbert's comic opera *Sweethearts* in 2001.

on February 18, 1952, with the Firestone Orchestra led by Howard Barlow. It's on the video *Eleanor Steber in Opera and Song.* VAI VHS. **1961 Robert Shaw Chorale.** The Robert Shaw Chorale and Orchestra perform the song "Sweethearts" on the album *The Immortal Victor Herbert.* RCA Victor LP. **1978 Beverly Sills/Sherrill Milnes.** Beverly Sills and Sherrill Milnes join in duet on "Sweethearts" on the album *Up in Central Park.* Julius Rudel conducts the New York City Opera. EMI LP. **1981 Gregg Smith Singers.** Rosalind Rees sings the role of Sylvia with Kevin Elliot as Prince Franz in this highlights recording of the comic opera by the Gregg Smith Singers. The other singers are Samantha Genton, Thomas Bogdan, Walter Richardson, Elsa Larsson and William Powell. Gregg Smith directs the singers and Carl Ebert conducts the Lake Placid Sinfonietta. MMG LP/CMG audiocassette. **1986 Eastman-Dryden Orchestra.** The Eastman-Dryden Orchestra, led by Donald Hunsberger, perform songs from the operetta on the album *Victor Herbert: L'Encore.* Arabesque CD. **2000 Elizabeth Futral/Steven White.** Elizabeth Futral and Steven White perform "Sweethearts" and "Pretty as a Picture" on the album *Sweethearts.* Rudolph Palmer conducts the Rudolph Palmer Singers and Robert Tweten plays piano. Newport Classics CD. **2001 Ohio Light Opera.** J. Lynn Thompson conducts the Ohio Light Opera Orchestra and Chorus in this revival of the operetta staged by Steven Daigle. Suzanne Woods, Cassidy King and John Pickle star with support from Robin Bricker, Ben Smith Alta Boover, Jonathan Stinson, Derek Parks, Patrick Howle, Bertha Curtis, Randall Umstad, Grant Knox and Justin Legris. Albany 2-CD box.

SWENSON, RUTH ANN *American soprano (1960–)*

Ruth Ann Swenson created the role of Belis in Conrad Susa's THE LOVE OF DON PERLIMPLIN at the PepsiCo Festival in Purchase, NY, in 1984. She sings EDGAR ALLAN POE's wife Virginia in a 1991 Lyric Opera of Chicago broadcast of Dominick Argento's opera THE VOYAGE OF EDGAR ALLAN POE and Marsinah in a 1991 recording of the Wright/Forrest KISMET with Samuel Ramey and Jerry Hadley. Swenson, born and brought up in Commack, NY, studied at Philadelphia's Academy of Vocal Arts. She began to sing professionally in San Francisco in 1983 and made her Metropolitan Opera debut in 1991.

THE SWING *1956 TV opera by Kastle*

A father tries to calm his jittery daughter on her wedding day by pushing her back and forth in a swing as he had when she was a child. It seems to work because when her mother comes out of the house, the bride is ready to go to her wedding. Leonard Kastle's 15-minute TV opera *The Swing*, libretto by the composer, was commissioned for the NBC women's program *The Home Show* and telecast on June 11, 1956. Norman Atkins was the father, Edith Gordon was the daughter, Marguerite Lewis was the mother and Arlene Dahl hosted the show. Lewis Ames produced and Garth Dietrich directed. Norman Paris conducted the NBC Opera Theatre Orchestra.

SYLVAN, SANFORD *American baritone (1953–)*

Sanford Sylvan created important roles in operas by John Adams. He played Chou En-lai in NIXON IN CHINA when it premiered at Houston Grand Opera in 1987 and he is featured on the telecast and recording. He played Leon Klinghoffer in THE DEATH OF KLINGHOFFER when it premiered in Brussels in 1991 and he is featured on its recording. He created a leading role in Philip Glass and Robert Moran's chamber opera THE JUNIPER TREE when it premiered at the American Repertory Theater in Cambridge, MA, in 1985 and he sang St. Ignatius in Virgil Thomson's opera FOUR SAINTS IN THREE ACTS when Robert Wilson staged it for Houston Grand Opera in 1996. He also gave the first performance of Adams' Walt Whitman-based work *The Wound Dresser*. Sylvan has been closely associated with Peter Sellars and sang in his modernized versions of the Da Ponte/Mozart operas.

THE SYSTEM *1974 opera by Bach*

American poet Edgar Allan seeks refuge from a storm in a bizarre old house. It turns out to be a an insane asylum run by the inmates who have taken over from the staff. After a time Edgar realizes that staff and inmates are interchangeable. Jan Bach's 50-minute one-act opera *The System* is a black comedy with a libretto by the composer loosely based on EDGAR ALLAN POE's story "The System of Doctor Tarr and Professor Fether." It premiered at Mannes College of Music in New York on March 5, 1974.

T

TABASCO *1894 opera by Chadwick*

The Bey of Tangier wants exciting new taste experiences and is enthralled by Tabasco sauce when an American introduces it. George Chadwick's burlesque opera *Tabasco*, libretto by R. A. Barnet, was a hit when it was premiered by the Boston Cadets in Boston on January 29, 1894. Thomas Q. Seabrook adapted the opera for his company and toured it to New York and the rest of America.

1992 New England Conservatory Orchestra. The Overture to the opera was performed in a concert at Jordan Hall in Boston by the New England Conservatory Orchestra under the direction of John Moriarty. It was recorded for the New England Conservatory of Music archive but is not currently available commercially.

TALE FOR A DEAF EAR *1957 opera by Bucci*

Laura and Tracy are married but love has died and they now argue bitterly. When Tracy suddenly dies of a heart attack, Laura regrets it and wishes him back. Three miracles from earlier eras in Italy, Germany and Scotland are presented and, as a fourth miracle, Tracy is restored to life. Nothing has changed, however, and after another bitter argument with Laura, he dies a second time for good. Mark Bucci's opera *Tale for a Deaf Ear*, libretto by the composer based on Elizabeth Enright's story *Moment Before the Rain*, premiered on August 5, 1957, at the Berkshire Music Center in the Tanglewood Festival with James Billings conducting the production by Boris Goldowsky. It was staged at the New York City Opera on April 6, 1958, with Patricia Neway as Laura, William Chapman as Tracy, Beverly Bowers as the Italian Woman, Lee Venora as the Scottish Girl, Richard Cassilly as the German Soldier and Arthur Newman as the Doctor. Michael Pollock directed and Arnold Gamson conducted.

1958 New York City Opera. Several parts of the opera performed by the New York City Opera with the cast as above were recorded on April 18, 1958, for use by the Voice of America. The tape is at the Library of Congress.

THE TALE OF GENJI *2000 opera by Miki*

Philandering Prince Genji is married to Aoi but he is having simultaneous affairs with his father's wife Fujitsobo and young Murasaki. His jealous former mistress Lady Rokujo kills all three women. Minoru Miki's opera *The Tale of Genji,* libretto in English by Colin Graham based on the classic novel by Lady Muraski, was commissioned by Opera Theater of St. Louis which premiered it on June 15, 2000, in a production by Graham. Mel Ulrich was Prince Genji, Jessica Miller was Aoi, Elisabeth Comeaux was Fujitsobo and Murasaki, Cheryl Rokujo was Lady Rokujo and the lady of Akashi, Andrew Wentzel was the Old Emperor and the Old Recluse, Richard Troxell was To-no-Chujo and Carleton Chambers was Suzaku. Setsu Asakura designed the sets and costumes, Kikushiro Onoe created the choreography and Steuart Bedford conducted the Opera Theater of St. Louis Orchestra and Chorus. The production was reprised in Japan.

THE TALE OF THE NUTCRACKER *1999 opera by Bohmler*

Adolescent Marie is in love with the Nutcracker Prince in a dream-like 1954 America but if she yields to her fantasy, she will never grow up. Craig Bohmler's opera *The Tale of the Nutcracker* is based on the E. T. A. Hoffmann story that inspired the Tchaikovsky ballet. Daniel Helfgot wrote the libretto with assistance on the lyrics by Mary Carol Warwick and Steve Mark Kohn. *Tale* was premiered by Opera San José on November 12, 1999, with Suzan Hanson as Marie and Brandon Jovanovich as the Prince. Yefim Maizel directed and Barbara Day Turner conducted the 14-piece orchestra. Bohmler's other operas include *The Harlot and the Monk* (1985/libretto by James Howley) and *The Achilles Heel* (1992/libretto by Mary Carol Warwick).

TALE OF THE SHIRT *1930 opera ensemble parody*

Groucho, Harpo and Chico Marx enjoyed poking fun at opera in their movies, most notably in *A Night at the Opera*, and they even performed a satirical American opera number in one film. The outlandish but delightful "Tale of the Shirt" is sung in the 1929 film *The Cocoanuts* to the music of the "Habanera" from *Carmen*. The lyrics revolve around repetition of the phrase "I want my shirt," after a man complains that he lost his shirt, and its effect grows in strength as a formidable chorus of well-wishers join in. Words and music to the songs in the film are credited to Irving Berlin, who created the source play with George S. Kaufman, but this number was probably a Marx Brothers innovation. Joseph Santley directed the film for Paramount.

TALE OF THE SUN GODDESS GOING INTO THE STONE HOUSE *1978 opera by Hovhaness*

Alan Hovhaness's mystical chamber opera *Tale of the Sun Goddess Going into the Stone House*, libretto by the composer, was first performed in Salinas, California, in 1978. It is based on a Japanese myth about a sun goddess and, like all of his works, has a strong spiritual element. It was apparently created for his wife, Japanese coloratura soprano Hinako Fujihara, as it calls for a very high voice.

1995 St. Thomas Center Chapel. Coloratura soprano Hinako Fujihara sings selections from the opera accompanied by flautist Scott Boff with the composer conducting the Northwest Sinfonia in a recording made at St. Thomas Center Chapel in Bothell, Washington, in January 1995. It's on an album called *Hovhaness Treasures* along with another vocal work by the composer, *Celestial Canticle for Coloratura Soprano and Piano.* Crystal CD.

TALES OF MALAMUD *1964 opera double-bill by Blitzstein*

Marc Blitzstein's *Tales of Malamud* consists of two one-act operas based on stories by Bernard Malamud, both left uncompleted at his death. The two operas, IDIOTS FIRST and THE MAGIC BARREL, were completed by Leonard Lehrman and staged.

THE TAMING OF THE SHREW   *1953 opera by Giannini*

Italy in the middle ages. Petruchio travels to Mantua in search of wealth and ends up marrying the shrew Katharina. She has a good dowry as her father wants to be rid of her so he can marry off his other daughters. Petruchio tames her to the surprise of her father. Vittorio Giannini's opera *The Taming of the Shrew*, libretto by Dorothy Fee and the composer based on the play by Shakespeare, was premiered in concert form at the Music Hall in Cincinnati on January 31, 1953/Robert Kirchner was Petruchio, Dorothy Short was Katharina, Walter Eyer was Baptista, Patricia Forquer was Bianca, Hal Dieffenwierth was Lucentio, Earl Rice was Tranio, John Maldrem was Biondello, Eugene Hines was Hortensio, Edgar Keenon was Gremio, Louis Linowitz was Vincentio, Paul Ross was Grumio and Fred Wygal was Curtis. Thor Johnson conducted the Cincinnati Symphony Orchestra. The opera attracted much more attention when it was televised by NBC Opera Theater in 1954. It was staged by New York City Opera in 1958 (with Walter Cassel as Petruchio and Phyllis Curtain as Katharina), by Kansas City Lyric Theater in 1969 and by Pacific Opera Victoria in Canada in 2001.

1954 NBC Opera Theatre. John Raitt stars as Petruchio opposite Susan Yager as Katharina in this TV production by NBC Opera Theatre. Sonia Stollin is Bianca, John Alexander is Lucentio, Donald Gramm is Hortensio and Leon Lishner is Baptista. It was produced by Samuel Chotzinoff, staged by Charles Polacheck, designed by William Molyneux and costumed by John Boxer. Artistic director Peter Herman Adler conducts the Symphony of the Air Orchestra and Kirk Browning directed the telecast on March 13, 1954. Video at MTR. **1969 Kansas City Lyric Theater.** Adair McGowen stars as Petruchio opposite Mary Jennings as Katharina in this recording of a Kansas City Lyric Theater production. Catherine Christensen is Bianca, Lowell Harris is Lucentio, Walter Hook is Hortensio, Robert Jones is Gremio, J. B. Davis is Baptista Charles Weedman is Grumio, William Powers is Lucentio's father Vincentio, David Holloway is Tranio, Brian Steel is Biondello and William Latimer is Curtis. Russell Patterson conducts the Kansas City Lyric Theater Orchestra. CRI LP/CD.

TAMKIN, DAVID   *American composer (1906–1975)*

David Tamkin's opera THE DYBBUK, libretto by his brother Alex Tamkin based on a 1920 Yiddish play by Saloman Ansky, was composed in 1931 and premiered by New York City Opera twenty years later, on October 4, 1951. His second opera *The Blue Plum Tree of Esau*, again with libretto by his brother, was composed in 1962. Tamkin was born in Russia but his parents moved to Portland, Oregon, when he was a child. After studying violin and composition and moving to Los Angeles, he became an orchestrator of movie scores for Hollywood, working mainly for Universal. His films range from quality pictures like *Letter from an Unknown Woman* to slapstick comedies like *Abbott and Costello Meet Frankenstein*.

TAMMANY; OR, THE INDIAN CHIEF   *1794 ballad opera by Hewitt*

Indian chieftain Tammany rescues his love Manana from the evil Ferdinand, one of Columbus's explorers. Ferdinand exacts his revenge by burning them alive in their home. James Hewitt's *Tammany, or The Indian Chief*, libretto by Anne Julia Kemble Hatton, is the first serious American opera with an American story and the first American opera with a libretto by a woman. It was a ballad opera, in the style of the time, and it premiered successfully at the John Street Theater in New York on March 3, 1794, and was then staged in Philadelphia and Boston. The libretto and one of its songs survive.

TAMU-TAMU   *1973 opera by Menotti*

An Indonesian refugee family appears mysteriously in the apartment of an American couple who have seen a photo of them in a newspaper. Gian Carlo Menotti's anthropological chamber opera, libretto by the composer in English and Indonesian, premiered at the Studebaker Theater in Chicago on September 5, 1973, during the International Congress of Anthropological and Ethnological Sciences. Robert J. Manzari was the American husband, Sylvia Davis was the American wife, Sung Kil Kim was the Indonesian husband Anonto, Sung Sook Lee was the Indonesian wife Radna, Theresa Teng Chen was the grandmother Nenek, Sumiko Mirashima was Indra, Ferlina Newyanti Darmodihardjo was Solema, Joseph Hutagalung was Kakek, Horas Hutagalung was Djoko, Douglas Perry was the Doctor and Samuel Terry was the Priest. Sandro La Ferla designed the sets and costumes and Christopher Keene conducted. The opera was reprised in Spoleto in Italy in 1974 with John Mauceri conducting and presented in New York in 1987.

TAN DUN   *American composer (1957–)*

Tan Dun's 1996 MARCO POLO, libretto by Paul Griffiths, was presented to great acclaim in Munich in 1996 and New York in 1997 and won many prizes including the Grawemeyer Award. It led to a commission to compose an opera for the Met ("Whatever I write, I treat as part of opera, " he says) Tan Dun was born in China but moved to New York to study music at Columbia. His 1989 *Nine Songs,* libretto by the composer, is based around poems by the 4th century poet B. C. Qu Yuan. In 1998 he composed new music for the 16th century Chinese opera PEONY PAVILION when the opera was staged by Peter Sellars. A condensed version was issued on CD as *Bitter Love.* Tan's opera *Tea* was premiered by Nederlandse Opera in Amsterdam in 2003. His *Ghost Opera,* performed around the world by the Kronos Quartet, is not an opera, though it is based on Chinese "spirit operas." His orchestral theater work *The Gate,* about three women who kill themselves for love, has operatic qualities. Tan reached his largest audience ever with is memorable score for Ang Lee's 2000 martial arts film *Crouching Tiger Hidden Dragon.*

TANGEMAN, NELL   *American mezzo-soprano (1917–1965)*

The tragic almost-forgotten mezzo-soprano Nell Tangeman created the role of Mother Goose in Igor Stravinsky's THE RAKE'S PROGRESS in Venice in 1951 and the role of Dinah in Leonard Bernstein's TROUBLE IN TAHITI at Brandeis University in 1952. Born in Columbus, Ohio, she studied violin at Ohio State but then switched to singing. She made her debut in 1945 in Cincinnati and was on the cutting edge of American music for a decade. She sang Jocasta in Stravinsky's *Oedipus Rex* in 1946 with Bernstein conducting and was the soloist in the premiere of Aaron Copland's *In the Beginning* in 1947. Ned Rorem, a close friend, wrote a number of songs for her, including the 1948 *Two Pieces.* Tangeman disappeared from the music scene in 1954 and was found murdered in Washington, DC, in 1965. She is not well represented on record despite her high reputation.

TANGO   *1986 opera by Rodriguez*

Robert Rodriguez' satiric one-act chamber opera *Tango,* libretto by the composer based on newspaper stories of the 1913–1914 periods concerning the dance, premiered in Dallas on January 29, 1986. The tango was so controversial in the years preceding World War I that it was condemned by Pope Pius X. Rodriguez' opera builds on that condemnation using the 1914 Papal announcement and newspaper comments as text. There are three roles: a tango dancer, a radio announcer and a Catholic Cardinal and all three are played by one person, a tenor who dances, sings and narrates. Part One of the opera uses articles from newspapers as text, Part Two is based on sermons and letters by Catholic clerics and Part Three is more stories from newspapers.

1999 Rafael Alvarez. Tenor Rafael Alvarez stars in the three roles in this recording of the opera made with the Voices of Change chamber orchestra. Composer Robert Rodriguez conducts. CRI Exchange CD.

TANIA   *1992 opera by Davis*

Heiress Patty Hearst is abducted by the Symbionese Liberation Army in 1974 and transmuted into the revolutionary Tania. Anthony Davis's surrealistic opera *Tania,* libretto by Michael John LaChiusa, mixes history with pop fantasy and consumerist satire including a love duet between Fidel Castro and Betty Ford. The opera premiered at the American Music Theater Festival in Philadelphia on June 17 1992. Cynthia Aaronson-Davis, who is Davis's wife, sang the role of Patty/Tania, Mark Doss was Symbionese leader Cinque, John Daniecki was Patty's husband/Che, Lynnen Yakes was Mom/Betty Ford, John Duykers was Dad/Fidel Castro, Claudia Rose Golde was Friend/Gabi, Steven Aiken was Teko, Freda Herseth was Fahizah, Ilya Speranza was Yolanda, Darynn Zimmer was Gelina and Kevin Deas was the Reporter. Christopher Alden directed, Paul Steinberg designed the set (which included five television monitors) and William McGlaughlin conducted the chamber orchestra.

1998 University of California San Diego. Cynthia Aaronson-Davis sings the role of Patty/Tania in this 1998 recording of the opera made at the University of California San Diego where the composer is a professor of music. Avery Brooks is Symbionese leader Cinque, Thomas Young is Dad/Fidel, Julie Randall-Osborn is Mom/Betty Ford, David Lee Brewer is Husband/Che, Carol Plantamura is Gaby, Philip Larson is Teko, Jana Campbell-Ellsworth is Galina and Priti Ghandi is Fahizah. Rand Steiger conducts the 16-piece instrumental ensemble Epistome. Koch International Classics CD.

TARQUIN   *1941 opera by Krenek*

Ernst Krenek's first American opera *Tarquin,* libretto by playwright Emmet Lavery, was premiered in concert form at Vassar College in Poughkeepsie, New York, on May 13, 1941. Scenes Two and Seven were presented complete with excerpts from other scenes. Emmet Lavery and John Pierce sang Marius in different scenes, Juliette Harvey, Elizabeth Muir and Elinor Shutts sang Corinna in different scenes, Richard Brooks was Cleon, Henry Noble McCracken was the Archbishop, Nikander Strelsky was the Chancellor, Charles Gordon Post was Bruno, Francis Matteson was the Reporter and Clair Leonard was Tonio. The composer played piano accompaniment. The opera received its first complete performance in Cologne in Germany on July 16, 1950, with Wolfgang von der Nahmer conducting. Felix Knäpper was Marius, Charlotte Hoffman-Pauels was Corinna, Karl Bernhoft was Cleon, Wilhelm Schirp was the Archbishop, Karl Schiebener was the Chancellor and Fritz Leo Liertz was the Reporter.

TARTUFFE   *1980 opera by Mechem*

France in 1660. Sanctimonious fraud Tartuffe ingratiates himself with wealthy Orgon through his apparent piety and then nearly destroys his family. Orgon wants daughter Mariane to marry Tartuffe until Orgon's wife Elmire exposes the scoundrel. Kirke Mechem's three-act opera *Tartuffe,* libretto by the composer based on the play by Molière, was premiered by San Francisco Opera in its American Opera Project series on May 27, 1980. John Del Carlo was Tartuffe, Thomas Hammons was Orgon, Susan Quittmeyer was Elmire, Roberta Cook was Mariane, Evelyn de la Rosa was Dorine, Robert Tate was Valère, Edward Huls was Damis, Leslie Richards was Madame Pernelle and Renée De Jarnatt was Flipote. David Agler conducted the orchestra. *Tartuffe* has become a popular opera with over a hundred productions by Arizona State University, Baton Rouge, Northwestern University, Pittsburgh and others. There is no commercial recording but videos of their productions were made by Opera St. Paul in 1984 and Opera Theater of San José in 1986. It was revived in 2001 by West Bay Opera Company in Palo Alto, CA.

TAYLOR, DEEMS   *American composer (1885–1966)*

Deems Taylor is best remembered today as music critic and long-time NBC radio opera commentator but he was considered America's most successful opera composer in the 1930s after premieres of two high-profile operas at the Met. THE KING'S HENCHMAN, libretto by poet Edna St. Vincent Millay based on a Saxon legend similar to *Tristan und Isolde,* premiered at the Met on February 17 1927, with Lawrence Tibbett in the main role. PETER IBBETSON, libretto by Constance Collier and the composer based on Gerald Du Maurier's novel, premiered at the Met on February 7, 1931, with Edward Johnson, Lucrezia Bori and Lawrence Tibbett in the principal roles. Both were hugely popular and became the most often performed American operas at the Met (*King's Henchman* was staged 14 times and Peter Ibbetson 16) but both fell out of fashion and are barely known today. Taylor was born in New York and studied at New York University where his first two music theater works were presented: the 1908 comic opera *Cap'n Kidd and Co* and the 1910 musical comedy *The Undergraduates.* Both had librettos by William Le Baron, later famous as the librettist of the hit

Composer Deems Taylor

show *Apple Blossoms*. Their third joint effort, the musical *The Echo*, about a waitress in a boarding house in love with a rich boarder, made it to The Globe Theater on Broadway in 1910 but only ran for two months. Taylor paired with a different librettist, J. M. Flagg, for the operetta *The Breath of Scandal* performed at Delmonico's in 1916. After his success at the Met in 1927, Taylor composed only two more operas. *Ramuntcho*, libretto by the composer, based on an 1897 novel by Pierre Loti, was premiered by Philadelphia Opera at the Academy of Music in 1942. The student-oriented *The Dragon*, libretto by the composer based on a play by Lady Gregory, was staged at New York University on February 6, 1958. Taylor also acted as Master of Ceremonies for Billy Rose's 1945 revue *Concert Varieties* in which he introduced Zero Mostel and Imogene Coca.

1941 There's Magic in Music. Deems Taylor plays himself in the operatic Paramount movie *There's Magic in Music* produced by his former librettist William Le Baron. He is shown holding a radio interview with Allan Jones about the National Music Camp at Interlochen when Jones begins to talk about an operatic burlesque performer named Toodles LaVerne (Susanna Foster). Andrew Stone directed the film for Paramount.

TAYLOR, RAYNER   *American composer (1747–1825)*

Raynor Taylor emigrated to the U.S. in 1791 with a young actress after beginning his career as a composer in London. He presented three of his comic operas at Annapolis in 1793: *Capocchio and Dorinna*, *The Gray Mare's the Best Horse* and *The Old Woman of Eighty-Three*. He premiered *The Shipwrecked Mariners Preserved*, libretto by Susan Rowson, in Baltimore in 1795 and *The Irish Taylor* in Charleston in 1796. He became an American citizen in 1809 and in 1814 composed his most important American opera, THE ETHIOP *or The Child of the Desert*. It premiered in Philadelphia on January 1, 1814, using a libretto by William Dimond which had previously been set by Henry Bishop. The complicated plot concerns a caliph in disguise and a Christian couple in Islamic Baghdad. *The Ethiop* was one of the earliest American operas to be staged and there is a recording of sections of it.

TAYMOR, JULIE   *American director/librettist (1954–)*

Julie Taymor, best known for producing Walt Disney's *The Lion King* on Broadway and Igor Stravinsky's *Oedipus Rex* in Japan, collaborated with composer Elliot Goldenthal on two innovative American music theatre works. *The Transposed Heads* (1986), libretto by Taymor and Sidney Goldfarb, was based on the Thomas Mann novel. The Obie-winning theatrical oratorio JUAN DARIEN: A CARNIVAL MASS was first performed in New York in 1988 and revived at Lincoln Center in 1996. For it she mixed fantastic puppets with live actors in a highly dramatic production that foreshadowed her success with *The Lion King*. Taylor, who was awarded a MacArthur Foundation "genius" award for her work in staging classic plays, has also staged operas in Houston, Los Angeles, Italy and Russia.

TEA   *2003 opera by Tan Dun*

An aristocratic monk in Kyoto recalls his doomed love affair with a princess while an iconic "Book of Tea" reveals true wisdom. Tan Dun's opera *Tea*, libretto in English by the composer, was premiered by Nederlandse Opera in Amsterdam in 2003. Haijink Fu took the part of the monk Seikyo, Nancy Allen Lundy was the Princess Lan, Christopher Gillett was her jealous brother and Steven Richardson was the Emperor. Jean Kálmán designed the set, Pierre Audi directed and Tan Dun conducted the chamber orchestra which featured three women percussionist playing while wandering through the audience area.

TEITELBAUM, RICHARD   *American composer (1939–)*

Richard Teitelbaum, who composes and performs with electronic instruments and microcomputer systems, has created and recorded a notable interactive opera. GOLEM, libretto by the composer based on a Jewish legend about a monster created by a rabbi, was premiered by the Heritage Chamber Orchestra in New York on March 14, 1989. Teitelbaum, a New York native, studied at Yale and in Italy with Luigi Nono. He became interested in the synthesizer and formed the performance group Musica Elettronica Viva. After further studies at Wesleyan University he formed the World Band which he has toured extensively.

TE KANAWA, KIRI   *New Zealand soprano (1944–)*

New Zealander Kiri Te Kanawa seems to like American music. She sang the title role in Samuel Barber's VANESSA for Monte Carlo Opera in 2001, sings American opera arias in her live concerts and has made operatic recordings of Richard Rodgers' SOUTH PACIFIC (1986), Leonard Bernstein's WEST SIDE STORY (1985) and Frederick Loewe's MY FAIR LADY (1987). Her recording of an aria from Bernard Herrmann's movie opera SALAMMBÔ, created for *Citizen Kane*, is particularly notable as is her delightful rendition of the satiric "Art Is Calling for Me (I Want to Be a Prima Donna)" from Victor Herbert's THE ENCHANTRESS. She has also recorded "Summertime" from George Gershwin's PORGY AND BESS, "You'll Never Walk Alone" from Rodgers' CAROUSEL, "Climb Ev'ry Mountain" from Rodgers' THE SOUND OF MUSIC, "It Never Was You" from Kurt Weill's KNICKERBOCKER HOLIDAY and several songs from Irving Berlin's ANNIE GET YOUR GUN. Te Kanawa began her career in New Zealand, rose to stardom in England and made her Metropolitan Opera debut in 1974.

THE TELEPHONE   *1947 opera by Menotti*

Ben wants to marry Lucy but his proposal is constantly interrupted by her talking on the telephone. He eventually decides to leave the house and phone in his proposal. Gian Carlo Menotti's one-act comic opera *The Telephone or L'amour à trois*, libretto by the composer, premiered at the Heckscher Theater in New York City on February 18, 1947. Marilyn Cotlow was Lucy and Frank Rogier was Ben while Leon Barzin conducted. The opera was written as a curtain raiser for *The Medium* when it opened on Broadway and one was one of the first operas presented on network television. LUCY'S ARIA ("Hello! Hello?")has become a popular recital piece for coloratura sopranos.

1947 Original Broadway cast. The original Broadway cast of *The Telephone* was recorded in 1947. Marilyn Cotlow is Lucy and Frank Rogier is Ben with Emanuel Balaban conducting the American Ballet Theater Orchestra. Columbia LP/Pearl CD. **1956 Eleanor Steber.** Eleanor Steber sings "Lucy's Aria" accompanied by Edwin Biltcliffe on piano. It's on her album *Eleanor Steber in Concert* 1956–1958. VAI CD. **1962 Liliane Berton/Jean-Christophe Benoit.** Liliane Berton is Lucy with Jean-Christophe Benoit in this recording of the opera made in France. Richard Blareau conducts the orchestra. RCA France LP. **1979 Kentucky Opera.** Paula Seibel is Lucy opposite Robert Orth as Ben in this recording by the stars of a 1978 Kentucky Opera production. Jorge Mester conducts the Louisville Orchestra. Louisville First Edition LP. **1992 Teatro San Marco.** Anne Victoria Banks sings Lucy with Gian Lucca Ricci as Ben in this recording made at the Teatro San Marco in Milan, Italy, in March 1992. Paolo Vaglieri conducts the

Milan Chamber Orchestra. Nuova Era CD. **1992 BBC Television.** Carole Farley gives a bravura performance as Lucy with Russell Smythe as Ben in this superb BBC TV Scotland production by Mike Newman. José Serebrier conducts the Scottish Chamber Orchestra. PolyGram VHS/London LD. **1994 New York Chamber Ensemble.** Jeanne Ommerle is Lucy and Richard Holmes is Ben on this recording made at Le Frak Concert Hall, Queens College, in New York City in May 1994. Stephen Rogers Radcliffe conducts the New York Chamber Ensemble. It's on the album *Happy Endings: Comic Chamber Operas.* Albany CD.

TELEVISION AND AMERICAN OPERA

American operas were telecast in the earliest days of television as live studio productions. The first four were all by Gian Carlo Menotti. THE OLD MAID AND THE THIEF, sung by the Hartford Opera Workshop, was telecast by General Electric's Schenectady station WRGB-TV in May 1943. THE TELEPHONE, sung by Curtis Institute of Music students, was telecast by NBC in May 1948. Later in 1948 there were telecasts of THE MEDIUM on both NBC and CBS with professional casts. American operas on TV became a regular feature in the 1950s, especially on NBC Opera Theater, which opened with Kurt Weill's DOWN IN THE VALLEY in 1950. Original operas began to be commissioned for TV following the success of Menotti's AMAHL AND THE NIGHT VISITORS on NBC in 1951. (For list of original TV operas, see "Operas Created for Television," below.) NET Opera began to telecast American operas in 1967 starting with Jack Beeson's LIZZIE BORDEN. After technical improvements made it possible to televise operas live from theaters, most telecasts were of stage productions. The first was Douglas Moore's THE BALLAD OF BABY DOE televised from New York City Opera in May 1976. In the 1980s and 1990s American operas were televised regularly from major opera houses and often issued on video. The following is a list of first television performances of selected American operas.

1943 Menotti, *The Old Maid and the Thief* (WRGB). 1948 Menotti, *The Telephone* (NBC). Menotti, *The Medium* (NBC and CBS). 1950 Weill, *Down in the Valley* (NBC). 1951 Menotti, *Amahl and the Night Visitors* (NBC). 1952 Bernstein, *Trouble in Tahiti* (NBC). 1953 Gershwin, *Blue Monday* (CBS). Martinů, *The Marriage* (NBC). 1954 Herrmann, *A Christmas Carol* (CBS). 1955 Foss, *Griffelkin* (NBC). Schumann, *The Mighty Casey* (CBS). 1956 Dello Joio, *The Trial at Rouen* (NBC). 1957 Moore, *The Ballad of Baby Doe* (ABC). 1959 Menotti, *Maria Golovin* (NBC). 1960 Copland, *The Second Hurricane* (CBS). 1961 Kastle, *Deseret* (NBC). 1962 Moore, *Gallantry* (CBS). Stravinsky, *The Flood* (CBS). 1963 Floyd, *The Sojourner and Mollie Sinclair* (NBC). 1965 Amram, *The Final Ingredient* (ABC). Menotti, *Martin's Lie* (CBS). 1967 Beeson, Lizzie Borden (NET). Laderman, *Galileo Galilei* (CBS). 1970 Beeson, *My Heart's in the Highlands* (NET). 1972 Pasatieri, *The Trail of Mary Lincoln* (NET). 1974 Henze,

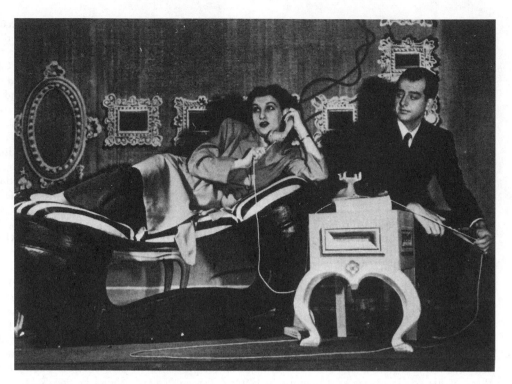

Marilyn Cotlow and Frank Rogier starred in the 1947 Broadway premiere of Gian Carlo Menotti's *The Telephone.*

Rachel La Cubana (NET). 1976 Moore, *The Ballad of Baby Doe* (PBS). 1979 Barber, *Vanessa* (PBS). Floyd, *Susannah* (WTIV). 1981 Floyd, *Willie Stark* (PBS). Still, *A Bayou Legend* (PBS). 1982 Hoiby, *Summer and Smoke* (PBS). 1986 Bernstein, *Candide* (PBS). 1991 Barber, *Antony and Cleopatra* (PBS). 1992 Corigliano, *The Ghosts of Versailles* (PBS). 1994 Susa, *The Dangerous Liaisons* (PBS). 1996 Picker, *Emmeline* (PBS). 1998 Previn, *A Streetcar Named Desire* (PBS). 1999 Drattell/Torke/Beaser, *Central Park* (PBS).

TELEVISION AND AMERICAN OPERETTAS

Classic American operettas began to appear on television in the 1950s when the TV audience started to expand. The television adaptations were often more respectful of the original operettas than the film versions and sometimes featured opera singers in principal roles. The list below includes TV and video versions of classic operettas and musicals featuring opera singers.

1951 NBC, *Mlle Modiste* (Herbert), Fritzi Scheff. 1950 NBC, *Babes in Toyland* (Herbert), Dennis King. 1954 NBC, *Babes in Toyland* (Herbert), Cook. 1958 CBS, *The Red Mill* (Herbert), Shirley Jones. 1960 NBC, *Babes in Toyland* (Herbert), S. Temple. 1965 NBC, *Naughty Marietta* (Herbert), Munsel. 1965 NBC, *The Desert Song* (Romberg), Eddy. 1967 ABC, *Carousel* (Rodgers), Patricia Neway. 1985 PBS, *West Side Story* (Bernstein), Te Kanawa. 1986 PBS, *Candide* (Bernstein), NY City Opera. 1986 NBC, *Babes in Toyland* (Herbert), Barrymore. 1986 PBS, *South Pacific* (Rodgers), Kiri Te Kanawa. 1987 PBS, *My Fair Lady* (Loewe), Kiri Te Kanawa. 1989 PBS, *Candide* (Bernstein), Anderson, Hadley. 1989 PBS, *The New Moon* (Herbert), NY City Opera.

Operas Created For Television: Television opera was created in America. Gian Carlo Menotti's AMAHL AND THE NIGHT VISITORS, commissioned by NBC, was the first, telecast on December 24, 1951, and its popularity led to many other commissions. In recent years American avant-garde composers have begun to create TV operas for video monitors rather than for broadcast television, Commissions for new TV operas have virtually disappeared in America, though they remain popular in Europe Listed below are notable American TV operas. See individual operas or composers for details.

1951 Menotti, AMAHL AND THE NIGHT VISITORS (NBC). 1953 Bucci, THE THIRTEEN CLOCKS (ABC). Martinů, THE MARRIAGE (NBC). Peter, THE PARROT (NBC). Wilder, MISS CHICKEN LITTLE (CBS). 1954 Giannini, THE TAMING OF THE SHREW (NBC). Gruenberg, *The Miracle of Flanders.* Gruenberg, *One Night of Cleopatra.* Herrmann, A CHRISTMAS CAROL (CBS). 1955 Foss, GRIFFELKIN (NBC). Herrmann, A CHILD IS BORN (CBS). Gruenberg, *The Delicate King.* 1956 Dello Joio, THE TRIAL AT ROUEN (NBC). Kastle, THE SWING (NBC). Simone, *The Emperor's New Clothes* (CBS). 1957 Hollingsworth, LA GRANDE BRETÈCHE (NBC). 1958 Johnson, THE THIRTEEN CLOCKS (ABC). Laderman, SARAH (CBS). Menotti, MARIA GOLOVIN (NBC but staged first). 1959 Hoiby, BEATRICE (WAVE-TV). Jones, THE CAGE (NBC). Woolen, THE DECORATOR (NBC). 1961 Kastle, DESERET (NBC). Jones, BREAK OF DAY (CBS). Strauss, THE ACCUSED (CBS). 1962 Antheil, CABEZA DE VACA (CBS). Stravinsky, THE FLOOD (CBS). 1963 Menotti, LABYRINTH (NBC). 1964 Menotti, MARTIN'S LIE (CBS). 1965 Amram, THE FINAL INGREDIENT (ABC). Bucci, THE HERO (NET). 1966 Kent, *A Room in Time* (WBAL). 1967 Laderman, THE TRIALS OF GALILEO (CBS). 1969 Kondorossy, *Shizuka's Dance* (Tokyo TV). 1970 Beeson, MY HEART'S IN THE HIGHLANDS (NET). 1972 Pasatieri, THE TRIAL OF MARY LINCOLN (CBS). Johnson, THE FOUR NOTE OPERA. 1973 Eaton, MYSHKIN (PBS). 1974 Henze, RACHEL LA CUBANA (NET). Lees, MEDEA IN CORINTH (CBS). 1975 Drew, *Mysterium.* 1976 Ashley, MUSIC WITH ROOTS IN THE AETHER (Paris). 1980 Ashley, PERFECT LIVES (The Kitchen). 1991 Ashley, IMPROVEMENT (Mills College). 1995 Ashley, EL/AFICIONADO (The Kitchen). 2004 John Adams opera commissioned by Channel 4.

TELEVISION OPERA DIRECTORS *American TV producers/directors*

The pioneering producers and directors of American operas on television have rarely received the recognition they deserve and are rarely listed in opera reference books. The first two were ROGER ENGLANDER and PAUL NICKELL, who began to present American operas on television in 1948. Englander produced and Nickell directed telecasts of Gian Carlo Menotti's THE TELEPHONE in May 1948 and Menotti's THE MEDIUM in October and December 1948. Englander later directed Menotti's THE OLD MAID AND THE THIEF (1953) and Aaron Copland's THE SECOND HURRICANE (1960). The other important pioneer is KIRK BROWNING, who directed dozens of American operas on TV for NBC Opera Theater beginning in 1950 with Kurt Weill's DOWN IN THE VALLEY. His premiere production of Menotti's AMAHL AND THE NIGHT VISITORS in 1951 was one of the great successes of TV opera and he went on to direct many other premieres. BRIAN LARGE, an Englishman who has become the leading TV opera director in recent years through his Metropolitan Opera telecasts, directed Carlisle Floyd's WILLIE STARK from Houston in 1981, John Adams' NIXON IN CHINA from Houston in 1988 and John Corigliano's THE GHOSTS OF VERSAILLES from the Met in 1991.

THE TELL-TALE HEART *American operas based on Poe story*

A young man kills his landlord and hides his body under the floor but becomes convinced the man's heart is still beating betraying his crime. There are five American one-act operas based on this famous 1843 story by EDGAR ALLAN POE.

1968 Leo Horácek. Leo Horácek's one-act opera *The Tell-Tale Heart*, libretto by Joseph Golz, was staged at Morgantown in West Virginia on August 7, 1968. **1979 Thomas Czerny-Hydzik.** Thomas Czerny-Hydzik's one-act opera *The Tell-Tale Heart*, libretto by the composer, was premiered by Prince George's Civic Opera in Largo, Maryland, Dec 27, 1979. **1982 Bruce Adolphe.** Bruce Adolphe's one-act opera *The Tell-Tale Heart*, libretto by the composer, adds a girlfriend to the story and uses Poe poems for lyrics. It premiered at the Opera Theatre of Boston on January 22, 1982, and was reprised by the New York Chamber Opera Company in 1988. **1999 David Bernstein.** David Bernstein's opera *The Tell-Tale Heart*, libretto by Charles Kondek, premiered at the University of Akron School of Music in Akron Ohio, on November 6, 1999, with baritone Alfred Anderson singing the role of the mad protagonist. It was staged with two other one-act operas by Bernstein/Kondek as *Poe 2, Hawthorne 1; An American Trilogy.* **1999 Adam Levowitz.** Adam Levowitz's chamber opera *The Tell-Tale Heart*, libretto by the composer based on the Poe story, was completed in 1999 but has not been staged.

TELSON, BOB *American composer (1956–)*

Composer Bob Telson and librettist Lee Breuer have created a number of unusual music theater works combining classical and poetic ideas with gospel and popular music forms. Their major success was the oratorio THE GOSPEL AT COLONUS, libretto based on Sophocles' play *Oedipus at Colonus*, which was premiered at the Brooklyn Academy of Music in 1983. The original cast included Morgan Freeman and the gospel group the Blind Boys of Alabama; it was recorded and telecast. Their first joint effort was SISTER SUZIE CINEMA, a "do-wop opera" based on dreams about the movies in which teenagers go into an empty movie theater and sing their fantasies in 1950s doo-wop style. This 23-minute work was premiered by the New Jersey *a cappella* quintet Fourteen Carat Soul at the Public Theater in New York in 1981. *The Warrior Ant,* based on Japanese theater techniques and featuring a range of music from Brazilian Samba and a Trinidad steel band to jazz, blues and gospel, was presented at the Composers' Showcase in New York in 1986 and at Spoleto Festival USA in 1988. Telson received an Oscar nomination for his score for the film *Bagdad Cafe.*

THE TEMPEST (1) *American operas based on Shakespeare play*

Prospero, formerly the Duke of Milan, has been illegally deposed and exiled and now lives on an isolated island with his daughter Miranda, the spirit Ariel and the monster Caliban. Prospero's foes are shipwrecked on the same island and the situation is resolved after Miranda falls in love with Prince Ferdinand, son of the King of Naples. Williams Shakespeare's play *The Tempest* has been the basis of over thirty operatic adaptations including five by American composers.

1970 Douglas Post. Douglas Post's operatic version of Shakespeare's *The Tempest*, libretto by the composer, was premiered in San Antonio in 1970. **1973 Alva Henderson.** Alva Henderson's opera *The Tempest*, libretto by the composer, was his second opera. It does not seem to have been performed. **1984 Peter Westergaard.** Peter Westergaard's three-act opera *The Tempest*, libretto by the composer, was premiered in the Opera Festival of New Jersey in Lawrenceville, NJ, on June 29, 1994. William Parcher sang the role of Prospero, Martha Elliot was Miranda, Maria Tegzes was Ariel, Michael Jones was Caliban, David Ronis was Trinculo, David

DuPont was Stephano, Thomas Sandri was Alonso, Michael Willson was Antonio and Frank Kelly was Ferdinand. Ron Kadri designed the sets, Christopher Mattaliano staged the opera and Michael Pratt conducted. **1985 John Eaton.** John Eaton's three-act grand opera *The Tempest*, libretto by critic Andrew Porter, was premiered by Santa Fe Opera on July 27, 1985. Timothy Noble sang the role of Prospero, Sally Wolf was Miranda, Susan Quittmeyer was Ariel, Ann Howard was Caliban, Colenton Freeman was Ferdinand, Gimi Beni was Stephano, Steven Richards was Trinculo, David Parsons was Alonzo, Joseph Frank was Antonio, John Stewart was Sebastian, Kevin Langan was Gonzalo,

Des Moines Metro Opera mounted the world premiere of Lee Hoiby's Shakespearean opera *The Tempest* in 1986. Photograph courtesy of Des Moines Metro Opera.

Melanie Helton was Iris, Lisa Turetsky was Ceres and Jean Kraft was Juno. Richard Bradshaw conducted The Santa Fe Opera Orchestra. Eaton used a variety of musical styles to characterize the roles, including jazz and electronic instruments. The opera was praised for its intellectual accomplishment and the quality of Porter's libretto.

THE TEMPEST (2)   *1986 opera by Hoiby*

Lee Hoiby's three-act opera *The Tempest*, libretto by Mark Shulgasser, was commissioned by Des Moines Metro Opera which premiered it at the Blank Performing Arts Center in Indianola, Iowa, on June 21, 1986. Peter Van Derick sang the role of Prospero, Carol Sparrow was Miranda, Constance Hauman was Ariel, Jacques Trussel was Caliban, and Kenneth Shaw was Ferdinand. Robert L. Larsen conducted. The opera was highly praised by critics and was successfully revived by Lyric Opera of Kansas City in 1988 and Dallas Opera in 1996. In Dallas Hauman and Trussel reprised their roles as Ariel and Caliban opposite Julian Patrick as Prospero, Joan Gibbons as Miranda and Gary Martin as Ferdinand. Hoiby's music is melodious and singer friendly and Caliban's tenor aria "BE NOT AFEARED" was praised by critic John Briggs of *Opera News* as "the most beautiful aria written into an American opera for nearly fifty years." Ariel's wordless coloratura aria VOCALISE has also become popular.

1997 Jacque Trussel. Jacque Trussel, who originated the role of Caliban, sings the tenor aria "Be not afeared" on his album *Sounds and Sweet Airs*. It was recorded in September 1997 at the Janácek Cultural Center in Haviov, Czech Republic, with Dennis Burkh conducting the Janáček Philharmonic Orchestra. Purchase Records CD.

THE TEMPLE DANCER   *1919 opera by Hugo*

The chief dancer in the Hindu temple of Mahadeo falls in love with a man of another religion and attempts to steal the jewels from the temple for him. The temple guard catches here but she seduces and poisons him. When she again seizes the jewels, she is struck dead by lightning. John Adam Hugo's one-act opera *The Temple Dancer,* libretto by Jutta Bell-Ranske based on her own story, premiered at the Metropolitan Opera on March 12, 1919. Florence Easton sang the role of the Temple Dancer, Morgan Kingston was the Temple Guard and Carl Schlegel was Yoga. Florence Glover, Lilyan Ogden and Jessie Rogge were the dancers, Joseph Novak designed the set, Richard Ordynski directed and Roberto Moranzi conducted the Met orchestra.

THE TENDER LAND   *1954 opera by Copland*

The American Midwest in the 1930s. Laurie lives on a farm with her mother and grandfather but dreams of escaping to a more exciting world. When two drifters arrive and are hired to work on the farm, she tries to persuade one of them to take her away. When he won't, she decides to leave alone. Aaron Copland's opera *The Tender Land,* libretto by Horace Everett (Eric Johns) was commissioned by Richard Rodgers and Oscar Hammerstein II for TV presentation. NBC turned it down, possibly for political reasons as it was the height of the McCarthy era and Copland was considered a leftist. Copland revised it for the stage and it was premiered at New York City Opera on April 1, 1954. Rosemary Carlos was Laurie, Norman Treigle was Grandpa Moss, Jean Handzlik was Ma Moss, Jon Crain was Martin, Andrew Gainey was Top, Adele Newton was Beth, Michael Pollock was Mr. Splinters, Mary Kreste was Mrs. Splinters, Teresa Gannon was Mrs. Jenks and Thomas Powell was Mr. Jenks. John Butler arranged the choreography, Jerome Robbins staged the opera and Thomas Schippers conducted. Copland revised the opera again after the premiere and this new version, presented at Oberlin College in Ohio on May 20, 1955, has become the standard version. Copland wanted the opera to be suitable for modest production groups and it has won wide acceptance at colleges and regional venues. A presentation at the Barbican in London in March 2000 was warmly welcomed.

1959 Boston Symphony Orchestra. Copland conducts the Boston Symphony Orchestra in a concert suite of *The Tender Land* featuring "Introduction and Love Music," "Party Scene" and "Finale: The Promise of Living." It's on the albums *Copland/Gould: Composers Conduct* (Sony CD) and *Copland: Appalachian Spring,*

The Tender Land (RCA CD). **1965 Lincoln Center.** Joy Clements sings Laurie with Copland conducting the New York Philharmonic and Choral Art Society in a concert version of the opera presented at Lincoln Center. Norman Treigle is Grandpa Moss, Claramae Turner is Ma Moss, Richard Cassilly is Martin, Richard Fredricks is Top, Kellis Miller is Mr. Splinter, Charlotte Povia is Mrs. Splinter, Don Jule is Mr. Jenks, Carolyn Friday is Mrs. Jenks and Sindee Richards is Beth. Columbia LP/Sony CD and Sony CD *A Copland Celebration Vol. 3.* **1978 Michigan Opera.** Karen Hunt sings Laurie with Frances Bible as Ma Moss and George Gaynes as Grandpa Moss in this televised production by Michigan Opera Theater. John Sandor is Martin, Charles Row is Top and Kim Harper and William Nolte take small roles. Copland conducts the Midland Festival Orchestra and Michigan Opera Theater Chorus, Eugene Loring arranged the choreography and Michael Montel staged the opera. Clark Santee directed the PBS telecast on August 28, 1979. House of Opera DVD/VHS. **1983 Helen-Kay Eberley.** Helen-Kay Eberley sings the aria "Thank You, Thank You All" from *The Tender Land* accompanied by pianist Donald Isaak on her album *American Girl.* Eb-Sko LP. **1985 Tanglewood Festival Choir.** The Tanglewood Festival Choir and Boston Pops Orchestra, conducted by John Williams, perform the finale of the opera, "The Promise of Living," on the album *John Williams: The Green Album.* Sony CD. **1987 Cincinnati Pops.** The Cincinnati Pops Orchestra, conducted by Eric Kunzel, performs the finale of the

opera, "The Promise of Living," on the album *Copland: Orchestral Works.* Telarc CD. **1990 Plymouth Music.** Elisabeth Comeaux sings Laurie in this recording of the opera with Philip Brunelle conducting the chorus and orchestra of the Plymouth Music Series in Minnesota. Janis Hardy is Ma Moss, LeRoy Lehr is Grandpa Moss, Dan Dressen is Martin, James Bohn is Top, Vern Sutton is Mr. Splinters, Agnes Smuda is Mrs. Splinters, Maria Jette is Beth, Merle Fristad is Mrs. Jenks and Sue Herber is Mrs. Jenks. Virgin Classics/Musical Heritage Society 2-CD box. **1992 Turtle Creek Chorale.** The Turtle Creek Chorale and Dallas Wind Symphony led by T. Seelig perform the finale of the opera, "The Promise of Living" on the album *Old American Songs.* Reference Recordings CD. **1992 Trammel Starks.** Electronic keyboard artist Trammel Starks performs "The Promise of Living" on his album *A Copland Portrait.* Pro Arte CD. **1995 James Sedares.** James Sedares conducts the Phoenix Symphony Orchestra in *The Tender Land* suite. It's on the album *Copland.* Koch International Classics CD. **1995 Dawn Upshaw.** Dawn Upshaw sings "Laurie's Song" accompanied by pianist David Zinman on her album *The World So Wide.* Nonesuch CD. **1997 Murry Sidlin.** Murry Sidlin conducts his New Music Ensemble in *The Tender Land* suite with singing by Monica Yunus and Robert MacNeil. Koch Classics CD. **1999 New Music Ensemble.** Susan Hanson sings the role of Laurie in a chamber version of the opera arranged by Murray Sidlin. Milagro Vargas is Ma Moss, Richard Zeller is Grandpa Moss, Robert MacNeil is Martin, Douglas Webster is Top, Amy Hansen is Beth, Scott Tuomi is Mr. Splinters, Christine Meadows is Mrs. Splinters, Janice Johnson is Mrs. Jenks and Kregg Arntson is Mr. Jenks. Sidlin, who made this arrangement for thirteen instruments with Copland's agreement, conducts the Third Angle New Music Ensemble and Choral Cross Ties. Koch International Classics CD. **2002 University of Kentucky Opera.** Students from the University of Kentucky Opera Theatre perform the opera in this recording made in Zlin in the Czech Republic. Andrea Jones is Laurie, Dawn Coon is Ma Moss, Benjamin Smolder is Grandpa Moss, Judson Perry is Martin and Michael Turay is Top. Kirk Trevor conducts the Bohuslav Martinů Philharmonic. Albany 2-CD box.

TENNESSEE   *American state (1796–)*

Tennessee has a wealth of opera companies in Chattanooga, Knoxville and Nashville but Memphis has been the main center of operatic activity and premieres. One of America's most popular operas, Carlisle Floyd's SUSANNAH, is set in Tennessee and has become more or less the state opera. Also set in Tennessee are Charles Friedman's MY DARLING' AIDA and William Mayer's A DEATH IN THE FAMILY. Tennessee-born opera people include baritone Gregg Baker (Memphis), composer Neely Bruce (Memphis), choreographer John Butler (Memphis), composer Kenton Coe, soprano Mary Costa (Knoxville), mezzo-soprano Mignon Dunn (Memphis), composer Sorrel Hayes (Memphis), baritone Eugene Holmes (Brownsville), soprano Grace Moore (Nough), composer Mary Carr Moore (Memphis), soprano Ruth Welting (Memphis) and soprano Dawn Upshaw (Nashville) and composer Clarence Cameron White (Clarksville).

Chattanooga: Edwin S. Lindsey's *Elizabeth and Leicester* premiered at the University of Chattanooga on April 21, 1936, and his *Hamlet,* based on the Shakespeare play, was staged there in 1952. Chattanooga Opera, founded in 1943, presented Carlisle Floyd's SUSANNAH in 1960 and reprised it in 1998. It commissioned Sorrell Hayes' *The Glass Woman* in 1989 and staged it in 1995. Other American productions include Seymour Barab's *The Toy Shop,* Gian Carlo Menotti's THE CONSUL, THE MEDIUM and THE

Aaron Copland's bucolic opera *The Tender Land* was premiered by New York City Opera in 1954.

OLD MAID AND THE THIEF, Douglas Moore's THE BALLAD OF BABY DOE and Stephen Paulus' THE VILLAGE SINGER.

Clarksville: Elizabeth Vercoe's HERSTORY III—*Jeanne de Lorraine*, a monodrama for mezzo-soprano based on poems about Joan of Arc, was commissioned by Austin Peay State University in Clarksville. It was created for mezzo Sharon Mabry, who premiered it in 1986.

Gatlinburg: Alan Hovhaness premiered two dance operas, *The Burning House* and *Wind Drum*, at Union College on August 23, 1964. William Berney premiered his folk opera *Dark of the Moon*, libretto by Howard Richardson set in the Great Smoky Mountains, in Gatlinburg in 1967.

Knoxville: Knoxville Opera, founded in 1978, presents its productions in the Tennessee Theater. It premiered Kenton Coe's *Rachel*, libretto by Anne Howard Bailey about Rachel and Andrew Jackson, on April 7, 1989. Other American productions include Leonard Bernstein's WEST SIDE STORY, Carlisle Floyd's SUSANNAH, Mitch Leigh's MAN OF LA MANCHA, Meredith Willson's THE MUSIC MAN, Frederick Loewe's MY FAIR LADY and Richard Rodgers' OKLAHOMA, THE SOUND OF MUSIC and SOUTH PACIFIC.

Martin: Ned Rorem's chamber opera FABLES, based on Marianne Moore's translations of fables by Jean de La Fontaine, premiered at the University of Tennessee in Martin on May 21, 1971.

Memphis: Opera Memphis at the University of Memphis, which began as Memphis Opera Theater in 1956, has been active in commissioning and presenting American operas at the National Center for Development of American Opera and the Orpheum Theater. Its artistic director is composer Michel Ching. Leonard Kastle's DESERET was given its first stage performance in 1976 following its TV premiere; Donald Freund's *The Bishop's Ghost*, libretto by Hall Peyton, was premiered on October 31, 1974; Christopher Drobny's *Touch and Go* was premiered in 1988; David Olney's *Light in August*, based on the William Faulkner novel, was premiered on February 12, 1993; John Baur's *The Vision of John Brown* was premiered on February 12, 1993; Michael Korie and Stewart Wallace's HOPPER'S WIFE was premiered in May 1994; Mike Reid's DIFFERENT FIELDS was commissioned by Opera Memphis, premiered in New York, and performed in Memphis on April 25, 1996; and Michael Ching's BUOSO'S GHOST, a sequel to Puccini's *Gianni Schicchi* using the same setting and cast, was premiered on January 25, 1997. The company has also staged George Gershwin's PORGY AND BESS, Leonard Kastle's DESERET, Mitch Leigh's MAN OF LA MANCHA, Frederick Loewe's MY FAIR LADY, Gian Carlo Menotti's THE MEDIUM and THE TELEPHONE and Richard Rodgers' SOUTH PACIFIC.

Nashville: Charles F. Bryan's *Singin' Billy*, libretto by Donald Davidson, premiered at Vanderbilt University in Nashville on April 23, 1952. Nashville Opera, founded in 1981 fifty years after its famous country cousin, the Grand Old Opry, presents productions at the Tennessee Performing Arts Center. Its American pro-

Scene from Memphis Opera's 2004 production of Michael Ching's opera *Corps of Discovery*. Photograph by William Moore, courtesy of Opera Memphis.

ductions have included Leonard Bernstein's TROUBLE IN TAHITI and George Gershwin's PORGY AND BESS.

THE TENOR   *1950 opera by Weisgall*

Opera tenor Gerardo is preparing for his role as Wagner's Tristan while recalling the many women who have fallen in love with him. His manager Maurice tells him he has to give up the married Helen to avoid scandal while he flirts with a girl in his dressing room. When Helen arrives and he rejects her, she kills herself. Hugo Weisgall's one-act opera *The Tenor,* libretto by Karl Shapiro

Hugo Weisgall's opera *The Tenor* was recorded in Vienna in 1958.

and Ernst Lert based on Frank Wedekind's play *Der Kammersänger* was premiered by the Peabody Opera Company in Baltimore on February 11 1951, with Richard Cassilly in the role of the egocentric tenor Gerardo.

1958 Vienna State Opera. Richard Cassilly stars as tenor Gerardo with Richard Cross as his manager Maurice in this recording made with the Vienna State Opera. Doris Young is the Young Girl, Dorothy Coulter is Helen, Chester Ludgin is the Valet and John Kuh is the Bellboy. Herbert Grossman conducts the Vienna State Opera Orchestra. Westminster/CRI LP and CD.

TER-ARUTUNIAN, ROUBEN   *American designer (1920–)*

Rouben Ter-Arutunian, who was the scene and costume designer for most NBC Opera Theatre productions, created designs for many American operas on television and stage. He designed the sets for the premieres of Lukas Foss's GRIFFELKIN (1955/NBC TV) Gian Carlo Menotti's MARIA GOLOVIN (1958/Brussels), Lee Hoiby's THE SCARF (1958/Spoleto), Norman Dello Joio's BLOOD MOON (1961), Igor Stravinsky's THE FLOOD (1962/CBS TV), Hans Werner Henze's RACHEL, LA CUBANA (1974/NET TV). He also designed the sets and costumes for the 1959 New York City Opera revival of Douglas Moore's THE DEVIL AND DANIEL WEBSTER. Ter-Arutunian, who was born in Tiflis, studied in Berlin and Vienna, and made his opera debut at New York City Opera in 1952.

TESTAMENT OF EVE   *1976 opera by Ivey*

Eve argues with the Serpent as she decides whether she should eat the fruit of the Tree of Knowledge and be expelled from the Garden of Eden. She heroically opts for knowledge over security. Jean Eichelberg Ivey's fascinating electronic opera *Testament of Eve*, libretto by the composer, was premiered in Baltimore on April 21, 1976, and reprised at Columbia University the same year. Eve is a mezzo-soprano, the Serpent's voice is on tape.

THE TESTAMENT OF FRANÇOIS VILLON   *1923 opera by Pound*

Fifteen century French poet-thief François Villon recalls his life in the shadow of the gallows. Ezra Pound's best-known opera *The Testament of François Villon* was created with the help of George Antheil and strong influence from troubadour music. Pound's libretto keeps Villon's poems in French but uses English for the dialogue. The opera was premiered in concert form at La Salle Pleyel in Paris in 1924, reprised in 1926, presented on radio by the BBC in 1932 and 1962, produced at the Spoleto Festival in 1963 and staged several times in recent years. The Western Opera Theater presented it in San Francisco in 1971 with Robert Hughes conducting. The Hamburg State Opera presented it in December 1973 as *Pound-Villon Testament* in a version by Hans Ludwig Hirsch with a cast that included Toni Blankenheim, Ursula Boese, Jutta-Renate Ihloff, Sigrid von Richtofen, Hanna Schwarz, Ude Krekow, Heinz Kruse and Kurt Marschner. Reinbert de Leeuw directed a ASKO-Ensemble production for the Holland Festival in 1980. The Cambridge Poetry Festival presented the opera in 1985 as *Villon* with a tie-in to a Pound exhibition at the Tate Gallery in London.

1971 Western Opera Theater. Robert Hughes conducts the Associated Students of the University of California orchestra in a Western Opera Theater production in San Francisco. The cast includes Philip Booth, John Duykers, Renée Blowers, Dorothy Barnhouse, Dan Parkerson, Wendy Hoggatt, Jaen Sharp, Sandra Bush and Lawrence Cooper. Fantasy Records LP. **1980 ASKO-Ensemble.** Reinbert de Leeuw conducts the ASKO-Ensemble and Chorus in a production of the opera at the Holland Festival. The cast includes Rita Dams, Jard van Nes, Harry Van der Kamp, Marius Van Altena, Lieuwe Visser, Charles van Tassel and Lucia Meeuwsen. The LP record sleeve pictures the cast sitting in chairs under a noose. ASKO LP. **2003 Ego Scriptor Cantilenae.** Excerpts from the opera are performed by the Western Opera Theater in 1971, the ASKO-Ensemble in 1980 and another group in 1992 on the compilation CD *Ego Scriptor Cantilenae: The Music of Ezra Pound*. It includes music by Pound taken from recordings made over a 30-year period. Other Minds CD.

TESTIMONY OPERA   *1945 movie opera by Fine*

An aria for an imaginary comic opera was created for Danny Kaye for the 1945 Goldwyn movie *Wonder Man*. Kaye is about to testify against a gangster who killed his brother. When the gangster's mob chases after him, he escapes onto an opera stage and sings his testimony as an aria to the district attorney in the audience. Sylvia Fine created the words and music for this bizarre aria. The opera singers on stage with Kaye are Noël Cravat, Nick Thompson, Nino Pipitone, and Baldo Minuti. Luis Alberni is the disturbed prompter, and Aldo Franchetti is the orchestra conductor. The film is on video.

TEXAS   *American state (1845–)*

Texas has two of the great opera companies of the world, Houston Grand Opera and Dallas Opera, and has premiered many notable operas. It has also produced a number of composers who are uniquely Texan, like Robert S. Rodriguez and Julia Smith. Texas-born opera people include choreographer Alvin Ailey (Rogers), tenor William Blankenship (Gatesville), baritone Jules Bledsoe (Waco), baritone John Boles (Greenville), composer Radie Britain (Silverton), mezzo-soprano Joyce Castle (Beaumont), soprano Dorothy Dow (Houston), tenor Bruce Ford (Lubbock), composer Scott Joplin (Texarkana), baritone Timothy Nolen (Rotan), composer Hannibal Peterson (Smithville) composer Harvey Schmidt (Dallas), composer Julia Smith (Denton), composer Robert X. Rodriguez (San Antonio), composer Kirk Theron (Alamo), tenor Neil Wilson (Abilene) director Robert Wilson (Waco). Operas set in Texas include George Antheil's CABEZA DE VACA, Jack Beeson's HELLO OUT THERE, Robert X. Rodriguez's THE RANSOM OF RED CHIEF, Harry Tierney's RIO RITA and Scott Warrender's Wagner parody DAS BARBECÜ.

Abilene: Abilene Opera, founded in 1980, usually presents three operas or comic operas every year at the Paramount Theater. In 1994 the company staged and videotaped Sigmund Romberg's THE STUDENT PRINCE.

Amarillo: Amarillo Opera, founded in 1988, presents productions at the Amarillo Civic Center Auditorium. Its American presentations have included Lucas Foss's THE JUMPING FROG OF CALAVERAS COUNTY, Mitchell LEIGH'S MAN OF LA MANCHA, Frederick Loewe's MY FAIR LADY and Wright/Forrest's KISMET.

Austin: Austin Lyric Opera, founded in 1987 and now the major opera company of the city, has staged Leonard Bernstein's CANDIDE, Jake Heggie's DEAD MAN WALKING, Carlisle Floyd's COLD SASSY TREE, Douglas Moore's THE BALLAD OF BABY DOE and André Previn's A STREETCAR NAMED DESIRE. Austin has been enjoying opera since 1871 when the Austin Opera House opened. Texas composer Julia Smith's *Cockcrow*, based on a Grimm tale, premiered at the Driskill Hotel on April 22, 1954, and her *Cynthia Parker*, based on a Texas legend, was staged by University of Texas-Austin Opera Theater on December 5, 1985. Dan Welcher's

Della's Gift, based on O Henry's THE GIFT OF THE MAGI, was premiered by the University in 1987 and Daron Hagen's BANDANNA, a Southwest version of the Othello story, in 1999.

Borger: Ruth Brush's folk opera *The Street Singers of Market Street* was premiered in Borger on February 16, 1965.

Corpus Christi: Lawrence Weiner's *Chipita Rodriguez*, libretto by Leo Carillo and John Wilson based on the true story of a woman who was hanged in Texas, was premiered by the Corpus Christi Symphony at the Bayfront Plaza Auditorium on April 3, 1982. Matt Doran's *The Committee* premiered at Del Mar College of Music on May 25, 1955.

Dallas: Sigmund Romberg's comic opera THE STUDENT PRINCE inaugurated the 5000-seat Fair Park Auditorium in Dallas on October 10, 1925. After it was remodeled in 1972 and renamed the Music Hall, it became the home of Dallas Opera. Dallas Opera, which was founded in 1957 with an inaugural concert by Maria Callas, focused on major international stars in its early years and did not present an American opera until 1978, Douglas Moore's THE BALLAD OF BABY DOE. Since then it has become a home for new American work. It premiered and televised Dominick Argento's THE ASPERN PAPERS, based on the Henry James story, in 1988 and has presented two other Argento operas, THE VOYAGE OF EDGAR ALLAN POE and THE DREAM OF VALENTINO. It commissioned Tobias Picker's opera THÉRÈSE RAQUIN, based on the novel by Emil Zola, and premiered it on November 30, 2001. Other American presentations include Samuel Barber's VANESSA, George Gershwin's PORGY AND BESS, Lee Hoiby's THE TEMPEST, Gian Carlo Menotti's AMELIA GOES TO THE BALL and THE MEDIUM, Igor Stravinsky's THE RAKE'S PROGRESS and Virgil Thomson's THE MOTHER OF US ALL. Dallas Opera has also worked with Texas composer Robert X. Rodriguez, who has premiered several operas in Dallas where he teaches. The children's opera MONKEY SEE, MONKEY DO, based on a folk tale, was commissioned by Dallas Opera and the Puppet Opera Theater and premiered on January 26, 1987. *Le Diable amoureux/The Devil in Love,* was televised by KERA-TV in Dallas on April 11, 1979. *Suor Isabella/Sister Isabella,* based on a *Decameron* story, premiered at the University of Texas on July 7, 1982. The semi-historical TANGO was staged on January 29, 1986. THE RANSOM OF RED CHIEF, based on the O. Henry story, was presented by Lyric Opera of Dallas in Mesquite near Dallas on October 10, 1986. Southern Methodist University has staged several American operas. Julia Smith's *The Stranger of Manzano*, libretto by J. W. Rogers, was presented on May 6, 1947, following its premiere in Denton. Jack Frederick Kilpatrick's *The Blessed Wilderness,* which concerns Native Americans in Georgia, was premiered there on April 18, 1959. Samuel Adler's *The Wrestler*, libretto by Judith Stampfer based on the story of Jacob in the Bible, was premiered there in 1972. Laurie Anderson's multi-media MOBY DICK was premiered there on April 29, 1999. Don Gillis's *The Libretto* was premiered at the National Opera Convention in Dallas in 1961. Neil Wolfe's BIRTH/DAY: THE FRANKENSTEIN MUSICAL, based on Mary Shelley's *Frankenstein,* was premiered by the Deep Ellum Opera Company at the Hickory Street Annex on October 15, 1994. Conrad Susa's church opera THE WISE WOMEN was premiered at the Dallas Convention of the American Guild of Organists in July 1994. Vincent McDermott's *Mata Hari*, libretto by Jan Baross, was premiered in Dallas in 1995.

Denton: Julia Smith was born in Denton and graduated from North Texas State University where she premiered two of her operas: *Cynthia Parker*, based on a Texas legend, on February 16, 1939; and *The Stranger of Manzano*, on May 1, 1946. Samuel Adler's popular

THE OUTCASTS OF POKER FLAT, based on the Bret Harte story, premiered at the University on June 8, 1962. George F. Root's 1857 "operatic cantata" THE HAYMAKERS was recorded by the North Texas State University Grand Chorus in 1979. Gian Carlo Menotti's comic opera THE HERO was staged at the University in 1987. The Denton Light Opera Company presents American operettas.

El Paso: Stanley Fletcher's *The Five Dollar Opera*, based on O Henry's story *The Whirligig of Life*, was premiered in El Paso on March 5, 1982. El Paso Opera, founded in 1992, presents repertory operas in the Abraham Chavez Theatre.

Fort Worth: Carl Venth, conductor of the Fort Worth Symphony Orchestra in its early years, premiered his ballet opera *The Rebel* in Fort Worth on May 29, 1926. Fort Worth Opera, founded in 1946, premiered Julia Smith's Christmas opera *The Shepherdess and the Chimney Sweep* on December 28, 1966, and Thomas Pasatieri's children's opera THE GOOSE GIRL on February 15, 1981. It has also staged Leonard Bernstein's CANDIDE, Gian Carlo Menotti's THE OLD MAID AND THE THIEF and THE TELEPHONE and Stephen Paulus's THE POSTMAN ALWAYS RINGS TWICE. Texas Wesleyan College premiered Don Gillis's THE GIFT OF THE MAGI, based on the O Henry story, on December 7, 1965. Samuel Adler's *The Lodge of Shadows*, a Native American version of the Orpheus legend, premiered in Fort Worth in 1988.

Houston: The innovative Houston Grand Opera, founded in 1956, is one of the world's finest and most adventurous opera companies. Noted for championing American opera, it commissioned and premiered twenty eight between 1974 and 2004 and recorded and telecast several of them. 1974 Thomas Pasatieri's THE SEAGULL. 1976 Carlisle Floyd's BILBY'S DOLL. 1981 Carlisle Floyd's WILLIE STARK. 1981 Henry Mollicone's STARBIRD. 1983 Leonard Bernstein's A QUIET PLACE. 1987 John Adam's NIXON IN CHINA. 1988 Philip Glass's THE MAKING OF THE REPRESENTATIVE FOR PLANET 8. 1989 Stewart Wallace's WHERE'S DICK? 1989 Michael Tippett's NEW YEAR. 1991 Meredith Monk's ATLAS. 1991 Carlisle Floyd's revised THE PASSION OF JONATHAN WADE. 1992 Robert L. Moran's DESERT OF ROSES. 1993 Craig Bohmler's THE ACHILLES HEEL. 1993 Mary Carol Warwick's TEXAS. 1994 Robert L. Moran's THE DRACULA DIARY. 1994 Noa Ain's revised THE OUTCAST. 1995 Stewart Wallace's HARVEY MILK. 1995 Sterling Tinsley's PUPPY AND THE BIG GUY. 1996 R. I. Gordon's THE TIBETAN BOOK OF THE DEAD. 1996 Daniel Catán's FLORENCIA EN EL AMAZONAS. 1997 Michael Daugherty's JACKIE O. 1998 Mary Carol Warwick's CINDERELLA IN SPAIN. 1998 Mark Adamo's LITTLE WOMEN. 1999 Tod Machover's RESURRECTION. 2000 Carlisle Floyd's COLD SASSY TREE. 2003 Rachel Portman's THE LITTLE PRINCE. 2004 Jake Heggie's THE END OF THE AFFAIR. Houston Grand Opera mounted the first professional production of Scott Joplin's TREEMONISHA in 1982 and recorded it for audio and video release. Its other American presentations include Irving Berlin's ANNIE GETS YOUR GUN, Leonard Bernstein's CANDIDE and TROUBLE IN TAHITI, Marc Blitzstein's REGINA, Carlisle Floyd's SUSANNAH, George Gershwin's PORGY AND BESS (with a Grammy-winning recording), Philip Glass's AKHNATEN, Philip Glass/Robert Moran's THE JUNIPER TREE, Victor Herbert's BABES IN TOYLAND, Jerome Kern's SHOW BOAT, Frederick Loewe's MY FAIR LADY, Gian Carlo Menotti's HELP, HELP, THE GLOBOLINKS and THE MEDIUM, Richard Rodgers' CAROUSEL, Robert X. Rodriguez's FRIDA: THE STORY OF FRIDA KAHLO, Bright Sheng's THE SONG OF MAJNUN, Stephen Sondheim's A LITTLE NIGHT MUSIC and SWEENEY TODD, John Philip Sousa's EL CAPITAN, Kurt Weill's STREET SCENE and Virgil Thomson's FOUR SAINTS IN THREE ACTS. The University of Houston premiered Michael Horvit's children's opera *Tomo* on November 21, 1968; Mary Warwick's THE LAST LEAF on April 27, 1988; and Ann Gebuhr's *Bonhoeffer,* about a German theologian executed for anti-Nazi activities, on May 19, 2000. It staged Conrad Susa's THE DANGEROUS LIAISONS at the Moore Opera Center in April 2000. Dominican College premiered Dawn Crawford's *The Pearl,* based on the John Steinbeck novel, in April 1972. Texas Opera Theater premiered two short operas on June 6, 1985, Michael Ching's *Leo, Opera in One Cat,* and Stewart Wallace's rock-oriented *Soap opera,* Peter Schickele's satirical *Hansel and Gretel and Ted and Alice,* described as an "opera in one unnatural act for bargain countertenor and beriberitone," was premiered in Houston in 1972. Stewart Wallace's mystic KABBALAH was presented in concert in Houston in June 1990 by DiverseWorks Artspace and the Jewish Community Center and recorded at Sugar Hill Studios. Houston Ebony Opera Guild, which stages operas with African American casts, produced a version of *La Bohème* set in Harlem during the Harlem Renaissance. Also located in Houston is the Opera in the Heights company.

Lubbock: John Gilbert premiered two one-act operas at Texas State Teacher's College in Lubbock, *A Mother's Requiem* on April 30, 1963, and *If This Be Madness* on April 21, 1964.

Mesquite: Robert X. Rodriguez's THE RANSOM OF RED CHIEF, based on the O. Henry story, was presented by Lyric Opera of Dallas in Mesquite on October 10, 1986.

San Antonio: Carl Venth's *La Vida de la Mission,* which is set in San Antonio, was premiered in the city on October 28, 1959, twenty years after the composer's death. Alan Hovhaness's *Blue Flame* was premiered there on December 15, 1959. Howard Hanson's MERRY MOUNT was revived in 1964 with Brian Sullivan and Beverly Sills in the leading roles. Douglas Post's operatic version of Shakespeare's THE TEMPEST was premiered in San Antonio in 1970. Theron Kirk's *The Lib: 393 B.C.,* women's lib in ancient Greece as seen by Aristophanes in *Lysistrata,* premiered at San Antonio College on May 5, 1972. San Antonio native Robert X. Rodriguez's *The Old Majestic* premiered at the University of Texas in San Antonio on May 28, 1988.

San Marcos: Mary Warwick's *Lealista,* based on Ernest Hemingway's play *The Fifth Column,* premiered at Southwest Texas State University in San Marcos on March 29, 1985.

Waco: Lyric Opera of Waco, founded in 1998, currently presents operas from the European repertory.

Wichita Falls: Robert X, Rodriguez's one-act *Le Diable amoureux/The Devil in Love,* was staged in Wichita Falls in 1982.

TEYTE, MAGGIE   *English soprano (1888–1976)*

English prima donna Maggie Teyte created a role in an American opera while performing in the United States during the 1910s. She sang the title role in Henry Hadley's BIANCA when it was premiered by the Society of American Singers at the Park Theater in New York in 1918. Teyte sang with Chicago Grand Opera from 1911 to 1914 and with Boston opera companies from 1914 to 1917.

THAT MORNING THING   *1970 opera by Ashley*

Robert Ashley's avant-garde opera *That Morning Thing,* libretto by the composer, was premiered at Ann Arbor on February 8, 1958, and revised for presentation at Mills College in Oakland, California, on December 8, 1970. Two of its components have been recorded: "She Was a Visitor" is a manifestation of the forming of rumor with a leader repeating the title sentence and other groups picking up the words and chanting them. "Purposeful Lady Slow Afternoon" revolves around a woman describing a sexual encounter to her friends in great detail with appropriate sounds.

1996 Automatic Writing. Ashley's CD album *Automatic Writing* includes the two recorded excerpts of the opera. "She Was a Visitor," performed by the Brandeis University Chamber Chorus conducted by Alvin Lucier, was recorded in 1967. "Purposeful Lady Slow Afternoon," performed by Mary Ashley, Cynthia Liddell, Barbara Lloyd and Mary Lucier, was recorded in 1971. The CD also includes the 1979 work *Automatic Writing.* Lovely Music CD.

THEBOM, BLANCHE   *American mezzo-soprano (1918–)*

Blanche Thebom created the role of Queen Elizabeth in Robert Middleton's opera COMMAND PERFORMANCE for the Boston Opera Group at Vassar College in 1961. She sings Baba the Turk on the 1953 Metropolitan Opera recording of Igor Stravinsky's THE RAKE'S PROGRESS and the Old Baroness on a recording of a 1965 Metropolitan Opera production of Samuel Barber's VANESSA. She can be seen singing "I Could Have Danced All Night," from Frederick Loewe's MY FAIR LADY, on a 1956 *Voice of Firestone* TV program. Thebom, born in Monessen, PA, studied with opera diva Margaret Matzenauer and began her 22-year career with the Metropolitan Opera in 1944.

THÉRÈSE RAQUIN   *2001 opera by Picker*

Thérèse Raquin and her lover kill her husband Camille and are not suspected of the crime. After they marry they are haunted by his ghost and growing guilt until eventually they kill themselves. Tobias Picker's opera *Thérèse Raquin,* libretto by Gene Scheer based on the 1867 novel by Emile Zola, was premiered by Dallas Opera on November 30, 2001. Sara Fulgoni was Thérèse, Richard Bernstein was her lover Laurent, Gordon Gietz was her husband Camille, Diana Soviero was Madame Lisette Raquin, Sheryl Woods was Suzanne Michaud, Gabor Andrasy was Olivier Michaud and Peter Kazaras was Monsieur Grivet. Marie-Jeanne Lecca designed the sets, Francesco Zambello directed and Graeme Jenkins conducted the Dallas Opera Orchestra. The opera, commissioned by Dallas in partnership with the Montreal and San Diego Opera companies, was reprised in San Diego in March 2002 with Kirstin Chávez as Thérèse, Christopher Maltman as Laurent, Josephine Barstow as Madame Raquin and Gordon Gietz again as Camille.

2001 Dallas Opera. Sara Fulgoni is Thérèse and Richard Bernstein is Laurent in this recording of the Dallas Opera premiere production made during performances in November and December 2002. Diana Soviero is Madame Raquin, Gordon Gietz is Camille, Sheryl Woods is Suzanne Michaud, Gabor Andrasy is Olivier Michaud and Peter Kazaras is Monsieur Grivet. Graeme Jenkins conducts the Dallas Opera Orchestra. Chandos 2-CD box.

THEYARD, HARRY   *American tenor (1939–)*

Harry Theyard created the role of Ezekiel Cheever in Robert Ward's THE CRUCIBLE at New York City Opera in 1961, Lt. Patrick in Carlisle Floyd's THE PASSION OF JONATHAN WADE at New York City Opera in 1962, Curley in Floyd's OF MICE AND MEN at Seattle Opera in 1970 and Dr. Arnek in Gian Carlo Menotti's THE MOST IMPORTANT MAN at New York City Opera in 1971. He sings Sam Polk in a live recording of a 1971 New York City Opera production of Floyd's *Susannah.* Theyard, who was born in New Orleans, made his debut at New York City Opera in 1965 singing Michele in Menotti's THE SAINT OF BLEECKER STREET.

THE THIEF AND THE HANGMAN   *1959 opera by Ellstein*

A convicted thief, who wants to plant the seed of the Tree of Life, finds his judges are as guilty as he is. Abraham Ellstein's allegorical one-act opera *The Thief and the Hangman,* libretto by Morton Wishengrad, premiered at the University of Ohio in Athens on January l7, 1959. It was presented on ABC television on October 15, 1961, and reprised in Salzberg, Austria, in November 1965. The music is atonal and fairly traditional with elements of dissonance.

1961 ABC Television. Frank Porretta stars as the Thief opposite Norman Atkins as the Hangman in this ABC Television production of the 30-minute opera on the *Directions '62* program. Rosalind Elias is the Narrator, Elaine Bonazzi is the Old one, John Macurdy is the Chamberlain and Ralph Herbert, Robert Trehy and Mark Chalta have supporting roles. Wiler Hance was the producer and Sylvan Levan conducted the orchestra. Telecast on October 15, 1961. Video at Library of Congress.

THE THIRTEEN CLOCKS *American music theater based on Thurber fable*

The clocks have stopped in the gloomy castle of the frigid and nasty Duke who has frozen time. Prince Zorn wants to win the hand of the Duke's beautiful (and warm) niece Princess Saralinda. With the help of the mysterious and usually invisible Golux, who is also a spy for the Duke, fulfills impossible tasks and wins the Princess. A monstrous being called the Todal takes charge of the Duke. Never trust a spy you cannot see. James Thurber's delightful 1944 fable *The Thirteen Clocks* has been the basis of three American music theater works.

1953 Mark Bucci. Mark Bucci's *The Thirteen Clocks*, libretto by the composer, Fred Sadoff and John Crilly, premiered on the Motorola TV Hour on ABC Television on December 29, 1953. Met soprano Roberta Peters was the Princess, John Raitt was the Prince, Basil Rathbone was the Duke and Cedric Hardwick was the Golux. Henry Brodkin produced, Al Lehman designed the costumes, Fred Stover designed the sets and Donald Richardson and Ralph Nelson directed. **1958 Mary Johnson.** Mary Johnson's operetta *The Thirteen Clocks*, libretto by Maritz and Norman Morgan and the composer based on the Thurber fable, was premiered at Hunter College in New York on March 18 1958, and telecast on ABC Television. **1983 Robert Chauls.** Robert Chauls' *The Thirteen Clocks*, libretto by Rhoda Levine based on the Thurber fable, was premiered in Waterford, CT, in May 1983.

THIS IS PROPHETIC *Soprano aria: Nixon in China (1987). Words: Alice Goodman. Music: John Adams*

President Nixon and Chairman Mao singing arias was one of the best things that ever happened to modern American opera as it changed ideas about what opera could be about. While Nixon's innocent aria "News has a kind of mystery" is exceptional, Pat Nixon's "This is prophetic" aria is equally memorable. While visiting the Summer Palace, she foresees a future when luxury will vanish and simple virtues will dominate. Let Gypsy Rose Lee kick off her party shoes, she says, let the expression on the face of the Statue of Liberty change, the Unknown Soldier has risen from his tomb. *Nixon in China*, which originated what has become known as the "CNN opera," revolves around President Nixon's 1972 visit to China and his meeting with Chairman Mao. It was premiered by Houston Grand Opera, was televised and is on CD. Carolann Page portrayed Pat Nixon in this production and introduced the aria. Dawn Upshaw includes it on her recital CD *The World So Wide*.

THOMAS, AUGUSTA *American composer (1964–)*

Augusta Thomas won the International Orpheus Prize in 1994 for her chamber opera LIGEIA, which was commissioned by Mstislav Rostropovich. The opera, libretto by Leslie Dunton-Downer based on the story by EDGAR ALLAN POE, was premiered at the Evian-les-Bains Festival in 1994 and staged at the Aspen Music Festival in 1995. Thomas, a native of New York, has taught at the Eastman School and served as composer-in-residence with the Chicago Symphony Orchestra. She composes instrumental works in many genres and several have been recorded.

THOMAS, EDWARD *American composer (1924–)*

Edward Thomas has composed four music theater works, two with librettos by Joe Masteroff. The best-known is his three-act folk opera DESIRE UNDER THE ELMS, based on the play by Eugene O'Neill, which was produced in its final form by New York Opera Repertory Theater in 1989, and recorded in 2002. *Six Wives,* based on the life and loves of the English King Henry VIII, was first performed at Waterford, CT, on August 14, 1986, and produced by the York Theater in New York in 1992. *Ballad for a Firing Squad,* a musical play about Mata Hari with libretto by Jerome Coopersmith and lyrics by Martin Charnin, was produced at the Theatre de Lys and revived at the York Theater. *Searching for Y*, libretto by Jon Marans, was staged in New York in 2000.

THOMAS, JOHN CHARLES *American baritone (1891–1960)*

John Charles Thomas created the role of Wrestling Bradford in the concert premiere of Howard Hanson's MERRY MOUNT in Ann Arbor, Michigan, on May 20, 1933. He sang on Broadway in Sigmund Romberg's MAYTIME in 1918, recorded its famous song "Will You Remember in 1922 and sang it for a Vitaphone film in 1927. Thomas, born in Meyersdale, Virginia, made his opera debut in Washington, D.C. in 1924 after his Broadway career and sang at the Metropolitan Opera from 1934 to 1943.

THOMAS, MICHAEL TILSON *American conductor (1944–)*

Michael Tilson Thomas conducted the premiere performance of Stanley Silverman's ELEPHANT STEPS at Tanglewood in 1968 and returned to conduct its recording in 1974. He is a strong advocate of the music of Leonard Bernstein and George Gershwin and has conducted several concerts and recordings of their work. His five albums devoted to Gershwin include three with excerpts from PORGY AND BESS: *Gershwin Live* (1983), *Classic Gershwin* (1987) and *Greatest Hits: Gershwin* (1994). He conducts the Los Angeles Philharmonic on the 1990 album *Essential Bernstein* and the London Symphony Orchestra on the 1992 operatic recording/video of ON THE TOWN. He conducted the National Symphony Orchestra in a 1982 concert celebrating the 100th anniversary of Igor Stravinsky. Tilson, who was born in Hollywood, studied at USC and began conducting while a student. He was made principal conductor of the London Symphony Orchestra in 1988 and was appointed music director of the San Francisco Symphony in 1995. Tilson is also a composer and his *From the Diary of Anne Frank* was premiered in Philadelphia in 1990 with Audrey Hepburn as narrator.

THOMAS, THOMAS L. *American baritone (1912–)*

Thomas L. Thomas usually featured songs from American operettas in his concert and radio shows. In 1939 he sang excerpts from NAUGHTY MARIETTA on a radio show released as a 78 album called *The Operetta World of Victor Herbert*. In 1952 he was featured in a radio highlights version of Jerome Kern's MUSIC IN THE AIR. He also sang American operetta songs on his *Voice of Firestone* television appearances in the 1950s. Thomas, who came to America from Wales with his family as a boy, won a Metropolitan Opera Auditions of the Air competition in 1937 and was given a contract with the Met but only sang there twice.

THOMPSON, HUGH   *American baritone/director (1915–)*

Hugh Thomson created the role of Bishop Cauchon, Joan of Arc's mortal enemy, in Norman Dello Joio's TV opera THE TRIAL AT ROUEN on NBC Opera Theatre in 1956 and the jealous husband Robert in Stanley Hollingsworth's TV opera LA GRANDE BRETÈCHE on NBC Opera Theatre in 1957. His work as director included a production of Gian Carl Menotti's *The Telephone*. Thompson, who was born in Tacoma, Washington, and studied at Juilliard, made his singing debut in Chicago in 1942 and his directing debut in St. Louis in 1955.

THOMPSON, RANDALL   *American composer (1899–1984)*

Randall Thompson is known primarily for his choral music but he also composed two operas. SOLOMON AND BALKIS, libretto by the composer based on Rudyard Kipling's fable *The Butterfly That Stamped*, was created for CBS Radio and broadcast on March 29, 1942. It was put on stage by a Harvard University opera group in Cambridge on April 14, 1942. THE NATIVITY ACCORDING TO ST. LUKE, libretto by R. Rowlands based on Luke's Gospel, was created to celebrate the 200th anniversary of Christ Church in Cambridge and was premiered there on December 13, 1961. Thompson, who was born in New York, studied at Harvard and the American Academy in Rome and taught music at Harvard from 1948 to 1965. His students included composers Leonard Bernstein and Lukas Foss.

THOMSON, VIRGIL   *American composer (1896–1989)*

Virgil Thomson's collaborations with avant-garde poet Gertrude Stein produced two remarkable operas. First came the shocking (for its time) FOUR SAINTS IN THREE ACTS (1934) which featured dozens of Spanish saints in more than three acts. It was a national scandal with its cellophane costumes, avant-garde staging, non-narrative libretto, much-mocked arias ("PIGEON ON THE GRASS, ALAS" became a popular catch-phrase) and, purely for the sake of diction (or so Thomson claimed), an all-black cast. It made Thomson and Stein famous and it essentially marked the beginning of modern American opera. Their second collaboration, THE MOTHER OF US ALL, did not make such an impact when it was staged in 1947 but there are critics today who consider it America's greatest opera. It is a pageant work revolving around women's suffrage leader Susan B. Anthony and other 19th century celebrities, and it features Thomson and Stein as characters. Thomson's final opera was the 1972 LORD BYRON, libretto by Jack Larson, composed for but not produced by the Met. It's the most straightforward of his operas and some critics think it is his best. Thomson was more than an opera composer, of course, and his large and varied output includes keyboard, orchestral, chamber, choral and vocal work. He was a major figure in ballet (*Filling Station, Parson Weems and the Cherry Tree*) and film music (*The Plow That Broke the Plains, Louisiana Story*). In his spare time he was an influential music critic.

1986 Virgil Thomson at 90. In John Huszar's fine documentary, Thomson guides the viewer along as he talks about his love of Paris, his friendships with artists like Picasso and Gertrude Stein, his film scores and his opera. There are filmed scenes of the 1934 "cellophane" production of *Four Saints in Three Acts* and photos and allusions to *The Mother of Us All* and *Lord Byron*. Librettist Jack Larson talks about working with Thomson on *Byron*, mezzo Betty Allen sings Thomson's setting of Stein's poem "Susie Asado" and an aria from *Four Saints* and there is an excerpt from the ballet *Filling Station*. *Virgil Thomson at 90* was telecast on November 30, 1986, and is on video. FilmAmerica VHS.

THREE AGAINST CHRISTMAS   *1964 opera by Imbrie*

An attempt to ban Christmas succeeds in its initial stages but eventually the holiday has to be brought back. Andrew Imbrie's comic opera *Three Against Christmas* (aka *Christmas in Peebles Town*), libretto by Richard Wincor, premiered at the University of California at Berkeley on December 3, 1964. Julian Patrick played the Troll, Thomas Hageman was Quibble and John Robert Dunlap was Drone. Robert Commanday conducted.

THE THREE HERMITS   *1997 church opera by Paulus*

A Russian bishop, sailing on the White Sea in the 19th century with his mother and two nuns, learns of three hermits living on an isolate island. He teaches them the Lord's Prayer to replace their simple chant but then discovers they can walk on water through the power of their faith. He decides they don't really need religious instruction from him. Stephen Paulus' church opera *The Three Hermits*, libretto by Michael Dennis Browne based on a story by Leo Tolstoy, was commissioned and premiered by the Motet Choir of the House of Hope Presbyterian Church in St. Paul, Minnesota, on April 24, 1997. James McKeel was the Bishop, Corby Welch, John Bitterman and Phil Jorgenson were the Three Hermits, Miriam Langsjoen was the Bishop's Mother, Esther Heideman was Sister Angelica, Vicki Johnson was Sister Miriam, Mark Schowalter was the Fisherman, James Wintle was the Captain and Marcia Laningham and Jon Harney were the Pilgrims. Thomas Lancaster conducted the choir and Saint Paul Sinfonietta Orchestra. The music is tonal and singer friendly and the opera is often compared to another American miracle opera, Gian Carlo Menotti's *Amahl and the Night Visitors*.

1997 Motet Choir, House of Hope. The opera was recorded by the Motet Choir of House of Hope Presbyterian Church in St. Paul, Minnesota, on April 29, 1997, with the premiere soloists. James McKeel is the Bishop, Corby Welch, John Bitterman and Phil Jorgenson are the Three Hermits, Miriam Langsjoen is the Bishop's Mother, Esther Heideman is Sister Angelica, Vicki Johnson is Sister Miriam, Mark Schowalter is the Fisherman, James Wintle is the Captain and Marcia Laningham and Jon Harney are the Pilgrims. Thomas Lancaster conducts the choir and Saint Paul Sinfonietta Orchestra. d'Note CD. **"Pilgrim's Hymn" recordings.** The final chorus of the opera, the "Pilgrims' Hymn," has become popular with choral groups and has been recorded by a number of groups including the St. Agnes High School Concert Chorale of St. Paul led by William E. White, the Greenville College Choir of North Carolina led by Jeffrey S. Wilson and the Dale Warland Singers led by Dale Warland.

THE THREE MUSKETEERS   *1928 operetta by Friml*

D'Artagnan and his Three Musketeer friends battle Cardinal Richelieu in the court of King Louis XIII as he woos Constance and helps the Queen. Rudolf Friml's operetta *The Three Musketeers*, libretto by William Anthony McGuire based on the Alexandre Dumas novel with lyrics by Clifford Grey and P. G. Wodehouse, premiered in New York on March 13, 1928. Dennis King played D'Artagnan, Vivienne Segal was Constance, Reginald

Owen was Richelieu, Clarence Derwent was Louis XIII, Vivienne Osborne was Lady De Winter, Detmar Poppen was Porthos, Douglass Dumbrille was Athos and Joseph Macaulay was Aramis. The most popular numbers were Aramis' "Ma Belle" and the Musketeer quartet's "March of the Musketeers."

1930 London cast. *The Three Musketeers* was staged in London in 1930 with Dennis King as D'Artagnan, Adrienne Brune as Constance, Arthur Wontner as Richelieu and Raymond Newell as Aramis. The cast album features King singing "Gascony" and "My Sword and I," King and Brune singing "Your Eyes" and "One Kiss," Raymond Newell and chorus singing "Ma Belle" and King and the Musketeers singing the "March of the Musketeers." Herman Finck conducts. Columbia 78s/Monmouth LP. **1930 Victor Light Opera.** The Victor Light Opera Company recorded a medley of songs from the operetta for a Victor 78. **1930 Columbia Light Opera.** The Victor Light Opera Companies recorded a medley of songs from the operetta for a Columbia 78. **1931 Rudolf Friml.** Rudolf Friml recorded a piano version of "March of the Musketeers" for a 78. It was reissued on the album *The Genius of Rudolf Friml.* Golden Crest LP. **1949 Robert Merrill.** Robert Merrill performs "Ma Belle" with an orchestra conducted by Spitalny. Pearl/Koch CD. **1951 Igor Gorin.** Igor Gorin sings "March of the Musketeers" backed by the Firestone Orchestra led by Howard Barlow on a 1951 *Voice of Firestone* telecast. It's on the video *Igor Gorin in Opera and Song.* VAI VHS. **1953 Leonard Warren.** Leonard Warren sings "March of the Musketeers" backed by the Firestone Orchestra led by Howard Barlow on a 1953 *Voice of Firestone* telecast. It's on the video *Leonard Warren in Opera and Song.* VAI VHS. **1960 Earl Wrightson/Lois Hunt.** Earl Wrightson and Lois Hunt duet on "Ma Belle" with an orchestra conducted by Frank DeVol on the album *A Night with Rudolf Friml.* Columbia LP.

THREE SISTERS   *1986 opera by Pasatieri*

Three sisters stagnate in a small 19th century Russian town yearning for their native Moscow. Olga, Masha and Irina dream of a new life but their hopes are destroyed by circumstance and their brother Andrei who mortgages their house and marries the shrewd Natasha. Thomas Pasatieri's two-act opera *Three Sisters,* libretto by Kenward Elmslie based on the 1901 play by Anton Chekhov, was premiered by Opera/Columbus at Columbus, Ohio, on March 13, 1986. The sisters were Patricia Wells as Masha, Maryanne Telese as Irena and Marvellee Cariaga as Olga. Stephen Dickson was Andrei, Marilyn Brustadt was Natasha, Jerold Siena was Fyodor, Louis Otey was Vershinin, Keith Olsen was the Baron, Steven Alexus Williams was Solyony, Willy Roy was Chebutkin, Randolph Locke was Vladimir, Rick Moon was Yakov and Irma Cooper was Nanna. Cal Stewart Kellogg conducted the Opera/Columbus Orchestra. This melodic opera was reprised in Russian in Moscow in October 1988 at the Moscow Musical Theater. (An earlier American opera based on the Chekhov play, Andrew Rudin's *Three Sisters,* libretto by William Ashbrook, was premiered by PRISM at Carnegie Hall in New York City on March 2, 1981.)

1986 Opera/Columbus. Patricia Wells, Maryanne Telese and Marvellee Cariaga star as the three sisters in this original cast recording of the opera made at the Palace Theater in Columbus on March 13, 1986. The other cast members are as above. Cal Stewart Kellogg conducts the Opera/Columbus Orchestra. Battery Records LP.

THREE SISTERS WHO ARE NOT SISTERS   *American operas based on Stein play*

Gertrude Stein's *Three Sisters Who Are Not Sisters* is a playful murder mystery that features three sisters who are not sisters and two brothers who are brothers. The three sisters are not sisters because they are orphans and don't have the same parents. It turns out they are all just children playing a game. The play, published in 1946 in *Gertrude Stein's First Reader* and described as a "melodrama," is popular with American composers. It has been used as a libretto three times and two versions have been recorded.

1953 David Ahlstrom. David Ahlstrom was the first American composer to set Stein's *Three Sisters Who Are Not Sisters* to music. His version premiered at the Cincinnati Conservatory in Cincinnati on March 1, 1953. **1969 Anna Sternberg.** Anna Sternberg composed her version for the Broadway show *Gertrude Stein's First Reader* which opened at the Astor Place Theater in New York on December 15, 1969. The premiere cast included Sandra Thornton Joy Garrett, Frank Giordano, Michael Anthony and the composer. It was recorded for an original cast album. Polydor LP. **1971 Ned Rorem.** Ned Rorem's version of *Three Sisters Who Are Not Sisters* was composed in 1968 on commission from the Met Opera Studio and intended for performance by children with piano accompaniment. It was premiered at the Student Opera Workshop at Temple University in Philadelphia on July 24, 1971, under the direction of Henry Butler. The After Dinner Opera company staged it three days later on July 27 at Lake Placid under the direction of Richard Flusser. It has been produced many times since and was recorded in 1994 by the Magic Circle Opera Ensemble. Carol Flamm is Helen, Andrea Matthews is Jenny, Mark Singer is Sylvester, Madeline Tsingopoulos is Ellen and Frederick Urrey is Samuel. Ray Evans Harrell conducts the Magic Circle Opera Orchestra and John Van Buskirk plays the piano. John Ostendorf produced the recording. Newport Classic CD.

THREE TALES   *2002 multi-media opera trilogy by Reich/Korot*

Three music/video "operas" examining three historically significant events of the 20th century that arose out of the growth of technology: the crash of the airship Hindenburg, the atom bomb tests on the Bikini atoll and the cloning of the sheep Dolly. Steve Reich's 120-minute multi-media opera *Three Tales,* libretto by the composer created with his wife, video artist Beryl Korot, premiered at the Spoleto Festival USA in Charleston, SC, on May 31, 2002. Reich and Korot presented their "documentary music video theater" in an abandoned Charleston theater, the Memminger Auditorium, with sixteen musicians and singers. Videos in the auditorium showed historical film, interviews, photographs and text as the operas were sung and played. Nick Mangano was the director and Brad Lubman was the conductor. The tales BIKINI and DOLLY were seen for the first time in this presentation, HINDENBURG was premiered in Spoleto in 1998. See their separate entries for full descriptions.

1998/2002 New York Studios. The three multi-media operas were recorded on CD and DVD in New York studios in 1998 and 2002 with the Synergy Vocals and The Steve Reich Ensemble. Bradley Lubman conducted *Bikini* and *Dolly,* Todd Reynolds conducted *Hindenburg.* Nonesuch Records DVD/CD.

THREE VISITATIONS   *1996 opera trilogy by Sherman*

Three people wait for a visitor who may bring death or salvation. Kim D. Sherman's *Three Visitations,* a trilogy of short operas with librettos by Paul Selig, was staged by New Music-Theatre Ensemble at the Southern Theater in Minneapolis in June 1996. In *A Long Island Dreamer* a pop singer (Nora Long) in a sound studio remembers how a rapist's face suddenly appeared in a motel window and changed her life. In *Red Tide* a teenager (Peter Vitale) waits on the beach for a lifeguard who saved his life many years before and is desperately needed now. In *Lamentations* a boy whose father has just died, perhaps murdered by his mother, waits in his apartment for an angel or for death. Karen C. Miller staged the trilogy.

THROUGH ROSES   *1980 monodrama by Neikrug*

A Jewish violinist survives his time in World War II German extermination camps by playing music as other prisoners walk to the gas chambers. After the war he finds he can still play the violin but the music of Bach and Beethoven has become discordant. Marc Neikrug's monodrama *Through Roses*, libretto by the composer based on a true story, premiered at the National Theatre in London in 1980 and was presented at the Kaufman Auditorium in New York on April 14, 1981.

1997 Maximilian Schell. Maximilian Schell stars as the Jewish violinist in an 80-minute film of the opera with Pinchas Zukerman playing the violin music. David Watkin was the cinematographer, Philip Traugott produced and Jurgen Flimm. directed.

THE THUNDER OF HORSES   *1995 opera by Franklin*

Orphan Long Arrow is adopted by the great warrior Heavy Runner who cures his deafness. When he is a young man, Heavy Runner sends him to find spirits who keep mysterious animals. After many adventures, he succeeds and bring a great gift back to his people — wild horses. Cary John Franklin's one-act children's opera *The Thunder of Horses*, libretto by Michael Patrick Albano based on the Blackfoot legend *The Story of the First Horses*, was premiered

Lawrence Tibbett shown on cover of *Musical America*.

by Opera Theatre of Saint Louis on June 10, 1995. Ryan Bell McAdams played Long Arrow, Katie Vagnino was Willow Flower, Lester Lynch was Heavy Runner and Devon Barnes was the Child. The opera was reprised by Madison Opera in 1996 and by Washington Opera in 1997.

THURBER, JAMES   *American writer (1894–1961)*

James Thurber, one of America's greatest humorists, was a mainstay of *The New Yorker* for many years. He was a splendid cartoonist and essayist but it is his gentle comic stories and fables that have inspired operas and music theater works, mostly in a lighter vein.

Many Moons (1943). 1962 Celius Dougherty's *Many Moons*, libretto by the composer. Premiere: Santa Fe, NM, July 1962. **The Secret Life of Walter Mitty (1939).** 1953 Charles Hamm's *The Secret Life of Walter Mitty*, libretto by composer. Premiere: Athens, Ohio, July 30, 1953. 1976 Lora Aborn's *The Secret Life of Walter Mitty*, libretto by composer. Premiere: October 1976. **The Thirteen Clocks (1950).** 1953 Mark Bucci's *The Thirteen Clocks*, libretto by Fred Sadoff, John Crilly, James Thurber and composer. Premiere: ABC Television, December 29, 1953. 1958 Mary Johnson's *The Thirteen Clocks*, libretto by Maritz and Norman Morgan. Premiere: Hunter College, New York, March 18, 1958. 1983 Robert Chauls' *The Thirteen Clocks*, libretto by Rhoda Levine. Premiere: Waterford, Connecticut, May 1983. **The Unicorn in the Garden (1940).** 1957 Russell Smith's *The Unicorn in the Garden*, libretto by James Thurber. Hartford CT, May 2, 1957.

TIBBETT, LAWRENCE   *American baritone (1896–1960)*

Lawrence Tibbett sang in more American operas at the Metropolitan Opera than any other singer and created roles in seven. He made the first recordings of PORGY AND BESS and he can be heard in recordings and radio broadcasts of many other American operas. Born in Bakersfield, California, he grew up in Los Angeles and began his film career in 1930 with *The Rogue Song*. He was the first American opera singer to became a movie star in the sound era and he finished his career singing leading roles on Broadway. The chronology of his career below shows how important he was to the development of American opera.

1923 Debut at the Hollywood Bowl and at the Met. 1925 Creates role of Cunnan in Frank Patterson's THE ECHO in Portland, Oregon. 1927 Creates role of King Eadgar in Deems Taylor THE KING'S HENCHMAN at the Met. 1931 Creates role of Colonel Ibbetson in Deems Taylor's PETER IBBETSON at the Met. 1931 Stars opposite Grace Moore in film of Sigmund Romberg's THE NEW MOON. 1933 Creates title role in Louis Gruenberg's THE EMPEROR JONES at the Met. 1934 Creates role of Wrestling Bradford in stage premiere of Howard Hanson's MERRY MOUNT at the Met. 1935 Creates role of Pasha in John Laurence Seymour's IN THE PASHA'S GARDEN at the Met. 1935 Makes first recordings of George Gershwin's PORGY AND BESS with Helen Jepson. 1937 Sings role of Count Guido Franceschini in Richard Hageman's CAPONSACCHI in its American premiere at the Met. 1950 Creates role of Colonel Norwood in Jan Meyerowitz's THE BARRIER at Columbia University and on Broadway. 1956 Takes over role of César from Ezio Pinza in Harold Rome's Broadway musical *Fanny*.

THE TIBETAN BOOK OF THE DEAD   *1996 opera by Gordon*

A dying soul makes an emotional spiritual journey on its way to being reborn. Ricky Ian Gordon's lyrical two-act opera *The Tibetan Book of the Dead: A Liberation Through Hearing*, libretto by

Jean-Claude van Italie based on his play derived from Tibetan scripture, was premiered by Houston Grand Opera Studio at Rice University on May 31, 1996. The featured singers were Frank Hernadez as Reader/Baritone, Eric Owen as Bass, Nicole Heaston as Soprano, John McVeigh as Tenor I, Gabriele Conzalez as Tenor II, Beth Clayton as Mezzo I, Jill Grove as Mezzo II and Jonita Lattimore as The Dying/The Dead. Allison Koturbash designed the sets, Marchus Stern directed and Charles Prince conducted the Houston Grand Opera Orchestra. The opera was recorded and broadcast on KUHF-FM in Houston and then reprised at the American Music Theater Festival, which had commissioned it with Houston.

TIERNEY, HARRY   American composer (1890–1965)

Harry Tierney, best known for his song "Alice Blue Gown" composed for the 1919 musical *Irene,* created an old-fashioned traditional operetta in 1927 at the request of producer Florenz Ziegfeld. RIO RITA was surprisingly popular and was quickly filmed. Tierney, born in Perth Amboy, NJ, created the music for many other Broadway shows, including *Up She Goes* (1922) and *Kid Boots* (1923).

TILLIE TELL   1945 "movie opera" by Skiles/Rossini

This bizarre "movie opera" is a hillbilly version of Rossini's *William Tell,* created for singer Judy Canova by Marlin Skiles who devised the new story and lyrics. It is featured in the 1945 Columbia movie *Hit the Hay,* where it is described as a "swing-comedy opera." It amazes the audience in the movie as much as it does us today. Canova plays a hillbilly girl whose mother was a popular opera singer. Canova has inherited her voice and demonstrates by singing arias from *The Barber of Seville* and *Martha.* She has had no training, however, and so most of the singing has been to the cows she milks. Opera tenor Mario Alvini (Fortunato Bonanova) is hired to coach her and does his best. After numerous mishaps, the audience is treated to the amazing production of *Tillie Tell.* Del Lord directed the film from a screenplay by Richard Weil and Charles R. Marion.

TIPPETT, MICHAEL   English composer (1905–1998)

Sir Michael Tippett's opera NEW YEAR, libretto by the composer set in Times Square on New Year's Eve, was premiered October 27, 1989, by Houston Grand Opera which commissioned it with Glyndebourne and BBC Television. Much of the opera's musical inspiration is American, especially the Broadway musical style. Tippett visited America for the first time in 1965 and was greatly influenced by what he saw and heard. His previous opera, *The Ice Break,* had also been set in America.

TITUS, ALAN   American baritone (1945–)

Alan Titus has made notable contributions to American opera and created six roles. He began with the small role of the Travelling Salesman in Lee Hoiby's SUMMER AND SMOKE at St. Paul Opera in June 1971 and became famous when he sang the role of the Celebrant in the premiere of Leonard Bernstein's MASS at the Kennedy Center in Washington, DC, in August 1971. He had a leading role in Thomas Pasatieri's TV opera THE TRIAL OF MARY LINCOLN in 1972, was one of Rachel's three lovers in Hans Werner Henze's TV opera RACHEL LA CUBANA on NET Opera in 1974, played Titus Thumb in Carlisle Floyd's BILBY'S DOLL at Houston Grand Opera in 1976 and portrayed the adult Pip in Dominick Argento's MISS HAVISHAM'S FIRE at New York City Opera in 1979. He can be heard in live recordings of two New York City Opera

production in 1978, as Harry Easter in Kurt Weill's STREET SCENE and as Etienne Grandet in Victor Herbert's NAUGHTY MARIETTA. Titus, born in New York City, made his debut in Washington in 1969.

"TO LEAVE, TO BREAK"   Quintet: Vanessa (1958). Words: Gian Carlo Menotti. Music: Samuel Barber.

"To Leave, To Break," the most famous quintet in American opera, was chosen, most appropriately, for presentation on the last night gala of the old Metropolitan Opera for it is introduced with the phrase "Who knows when I shall see this house again!" In Samuel Barber's opera *Vanessa*, libretto by Gian Carlo Menotti, it is sung in the final scene as Vanessa prepares to leaves her mansion forever with her young lover Anatol. It was introduced in the 1958 Met premiere by Eleanor Steber as Vanessa, Rosalind Elias as Erika, Regina Resnik as the Old Baroness, Nicolai Gedda as Anatol and Giorgio Tozzi as the Doctor. They speak of hoping, dreaming, weeping, remembering and loving and they say goodbye. It is sung by the premiere cast on the 1958 recording of the opera with Dimitri Mitropoulos conducting the Metropolitan Opera Orchestra. On the 1965 live recording of a Met broadcast, it is sung by Mary Costa as Vanessa, Rosalind Elias as Erika, Blanche Thebom as the Old Baroness, John Alexander as Anatol and Giorgio Tozzi as the Doctor with William Steinberg conducting. In a 1978 Spoleto Festival USA recording, it is sung by Johanna Meier as Vanessa, Katherine Ciesinski as Erika, Alice Garrott as the Old Baroness, Henry Price as Anatol and Irwin Densen as the Doctor with Christopher Keene conducting. In a 1992 Seattle Opera production, it is sung by Sherry Greenawald as Vanessa, Kimberly Barber as Erika, Shirley Nadler as the Old Baroness, Paul Charles Clark as Anatol and Charles Stilwell as the Doctor. In a 2004 Ukrainian studio recording, it is sung by Ellen Chickering as Vanessa, Andrea Matthews as Erika, Marion Dry as the Old Baroness, Ray Bauwens as Anatol and Richard Conrad as the Doctor. The quintet is also a high point of the 2004 Leonard Slatkin-led recording with Susan Graham.

"TO THIS WE'VE COME"   Soprano aria: The Consul (1950). Words and Music: Gian Carlo Menotti.

The famous anti-bureaucratic aria, "To this we've come...Papers, papers, papers" is sung in despair by the opera's heroine as the impersonal forces of bureaucracy wear her down. She is desperate to get a visa so she can leave a police state and join her husband abroad. When it seems impossible, she bursts out with this diatribe and fills out her last form saying her occupation is waiting and her eyes are the color of tears. Menotti's opera *The Consul*, which premiered at the height of the cold war, is set in Europe in the late 1940s and tells the story of Magda, the wife of a freedom fighter. The aria was introduced by Patricia Neway in the 1950 premiere in Philadelphia and was sung by her in the Broadway run and on the cast album. It is sung by Loris Synan as Magda in a videotaped 1962 Australian TV production, by Melita Muszely in a 1963 recording of a Vienna Volksoper production, by Virginia Zeani in a 1972 recording of a Spoleto Festival production. by Olivia Stapp in a recording 1974 New York City Opera production, by Marvellee Cariaga in a recorded 1977 Spoleto Festival USA production. by Martine Surrais in a 1988 recording of a French production. by Susan Bullock in the 1998 Spoleto Festival recording and by Beverly O'Regan Thiele on a 1998 recording by the Berkshire Opera company. "To This We've Come" is one of four American opera arias analyzed in Martial Singher's superb *An Interpretive Guide to Operatic Arias.*

TOCH, ERNST   *American composer (1887–1964)*

Ernst Toch's last opera, THE LAST TALE, was created in America in 1962 long after he had fled from the Nazis in Germany. He settled in southern California in the 1930s, where he taught music at USC and wrote scores for the movies. He won three Oscar nomination for his scores and was awarded the Pulitzer Prize for Music in 1956 for his Third Symphony. Toch had first become known in Europe for his fairytale opera, *The Princess and the Pea,* which premiered in Germany in 1927. He completed two more operas in Germany but then stopped until *The Last Tale,* a political version of a story Scheherazade tells in the *Arabian Nights.* It was never staged in America but was premiered in Germany in 1995, thirty years after Toch's death.

TOM SAWYER   *1989 children's opera by Owen*

Tom Sawyer and his friend Becky Thatcher get lost in a cave during a school trip and recall their recent adventures. Richard Owen's children's opera *Tom Sawyer,* libretto by the composer based on the Mark Twain novel, was premiered by Cynthia Auerbach's Children's Opera Theater at the Manhattan School of Music in New York on April 9, 1989. All the performers were children with Richard Owen Jr. playing Tom Sawyer and Lee Franklin as Becky. Carol Macauly conducted the Manhattan School Preparatory Division Chorus and Orchestra.

1989 Children's Opera Theater. Richard Owen Jr. as Tom Sawyer and Lee Franklin as Becky Thatcher lead the cast in this recording of the premiere performance by Cynthia Auerbach's Children's Opera Theater at the Manhattan School of Music in New York on April 9, 1989. Carol Macauly conducts the Manhattan School Preparatory Division Chorus and Orchestra. Aurora audiocassette.

TOM-TOM   *1932 pageant opera by Graham*

The story of African Americans' long journey from Africa to the American South to Harlem. In the course of their journeying. the tom-tom becomes their voice, Shirley Graham's three-act sixteen-scene pageant opera TOM-TOM, libretto by the composer, was premiered on stage by the Cleveland Opera Company at Cleveland Stadium on June 30, 1932, after being previewed in excerpt form on NBC radio on June 26, 1932. It was a truly grandiose production, featuring 500 singers, dancers and musicians. Jules Bledsoe, who created the role of Joe in *Show Boat,* sang the principal role of Voodoo Man, Charlotte Murray was the Mother, Lillian Cowan was the Girl, Luther King was the Boy, Hazel Walker was the Mammy and Augustine Grist was the Leader/Preacher/Captain. *Tom-Tom* was the first dramatic opera by an African American woman to be produced on stage. It had originated as a one-act play and was turned into an opera by Graham for the Cleveland summer program *Theatre of Nations* on a commission by Lawrence Higgins. The libretto is available in the anthology *Roots of African American Drama* (Wayne State University Press, 1991) but there is no recording.

TONKIN   *1994 opera by Cummings*

An American man comes to Vietnam in 1945 and decides to stay on. A Vietnamese girl becomes disillusioned with communism. Ho Chi Minh tries to unite the country. The Vietnam War grows out of an incident in Tonkin in 1964. Conrad Cummings' opera *Tonkin,* libretto by Thomas Bird and Robert T. Jones, was one of the first operas to deal with the Vietnam War. It was premiered by OperaDelaware on December 4, 1994, in Wilmington in a production by Harry Silverstein. Matthew Lord sang the role of the American, Peggy Kriha was the Vietnamese girl and Perry Ward was Ho Chi Minh. David Lawton conducted the OperaDelaware Orchestra.

TOO MANY SOPRANOS   *2000 opera by Penhorwood*

Four opera divas arrive in Heaven and are outraged at having to audition for St. Peter before they can sing in the heavenly choir. There are very few places open as there are too many sopranos in Heaven and not enough tenors and basses (they usually go to Hell). St. Peter invokes a Redemption Clause in an attempt to upgrade the choir. The sopranos are told they can bring back as many tenors and basses as they want from Hell and get into the choir if they perform a selfless deed. Edwin Penhorwood's two-act comic opera *Too Many Sopranos,* libretto by Miki Thompson, was premiered by Cedar Rapids Opera Theatre on June 16, 2000. Baritone Kyle Ketelsen was St. Peter, Twyla Robinson was Madame Pompous, Kathryn Chambers was Dame Woeful, Robin Blitch Wiper was a Diva and Kerrin Dunbar Hightower was Sandman. Vince Liotta staged the opera and Daniel Kleinknecht conducted. The opera has been published but there is no recording.

TORKE, MICHAEL   *American composer (1961–)*

Michael Torke's one-act opera *Strawberry Fields,* libretto by A. R. Gurney, was the second opera in the CENTRAL PARK trilogy. It was premiered at Glimmerglass Opera on August 8, 1999, and then staged at New York City Opera. The collaboration apparently worked well as their second opera, the full-length *House of Mirth* based on the novel by Edith Wharton, is to be staged by New York City Opera. Torke, who was born in Milwaukee and studied at the Eastman School of Music, had earlier created the one-act opera *The Directions* (1986) based on his own *The Yellow Pages.*

TOUSSAINT BEFORE THE SPIRITS   *2003 opera by Ruehr*

François Toussaint L'Ouverture leads a revolution against the French in Haiti but is captured in 1803 and imprisoned in a fortress by Napoleon. He is visited in his prison cell by voodoo spirits and the accusing ghost of his godson Moyse, whom he had had executed. Elene Ruehr's 45-minute opera *Toussaint Before the Spirits,* libretto by Madison Smart Bell and Elizabeth Spires, was premiered by Opera Boston on June 7, 2003, at the Tower Auditorium of the Massachusetts College of Art. The opera was created for baritone Stephen Salters, who portrayed Toussaint, while tenor Ramón Digg played Moyse and Alison Buchanan provided the voice of the various Spirits. Nicola Hawkins choreographed the opera and Gil Rose conducted the chamber orchestra.

THE TOWER   *1957 opera by Levy*

King Solomon puts his daughter in prison following a prophecy that she will marry the poorest man in the kingdom. The ultra-poor Joash gets thrown into the same prison, marries the Princess and is, perforce, accepted by the King as his son-in-law. Marvin Davy Levy's one-act comic opera *The Tower,* libretto by Townsend Brewster, was premiered by Santa Fe Opera on August 2, 1957. William McGrath was King Solomon, Carol Bergey was the Princess, Peter Binder was Joash, Regina Sarfaty was the Nurse, Joan Carroll was the Maidservant and Robert Rue was the Young Prophet. Levy staged the opera and Robert Baustion conducted the Santa Fe Opera Orchestra.

THE TOWN OF GREED   *1997 opera by Balada*

Johnny, the boss of the town of Greed, sells its oil, uranium and plutonium to companies around the world and works with the

Mafia to get rid of opponents. He has become very rich. When he has sold everything, however, the townspeople turn against him and are ready to hang him. A Wall Street Man, who has bought the area to use as a toxic dump, arrives and shoots him as a troublemaker. Leonardo Balada's one-act chamber opera *The Town of Greed,* libretto by the composer in English, Spanish and Catalan based on an idea by Akram Midani and the composer, is a sequel to Balada's 1982 opera HANGMAN, HANGMAN! In that opera Johnny was to be hanged for stealing a horse but was saved by a rich man. The sequel takes place twenty years. It was premiered in its English version at Kresge Recital Hall at Carnegie Mellon University in Pittsburgh in April 2002 and in its Spanish version at the Teatro de la Zarzuela in Madrid in October 2003.

2001 Carnegie Mellon Opera Theater. Colman Pierce conducts the Carnegie Mellon University Contemporary Ensemble and Pittsburgh Camerata in a recording made at Kresge Recital Hall at Carnegie Mellon University in April 2001. James Longmire is Johnny, Ja-Nae Duane is the Secretary, Robert Frankenberry is Mr. Rich and Wall Street Man, Jim Means is Mr. Rot, Gary Koehler is Mr. Rat, Paul Nicolaysen is Mr. Wreck, Roy Matway is Mr. Rip, Kenn Kumpf is Mr. Rude, Craig Raymaley is the Ambassador and Tokopoko, Adrian Rollert is Mr. Capotte, Natalya Kraevsky is the Sweetheart, Petra Dierkes-Thruns is the Queen's Secretary, Rose Dorsey is the King's Secretary, Elizabeth Sederburg is Mother, Robert Fire is Father, Patrick Jacobs is Sheriff, Stephen Neely is he Hangman and Linda Shaw is the rich Irishman's Secretary. Naxos CD.

TOZZI, GIORGIO   *American bass-baritone (1923–)*

Giorgio Tozzi created the role of the Doctor in Samuel Barber's VANESSA at the Metropolitan Opera in 1958 and then recorded it and sang it in revivals. He played the role of Melchior in a 1979 film of Gian Carlo Menotti's AMAHL AND THE NIGHT VISITORS, which is on video and CD. He recorded Rudolf Friml's ROSE MARIE and Sigmund Romberg's THE DESERT SONG in 1958 and THE STUDENT PRINCE in 1962. He provided the singing voice for Rossano Brazzi in the 1958 film of Richard Rodgers' SOUTH PACIFIC and sang the role on stage at Lincoln Center in 1967. He sang the operatic lead of Tony in the revival of Frank Loesser's THE MOST HAPPY FELLA at New York City Opera in 1991. Tozzi, who was born in Chicago, studied with Rosa Raisa and Giacomo Rimini and made his debut in Chicago in 1948. He began to sing at the Metropolitan Opera in 1955.

TRANSATLANTIC   *1928 opera by Antheil*

An American presidential candidate in a 1920s election is backed by a corrupt oil millionaire who attempts to control him through a seductive woman. George Antheil's opera *Transatlantic: or, The People's Choice* was premiered by Frankfurt State Opera in Germany on May 25, 1930. It was a predecessor of the CNN docu-opera as the first opera to portray contemporary American life. It utilizes jazz, tango and other forms of popular flapper-esque music of the period and features rapid cinematic-style scene changes. Parallels with ancient Greece are evoked by the characters names; the candidate is named Hector, the millionaire is named Ajax, the woman is called Helen, etc. Frankfurt gave the opera an elaborate production with four stages, an ocean liner and a movie screen for the rapid thirty scenes of the last act (movie created by Fernand Leger). Herbert Graf staged the opera and William Steinberg conducted. It was a great success but the rise of Hitler blocked further productions in Germany and the Depression made it too expensive for American opera houses. A revised version was pre-

sented by Encompass Music Theater in Trenton, New Jersey in 1981 but the opera was not fully staged in America until 1998 when Minnesota Opera gave it a major production.

1994 Marthanne Verbit. The Tango from *Transatlantic* is played by pianist Marthanne Verbit on the album *Bad Boy of Music,* which features music by Antheil. The other pieces are "Airplane Sonata," "La femme 100 têtes," "Sonata Sauvage," "Little Shimmy" and "Valentine Waltzes." Albany CD. **1998 Minnesota Opera.** Sherrill Milnes stars as oil baron Ajax in the 1998 Minnesota Opera production of *Transatlantic*. Karl Daymond is presidential candidate Hector, Juliana Rambaldi is mysterious Helen, Mark Calkins is gigolo husband Jason, Dennis Petersen is campaign manager Leo and Jane Thorngren is flapper Gladys. John Conklin designed the elaborate constructivist set, James Robinson staged the opera and David Agler conducted the orchestra. The opera was taped and broadcast on Minnesota Public Radio on June l4 but has not been released on CD.

TRANSFORMATIONS   *1973 opera by Susa*

Grimm fairy tales are transformed into autobiography by poet Anne Sexton as she examines the darker aspects of her life, including incest and adultery. The reinterpreted stories include *Snow White and the Seven Dwarfs* (difficult relationship with mother) and *The Sleeping Beauty* (possible incest with father) and feature a princess, prince, good fairy, witch, king and wizard. Conrad Susa's opera *Transformations,* libretto by the composer based on Sexton's poetic versions of the fairy tales, was premiered by Minnesota Opera in Minneapolis on May 5, 1973. Catherine Malfitano played the Princess, Robert Israel designed the sets and costumes and Philip Brunelle conducted. *Transformations* features eight performers singing in musical styles that reference pop styles of the 1940s and 1950s. It has become one of the most frequently performed modern American operas with productions in Aspen, Kansas City, Miami, New York, Spoleto and Wolf Trap. In 1997 there were productions by Opera Theater of St Louis, with Sheri Greenawald as Sexton, and Lyric Opera of Cleveland, with Susan Russell in the role. Sexton committed suicide in 1974, one year after the premiere of the opera.

1973 Minnesota Opera. Minnesota Opera's premiere performance of *Transformations,* conducted by Philip Brunelle with Catherine Malfitano as the Princess, was recorded and broadcast by National Public Radio. It has been transferred onto LP records but they have not been made commercially available. **1978 Minnesota Opera.** Barbara Brandt portrays Anne Sexton and the Witch in this Minnesota Opera production by H. Wesley Balk with sets and costumes by Robert Israel. Marsha Hunter is the Princess, Janis Hardy is the Good Fairy, Michael Riley is the King, Vern Sutton is the Wizard, William Wahman is the Prince, Stanley Wexler is the Neighboring King and Yale Marshall is the Magic Object. Philip Brunelle conducts the Minnesota Opera Orchestra. The opera was directed for video by Lynwood King and telecast on August 14, 1978. Video at MTR.

THE TRANSPOSED HEADS   *1954 opera by Glanville-Hicks*

India in ancient times. Hindu Shridaman cuts off his head as a sacrifice in homage to the death goddess Kali. His friend Nanda blames himself for the tragedy because of his love for Shridaman's wife Sita, so he also beheads himself. Sita prays to Kali to restore them both to life and her prayer is answered but their heads get transposed when they are revived. Death for all three seems to be the only answer. Peggy Glanville-Hicks chamber opera *The Trans-*

posed Heads, libretto by the composer based on the Thomas Mann novel, was commissioned by the Louisville Philharmonic Society and premiered by Kentucky Opera In Louisville on April 3, 1954. Monas Harlan sang Shridaman, William Pickett was Nanda, Audrey Nossaman was Sita and David Anderson was the voice of Kali. Moritz Bomhard designed the sets, staged the production and conducted the Louisville Orchestra. Glanville-Hicks incorporates Hindi music and rhythms into the score. The opera was reprised in New York in 1958, in Sydney in 1970 and 1984 and in Adelaide in 1986. (Another American opera titled *The Transposed Heads* based on the Mann novel was composed in 1986 by Elliot Goldenthal to a libretto by Julie Taymor.)

1954 Kentucky Opera. Monas Harlan is Shridaman, William Pickett is Nanda and Audrey Nossaman is Sita in this original cast Kentucky Opera recording of the opera. Robert Whitney replaces Bomhard as conductor of the Louisville Orchestra. Louisville First Edition Records LP. **1984 ABC, Perth.** Gerald English is Shridaman, Michael Leighton-Jones is Nanda and Genty Stevens is Sita in this recording made at the Australian Broadcasting Corporation (ABC) studios in Perth in September 1984 in the presence of the composer. Maggie King is the voice of Kali with Raymond Long as the narrator Kamadamana. David Measham conducts the West Australian Symphony Orchestra and Festival Chorus. The recording was broadcast on November 29, 1994. ABC Classics CD.

TRAUBEL, HELEN *American soprano (1899–1972)*

Wagnerian soprano Helen Traubel made her Metropolitan Opera debut in 1937 creating the role of Mary Rutledge in Walter Damrosch's THE MAN WITHOUT A COUNTRY. The composer had been so impressed when he heard her sing the *Tristan und Isolde* Liebestod in a concert that he wrote the part specifically for her. She plays the restaurant owner in the 1954 Sigmund Romberg film biography *Deep in My Heart* and performs songs from THE NEW MOON and BLUE PARADISE. She created the role of brothel owner Madame Fauna in Rodgers and Hammerstein's musical *Pipe Dream* on Broadway in 1955 and performed its hit number "Sweet Thursday." Traubel, who was born in St. Louis and began singing concerts in 1923, had grandeur as well as a remarkable voice so her Wagnerian career quickly took off at the Met where she remained until 1953.

THE TRAVELLERS *1967 opera by Hovhaness*

An elderly couple, seated in the compartment of a train, hear a knock at the door. A man and a woman enter and the older couple vanish out a window. The man and the woman talk about their wedding, their life to come and their eventual death. They begin to dance but gradually become tired. There is a knock on the door and a younger couple appear. The man and the woman open the window and vanish. Alan Hovhaness's symbolic 18-minute opera *The Travellers,* libretto by the composer, premiered at Foothill College in Los Altos, California, on April 22, 1967.

TRAVELS *1995 opera by Bond*

Gull travels around an absurdist world visiting places like the Coming-Soon-Kingdom and the Laboratory for the Redesign of the Mind. He finds money-oriented religions, chemical craziness and macho cults while his own brother becomes his chief rival. Victoria Bond's satirical opera *Travels,* a contemporary version of Jonathan Swift's *Gulliver's Travels* composed to libretto by Ann Goethe, is a revision of her 1988 opera *Gulliver.* It was premiered by Opera Roanoke in Virginia on May 18, 1995, with baritone

Nicolas Loren as Gull, tenor Dean Anthony as his brother, Diana Walker as Gull's girlfriend, Robert Osborne as his father and Margaret Lisi as his mother. Jonathan Alan Arak directed, Frank Ludwig designed the sets and Bond conducted.

TRAVIS, ROY *American composer (1922–)*

Roy Travis has composed two operas based on Greek tragedies. THE PASSION OF OEDIPUS, libretto by the composer loosely based on Sophocles' play *Oedipus Rex,* premiered at UCLA in Los Angeles on November 8, 1968. *The Black Bacchants,* libretto by the composer loosely based on Euripides' play *The Bacchae* and incorporating West African rhythms, was composed in 1982. Travis, a New York-native who studied with Otto Luening in the U.S. and with Darius Milhaud in Paris, taught at Mannes College and UCLA. His orchestra work *Collage* has been performed by a number of symphony orchestras.

A TREE ON THE PLAINS *1942 "folk opera" by Bacon*

Ernst Bacon's folk opera *A Tree on the Plains,* libretto by Paul Horgan, is a folksy tale about life on the prairie. When neighbors gather for the funeral of Corrie Mae's grandfather, cowboy Lou tries to get her to marry him. Her brother Buddy leaves for a more urban life, a storm breaks a drought, Mom and Pop become contented and the Reverend marries Corrie and Lou. The opera was premiered at Converse College in Spartanburg, South Carolina, on May 2, 1942, where Bacon was teaching. It was presented at St. Bartholomew's Church in New York on May 5, 1945, at Stanford in 1947 and at Stanford again in 1958 in revised form. It received the Bispham Medal in 1946.

TREEMONISHA *1911 opera by Joplin*

A group of former slaves have made a home for themselves on a remote Arkansas plantation in 1884, twenty years after the Civil War. Eighteen-year-old Treemonisha, the foundling daughter of Monisha and Ned, so named because she was found under a tree, fights evil magicians who are trying to exploit the community and is kidnapped by them. She is rescued by Remus and the opera ends in forgiveness with the ensemble A REAL SLOW DRAG and its refrain "Marching Onward." Scott Joplin's ragtime opera *Treemonisha,* libretto by the composer, was self-published in 1911 and "premiered" in a rehearsal hall in Harlem with piano accompaniment. The tryout production, paid for by the composer, was a flop and hastened Joplin's death in an asylum two years later. *Treemonisha* was forgotten until 1970 when it was rediscovered by Vera Brodsky Lawrence and published by the New York Public Library. It was presented in concert form by the Atlanta Symphony at Morehouse College, Atlanta, on January 28, 1972; Robert Shaw conducted an orchestration made by T. J. Anderson with the singing by Alpha Floyd, Louise Park, Seth McCoy and Simon Estes. The opera was presented at Wolf Trap later the same year with orchestration by William Bolcom and Paul Hill conducting. *Treemonisha* won a posthumous Pulitzer Prize for Joplin in 1974 and was fully staged for the first time in May 1975 by Houston Grand Opera. Gunther Schuller wrote another orchestration and conducted the production by Frank Corsaro. Carmen Balthrop played Treemonisha, Betty Allen was Monisha, Willard White was Ned and Curtis Rayam was Remus. The opera continues to be staged and appears to have entered the repertory. A particularly successful production was produced by Opera Theater of St. Louis in 2000 with Christina Clark as Treemonisha. Monisha's aria THE SACRED TREE has become popular in its own right as a recital piece.

1972 Atlanta Symphony. The Atlanta Symphony Orchestra

concert performance of *Treemonisha* was broadcast on NPR Radio January 27, 1972, from Morehouse College in Atlanta. The featured singers are Alpha Floyd, Louise Park, Seth McCoy and Simon Estes. Robert Shaw conducts the orchestration by Thomas J. Anderson. The broadcast was recorded and is on audiocassette. **1974 Richard Zimmerman.** American pianist Richard Zimmerman recorded the original unorchestrated piano version of *Treemonisha* without vocals in 1974. Zimmerman, who specializes in ragtime, has recorded all of Scott Joplin's music for CDs. On CD. **1975 Houston Grand Opera.** Houston Grand Opera's recording of *Treemonisha* features Carmen Balthrop as Treemonisha, Betty Allen as Monisha, Willard White as Ned, Ben Harney as Zodzetrick, Curtis Rayam as Remus, Kenneth Hicks as Andy, Cora Johnson as Lucy, Dorceal Duckens as Luddud, Dwight Ransom as Cephus, Raymond Bazemore as Simon and Edward Pierson as Parson Alltalk. Gunther Schuller, who arranged and orchestrated the opera, conducts the Houston Grand Opera Orchestra and Chorus. DG 2-LP set/2-CD set. **1982 Houston Grand Opera.** The Houston Grand Opera video is different from the Houston Grand Opera recording with changes in singers and conductor. Carmen Balthrop still plays Treemonisha but Delores Ivory is Monisha, Dorceal Duckens is Ned, Obba Babatunde is Zodzetrick and Ray Jacobs is Parson Alltalk. Curtis Rayam remains as Remus, Kenneth Hicks as Andy and Cora Johnson as Lucy. John DeMain conducts the Houston Grand Opera Orchestra using Gunther Schuller's orchestration. Franco Colavecchia designed the sets and costumes. Mabel Robinson created the choreography and Frank Corsaro directed. The opera was telecast on PBS in the *Great Performances* series on February 2, 1982. Kultur/Home Vision/VAI VHS. **1985 Original piano version.** Valerie Stewart sings the role of Treemonisha in a performance of the original version of the opera with piano accompaniment. Marion Lowe is Monisha, Colin Gamage is Remus and Anthony Watts is Zodzetrick and conducts. Adrian David plays the piano. Rare Recorded Edition 2-LP set. **1986 Jessye Norman.** Jessye Norman leads a staged performance of "A Real Slow Drag" at the Royal Opera House in London on April 21, 1986, with Lisa Casteen and ensemble joining her in singing "Marching Onward." It's part of a Royal Gala evening with Edward Downes conducting the Royal Opera House Orchestra. Video at MPRC in London.

THE TREES ON THE MOUNTAIN　*Soprano aria: Susannah (1955). Words and music: Carlisle Floyd.*

"The Trees on the Mountains Are Cold and Bare" is sung by 18-year-old Susannah alone on her porch soon after she has been condemned in church as a sinner. Her "sin" was being caught bathing in a creek in the nude by the church elders. Her song is heard by the preacher Blitch who says he has come to talk to her about her "soul" but turns out to be more interested in her body. The folk-like song was introduced on stage in Carlisle Floyd's *Susanna* by Phyllis Curtin when the opera was premiered at Florida State University in Tallahassee in 1955 and reprised by her in 1956 at New York City Opera. There is no recording of these performances but Curtin was recorded singing the opera and aria in a production in New Orleans in 1962. Joy Clements sings it on a recording of 1965 New York City Opera production, Maralin Niska on a recording of a 1971 New York City Opera production, Nancy Shade on a recording of 1974 Kentucky Opera production, Diana Soviero on a 1975 Houston Grand Opera production and Jean Herzberg on a video of a 1979 Indiana Opera production. Helen-Kay Eberley features it on her 1983 recital album *American Girl*, Cheryl Studer sings it on the 1992 Lyons Opera recording of the

complete opera, Renée Fleming features it on her 1999 recital album *I Want Magic* and Nancy Gustafson sings it on a recording of a 2001 Geneva Opera production.

TREIGLE, NORMAN　*American bass-baritone (1927–1975)*

Norman Treigle created important roles in six American operas. He was Grandpa Moss in Aaron Copland's THE TENDER LAND in 1956, William Jennings Bryan in Douglas Moore's THE BALLAD OF BABY DOE in 1956, the Reverend John Hale in Robert Ward's THE CRUCIBLE in 1961, Judge Townsend in Carlisle Floyd's THE PASSION OF JONATHAN WADE in 1962, the Sojourner in Floyd's THE SOJOURNER AND MOLLIE SINCLAIR in 1963 and Markheim in Floyd's MARKHEIM in 1966. He took over the role of the tortured preacher Owen Blitch in Floyd's *Susannah* when it came to the New York City Opera in 1955 and can be heard in the role on record. Treigle came to the New York City Opera in 1953 after beginning his career in his native New Orleans and sang principal bass-baritone roles there for twenty years.

TRENTINI, EMMA　*Italian soprano (1885–1959)*

Diminutive soprano Emma Trentini came to America to sing for impresario Oscar Hammerstein in his Manhattan Opera House and was a big hit as Musetta. When his opera house folded, Hammerstein commissioned Victor Herbert to compose the comic opera NAUGHTY MARIETTA for her. Herbert devised memorable coloratura-style arias like "Italian Street Song" and Trentini created the role of Marietta when the operetta premiered on Broadway in 1910. Herbert refused to work with her any further because of her difficult temperament so Hammerstein hired Rudolf Friml to take over. Friml composed *The Firefly* for her and she created the role of streetsinger/opera diva Nina on Broadway in 1912 and sings the hits "Giannina Mia" and "Love Is Like a Firefly." Trentini, who was born in Mantua, became more and more difficult to work with after her early success and her career never developed. She returned to Italy in 1914.

THE TRIAL AT ROUEN　*1956 TV opera by Dello Joio*

Joan of Arc is tried for heresy at Rouen in 1431. Sympathetic Friar Julien urges Joan to submit while Bishop Cauchon seems intent on destroying her. She is condemned to death and burned at the stake. Norman Dello Joio's two-act opera *The Trial at Rouen*, libretto by the composer, was telecast on April 8, 1956 by NBC Opera Theatre. Elaine Malbin sang the role of Joan, Hugh Thompson played her antagonist Bishop Cauchon and Chester Watson was the kindly Friar Julien. The cast also included Paul Ukena, Loren Driscoll, Carole O'Hara and R. W. Barry. There are three choruses representing the inquisitors, the people and Joan's heavenly voices. Trew Hocker designed the sets, Noel Polacheck designed the costumes, Samuel Chotzinoff directed and Peter Herman Adler conducted the Symphony of the Air Orchestra. Kirk Browning directed the telecast. The opera grew out of an earlier one that was staged at Sarah Lawrence College in 1950 as *The Trial of Joan*. Dello Joio withdrew that opera and wrote a new libretto and score for NBC. He revised it a third time for the stage and it was produced by New York City Opera in 1959 with the title THE TRIUMPH OF ST. JOAN.

THE TRIAL OF LUCULLUS　*1947 opera by Sessions*

Roman general Lucius Lucullus (114–57 BC), who conquered much of the East for Rome, is tried by the dead in the underworld for slaughtering thousands of soldiers and civilians. Roger Sessions' pacifist one-act opera *The Trial of Lucullus,* based on a radio play by Bertolt Brecht, was premiered by the Drama Department of the University of California at Berkeley at Wheeler Auditorium on April 18, 1947.

THE TRIAL OF MARY LINCOLN   *1972 TV opera by Pasatieri*

Abraham Lincoln's widow Mary is forced to undergo a trial in 1875 to determine her sanity. It has been arranged by her son Robert who wants to put in an asylum. During the trial she remembers her life with her husband. Thomas Pasatieri's 60-minute television opera *The Trial of Mary Lincoln,* libretto by Anne Howard Bailey based on true events, was premiered on February 26, 1972, on NET Opera Theatre. Elaine Bonazzi sang the demanding central role of Mary Lincoln, Wayne Turnage was her son Robert, Carole Bogard was her sister Elizabeth, Chester Watson was Leonard Swett, Louise Parker was her dressmaker and Julian Patrick was Lincoln's clerk. Also in the strong cast were Alan Titus, Lizabeth Pritchett, Mark Howard and Robert Owen Jones. William Ritman designed the sets and producer Peter Herman Adler conducted the Boston Symphony Orchestra. Pasatieri and Bailey designed the opera for TV techniques, including flashbacks and voice-overs with Lincoln as an offstage voice. Kirk Browning directed the telecast which won an Emmy. Opera Dubs VHS/video at MTR.

THE TRIAL OF THE GYPSY   *1978 dramatic cantata by Menotti*

A gypsy boy is accused of theft and sorcery. When he predicts misfortunes for his judges, they run off and leave him to go free. Gian Carlo Menotti's half-hour dramatic children's cantata *The Trial of the Gypsy,* libretto by the composer, premiered at Alice Tully Hall in Lincoln Center on May 24, 1978. Boy soprano André Hardmon was the Gypsy and boy altos Ivan Bonilla, James Byrd and Sean Sirmans were the Judges. Terence Shook led the Newark Boys' Chorus and Barbara Chernichowski provided the piano accompaniment.

THE TRIALS OF GALILEO   *1967 opera by Laderman*   See *GALILEO GALILEI (1)*

TRIPLE-SEC   *1929 opera by Blitzstein*

Lord Silverside is about to get married when a strange woman arrives and says she is already married to him. Bride-to-be Lady Betty faints. Marc Blitzstein's first opera *Triple-Sec,* libretto by Ronald Jeans, was premiered in the ballroom of the Bellevue Stratford Hotel in Philadelphia on May 6, 1929. The 15-minute opera was exceptionally well received because of the novelty of its Dada-like staging. The conceit is that the audience members are eating and drinking champagne while watching the opera and get so drunk they eventually see the characters on stage in triplicate.

THE TRIUMPH OF ST. JOAN   *1959 opera by Dello Joio*

Joan of Arc is on trial at Rouen in 1431. Friar Julien saves Joan from a drunken jailer and is urged by Bishop Cauchon to persuade her to wear women's clothes. She is tried, recants in a moment of weak-

ness, changes her mind and is condemned to be burned at the stake. Norman Dello Joio's opera about the Maid of Orleans has had three incarnations. The final version for New York City Opera is *The Triumph of St. Joan,* libretto by the composer, which premiered on April 16, 1959, and won the New York Music Critics Circle Award. Lee Venora portrayed St. Joan, Mack Harrell was Bishop Cauchon, Chester Watson was Friar Julien, Arnold Vokaitis was the Kind Inquisitor, Jack DeLon was the Stern Inquisitor, Frank Porretta was the Sentry and Regina Sarfaty, Jacqueline Moody and Sharon Williams were Joan's Heavenly Voices. José Quintero staged the opera, David Hays designed the sets and lighting and Herbert Grossman conducted. The original version of the opera was presented at Sarah Lawrence College in 1950 as *The Trial of Joan,* the second on NBC television in 1956 as THE TRIAL AT ROUEN.

TROUBLE IN TAHITI   *1952 opera by Bernstein*

A Greek chorus–like jazz trio sings of the joys and tribulations of married life in the middle-class suburbs as Dinah and Sam have a breakfast row. The trio continue to comment on the couple's life as he does some office work and plays handball at the gym while she visits her psychiatrist and enjoys (somewhat shamefully) a movie called *Trouble in Tahiti.* In the evening they go to the same movie which Dinah can't say she had seen in the afternoon. Leonard Bernstein's *Trouble in Tahiti,* libretto by the composer, premiered at the Ullman Amphitheatre at Brandeis University in Waltham, Massachusetts, on June 12, 1952. Nell Tangeman played Dinah, Seymour Lipkin was Sam and the composer conducted. It was overshadowed by the premiere on the same night of Marc Blitzstein's version of *The Three-Penny Opera.* It attracted more attention when

This famous 1953 recording of Leonard Bernstein's *Trouble in Tahiti,* now a Newport Classic CD, helped the opera gain wider recognition.

it was presented on NBC Television on November 16, 1952, with Beverly Wolff as Dinah and David Atkinson as Sam. The first New York stage production was in 1955 at The Playhouse with Alice Ghostly as Dinah and John Tyers as Sam. Wolff and Atkinson were the stars when it was staged by New York City Opera in 1958. *Trouble in Tahiti* was later incorporated into Bernstein's opera A QUIET PLACE as a flashback after the death of Dinah but it continues to enjoy a sparkling life of its own. Dinah's aria "WHAT A MOVIE" has become a popular recital piece for sopranos.

1952 Brandeis University. The premiere of the opera at Brandeis University on June 12, 1952, was filmed and some of the footage has been restored. Nell Tangeman is Dinah, Seymour Lipkin is Sam and Leonard Bernstein conducts. The scenes are included as an extra on the DVD of the 2001 BBC Wales production of the opera. BBC/Opus Arte DVD. **1952 NBC Opera.** Beverly Wolff is Dinah and David Atkinson is Sam in this 45-minute black-and-white television production with the jazzy trio played by Constance Brigham, Robert Kole and William Harder. Leonard Bernstein conducts the NBC Orchestra. Samuel Chotzinoff and Charles Polacheck produced and Kirk Browning directed the telecast on November 16, 1952. Video at MTR. **1953 MGM recording.** Beverly Wolff is Dinah and David Atkinson is Sam in this MGM recording of the opera but the other performers are different from the NBC telecast. The jazzy trio singers are Miriam Workman, Robert Bolinger and Earl Rogers. Arthur Winograd conducts the MGM Orchestra. MGM-Helidor LP/Polygram CD. **1973 London Weekend Television.** Nancy Williams is Dinah with Julian Patrick as Sam in this inventive British TV adaptation. Antonia Butler, Michael Clark and Mark Brown are the Trio. The singers perform in front of animated drawn sets with production designs by Eileen Diss and graphic sequences by Pat Gavin. Leonard Bernstein leads the London Symphonic Wind Ensemble. David Griffiths produced and Bill Hays directed the 45-minute video for London Weekend Television. Columbia LP/Sony CD/Kultur VHS. **1973 Hollywood Bowl.** Evelyn Lear sings Dinah with Thomas Stewart as Sam in a Hollywood Bowl presentation recorded live on July 24, 1973. James Levine conducts. Live Opera audiocassette. **1986 Vienna State Opera.** Wendy White is Dinah with Edward Crafts as Sam in the *Trouble in Tahiti* section of *A Quiet Place* in the Vienna State Opera production. The Trio are Louise Edeiken, Mark Thomsen and Kurt Ollmann. Leonard Bernstein conducts the ORF Austrian Radio Symphony Orchestra. The opera is included on the anthology album *Centenary Collection Vol. 6 (1978–1987)*. Uni-Deutsche CD set. **1995 Dawn Upshaw.** Dawn Upshaw sings the aria "What a Movie" accompanied by pianist David Zinman on her album *The World So Wide*. Nonesuch CD. **1995 Monique Haas.** Pianist Monique Haas performs the aria "What a Movie" on her album *Monique Haas*. Polygram CD. **1998 Manhattan School of Music.** Elizabeth Shammash is Dinah and Samuel Hepler is Sam in a Manhattan School of Music Opera Theater production recorded live in December 1998. The trio are Danielle Martin, Micah Olson and Bryan Montemarano. Glen Barton Cortese conducts the Manhattan School of Music Opera Orchestra. Newport Classics CD. **2001 BBC Wales.** Stephanie Novacek is Dinah with Karl Daymond as Sam in an outstanding studio production filmed by BBC Wales. The trio are Thomas Randle, Mary Hegarty and Toby Stafford Allen. Amir Hosseinpour choreographed the production with Paul Daniel conducting the City of London Sinfonia. Director Tom Cairns and producer Fiona Morris re-imagine the settings of the opera with a brash 1950s look while the protagonists sing while engaged in work and play. Extra silent characters are added including their son, Sam's secretary and Dinah's psychiatrist. The DVD extras includes footage of the 1952 premiere and interviews with biographer Humphrey Burton and conductor Daniel. Telecast on December 26, 2001. BBC/Opus Arte DVD.

TROUBLED ISLAND   *1941 opera by Still*

Haiti at the beginning of the 19th century. Jean Jacques Dessalines leads the slaves in a revolution against their French masters and proclaims himself Emperor. He abandons his wife Azelia and makes his mistress Claire the Empress but Claire plots with her lover Vuval and General Stenio to overthrow Dessalines. He is killed by Vuval but only Azelia weeps for him. William Grant Still's opera *Troubled Island*, libretto by Langston Hughes, was completed in 1941 but not staged until March 31, 1949, when it was premiered by New York City Center Opera. Robert Weede played Dessalines, Marie Powers was Azelia, Helena Bliss was Claire, Richard Charles was Vuval, Arthur Newman was Stenio, Robert McFerrin was the voodoo priest Mamaloi and Frances Bible played the Mango Vendor and a Servant. H. A. Condell designed the sets, Eugene Bryden directed and Laszlo Halasz conducted. Excerpts from the opera were broadcast on WOR radio in 1943.

1949 New York City Center Opera. The opera was recorded at a New York City Center Opera dress rehearsal in 1949 with the premiere cast as above. The recording, made by the. State Department, was broadcast by the Voice of America and WNYC and distributed overseas. Audiocassettes can be obtained from William Grant Still Music, 4 South San Francisco Street, Suite 422, Flagstaff, Arizona.

TROYANOS, TATIANA   *American mezzo-soprano (1938–1993)*

Tatiana Troyanos created the role of Queen Isabella in Philip Glass's opera THE VOYAGE at the Metropolitan Opera in 1992 and sang one of the major roles in the premiere of Gunther Schuller's THE VISITATION at Hamburg's Staatsoper in 1966. She sings Anita in the 1996 operatic recording and "making of" video of Leonard Bernstein's WEST SIDE STORY. On stage she had sung Baba the Turk in Igor Stravinsky's *The Rake's Progress* Troyanos, born in New York City, made her debut in 1963 at New York City Opera after playing a chorus nun in Richard Rodgers' THE SOUND OF MUSIC on Broadway for two years. She sang in Hamburg for ten years before her Met debut in 1976. Her untimely death at the age of 54 cut short a remarkable career.

TRUSSEL, JACQUE   *American tenor (1943–)*

Jacque (aka Jack) Trussel created the role of Dr. Dorn in Pasatieri's THE SEAGULL for Houston Grand Opera in 1974, the demon-esque Shad in Carlisle Floyd's BILBY'S DOLL for Houston Grand Opera in 1976 and the monstrous Caliban in Lee Hoiby's THE TEMPEST for Des Moines Metro Opera in 1986. He sings Octavius in a taped 1991 Lyric Opera of Chicago production of Samuel Barber's ANTONY AND CLEOPATRA, and Captain Dick in a taped 1978 New York City Opera production of Victor Herbert's NAUGHTY MARIETTA Trussel, born in San Francisco, studied at Ball State University and made his debut at the Oberlin Festival in 1970. His recital album *Sounds and Sweet Airs*, recorded in 1997 in the Czech Republic, includes the aria "BE NOT AFEARED" from *The Tempest* and the aria "The breaking of so great a thing" from *Antony and Cleopatra*.

TUCKER, RICHARD   *American tenor (1913–1975)*

Richard Tucker can be heard and seen performing arias from four

American operettas. He recorded "Softly, as in a Morning Sunrise" from Sigmund Romberg's THE NEW MOON in 1951. When he appeared on the *Voice of Firestone* TV program in 1957, he performed "Serenade" from Romberg's THE STUDENT PRINCE and "Neapolitan Love Song" from Victor Herbert's THE PRINCESS PAT. He sings the role of the Padre opposite Marilyn Horne on a 1965 recording of Mitch Leigh's MAN OF LA MANCHA. Tucker, born in Brooklyn, made his debut in 1943 with Salmaggi Opera in New York and began to sing at the Met in 1945.

TURNER, CLARAMAE   *American contralto (1920–)*

Gian Carlo Menotti chose Claramae Turner to create the title role of Madame Flora in THE MEDIUM at Columbia University in 1946. She did not take the role on to Broadway, but she did re-create it for NBC television in 1959. She also created the role of Diana Orsini in Alberto Ginastera's BOMARZO at Washington Opera in 1967 and is heard on the cast recording. She sings the role of Ma Moss in Aaron Copland's 1965 Lincoln Center recording of his opera *The Tender Land*. She plays Nettie in the 1956 film of Richard Rodgers' CAROUSEL and reprised the role in the operatic 1962 recording. On stage she sang Miss Todd in Menotti's THE OLD MAID AND THE THIEF, August Tabor in Douglas Moore's THE BALLAD OF BABY DOE and the Old Woman in Raffaelo De Banfield's LORD BYRON'S LOVE LETTER. Turner, born in Dinuba, California, studied in San Francisco and New York and began her career in the chorus of the San Francisco Opera. She made her official debut in San Francisco in 1945 and began to sing at the Met in 1946.

TWAIN, MARK   *American writer (1835–1910)*

Mark Twain (penname of Samuel Langhorne Clemens) was a master of many genres including travelogues, essays and short stories but is especially treasured for his novels *The Adventures of Tom Sawyer* and *Adventures of Huckleberry Finn*. There are a number of operas and music theater works based on both these novels as well as some based on other stories. The most popular Twain opera is probably Lukas Foss's 1949 THE JUMPING FROG OF CALAVERAS COUNTY while the best-known music theater work seems to be Roger Miller's Tony award-winning Broadway musical *Big River,* based on *Huckleberry Finn.*

Adventures of Huckleberry Finn (1885). 1957 Jack Urbont's *Livin' the Life,* libretto by Bruce Geller and Dale Wasserman. Premiere: Phoenix Theater, NY, April 27, 1957. 1971 Hall Overton's *Huckleberry Finn,* libretto by J. Stamfer. Premiere: Juilliard School of Music, NY, May 20, 1971. 1981 Leslie Dweir's *The Raft,* libretto by Bill Thompson. Premiere: Huntington Station, NY October 19, 1985. 1983 Bruce Pomahac's *Huck and Jim on the Mississippi,* libretto by Joshua Logan. Premiere: Florida Atlantic University, November 11, 1983. 1985 Roger Miller's *Big River,* libretto by William Hauptmann and composer. Opened on Broadway on April 25, 1985. 1985 John Stuart Braden's *Downriver,* libretto by Jeff Tanborinio.

The Adventures of Tom Sawyer (1876). 1953 Jonathan Elkus's *Tom Sawyer,* libretto by composer. Premiere: San Francisco Boy's Chorus, May 22, 1953. 1966 Martin Kalmanoff's *Huck Finn and Tom Sawyer,* libretto by composer. Premiere: New York City, October 15, 1966. 1989 Richard Owen's *Tom Sawyer,* libretto by composer. Premiere: Manhattan School of Music, NY, April 9, 1989.

The Jumping Frog of Calaveras County (1865). 1950 Lukas Foss's THE JUMPING FROG OF CALAVERAS COUNTY, libretto by Jean Karsavina. Premiere: Bloomington, Indiana, May 18, 1950.

The Man Who Corrupted Hadleyberg (1900). 1987 Roger L. Nelson's *The Man Who Corrupted Hadleyberg,* libretto by Kate Pogue.

The Million Pound Bank-Note (1893). 1965 William Goldstein's *A Total Sweet Story,* libretto by Marvin Shofer. Premiere: Music Theater Group, New York, March 8, 1988

The Prince and the Pauper (1882). 1955 Arnold Black's *The Prince and the Pauper,* libretto by composer. Premiere: Duxbury, Massachusetts, August 26, 1955. 1989 Matthew Granovetter's *The Prince and the Pauper,* libretto by Patricia Sternberg and the composer.

TWELFTH NIGHT   *1968 opera by Amram*

Viola is shipwrecked and disguises herself as a boy to become the page of Duke Orsino. with whom she falls in love. She bears messages of love from him to Olivia. who falls in love with her. Viola's twin brother Sebastian appears and the situation becomes rather complicated. The comic figures include the ambitious steward Malvolio, the clever fool Feste, the drunken Sir Toby Belch, the scheming maid Maria and the foolish Sir Andrew Aguecheek. David Amran's opera *Twelfth Night,* libretto by Joseph Papp based on the Shakespeare comedy, was presented at the Lake George Opera Festival in Glen Falls, New York, on August 1, 1968. Marcia Baldwin took the role of Viola, Sean Barker was Orsino, Carolyn Heafner was Olivia, Philip Smith was Sebastian, Richard Allen was Malvolio, Robert Falk was Sir Toby Belch, William Brown was Feste, Richard Levitt was Sir Andrew Aguecheek and Martha Williford was Maria. Adelaide Bishop directed and Paul Calloway conducted. Amran's arias, duets and ensembles are traditional but highly entertaining and carry the story forward rapidly.

TWENTY TWO (TAKER OF THE TOTAL CHANCE)   *2003 opera by Chase*

Nicolas Francis Chase's one-act avant-garde opera *Twenty Two (Taker of the Total Chance),* libretto by Anne Haround, was premiered at Long Beach Opera in California on June 8, 2003, in a program titled "Seven Small Operas." Kerry Walsh and Tannic Ling starred in this surrealist dreamlike non-narrative work.

U

UNCLE TOM'S CABIN   *American operas based on Stowe novel*

Uncle Tom is sold by a Kentucky owner because of debt but young Eliza refuses to be bought and runs away to Canada with her child. Tom gets a kindly owner at first and makes friends with little Eva and her black friend Topsy who "just growed." Later Tom is sold to brutal Simon Legree, a cotton plantation owner who has Tom beaten to death. Harriet Beecher Stowe's novel *Uncle Tom's Cabin* (1852*),* one of the most influential novels ever written, caused a huge increase in the opposition to slavery. Equally influential was a melodramatic play version by George Akin which helped forge iconic images of Uncle Tom, Simon Legree, Topsy and Eliza escaping over a frozen river. The first opera based on the novel was staged in Italy one year after it was published, Paolo Giorza's *La Capanna dello zio Tom,* but the first American opera was not composed until 1882, long after the Civil War. There were film versions of the story as early as 1903 and a famous musical starring the Duncan Sisters as Topsy and Eva. American operas based on the novel are listed below.

1882 Caryl Florio. Caryl Florio's *Uncle Tom's Cabin,* libretto by the composer, was the first American opera to use the novel as source. It was premiered in Philadelphia in 1882. **1883 Harrison Millard.** Harrison Millard's *Uncle Tom's Cabin*, libretto by the composer based on the novel, was premiered in Toronto, Canada, in 1883. **1928 Leslie Grossmith.** Leslie Grossmith's *Uncle Tom's Cabin*, libretto by the composer based on the novel, was staged in 1928 and awarded the Bispham Memorial Medal in 1932. **1966 Avery Claflin.** Avery Claflin's *Uncle Tom's Cabin*, libretto by D. Claflin based on the novel, was premiered at the Metropolitan Opera Studio in New York in 1964.

UNDER THE ARBOR　*1992 opera by Greenleaf*

Rural Alabama in 1943. Hallelujah Jernigan and Robert Patterson Lee discover love and sex during their meetings on the banks of the Chattahoochee River. Southern attitudes about race, religion and voodoo color their relationship as they learns about guilt as well as love. Robert Greenleaf's opera *Under the Arbor,* libretto by Marian Motley Carcache based on her short story, premiered in October 1992 at the Civic Center Concert Hall in Birmingham, Alabama. Sunny Joy Langton played Hallie, Mark Calkins was Robert, Carmen Balthrop was Annie, Vanessa Ayers was Duck, Ruby Hinds was Madame Queen, Tichina Vaughn was Mattie, Claudia Cummings was Miss Nell and Bruce Hall was Papa Brown. David Gately directed, Bob Cooley produced and Paul Polivnick conducted the Alabama Symphony Orchestra.

1993 Birmingham Civic Center. Sunny Joy Langton and Mark Calkins star as the lovers Hallie and Robert in the videotaped premiere production of the opera at the Civic Center Concert Hall in Birmingham, Alabama. The other cast members are as above. Paul Polivnick conducts the Alabama Symphony Orchestra. Bruce Kuerten directed the 112-minute video which was telecast on PBS. Kultur VHS.

UNDER THE DOUBLE MOON　*1989 opera by Davis*

In the far future on the planet Udine, a dying empress needs to use the telepathic twins Xola and Tarj to prolong her life. She sends the Inspector to get them but the sea creature Gaxulta, who is their real father, saves them. He is joined in the sea by their mother Kanaxa and the children set out on their own. Anthony Davis's impressionistic opera *Under the Double Moon,* libretto by science-fiction writer Deborah Atherton, was commissioned by Opera Theater of St. Louis which premiered it on June 15, 1989. Ai-Lan Zhu was Xola, Eugene Perry was Tarj, Cynthia Clarey was Kanaxa, Jake Gardner was Gaxulta, Thomas Young was the Inspector and John Duykers was fisherman Krillig. Rhoda Levine directed and William McLaughlin conducted. Davis says he used Balinese music as inspiration for the outer space sounds he uses in the opera.

THE UNICORN, THE GORGON AND THE MANTICORE　*1956 madrigal opera by Menotti*

The Man in the Castle, who lives apart, joins the villagers in their Sunday promenade leading a Unicorn. Soon the Count and Countess and then everyone else has to have one. When he promenades with a Gorgon, everyone again copies him. Finally he appears with a Manticore and warns that it is a dangerous creature but everyone still imitates him. When the Man does not appear at a Sunday promenade, the people go to his castle and find him lying on his deathbed with his animals by his side. Gian Carlo Menotti's allegorical *The Unicorn, the Gorgon and the Manticore or, The Three Sundays of a Poet,* libretto by the composer inspired by Orazio Vecchi's 1597 *L'Amfiparnasso,* is described by its creator as a "madrigal fable," a combination of chamber opera, ballet and

oratorio with singers and dancers. It was commissioned by the Elizabeth Sprague Coolidge Foundation and premiered at the Coolidge Auditorium at the Library of Congress on October 19, 1956. Swen Swenson was the Poet, Talley Beatty was the Unicorn, John Renn was the Gorgon, Dorothy Ethridge was the Manticore, Loren Hightower was the Count, Gemze was the Countess, John Foster was the Doctor, Ethel Martin was the Doctor's Wife, Jack Leigh was the Mayor and Lee Becker was the Mayor's wife. Robert Fletcher designed the fantastic costumes for the animals, John Butler created the choreography, Menotti directed and Paul Callaway conducted. *Unicorn* was reprised by New York City Ballet on January 15, 1957, with Nicholas Magallens as the Poet, Arthur Mitchell as the Unicorn, Eugene Tanner as the Gorgon and Richard Thomas as the Manticore. Thomas Schippers conducted.

1956 Thomas Schippers. Thomas Schippers conducts the Paul Hill Chorale and University of Michigan Orchestra and Chorus in a recording made in Europe with the New York City Ballet. The soloists are sopranos Betty Hodges and Hallie Nowland, contralto Mary Hensley and tenor Frank Karian. Angel LP. **1968 Charles Byers.** Charles Byers conducts the University of Colorado University Singers in a recording of *Unicorn* made during a concert on May 6 1968. Century Records LP. **1970 William Wells.** William Wells conducts the Carlton College Chamber Singers and Orchestra in a live performance of *Unicorn* at Skinner Chapel on

Gian Carlo Menotti's *The Unicorn, the Gorgon and the Manticore* was produced in New York in 1957 with Arthur Mitchell as the Unicorn, Eugene Tanner as the Gorgon and Richard Thomas as the Manticore.

April 17, 1970, The soloists are soprano Margaret Howell, mezzo-soprano Polly Detels and contralto Roxanne Frederickson. Carlton LP. **1978 Paul Hill.** Paul Hill conducts the Paul Hill Chorale and Orchestra in a recording of *Unicorn* made in 1978. Golden Crest LP. **1979 Thomas Hilbish.** Thomas Hilbish conducts the University of Michigan Chamber Choir and Orchestra in a recording of *Unicorn* made at Hill Auditorium at the University of Michigan in 1979. University of Michigan Records LP. **1980 Marietta Cheng.** Marietta Cheng conducts the Colgate University Chorus and Orchestra in a recording of *Unicorn* made at Colgate in 1980. Redwood Records LP. **1997 Donald Teeters.** Donald Teeters leads the Boston Cecilia Chorus and Chamber Ensemble in a recording of *Unicorn* made in January 1997 following a 1996 stage production. The soloists are sopranos Andrea Matthews and Susan Trout and contraltos Elizabeth Anker and Marylène Altierei. Newport Classics CD.

UNITED STATES   *1982 multi-media work by Anderson*
Laurie Anderson's multi-media work *United States* is essentially an experimental opera in disguise with 78 separate performance pieces. It is best known for the avant-garde aria "O Superman (for Massenet)" which became a commercial hit in England. *United States* premiered at the Brooklyn Academy of Music on February 3, 1982, and was then presented with great success at a festival in Holland. It consists of four parts (Transportation, Politics Money, Love) examined through words and music. There is no narrative per se but the whole is an effective description of American society and culture.

1985 United States Live. Anderson's four-part multi-media work was recorded live over four days in February 1983 at the Brooklyn Academy of Music. This was the premiere of the work in its final form. Supporting Anderson are soprano Shelley Karson and instrumentalists Ann DeMarinis, Chuck Fisher, Bill Obrecht and David Van Tieghem. Warner Brothers CD/cassette box.

UP IN CENTRAL PARK   *1945 operetta by Romberg*
Central Park in Manhattan is the focal point of this operetta set in the 1870s when Tammany Hall controlled the city. Boss Tweed, who is organizing a crooked election, drafts new Irish immigrant Timothy Moore for multiple vote duty. His daughter Rosie becomes romantically involved with investigative New York Times reporter John Matthews but marries a Tweed crony to advance her singing career. After she is betrayed by him and Matthews exposes a Tweed scheme, the lovers are reunited. Sigmund Romberg's operetta *Up in Central Park,* libretto by Dorothy and Herbert Fields, premiered at the New Century Theatre in New York City on January 27, 1945, in a splendid Mike Todd production. Maureen Cannon was Rosie Moore, Wilbur Evans was John Matthews and Noah Beery was Boss Tweed while Betty Bruce. Maurice Burke and Robert Rounseville added strong support. The most popular number was the "Courier and Ives ballet" skating sequence in Central Park choreographed by Helen Tamaris, while the hit song was the duet "Close as Pages in a Book."

1945 Original cast. Wilbur Evans of the original Broadway cast, Met soprano Eileen Farrell and Broadway star Celeste Holm are featured in this recording of highlights from the operetta. Max Meth leads the chorus and orchestra of the original stage production. Decca LP. **1945 Radio broadcast.** Met soprano Patrice Munsel, Jack Smith, William Tabbert and Audrey Marsh are featured in a radio broadcast of highlights from the operetta. Al Goodman conducts the Orchestra. The broadcast was recorded for a V-Disc and later issued on an LP. **1948 Universal film.** Deanna Durbin

plays Rosie Moore in this movie version of the operetta. She falls in love with crusading reporter Dick Haymes and gets to sing the best songs. Vincent Price plays Boss Tweed, Tom Powers is Rogan and Albert Sharp is Timothy Moore. Karl Tunberg wrote the script and William Seiter directed for Universal-International. Premiere Opera VHS. **1950 Robert Merrill/Jeanette MacDonald.** Robert Merrill and Jeanette MacDonald join in duets from the operetta, including "The Fireman's Bride." Their songs are on the 1993 album *Change Partners.* Box Office CD. **1978 Beverly Sills/Sherrill Milnes.** Soprano Beverly Sills and baritone Sherrill Milnes join in duet on "'Close as Pages in a Book" and "The Fireman's Bride" on the album *Up in Central Park.* Julius Rudel conducts the New York City Opera Orchestra. EMI Angel LP. **1985 Sherrill Milnes/Julia Migenes.** Baritone Sherrill Milnes duets with soprano Julia Migenes on "Close as Pages in a Book" in a concert taped in Berlin for TV. Anton Guadagno conducts the London Symphony Orchestra on *Sherrill Milnes All-Star Gala.* VAI VHS. **1993 Barbara Cook.** Barbara Cook recorded two songs from *Up in Central Park,* Rosie's sweet ballad "April Snow" and the love duet "Close as Pages in a Book" for her album in tribute to lyricist Dorothy Fields titled *Close as Pages in a Book.* DRG CD. **1995 Maxine Sullivan.** Maxine Sullivan sings "Close as Pages in a Book" accompanied by jazz clarinetist Bob Wilber on their album *Close as Pages in a Book.* Audiophile CD.

UPPMAN, THEODOR   *American baritone (1920–)*
Theodor Uppman created important roles in five American operas. He was the Innkeeper in Bernard Herrmann's TV opera A CHILD IS BORN on CBS in 1955, Jonathan Wade in Carlisle Floyd's THE PASSION OF JONATHAN WADE at New York City Opera in 1962, Victor in Heitor Villa-Lobos' YERMA at Santa Fe Opera in 1971, Juan in Thomas Pasatieri's THE BLACK WIDOW in Seattle in 1972 and Bill in Leonard Bernstein's A QUIET PLACE at Houston Grand Opera in 1983. Uppman, born in San Jose, California, studied at the Curtis Institute and at USC. He made his debut at New York City Opera in 1948 and is best known for creating the title role in Benjamin Britten's *Billy Budd.*

UPSHAW, DAWN   *American soprano (1960–)*
Dawn Upshaw has recorded albums of arias from American operas as well as creating roles in them. She played Mary in the revised version of William Mayer's A DEATH IN THE FAMILY at St. Louis Opera in 1986, Daisy in the premiere of John Harbison's THE GREAT GATSBY at the Metropolitan Opera in 1999, Mary in John Adams' EL NIÑO in Paris in 2000 and Catalan actress Margarita Sixrgu in Osvaldo Golijov's chamber opera AINADAMAR at Tanglewood in 2003. Her 1995 album *The World So Wide* features arias from eight American operas: John Adams' NIXON IN CHINA, Samuel Barber's ANTONY AND CLEOPATRA, Leonard Bernstein's TROUBLE IN TAHITI, Aaron Copland's THE TENDER LAND, Carlisle Floyd's SUSANNAH, Tania León's SCOURGE OF HYACINTHS, Douglas Moore's THE BALLAD OF BABY DOE and Kurt Weill's STREET SCENE. Her 1994 album *I Wish It So* features American music theater songs from Bernstein's CANDIDE and WEST SIDE STORY, Marc Blitzstein's JUNO, REUBEN, REUBEN, and NO FOR AN ANSWER, Weill's LADY IN THE DARK, LOST IN THE STARS and ONE TOUCH OF VENUS and STEPHEN SONDHEIM musicals. Her 1989 album *Knoxville: Summer of 1915* includes arias from Gian Carlo Menotti's THE OLD MAID AND THE THIEF and Igor Stravinsky's THE RAKE'S PROGRESS. She sings Anne Trulove on three versions of THE RAKE'S PROGRESS: on video in 1992 and on CD in 1996 at Aix-in-Provence and on video in 1996 at Salzburg. Upshaw, born

in Nashville, Tennessee, studied at the Manhattan School of Music and made her debut there in 1983.

UTAH *American state (1896–)*

Utah has a long history of producing operas dealing with its history and the life of the Native American who were there when the Mormon settlers arrived in the 19th century. Its major opera company is Utah Opera in Salt Lake City; it commissioned David Carlson's DREAMKEEPERS to celebrate the centennial of Utah statehood in 1996.

Logan: Utah Festival Opera, founded in 1993, presents a summer season of opera and operetta in Logan in the Cache Valley in northern Utah. American presentations have included Carlisle Floyd's SUSANNAH, Victor Herbert's NAUGHTY MARIETTA, Frank Loesser's *Greenwillow*, Henry Mollicone's COYOTE TALES, Richard Rodgers' THE SOUND OF MUSIC and Sigmund Romberg's THE DESERT SONG.

Ogden: Mark Bucci's *Triad* was premiered at Weber State College in Ogden in 1971.

Provo: Three operas have premiered at Brigham Young University in Provo. William F. Hanson's *Tam-Man-Nacup,* about Uintah Indian life, was staged in 1928, while his *The Bleeding Heart of Timpanogas* was presented in 1937. John Laurence Seymour's *Ramona,* libretto by Henry C. Tracy based on the novel by Helen Hunt Jackson, was premiered on November 11, 1970.

Salt Lake City: Utah Opera was founded in Salt Lake City in 1978 by tenor Glade Peterson. Most of its productions are from the Italian repertory but it has staged Gian Carlo Menotti's AMAHL AND THE NIGHT VISITORS (three times), Douglas Moore's THE BALLAD OF BABY DOE and Sigmund Romberg's THE STUDENT PRINCE. David Carlson's DREAMKEEPERS, libretto by Aden Ross, was commissioned to celebrate Utah centennial as a state and premiered in 1996 with a cast headed by Juliana Gondek.

Vernal: William F. Hanson's five-act *The Sun Dance,* libretto by the composer about the Sioux people, was premiered by Uintah Academy's music department in Vernal on February 20 1913.

V

THE VAGABOND KING *1925 operetta by Friml*

Poet-thief François Villon becomes king for a day in 15th century France, defeats the enemy Burgundians and wins the hand of haughty aristocrat Lady Katherine, Rudolf Friml's last notable stage operetta, *The Vagabond King,* libretto by Brian Hooker and W. H. Post based on Justin McCarthy's play *If I Were King,* opened at the Casino Theater in New York on September 21, 1925, with Dennis King as Villon, Carolyn Thompson as Lady Katherine and Jane Carroll as the self-sacrificing Huguette. The hit songs were "Only a Rose" and "Song of the Vagabonds."

1925 Rudolf Friml. Rudolf Friml recorded piano versions of songs from the operetta in 1925 and 1929, including "Song of the Vagabonds," "Huguette Waltz," "Some Day," "Love Me Tonight" and "Only a Rose." They're on several albums including *The Genius of Rudolf Friml.* Golden Crest LP. **1927 Original Cast.** Original cast member Dennis King (Vil-

lon) recorded "Song of the Vagabonds" and Carolyn Thompson (Lady Katherine) recorded "Only a Rose" for a Victor 78. The recordings have been reissued on various albums. **1927 London Cast.** Original London cast members recorded highlights from the operetta in 1927. Derek Oldham (Villon) and Winnie Melville (Katherine) sing "Love Me Tonight" and "Only a Rose" while Norah Blaney (Huguette) sings "Huguette Waltz" and "Love for Sale." They're on the album *Rudolph Friml in London.* World Record Club LP. **1929 Richard Crooks.** Richard Crooks recorded the song "Only a Rose" with the Berlin State Opera Orchestra. It's included on the album *Only a Rose—The Art of Richard Crooks in Song.* Pearl/Koch CD. **1930 Paramount film.** The first film of the operetta features Dennis King as Villon repeating the role he originated on stage. Jeanette MacDonald plays his lady love Katherine and Lillian Roth is Huguette. Ludwig Berger directed for Paramount. The film was made in a fragile early two-color Technicolor process and was almost lost, but it has now been beautifully restored by the UCLA Film and Television Archive. The soundtrack is on a Vertinge LP. **1935 Charles Kullman.** Charles Kullman starred in a radio broadcast of an abridged version of the operetta on April 21, 1935. It was recorded and issued on tape. Live Opera audiocassette. **1937 Jussi Björling.** Jussi Björling recorded "Only a Rose" with the Stockholm Opera Orchestra led by Nils Grevillius. It's on several albums including *Jussi Björling*

Dennis King starred in the stage and film versions of Rudolf Friml's operetta *The Vagabond King.*

Vol. 2: Operetta and Song (1929–1938). Pearl/Koch CD. **1940 Southern California Light Opera.** The Southern California Light Opera Orchestra and Chorus recorded highlights from *The Vagabond King* as a radio transcription for the WPA Federal Music Project. There is a recording at the Library of Congress. **1940 Anne Ziegler/Webster Booth.** Anne Ziegler and Webster Booth, the MacDonald and Eddy of England, sing "Only a Rose" for a 78. It's on their album *The Golden Age of Anne Ziegler and Webster Booth*. EMI LP. **1946 Gladys Swarthout.** Gladys Swarthout sings "Only a Rose" on a 1946 radio broadcast. It's on the album *Gladys Swarthout: Favorites from the Musical Theatre*. Take Two LP. **1950 Gordon MacRae/Lucille Norman.** Gordon MacRae and Lucille Norman perform a highlights version of the operetta with the orchestra conducted by Paul Weston. Capitol LP. **1950 Eric Wrightson/Frances Greer.** Eric Wrightson and Frances Greer perform highlights from the operetta with the orchestra conducted by Al Goodman. RCA Victor LP. **1951 Frances Bible/Alfred Drake.** New York City Opera mezzo-soprano Frances Bible, Broadway baritone Alfred Drake and soprano Mimi Benzel perform a highlights version of the operetta with Jay Blackton conducting the orchestra. Decca LP. **1952 Dorothy Kirsten/Gordon MacRae.** Dorothy Kirsten and Gordon MacRae perform a highlights radio version of the operetta. Demand Performance audiocassette. **1956 Paramount film.** Oreste stars as Villon with Kathryn Grayson as Katherine in this movie version of the operetta. Oreste sings well but he has little screen charisma, and the film was not a hit. Rita Moreno is Huguette and Walter Hampden is King Louis XI. Robert Burks photographed this VistaVision spectacular and Michael Curtis directed for Paramount. **1956 Oreste/Jean Fenn.** Tenor Oreste, who starred in the 1956 Paramount film of the operetta, and Met soprano Jean Fenn sing twelve selections from the film of the operetta, including three tunes written for the screen version. Henri René conducts. RCA Victor LP. **1959 Mario Lanza/Judith Raskin.** Mario Lanza and Judith Raskin perform a highlights version of the operetta with Constantine Callinicos conducting the orchestra. RCA Victor LP/CD. **1960 Earl Wrightson/Lois Hunt.** Baritone Earl Wrightson and soprano Lois Hunt sing "Song of the Vagabonds," "Only a Rose," "Love Me Tonight" and "Some Day" with an orchestra conducted by Frank DeVol. The selections are on the album *A Night with Rudolf Friml*. Columbia LP. **1960 John Hanson/Jane Fyffe.** John Hanson and Jane Fyffe perform selections from the operetta on this British album with orchestra conducted by Peter Knight. Pye LP. **1961 Jan Cerveka.** Jan Cerveka conducts the orchestra and cast in this highlights recording of the operetta featuring singers Edwin Steffe, Lissa Gray, Dorothy Dorow, John Larsen and Freda Larsen. World Record Club LP. **1962 Rosalind Elias/William Lewis.** Rosalind Elias sings Huguette opposite William Lewis as Villon and Sara Endich as Katherine in this highlights recording. Lehman Engel conducts the orchestra and chorus for the Reader's Digest *Treasury of Great Operettas*. RCA LP box set. **1986 Teresa Ringholz.** Teresa Ringholz and the Eastman-Dryden Orchestra, led by Donald Hunsberger, perform "Song of the Vagabonds," "Only a Rose" and the "Huguette Waltz" on the album *Rudolf Friml: Chansonette*. Arabesque LP/CD. **1993 Jerry Hadley.** Jerry Hadley sings "Song of the Vagabonds" on his album *Golden Days* with Paul Gemignani conducting the American Theatre Orchestra. BMG RCA Victor CD.

VALENTE, BENITA   *American soprano (1937–)*

Benita Valente has championed the work of modern American composers for over four decades. She sang the role of Peony in Ned Rorem's A CHILDHOOD MIRACLE in a televised production in Philadelphia in 1956 while still a student at the Curtis Institute and she created the role of Melody Cardwell in Leslie Savoy Burrs VANQUI for Opera/Columbus in 1999. When she toured with Sarah Caldwell's American National Opera Company she sang Anne Trulove in Igor Stravinsky's *The Rake's Progress*. John Harbison composed *The Reawaking* for her to sing with the Juilliard Quartet and she also premiered David Del Tredici's *Night Conjure-Verse* and William Bolcom's cantata *Let Evening Come*. Valente, born in Delcano, California, studied with Lotte Lehman and at the Curtis Institute and made her stage debut in Freiburg, Germany, in 1962.

VALENTINE, MAY   *American conductor*

May Valentine was one of the first women to produce and conduct American comic opera, beginning with a production of Reginald De Koven's ROBIN HOOD at the Park Theater in New York which she conducted when she was nineteen. She organized and toured comic operas with the May Valentine Opera Company, presenting mainly Gilbert and Sullivan, but also comic operas by De Koven and Victor Herbert. The company continued to travel as a road show into the 1920s.

VALIS   *1987 opera by Machover*

Science fiction writer Philip K. Dick has a bizarre "pink light experience," a mystical, possibly extraterrestrial, revelation that transforms him into a mirror self he calls Horselover Fat. VALIS is an acronym for "Vast Active Living Intelligence System." Tod Machover's multi-media opera *VALIS*, libretto by Catherine Ikam, Bill Raymond and the composer based on an autobiographical novel by Philip K. Dick. was commissioned by IRCAM and premiered at the Pompidou Center in Paris in 1987. Olivier Angèle was Horselover Fat/Philip K. Dick, Sophie Marin-Degor was Gloria, Terry Edwards was Dr. Stone, Mary King was Linda Lampton, Daryl Runswick was Eric Lampton and Anne Azéma was Sophia. Emma Stephenson played keyboards, Daniel Ciampolini performed the percussion and Todd Machover was the conductor. **1988 MIT Experimental Media Facility.** The final version of *VALIS* was recorded at MIT's Experimental Media Facility in February 1988 with Patrick Mason as Horselover Fat/Philip K. Dick, Janice Felty as Gloria, Terry Edwards as Dr. Stone, Anne Azéma as Sophia, Daryl Runswich as Eric Lampton, Mary King as Linda Lampton, Thomas Bogdan as Gesegnet Song and Arnaud Petit as Exegesis 1 and 2. Emma Stephenson plays piano and keyboards, Daniel Ciampolini plays percussion and Todd Machover is the conductor. Bridge CD.

VAN DE VATE, NANCY   *American composer (1930–)*

Nancy Van de Vate, who founded the International League of Women Composers, has written a number of works for the stage. The chamber opera *In the Shadow of the Glen*, libretto by the composer based on the play by John Millington Synge, was premiered in Tupelo, Mississippi, on February 8, 1960. The chamber opera *The Death of the Hired Man*, libretto by the composer based on the Robert Frost poem, was completed in 1960. The theater piece *A Night in the Royal Ontario Museum*, composed for soprano and tape, was premiered in Washington, DC, April 13, 1984. *The Saga of Cocaine Lil*, a theater piece for mezzo-soprano, four singers and percussion, premiered in Frankfurt, Germany, on April 20, 1988. *All Quiet on the Western Front*, libretto by the composer based on the novel by Erich Maria Remarque, and *Where the Cross Is Made*, libretto by the composer based on the play by Eugne O'Neill, are both works in progress Van de Vate, born in Plainfield, New Jersey, studied at Eastman House and Wellesley. She has taught at several universities, including Mississippi and Hawaii.

VANESSA *1958 opera by Barber*

Wealthy aristocrat Vanessa, her niece Erika and her mother the Old Baroness live a lonely existence on an isolated estate in the far north. Vanessa is expecting the return of her lover Anatol, who had jilted her twenty years before. The man who actually arrives is her old lover's son, a fortune hunter in search of a wealthy wife. On the night of his arrival, after Vanessa has gone to bed disappointed and despairing, he seduces Erika. Their relationship goes wrong, and he leaves the estate with Vanessa as his bride. Erika and the Old Baroness settle into renewed lonely isolation. Samuel Barber's *Vanessa*, libretto by Gian Carlo Menotti inspired by the stories of Isak Dinesen, premiered at the Metropolitan Opera on January 15, 1958. Eleanor Steber was Vanessa, Rosalind Elias was her niece Erika, Nicolai Gedda was Anatol, Regina Resnik was the Old Baroness, Giorgio Tozzi was the Doctor, George Cehanovsky was the Major-Domo and Robert Nagy was the Footman. Dimitri Mitropoulos conducted the Metropolitan Opera Orchestra and Chorus. The opera won wide acceptance and was awarded the Pulitzer Prize for Music. It continues to be revived, including a notable production by Opéra de Monte Carlo with original cast member Rosalind Elias as the Old Baroness, Kiri Te Kanawa as Vanessa, Lucy Schauffer as Erika and David Maxwell Anderson as Anatol.

1958 Metropolitan Opera recording. The opera was recorded by the original Metropolitan Opera cast at the Manhattan Center in New York during February–April 1958. Eleanor Steber is Vanessa, Rosalind Elias is Erika, Nicolai Gedda is Anatole, Regina Resnik is the Old Baroness, Giorgio Tozzi is the Doctor, George Cehanovsky is the Major-Domo and Robert Nagy is the Footman. Dimitri Mitropoulos conducts the Metropolitan Opera Orchestra and Chorus. RCA Victor LP/CD box. **1958 Metropolitan Opera broadcast.** The opera was broadcast from the Metropolitan Opera on February 1, 1958, with the original cast. Eleanor Steber is Vanessa, Rosalind Elias is Erika, Nicolai Gedda is Anatole, Regina Resnik is the Old Baroness and Giorgio Tozzi is the Doctor. Dimitri Mitropoulos conducts the Metropolitan Opera Orchestra and Chorus. The broadcast, recorded off air, is on an Omega Opera Archives CD. **1958 Salzberg Festival.** The opera was broadcast from the Salzberg Festival in Austria on August 16, 1958, with the original cast. Eleanor Steber is Vanessa, Rosalind Elias is Erika, Nicolai Gedda is Anatole, Regina Resnik is the Old Baroness and Giorgio Tozzi is the Doctor. Dimitri Mitropoulos conducts. The broadcast, recorded off air, is on an Omega Opera Archives CD. **1959 André Kostelanetz.** André Kostelanetz conducts the New York Philharmonia Orchestra in the Act IV Intermezzo performed after a dra-

matic scene between Erika and the Old Baroness. It's on the album *Spirit of '76.* Columbia LP. **1960 Thomas Schippers.** Thomas Schippers conducts the Columbia Symphony Orchestra in the Act IV Intermezzo of the opera on the album *Orchestral Music from the Opera.* Columbia Masterworks LP. **1965 Metropolitan Opera.** Mary Costa sings the role of Vanessa in an April, 3, 1965, broadcast of the Metropolitan Opera revival. Rosalind Elias is Erika, Blanche Thebom is the Old Baroness, John Alexander is Anatol and Giorgio Tozzi is the Doctor. William Steinberg conducts the Metropolitan Opera Orchestra. Off-air recording on Omega Opera Archives CD. **1967 Leontyne Price.** Leontyne Price sings Vanessa's aria "He has come, he has come!...Do not utter a word" with Francesco Molinari Prandelli conducting the RCA Italian Opera Orchestra. The aria is on several CD albums including RCA's *The Essential Leontyne Price: Great Soprano Arias* and *The Prima Donna Collection.* **1969 L. Ivanova.** Soviet soprano L. Ivanova sings the Doctor's folk song style aria "Under the willow tree" on the Soviet album *Songs by Samuel Barber.* Melodiya LP. **1978 Spoleto Festival, USA.** Johanna Meier is Vanessa, Henry Price is Anatol and Katherine Ciesinski is Erika in this Gian Carlo Menotti production filmed at the Spoleto Festival USA in Charleston in May 1978. Alice Garrott is the Old Baroness, Irwin Densen is the Doctor and William Bender is Nicholas. Christopher Keene conducts the Spoleto Festival Orchestra. Kirk Browning directed the video telecast by South Carolina Educational Television in the *Great Performances* series on January 31, 1979. Premiere Opera and Lyric VHS/New York Public Library video/Live Opera audiocassette. **1983 Helen-Kay Eberley.** American soprano Helen-Kay Eberley sings Vanessa's aria "Do not utter a word" on her album *American Girl.* She is accompanied by pianist Donald Isaak. Eb-Sko LP. **1991 Frederica von Stade.** Frederica von Stade sings Erika's aria "Must the winter come so soon?" at a televised concert at Lincoln Center ON November 10, 1991. James Conlon conducts members of the Metropolitan Opera Orchestra in the program *A Salute to American Music.* RCA Victor CD. **1992**

Samuel Barber's opera *Vanessa* was staged in 2001 by Des Moines Metro Opera. Photograph courtesy of Des Moines Metro Opera.

Roberta Alexander. Soprano Roberta Alexander performs two arias from *Vanessa* on her album *Barber: Songs and Arias* with Edo de Waart conducting the Nederlands Radio Philharmonic Orchestra. Etcetera CD. **1992 Cambridge University Chamber Choir.** The Cambridge University Chamber Choir performs the Doctor's folk-like "Under the willow tree" on their album *Barber — Choral Music.* Timothy Brown conducts. Gamut Classics CD. **1999 Denyce Graves.** Mezzo-soprano Denyce Graves sings Erika's aria "Must the winter come so soon?" on her 1999 album *Voce di Donna.* She is accompanied by the Munich Radio Orchestra led by Maurizio Barbacini. RCA Red Seal CD. **1999 Renée Fleming.** Renée Fleming sings Vanessa's aria "Do not utter a word" on her album *I Want Magic: American Opera Arias.* She is accompanied by James Levine conducting the Metropolitan Opera Orchestra. London Classics CD. **1999 Seattle Opera.** Sherry Greenawald sings the role of Vanessa on a broadcast of a Seattle Opera production. Kimberly Barber is Erika, Shirley Nadler is the Old Baroness, Paul Charles Clark is Anatol, Charles Stilwell is the Doctor and Archie Drake is the Major Domo. Yves Abel conducts the Seattle Opera Orchestra. Classic Opera audiocassette. **2003 Washington Opera Commentary.** Saul Lilienstein analyses *Vanessa* on this recording in the Washington Opera *Commentaries on CD* series. Washington Opera CD. **2004 Ukraine recording.** Gil Rose conducts the National Symphony Orchestra of the Ukraine and the Ukrainian National Capella "Dumka" in this excellent studio recording. Ellen Chickering sings Vanessa, Andrea Matthews is Erika, Marion Dry is the Old Baroness, Ray Bauwens is Anatol, Richard Conrad is the Doctor and Philip Lima is the Major Domo. Naxos 2-CD box. **2004 Barbican.** Susan Graham plays Erika opposite Christine Brewer as Vanessa, William Burden as Anatol and Catherine Wyn-Rogers as the Old Baroness in this acclaimed British studio recording based on a Barbican performance. Leonard Slatkin leads the BBC Singers and Orchestra. Chandos SACD.

VAN ETTEN, JANE   *American composer (1871–?)*

Jane Van Etten was one of the first American woman composers to have an opera produced by a regular opera company. Her one-act GUIDO FERRANTI, libretto by Elsie M. Wilbor based on Oscar Wilde's play *The Duchess of Padua,* was premiered by the Century Opera Company at the Auditorium Chicago on December 29, 1914, and awarded the David Bispham Memorial Medal for an American opera. Van Etten, who was born in St. Paul, Minnesota, studied music in New York, Paris and London and made her debut singing Siébel in *Faust* at Drury Lane in London in 1895. After her marriage in 1901, she gave up singing for composing.

VAN GROVE, ISAAC   *American composer/conductor (1892–1979)*

Isaac Van Grove, who was awarded the David Bispham Memorial Medal in 1925 for an opera about Mozart's last days, waited thirty years to write six more, all religious. The award winner was the two-act *The Music Robber,* libretto by Richard Stokes, which premiered in its final form by Cincinnati Opera on July 4, 1926. It featured Forrest Lamont as Mozart and Kathryne Browne as Constanze with the composer conducting. The six religious operas were created for summer performances in Arkansas. *The Other Wise Man,* libretto by the composer, was presented in Bentonville, Arkansas, on July 14, 1959. It tells the story of a fourth wise man on his way to Bethlehem who gives his gifts of jewels away before he arrives; he has good reasons. It was reprised at the Opera in the Ozarks festival at Inspiration Point Fine Arts Colony in Eureka Springs, Arkansas, where his other operas were staged. *The Shining Chalice,*

libretto by Janice Lovoos based on her play about a boy in the Middle Ages who makes a chalice for a blind Crusader king, premiered July 30, 1964. *Ruth,* libretto by Lovoos, was staged on July 22, 1966. *The Prodigal, His Wandering Years,* libretto by Lovoos, was performed July 18, 1976. Also presented in Eureka Springs were *Miracles of Our Lady* and *Noe's Fludde.* Van Grove, who was born in Philadelphia, studied at the Chicago Musical College and was a conductor with the Chicago Civic Opera Company for five seasons in the 1920s; he later conducted in Columbus and Cincinnati.

VANQUI   *1999 opera by Burrs*

Runaway slave Prince is killed during a revolt and his wife Vanqui is sold to a plantation where she is murdered. They become spirits "riding the wind," searching for each other and meeting African American heroes and heroines like Nat Turner and Harriet Tubman during the slavery period. African American composer Leslie Savoy Burrs opera *Vanqui,* libretto by John A. Williams based on Virginia Hamilton's book *Many Thousands Gone,* was commissioned by Opera/Columbus in 1993. It was premiered in concert form in Columbus on February 27, 1999, with Carmen Balthrop as Vanqui, Michael Forest as Prince, Pamela Dillard as Garner/Moremi, Benita Valente as Melody Cardwell, Reginald Pindellas as Nat Turner and William Florescu as John Brown. They were supported by the Raise Mass Choir and Opera Columbus Orchestra conducted by Gary Sheldon with augmentation from the African American ensemble Chakaba. The opera was fully staged by the company on October 15 with Balthrop as Vanqui and Roderick Dixon as Prince.

VARGAS, MILAGRO   *American mezzo-soprano (1956–)*

Milagro Vargas created the role of Nefertiti in Philip Glass's AKHNATEN at the Stuttgart State Opera in 1984 and sings the role on the recording. She sings Ma Moss in the 1999 New Music Ensemble recording of Aaron Copland's THE TENDER LAND and reprised the role on stage in 2000 with the Cabrillo Music Festival. Vargas, a native New Yorker, studied at Oberlin and Eastman House. She was a soloist with the Stuttgart Opera from 1983 to 1992 and joined the University of Oregon School of Music faculty in 1992.

VARNAY, ASTRID   *American soprano (1918–)*

Astrid Varnay created the role of Telea in Gian Carlo Menotti's THE ISLAND GOD at the Metropolitan Opera in 1942. She sings the part of the Old Woman in a 1955 recording of Raffaelo de Banfield's LORD BYRON'S LOVE LETTER and the part of Mother Goose in a 1983 recording of Igor Stravinsky's THE RAKE'S PROGRESS. Varnay was born in Stockholm but her family emigrated to America when she was a child. She studied privately in New York and made her debut at the Met in 1941 as Sieglinde.

THE VEIL   *1950 opera by Rogers*

Lucinda has been put in an insane asylum by her brother so he can control her fortune. Dr Keane believes in her sanity but Dr. Betts, who is in charge, falls in love with Lucinda and forces her to undergo a mock marriage ceremony wearing a bridal veil. As Keane attempts to rescue her, she is strangled by Betts. Bernard Rogers' macabre 70-minute one-act opera *The Veil,* libretto by Robert Lawrence. was premiered at Indiana University in Bloomington on May 18, 1950. The music is mostly gloomy and atonal.

VENUS IN AFRICA   *1957 opera by Antheil*

George Antheil's one-act opera *Venus in Africa,* libretto by M. Dyne, was premiered at the University of Denver in Colorado on

May 24, 1957. Marilyn Winters sang the role of Yvonne, Richard Schleffer was Charles and Winifred Magoun was the Girl. Waldo Williams conducted the orchestra.

VERA OF LAS VEGAS   *1996 "cabaret opera" by Hagen*

Dumdum and Taco, who are IRA volunteers on the run, are hiding out in Las Vegas. They are tricked and conned by Doll, a rogue INS agent/stewardess, and her friend Vera, an African American transvestite, There is plenty of deception all round. Daron Eric Hagen's "nightmare cabaret opera" *Vera of Las Vegas*, libretto by Paul Muldoon, was commissioned by the University of Nevada Las Vegas Opera Theater and premiered at the Artemus W. Ham Concert Hall in Las Vegas on March 8, 1996. Carolann Page was Doll, Charles Maxwell was Vera, Paul Kreider was Dumdum and Patrick Jones was Taco. Hagen conducted the University of Nevada Las Vegas Opera Theater Chorus and Orchestra. The score features guitars, synthesizer and orchestra vocalists in addition to normal instruments.

1996 University of Nevada Las Vegas Opera Theater. Carolann Page is Doll, Charles Maxwell is Vera, Paul Kreider is Dumdum and Patrick Jones is Taco in this live recording of the opera made at the University of Nevada Las Vegas on 8, 9 and 10 March 1996. Hagen conducts the University of Nevada Las Vegas Opera Theater Chorus and Orchestra. CRI CD.

VERMONT   *American state (1791–)*

Vermont has opera companies in Montpelier and Norwich but does not have a strong opera tradition. However, opera composer Otto Luening was director of music at Bennington College from 1934 to 1944 and he helped make it into a center for new music. Operas set in Vermont include Stephen Paulus's THE VILLAGE SINGER, based on a Mary Wilkins Freeman story about a singer in a Vermont church who does not want to be replaced.

Bennington. Jack Serulnikoff's one-act *This Evening* was premiered at Bennington College on June 20, 1960. **Montpelier.** Vermont Opera Theater, which presents operas from the standard repertory, is based in Montpelier. **Norwich.** Opera North, a community opera company founded in 1981 and supported by the adjacent cities of Norwich in Vermont and Lebanon in New Hampshire, produces operas at the Lebanon Opera House. It has staged Domenick ARGENTO'S THE BOOR, Carlisle Floyd's SUSANNAH, Henry Mollicone's THE FACE ON THE BARROOM FLOOR and Gian Carlo Menotti's THE MEDIUM.

VERRALL, JOHN   *American composer (1908–)*

John Verrall, who based his music on a nine-note scale of his own devising, composed three operas using this unique system. All three were premiered at the University of Washington in Seattle where they were produced and directed by John Chapple. *The Cowherd and the Sky Maiden*, libretto by E. Shepherd based on a Chinese legend, was staged on January 17, 1952. *The Wedding Knell*, libretto by the composer based on the story by Nathaniel Hawthorne, premiered December 5, 1952. *Three Blind Mice,* libretto by G. Hughes, was presented May 22, 1955. Verrall was born in Britt, Iowa, and studied in London and Budapest and with Aaron Copland and Roy Harris. He taught at the University of Washington from 1948 to 1973 and his students included opera composer William Bolcom. Verrall also composed chamber and orchestral pieces and even a film score.

VERRETT, SHIRLEY   *American mezzo-soprano/soprano (1931–)*

Shirley Verrett began to sing with New York City Opera in 1958 using the name Shirley Carter and her first role was that of Irina in Kurt Weill's LOST IN THE STARS. She created the title role of Queen Athaliah in Hugo Weisgall's ATHALIAH for the Concert Opera Association at the Philharmonic Hall in New York in 1964 and she sings Netti in the 1994 Lincoln Center recording of Richard Rodgers' CAROUSEL. Verrett, who was born in New Orleans, studied at Juilliard and made her debut in Yellow Springs, Ohio, in 1957. She began to sing at the Met in 1968 moving from mezzo roles to soprano parts like Tosca and Aida. She is best known, however, for her performances as Carmen.

VIDE COR MEUM   *2001 American "movie opera"*

Patrick Cassidy created a mini-opera called *Vide Cor Meum* (See Your Heart) for the film *Hannibal* with a libretto based on Dante's *La Vita Nuova;* in it he describes his first attempts at poetry and his famous meeting with Beatrice. This MOVIE OPERA is staged by Cassidy and Hans Zimmer in period costume in a palace in Florence, Italy, as if it were one of the early operas created by the Camerata around 1600. Bruno Lazzaretti sings the role of Dante and Danielle de Niese is Beatrice with the music played by the Lyndhurst Orchestra led by Gavin Greenaway. Only about a minute or so of the opera is seen, but there is more on the film soundtrack album. Attending the performance are serial killer Hannibal Lecter (Anthony Hopkins) and the policeman who is trying to catch him (Giancarlo Giannini). The film is a sequel to *The Silence of the Lambs* and carries on the gruesome adventures of Lecter. Ridley Scott directed from a screenplay by David Mamet and Steven Zaillian based on the novel by Thomas Harris.

VIENNESE NIGHTS   *1930 screen operetta by Romberg*

Vienna in 1879. Elsa, a beautiful young woman who works in a shop, is in love with Otto, a struggling composer. but misunderstandings cause her to marry Franz, a baron's son. In 1890 they meet again in New York and almost resume their romance. Finally, in 1930, Elsa's granddaughter Barbara finds happiness with Otto's grandson, also a composer. Sigmund Romberg's bittersweet *Viennese Nights,* libretto by Oscar Hammerstein II, was the first of two operettas the pair wrote for Warner Brothers following the success of THE DESERT SONG. Vivienne Segal is Elsa, Alexander Gray is Otto and his grandson, Walter Pidgeon is Franz, Bert Roach is Gus and Alice Day is Barbara. James Van Trees was the cinematographer, Louis Silvers was the music director and Alan Crosland directed. The most popular song was "You Will Remember Vienna." *Viennese Nights* was not a success so Romberg and Hammerstein were only allowed to create one other screen operetta for Warner Bros., *Children of Dreams* (1931), a lost movie.

A VIEW FROM THE BRIDGE   *1999 opera by Bolcom*

Eddie and Beatrice Carbone, who live in a Brooklyn Italian community in the 1950s, maintain a strong Sicilian identity. Eddie becomes obsessed with his wife's Americanized niece Catherine and, when she falls in love with illegal immigrant Rodolpho, betrays him to the authorities. Sicily's code of honor demands a fight to the death. William Bolcom's opera *A View from the Bridge,* libretto by Arnold Weinstein and Arthur Miller based on Miller's play, was premiered by Lyric Opera of Chicago on October 9, 1999. Kim Josephson was Eddie Carbone, Catherine Malfitano was Beatrice, Juliana Rambaldi was Catherine, Timothy Nolen was Alfieri, Gregory Turay was Rodolpho, Mark McCrory was Marco, Dale Travis was Louis, Jeffrey Picón was Mike, Marlin Miller was Tony, Gale Scott Bower was the First Officer, Michael Sommese was Second Officer. Gwendolyn Brown was Old Woman, Ronald Watkins was Man and Sheryl Veal was Woman. Santa Loquasto designed sets and costumes, Frank Galalt directed and Dennis Russell Davies conducted Chicago Lyric Opera Chorus and Orchestra. The opera was exceptionally well reviewed and was reprised by the Metropolitan Opera in New York in 2003 with Josephson again playing Eddie Carbone, Malfitano as Beatrice and Turay as Rodolpho but with Isabel Bayrakdraian as Catherine.

1999 Lyric Opera of Chicago. The opera was recorded live at the Lyric Opera in October/November 1999, broadcast nationally on May 13, 2000, and released on CD in 2001. Kim Josephson is Eddie, Catherine Malfitano is Beatrice, Juliana Rambaldi is Catherine, Timothy Nolen is Alfieri, Gregory Turay is Rodolpho, Mark McCrory is Marco, Dale Travis is Louis, Marlin Miller is Tony, Jeffrey Picón is Mike. Gale Scott Bower is First Officer, Michael Sommese is Second Officer, Gwendolyn Brown is Old Woman, Ronald Watkins is Man and Sheryl Veal is Woman. Dennis Russell Davies conducts Chicago Lyric Opera Chorus and Orchestra. New World 2-CD box. **1999 Lyric Opera of Chicago Commentary.** Critical analysis of *A View from the Bridge* By Roger Pines with comments from composer William Bolcom in the *Women's Board of Lyric Opera* series. It features plot summary, musical excerpts, composer biography and social and historical background. Lyric Opera Commentaries audiocassette.

VILLA-LOBOS, HEITOR   *Brazilian composer (1887–1959)*

Heitor Villa-Lobos, the leading Brazilian composer of the 20th century, created two operas on American commissions that premiered in the U.S. The light opera MAGDALENA, composed while he was living in New York, has a libretto by Robert Wright and George Forrest, the creators of *Kismet* and *Song of Norway*. It premiered in Los Angeles in 1947 and had a Broadway run. The tragic opera YERMA, based on a Lorca play, was commissioned by John Blankenship of St. Lawrence College and was to have been staged with an all-black cast in 1956. The production was called off and the opera was not staged until after the composers' death. It was premiered by Santa Fe Opera on August 12, 1971, with Frederica von Stade in the leading role.

THE VILLAGE   *1995 opera by Mandelbaum*

A young Jewish boy named Daniel Cohen is hidden by the Catholic Bernaud family in a French village from 1942 to 1944. Letters from his mother explain what is happening. Joel Mandelbaum's three-act opera *The Village*, libretto by poet Susan Fox based on her husband's experiences as a child, premiered at the Queens College Theater on Long Island on March 25, 1995. Nine-year-old Zachary Wissner-Gross sang the role of David Cohen, Mary Beth Cunningham was his mother, Korby Myrick was Mrs. Bernaud, Gina Jones was her daughter Sophie, Arthur Francesco was the baker, Sean Banayan was the baker's son, Eric Thomas was the mayor, Rufus Hallmark was the priest, Robert Campbell was the villager and Arizeder Urreiztieta was the German officer. Susan Einhort staged the opera and Doris Lang Kosloff conducted the Queens College Orchestra and Chorus.

THE VILLAGE SINGER   *1979 opera by Paulus*

Candace Whitcomb, a woman in her 60s who has been the soloist in her church for 40 years, is replaced by the young singer Alma Way. She refuses to accept the change gracefully and begins to compete with her replacement by continuing to sing during services. Stephen Paulus' 60-minute chamber opera *The Village Singer*, libretto by Michael Browne based on a story by Mary

Wilkins Freeman, was premiered by Opera Theater of St. Louis on June 9, 1979. Pauline Tinsley was Candace, Elizabeth Pruett was Alma, Marc Embree was choir director William Emmons, Jerry Hadley was Todd Wilkins, David Hillman was Wilson Ford, Fredda Rakusin was Nancy Ford, Brenda Warren was Jenny Carr, Carolee Coomb-Stacy was Minnie Lansing, Paul Barrientos was Brent Freeman, and Melvin Lowery was the Rev, Pollard. Maxine Willi Klein designed the sets, Colin Grahm directed and C. William Harwood conducted. This was Paulus's first opera and the beginning of a long collaboration with Opera Theater of St. Louis. *The Village Singer*, which is lyrical and tonal, incorporates a number of traditional hymns into the score. It has been revived many times, including productions in Chattanooga, Charlottetown, Denver, Eureka Springs, Madison, Minneapolis, New York, Santa Barbara and Wilmington.

VIRGIL'S DREAM   *1967 opera by Colgrass*

Virgil, a seven-year-old music prodigy, has his dream of future success insured. The insurance company trains him for his concert career but discovers that he is shrinking. At his debut in Carnegie Hall ten years later, he shrinks away to nothing. Michael Colgrass's opera *Virgil's Dream*, libretto by the composer, premiered at the Brighton Festival in England in April 1967. Virgil is not seen but is portrayed by four on-stage musicians, one of whom is a percussionist. The singing roles are Virgil's mother and three insurance company officials. The opera was reprised at Xavier University in New Orleans in 1972 and produced in New York in 1976.

VIRGINIA   *American state (1788–)*

Virginia is home to a number of opera festivals and companies, including Virginia Opera of Norfolk, one of the fifteen largest in the U.S. Virginia-born opera people include soprano Roberta Alexander (Lynchburg), librettist Edward Albee, composer Alvin Carmines (Hampton), mezzo-soprano Cynthia Clarey (Smithfield), composer Charles Hamm (Charlottesville), librettist John Latouche (Richmond), baritone John Charles Thomas (Meyersdale), soprano Camilla Williams (Danville) and composer Maurice Wright (Front Royal). Operas set in Virginia include Seymour Barab's PHILIP MARSHALL, based on Dostoevsky's novel *The Idiot* transposed to Virginia.

Alexandria: Alexandria is the home of Capital City Opera which presents operas from the standard repertory.

Arlington: Alma Grace Miller's *The Whirlwind* premiered at Washington-Lee Auditorium on September 24, 1953. Opera Theater of Northern Virginia, located in Arlington, was founded in 1961. Its adventurous American opera presentations have included George Gershwin's BLUE MONDAY, Victor Herbert's MADELEINE, Charles Strouse's NIGHTINGALE and the premiere of M. Hull's *Nancy*. Opera Music Theater International is based in Arlington.

Bristol: Charles Hamm's *The Salesgirl* was premiered at Virginia Intermont College on March 1, 1955.

Charlottesville: Ash Lawn Opera Festival, started in 1978, is held near Charlottesville at Ash Lawn-Highland, the historic home of President James Monroe. It began presenting American opera when it premiered Judith Shatin's one-act *Follies and Fancies,* based on Molière's *Les Précieuses Ridicules,* on August 14, 1981. Other American presentations have included Mark Adamo's LITTLE WOMEN, Aaron Copland's THE TENDER LAND, Frederick Loewe's CAMELOT, Gian Carlo Menotti's THE TELEPHONE, Henry Mollicone's THE FACE ON THE BARROOM FLOOR, Richard Rodgers' CAROUSEL and SOUTH PACIFIC and Meredith Willson's THE MUSIC MAN.

Norfolk: Francesco Fanciulli's opera *Priscilla, the Maid of Plymouth*, based on Longfellow's narrative poem *The Courtship of Miles Standish*, was premiered in Norfolk on November 1, 1901, and taken on tour (Fanciulli was John Philip Sousa's successor at leader of the Marine Band). Virginia Opera, the state's leading opera company, has premiered and recorded most of Thea Musgrave's operas; her husband Peter Mark is the company director. MARY, QUEEN OF SCOTS, was staged on March 29, 1978, and then recorded. A CHRISTMAS CAROL, based on the Dickens tale, was premiered December 7, 1979, and recorded. HARRIET, THE WOMAN CALLED MOSES, about an African American slave who helped free other slaves, was premiered on March 1, 1985. SIMÓN BOLÍVAR, about the South American liberator, was premiered on January 29, 1995. The company also premiered Michael Ching's CUE 67 on January 24, 1992, in a double bill with Gian Carlo Menotti's THE MEDIUM. It has staged Leonard Bernstein's WEST SIDE STORY, Aaron Copland's THE TENDER LAND, George Gershwin's PORGY AND BESS, Mitch Leigh's MAN OF LA MANCHA and Menotti's AMAHL AND THE NIGHT VISITORS. Sherman Krane's one-act opera *The Giant's Garden* was premiered at William and Mary College on March 12, 1960. Robert Kelly's folk opera *Tod's Gal* was premiered at Old Dominion University on January 8, 1971.

Richmond: Allan Blank's *The Noise*, based on a surrealistic story by Boris Vian, premiered at Virginia Commonwealth University, where Blank was teaching, in April 1986.

Roanoke: Arthur Kreutz's "folk opera" SOURWOOD MOUNTAIN was staged in Roanoke in 1959. Opera Roanoke, which began in 1976 as Southwest Virginia Opera, opened with an American opera, Gian Carlo Menotti's THE CONSUL. It premiered Milton Granger's one-act opera *The Proposal* on November 1, 1988, after it had won a National Opera Association competition. It premiered Victoria Bond's *Travels*, a contemporary version of *Gulliver's Travels*, on May 18, 1995. The company's other American music theater productions include Victor Herbert's NAUGHTY MARIETTA, Douglas Moore's THE BALLAD OF BABY DOE, Sigmund Romberg's THE STUDENT PRINCE, Stephen Sondheim's SWEENEY TODD and Wright-Forrest's KISMET. Hollins College in Roanoke has premiered several other operas by Milton Granger: *Troy NY, 1869*, in November 1977, *The Great Man's Widow* and *Sparkplugs* in November 1986, *The Queen Bee* in November 1987 and *O Henry's Christmas Carol* in December 1988.

Vienna: The Wolf Trap Opera company has created an international reputation for its quality productions and strong American opera programming. Inaugurated in 1971, it premiered Thomas Pasatieri's SIGNORE DELUSO, based on Molière's *Sganarelle*, at the Madeira School on July 17, 1974, in a double bill with the composer's church opera CALVARY. It premiered Stephen Douglas Burton's *The Duchess of Malfi*, based on the play by John Webster, on August 18, 1978. The company's other American productions include Dominick Argento's POSTCARD FROM MOROCCO, Marc Blitzstein's REGINA, Victor Giannini's THE TAMING OF THE SHREW, Scott Joplin's TREEMONISHA, Frank Loesser's THE MOST HAPPY FELLA, Gian Carlo Menotti's THE MEDIUM, THE SAINT OF BLEECKER STREET and THE TELEPHONE, Cole Porter's KISS ME KATE, Richard Rodger's THE KING AND I, Stephen Sondheim's A LITTLE NIGHT MUSIC, Conrad Susa's TRANSFORMATIONS, Robert Ward's THE CRUCIBLE, Kurt Weill's DOWN IN THE VALLEY and the Wright/Forrest KISMET. Wolf Trap has also hosted other opera companies which stage American operas, including Minneapolis Center Opera which presented John Gessner's *Faust Counter Faust* and Virgil Thomson's THE MOTHER OF US ALL.

A VISIT TO THE COUNTRY   *1987 opera by Wargo*

A once-wealthy woman landowner tries to save her estate by marrying her younger sister to a rich lawyer. It doesn't work out. Richard Wargo's bittersweet one-act opera *A Visit to the Country*, libretto by the composer based on a Chekhov story, was commissioned by Greater Miami Opera which premiered it in 1987. It was staged as the second part of Wargo's A CHEKHOV TRILOGY in 1993. In 1996 the Philadelphia Academy of Vocal Arts Opera Theater presented a much-praised production by Dorothy Danner with Megan Dey-Toth, Hugh Smith and Amy Schroeder in the principal roles.

THE VISITATION   *1966 opera by Schuller*

Black student Carter Jones is threatened by the white men in his small Southern town. After a flirtation with white neighbor Miss Hampton, he is put on trial and nearly hanged. He asks for help but no one will do anything; finally he is beaten and killed. Gunther Schuller's three-act opera *The Visitation*, libretto by the composer loosely based on Franz Kafka's novel *The Trial*, was premiered by Hamburg's Staatsoper on October 12, 1966. American baritone McHenry Boatwright sang the role of Carter Jones with strong support from Jeanette Scovotti as Miss Hampton, Simon Estes as Uncle Albert, Tatiana Troyanos, Tom Krause, Felicia Weather, Heinz Blankenburg, Kim Borg, Helmut Melcher, Peter Roth Ehrang, Carl Schultz and William de Valentine. Schuller himself conducted. The opera opens and closes with Bessie Smith's recording of "Nobody Knows You When You're Down and Out" and mixes jazz and blues with modernist classical devices, serial techniques and quarter tones. Schuller has also written an orchestral suite based on the opera.

"VOCALISE"   *Soprano aria: The Tempest (1986). Music: Lee Hoiby.*

The spirit Ariel is alone and suspended from a cloud on a remote island ruled by the shipwrecked Prospero. He sings of his feelings about the night and the moon. "Vocalise," a wordless coloratura aria for soprano with music by Lee Hoiby, is featured in his 1986 opera *The Tempest* based on the play by Shakespeare. It was introduced on stage by Constance Hauman at the beginning of the second scene of Act II. Robert Larsen and Martha Gerhart feature it in their book *Coloratura Arias for Sopranos* (2002/G. Schirmer).

THE VOICE OF FIRESTONE   *NBC radio/TV music programs (1928–1963)*

The Voice of Firestone started as an NBC radio show featuring popular music. In later years, and especially after it became a television show in 1949, it features opera singers who sometimes performed arias from American operas and operettas. Arias from PORGY AND BESS, for example, were sung on the TV program by Eleanor Steber and Jerome Hines while Risë Stevens, Roberta Peters, George London, Patrice Munsel and Robert Merrill sang arias from NAUGHTY MARIETTA. In 1963 Hines presented a ten-minute excerpt from the sacred opera I AM THE WAY which he had composed. The Firestone Orchestra was usually conducted by Howard Barlow, long an advocate of American operatic music. Selections from kinescopes of telecast have been issued on VAI video while radio broadcasts can be heard at the Museum of Television and Radio.

VOICES OF LIGHT   *1994 opera by Einhorn*

Joan of Arc, tried for heresy after she leads the French to victory over the English, is burned at the stake in 1431. Richard

Einhorn's opera/oratorio *Voices of Light*, libretto by the composer based on medieval texts, was composed to be sung with Carl Dreyer's 1928 silent film *La Passion de Jeanne d'Arc*. There are four soloists with two singers performing the role of Joan. *Voices of Light* was premiered in Northampton, MA, in February 1994, by the Arcadia Players conducted by Margaret Irwin-Brandon. Dreyer's classic film, which stars Falconetti as Joan, is based on transcripts of her trial. The opera was reprised at the Brooklyn Academy of Music in 1994 and presented at the Hollywood Bowl in 1995.

1995 Anonymous Four. The Anonymous Four are the voice of Joan on this recording of the opera made in Holland with the Netherlands Radio Choir and Netherlands Radio Philharmonic. conducted by Steven Mercurio. The Anonymous Four (Ruth Cunningham, Marsha Genensky, Susan Hellauer and Johanna Rose) are partnered with soprano Susan Narucki, alto Corrie Pronk, tenor Frank Hameleers and bass-baritone Henk van Heijnsbergen. Sony Classical CD. **2000 Criterion DVD.** The DVD version of the Dreyer opera features Einhorn's oratorio as the soundtrack for the film. Falconetti stars as Joan and gives one of the most harrowing performances ever filmed. Criterion DVD.

VOLPONE   *American operas based on Jonson play*

Volpone, a rich Venetian conman, the fox of the title, works with his servant Mosca on schemes to swindle unlikable victims. Ben Jonson's play *Volpone*, written in 1605, has been very popular on stage and attracted a number of opera composers. The original plot, often altered in modern versions, features Volpone in a scheme to defraud his neighbors by pretending he is near death. Two American operas based on the play are listed below. A film version titled *The Honey Pot* was produced in 1967 with Rex Harrison as the Venetian swindler.

1953 George Antheil. George Antheil's three-act opera *Volpone*, libretto by Albert Perry based on the play by Ben Jonson, was premiered by the Opera Workshop of the University of Southern California in Los Angeles on January 9, 1953. Paul Keast was Volpone, Caesar Curzi was Mosca, Marilyn Hall was Celia, Francis Barnes was Corvine, Phyllis Althof was Pepita and Grace-Lynne Martin was Nina. Carl Ebert was director and Wolfgang Martin conducted the orchestra. *Volpone* is considered by critics to be Antheil's most successful later opera, full of comic invention and attractive melodies. **2004 John Musto.** John Musto's opera *Volpone*, libretto by Mark Campbell based on Ben Jonson's play which follows the original story fairly closely, was premiered by Wolf Trap Opera on March 10, 2004. Joshua Winograde played Volpone, Joseph Kaiser was Mosca, Ryan Taylor was lawyer Voltore, Ross Hauck was Bonario, Jason Ferrante was Corbaccio, Sarah Wolfson was Celia, Adriana Zabala was Erminella, and Wendy Hill was Corvina. Erhard Rom designed the sets, Leon Major directed and Michael Barrett conducted.

VON STADE, FREDERICA   *American mezzo-soprano (1945–)*

Frederica von Stade created major roles in five American operas and sang in operatic recordings of three musicals. She was Maria in Heitor Villa-Lobos YERMA at Santa Fe Opera in 1971, Nina in Thomas Pasatieri's THE SEAGULL at Houston Grand Opera in 1974, Tina in Domenick Argento's THE ASPERN PAPERS, at Dallas Opera in 1988, Marquise de Merteuil in Conrad Susa's THE DANGEROUS LIAISONS at San Francisco Opera in 1994 and the Mother of condemned killer Joseph in Jake Heggie's DEAD MAN WALKING at San Francisco Opera in 2000. She sings the role of Maria in the 1987 recording of Richard Rodgers' THE SOUND OF MUSIC, Mag-

nolia in the 1988 recording of Jerome Kern's SHOW BOAT and Claire in the 1992 recording of Leonard Bernstein's ON THE TOWN. She sang Erika's aria "Must the Winter Come So Soon?" from Samuel Barber's VANESSA in a televised Lincoln Center concert in 1991 and starred in a Houston Grand Opera production of Stephen Sondheim's A LITTLE NIGHT MUSIC in 1999. Von Stade, born in Somerville, NJ, studied at Mannes College of Music in New York and made her debut at the Metropolitan Opera in 1970.

VOODOO   *1928 opera by Freeman*

Incidents in the life of African American ex-slaves on a plantation in Louisiana after the Civil War. Harry Lawrence Freeman's opera *Voodoo*, libretto by the composer, was broadcast in a 30-minute highlights version on WGBS Radio in New York City on May 20, 1928, the first American opera to premiere on radio. Freeman's Negro Grand Opera Company staged the complete three-act opera at the Palm Garden in New York on September 10, 1928.

THE VOYAGE   *1992 opera by Glass*

A scientist in a wheelchair descends from the skies and meditates on the idea of exploration. During a long ago Ice Age humans on a spaceship make a forced landing on Earth. In 1492 Columbus remembers Queen Isabella of Spain as his ship Santa Maria approaches land after 32 days at sea. In the year 2092 space and earth twins rediscover their origins and start another voyage of discovery. Philip Glass's three-act opera *The Voyage*, libretto by David Henry Hwang based on a story by the composer, premiered at the Metropolitan Opera on October 12, 1992. It was commissioned by the Met to celebrate the 500th anniversary of Columbus's discovery of America. Douglas Perry was Scientist/First Mate, Patricia Schuman was Commander, Tatiana Troyanos was Queen Isabella, Timothy Noble was Columbus, Kaaren Erickson was Ship's Doctor/Space Twin #1, Julien Robbins was Second Mate/Space Twin #2, Jane Shaulis was Earth Twin #1 and Jan Opalach was Earth Twin #2. Robert Israel designed the sets, David Pountney directed the production and Bruce Ferden conducted the Metropolitan Opera Orchestra. The production was reprised by the Met on April 6, 1996, with Philip Creech as Scientist/First Mate, Patricia Schuman as Commander, Sally Burgess as Queen Isabella and Timothy Noble as Columbus. Dennis Russell Davies conducted.

1992 Metropolitan Opera. The opera premiere was broadcast on October 12, 1992, with the cast as above headed by Douglas Perry, Patricia Schuman, Tatiana Troyanos and Timothy Noble. Bruce Ferden conducted. The broadcast lasted 195 minutes with Glass being interviewed during an intermission. Recording at New York Public Library for the Performing Arts. **1996 Metropolitan Opera.** The opera was broadcast a second time on April 6, 1992, with cast as above headed by Philip Creech, Patricia Schuman, Sally Burgess and Timothy Noble. Dennis Russell Davies conducted. Glass and Davies were interviewed during the intermissions. Recording at New York Public Library for the Performing Arts. **1996 Vienna Radio Symphony.** The "Mechanical Ballet" from *The Voyage* is performed by the Vienna Radio Symphony Orchestra in a recording made in September 1996. It's on the 2000 Glass album *Symphony No. 3*. Electra Nonesuch CD.

THE VOYAGE OF EDGAR ALLAN POE   *1976 opera By Argento*

Edgar Allan Poe boards a phantom ship in 1849 on the night of his death and his past life is shown in flashbacks. Dominick Argento's opera *The Voyage of Edgar Allan Poe*, libretto by Charles Nolte based on Poe's writings, was premiered by Minnesota Opera

Studio in St. Paul on April 24, 1976, with George Livings as Poe and Karen Hunt as Virginia Poe. Most of the cast played multiple roles. Barbara Brandt was Mrs. Poe/Ballad Singer, Vern Sutton was Doctor/Wedding Guest/Passenger, Kathryn Asman was Nancy/ Mrs. Clemm, John Brandstetter was Griswold/Captain/Mr. Allan, Rose Taylor was Granny Poe/Mrs. Allan, Peter Strummer was Theater Director/M. Dupin, Linda Smith-Collins was Rosy and Philip Jore was Willie. Philip Brunelle conducted the Minnesota Opera Studio orchestra and University of Minnesota Chamber Singers. The premiere was recorded and videotaped but is not available commercially. The opera was reprised in Chicago in 1991 and in Dallas in 1992.

1990 Lyric Opera of Chicago Commentary. Critical analysis of *The Voyage of Edgar Allan Poe* by Alfred Glasser and Frank Galati in the *Women's Board of Lyric Opera* series. It includes plot summary, musical excerpts, composer biography and social and historical background. Lyric Opera Commentaries audiocassette. **1991 Lyric Opera of Chicago.** Donald Kaasch plays Poe in a radio broadcast of the opera performed by the Lyric Opera of Chicago. John Duykers was the Doctor, Richard Stilwell was Griswold, Winifred Faix Brown was Mrs. Poe, Phyllis Pancella was Mrs. Clemm, Jane Shaulis was Mrs. Allan, Stephen West was Theater Director and Ruth Ann Swenson was Virginia Poe. Christopher Keene conducted. The opera was broadcast on May 25, 1991. On audiocassette. **2000 Minnesota Orchestra.** Chad Telton is the featured tenor in a sixteen-minute suite from *The Voyage of Edgar Allan Poe* titled "Le Tombeau d'Edgar Poe." Eiji Oue conducts the Minnesota Orchestra on the album *Valentino Dances*. Reference Recordings CD.

Dominick Argento's imaginative opera *The Voyage of Edgar Allan Poe* was premiered by Minnesota Opera in 1976.

W

THE W. OF BABYLON   *1975 opera by Wuorinen*

A sexy Marquise and an open-minded Chinese Princess misbehave in a French chateau in 1685. Charles Wuorinen's two-act "baroque burlesque opera" *The W. of Babylon: or, The Triumph of Love over Moral Depravity,* libretto by Renaud Charles Bruce, was commissioned by the National Opera Institute for the Light Fantastic Players. It was premiered in an incomplete version at the Manhattan School of Music in New York on December 15, 1975, and the final version was premiered by San Francisco Orchestra in a concert version on January 20, 1989.

WADSWORTH, STEPHEN   *American librettist/director (1953–)*

Stephen Wadsworth is best known as an opera director but he also writes librettos. The first was Jonathan Sheffer's *The Mistake*, a tale about a soprano backstage during an intermission, which was premiered by Central City Opera in 1981. The best-known is the libretto he wrote for Leonard Bernstein's last opera A QUIET PLACE, premiered by Houston Grand Opera in 1983. Wadsworth also directed the opera when it was staged at La Scala and Vienna in 1986. He directed the premiere of Daron Hagen's SHINING BROW at Madison Opera in 1993 and the premiere Peter Lieberson's' ASHOKA'S DREAM at Santa Fe Opera in 1997. Wadsworth, born in Mt. Kisko, NY, began his operatic career as stage and artistic director of Skylight Opera in Milwaukee. He wrote a number of music theater work for Skylight, including *Bernstein Revued* in 1986.

WAITS, TOM   *American composer/singer (1949)*

Singer-songwriter Tom Waits teamed up with producer Robert Wilson and writer William S. Burrough to create the cabaret opera THE BLACK RIDER. It was premiered at the Thalia Theater in Hamburg in 1990 and was presented with the same cast at the Brooklyn Academy of Music in 1994. He teamed with Wilson again for the musical *Alice*, music and lyrics by Waits and Kathleen Brennan with book by Paul Schmidt. It was performed at the Thalia in 1992 and presented at BAM in 1995. Their third collaboration was *Woyzeck*, based on George Büchner's play, which was premiered in Copenhagen, Denmark, in 2002 at the Betty Nansen Theatre and then presented at BAM with the Danish cast. Waits, born in Pomona, CA, became widely known in the 1970s when he began recording his bleak, poetic songs. He has also composed scores for films and was nominated for an Oscar for his score for Francis Ford Coppola's *One from the Heart*.

WALKER, MARGARET   *American novelist/poet (1915–)*

Margaret Walker became known for her poetry following the

publication of *For My People* in 1942. Her 1965 novel *Jubilee,* based on the life of her great grandmother and her progression from slavery to freedom, provided the basis for an African American opera. Ulysses Kay's three-act JUBILEE, libretto by Donald Dorr, was premiered at Jackson State University in 1976.

WALLACE, STEWART   *American composer (1960–)*

Stewart Wallace and his librettist collaborator Michael Korie have created four notable operas. WHERE'S DICK, libretto by Korie based loosely on the comic strip *Dick Tracy,* was premiered by Houston Grand Opera in May 1989. KABBALAH, libretto by Korie in the form of a dramatized ritual based on mystical Jewish texts, was premiered by Dance Theater Workshop at the Brooklyn Academy of Music in November 1989. HARVEY MILK, libretto by Korie about the killing of a gay San Francisco public official by a homophobe, was commissioned by Houston Grand Opera and premiered in Houston in January 1995. HOPPERS' WIFE, libretto by Korie about artist Edward Hopper, gossip columnist Hedda Hopper and actress Ava Gardner and their imagined adventures together in Hollywood in the 1940s, was premiered by Long Beach Opera in June 1997. Wallace's first opera was the rock-oriented *Soapopera,* libretto by Jim Morgan, which was premiered by Texas Opera Theater in Houston on June 6, 1985. He has also composed the opera *Yiddisher Teddy Bears,* libretto by Richard Foreman inspired by klezmer music, which is set in New York's Lower East Side at the turn of the century. Wallace was born in Philadelphia but grew up in Houston and studied at the University of Texas.

WALLER, JUANITA   *American soprano (1939–)*

Juanita Waller created the role of Aurore in William Grant Still's A BAYOU LEGEND when it was premiered by Opera/South in Jackson, Mississippi, in 1974 and she sings the role on the telecast. She has also sung Bess in a production of George Gershwin's *Porgy and Bess.* Waller, born in Pittsburgh, PA, studied at Carnegie-Mellon University and made her debut in Bremen, Germany.

WARD, EDWARD   *American composer (1896–?)*

Edward Ward composed the movie operas AMOUR ET GLOIRE and LE PRINCE MASQUE DE LA CAUCASIE to librettos by George Waggner. Both are elaborately staged in French translations in the Paris Opera in the 1943 MGM opera film *The Phantom of the Opera.* Ward, born in St. Louis, Missouri, studied at the Beethoven School of Music and wrote scores for several Hollywood films and a stage musical.

WARD, ROBERT   *American composer (1917–)*

Robert Ward won the Pulitzer Prize in 1962 for his opera THE CRUCIBLE, libretto by his frequent collaborator Bernard Stambler based on the play by Arthur Miller equating the witch hunts of 17th century Puritan Salem with the Communist hysteria of the 1950s McCarthy era. It was premiered by New York City Opera, recorded and telecast and is frequently revived. Ward's first opera was HE WHO GETS SLAPPED, libretto by Stambler based on Leonid Andreyev's play about a sad circus clown, which premiered at the Juilliard School of Music in 1956 and was reprised at New York City Opera in 1959. THE LADY FROM COLORADO, libretto by Stambler based on a novel by Homer Croy, was premiered in Central City, Colorado, in 1964, but later revised and staged as *Lady Kate.* CLAUDIA LEGARE, libretto by Stambler based on Henrik Ibsen's play *Hedda Gabler* transposed to the American South after the Civil War, was premiered by Minnesota Opera in Minneapolis in 1978. ABELARD AND HELOISE, libretto by Jan Hartman telling the

story of the medieval scholar lovers, was premiered by Charlotte Opera in 1982. MINUTES TILL MIDNIGHT, libretto by Daniel Lang about a scientist concerned with the nuclear threat, was premiered by Greater Miami Opera in 1982. ROMAN FEVER, libretto by Roger Brunyate based on an Edith Wharton story, was premiered by Triangle Opera on June 9, 1993, at Duke University in Durham, NC, and recorded by the Manhattan School in 2001. The church opera *Images of God,* libretto by Susan Chapek and Stuart C. Henry, which features singers, actors, a choir, a minister and organ music, premiered at Duke University Chapel February 19, 1989. Ward, born in Cleveland, Ohio, studied with Howard Hanson and Bernard Rogers at Eastman and Juilliard. He taught at Juilliard for ten years after World War II and at Duke from 1978 to 1987.

WARFIELD, WILLIAM   *American bass (1920–2002)*

William Warfield created the role of Cal in Marc Blitzstein's REGINA in Boston in 1949 and then sang it on Broadway for its run. He played the role of Joe in the 1951 MGM movie of Jerome Kern's SHOW BOAT and sang a justly famous version of "Ol' Man River;" the film is on DVD/VHS and the soundtrack on LP/CD. He also sings Joe on 1962 studio and 1966 Lincoln Center recordings. In 1952 and 1953 he toured Europe in George Gershwin's PORGY AND BESS, singing Porgy to Leontyne Price's Bess, and they recorded it in 1963. He married Price in 1952 but they separated after six years and were divorced in 1972. Warfield was not in the 1953 Broadway production of *Porgy and Bess* (he was on a concert tour) but performed in it there in 1961 and at the Vienna Volksopera in 1971. He made his stage debut in a touring production of Harold Rome's musical *Call Me Mister* in 1947, his Broadway debut in *Regina* in 1949 and his recital debut at Town Hall in New York in 1950. He won a Grammy in 1984 for his narration of Copland's *A Lincoln Portrait.* He became a professor of music at the University of Illinois in 1975 but continued to perform into the 1990s, including singing in productions of *Porgy and Bess* and *Show Boat.* Warfield, who was born in West Helena, Arkansas, and raised in Rochester, NY, studied music at the Eastman School.

WARGO, RICHARD   *American composer (1957–)*

Richard Wargo, a native of Scranton, PA, is best known for A CHEKHOV TRILOGY, three one-act operas based on stories by Anton Chekhov presented together for the first time in 1993. The poignant THE SEDUCTION OF A LADY, libretto by the composer based on Neal Simon's play *The Good Doctor* derived from a Chekhov story, was first performed by the National Institute for Music Theater in New York in 1984 and officially premiered by Florida State University in 1985. The comic THE MUSIC SHOP, libretto by the composer based on the Chekhov story *Forgot,* was first performed by Minnesota Opera in Minneapolis in 1984. The bittersweet A VISIT TO THE COUNTRY, libretto by the composer based on a Chekhov story, was commissioned by Greater Miami Opera which premiered it in 1987. Wargo's opera BALLYMORE, libretto by the composer based on Brian Friel's Irish play duo *Lovers,* was premiered by Skylight Opera Theater in 1999. Wargo's earlier operas include *The Crystal Mirror,* libretto by the composer based on Nathaniel Hawthorne's story *Dr. Heidegger's Experiment,* which was presented at the Eastman School of Music in Rochester, NY, on April 28, 1979, and *The River Flow,* composed in 1982.

WARING, KATE   *American composer (1953–)*

Kate Waring has had both of her operas produced. The chamber opera *Rapunzel,* libretto by Rudiger Gollnick based on a

Grimm fairytale, was premiered in Bonn, Germany, on November 7, 1989. The children's opera *A. B. C. America Before Columbus*, libretto by Joseph Robinette, was commissioned by Opera-Delaware which premiered it in March 1993. Waring is a native of Alexandria, Louisiana.

WARREN, LEONARD   *American baritone (1911–1960)*

Leonard Warren created the role of the worshiper Ilo in Gian Carlo Menotti's THE ISLAND GOD at the Metropolitan Opera in 1942. He can be seen in performance on TV in 1949 on the *Voice of Firestone* singing "Will You Remember" from Sigmund Romberg's MAYTIME and in 1953 singing the "March of the Musketeers" from Rudolf Friml's THE THREE MUSKETEERS. Warren, who was born in the Bronx, studied in Italy and made his debut at the Met in 1939. He made it home for 21 years and actually died on the Met stage while singing *La Forza del Destino* in 1960.

Baritone Leonard Warren

WARREN, ROBERT PENN   *American novelist/poet (1905–1989)*

Robert Penn Warren won the Pulitzer Prize twice, once for poetry, once for fiction, and was one of the most influential writers of his time. He is best known today for his 1946 Pulitzer Prize-winning novel *All the King's Men*, the story of a populist Southern politician loosely based on the life of Huey Long. It became a successful play and an Oscar-winning movie. Composer Carlisle Floyd's turned it into the opera WILLIE STARK, premiered at Houston Grand Opera in 1981 and nationally telecast.

THE WARRIOR   *1947 opera by Rogers*

A retelling of the Biblical story of Jewish warrior Samson and his seducer Delilah. Bernard Rogers' grand opera *The Warrior*, libretto by Norman Corwin, premiered at the Metropolitan Opera on January 11, 1947. Mack Harrell sang the role of Samson, Regina Resnik was Delilah, Kenneth Schön was the Officer, Irene Jordan was the Boy and the Philistine Lords were Felix Knight, Anthony Marlowe, John Baker and Osie Hawkins. Samuel Leve designed the set, Herbert Graf directed and Max Rudolf conducted the Metropolitan Opera Orchestra.

1947 Metropolitan Opera. Mack Harrell stars as Samson opposite Regina Resnik as Delilah in this off-air recording of the radio broadcast of the premiere performance on January 11, 1947. Omega Opera Archives CD.

WASHINGTON   *American state (1889–)*

Washington has a long tradition of welcoming American operas. Mary Carr Moore's comic opera *The Oracle* was presented in Seattle in January 1902 following its premiere in San Francisco. Her grand opera NARCISSA, one of the first dramatic operas written and staged by an American woman, was premiered at the Moore Theater in Seattle on April 22, 1912. Gerard Tonning premiered four of his operas at the same theater: *Leif Ericsson* in 1910, *In Old New England* in 1913, *All in a Garden Fair* in 1913 and *Blue Wing* in 1917. George Hager's *Pan* was premiered at the Cornish School on April 21, 1922. Washington-born opera people include composer Joyce Barthelson (Yakima), composer Harold Blumenfeld (Seattle), composer William Bolcom (Seattle), soprano Kaaren Erickson (Seattle), choreographer Mark Morris (Seattle) and composer Earl Robinson (Seattle),

Bellvue: Allen Shawn's children's opera *The Ant and the Grasshopper*, libretto by Penny Orloff, was commissioned and premiered by Chaspen Opera in Bellvue. The company presents Gian Carlo Menotti's *Amahl and the Night Visitors* every December as a Christmas special.

Bremerton: Kitsap Opera in Bremerton, founded in 1992, presents fully-staged operas and operettas from the classical repertory for the West Sound community.

Pullman: William Brandt's *No Neutral Ground*, about an incident in the American Civil War, was premiered at Washington State University in Pullman in 1961.

Richland: Washington East Opera, located in Richland, presents operas from the standard repertory.

Seattle: The University of Washington in Seattle, founded in 1861, has been welcoming American operas for many years, starting with the premiere of Charles Lawrence's *Atsumori* on December 11, 1929 (it was revived in 1954). John Verrall premiered three operas at the university in the 1950s: *The Cowherd and the Sky Maiden* in 1952; *The Wedding Knell*, based on a Hawthorne story, in 1952; and *Three Blind Mice* in 1955. Gerald Kechley premiered two of his operas there, *The Beckoning Fair One* in 1954 and THE GOLDEN LION in 1959. Dorothy Hokanson's *Undine* was premiered at the University in 1958. Robert Moran's *Night Passage*, about gay men fleeing England after the Oscar Wilde trial, was commissioned by the Seattle Men's Chorus and premiered on April 17, 1995, at the University. The first Washington opera company was founded in Seattle in 1914, the short-lived Standard Grand Opera Company. Seattle Opera, the major company today, was founded in 1964 and has premiered several American operas. Carlisle Floyd's OF MICE AND MEN, based on the Steinbeck novel, was premiered in 1970; Thomas Pasatieri's CALVARY, based on the Yeats play, in 1971; The Who's rock opera *Tommy* was given its first professional stage performance by Settle Opera in 1971; Pasatieri's THE BLACK WIDOW, based on a Miguel de Unamuno's novella, was premiered in 1972; and Scott Warrender's DAS BARBECÜ, a satire on the Ring cycle set in Texas, was premiered in 1993. The company has also staged Samuel Barber's VANESSA, Carlisle Floyd's THE PASSION OF JONATHAN WADE, George Gershwin's PORGY AND BESS, Philip Glass's SATYAGRAHA, Pasatieri's THE SEAGULL and Douglas Moore's THE BALLAD OF BABY DOE. Seattle Opera commissioned Leonard Kastle's three-act opera *The Pariahs*, about early American whalers, premiered in Albany, NY, in 1985; and it co-commissioned Daniel

Catán's FLORENCIA EN EL AMAZONAS, premiered by Houston Grand Opera in 1996. Lockrem Johnson's *A Letter to Emily,* based on the life of Emily Dickinson, was premiered at the Cornish School of Music in Seattle on April 24, 1951. Lou Harrison's *Jephtha's Daughter* was premiered at Cabrillo College on March 9, 1963. Erling Wold's *Sub Pontio Pilato* was premiered in Seattle in 1999 and Jarrad Powell's *Kali* was staged in Seattle in 2000. Philip Glass's IN THE PENAL COLONY, based on the Kafka story, was premiered by A Contemporary Theatre on September 28, 2000. Seattle Symphony presented a concert performance of Howard Hanson's rarely-seen opera MERRY MOUNT in 1996, with a cast headed by Richard Zeller and Lauren Flanigan, and presented a concert performance of Deems Taylor's equally rare PETER IBBETSON in 1999, with a cast headed by Anthony Griffey and Lauren Flanigan. Arias from David Diamond's unstaged *The Noblest Game* were sung in a Symphony showcase in 1998 by Juliana Gondek.

Spokane: Spokane Opera presents its productions of operas from the standard repertory at the Metropolitan Performing Arts Center.

Tacoma: Adeline Appleton's *The Witches' Well,* libretto by Percy David, premiered at the Tacoma Hotel in May 1928. Tacoma Opera, founded in 1968, premiered Carol Sam's *The Pied Piper of Hamelin* on November 6, 1993, and Daron Hagen's monodrama *Madness and Sorrow* on January 31, 1997. Its other American productions include Rudolf Friml's THE VAGABOND KING and Gian Carlo Menotti's AMAHL AND THE NIGHT VISITORS.

WASHINGTON SQUARE   *1976 opera by Pasatieri*

New York City in the 19th century, Catherine Sloper lives Washington Square area with her doctor father and her aunt. She is courted by fortune hunter Morris Townsend, but he abandons her when her father threatens to disinherit her. After the father's death, Morris returns but Catherine turns him away, opting to stay a spinster. Thomas Pasatieri's three-act opera *Washington Square,* libretto by Kenward Elmslie based on the novel by Henry James, was commissioned by Michigan Opera Theater which premiered it on January 10, 1976. Catherine Malfitano was Catherine Sloper, Richard Cross was Dr. Austin Sloper, Brent Ellis was Morris Townsend, Elaine Bonazzi was Lavinia Davenport, Sheri Greenawald was Marian Harrington, Elsie Inselman was Elizabeth Harrington, Ronald Raines was Arthur Townsend and Dolores Strazicich was Mrs. Montgomery. Santo Loquasto designed the sets, Nikos Psacharopoulos directed and Henry Holt conducted the orchestra. The opera was reprised by New York Lyric Opera in 1977 and Augusta Opera in 1979 and was presented in a summer opera festival in Germany in 1995. (Michael Cunningham has also composed an opera based on the Henry James novel, *Catherine Sloper of Washington Square,* premiered athe the University of Wisconsin in Eau Claire in 1978).

1977 CBS Television. Catherine Malfitano, Brent Ellis and Elaine Bonazzi, who created the roles in the opera, perform the "Carriage Scene" from *Washington Square* on the CBS Camera Three television pro-gram *The Operas of Thomas Pasatieri.* Roger Englander directed the half-hour telecast for the Camera Three series. Videos at MTR and New York State Education Department. **1979 Abbeville Opera.** Maryanne Telese, who created the role of Irena in Pasatieri's opera *The Three Sisters,* sings the role of Catherine Sloper in a live recording made of a 1979 production of *Washington Square* in Abbeville, South Carolina. M. Cooper was Dr. Sloper, J. Stevens was Morris and D. Hess conducted. Live Opera audiocassette.

A WATER BIRD TALK   *1974 opera by Argento*

A henpecked lecturer becomes confused during his talk and mixes tobacco with water fowl while exposing his life with a domineering wife, who is watching from the wings. Dominick Argento's chamber opera for baritone *A Water Bird Talk,* libretto by the composer based Anton Chekhov's story "On the Harmfulness of Tobacco" and John James Audubon's book *The Birds of America,* was premiered by New Opera Theatre at the Brooklyn Academy of Music on May 19, 1977. Vern Sutton was the lecturer, Ian Strasfogel was the stage director and Philip Brunelle conducted the Orpheus Chamber Ensemble.

1996 Maryland Opera. John Shirley-Quick plays the frustrated lecturer in this recording of the opera made at the Gordon Center for the Performing Arts in Owings Mills, Maryland, in August 1996. He is accompanied by the Sinfonia of St. Cecilia conducted by Sara Watkins. Koch CD. **1996 Manhattan Chamber Orchestra.** Vern Sutton takes the role of the confused lecturer in this recording of the opera made in New York, He is supported by the Manhattan Chamber Orchestra led by Richard Auldon Clark. Newport Classics CD.

WATER! WATER!   *1961 opera by Partch*

In the mythical city of Santa Mystiana there is a horrible drought. The Mayor hires a jazz musician who is said to be able to bring rain through his collaboration with water witches. Rains do come but they won't stop and soon there is disastrous flooding.

Elaine Bonazzi, Richard Cross and Elsie Inselman in Thomas Pasatieri's opera *Washington Square.* Photograph by Dirk Bakker, courtesy of Michigan Opera Theatre.

The Mayor put the musician and witches on trial. Harry Partch's experimental *Water! Water!*, libretto by the composer who called it as "an intermission with prologues and epilogues," premiered at the University of Illinois in Urbana on March 2, 1962. John Garvey was the Conductor and jazz soloist; Cynthia Swartz was the Mayor, Scott Meland was Arthur, God of Rain; Alan Gossard was Phoebus the Disk Jockey; Jane Daily was the Spoleto Singer/Wanda the Water Witch; Paul Cooper was the Producer, Patrick Day was Clarence; Steven Allen was Aquarius, Kathleen Roche was the Visitor from Alabama, Carolyn Burrill was Pura and Nina Cutler and Stephen Farish were the Water Criers. John Garvey conducted the university orchestra and chorus.

1962 Gate 5 Ensemble. Excerpts from the opera were recorded at the Studebaker Theater in Chicago on March 17, 1962, soon after the Urbana premiere. Several student performers were not available so their parts were sung by principals. John Garvey conducts the Gate 5 Ensemble. Only 38 minutes of the opera was recorded and they are included in the CRI CD *The Harry Partch Collection, Volume 3*.

WATSON, CHESTER   *American bass (1911–1979)*

Chester Watson created the role of the First Police Agent in Gian Carlo Menotti's THE CONSUL in Philadelphia and on Broadway in 1950, an unnamed role in Darrell Peter's THE PARROT on NBC television in 1953 and Palivec/General von Schwarzburg in Robert Kurka's THE GOOD SOLDIER SCHWEIK at New York City Opera in 1958. He created Friar Julien in Norman Dello Joio's THE TRIAL AT ROUEN on NBC Television in 1956 and reprised the role in the revised, renamed stage version THE TRIUMPH OF ST. JOAN at New York City Opera in 1959. Back on television he created the Minister in Marc Bucci's THE HERO on NET in 1965 and Leonard Swett in Thomas Pasatieri's THE TRIAL OF MARY LINCOLN on NBC in 1972. Watson, who born in Brooklyn, was also a popular concert singer.

WAYDITCH, GABRIEL VON   *American composer (1888–1969)*

Gabriel Von Wayditch is a little known composer who set an operatic record by composing fourteen full-scale operas in the South Bronx, the largest body of opera music created by a single composer in the 20th century. His major work, *The Heretics*, which he worked on from 1948 to his death in 1969, is the longest traditional opera ever written, according to the *Guinness Book of World Records*; it has an orchestral score of 2870 pages and would last over eight and one-half hours if staged. Wayditch's music is tonal but extremely complex and dense and requires very large orchestras, over 100 instruments. His librettos, which he wrote in Hungarian, are abstruse and metaphysical and hard to summarize. His production requirements are immense with elaborate sets and countless scene changes. As Wayditch made no compromises with the realities of performance, it is hardly surprising that his operas have rarely been performed. Two early, relatively short, one-act operas are on CD. THE CALIPH'S MAGICIAN was recorded in Budapest by the Budapest National Opera in 1975 and JESUS BEFORE HEROD was recorded in English at a concert by the San Diego Symphony in 1979. The four-hour opera *Horus* (1931) was staged by Philadelphia's La Scala Opera Company on January 5, 1939, with Fritz Mahler conducting. Wayditch's other operas are *Anthony of Padua, Buddha, The Catacombs, Maria Magdalena, Maria Tesztver, Neptune's' Daughter, Nereida, Opium Dreams, Sahara* and *The Venus Dwellers*. Wayditch, who was born in Budapest, studied at the Royal Academy of Music and emigrated with his family to the United States in 1911. He was a highly respected concert pianist and made his living by playing with a trio on radio and giving private music lessons. The rest of his time was devoted to composing his huge operas in the Bronx. His son has set up a foundation to promote his music.

A WEDDING   *2004 opera by Bolcom*

A lavish wedding party. The groom is old money from Illinois, the bride is nouveau-riche from Kentucky and the bride's mother and the groom's uncle are making plans to run off together. Meanwhile the groom's sister is having an affair with the butler, a socialist aunt is about to shock everyone with her radical ideas and a long lost uncle from Italy is about to reveal secrets of the past. William Bolcom's satirical opera *A Wedding*, libretto by Robert Altman based on his 1978 film, was premiered by Lyric Opera of Chicago on December 11, 2004. Lauren Flanigan played Tulip, Catherine Malfitano was Victoria, Jerry Hadley was Luigi, Mark Delavan was Snooks, Kathryn Harries was Nettie, Timothy Nolen was William Williamson, Jake Gardner was Jules, Mark S. Doss was Randolph, Cynthia Lawrence was Candace, Anna Christy was Muffin, Patrick Miller was Dino, David Cangelosi was Uncle Donato, Beth Clayton was Antonia, Patricia Risley was Diana , Maria Kanyova was Rita and Brian Leerhuber was Breedley. Robin Wagner designed the sets, Dona Granata designed the costumes, Patricia Birch arranged the choreography, Robert Altman staged the production and Dennis Russell Davies conducted the Lyric Opera of Chicago Orchestra and Chorus.

WEEDE, ROBERT   *American baritone (1903–1972)*

Metropolitan Opera baritone Robert Weede is best known for creating the title role of the wine farmer Tony in Frank Loesser's 1956 "quasi-opera" THE MOST HAPPY FELLA, a performance that can be heard on the original cast album. Before that he had created major roles in two notable American operas. He was the thief Bob in Gian Carlo Menotti's THE OLD MAID AND THE THIEF when it premiered on NBC radio in 1939, and he was the slave rebellion leader Jean Jacques Dessalines in William Grant Still's *Troubled Island* at New York City Opera in 1949. On a lighter note he played Santa Clause in a 1950 NBC television production of Victor Herbert's BABES IN TOYLAND. Weede, who was born in Baltimore, studied at the Eastman School of Music and in Milan. He made his debut at the Met in 1937 and continued to sing there until 1947.

WEILL, KURT   *American composer (1900–1950)*

Kurt Weill became one of the great American opera/music theater composers after leaving Nazi Germany and emigrating to American in the late 1930s. His Broadway opera STREET SCENE and his folk opera DOWN IN THE VALLEY are among the finest American operas and his cabaret operas, operettas and musicals have been embraced by opera companies. His first American stage work was the anti-war cabaret opera JOHNNY JOHNSON, libretto by Paul Green, which premiered in New York in 1936 at the Group Theatre. Next was the Jewish/Biblical pageant drama THE ETERNAL ROAD, original libretto by Franz Werfel, staged by Max Reinhardt at the Manhattan Opera House in 1937. KNICKERBOCKER HOLIDAY, libretto by Maxwell Anderson satirizing the nefarious activities of Peter Stuyvesant in Manhattan in 1647, premiered in New York in 1938 with Walter Huston as Peter singing "September Song." The patriotic scenic cantata *The Ballad of Magna Carta*, libretto by Maxwell Anderson for tenor, bass and chorus, was broadcast on CBS Radio in 1940. LADY IN THE DARK, libretto by

Robert Altman, director and librettist of the opera *A Wedding*, is shown directing the film on which is was based.

Moss Hart with lyrics by Ira Gershwin using surrealistic dream sequences to tell the story of a woman undergoing psychoanalysis, opened in New York in 1941 with Gertrude Lawrence as star and became Weill's biggest stage success. ONE TOUCH OF VENUS, libretto by S. J. Perlman and Ogden Nash about a sexy statue of Venus that comes to life, premiered in New York in 1943 with Mary Martin. The Broadway opera THE FIREBRAND OF FLORENCE, libretto by S. J. Mayer with lyrics by Ira Gershwin describing the adventures of artist Benvenuto Cellini, premiered in New York in 1945. The l2-minute "movie opera" COLUMBUS, libretto by Ira Gershwin, was created for the 1945 film *Where Do We Go from Here?* The Broadway opera STREET SCENE, libretto by Elmer Rice based on his play with lyrics by Langston Hughes telling the tragic story of a family of New York tenement dwellers, opened in New York in 1947. Weill considered it his best work and many critics rank it alongside PORGY AND BESS. The folk opera DOWN IN THE VALLEY, libretto by Arnold Sundgaard based on the ballad "Down in the Valley," was composed in 1945 as a radio opera but never broadcast so Weill rewrote it for the stage and premiered it at Indiana University in 1948. The vaudeville LOVE LIFE, libretto by A. J. Lerner about a married couple seen in different eras in American history, premiered in 1948. LOST IN THE STARS, libretto by Maxwell Anderson about race problems in South Africa based on Alan Paton's novel *Cry the Beloved Country*, premiered in New York in 1949. Weill was working on the musical *Huckleberry Finn* with Maxwell Anderson when he died of a heart attack in 1950 at the age of 50. His reputation as one of the great composers of the 20th century continues to rise as his stage works are revived and recorded. Weill was born in Dessau, Germany, the son of a cantor, and first became known as a composer in Berlin in the late 1920s collaborating with Bertolt Brecht on *The Threepenny Opera* and other works. His wife Lotta Lenya sang in many of his stage production, most notably in *The Threepenny Opera,* and promoted and recorded his songs after his death. The Kurt Weill Foundation for Music has also been instrumental in encouraging interest in his music. There are many collections of Weill songs on LP and CD. Some of them are described below.

1943/45 Tryout: Kurt Weill and Ira Gershwin. Kurt Weill and Ira Gershwin perform sequences from the film *Where Do We Go from Here?*, including the mini-opera *Columbus,* and Weill sings numbers from *One Touch of Venus* on the album *Tryout: A Series of Private Rehearsal Recordings.* Heritage LP/DRG CD. **1964 Lotte Lenya.** Lotte Lenya appears on the Camera Three program *Broadway Years of Kurt Weill* and sings material from *One Touch of Venus, Lady in the Dark, Knickerbocker Holiday, Street Scene* and *The Firebrand of Florence.* Jack Landau directed the telecast on WCBS on October 28, 1964. Video at MTR. **1972 Berlin to Broadway with Kurt Weill.** The off-Broadway revue *Berlin to Broadway with Kurt Weill, A Musical Voyage* features Broadway opera songs by Weill. Paramount LP. **1981 Kurt Weill Revisited.** Lesser known Weill songs are featured on two albums in Ben Bagley's *Revisited* series. Paula Lawrence, Ann Miller, John Reardon, Chita Rivera, Arthur Siegel and Jo Sullivan perform on the first album and Ellen Burstyn, Nell Carter, Blossom Dearie, Tammy Grimes, Estelle Parsons, John Reardon, Arthur Siegel and Jo Sullivan sing on the second. Painted Smiles LPs/CDs. **1986 Teresa Stratas.** Teresa Stratas performs Weill songs on the album *Stratas Sings Weill* with Gerard Schwarz conducting the Y Chamber Orchestra. Nonesuch LP/CD. **1988 Ute Lemper.** Ute Lemper performs songs by Weill on two albums, *Ute Lemper Sings Kurt Weill, Volumes 1 and 2,* with Berlin orchestras led by John Mauceri. London/Decca CD. **1992 Carole Farley.** Carole Farley sings Weill tunes accompanied by Roger Vignoles on the album *Kurt Weill Songs.* ASV CD. **1992 Angelina Réaux.** Angelina Réaux performs Weill songs accompanied by pianist Robert Kapilow on the album *Songs of Kurt Weill.* Koch CD. **1992 Ute Lemper.** Ute Lemper performs numbers from *One Touch of Venus, Lady in the Dark* and *Lost in the Stars* at Les Bouffes du Nord in Paris on the video *Ute Lemper Sings Kurt Weill.* Jeff Cohen plays piano. London VHS. **1995 Anne Sofie von Otter.** Anne Sofie von Otter sings Weill on the album *Speak Low: Songs by Kurt Weill*. John Eliot Gardiner conducts the North Germany Radio Symphony Orchestra. DG CD. **1996 Steven Kimbrough.** Steven Kimbrough sings Weill on the album *Kurt Weill on Broadway*. Victor Symonteete conducts the Cologne West German Radio Orchestra. Koch Schwann CD. **1997 Kurt Weill: From Berlin to Broadway I and II.** This four-CD set features rare material from Weill shows, including *Knickerbocker Holiday, Lady in the Dark* and *One Touch of Venus*. Pearl CDs. **1997 Kurt Weill on Broadway.** Thomas Hampson, Elizabeth Futral, Jerry Hadley and Jeanne Lehman sing Weill on the album *Kurt Weill on Broadway*. John McGlinn conducts the London Sinfonietta. EMI Classics CD. **2000 Kurt Weill: The Centennial.** Top singers perform their favorite Weill songs in this centennial tribute to Weill staged in Los Angeles on November 4, 2000. LML Music 2-CD box. **2000 Urs Affolter.** Urs Affolter sings Weill tunes on the album *Stay Well: Urs Affolter Sings Kurt Weill* accompanied by Uli Kofler. Antes CD. **2002 Center City Brass Quintet.** The Center City Brass Quintet plays songs from Weill's musicals on the album *From Berlin to Broadway*. Chandos CD.

WEINER, LAZAR   *American composer (1897–1982)*

Lazar Weiner, a leading figure in Jewish and Yiddish music in New York in his lifetime, composed a number of religious cantatas and Yiddish musical comedies and a notable opera. THE GOLEM, libretto by R. Smolover, is the story of a rabbi in medieval Prague who creates a giant creature to protect the Jewish people. The legend is based on folklore about Rabbi Lowe, said to have created the Golem in 1580. The opera was premiered at the Jewish Community Center in White Plains, NY, on January 13, 1957, and was reprised in New York City at the 92nd Street Y in 1981. Weiner, who was born in Kiev, emigrated to America in 1914.

WEISGALL, HUGO   *American composer (1912–1997)*

Hugo Weisgall, one of America's most important opera composers, created a number of dramatic stage works based on notable plays and featuring strong atonal music. THE TENOR, libretto by Karl Shapiro and Ernst Lert based on Frank Wedekind's play *Der Kammersänger* about an egotistical opera singer, was premiered by

Composer Hugo Weisgall pictured on CRI CD.

the Peabody Opera Company in Baltimore in 1951. THE STRONGER, libretto by Richard Hart based on a Strindberg play about a confrontation between two women, was premiered by the Baltimore-based Hilltop Opera Company in 1952; it is his most frequently performed opera. SIX CHARACTERS IN SEARCH OF AN AUTHOR, libretto by Denis Johnston based on the play by Luigi Pirandello about fictional people looking for someone to tell their story, was premiered at New York City Opera on April 26, 1959. PURGATORY, libretto by the composer based on an allegorical play by William Butler Yeats about guilt and old age, was first performed at the Library of Congress in Washington in 1961. THE GARDENS OF ADONIS, libretto by John Olon-Scrymgeour based on an André Obey play and Shakespeare's poem *Venus and Adonis*, was premiered in 1992 by Opera/Omaha. ATHALIAH, libretto by R. F. Goldman based on play by Racine about a usurper Queen, was presented by the Concert Opera Association at the Philharmonic Hall in New York in 1964. NINE RIVERS FROM JORDAN, libretto by Denis Johnston based on his symbolic novel, was premiered by New York City opera in 1968. JENNY, OR THE HUNDRED NIGHTS, libretto by John Hollander based on a Noh play by Yukio Mishima about an old woman and a photographer, premiered at the American Opera Center at Juilliard in 1976. WILL YOU MARRY ME?, libretto by Charles Kondek based on Alfred Sutro's *A Marriage Has Been Arranged*, was premiered in New York in 1989. ESTHER, libretto by Charles Kondek based on the Biblical story about a Persian Queen who saved the Jews, was premiered by New York City Opera in 1993. Weisgall, a descendent of four generations of cantors, was born in Czechoslovakia and came to the U.S. in 1920 with his parents. He studied at the Peabody Conservatory, the Curtis Institute and John Hopkins University and with Roger Sessions and Fritz Reiner. He taught at John Hopkins, Queens College and the Juilliard School and founded the Hilltop Opera Company in Baltimore.

WELFARE: THE OPERA   *2004 opera by Pickett*

The terrors, torment and absurdities of a New York City welfare office as those who most desperately need help struggle to survive an implacable bureaucracy. Seven actor/singers portray eighteen people featured in Frederick Wiseman's 1975 documentary film *Welfare* and describe their situations in arias, duets and ensemble pieces. Lenny Pickett's *Welfare: The Opera*, libretto by poet David Slavitt, was premiered by American Opera Projects on May 27, 2004, at the Dance Theater Workshop in New York City. Wiseman, who directed the production, shot a new documentary at each performance with the new video images projected onto a screen and intercut with scenes from the original film. The actor/singers were Amy Van Roekel (soprano) Stephanie Woodling (mezzo) La'Shelle Allen (contralto) Jimmy Justice (tenor) James Archie Worley (tenor) Michael Zegarski (baritone) and Jack Wadell (bass). Doug Elkin created the choreography and Steven Osgood conducted the nine-piece band with composer Pickett playing the saxophone The score is a mixture of musical styles, including opera, jazz, gospel and blues.

WELLES, ORSON   *American director (1915–1985)*

Orson Welles directed the premieres of two notable American operas in 1937. The first was Aaron Copland's THE SECOND HURRICANE; it was staged without fanfare in a New York City high school and attracted little media attention. The second was Marc Blitzstein's THE CRADLE WILL ROCK; it was premiered despite government attempts to block it and this foiled attempt at censorship helped make it one of the major media events of the era. The sponsoring

Federal Theatre Project had decided the opera was a political hot potato, which they didn't want staged, so they arranged to close the Maxine Elliott Theater where it was to premiere. Welles and producer John Houseman found another theater and led the cast and audience to it. As the actors couldn't go on stage because of union restrictions and there was no orchestra, Welles told the performers to sing from their seats in the auditorium while Blitzstein played piano accompaniment on the stage. After young Olive Stanton, playing Moll, stood up and sang NICKEL UNDER THE FOOT, the other performers were inspired. The evening was a triumph and the opera went onto a long run. This premiere is the central scene in the film *Cradle Will Rock* in which Angus Macfadyen plays the director. In 1940 Welles moved to Hollywood and commissioned one of the most famous arias in American opera. He asked composer Bernard Hermann to create it for the "movie opera" SALAMMBÔ, featured in his film *Citizen Kane*. Welles, born in Kenosha, Wisconsin, never made another film featuring an opera scene but his portrayal of Falstaff in *Chimes at Midnight* (1966) has operatic resonance.

Orson Welles as he appeared in *Citizen Kane*.

WELLS, JEFFREY *American bass-baritone (1955–)*

Jeffrey Welles sings Anthony opposite the Cleopatra of Esther Hinds in Gian Carlo Menotti's revised version of Samuel Barber's ANTONY AND CLEOPATRA in a recording made at the 1983 Spoleto Festival in Italy. In 1982 he had sung the role of John Sorel in Menotti's *The Consul*. Wells, born in Baton Rouge, LA, studied at Louisiana State and Southeastern Louisiana universities. He began to sing at New York City Opera in 1980 and at the Metropolitan Opera in 1989, and is particularly noted for his performances in Russian operas.

WELLS, PATRICIA *American soprano (1941–)*

Patricia Wells has created the role of Masha twice in American operas based on plays by Chekhov. She was Masha for the first time in Thomas Pasatieri's THE SEAGULL at Houston Grand Opera in 1974 and she was Masha again in Pasatieri's THREE SISTERS at Opera/Columbus in 1986. She has also sung the title role in Carlisle Floyd's SUSANNAH. Wells, who was born in Ruston, LA, and studied at Juilliard, made her debut in 1963 at Shreveport Opera in Louisiana.

WELTING, RUTH *American soprano (1949–1999)*

Coloratura soprano Ruth Welting stars as Baby Doe in the 1976 New York City Opera telecast of Douglas Moore's THE BALLAD OF BABY DOE, one of the first *Live from Lincoln Center* television broadcasts. She also sang Kitty in a production of Gian Carlo Menotti's THE LAST SAVAGE. Welting, who was born in Memphis, Tennessee, studied in Rome and Paris and made her debut at New York City Opera in 1970. She sang a wide variety of roles at the Metropolitan Opera from 1976 to 1994 and then quit singing so she could attend Syracuse University and take a liberal arts degree. She graduated in 1998 and was doing post-graduate work when she died of cancer.

WERNICK, RICHARD *American composer (1934–)*

Boston-born Richard Wernick, who won the Pulitzer Prize for Music in 1977 for *Visions of Wonder and Terror* based on texts from the Bible and the Koran, has written only one opera. *Maggie*, based on Stephen Crane's 1893 novel *Maggie: A Child of the Street*, is, like *Visions,* concerned with suffering and redemption. Completed in 1959, it tells the story of a young prostitute who commits suicide. Wernick, who studied at Brandeis and Mills and with Aaron Copland and Leonard Bernstein, has also composed ballets and set poems by E. E. Cummings.

WERRENRATH, REINALD *American baritone (1883–1953)*

Reinald Werrenrath, a popular recording artist for Victor in the early years of the record industry, sang at the Metropolitan Opera from 1919 to 1921. He recorded the aria "Alvarado's Serenade" from Victor Herbert's dramatic opera *Natoma* in 1912 and followed it with songs from four of Herbert's comic operas, SWEETHEARTS in 1913, PRINCESS PAT in 1916, THE FORTUNE TELLER in 1920 and

Baritone Reinald Werrenrath

DREAM GIRL in 1924. He also recorded numbers from Reginald De Koven's ROBIN HOOD and Sigmund Romberg's BLOSSOM TIME. Werrenrath, who was born in Brooklyn and studied with Victor Maurel, made his operatic debut in 1907. He can be seen performing popular songs in a 1928 Vitaphone short.

WEST OF WASHINGTON SQUARE   *1988 opera by Henderson*   See THE LAST LEAF

WEST SIDE STORY   *1957 operatic musical by Bernstein*

The "Hell's Kitchen" area of Manhattan's West side in the 1950s where youth gangs dispute control with fights called "rumbles." The Italian Jets are led by Riff and the Puerto Rican Sharks by Bernardo. Tony, the former leader of the Jets, is trying to escape from gang life. He meets Bernardo's sister Maria at a dance and they fall in love. When he tries to break up a rumble and ends up killing Bernardo, he knows their love affair is doomed. A Shark kills Tony in revenge and Maria mourns over his body. Leonard Bernstein's operatic musical *West Side Story,* libretto by Arthur Laurents based loosely on Shakespeare's *Romeo and Juliet* with lyrics by Stephen Sondheim, premiered at the National Theater in Washington, D.C., on August 19, 1957, and opened at the Winter Garden in New York on September 26, 1957. Carol Lawrence was Maria, Larry Kert was Tony, Chita Rivera was Anita, Michael Calin

Leonard Bernstein's operatic musical *West Side Story* was filmed in 1961 with Natalie Wood as Maria.

was Riff, Marilyn Cooper was Rosalia, Reri Grist (who later had a notable opera career) was Consuelo, Ken LeRoy was Bernardo, Carmen Guiterrez was Teresita, Elizabeth Taylor was Francisca, Eddie Roll was Action and Grover Dale was Snowboy. Jerome Robbins directed the production and choreographed it with Peter Gennaro, Harold Prince produced with Robert Griffith and Max Goberman conducted the orchestra. The magnificence of Bernstein's music is matched by the glory of Sondheim's lyrics. Many of the songs are close to being operatic arias, especially "SOMEWHERE" which is usually performed by an opera singer (Reri Grist in the premiere production). *West Side Story,* which has started to enter the opera house repertory and be recorded by opera singers, has been revived many times, including a Lincoln Center production in 1968 and a Minskoff Theater production in 1980.

1957 Original cast. Carol Lawrence is Maria, Tony Kert is Tony and Chita Rivera is Anita in the original cast recording of *West Side Story.* Reri Grist is Consuelo, Michael Calin is Riff, Marilyn Cooper is Rosalia, Ken LeRoy is Bernardo, Carmen Guiterrez is Teresita, Eddie Roll is Action and Grover Dale is Snowboy. Max Goberman conducts. Columbia LP/Sony CD. **1961 Columbia film.** The superb film version of *West Side Story,* adapted for the screen by Ernest Lehman, was brilliantly directed by Robert Wise and Jerome Robbins. The opening helicopter shot and gang dance sequence choreographed by Robbins are especially memorable. Natalie Wood plays Maria with Marni Nixon doing her singing, Richard Beymer plays Tony with Jim Bryant doing his singing, Rita Moreno plays Anita with parts of her singing done by Marni Nixon and Betty Wand, Russ Tamblyn is Riff, George Chakiris is Bernardo and Tucker Smith is Ice. Johnny Green conducted the orchestra, Daniel Fapp was the cinematographer and Boris Leven was the art director. The film won six Academy Awards, including Best Picture and Best Director. Soundtrack on Columbia LP and Sony CD. Film on Sony DVD and VHS. **1985 The Making of West Side Story.** *The Making of West Side Story* is a documentary about a recording session under the direction of Leonard Bernstein. Kiri Te Kanawa has the role of Maria, José Carreras is Tony, Tatiana Troyanos is Anita and Kurt Ollmann is Riff. Te Kanawa sounds splendid and is much appreciated by Bernstein but Carreras has difficulties and seems badly miscast. Christopher Swann directed the film. DG DVD/VHS. **1985 Kiri Te Kanawa/José Carreras.** Kiri Te Kanawa is Maria with José Carreras as Tony in this recording directed and conducted by Leonard Bernstein. Tatiana Troyanos is Anita, Kurt Ollmann is Riff, Marilyn Horne sings "Somewhere," Louise Edeiken is Rosalia, Stella Zambalis is Consuela, Angela Reaux is Francisca, David Livingston is Action, Marty Nelson in Diesel, Stephen Bogardus is Baby John, Peter Thom is A-rab, Todd Lester is Snowboy and Richard Harrell is Bernardo. DG CD. **1993 Barbara Bonney/Michael Ball.** Barry Wordsworth conducts the Royal Philharmonic Orchestra and Chorus in this recording of the musical. Barbara Bonney sings Maria, Michael Ball is Tony, and La Verne Williams is Anita. Warner Classic CD. **1993 Tinuke Olafimihan/Paul Manual.** This recording of the musical is based on a 1992 London stage production, with the addition of Tinuke Olafimihan as Maria and Sally Burgess as the girl who sings "Somewhere." Paul Manual is Tony, Caroline O'Connor is Anita, Nicolas Warford is Riff and Nick Ferranti is Bernardo. John Owen Edwards conducts the National Symphony Orchestra. TER CD box. **1994 Kiri Te Kanawa.** Kiri Te Kanawa sings "Somewhere" on her album *Kiri!— Her Greatest Hits.* Stephen Barlow conducts the London Symphony Orchestra. London Classics CD and Video. **1998 Renée Fleming/Placido Domingo.** Renée Fleming and Placido Domingo duet on "Tonight" and Fleming sings "Somewhere" on their recital album *Prelude to a Kiss*. Daniel Barenboim conducts the Chicago Symphony Orchestra. Decca/London CD

WEST VIRGINIA *American state (1863–)*

West Virginia is without a permanent opera company but its universities and colleges are operatically active and have premiered a number of operas. One of the most unusual was Judith Shatin's folk opera COAL, based on West Virginia coal mining songs. West Virginia-born opera people include composer George Crumb (Charleston), soprano Phyllis Curtin (Clarksburg) and soprano Eleanor Steber (Wheeling). Vittorio Giannini's radio opera BLENNERHASSETT is set in West Virginia.

Charleston: The Lilliput Opera Orchestra, founded in 1979 but now inactive, presented a number of American music theater works including *Riverboat Man*, George Kleinsinger's ARCHY AND MEHITABEL and Gian Carlo Menotti's THE MEDIUM. The West Virginia Symphony Orchestra in Charleston also presents an occasional opera.

Institute: Grant Still's opera HIGHWAY 1, U.S.A. was staged at West Virginia State College in Institute in 1974. Composer T. J. Anderson studied at the College.

Morgantown: Leo Horacek's THE TELL-TALE HEART, libretto by Joseph Golz based on the EDGAR ALLAN POE story, was premiered at West Virginia University in Morgantown on August 7, 1968.

Shepherdstown: Judith Shatin's Appalachian-style folk opera COAL, based on West Virginia coal mining songs, was premiered at Shepherd College in Shepherdstown on November 12, 1995.

WESTERGAARD, PETER *American composer (1931–)*

Peter Westergaard, a music theorist as well as a notable composer, has written three operas. *Charivari*, libretto by the composer, was performed at Cambridge, MA, on May 13, 1953. MR. AND MRS. DISCOBBOLOS, libretto by the composer based on a poem by Edward Lear about two people sitting on a wall, premiered at Columbia University in 1966. THE TEMPEST, libretto by the composer based on the Shakespeare play, was premiered by Opera Festival of New Jersey in 1994. Westergaard has also composed a number of dramatic cantatas, including *The Plot Against the Giant* (1956), based on the Wallace Stevens poem; *A Refusal to Mourn the Death of a Child by Fire in London* (1958), based on the Dylan Thomas poem; and *Leda and the Swan* (1961), based on the W. B. Yeats poem. Westergaard, who was born in Champaign, Illinois, studied at Harvard and Princeton and in Paris and Germany and with Milton Babbitt, Darius Milhaud, Walter Piston and Roger Sessions. He later taught at Princeton and wrote an influential book on tonal music. He composed his operas to a 12-tone polyphony system of his own invention.

"WHAT A MOVIE" *Soprano aria: Trouble in Tahiti (1952). Words and Music: Leonard Bernstein.*

"What a Movie" is the opera aria as film criticism. A bored housewife goes to see a "terrible awful" movie called *Trouble in Tahiti* and describes the plot in caustic but amusing detail. It would bore a four-year-old, she claims, but she is fascinated by it and tells us it features a beautiful princess wearing a tiny sarong, a handsome American flyer and a volcanic curse if it rains on their marriage. "What a Movie," featured in Leonard Bernstein's satirical 1952 opera TROUBLE IN TAHITI, has some of Bernstein's cleverest lyrics and is a showcase for the soprano who performs it. Nell Tangeman introduced it on stage in the June 1952 premiere at

Brandeis University but it did not really get noticed until Beverly Wolff performed it in an NBC TV production in November 1952 and recorded it in 1953. Alice Ghostly sang it in a 1955 production at The Playhouse and Wolff reprised it at New York City Opera in 1958. Nancy Williams sings it in a videotaped 1973 British television production, Evelyn Lear sings it on a live recording of a Hollywood Bowl production in 1973, Wendy White performs it in a recorded 1985 Vienna State Opera production, Dawn Upshaw sings it on her 1995 recital album, pianist Monique Haas performs it on her 1995 recital album, Elizabeth Shammash sings it on a 1998 Manhattan School of Music Opera Theater recording of the opera and Stephanie Novacek performs it on the superb 2001 BBC Wales TV version.

"WHAT GOOD WOULD THE MOON BE?" *Soprano aria : Street Scene (1947). Words: Langston Hughes. Music: Kurt Weill.*

One of the most affecting arias from Weill's great Broadway opera is the plaintive lament "What good would the moon be?" sung by young Rose Maurrant after she has been propositioned by a slick suitor. She feel that wealth without love wouldn't really satisfy her, that diamonds are beautiful but cold. Anne Jeffreys introduced the aria on Broadway in the 1947 premiere and sings it on the original cast album. Catherine Malfitano is the singer in a recording of a 1978 New York City Opera production and in a televised production in 1979. On the 1991 Scottish Opera recording of the opera it is sung by Angelina Reaux. Janis Kelly sings it on the 1992 English National Opera recording of the opera but Lesley Garrett sings it in the videotaped 1992 English National Opera telecast and on her 1992 recital album *Prima Donna*. Teri Hansen performs it on the DVD of the telecast of the 1994 Houston Grand Opera production from the Theater des Westerns in Berlin.

WHAT HAPPENED *1963 music theater work by Carmine*

No characters, no setting and no plot are featured in this unusual music theater work that utilizes singers, dancers and actor in a non-linear Gertrude Stein way. Alvin Carmine's 32-minute *What Happened*, libretto by Stein, was premiered at the Judson Poets Theatre in the Judson Memorial Church in New York City in 1963 in a production by Lawrence Kornfeld. The performers included Yvonne Rainer, Lucinda Childs, Aileen Passloff, Arlene Rothlein and Joan Baker. *What Happened* was so popular it was revived five times and went on to win five OBIE awards.

WHAT MEN LIVE BY *1953 TV opera by Martinů*

God punishes an errant angel by forced him to live on earth with a poor peasant shoemaker until he learns the three great truths that men live by. Bohuslav Martinů's 55-minute television opera *What Men Live By*, libretto by the composer based on an 1881 short story by Leo Tolstoy, premiered on television in New York in May 1953. The opera was later staged at Opera in the Ozarks, the summer festival at the Inspiration Point Fine Arts Colony in Eureka Springs, Arkansas.

WHAT NEXT? *1999 opera by Carter*

Six people are involved in an absurd car accident and end up wondering what next. Rose is a coloratura soprano bride, her bridegroom Harry/Larry is a clown, Stella is an astronomer, Mama is a mother, Zen is her philosophic ex-husband and Kid is a 12-year-old who wants candy. Elliot Carter's 40-minute opera *What Next?*, written at the age of 91 to a libretto by music critic Paul Griffiths, was seen by critics as Ionesco-like though Carter says his model was actually Jacque Tati's car crash comedy film *Traffic*. Daniel Barenboim persuaded Carter to write the opera which premiered at Berlin's Staatsoper Unter den Linden on September 16, 1999, with Barenboim conducting. Simone Nold was soprano Rose, Hanno Mueller-Brachmann was Harry/Larry, Lynne Dawson was Mother, William Joyner was Zen, Hilary Summers was Stella and Michael John Divine was the Kid. The opera was reprised at Carnegie Hall in New York on March 5, 2000, with the same cast, orchestra and conductor.

2001 Concertgebouw, Amsterdam. Peter Eötvös conducts the Netherlands Radio Chamber Orchestra in a production of the opera recorded live at the Concertbegouw in Amsterdam on September 9, 2001. Valdine Anderson is Rose, Dean Elzinga is Harry, Sarah Leonard is Mama, William Joyner is Zen, Hilary Summers is Stella and Emanuel Hoogeveen is the Kid. ECM New Series CD.

WHAT PRICE CONFIDENCE   *1946 opera by Krenek*

Two free-thinking couples in Victorian England, decide to test each other's confidence. One makes as assignation in the British Museum, another attempts to jump from Waterloo Bridge. They end up by exchanging partners. Ernst Krenek's 12-tone comic chamber opera *What Price Confidence?*, libretto by the composer, was composed in 1946 for singers from the Metropolitan Opera. They asked for a chamber opera for four singers that could be presented with piano in a small theater but they never performed it. It was finally premiered at the Stadttheater in Saarbrücken, Germany, on May 23, 1962, in a German translation. Waltraud Schatzl was Gloria, Heidi Ferch was Vivian, Phil Sona was Richard and Hans Riediker was Edwin. Werner Wilke conducted. The opera, which received its American premiere in 1968, was revived in 2000 by the Elysium: Between Two Continents company at the Riverside Church in Manhattan. The singers were Joshua Parrillo, Julia Koci, Christopher Pfund and Anne Duraski, Gregori H. von Lëitis directed and John W. Simmons played the piano.

WHEELER, HUGH   *American librettist/novelist (1912–1987)*

Hugh Wheeler led a double life under two names; as Wheeler, he was a successful Broadway playwright/librettist writing words for Leonard Bernstein and Stephen Sondheim while as Patrick Quentin he was an equally successful mystery writer. He created the libretto for Sondheim's A LITTLE NIGHT MUSIC (1973), based on a screenplay by Ingmar Bergman, and the libretto of Sondheim's SWEENEY TODD (1979), based on a play by Christopher Bond. He also worked on the libretto for Sondheim's *Pacific Overtures*, wrote the revised libretto of Bernstein's CANDIDE for its 1979 revival and wrote the revised libretto of Sigmund Romberg's THE STUDENT PRINCE for its 1980 revival. His last libretto was for the musical *Meet Me in St. Louis*, based on the MGM film. Wheeler, born and educated in England, came to America in 1934 and served in the U. S. Army during the war. His best known books as a mystery writer are the *Puzzle* novels beginning with the 1936 *A Puzzle for Fools*. He won an Edgar award in 1962 for a collection of his stories.

WHEN LILACS LAST IN THE DOORYARD BLOOMED   *1971 cantata by Sessions*

Walt Whitman, who was an opera enthusiast, said he used "the method of the Italian opera" to write his poem about Lincoln's assassination, *When Lilacs Last in the Dooryard Bloomed*. Roger Sessions used Whitman's poem as the libretto for his cantata dedicated "To the memory of Martin Luther King Jr. and Robert F. Kennedy." It was commissioned by the University of California, Berkeley, and first performed at Berkeley on May 23, 1971, with James Cunningham leading the University Symphony Orchestra and Chorus. The soloists were soprano Helene Joseph, contralto Stephanie Friedman and baritone Allen Shearer. Some critics consider this cantata to be Sessions' greatest work.

1977 Tanglewood Festival. Soprano Esther Hinds, mezzo-soprano Florence Quivar and baritone Dominic Cossa are the soloists with the Tanglewood Festival Chorus in this performance of the cantata recorded live at Symphony Hall in Boston. John Oliver leads the chorus and Seiji Ozawa conducts the Boston Symphony Orchestra. New World LP/CD.

WHERE THE WILD THINGS ARE   *1980 children's opera by Knussen*

Bad boy Max, who has misbehaved and been sent to bed without supper, imagines how to escape. He mentally turns his room in a wild forest and takes a boat to an island where the monstrous Wild Things live. He takes charge of their revels and has a good time before they turn against him and chase him home. Oliver Knussen's children's opera *Where the Wild Things Are*, libretto by American Maurice Sendak based on his popular book, was premiered in a preliminary version at the Théâtre de La Monnaie in Brussels on November 28, 1980, with sets and costumes designed by Sendak. The revised, definitive version was premiered by Glyndebourne Touring Opera in London on January 9, 1984, and then presented at the Glyndebourne Festival. Karen Beardsley played Max with Mary King as Mama. The Wild Things were sung and danced by Mary King, Jenny Weston, Hugh Hetherington, Perry Davey, Jeremy Munro, Cenzig Saner, Stephen Rhys-Williams, Brian Andrew, Andrew Gallagher, Bernard Bennett and Mike Gallant. Knussen conducted and Frank Corsaro directed. *Where the Wild Things Are* is often paired with the other Sendak/Knussen children's opera HIGGLETY PIGGLETY POP!

1984 Glyndebourne Festival. Rosemary Hardy sings the role of Max in this recording with Oliver Knussen conducting the London Sinfonietta. Mary King is Mama and Tzippy, Hugh Hetherington is Wild Thing with a Beard and Goat Wild Thing, Stephen Richards is Wild Thing with Horns and Rooster Wild Thing and Andrew Gallacher is Bull Wild Thing. Unicorn LP/Arabesque CD.

1985 Glyndebourne Festival. This visually delightful Glyndebourne Festival video showcases Sendak's imaginative characters, costumes and sets. Karen Beardsley is Max with support from Mary King as Mama, Jenny Weston, Hugh Hetherington, Perry Davey, Jeremy Munro. Oliver Knussen conducts the London Sinfonietta. Frank Corsaro staged the production and Christopher Swann directed the video. DVD/Home Vision VHS/Pioneer Artists LD.

1999 Glyndebourne Festival. Lisa Saffer is Max in this recording made by a Glyndebourne Festival cast at the EMI Abbey Road Studios in London in March 1999. Mary King is Mama and Tzippy, Christopher Gillett is Wild Thing with a Beard and Goat Wild Thing, Davis Wilson-Johnson is Rooster Wild Thing, Quentin Hayes is Wild Thing with Horns and Stephen Richardson is Bull Wild Thing. Oliver Knussen conducts the London Sinfonietta. DG 2-CD set with *Higglety Pigglety Pop!*

WHERE'S DICK?   *1989 opera by Wallace*

Where's Dick takes place on Christmas Eve in a city overflowing with crooks and seems to have been modeled on the comic strip *Dick Tracy*. Young detective Junior has a series of violent, sexy adventures as he searches for his hero Dick. Stewart Wallace's three-act opera *Where's Dick?*, libretto by Michael Korie, was commissioned by Opera/Omaha which presented it in workshop form in 1987. It was premiered officially by Houston Grand Opera on May 24, 1989. Henry Stram was Junior, Matthew Lord was Sterling Tarnish, Angelina Réaux was Baby Snowflake, Mary McClain was Mouth, Daryl Henriksen was Rev. J. J. Newbright, Joyce Castle was Mrs. Heimlich, Randall K. Wong was Boldface Headlines, Wilbur Pauley was Santa, Consuelo Hill was Chief Blowhard, Ken Jennings was Stump Tower, Cindy Benson was Ma Paddle, Natalie Oliver was Sister Immacula, Karen Patricia McVoy was Fate Spritely, Charles Workman was Stainless Tarnish, and Little Willie played himself. Richard Foreman designed the sets and staged the production while John De Main conducted the Houston Grand Opera Orchestra. The score includes many references to popular music.

WHITE, CAROLINA   *American soprano (1886–1961)*

Carolina White, a major star at the Chicago Opera from 1910 to 1914, sang the role of Barbara in the 1913 Chicago premiere of Victor Herbert's opera NATOMA and recorded its aria "Spring Song" for Columbia. She sang the role of Minnie in the Chicago premiere of Puccini's *La fanciulla del West* on December 27, 1910, only two weeks after its premiere in New York. She was discovered by Enrico Caruso when he came to Chicago to sing the role of Dick Johnson in *Fanciulla* and he later chose her to act in his 1918 film *My Cousin*. White, who began her career in Italy after studies in Boston, made her debut at San Carlo in Naples in 1908 and married her music coach Paolo Longone. She sang in operetta and vaudeville after 1914 and retired from the stage in 1922.

WHITE, CLARENCE CAMERON   *American composer (1880–1960)*

Clarence Cameron White won the David Bispham Medal in 1932 for his three-act opera OUANGA!, libretto by John F. Matheus. Based on a Haitian historical episode, it was presented in partial form in Chicago in 1932, in concert form in 1941, on stage in South Bend, Indiana, in 1949 and at the Metropolitan Opera in 1956. White's only other opera was *A Carnival Romance,* libretto by the composer, completed in 1952. Both operas incorporate Haitian, Creole and African American rhythms and melodies. White, who was born in Clarkesville, Tennessee, studied at Howard University, Oberlin Conservatory and the Juilliard School and in Paris and London. He was an excellent violinist and for many years combined concert tours as a violinist with his teaching work.

WHITE, E. B.   *American humor writer (1899–1985)*

E. B. White is nearly as famous for his children's novels as for his humorous articles in *The New Yorker. Stuart Little* (1945) and *Charlotte's Web* (1952) have both been turned into popular films and *Charlotte's Web* was turned into an opera by Lee Ahlin. It was premiered by the American Stage company in St. Petersburg, Florida, on October 20, 1988. White, born in Mt. Vernon, NY, studied at Cornell and began to write for *The New Yorker* in the 1920s.

WHITE, WILLARD   *American bass (1946–)*

Willard White, a powerful singer with a resonant voice, has made major contributions to American opera. Most famously he sings the role of Porgy in the influential 1976 Lorin Maazel/Cleveland Orchestra recording of George Gershwin's PORGY AND BESS and he reprised the role in Simon Rattle/Trevor Nunn's 1987 recording/film of a Glyndebourne Festival production. He has

created roles in three American operas. He was Jim in Hall Overton's *Huckleberry Finn* at the Juilliard School of Music in 1971, Ned in the first staged performance of Scott Joplin's TREEMONISHA at Houston Grand Opera in 1975 and Joseph/Herod in John Adams' EL NIÑO in Paris in 2000. He plays King Balthazar in the 1978 film of Gian Carlo Menotti's AMAHL AND THE NIGHT VISITORS and the King of Clubs in the 1982 Glyndebourne Festival video of Sergei Prokofiev's THE LOVE OF THREE ORANGES. White, who was born in St. Catherine, Jamaica, studied at Juilliard and with Giorgio Tozzi. He made his debut in 1974 with Washington Opera.

THE WHITE BIRD   *1922 opera by Carter*

Reginald and wife Elinor live on an estate by a lake in the Adirondacks. When he discovers that she has fallen in love with his forester Basil, he arranges for her to be "accidentally" killed by her lover. Ernest Carter's opera *The White Bird,* libretto by Brian Hooker, was presented in concert on May 23, 1922, in New York at the Carnegie Chamber Music Hall and staged at the Studebaker Theater in Chicago on March 6, 1924. Ward Pound played Reginald, Hazel Eden was Elinor and Bryce Talbot was Basil. Leroy N. Wetzel conducted. *The White Bird* was staged at the Städtische Theater in Osnabrück, Germany, on November 15, 1927, one of the first American operas to be produced in Europe.

WHITE EAGLE   *1927 operetta by Friml*

An English aristocrat goes to the American West using the name Jim Carson and marries Indian princess Silverwing. When he inherits his family title, she kills herself in the mistaken belief this will help him. Rudolf Friml's operetta *White Eagle,* libretto by Brian Hooker and W. H. Post, is based on Edwin Milton Royle's 1905 play *The Squaw Man.* It premiered at the Casino Theater in New York on December 26, 1927, with Allen Prior as Jim and Marion Keeler as Silverwing. The hit song from the show was "Give Me One Hour." The play *The Squaw Man* has been filmed four times, mostly famously by Cecil B. DeMille in 1914 as the first Hollywood feature.

1940 Rudolf Friml. The composer play a piano version of "Give Me One Hour" from *White Eagle.* It on the Schirmer 78 album *Rudolf Friml in Person.* **1942 Gladys Swarthout.** Met soprano Gladys Swarthout took time out from singing Carmen in 1942 to record "Give Me One Hour" from *White Eagle.* It's on her album *Gladys Swarthout in Arias and Song.* OASI CD. **1960 Earl Wrightson/Lois Hunt.** Baritone Earl Wrightson and soprano Lois Hunt sing "Give Me One Hour" with orchestra conducted by Frank DeVol. The song is on the album *A Night with Rudolf Friml.* Columbia LP.

WHITE RAVEN   *1998 opera by Glass*

White Raven celebrates "discoveries" by Portuguese explorers from the expeditions of Vasco de Gama to modern-day missions to the moon and future explorations of the universe. It takes its title from the Greek myth in which Apollo turns a white crow black and the bird becomes a messenger of misfortune. Philip Glass's five-act *White Raven* (Corvo Branco), libretto by Portuguese writer Luísa Costa Gomes in Portuguese and the language of the audience and devised for the stage by Robert Wilson, was premiered at Teatro Camões in Lisbon, Portugal, on September 25, 1998. It is scored for sixteen soloists (seven women, eight men and a narrator ("the writer"), chorus, corps de ballet, and orchestra. The premiere cast included American singers Susan Hanson as Raven 1, Maria Jonas as Raven 2 and John Duykers. Dennis

Russell Davies conducted the Orquesta Sinfónica Portuguesa and Coro do Teatro Nacional São Carlos and Wilson directed. The opera was commissioned by the Portuguese for the World Expo '98 in Lisbon and Teatro Real in Madrid. *Act V* of the opera, which opens with "the writer" as a pilot describing the historic first over-water air flight from Lisbon, had its American premiere in a concert version on February 27, 2000, at Carnegie Hall. It was performed by the American Composers Orchestra with Robert Wilson as narrator and Susan Hanson and Maria Jonas (who created the roles) as the ravens. The full opera was premiered at Lincoln Center in New York on July 10, 2001.

WHITE WINGS   *1949 opera by Moore*

The Inch family company White Wings is facing ruin in 1895 because the automobile is about to replace the horse and they have made their money in street cleaning. Inch heir Archie loves Mary, but she despises horses and loves cars which her father has started to manufacture. They are reconciled when the last horse in town is shot, Archie become a taxi driver and his father buys a garbage truck. Douglas Moore's satirical three-act opera *White Wings,* libretto by the composer based on the play by Philip Barry, premiered at the Hartt School in Hartford, Connecticut, on February 9, 1949.

WHITEHILL, CLARENCE   *American bass-baritone (1871–1932)*

Clarence Whitehill sang a leading role in the first American opera ever presented at the Metropolitan Opera in New York. He played the Old One in Frederick Converse's THE PIPE OF DESIRE, staged at the Met on March 18, 1910. Whitehill, who was born in Parnell, Iowa, studied in Paris and made his debut in Brussels in 1898. He was known primarily for performing Wagnerian roles and continued to sing at the Met until 1932.

WHITTIER, JOHN GREENLEAF   *American writer (1807–1892)*

John Greenleaf Whittier is best known for poems like "Barbara Frietchie" but he also wrote a large number of stories about his native New England. Robert James Haskin's one-act opera *Cassandra Southwick,* libretto by John Koppenhaver, is based on a Whittier story about Quakers and Puritans. It premiered in Springfield, Ohio, January 24 1964.

THE WIFE OF MARTIN GUERRE   *1956 opera by Bergsma*

Martin Guerre leaves his 15th century village in the French Pyrenees to become a soldier and returns after eight years a better and somewhat different man. His wife Bertrande suspects he is an imposter and takes legal action after three years. After a trial he is condemned to be hanged but then the real Martin Guerre returns. William Bergsma's two-hour opera *The Wife of Martin Guerre,* libretto by Janet Lewis based on her novel, was premiered at the Juilliard School of Music in New York on February 15, 1956. Mary Judd played Martin Guerre's wife Bertrande, Regina Sarfaty was the servant Catherine, Stephen Harbachick was the man claiming to be Martin Guerre, Lynne Clark was Diane, Anna Maria Saritelli was Annette, Lyn Clarke was Sanxi, John Parella was Pierre, Guy Baker was Father Antoine and Frank Porretta was the Steward. Frederic Cohen directed the production and Frederick Waldman conducted the Juilliard School chamber orchestra. Bergsma's score for the opera is dissonant but lyrical.

1956 Juilliard School. Mary Judd is Martin Guerre's wife Bertrande, Regina Sarfaty is the servant Catherine and Stephen Harbachick is the imposter Martin Guerre in this original cast recording of scenes from the opera. John Parella is Pierre, Lynne Clark is Diane and Sanxi, Annamaria Saritelli is Annette, Guy Baker is Father Antoine and Frank Porretta is the Steward. Frederick Waldman conducts the Juilliard School chamber orchestra. CRI LP.

WIGGLESWORTH, FRANK   *American composer (1918–)*

Frank Wigglesworth composed two operas based around the projection of illustrated slides. *The Willowdale Handcar: or, The Return of the Black Doll,* libretto and slides by macabre humorist Edward Gorey, was premiered in New York on May 28, 1969, and reprised by After Dinner Opera at Lincoln Center on March 16, 1973. It involves three people on a wondrous trip by railroad handcar through a fantastic Gorey-esque landscape. *The Police Log of the Chronicle,* libretto by the composer based on materials in the Ipswich, MA, police log with slides by Anne Parker, was premiered by the New School Opera Workshop in New York on February 10, 1984. It describes what the police experience in a small town and how their problems are solved. Wigglesworth, a native of Boston, studied at Columbia where he later taught for forty years. He also wrote the musical play *Between the Atoms and the Stars.*

WILCOX, CAROL   *American soprano (1945–)*

Carol Ann Wilcox created the role of the opera diva Aurelia Trentoni in Jack Beeson's CAPTAIN JINKS OF THE HORSE MARINES at Lyric Opera of Kansas City in 1975 and she sings the role on the 1976 recording. She created Rachel Lockhart in Beeson's DR. HEIDEGGER'S FOUNTAIN OF YOUTH at the National Arts Club in New York in 1978 and is featured on its recording. She has also sung Abigail in Robert Ward's THE CRUCIBLE. Wilcox, born in Antioch, California, studied at the University of Kansas and the Manhattan School of Music. She made her debut in 1970 at the Metropolitan Opera Studio.

THE WILD PARTY   *2000 music-theater work by LaChiusa*

The irrepressible Queenie and her clown lover Burrs throw a wild party in New York in the late 1920s with liquor, drugs, jazz, flappers and wide-open sex as part of the mix. The party get more and more frenetic but when Queenie falls in love with another man, Burrs tries to kill him. Michael John LaChiusa's music-theater work *The Wild Party,* libretto by the composer based on Joseph Moncure March's 1928 narrative poem, premiered at the Virginia Theater on Broadway on April 13, 2000. Toni Collette was Queenie, Mandy Patinkin was Burrs, Eartha Kitt was Dolores, Marc Kudisch was Jackie, Jane Summerhays was Miss Madeleine True, Sally Murphy was Sally, Norm Lewis was Eddie Mackrel, Leah Hocking was Mae, Brooke Sunny Moriber was Nadine, Nathan Lee Graham was Phil D'Armano, Michael McElroy was Oscar D'Armano, Adam Grupper was Gold, Stuart Zagnit was Goldberg, Yancey Arias was Black and Tony Pinkins was Kate. Todd Ellison was the conductor and George C. Wolfe directed. *The Wild Party* has been described as *The Threepenny Opera* for the bathtub gin set and was hailed by some critics as the most imaginative Broadway score for years.

2000 Original cast. Toni Collette as Queenie, Mandy Patinkin as Burrs and Eartha Kitt as Dolores star in the original cast album of *The Wild Party* recorded in April 2000 at the Sony Studios in New York. The rest of the cast are as above. Todd Ellison conducts. Decca CD.

WILDER, ALEC   *American composer (1907–1980)*

Alec Wilder, who is best known as a songwriter and music critic, also composed operas. He started in 1946 with the children's operas *The Churkendoose* and *Hermine Ermine in Rabbit Town,* both with librettos by B. R. Berenberg. In 1952 he began a twenty-year partnership with librettist Arnold Sundgaard that resulted in eight operas and a musical. *The Lowland Sea* premiered at Montclair State College in New Jersey on May 8, 1952. SUNDAY EXCURSION, a popular curtain raiser focusing on young people traveling on a New York Sunday excursion train in 1910, premiered in New York City in 1953. *Cumberland Fair* was performed at Montclair State College on May 22, 1953. *Kittiwake Island* was presented at Interlochen on August 7, 1954, and was staged off-Broadway in New York in 1960 with Kathleen Murray and Lainie Kazan. *The Long Way* was premiered in Nyack, NY, on June 3, 1955. *The Impossible Forest* was presented at Westport, CT, on July 13, 1958. THE OPENING, a post-modern story about problems on the opening night of a play, premiered at the New England Conservatory in Boston in 1969. *The Truth about Windmills* was performed in Rochester, NY, on October 14, 1973. The musical *Nobody's Earnest,* based on Oscar Wilde's play *The Importance of Being Earnest,* was premiered in Williamsburg, MA, in June 1974. Wilder's third librettist partner was William Engvick with whom he created three operas. Their "musical fable" MISS CHICKEN LITTLE, in which the Fox takes advantage of the fowl's gullibility, was telecast by CBS on December 27, 1953. *The Long Way* was first staged at Nyack, NY, June 3, 1955, and then revised and staged as *Ellen* in 1964. Their children's opera *Racketty Packetty House* was created in 1967. Wilder, who was born in Rochester, NY, and studied at Eastman School, was highly successful as a songwriter with songs recorded by Bing Crosby, Frank Sinatra and Mabel Mercer among others. His 1972 book *American Popular Song* is one of the definitive studies of the genre. Surprisingly there are no recording of his operas.

Original cast album for Michael John LaChiusa's *The Wild Party,* which has been described as *The Threepenny Opera* for the bathtub gin set.

WILDER, THORNTON   *American writer (1897–1975)*

Thornton Wilder won the Pulitzer Prize in 1927 for his novel *The Bridge of San Luis Rey,* in 1938 for his play *Our Town* and in 1942 for his play. He wrote the libretto for Paul Hindemith's 1961 opera THE LONG CHRISTMAS DINNER, about an American family having dinner for ninety years, using his own play as source. THE BRIDGE OF SAN LUIS REY was turned into an opera by composer/librettist Paula Kimper and premiered by American Opera Projects at The Lighthouse in New York City in 2002.

WILL YOU MARRY ME?   *1989 opera by Kondek*

A man and a woman meet at a party. As their parents expect them to get engaged, they try to behave as badly as possible towards each other. As they talk they discover good qualities in each other and decided to marry after all. Hugo Weisgall's one-act opera *Will You Marry Me?,* libretto by Charles Kondek based on Alfred Sutro's play *A Marriage Has Been Arranged,* was premiered by the Opera Ensemble of New York on March 8, 1989. Andrea Broido was the woman, David Trombley was the man, Charles Kondek directed and Donald W. Johnston conducted the chamber orchestra. The music reflects the dance of their courtship which is reflected in off-stage dance music. *Will You Marry Me?* was composed to be presented in a trilogy with Weisgall's other one-act operas, *The Stronger* and *Purgatory.*

WILLIAM PENN   *1975 opera by Cascarino*

Quaker William Penn is persecuted for his religious beliefs and emigrates to America in 1682 to found the tolerant state of Pennsylvania and the city of Philadelphia. Romeo Cascarino's historical opera *William Penn,* libretto by the composer based on texts by Penn, was begun in 1950 as a choral work, premiered in a concert version in 1975 and fully staged on October 24, 1982, at the Academy of Music in Philadelphia to celebrate the 300th anniversary of the founding of the city. John Cheek was William Penn, Dolores Ferraro was Gulielma Penn, Roy Wilbur was Kent, Robert Mattern was Parry, Katherine Ritz was Rhoda, Michael Fiacco was Thomas, Andrea Jaber was Mariah, Gary Michael was Sidney, Phyllis Demetropoulos was Anne, Kenneth Garner was Richard, Jane Peterson was Charlotte, Lucas Ernst was the Stranger and Richard Pendergraph was King Taminent. Christofer Macatsoris conducted the Thomas Jefferson University Choir, Philadelphia Singers and Philadelphia Chamber Orchestra.

1982 Academy of Music. The stage premiere of the operas was recorded live at the Academy of Music in Philadelphia on October 24 and 29, 1982. John Cheek portrays William Penn, Dolores Ferraro (the composer's wife) is Gulielma Penn, Roy Wilbur is Kent, Robert Mattern is Parry and the rest of the cast are as listed above. Christofer Macatsoris conducts the Thomas Jefferson University Choir, Philadelphia Singers and Philadelphia Chamber Orchestra. RC CD.

WILLIAMS, CAMILLA   *American soprano (1922–)*

Camilla Williams sings Bess opposite Lawrence Winters as Porgy in a famous 1951 recording of George Gershwin's PORGY AND BESS said at the time to be the "first complete recording" (it was released on three 10-inch LPs). She also recorded "Summertime" for an RCA Victor 78 and she played Annina in the Vienna State Opera production of Gian Carlo Menotti's THE SAINT OF BLEECKER STREET. Williams, who was born in Danville, Virginia, and studied at Virginia State College, was one of the first African American singers to perform at New York City Opera, making her debut in 1946 as Madama Butterfly.

WILLIAMS, NANCY   *American mezzo-soprano (1936–)*

Nancy Williams created the role of Mrs. Bassett in Lee Hoiby's SUMMER AND SMOKE at St. Paul Opera in 1971. She plays Dinah opposite Julian Patrick in the 1973 London Weekend Television production of Leonard Bernstein's TROUBLE IN TAHITI, which is on CD and video. She has sung Raquel in Thomas Pasatieri's THE BLACK WIDOW, the Announcer in Douglas Moore's GALLANTRY, the Mother in Gian Carlo Menotti's AMAHL AND THE NIGHT VISITORS, Elizabeth Proctor in Robert Ward's THE CRUCIBLE and Baba the Turk in Igor Stravinsky's THE RAKE'S PROGRESS. Williams, who was born in Cleveland, Ohio, and studied in Pittsburgh and New York, made her debut at New England Opera Theater in 1958.

WILLIAMS, TENNESSEE   *American playwright (1911–1983)*

Tennessee Williams became one of America's best-known playwrights after the Broadway success of *The Glass Menagerie* (1944) and *A Streetcar Named Desire* (1947). His plays and stories have inspired a number of operas and he wrote an original libretto for one of them The best known is André Previn's A STREETCAR NAMED DESIRE which premiered at San Francisco Opera in 1998. Operas and their composers and librettists are listed below.

I Rise in Flame, Cried the Phoenix (1951). Thomas Flanagan's *I Rise in Flame, Cried the Phoenix*, libretto by the composer. Premiere: Golden Fleece, New York, Feb 7, 1980. **The Lady of Larkspur Lotion (1938).** Robert Convey's *The Lady of Larkspur Lotion*, libretto by the composer. Premiere: Spoleto Festival, Italy, July 15, 1980, with Gail Blache-Gill as the Lady. **Lord Byron's Love Letter (1955).** Raffaelo de Banfield's LORD BYRON'S LOVE LETTER, libretto by Tennessee Williams. Premiere: Tulane University, January 17, 1955. **A Streetcar Named Desire (1947).** André Previn's A STREETCAR NAMED DESIRE, libretto by Philip Littell. Premiere: San Francisco Opera, September 19, 1998. **Summer and Smoke (1948).** Lee Hoiby's SUMMER AND SMOKE, libretto by Lanford Wilson. Premiere: St. Paul Opera, St. Paul, June 19, 1971.

WILLIAMS, WILLIAM CARLOS   *American poet/ playwright (1883–1963)*

William Carlos Williams, one of America's greatest poets, also wrote stories and plays. His play *The First President*, a fantasy on the life of George Washington, was published in 1961 and turned into an opera in 1964. Theodore Harris's *The First President*, libretto based on the play, premiered at Fairleigh Dickinson University in Rutherford, NJ. Williams was born in Rutherford, NJ, and spent most of life there working as a doctor.

WILLIE STARK   *1981 opera by Floyd*

Willie Stark, the corrupt but popular governor of a Southern state in the 1930s, is about to be impeached by the state legislature. Stark's idealistic assistant Jack attempts to get support for Stark from his father Judge Burton but is turned down. After Stark digs up dirt from the judge's past and threatens to reveal it, the judge kills himself. Jack's girl Anne leaves him for Stark who promises to marry her. Jack goes crazy and shoots Stark at a celebratory rally and is killed by a bodyguard. Carlisle Floyd's opera *Willie Stark*, libretto by the composer based on Robert Penn Warren's novel *All The King's Men*, was premiered by Grand Opera Houston in Houston on April 24, 1981. Timothy Nolen played Willie Stark, Alan Kays was Jack, Jan Curtiz was streetwise floozy Sadie Burke, Julia Conwell was Jack's girl Anne Stanton, David Vos-

burgh was "Tiny" Duffy, Robert Moulson was Sugar Boy, Donald Bess was the Mayor, Don Garrard was Judge Burden, Herbert Wilkerson was George William, Lisa de la Reza was Lucy Stark, Lynn Griebling was Mrs. Stark, Rodney Stenborg was Hugh, Bruce Ford was Jeff, Raydon Vaught was the Reporter and Lowell Thomas was the Radio Commentator. Eugene Lee designed the sets, Judith Dolan designed the costumes, Harold Prince directed and John DeMain conducted the Houston Grand Opera Orchestra. The Pulitzer Prize-winning novel that inspired the opera, based on the life of Louisiana Governor Huey Long, was made into a film in 1949 with Broderick Crawford as Willie Stark.

1981 Houston Grand Opera. Timothy Nolen is Willie Stark and Alan Clark is Jack in this videotaped telecast of the Houston Grand Opera premiere production. The cast members are as above with John DeMain conducting. TV director Brian Large taped the opera without an audience so he could place cameras in the auditorium and on the stage. Premiere Opera VHS/Live Opera audiocassette. Video at MTR.

WILLOW SONG   *Soprano aria : The Ballad of Baby Doe (1956). Words: John Latouche. Music: Douglas Moore*

The touching "Willow Song," with its antecedents in the operas of Verdi and Rossini, is the first aria sung by Baby Doe McCourt, a young woman just arrived in a small mining town in Colorado in 1880. She sits at the piano in the Clarendon Hotel in Leadville and tells of her loneliness in a simple, charming way, beginning with the phrase "Willow, where we met together." Silver millionaire Horace Tabor hears her singing and is charmed; their tragic love story begins. The aria was introduced at the Central City Opera House premiere in 1956 by soprano Dolores Wilson but it was Beverly Sills who became famous singing it in the New York City Opera production and cast album. Virginia Copeland and Ruth Welting perform it in televised productions, Jan Grissom sings it on a 1997 Central City cast recording and Dawn Upshaw and Helen-Kay Eberley feature it on their albums of American arias. The "Willow Song," like *The Ballad of Baby Doe* which has been in the American opera repertory for half a century, seems likely to endure. It is included in Richard Walters' compilation *Opera American Style: Arias for Soprano.*

THE WILLOW TREE   *1932 radio opera by Cadman*

Gordon is loved by Donatella and all goes well until beautiful Alison arrives and wins him away. When Gordon and Alison arrange a rendezvous under a willow tree, Donatella and her father Pietro spy on them and Pietro kills Gordon. Charles Wakefield Cadman's 23-minute opera *The Willow Tree*, libretto by Nelle Richmond Eberhart, premiered on NBC Radio on October 3, 1932, as the first opera written expressly for radio. The singers were Muriel Wilson, Veronica Wiggins, Frederick Hufsmith and Theodore Webb. Cesare Sodero conducted the NBC National Grand Opera Orchestra. *The Willow Tree* has been staged by Opera in the Ozarks, the summer festival at Inspiration Point Fine Arts Colony in Eureka Springs, Arkansas.

WILLSON, MEREDITH   *American composer (1902–1984)*

Meredith Willson created one of the great American musicals, THE MUSIC MAN, an outpouring of melodic nostalgia for his Iowa childhood. He was born in Mason City, Iowa, the inspiration for the musical's setting of River City, and studied music at Juilliard and with composer Henry Hadley while playing flute in the New York Philharmonic. He worked in radio, television and film (his movie scores include Charlie Chaplin's *The Great Dictator*) and turned to the musical stage in 1957 with *The Music Man*, the story of a irresistible conman who sells musical instruments in small towns. It was followed by the popular *The Unsinkable Molly Brown* in 1960 and the less successful *Here's Love*, based on the film *Miracle on 34th Street*, in 1963. His light opera *1491* was premiered by Los Angeles Opera at the Chandler Pavilion in Los Angeles in 1969.

WILSON, LANFORD   *American librettist/playwright (1937–)*

Lanford Wilson, who won the Pulitzer Prize for Drama for his 1979 play *Talley's Folley,* wrote the libretto for Lee Hoiby's opera SUMMER AND SMOKE based on the play by Tennessee Williams. It was commissioned by St. Paul Opera which premiered it in 1971. Wilson, who was born in Lebanon, Missouri, made his reputation in the 1960s in off-Broadway theater and increased it in the 1970s with larger ensemble plays in the tradition of Williams.

WILSON, NEIL   *American tenor (1956–2000)*

Neil Wilson created the role of Dog in Henry Mollicone's STARBIRD for Texas Opera Theater in Houston in 1981. Wilson, born in Abilene Texas, made his debut in 1980 at Wolf Trap. He sang at the Metropolitan Opera for five years and was also popular with German opera houses.

WILSON, ROBERT   *American designer/director (1941–)*

Robert Wilson calls many of his avant-garde stage productions "operas" and has worked with several composers on notable music theater works. He staged and wrote the librettos for three "operas" with music by Alan Lloyd: the 12-hour "silent opera" *The Life and Times of Joseph Stalin* in 1973, *A Letter for Queen Victoria* in 1974 and *Death, Destruction and Detroit* in 1979. His first collaboration with Philip Glass was on EINSTEIN ON THE BEACH; it premiered at the Avignon Theatre Festival in France in 1976 and was then staged at opera houses in Europe and at the Met. They next worked together on THE CIVIL WARS: *a tree is best measured when it is down,* which was planned for the 1984 Los Angeles Olympics Arts Festival but became so costly only two parts were produced. Their multi-media opera MONSTERS OF GRACE, premiered in 1998 at UCLA's Melnitz Hall in Los Angeles, incorporated digital 3-D imagery. Wilson has also worked on music theater works with Tom Waits. The cabaret opera THE BLACK RIDER was premiered in

Director Robert Wilson

Hamburg in 1990 and reprised at the Brooklyn Academy of Music in 1994; *Alice,* music and lyrics by Waits and Kathleen Brennan, book by Paul Schmidt, was staged at the Thalia in 1992 and BAM in 1995; and *Woyzeck,* based on George Büchner's play, was premiered in Copenhagen in 2002 and reprised at BAM. In addition he staged Tania León's *The Golden Windows* and SCOURGE OF HYACINTHS in Europe, produced Virgil Thomson's classic FOUR SAINTS IN THREE ACTS for Houston Grand Opera in 1996 and staged Gertrude Stein's DOCTOR FAUSTUS LIGHTS THE LIGHTS with music by Hans Peter Kuhn at Lincoln Center in July 1992. Wilson, who was born in Waco, Texas, studied at the University of Texas and graduated with a degree in architecture from the Pratt Institute in Brooklyn in 1965.

THE WIND REMAINS   *1943 zarzuela opera by Bowles*

A man courts a woman who can't seem to make up her mind. Paul Bowles zarzuela-style opera *The Wind Remains*, libretto by the composer (original version by William Saroyan), is based on Federico Garcia Lorca's play "Asi que pasen cinco años." It is not strong on narrative and we never know whether love wins out, though dancers comment on the action through mime. The music is a mix of jazz, Latino and American styles with the singers accompanied by flute-like wind instruments, harp, bells and guitar It premiered at the Museum of Modern Art in New York on March 30, 1943, with Leonard Bernstein conducting and Merce Cunningham in charge of the choreography.

1995 EOS Ensemble. Mezzo-soprano Lucy Schaufer is the woman being wooed and tenor Carl Halvorson is the would-be seducer in this 23-minute recording of the opera made at the Manhattan Center Studios in September 1995. Jonathan Sheffer conducts the EOS Ensemble on the album *The Music of Paul Bowles.* RCA Victor CD.

WINDSTORM IN BUBBLELAND   *1980 children's TV opera by Rogers*

The peace of Bubbleland, where bubbles and bubble people are prized, is threatened by a nasty wind. A banana-boat captain and his friends build a wall to protect it. Fred Rogers' children's TV opera *Windstorm in Bubbleland*, libretto by the composer, was premiered on PBS on May 19, 1980. Baritone John Reardon and tenor Francois Clemmons did most of the singing with support from Betty Aberlin, Joe Negri, Don Brocket and a group of puppets. The educational opera was created for the kids program *Mister Rogers' Neighborhood.*

THE WINGS OF THE DOVE   *1961 opera by Moore*

Kate Croy loves Miles Dunstan and wants to marry him but her father Homer has gambled away the family fortune. Kate arranges for rich but frail American heiress Milly Theale to marry Miles believing she will die soon and Miles will inherit her money. Lord Mark tells Milly about the plot but they are reconciled before Milly dies leaving him her fortune. Miles says he will marry Kate if she will give up the money but she refuses. Milly is the white dove shadowing them. Douglas Moore's two-act opera *The Wings of the Dove,* libretto by Ethan Ayer based on the novel by Henry James, was commissioned by Julius Rudel for New York City Opera where it premiered on October 12, 1961. Regina Sarfaty sang the role of Kate, John Reardon was Miles, Dorothy Coulter was Milly, Norman Kelley was Lord Mark, Martha Lipton was Aunt Maud, Paul Ukena was Homer, Mary LeSawyer was Susan, Richard Fredericks was Steffens, Maurice Stern was the Lecturer and Fredric Milstein was Giuliano. Donald Oenslager designed the sets, Patton

Campbell designed the costumes, Christopher West directed and Julius Rudel conducted.

WINONA   *1926 opera by Bimboni*

Native Americans Winona and Chatonska are in love but when he leaves a hunt in order to meet with her, he is branded a coward by her uncle Wabashaw. When her uncle tries to force her to marry Matosapa, she jumps to her death from a high ledge. Alberto Bimboni's three-act opera *Winona*, libretto by Perry Williams based on a Sioux Indian legend, was premiered by the American Grand Opera Company in Portland, Oregon, on November ll, 1926, with Bimboni conducting. Minna Pelz was Winona, J. McMillan Muir was Chatonska, Alice Price Moore was Winona's friend Weeko, A. K. Houghton was Matosapa and William Fraser Robertson was Wabashaw. The opera was revived in Minneapolis in 1928 where it was praised for incorporating elements of Native American music in its score. It was awarded the David Bispham Medal that year.

WINTERS, LAWRENCE   *American bass-baritone (1915–1965)*

Lawrence Winters made his operatic debut singing the role of slave revolution leader Jean Jacques Dessalines in Clarence Cameron White's OUANGA in 1941 at the New School for Social Research and began to sing with New York City Opera in 1948. He created the role of the Messenger in David Tamkin's THE DYBBUK at New York City Opera in 1951 and his other roles at NYCO included King Melchior in Gian Carlo Menotti's AMAHL AND THE NIGHT VISITORS (1952), Stephen Kumalo in Kurt Weill's LOST IN THE STARS (1958) and Porgy in George Gershwin's PORGY AND BESS (1962). He recorded the role of Porgy in 1953 for an album with three 12-inch LPs, said at the time to be first complete recording and he recorded the role Daniel Webster in Douglas Moore's THE DEVIL AND DANIEL WEBSTER in 1957 with the Festival Choir. He has also sung the role of Joe in Jerome Kern's *Show Boat*. Winters, born in Kings Creek, South Carolina, studied at Howard University and with Porgy creator Todd Duncan. In addition to NYCO, he sang at San Francisco Opera and Hamburg State Opera.

A WINTER'S TALE   *1974 opera by Harbison*

King Leontes, jealous of Queen Hermione, suspects her of having an affair with rival King Polixenes. He sends her to prison where she gives birth to a baby girl and dies. The baby girl, named Perdita, is banished from the kingdom. She returns sixteen years with Prince Florizel, son of rival Polixenes, whom she loves. Leontes welcomes his lost child and a statue of his queen comes to life. She forgives him and embraces Perdita. John Harbison's two-act opera *A Winter's Tale*, libretto by the composer based on the play by Shakespeare, was premiered on August 20, 1979, by San Francisco Opera's American Opera Project. David Arnold sang the role of Leontes, Susan Quittmeyer was Hermione, David Koch was Polixenes, Ellen Kerrigan was Perdita, Tonio Di Paolo was Florizel, Gwendolyn Jones was Paulina, John Miller was Time, William Pisenti was the Shepherd, Daniel De Jarnett was Mamillius, William Mallory was Camillo and Robert Tate was Antigonus. The action is highly stylized, almost ritualistic, with six pantomime dumbshows advancing the action when needed. A revised version was staged by Aspen Opera Theater in 1997.

WISCONSIN   *American state (1848–)*

Wisconsin has been a center of musical culture since the 19th century, especially Milwaukee which became famous for the quality of its German singing groups. The first American opera premiered in Wisconsin was Edward Sobolewski's three-act MOHEGA, *The Flower of the Forest*, about a Native American woman who loved a Revolutionary war hero; it was produced in German at Albany Hall in Milwaukee on October 11, 1859. Another grand opera with a Native American heroine, Willard Patton's *Pocahontas*, was premiered at the Hotel Radisson in Milwaukee on January 4, 1911. Eleanor Everest Freer's *A Legend of Spain* premiered at Marwood Studios in Milwaukee on June 19, 1931. Milwaukee remains the center of operatic activity in Wisconsin today, with two innovative companies, but Madison and the universities are also active. Skylight Opera in Milwaukee has one of the strongest American opera/music theater programs in the U.S. Wisconsin-born opera people include bass-baritone Donald Gramm (Milwaukee), composer Daron Eric Hagen (Milwaukee), composer Lee Hoiby (Madison), composer Otto Luening (Milwaukee), baritone Kurt Ollmann (Racine), composer Herbert Stothart (Milwaukee) and director Orson Welles (Kenosha). Conrad Susa's grim opera BLACK RIVER: *a Wisconsin Idyll*, based on Michael Vesy's photographic book *Wisconsin Death Trip*, takes place in Wisconsin.

Appleton: La Vahn Maesch's *The Grandmother and the Witch* was premiered at the First Congregational Church in Appleton in November 1972.

Eau Claire: Michael Cunningham has premiered three operas at the University of Wisconsin in Eau Claire: *Figg and Bean*, based on a story by John Madison Morton, on March 7, 1975; *Catherine Sloper of* WASHINGTON SQUARE, based on the novel by Henry James, on March 31, 1978; and *Dorian Gray*, based on the novel by Oscar Wilde, on January 25, 1985.

Green Bay: Pamiro Opera, which describes itself as the "Northeast Wisconsin regional opera company," has a strong interest in American opera. Its productions have included Seymour Barab's *Little Red Riding Hood* and Gian Carlo Menotti's AMAHL AND THE NIGHT VISITORS.

Madison: Madison Opera, founded in 1963, premiered Daron Hagen's SHINING BROW, the story of Frank Lloyd Wright, on April 21, 1993. It's other American presentations include Leonard Bernstein's CANDIDE, Lukas Foss's THE JUMPING FROG OF CALAVERAS COUNTY, John Franklin's children's opera THE THUNDER OF HORSES, Mitch Leigh's MAN OF LA MANCHA, Gian Carlo Menotti's AMAHL AND THE NIGHT VISITORS, AMELIA GOES TO THE BALL and HELP, HELP, THE GLOBOLINKS!, Douglas Moore's THE BALLAD OF BABY DOE, Stephen Paulus's THE VILLAGE SINGER, Cole Porter's KISS ME KATE, Richard Rodgers' CAROUSEL, Peter Schickele's A LITTLE NIGHTMARE MUSIC and THE STONED GUEST, Harvey Schmidt's *The Fantasticks*, and Stephen Sondheim's A LITTLE NIGHT MUSIC and *Side by Side by Sondheim*. David Bishop's ESPERANZA, based on Michael Wilson's screenplay for the 1953 film *Salt of the Earth*, premiered at the University of Wisconsin's Music Hall in Madison on August 25, 2000.

Milwaukee: Florentine Opera began in 1951 with a production of Gian Carlo Menotti's THE TELEPHONE. It mounted the American premiere of Lowell Liebermann's THE PICTURE OF DORIAN GRAY, based on the Oscar Wilde novel, on February 5, 1999. Its other American productions have included George Gershwin's PORGY AND BESS, Menotti's THE CONSUL and Douglas Moore's THE BALLAD OF BABY DOE. Arthur Penn premiered his one-act comic opera *Ladies' Aid* in Milwaukee in 1955. Roger Reynolds' *The Emperor of Ice Cream*, based on Wallace Stevens's poem, was presented at the University of Wisconsin in Milwaukee on November 17, 1965. Jonathan Elkus premiered two classical one-act operas at the University on November 13, 1970: MEDEA, based on the play by Euripides, and *Helen of Egypt,* based on an epic poem by Hilda Doolittle. Gian Carlo Menotti's highly biographical cantata LANDSCAPES AND REMEMBRANCES was commissioned by Milwaukee's Bel Canto Chorus and premiered and telecast May l4, 1976, at the Milwaukee Performing Arts Center. Skylight Opera Theater, founded in 1959, presents a an eclectic mixture of operas, operettas and musicals and has devoted much of its production to American work. It co-commissioned Richard Wargo's BALLYMORE which it premiered on January 29, 1999. Director Francesca Zambello was co-artistic director of the company from 1985 to 1990 before beginning her international career and baritone Kurt Ollmann began his career there. Skylight's many American productions include Domenick Argento's POSTCARD FROM MOROCCO, Leonard Bernstein's CANDIDE, TROUBLE IN TAHITI and WEST SIDE STORY, Marc Blitzstein's THE CRADLE WILL ROCK and REGINA, Stephen Flaherty's *Once on This Island,* Carlisle Floyd's FLOWER AND HAWK and SUSANNAH, Lukas Foss's GRIFFELKIN and THE JUMPING FROG OF CALAVERAS COUNTY, Rudolf Friml's THE VAGABOND KING, Adam Guettel's operatic musical FLOYD COLLINS, Victor Herbert's NAUGHTY MARIETTA and THE RED MILL, Robert Kurka's THE GOOD SOLDIER SCHWEIK, Mitch Leigh's MAN OF LA MANCHA, Frank Loesser's *Guys and Dolls,* Gian Carlo Menotti's THE EGG, THE MEDIUM and THE SAINT OF BLEECKER STREET, Douglas Moore's THE DEVIL AND DANIEL WEBSTER, Jerome Moross's GENTLEMEN, BE SEATED, Thea Musgrave's HARRIET, THE WOMAN CALLED MOSES, Thomas Pasatieri's THE BLACK WIDOW, Rachel Portman's THE LITTLE PRINCE, Richard Rodgers' OKLAHOMA!, Sigmund Romberg's BLOSSOM TIME, THE DESERT SONG and THE STUDENT PRINCE, Harvey Schmidt's THE FANTASTICKS, Stephen Sondheim's A LITTLE NIGHT MUSIC and SWEENEY TODD, Charles Strouse's children's opera NIGHTINGALE, John Philip Sousa's EL CAPITAN and *The Free Lance,* Igor Stravinsky's THE RAKE'S PROGRESS, Virgil Thomson's THE MOTHER OF US ALL, Richard Wargo's A CHEKHOV TRILOGY, Kurt Weill's DOWN IN THE VALLEY and LOST IN THE STARS and Hugo Weisgall's THE STRONGER.

Stevens Point: Ronald Combs' *The Monkey's Paw,* based on the story by W. W. Jacobs, premiered at the University of Wisconsin in Stevens Point in February 1974.

THE WISE WOMEN   *1994 church opera by Susa*

Three Wise Women (Maiden, Goodwife, Crone) and Three Wise Men (Youth, Husband, Old Man) follow a tri-partite star towards Bethlehem. The men think the King they seek will be an adult, the women think it will be a baby and because of this disagreement, the men go on alone. The Holy Family is transported to the women in a vision and later the women teach the men about the greatest gift for a child—love. Conrad Susa's 50-minute church opera *The Wise Women,* libretto by Philip Littell (who also wrote the libretto for Susa's *The Dangerous Liaisons*), was commissioned by the American Guild of Organists for their Dallas Convention in July 1994 and features two organs in its eight-instrument score. Virginia Dupuy played the Crone and Philip Brunelle conducted the organs and chamber orchestra.

1996 Civic Opera Theater. The Three Wise Women are Kelly Etter (Maiden), Amy Lynn Rosine (Goodwife) and Margaret Hauber (Crone) in this performance of the opera by the Civic Opera Theater of Kansas City. The Three Wise Men are Stanley Jackson (Youth), Michael B. Lanman (Husband), and Todd Berry (Old Man). Cathy McNown, Sylvia Stoner and Paul Votabva Resch portrayed the tri-partite Star, Braxton Jensen was Baby Jesus, Nina Witt was Mary, John Landry was Joseph and Mary Landry

was Mary Queen of Heaven. The Angels, Shepherds, Animals, Retinue, Acolytes and Secret Service Men were portrayed by chorus singers. John Obetz played the grand organ, Laura Burkhart designed the set, Linda Ade Brand directed the opera and Charles Bruffy conducted the chamber orchestra and Grace and Holy Trinity Episcopal Cathedral Chancel Choir. The opera was videotaped live at the Temple of the Reorganized Church of Jesus Christ of Latter Day Saints in Independence, Missouri, in December 1996, and presented on Kansas City Public Television. KCPT VHS.

THE WISH   *1955 opera by Antheil*

Rick brings Harriet and Josh a cake to celebrate their fourth wedding anniversary. Rick is secretly in love with Harriet but she refuses him; he becomes deranged and kills her. Josh and Harriet celebrate their anniversary in a restaurant but she turns out to be a ghost. Rick confesses the murder to Josh. George Antheil's macabre one-act opera *The Wish,* libretto by the composer, was premiered by Kentucky Opera at Louisville on April 3, 1955. Charme Riesley was Harriet, William Pickett was husband Josh, Farrold Stephens was friend Rick, Joyce Tisdale was landlady Mrs. Burnett, Richard Dales was restaurant owner Alberto, Robert Fischer was policeman Pat, Russell Hedger was the blind man and Ben Weiss and Virginia Guerney were the Dancers. Moritz Bombard staged the production, designed the set and conducted the Louisville Orchestra. *The Wish* was one of six American operas commissioned by Louisville Orchestra in the 1950s with Rockefeller Foundation funds.

1955 Kentucky Opera. The Kentucky Opera premiere performance was recorded with the cast as listed above headed by Charme Riesley as Harriet, William Pickett as Josh and Farrold Stephens as Rick. Moritz Bomhard conducts the Louisville Orchestra. Louisville First Edition Records LP.

WISTER, OWEN   *American writer/composer (1860–1938)*

Owen Wister, the progenitor of western fiction, was also an opera composer and librettist. His 1902 novel *The Virginian* made him famous. especially through its many stage and movie versions, and he is credited with creating many of the conventions and cliches associated with the Western genre (like "Smile when you call me that, stranger"). His first opera was *La Serenade,* performed in Boston in 1883. It was followed by *Montezuma* (1884) and *Charlemagne* (1890), neither of which seem to have been staged. His last and most popular opera was the prohibition-inspired *Watch Your Thirst: A Dry Opera in Three Acts* published in 1923 and premiered in Boston in 1924.

A WITCH OF SALEM   *1925 opera by Cadman*

Salem, Massachusetts in 1692 during the Puritan witch trials. Sheila is in love with Arnold but he loves Claris so she accuses Claris of witchcraft to get rid of her. She recants at the last moment after a kiss from Arnold and takes Claris's place on the gallows. Charles Cadman's opera *A Witch of Salem,* libretto by Nellie Richmond Eberhard, was premiered by Chicago Civic Opera on December 8, 1926. Irene Pavloska sang the role of Sheila, Eidé Norena was Claris, Charles Hackett was Arnold, José Mojica was Deacon Fairfield, Howard Preston was Nathaniel and Helen Freund was Elizabeth. Henry G. Weber conducted. The opera was revived in 1928 and staged in Chicago and Los Angeles and then presented on radio. It was broadcast by NBC's National Grand Opera Company on June 13, 1928, with Cesare Sodero conducting the Grand Opera Orchestra.

WITHERSPOON, HERBERT   *American bass (1873–1935)*

Herbert Witherspoon sang in the first two American operas presented at the Metropolitan Opera. He played the Gnome in Frederick Converse's THE PIPE OF DESIRE in 1910 and he created the role of Arth in Horatio Parker's MONA in 1912. Witherspoon, who was born in Buffalo, NY, and studied at Yale, made his debut with the Castle Square Opera Company in New York in 1898 and began to sing at the Met in 1908. He succeeded Giulio Gatti-Casazza as general manager of the Met om 1935 but died a month later of a heart attack.

THE WIZARD OF THE NILE   *1895 comic opera by Herbert*

During a drought in ancient Egypt an itinerant Persian magician named Kibosh is hired by King Ptolemy to create rain. When he brings so much rain it causes floods, he gets thrown in prison. Meanwhile Princess Cleopatra has become romantically involved with her music teacher Ptarmigan. Victor Herbert's comic opera *The Wizard of the Nile*, libretto by Harry B. Smith, premiered at the Grand Opera House in Wilkes-Barres, PA, on September 26, 1895, and opened in New York at the Casino Theater on November 4. Frank Daniels played Kibosh, Louise Royce was his apprentice Abydos, Walter Allen was Ptolemy, Dorothy Morton was Cleopatra, Edwin Isham was Ptarmigan and Mary Palmer was Ptolemy's wife Simoona. *Wizard* was produced by the Frank Daniels Opera Company and staged by Napier Lothian, Jr. with Frank Palma conducting. Afterwards it became an international success and was staged in England, Austria, Germany and Hungary.

1909 Victor Herbert. Composer Victor Herbert leads his orchestra in a selection of songs from *The Wizard of the Nile* for an Edison 78 record. **1950 Schenectady Light Opera.** Emerson Smith stars as Kibosh in a live recording of a concert version of the opera presented by the Schenectady Light Opera Company in May 1950. Peggy Coe is Abydos, Dick Babbit is Ptolemy, Julie Scherk is Simoona, Sylvia Horowitrz is Cleopatra, Ed Curry is Ptarmigan, Hal Eidlebuss is Cheops, Cynthia Brooks is Obeliska, Barbara Gervais is Netooris, Florence Jones is Memphis and Marge Turpin is Merza. Edward J. Hatfield Jr. leads the Schenectady Light Opera Company Chorus and Orchestra. The album, called *A Concert Performance of The Wizard of the Nile*, features twenty-four numbers from the show. It was recorded on acetate discs and released on a CD by AEI in 1999.

WNYC RADIO   *New York radio station*

WNYC Radio in New York City presented a dozen short American operas between 1945 and 1968, most of them premieres, and they were broadcast nationally through the Mutual Broadway System. Seven of them were written by Brooklyn composer Martin Kalmanoff.

1945 Robert Russell Bennett, THE ENCHANTED KISS. 1947 Julia Smith, *The Gooseherd and the Goblin.* 1948 Salvatore Virzi, *Sulamita.* 1949 Martin Kalmanoff, *Fit for a King.* 1951 Martin Kalmanoff, *Noah and the Stowaway.* 1952 Martin Kalmanoff, THE EMPTY BOTTLE. 1953 Martin Kalmanoff, GODIVA. 1954 Beatrice Laufer, ILE. 1955 Martin Kalmanoff, THE DELINQUENTS. 1956 Martin Kalmanoff, OPERA, OPERA. 1958 Mildred Kayden, *Mardi Gras.* 1964 Herbert Hausfrecht, *A Pot of Broth.* 1968 Martin Kalmanoff, *The Audition.*

WOLFF, BEVERLY   *American mezzo-soprano (1928–)*

Dramatic mezzo-soprano Beverly Wolff has made important contributions to American opera. She sang Dinah in the 1952 NBC TV production and recording of Leonard Bernstein's TROUBLE IN TAHITI and it was this production that finally attracted attention to the opera. She reprised the role on stage in 1958 at New York City Opera. She created the role of the Executive Director in Gian Carlo Menotti's LABYRINTH on NBC Television in 1963, Carry Nation in Douglas Moore's CARRY NATION at the University of Kansas in Lawrence in 1966, Leona in Menotti's THE MOST IMPORTANT MAN at New York City Opera in 1971 and the title role in Ned Rorem's BERTHA at Alice Tully Hall in New York in 1973. She sang Desideria in the New York City Opera production of Menotti's THE SAINT OF BLEECKER STREET in 1965 and has also sung Erika in Samuel Barber's VANESSA and Elizabeth Proctor in Robert Ward's THE CRUCIBLE. Wolff, who was born in Atlanta and studied there and in Philadelphia, made her debut at New York City Opera in 1960.

THE WOMAN AT OTOWI CROSSING   *1995 opera by Paulus*

Helen Chalmers, who runs a tearoom in New Mexico in the 1940s, becomes a nurturing mother figure to Native Americans and scientists of the Manhattan Project creating the atomic bomb. She tries to reconcile their contrasting worlds and has difficult relationships with her lover, her daughter and the FBI. Stephen Paulus' opera *The Woman at Otowi Crossing*, libretto by Joan Vail Thorne based on a novel by Frank Waters, was premiered by Opera Theater of Saint Louis on June 17, 1995. Sheri Greenawald starred as Helen, Kimm Julian was her lover, Christine Abrahams was her daughter, Andrew Wentzel and Grant Youngblood were the Native Americans and Richard Troxell, John Stephens, Paul D. Bustin and James Martin were the Scientists. Derek McLane designed the set, Colin Graham directed and Richard Buckley conducted.

THE WOMEN IN THE GARDEN   *1978 chamber opera by Fine*

Gertrude Stein, Isadora Duncan, Virginia Woolf and Emily Dickinson get together to discuss their lives, work and problems. Vivian Fine's feminist opera *The Women in the Garden*, libretto by the composer based on the writings of the four women, was premiered by the Port Costa Players in San Francisco on December 2, 1978, and reprised at the San Francisco Opera Center in 1982. The opera is composed five singers, the fifth being a tenor who sings all the male roles.

WOMEN OPERA COMPOSERS

Women opera composers have made important contributions to the growth and development of American opera. MARY ANN POWNALL wrote the songs for the ballad opera *Needs Must* in 1793, the first ballad opera created by a woman in America. ABBIE GERRISH-JONES created the four-act romantic opera *Priscilla* in 1887, the first American opera with libretto and score by a woman. EMMA STEINER's comic opera *Fleurette* was staged in San Francisco in 1889. MARY CARR MOORE began her opera career starring in her light opera *The Oracle* in San Francisco in 1894. JANE VAN ETTEN had her opera *Guido Ferranti* premiered by the Century Opera Company in Chicago in 1914. ELEANOR EVEREST FREER created the Bispham Memorial Medal in 1924 to honor American opera composers. SHIRLEY GRAHAM. the first African American woman to have an opera produced on stage, premiered her grandiose *Tom-Tom* in Cleveland in 1932. PEGGY GLANVILLE-HICKS attracted a lot of attention with her opera *Nausicaa* in 1961. THEA MUSGRAVE has become one of the best known American composers with operas like *Harriet, the Woman Called Moses* (1985). Avant-garde women composers have also become important, most notably MEREDITH MONK, LAURIE ANDERSON and ALICE SHIELDS. Other women composers with entries in this encyclopedia include LORA ABORN, NOA AIN, BETH ANDERSON, JOYCE BARTHELSON, AMY MARCY BEACH, VICTORIA BOND, TINA DAVIDSON, VIVIEN FINE, ELEANOR EVEREST FREER, MARGARET GARWOOD, JANICE GITECK, PEGGY GLANVILLE-HICKS, SORREL HAYES, JEAN EICHELBERG IVEY, BETSY JOLAS, EVA JESSYE, JOAN LA BARBARA, LIBBY LARSEN. BEATRICE LAUFER, TANIA LEÓN, DOROTHY RUDD MOORE, POLLY PEN, JULIA PERRY, RACHEL PORTMAN, JULIA SMITH, NANCY HAYES and KATE WARING.

WOMEN OPERA LIBRETTISTS

Women have been writing librettos for American operas since colonial times, including many famous poets and novelists. ANN JULIA KEMBLE HATTON and SUSANNA ROWSON were the first. Hatton collaborated with Mary Ann Pownall on the ballad opera *Needs Must* (1793), the first ballad opera created by women in America, and with James Hewitt on *Tammany* (1794), the first serious American opera with an American story. Rowson wrote the librettos for two operas by Alexander Reinagle. *Slaves in Algiers* (1794) and *The Volunteers* (1795). RIDA JOHNSON YOUNG was the queen of operetta librettists at the beginning of the 20th century, working with Victor Herbert on NAUGHTY MARIETTA, Sigmund Romberg on *Maytime*, Rudolf Friml and Jerome Kern. Songwriter DOROTHY FIELD wrote librettos for Romberg and Irving Berlin. NELLE RICHMOND EBERHART wrote the librettos for Charles Wakefield Cadman's operas, most notably *Shanewis* which was staged at the Metropolitan Opera in 1918. Poet EDNA ST. VINCENT MILLAY wrote the libretto for Deems Taylor's opera *The King's Henchman*, staged at the Met in 1927. VERNA ARVEY wrote the librettos for the operas composed by her husband William Grant Still. LUCILLE FLETCHER wrote the libretto for husband Bernard Herrmann's 1951 opera *Wuthering Heights* based on the novel by Emily Bronte. The most influential librettist was Gertrude Stein whose librettos and plays have inspired dozen of composers, most notably *Four Saints in Three Acts* (1934) and *The Mother of Us All* (1947), created in collaboration with composer Virgil Thomson. BETTY COMDEN wrote the book for Leonard Bernstein's *On the Town* with Adolph Green while Lillian Hellman wrote the libretto for Leonard Bernstein's *Candide* (1956) but probably wished she hadn't as it caused so much controversy. Laura Harrington wrote the libretto for Tod Machover's *Resurrection*, based on the epic Tolstoy novel, which was premiered at Houston Grand Opera in 1999. Novelist Joyce Carol Oates wrote the libretto for John Duffy's 1997 opera *Black Water* and director Julie Taymor wrote librettos for two operas by composer Elliot Goldenthal.

WONDERFUL TOWN   *1953 musical by Bernstein*

Two sisters from Ohio find how wonderfully romantic life in New York can be. Leonard Bernstein's musical *Wonderful Town*, which appears to be entering the opera repertory, has lyrics by Betty Comden and Adolph Green and a libretto by Joseph Field and Jerome Chodorov based on their 1940 play *My Sister Eileen* derives from Ruth McKinney stories. It premiered at the Winter Garden in New York on February 25, 1953, with Rosalind Russell as Ruth, Edie Adams as sister Eileen and George Gaynes as Ruth's love interest Bob. George Abbott directed and Lehman Engel conducted. *Wonderful Town* was a big success in both New York and London and has been revived many times since, often by light

opera companies. It was presented by New York City Opera in 1994 with Kay McClelland and Crista Moore as the sisters.

1953 Original cast. Rosalind Russell and Edie Adams star as the sisters in the original cast album with support from George Gaynes, Delbert Anderson, Warren Galjour, Jordan Bentley and Cris Alexander. Lehman Engel conducts. Decca LP/MCA CD. **1958 CBS Television.** Rosalind Russell reprises her role as Ruth in this TV version of the musical with Jacquelyn McKeever as Eileen and Sidney Chaplin as boyfriend Bob. Lending support are Cris Alexander, Jordan Bentley and Sam Kirkham. Mel Ferber directed and Lehman Engel conducted. The musical was telecast November 30, 1958, and the soundtrack was issued as a Columbia LP. **1998 London recording.** Audra McDonald sings Eileen, Kim Criswell is Ruth and Thomas Hampson is Bob in this London recording. Simon Rattle conducts the London Voices and the Birmingham Contemporary Music Group. EMI CD.

THE WOODLANDERS   *1985 opera by Paulus*

The serenity of the English villager of Little Hintock is disrupted by three newcomers: Grace Melbury, who was born in the town but has been away studying; Edred Fitzpiers, a young doctor doing research; and Mrs. Felice Charmond, a woman of social standing. Grace marries Edred but takes up with her childhood sweetheart Giles when her husband gets involved with Felice. The people of the village remain as solidly rooted as their trees. Stephen Paulus' three-act opera *The Woodlanders*, libretto by Colin Graham based on the novel by Thomas Hardy, was premiered by Opera Theatre of St. Louis on June 13, 1985. Carol Gale was Grace Melbury, Mark Thomsen was Dr. Edred Fitzpiers, Lisbeth Lloyd was Mrs. Felice Charmond, James McGuire was Giles Winterbourne, Cory Miller was Marty South, Joanna Levy was Grammer Oliver, Thomas Arnold was Old Tim Tange, Reginald Unterseher was Young Tim Tange, John McGhee was Robert Creedle, Dan Sullivan was George Melbury, Stephen Morton was Tincott, Stephen Kirchgraber was John Upjohn and Gregory Newton was Rob Slatters. Richard Buckley conducted the orchestra.

WOODS, SHERYL   *American soprano (1951–)*

Sheryl Woods has specialized in singing the heroines of modern American operas. She has portrayed Celia in Floyd's THE PASSION OF JONATHAN WADE in Houston, Susannah in Floyd's SUSANNAH at Lake George, Blanche DuBois in Previn's A STREETCAR NAMED DESIRE in San Diego and New Orleans, Susanne in Picker's THÉRÈSE RAQUIN in Dallas and San Diego, Mrs. Patrick De Rocher in Heggie's DEAD MAN WALKING, and Birdie in Blitzstein's REGINA. Woods is a graduate of the University of Cincinnati Conservatory of Music.

WOOLF, BENJAMIN E.   *American librettist/composer (1836–1901)*

Benjamin Edward Woolf wrote librettos for over thirty Boston stage shows and composed music for three more. Most of his librettos were for composer Julius Eichberg, and their opéra bouffe THE DOCTOR OF ALCANTARA was the most successful early American comic opera. Following its premiere at the Boston Museum on April 7, 1862, (Woolf was conductor of the Museum's orchestra from 1859 to 1964), it was staged around America, Britain and Australia. It was the first American opera to be staged by an African American opera company, the Original Colored American Opera Troupe of Washington, D.C., which presented it in Washington and Philadelphia in 1873. Eichberg's other comic operas with librettos by Woolf, all first performed in Boston, were *A Night in*

Rome (1864), *The Rose of Tyrol* (1865) and *The Two Cadis* (1868). Woolf's comic operas for which he wrote the music were also premiered in Boston: *Lawn Tennis; or, Jjakh and Djill*, libretto by the composer, in 1880; *Pounce and Company*, libretto by the composer, in 1883; and *Westward Ho!*, libretto by Richard Ware, in 1894. Woolf was a important music critic as well, writing regularly for the *Boston Globe* and *Boston Herald*.

THE WORLD IS ROUND   *1993 opera by Sellars*

Rose, who is a rose who is a rose, learns about the ways of the world and finds her own identity after climbing a symbolic mountain. James Sellars' chamber opera *The World Is Round*, libretto by Juanita Rockwell based on a 1939 children's book by Gertrude Stein, was premiered by Company One Theater at the Aetna Theater at the Wadsworth Atheneum in Hartford, Connecticut, on April 22, 1993. Karen Holvik sang the role of Rose and Ginny Meader was the Moon. The other roles, including a trio of owls, were performed by Jeanne Moniz, Steven Goldstein and Jonathan Hays. Sarah Edkins designed the sets, librettist Rockwell directed and Kyle Swann conducted.

WRIGHT, MAURICE   *American composer (1949–)*

Maurice Wright, best known for his electronic music, also composed two operas. *The Fifth String*, libretto by the composer based on a novel by John Philip Sousa, was composed for a standard chamber orchestra and completed in 1980. It was followed by the more electronic *The Trojan Conflict*, libretto by the composer based on Homer's *Iliad*, which tells the story of the Trojan War through television news reports. Zeus plays cello in an acoustic instrument quartet and watches the war on TV while contrasting music is played by a quartet of synthesizers. There are arias for Achilles, Paris, Aphrodite and the other participants in the war. *The Trojan Conflict* was commissioned by the Philadelphia Network of Music and premiered at the Painted Bride Arts Center in Philadelphia on April 2, 1989. Wright, who was born in Front Royal, VA, studied at Duke and Columbia and taught at Columbia, Boston and Temple. In addition to his electronic, chamber and vocal work, he has written scores for three films about modern artists.

WRIGHT, ROBERT   *American composer*   See GEORGE FORREST

A WRINKLE IN TIME   *1992 opera by Larsen*

Meg Murry, teenage daughter of atomic scientist Dr Murry who has disappeared on a secret mission, sets out to rescue him from alien villains holding him captive in a fifth dimensional world. Meg and her friends travel through time and space to the planet Camzotz and rescue her father from an evil brain. Libby Larsen's 60-minute opera *A Wrinkle in Time*, libretto by Walter Green based on the 1963 children's fantasy novel by Madeleine L'Engle, was commissioned by OperaDelaware Family Opera Theater in Wilmington which premiered it on March 27, 1992. Andrea Brown played the heroine Meg Murry, Matthew Harrigan was her nine-year-old brother Charles Wallace and Andrew Rumbaugh was teenage friend Calvin. Debra Field was Mother, David Price was the scientist Father, Andrew Wagner was the principal Mr. Jenkins and evil Man with Red Eyes in the Fifth Dimension while Joy Vandever, Lorie Gratis and Charlene Campbell played the delightful trio of witches. Leland Kimball designed the sets and directed while Evelyn Swensson conducted the chamber orchestra which featured electronic and acoustic instruments.

WUORINEN, CHARLES   *American composer (1938–)*

Charles Wuorinen, who won the Pulitzer Prize in 1970 for his synthesizer composition *Time's Encomium*, is best known for twelve-tone concert music but he has also composed several theatrical works. DR. FAUSTUS LIGHTS THE LIGHTS, a setting of the Gertrude Stein play for narrator and chamber orchestra, was performed in 1957. THE POLITICS OF HARMONY, a serial-derived masque with libretto by Richard Monaco based on an old Chinese tale, was premiered in New York October 28, 1968. THE W. OF BABYLON: *or, The Triumph of Love over Moral Depravity*, libretto by Renaud Charles Bruce, is a two-hour "baroque burlesque opera" about an frolicsome octet misbehaving in a 17th century French chateau; Light Fantastic Players premiered it the Manhattan School of Music in New York on December 15, 1975. *The Magic Art*, an instrumental masque after Purcell, was composed in 1979. *Haroun and the Sea of Stories*, libretto by James Fenton based on the novel by Salman Rushdie, was commissioned by New York City Opera in 2004. Wuorinen was born in New York and studied at Columbia University with opera composers Jack Beeson and Otto Luening.

WUORNOS   *2001 opera by Lucero*

Aileen Wuornos, the only known female serial killer, murders seven men while working as a prostitute in Florida. She is arrested in 1991, convicted of the crimes and executed. Carla Lucero's opera *Wuornos*, libretto by the composer, was premiered at San Francisco's Yerba Buena Center for the Arts in June 2001. Wuornos has also inspired three movies; Charlize Theron won an Oscar for portraying her in *Monster* (2003).

WUTHERING HEIGHTS (1)   *1951 opera by Herrmann*

Cathy Earnshaw and Heathcliff are star-crossed lovers whose passion ends in tragedy on the moors of 19th century Yorkshire. Bernard Herrmann's four-act opera *Wuthering Heights*, libretto by Lucille Fletcher based on the novel by Emily Brontë, is his most ambitious work but it was not staged during his lifetime. Portland Opera presented the first stage production, effectively the world premiere, on November 6, 1982, under the direction of Malcolm Fraser. Victor Braun was Heathcliff, Barrie Smith was Cathy,

Bernard Herrmann recorded his opera *Wuthering Heights* in London in 1966, but it was not staged until 1982.

Chester Ludgin was Hindley, Alyce Rogers was Isabella, John Walker was Edgar and Geraldine Decker was Nelly. Carey Wong designed the sets and Stefan Minde conducted the orchestra.

1966 London studio recording. Morag Beaton sings Cathy with Donald Bell as Heathcliff in this recording made in England under the supervision of the composer conducting the Pro Arte Orchestra. John Kitchiner is Hindley, Pamela Bowden is Isabel, Joseph Ward is Edgar, Elizabeth Bainbridge is Nelly, Michael Rippon is Joseph, David Kelly is Mr. Lockwood and the Elizabethan Singers are the Carolers. Unicorn and Pye 4-LP set/Unicorn 3-CD set. **1999 Renée Fleming.** Renée Fleming sings the aria "I Have Dreamt" from *Wuthering Heights* on her recital album *I Want Magic.* She is accompanied by James Levine conducting the Metropolitan Opera Orchestra. London Classics CD.

WUTHERING HEIGHTS (2)   *1958 opera by Floyd*

Carlisle Floyd's three-act opera *Wuthering Heights*, libretto by the composer based on Emily Brontë's novel about the star-crossed lovers Cathy and Heathcliff, was premiered by Santa Fe Opera on July 16, 1958. Phyllis Curtin was Cathy, Robert Trehy was Heathcliff, Regina Sarfaty was Nelly, Loren Driscoll was Edgar, Mildred Allen was Isabella, Davis Cunningham was Hindley, John Macurdy was Earnshaw, Elaine Bonazzi was Mrs. Linton and David Beckwith was Mr. Linton. Irving Gutman staged the opera and John Crosby conducted. It was presented in a revised version by New York City Opera on April 9, 1959, with Curtin again as Cathy but with John Reardon as Heathcliff, Patricia Neway as Nelly and Frank Porretta as Edgar. Patton Campbell designed the sets, Delbert Mann directed and Julius Rudel conducted. It was revived by Boston Lyric Opera in 1993 with Joan Gibbons as Cathy and Jeff Mattsey as Heathcliff and presented in New York City in 2001 in concert format.

WYMETAL, WILHELM VON   *American opera director (1862–1937)*

Wilhelm von Wymetal staged the premieres of two American operas at the Metropolitan Opera, both composed by Deems Taylor, PETER IBBETSON in 1931 and THE KING'S HENCHMAN in 1927. Wymetal, who was born a baron in Austria, directed opera in Europe before coming to the Met in 1922 where he staged 49 productions before retiring in 1935. His son Wilhelm von Wymetal Jr. also directed operas at the Met.

WYMETAL, WILHELM VON, JR.   *American opera director (1890–1970)*

Wilhelm von Wymetal Jr. staged the premiere of two American operas at the Met and directed three "movie operas." The son of Baron Wilhelm von Wymetal, he called himself William when he worked in movies and Wilhelm when he worked in opera. At the Metropolitan Opera he directed the premieres of Howard Hanson's MERRY MOUNT in 1933 and John Laurence Seymour's IN THE PASHA'S GARDEN in 1935. In Hollywood he staged the movie opera CZARITA in *Maytime* (1937) and wrote lyrics for and staged the movie operas AMOUR ET GLOIRE and LE PRINCE MASQUE DE LA CAUCASIE in *The Phantom of the Opera* (1943). He staged opera sequences for several other movies, including *San Francisco* (1936), *Moonlight Murder* (1936) and *I'll Take Romance* (1937). He was managing director of the Pittsburgh Civic Light Opera from 1947 to 1968.

WYOMING   *American state (1893–)*

Wyoming's capitol city Cheyenne was founded in 1867 and English cattle barons tried to make it seem cultural by opening a thousand-seat opera house in 1882. A second opera house was built in Rock Springs but opera never became popular in the state. Owen Wister, author of *The Virginian,* the Wyoming novel that began the Western fiction tradition, was also an opera composer, but then he was an Easterner who only came for visits. George Hufsmith's opera *Sweetwater Lynching (The Battle of Cattle Kate),* based on real events, was premiered in Laramie on March 2, 1976. Jarod Shaffer Tate's ballet musical *Winter Moons* was performed around the state in 1992. Opera singers made occasional stopovers. Wagnerian contralto Ernestine Schumann-Heink gave a concert at the Wyoming State Fairgrounds in Douglas on July 24, 1924. Marian Anderson sang at the University of Wyoming in 1954. Marilyn Horne fulfilled her goal of singing in all fifty states performing in Laramie in September 1999.

Casper: Pat Mendoza's folk opera *Song of the Plains* was staged in Casper in 1993.

Cheyenne: The Cheyenne Opera House was opened on May 25, 1882, with Edmund Audran's *Olivette* performed by the touring Comly-Barton Opera Company. The Wyoming Opera Guild presented Kurt Weill's DOWN IN THE VALLEY in 1955.

Laramie: George Hufsmith's opera *Sweetwater Lynching (The Battle of Cattle Kate),* based on an incident during the Wyoming cattle war, was created for the 1976 Bicentennial and premiered in Laramie on March 2, 1976. It tells the story of Cattle Kate and Jim Averell, who are also featured in the 1980 movie *Heaven's Gate.* The incident was also the subject of the first Wyoming ballet, *The Lynching of Cattle Kate,* which premiered at the University of Wyoming in 1989.

X

X, THE LIFE AND TIMES OF MALCOLM X   *1986 opera by Davis*

Malcolm Little's father is killed by the Ku Klux Klan. He grow up to be the charismatic Black Muslim leader Malcolm X but is

Anthony Davis's powerful opera *X, the Life and Times of Malcolm X* was recorded in New York in 1992.

assassinated. Anthony Davis's opera *X, the Life and Times of Malcolm X,* libretto by Thulani Davis based on a story by Christopher Davis, was developed by the American Music Theater Festival and had its first full-length production with orchestra in Philadelphia on October 9, 1985. It was officially premiered at New York City Opera on September 28, 1986, in a production by Rhoda Levine with Christopher Keene conducting. Ben Holt sang Malcolm X, Thomas Young was Street and Elijah, Priscilla Baskerville was Louise and Betty, Marietta Simpson was Ella and Muslim, Mark S. Doss was Reginald and Armond Presley was Young Malcolm. The opera, which incorporates elements of popular music from swing and jazz to rap, was warmly received by critics.

1992 New York recording. Eugene Perry takes over the role of Malcolm X for this recording of the opera produced in New York in 1992 by Max Wilcox with some of the original cast members. Thomas Young is Street and Elijah, Priscilla Baskerville is Louise and Betty, Hilda Harris is Ella, Herbert Perry is Reginald, Cynthia Aaronson is Social Worker and Reporter, child tenor Timothy D. Price is Young Malcolm, Raymond Bazemore is Preacher and John Daniecki, Ronald Edwards and Richard Byrne takes small roles. William Henry Curry conducts the Orchestra of St. Luke's and the group Episteme. Gramavision CD box.

Y

YAVELOW, CHRISTOPHER   *American composer (1950–)*
Christopher Yavelow's one-act opera COUNTDOWN, created with the help of an Apple Macintosh computer on a commission from the Boston Lyric Opera Company, was premiered in Boston on February 12, 1987. The music is played by a Digital Music Workstation. Yavelow, who was born in Cambridge, Massachusetts, also composed the 1993 three-act opera *The Passion of Vincent Van Gogh,* libretto by Monique Yavelow.

YEATES, RAY   *American tenor (1909–)*
Ray Yeates created the roles of Nelson and the Crab Man in the premiere of George Gershwin's PORGY AND BESS in Boston and New York in 1935 and he sang in the 1953 Broadway revival starring Leontyne Price directed by Robert Breen. Yeates was born in North Carolina.

YEHU: A CHRISTMAS LEGEND   *1974 opera by Zador*
Yehu, a soldier in King Herod's army who is afflicted with leprosy, is ordered home to Bethlehem to take the census. His parents Rachel and Simon offer a poor couple their barn for the night as the woman is expecting a child. When they discover Herod's soldiers have been ordered to kill all the infants in Bethlehem, they plead with Yehu to spare the baby in their barn but he refuses and goes out to the barn. When he returns. he tells them that he was unable to harm the child and his leprosy is cured. Eugene Zador's one-act religious opera *Yehu: A Christmas Legend,* libretto by Anna Egyud, was premiered by the Municipal Art Department of the Bureau of Music in Los Angeles on December 21, 1974.

THE YELLOW WALLPAPER   *1992 opera by Perera*
Charlotte is taken by her doctor husband to a colonial house in rural Connecticut and thinks she has arrived in paradise. Later, when she becomes ill with "nervous depression," he confines her in a room in the house with yellow wallpaper. Slowly she begins to go mad. Ronald Perera's opera *The Yellow Wallpaper,* libretto by Constance Congdon based on the famous novella by Charlotte Perkins Gilman, was premiered at Smith College in Northampton, MA, on May 17, 1989. It was revived in a more elaborate production by Mark Harrison at the John Brownlee Opera Theater at the Manhattan School of Music on December 9, 1992. Peggy Kriha sang the role of Charlotte, Kyle Portmiller was her husband John, Pamela Moore was her husband's sister Jennie, Charles Bressler was Dr. Silas Weir, Red Nelman was Ed and Lee Ann Hutchinson was the Woman in the Wall. David Gilbert was the conductor. The opera was reprised by OperaDelaware in 1993.

YERMA   *1971 opera by Villa-Lobos*
Yerma, who lives in a small Spanish village, is desperate to have a child. Her husband Juan is not interested and she is tempted by former lover Victor. When her husband follows her to a fertility shrine, she is outraged and kills him. Heitor Villa-Lobos opera *Yerma,* libretto based on a 1934 play by Federico García Lorca, was commissioned by John Blankenship, the director of drama at St. Lawrence College in New York. It was to have been premiered by Blankenship with an LL African American cast in 1956 but the production was called off. It was finally premiered, after the composer's death, on August 12, 1971, by Santa Fe Opera. Frederica von Stade sang the role of Maria and Theodor Uppman was Victor. The opera was later staged in London and Rio de Janeiro.

YOUMANS, VINCENT   *American composer (1898–1946)*
Vincent Youmans wrote the score for a dozen notable musicals including the enduring classics *No, No, Nanette* (1925), with its hit song "Tea for Two," and *Hit the Deck* (1927). His last score was for the 1933 RKO film *Flying Down to Rio* which made a star of Fred Astaire and Ginger Rogers. Youmans, who was born in New York, learned the music business by working as a piano salesman and song plugger. He began composing while serving in the Navy in World War I and his first musical, *Too Little Girls in Blue,* was staged in 1921.

YOUNG, RIDA JOHNSON   *American librettist (1866–1926)*
Rida Johnson Young wrote thirty-four plays and musical comedies including the librettos and lyrics for Victor Herbert's NAUGHTY MARIETTA and THE DREAM GIRL, Sigmund Romberg's MAYTIME and *Her Soldier Boy,* Rudolf Friml's *Sometime* and Jerome Kern's *The Red Petticoat.* The Baltimore native began her stage career with a hit play, the 1906 *Brown of Harvard,* and was one of the most popular librettists and lyricists on Broadway in the 1910s. Her classic songs include "Ah, Sweet Mystery of Life," "I'm Falling in Love with Someone," "Tramp, Tramp, Tramp," "Will You Remember" and "Mother Machree."

YOUNG, THOMAS J.   *American tenor (1960–)*
Thomas Young has played an important role in the operas of Anthony Davis and John Adams and created roles in four of them. He made his debut as Street and Elijah in X, THE LIFE AND TIMES OF MALCOLM X at New York City Opera in 1986 and sings both roles on the cast recording. He created the role of the Inspector in Davis's UNDER THE DOUBLE MOON in St. Louis in 1989 and the Trickster God in Davis's AMISTAD in Chicago in 1997. For Adams he created the role of Molqi in THE DEATH OF KLINGHOFFER in Brussels in 1991 and later sang the part of Jonathan Rumor. He has also sung the role of Sportin' Life in George Gershwin's PORGY AND BESS. Young, who was born in Cleveland, studied at the Cleveland Institute of Music and USC and first sang with Opera Ebony.

YOUNG CAESER   *1971 puppet opera by Harrison*

Young Julius Caesar conquers Bithynia and gets seduced by King Nicomedes. Lou Harrison's gay puppet opera *Young Caeser,* libretto by Robert Gordon, was premiered at Pasadena, CA, on November 5, 1971. It was created for nine singers, four speakers and a medley of invented instruments built by Harrison's friend William Colvig. The singers sit in the pit with the orchestra in front of the puppets.

YOUNG GOODMAN BROWN   *1970 opera by Mollicone*

A Puritan goes into the forest to meet a Stranger and finds himself involved in a witches' Sabbath. Members of his religious community seem to be present, including his wife Faith. When he tells her to resist, the scene dissolves and he is alone. Henry Mollicone's allegorical one-act opera *Young Goodman Brown,* libretto by John S. Bowman and the composer based on the story by Nathaniel Hawthorne, premiered at the Lake George Opera Festival in Glen Falls, NY, in summer 1970. Philip Booth played the Stranger.

YOUR MONEY MY LIFE GOODBYE   *1998 opera by Ashley*

Robert Ashley's avant-garde electronic opera *Your Money My Life Goodbye,* libretto by the composer about the life of Ms. Ona, was premiered at the Kitchen in 1998.

1998 Original Cast recording. The original cast album features Joan La Barbara, Jacqueline Humbert, Thomas Buckner, Thomas Hamilton, Sam Ashley and the composer. Lovely Music CD.

YULE, DON   *American bass (1935–)*

Don Yule created small roles in three operas at New York City Opera while he was a member of the company. He was the Stableboy in Ned Rorem's MISS JULIE in 1965, the Leader of the Bedouins in Hugo Weisgall's NINE RIVERS FROM JORDAN in 1968 and Professor Grippel in Gian Carlo Menotti's THE MOST IMPORTANT MAN in 1971. Yule made his debut at New York City Opera in 1960 singing the role of Gluttony in Hugo Weisgall's SIX CHARACTERS IN SEARCH OF AN AUTHOR.

Z

ZADOR, EUGENE   *American composer (1894–1977)*

Eugene Zador composed five operas after emigrating to America from Hungary in 1939. The radio opera *Christopher Columbus,* libretto by J. Mohácsi, was broadcast on NBC on October 8, 1939. *The Virgin and the Fawn,* libretto by L. Zilahy, was staged in Los Angeles in 1964. THE MAGIC CHAIR, libretto by George Jellinek based on a play by Karinthy, premiered in Baton Rouge in 1966. *The Scarlet Mill,* libretto by Jellinek based on a play by Molnar, premiered at Brooklyn College Opera in 1968. YEHU: A CHRISTMAS LEGEND, libretto by Anna Egyud, premiered in Los Angeles in 1974. Zador, who was born in Bátaszék, taught music in Vienna and Budapest before coming to America to work as an orchestrator in Hollywood. His unproduced 1928 Hungarian opera *The Inspector General,* based on the story by Gogol, was premiered in Los Angeles in 1971.

ZAMBELLO, FRANCESCA   *American stage director (1956–)*

Francesca Zambello directed the premiere of Carly Simon's "family opera" ROMULUS HUNT in New York in 1993, the premiere of Tobias Picker's EMMELINE for Santa Fe Opera in July 1996 and the premiere of Daniel Catán's FLORENCIA EN EL AMAZONAS for Houston Grand Opera in October 1996. She directed the American premiere of Philip Glass film-based opera ORPHÉE for the American Repertory Theater in Cambridge in 1993, Kurt Weill's STREET SCENE for Houston Grand Opera in 1994, Benjamin Britten's PAUL BUNYAN for the Royal Opera House in London in 1999 and Carlisle Floyd's OF MICE AND MEN for the Bregenz Festival in 2001. Zambello, who was born in New York City, studied with Jean-Pierre Ponnelle after graduating from Colgate. She was co-artistic director of the Skylight Opera Theater In Milwaukee from 1985 to 1990 before beginning her international career.

ZEFFIRELLI, FRANCO   *Italian director/designer/librettist (1923–)*

Franco Zeffirelli wrote the libretto for Anthony Barber's ANTHONY AND CLEOPATRA and staged the opera in a grandiose manner as the opening program of the new Metropolitan Opera House in 1966. It was a disaster and much of the blame was directed at Zeffirelli for his over-elaborate staging and over-complicated libretto. Barber never wrote another opera though he later revised and simplified the libretto of *Anthony and Cleopatra* with the help of Gian Carlo Menotti. Zeffirelli, a hugely popular director of European operas at the Met, has had no other connection with American opera.

ZEISL, ERIC   *American composer (1905–1959)*

Eric Zeisl spent the last twenty years of his life working on his Hebraic opera masterwork *Job: The Story of a Simple Man.* Based on a novel by Joseph Roth, it explores the suffering of modern Jews through the story of a Job-like Jewish schoolteacher. Austrian-born Zeisl could draw on his own experiences as he had fled to America from the Nazis in the late 1930s. He settled in Los Angeles in 1941 writing music for MGM movies and teaching at Los Angeles City College while working on his opera. *Job* (or *Hiob*), composed to a libretto by Hans Kafka, was never finished but impressive excerpts from it were presented in Los Angeles in 1957. Malcolm S. Cole gives a fascinating description of the evolution of this lost work in the Winter 1992 edition of *Opera Quarterly.*

ZENOBIA   *1905 opera by Coerne*

The first American opera staged in Europe was Louis Adolphe Coerne's three-act *Zenobia,* libretto by Oscar Stein, which was premiered at the Stadttheater in Bremen, Germany, on December 1, 1905. It tells the story of Zenobia, Queen of Palmyra in Syria in the third century. After her defeat by the Roman army, Emperor Aurelian offers to make her his consort. She prefers death by the side of the man she loves. The Bremen premiere cast featured Miss Gerstorfer as Zenobia and Mr. Vogl as Aurelian with Egon Pollak conducting. The music was reportedly somewhat in a Wagnerian mode but the opera has never been staged in America.

Bibliography

This selective bibliography of books related to American opera may be helpful to those interested in obtaining more information about American operas and operettas. It does not include librettos, scores, source literary works or general studies that include references to American opera. The most useful complete bibliographical guide is Guy A. Marco's *Opera: A Research and Information Guide*. The best continuing source of information about new American operas is Opera America and its many publications. American opera productions and recordings are reviewed regularly in *BBC Music Magazine, Gramophone, Opera, Opera News, Opera Now* and *Opera Quarterly,*

Operas and Operettas

Alpert, Hollis. *The Life and Times of Porgy and Bess.* Alfred A. Knopf, 1990

Baxter, Joan. *Television Musicals.* McFarland, 1997.

Bloom, Ken. *American Song: Musical Theater Companion 1900–1984.* Facts on File, 1985.

Blum, Daniel. *A Pictorial Treasury of Opera in America.* Grosset & Dunlap, 1954.

Bordman, Gerald. *American Operetta, from* H.M.S. Pinafore *to* Sweeney Todd. Oxford, 1981.

Boroff, Edith. *American Operas: A Checklist.* Harmonie Park Press, 1992.

Bradley, Edwin M. *The First Hollywood Musicals.* McFarland, 1996.

Burke, John. *The Legend of Baby Doe.* University of Nebraska Press, 1974.

Cavendish, Thomas Hamilton. *Folk Music in Selected 20th Century American Operas.* Florida State University Ph.D. dissertation. University Microfilms, 1967.

Chase, Gilbert. *America's Music, from the Pilgrims to Present.* University of Illinois Press, 1987.

Davis, Ronald L. *A History of Opera in the American West.* Prentice-Hall, 1965.

Dizikes, John. *Opera in America: A Cultural History.* Yale University Press, 1993.

Drummond, Andrew. *American Opera Librettos.* Scarecrow, 1972.

Eaton, Quaintance. *Opera Production: A Handbook.* University of Minnesota Press, 1962.

_____. *Opera Production II: A Handbook.* University of Minnesota Press 1974.

Gänzl, Kurt. *The Blackwell Guide to the Musical Theater on Record.* Blackwell, 1990.

_____. *The Encyclopedia of the Musical Theatre.* Blackwell, 1994.

_____. *Gänzl's Book of the Musical Theatre.* Schirmer, 1989.

Glasser, Alfred (editor). *The Lyric Opera Companion.* Andrews McMeel, 1991.

Green, Stanley. *Encyclopedia of the Musical.* Cassell, 1977.

Griffiths, Paul. *Encyclopedia of 20th Century Music.* Thames and Hudson, 1986.

Hamilton, David. *The Metropolitan Opera Encyclopedia.* Simon and Schuster, 1987.

Hipsher, Edward Ellsworth. *American Opera and Its Composers.* Theodore Presser, 1927.

Hischak, Thomas S. *The American Musical Theatre Song Encyclopedia.* Greenwood, 1995.

Hitchcock, H. Wiley, and Stanley Sadie (editors). *The New Grove Dictionary of American Music* (4 vols.). Macmillan, 1986.

Holden, Amanda (editor). *The New Penguin Opera Guide.* Penguin Books, 2001.

Howard, John Tasker. *Our American Music, Three Hundred Years of It.* Crowell, 1965.

_____. *Our Contemporary Composers: American Music in the 20th Century.* Crowell, 1941.

Hughes, Gervase. *Composers of Operetta.* St. Martin's Press, 1962.

Johnson, H. Earle. *Operas on American Subjects.* Coleman-Ross, 1964.

Kirk, Elise K. *American Opera.* University of Illinois Press, 2001

Kornick, Rebecca Hodell. *Recent American Opera: A Production Guide.* Columbia, 1991.

Lebrecht, Norman. *Companion to 20th Century Music.* Simon & Schuster, 1992.

Levin, Monroe. *Clues to American Music.* Starrhill Press, 1992.

Machlis, Joseph. *Introduction to Contemporary Music.* Norton, 1961.

Marco, Guy A. *Opera: A Research and Information Guide.* Garland, 2001.

Martin, George. *The Opera Companion to Twentieth Century Opera.* Dodd, Mead, 1997

_____. *Twentieth Century Opera: A Guide.* Limelight Editions, 1999.

Mates, Julian. *The American Musical Stage Before 1800.* Greenwood, 1962.

Mattfeld, Julius. *A Handbook of American Opera Premieres 1731–1962.* Information Service Detroit, 1963.

_____. *A Hundred Years of Grand Opera in New York 1825–1925.* New York Public Library, 1927.

McSpadden, J. Walker. *Operas and Musical Comedies.* Crowell, 1946.

Morton, Brian. *The Blackwell Guide to Recorded Contemporary Music.* Blackwell, 1996.

Opera America. *Annual Field Reports, Registers, Schedules of Performances.*

Raymond, Jack. *Show Music on Record.* Smithsonian Institution Press, 1992.

Rich, Maria (editor). *Directory of Contemporary Operas and Music Theater Works 1967–1975 and 1980–1989.* Central Opera Service, 1976 and 1990.

Rockwell, John. *All American Music.* Alfred A. Knopf, 1983.

Rous, Samuel Holland. *The Victrola Book of the Opera.* Victor Talking Machine, 1917.

Sadie, Stanley (editor). *The New Grove Dictionary of Opera.* Macmillan, 1992.

Schliefer, Martha Furman. *American Opera and Music for the Stage.* G. K. Hall, 1990.

Sonneck, Oscar G. *Early Opera in America.* G. Schirmer, 1915.

Struble, John Warthien. *The History of American Classical Music.* Facts on File, 1995.

Smith, Duane A. *The Ballad of Baby Doe.* University Press of Colorado, 2002.

Traubner, Richard. *Operetta: A Theatrical History.* Doubleday, 1983.

Virga, Patricia H. *The American Opera to 1790.* UMI Research Press, 1982.

Watson, Steven. *Prepare for Saints.* Random House, 1996.

Composers, Librettists and Singers

Alda, Frances. *Men, Women and Tenors.* AMS, 1937.

Ammer, Christine. *Unsung: A History of Women in American Music.* Greenwood, 1980.

Antheil, George. *Bad Boy of Music.* Doubleday, 1945.

Ardoin, John. *The Stages of Menotti.* Doubleday, 1985.

Auden, W. H. *The Dyer's Hand and Other Essays.* Vintage Books, 1968.

Austin, William, et al. (editors). *The New Grove 20th Century American Masters.* Norton, 1988.

Banfield, Stephen. *Sondheim's Broadway Musicals.* University of Michigan Press, 1993.

Block, Adrienne Fried. *Amy Beach, Passionate Victorian.* Oxford University Press, 1998.

Bloomfield, Arthur. *Frederick Shepherd Converse (1871–1940).* Scarecrow, 1994.

Bowles, Garrett H. *Ernest Krenek: A Bio-Bibliography.* Greenwood, 1989.

Brinnin, John Malcolm. *Selected Operas and Plays of Gertrude Stein.* University of Pittsburgh Press, 1970.

Collier, James Lincoln. *Duke Ellington.* Oxford University Press, 1987.

Copland, Aaron, and Vivian Perlis. *Copland Since 1943.* St. Martin's Press, 1989.

Cross, Jonathan. *The Cambridge Companion to Stravinsky.* Cambridge University Press. 2003.

Cummings, David M. *International Who's Who in Music.* International Who's Who, 1990.

Davis, Peter G. *The American Opera Singer.* Doubleday, 1997.

Dean, Phillip Hayes. *Paul Robeson.* Doubleday, 1978.

Drew, David. *Kurt Weill: A Handbook.* University of California Press, 1987.

Ewen, David. *Musicians Since 1900: Performers in Concert and Opera.* Wilson, 1978.

Farkas, Andrew. *Lawrence Tibbett, Singing Actor.* Amadeus Press, 1981.

Fisher, Margaret. *Ezra Pound's Radio Operas.* MIT Press, 2002.

Freedland, Michael. *Jerome Kern: A Biography.* Robson, 1978.

Fuller, Sophie. *The Pandora Guide to Women Composers.* HarperCollins, 1994.

Garofalo, Robert J. *Frederick Shepherd Converse (1870–1940).* Scarecrow, 1994.

Gilbert, Steven E. *The Music of Gershwin.* Yale University Press, 1995.

Gordon, Eric A. *Mark the Music: The Life and Work of Marc Blitzstein.* St. Martin's Press, 1989.

Goss, Madeleine. *Modern Music Makers: Contemporary American Composers.* Dutton, 1952.

Grieb, Lyndal. *The Operas of Gian Carlo Menotti, 1937–1972.* Scarecrow, 1974.

Griffiths, Paul. *Encyclopaedia of 20th-Century Music.* Thames and Hudson, 1986.

Hayes, Deborah. *Peggy Glanville-Hicks: A Bio-Bibliography.* Greenwood, 1990.

Hennessee, Don. *Samuel Barber: A Bio-Bibliography.* Greenwood, 1985.

Heyman, Barbara B. *Samuel Barber: The Composer and His Music.* Oxford University Press, 1992.

Hillier, Paul (editor). *Steve Reich: Writing on Music 1965–2000.* Oxford University Press, 2002.

Hixon, Donald L. *Thea Musgrave: A Bio-Bibliography.* Greenwood, 1984.

Horowitz, Joseph. *The Virgil Thomson Centenary 1896–1996.* Finlay Brothers, 1996.

Howard, John Tasker. *American Opera and Its Composers.* Da Capo, 1978.

Jones, Robert T. (editor) *Music by Philip Glass.* Harper & Row, 1987.

Jowitt, Deborah. *Meredith Monk.* Johns Hopkins University Press, 1997.

Kostelanetz, Richard. *John Cage (ex)plain(ed).* Schirmer Books, 1996.

_____. *Writing on Glass.* Schirmer Books, 1997.

Kreitner, Kenneth. *Robert Ward: A Bio-Bibliography.* Greenwood, 1988.

Kutsch, K. J., and Leo Riemens. *A Concise Dictionary of Singers.* Chilton, 1969.

_____, and _____. *Unvergängliche Stimmen Sangerlexikon.* Francke, 1975.

Luening, Otto. *The Odyssey of an American Composer.* Scribner, 1980.

Machlis, Joseph. *American Composers of Our Time.* Crowell, 1963.

Mangan, Timothy, and Irene Herrmann. *Paul Bowles on Music.* University of California Press, 2003.

Meckna, Michael. *Virgil Thomson: A Bio-Bibliography.* Greenwood, 1986.

Orrey, Leslie. *Charles T. Griffes: The Life of an American Composer.* Alfred A, Knopf, 1984.

Page, Tim, and Vanessa Weeks. *Selected Letters of Virgil Thomson.* Summit Books, 1988.

Perone, James E. *Howard Hanson: A Bio-Bibliography.* Greenwood, 1993.

Perone, Karen L. *Lukas Foss: A Bio-Bibliography.* Greenwood, 1991.

Pollack, Howard. *Aaron Copland: The Life and Work of an Uncommon Man.* Holt, 1999.

Purdy, Claire Lee. *Victor Herbert, American Music-Master.* Julian Messner, 1944.

Rich, Maria F. *Who's Who in Opera.* Arno Press, 1976.

Rimler, Walter. *A Gershwin Companion.* Popular Culture, 1981.

Rorem, Ned: *Knowing When to Stop: A Memoir.* Simon & Schuster, 1994.

_____. *Other Entertainment. Collected Pieces.* Simon & Schuster, 1996.

_____. *Paris and New York Diaries of Ned Rorem 1951–1961.* North Point, 1983.

Rosenwald, Hans, et al. (editors). *Who Is Who in Music 1941.* Lee Stern Press, 1941.

Ruttencutter, Helen Drees. *Previn.* St. Martin's, 1985.

Sadie, Julie Anne, and Rhian Samuel. *The Norton/Grove Dictionary of Women Composers.* W.W. Norton, 1995.

St. Louis Municipal Opera: 50 Golden Years 1919–1968. St. Louis Opera, 1968.

Sander, Ronald. *The Days Grow Short: The Life and Music of Kurt Weill.* Holt, Rinehart, 1980.

Secrest, Meryle. *Leonard Bernstein: A Life.* Alfred A. Knopf, 1994.

Seeger, Horst. *Opernlexikon.* Florian Noetzel Verlag, 1989.

Sheean, Vincent. *The Amazing Oscar Hammerstein.* Weidenfeld and Nicolson, 1956.

Skowronski, JoAnn. *Aaron Copland: A Bio-Bibliography.* Greenwood, 1985.

Slonimsky, Nicolas. *The Concise Baker's Biographical Dictionary of Musicians.* Schirmer, 1988.

Smith, Eric Ledell. *Blacks in Opera.* McFarland, 1995.

Stein, Gertrude. *Operas and Plays.* Station Hill Arts, 1987.

Stewart, John L. *Ernest Krenek: The Man and His Music.* University of California Press, 1991.

Still, Judith Anne, Michael J. Dabrishus and Carolyn L. Quin. *William Grant Still: A Bio-Bibliography.* Greenwood, 1996.

Stravinsky, Igor, and Robert Craft. *Memories and Commentaries.* Faber & Faber, 2002.

Stravinsky, Théodore, and Denise Stravinsky. *Catherine & Igor Stravinsky.* Schirmer, 2004.

Taylor, Deems. *The Well Tempered Listener.* Simon & Schuster, 1942.

Teasdale, May Silva. *Handbook of 20th Century Opera.* Dutton, 1938.

Thompson, Oscar. *The American Singer: A Hundred Years of Success in Opera.* Dial, 1937.

Thomson, Virgil. *Virgil Thomson: An Autobiography.* Alfred A. Knopf, 1966.

_____. *A Virgil Thomson Reader.* Dutton, 1981.

Tommasini, Anthony. *Virgil Thomson: Composer on the Aisle.* W. W. Norton, 1997.

Upton, William Treat. *William Henry Fry.* Crowell, 1954.

Van Vechten, Carl. *Selected Writings of Gertrude Stein.* Vintage Books, 1972.

Walsh, Stephen. *The Music of Stravinsky.* Routledge, 1988.

Waters, Edward N. *Victor Herbert: A Life in Music.* Macmillan, 1955.

White, Eric Walter. *Stravinsky: The Composer and His Works.* Faber & Faber, 1979.

Whitesitt, Linda. *The Life and Music of George Antheil, 1900–1959.* UMI Research, 1983.

Wlaschin, Ken. *Gian Carlo Menotti on Screen.* McFarland, 1999.

Wood, Bret. *Orson Welles: A Bio-Bibliography.* Greenwood, 1990.

Wyatt, Robert, and John Andrew Johnson. *The George Gershwin Reader.* Oxford University Press, 2004.

Yellin, Victor Fell. *Chadwick, Yankee Composer.* Smithsonian Institution Press, 1990.

Zadan, Craig. *Sondheim & Co.* Macmillan, 1974.

Zaimont, Judith, and Karen Famera. *Contemporary Concert Music by Women.* Greenwood, 1981.

Opera Houses and Companies

Bloomfield, Arthur. *The San Francisco Opera 1922–1978.* Comstock, 1978.

Davis, Ronald L. *Opera in Chicago, 1850–1965.* Appleton-Century, 1966.

Dedmon, Emmett. *Fabulous Chicago.* Random House, 1953.

Eaton, Quaintance. *The Boston Opera Company.* Appleton-Century, 1965.

Fitzgerald, Gerald (editor). *Annals of the Metropolitan Opera: Complete Chronicle of Performances and Artists* (2 vols.). G. K. Hall, 1989.

Gruber, Paul. The *Metropolitan Opera Guide to Recorded Opera.* Norton, 1993.

Kolodin, Irving. *The Story of the Metropolitan Opera 1883–1950.* Alfred A. Knopf, 1953.

Koopal, Grace G. *Miracle of Music: The History of the Hollywood Bowl.* Toberman, 1972.

McKenna, Harold J. (editor). New York City Opera Sings. Richard Rosen Press, 1981.

Moore, Edward. *Forty Years of Opera in Chicago.* Horace Liveright, 1930.

Morrissey, Lee. *The Kitchen Turns Twenty: A Retrospective Anthology.* The Kitchen, 1992.

Rich, Alan. *American Voice: Houston Grand Opera Celebrates 25 World Premieres.* Houston Grand Opera, 2000.

Scott, Eleanor. *The First Twenty Years of the Santa Fe Opera.* Sunstone Press, 1976.

Sokol, Martin L. *The New York City Opera: An American Adventure.* Macmillan, 1981.

Struble, John Warthen. *The Golden Horseshoe: The Life and Times of the Metropolitan Opera House.* Viking, 1965.

Thierstein, Eldred A. *Cincinnati Opera, from Zoo to Music Hall.* Deerstone Books, 1995.

Zietz, Karyl Lynn: *National Trust Guide to Great Opera Houses in America.* Wiley, 1996.

_____. *Opera Companies and Houses of the United States.* McFarland, 1995.

Index

Entries in SMALL CAPITALS are subject entries listing multiple operas.

439